W9-CKH-709

CONNECT FEATURES

Intelligent Response Technology

Intelligent Response Technology (IRT) is a redesigned student interface for our end-of-chapter assessment content. In addition to a streamlined interface, IRT provides improved answer acceptance to reduce students' frustration with formatting issues (such as rounding).

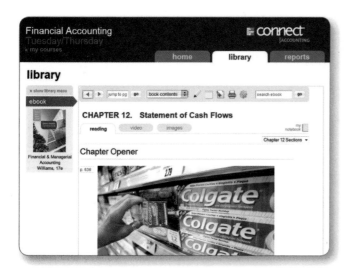

eBook

Connect Plus includes an eBook that allows you to share your notes with your students. Your students can insert and review their own notes, highlight the text, and search for specific information. Using an eBook with Connect Plus gives your students a complete digital solution that allows them to access their materials from any computer.

Tegrity

Make your classes available anytime, anywhere. With simple, one-click recording, students can search for a word or phrase and be taken to the exact place in your lecture that they need to review.

EASY TO USE

Learning Management System Integration

McGraw-Hill Campus is a one-stop teaching and learning experience available to use with any learning management system. McGraw-Hill Campus provides single sign-on to faculty and students for all McGraw-Hill material and technology from within the school website. McGraw-Hill Campus also allows instructors instant access to all supplements and teaching materials for all McGraw-Hill products.

Blackboard users also benefit from McGraw-Hill's industry-leading integration, providing single sign-on to access all Connect assignments and automatic feeding of assignment results to the Blackboard grade book.

The **Best** of **Both Worlds**

POWERFUL REPORTING

Connect generates comprehensive reports and graphs that provide instructors with an instant view of the performance of individual students, a specific section, or multiple sections. Since all content is mapped to learning objectives, Connect reporting is ideal for accreditation or other administrative documentation.

| At a Glance Insights | Assignment Results & Statistics Reports | Student Performance Reports | Item Analysis Reports | Category Analysis Reports | At-Risk Student Reports | LearnSmart Reports |

16TH EDITION

Financial Accounting

JAN R. WILLIAMS
University of Tennessee

SUSAN F. HAKA
Michigan State University

MARK S. BETTNER
Bucknell University

JOSEPH V. CARCELLO
University of Tennessee

Mc
Graw
Hill
Education

FINANCIAL ACCOUNTING, SIXTEENTH EDITION

Published by McGraw-Hill Education, 2 Penn Plaza, New York, NY 10121. Copyright © 2015 by McGraw-Hill Education. All rights reserved. Printed in the United States of America. Previous editions © 2012, 2010, and 2008. No part of this publication may be reproduced or distributed in any form or by any means, or stored in a database or retrieval system, without the prior written consent of McGraw-Hill Education, including, but not limited to, in any network or other electronic storage or transmission, or broadcast for distance learning.

Some ancillaries, including electronic and print components, may not be available to customers outside the United States.

This book is printed on acid-free paper.

1 2 3 4 5 6 7 8 9 0 DOW/DOW 1 0 9 8 7 6 5 4

ISBN 978-0-07-786238-1
MHID 0-07-786238-4

Senior Vice President, Products & Markets: *Kurt L. Strand*
Vice President, Content Production & Technology Services: *Kimberly Meriwether David*
Managing Director: *Tim Vertovec*
Executive Brand Manager: *Steve Schuetz*
Executive Director of Development: *Ann Torbert*
Development Editor: *Rebecca Mann*
Director of Digital Content: *Patricia Plumb*
Digital Development Editor: *Julie Hankins*
Senior Marketing Manager: *Kathleen Klehr*
Director, Content Production: *Terri Schiesl*
Content Project Manager: *Angela Norris*
Content Project Manager: *Brian Nacik*
Senior Buyer: *Michael R. McCormick*
Design: *Srdjan Savanovic*
Cover Image: © *Giorgio Fochesato/Getty Images*
Icon Images: © *Tom Grill/Getty Images (Internet);* © *Tom Grill/Getty Images (Financial Analysis and Decision Making);* © *Solomonkein/Shutterstock (International Case in Point);* © *Maksim Kabakou/Shutterstock (marginal notes icon)*
Content Licensing Specialist: *Joanne Mennemeier*
Typeface: *10/12 Times Roman*
Compositor: *Laserwords Private Limited*
Printer: *R. R. Donnelley*

All credits appearing on page or at the end of the book are considered to be an extension of the copyright page.

Library of Congress Cataloging-in-Publication Data

Williams, Jan R.
    Financial accounting / Jan R. Williams, University of Tennessee, Susan F. Haka, Michigan State University,
    Mark S. Bettner, Bucknell University, Joseph V. Carcello, University of Tennessee.
    —16th edition.
    pages cm
    Revised edition of: Financial accounting / Jan R. Williams . . . [et al.]. 15th ed.
    ISBN 978-0-07-786238-1 (alk. paper)—ISBN 0-07-786238-4 (alk. paper)
    1. Accounting. I. Title.
HF5636.W7254 2015
657—dc23   2013041567

The Internet addresses listed in the text were accurate at the time of publication. The inclusion of a website does not indicate an endorsement by the authors or McGraw-Hill Education, and McGraw-Hill Education does not guarantee the accuracy of the information presented at these sites.

www.mhhe.com

To Ben and Meg Wishart and Asher, Lainey, and Lucy Hunt, who have taught me the joys of being a grandfather.

—Jan R. Williams

For Cliff, Abi, and my mother, Fran.

—Susan F. Haka

To my parents, Fred and Marjorie.

—Mark S. Bettner

To Terri, Stephen, Karen, and Sarah, whose sacrifices enabled me to participate in writing this book. Thank you—I love you!

—Joseph V. Carcello

Jan R. Williams is Dean and Professor Emeritus of the College of Business Administration at the University of Tennessee—Knoxville, where he has been a faculty member since 1977. He received a BS degree from George Peabody College, an MBA from Baylor University, and a PhD from the University of Arkansas. He previously served on the faculties at the University of Georgia and Texas Tech University. A CPA in Tennessee and Arkansas, Dr. Williams is also the coauthor of three books and has published over 70 articles on issues of corporate financial reporting and accounting education. He served as president of the American Accounting Association in 1999–2000 and has been actively involved in Beta Alpha Psi, the Tennessee Society of CPAs, the American Institute of CPAs, and AACSB International—the Association to Advance Collegiate Schools of Business—the accrediting organization for business schools and accounting programs worldwide. He served as chair of the Board of Directors of AACSB International in 2011 through 2012. He retired from the University of Tennessee in 2013, and remains active in several business and accounting professional organizations.

Susan F. Haka is the Senior Associate Dean for Academic Affairs and Research in the Broad College of Business and the EY Professor of Accounting in the Department of Accounting and Information Systems at Michigan State University. Dr. Haka received her PhD from the University of Kansas and a master's degree in accounting from the University of Illinois. She served as president of the American Accounting Association in 2008–2009 and has previously served as president of the Management Accounting Section. Dr. Haka is active in editorial processes and has been editor of *Behavioral Research in Accounting* and an associate editor of *Journal of Management Accounting Research, Accounting Horizons, The International Journal of Accounting,* and *Contemporary Accounting Research.* Dr. Haka has been honored by Michigan State University with several teaching and research awards, including both the university-wide Teacher-Scholar and Distinguished Faculty awards. In 2012, Dr. Haka was honored with the Outstanding Accounting Educator Award from the American Accounting Association.

Mark S. Bettner is the Christian R. Lindback Chair of Accounting & Financial Management at Bucknell University. Dr. Bettner received his PhD in business administration from Texas Tech University and his MS in accounting from Virginia Tech University. In addition to his work on *Financial Accounting* and *Financial & Managerial Accounting,* he has written many ancillary materials, published in scholarly journals, and presented at academic and practitioner conferences. Professor Bettner is also on the editorial advisory boards of several academic journals, including the *International Journal of Accounting and Business Society* and the *International Journal of Business and Accounting,* and has served as a reviewer for several journals, including *Advances in Public Interest Accounting, Essays in Economics and Business History, Critical Perspectives on Accounting,* and *International Journal on Critical Accounting.* Professor Bettner also offers professional development courses for the Pennsylvania Bankers Association.

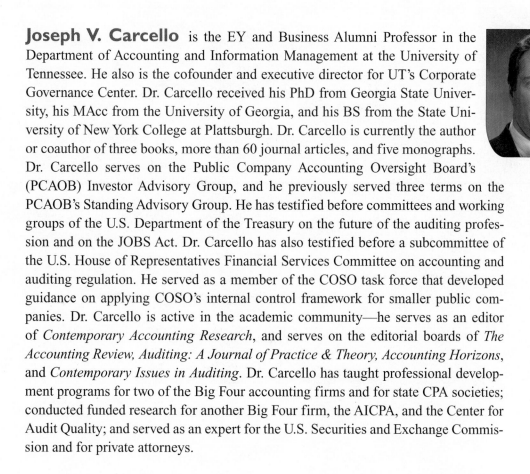

Joseph V. Carcello is the EY and Business Alumni Professor in the Department of Accounting and Information Management at the University of Tennessee. He also is the cofounder and executive director for UT's Corporate Governance Center. Dr. Carcello received his PhD from Georgia State University, his MAcc from the University of Georgia, and his BS from the State University of New York College at Plattsburgh. Dr. Carcello is currently the author or coauthor of three books, more than 60 journal articles, and five monographs. Dr. Carcello serves on the Public Company Accounting Oversight Board's (PCAOB) Investor Advisory Group, and he previously served three terms on the PCAOB's Standing Advisory Group. He has testified before committees and working groups of the U.S. Department of the Treasury on the future of the auditing profession and on the JOBS Act. Dr. Carcello has also testified before a subcommittee of the U.S. House of Representatives Financial Services Committee on accounting and auditing regulation. He served as a member of the COSO task force that developed guidance on applying COSO's internal control framework for smaller public companies. Dr. Carcello is active in the academic community—he serves as an editor of *Contemporary Accounting Research*, and serves on the editorial boards of *The Accounting Review, Auditing: A Journal of Practice & Theory, Accounting Horizons*, and *Contemporary Issues in Auditing*. Dr. Carcello has taught professional development programs for two of the Big Four accounting firms and for state CPA societies; conducted funded research for another Big Four firm, the AICPA, and the Center for Audit Quality; and served as an expert for the U.S. Securities and Exchange Commission and for private attorneys.

REACHING GREAT HEIGHTS BEGINS WITH A SOLID BASE

As our eyes are drawn upward to the skyline of great cities, it's important to remember that these impressive constructions are able to reach such heights only because their foundations are strong. In much the same way, being successful in the business world begins with fundamental courses like financial accounting. It is only when students have a firm grasp of concepts like the accounting cycle that they have a base on which to stand, a strong foundation on which to grow.

In this edition, as before, the Williams team has revised the text with a keen eye toward the principle of helping students establish the foundation they will need for future success in business. However, through new coverage of International Financial Reporting Standards and a revised globalization chapter, the Williams book also introduces students to larger themes and evolving concerns. This dual emphasis allows students to keep their eyes trained upward even as they become solidly grounded in accounting fundamentals.

The Williams book continues to rest on a bedrock of four key components:

Balanced Coverage. The 16th edition of Williams provides the most balanced coverage of financial topics on the market. By giving equal weight to financial topics, the authors emphasize the need for a strong foundation in accounting.

> "This is a **well balanced textbook** that encompasses many issues, yet provides them in a precise, readable, and orderly fashion to students. The extent of the real-world examples makes this edition **clearly a superior choice.**"
>
> *Hossein Noorian,*
> *Wentworth Institute*

> "**Excellent book!** Explains difficult subjects in easy-to-understand terms."
>
> *Naser Kamleh, Wallace*
> *Community College*

Clear Accounting Cycle Presentation. In the first five chapters of *Financial Accounting,* the authors present the Accounting Cycle in a clear, graphically interesting four-step process. Central to this presentation is the dedication of three successive chapters to three key components of the cycle: recording entries (Chapter 3), adjusting entries (Chapter 4), and closing entries (Chapter 5). The Williams team places easy-to-read margin notes explaining each equation used in particular journal entries.

Student Motivation. The Williams team has put together a market-leading student package that will not only motivate your students, but help you see greater retention rates in your accounting courses. Vital pieces of technology supplement the core curriculum covered in the book: McGraw-Hill *Connect Accounting* uses end-of-chapter material pulled directly from the textbook to create static and algorithmic questions that can be used for homework and practice tests; and the Online Learning Center provides supplemental tools for both students and instructors.

> "This textbook is current and very interactive. It brings in excellent "real-world" applications for the students to use in applying the concepts. It has **excellent student and instructor resources.** Some of the resources would be especially valuable for instructors teaching online."
>
> *Karen Mozingo, Pitt*
> *Community College*

> "The text is excellent. **I wish the texts had been this well written** when I was a student!"
>
> *Mark Anderson, Bob Jones University*

Problem-Solving Skills. *Financial Accounting* challenges your students to think about real-world situations and put themselves in the role of the decision maker through Case in Point, Your Turn, and Ethics, Fraud, & Corporate Governance boxes. Students reference the Home Depot Financial Statements—included in the text as an appendix—to further hone problem-solving skills by evaluating real world financial data. The authors show a keen attention to detail when creating high-quality end-of-chapter material, such as the Critical Thinking Cases and Problems, ensuring that all homework is tied directly back to chapter learning objectives.

How Does **Williams** Help Students
Step-by-Step Process for the Accounting Cycle

Financial Accounting was the FIRST text to illustrate Balance Sheet and Income Statement transactions using the four-step process described below. This hallmark coverage has been further revised and refined in the 16th edition.

The Williams team breaks down the Accounting Cycle into three full chapters to help students absorb and understand this material: recording entries (Chapter 3), adjusting entries (Chapter 4), and closing entries (Chapter 5). Transactions are demonstrated visually to help students conquer recording transactions by showing the **four steps in the process:**

1 **Analysis**—shows which accounts are recorded with an increase/decrease.

2 **Debit/Credit Rules**—helps students to remember whether the account should be debited/credited.

3 **Journal Entry**—shows the result of the two previous steps.

4 **Ledger T-Accounts**—shows students what was recorded and where.

The Williams team puts the Accounting Equation **(A = L + OE)** in the margin by transaction illustrations to show students the big picture!

Build a Strong Foundation?
Robust End-of-Chapter Material

Brief Exercises supplement the exercises with shorter, single-concept exercises that test the basic concepts of each chapter. These brief exercises give instructors more flexibility in their homework assignments.

An Alternate Problem Set provides students with even more practice on important concepts.

Six **Comprehensive Problems**, ranging from two to five pages in length, present students with real-world scenarios and challenge them to apply what they've learned in the chapters leading up to them.

Defined **Key Terms** and **Self-Test Questions** review and reinforce chapter material.

Demonstration Problems and their solutions allow students to test their knowledge of key points in the chapters.

Critical Thinking Cases and **Problems** put students' analytical skills to the test by having them think critically about key concepts from the chapter and apply them to business decisions. **TWO** sets of Problems and a full set of Exercises in EACH chapter give *Financial Accounting* the edge in homework materials.

Ethics Cases in *each* chapter challenge students to explore the ethical impact of decisions made in business.

The **2012 Home Depot Financial Statements** are included in Appendix A. Students are referred to key aspects of the 10-K in the text material and in end-of-chapter material to illustrate actual business applications of chapter concepts.

Connect Accounting System

Ethical

Group Activities

Writing

Internet

International

The Williams Pedagogy Helps

➤ High-profile companies frame each chapter discussion through the use of dynamic **CHAPTER OPENER** vignettes. Students learn to frame the chapter's topic in a real-world scenario.

▼ **YOUR TURN** boxes challenge students with ethically demanding situations. They must apply what they've learned in the text to situations faced by investors, creditors, and managers in the real world.

 YOUR TURN | You as a Financial Advisor

Assume that you are the financial advisor for a recently retired investor. Your client wants to invest her savings in such a way as to receive a stable stream of cash flow every year throughout her retirement. She has expressed concern to you regarding the volatility of long-term bond prices when interest rates fluctuate.

If your client invests her savings in a variety of long-term bonds and holds these bonds until maturity, will interest rate fluctuations affect her annual cash flow during her retirement years?

(See our comments on the Online Learning Center website.)

CHAPTER 2

Basic Financial Statements

AFTER STUDYING THIS CHAPTER, YOU SHOULD BE ABLE TO:

Learning Objectives

LO2-1 Explain the nature and general purposes of financial statements.

LO2-2 Explain certain accounting principles that are important for an understanding of financial statements and how professional judgment by accountants may affect the application of those principles.

LO2-3 Demonstrate how certain business transactions affect the elements of the accounting equation: Assets = Liabilities + Owners' Equity.

LO2-4 Explain how the statement of financial position, often referred to as the balance sheet, is an expansion of the basic accounting equation.

LO2-5 Explain how the income statement reports an enterprise's financial performance for a period of time in terms of the relationship of revenues and expenses.

LO2-6 Explain how the statement of cash flows presents the change in cash for a period of time in terms of the company's operating, investing, and financing activities.

LO2-7 Explain how the statement of financial position (balance sheet), income statement, and statement of cash flows relate to each other.

LO2-8 Explain common forms of business ownership—sole proprietorship, partnership, and corporation—and demonstrate how they differ in terms of their statements of financial position.

LO2-9 Discuss the importance of financial statements to a company and its investors and creditors and why management may take steps to improve the appearance of the company in its financial statements.

> "Lots of eye appeal and in-depth coverage. **Students will love it.**"
>
> *James Specht, Concordia College*

➤ **EXHIBITS** illustrate key concepts in the text.

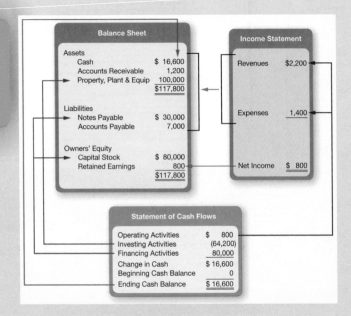

Students Reach Great Heights

© Tony Avelar/Bloomberg via Getty Images

INTEL

Intel was created in 1968 with a vision of providing semi-conductor memory products. By 1971, the company introduced the world's first microprocessor. Today Intel supplies the computing and communications industries with chips, boards, and systems building blocks that are the ingredients of computers and servers as well as networking and communications products. These industries use Intel's products to create advanced computing and communications systems. Intel states that its mission is to be the preeminent building block supplier in the worldwide Internet economy.

Technology-based companies like Intel operate in highly competitive markets and continuously intro-duce new products. In a recent corporate information communication on the company's website, manage-ment explains the importance of meeting the needs of customers: "Our goal is to be the preeminent provider of semiconductor chips and platforms for the world-wide digital economy . . . We offer products at various levels of integration, to allow our customers flexibility in creating computing and communications systems. The substantial majority of our revenue is from the sale of microprocessors and chipsets."

Modern-day historians agree that we have moved from the industrial age to the information age. Compa-nies like Intel, Microsoft, and Cisco Systems are major players in this transformation of business. Information-age companies rely more heavily on intellectual capital, research and development, and other intangibles that were less important for companies whose focus was heavy manufacturing or, even earlier in our history, pri-marily agricultural. ∎

"Williams is a great text overall. It provides excellent and accurate coverage of the accounting principles curriculum. Students like it better than any other text I have used. A few years ago I was in a situation where I had to use a different text, since I took over a class for another teacher at the last minute. Students were getting the Williams text on their own and I saw immediate improvement in their understanding and grades across the board. Williams comes through again and again, where other texts fall hopelessly short."

Malcolm E White, Columbia College

CASE IN POINT

© Digital Vision/Alamy

How long does a building last? For pur-poses of computing depreciation expense, most companies estimate about 30 or 40 years. Yet the Empire State Building was built in 1931, and it's not likely to be torn down anytime soon. As you might guess, it often is difficult to estimate in advance just how long depreciable assets may remain in use.

▲ **CASE IN POINT** boxes link accounting concepts in the chapter to their use in the real world. These examples often present an international scenario to expose students to accounting practices around the world.

Ethics, Fraud, & Corporate Governance

A major outgrowth from the business failures amid allega-tions of fraudulent financial reporting discussed in the last chapter was the passage of the Sarbanes-Oxley Act of 2002. This Act was signed into law by President George W. Bush on July 30, 2002. The Sarbanes-Oxley Act (hereafter SOX or the Act) is generally viewed as the most far-reaching piece of securities legislation since the original Securities Acts were passed in the 1930s.

One of the major requirements of this legislation is for CEOs and CFOs to certify the accuracy of their company's financial statements. The CEOs and CFOs of all public com-panies must certify on an annual and quarterly basis that they (1) have reviewed their company's financial statements, (2) are not aware of any error or omission that would make the financial statements misleading, and (3) believe that the financial statements fairly present in all material respects the company's financial condition (balance sheet) and results of operations (income statement). There is some evidence that this certification requirement is affecting corporate behavior. For example, a former CFO of HealthSouth (Weston Smith, shown to the right) contacted federal authorities about the

© Gary Tramontina/Bloomberg via Getty Images

massive (alleged) accounting fraud at that company because he was not willing to certify that HealthSouth's financial statements were materially accurate.

◀ **ETHICS, FRAUD, & CORPORATE GOVER-NANCE** boxes discuss the accounting scandals of recent years that have sparked such comprehensive legis-lation as Sarbanes-Oxley. The inclusion of EFCG boxes in each chapter offers instructors the opportunity to bring complex accounting and ethical issues into the classroom.

Leading Technology Extends Learning

MCGRAW-HILL *CONNECT ACCOUNTING*

Get *Connect Accounting*. Get Results.

McGraw-Hill *Connect Accounting* is a digital teaching and learning environment that gives students the means to better connect with their coursework, with their instructors, and with the important concepts that they will need to know for success now and in the future. With *Connect Accounting*, instructors can deliver assignments, quizzes, and tests easily online. Students can practice important skills at their own pace and on their own schedule.

Online Assignments

Connect Accounting helps students learn more efficiently by providing feedback and practice material when they need it, where they need it. *Connect Accounting* grades homework automatically and gives immediate feedback on any questions students may have missed.

Intelligent Response Technology (IRT)

IRT is a redesigned student interface for our end-of-chapter assessment content. The benefits include improved answer acceptance to reduce students' frustration with formatting issues (such as rounding); and a general journal application that looks and feels more like you would find in a general ledger software package.

Student Library

The *Connect Accounting* Student Library gives students access to additional resources such as recorded lectures, online practice materials, an eBook, and more.

Beyond the Classroom

MCGRAW-HILL *CONNECT ACCOUNTING* FEATURES

Connect Accounting offers a number of powerful tools and features to make managing assignments easier, so faculty can spend more time teaching.

Simple Assignment Management and Smart Grading

With *Connect Accounting*, creating assignments is easier than ever, so instructors can spend more time teaching and less time managing.

- Create and deliver assignments easily with selectable end-of-chapter questions and Test Bank items.
- Go paperless with the eBook and online submission and grading of student assignments.
- Have assignments scored automatically, giving students immediate feedback on their work and side-by-side comparisons with correct answers.
- Access and review each response; manually change grades or leave comments for students to review.
- Reinforce classroom concepts with practice tests and instant quizzes.

Student Reporting

Connect Accounting keeps instructors informed about how each student, section, and class is performing, allowing for more productive use of lecture and office hours. The progress-tracking function enables you to:

- View scored work immediately and track individual or group performance with assignment and grade reports.
- Access an instant view of student or class performance relative to learning objectives.
- Collect data and generate reports required by many accreditation organizations, such as AACSB and AICPA.

Instructor Library

The *Connect Accounting* Instructor Library is a repository for additional resources to improve student engagement in and out of class. You can select and use any asset that enhances your lecture. The *Connect Accounting* Instructor Library includes access to the eBook version of the text, slide presentations, Solutions Manual, Instructor's Manual, and Test Bank. The *Connect Accounting* Instructor Library also allows you to upload your own files.

MCGRAW-HILL *CONNECT PLUS ACCOUNTING*

 McGraw-Hill reinvents the textbook learning experience for the modern student with *Connect Plus Accounting*. A seamless integration of an eBook and *Connect Accounting*, *Connect Plus Accounting* provides all of the *Connect Accounting* features plus the following:

- An integrated eBook, allowing for anytime, anywhere access to the textbook.
- Media-rich capabilities like highlighting and sharing notes.
- Dynamic links between the problems or questions you assign to your students and the location in the eBook where that concept is covered.
- A powerful search function to pinpoint key concepts for review.

In short, *Connect Plus Accounting* offers students powerful tools and features that optimize their time and energy, enabling them to focus on learning.

For more information about *Connect Plus Accounting*, go to www.mcgrawhillconnect.com, or contact your local McGraw-Hill sales representative.

TEGRITY CAMPUS: LECTURES 24/7

Tegrity Campus is a service that makes class time available 24/7 by automatically capturing every lecture. With a simple one-click start-and-stop process, you capture all computer screens and corresponding audio in a format that is easily searchable, frame by frame. Students can replay any part of any class with easy-to-use browser-based viewing on a PC, Mac, iPod, or other mobile device.

Educators know that the more students can see, hear, and experience class resources, the better they learn. In fact, studies prove it. Tegrity Campus's unique search feature helps students efficiently find what they need, when they need it, across an entire semester of class recordings. Help turn your students' study time into learning moments immediately supported by your lecture. With Tegrity Campus, you also increase intent listening and class participation by easing students' concerns about note-taking. Tegrity Campus will make it more likely you will see students' faces, not the tops of their heads.

To learn more about Tegrity, watch a 2-minute Flash demo at http://tegritycampus.mhhe.com.

> *Students like the flexibility that Connect offers . . . They can complete their work and catch up on lectures anytime and anywhere.*
>
> —*Professor Lisa McKinney, M.T.A., CPA, University of Alabama*

MCGRAW-HILL CAMPUS

 McGraw-Hill Campus™ is a new one-stop teaching and learning experience available to users of any learning management system. This institutional service allows faculty and students to enjoy single sign-on (SSO) access to all McGraw-Hill Higher Education materials, including the award-winning McGraw-Hill *Connect* platform, directly from within the institution's website. McGraw-Hill Campus provides faculty with instant access to teaching materials (e.g., eTextbooks, Test Banks, PowerPoint slides, animations, and learning objects), allowing them to browse, search, and use any ancillary content in our vast library. Students enjoy SSO access to a variety of free products (e.g., quizzes, flash cards, and presentations) and subscription-based products (e.g., McGraw-Hill *Connect*). With McGraw-Hill Campus, faculty and students will never need to create another account to access McGraw-Hill products and services.

Custom Publishing through Create

McGraw-Hill Create™ is a self-service website that allows instructors to create custom course materials by drawing upon McGraw-Hill's comprehensive cross-disciplinary content. Instructors can add their own content quickly and easily and tap into other rights-secured third party sources as well, then arrange the content in a way that makes the most sense for their course. Instructors can even personalize their book with the course name and information and choose the best format for their students—color print, black-and-white print, or an eBook.

Through Create, instructors can

- Select and arrange the content in a way that makes the most sense for their course.
- Combine material from different sources and even upload their own content.
- Choose the best format for their students—print or eBook.
- Edit and update their course materials as often as they'd like.

Begin creating now at www.mcgrawhillcreate.com.

 COURSESMART

Learn Smart. Choose Smart.

CourseSmart is a way for faculty to find and review eTextbooks. It's also a great option for students who are interested in accessing their course materials digitally and saving money.

CourseSmart offers thousands of the most commonly adopted textbooks across hundreds of courses from a wide variety of higher education publishers. It is the only place for faculty to review and compare the full text of a textbook online, providing immediate access without the environmental impact of requesting a print exam copy.

With the CourseSmart eTextbook, students can save up to 45 percent off the cost of a print book, reduce their impact on the environment, and access powerful web tools for learning. CourseSmart is an online eTextbook, which means users access and view their textbook online when connected to the Internet. Students can also print sections of the book for maximum portability. CourseSmart eTextbooks are available in one standard online reader with full text search, notes and highlighting, and e-mail tools for sharing notes between classmates. For more information on CourseSmart, go to www.coursesmart.com.

Supplements for *Financial Accounting*

A strong foundation needs support.

Financial Accounting authors Williams, Haka, Bettner, and Carcello know that every component of the learning package must be integrated and supported by strong ancillaries. Instructors and students have a wealth of material at their fingertips to help make the most of a challenging course in accounting.

Online Learning Center (OLC)
www.mhhe.com/williamsfinancial16e

The Online Learning Center (OLC) that accompanies *Financial Accounting* provides a wealth of extra material for both instructors and students. With content specific to each chapter of the book, the Williams OLC doesn't require any building or maintenance on your part.

A secure **Instructor Resource Center** stores your essential course materials to save you prep time before class. The **Instructor's Manual, Solutions Manual, PowerPoint presentations,** and **Testbank** are now just a couple of clicks away.

The OLC website also serves as a doorway to McGraw-Hill's other technology solutions.

Instructor's Resource Manual
Available on the OLC

This manual provides for each chapter: (1) a chapter summary detailing what has changed, new problems that have been added, and author suggestions on how to incorporate new material; (2) brief topical outline; (3) sample "10-minute quizzes" designed to test the basic concepts in each chapter; and (4) suggestions for group, Internet, and other class exercises to supplement the material in the book.

Solutions Manual
Available on the OLC

The Solutions Manual includes detailed solutions for every question, exercise, problem, and case in the text.

Testbank
Available on the OLC

This comprehensive Testbank contains over 3,000 problems and true/false, multiple-choice, and essay questions. Included in this edition are written explanations to the solutions—making it easier than ever for you to see where students have gone wrong in their calculations.

Assurance of Learning Ready

Many educational institutions today are focused on the notion of assurance of learning, an important element of some accreditation standards. *Financial Accounting,* 16e, is designed specifically to support your assurance of learning initiatives with a simple, yet powerful, solution.

Each testbank question for *Financial Accounting,* 16e, maps to a specific chapter learning outcome/objective listed in the text. You can use our testbank software, *EZ Test,* and *EZ Test Online,* or in *Connect Accounting* to easily query for learning outcomes/objectives that directly relate to the learning objectives for your course. You can then use the reporting features of *EZ Test* or in *Connect Accounting* to aggregate student results similar fashion, making the collection and presentation of assurance of learning data simple and easy.

AACSB Statement

McGraw-Hill Education is a proud corporate member of AACSB International. Understanding the importance and value of AACSB accreditation, *Financial Accounting,* 16e, recognizes the curricula guidelines detailed in AACSB standards for business accreditation by connecting selected questions in the text and testbank to six of the general knowledge and skill guidelines found in the AACSB standards.

The statements contained in *Financial Accounting,* 16e, are provided only as a guide for the users of this text. The AACSB leaves content coverage and assessment within the purview of individual schools, the mission of the school, and the faculty. While *Financial Accounting,* 16e, and its teaching package make no claim of any specific AACSB qualification or evaluation, we have, within *Financial Accounting,* 16e, labeled selected questions according to six of the general knowledge and skills areas.

STUDENT SUPPLEMENTS

Online Learning Center (OLC)
www.mhhe.com/williamsfinancial16e

The OLC is full of resources for students, including: Online Quizzes and PowerPoint Presentations.

What's New about the 16th Edition of *Financial Accounting?*

The following list of revisions is a testament to the enthusiastic response of dozens of reviewers who contributed their considerable expertise. In doing so they have helped make the 16th edition of *Financial Accounting* the best book of its kind.

Chapter 1:

- New chapter opener using Hewlett-Packard
- Updated Case in Point using Sony
- Briefly covered the new COSO framework on internal control (*Internal Control–Integrated Framework: 2013*)
- Briefly covered the SEC Report on incorporating IFRS into the financial reporting system for U.S. public companies
- Briefly discussed the managerial role of the chief accounting officer
- Extended the discussion of the importance of accounting for non-accounting majors in response to reviewer feedback
- Revised end-of-chapter material

Chapter 2:

- Updated chapter opener to include new data for Intel
- Added an explanation about the order in which assets are presented in the balance sheet and then revised the EOC material accordingly. This is a small but important change and one triggered by user input
- Revised end-of-chapter material

Chapter 3:

- Updated chapter opener to include new data for Kraft Foods Group, Inc.
- Updated in-chapter illustration to include new data for Walmart
- Updated and streamlined Ethics, Fraud, & Corporate Governance boxed feature
- Revised end-of-chapter material

Chapter 4:

- New chapter opener using Royal Caribbean Cruises, LTD.
- Updated in-chapter illustration to include new data for the New York Times
- Updated two Case in Point boxes
- Revised end-of-chapter material

Chapter 5:

- Updated chapter opener to include new data for Best Buy

- Incorporated a number of suggestions from adopters, including:
  - Providing a more detailed discussion of the closing process
  - Better articulating the relationship between the income statement and balance sheet
  - Introducing and briefly explaining a classified balance sheet
- Revised end-of-chapter material

Chapter 6:

- Updated chapter opener to include new data for Saks, Inc.
- Brief coverage of the SEC whistleblower "bounty" program under the Dodd-Frank Act in the EFCG case
- Revised end-of-chapter material

Chapter 7:

- New chapter opener using Apple, Inc.
- Wrote a new Ethics, Fraud, and Corporate Governance case based on SEC AAER #2673
- Added a new learning objective covering internal controls over accounts receivable based on reviewer suggestion
- Wrote a new International Case in Point based on IFRS No. 9
- Revised end-of-chapter material

Chapter 8:

- New chapter opener using Belk, Inc.
- Target illustration in text updated
- Revised end-of-chapter material including updating and replacing real company data
- Comprehensive Problem 2 refreshed

Chapter 9:

- Updated chapter opener to include new data for United Parcel Service
- Updated references to the financial statements of all real companies
- Revised end-of-chapter material

Chapter 10:

- New chapter opener using Procter & Gamble Company

- Significant revision within the chapter, both text and end-of-chapter material, to more reasonable (i.e., lower) interest rates to better reflect our current and projected economic climate
- Revised end-of-chapter material

Chapter 11:

- Updated chapter opener to include new data for Target Corporation
- Updated all real company references
- Revised end-of-chapter material

Chapter 12:

- New chapter opener using Colgate-Palmolive
- Briefly covered the new FASB standard on the reporting of comprehensive income, requiring either a combined statement of Income and Comprehensive Income or separate statements of Income and Comprehensive Income
- Revised end-of-chapter material

Chapter 13:

- New chapter opener using Pepsi Co.
- Revised end-of-chapter material

Chapter 14:

- Updated chapter opener to include new data for Johnson & Johnson
- Updated all real company references
- Revised end-of-chapter material

Chapter 15:

- Updated chapter opener on IASB and IFRS
- Updated Exhibit 15-1 to include changes of the number of multinational companies
- Updated Exhibits 15-4 through 15-7 for international changes and exchange rates
- Replaced Ethics, Fraud, & Corrupt Governance for more recent Foreign Corrupt Practices Act example
- Changed demonstration problem with more current exchange rates
- Revised end-of-chapter material

We are grateful . . .

We would like to acknowledge the following individuals for their help in developing some of the text's supplements: Barbara Muller, Arizona State University; LuAnn Bean, Florida Technical Institute; Helen Roybark, Radford University; Teri Zuccaro, Clarke University; Teressa Farough; and the team at ANSR Source.

We appreciate the expert attention given to this project by the staff at McGraw-Hill Education, especially Tim Vertovec, Managing Director; Steve Schuetz, Executive Brand Manager; Rebecca Mann, Development Editor; Julie Hankins, Digital Development Editor; Michelle Nolte, Senior Marketing Manager; Kathleen Klehr, Senior Marketing Manager; Angela Norris, Content Project Manager; Brian Nacik, Content Project Manager; Joanne Mennemeier, Content Licensing Specialist; Srdjan Savanovic, Senior Designer; and Michael McCormick, Senior Buyer.

Sincerely,

Jan R. Williams, Susan F. Haka, Mark S. Bettner, and Joseph V. Carcello

Acknowledgments

Many of our colleagues reviewed *Financial Accounting*. Through their time and effort, we are able to continually improve and update the book to meet the needs of students and professors. We sincerely thank each of you for your valuable time and suggestions.

Editorial Review Board

Mark Anderson, *Southern Polytechnic State University*

Cynthia Ash, *Davenport University*

Marjorie Ashton, *Truckee Meadows Community College*

Elenito Ayuyao, *Los Angeles City College*

Walter Baggett, *Manhattan College*

Sharla Bailey, *Southwest Baptist University*

Jill Bale, *Doane College*

Scott Barhight, *Northampton County Area Community College*

William Barze, *St. Petersburg Junior College*

John Bayles, *Oakton Community College*

Janet Becker, *University of Pittsburg*

Rob Beebe, *Morrisville State College*

Kim Belden, *Daytona Beach Community College*

Gerard Berardino, *Community College of Allegheny County*

Teri Bernstein, *Santa Monica College*

Dan Biagi, *Walla Walla Community College*

Margaret Black, *San Jacinto College North*

Cynthia Bolt-Lee, *The Citadel*

Susan Borkowski, *La Salle University*

Sue Van Boven, *Paradise Valley Community College*

Nancy Boyd, *Middle Tennessee State University*

Benoit Boyer, *Sacred Heart University*

Sallie Branscom, *Virginia Western Community College*

Russell Bresslauer, *Chabot College*

Nat R. Briscoe, *Northwestern State University*

R. E. Bryson, *University of Alabama*

Bryan Burks, *Harding University*

Priscilla Burnaby, *Bentley College*

Sandra Byrd, *Missouri State University*

Loring Carlson, *Western New England College*

Brenda Catchings, *Augusta Technical College*

James J. Chimenti, *Jamestown Community College*

Steven L. Christian, *Jackson Community College*

David Chu, *College of the Holy Cross*

Stanley Chu, *Borough Manhattan Community College*

Carol Collinsworth, *University of Texas at Brownsville*

Christie L. Comunale, *Long Island University*

Jennie Conn, *Louisiana State University–Alexandria*

Joan Cook, *Milwaukee Area Technical College*

William Cravey, *Jersey City State College*

Chris Crosby, *York Technical College*

Christine M. Cross, *James A. Rhodes State College*

Marcia Croteau, *University of Maryland Baltimore County*

Ana M. Cruz, *Miami–Dade Community College*

Brian Curtis, *Raritan Valley Community College*

Steve Czarsty, *Mary Washington College*

Robert Daily, *El Camino College*

Anthony Daly-Leonard, *Delaware County Community College*

Judy Daulton, *Piedmont Technical College*

Amy David, *Queens College*

Larry Davis, *Southwest Virginia County College*

Mary B. Davis, *University of Maryland Baltimore County*

Scott Davis, *High Point University*

Vaun Day, *Central Arizona College*

Keren H. Deal, *Auburn University*

Laura DeLaune, *Louisiana State University–Baton Rouge*

Victoria Doby, *Villa Julie College*

Carlton Donchess, *Bridgewater State College*

Jim Dougher, *DeVry University*

Steve Driver, *Horry–Georgetown Tech*

Pamela Druger, *Augustana College*

Anita Ellzey, *Hartford Community College*

Emmanuel Emenyonu, *Sacred Heart University*

David Erlach, *CUNY–Queens College*

Paul Everson, *Northern State University*

Kel-Ann S. Eyler, *Brenau University*

Carla Feinson, *Bethune–Cookman College*

Calvin Fink, *Daytona Beach Community College*

Brother Gerald Fitzgerald, *LaSalle University*

Ralph Fritsch, *Midwestern State University*

Mark Fronke, *Cerritos College*

Mike Fujita, *Leeward Community College*

John Gabelman, *Columbus State Community College*

Mary Lou Gamma, *East Tennessee State University*

Peter Gilbert, *Thomas College*

Tony Greig, *Purdue University–West Lafayette*

Betty Habiger, *New Mexico State University at Grants*

Penny Hanes, *Mercyhurst College*

Richard Hanna, *Ferris State University*

Stephen Hano, *Rockland Community College*

Heidi Hansel, *Kirkwood Community College*

MAJ Charles V. Hardenbergh, *Virginia Military Institute*

Sara Harris, *Arapahoe Community College*

Carolyn J. Hays, *Mt. San Jacinto College*

Lyle Hicks, *Danville Area Community College*

Jeannelou Hodgens, *Florence–Darlington Technical College*

Merrily Hoffman, *San Jacinto College Central*

Michael Holland, *Valdosta State University*

Mary L. Hollars, *Vincennes University*

Patricia H. Holmes, *Des Moines Areo Community College*

Michael Holt, *Eastern Nazarene College*

Evelyn Honaker, *Walters State Community College*

Steven Hornik, *University of Central Florida*

Christine Irujo, *Westfield State College*

Gregory Iwaniuk, *Lake Michigan College*

Jeff Jackson, *San Jacinto College Central*

Dave Jensen, *Bucknell University*

Leo Jubb, *Essex Community College*

David Junnola, *Eastern Michigan University*

Jeffrey Kahn, *Woodbury University*

Naser Kamleh, *Wallace Community College*

Khondkar Karim, *Monmouth University*

James Kennedy, *Texas A&M University*

Jane Kingston, *Piedmont Virginia Community College*

Carol Klinger, *Queens College of CUNY*

Ed Knudson, *Linn Benton Community College*

Samuel Kohn, *Empire State College*

Charles Konkol, *University of Wisconsin–Milwaukee*

Raymond Krasniewski, *Ohio State University*

Tara Laken, *Joliet Junior College*

Rosemary Lanahan, *Schenectady County Community College*

David Lardie, *Tunxis Community College*

Bill Lasher, *Jamestown Community College*

Dr. Martin Lecker, *Rockland Community College*

Suk Jun Lee, *Chapman University*

Adena Lejune, *Louisiana State University*

Annette M. Leps, *Goucher College*

Eric Lewis, *Union College*

Ralph Lindeman, *Kent State University*

Philip Little, *Western Carolina University*

Susan Logorda, *Lehigh Carbon Community College*

J. Thomas Love, *Walters State Community College*

Don Lucy, *Indian River Community College*

Marie Main, *Columbia College–Marysville*

Linda L. Mallory, *Central Virginia Community College*

Ken Mark, *Kansas City Kansas Community College*

Dewey Martin, *Husson College*

Nicholas Marudas, *Auburn University Montgomery*

Terri Meta, *Seminole Community College*

Josie Miller, *Mercer Community College*

Merrill Moore, *Delaware Tech & Community College*

Michelle Moshier, *University at Albany*

Deborah Most, *Dutchess Community College*

Haim Mozes, *Fordham University*

Karen Mozingo, *Pitt Community College*

Tom Nagle, *Northland Pioneer College*

Hossein Noorian, *Wentworth Institute of Technology*

Frank Olive, *Nicholas College*

Bruce Oliver, *Rochester Institute of Technology*

Rudy Ordonez, *LA Mission College*

Ginger Parker, *Creighton University*

Yvonne Phang, *Borough of Manhattan Community College*

Timothy Prindle, *Des Moines Area Community College*

Matthew B. Probst, *Ivy Tech Community College*

Michael Prockton, *Finger Lakes Community College*

Holly Ratwani, *Bridgewater College*

Chris Rawlings, *Bob Jones University*

Gary Reynolds, *Ozard Technical College*

Laura Rickett, *Kent State University*

Renee Rigoni, *Monroe Community College*

Earl Roberts, *Delaware Tech & Community College*

Julie Rosenblatt, *Delaware Tech & Community College*

Bob Rothenberg, *SUNY–Oneonta*

Victoria Rymer, *University of Maryland*

Benjamin L. Sadler, *Miami–Dade Community College*

Francis A. Sakiey, *Mercer County Community College*

Marcia Sandvold, *Des Moines Area Community College*

Richard Sarkisian, *Camden County College*

Mary Jane Sauceda, *University of Texas at Brownsville*

Linda Schain, *Hofstra University*

Lauran Schmid, *University of Texas at Brownsville*

Mike Schoderbek, *Rutgers University–New Brunswick*

Monica Seiler, *Queensborough Community College*

Joseph W. Sejnoha, *Mount Mary College*

Randall Serrett, *University of Houston–Downtown*

Rajewshwar D. Sharma, *Livingstone College*

Carlo Silvestini, *Gwynedd–Mercy College*

Kimberly D. Smith, *County College of Morris*

Warren Smock, *Ivy Tech Community College*

James Specht, *Concordia College–Moorhead*

Stan Stanley, *Skagit Valley College*

Jim Stanton, *Mira Costa College*

Robert Stilson, *CUNY*

Carolyn Strickler, *Ohlone College*

Barbara Sturdevant, *SUNY*

Gene Sullivan, *Liberty University and Central Virginia Community College*

Mary Ann Swindlehurst, *Carroll Community College*

Larry Tartaglino, *Cabrillo College*

Martin Taylor, *University of Texas at Arlington*

Anne Tippett, *Tarrant County College South*

Bruce Toews, *Walla Walla College*

Cynthia Tomes, *Des Moines Area Community College*

Robin D. Turner, *Rowan–Cabarrus Community College*

Don Van Gieson, *Kapiolani Community College*

Marcia R. Veit, *University of Central Florida*

Shane Warrick, *Southern Arkansas University*

Dr. Michael P. Watters, *Henderson State University*

Malcolm White, *Columbia College–Marysville*

Lisa Wilhite, CPA, *Bevill State Community College*

Andy Williams, *Edmonds Community College*

Harold Wilson, *Middle Tennessee State University*

Steve Willits, *Bucknell University*

Michael Yampuler, *University of Houston*

Teri Yohn, *Georgetown University*

Brief Contents

1 Accounting: Information for Decision Making 2
2 Basic Financial Statements 38
3 The Accounting Cycle: Capturing Economic Events 86
4 The Accounting Cycle: Accruals and Deferrals 140
5 The Accounting Cycle: Reporting Financial Results 192

   COMPREHENSIVE PROBLEM 1: Susquehanna Equipment Rentals 243

6 Merchandising Activities 246
7 Financial Assets 288
8 Inventories and the Cost of Goods Sold 340

   COMPREHENSIVE PROBLEM 2: Music-Is-Us, Inc. 383

9 Plant and Intangible Assets 386
10 Liabilities 430
11 Stockholders' Equity: Paid-In Capital 484

   COMPREHENSIVE PROBLEM 3: Springdale Retail, Inc. 521

12 Income and Changes in Retained Earnings 522
13 Statement of Cash Flows 564
14 Financial Statement Analysis 622

   COMPREHENSIVE PROBLEM 4: Home Depot, Inc. 682

15 Global Business and Accounting 684

   APPENDIX A: Home Depot 2012 Financial Statements . . . . A
   APPENDIX B: The Time Value of Money: Future Amounts and Present Values . . . . B
   INDEX I

Contents

1 ACCOUNTING: INFORMATION FOR DECISION MAKING

Accounting Information: A Means to an End   **4**
Accounting from a User's Perspective   5
Types of Accounting Information   5

Accounting Systems   **6**
Determining Information Needs   7
The Cost of Producing Accounting Information   8
Basic Functions of an Accounting System   8
Who Designs and Installs Accounting Systems?   8
Components of Internal Control   8

Financial Accounting Information   **10**
External Users of Accounting Information   10
Objectives of External Financial Reporting   10
Characteristics of Externally Reported Information   13

Management Accounting Information   **14**
Users of Internal Accounting Information   14
Objectives of Management Accounting Information   15
Characteristics of Management Accounting Information   16

Integrity of Accounting Information   **17**
Institutional Features   17
Professional Organizations   20
Competence, Judgment, and Ethical Behavior   22

Careers in Accounting   **24**
Public Accounting   24
Management Accounting   25
Governmental Accounting   25
Accounting Education   26
What about Bookkeeping?   26
Accounting as a Stepping-Stone   26
But What about Me? I'm Not an Accounting Major   26

Ethics, Fraud, & Corporate Governance   **27**
Concluding Remarks   **27**
End-of-Chapter Review   **29**
Assignment Material   **32**

2 BASIC FINANCIAL STATEMENTS

Introduction to Financial Statements   **40**
A Starting Point: Statement of Financial Position   **41**
Assets   42

Liabilities   44
Owners' Equity   45
The Accounting Equation   45
The Effects of Business Transactions: An Illustration   46
Effects of These Business Transactions on the Accounting Equation   50

Income Statement   **51**
Statement of Cash Flows   **53**
Relationships among Financial Statements   **54**
Financial Analysis and Decision Making   **57**
Forms of Business Organization   **57**
Sole Proprietorships   57
Partnerships   58
Corporations   58
Reporting Ownership Equity in the Statement of Financial Position   58

The Use of Financial Statements by External Parties   **59**
The Need for Adequate Disclosure   60
Management's Interest in Financial Statements   60

Ethics, Fraud, & Corporate Governance   **61**
Concluding Remarks   **62**
End-of-Chapter Review   **63**
Assignment Material   **66**

3 THE ACCOUNTING CYCLE: CAPTURING ECONOMIC EVENTS

The Accounting Cycle   **88**
The Role of Accounting Records   88

The Ledger   **88**
The Use of Accounts   **89**
Debit and Credit Entries   **89**
Double-Entry Accounting—The Equality of Debits and Credits   90

The Journal   **91**
Posting Journal Entries to the Ledger Accounts (and How to "Read" a Journal Entry)   92

Recording Balance Sheet Transactions: An Illustration   **92**
Ledger Accounts after Posting   **96**
What Is Net Income?   **98**
Retained Earnings   98
The Income Statement: A Preview   98

Revenue	100
Expenses	100
The Accrual Basis of Accounting	102
Debit and Credit Rules for Revenue and Expenses	102
Dividends	**103**
Recording Income Statement Transactions: An Illustration	**103**
The Journal	109
February's Ledger Balances	**109**
The Trial Balance	**111**
Uses and Limitations of the Trial Balance	112
Concluding Remarks	**112**
The Accounting Cycle in Perspective	112
Ethics, Fraud, & Corporate Governance	**113**
End-of-Chapter Review	**114**
Assignment Material	**119**

4 THE ACCOUNTING CYCLE: ACCRUALS AND DEFERRALS

Adjusting Entries	**142**
The Need for Adjusting Entries	142
Types of Adjusting Entries	142
Adjusting Entries and Timing Differences	143
Characteristics of Adjusting Entries	143
Year-End at Overnight Auto Service	145
Converting Assets to Expenses	145
The Concept of Depreciation	148
Converting Liabilities to Revenue	151
Accruing Unpaid Expenses	152
Accruing Uncollected Revenue	154
Accruing Income Taxes Expense: The Final Adjusting Entry	155
Adjusting Entries and Accounting Principles	**156**
The Concept of Materiality	157
Effects of the Adjusting Entries	158
Concluding Remarks	**160**
Ethics, Fraud, & Corporate Governance	**161**
End-of-Chapter Review	**162**
Assignment Material	**167**

5 THE ACCOUNTING CYCLE: REPORTING FINANCIAL RESULTS

Preparing Financial Statements	**194**
The Income Statement	194
The Statement of Retained Earnings	197
The Balance Sheet	197
Relationships among the Financial Statements	**198**
Drafting the Notes That Accompany Financial Statements	198
What Types of Information Must Be Disclosed?	199
Closing the Temporary Accounts	**200**
Closing Entries for Revenue Accounts	201
Closing Entries for Expense Accounts	202
Closing the Income Summary Account	203
Closing the Dividends Account	203
Summary of the Closing Process	**204**
After-Closing Trial Balance	**205**
A Last Look at Overnight: Was 2015 a Good Year?	205
Financial Analysis and Decision Making	**206**
Preparing Financial Statements Covering Different Periods of Time	207
Ethics, Fraud, & Corporate Governance	**208**
Concluding Remarks	**208**
Supplemental Topic: The Worksheet	**209**
Isn't This Really a Spreadsheet?	209
How Is a Worksheet Used?	209
The Mechanics: How It's Done	209
What If: A Special Application of Worksheet Software	212
End-of-Chapter Review	**213**
Assignment Material	**217**
COMPREHENSIVE PROBLEM 1	
Susquehanna Equipment Rentals	**243**

6 MERCHANDISING ACTIVITIES

Merchandising Companies	**248**
The Operating Cycle of a Merchandising Company	248
Income Statement of a Merchandising Company	249
Accounting System Requirements for Merchandising Companies	250
Two Approaches Used in Accounting for Merchandise Inventories	251
Perpetual Inventory Systems	**251**
Taking a Physical Inventory	253
Closing Entries in a Perpetual Inventory System	254
Periodic Inventory Systems	**254**
Operation of a Periodic Inventory System	254
Closing Process in a Periodic Inventory System	255

Comparison of Perpetual and Periodic Inventory Systems	257	
Selecting an Inventory System	258	
Transactions Relating to Purchases	**259**	
Credit Terms and Cash Discounts	259	
Returns of Unsatisfactory Merchandise	261	
Transportation Costs on Purchases	261	
Transactions Relating to Sales	**262**	
Sales Returns and Allowances	262	
Sales Discounts	263	
Delivery Expenses	263	
Accounting for Sales Taxes	264	
Modifying an Accounting System	**264**	
Special Journals Provide Speed and Efficiency	264	
Financial Analysis and Decision Making	**265**	
Ethics, Fraud, & Corporate Governance	**266**	
Concluding Remarks	**266**	
End-of-Chapter Review	**267**	
Assignment Material	**271**	

7 FINANCIAL ASSETS

How Much Cash Should a Business Have?	290
The Valuation of Financial Assets	290
Cash	**291**
Reporting Cash in the Balance Sheet	291
Cash Management	292
Internal Control over Cash	292
Bank Statements	293
Reconciling the Bank Statement	293
Short-Term Investments	**297**
Accounting for Marketable Securities	**298**
Purchase of Marketable Securities	298
Recognition of Investment Revenue	298
Sale of Investments	298
Adjusting Marketable Securities to Market Value	299
Accounts Receivable	**300**
Internal Control over Receivables	301
Uncollectible Accounts	301
The Allowance for Doubtful Accounts	303
Writing Off an Uncollectible Account Receivable	303
Monthly Estimates of Credit Losses	304
Recovery of an Account Receivable Previously Written Off	306
Direct Write-Off Method	307
Factoring Accounts Receivable	307
Credit Card Sales	308

Notes Receivable and Interest Revenue	**309**
Nature of Interest	309
Accounting for Notes Receivable	310
Financial Analysis and Decision Making	**311**
Ethics, Fraud, & Corporate Governance	**313**
Concluding Remarks	**313**
End-of-Chapter Review	**314**
Assignment Material	**318**

8 INVENTORIES AND THE COST OF GOODS SOLD

Inventory Defined	342
The Flow of Inventory Costs	**342**
Which Unit Did We Sell?	343
Data for an Illustration	343
Specific Identification	344
Cost Flow Assumptions	344
Average-Cost Method	344
First-In, First-Out Method	345
Last-In, First-Out Method	346
Evaluation of the Methods	347
Do Inventory Methods Really Affect Performance?	349
The Principle of Consistency	349
Just-in-Time (JIT) Inventory Systems	349
Taking a Physical Inventory	**351**
Recording Shrinkage Losses	351
LCM and Other Write-Downs of Inventory	351
The Year-End Cutoff of Transactions	352
Periodic Inventory Systems	353
International Financial Reporting Standards	356
Importance of an Accurate Valuation of Inventory	357
Techniques for Estimating the Cost of Goods Sold and the Ending Inventory	358
The Gross Profit Method	358
The Retail Method	359
"Textbook" Inventory Systems Can Be Modified . . . and They Often Are	359
Financial Analysis and Decision Making	**360**
Ethics, Fraud, & Corporate Governance	**361**
Concluding Remarks	**361**
End-of-Chapter Review	**362**
Assignment Material	**365**
COMPREHENSIVE PROBLEM 2	
Music-Is-Us, Inc.	**383**

9 PLANT AND INTANGIBLE ASSETS

Plant Assets as a "Stream of Future Services"	388
Major Categories of Plant Assets	388
Accountable Events in the Lives of Plant Assets	388
Acquisitions of Plant Assets	**388**
Determining Cost: An Example	389
Some Special Considerations	389
Capital Expenditures and Revenue Expenditures	390
Depreciation	**391**
Allocating the Cost of Plant and Equipment over the Years of Use	391
Causes of Depreciation	392
Methods of Computing Depreciation	392
The Straight-Line Method	393
The Declining-Balance Method	395
Which Depreciation Methods Do Most Businesses Use?	397
Financial Statement Disclosures	398
The Impairment of Plant Assets	399
Other Depreciation Methods	**399**
The Units-of-Output Method	399
MACRS	400
Sum-of-the-Years' Digits	400
Decelerated Depreciation Methods	400
Depreciation Methods in Use: A Survey	400
Disposal of Plant and Equipment	**400**
Gains and Losses on the Disposal of Plant and Equipment	401
Trading in Used Assets for New Ones	402
International Financial Reporting Standards	402
Intangible Assets	**403**
Characteristics	403
Operating Expenses versus Intangible Assets	403
Amortization	403
Goodwill	403
Patents	406
Trademarks and Trade Names	406
Franchises	406
Copyrights	407
Other Intangibles and Deferred Charges	407
Research and Development (R&D) Costs	407
Financial Analysis and Decision Making	**407**
Natural Resources	**408**
Accounting for Natural Resources	408
Depreciation, Amortization, and Depletion—A Common Goal	409
Plant Transactions and the Statement of Cash Flows	**409**
Ethics, Fraud, & Corporate Governance	**410**
Concluding Remarks	**410**
End-of-Chapter Review	**411**
Assignment Material	**414**

10 LIABILITIES

The Nature of Liabilities	432
Current Liabilities	**433**
Accounts Payable	433
Notes Payable	433
The Current Portion of Long-Term Debt	434
Accrued Liabilities	435
Payroll Liabilities	435
Unearned Revenue	437
Long-Term Liabilities	**437**
Maturing Obligations Intended to Be Refinanced	437
Installment Notes Payable	438
Bonds Payable	440
What Are Bonds?	440
Tax Advantage of Bond Financing	442
Accounting for Bonds Payable	442
Bonds Issued at a Discount or a Premium	444
Accounting for a Bond Discount: An Illustration	445
Accounting for a Bond Premium: An Illustration	447
Bond Discount and Premium in Perspective	450
The Concept of Present Value	450
Bond Prices after Issuance	451
Early Retirement of Bonds Payable	452
Estimated Liabilities, Loss Contingencies, and Commitments	**453**
Estimated Liabilities	453
Loss Contingencies	453
Commitments	454
Evaluating the Safety of Creditors' Claims	**454**
Methods of Determining Creditworthiness	455
How Much Debt Should a Business Have?	455
Financial Analysis and Decision Making	**456**
Ethics, Fraud, & Corporate Governance	**457**
Special Types of Liabilities	**457**
Lease Payment Obligations	457
Operating Leases	457
Capital Leases	458

Liabilities for Pensions and Other
Postretirement Benefits 458

Deferred Income Taxes 460

Concluding Remarks **461**

End-of-Chapter Review **462**

Assignment Material **467**

11 STOCKHOLDERS' EQUITY: PAID-IN CAPITAL

Corporations **486**

Why Businesses Incorporate 486

Publicly Owned Corporations 487

Formation of a Corporation **488**

Stockholder Records in a Corporation 490

Paid-In Capital of a Corporation **490**

Authorization and Issuance of Capital Stock 490

Common Stock and Preferred Stock 492

Characteristics of Preferred Stock 493

Book Value per Share of Common Stock 495

Market Value **496**

Market Price of Preferred Stock 497

Market Price of Common Stock 498

Book Value and Market Price 498

Stock Splits 498

Treasury Stock **499**

Recording Purchases of Treasury Stock 499

Reissuance of Treasury Stock 499

Stock Buyback Programs 501

Financial Analysis and Decision Making **501**

Ethics, Fraud, & Corporate Governance **502**

Concluding Remarks **502**

End-of-Chapter Review **503**

Assignment Material **506**

COMPREHENSIVE PROBLEM 3
Springdale Retail, Inc. **521**

12 INCOME AND CHANGES IN RETAINED EARNINGS

Reporting the Results of Operations **524**

Developing Predictive Information 524

Reporting Irregular Items: An Illustration 524

Continuing Operations 524

Discontinued Operations 525

Extraordinary Items 525

Earnings per Share (EPS) 527

Financial Analysis and Decision Making **529**

Other Transactions Affecting Retained Earnings **530**

Cash Dividends 530

Dividend Dates 531

Liquidating Dividends 532

Stock Dividends 532

Statement of Retained Earnings 534

Prior Period Adjustments 535

Comprehensive Income 536

Statement of Stockholders' Equity 536

Stockholders' Equity Section of the Balance Sheet 537

Ethics, Fraud, & Corporate Governance **538**

Concluding Remarks **539**

End-of-Chapter Review **540**

Assignment Material **544**

13 STATEMENT OF CASH FLOWS

Statement of Cash Flows **566**

Purposes of the Statement 566

Example of a Statement of Cash Flows 566

Classification of Cash Flows 566

Preparing a Statement of Cash Flows **569**

Operating Activities 570

Investing Activities 570

Financing Activities 571

Cash and Cash Equivalents 571

Cash Flows from Operating Activities 572

Cash Payments for Merchandise and for Expenses 573

Cash Flows from Investing Activities 575

Cash Flows from Financing Activities 577

Relationship between the Statement of Cash Flows and the Balance Sheet 578

Reporting Operating Cash Flows by the Indirect Method 579

Reconciling Net Income with Net Cash Flows 580

The Indirect Method: A Summary 581

Indirect Method May Be Required in a Supplementary Schedule 581

The Statement of Cash Flows: A Second Look 581

Financial Analysis and Decision Making **583**

Managing Cash Flows **584**

Budgeting: The Primary Cash Management Tool 585

What Priority Should Managers Give to Increasing Net Cash Flows? 585

Some Strategies for Permanent Improvements
in Cash Flow 586

Ethics, Fraud, & Corporate Governance **587**

**A Worksheet for Preparing a
Statement of Cash Flows** **587**

Data for an Illustration 587

The Worksheet 588

Entry 590

Concluding Remarks **591**

End-of-Chapter Review **593**

Assignment Material **598**

14 FINANCIAL STATEMENT ANALYSIS

Financial Statements Are Designed for Analysis 624

Tools of Analysis **625**

Dollar and Percentage Changes 625

Trend Percentages 626

Component Percentages 627

Ratios 627

Standards of Comparison 627

Quality of Earnings 628

Quality of Assets and the Relative
Amount of Debt 629

Measures of Liquidity and Credit Risk **629**

A Classified Balance Sheet 629

Working Capital 631

Current Ratio 631

Quick Ratio 632

Debt Ratio 632

Evaluating Financial Ratios 632

Liquidity, Credit Risk, and the Law 634

Measures of Profitability **634**

Classifications in the Income Statement 635

Multiple-Step Income Statements 636

Earnings per Share 638

Price-Earnings Ratio 638

Single-Step Income Statements 639

Evaluating the Adequacy of Net Income 639

Return on Investment (ROI) 639

Return on Assets (ROA) 640

Return on Equity (ROE) 640

**Comprehensive Illustration:
Seacliff Company** **641**

Analysis by Common Stockholders 644

Return on Investment (ROI) 646

Leverage 647

Analysis by Long-Term Creditors 648

Analysis by Short-Term Creditors 648

Cash Flow Analysis 652

Usefulness of Notes to Financial Statements 653

International Financial Reporting Standards 653

Summary of Analytical Measurements 654

Ethics, Fraud, & Corporate Governance **656**

Concluding Remarks **656**

End-of-Chapter Review **658**

Assignment Material **662**

COMPREHENSIVE PROBLEM 4
Home Depot, Inc. 682

15 GLOBAL BUSINESS AND
ACCOUNTING

Globalization **686**

**Environmental Forces
Shaping Globalization** **688**

Political and Legal Systems 688

Economic Systems 689

Culture 689

Technology and Infrastructure 690

**Harmonization of Financial Reporting
Standards** **691**

International Financial Reporting
Standards: Adoption or Convergence 691

Foreign Currencies and Exchange Rates **693**

Exchange Rates 693

Accounting for Transactions with Foreign
Companies 694

Currency Fluctuations—Who Wins
and Who Loses? 698

Consolidated Financial Statements That Include
Foreign Subsidiaries 700

Global Sourcing **700**

Foreign Corrupt Practices Act 702

Ethics, Fraud, & Corporate Governance **703**

Concluding Remarks **703**

End-of-Chapter Review **704**

Assignment Material **707**

A HOME DEPOT 2012 FINANCIAL
STATEMENTS A

B THE TIME VALUE OF MONEY:
FUTURE AMOUNTS AND
PRESENT VALUES B

The Concept **B-1**
Relationships between Present Values and Future
Amounts B-1
Compound Interest B-2
Applications of the Time Value of Money Concept B-2
Future Amounts **B-2**
The Tables Approach B-3
The Future Amount of an Annuity B-4
Interest Periods of Less Than One Year B-6

Present Values **B-6**
Using Present Value Tables B-7
What Is the Appropriate Discount Rate? B-7
The Present Value of an Annuity B-8
Discount Periods of Less Than One Year B-10
Valuation of Financial Instruments **B-10**
Interest-Bearing Receivables
and Payables B-10
"Non-Interest-Bearing" Notes B-10
Market Prices of Bonds B-12
Capital Leases B-13
Obligations for Postretirement Benefits B-14
Assignment Material **B-14**
Index I

Financial Accounting

CHAPTER 1

Accounting

Information for Decision Making

AFTER STUDYING THIS CHAPTER, YOU SHOULD BE ABLE TO:

Learning Objectives

LO1-1 Discuss accounting as the language of business and the role of accounting information in making economic decisions.

LO1-2 Discuss the significance of accounting systems in generating reliable accounting information and understand the five components of internal control.

LO1-3 Explain the importance of financial accounting information for external parties—primarily investors and creditors—in terms of the objectives and the characteristics of that information.

LO1-4 Explain the importance of accounting information for internal parties—primarily management—in terms of the objectives and the characteristics of that information.

LO1-5 Discuss elements of the system of external and internal financial reporting that create integrity in the reported information.

LO1-6 Identify and discuss several professional organizations that play important roles in preparing and communicating accounting information.

LO1-7 Discuss the importance of personal competence, professional judgment, and ethical behavior on the part of accounting professionals.

LO1-8 Describe various career opportunities in accounting.

© The McGraw-Hill Companies, Inc./Christopher Kerrigan, photographer

HEWLETT-PACKARD

Hewlett-Packard (HP) was founded by Bill Hewlett and Dave Packard in 1939 in a garage. Over the years, HP grew to be become a multinational information technology company, with revenues and assets of well over $100 billion. HP has often grown in recent years by acquiring other companies. Just as an individual is making an investment when he or she buys shares of stock, a corporation is making a much larger investment when it buys an entire company. And, just as reliable financial information is critical to individuals when making investment decisions, it is equally important when one company is considering buying another company.

In 2011, HP bought the British software company, Autonomy, for over $11 billion. Just a year later, HP wrote down the value of its investment in Autonomy by $8.8 billion. HP alleged that the write-down was due to its having overpaid, a result of Autonomy willfully overstating its revenues, margins (revenues − cost of sales), and growth rate prior to the acquisition. HP claims that approximately $5 billion of the $8.8 billion write-off is due to the alleged accounting improprieties. Autonomy and its founder Mike Lynch strongly deny HP's accusations. Autonomy claims that its accounting practices were permissible under international accounting standards, which it followed given its location in the UK, and which differed from U.S. accounting standards. Given the magnitude and seriousness of these charges, securities regulators and law enforcement agencies in both the United States and United Kingdom are investigating.

(continued)

Before buying another company, the purchaser typically performs due diligence procedures, including reviewing and evaluating the target company's financial results. HP ostensibly performed extensive due diligence procedures, including relying on Autonomy's auditor and another accounting firm that HP hired to perform due diligence procedures; both of these accounting firms are very large international firms. In addition, a number of prominent law and investment banking firms were retained by HP to vet the proposed acquisition. It has been reported that advisors on both sides of this deal earned over $60 million. Yet, if HP's allegations are ultimately proven true, these advisors did not appear to discover the accounting improprieties. Regardless of the ultimate veracity of HP's allegations, the Autonomy acquisition clearly has to be labeled as a failure, and HP's shareholders are the ones left holding the bag— HP's stock price declined by over 58 percent from the time when the Autonomy deal was announced until shortly after the alleged accounting improprieties were made public. ∎

Understanding and using accounting information is an important ingredient of any business undertaking. Terms such as sales revenue, net income, cost, expense, operating margin, and cash flow have clearly defined meanings and are commonly used in business-related communications. Although the precise meaning of these terms may be unfamiliar to you at this point, to become an active participant in the business world, you must gain a basic understanding of these and other accounting concepts. Our objective in this book is to provide those who both use and prepare accounting information with that basic understanding.

Information that is provided to external parties who have an interest in a company is sometimes referred to as financial accounting information. Information used internally by management and others is commonly referred to as managerial accounting information. Whereas these two types of information have different purposes and serve different audiences, they have certain attributes in common. For example, both financial and managerial accounting require the use of judgment and information prepared for either purpose should be subject to the company's system of internal control. Financial accounting concepts are critical in order to understand the financial condition of a business enterprise. Determining a company's net income by subtracting its expenses from its revenue is a particularly important part of financial reporting today. This may appear to be a simple process of keeping accounting records and preparing reports from those records, but a great deal of judgment is required. For example, when should the cost of acquiring a resource that is used for several years be recognized as an expense in the company's financial statements? What information is particularly useful for management, but not appropriate for public distribution because of the potential competitive disadvantage that might result? These are among the many complex issues that business faces on a day-to-day basis and which have a critical impact on the company's responsibility to its owners, creditors, the government, and society in general.

As we begin the study of accounting, keep in mind that business does not exist solely to earn a return for its investors and creditors that supply a company's financial resources. Business also has a responsibility to operate in a socially responsible manner and to balance its desire for financial success within this broader social responsibility. We begin our development of these ideas in this chapter, and continue their emphasis throughout this text.

Accounting Information: A Means to an End

The primary objective of accounting is to provide information that is useful for decision-making purposes. From the very start, we emphasize that accounting is *not an end,* but rather it is *a means to an end.* The final product of accounting information is the decision that is enhanced by the use of that information, whether the decision is made by owners, management, creditors, governmental regulatory bodies, labor unions, or the many other groups that have an interest in the financial performance of an enterprise.

Because accounting is widely used to describe all types of business activity, it is sometimes referred to as the *language of business.* Costs, prices, sales volume, profits, and return on investment are all accounting measurements. Investors, creditors, managers, and others who have a financial interest in an enterprise need a clear understanding of accounting terms and concepts if they are to understand and communicate about the enterprise. While our primary orientation in this text is the use of accounting information in business, from time to time we emphasize that accounting information is also used by governmental agencies, nonprofit organizations, and individuals in much the same manner as it is by business organizations.

L01-1

LEARNING OBJECTIVE
Discuss accounting as the language of business and the role of accounting information in making economic decisions.

ACCOUNTING FROM A USER'S PERSPECTIVE

Many people think of accounting as simply a highly technical field practiced only by professional accountants. In reality, nearly everyone uses accounting information daily. Accounting information is the means by which we measure and communicate economic events. Whether you manage a business, make investments, or monitor how you receive and use your money, you are working with accounting concepts and accounting information.

Our primary goal in this book is to develop your ability to understand and use accounting information in making economic decisions. To do this, you need to understand the following:

- The nature of economic activities that accounting information describes.
- The assumptions and measurement techniques involved in developing accounting information.
- The information that is most relevant for making various types of decisions.

Exhibit 1–1 illustrates how economic activities flow into the accounting process. The accounting process produces accounting information used by decision makers in making economic decisions and taking specific actions. These decisions and actions result in economic activities that continue the cycle.

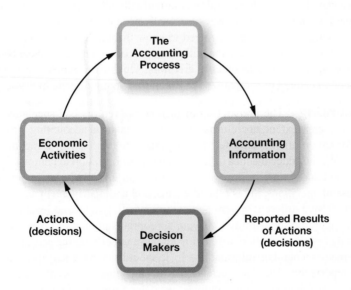

EXHIBIT 1-1
The Accounting Process

Accounting links decision makers with economic activities—and with the results of their decisions

TYPES OF ACCOUNTING INFORMATION

Just as there are many types of economic decisions, there are also many types of accounting information. The terms *financial accounting, management accounting,* and *tax accounting* often are used in describing three types of accounting information that are widely used in the business community.

Financial Accounting

Financial accounting refers to information describing the financial resources, obligations, and activities of an economic entity (either an organization or an individual). Accountants use the term *financial position* to describe an entity's financial resources and obligations at a point in time and the term *results of operations* to describe its financial activities during the year.

CASE IN POINT

In Sony Corporation's 2012 financial statements to owners, financial position is presented as consisting of ¥13,295 trillion in assets (including cash, inventories, property, and equipment), with obligations against those assets of ¥10,805 trillion. This leaves ¥2,490 trillion as the owners' interest in those assets. In the same report, results of operations indicate that Sony had a net loss (expenses exceeded revenues) of ¥456 billion for the year ending March 31, 2012.

Financial accounting information is designed primarily to assist investors and creditors in deciding where to place their scarce investment resources. Such decisions are important to society, because they determine which companies and industries will receive the financial resources necessary for growth.

Financial accounting information also is used by managers and in income tax returns. In fact, financial accounting information is used for so many different purposes that it often is called "general-purpose" accounting information.

Management Accounting

Management (or managerial) **accounting** involves the development and interpretation of accounting information intended *specifically to assist management* in operating the business. Managers use this information in setting the company's overall goals, evaluating the performance of departments and individuals, deciding whether to introduce a new line of products, and making virtually all types of managerial decisions.

A company's managers and employees constantly need information to run and control daily business operations. For example, they need to know the amount of money in the company's bank accounts; the types, quantities, and dollar amounts of merchandise in the company's warehouse; and the amounts owed to specific creditors. Much management accounting information is financial in nature but is organized in a manner relating directly to the decision at hand.

Tax Accounting

The preparation of income tax returns is a specialized field within accounting. To a great extent, tax returns are based on financial accounting information. However, the information often is adjusted or reorganized to conform with income tax reporting requirements. We introduce the idea of tax accounting information to contrast it with financial and management accounting information. Although tax information is important for a company's successful operations and is related to financial and management accounting information, it results from a different system and complies with specialized legal requirements that relate to a company's responsibility to pay an appropriate amount of taxes. Laws and regulations governing taxation are often different from those underlying the preparation of financial and management accounting information, so it should not be a surprise that the resulting figures and reports are different. Because the focus of this text is introductory accounting, and because tax accounting is quite complex, we defer coverage of tax accounting subjects to subsequent accounting courses.

LO1-2

LEARNING OBJECTIVE
Discuss the significance of accounting systems in generating reliable accounting information and understand the five components of internal control.

Accounting Systems

An **accounting system** consists of the personnel, procedures, technology, and records used by an organization (1) to develop accounting information and (2) to communicate this information to decision makers. The design and capabilities of these systems vary greatly from one organization to another. In small businesses, accounting systems may consist of little more than a cash register, a checkbook, and an annual trip to an income tax preparer. In large businesses, accounting systems include computers, highly trained personnel, and accounting reports that affect the daily operations of every department. But in every case, the basic purpose of the accounting system remains the same: *to meet the organization's needs for information as efficiently as possible.*

Many factors affect the structure of the accounting system within a particular organization. Among the most important are (1) the company's *needs for accounting information* and (2) the *resources available* for operation of the system.

Describing accounting as an information system focuses attention on the information accounting provides, the users of the information, and the support for financial decisions that is provided by the information. These relationships are depicted in Exhibit 1–2. While some of the terms may not be familiar to you at this early point in your study of business and accounting, you will be introduced to them more completely as we proceed through this textbook and as you undertake other courses in business and accounting. Observe, however, that the information system produces the information presented in the middle of the diagram—financial position, profitability, and cash flows. This information meets the needs of users of the information—investors, creditors, managers, and so on—and supports many kinds of financial decisions—performance evaluation and resource allocation, among others. These relationships are consistent with what we have already learned—namely, that accounting information is intended to be useful for decision-making purposes.

EXHIBIT 1–2

Accounting as an Information System

DETERMINING INFORMATION NEEDS

The types of accounting information that a company develops vary with such factors as the size of the organization, whether it is publicly owned, and the information needs of management. The need for some types of accounting information may be prescribed by law. For example, income tax regulations require every business to have an accounting system that can measure the company's taxable income and explain the nature and source of every item in the company's income tax return. Federal securities laws require publicly owned companies to prepare financial statements in conformity with generally accepted accounting principles. These statements must be filed with the Securities and Exchange Commission, distributed to stockholders, and made available to the public.

Other types of accounting information are required as matters of practical necessity. For example, every business needs to know the amounts owed to it by each customer and the amounts owed by the company to each creditor. Although much accounting information clearly is essential to business operations, management still has many choices as to the types and amount of accounting information to be developed. For example, should the accounting system of a department store measure separately the sales of each department and of different types of merchandise? The answer to such questions depends on *how useful* management considers the information to be and the *cost* of developing the information.

THE COST OF PRODUCING ACCOUNTING INFORMATION

Accounting systems must be *cost-effective*—that is, the value of the information produced should exceed the cost of producing it. Management has no choice but to produce the types of accounting reports required by law or contract. In other cases, however, management may use *cost-effectiveness* as a criterion for deciding whether or not to produce certain information.

In recent years, the development and installation of computer-based information systems have increased greatly the types and amount of accounting information that can be produced in a cost-effective manner.

BASIC FUNCTIONS OF AN ACCOUNTING SYSTEM

In developing information about the activities of a business, every accounting system performs the following basic functions:

1. *Interpret and record* the effects of business transactions.
2. *Classify* the effects of similar transactions in a manner that permits determination of the various *totals* and *subtotals* useful to management and used in accounting reports.
3. *Summarize and communicate* the information contained in the system to decision makers.

The differences in accounting systems arise primarily in the manner, frequency, and speed with which these functions are performed.

In our illustrations, we often assume the use of a simple manual accounting system. Such a system is useful in illustrating basic accounting concepts, but it is too slow and cumbersome to meet the needs of most business organizations. In a large business, transactions may occur at a rate of several hundred or several thousand per hour. To keep pace with such a rapid flow of information, these companies must use accounting systems that are largely computer-based. The underlying principles within these systems are generally consistent with the basic manual system we frequently refer to in this text. Understanding manual systems allows users to understand the needs that must be met in a computerized system.

WHO DESIGNS AND INSTALLS ACCOUNTING SYSTEMS?

The design and installation of large accounting systems is a specialized field. It involves not just accounting, but expertise in management, information systems, marketing, and—in many cases—computer programming. Thus accounting systems generally are designed and installed by a team of people with many specialized talents.

Large businesses have a staff of systems analysts, internal auditors, and other professionals who work full-time in designing and improving the accounting system. Medium-size companies often hire a CPA firm to design or update their systems. Small businesses with limited resources often purchase one of the many packaged accounting systems designed for small companies in their line of business. These packaged systems are available through office supply stores, computer stores, and software manufacturers.

COMPONENTS OF INTERNAL CONTROL[1]

In developing its accounting system, an organization also needs to be concerned with developing a sound system of internal control. **Internal control** is a process designed to provide

---

[1] The information in this section is taken from *Internal Control–Integrated Framework: 2013,* Committee of Sponsoring Organizations of the Treadway Commission, May 2013.

reasonable assurance that the organization produces reliable financial reports, complies with applicable laws and regulations, and conducts its operations in an efficient and effective manner. A company's board of directors, its management, and other personnel are charged with developing and monitoring internal control. The five components of internal control, as discussed in *Internal Control–Integrated Framework: 2013* (Committee of Sponsoring Organizations of the Treadway Commission), are the *control environment, risk assessment, control activities, information and communication,* and *monitoring activities.*

An organization's **control environment** is the foundation for all the other elements of internal control, setting the overall tone for the organization. Factors that affect a company's control environment are: (1) the organization's commitment to integrity and ethical values, (2) the independence of the board of directors from management, and the board's oversight of internal control, (3) management assignment, with board oversight, of appropriate levels of authority and responsibility, (4) an organizational commitment to attract, develop, and retain competent individuals, and (5) individuals being held accountable for the performance of their control responsibilities. The control environment is particularly important because fraudulent financial reporting often results from an ineffective control environment.

Risk assessment involves identifying, analyzing, and managing those risks that pose a threat to the achievement of the organization's objectives. For example, a company should assess the risks that might prevent it from preparing reliable financial reports and then take steps to minimize those risks. The situation described in the chapter opener involving **Hewlett-Packard and Autonomy** provides an example of where that firm's risk assessment procedures failed.

Control activities are the policies and procedures that management puts in place to address the risks identified during the risk assessment process. Examples of control activities include approvals, authorizations, verifications, reconciliations, reviews of operating performance, physical safeguarding of assets, and segregation of duties.

Information and communication involves developing information systems to capture and communicate operational, financial, and compliance-related information necessary to run the business. Effective information systems capture both internal and external information. In addition, an effective control system is designed to facilitate the flow of information downstream (from management to employees), upstream (from employees to management), and across the organization. Employees must receive the message that top management views internal control as important, and they must understand their role in the internal control system and the roles of others.

All internal control systems need to be monitored. **Monitoring activities** enable the company to evaluate the effectiveness of its system of internal control over time. Monitoring activities are generally accomplished through ongoing management and supervisory activities, as well as by periodic separate evaluations of the internal control system. Most large organizations have an internal audit function, and the activities of internal audit represent separate evaluations of internal control. In fact, the NYSE requires all listed companies to maintain an internal audit function.

As a result of the large financial frauds at **Enron** and **WorldCom**, the U.S. Congress passed, and President George W. Bush signed, the **Sarbanes-Oxley Act** (SOX) of 2002. SOX has been described as the most far-reaching securities law since the 1930s. One of the SOX requirements is that public companies issue a yearly report indicating whether they have an effective system of internal control over financial reporting. In essence, management must indicate whether the entity's internal control system provides reasonable assurance that financial statements will be prepared in accordance with laws and regulations governing financial reporting. In addition for all but the smallest public companies, the company's external auditor must issue its own report as to whether the auditor believes that the company's internal control system is effective. These requirements are contained in Section 404 of SOX; therefore, many businesspeople describe the above process as the 404 certification and the audit under Section 404. This certification process has been extremely expensive and time-consuming, and some businesspeople believe that the costs associated with this certification requirement exceed the benefits.

Financial Accounting Information

L01-3

LEARNING OBJECTIVE
Explain the importance of financial accounting information for external parties—primarily investors and creditors—in terms of the objectives and the characteristics of that information.

Financial accounting is an important subject for students who need only an introduction to the field of accounting, as well as for students who will pursue accounting as a major and take many additional accounting courses. Financial accounting provides information about the financial resources, obligations, and activities of an enterprise that is intended for use primarily by external decision makers—investors and creditors.

EXTERNAL USERS OF ACCOUNTING INFORMATION

What do we mean by *external users* and who are they? **External users** of accounting information are individuals and other enterprises that have a current or potential financial interest in the reporting enterprise, but that are not involved in the day-to-day operations of that enterprise. External users of financial information may include the following:

- Owners
- Creditors
- Potential investors
- Labor unions
- Governmental agencies
- Suppliers
- Customers
- Trade associations
- General public

Each of these groups of external decision makers requires unique information to be able to make decisions about the reporting enterprise. For example, customers who purchase from the enterprise need information to allow them to assess the quality of the products they buy and the faithfulness of the enterprise in fulfilling warranty obligations. Governmental agencies such as the Federal Trade Commission may have an interest in whether the enterprise meets certain governmental regulations that apply. The general public may be interested in the extent to which the reporting enterprise is socially responsible (for example, does not pollute the environment).

Providing information that meets the needs of such a large set of diverse users is difficult, if not impossible, in a single set of financial information. Therefore, external financial reporting is primarily used by two groups—investors and creditors. As you will soon see, investors are individuals and other enterprises that own the reporting enterprise. Creditors, on the other hand, are individuals and other enterprises to whom the reporting entity owes money, goods, or services. For example, a commercial bank may have loaned money to the reporting enterprise, or a supplier may have permitted the reporting enterprise to purchase goods and to pay for those goods later. Our assumption is that by meeting the financial information needs of investors and creditors, we provide information that is also useful to many other users of financial information.

For these reasons, we sometimes refer to investors and creditors as the primary external financial information users. When you see references like these, keep in mind that we are talking about both current investors and creditors and those individuals and other enterprises that may become investors and creditors in the future.

OBJECTIVES OF EXTERNAL FINANCIAL REPORTING

If you had invested in a company, or if you had loaned money to a company, what would be your primary financial interest in the company? You probably would be interested in two things, both of which make up the company's **cash flow prospects.** You would be interested in the return to you at some future date of the amount you had invested or loaned. We refer to this as the **return *of* your investment.** In addition, you would expect the company to pay you something for the use of your funds, either as an owner or a creditor. We refer to this as the **return *on* your investment.** Information that is useful to you in making judgments about the company's ability to provide you with what you expect in terms of the return *of* your funds as well as a return *on* your funds while you do not have use of them is what we mean by information about *cash flow prospects.*

Assume that you have a friend who wants to start a business and needs some help getting the money required to rent space and acquire the needed assets to operate the business (for

YOUR TURN   You as a Creditor

You are a loan officer at a bank that makes small loans to individuals to help finance purchases such as automobiles and appliances. You are considering an application from a young woman who needs to purchase a new car. She is requesting a loan of $10,000 which, when combined with the trade-in value of her old car, will allow her to meet her needs. What are your expectations with regard to repayment of the loan, and what information would help you decide whether she is a good credit risk for your bank?

(See our comments on the Online Learning Center website.)

example, delivery truck, display fixtures) and pay employees for their work before the doors open and customers begin paying for the products the company plans to sell. You are in a financially strong position and agree to loan your friend $100,000. Your intent is not to be a long-term investor or co-owner of the business, but rather to help your friend start his company and at the same time earn a return on the funds you have loaned him. Assume further that you agree to let your friend have the use of your $100,000 for one year and, if you had not loaned this amount to him, you could have earned an 8 percent return by placing your money in another investment.

In addition to wanting to help a friend, you are interested in knowing how much risk you are taking with regard to your $100,000. You expect your friend to pay that $100,000 back, and to also pay you an additional amount of $8,000 ($100,000 × 8%) for his use of your money. The total return of your investment ($100,000) back to you one year later, added to the amount you expect to receive for his having used your money for a year ($8,000), is shown in Exhibit 1–3.

EXHIBIT 1–3
Investment Analysis

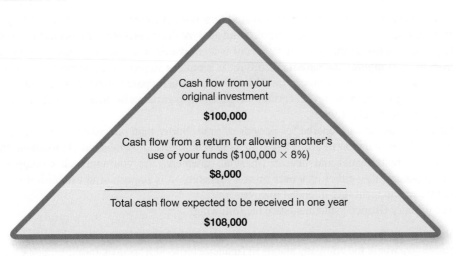

Cash flow from your original investment

$100,000

Cash flow from a return for allowing another's use of your funds ($100,000 × 8%)

$8,000

Total cash flow expected to be received in one year

$108,000

Providing information for you to assess your friend's ability to meet his cash flow commitment to you is essentially what financial reporting is about. You need information to assess the risk you are taking and the prospects that your friend will be able to deliver $108,000 to you one year from the time you loan him the $100,000. While this is a relatively simple example, it sets the stage for your understanding of the kinds of information that will help you make this important investment decision.

The accounting profession has identified certain objectives of external financial reporting to guide its efforts to refine and improve the reporting of information to external decision makers. These general objectives are displayed in Exhibit 1–4 and are best understood if studied from the bottom up—from general to specific.[2]

EXHIBIT 1–4

Objectives of Financial
Reporting: Building from the
General to the Specific

> Provide specific information about
> economic resources, claims to resources,
> and changes in resources and claims.

> Provide information useful in assessing the amount,
> timing, and uncertainty of future cash flows.

> Provide general information useful in making investment and credit decisions.

The first objective is the most general and is to provide information that is useful in making investment and credit decisions. As we indicated earlier, investors and creditors are the primary focus of external financial reporting. We believe that, by meeting the information needs of investors and creditors, we provide general information that is also useful to many other important financial statement users.

The second objective, which is more specific than the first, is to provide information that is useful in assessing the amount, timing, and uncertainty of future cash flows. As we discussed earlier, investors and creditors are interested in future cash flows to them, so an important objective of financial reporting is to provide general information that permits that kind of analysis.

The most specific objective of external financial reporting is to provide information about the enterprise's resources, claims to those resources, and how both the resources and claims to resources change over time. An enterprise's resources are often referred to as *assets,* and the primary claims to those resources are the claims of creditors and owners, known as liabilities and owners' equity.

One of the primary ways investors and creditors assess whether an enterprise will be able to make future cash payments is to examine and analyze the enterprise's financial statements. In the general sense of the word, a statement is simply a declaration of something believed to be true. A **financial statement,** therefore, is simply a monetary declaration of what is believed to be true about an enterprise. When accountants prepare financial statements, they are describing in financial terms certain attributes of the enterprise that they believe fairly represent its financial activities.

Financial statements prepared for periods of time shorter than one year (for example, for three months or one month) are referred to as *interim financial statements.* Throughout this text, we use both annual and interim financial statements. As you approach a company's financial statements—either as a user or as a preparer—it is important to establish the time period those statements are intended to cover.

The primary financial statements are the following:

- *Statement of financial position (balance sheet).* The **balance sheet** is a position statement that shows where the company stands in financial terms at a specific date.
- *Income statement.* The **income statement** is an activity statement that shows details and results of the company's profit-related activities for a period of time (for example, a month, quarter [three months], or year).
- *Statement of cash flows.* The **statement of cash flows** is an activity statement that shows the details of the company's activities involving cash during a period of time.

---

[2] FASB *Statement of Financial Accounting Concepts No. 1,* "Objectives of Financial Reporting by Business Enterprises" (Norwalk, Conn.: 1978), p. 4.

The names of the three primary financial statements are descriptive of the information you find in each. The **statement of financial position,** or balance sheet, for example, is sometimes described as a snapshot of the business in financial or dollar terms (that is, what the enterprise looks like at a specific date). An income statement is an activity statement that depicts the profitability of an enterprise for a designated period of time. The statement of cash flows is particularly important in understanding an enterprise for purposes of investment and credit decisions. As its name implies, the statement of cash flows depicts the ways cash has changed during a designated period. While the interest of investors and creditors is in cash flows to themselves rather than to the enterprise, information about cash activity of the enterprise is considered to be an important signal to investors and creditors.

At this early stage in your study of accounting, you are not expected to understand these financial statements or how they precisely help you assess the cash flow prospects of a company. The statement of financial position (balance sheet), income statement, and statement of cash flows are introduced more fully to you in the next chapter. Thereafter, you will learn a great deal about how these statements are prepared and how the information contained in them can be used to help you understand the underlying business activities they represent.

CHARACTERISTICS OF EXTERNALLY REPORTED INFORMATION

Financial information that is reported to investors, creditors, and others external to the reporting enterprise has certain qualities that must be understood for the information to have maximum usefulness. Some of these qualities are discussed in the following paragraphs.

Financial Reporting—A Means   As we learned in the introduction to this chapter, financial information is a means to an end, not an end in and of itself. The ultimate outcome of providing financial information is to improve the quality of decision making by external parties. Financial statements themselves are simply a means by which that end is achieved.

Financial Reporting versus Financial Statements   Financial reporting is broader than financial statements. Stated another way, financial statements are a subset of the total information encompassed by financial reporting. Investors, creditors, and other external users of financial information learn about an enterprise in a variety of ways in addition to its formal financial statements (for example, press releases sent directly to investors and creditors, articles in *The Wall Street Journal,* and more recently, open communications via the Internet). Serious investors, creditors, and other external users take advantage of many sources of information that are available to support their economic decisions about an enterprise.

Historical in Nature   Externally reported financial information is generally historical in nature. It looks back in time and reports the results of events and transactions that already have occurred. While historical information is very useful in assessing the future, the information itself is more about the past than it is about the future. However, in recent years, accounting standard setters are requiring greater use of fair values, rather than historical costs, in measuring assets and liabilities.

Inexact and Approximate Measures   Externally reported financial information may have a look of great precision, but in fact much of it is based on estimates, judgments, and assumptions that must be made about both the past and the future. For example, assume a company purchases a piece of equipment for use in its business. To account for that asset and to incorporate the impact of it into the company's externally reported financial information, some assumptions must be made about how long it will be used by the company—how many years it will be used, how many machine-hours it will provide, and so on. The fact that a great deal of judgment underlies most accounting information is a limitation that is sometimes misunderstood.

General-Purpose Assumption   As we have already mentioned, we assume that, by providing information that meets the needs of investors and creditors, we also meet the information needs of other external parties. We might be able to provide superior information if we were to treat each potential group of external users separately and prepare different information for each group. This approach is impractical, however, and we instead opt for preparing what is referred to as **general-purpose information** that we believe is useful to multiple user groups (that is, "one size fits all").

Usefulness Enhanced via Explanation   The accounting profession believes that the value of externally reported financial information is enhanced by including explanations from management. This information is often nonquantitative and helps to interpret the financial numbers that are presented. For this reason, financial information, including financial statements, is accompanied by a number of notes and other explanations that help explain and interpret the numerical information.

Management Accounting Information

LO1-4

LEARNING OBJECTIVE
Explain the importance of accounting information for internal parties—primarily management—in terms of the objectives and the characteristics of that information.

Internal decision makers employed by the enterprise, often referred to as management, create and use internal accounting information not only for exclusive use inside the organization but also to share with external decision makers. For example, in order to meet a production schedule, a producer may design an accounting information system for suppliers detailing its production plans. The producer shares this information with its supplier companies so that they can help the producer meet its objectives. Thus, although the creator and distributor of the accounting information is an internal decision maker, the recipient of the information is, in this case, an external decision maker. Other types of accounting information, however, are not made available to external decision makers. Long-range plans, research and development results, capital budget details, and competitive strategies typically are closely guarded corporate secrets.

USERS OF INTERNAL ACCOUNTING INFORMATION

Every employee of the enterprise uses internal accounting information. From basic labor categories to the chief executive officer (CEO), all employees are paid, and their paychecks are generated by the accounting information system. However, the amount of use and, in particular, the involvement in the design of accounting information systems vary considerably. Examples of **internal users** of accounting information systems are as follows:

- Board of directors
- Chief executive officer (CEO)
- Chief financial officer (CFO)
- Vice presidents (information services, human resources, ethics, and so forth)

- Business unit managers
- Plant managers
- Store managers
- Line supervisors

Employees have different specific goals and objectives that are designed to help the enterprise achieve its overall strategies and mission. Looking at the typical, simple organization chart in Exhibit 1–5, you can see that the information created and used by various employees will differ widely. All enterprises follow rules about the design of their accounting information systems to ensure the integrity of accounting information and to protect the enterprise's assets. There are no rules, however, about the type of internal reports or the kind of accounting information that can be generated. A snapshot look inside a firm will demonstrate the diversity of accounting information generated and used in the decision-making processes of employees.

Many enterprises use a database warehousing approach for the creation of accounting information systems. This approach, coupled with user-friendly software, allows management and other designated employees access to information to create a variety of accounting reports, including required external financial reports. For example, detailed cost information about a production process is used by the production line supervisor to help control production costs. A process design engineer, when considering the best configuration of equipment and employees, uses the same information to reduce costs or to increase efficiency. Finally, production-related cost information appears in the external financial statements used by investors and creditors.

EXHIBIT 1–5 Typical Simple Organization Chart

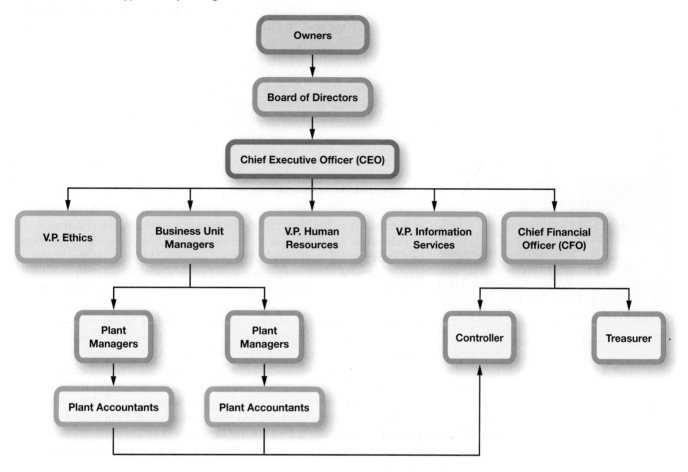

OBJECTIVES OF MANAGEMENT ACCOUNTING INFORMATION

Each enterprise has implicit and explicit goals and objectives. Many enterprises have a mission statement that describes their goals. These goals can vary widely among enterprises ranging from nonprofit organizations, where goals are aimed at serving specified constituents, to for-profit organizations, where goals are directed toward maximizing the owners' objectives. For example, the **American Cancer Society**, a nonprofit organization, has the following mission:

> The American Cancer Society is the nationwide community-based voluntary health organization dedicated to eliminating cancer as a major health problem by preventing cancer, saving lives, and diminishing suffering from cancer, through research, education, advocacy, and service.[3]

Procter & Gamble, a for-profit, global producer of consumer products, has the following purpose:

> We will provide branded products and services of superior quality and value that improve the lives of the world's consumers, now and for generations to come. As a result, consumers will reward us with leadership sales, profit, and value creation, allowing our people, our shareholders, and the communities in which we live and work to prosper.[4]

---

[3] www.cancer.org.

[4] www.pg.com.

Procter & Gamble's annual report to shareholders provides more detail on how the company will achieve its mission. Procter & Gamble's long-term track record of success is based on a time-tested business model that was explained in P&G's annual letter to its shareholders and includes:

- Discover meaningful insights into what consumers need and want.
- Translate those insights into noticeably superior products.
- Communicate product superiority through advertising that includes compelling claims, performance demonstrations, and superior benefit visuals.
- Price products so that consumers experience superior overall value.[5]

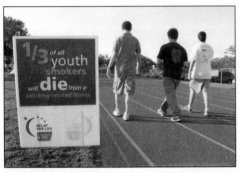

© Stephanie Bartelt/Alamy

The constituents of these organizations receive external financial information that helps them assess the progress being made in achieving these goals and objectives. In the case of Procter & Gamble, quarterly and annual information is provided to shareholders. The American Cancer Society is required to report its activities and financial condition to regulators. Providing constituents evaluative information is only one objective of accounting systems.

Enterprises design and use their internal accounting information systems to help them achieve their stated goals and missions. Multiple reports, some as part of the normal reporting process and some that are specially constructed and designed, are produced and distributed regularly. To motivate managers to achieve organizational goals, the internal accounting system is also used to evaluate and reward decision-making performance. When the accounting system compares the plan or budget to the actual outcomes for a period, it creates a signal about the performance of the employee responsible for that part of the budget. In many enterprises management creates a reward system linked to performance as measured by the accounting system.

Thus the objectives of accounting systems begin at the most general level with the objectives and mission of the enterprise. These general organizational goals create a need for information. The enterprise gathers historical and future information from both inside the enterprise and external sources. This information is used by the decision makers who have authority over the firm's resources and who will be evaluated and rewarded based on their decision outcomes.

CHARACTERISTICS OF MANAGEMENT ACCOUNTING INFORMATION

The accounting information created and used by management is intended primarily for planning and control decisions. Because the goal of creating and using management accounting information differs from the reasons for producing externally reported financial information, its characteristics are different.

Both the processes used to create financial accounting reports and the structure of those reports significantly impact management strategy. For example, because external financial reporting standards require companies to include pension-related obligations on their financial statements, management monitors those obligations closely. These pension-related obligations impact labor negotiations and labor-related corporate strategies.

Another example is that the processes necessary to create required external financial reports have historically determined the type of accounting information available inside of companies for internal decision making. Most plants within companies are organized as profit centers where plant-related financial statements mirror those necessary for external reporting purposes.

As you read the chapters of this book, we will remind you about how financial reporting has an impact on and is impacted by management strategies. The following paragraphs identify internal accounting information characteristics.

Importance of Timeliness   In order to plan for and control ongoing business processes, accounting information needs to be timely. The competitive environment faced by many enterprises demands immediate access to information. Enterprises are responding to this demand by creating computerized databases that link to external forecasts of industry

---

[5] Procter & Gamble, 2012 Annual Report, Letter to Shareholders.

associations, to their suppliers and buyers, and to their constituents. Time lines for the development and launch of new products and services are becoming shorter and shorter, making quick access to information a priority.

In addition to needing timely information for planning purposes, enterprises are constantly monitoring and controlling ongoing activities. If a process or activity goes out of control, the enterprise can incur significant costs. For example, recalls of products can be very expensive for a company. If the company can monitor processes and prevent low-quality or defective products from reaching its customers, it can experience significant savings.

Identity of Decision Maker Information that is produced to monitor and control processes needs to be provided to those who have decision-making authority to correct problems. Reporting scrap and rework information to line workers without providing them the responsibility for fixing the process is counterproductive. However, a self-directed work team that has been assigned decision-making responsibility over equipment and work-related activities can have a significant impact on rework and scrap if team members control the process causing the problems.

Oriented toward the Future Although some accounting information, like financial accounting information, is historical in nature, the purpose in creating and generating it is to affect the future. The objective is to motivate management to make future decisions that are in the best interest of the enterprise, consistent with its goals, objectives, and mission.

Measures of Efficiency and Effectiveness Accounting information measures the efficiency and effectiveness of resource usage. By comparing the enterprise's resource inputs and outputs with measures of competitors' effectiveness and efficiency, an assessment can be made of how effective management is in achieving the organization's mission. The accounting system uses money as a common unit to achieve these types of comparisons.

Management Accounting Information—A Means As with financial accounting information, management accounting information is a means to an end, not an end in and of itself. The ultimate objective is to design and use an accounting system that helps management achieve the goals and objectives of the enterprise.

Integrity of Accounting Information

What enables investors and creditors to rely on financial accounting information without fear that the management of the reporting enterprise has altered the information to make the company's performance look better than it actually was? How can management be sure that internally generated information is free from bias that might favor one outcome over another? The word **integrity** refers to the following qualities: complete, unbroken, unimpaired, sound, honest, and sincere. Accounting information must have these qualities because of the significance of the information to individuals who rely on it in making important financial decisions.

The integrity of accounting information is enhanced in three primary ways. First, certain institutional features add significantly to the integrity of accounting information. These features include standards for the preparation of accounting information, an internal control structure, and audits of financial statements. Second, several professional accounting organizations play unique roles in adding to the integrity of accounting information. Finally, and perhaps most important, is the personal competence, judgment, and ethical behavior of professional accountants. These three elements of the accounting profession come together to ensure that users of accounting information—investors, creditors, managers, and others—can rely on the information to be a fair representation of what it purports to represent.

L01-5

LEARNING OBJECTIVE
Discuss elements of the system of external and internal financial reporting that create integrity in the reported information.

INSTITUTIONAL FEATURES

Standards for the Preparation of Accounting Information Accounting information that is communicated externally to investors, creditors, and other users must be prepared in accordance with standards that are understood by both the preparers and users of that information. We call these standards **generally accepted accounting principles,** often shortened to GAAP. These principles provide the general framework for determining what information is included in financial statements and how this information is to be prepared and presented. GAAP includes broad principles of measurement and presentation, as well as detailed rules that are used by professional accountants in preparing accounting information and reports.

Accounting principles are not like physical laws; they do not exist in nature waiting to be discovered. Rather, they are developed by people, in light of what we consider to be the most important objectives of financial reporting. In many ways, accounting principles are similar to the rules established for an organized sport, such as baseball or basketball. For example, accounting principles, like sports rules:

- Originate from a combination of tradition, experience, and official decree.
- Require authoritative support and some means of enforcement.
- Are sometimes arbitrary.
- May change over time as shortcomings in the existing rules come to light.
- Must be clearly understood and observed by all participants in the process.

Accounting principles vary somewhat from country to country. The phrase "generally accepted accounting principles (GAAP)" refers to the accounting concepts in use in the United States. The International Accounting Standards Board (IASB) is currently attempting to establish greater uniformity among the accounting principles in use around the world in order to facilitate business activity that increasingly is carried out in more than one country.

In the United States, three organizations are particularly important in establishing accounting principles—the Securities and Exchange Commission (SEC), the Financial Accounting Standards Board (FASB), and the International Accounting Standards Board (IASB).

Securities and Exchange Commission   The **Securities and Exchange Commission** is a governmental agency with the *legal power* to establish accounting principles and financial reporting requirements for publicly owned corporations. In the past, the SEC has generally adopted the recommendations of the FASB (discussed below), rather than develop its own set of accounting principles. Thus, accounting principles continue to be developed in the private sector but are given the *force of law* since the SEC looks to the FASB to develop accounting standards in the United States.

To ensure widespread acceptance of new accounting standards, the FASB *needs the support* of the SEC. Therefore, the two organizations work closely together in developing new accounting standards. The SEC also reviews the financial statements of publicly owned corporations to ensure compliance with its reporting requirements. In the event that a publicly owned corporation fails to comply with these requirements, the SEC may initiate legal action against the company and the responsible individuals. Thus the SEC enforces compliance with generally accepted accounting principles that are established primarily by the FASB.

Financial Accounting Standards Board   Today, the most authoritative source of generally accepted accounting principles is the **Financial Accounting Standards Board.** The FASB is an independent rule-making body, consisting of seven members from the accounting profession, industry, financial statement users, and accounting education. Lending support to these members are an advisory council and a large research staff.

The FASB has compiled all of its standards, and those of its predecessors, in an Accounting Standards Codification. The FASB periodically issues updates to its codification. The codification represents official expressions of generally accepted accounting principles.

In addition to maintaining the Accounting Standards Codification, the FASB has completed a project describing a *conceptual framework* for financial reporting. This conceptual framework sets forth the FASB's views as to the:

- Objectives of financial reporting.
- Desired characteristics of accounting information (such as relevance, verifiability, and understandability).
- Elements of financial statements.

- Criteria for deciding what information to include in financial statements.
- Valuation concepts relating to financial statement amounts.

The primary purpose of the conceptual framework is to provide guidance to the FASB in developing new accounting standards, which are issued as updates to the codification. By making each new standard consistent with this framework, the FASB believes that the Accounting Standards Codification resolves accounting problems in a logical and consistent manner.

The FASB is part of the private sector of the economy—*it is not a governmental agency.* The development of accounting principles in the United States traditionally has been carried out in the private sector, although the government, acting through the SEC, exercises considerable influence.

International Accounting Standards Board   When an enterprise operates beyond the borders of its own country, differences in financial reporting practices between countries can pose significant problems. For example, when a company buys or sells products in another country, the lack of comparability of accounting information can create uncertainties. Similarly, cross-border financing, where companies sell their securities in the capital markets of another country, is increasingly popular. Business activities that cross borders create the need for more comparable information between companies that reside in different countries.

As a result of increasing cross-border activities, efforts are under way to harmonize accounting standards around the world. The **International Accounting Standards Board (IASB)** is playing a leading role in the harmonization process. The London-based IASB is an elite panel of professionals with deep knowledge of accounting methods used in the most vibrant capital markets.

The IASB issues *International Financial Reporting Standards (IFRSs).* European Union countries, Australia, and Canada, among over 100 other countries, require listed companies to follow IASB standards. Most important, the SEC accepts financial statements prepared using IASB standards from foreign companies that are cross-listed on a U.S. stock exchange. In addition, the AICPA, which essentially has jurisdiction over private company reporting, accepts either FASB standards or IASB standards as authoritative sources of accounting principles.

In early 2010, the SEC issued a Statement in Support of Convergence and Global Accounting Standards. This SEC statement reaffirms the SEC's belief that a single set of high-quality, global accounting standards is in the best interests of investors, and also reaffirms the SEC's belief that IFRS as issued by the IASB is the set of standards best positioned to fill this role. However, in 2012 the SEC issued an extensive report on requiring U.S. public companies to use IFRS. Although the SEC report concluded that IASB standards are generally viewed as high quality, there remain significant obstacles to adopting IASB standards in the United States, including the IASB's dependence on funding from the major accounting firms. In addition, a number of U.S. companies indicated that adopting IFRS could be among the largest accounting-related costs ever imposed on the private sector.[6]

CASE IN POINT

If the United States moves to IFRS, it likely would require significant changes to accounting systems, controls, and procedures. For example, IFRS requires that an entity account for similar transactions in an identical manner regardless of where the transaction occurs in the entity, a requirement that does not exist under U.S. GAAP. Therefore, if IFRS becomes mandatory for U.S. public companies, companies would have to develop a listing of all of their transactions and how they are accounted for throughout the entity.

[6] United States Securities and Exchange Commissions Office of the Chief Accountant, *Work Plan for the Consideration of Incorporating International Financial Reporting Standards into the Financial Reporting System for U.S. Issuers,* July 2012.

Public Company Accounting Oversight Board   The **Public Company Accounting Oversight Board (PCAOB)** is a quasi-governmental body charged with oversight of the public accounting profession. The Board was created as a result of the Sarbanes-Oxley Act of 2002 and began operations in the spring of 2003.

The PCAOB has extensive powers in overseeing the accounting profession. As stated earlier in the chapter, any accounting firm wishing to audit a public company must register with the PCAOB. The PCAOB sets auditing standards for audits of publicly traded companies, an activity that previously was performed by the accounting profession. The Board also inspects the quality of audits performed by public accounting firms and conducts investigations and administers penalties when substandard audit work is alleged.

The PCAOB is headquartered in Washington, D.C., and has regional offices in major cities throughout the United States. The PCAOB has five members who serve a five-year term and are eligible to be reappointed once. No more than two members of the Board can be certified public accountants. The Board also maintains a large and well-qualified staff. The PCAOB is funded by a mandatory assessment on publicly traded companies. The assessment is a function of the company's market value relative to overall stock market value in the United States.

Audits of Financial Statements   What assurance do outsiders have that the financial statements issued by management provide a complete and reliable picture of the company's financial position and operating results? In large part, this assurance is provided by an *audit* of the company's financial statements, performed by a firm of *certified public accountants (CPAs)*. These auditors are experts in the field of financial reporting and are *independent* of the company issuing the financial statements.

An **audit** is an *investigation* of a company's financial statements, designed to determine the fairness of these statements. Accountants and auditors use the term *fair* in describing financial statements that are reliable and complete, conform to generally accepted accounting principles, and are *not misleading*.

In the auditing of financial statements, generally accepted accounting principles are the standard by which those statements are judged. For the auditor to reach the conclusion that the financial statements are fair representations of a company's financial position, results of operations, and cash flows, the statements must comply in all important ways with generally accepted accounting principles.

Legislation   As discussed previously, Congress passed the Sarbanes-Oxley Act in 2002. Among the more important provisions of Sarbanes-Oxley is the creation of the Public Company Accounting Oversight Board described earlier in this chapter. Another important provision of the Act is to ban auditors from providing many nonaudit services for their audit clients on the assumption that those services interfere with the objectivity required of auditors in rendering opinions regarding financial statements upon which investors and creditors rely. Sarbanes-Oxley also places additional responsibilities on corporate boards of directors and audit committees with regard to their oversight of external auditors, and it places responsibility on chief executive officers and chief financial officers of companies to certify the fairness of the company's financial statements.

PROFESSIONAL ORGANIZATIONS

LO1-6

LEARNING OBJECTIVE
Identify and discuss several
professional organizations
that play important roles in
preparing and communicating
accounting information.

Several professional accounting organizations play an active role in improving the quality of accounting information that is used by investors, creditors, management, and others. In addition to the Securities and Exchange Commission, Financial Accounting Standards Board, and International Accounting Standards Board discussed earlier, the American Institute of CPAs, the Institute of Management Accountants, the Institute of Internal Auditors, the American Accounting Association, and the Committee of Sponsoring Organizations of the Treadway Commission are particularly important.

American Institute of CPAs (AICPA)   The **American Institute of CPAs** is a professional association of certified public accountants. Its mission is to provide members with the resources, information, and leadership to enable them to provide valuable services in the highest professional manner to benefit the public, employers, and clients.[7] The AICPA participates in many aspects of the accounting profession. The AICPA conducts accounting research and works closely with the FASB in the establishment and interpretation of generally accepted accounting principles. In fact, prior to the establishment of the FASB, the AICPA had primary responsibility for the establishment of accounting principles. The AICPA's Auditing Standards Board has developed the standards by which audits of private companies are conducted, and the PCAOB has accepted many of these standards for audits of public companies. The AICPA also issues standards for the conduct of other professional services. Finally, the AICPA is responsible for the preparation and grading of the CPA examination, which is discussed later in this chapter.

Institute of Management Accountants (IMA)

The mission of the **Institute of Management Accountants** is to provide a forum for research, practice development, education, knowledge sharing, and the advocacy of the highest ethical and best business practices in management accounting and finance.[8] The IMA is recognized by the financial community as a respected organization that influences the concepts and ethical practice of management accounting and financial management. The IMA sponsors a number of educational activities for its members, including national seminars and conferences, regional and local programs, self-study courses, and in-house and online programs. The IMA offers a certification program—the Certified Management Accountant (CMA). This designation testifies to the individual's competence and expertise in management accounting and financial management.

Institute of Internal Auditors (IIA)

With more than 175,000 members in over 100 countries, the **Institute of Internal Auditors** is the primary international professional association dedicated to the promotion and development of the practice of internal auditing.[9] It provides professional development through the Certified Internal Auditor® Program and leadingedge conferences and seminars; research through the IIA Research Foundation on trends, best practices, and other internal auditing issues; guidance through the *Standards for the Professional Practice of Internal Auditing;* and educational products on virtually all aspects of the profession. The IIA also provides audit specialty services and industry-specific auditing programs, as well as quality assurance reviews and benchmarking services.

American Accounting Association (AAA)

Membership in the **American Accounting Association** is made up primarily of accounting educators, although many practicing accountants are members as well. The mission of the AAA includes advancing accounting education and research, as well as influencing accounting practice. The focus of many of the AAA's activities is on improving accounting education by better preparing accounting professors and on advancing knowledge in the accounting discipline through research and publication. An important contribution of the AAA to the integrity of accounting information is its impact through accounting faculty on the many students who study accounting in college and subsequently become professional accountants.

Committee of Sponsoring Organizations of the Treadway Commission (COSO)

COSO is a voluntary private sector organization dedicated to providing thought leadership through the development of comprehensive frameworks and guidance on enterprise risk management, internal control, and fraud deterrence designed to improve organizational performance and governance and to reduce the extent of fraud in organizations.[10] COSO was originally formed in 1985 to sponsor the National Commission on Fraudulent Financial Reporting (chaired by former SEC Commissioner James C. Treadway, Jr.). The National Commission on Fraudulent Financial Reporting studied the causal factors that lead to fraudulent financial reporting and made a series of recommendations for improving financial reporting, auditing, and accounting education. The original sponsors of the National

---

[7] www.aicpa.org.

[8] www.imanet.org.

[9] www.theiia.org.

[10] www.coso.org.

Commission on Fraudulent Financial Reporting, and the current sponsors of COSO, are the AAA, the AICPA, Financial Executives International, the IIA, and the IMA.

COSO is best known for its work in developing the standards for evaluating internal control—particularly internal control over financial reporting. As a result of the Sarbanes-Oxley Act, public companies now need to evaluate the effectiveness of their internal control over financial reporting on a yearly basis, as well as have their auditors separately report on the auditors' evaluation of the effectiveness of internal control over financial reporting. The standard for evaluating the effectiveness of internal control over financial reporting is contained in COSO's 2013 publication, *Internal Control–Integrated Framework: 2013.*

COMPETENCE, JUDGMENT, AND ETHICAL BEHAVIOR

L01-7

LEARNING OBJECTIVE
Discuss the importance of personal competence, professional judgment, and ethical behavior on the part of accounting professionals.

Preparing and presenting accounting information is not a mechanical task that can be performed entirely by a computer or even by well-trained clerical personnel. A characteristic common to all recognized professions, including medicine, law, and accounting, is the need for competent individual practitioners to solve problems using their professional judgment and applying strong ethical standards. The problems encountered in the practice of a profession are often complex, and the specific circumstances unique. In many cases, the well-being of others is directly affected by the work of a professional.

To illustrate the importance of competence, professional judgment, and ethical behavior in the preparation of financial statements, consider the following complex issues that must be addressed by the accountant:

- At what point should an enterprise account for transactions that continue over a long period of time, such as a long-term contract to construct an interstate highway?
- What constitutes adequate disclosure of information that would be expected by a reasonably informed user of financial statements?
- At what point are a company's financial problems sufficient to question whether it will be able to remain in business for the foreseeable future, and when should that information be communicated to users of its financial statements?
- When have efforts by management to improve (that is, "window dress") its financial statements crossed a line that is inappropriate, making the financial statements actually misleading to investors and creditors?

Judgment always involves some risk of error. Some errors in judgment result from carelessness or inexperience on the part of the preparer of financial information or the decision maker who uses that information. Others occur simply because future events are uncertain and do not work out as expected when the information was prepared.

If the public is to have confidence in the judgment of professional accountants, these accountants first must demonstrate that they possess the characteristic of *competence.* Both the accounting profession and state governments have taken steps to assure the public of the technical competence of **certified public accountants** (CPAs). CPAs are licensed by the states, in much the same manner as states license physicians and attorneys. The licensing requirements vary somewhat from state to state, but in general, an individual must be of good character, have completed 150 semester hours of college work with a major in accounting, pass a rigorous examination, and have accounting experience. In addition, most states require all CPAs to spend at least 40 hours per year in continuing professional education throughout their careers.

Management accountants are not required to be licensed as CPAs. However, they voluntarily may earn a **Certified Management Accountant** (CMA) or a **Certified Internal Auditor** (CIA) as evidence of their professional competence. These certifications are issued by the IMA and the IIA, and signify competence in management accounting and internal auditing, respectively. The requirements for becoming a CMA and CIA are similar to those for becoming a CPA.

Integrity in accounting requires honesty and a strong commitment to ethical conduct—doing the right thing. For a professional accountant, ethical behavior is just as important as competence. However, it is far more difficult to test or enforce.

Many professional organizations have codes of ethics or professional conduct that direct the activities of their members. The AICPA, for example, has a code of professional conduct that expresses the accounting profession's recognition of its responsibilities to the public, to clients, and to colleagues. The principles included in the code guide AICPA members in the performance of their professional responsibilities. This code expresses the basic tenets of ethical and professional behavior and is enforced in conjunction with state professional societies of CPAs, although state regulatory boards take precedence in regulating the CPA license.

Exhibit 1–6 contains excerpts from the AICPA code of professional conduct. One of the principles expressed in the AICPA's code of professional conduct is the commitment of CPAs

---

YOUR TURN · You as a Professional Accountant

You are a professional accountant working for a public accounting firm and find yourself in a difficult situation. You have discovered some irregularities in the financial records of your firm's client. You are uncertain whether these irregularities are the result of carelessness on the part of the company's employees or represent intentional steps taken to cover up questionable activities. You approach your superior about this and she indicates that you should ignore it. Her response is, "These things happen all of the time and usually are pretty minor. We are on a very tight time schedule to complete this engagement, so let's just keep our eyes on our goal of finishing our work by the end of the month." What would you do?

(See our comments on the Online Learning Center website.)

EXHIBIT 1–6

Excerpts from the AICPA Code of Professional Conduct

Preamble

These Principles of the Code of Professional Conduct of the American Institute of Certified Public Accountants express the profession's recognition of its responsibilities to the public, to clients, and to colleagues.[11] They guide members in the performance of their professional responsibilities and express the basic tenets of ethical and professional conduct. The Principles call for an unswerving commitment to honorable behavior, even at the sacrifice of personal advantage.

Articles

I. Responsibilities

In carrying out their responsibilities as professionals, members should exercise sensitive professional and moral judgments in all their activities.

II. The Public Interest

Members should accept the obligation to act in a way that will serve the public interest, honor the public trust, and demonstrate commitment to professionalism.

III. Integrity

To maintain and broaden public confidence, members should perform all professional responsibilities with the highest sense of integrity.

IV. Objectivity and Independence

A member should maintain objectivity and be free of conflicts of interest in discharging professional responsibilities. A member in public practice should be independent in fact and appearance when providing auditing and other attestation services.

V. Due Care

A member should observe the profession's technical and ethical standards, strive continually to improve competence and the quality of services, and discharge professional responsibility to the best of the member's ability.

VI. Scope and Nature of Services

A member in public practice should observe the Principles of the Code of Professional Conduct in determining the scope and nature of services to be provided.

to the public interest, shown in Article II. The public interest is defined as the collective well-being of the community of people and institutions the profession serves. Other principles emphasize the importance of integrity, objectivity, independence, and due care in the performance of one's duties.

Expectations of ethical conduct are also important for other accountants. The IMA has a code of conduct for management accountants, as does the IIA for internal auditors.

Users of accounting information—both external and internal—recognize that the reliability of the information is affected by the competence, professional judgment, and ethical standards of accountants. While the institutional features and professional organizations that were discussed earlier are important parts of the financial reporting system, the personal attributes of competence, professional judgment, and ethical behavior ultimately ensure the quality and reliability of accounting information.

In this text, we address the topic of ethical conduct primarily through questions, exercises, problems, and cases that emphasize the general concepts of honesty, fairness, and adequate disclosure. Most chapters include assignment material in which you are asked to make judgment calls in applying these concepts. (These assignments are identified by the scales of justice logo appearing in the margin.)

Careers in Accounting

L01-8

LEARNING OBJECTIVE
Describe various career
opportunities in accounting.

Accounting—along with such fields as architecture, engineering, law, medicine, and theology—is recognized as a profession. What distinguishes a profession from other disciplines? There is no single recognized definition of a profession, but all of these fields have several characteristics in common.

First, all professions involve a complex and evolving body of knowledge. In accounting, the complexity and the ever-changing nature of the business world, financial reporting requirements, management's demands for increasingly complex information, and income tax laws certainly meet this criterion.

Second, in all professions, practitioners must use their professional judgment to resolve problems and dilemmas. Throughout this text, we will point out situations requiring accountants to exercise professional judgment.

Of greatest importance, however, is the unique responsibility of professionals *to serve the public's best interest, even at the sacrifice of personal advantage.* This responsibility stems from the fact that the public has little technical knowledge in the professions, yet fair and competent performance by professionals is vital to the public's health, safety, or well-being. The practice of medicine, for example, directly affects public health, while engineering affects public safety. Accounting affects the public's well-being in many ways, because accounting information is used in the allocation of economic resources throughout society. Thus, accountants have a basic social contract to avoid being associated with misleading information.

Accountants tend to specialize in specific fields, as do the members of other professions. Career opportunities in accounting may be divided into four broad areas: (1) public accounting, (2) management accounting, (3) governmental accounting, and (4) accounting education.

PUBLIC ACCOUNTING

Certified public accountants offer a variety of accounting services to the public. These individuals may work in a CPA firm or as sole practitioners.

The work of public accountants consists primarily of auditing financial statements, income tax work, and management advisory services (management consulting).

Management advisory services extend well beyond tax planning and accounting matters; CPAs advise management on such diverse issues as international mergers, manufacturing processes, and the introduction of new products. CPAs assist management because *financial considerations enter into almost every business decision.*

---

[11] **www.aicpa.org.**

A great many CPAs move from public accounting into managerial positions with organizations. These "alumni" from public accounting often move directly into such top management positions as controller, treasurer, or chief financial officer.

The CPA Examination   To become a CPA, a person must meet several criteria, including an extensive university education requirement, passing the CPA examination, and meeting a practice experience requirement. CPA certificates are granted by 55 legal jurisdictions (50 U.S. states, Guam, Puerto Rico, the Virgin Islands, Washington, D.C., and the Mariana Islands). The CPA examination is a rigorous examination that covers a variety of accounting and business subjects that allow candidates to demonstrate their knowledge and skills in areas believed important for protecting the public. The exam is computer-based and is offered at many testing centers throughout the United States.

MANAGEMENT ACCOUNTING

In contrast to the public accountant who serves many clients, the management accountant works for one enterprise. Management accountants develop and interpret accounting information designed specifically to meet the various needs of management.

The chief accounting officer of an organization usually is called the *chief accounting officer (CAO)* or *controller.* The term *controller* has been used to emphasize the fact that one basic purpose of accounting data is to aid in controlling business operations. The CAO or controller is part of the top management team, which is responsible for running the business, setting its objectives, and seeing that these objectives are met. For example, only three corporate officers are required to sign the Form 10-K that public companies file yearly with the Securities and Exchange Commission—the CEO, the CFO, and the chief accounting officer (CAO).

In addition to developing information to assist managers, management accountants are responsible for operating the company's accounting system, including the recording of transactions and the preparation of financial statements, tax returns, and other accounting reports. Because the responsibilities of management accountants are so broad, many areas of specialization have developed. Among the more important are financial forecasting, cost accounting, and internal auditing.

GOVERNMENTAL ACCOUNTING

Governmental agencies use accounting information in allocating their resources and in controlling their operations. Therefore, the need for management accountants in governmental agencies is similar to that in business organizations.

The GAO: Who Audits the Government?   The **Government Accountability Office** (GAO) audits many agencies of the federal government, as well as some private organizations doing business with the government. The GAO reports its findings directly to Congress, which, in turn, often discloses these findings to the public.

GAO investigations may be designed either to evaluate the efficiency of an entity's operations or to determine the fairness of accounting information reported to the government.

The IRS: Audits of Income Tax Returns   Another governmental agency that performs extensive auditing work is the **Internal Revenue Service** (IRS). The IRS handles the millions of income tax returns filed annually by individuals and business organizations and frequently performs auditing functions to verify data contained in these returns.

The SEC: The "Watchdog" of Financial Reporting   The SEC works closely with the FASB in establishing generally accepted accounting principles. Most publicly owned corporations must file audited financial statements with the SEC each year. If the SEC believes that a company's financial statements are deficient in any way, it conducts an investigation. If the SEC concludes that federal securities laws have been violated, it initiates legal action against the reporting entity and responsible individuals.

Many other governmental agencies, including the FBI, the Treasury Department, and the FDIC (Federal Deposit Insurance Corporation), use accountants to audit compliance with governmental regulations and to investigate suspected criminal activity. People beginning their careers in governmental accounting often move into top administrative positions.

ACCOUNTING EDUCATION

Some accountants, including your instructor and the authors of this textbook, have chosen to pursue careers in accounting education. A position as an accounting faculty member offers opportunities for teaching, research, consulting, and an unusual degree of freedom in developing individual skills. Accounting educators contribute to the accounting profession in many ways. One, of course, lies in effective teaching; second, in publishing significant research findings; and third, in influencing top students to pursue careers in accounting.

WHAT ABOUT BOOKKEEPING?

Some people think that the work of professional accountants consists primarily of bookkeeping. Actually, it doesn't. In fact, many professional accountants do *little or no* book-keeping. **Bookkeeping** is the clerical side of accounting—the recording of routine transactions and day-to-day record keeping. Today such tasks are performed primarily by computers and skilled clerical personnel, not by accountants.

Professional accountants are involved more with the *interpretation and use* of accounting information than with its actual preparation. Their work includes evaluating the efficiency of operations, resolving complex financial reporting issues, forecasting the results of future operations, auditing, tax planning, and designing efficient accounting systems. There is very little that is "routine" about the work of a professional accountant.

A person might become a proficient bookkeeper in a few weeks or months. To become a professional accountant, however, is a far greater challenge because this requires more than understanding the bookkeeping systems. It requires years of study, experience, and an ongoing commitment to keeping current.

We will illustrate and explain a number of bookkeeping procedures in this text, particularly in the next several chapters. But teaching bookkeeping skills is *not* our goal; the primary purpose of this text is to develop your abilities to *understand and use* accounting information in today's business world.

ACCOUNTING AS A STEPPING-STONE

We have mentioned that many professional accountants leave their accounting careers for key positions in management or administration. An accounting background is invaluable in such positions, because top management works continuously with issues defined and described in accounting terms and concepts.

An especially useful stepping-stone is experience in public accounting. Public accountants have the unusual opportunity of getting an inside look at many different business organizations, which makes them particularly well suited for top management positions in other organizations.

BUT WHAT ABOUT ME? I'M NOT AN ACCOUNTING MAJOR

Most students who use this book are not accounting majors. However, the study of accounting is still important to you. You need to understand accounting concepts, both for your professional careers and for many aspects of your personal life. Accounting is the language of business, and trying to run a business without understanding accounting information is analogous to trying to play sports without understanding the rules. Finance students need to understand accounting concepts if they seek positions in investment banking, consulting, or in corporate America as a financial analyst. Approximately 50 percent of the chief financial officers of large U.S. corporations have a background in accounting. A management student seeking a career as a management trainee—with the ultimate goal of running a corporation or a corporate division—needs to understand accounting in order to be able to run, control, and evaluate the performance of a business unit. For example, the CEO, who holds the top management position, must certify the accuracy of the company's financial statements on a quarterly and yearly basis. The Sarbanes-Oxley Act imposes severe civil and criminal sanctions on CEOs who certify their company's financial statements if the CEO knows, or should have known, that the financial statements are materially misstated. Marketing students often take positions in sales. It is imperative that marketing students understand the principles of revenue recognition, as well as the obligations of a public company under the U.S. securities laws. A lack of

Ethics, Fraud, & Corporate Governance

The early 2000s was a time of unprecedented business failures amid allegations of fraudulent financial reporting that include corporations that have now become household names—Enron, WorldCom, HealthSouth, Adelphia Communications, Tyco, and Qwest, among others. These problems are not exclusively a problem with financial reporting in the United States, as evidenced by fraud allegations at Parmalat, a large Italian company.

Fraud typically is perpetrated by senior management; for example, a 2010 study indicates that the company's chief executive officer and/or chief financial officer is involved in 89 percent of the fraud-related enforcement actions brought by the Securities and Exchange Commission. Committing fraud, an illegal act, obviously suggests a serious lack of ethical awareness and ethical sensitivity on the part of the perpetrators. Another feature of many frauds is that the company where the fraud occurred had a weak corporate governance environment. **Corporate governance** entails corporate structures and processes for overseeing the company's affairs, including oversight by the board of directors of the actions of top management to ensure that the company is being managed with the best interests of shareholders in mind.

In each chapter, we will discuss common fraud-related schemes relevant to the material covered in that chapter, ethical quandaries and challenges faced by businesspeople, or efforts to improve corporate governance and by extension the quality of accounting information in the United States.

© AP Photo/Adam Rountree

Dennis Kozlowski, the former CEO of Tyco, leaves court upon his conviction for conspiracy, securities fraud, and falsifying records. Kozlowski was sentenced to 8⅓ to 25 years in prison. A failure to understand and apply securities laws exposes management to great personal and professional risk.

this understanding has led many a marketing/sales executive to become involved in improper revenue recognition schemes. Many of these executives have been subject to civil and criminal prosecution.

Finally, accounting knowledge is helpful in many aspects of your personal lives. Accounting concepts are integral to such everyday decisions as personal budgeting, retirement and college planning, lease versus buy decisions, evaluation of loan terms, and evaluation of investment opportunities. Since accounting skills are designed to help you make better economic decisions, you will be using these skills for the rest of your life. The only question is the degree of skill with which you will apply these concepts. Unfortunately, there is substantial evidence that most Americans have a low level of skill when it comes to applying accounting or financial concepts. For example, a recent study by the Securities and Exchange Commission found that "retail investors have a weak grasp of elementary financial concepts and lack critical knowledge of ways to avoid investment fraud."[12]

Concluding Remarks

In this chapter, we have established a framework for your study of accounting. You have learned how financial accounting provides information for external users, primarily investors and creditors, and how accounting provides information for internal management. We have

---

[12] U.S. Securities and Exchange Commission, *Study Regarding Financial Literacy Among Investors,* August 2012.

established the importance of integrity in accounting information and have learned about several things that build integrity. Looking ahead, in Chapter 2 we begin to look in greater depth at financial accounting and, more specifically, financial statements. You will be introduced to the details of the three primary financial statements that provide information for investors and creditors. As the text progresses, you will learn more about the important information that these financial statements provide and how that information is used to make important financial decisions.

END-OF-CHAPTER REVIEW

SUMMARY OF LEARNING OBJECTIVES

LO1-1 **Discuss accounting as the language of business and the role of accounting information in making economic decisions.** Accounting is the means by which information about an enterprise is communicated and, thus, is sometimes called the language of business. Many different users have need for accounting information in order to make important decisions. These users include investors, creditors, management, governmental agencies, labor unions, and others. Because the primary role of accounting information is to provide useful information for decision-making purposes, it is sometimes referred to as a means to an end, with the end being the decision that is helped by the availability of accounting information.

LO1-2 **Discuss the significance of accounting systems in generating reliable accounting information and understand the five components of internal control.** Information systems are critical to the production of quality accounting information on a timely basis and the communication of that information to decision makers. While there are different types of information systems, they all have one characteristic in common—to meet the organization's needs for accounting information as efficiently as possible. Per the COSO framework, the five elements of internal control are: (1) control environment, (2) risk assessment, (3) control activities, (4) information and communication, and (5) monitoring activities.

LO1-3 **Explain the importance of financial accounting information for external parties—primarily investors and creditors—in terms of the objectives and the characteristics of that information.** The primary objectives of financial accounting are to provide information that is useful in making investment and credit decisions; in assessing the amount, timing, and uncertainty of future cash flows; and in learning about the enterprise's economic resources, claims to resources, and changes in claims to resources. Some of the most important characteristics of financial accounting information are: It is a means to an end, it is historical in nature, it results from inexact and approximate measures of business activity, and it is based on a general-purpose assumption.

LO1-4 **Explain the importance of accounting information for internal parties—primarily management—in terms of the objectives and the characteristics of that information.** Accounting information is useful to the enterprise in achieving its goals, objectives, and mission; assessing past performance and future directions; and evaluating and rewarding decision-making performance. Some of the important characteristics of internal accounting information are its timeliness, its relationship to decision-making authority, its future orientation, its relationship to measuring efficiency and effectiveness, and the fact that it is a means to an end.

LO1-5 **Discuss elements of the system of external and internal financial reporting that create integrity in the reported information.** Integrity of financial reporting is important because of the reliance that is placed on financial information by users both outside and inside the reporting organization. Important dimensions of financial reporting that work together to ensure integrity in information are institutional features (accounting principles, internal structure, audits, and legislation); professional organizations (the AICPA, IMA, IIA, AAA); and the competence, judgment, and ethical behavior of individual accountants.

LO1-6 **Identify and discuss several professional organizations that play important roles in preparing and communicating accounting information.** The FASB, IASB, PCAOB, and SEC are important organizations in terms of standard setting in the United States. The FASB and IASB are private-sector organizations that establish accounting standards for public and private companies. The PCAOB sets auditing standards and oversees accounting firms. The SEC is a governmental entity that oversees U.S. public companies and the capital markets.

LO1-7 **Discuss the importance of personal competence, professional judgment, and ethical behavior on the part of accounting professionals.** Personal competence and professional judgment are, perhaps, the most important factors in ensuring the integrity of financial information. Competence is demonstrated by one's education and professional certification (CPA, CMA, CIA). Professional judgment is important because accounting information is often based on inexact measurements and assumptions are required. Ethical behavior refers to the quality of accountants being motivated to "do the right thing."

LO1-8 **Describe various career opportunities in accounting.** Accounting opens the door to many career opportunities. Public accounting is the segment of the profession where professionals offer audit, tax, and consulting services. Management, or managerial, accounting refers to that segment of the accounting profession where professional accountants work for individual companies in a wide variety of capacities. Many accountants work for governmental agencies. Some accountants choose education as a career and work to prepare students for future careers in one of the other segments of the accounting profession. While keeping detailed records (that is, bookkeeping) is a part of accounting, it is not a distinguishing characteristic of a career in accounting; in fact, many accounting careers involve little or no bookkeeping. Accounting skills are important to nonaccounting majors and to all students in their personal lives.

Key Terms Introduced or Emphasized in Chapter 1

accounting system (p. 6)   The personnel, procedures, devices, and records used by an organization to develop accounting information and communicate that information to decision makers.

American Accounting Association (p. 21)   A professional accounting organization consisting primarily of accounting educators that is dedicated to improving accounting education, research, and practice.

American Institute of CPAs (p. 20)   A professional accounting organization of certified public accountants that engages in a variety of professional activities, including establishing auditing standards for private companies, conducting research, and preparing and grading the CPA exam.

audit (p. 20)   An investigation of financial statements designed to determine their fairness in relation to generally accepted accounting principles.

balance sheet (p. 12)   A position statement that shows where the company stands in financial terms at a specific date. (Also called the statement of financial position.)

bookkeeping (p. 26)   The clerical dimension of accounting that includes recording the routine transactions and day-to-day record keeping of an enterprise.

cash flow prospects (p. 10)   The likelihood that an enterprise will be able to provide an investor with both a return on the investor's investment and the return of that investment.

Certified Internal Auditor (p. 22)   A professional designation issued by the Institute of Internal Auditors signifying expertise in internal auditing.

Certified Management Accountant (p. 22)   A professional designation issued by the Institute of Management Accountants signifying expertise in management accounting.

Certified Public Accountant (p. 22)   An accountant who is licensed by a state after meeting rigorous education, experience, and examination requirements.

Committee of Sponsoring Organizations of the Treadway Commission (COSO) (p. 21)   A voluntary private-sector organization dedicated to improving the quality of financial reporting through enterprise risk management, effective internal control, and fraud deterrence.

control activities (p. 9)   Policies and procedures that management puts in place to address the risks identified during the risk assessment process.

control environment (p. 9)   The foundation for all the other elements of internal control, setting the overall tone for the organization.

corporate governance (p. 27)   Includes the corporate structures and processes for overseeing a company's affairs, for example, the board of directors and the company's internal control processes.

external users (p. 10)   Individuals and other enterprises that have a financial interest in the reporting enterprise but that are not involved in the day-to-day operations of that enterprise (e.g., owners, creditors, labor unions, suppliers, customers).

financial accounting (p. 6)   Providing information about the financial resources, obligations, and activities of an economic entity that is intended for use primarily by external decision makers—investors and creditors.

Financial Accounting Standards Board (FASB) (p. 18)   A private-sector organization that is responsible for determining generally accepted accounting principles in the United States.

financial statement (p. 12)   A monetary declaration of what is believed to be true about an enterprise.

general-purpose information (p. 14)   Information that is intended to meet the needs of multiple users that have an interest in the financial activities of an enterprise rather than tailored to the specific information needs of one user.

generally accepted accounting principles (GAAP) (p. 18)   Principles that provide the framework for determining what information is to be included in financial statements and how that information is to be presented.

Government Accountability Office (p. 25)   A federal government agency that audits many other agencies of the federal government and other organizations that do business with the federal government and reports its findings to Congress.

income statement (p. 12)   An activity statement that shows details and results of the company's profit-related activities for a period of time.

information and communication (p. 9)   The organization's process for capturing operational, financial, and compliance-related information necessary to run the business, and communicating that information downstream (from management to employees), upstream (from employees to management), and across the organization.

Institute of Internal Auditors (p. 21)   A professional accounting organization that is dedicated to the promotion and development of the practice of internal auditing.

Institute of Management Accountants (p. 21)   A professional accounting organization that intends to influence the concepts and ethical practice of management accounting and financial management.

integrity (p. 17)   The qualities of being complete, unbroken, unimpaired, sound, honest, and sincere.

internal control (p. 8)   A process designed to provide reasonable assurance that the organization produces reliable financial reports, complies with applicable laws and regulations, and conducts its operations in an efficient and effective manner.

Internal Revenue Service (p. 25)   A government organization that handles millions of income tax returns filed by individuals and businesses and performs audit functions to verify the data contained in those returns.

internal users (p. 14)   Individuals who use accounting information from within an organization (for example, board of directors, chief financial officer, plant managers, store managers).

International Accounting Standards Board (IASB) (p. 19)   The group responsible for creating and promoting *International Financial Reporting Standards (IFRSs)*.

management accounting (p. 6)   Providing information that is intended primarily for use by internal management in decision making required to run the business.

monitoring activities (p. 9)   The process of evaluating the effectiveness of an organization's system of internal control over time, including both ongoing management and supervisory activities and periodic separate evaluations.

Public Company Accounting Oversight Board (PCAOB) (p. 20)   A quasi-governmental body charged with oversight of the public accounting profession. The PCAOB sets auditing standards for audits of publicly traded companies.

return of investment (p. 10)   The repayment to an investor of the amount originally invested in another enterprise.

return on investment (p. 10)   The payment of an amount (interest, dividends) for using another's money.

risk assessment (p. 9)   A process of identifying, analyzing, and managing those risks that pose a threat to the achievement of the organization's objectives.

Sarbanes-Oxley Act (p. 9)   A landmark piece of securities law, designed to improve the effectiveness of corporate financial

reporting through enhanced accountability of auditors, audit committees, and management.

Securities and Exchange Commission (SEC) (p. 18)   A governmental organization that has the legal power to establish accounting principles and financial reporting requirements for publicly held companies in the United States.

statement of cash flows (p. 12)   An activity statement that shows the details of the company's activities involving cash during a period of time.

statement of financial position (p. 13)   Also called the balance sheet.

Demonstration Problem

Find the Intel Corporation annual 10-K report from 2012 at the following Internet address (www.intc.com/secfiling.cfm?filingID=1193125-13-65416) to answer the following questions:

a. Name the titles of the financial reports in the Intel Corp. annual report that provide specific information about economic resources, claims to resources, and changes in resources and claims.

b. Name three other sections from Intel's 2012 annual report that provide information useful in assessing the amount, timing, and uncertainty of future cash flows.

c. Which main categories of other general information are useful in making investment and credit decisions?

Solution to the Demonstration Problem

a. • Intel Corporation
     Consolidated Balance Sheets

  • Intel Corporation
     Consolidated Statements of Stockholders' Equity

  • Intel Corporation
     Consolidated Statements of Income

  • Intel Corporation
     Consolidated Statements of Cash Flows

b. • Management's Discussion and Analysis of Financial Condition and Results of Operations

  • Quantitative and Qualitative Disclosures about Market Risk

  • Notes to the Consolidated Financial Statements

c. • Business Discussion

  • Management's Discussion and Analysis of Financial Condition and Results of Operations that contains general discussions about strategy, results of operations, business outlook, and liquidity and capital resources

  • Report of the Independent Registered Public Accounting Firm

Self-Test Questions

The answers to these questions appear on page 37.

1. Which of the following does *not* describe accounting?

  a. Language of business.

  b. Is an end rather than a means to an end.

  c. Useful for decision making.

  d. Used by business, government, nonprofit organizations, and individuals.

2. To understand and use accounting information in making economic decisions, you must understand:

   a. The nature of economic activities that accounting information describes.

   b. The assumptions and measurement techniques involved in developing accounting information.

   c. Which information is relevant for a particular type of decision that is being made.

   d. All of the above.

3. Purposes of an accounting system include all of the following *except:*

   a. Interpret and record the effects of business transactions.

   b. Classify the effects of transactions to facilitate the preparation of reports.

   c. Summarize and communicate information to decision makers.

   d. Dictate the specific types of business transactions that the enterprise may engage in.

4. External users of financial accounting information include all of the following *except:*

   a. Investors.

   b. Labor unions.

   c. Line managers.

   d. General public.

5. Objectives of financial reporting to external investors and creditors include preparing information about all of the following *except:*

   a. Information used to determine which products to produce.

   b. Information about economic resources, claims to those resources, and changes in both resources and claims.

   c. Information that is useful in assessing the amount, timing, and uncertainty of future cash flows.

   d. Information that is useful in making investment and credit decisions.

6. Financial accounting information is characterized by all of the following *except:*

   a. It is historical in nature.

   b. It sometimes results from inexact and approximate measures.

   c. It is factual, so it does not require judgment to prepare.

   d. It is enhanced by management's explanation.

7. Which of the following is *not* a user of internal accounting information?

   a. Store manager.

   b. Chief executive officer.

   c. Creditor.

   d. Chief financial officer.

8. Characteristics of internal accounting information include all of the following *except:*

   a. It is audited by a CPA.

   b. It must be timely.

   c. It is oriented toward the future.

   d. It measures efficiency and effectiveness.

9. Which of the following are important factors in ensuring the integrity of accounting information?

   a. Institutional factors, such as standards for preparing information.

   b. Professional organizations, such as the American Institute of CPAs.

   c. Competence, judgment, and ethical behavior of individual accountants.

   d. All of the above.

10. The code of conduct of the American Institute of Certified Public Accountants includes requirements in which of the following areas?

    a. The Public Interest.

    b. Objectivity.

    c. Independence.

    d. All of the above.

ASSIGNMENT MATERIAL   **Discussion Questions**

1. Accounting is sometimes described as the language of business. What is meant by this description?

2. When you invest your savings in a company, what is the difference between the return *on* your investment and the return *of* your investment?

3. Going from general to specific, what are the three primary objectives of financial accounting information?

4. What are the three primary financial statements with which we communicate financial accounting information?

5. Is externally reported financial information always precise and accurate?

6. Is internal accounting information primarily historical or future-oriented? How does that compare with financial accounting information?

7. What is meant by *generally accepted accounting principles,* and how do these principles add to the integrity of financial accounting information?

8. What is the definition of *internal control,* and what are the five components of COSO's internal control framework?

9. What is an *audit,* and how does it add to the integrity of accounting information?

10. What is meant by the professional designations *CPA, CMA,* and *CIA,* and how do these designations add to the integrity of accounting information?

11. Why was the Sarbanes-Oxley legislation passed in 2002, and what are its implications for the accounting profession?

12. What is the Financial Accounting Standards Board (FASB), and what is its role in external financial reporting?

13. What is the Securities and Exchange Commission (SEC), and what is its role in external financial reporting?

14. What is the role of the Public Company Accounting Oversight Board in the audit of financial statements?

15. What is the International Accounting Standards Board (IASB), and what are its objectives?

Brief Exercises

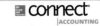

BRIEF EXERCISE 1.1
Users of Information

List four external users of accounting information.

BRIEF EXERCISE 1.2
Components of Internal Control

Match the terms on the left with the descriptions on the right. Each description should be used only once.

Term	Description
_____ Control environment	a. Policies and procedures put in place by management to address the risks identified during the risk assessment process.
_____ Risk assessment	
_____ Control activities	b. A process, involving both ongoing activities and separate evaluations, that enables an organization to evaluate the effectiveness of its system of internal control over time.
_____ Information and communication	
_____ Monitoring activities	c. The foundation for all the other elements of internal control, setting the overall tone for the organization.
	d. The process of capturing and communicating operational, financial, and compliance-related information.
	e. Identifying, analyzing, and managing those risks that pose a threat to the achievement of the organization's objectives.

BRIEF EXERCISE 1.3
Inexact or Approximate Measures

Why does accounting rely on inexact or approximate measures?

BRIEF EXERCISE 1.4
Standards for the Preparation of Accounting Information

What are the two primary organizations in the United States that are responsible for setting standards related to the preparation of accounting information?

BRIEF EXERCISE 1.5
FASB Conceptual Framework

The FASB's conceptual framework sets forth the Board's views on which topics?

BRIEF EXERCISE 1.6
Public Company Accounting Oversight Board (PCAOB)

Use the web to find the home page of the PCAOB. What are the four primary activities of the PCAOB?

BRIEF EXERCISE 1.7
Committee of Sponsoring Organizations (COSO)

Who are the sponsoring organizations of COSO, and what is COSO best known for doing?

BRIEF EXERCISE 1.8
Professional Certifications in Accounting

List three professional certifications offered in accounting and the organizations that offer them.

BRIEF EXERCISE 1.9
AICPA Code of Professional Conduct

Match the terms on the left with the descriptions on the right. Each description should be used only once.

Term	Description
_____ Responsibilities	a. A member in public practice should observe the Principles of the Code of Professional Conduct in determining the scope and nature of services to be provided.
_____ The Public Interest	
_____ Integrity	b. To maintain and broaden public confidence, members should perform all professional responsibilities with the highest sense of integrity.
_____ Objectivity and Independence	
_____ Due Care	c. A member should maintain objectivity and be free of conflicts of interest in discharging professional responsibilities. A member in public practice should be independent in fact and appearance when providing auditing and other attestation services.
_____ Scope and Nature of Services	
	d. Members should accept the obligation to act in a way that will serve the public interest, honor the public trust, and demonstrate commitment to professionalism.
	e. In carrying out their responsibilities as professionals, members should exercise sensitive professional and moral judgments in all their activities.
	f. A member should observe the profession's technical and ethical standards, strive continually to improve competence and the quality of service, and discharge professional responsibility to the best of the member's ability.

BRIEF EXERCISE 1.10
Personal Benefits of Accounting Skills

List three accounting-related skills that are useful to many people in their personal lives.

Exercises

LOI-1
EXERCISE 1.1
You as a User of Accounting Information

Identify several ways in which *you* currently use accounting information in your life as a student. Also identify several situations in which, while you are still a student, you might be required to supply financial information about yourself to others.

LOI-3, LOI-4
EXERCISE 1.2
Users of Accounting Information

Boeing Company is the largest manufacturer of commercial aircraft in the United States and is a major employer in Seattle, Washington. Explain why each of the following individuals or organizations would be interested in financial information about the company.

a. **California Public Employees Retirement System**, one of the world's largest pension funds.

b. **China Airlines**, a rapidly growing airline serving the Pacific Rim.

c. Henry James, a real estate investor considering building apartments in the Seattle area.

d. **Boeing's** management.

e. **International Association of Machinists and Aerospace Workers**, a labor union representing many **Boeing** employees.

LOI-3
EXERCISE 1.3
What Is Financial Reporting?

A major focus of this course is the process of financial reporting.

a. What is meant by the term *financial reporting?*

b. What are the principal accounting reports involved in the financial reporting process? In general terms, what is the purpose of these reports?

c. Do all business entities engage in financial reporting? Explain.

d. How does society benefit from the financial reporting process?

LOI-6
EXERCISE 1.4
Generally Accepted Accounting Principles

Generally accepted accounting principles play an important role in financial reporting.

a. What is meant by the phrase *generally accepted accounting principles?*

b. What are the major sources of these principles?

c. Is there a single comprehensive list of generally accepted accounting principles? Explain.

d. What types of accounting reports are prepared in conformity with generally accepted accounting principles?

LOI-6
EXERCISE 1.5
Accounting Organizations

Describe the roles of the following organizations in establishing generally accepted accounting principles:

a. The FASB   **b.** The AICPA   **c.** The SEC

From which of these organizations can you most easily obtain financial information about publicly owned companies?

LOI-3
EXERCISE 1.6
Investment Return

You recently invested $15,000 of your savings in a security issued by a large company. The security agreement pays you 8 percent per year and has a maturity three years from the day you purchased it. What is the total cash flow you expect to receive from this investment, separated into the return on your investment and the return of your investment?

LOI-3 through LOI-5, LOI-7
EXERCISE 1.7
Accounting Terminology

Match the terms on the left with the descriptions on the right. Each description should be used only once.

Term	Description
_____ Financial accounting	a. Statement of financial position (balance sheet), income statement, statement of cash flows.
_____ Management accounting	b. The segment of the accounting profession that relates to providing audit, tax, and consulting services to clients.
_____ Financial reporting	c. The area of accounting that refers to providing information to support external investment and credit decisions.
_____ Financial statements	d. The procedural aspect of accounting that involves keeping detailed records of business transactions, much of which is done today by computers.
_____ General-purpose assumption	e. Procedures and processes within an organization that ensure the integrity of accounting information.
_____ Integrity	
_____ Internal control	f. A broad term that describes all information provided to external users, including but not limited to financial statements.
_____ Public accounting	g. The area of accounting that refers to providing information to support internal management decisions.
_____ Bookkeeping	h. The fact that the same information is provided to various external users, including investors and creditors.
	i. An important quality of accounting information that allows investors, creditors, management, and other users to rely on the information.

LOI-6
EXERCISE 1.8
Accounting Organizations

Match the organizations on the left with the functions on the right. Each function should be used only once.

Organization	Function
_____ Institute of Internal Auditors	a. The group that creates and promotes International Financial Reporting Standards (IFRSs).
_____ Securities and Exchange Commission	b. Professional association of Certified Public Accountants.
_____ American Institute of CPAs	c. Organization consisting primarily of accounting educators that encourages improvements in teaching and research.
_____ Institute of Management Accountants	d. International organization dedicated to the advancement of internal auditing.
_____ Financial Accounting Standards Board	e. Private-sector organization that establishes accounting standards.
_____ American Accounting Association	f. The body charged with setting auditing standards for audits of public companies.
_____ Public Company Accounting Oversight Board	g. Organization dedicated to providing members personal and professional development opportunities in the area of management accounting.
_____ International Accounting Standards Board	h. Government agency responsible for financial reporting by publicly held companies.

LOI-3, LOI-4

EXERCISE 1.9

Financial and Management Accounting

The major focus of accounting information is to facilitate decision making.

a.   As an investor in a company, what would be your primary objective?

b.   As a manager of a company, what would be your primary objective?

c.   Is the same accounting information likely to be equally useful to you in these two different roles?

LOI-4

EXERCISE 1.10

Management Accounting Information

Internal accounting information is used primarily for internal decision making by an enterprise's management.

a.   What are the three primary purposes of internal accounting information?

b.   Which of these is the most general and which is the most specific?

c.   Give several examples of the kinds of decisions that internal accounting information supports.

LOI-6

EXERCISE 1.11

Accounting Organizations

Describe which professional organization(s) would most likely be of greatest value to you if your position involved each of the following independent roles:

a.   Accounting educator.

b.   Management accountant.

c.   Certified public accountant.

LOI-5

EXERCISE 1.12

Purpose of an Audit

Audits of financial statements are an important part of the accounting process to ensure integrity in financial reporting.

a.   What is the purpose of an audit?

b.   As an external user of accounting information, what meaning would you attach to an audit that concludes that the financial statements are fairly presented in conformity with generally accepted accounting principles?

c.   Would your interest in investing in this same company be affected by an auditor's report that concluded the financial statements were *not* fairly presented? Why or why not?

LOI-5

EXERCISE 1.13

Audits of Financial Statements

The annual financial statements of all large, publicly owned corporations are audited.

a.   What is an audit of financial statements?

b.   Who performs audits?

c.   What is the purpose of an audit?

LOI-7

EXERCISE 1.14

Ethics and Professional Judgment

Ethical conduct and professional judgment each play important roles in the accounting process.

a.   In general terms, explain why it is important to society that people who prepare accounting information act in an ethical manner.

b.   Identify at least three areas in which accountants must exercise *professional judgment,* rather than merely relying on written rules.

LOI-8

EXERCISE 1.15

Careers in Accounting

Four accounting majors, Maria Acosta, Kenzo Nakao, Helen Martin, and Anthony Mandella, recently graduated from Central University and began professional accounting careers. Acosta entered public accounting, Nakao became a management accountant, Martin joined a governmental agency, and Mandella (who had completed a graduate program) became an accounting faculty member.

Assume that each of the four graduates was successful in his or her chosen career. Identify the types of accounting *activities* in which each of these graduates might find themselves specializing several years after graduation.

LOI-1, LOI-3, LOI-5

EXERCISE 1.16

Home Depot, Inc. General and Specific Information

Locate the **Home Depot, Inc.**, 2012 financial statements in Appendix A of this text. Briefly peruse the financial statements and answer the following questions:

a.   Name the titles of each of **Home Depot**'s financial statements that provide specific information about economic resources, claims to resources, and changes in resources and claims.

b.   Name three other sections from **Home Depot**'s 2012 financial statements that might be useful to a potential investor or creditor.

*Due to the introductory nature of this chapter and the conceptual nature of its contents, no items labeled **Problems** are included. In all future chapters, you will find two problem sets, A and B, that generally include computations, are more complex, and generally require more time to complete than the Exercises.*

Critical Thinking Cases

LOI-5

CASE 1.1

Reliability of Financial
Statements

In the mid-2000s, Fannie Mae was in severe financial difficulty and desperately needed additional capital for the company to survive. What factors prevented Fannie Mae from simply providing potential lenders with misleading financial statements to make the company look like a risk-free investment?

LOI-3

CASE 1.2

Objectives of Financial
Accounting

Divide into groups as instructed by your professor and discuss the following:

a. How does the description of accounting as the "language of business" relate to accounting as being useful for investors and creditors?

b. Explain how the decisions you would make might differ if you were an external investor or a member of an enterprise's management team.

LOI-2

CASE 1.3

Accounting Systems

You are employed by a business consulting firm as an information systems specialist. You have just begun an assignment with a startup company and are discussing with the owner her need for an accounting system. How would you respond to the following questions from the owner?

a. What is the meaning of the term *accounting system?*

b. What is the purpose of an accounting system and what are its basic functions?

c. Who is responsible for designing and implementing an accounting system?

LOI-7

CASE 1.4

Codes of Ethics

Assume you have recently completed your college degree with a major in accounting and have accepted a position on the accounting staff of a large corporation. Your supervisor suggests that in preparing for your first day on the job, you become familiar with the basic principles included in the code of ethics of the Institute of Management Accountants. Briefly explain what you learn as you study the code and how it might affect your behavior on your new job. (Use the IMA's website to obtain access to the IMA's Code of Ethics.)

LOI-6, LOI-7

INTERNET CASE 1.5

Accessing Information
on the Internet

The Internet is a good place to get information that is useful to you in your study of accounting. For example, you can find information about accounting firms, standard setters, and regulators.

Instructions

a. The largest U.S. accounting firms are referred to as the Big 4—Deloitte, Ernst & Young, KPMG, and PwC. Find the Internet sites of these four firms and learn what you can about the types of services provided by the firm.

b. The Public Company Accounting Oversight Board (PCAOB) was created by the Sarbanes-Oxley Act to oversee auditors of public companies. Find the PCAOB's Internet site and learn what you can about the PCAOB's four major activities.

c. The Financial Accounting Standards Board (FASB) is the designated accounting standard setter in the U.S. Find the FASB's Internet site and identify the FASB's board members including a brief description of their backgrounds.

d. The International Accounting Standards Board (IASB) is the body that issues International Financial Reporting Standards. Find the IASB's Internet site and identify the IASB's board members including a brief description of the backgrounds of five board members.

Internet sites are time and date sensitive. It is the purpose of these exercises to have you explore the Internet. You may need to use the Yahoo! search engine www.yahoo.com (or another favorite search engine) to find a company's current web address.

Answers to Self-Test Questions

1. b   **2.** d   **3.** d   **4.** c   **5.** a   **6.** c   **7.** c   **8.** a
9. d   **10.** d

CHAPTER 2

Basic Financial Statements

AFTER STUDYING THIS CHAPTER, YOU SHOULD BE ABLE TO:

Learning Objectives

LO2-1 Explain the nature and general purposes of financial statements.

LO2-2 Explain certain accounting principles that are important for an understanding of financial statements and how professional judgment by accountants may affect the application of those principles.

LO2-3 Demonstrate how certain business transactions affect the elements of the accounting equation: Assets = Liabilities + Owners' Equity.

LO2-4 Explain how the statement of financial position, often referred to as the balance sheet, is an expansion of the basic accounting equation.

LO2-5 Explain how the income statement reports an enterprise's financial performance for a period of time in terms of the relationship of revenues and expenses.

LO2-6 Explain how the statement of cash flows presents the change in cash for a period of time in terms of the company's operating, investing, and financing activities.

LO2-7 Explain how the statement of financial position (balance sheet), income statement, and statement of cash flows relate to each other.

LO2-8 Explain common forms of business ownership—sole proprietorship, partnership, and corporation—and demonstrate how they differ in terms of their statements of financial position.

LO2-9 Discuss the importance of financial statements to a company and its investors and creditors and why management may take steps to improve the appearance of the company in its financial statements.

© Tony Avelar/Bloomberg via Getty Images

INTEL

Intel was created in 1968 with a vision of providing semi-conductor memory products. By 1971, the company introduced the world's first microprocessor. Today Intel supplies the computing and communications industries with chips, boards, and systems building blocks that are the ingredients of computers and servers as well as networking and communications products. These industries use Intel's products to create advanced computing and communications systems. Intel states that its mission is to be the preeminent building block supplier in the worldwide Internet economy.

Technology-based companies like Intel operate in highly competitive markets and continuously introduce new products. In a recent corporate information communication on the company's website, management explains the importance of meeting the needs of customers: "Our goal is to be the preeminent provider of semiconductor chips and platforms for the worldwide digital economy . . . We offer products at various levels of integration, to allow our customers flexibility in creating computing and communications systems. The substantial majority of our revenue is from the sale of microprocessors and chipsets."

Modern-day historians agree that we have moved from the industrial age to the information age. Companies like Intel, Microsoft, and Cisco Systems are major players in this transformation of business. Information-age companies rely more heavily on intellectual capital, research and development, and other intangibles that were less important for companies whose focus was heavy manufacturing or, even earlier in our history, primarily agricultural. ∎

If you were a person with considerable wealth who wanted to invest in a forward-looking company in today's information age, how would you know whether **Intel** or any other company is a wise investment? What information would you seek out to help you decide where to place your investment dollars? A primary source of financial information is a company's financial statements. These statements, which are prepared at least once a year and in many cases more frequently, provide insight into the current financial status of the company and how successful the company has been in meeting its financial goals. In this chapter, you are introduced to the three primary financial statements—the statement of financial position (often referred to as the balance sheet), the income statement, and the statement of cash flows. Combined with information presented in notes and other accompanying presentations, these financial statements provide for investors, creditors, and other interested parties a wealth of useful information. In fact, financial information is what this entire textbook is about, and in this chapter you receive your initial introduction to how financial statements come about and how they may be used to better understand a company.

Introduction to Financial Statements

In Chapter 1, we learned that investors and creditors are particularly interested in cash flows that they expect to receive in the future. Creditors, for example, are interested in the ability of an enterprise, to which they have made loans or sold merchandise on credit, to meet its payment obligations, which may include payment of interest. Similarly, investors are interested in the market value of their stock holdings, as well as dividends that the enterprise will pay to them while they own the stock.

One of the primary ways investors and creditors assess the probability that an enterprise will be able to make future cash payments is to study, analyze, and understand the enterprise's financial statements. As discussed in Chapter 1, a **financial statement** is simply a declaration of what is believed to be true about an enterprise, communicated in terms of a monetary unit, such as the dollar. When accountants prepare financial statements, they are describing in financial terms certain attributes of the enterprise that they believe fairly represent its financial activities.

In this chapter, we introduce three primary financial statements:

- Statement of financial position (often referred to as the balance sheet)
- Income statement
- Statement of cash flows

In introducing these statements, we use the form of business ownership referred to as a *corporation*. The corporation is a unique form of organization that allows many owners to combine their resources into a business enterprise that is larger than would be possible based on the financial resources of a single owner or a small number of owners. While businesses of any size may be organized as corporations, most large businesses are corporations because of their need for a large amount of capital that the corporate form of business organization makes possible. Later in this chapter we introduce two other forms of business organization—the sole proprietorship and the partnership—which are alternatives to the corporate form for some business enterprises.

LO2-1

LEARNING OBJECTIVE
Explain the nature and general purposes of financial statements.

The names of the three primary financial statements describe the information you find in each. The **statement of financial position,** or **balance sheet,** is a financial statement that describes where the enterprise stands at a specific date. It is sometimes described as a snapshot of the business in financial or dollar terms (that is, what the enterprise "looks like" at a specific date).

As businesses operate, they engage in transactions that create revenues and incur expenses that are necessary to earn those revenues. An **income statement** is an activity statement that shows the revenues and expenses for a designated period of time. Revenues already have resulted in positive cash flows, or are expected to do so in the near future, as a result of transactions with customers. For example, a company might sell a product for $100. This revenue transaction results in an immediate positive cash flow into the enterprise if the customer pays cash at the time of the transaction. An expected future cash flow results if it is a credit transaction in which payment is to be received later. Expenses have the opposite effect in that they result in an immediate cash flow *out* of the enterprise (if a cash transaction) or an expected future flow of cash out of the enterprise (if a credit transaction). For example, if a company incurs a certain expense of $75 and pays it at that time, an immediate cash outflow takes place. If payment is delayed until some future date, the transaction represents an expected future cash outflow. Revenues result in **positive cash flows**—either past, present, or future—while expenses result in **negative cash flows**—either past, present, or future. *Positive* and *negative* indicate the directional impact on cash. The term *net income* (or *net loss*) is simply the difference between all of an enterprise's revenues and expenses for a designated period of time.

The **statement of cash flows** is particularly important in understanding an enterprise for purposes of investment and credit decisions. As its name implies, the statement of cash flows shows the ways cash changed during a designated period—the cash received from revenues and other transactions as well as the cash paid for certain expenses and other acquisitions during the period. While the primary focus of investors and creditors is on cash flows to themselves rather than to the enterprise, information about cash activity of the enterprise is an important signal to investors and creditors about the prospects of future cash flows to them.

A Starting Point: Statement of Financial Position

All three financial statements contain important information, but each includes different information. For that reason, it is important to understand all three financial statements and how they relate to each other. The way they relate is sometimes referred to as **articulation,** a term we will say more about later in this chapter.

A logical starting point for understanding financial statements is the statement of financial position, also called the balance sheet. The purpose of this financial statement is to demonstrate where the company stands, in financial terms, at a specific point in time. As we will see later in this chapter, the other financial statements relate to the statement of financial position and show how important aspects of a company's financial position change over time. Beginning with the statement of financial position also allows us to understand certain basic accounting principles and terminologies that are important for understanding all financial statements.

Every business prepares a balance sheet at the end of the year, and many companies prepare one at the end of each month, week, or even day. It consists of a listing of the assets, the liabilities, and the owners' equity of the business. The *date* is important, as the financial position of a business may change quickly. Exhibit 2–1 shows the financial position of Vagabond Travel Agency at December 31, 2015.

EXHIBIT 2–I

Statement of Financial Position

 A balance sheet shows financial position at a specific date

VAGABOND TRAVEL AGENCY STATEMENT OF FINANCIAL POSITION DECEMBER 31, 2015				
Assets		**Liabilities & Owners' Equity**		
Cash.	$ 22,500	Liabilities:		
Notes Receivable	10,000	Notes Payable.	$ 41,000	
Accounts Receivable	60,500	Accounts Payable.	36,000	
Supplies	2,000	Salaries Payable	3,000	$ 80,000
Office Equipment	15,000	Owners' equity:		
Building	90,000	Capital Stock	$150,000	
Land	100,000	Retained Earnings.	70,000	220,000
Total	$300,000	Total		$300,000

Let us briefly describe several features of the statement of financial position, using Exhibit 2–1 as an example. First, the heading communicates three things: (1) the name of the business, (2) the name of the financial statement, and (3) the date. The body of the balance sheet consists of three distinct sections: *assets, liabilities,* and *owners' equity.*

Notice that cash is listed first among the assets, followed by notes receivable, accounts receivable, supplies, and any other assets that will *soon be converted into cash or used up in business operations.* Following these assets are the more permanent assets, such as equipment, buildings, and land.

Moving to the right side of the balance sheet, liabilities are shown before owners' equity. Each major type of liability (such as notes payable, accounts payable, and salaries payable) is listed separately, followed by a figure for total liabilities.

Owners' equity is separated into two parts—capital stock and retained earnings. Capital stock represents the amount that owners originally paid into the company to become owners. It consists of individual shares and each owner has a set number of shares. Notice in this illustration that capital stock totals $150,000. This means that the assigned value of the shares held by owners, multiplied by the number of shares, equals $150,000. For example, assuming an assigned value of $10 per share, there would be 15,000 shares ($10 × 15,000 = $150,000). Alternatively, the assigned value might be $5 per share, in which case there would be 30,000 shares ($5 × 30,000 = $150,000). The retained earnings component of owners' equity is the accumulated earnings of previous years that remain within the enterprise. Retained earnings is considered part of the equity of the owners and serves to enhance their investment in the business.

Finally, notice that the amount of total assets ($300,000) is *equal* to the total amount of liabilities and owners' equity (also $300,000). This relationship *always exists*—in fact, the *equality of these totals* is why this financial statement is frequently called a *balance* sheet.

The Concept of the Business Entity
Generally accepted accounting principles require that financial statements describe the activities of a specific economic entity. This concept is called the *entity principle.*

LO2-2

LEARNING OBJECTIVE
Explain certain accounting principles that are important for an understanding of financial statements and how professional judgment by accountants may affect the application of those principles.

A **business entity** is an economic unit that engages in identifiable business activities. For accounting purposes, the business entity is regarded as *separate from the personal activities of its owners.* For example, Vagabond is a business organization operating as a travel agency. Its owners may have personal bank accounts, homes, cars, and even other businesses. These items are not involved in the operation of the travel agency and do not appear in Vagabond's financial statements.

If the owners were to commingle their personal activities with the transactions of the business, the resulting financial statements would fail to describe clearly the financial activities of the business organization. Distinguishing business from personal activities of the owners may require judgment by the accountant.

ASSETS

Assets are economic resources that are owned by a business and are expected to benefit future operations. In most cases, the benefit to future operations comes in the form of positive future cash flows. The positive future cash flows may come directly as the asset is converted into cash (collection of a receivable) or indirectly as the asset is used in operating the business to create other assets that result in positive future cash flows (buildings and land used to manufacture a product for sale). Assets may have definite physical characteristics such as buildings, machinery, or an inventory of merchandise. On the other hand, some assets exist not in physical or tangible form, but in the form of valuable legal claims or rights; examples are amounts due from customers, investments in government bonds, and patent rights held by the company.

One of the most basic and at the same time most controversial problems in accounting is determining the correct dollar amount for the various assets of a business. At present, generally accepted accounting principles call for the valuation of some assets in a balance sheet at *cost,* rather than at their current value. The specific accounting principles supporting cost as the basis for asset valuation are discussed below.

The Cost Principle   Assets such as land, buildings, merchandise, and equipment are typical of the many economic resources that are required in producing revenue for the business. The prevailing accounting view is that such assets should be presented in the statement of financial position at their cost. When we say that an asset is shown at its *historical cost,* we mean the original amount the business entity paid to acquire the asset. This amount may be different from what it would cost to purchase the same asset today or the amount that would be received if the asset were sold today.

For example, let us assume that a business buys a tract of land for use as a building site, paying $100,000 in cash. The amount to be entered in the accounting records for the asset is the cost of $100,000. If we assume a booming real estate market, a fair estimate of the market value of the land 10 years later might be $250,000. Although the market price or economic value of the land has risen greatly, the amount shown in the company's accounting records and in its balance sheet would continue unchanged at the cost of $100,000. This policy of accounting for many assets at their cost is often referred to as the **cost principle** of accounting.

Exceptions to the cost principle are found in some of the most liquid assets (that is, assets that are expected to soon become cash). Amounts receivable from customers are generally included in the balance sheet at their *net realizable value,* which is an amount that approximates the cash that is expected to be received when the receivable is collected. Similarly, certain investments in other enterprises are included in the balance sheet at their current market value if management's plan includes conversion into cash in the near future.

In reading a balance sheet, it is important to keep in mind that the dollar amounts listed for many assets do not indicate the prices at which the assets could be sold or the prices at which they could be replaced. A frequently misunderstood feature of a balance sheet is that it *does not* show how much the business currently is worth, although it contains valuable information in being able to calculate such a value.

The Going-Concern Assumption   *Why* don't accountants change the recorded amounts of assets to correspond with changing market prices for these properties? One reason is that assets like land and buildings are being used to house the business and were acquired for *use* and not for resale; in fact, these assets usually could not be sold without disrupting the business. The balance sheet of a business is prepared on the assumption that the business is a continuing enterprise, or a **going concern.** Consequently, the present estimated prices at which assets like land and buildings could be sold are of less importance than if these properties were intended for sale. These are frequently among the largest dollar amounts of a company's assets. Determining that an enterprise is a going concern may require judgment by the accountant.

The Objectivity Principle   Another reason for using cost rather than current market values in accounting for many assets is the need for a definite, factual basis for valuation. The cost of land, buildings, and many other assets that have been purchased can be definitely determined. Accountants use the term *objective* to describe asset valuations that are factual and can be verified by independent experts. For example, if land is shown on the balance sheet at cost, a CPA who performed an audit of the business would be able to find objective evidence that the land was actually measured at the cost incurred in acquiring it. On the other

YOUR TURN   You as a Home Owner

First, assume you have owned your home for 10 years and need to report the value of your home to the city assessor for real estate tax assessment purposes. What information would you provide? Second, assume you are planning to sell your home. What type of information would you provide to potential buyers? What ethical issues arise in these two situations that the objectivity principle helps address?

(See our comments on the Online Learning Center website.)

hand, estimated market values for assets such as buildings and specialized machinery are not factual and objective. Market values are constantly changing, and estimates of the prices at which assets could be sold are largely a matter of judgment.

At the time an asset is acquired, the cost and market value are usually the same. With the passage of time, however, the current market value of assets is likely to differ considerably from its historical cost. As you will learn, for some assets we adjust the amount in the balance sheet as the value changes. For other assets, we retain historical cost as the basis of the asset in the balance sheet.

The Stable-Dollar Assumption   A limitation of measuring assets at historical cost is that the value of the monetary unit or dollar is not always stable. **Inflation** is a term used to describe the situation where the value of the monetary unit decreases, meaning that it will purchase less than it did previously. **Deflation,** on the other hand, is the opposite situation in which the value of the monetary unit increases, meaning that it will purchase more than it did previously. Typically, countries like the United States have experienced inflation rather than deflation. When inflation becomes severe, historical cost amounts for assets lose their relevance as a basis for making business decisions.

Accountants in the United States prepare financial statements under an assumption that the dollar is a stable unit of measurement, as is the gallon, the acre, or the mile. The cost principle and the **stable-dollar assumption** work well in periods of stable prices but are less satisfactory under conditions of rapid inflation. For example, if a company bought land 20 years ago for $100,000 and purchased a second similar tract of land today for $500,000, the total cost of land shown by the accounting records would be $600,000 following the historical cost principle. This treatment ignores the fact that dollars spent 20 years ago had greater purchasing power than today's dollar. Thus the $600,000 total for the cost of land is a mixture of two "sizes" of dollars with different purchasing power.

INTERNATIONAL CASE IN POINT

Many countries experience prolonged and serious inflation. Inflation can undermine the stable-currency assumption. Accounting rules have been designed in some foreign countries to address the impact of inflation on a company's financial position. For example, Mexican corporate law requires Mexican companies to adjust their balance sheets to current purchasing power by using indexes provided by the government. Because inflation is significant, the indexes are used to devalue the Mexican currency (pesos) to provide a more transparent representation of the company's financial condition.

After much research into this problem, at one time the FASB required on a trial basis that large corporations annually disclose financial data adjusted for the effects of inflation. At the present time, this disclosure is optional, as judged appropriate by the accountant who prepares the financial statements.

LIABILITIES

Liabilities are financial obligations or debts. They represent negative future cash flows for the enterprise. The person or organization to whom the debt is owed is called a **creditor.**

All businesses have liabilities; even the largest and most successful companies often purchase merchandise, supplies, and services "on account." The liabilities arising from such purchases are called *accounts payable.* Many businesses borrow money to finance expansion or the purchase of high-cost assets and pay for them over time. When obtaining a loan, the borrower usually must sign a formal note payable. A *note payable* is a written promise to repay the amount owed by a particular date and usually calls for the payment of interest as well.

Accounts payable, in contrast to notes payable, involve no written promises and generally do not call for interest payments. In essence, a note payable is a *more formal* arrangement than an account payable, but they are similar in that both require the company to make payment in the future.

Liabilities are usually listed in the order in which they are expected to be repaid.[1] Liabilities that are similar may be combined to avoid unnecessary detail in the financial statement. For example, if a company had several expenses payable at the end of the year (for example, wages, interest, taxes), it might combine these into a single line called *accrued expenses.* The word *accrued* is an accounting term communicating that the payment of certain expenses has been delayed or deferred.

Liabilities represent claims against the borrower's assets. As we shall see, the owners of a business *also* have claims on the company's assets. But in the eyes of the law, creditors' claims *take priority* over those of the owners. This means that creditors are entitled to be *paid in full,* even if such payment would exhaust the assets of the business and leave nothing for its owners.

OWNERS' EQUITY

Owners' equity represents the *owners' claims* on the assets of the business. Because liabilities or creditors' claims have legal priority over those of the owners, owners' equity is a *residual amount.* If you are the owner of a business, you are entitled to assets that are left after the claims of creditors have been satisfied in full. Therefore, owners' equity is always equal to *total assets minus total liabilities.* For example, using the data from the illustrated balance sheet of Vagabond Travel Agency (Exhibit 2–1):

Vagabond has total assets of.	$300,000
And total liabilities of	(80,000)
Therefore, the owners' equity must be.	$220,000

Owners' equity does *not* represent a specific claim to cash or any other particular asset. Rather, it is the owners' overall financial interest in the entire company.

Increases in Owners' Equity The owners' equity in a business comes from two primary sources:

1. *Investments of cash or other assets* by owners.
2. *Earnings* from profitable operation of the business.

Decreases in Owners' Equity Decreases in owners' equity also are caused in two ways:

1. *Payments of cash or transfers of other assets* to owners.
2. *Losses* from unprofitable operation of the business.

Accounting for payments to owners and net losses are addressed in later chapters.

THE ACCOUNTING EQUATION

A fundamental characteristic of every statement of financial position is that the total for assets always equals the total of liabilities plus owners' equity. This agreement or balance of total assets with the total of liabilities and owners' equity is the reason for calling this financial statement a *balance sheet.* But *why* do total assets equal the total of liabilities and owners' equity?

The dollar totals on the two sides of the balance sheet are always equal because they represent *two views of the same business.* The listing of assets shows us what things the business

L02-3

LEARNING OBJECTIVE
Demonstrate how certain business transactions affect the elements of the accounting equation:

Assets = Liabilities + Owners' Equity.

---

[1] Short-term liabilities generally are those due within one year. Long-term liabilities are shown separately in the balance sheet, after the listing of all short-term liabilities. Long-term liabilities are addressed in Chapter 10.

owns; the listing of liabilities and owners' equity tells us who supplied these resources to the business and how much each group supplied. Everything that a business owns has been supplied to it either by creditors or by the owners. Therefore, the total claims of the creditors plus the claims of the owners always equal the total assets of the business.

The equality of the assets on the one hand and the claims of the creditors and the owners on the other hand is expressed in the following **accounting equation:**

The accounting equation

$$\text{Assets} = \text{Liabilities} + \text{Owners' Equity}$$
$$\$300{,}000 = \$80{,}000 \quad + \$220{,}000$$

The amounts listed in the equation were taken from the balance sheet illustrated in Exhibit 2–1. The balance sheet is simply a detailed statement of this equation. To illustrate this relationship, compare the balance sheet of Vagabond Travel Agency with the above equation.

Every business transaction, no matter how simple or how complex, can be expressed in terms of its effect on the accounting equation. A thorough understanding of the equation and some practice in using it are essential to the student of accounting.

Regardless of whether a business grows or contracts, the equality between the assets and the claims on the assets is always maintained. Any increase in the amount of total assets is necessarily accompanied by an equal increase on the other side of the equation—that is, by an increase in either the liabilities or the owners' equity. Any decrease in total assets is necessarily accompanied by a corresponding decrease in liabilities or owners' equity. The continuing equality of the two sides of the accounting equation can best be illustrated by taking a new business as an example and observing the effects of various transactions.

THE EFFECTS OF BUSINESS TRANSACTIONS: AN ILLUSTRATION

How does a statement of financial position come about? What has occurred in the past for it to exist at any point in time? The statement of financial position is a picture of the results of past business transactions that has been captured by the company's information system and organized into a concise financial description of where the company stands at a point in time. The specific items and dollar amounts are the direct results of the transactions in which the company has engaged. The balance sheets of two separate companies would almost always be different due to the unique nature, timing, and dollar amounts of each company's business transactions.

© Getty Images/Stockbyte

To illustrate how a balance sheet comes about, and later to show how the income statement and statement of cash flows relate to the balance sheet, we use an example of a small auto repair business, Overnight Auto Service.

The Business Entity   Assume that Michael McBryan, an experienced auto mechanic, opens his own automotive repair business, Overnight Auto Service. A distinctive feature of Overnight's operations is that all repair work is done at night. This strategy offers customers the convenience of dropping off their cars in the evening and picking them up the following morning.

Operating at night also enables Overnight to minimize labor costs. Instead of hiring full-time employees, Overnight offers part-time work to mechanics who already have day jobs at major automobile dealerships. This eliminates the need for costly employee training programs and for such payroll fringe benefits as group health insurance and employees' pension plans, benefits usually associated with full-time employment.

Overnight's Accounting Policies   McBryan has taken several courses in accounting and maintains Overnight's accounting records himself. He knows that small businesses such as his are not required to prepare formal financial statements, but he prepares them anyway. He believes they will be useful to him in running the business. In addition, if Overnight is successful, McBryan plans to open more locations. He anticipates needing to raise substantial amounts of capital from investors and creditors. He believes that the financial history provided by a series of monthly financial statements will be helpful in obtaining investment capital.

The Company's First Transaction   McBryan officially started Overnight on January 20, 2015. On that day, he received a charter from the state to begin a small, closely held corporation whose owners consisted of himself and several family members. Capital stock issued to these investors included 8,000 shares at $10 per share. McBryan opened a bank account in the name of Overnight Auto Service, into which he deposited the $80,000 received from the issuance of the capital stock.

This transaction provided Overnight with its first asset—Cash—and also created the initial owners' equity in the business entity. See the balance sheet showing the company's financial position after this initial transaction in Exhibit 2–2.

OVERNIGHT AUTO SERVICE
BALANCE SHEET
JANUARY 20, 2015

Assets		Owners' Equity	
Cash......................	$80,000	Capital Stock	$80,000

EXHIBIT 2–2
Balance Sheet, Jan. 20

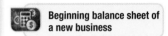
Beginning balance sheet of a new business

Overnight's next two transactions involved the acquisition of a suitable site for its business operations.

Purchase of an Asset for Cash   Representing the business, McBryan negotiated with both the City of Santa Teresa and the Metropolitan Transit Authority (MTA) to purchase an abandoned bus garage. (The MTA owned the garage, but the city owned the land.)

On January 21, Overnight purchased the land from the city for *$52,000 cash*. This transaction had two immediate effects on the company's financial position: first, Overnight's cash was reduced by $52,000; and second, the company acquired a new asset—Land. We show the company's financial position after this transaction in Exhibit 2–3.

OVERNIGHT AUTO SERVICE
BALANCE SHEET
JANUARY 21, 2015

Assets		Owners' Equity	
Cash......................	$28,000	Capital Stock	$80,000
Land......................	52,000		
Total	$80,000	Total	$80,000

EXHIBIT 2–3
Balance Sheet, Jan. 21

Balance sheet totals unchanged by purchase of land for cash

Purchase of an Asset and Financing Part of the Cost   On January 22, Overnight purchased the old garage building from Metropolitan Transit Authority for *$36,000*. Overnight made a cash down payment of *$6,000* and issued a 90-day non-interest-bearing note payable for the *$30,000* balance owed.

As a result of this transaction, Overnight had (1) $6,000 less cash; (2) a new asset, Building, which cost $36,000; and (3) a new liability, Notes Payable, in the amount of $30,000. This transaction is reflected in Exhibit 2–4.

Once a company has multiple assets and liabilities, the question arises as to the proper order of the items in the statement of financial position. Assets are ordinarily presented in their order of "permanence," starting with cash. Next are other assets that are close to cash (e.g., receivables from customers), followed by more permanent assets like equipment, buildings, and land, which is considered the most permanent asset. Liabilities are usually presented in the order in which they become due. We discuss the subject of "classified balance sheets" later in this text.

EXHIBIT 2–4

Balance Sheet, Jan. 22

Totals increased equally by debt incurred in acquiring assets

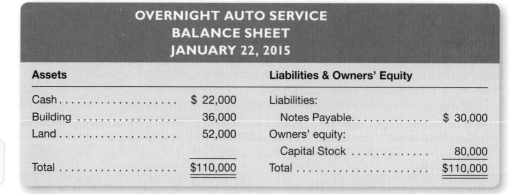

OVERNIGHT AUTO SERVICE
BALANCE SHEET
JANUARY 22, 2015

Assets		Liabilities & Owners' Equity	
Cash...................	$ 22,000	Liabilities:	
Building	36,000	Notes Payable.............	$ 30,000
Land....................	52,000	Owners' equity:	
		Capital Stock	80,000
Total	$110,000	Total	$110,000

Purchase of an Asset on Account   On January 23, Overnight purchased tools and automotive repair equipment from Snappy Tools. The purchase price was *$13,800,* due within 60 days. After this purchase, Overnight's financial position is depicted in Exhibit 2–5.

EXHIBIT 2–5

Balance Sheet, Jan. 23

Totals increased equally by debt incurred in acquiring assets

OVERNIGHT AUTO SERVICE
BALANCE SHEET
JANUARY 23, 2015

Assets		Liabilities & Owners' Equity	
Cash....................	$ 22,000	Liabilities:	
Tools and Equipment	13,800	Notes Payable...........	$ 30,000
Building	36,000	Accounts Payable........	13,800
Land.....................	52,000	Total liabilities	$ 43,800
		Owners' equity:	
		Capital Stock	80,000
Total	$123,800	Total	$123,800

Sale of an Asset   After taking delivery of the new tools and equipment, Overnight found that it had purchased more than it needed. Ace Towing, a neighboring business, offered to buy the excess items. On January 24, Overnight sold some of its new tools to Ace for *$1,800,* a price equal to Overnight's cost.[2] Ace made no down payment but agreed to pay the amount due within 45 days. This transaction reduced Overnight's tools and equipment by $1,800 and created a new asset, Accounts Receivable, for that same amount. A balance sheet as of January 24 appears in Exhibit 2–6.

EXHIBIT 2–6

Balance Sheet, Jan. 24

No change in totals by sale of assets at cost

OVERNIGHT AUTO SERVICE
BALANCE SHEET
JANUARY 24, 2015

Assets		Liabilities & Owners' Equity	
Cash....................	$ 22,000	Liabilities:	
Accounts Receivable	1,800	Notes Payable...........	$ 30,000
Tools and Equipment	12,000	Accounts Payable........	13,800
Building	36,000	Total liabilities	$ 43,800
Land.....................	52,000	Owners' equity:	
		Capital Stock	80,000
Total	$123,800	Total	$123,800

---

[2] Sales of assets at prices above or below cost result in gains or losses. Such transactions are discussed in later chapters.

Collection of an Account Receivable On January 26, Overnight received $600 from Ace Towing as partial settlement of its account receivable from Ace. This transaction caused an increase in Overnight's cash but a decrease of the same amount in accounts receivable. This transaction converts one asset into another of equal value; there is no change in the amount of total assets. After this transaction, Overnight's financial position is summarized in Exhibit 2–7.

EXHIBIT 2–7

Balance Sheet, Jan. 26

OVERNIGHT AUTO SERVICE
BALANCE SHEET
JANUARY 26, 2015

Assets		Liabilities & Owners' Equity	
Cash	$ 22,600	Liabilities:	
Accounts Receivable	1,200	Notes Payable	$ 30,000
Tools and Equipment	12,000	Accounts Payable	13,800
Building	36,000	Total liabilities	$ 43,800
Land	52,000	Owners' equity:	
		Capital Stock	80,000
Total	$123,800	Total	$123,800

Totals unchanged by collection of a receivable

Payment of a Liability On January 27, Overnight made a partial payment of $6,800 on its account payable to Snappy Tools. This transaction reduced Overnight's cash and accounts payable by the same amount, leaving total assets and the total of liabilities plus owners' equity in balance. Overnight's balance sheet at January 27 appears in Exhibit 2–8.

EXHIBIT 2–8

Balance Sheet, Jan. 27

OVERNIGHT AUTO SERVICE
BALANCE SHEET
JANUARY 27, 2015

Assets		Liabilities & Owners' Equity	
Cash	$ 15,800	Liabilities:	
Accounts Receivable	1,200	Notes Payable	$ 30,000
Tools and Equipment	12,000	Accounts Payable	7,000
Building	36,000	Total liabilities	$ 37,000
Land	52,000	Owners' equity:	
		Capital Stock	80,000
Total	$117,000	Total	$117,000

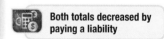

Both totals decreased by paying a liability

Earning of Revenue By the last week in January, McBryan had acquired the assets Overnight needed to start operating, and he began to provide repair services for customers. Rather than recording each individual sale of repair services, he decided to accumulate them and record them at the end of the month. Sales of repair services for the last week of January were $2,200, all of which was received in cash.

Earning of revenue represents the creation of value by Overnight. It also represents an increase in the financial interest of the owners in the company. As a result, cash is increased by $2,200 and owners' equity is increased by the same amount. To distinguish owners' equity that is earned from that which was originally invested by the owners, the account *Retained Earnings* is used in the owners' equity section of the balance sheet. The balance sheet in Exhibit 2–9, as of January 31, reflects the increase in assets (cash) and owners' equity (retained earnings) from the revenue earned and received in cash during the last week of January, but before the payment of expenses (see next section).

EXHIBIT 2–9

Balance Sheet, Jan. 31

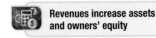

Revenues increase assets and owners' equity

OVERNIGHT AUTO SERVICE
BALANCE SHEET
JANUARY 31, 2015

Assets		Liabilities & Owners' Equity		
Cash	$ 18,000	Liabilities:		
Accounts Receivable	1,200	Notes Payable	$ 30,000	
Tools and Equipment	12,000	Accounts Payable	7,000	
Building	36,000	Total liabilities		$ 37,000
Land	52,000	Owners' equity:		
		Capital Stock	$ 80,000	
		Retained Earnings	2,200	$ 82,200
Total	$119,200	Total		$119,200

L02-4

LEARNING OBJECTIVE

Explain how the statement of financial position, often referred to as the balance sheet, is an expansion of the basic accounting equation.

Payment of Expenses In order to earn the $2,200 of revenue that we have just recorded, Overnight had to pay some operating expenses, namely utilities and wages. McBryan decided to pay all operating expenses at the end of the month. For January, he owed $200 for utilities and $1,200 for wages to his employees, a total of $1,400, which he paid on January 31. Paying expenses has an opposite effect from revenues on the owners' interest in the company—their investment is reduced. Of course, paying expenses also results in a decrease of cash. The January 31 balance sheet, after the payment of utilities and wages, is presented in Exhibit 2–10.

EXHIBIT 2–10

Balance Sheet, Jan. 31

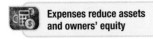

Expenses reduce assets and owners' equity

OVERNIGHT AUTO SERVICE
BALANCE SHEET
JANUARY 31, 2015

Assets		Liabilities & Owners' Equity		
Cash	$ 16,600	Liabilities:		
Accounts Receivable	1,200	Notes Payable	$ 30,000	
Tools and Equipment	12,000	Accounts Payable	7,000	
Building	36,000	Total liabilities		$ 37,000
Land	52,000	Owners' equity:		
		Capital Stock	$ 80,000	
		Retained Earnings	800	80,800
Total	$117,800	Total		$117,800

Notice that the expenses of $1,400 ($200 for utilities and $1,200 for wages) reduce the amount of retained earnings in the balance sheet. That balance was formerly $2,200, representing the revenues for the last week of January. It is now $800, representing the difference between the revenues for the last week of January and the $1,400 of expenses that Overnight incurred during the same period of time. From this illustration we can see that revenues enhance or increase the financial interest of owners while expenses diminish or reduce the interest of owners. In a corporation, the net effect of this activity is reflected in the balance sheet as retained earnings.

EFFECTS OF THESE BUSINESS TRANSACTIONS ON THE ACCOUNTING EQUATION

As we learned earlier, the statement of financial position, or balance sheet, is a detailed expression of the accounting equation:

$$\text{Assets} = \text{Liabilities} + \text{Owner's Equity}$$

As we have progressed through a series of business transactions, we have illustrated the effects of Overnight's January transactions on the statement of financial position.

To review, Overnight's transactions during January were as follows, with the resulting balance sheet indicated in parentheses:

Jan. 20 Michael McBryan started the business by depositing $80,000 received from the sale of capital stock in a company bank account (Exhibit 2–2).

Jan. 21 Purchased land for $52,000, paying cash (Exhibit 2–3).

Jan. 22 Purchased a building for $36,000, paying $6,000 in cash and issuing a note payable for the remaining $30,000 (Exhibit 2–4).

Jan. 23 Purchased tools and equipment on account, $13,800 (Exhibit 2–5).

Jan. 24 Sold some of the tools at a price equal to their cost, $1,800, collectible within 45 days (Exhibit 2–6).

Jan. 26 Received $600 in partial collection of the account receivable from the sale of tools (Exhibit 2–7).

Jan. 27 Paid $6,800 in partial payment of an account payable (Exhibit 2–8).

Jan. 31 Received $2,200 of sales revenue in cash (Exhibit 2–9).

Jan. 31 Paid $1,400 of operating expenses in cash—$200 for utilities and $1,200 for wages (Exhibit 2–10).

The expanded accounting equation in Exhibit 2–11 shows the effects of these transactions on the accounting equation. The effect of each transaction is shown in red. Notice that the "balances," shown in black, are the amounts appearing in Overnight's balance sheets in Exhibits 2–2 through 2–10. Notice also that the accounting equation is in balance after each transaction.

While this table represents the impact of Overnight's transactions on the accounting equation, and on its financial position as shown in its balance sheet, we can now learn how the income statement and statement of cash flows enter the picture. Specifically, the income statement is a separate financial statement that shows how the statement of financial position changed as a result of its revenue and expense transactions. The statement of cash flows shows how the company's cash increased and decreased during the period.

 Multiple transactions significantly change the enterprise's financial position

Income Statement

The income statement is a summarization of the company's revenue and expense transactions for a period of time. The income statement is particularly important for the company's owners, creditors, and other interested parties to understand. Ultimately the company will succeed or fail based on its ability to earn revenues in excess of its expenses. Once the company's assets are acquired and business commences, revenues and expenses are important dimensions of the company's operations. **Revenues** are increases in the company's assets from its profit-directed activities, and they result in positive cash flows. **Expenses** are decreases in the company's assets from its profit-directed activities, and they result in negative cash flows. *Net income* is the difference between the revenues and expenses for a specified period of time. Should a company find itself in the undesirable situation of having expenses greater than revenues, we call the difference a *net loss.*

Overnight's income statement for January 20–31 is relatively simple because the company did not have a large number of complex revenue and expense transactions.[3] Taking information directly from the Retained Earnings column in Exhibit 2–11, and separating the total expenses of $1,400 into wages of $1,200 and utilities of $200, we can prepare the company's income statement as shown in Exhibit 2–12.

LO2-5

LEARNING OBJECTIVE
Explain how the income statement reports an enterprise's financial performance for a period of time in terms of the relationship of revenues and expenses.

---

[3] In this illustration, only revenue and expense transactions change the amount of owners' equity from the original $80,000 investment of the owner. Examples of other events and transactions that affect the amount of owners' equity, but that are *not included in net income,* are the sale of additional shares of capital stock and the payment of dividends to shareholders. These subjects are covered in later chapters.

EXHIBIT 2–11 Expanded Accounting Equation

OVERNIGHT AUTO SERVICE
EXPANDED ACCOUNTING EQUATION
JANUARY 20–31, 2015

	Assets					=	Liabilities		+	Owners' Equity	
	Cash	+ Accounts Receivable	+ Tools and Equipment	+ Building	+ Land	=	Notes Payable	+ Accounts Payable	+	Capital Stock	Retained Earnings
Jan. 20	$80,000					=				$80,000	
Balances	$80,000					=				$80,000	
Jan. 21	−52,000				+$52,000	=					
Balances	$28,000				$52,000	=				$80,000	
Jan. 22	−6,000			+$36,000		=	+$30,000				
Balances	$22,000			$36,000	$52,000	=	$30,000			$80,000	
Jan. 23			+$13,800			=		+$13,800			
Balances	$22,000		$13,800	$36,000	$52,000	=	$30,000	$13,800		$80,000	
Jan. 24		+$1,800	−1,800			=					
Balances	$22,000	$1,800	$12,000	$36,000	$52,000	=	$30,000	$13,800		$80,000	
Jan. 26	+600	−600				=					
Balances	$22,600	$1,200	$12,000	$36,000	$52,000	=	$30,000	$13,800		$80,000	
Jan. 27	−6,800					=		−6,800			
Balances	$15,800	$1,200	$12,000	$36,000	$52,000	=	$30,000	$7,000		$80,000	
Jan. 31	+2,200					=					+$2,200
Jan. 31	−1,400					=					−1,400
Balances	$16,600	$1,200	$12,000	$36,000	$52,000	=	$30,000	$7,000		$80,000	$ 800

Statement of Cash Flows

Income Statement

OVERNIGHT AUTO SERVICE INCOME STATEMENT FOR THE PERIOD JANUARY 20 – 31, 2015		
Sales Revenues		$2,200
Operating expenses:		
Wages	$1,200	
Utilities	200	1,400
Net Income		$ 800

EXHIBIT 2–12

Income Statement

 An income statement displays revenues and expenses for a period of time

Notice that the heading for the income statement refers to a *period* of time rather than a *point* in time, as was the case with the balance sheet. The income statement reports on the financial performance of the company in terms of earning revenue and incurring expenses *over a period of time* and explains, in part, how the company's financial position changed between the beginning and ending of that period.

Statement of Cash Flows

In Chapter 1, we established the importance of cash flows to investors and creditors and that the cash flows of the company are an important consideration in investors' and creditors' assessments of cash flows to them. As a result, a second set of information that is particularly important concerning how a company's financial position changed between two points in time is cash flow information.

We can use the entire Cash column of the analysis in Exhibit 2–11 to create a statement of cash flows for Overnight Auto Service. The statement classifies the various cash flows into three categories—operating, investing, and financing—and relates these categories to the beginning and ending cash balances. Cash flows from **operating activities** are the cash effects of revenue and expense transactions that are included in the income statement.[4] Cash flows from **investing activities** are the cash effects of purchasing and selling assets, such as land and buildings. Cash flows from **financing activities** are the cash effects of the owners investing in the company and creditors loaning money to the company and the repayment of either or both.

The statement of cash flows for Overnight Auto Service for the period January 20–31 is presented in Exhibit 2–13.

Notice that the operating, investing, and financing categories include both positive and negative cash flows. (The negative cash flows are in parentheses.) Also notice that the combined total of the three categories of the statement (increase of $16,600) explains the total change in cash from the beginning to the end of the period. On January 20, the beginning balance was zero because the company was started on that day. Several transactions and parts of transactions had no cash effects and, therefore, are not included in the statement of cash flows. For example, on January 22, Overnight purchased a building for $36,000, only $6,000 of which was paid in cash. The remaining $30,000 is not included in the statement of cash flows because it did not affect the amount of cash at the time the building was purchased. Similarly, on January 23, Overnight purchased tools and equipment for $13,800, paying no cash at that time. That transaction has no cash effect on January 23, although the cash payment of $6,800 on January 27, which is a continuation of that transaction, did affect cash and is included in the statement of cash flows. Transactions that did not affect cash are called *noncash investing and*

L02-6

LEARNING OBJECTIVE
Explain how the statement of cash flows presents the change in cash for a period of time in terms of the company's operating, investing, and financing activities.

---

[4] In this illustration, net cash amounts provided by operating activities and net income are equal. This is because all of Overnight Auto Service's revenues and expenses were cash transactions. This will not always be the case. As we learn more about the accrual method of accounting, you will see that revenues and expenses may be recorded in a different accounting period than the period when cash is received or paid. This will cause net income and net cash from operating activities to be different amounts.

EXHIBIT 2–13

Statement of Cash Flows

OVERNIGHT AUTO SERVICE STATEMENT OF CASH FLOWS FOR THE PERIOD JANUARY 20 – 31, 2015			
Cash flows from operating activities:			
Cash received from revenue transactions	$ 2,200		
Cash paid for expenses	(1,400)		
Net cash provided by operating activities		$ 800	
Cash flows from investing activities:			
Purchase of land.	$(52,000)		
Purchase of building.	(6,000)		
Purchase of tools	(6,800)		
Sale of tools	600		
Net cash used by investing activities		(64,200)	
Cash flows from financing activities:			
Sale of capital stock		80,000	
Increase in cash for the period.		$16,600	
Beginning cash balance, January 20, 2015		-0-	
Ending cash balance, January 31, 2015		$16,600	

A statement of cash flows shows how cash changed during the period

CASE IN POINT

It is not unusual for a company to report an increase in cash from operating activities, but a decrease in the total amount of cash. This outcome results when more cash is used for investing and financing activities than is generated from operations. For example, in 2010 Carnival Corporation, which owns and operates cruise lines, reported cash *provided by* operating activities of over $3.8 billion but a *decrease* in total cash of $109 million. This was due primarily to large expenditures for property and equipment, such as cruise ships, which are presented as investing activities in the company's statement of cash flows. In addition, Carnival used a large amount of cash to reduce its debt.

financing transactions. In a formal statement of cash flows, these transactions are required to be noted as we explain later in this text, even though they do not affect the actual flow of cash into and out of the company.

Relationships among Financial Statements

LO2-7

LEARNING OBJECTIVE
Explain how the statement of financial position (balance sheet), income statement, and statement of cash flows relate to each other.

As our discussion of Overnight Auto Service indicates, the statement of financial position (balance sheet), the income statement, and the statement of cash flows are all based on the same transactions, but they present different "views" of the company. They should not be thought of as alternatives to each other; rather, all are important in terms of presenting key financial information about the company.

The diagram in Exhibit 2–14 explains how the three financial statements relate to the period of time they cover. The horizontal line represents time (for example, a month or a year). At the beginning and ending points in time, the company prepares a statement of financial position (balance sheet) that gives a static look in financial terms of where the company stands. The other two financial statements—the income statement and the statement of cash flows—cover the intervening *period of time* between the two balance sheets and help explain important changes that occurred during the period.

Date at beginning
of period

Time

Date at end
of period

Statement of
financial position
(Balance sheet)

Income statement
Statement of cash flows

Statement of
financial position
(Balance sheet)

EXHIBIT 2–14
Financial Reporting
Time Line

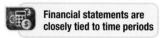
Financial statements are
closely tied to time periods

If we understand where a company stands financially at two points in time, and if we understand the changes that occurred during the intervening period in terms of the company's profit-seeking activities (income statement) and its cash activities (statement of cash flows), we know a great deal about the company that is valuable in assessing its future cash flows—information that is useful to investors, creditors, management, and others.

Because the balance sheet, income statement, and statement of cash flows are derived from the same underlying financial information, they are said to "articulate," meaning that they relate closely to each other. The diagram in Exhibit 2–15 indicates relationships that we have discussed in this chapter as we have introduced these three important financial statements. The dollar amounts are taken from the Overnight Auto Service example presented earlier in this chapter. In the balance sheet, the property, plant, and equipment amount of $100,000 represents the total of land ($52,000), building ($36,000), and tools and equipment ($12,000).

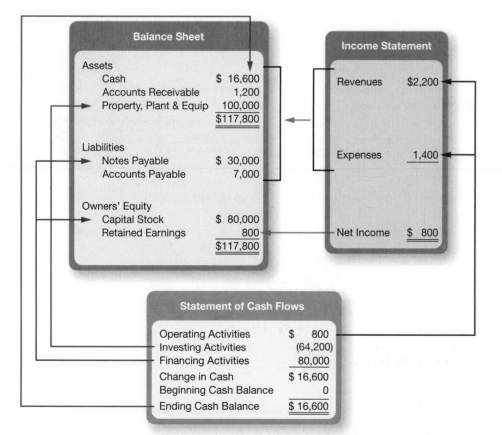

EXHIBIT 2–15
Financial Statement
Articulation

Balance Sheet	
Assets	
Cash	$ 16,600
Accounts Receivable	1,200
Property, Plant & Equip	100,000
	$117,800
Liabilities	
Notes Payable	$ 30,000
Accounts Payable	7,000
Owners' Equity	
Capital Stock	$ 80,000
Retained Earnings	800
	$117,800

Income Statement	
Revenues	$2,200
Expenses	1,400
Net Income	$ 800

Statement of Cash Flows	
Operating Activities	$ 800
Investing Activities	(64,200)
Financing Activities	80,000
Change in Cash	$ 16,600
Beginning Cash Balance	0
Ending Cash Balance	$ 16,600

Financial statements
are based on the same
underlying transactions

The balance sheet represents an expansion of the accounting equation and explains the various categories of assets, liabilities, and owners' equity. The income statement explains changes in financial position that result from profit-generating transactions in terms of revenue and expense transactions. The resulting number, net income, represents an addition to the owners' equity in the enterprise. The statement of cash flows explains the ways cash increased and decreased during the period in terms of the enterprise's operating, investing, and financing activities.

While these three key financial statements present important information, they do not include all possible information that might be presented about a company. For example, look again at Overnight's activities during the latter part of January. We could have prepared a separate financial statement on how liabilities changed or how the Tools and Equipment asset account changed. There is also important nonfinancial information that underlies the statement of financial position, the income statement, and the statement of cash flows that could be presented and that would benefit users of the statements. Accountants have developed methods of dealing with these other types of information, which we will learn about later in this text. At this point, we have focused our attention on the three primary financial statements that companies most often use to describe the activities that are capable of being captured in financial terms.

Financial reporting, and financial statements in particular, can be thought of as a lens through which you can view a business. (See Exhibit 2–16.) A lens allows you to see things from a distance that you would not otherwise be able to see; it also allows you to focus in greater detail on certain aspects of what you are looking at. Financial information, and particularly financial statements, allows you to do just that—focus in on certain financial aspects of the enterprise that are of particular interest to you in making important investing and credit decisions. Financial reporting encompasses financial statements, but it is not limited to financial statements.

EXHIBIT 2–16

Financial Reporting and
Financial Statements

FINANCIAL ANALYSIS and Decision Making

Relationships among the three primary financial statements provide the opportunity to learn a great deal about a company by bringing information together in a meaningful way. In fact, some people believe that relationships in the financial statements are as important as the actual dollar figures in those statements.

For example, take another look at the balance sheet in Exhibit 2–10. Notice that the company has $16,600 of cash and $1,200 of accounts receivable, a total of $17,800 in what are sometimes referred to as *current* assets, denoting that they either are cash or will soon become cash. Now look at the liabilities in the balance sheet and notice that the company has notes payable of $30,000 and accounts payable of $7,000 for a total of $37,000 of liabilities. Because both types of liabilities are current liabilities, meaning that they will be due in the near future and can be expected to require the use of current assets, Overnight Auto Service will have difficulty paying them because it does not have enough liquid assets to cover its liabilities. The company may need to seek additional capital or long-term financing of the $30,000 note payable on the building. The relationship of current assets to current liabilities is called the *current ratio*. For Overnight Auto Service it is a low .48 ($17,800 divided by $37,000). This means that Overnight Auto Service has only 48 cents available for every $1 of liabilities that will come due in the near future. On the other hand, if the $30,000 notes payable resulting from the building purchase is not due in the near future, the company's liquidity is much stronger and the company may have sufficient time to bring in enough cash through its operations to pay the note when it is due.

While the above refers exclusively to information found in the balance sheet, key information from one financial statement often is combined with information from another financial statement. For example, we may be interested in knowing the amount of cash provided by operations (cash flow statement) relative to the amount of a company's currently maturing liabilities (balance sheet). Or we might want to compare a company's net income (income statement) with the investment in assets (balance sheet) that were used to generate that income.

Many of the chapters in this text introduce you to various types of financial analysis. We build on those introductory discussions in Chapter 14, Financial Statement Analysis, in which we provide a comprehensive treatment of how financial statements are used to inform investors and creditors.

YOUR TURN   You as a Creditor

Assume that you are a financial analyst for a potential supplier to Overnight Auto Service. Overnight wants to buy goods from your company on credit. What factors might you consider in deciding whether to extend credit to Overnight?

(See our comments on the Online Learning Center website.)

Forms of Business Organization

In the United States, most business enterprises are organized as *sole proprietorships, partnerships,* or *corporations.* Generally accepted accounting principles can be applied to the financial statements of all three forms of organization.

SOLE PROPRIETORSHIPS

An unincorporated business owned by one person is called a **sole proprietorship.** Often the owner also acts as the manager. This form of business organization is common for small retail stores, farms, service businesses, and professional practices in law, medicine, and accounting. In fact, the sole proprietorship is the most common form of business organization in our economy.

From an accounting viewpoint, a sole proprietorship is regarded as a business entity *separate from the other financial activities of its owner.* From a legal viewpoint, however, the business and its owner are not regarded as separate entities. Thus, *the owner is personally liable*

LO2-8

LEARNING OBJECTIVE
Explain common forms of business ownership—sole proprietorship, partnership, and corporation—and demonstrate how they differ in terms of their statements of financial position.

for the debts of the business. If the business encounters financial difficulties, creditors can force the owner to sell his or her personal assets to pay the business debts. While an advantage of the sole proprietorship form of organization is its simplicity, this *unlimited liability* feature is a disadvantage to the owner.

PARTNERSHIPS

An unincorporated business owned by two or more persons voluntarily acting as partners (co-owners) is called a **partnership.** Partnerships, like sole proprietorships, are widely used for small businesses. In addition, some large professional practices, including CPA firms and law firms, are organized as partnerships. As in the case of the sole proprietorship, the owners of a partnership are personally responsible for all debts of the business. From an accounting standpoint, a partnership is viewed as a business entity separate from the personal affairs of its owners.[5] A benefit of the partnership form over the sole proprietorship form is the ability to bring together larger amounts of capital investment from multiple owners.

CORPORATIONS

A **corporation** is a type of business organization that is recognized *under the law* as an entity separate from its owners. Therefore, the owners of a corporation are *not* personally liable for the debts of the business. These owners can lose no more than the amounts they have invested in the business—a concept known as *limited liability.* This concept is one of the principal reasons that corporations are an attractive form of business organization to many investors. Overnight Auto Service, the company used in our illustrations, is a corporation.

Ownership of a corporation is divided into transferable shares of capital stock, and the owners are called **stockholders** or shareholders. Stock certificates are issued by the corporation to each stockholder showing the number of shares that he or she owns. The stockholders are generally free to sell some or all of these shares to other investors at any time. This *transferability of ownership* adds to the attractiveness of the corporate form of organization, because investors can more easily get their money out of the business. Corporations offer an even greater opportunity than partnerships to bring together large amounts of capital from multiple owners.

There are many more sole proprietorships and partnerships than corporations, but most large businesses are organized as corporations. Thus, corporations are the dominant form of business organization in terms of the *dollar volume* of business activity. Of the three types of business, corporations are most likely to distribute financial statements to investors and other outsiders.

REPORTING OWNERSHIP EQUITY IN THE STATEMENT OF FINANCIAL POSITION

Assets and liabilities are presented in the same manner in the statement of financial position of all three types of business organization. Some differences arise, however, in the presentation of the ownership equity.

Sole Proprietorships   A *sole proprietorship* is owned by only one person. Therefore, the owner's equity section of the balance sheet includes only one item—the equity of the owner. If Overnight Auto Service had been organized as a sole proprietorship with Michael McBryan the owner, owner's equity in the January 31 balance sheet would appear as follows:

Ownership equity in a sole proprietorship

Owner's equity:
    Michael McBryan, Capital. $80,800

Partnerships   A *partnership* has two or more owners. Accountants use the term *partners' equity* instead of owners' equity and usually list separately the amount of each partner's equity in the business. If, for example, Michael McBryan had been in partnership with his

---

[5] Creditors of an unincorporated business often ask to see the *personal* financial statements of the business owners, as these owners ultimately are responsible for paying the debts of the business.

sister, Rebecca McBryan, in Overnight Auto Service, and if each had contributed an equal amount of cash ($40,000) and had shared equally in the net income ($400), the partners' equity section of the balance sheet would have been presented as follows:

Partners' equity:
Michael McBryan, Capital. $40,400
Rebecca McBryan, Capital.   40,400
    Total partners' equity. $80,800

 . . . in a partnership

Corporations   In a business organized as a *corporation,* it is *not* customary to show separately the equity of each stockholder. In the case of large corporations, this clearly would be impractical because these businesses may have *several million* individual stockholders (owners).

We return to our original assumption that Overnight Auto Service is organized as a corporation. Owners' equity (also referred to as **stockholders' equity** or shareholders' equity) is presented in two amounts—capital stock and retained earnings. This section of the balance sheet appears as follows:

Owners' equity:
Capital Stock $80,000
Retained Earnings.   800
    Total stockholders' equity $80,800

 . . . and in a corporation

Capital stock represents the amount that the stockholders originally invested in the business in exchange for shares of the company's stock. **Retained earnings,** in contrast, represents the increase in owners' equity that has accumulated over the years as a result of profitable operations.

The Use of Financial Statements by External Parties

As we learned in Chapter 1, investors and creditors use financial statements in making *financial decisions*—that is, in selecting those companies in which they will invest resources or to which they will extend credit. For this reason, financial statements are designed primarily to meet the needs of creditors and investors. Two factors of particular concern to creditors and investors are the *liquidity* and *profitability* of a business organization.

Creditors are interested in **liquidity**—the ability of the business to pay its debts as they come due. Liquidity is critical to the very survival of a business organization—a business that is not liquid may be forced into bankruptcy by its creditors. Once bankrupt, a business may be forced by the courts to stop its operations, sell its assets (for the purpose of paying its creditors), and eventually go out of existence.

Investors also are interested in the liquidity of a business organization, but often they are even more interested in its profitability. *Profitable operations increase the value of the owners' equity* in the business. A company that continually operates unprofitably will eventually exhaust its resources and be forced out of existence. Therefore, most users of financial statements study these statements carefully for clues to the company's liquidity and future profitability.

The Short Run versus the Long Run   In the short run, liquidity and profitability may be independent of each other. A business may be operating profitably but nevertheless run out of cash needed to meet its obligations. On the other hand, a company may operate unprofitably during a given year yet still have enough cash from previous periods to pay its bills and remain liquid.

Over a longer term, however, liquidity and profitability go hand in hand. If a business is to survive, it must remain liquid and, in the long run, must operate profitably.

Evaluating Short-Term Liquidity   As discussed earlier in this chapter, one key indicator of short-term liquidity is the relationship between an entity's *liquid* assets and the liabilities requiring payment *in the near future.* By studying the nature of a company's assets, and the amounts and due dates of its liabilities, users of financial statements often may anticipate whether the company is likely to have difficulty in meeting its upcoming obligations. This simple type of analysis meets the needs of many *short-term* creditors. Evaluating long-term debt-paying ability is a more difficult matter and is discussed in later chapters.

In studying financial statements, users should *always* read the accompanying notes and the auditors' report.

THE NEED FOR ADEQUATE DISCLOSURE

The concept of adequate **disclosure** is an important generally accepted accounting principle. Adequate disclosure means that users of financial statements are informed of all information *necessary for the proper interpretation* of the statements. Adequate disclosure is made in the body of the financial statements and in *notes* accompanying these statements. It is not unusual to find a series of notes to financial statements that are longer than the statements themselves.

Among the events that may require disclosure in notes to the financial statements are occurrences after the date of the financial statements. For example, assume that Overnight Auto Service's building is destroyed by fire on February 2, and that Michael McBryan is using the financial statements to acquire additional financing for the business after that date. Assume also that McBryan has less insurance on the building than will be needed to replace it. Users of the financial statements, such as bankers who might be considering lending money to Overnight, must be informed of this important "subsequent event." This disclosure usually would be done with a note like the following:

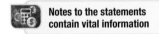
Notes to the statements contain vital information

> *Note 7: Events occurring after the financial statement date*
> The building included in the January 31 statement of financial position at $36,000 was destroyed by fire after the reporting period covered by the December 31 statement of financial position. While the company has insurance on this facility, management expects to recover only approximately $30,000 of the loss.

In addition to important subsequent events, many other situations may require disclosure in notes to the financial statements. Examples include unsettled lawsuits against the company, due dates of major liabilities, assets pledged as collateral to secure loans, amounts receivable from officers or other "insiders," and contractual commitments requiring large future cash outlays.

There is no single comprehensive list of the items and events that may require disclosure. As a general rule, a company should disclose all financial information that a reasonably informed person would consider *necessary for the proper interpretation* of the financial statements. Events that clearly are unimportant *do not* require disclosure. Determining information that should be disclosed in financial statements is another situation that requires significant judgment on the part of the accountant.

MANAGEMENT'S INTEREST IN FINANCIAL STATEMENTS

LO2-9

LEARNING OBJECTIVE
Discuss the importance of financial statements to a company and its investors and creditors and why management may take steps to improve the appearance of the company in its financial statements.

While we have emphasized the importance of financial statements to investors and creditors, the management of a business organization is vitally concerned with the financial position of the business and with its profitability and cash flows. Therefore, management is anxious to receive financial statements as frequently and as quickly as possible so that it may take action to improve areas of weak performance. Most large organizations provide managers with financial statements on at least a monthly basis. With modern technology, financial statements prepared on a weekly, daily, or even hourly basis are possible.

Managers have a special interest in the *annual* financial statements, because these statements are used by decision makers outside of the organization. For example, if creditors view the annual financial statements as strong, they will be more willing to extend credit to the business than if they regard the company's financial statements as weak. Management is concerned with its ability to obtain the funds it needs to meet its objectives, so it is particularly interested in how investors and creditors react to the company's financial statements.

A strong statement of financial position is one that shows relatively little debt and large amounts of liquid assets relative to the liabilities due in the near future. A strong income statement is one that shows large revenues relative to the expenses required to earn the revenues. A strong statement of cash flows is one that not only shows a strong cash balance but also indicates that cash is being generated by operations. Demonstrating that these positive characteristics of the company are ongoing and can be seen in a series of financial statements is particularly helpful in creating confidence in the company on the part of investors and creditors. Because of the importance of the financial statements, management may take steps that are specifically intended to improve the company's financial position and financial performance. For example, cash purchases of assets may be delayed until the beginning of the next accounting period so that large amounts of cash will be included in the statement of financial position and the statement of cash flows. On the other hand, if the company is in a particularly strong cash position, liabilities due in the near future may be paid early, replaced with longer-term liabilities, or even replaced by additional investments by owners to communicate that future negative cash flows will not be as great as they might otherwise appear.

These actions are sometimes called **window dressing**—measures taken by management to make the company appear as strong as possible in its financial statements. Users of financial statements should realize that, while the financial statements are fair representations of the financial position at the end of the period and financial performance during the period, they may not necessarily describe the typical financial situation of the business throughout the entire financial reporting period. In its annual financial statements, in particular, management tries to make the company appear as strong as is reasonably possible. As a result, many creditors regard more frequent financial statements (for example, quarterly or even monthly) as providing important additional information beyond that in the annual financial statements. The more frequently financial statements are presented, the less able management is to window-dress and make a company look financially stronger than it actually is.

Ethics, Fraud, & Corporate Governance

A major outgrowth from the business failures amid allegations of fraudulent financial reporting discussed in the last chapter was the passage of the Sarbanes-Oxley Act of 2002. This Act was signed into law by President George W. Bush on July 30, 2002. The Sarbanes-Oxley Act (hereafter SOX or the Act) is generally viewed as the most far-reaching piece of securities legislation since the original Securities Acts were passed in the 1930s.

One of the major requirements of this legislation is for CEOs and CFOs to certify the accuracy of their company's financial statements. The CEOs and CFOs of all public companies must certify on an annual and quarterly basis that they (1) have reviewed their company's financial statements, (2) are not aware of any error or omission that would make the financial statements misleading, and (3) believe that the financial statements fairly present in all material respects the company's financial condition (balance sheet) and results of operations (income statement). There is some evidence that this certification requirement is affecting corporate behavior. For example, a former CFO of **HealthSouth** (Weston Smith, shown to the right) contacted federal authorities about the

© Gary Tramontina/Bloomberg via Getty Images

massive (alleged) accounting fraud at that company because he was not willing to certify that **HealthSouth**'s financial statements were materially accurate.

Concluding Remarks

Throughout this text, we emphasize how accounting information is the basis for business decisions. In this chapter, you have been introduced to business transactions and how they are combined and presented in the form of three basic financial statements—the statement of financial position (balance sheet), the income statement, and the statement of cash flows. These financial statements constitute some of the primary products of the accountant's work, and they provide investors, creditors, and other parties with pertinent information that is useful for decision making.

As you continue your study of financial accounting, in Chapter 3 you will learn how business transactions are actually recorded, how they move through an accounting system, and how they eventually lead to the preparation of financial statements. The foundation you have received in Chapter 2 will be helpful to you as we move into a more sophisticated discussion of business transactions and how they impact a company's financial position, results of operations, and cash flows.

END-OF-CHAPTER REVIEW

LO2-1   Explain the nature and general purposes of financial statements. Financial statements are presentations of information in financial terms about an enterprise that are believed to be fair and accurate. They describe certain attributes of the enterprise that are important for decision makers, particularly investors (owners) and creditors.

LO2-2   Explain certain accounting principles that are important for an understanding of financial statements and how professional judgment by accountants may affect the application of those principles. Accountants prepare financial statements by applying a set of standards or rules referred to as generally accepted accounting principles. Consistent application of these standards permits comparisons between companies and between years of a single company. Generally accepted accounting principles allow for significant latitude in how certain transactions should be accounted for, meaning that professional judgment is particularly important.

LO2-3   Demonstrate how certain business transactions affect the elements of the accounting equation: Assets = Liabilities + Owners' Equity. Business transactions result in changes in the three elements of the basic accounting equation. A transaction that increases total assets must also increase total liabilities and owners' equity. Similarly, a transaction that decreases total assets must simultaneously decrease total liabilities and owners' equity. Some transactions increase one asset and reduce another. Regardless of the nature of the specific transaction, the accounting equation must stay in balance at all times.

LO2-4   Explain how the statement of financial position, often referred to as the balance sheet, is an expansion of the basic accounting equation. The statement of financial position, or balance sheet, presents in detail the elements of the basic accounting equation. Various types of assets are listed and totaled. The enterprise's liabilities are listed, totaled, and added to the owners' equity. The balancing feature of this financial statement is one of its dominant characteristics because the statement is simply an expansion of the basic accounting equation.

LO2-5   Explain how the income statement reports an enterprise's financial performance for a period of time in terms of the relationship of revenues and expenses. Revenues are created as the enterprise provides goods and services for its customers. Many expenses are required to be able to provide those goods and services. The difference between the revenues and expenses is net income or net loss.

LO2-6   Explain how the statement of cash flows presents the change in cash for a period of time in terms of the company's operating, investing, and financing activities. Cash is one of the most important assets, and the statement of cash flows shows in detail how the enterprise's cash balance changed between the beginning and end of the accounting period. Operating activities relate to ongoing revenue and expense transactions. Investing activities relate to the purchase and sale of various types of assets (for example, land, buildings, and equipment). Financing activities describe where the enterprise has received its debt and equity financing. The statement of cash flows combines information about all of these activities into a concise statement of changes in cash that reconciles the beginning and ending cash balances.

LO2-7   Explain how the statement of financial position (balance sheet), income statement, and statement of cash flows relate to each other. The three primary financial statements are based on the same underlying transactions. They are not alternatives to each other, but rather represent three different ways of looking at the financial activities of the reporting enterprise. Because they are based on the same transactions, they "articulate" with each other.

LO2-8   Explain common forms of business ownership—sole proprietorship, partnership, and corporation—and demonstrate how they differ in terms of their statements of financial position. Owners' equity is one of three major elements in the basic accounting equation. Regardless of the form of organization, owners' equity represents the interest of the owners in the assets of the reporting enterprise. For a sole proprietorship, owner's equity consists of the interest of a single owner. For a partnership, the ownership interests of all partners are added together to determine the total owners' equity of the enterprise. For a corporation, which may have many owners, the total contribution to the enterprise represents its owners' equity. In all cases, the enterprise's net income is added to owners' equity.

LO2-9   Discuss the importance of financial statements to a company and its investors and creditors and why management may take steps to improve the appearance of the company in its financial statements. Financial statements are particularly important for investors and creditors in their attempts to evaluate future cash flows from the enterprise to them. Management is interested in the enterprise looking as positive as possible in its financial statements and may take certain steps to improve the overall appearance of the enterprise. A fine line, however, exists between the steps management can take and the steps that are unethical, or even illegal.

Key Terms Introduced or Emphasized in Chapter 2

accounting equation (p. 46)   Assets are equal to the sum of liabilities plus owners' equity.

articulation (p. 41)   The close relationship that exists among the financial statements that are prepared on the basis of the same underlying transaction information.

assets (p. 42)   Economic resources owned by an entity.

balance sheet (p. 40)   The financial statement showing the financial position of an enterprise by summarizing its assets, liabilities, and owners' equity at a point in time. Also called the statement of financial position.

business entity (p. 42)   An economic unit that controls resources, incurs obligations, and engages in business activities.

capital stock (p. 59)   Transferable units of ownership in a corporation.

corporation (p. 58)   A business organized as a separate legal entity and chartered by a state, with ownership divided into transferable shares of capital stock.

cost principle (p. 43)   The widely used principle of accounting for assets at their original cost to the current owner.

creditor (p. 44)   A person or organization to whom debt is owed.

deflation (p. 44)   A decline in the general price level, resulting in an increase in the purchasing power of the monetary unit.

disclosure (p. 60)   The accounting principle of providing with financial statements any financial and other facts that are necessary for proper interpretation of those statements.

expenses (p. 51)   Past, present, or future reductions in cash required to generate revenues.

financial statement (p. 40)   A declaration of information believed to be true and communicated in monetary terms.

financing activities (p. 53)   A category in the statement of cash flows that reflects the results of debt and equity financing transactions.

going-concern assumption (p. 43)   An assumption by accountants that a business will operate in the foreseeable future unless specific evidence suggests that this is not a reasonable assumption.

income statement (p. 40)   An activity statement that subtracts from the enterprise's revenue those expenses required to generate the revenues, resulting in a net income or a net loss.

inflation (p. 44)   An increase in the general price level, resulting in a decline in the purchasing power of the monetary unit.

investing activities (p. 53)   A category in the statement of cash flows that reflects the results of purchases and sales of assets, such as land, buildings, and equipment.

liabilities (p. 44)   Debts or obligations of an entity that resulted from past transactions. They represent the claims of creditors on the enterprise's assets.

liquidity (p. 59)   Having the financial ability to pay debts as they become due.

negative cash flows (p. 41)   A payment of cash that reduces the enterprise's cash balance.

operating activities (p. 53)   A category in the statement of cash flows that includes the cash effects of all revenues and expenses included in the income statement.

owners' equity (p. 45)   The excess of assets over liabilities. The amount of the owners' investment in the business, plus profits from successful operations that have been retained in the business.

partnership (p. 58)   An unincorporated form of business organization in which two or more persons voluntarily associate for purposes of carrying out business activities.

positive cash flows (p. 41)   Increases in cash that add to the enterprise's cash balance.

retained earnings (p. 59)   The portion of stockholders' equity that has accumulated as a result of profitable operations.

revenues (p. 51)   Increases in the enterprise's assets as a result of profit-oriented activities.

sole proprietorship (p. 57)   An unincorporated business owned by a single individual.

stable-dollar assumption (p. 44)   An assumption by accountants that the monetary unit used in the preparation of financial statements is stable over time or changes at a sufficiently slow rate that the resulting impact on financial statements does not distort the information.

statement of cash flows (p. 41)   An activity statement that explains the enterprise's change in cash in terms of its operating, investing, and financing activities.

statement of financial position (p. 40)   Same as balance sheet.

stockholders (p. 58)   Owners of capital stock in a corporation.

stockholders' equity (p. 59)   The owners' equity of an enterprise organized as a corporation.

window dressing (p. 61)   Measures taken by management specifically intended to make a business look as strong as possible in its balance sheet, income statement, and statement of cash flows.

Demonstration Problem

Account balances for Crystal Auto Wash at September 30, 2015, are shown below. The figure for retained earnings is not given, but it can be determined when all the available information is assembled in the form of a balance sheet.

Accounts Payable	$14,000	Land	$68,000
Accounts Receivable	800	Machinery & Equipment	65,000
Buildings	52,000	Notes Payable (due in	
Cash	9,200	30 days)	29,000
Capital Stock	100,000	Salaries Payable	3,000
Retained Earnings	?	Supplies	400

Instructions

a. Prepare a balance sheet at September 30, 2015.

b. Does this balance sheet indicate that the company is in a strong financial position? Explain briefly.

c. How would an income statement and a statement of cash flows allow you to better respond to part **b**?

Solution to the Demonstration Problem

a.

CRYSTAL AUTO WASH
BALANCE SHEET
SEPTEMBER 30, 2015

Assets		Liabilities & Owners' Equity	
Cash	$ 9,200	Liabilities:	
Accounts Receivable	800	Notes Payable	$ 29,000
Supplies	400	Accounts Payable	14,000
Machinery & Equipment.	65,000	Salaries Payable	3,000
Buildings.	52,000	Total liabilities	$ 46,000
		Owners' equity:	
Land	68,000	Capital Stock	$100,000
		*Retained Earnings	49,400
Total	$195,400	Total	$195,400

*Computed as $195,400 (total assets) − $46,000 (total liabilities) − $149,400 (owners' equity); $149,400 − $100,000 (capital stock) = $49,400.

b. The balance sheet indicates that Crystal Auto Wash is in a *weak* financial position. The only liquid assets—cash and receivables—total only $10,000, but the company has *$46,000* in liabilities due in the near future.

c. An income statement for Crystal Auto Wash would show the company's revenues and expenses for the period (month, quarter, or year) ending on the date of the balance sheet, September 30, 2015. This information would be helpful in determining whether the company is successful in selling its auto wash services at an amount that exceeds its cost of providing those services, something the company must do to remain in business and be successful. The statement of cash flows for the same period as the income statement would show where the company's cash came from and where it went in terms of its operating, investing, and financing activities. This information would be particularly helpful in assessing the strength of the company's ability to satisfy its obligations as they come due in light of the relatively weak balance sheet.

Self-Test Questions

The answers to these questions appear on page 85.
Note: In order to review as many chapter concepts as possible, some self-test questions include *more than one* correct answer. In these cases, you should indicate *all* of the correct answers.

1. A set of financial statements:

a. Is intended to assist users in evaluating the financial position, profitability, and future prospects of an entity.

b. Is intended to substitute for filing income tax returns to the Internal Revenue Service in determining the amount of income taxes owed by a business organization.

c. Includes notes disclosing information necessary for the proper interpretation of the statements.

d. Is intended to assist investors and creditors in making decisions involving the allocation of economic resources.

2. Which of the following statements is (are) *not* consistent with generally accepted accounting principles relating to asset valuation?

a. Most assets are originally recorded in accounting records at their cost to the business entity.

b. Subtracting total liabilities from total assets indicates what the owners' equity in the business is worth under current market conditions.

c. Accountants assume that assets such as office supplies, land, and buildings will be used in business operations rather than sold at current market prices.

d. Accountants prefer to base the valuation of assets on objective, verifiable evidence rather than upon appraisals or personal opinions.

3. Waterworld Boat Shop purchased a truck for $12,000, making a down payment of $5,000 cash and signing a $7,000 note payable due in 60 days. As a result of this transaction:

   a. Total assets increased by $12,000.

   b. Total liabilities increased by $7,000.

   c. From the viewpoint of a short-term creditor, this transaction makes the business more liquid.

   d. This transaction had no immediate effect on the owners' equity in the business.

4. A transaction caused a $15,000 *decrease* in both total assets and total liabilities. This transaction could have been:

   a. Purchase of a delivery truck for $15,000 cash.

   b. An asset with a cost of $15,000 destroyed by fire.

   c. Repayment of a $15,000 bank loan.

   d. Collection of a $15,000 account receivable.

5. Which of the following is (are) correct about a company's balance sheet?

   a. Displays sources and uses of cash for the period.

   b. Is an expansion of the basic accounting equation: Assets = Liabilities + Owners' Equity.

   c. Is sometimes referred to as a statement of financial position.

   d. It is unnecessary if both an income statement and statement of cash flows are available.

6. Which of the following would you expect to find in a correctly prepared income statement?

   a. Cash balance at the end of the period.

   b. Revenues earned during the period.

   c. Contributions by the owner during the period.

   d. Expenses incurred during the period to earn revenues.

7. What information would you find in a statement of cash flows that you would not be able to get from the other two primary financial statements?

   a. Cash provided by or used in financing activities.

   b. Cash balance at the end of the period.

   c. Total liabilities due to creditors at the end of the period.

   d. Net income.

8. Which of the following statements relating to the role of professional judgment in the financial reporting process is (are) true?

   a. Different accountants may evaluate similar situations differently.

   b. The determination of which items should be disclosed in notes to financial statements requires professional judgment.

   c. Once a complete list of generally accepted accounting principles is prepared, judgment by accountants will no longer enter into the financial reporting process.

   d. The possibility exists that professional judgment later may prove to have been incorrect.

ASSIGNMENT MATERIAL Discussion Questions

1. In broad general terms, what is the purpose of accounting?

2. Why is a knowledge of accounting terms and concepts useful to persons other than professional accountants?

3. In general terms, what are revenues and expenses? How are they related in the determination of an enterprise's net income or net loss?

4. Why is the statement of financial position, or balance sheet, a logical place to begin a discussion of financial statements?

5. What is the basic accounting equation? Briefly define the three primary elements in the equation.

6. Why is the going-concern assumption an important consideration in understanding financial statements?

7. Can a business transaction cause one asset to increase without affecting any other asset, liability, or owners' equity?

8. Give an example of business transactions that would:

   a. Cause one asset to increase and another asset to decrease, with no effect on either liabilities or owners' equity.

   b. Cause both total assets and liabilities to increase with no effect on owners' equity.

9. What is meant by the terms *positive cash flows* and *negative cash flows?* How do they relate to revenues and expenses?

10. What are the three categories commonly found in a statement of cash flows, and what is included in each category?

11. What is meant by the statement that the financial statements *articulate?*

12. What is meant by the term *adequate disclosure,* and how do accountants fulfill this requirement in the preparation of financial statements?

13. What is meant by the term *window dressing* when referring to financial statements?

14. What are the characteristics of a strong income statement?

15. What are the characteristics of a strong statement of cash flows?

Brief Exercises

LO2-3 **BRIEF EXERCISE 2.1** Recording Transactions	Walters Company purchased a piece of machinery on credit for $20,000. Briefly state the way this transaction affects the company's basic accounting equation.
LO2-3 **BRIEF EXERCISE 2.2** Recording Transactions	Foster, Inc., purchased a truck by paying $5,000 and borrowing the remaining $30,000 required to complete the transaction. Briefly state how this transaction affects the company's basic accounting equation.
LO2-4 **BRIEF EXERCISE 2.3** Computing Retained Earnings	Bosh Company's assets total $155,000 and its liabilities total $85,000. What is the amount of Bosh's retained earnings if its capital stock amounts to $50,000?
LO2-4 **BRIEF EXERCISE 2.4** Computing Total Liabilities	White Company's assets total $780,000 and its owners' equity consists of capital stock of $500,000 and retained earnings of $150,000. Does White Company have any outstanding liabilities and, if so, what is the total amount of its liabilities?
LO2-5 **BRIEF EXERCISE 2.5** Computing Net Income	Wiley Company had total revenues of $300,000 for a recent month. During the month the company incurred operating expenses of $205,000 and purchased land for $55,000. Compute the amount of Wiley's net income for the month.
LO2-5 **BRIEF EXERCISE 2.6** Computing Net Income	Wexler, Inc.'s income statement showed total expenses for the year to be $50,000. If the company's revenues for the year were $135,000 and its year-end cash balance was $35,000, what was Wexler's net income for the year?
LO2-6 **BRIEF EXERCISE 2.7** Computing Change in Cash	Wilkes Company had the following transactions during the current year: • Earned revenues of $100,000 and incurred expenses of $56,000, all in cash. • Purchased a truck for $25,000. • Sold land for $10,000. • Borrowed $15,000 from a local bank. What was the total change in cash during the year?
LO2-8 **BRIEF EXERCISE 2.8** Alternative Forms of Equity	Solway Company is a sole proprietorship whose owner, Joe Solway, has an equity interest of $50,000. Had Solway been a partnership rather than a sole proprietorship, and the two equal partners were Joe and his brother Tom, how would the $50,000 owners' equity be presented in the company's balance sheet?
LO2-8 **BRIEF EXERCISE 2.9** Alternative Forms of Equity	Repeat Brief Exercise 2.8, except assume that rather than being a sole proprietorship or a partnership, Solway Company is organized as a corporation with capital stock of $40,000. How would the $50,000 of owners' equity be presented in the company's balance sheet?
LO2-7 **BRIEF EXERCISE 2.10** Articulation of Financial Statements	Ben Washington, sole owner of Washington Mattress Company, has an ownership interest in the company of $50,000 at January 1, 2015. During that year, he invests an additional $20,000 in the company and the company reports a net income of $25,000. Determine the balance of owner's equity that will appear in the statement of financial position at the end of the year, and explain how the amount of net income articulates with that figure in the balance sheet.

Exercises

LO2-3 **EXERCISE 2.1** The Nature of Assets and Liabilities	Assets and liabilities are important elements of a company's financial position. **a.** Define *assets*. Give three examples of assets other than cash that might appear in the balance sheet of (1) **American Airlines** and (2) a professional sports team, such as the **Boston Red Sox**. **b.** Define *liabilities*. Give three examples of liabilities that might appear in the balance sheet of (1) **American Airlines** and (2) a professional sports team, such as the **Boston Red Sox**.

LO2-4

EXERCISE 2.2

Preparing a Balance Sheet

The night manager of Willis Transportation Service, who had no accounting background, prepared the following balance sheet for the company at February 28, 2015. The dollar amounts were taken directly from the company's accounting records and are correct. However, the balance sheet contains a number of errors in its headings, format, and the classification of assets, liabilities, and owners' equity.

WILLIS TRANSPORTATION SERVICE MANAGER'S REPORT 8 P.M. THURSDAY			
Assets		**Owners' Equity**	
Capital Stock	$ 92,000	Accounts Receivable	$ 70,000
Retained Earnings	62,000	Notes Payable	288,000
Cash.	79,000	Supplies	14,000
Building	80,000	Land	70,000
Automobiles.	165,000	Accounts Payable	36,000
	$478,000		$478,000

Prepare a corrected balance sheet. Include a proper heading.

LO2-4

EXERCISE 2.3

Preparing a Balance Sheet

The balance sheet items of Kiner Company as of December 31, 2011, follow in random order. You are to prepare a balance sheet for the company, using a similar sequence for assets as illustrated in Exhibit 2–9. You must compute the amount for Retained Earnings.

Land	$90,000	Office Equipment	$ 12,400
Accounts Payable	43,800	Building	210,000
Accounts Receivable	56,700	Capital Stock	88,000
Cash.	36,300	Notes Payable	207,000
		Retained Earnings	?

LO2-2

EXERCISE 2.4

Accounting Principles and Asset Valuation

The following cases relate to the valuation of assets. Consider each case independently.

a. World-Wide Travel Agency has office supplies costing $1,400 on hand at the balance sheet date. These supplies were purchased from a supplier that does not give cash refunds. World-Wide's management believes that the company could sell these supplies for no more than $500 if it were to advertise them for sale. However, the company expects to use these supplies and to purchase more when they are gone. In its balance sheet, the supplies were presented at $500.

b. Perez Corporation purchased land in 1957 for $40,000. In 2015, it purchased a similar parcel of land for $300,000. In its 2015 balance sheet, the company presented these two parcels of land at a combined amount of $340,000.

c. At December 30, 2015, Felix, Inc., purchased a computer system from a mail-order supplier for $14,000. The retail value of the system—according to the mail-order supplier—was $20,000. On January 7, however, the system was stolen during a burglary. In its December 31, 2015, balance sheet, Felix showed this computer system at $14,000 and made no reference to its retail value or to the burglary. The December balance sheet was issued in February 2016.

In each case, indicate the appropriate balance sheet amount of the asset under generally accepted accounting principles. If the amount assigned by the company is incorrect, briefly explain the accounting principles that have been violated. If the amount is correct, identify the accounting principles that justify this amount.

LO2-3

EXERCISE 2.5

Using the Accounting Equation

Compute the missing amounts in the following table:

	Assets	= Liabilities	+ Owners' Equity
a.	$635,000	$342,000	?
b.	?	562,500	$610,000
c.	307,500	?	187,200

LO2-3

EXERCISE 2.6

The Accounting Equation

A number of business transactions carried out by Smalling Manufacturing Company are as follows:

a. Borrowed money from a bank.

b. Sold land for cash at a price equal to its cost.

c. Paid a liability.

d. Returned for credit some of the office equipment previously purchased on credit but not yet paid for. (Treat this the opposite of a transaction in which you purchased office equipment on credit.)

e. Sold land for cash at a price in excess of cost. (Hint: The difference between cost and sales price represents a gain that will be in the company's income statement.)

f. Purchased a computer on credit.

g. The owner invested cash in the business.

h. Purchased office equipment for cash.

i. Collected an account receivable.

Indicate the effects of each of these transactions on the total amounts of the company's assets, liabilities, and owners' equity. Organize your answer in tabular form, using the following column headings and the code letters **I** for increase, **D** for decrease, and **NE** for no effect. The answer for transaction **a** is provided as an example:

Transaction	Assets	=	Liabilities	+	Owners' Equity
(a)	I		I		NE

LO2-3

EXERCISE 2.7

Effects of Business Transactions

For each of the following categories, state concisely a transaction that will have the required effect on the elements of the accounting equation.

a. Increase an asset and increase a liability.

b. Decrease an asset and decrease a liability.

c. Increase one asset and decrease another asset.

d. Increase an asset and increase owners' equity.

e. Increase one asset, decrease another asset, and increase a liability.

LO2-8

EXERCISE 2.8

Forms of Business Organization

Spencer Software Company has assets of $850,000 and liabilities of $460,000.

a. Prepare the owners' equity section of the company's balance sheet under each of the following *independent* assumptions:

    1. The business is organized as a sole proprietorship, owned by Johanna Spencer.

    2. The business is organized as a partnership, owned by Johanna Spencer and Mikki Yato. Spencer's equity amounts to $240,000.

    3. The business is a corporation with 27 stockholders, each of whom originally invested $10,000 in exchange for shares of the company's capital stock. The remainder of the stockholders' equity has resulted from profitable operation of the business.

b. Assume that you are a loan officer at Security Bank. Spencer Software Company has applied to your bank for a large loan to finance the development of new products. Does it matter to you whether Spencer is organized as a sole proprietorship, a partnership, or a corporation? Explain.

LO2-9

EXERCISE 2.9

Factors Contributing to Solvency

Explain whether each of the following balance sheet items increases, reduces, or has no direct effect on a company's ability to pay its obligations as they come due. Explain your reasoning.

a. Cash.

b. Accounts Payable.

c. Accounts Receivable.

d. Capital Stock.

LO2-2

EXERCISE 2.10

Professional Judgment

Professional judgment plays a major role in the practice of accounting.

a. In general terms, explain why judgment enters into the accounting process.

b. Identify at least three situations in which accountants must rely on their professional judgment, rather than on official rules.

LO2-6

EXERCISE 2.11

Statement of Cash Flows

During the month of October 2015, Weller Company had the following transactions:

1. Revenues of $12,000 were earned and received in cash.

2. Bank loans of $3,000 were paid off.

3. Equipment of $2,500 was purchased for cash.

4. Expenses of $7,600 were paid.

5. Additional shares of capital stock were sold for $7,500 cash.

Assuming that the cash balance at the beginning of the month was $7,450, prepare a statement of cash flows that displays operating, investing, and financing activities and that reconciles the beginning and ending cash balances.

LO2-5

EXERCISE 2.12

Income Statement

Jiminez, Inc., had the following transactions during the month of March 2015. Prepare an income statement based on this information, being careful to include only those items that should appear in that financial statement.

1. Cash received from bank loans was $10,000.

2. Revenues earned and received in cash were $9,850.

3. Dividends of $4,000 were paid to stockholders.

4. Expenses incurred and paid were $5,465.

LO2-5

EXERCISE 2.13

Income Statement

An inexperienced accountant for Prestwick Company prepared the following income statement for the month of August 2015:

PRESTWICK COMPANY		
AUGUST 31, 2015		
Revenues:		
Services provided to customers............................	$17,000	
Investment by stockholders	5,000	
Loan from bank	15,000	$37,000
Expenses:		
Payments to long-term creditors	$11,700	
Expenses required to provide services to customers	7,800	
Purchase of land.......................................	16,000	35,500
Net income...		$ 1,500

Prepare a revised income statement in accordance with generally accepted accounting principles.

LO2-6

EXERCISE 2.14

Statement of Cash Flows

On the basis of the information for Prestwick Company in Exercise 2.13, prepare a statement of cash flows in a form consistent with generally accepted accounting principles. You may assume all transactions were in cash and that the beginning cash balance was $7,200.

LO2-9

EXERCISE 2.15

Window Dressing Financial Statements

Prepare a two-column analysis that illustrates steps management might take to improve the appearance of its company's financial statements. In the left column, briefly identify three steps that might be taken. In the right column, briefly describe for each step the impact on the balance sheet, income statement, and statement of cash flows. If there is no impact on one or more of these financial statements, indicate that.

LO2-4 through LO2-6

EXERCISE 2.16

Home Depot, Inc.
Financial Statements

Locate the balance sheet, income statement, and statement of cash flows of Home Depot, Inc., in Appendix A of your text. Review those statements and then respond to the following for the year ended February 3, 2013 (fiscal year 2012).

a.   Did the company have a net income or net loss for the year? How much?

b.   What were the cash balances at the beginning and end of the year? What were the most important causes of the cash decrease during the year? (Treat "cash equivalents" as if they were cash.)

c.   What are the two largest assets and two largest liabilities included in the company's balance sheet at the end of the year?

LO2-5

EXERCISE 2.17

Assessing Financial Results

McKesson Corporation's annual report for the year ended March 31, 2012, includes income statements for three years: ending on March 31, 2010, 2011, and 2012. Net income for these three years is as follows (all in millions): $1,263 (2010), $1,202 (2011), and $1,403 (2012). Further analysis of the same income statements reveals that revenues were the following amounts for these same years (all in millions): $108,702 (2010), $112,084 (2011), and $122,734 (2012). State each year's net income as a percentage of revenues and comment briefly on the trend you see over the three-year period.

Problem Set A

LO2-4

PROBLEM 2.1A

Preparing and Evaluating a Balance Sheet

Listed below in random order are the items to be included in the balance sheet of Rocky Mountain Lodge at December 31, 2015:

Equipment	$ 39,200	Buildings	$500,000
Land	425,000	Capital Stock	135,000
Accounts Payable	54,800	Cash	31,400
Accounts Receivable	10,600	Furnishings	58,700
Salaries Payable	33,500	Snowmobiles	15,400
Interest Payable	12,000	Notes Payable	620,000
		Retained Earnings	?

Instructions

a. Prepare a balance sheet at December 31, 2015. Include a proper heading and organize your balance sheet similar to Exhibit 2–9. You will need to compute the amount to be shown for Retained Earnings.

b. Assume that no payment is due on the notes payable until 2017. Does this balance sheet indicate that the company is in a strong financial position as of December 31, 2015? Explain briefly.

LO2-3

PROBLEM 2.2A

Interpreting the Effects of Business Transactions

The following six transactions of Memphis Moving Company, a corporation, are summarized in equation form, with each of the six transactions identified by a letter. For each of the transactions **(a)** through **(f)** write a separate statement explaining the nature of the transaction. For example, the explanation of transaction **(a)** could be as follows: Purchased equipment for cash at a cost of $3,200.

			Assets				=	Liabilities	+	Owners' Equity
	Cash	+	Accounts Receivable	+ Equipment +	Building +	Land	=	Accounts Payable	+	Capital Stock
Balances	$26,000	$39,000	$36,000	$110,000	$45,000		$42,000		$214,000
(a)	−3,200		+3,200						
Balances	$22,800	$39,000	$39,200	$110,000	$45,000		$42,000		$214,000
(b)	+900	−900							
Balances	$23,700	$38,100	$39,200	$110,000	$45,000		$42,000		$214,000
(c)	−3,500		+13,500				+10,000		
Balances	$20,200	$38,100	$52,700	$110,000	$45,000		$52,000		$214,000
(d)	−14,500						−14,500		
Balances	$ 5,700	$38,100	$52,700	$110,000	$45,000		$37,500		$214,000
(e)	+15,000								+15,000
Balances	$20,700	$38,100	$52,700	$110,000	$45,000		$37,500		$229,000
(f)			+7,500				+7,500		
Balances	$20,700	$38,100	$60,200	$110,000	$45,000		$45,000		$229,000

LO2-3

PROBLEM 2.3A

Recording the Effects of Transactions

Maxwell Communications was organized on December 1 of the current year and had the following account balances at December 31, listed in tabular form:

	Assets				=	Liabilities		+	Owners' Equity
Cash	+	Office Equipment	+	Building	+	Land	=	Notes Payable	+	Accounts Payable	+	Capital Stock
Balances	$37,000		$51,250		$125,000		$95,000		$80,000		$28,250		$200,000

Early in January, the following transactions were carried out by Maxwell Communications:

1. Sold capital stock to owners for $35,000.
2. Purchased land and a small office building for a total price of $90,000, of which $35,000 was the value of the land and $55,000 was the value of the building. Paid $22,500 in cash and signed a note payable for the remaining $67,500.
3. Bought several computer systems on credit for $9,500 (30-day open account).
4. Obtained a loan from Capital Bank in the amount of $20,000. Signed a note payable.
5. Paid the $22,250 account payable due as of December 31.

Instructions

a. List the December 31 balances of assets, liabilities, and owners' equity in tabular form as shown.

b. Record the effects of each of the five transactions in the format illustrated in Exhibit 2–11. Show the totals for all columns after each transaction.

LO2-3

PROBLEM 2.4A

An Alternate Problem on Recording the Effects of Transactions

The items making up the balance sheet of Phillips Truck Rental at December 31 are listed below in tabular form similar to the illustration of the accounting equation in Exhibit 2–11.

	Assets						=	Liabilities		+	Owners' Equity
Cash	+	Accounts Receivable	+	Office Equipment	+	Trucks	=	Notes Payable	+	Accounts Payable	+	Capital Stock
Balances	$9,500		$13,900		$3,800		$68,000		$20,000		$10,200		$65,000

During a short period after December 31, Phillips Truck Rental had the following transactions:

1. Bought office equipment at a cost of $2,700. Paid cash.
2. Collected $4,000 of accounts receivable.
3. Paid $3,200 of accounts payable.
4. Borrowed $10,000 from a bank. Signed a note payable for that amount.
5. Purchased two trucks for $30,500. Paid $15,000 cash and signed a note payable for the balance.
6. Sold additional stock to investors for $85,000.

Instructions

a. List the December 31 balances of assets, liabilities, and owners' equity in tabular form as shown above.

b. Record the effects of each of the six transactions in the preceding tabular arrangement. Show the totals for all columns after each transaction.

LO2-4

PROBLEM 2.5A

Preparing a Balance Sheet;
Effects of a Change in Assets

HERE COME THE CLOWNS! is the name of a traveling circus. The ledger accounts of the business at June 30, 2015, are listed here in alphabetical order:

Accounts Payable	$ 26,100	Notes Payable	$180,000
Accounts Receivable	7,450	Notes Receivable	9,500
Animals	189,060	Props and Equipment	89,580
Cages	24,630	Retained Earnings	27,230
Capital Stock	300,000	Salaries Payable	9,750
Cash	?	Tents	63,000
Costumes	31,500	Trucks & Wagons	105,840

Instructions

a. Prepare a balance sheet by using these items and computing the amount of Cash at June 30, 2015. Organize your balance sheet similar to the one illustrated in Exhibit 2–10. Include a proper balance sheet heading.

b. Assume that late in the evening of June 30, after your balance sheet had been prepared, a fire destroyed one of the tents, which had cost $14,300. The tent was not insured. Explain what changes would be required in your June 30 balance sheet to reflect the loss of this asset.

LO2-4

PROBLEM 2.6A

Preparing a Balance
Sheet—A Second Problem

The following list of balance sheet items are in random order for Alexander Farms, Inc., at September 30, 2015:

Land	$490,000	Fences and Gates	$ 33,570
Barns and Sheds	78,300	Irrigation System	20,125
Notes Payable	330,000	Cash	16,710
Accounts Receivable	22,365	Livestock	120,780
Citrus Trees	76,650	Farm Machinery	42,970
Accounts Payable	77,095	Retained Earnings	?
Property Taxes Payable	9,135	Wages Payable	5,820
Capital Stock	290,000		

Instructions

a. Prepare a balance sheet by using these items and computing the amount for Retained Earnings. Use a sequence of assets similar to that illustrated in Exhibit 2–10. (After "Barns and Sheds," you may list the remaining assets in any order.) Include a proper heading for your balance sheet.

b. Assume that on September 30, immediately after this balance sheet was prepared, a tornado completely destroyed one of the barns. This barn had a cost of $14,000 and was not insured against this type of disaster. Explain what changes would be required in your September 30 balance sheet to reflect the loss of this barn.

LO2-3, LO2-4, LO2-6

PROBLEM 2.7A

Preparing a Balance Sheet
and Statement of Cash
Flows; Effects of Business
Transactions

The balance sheet items for Franklin Bakery (arranged in alphabetical order) were as follows at August 1, 2015. (You are to compute the missing figure for Retained Earnings.)

Accounts Payable	$16,200	Equipment and Fixtures	$44,500
Accounts Receivable	11,260	Land	67,000
Building	84,000	Notes Payable	74,900
Capital Stock	80,000	Salaries Payable	8,900
Cash	6,940	Supplies	7,000

During the next two days, the following transactions occurred:

Aug. 2 Additional capital stock was sold for $25,000. The accounts payable were paid in full. (No payment was made on the notes payable or salaries payable.)

Aug. 3 Equipment was purchased at a cost of $7,200 to be paid within 10 days. Supplies were purchased for $1,250 cash from a restaurant supply center that was going out of business. These supplies would have cost $1,890 if purchased through normal channels.

Instructions

a. Prepare a balance sheet at August 1, 2015.

b. Prepare a balance sheet at August 3, 2015, and a statement of cash flows for August 1–3. Classify the payment of accounts payable and the purchase of supplies as operating activities.

c. Assume the notes payable do not come due for several years. Is Franklin Bakery in a stronger financial position on August 1 or on August 3? Explain briefly.

LO2-4 through LO2-6

PROBLEM 2.8A

Preparing Financial Statements; Effects of Business Transactions

The balance sheet items of The Soda Shop (arranged in alphabetical order) were as follows at the close of business on September 30, 2015:

Accounts Payable	$ 8,500	Furniture and Fixtures	20,000
Accounts Receivable	1,250	Land	$55,000
Building	45,500	Notes Payable	?
Capital Stock	50,000	Retained Earnings	4,090
Cash	7,400	Supplies	3,440

The transactions occurring during the first week of October were:

Oct. 3   Additional capital stock was sold for $30,000. The accounts payable were paid in full. (No payment was made on the notes payable.)

Oct. 6   More furniture was purchased on account at a cost of $18,000, to be paid within 30 days. Supplies were purchased for $1,000 cash from a restaurant supply center that was going out of business. These supplies would have cost $1,875 if purchased under normal circumstances.

Oct. 1–6   Revenues of $5,500 were earned and received in cash. Expenses required to earn the revenues of $4,000 were incurred and paid in cash.

Instructions

a. Prepare a balance sheet at September 30, 2015. (You will need to compute the missing figure for Notes Payable.)

b. Prepare a balance sheet at October 6, 2015. Also prepare an income statement and a statement of cash flows for the period October 1–6, 2015. In your statement of cash flows, treat the purchase of supplies and the payment of accounts payable as operating activities.

c. Assume the notes payable do not come due for several years. Is The Soda Shop in a stronger financial position on September 30 or on October 6? Explain briefly.

LO2-4, LO2-8

PROBLEM 2.9A

Preparing a Balance Sheet; Discussion of Accounting Principles

Anita Spencer is the founder and manager of Spencer Playhouse. The business needs to obtain a bank loan to finance the production of its next play. As part of the loan application, Anita Spencer was asked to prepare a balance sheet for the business. She prepared the following balance sheet, which is arranged correctly but which contains several errors with respect to such concepts as the business entity and the valuation of assets, liabilities, and owner's equity.

SPENCER PLAYHOUSE
BALANCE SHEET
SEPTEMBER 30, 2015

Assets		Liabilities & Owner's Equity	
Cash	$ 21,900	Liabilities:	
Accounts Receivable	132,200	Accounts Payable	$ 6,000
Props and Costumes	3,000	Salaries Payable	29,200
Theater Building	27,000	Total liabilities	$ 35,200
Lighting Equipment	9,400	Owner's equity:	
Automobile	15,000	Anita Spencer, Capital	173,300
Total	$208,500	Total	$208,500

In discussions with Anita Spencer and by reviewing the accounting records of Spencer Playhouse, you determine the following facts:

1. The amount of cash, $21,900, includes $15,000 in the company's bank account, $1,900 on hand in the company's safe, and $5,000 in Anita Spencer's personal savings account.

2. The accounts receivable, listed as $132,200, include $7,200 owed to the business by Artistic Tours. The remaining $125,000 is Anita Spencer's estimate of future ticket sales from September 30 through the end of the year (December 31).

3. Anita Spencer explains to you that the props and costumes were purchased several days ago for $18,000. The business paid $3,000 of this amount in cash and issued a note payable to Actors' Supply Co. for the remainder of the purchase price ($15,000). As this note is not due until January of next year, it was not included among the company's liabilities.

4. Spencer Playhouse rents the theater building from Kievits International at a rate of $3,000 a month. The $27,000 shown in the balance sheet represents the rent paid through September 30 of the current year. Kievits International acquired the building seven years ago at a cost of $135,000.

5. The lighting equipment was purchased on September 26 at a cost of $9,400, but the stage manager says that it isn't worth a dime.

6. The automobile is Anita Spencer's classic 1978 Jaguar, which she purchased two years ago for $9,000. She recently saw a similar car advertised for sale at $15,000. She does not use the car in the business, but it has a personalized license plate that reads "PLAHOUS."

7. The accounts payable include business debts of $3,900 and the $2,100 balance of Anita Spencer's personal Visa card.

8. Salaries payable include $25,000 offered to Mario Dane to play the lead role in a new play opening next December and $4,200 still owed to stagehands for work done through September 30.

9. When Anita Spencer founded Spencer Playhouse several years ago, she invested $20,000 in the business. However, Live Theatre, Inc., recently offered to buy her business for $173,300. Therefore, she listed this amount as her equity in the above balance sheet.

Instructions

a. Prepare a corrected balance sheet for Spencer Playhouse at September 30, 2015.

b. For each of the nine numbered items above, explain your reasoning in deciding whether or not to include the items in the balance sheet and in determining the proper dollar valuation.

LO2-2, LO2-4

PROBLEM 2.10A

Preparing a Balance Sheet; Discussion of Accounting Principles

Big Screen Scripts is a service-type enterprise in the entertainment field, and its manager, William Pippin, has only a limited knowledge of accounting. Pippin prepared the following balance sheet, which, although arranged satisfactorily, contains certain errors with respect to such concepts as the business entity and asset valuation. Pippin owns all of the corporation's outstanding stock.

BIG SCREEN SCRIPTS
BALANCE SHEET
NOVEMBER 30, 2015

Assets		Liabilities & Owner's Equity	
Cash	$ 5,150	Liabilities:	
Notes Receivable	2,700	Notes Payable	$ 67,000
Accounts Receivable	2,450	Accounts Payable	35,805
Land	70,000	Total liabilities	$102,805
Building	54,320	Owner's equity:	
Office Furniture.	8,850	Capital Stock	5,000
Other Assets.	22,400	Retained Earnings.	58,065
Total	$165,870	Total	$165,870

In discussion with Pippin and by inspection of the accounting records, you discover the following facts:

1. The amount of cash, $5,150, includes $3,400 in the company's bank account, $540 on hand in the company's safe, and $1,210 in Pippin's personal savings account.

2. One of the notes receivable in the amount of $500 is an IOU that Pippin received in a poker game several years ago. The IOU is signed by "B.K.," whom Pippin met at the game but has not heard from since.

3. Office furniture includes $2,900 for a Persian rug for the office purchased on November 20. The total cost of the rug was $9,400. The business paid $2,900 in cash and issued a note payable to Zoltan Carpet for the balance due ($6,500). As no payment on the note is due until January, this debt is not included in the liabilities above.

4. Also included in the amount for office furniture is a computer that cost $2,525 but is not on hand because Pippin donated it to a local charity.

5. The "Other Assets" of $22,400 represent the total amount of income taxes Pippin has paid the federal government over a period of years. Pippin believes the income tax law to be unconstitutional, and a friend who attends law school has promised to help Pippin recover the taxes paid as soon as he passes the bar exam.

6. The asset "Land" was acquired at a cost of $39,000 but was increased to a valuation of $70,000 when one of Pippin's friends offered to pay that much for it if Pippin would move the building off the lot.

7. The accounts payable include business debts of $32,700 and the $3,105 balance owed on Pippin's personal MasterCard.

Instructions

a. Prepare a corrected balance sheet at November 30, 2015.

b. For each of the seven numbered items above, use a separate numbered paragraph to explain whether the treatment followed by Pippin is in accordance with generally accepted accounting principles.

Problem Set B

LO2-4

PROBLEM 2.1B

Preparing and Evaluating a Balance Sheet

Listed below in random order are the items to be included in the balance sheet of Tri-State Lodge at December 31, 2015:

Equipment	$ 9,000	Buildings	$430,000
Land	140,000	Capital Stock	?
Accounts Payable	27,400	Cash	9,100
Accounts Receivable	3,300	Furnishings	22,600
Salaries Payable	13,200	Notes Payable	217,000
Interest Payable	4,000	Retained Earnings	225,400

Instructions

a. Prepare a balance sheet at December 31, 2015. Include a proper heading and organize your balance sheet similar to the illustrations shown in Chapter 2. You will need to compute the amount to be shown for Capital Stock.

b. Assume that no payment is due on the notes payable until 2017. Does this balance sheet indicate that the company is in a strong financial position as of December 31, 2015? Explain briefly.

LO2-3

PROBLEM 2.2B

Interpreting the Effects of Business Transactions

Six transactions of Prosperity Company, a corporation, are summarized below in equation form, with each of the six transactions identified by a letter. For each of the transactions (**a**) through (**f**) write a separate statement explaining the nature of the transaction. For example, the explanation of transaction (**a**) could be as follows: Purchased furniture for cash at a cost of $800.

	Assets					=	Liabilities	+	Owners' Equity
	Cash	+	Accounts Receivable	+ Furniture +	Building +	Land =	Accounts Payable	+	Capital Stock
Balances	$ 9,000		$30,000	$10,000	$90,000	$40,000	$30,000		$149,000
(a)	−800			+800					
Balances	$ 8,200		$30,000	$10,800	$90,000	$40,000	$30,000		$149,000
(b)	+500		−500						
Balances	$ 8,700		$29,500	$10,800	$90,000	$40,000	$30,000		$149,000
(c)	−3,000			+5,000			+2,000		
Balances	$ 5,700		$29,500	$15,800	$90,000	$40,000	$32,000		$149,000
(d)	−2,000						−2,000		
Balances	$ 3,700		$29,500	$15,800	$90,000	$40,000	$30,000		$149,000
(e)	+10,000								+10,000
Balances	$13,700		$29,500	$15,800	$90,000	$40,000	$30,000		$159,000
(f)				+3,000			+3,000		
Balances	$13,700		$29,500	$18,800	$90,000	$40,000	$33,000		$159,000

LO2-3

PROBLEM 2.3B

Recording the Effects of Transactions

Delta Corporation was organized on December 1 of the current year and had the following account balances at December 31, listed in tabular form:

	Assets				=	Liabilities		+	Owners' Equity
	Cash	+	Office Equipment	+ Building +	Land =	Notes Payable	+ Accounts Payable	+	Capital Stock
Balances	$12,000		$41,300	$66,000	$80,000	$42,000	$7,300		$150,000

Early in January, the following transactions were carried out by Delta Corporation:

1. Sold capital stock to owners for $40,000.
2. Purchased land and a small office building for a total price of $80,000, of which $30,000 was the value of the land and $50,000 was the value of the building. Paid $10,000 in cash and signed a note payable for the remaining $70,000.
3. Bought several computer systems on credit for $8,000 (30-day open account).
4. Obtained a loan from 2nd Bank in the amount of $12,000. Signed a note payable.
5. Paid $6,000 of account payable due as of December 31.

Instructions

a. List the December 31 balances of assets, liabilities, and owners' equity in tabular form as shown above.
b. Record the effects of each of the five transactions in the format illustrated in Chapter 2 of the text. Show the totals for all columns after each transaction.

LO2-3

PROBLEM 2.4B

An Alternate Problem on Recording the Effects of Transactions

The items making up the balance sheet of Maxx Trucking at December 31 are listed below in tabular form similar to the illustration of the accounting equation in Chapter 2 of the text.

	Assets				=	Liabilities		+	Owners' Equity
	Cash	+ Accounts Receivable	+ Office Equipment	+ Trucks =	Notes Payable	+ Accounts Payable	+	Capital Stock
Balances	$4,700	$8,300	$3,000	$72,000	$10,000	$8,000		$70,000

During a short period after December 31, Maxx Trucking had the following transactions:

1. Bought office equipment at a cost of $2,600. Paid cash.
2. Collected $2,500 of accounts receivable.
3. Paid $2,000 of accounts payable.
4. Borrowed $5,000 from a bank. Signed a note payable for that amount.
5. Purchased three trucks for $60,000. Paid $5,000 cash and signed a note payable for the balance.
6. Sold additional stock to investors for $25,000.

Instructions

a. List the December 31 balances of assets, liabilities, and owners' equity in tabular form as shown above.

b. Record the effects of each of the six transactions in the tabular arrangement illustrated above. Show the totals for all columns after each transaction.

LO2-4

PROBLEM 2.5B

Preparing a Balance Sheet; Effects of a Change in Assets

Circus World is the name of a traveling circus. The ledger accounts of the business at June 30, 2015, are listed here in alphabetical order:

Accounts Payable	$ 25,000	Notes Payable	$115,000
Accounts Receivable	5,600	Notes Receivable	1,200
Animals	310,000	Props and Equipment	108,000
Cages	15,000	Retained Earnings	89,000
Capital Stock	400,000	Salaries Payable	1,250
Cash	?	Tents	40,000
Costumes	16,000	Trucks & Wagons	125,300

Instructions

a. Prepare a balance sheet by using these items and computing the amount of Cash at June 30, 2015. Include a proper balance sheet heading.

b. Assume that late in the evening of June 30, after your balance sheet had been prepared, a fire destroyed one of the tents, which had cost $10,000. The tent was not insured. Explain what changes would be required in your June 30 balance sheet to reflect the loss of this asset.

LO2-4

PROBLEM 2.6B

Preparing a Balance Sheet—A Second Problem

Shown below in random order is a list of balance sheet items for Maple Valley Farms at September 30, 2015:

Land	$ 50,000	Fences and Gates	$14,100
Barns and Sheds	19,100	Irrigation System	10,200
Notes Payable	65,000	Cash	9,300
Accounts Receivable	15,000	Livestock	5,000
Apple Trees	84,000	Farm Machinery	20,000
Accounts Payable	8,100	Retained Earnings	?
Property Taxes Payable	4,700	Wages Payable	1,200
Capital Stock	100,000		

Instructions

a. Prepare a balance sheet by using these items and computing the amount for Retained Earnings. Use a sequence of assets similar to that illustrated in Chapter 2 of the text. Include a proper heading for your balance sheet.

b. Assume that on September 30, immediately after this balance sheet was prepared, a tornado completely destroyed one of the barns. This barn had a cost of $4,500 and was not insured against this type of disaster. Explain what changes would be required in your September 30 balance sheet to reflect the loss of this barn.

LO2-3, LO2-4, LO2-6
PROBLEM 2.7B
Preparing a Balance Sheet and Statement of Cash Flows; Effects of Business Transactions

The balance sheet items for Collier Butcher Shop (arranged in alphabetical order) were as follows at July 1, 2015. (You are to compute the missing figure for Retained Earnings.)

Accounts Payable	$ 7,000	Equipment and Fixtures	$25,000
Accounts Receivable	8,200	Land	50,000
Building	90,000	Notes Payable	40,000
Capital Stock	100,000	Salaries Payable	3,700
Cash	4,100	Supplies	7,000

During the next few days, the following transactions occurred:

July 4   Additional capital stock was sold for $30,000. The accounts payable were paid in full. (No payment was made on the notes payable or salaries payable.)

July 5   Equipment was purchased at a cost of $6,000 to be paid within 10 days. Supplies were purchased for $1,000 cash from a restaurant supply center that was going out of business. These supplies would have cost $2,000 if purchased through normal channels.

Instructions

a.   Prepare a balance sheet at July 1, 2015.

b.   Prepare a balance sheet at July 5, 2015, and a statement of cash flows for July 1–5. Classify the payment of accounts payable and the purchase of supplies as operating activities.

c.   Assume the notes payable do not come due for several years. Is Collier Butcher Shop in a stronger financial position on July 1 or on July 5? Explain briefly.

LO2-4 through LO2-6
PROBLEM 2.8B
Preparing Financial Statements; Effects of Business Transactions

The balance sheet items of The Sweet Shop (arranged in alphabetical order) were as follows at the close of the business on September 30, 2015:

Accounts Payable	$ 6,800	Furniture and Fixtures	$ 9,000
Accounts Receivable	5,000	Land	72,000
Building	80,000	Notes Payable	?
Capital Stock	100,000	Retained Earnings	19,100
Cash	6,900	Supplies	3,000

The transactions occurring during the first week of October were:

Oct. 3   Additional capital stock was sold for $30,000. The accounts payable were paid in full. (No payment was made on the notes payable.)

Oct. 6   Furniture was purchased on account at a cost of $8,000, to be paid within 30 days. Supplies were purchased for $900 cash from a restaurant supply center that was going out of business. These supplies would have cost $2,000 if purchased under normal circumstances.

Oct. 1–6   Revenues of $8,000 were earned and received in cash. Expenses required to earn the revenues of $3,200 were incurred and paid in cash.

Instructions

a.   Prepare a balance sheet at September 30, 2015. (You will need to compute the missing figure for Notes Payable.)

b.   Prepare a balance sheet at October 6, 2015. Also prepare an income statement and a statement of cash flows for the period October 1–6, 2015. In your statement of cash flows, treat the purchase of supplies and the payment of accounts payable as operating activities.

c.   Assume the notes payable do not come due for several years. Is The Sweet Shop in a stronger financial position on September 30 or on October 6? Explain briefly.

Howard Jaffe is the founder and manager of Old Town Playhouse. The business wishes to obtain a bank loan to finance the production of its next play. As part of the loan application, Jaffe was asked to prepare a balance sheet for the business. He prepared the following balance sheet, which is arranged correctly but which contains several errors with respect to such concepts as the business entity and the valuation of assets, liabilities, and owner's equity.

OLD TOWN PLAYHOUSE
BALANCE SHEET
SEPTEMBER 30, 2015

Assets		Liabilities & Owner's Equity	
Cash	$ 19,400	Liabilities:	
Accounts Receivable	150,200	Accounts Payable.	$ 7,000
Props and Costumes	3,000	Salaries Payable	32,000
Theater Building	26,000	Total Liabilities.	$ 39,000
Lighting Equipment	10,000	Owner's Equity:	
Automobile.	15,000	Howard Jaffe,	
		Capital.	184,600
Total	$223,600	Total	$223,600

In discussions with Jaffe and by reviewing the accounting records of Old Town Playhouse, you discover the following facts:

1. The amount of cash, $19,400, includes $16,000 in the company's bank account, $2,400 on hand in the company's safe, and $1,000 in Jaffe's personal savings account.

2. The accounts receivable, listed as $150,200, include $10,000 owed to the business by Dell, Inc. The remaining $140,200 is Jaffe's estimate of future ticket sales from September 30 through the end of the year (December 31).

3. Jaffe explains to you that the props and costumes were purchased several days ago for $18,000. The business paid $3,000 of this amount in cash and issued a note payable to Ham's Supply Co. for the remainder of the purchase price ($15,000). As this note is not due until January of next year, it was not included among the company's liabilities.

4. Old Town Playhouse rents the theater building from Time International. The $26,000 shown in the balance sheet represents the rent paid through September 30 of the current year. Time International acquired the building seven years ago at a cost of $180,000.

5. The lighting equipment was purchased on September 26 at a cost of $10,000, but the stage manager says that it isn't worth a dime.

6. The automobile is Jaffe's classic 1935 Ford, which he purchased two years ago for $12,000. He recently saw a similar car advertised for sale at $15,000. He does not use the car in the business, but it has a personalized license plate that reads "OTPLAY."

7. The accounts payable include business debts of $6,000 and the $1,000 balance of Jaffe's personal Visa card.

8. Salaries payable include $30,000 offered to Robin Needelman to play the lead role in a new play opening next December and $2,000 still owed to stagehands for work done through September 30.

9. When Jaffe founded Old Town Playhouse several years ago, he invested $20,000 in the business. However, New Theatre, Inc., recently offered to buy his business for $184,600. Therefore, he listed this amount as his equity in the above balance sheet.

Instructions

a. Prepare a corrected balance sheet for Old Town Playhouse at September 30, 2015.

b. For each of the nine numbered items above, explain your reasoning for deciding whether or not to include the items in the balance sheet and in determining the proper dollar valuation.

LO2-2, LO2-4
PROBLEM 2.10B

Preparing a Balance Sheet;
Discussion of Accounting
Principles

Star Scripts is a service-type enterprise in the entertainment field, and its manager, Joe Smartt, has only a limited knowledge of accounting. Joe prepared the following balance sheet, which, although arranged satisfactorily, contains certain errors with respect to such concepts as the business entity and asset valuation. Joe owns all of the corporation's outstanding stock.

STAR SCRIPTS
BALANCE SHEET
NOVEMBER 30, 2015

Assets		Liabilities & Owner's Equity	
Cash	$ 5,000	Liabilities:	
Notes Receivable	4,000	Notes Payable	$ 65,000
Accounts Receivable	3,000	Accounts Payable	32,000
Land	60,000	Total Liabilities	$ 97,000
Building	75,000	Owner's Equity:	
Office Furniture	9,600	Capital Stock	10,000
Other Assets	25,000	Retained Earnings	74,600
Total	$181,600	Total	$181,600

In discussion with Joe and by inspection of the accounting records, you discover the following facts:

1. The amount of cash, $5,000, includes $2,000 in the company's bank account, $1,200 on hand in the company's safe, and $1,800 in Joe's personal savings account.

2. One of the notes receivable in the amount of $600 is an IOU that Joe received in a poker game five years ago. The IOU is signed by "G.W.," whom Joe met at the game but has not heard from since.

3. Office furniture includes $2,500 for an Indian rug for the office purchased on November 15. The total cost of the rug was $10,000. The business paid $2,500 in cash and issued a note payable to Jana Interiors for the balance due ($7,500). As no payment on the note is due until January, this debt is not included in the liabilities above.

4. Also included in the amount for office furniture is a computer that cost $800 but is not on hand because Joe donated it to a local charity.

5. The "Other Assets" of $25,000 represent the total amount of income taxes Joe has paid the federal government over a period of years. Joe believes the income tax law to be unconstitutional, and a friend who attends law school has promised to help Joe recover the taxes paid as soon as he passes the bar exam.

6. The asset "Land" was acquired at a cost of $15,000 but was increased to a valuation of $60,000 when one of Joe's friends offered to pay that much for it if Joe would move the building off the lot.

7. The accounts payable include business debts of $30,000 and the $2,000 balance owed on Joe's personal MasterCard.

Instructions

a. Prepare a corrected balance sheet at November 30, 2015.

b. For each of the seven numbered items above, use a separate numbered paragraph to explain whether the treatment followed by Joe is in accordance with generally accepted accounting principles.

Critical Thinking Cases

LO2-4
CASE 2.1
Content of a Balance Sheet

You are asked to prepare a balance sheet for a *hypothetical* business entity of your choosing (or specified by your instructor). Include in your balance sheet the types of assets and liabilities that you think the entity might have, and show these items at what you believe would be realistic dollar amounts. Make reasonable assumptions with regard to the company's capital stock and retained earnings.

Note: The purpose of this assignment is to help you consider the types of assets and liabilities required for the operations of a specific type of business. You should complete this assignment *without* referring to an actual balance sheet for this type of business.

LO2-4 through LO2-6
CASE 2.2
Using Financial Statements

Obtain from the library the *annual report* of a well-known company (or a company specified by your instructor).

Instructions

From the balance sheet, income statement, statement of cash flows, and notes to the financial statements, answer the following:

a. What are the largest assets included in the company's balance sheet? Why would a company of this type (size and industry) have a large investment in this particular type of asset?

b. In a review of the company's statement of cash flows:
    1. What are the primary sources and uses of cash from investing activities?
    2. Did investing activities cause the company's cash to increase or decrease?
    3. What are the primary sources and uses of cash from financing activities?
    4. Did financing activities cause the company's cash to increase or decrease?

c. In a review of the company's income statement, did the company have a net income or a net loss for the most recent year? What percentage of total revenues was that net income or net loss?

d. Select three items in the notes accompanying the financial statements and explain briefly the importance of these items to people making decisions about investing in, or extending credit to, this company.

e. Assume that you are a lender and this company has asked to borrow an amount of cash equal to 10 percent of its total assets, to be repaid in 90 days. Would you consider this company to be a good credit risk? Explain.

LO2-4
CASE 2.3
Using a Balance Sheet

Moon Corporation and Star Corporation are in the same line of business and both were recently organized, so it may be assumed that the recorded costs for assets are close to current market values. The balance sheets for the two companies are as follows at July 31, 2015:

MOON CORPORATION **BALANCE SHEET** **JULY 31, 2015**				
Assets		**Liabilities & Owners' Equity**		
Cash	$ 18,000	Liabilities:		
Accounts Receivable . .	26,000	Notes Payable		
Office Equipment	1,200	(due in 60 days)		$ 12,400
Building	38,000	Accounts Payable		9,600
Land	37,200	Total liabilities		$ 22,000
		Stockholders' equity:		
		Capital Stock	$60,000	
		Retained Earnings . . .	38,400	98,400
Total	$120,400	Total		$120,400

STAR CORPORATION
BALANCE SHEET
JULY 31, 2015

Assets		Liabilities & Owners' Equity		
Cash	$ 4,800	Liabilities:		
Accounts Receivable . . .	9,600	Notes Payable		
Office Equipment	12,000	(due in 60 days)		$ 22,400
Building	60,000	Accounts Payable.		43,200
Land	96,000	Total liabilities		$ 65,600
		Stockholders' equity:		
		Capital Stock	$72,000	
		Retained Earnings.	44,800	116,800
Total	$182,400	Total		$182,400

Instructions

a. Assume that you are a banker and that each company has applied to you for a 90-day loan of $12,000. Which would you consider to be the more favorable prospect? Explain your answer fully.

b. Assume that you are an investor considering purchasing all the capital stock of one or both of the companies. For which business would you be willing to pay the higher price? Do you see any indication of a financial crisis that you might face shortly after buying either company? Explain your answer fully. (For either decision, additional information would be useful, but you are to reach your decision on the basis of the information available.)

LO2-6

CASE 2.4

Using Statements of Cash Flows

John Marshall is employed as a bank loan officer for First State Bank. He is comparing two companies that have applied for loans, and he wants your help in evaluating those companies. The two companies—Morris, Inc., and Walker Company—are approximately the same size and had approximately the same cash balance at the beginning of 2013. Because the total cash flows for the three-year period are virtually the same, John is inclined to evaluate the two companies as equal in terms of their desirability as loan candidates.

Abbreviated information (in thousands of dollars) from Morris, Inc., and Walker Company is as follows:

	Morris, Inc.			Walker Company		
	2013	2014	2015	2013	2014	2015
Cash flows from:						
Operating activities	$10	$13	$15	$ 8	$3	$(2)
Investing activities	(5)	(8)	(10)	(7)	(5)	8
Financing activities	8	(3)	1	12	4	-0-
Net from all activities	$13	$ 2	$ 6	$13	$2	$ 6

Instructions

a. Do you agree with John's preliminary assessment that the two companies are approximately equal in terms of their strength as loan candidates? Why or why not?

b. What might account for the fact that Walker Company's cash flow from financing activities is zero in 2015?

c. Generally, what would you advise John with regard to using statements of cash flows in evaluating loan candidates?

LO2-4

CASE 2.5

Ethics and Window
Dressing

The date is November 18, 2015. You are the chief executive officer of Omega Software—a publicly owned company that is currently in financial difficulty. Omega needs new large bank loans if it is to survive.

You have been negotiating with several banks, but each has asked to see your 2015 financial statements, which will be dated December 31. These statements will, of course, be audited. You are now meeting with other corporate officers to discuss the situation, and the following suggestions have been made:

1. "We are planning to buy WordMaster Software Co. for $8 million cash in December. The owners of WordMaster are in no hurry; if we delay this acquisition until January, we'll have $8 million more cash at year-end. That should make us look a lot more solvent."

2. "At year-end, we'll owe accounts payable of about $18 million. If we were to show this liability in our balance sheet at half that amount—say, $9 million—no one would know the difference. We could report the other $9 million as stockholders' equity and our financial position would appear much stronger."

3. "We owe Delta Programming $5 million, due in 90 days. I know some people at Delta. If we were to sign a note and pay them 10 percent interest, they'd let us postpone this debt for a year or more."

4. "We own land that cost us $2 million but today is worth at least $6 million. Let's show it at $6 million in our balance sheet, and that will increase our total assets and our stockholders' equity by $4 million."

Instructions

Separately evaluate each of these four proposals to improve Omega Software's financial statements. Your evaluations should consider ethical and legal issues as well as accounting issues.

LO2-9

CASE 2.6

Public Company
Accounting Oversight
Board

The Public Company Accounting Oversight Board (PCAOB) is a direct outcome of the Sarbanes-Oxley Act of 2002. This is considered one of the most significant pieces of legislation to have ever been enacted in terms of financial reporting in several decades. To respond to the instructions in this case, use the methodology of your choice to locate the Web site of the PCAOB.

Instructions

a. State the mission of the PCAOB.

b. Access the category "About Us" and list the names of the members of the PCAOB.

c. Access the category "Enforcement" and describe the authority the PCAOB has been granted by the Sarbanes-Oxley Act of 2002.

d. Access the category "Standards" and describe the responsibility of the PCAOB to establish standards that impact corporate financial reporting.

LO2-4, LO2-5

INTERNET CASE 2.7

Gathering Financial
Information

This assignment introduces you to EDGAR, the Securities and Exchange Commission's database of financial information about publicly owned companies. The SEC maintains EDGAR to increase the efficiency of financial reporting in the American economy and also to give the public free and easy access to information about publicly owned companies.

Instructions

Access EDGAR at the following Internet address: www.sec.gov. Study the website enough to be able to access the financial statements of **Cisco Systems, Inc.** Locate the company's most recent 10Q (quarterly) report.

a. What is the business address of Cisco Systems?

b. Locate the balance sheet in Form 10Q and determine whether the amount of the company's cash (and cash equivalents) increased or decreased in the most recent quarter.

c. Locate the income statement (called the "statement of operations"). What was the company's net income for the most recent quarter? Is that amount higher or lower than in the previous quarter?

d. Analyze the statement of cash flows. How much cash was provided by operations to date for the current year?

e. While you are in EDGAR, pick another company that interests you and learn more about it by studying that company's information. Be prepared to tell the class which company you selected and explain what you learned.

Internet sites are time and date sensitive. It is the purpose of these exercises to have you explore the Internet. You may need to use the Yahoo! search engine www.yahoo.com *(or another favorite search engine) to find a company's current web address.*

Answers to Self-Test Questions

1. a, c, d   **2.** b   **3.** b, d   **4.** c   **5.** b, c   **6.** b, d   **7.** a   **8.** a, b, d

CHAPTER 3

The Accounting Cycle
Capturing Economic Events

AFTER STUDYING THIS CHAPTER, YOU SHOULD BE ABLE TO:

Learning Objectives

LO3-1 Identify the steps in the accounting cycle and discuss the role of accounting records in an organization.

LO3-2 Describe a ledger account and a ledger.

LO3-3 Understand how balance sheet accounts are increased or decreased.

LO3-4 Explain the double-entry system of accounting.

LO3-5 Explain the purpose of a journal and its relationship to the ledger.

LO3-6 Explain the nature of *net income, revenue,* and *expenses.*

LO3-7 Apply the *realization* and *matching* principles in recording revenue and expenses.

LO3-8 Understand how revenue and expense transactions are recorded in an accounting system.

LO3-9 Prepare a trial balance and explain its uses and limitations.

LO3-10 Distinguish between accounting cycle procedures and the *knowledge* of accounting.

© Dennis MacDonald/Alamy

KRAFT FOODS GROUP, INC.

Capturing the economic events of a *kool-Aid*™ stand is a fairly simple process. In fact, for most *kool-Aid*™ stands, a small notebook, a sharp pencil, and an empty shoebox may serve as a complete information system.

Capturing the economic activities of Kraft Foods Group, Inc.—one of the largest food companies in the world and the maker of *kool-Aid*™—is an entirely different matter. This corporate giant controls nearly $24 billion in total assets, earns more than $18 billion in annual revenue, and generates in excess of $3 billion in annual net cash flow from its operating activities. Employing nearly 24,000 people, and managing

hundreds of manufacturing facilities and thousands of warehouses and distribution centers, Kraft Foods Group, Inc., must somehow capture the complex business transactions of its worldwide operations.

From *kool-Aid*™ stands to multinational corporations, efficiently and effectively capturing economic events—such as sales orders and raw material purchases—is absolutely essential for survival. Most enterprises use computer systems to account for these activities. Very few still use paper ledgers and handwritten journals to record daily activities and transactions. ■

Although Overnight Auto Service engaged in several business transactions in the previous chapter, we did not illustrate how these events were captured by Overnight for use by management and other interested parties. This chapter demonstrates how accounting systems record economic events related to a variety of business transactions.

The Accounting Cycle

LO3-1

LEARNING OBJECTIVE
Identify the steps in the accounting cycle and discuss the role of accounting records in an organization.

In Chapter 2, we illustrated several transactions of Overnight Auto Service that occurred during the last week in January 2015. We prepared a complete set of financial statements immediately following our discussion of these transactions. For practical purposes, businesses do not prepare new financial statements after every transaction. Rather, they accumulate the effects of individual transactions in their *accounting records.* Then, at regular intervals, the data in these records are used to prepare financial statements, income tax returns, and other types of reports.

The sequence of accounting procedures used to record, classify, and summarize accounting information in financial reports at regular intervals is often termed the **accounting cycle.** The accounting cycle begins with the initial recording of business transactions and concludes with the preparation of a complete set of formal financial statements. The term *cycle* indicates that these procedures must be repeated continuously to enable the business to prepare new, up-to-date financial statements at reasonable intervals.

The accounting cycle generally consists of eight specific steps. In this chapter, we illustrate how businesses (1) journalize (record) transactions, (2) post each journal entry to the appropriate ledger accounts, and (3) prepare a trial balance. The remaining steps of the cycle will be addressed in Chapters 4 and 5. They include (4) making end-of-period adjustments, (5) preparing an adjusted trial balance, (6) preparing financial statements, (7) journalizing and posting closing entries, and (8) preparing an after-closing trial balance.

THE ROLE OF ACCOUNTING RECORDS

The cyclical process of collecting financial information and maintaining accounting records does far more than facilitate the preparation of financial statements. Managers and employees of a business frequently use the information stored in the accounting records for such purposes as:

1. Establishing **accountability** for the assets and/or transactions under an individual's control.
2. Keeping track of routine business activities—such as the amounts of money in company bank accounts, amounts due from credit customers, or amounts owed to suppliers.
3. Obtaining detailed information about a particular transaction.
4. Evaluating the efficiency and performance of various departments within the organization.
5. Maintaining documentary evidence of the company's business activities. (For example, tax laws require companies to maintain accounting records supporting the amounts reported in tax returns.)

The Ledger

LO3-2

LEARNING OBJECTIVE
Describe a ledger account and a ledger.

An accounting system includes a separate record for each item that appears in the financial statements. For example, a separate record is kept for the asset cash, showing all increases and decreases in cash resulting from the many transactions in which cash is received or paid. A similar record is kept for every other asset, for every liability, for owners' equity, and for every revenue and expense account appearing in the income statement.

The record used to keep track of the increases and decreases in financial statement items is termed a "ledger account" or, simply, an **account.** The entire group of accounts is kept together in an accounting record called a **ledger.** Exhibit 3–8 on page 110 illustrates the ledger of Overnight Auto Service.

The Use of Accounts

An account is a means of accumulating in one place all the information about changes in specific financial statement items, such as a particular asset or liability. For example, the Cash account provides a company's current cash balance, a record of its cash receipts, and a record of its cash disbursements.

In its simplest form, an account has only three elements: (1) a title; (2) a left side, which is called the *debit* side; and (3) a right side, which is called the *credit* side. This form of an account, illustrated below and on the following page, is called a *T account* because of its resemblance to the letter "T." In a computerized system, of course, the elements of each account are stored and formatted electronically. More complete forms of accounts will be illustrated later.

Title of Account	
Left or Debit Side	Right or Credit Side

 A T account—a ledger account in its simplest form

Debit and Credit Entries

An amount recorded on the left, or debit, side of an account is called a **debit,** or a debit entry. Likewise, any amount entered on the right, or credit, side is called a **credit,** or a credit entry. In simple terms, debits refer to the left side of an account, and credits refer to the right side of an account.

To illustrate the recording of debits and credits in an account, let us go back to the eight cash transactions of Overnight Auto Service, described in Chapter 2. When these cash transactions are recorded in the Cash account, the receipts are listed on the debit side, and the payments are listed on the credit side. The dates of the transactions may also be listed, as shown in the following illustration:

Cash			
1/20	80,000	1/21	52,000
1/26	600	1/22	6,000
1/31	2,200	1/27	6,800
		1/31	200
		1/31	1,200
1/31 Balance	16,600		

 Cash transactions entered in ledger account

Each debit and credit entry in the Cash account represents a cash receipt or a cash payment. The amount of cash owned by the business at a given date is equal to the *balance* of the account on that date.

Determining the Balance of a T Account   The balance of an account is the difference between the debit and credit entries in the account. If the debit total exceeds the credit total, the account has a *debit balance;* if the credit total exceeds the debit total, the account has a *credit balance.*

In our illustrated Cash account, a line has been drawn across the account following the last cash transaction recorded in January. The total cash receipts (debits) recorded in January amount to $82,800, and the total cash payments (credits) amount to $66,200. By subtracting the credit total from the debit total ($82,800 − $66,200), we determine that the Cash account has a debit balance of *$16,600* on January 31.

This debit balance is entered in the debit side of the account just below the line. In effect, the line creates a "fresh start" in the account, with the month-end balance representing the *net result* of all the previous debit and credit entries. The Cash account now shows the amount of cash owned by the business on January 31. In a balance sheet prepared at this date, Cash in the amount of $16,600 would be listed as an asset.

Debit Balances in Asset Accounts   In the preceding illustration of a Cash account, increases were recorded on the left, or debit, side of the account and decreases were recorded on the right, or credit, side. The increases were greater than the decreases and the result was a debit balance in the account.

All asset accounts *normally have debit balances.* It is hard to imagine an account for an asset such as land having a credit balance, as this would indicate that the business had disposed of more land than it had ever acquired. (For some assets, such as cash, it is possible to acquire a credit balance—but such balances are only *temporary.*)

The fact that assets are located on the *left* side of the balance sheet is a convenient means of remembering the rule that an increase in an asset is recorded on the *left* (debit) side of the account and an asset account normally has a debit *(left-hand)* balance.

LO3-3

LEARNING OBJECTIVE
Understand how balance sheet accounts are increased or decreased.

Asset accounts normally have debit balances

Any Asset Account	
Debit (to record an increase)	Credit (to record a decrease)

Credit Balances in Liability and Owners' Equity Accounts   Increases in liability and owners' equity accounts are recorded by credit entries and decreases in these accounts are recorded by debits. The relationship between entries in these accounts and their position on the balance sheet may be summed up as follows: (1) liabilities and owners' equity belong on the *right* side of the balance sheet, (2) an increase in a liability or an owners' equity account is recorded on the *right* (credit) side of the account, and (3) liability and owners' equity accounts normally have credit *(right-hand)* balances.

Liability and owners' equity accounts normally have credit balances

Any Liability Account or Owners' Equity Account	
Debit (to record a decrease)	Credit (to record an increase)

Concise Statement of the Debit and Credit Rules   The use of debits and credits to record changes in assets, liabilities, and owners' equity may be summarized as follows:

Debit and credit rules

Asset Accounts	Liability & Owners' Equity Accounts
Normally have debit balances. Thus, increases are recorded by debits and decreases are recorded by credits.	Normally have credit balances. Thus, increases are recorded by credits and decreases are recorded by debits.

DOUBLE-ENTRY ACCOUNTING—THE EQUALITY OF DEBITS AND CREDITS

The rules for debits and credits are designed so that *every transaction is recorded by equal dollar amounts of debits and credits.* The reason for this equality lies in the relationship of the debit and credit rules to the accounting equation:

$$\text{Assets} = \text{Liabilities} + \text{Owners' Equity}$$

$$\textbf{Debit Balances} = \textbf{Credit Balances}$$

If this equation is to remain in balance, any change in the left side of the equation (assets) *must be accompanied by an equal change* in the right side (either liabilities or owners' equity). According to the debit and credit rules that we have just described, increases in the left side of the equation (assets) are recorded by *debits,* while increases in the right side (liabilities and owners' equity) are recorded by *credits,* as illustrated below:

LO3-4

LEARNING OBJECTIVE
Explain the double-entry system of accounting.

Assets		=	Liabilities		+	Owners' Equity	
Debit to increase (+)	Credit to decrease (−)		Debit to decrease (−)	Credit to increase (+)		Debit to decrease (−)	Credit to increase (+)

This system is often called **double-entry accounting.** The phrase *double-entry* refers to the need for both *debit entries* and *credit entries,* equal in dollar amount, to record every transaction. Virtually every business organization uses the double-entry system regardless of whether the company's accounting records are maintained manually or by computer. Later in this chapter, we will see that the double-entry system allows us to measure net income at the same time we record the effects of transactions on the balance sheet accounts.

The Journal

LO3-5

LEARNING OBJECTIVE
Explain the purpose of a journal and its relationship to the ledger.

In the preceding discussion we illustrated how the debit and credit rules of double-entry accounting are applied in the recording of economic events. Using T accounts, we stressed the effects that business transactions have on individual asset, liability, and owners' equity accounts that comprise a company's general ledger. It is important to realize, however, that transactions are rarely recorded *directly* in general ledger accounts. In an actual accounting system, the information about each business transaction is *initially* recorded in an accounting record called the **journal.** This information is *later* transferred to the appropriate accounts in the general ledger.

The journal is a chronological (day-by-day) record of business transactions. At convenient intervals, the debit and credit amounts recorded in the journal are transferred (posted) to the accounts in the ledger. The updated ledger accounts, in turn, serve as the basis for preparing the company's financial statements.

To illustrate the most basic type of journal, called a **general journal,** let us examine the very first business transaction of Overnight Auto Service. Recall that on January 20, 2015, the McBryan family invested $80,000 in exchange for capital stock. Thus, the asset Cash increased by $80,000, and the owners' equity account Capital Stock increased by the same amount.

Applying the debit and credit rules discussed previously, we know that increases in assets are recorded by debits, whereas increases in owners' equity are recorded by credits. As such, this event requires a *debit* to Cash and a *credit* to Capital Stock in the amount of $80,000. The transaction is recorded in the company's general journal as illustrated in Exhibit 3–1. Note the basic characteristics of this general journal entry:

1. The name of the account debited (Cash) is written first, and the dollar amount to be debited appears in the left-hand money column.
2. The name of the account credited (Capital Stock) appears below the account debited and is indented to the right. The dollar amount appears in the right-hand money column.
3. A brief description of the transaction appears immediately below the journal entry.

Accounting software packages automate and streamline the way in which transactions are recorded. However, recording transactions manually—without a computer—is an effective way to conceptualize the manner in which economic events are captured by accounting systems and subsequently reported in a company's financial statements.

EXHIBIT 3–1

Recording a Transaction in the General Journal

GENERAL JOURNAL			
Date	**Account Titles and Explanation**	**Debit**	**Credit**
2015			
Jan. 20	Cash	80,000	
	Capital Stock		80,000
	Owners invest cash in the business.		

A familiarity with the general journal form of describing transactions is just as essential to the study of accounting as a familiarity with plus and minus signs is to the study of mathematics. The journal entry is a *tool* for *analyzing* and *describing* the impact of various transactions on a business entity. The ability to describe a transaction in journal entry form requires an understanding of the nature of the transaction and its effect on the financial position of the business.

POSTING JOURNAL ENTRIES TO THE LEDGER ACCOUNTS (AND HOW TO "READ" A JOURNAL ENTRY)

We have made the point that transactions are recorded *first* in the journal. Ledger accounts are updated *later,* through a process called **posting.** (In a computerized system, postings often occur instantaneously, rather than later.)

Posting simply means *updating the ledger accounts* for the effects of the transactions recorded in the journal. Viewed as a mechanical task, posting basically amounts to performing the steps you describe when you "read" a journal entry aloud.

Consider the first entry appearing in Overnight's general journal. If you were to read this entry aloud, you would say: "Debit Cash, $80,000; credit Capital Stock, $80,000." That's precisely what a person posting this entry should do: Debit the Cash account for $80,000, and credit the Capital Stock account for $80,000.

The posting of Overnight's first journal entry is illustrated in Exhibit 3–2. Notice that no new information is recorded during the posting process. Posting involves copying into the ledger accounts information that *already has been recorded in the journal.* In manual accounting systems, this can be a tedious and time-consuming process, but in computer-based systems, it is done instantly and automatically. In addition, computerized posting greatly reduces the risk of errors.

EXHIBIT 3–2

Posting a Transaction From the Journal to Ledger Accounts

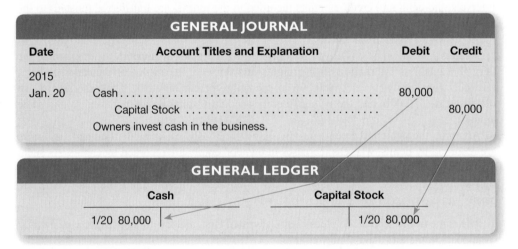

Recording Balance Sheet Transactions: An Illustration

To illustrate how to use debits and credits for recording transactions in accounts, we return to the January transactions of Overnight Auto Service. At this point, we discuss only those transactions related to changes in the company's financial position and reported directly in its balance sheet. The revenue and expense transactions that took place on January 31 will be addressed later in the chapter.

Each transaction from January 20 through January 27 is analyzed first in terms of increases in assets, liabilities, and owners' equity. Second, we follow the debit and credit rules for entering these increases and decreases in specific accounts. Asset ledger accounts are shown on the left side of the analysis; liability and owners' equity ledger accounts are shown on the right side. For convenience in the following transactions, both the debit and credit figures for the transaction under discussion are shown in *red*. Figures relating to earlier transactions appear in *black*.

Jan. 20   Michael McBryan and family invested $80,000 cash in exchange for capital stock.

Jan. 21   Representing Overnight, McBryan negotiated with both the City of Santa Teresa and Metropolitan Transit Authority (MTA) to purchase an abandoned bus garage. (The city owned the land, but the MTA owned the building.) On January 21, Overnight Auto Service purchased the land from the city for $52,000 cash.

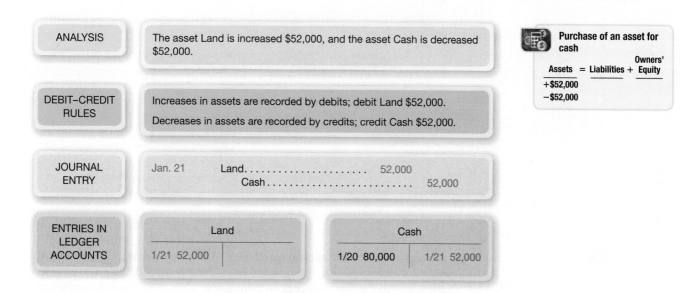

Jan. 22   Overnight completed the acquisition of its business location by purchasing the abandoned building from the MTA. The purchase price was $36,000; Overnight made a $6,000 cash down payment and issued a 90-day, non-interest-bearing note payable for the remaining $30,000.

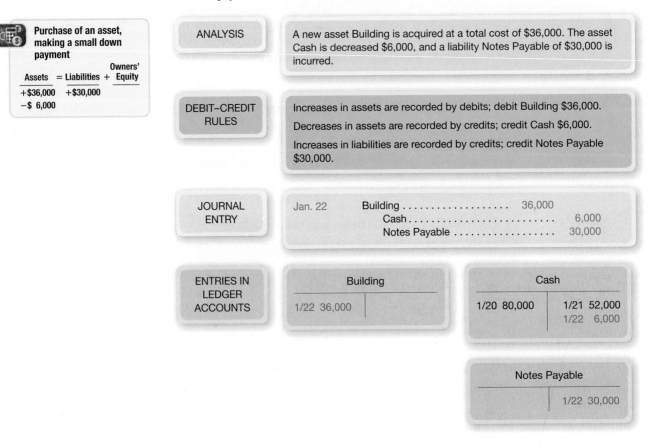

Jan. 23   Overnight purchased tools and equipment on account from Snappy Tools. The purchase price was $13,800, due in 60 days.

Jan. 24   Overnight found that it had purchased more tools than it needed. On January 24, it sold the excess tools on account to Ace Towing at a price of $1,800. The tools were sold at a price equal to their cost, so there was no gain or loss on this transaction.

ANALYSIS	Since the tools are sold at cost, there is no gain or loss on this transaction. An asset Accounts Receivable is acquired in the amount of $1,800; the asset Tools and Equipment is decreased $1,800.	Credit sale of an asset (with no gain or loss)

Credit sale of an asset (with no gain or loss)

Assets	=	Liabilities	+	Owners' Equity
+$1,800				
−$1,800				

DEBIT–CREDIT RULES	Increases in assets are recorded by debits; debit Accounts Receivable $1,800. Decreases in assets are recorded by credits; credit Tools and Equipment $1,800.

JOURNAL ENTRY	Jan. 24 Accounts Receivable . . . . 1,800 Tools and Equipment 1,800

ENTRIES IN LEDGER ACCOUNTS	**Accounts Receivable** 1/24 1,800	**Tools and Equipment** 1/23 13,800 │ 1/24 1,800

Jan. 26 Overnight received $600 in partial collection of the account receivable from Ace Towing.

Collection of an account receivable

Assets	=	Liabilities	+	Owners' Equity
+$600				
−$600				

ANALYSIS	The asset Cash is increased $600, and the asset Accounts Receivable is decreased $600.

DEBIT–CREDIT RULES	Increases in assets are recorded by debits; debit Cash $600. Decreases in assets are recorded by credits; credit Accounts Receivable $600.

JOURNAL ENTRY	Jan. 26 Cash. . . . . 600 Accounts Receivable 600

ENTRIES IN LEDGER ACCOUNTS	**Cash** 1/20 80,000 │ 1/21 52,000 1/26 600 │ 1/22 6,000	**Accounts Receivable** 1/24 1,800 │ 1/26 600

Jan. 27 Overnight made a $6,800 partial payment of its account payable to Snappy Tools.

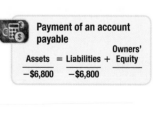

Payment of an account payable

Assets	=	Liabilities	+	Owners' Equity
−$6,800		−$6,800		

ANALYSIS	The liability Accounts Payable is decreased $6,800, and the asset Cash is decreased $6,800.

DEBIT–CREDIT RULES	Decreases in liabilities are recorded by debits; debit Accounts Payable $6,800. Decreases in assets are recorded by credits; credit Cash $6,800.

JOURNAL ENTRY	Jan. 27 Accounts Payable . . . . 6,800 Cash 6,800

ENTRIES IN LEDGER ACCOUNTS	**Accounts Payable** 1/27 6,800 │ 1/23 13,800	**Cash** 1/20 80,000 │ 1/21 52,000 1/26 600 │ 1/22 6,000 │ 1/27 6,800

Ledger Accounts after Posting

The seven journal entries made by Overnight Auto Service from January 20 through January 27 are summarized in Exhibit 3–3.

EXHIBIT 3–3

General Journal Entries:
January 20 Through 27

OVERNIGHT AUTO SERVICE
GENERAL JOURNAL
JANUARY 20–27, 2015

Date	Account Titles and Explanation	Debit	Credit
2015			
Jan. 20	Cash...	80,000	
	Capital Stock.................................		80,000
	Owners invest cash in the business.		
21	Land..	52,000	
	Cash..		52,000
	Purchased land for business site.		
22	Building...	36,000	
	Cash..		6,000
	Notes Payable..................................		30,000
	Purchased building from the MTA. Paid part cash; balance payable within 90 days.		
23	Tools and Equipment...............................	13,800	
	Accounts Payable...............................		13,800
	Purchased tools and equipment on credit from Snappy Tools. Due in 60 days.		
24	Accounts Receivable..............................	1,800	
	Tools and Equipment..........................		1,800
	Sold unused tools and equipment at cost to Ace Towing.		
26	Cash...	600	
	Accounts Receivable...........................		600
	Collected part of account receivable from Ace Towing.		
27	Accounts Payable.................................	6,800	
	Cash..		6,800
	Made partial payment of the liability to Snappy Tools.		

After all of the journal entries in Exhibit 3–3 have been posted, Overnight's ledger accounts appear as shown in Exhibit 3–4. The accounts are arranged in the same order as in the balance sheet—that is, assets first, followed by liabilities and owners' equity accounts. Each ledger account is presented in what is referred to as a *running balance* format (as opposed to simple T accounts). You will notice that the running balance format does not indicate specifically whether a particular account has a debit or credit balance. This causes no difficulty, however, because we know that asset accounts normally have debit balances, and liability and owners' equity accounts normally have credit balances.

In the ledger accounts in Exhibit 3–4, we have not yet included any of Overnight's revenue and expense transactions discussed in Chapter 2. All of the company's revenue and expense transactions took place on January 31. Before we can discuss the debit and credit rules for revenue and expense accounts, a more in-depth discussion of *net income* is warranted.

CASH

Date	Debit	Credit	Balance
2015			
Jan. 20	80,000		80,000
21		52,000	28,000
22		6,000	22,000
26	600		22,600
27		6,800	15,800

ACCOUNTS RECEIVABLE

Date	Debit	Credit	Balance
2015			
Jan. 24	1,800		1,800
26		600	1,200

TOOLS AND EQUIPMENT

Date	Debit	Credit	Balance
2015			
Jan. 23	13,800		13,800
24		1,800	12,000

BUILDING

Date	Debit	Credit	Balance
2015			
Jan. 22	36,000		36,000

LAND

Date	Debit	Credit	Balance
2015			
Jan. 21	52,000		52,000

NOTES PAYABLE

Date	Debit	Credit	Balance
2015			
Jan. 22		30,000	30,000

ACCOUNTS PAYABLE

Date	Debit	Credit	Balance
2015			
Jan. 23		13,800	13,800
27	6,800		7,000

CAPITAL STOCK

Date	Debit	Credit	Balance
2015			
Jan. 20		80,000	80,000

EXHIBIT 3–4
Ledger Showing
Transactions

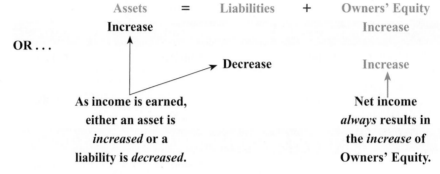

What Is Net Income?

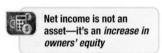

LO3-6

LEARNING OBJECTIVE
Explain the nature of *net income, revenue,* and *expenses.*

As previously noted, **net income** is *an increase in owners' equity resulting from the profitable operation of the business.* Net income does not consist of any cash or any other specific assets. Rather, net income is a *computation* of the overall effects of many business transactions on *owners' equity.* The effects of net income on the basic accounting equation are illustrated as follows:

Net income is not an asset—it's an *increase in owners' equity*

Assets	=	Liabilities	+	Owners' Equity
Increase				**Increase**

OR...

↑

↗ **Decrease**

Increase

↑

As income is earned, either an asset is *increased* or a liability is *decreased.*

Net income *always* results in the *increase* of Owners' Equity.

Our point is that net income represents an *increase in owners' equity* and has no direct relationship to the types or amounts of assets on hand. Even a business operating at a profit may run short of cash.

In the balance sheet, the changes in owners' equity resulting from profitable or unprofitable operations are reflected in the balance of the stockholders' equity account, *Retained Earnings.* The assets and liabilities of the business that change as a result of income-related activities appear in their respective sections of the balance sheet.

RETAINED EARNINGS

As illustrated in Chapter 2, the Retained Earnings account appears in the stockholders' equity section of the balance sheet. Earning net income causes the balance in the Retained Earnings account to increase. However, many corporations follow a policy of distributing to their stockholders some of the resources generated by profitable operations. Distributions of this nature are termed **dividends,** and they reduce both total assets and stockholders' equity. The reduction in stockholders' equity is reflected by decreasing the balance of the Retained Earnings account.

The balance in the **Retained Earnings** account represents the total net income of the corporation over the *entire lifetime* of the business, less all of the dividends to its stockholders. In short, retained earnings represent the earnings that have been *retained* by the corporation to finance growth. Some of the largest corporations have become large by consistently retaining in the business most of the resources generated by profitable operations. For instance, a recent annual report of **Walmart Stores, Inc.,** shows total stockholders' equity of $76 billion. Of this amount, retained earnings of nearly $69 billion account for over 90 percent of the company's total equity.

© The McGraw-Hill Companies, Inc./John Flournoy, photographer

THE INCOME STATEMENT: A PREVIEW

An **income statement** is a financial statement that summarizes the profitability of a business entity for a specified period of time. In this statement, net income is determined by comparing *sales prices* of goods or services sold during the period with the *costs* incurred by the business in delivering these goods or services. The technical accounting terms for these components of net income are **revenue** and **expenses.** Therefore, accountants say that net income is equal to *revenue minus expenses.* Should expenses exceed revenue, a **net loss** results.

A sample income statement for Overnight Auto Service for the year ended December 31, 2015, is shown in Exhibit 3–5. In Chapter 5, we show exactly how this income statement was developed from the company's accounting records. For now, however, the illustration will assist us in discussing some of the basic concepts involved in measuring net income.

OVERNIGHT AUTO SERVICE INCOME STATEMENT FOR THE YEAR ENDED DECEMBER 31, 2015		
Revenue:		
Repair service revenue		$172,000
Rent revenue earned		3,000
Total revenue		$175,000
Expenses:		
Advertising	$ 3,900	
Salaries and wages	58,750	
Supplies	7,500	
Depreciation: building	1,650	
Depreciation: tools and equipment	2,200	
Utilities	19,400	
Insurance	15,000	
Interest	30	108,430
Income before income taxes		$ 66,570
Income taxes		26,628
Net income		$ 39,942

EXHIBIT 3–5

A Preview of Overnight's Income Statement

Income Must Be Related to a Specified Period of Time   Notice that our sample income statement covers a *period of time*—namely, the year 2015. A balance sheet shows the financial position of a business at a *particular date.* We cannot evaluate net income unless it is associated with a specific time period. For example, if an executive says, "My business earns a net income of $10,000," the profitability of the business is unclear. Does it earn $10,000 per week, per month, or per year?

CASE IN POINT

The late J. Paul Getty, one of the world's first billionaires, was once interviewed by a group of business students. One of the students asked Getty to estimate the amount of his income. As the student had not specified a time period, Getty decided to have some fun with his audience and responded, "About $11,000." He paused long enough to allow the group to express surprise over this seemingly low amount, and then completed his sentence, "an hour."

Accounting Periods   The period of time covered by an income statement is termed the company's **accounting period.** To provide the users of financial statements with timely information, net income is measured for relatively short accounting periods of equal length. This concept, called the **time period principle,** is one of the underlying accounting principles that guide the interpretation of financial events and the preparation of financial statements.

The length of a company's accounting period depends on how frequently managers, investors, and other interested people require information about the company's performance.

Every business prepares annual income statements, and most businesses prepare quarterly and monthly income statements as well. (Quarterly statements cover a three-month period and are prepared by all large corporations for distribution to their stockholders.)

The 12-month accounting period used by an entity is called its **fiscal year.** The fiscal year used by most companies coincides with the calendar year and ends on December 31. Some businesses, however, elect to use a fiscal year that ends on some other date.

For example, **The Walt Disney Company** ends its fiscal year on September 30. Why? For one reason, September and October are relatively slow months at the company's theme parks. Furthermore, September financial statements provide timely information about the preceding summer, which is the company's busiest season. Most large retailers, such as **Walmart** and **JCPenney**, end their fiscal years at the end of January, after the rush of the holiday season. Many choose the last Saturday of January as their cutoff, which results in an exact 52-week reporting period approximately five out of every six years.

Let us now explore the meaning of the accounting terms *revenue* and *expenses* in more detail.

REVENUE

Revenue always causes an *increase* in owners' equity

Revenue is the price of goods sold and services rendered during a given accounting period. Earning revenue causes owners' equity to increase. When a business renders services or sells merchandise to its customers, it usually receives cash or acquires an account receivable from the customer. The inflow of cash and receivables from customers increases the total assets of the company; on the other side of the accounting equation, owners' equity increases to match the increase in total assets. Thus, revenue is the gross *increase in owners' equity* resulting from operation of the business.

Various account titles are used to describe different types of revenue. For example, a business that sells merchandise rather than services, such as **Walmart** or **General Motors**, uses the term *Sales* to describe its revenue. In the professional practices of physicians, CPAs, and attorneys, revenue usually is called *Fees Earned.* A real estate office, however, might call its revenue *Commissions Earned.*

Overnight Auto Service's income statement reveals that the company records its revenue in two separate accounts: (1) *Repair Service Revenue* and (2) *Rent Revenue Earned.* A professional sports team might also have separate revenue accounts for *Ticket Sales, Concessions Revenue,* and *Revenue from Television Contracts.* Another type of revenue common to many businesses is *Interest Revenue* (or Interest Earned), stemming from the interest earned on bank deposits, notes receivable, and interest-bearing investments.

LO3-7

LEARNING OBJECTIVE
Apply the *realization* and *matching* principles in recording revenue and expenses.

The Realization Principle: When to Record Revenue   When should revenue be recognized? In most cases, the **realization principle** indicates that revenue should be recognized *at the time goods are sold or services are rendered.* At this point, the business has essentially completed the earnings process, and the sales value of the goods or services can be measured objectively. At any time prior to the sale, the ultimate value of the goods or services sold can only be estimated. After the sale, the only step that remains is to collect from the customer, usually a relatively certain event.

To illustrate, assume that on July 25 a radio station contracts with a car dealership to air a series of one-minute advertisements during August. If all of the agreed-upon ads are aired in August, but payment for the ads is not received until September, in which month should the station recognize the advertising revenue? The answer is August, the month in which it *rendered the services* that earned the advertising revenue. In other words, revenue is recognized when it is *earned,* without regard to when a contract is signed or when cash payment for providing goods or services is received.

EXPENSES

Expenses are the costs of the goods and services used up in the process of earning revenue. Examples include the cost of employees' salaries, advertising, rent, utilities, and the depreciation of buildings, automobiles, and office equipment. All these costs are necessary to attract and serve customers and thereby earn revenue. Expenses are often called the "costs of doing business," that is, the cost of the various activities necessary to carry on a business.

An expense always causes a *decrease in owners' equity.* The related changes in the accounting equation can be either (1) a decrease in assets or (2) an increase in liabilities. An expense reduces assets if payment occurs at the time that the expense is incurred. If the expense will not be paid until later, as, for example, the purchase of advertising services on account, the recording of the expense will be accompanied by an increase in liabilities.

 Expenses always cause a *decrease* in owners' equity

The Matching Principle: When to Record Expenses

A significant relationship exists between revenue and expenses. Expenses are incurred for the *purpose of producing revenue.* In the measurement of net income for a period, revenue should be offset by *all the expenses incurred in producing that revenue.* This concept of offsetting expenses against revenue on a basis of cause and effect is called the **matching principle.**

Timing is an important factor in matching (offsetting) revenue with the related expenses. For example, in the preparation of monthly income statements, it is important to offset this month's expenses against this month's revenue. We should not offset this month's expenses against last month's revenue because there is no cause and effect relationship between the two.

Assume that the salaries earned by a company's marketing team for serving customers in July are not paid until early August. In which month should these salaries be regarded as expenses—July or August? The answer is July, because July is the month in which the marketing team's services *helped to produce revenue.* Just as revenue and cash receipts are not one and the same, expenses and cash payments are not identical. In fact, the cash payment of an expense may occur before, after, or in the same period that revenue is earned. In deciding when to report an expense in the income statement, the critical question is, "In what period does the cash expenditure help to produce revenue?"—*not,* "When does the payment of cash occur?"

Expenditures Benefiting More Than One Accounting Period

Many expenditures made by a business benefit two or more accounting periods. Fire insurance policies, for example, usually cover a period of 12 months. If a company prepares monthly income statements, a portion of the cost of such a policy should be allocated to insurance expense each month that the policy is in force. In this case, apportionment of the cost of the policy by months is an easy matter. If the 12-month policy costs $2,400, for example, the insurance expense for each month amounts to $200 ($2,400 cost ÷ 12 months).

Not all transactions can be divided so precisely by accounting periods. The purchase of a building, furniture and fixtures, machinery, a computer, or an automobile provides benefits to the business over all the years in which such an asset is used. No one can determine in advance exactly how many years of service will be received from such long-lived assets. Nevertheless, in measuring the net income of a business for a period of one year or less, accountants must *estimate* what portion of the cost of the building and other long-lived assets is applicable to the current year. Since the allocations of these costs are estimates rather than precise measurements, it follows that income statements should be regarded as useful *approximations* of net income rather than as absolutely correct measurements.

For some expenditures, such as those for employee training programs, it is not possible to estimate objectively the number of accounting periods over which revenue is likely to be produced. In such cases, generally accepted accounting principles require that the expenditure be charged *immediately to expense.* This treatment is based upon the accounting principle of **objectivity** and the concept of **conservatism.** Accountants require *objective evidence* that an expenditure will produce revenue in future periods before they will view the expenditure as creating an asset. When this objective evidence does not exist, they follow the conservative practice of recording the expenditure as an expense. *Conservatism,* in this context, means applying the accounting treatment that results in the *lowest* (most conservative) estimate of net income for the current period.

INTERNATIONAL CASE IN POINT

International financial reporting standards (IFRSs) differ significantly from U.S. GAAP with respect to costs that are expensed immediately and costs that are capitalized. For example, IFRS 38 allows development costs to be capitalized if certain criteria are met, but under U.S. GAAP these same costs would need to be expensed in the period in which they occur. Alternatively, idle capacity and spoilage costs need to be expensed immediately under IFRS 2, but U.S. GAAP allows these costs to be capitalized in inventory. The FASB and the IASB have made an agreement to work toward eliminating differences between international accounting standards and GAAP over the next several years.

THE ACCRUAL BASIS OF ACCOUNTING

The policy of recognizing revenue in the accounting records when it is *earned* and recognizing expenses when the related goods or services are *used* is called the **accrual basis of accounting.** The purpose of accrual accounting is to measure the profitability of the *economic activities conducted* during the accounting period.

The most important concept involved in accrual accounting is the *matching principle.* Revenue is offset with all of the expenses incurred in generating that revenue, thus providing a measure of the overall profitability of the economic activity.

An alternative to the accrual basis is called *cash basis accounting.* Under cash basis accounting, revenue is recognized when cash is collected from the customer, rather than when the company sells goods or renders services. Expenses are recognized when payment is made, rather than when the related goods or services are used in business operations. The cash basis of accounting measures the amounts of cash received and paid out during the period, but it does *not* provide a good measure of the *profitability of activities* undertaken during the period.

Exhibit 3–6 illustrates that, under the accrual basis of accounting, cash receipts or disbursements may occur *prior to* or *after* revenue is earned or an expense is incurred.

EXHIBIT 3–6

Cash Flow Versus Income
Statement Recognition

DEBIT AND CREDIT RULES FOR REVENUE AND EXPENSES

We have stressed that revenue increases owners' equity and that expenses decrease owners' equity. The debit and credit rules for recording revenue and expenses in the ledger accounts are a natural extension of the rules for recording changes in owners' equity. The rules previously stated for recording increases and decreases in owners' equity are as follows:

- *Increases* in owners' equity are recorded by *credits.*
- *Decreases* in owners' equity are recorded by *debits.*

This rule is now extended to cover revenue and expense accounts:

- *Revenue* increases owners' equity; therefore, revenue is recorded by *credits.*
- *Expenses* decrease owners' equity; therefore, expenses are recorded by *debits.*

Dividends

A dividend is a distribution of assets (usually cash) by a corporation to its stockholders. In some respects, dividends are similar to expenses—they reduce both the assets and the owners' equity in the business. However, *dividends are not an expense, and they are not deducted from revenue in the income statement.* The reason why dividends are not viewed as an expense is that these payments do not serve to generate revenue. Rather, they are a *distribution of profits* to the owners of the business.

Since the declaration of a dividend reduces stockholders' equity, the dividend could be recorded by debiting the Retained Earnings account. However, a clearer record is created if a separate Dividends account is debited for all dividends to stockholders. The reporting of dividends in the financial statements will be illustrated in Chapter 5.

The debit–credit rules for revenue, expenses, and dividends are summarized below:

Owners' Equity	
Decreases **recorded by** Debits	Increases **recorded by** Credits
Expenses decrease owners' equity	**Revenue increases owners' equity**
Expenses **are recorded by** Debits	Revenue **is recorded by** Credits
Dividends reduce owners' equity	
Dividends **are recorded by** Debits	

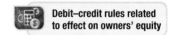

Debit–credit rules related to effect on owners' equity

Recording Income Statement Transactions: An Illustration

In Chapter 2, we introduced Overnight Auto Service, a small auto repair shop formed on January 20, 2015. Early in this chapter, we journalized and posted all of Overnight's balance sheet transactions through January 27. At this point we will illustrate the manner in which Overnight's January income statement transactions were handled and continue into February with additional transactions.

Three transactions involving revenue and expenses were recorded by Overnight on January 31, 2015. The following illustrations provide an analysis of each transaction.

Jan. 31   Recorded revenue of $2,200, all of which was received in cash.

LO3-8

LEARNING OBJECTIVE
Understand how revenue and expense transactions are recorded in an accounting system.

Jan. 31 Paid employees' wages earned in January, $1,200.

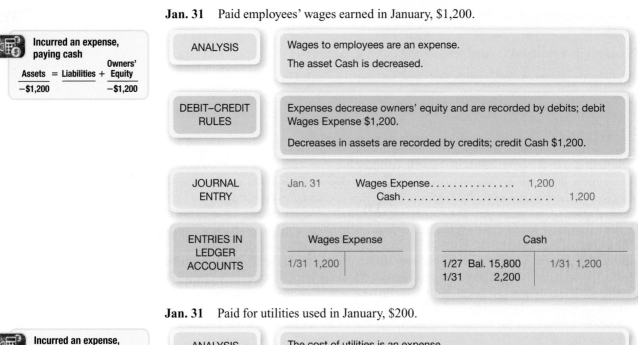

ANALYSIS
Wages to employees are an expense.
The asset Cash is decreased.

DEBIT–CREDIT RULES
Expenses decrease owners' equity and are recorded by debits; debit Wages Expense $1,200.
Decreases in assets are recorded by credits; credit Cash $1,200.

JOURNAL ENTRY
Jan. 31   Wages Expense.............. 1,200
                 Cash........................... 1,200

ENTRIES IN LEDGER ACCOUNTS

Wages Expense		Cash	
1/31 1,200		1/27 Bal. 15,800	1/31 1,200
		1/31 2,200	

Jan. 31 Paid for utilities used in January, $200.

ANALYSIS
The cost of utilities is an expense.
The asset Cash is decreased.

DEBIT–CREDIT RULES
Expenses decrease owners' equity and are recorded by debits; debit Utilities Expense $200.
Decreases in assets are recorded by credits; credit Cash $200.

JOURNAL ENTRY
Jan. 31   Utilities Expense 200
                 Cash 200

ENTRIES IN LEDGER ACCOUNTS

Utilities Expense		Cash	
1/31 200		1/27 Bal. 15,800	1/31 1,200
		1/31 2,200	1/31 200

Having analyzed and recorded all of Overnight's January transactions, next we focus upon the company's February activities. Overnight's February transactions are described, analyzed, and recorded as follows:

Feb. 1 Paid *Daily Tribune* $360 cash for newspaper advertising to be run during February.

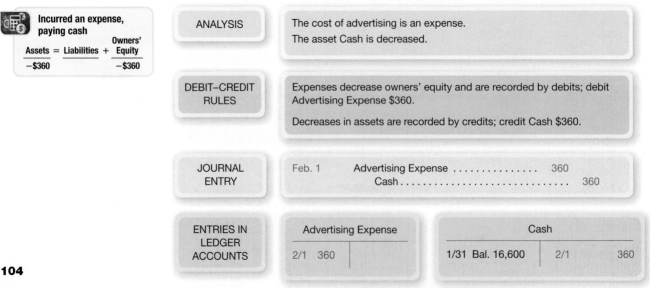

ANALYSIS
The cost of advertising is an expense.
The asset Cash is decreased.

DEBIT–CREDIT RULES
Expenses decrease owners' equity and are recorded by debits; debit Advertising Expense $360.
Decreases in assets are recorded by credits; credit Cash $360.

JOURNAL ENTRY
Feb. 1   Advertising Expense 360
                 Cash........................... 360

ENTRIES IN LEDGER ACCOUNTS

Advertising Expense		Cash	
2/1 360		1/31 Bal. 16,600	2/1 360

Feb. 2 Purchased radio advertising from KRAM to be aired in February. The cost was
$470, payable within 30 days.

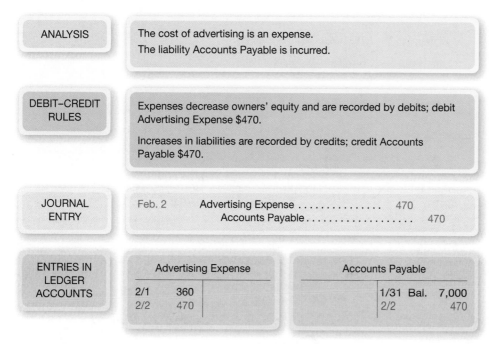

| ANALYSIS | The cost of advertising is an expense.
The liability Accounts Payable is incurred. |

Incurred an expense to be paid later

Assets	=	Liabilities	+	Owners' Equity
		+$470		−$470

| DEBIT–CREDIT RULES | Expenses decrease owners' equity and are recorded by debits; debit Advertising Expense $470.

Increases in liabilities are recorded by credits; credit Accounts Payable $470. |

| JOURNAL ENTRY | Feb. 2   Advertising Expense 470
              Accounts Payable .... 470 |

ENTRIES IN LEDGER ACCOUNTS

Advertising Expense			Accounts Payable	
2/1	360		1/31 Bal.	7,000
2/2	470		2/2	470

Feb. 4 Purchased various shop supplies (such as grease, solvents, nuts, and bolts) from
CAPA Auto Parts; the cost was $1,400, due in 30 days. These supplies are expected
to meet Overnight's needs for *three or four months.*

| ANALYSIS | As these supplies will last for several accounting periods, they are an asset, not an expense of February.[1]
A liability is incurred. |

When a purchase clearly benefits future accounting periods, it's an asset, not an expense

Assets	=	Liabilities	+	Owners' Equity
+$1,400		+$1,400		

| DEBIT–CREDIT RULES | Increases in assets are recorded by debits; debit Shop Supplies $1,400.

Increases in liabilities are recorded by credits; credit Accounts Payable $1,400. |

| JOURNAL ENTRY | Feb. 4   Shop Supplies 1,400
              Accounts Payable .... 1,400 |

ENTRIES IN LEDGER ACCOUNTS

Shop Supplies			Accounts Payable	
2/4	1,400		1/31 Bal.	7,000
			2/2	470
			2/4	1,400

---

[1] If the supplies are expected to be used within the *current* accounting period, their cost may be debited
directly to the Supplies Expense account, rather than to an asset account.

Feb. 15   Collected $4,980 cash for repairs made to vehicles of Airport Shuttle Service.

Feb. 28   Billed Harbor Cab Co. $5,400 for maintenance and repair services Overnight provided in February. The agreement with Harbor Cab calls for payment to be received by March 10.

Feb. 28   Paid employees' wages earned in February, $4,900.

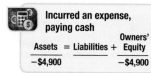

Incurred an expense, paying cash

Assets	= Liabilities +	Owners' Equity
−$4,900		−$4,900

ANALYSIS	Wages to employees are an expense. The asset Cash is decreased.
DEBIT–CREDIT RULES	Expenses decrease owners' equity and are recorded by debits; debit Wages Expense $4,900. Decreases in assets are recorded by credits; credit Cash $4,900.
JOURNAL ENTRY	Feb. 28 Wages Expense . . . . 4,900 Cash 4,900

ENTRIES IN LEDGER ACCOUNTS

Wages Expense

1/31	Bal. 1,200	
2/28	4,900	

Cash

1/31	Bal. 16,600	2/1	360
2/15	4,980	2/28	4,900

YOUR TURN — You as Overnight Auto Service's Accountant

Your good friend, Fred Jonas, is the manager of Harbor Cab Co. Your family and Fred's family meet frequently outside of your respective workplaces for fun. At a recent barbecue, Fred asked you about the amount of repair services rendered by Overnight Auto to Airport Shuttle Services in February. Airport Shuttle Services competes with Harbor Cab Co. for fares to and from the airport. What should you say to Fred?

(See our comments on the Online Learning Center website.)

Feb. 28   Recorded $1,600 utility bill for February. The entire amount is due March 15.

Feb. 28   Overnight Auto Services declares and pays a dividend of 40 cents per share to the owners of its 8,000 shares of capital stock—a total of $3,200.[2]

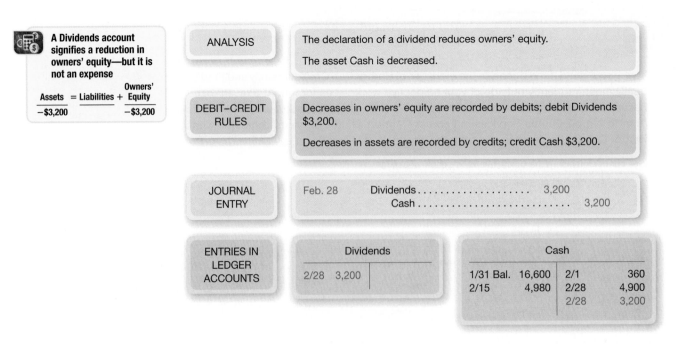

---

[2] As explained earlier, dividends are not an expense. In Chapter 5, we will show how the balance in the Dividends account eventually reduces the amount of Retained Earnings reported in the owners' equity section of the balance sheet.

THE JOURNAL

In our illustration, journal entries were shown in a very abbreviated form. The actual entries made in Overnight's journal appear in Exhibit 3–7. Notice that these formal journal entries include short *explanations* of the transactions, which include such details as the terms of credit transactions and the names of customers and creditors.

Date	Account Titles and Explanation	Debit	Credit
OVERNIGHT AUTO SERVICE GENERAL JOURNAL JANUARY 31–FEBRUARY 28, 2015			
2015			
Jan. 31	Cash...	2,200	
	Repair Service Revenue		2,200
	Repair services rendered to various customers.		
31	Wages Expense	1,200	
	Cash		1,200
	Paid all wages for January.		
31	Utilities Expense................................	200	
	Cash		200
	Paid all utilities for January.		
Feb. 1	Advertising Expense	360	
	Cash		360
	Purchased newspaper advertising from *Daily Tribune* to run in February.		
2	Advertising Expense	470	
	Accounts Payable		470
	Purchased radio advertising on account from KRAM; payment due in 30 days.		
4	Shop Supplies	1,400	
	Accounts Payable		1,400
	Purchased shop supplies on account from CAPA; payment due in 30 days.		
15	Cash...	4,980	
	Repair Service Revenue		4,980
	Repair services rendered to Airport Shuttle Service.		
28	Accounts Receivable	5,400	
	Repair Service Revenue		5,400
	Billed Harbor Cab for services rendered in February.		
28	Wages Expense	4,900	
	Cash		4,900
	Paid all wages for February.		
28	Utilities Expense	1,600	
	Accounts Payable		1,600
	Recorded utility bill for February.		
28	Dividends......................................	3,200	
	Cash		3,200
	Paid cash dividend of 40 cents per share on 8,000 shares of capital stock owned by the McBryan family.		

EXHIBIT 3–7

General Journal Entries: January 31 Through February 28

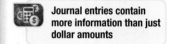 Journal entries contain more information than just dollar amounts

February's Ledger Balances

After posting all of the January and February transactions, Overnight's ledger accounts appear as shown in Exhibit 3–8. To conserve space, we have illustrated the ledger in T account form and have carried forward each account's summary balance from January 31. For convenience,

EXHIBIT 3–8 Overnight Auto Service's Ledger Accounts

OVERNIGHT AUTO SERVICE
THE LEDGER

Asset Accounts

Cash

	Debit		Credit
1/31 Bal.	16,600	2/1	360
2/15	4,980	2/28	4,900
		2/28	3,200
Bal. $13,120			

Accounts Receivable

	Debit
1/31 Bal.	1,200
2/28	5,400
Bal. $6,600	

Shop Supplies

	Debit
1/31 Bal.	0
2/4	1,400
Bal. $1,400	

Tools and Equipment

	Debit
1/31 Bal.	12,000
Bal. $12,000	

Building

	Debit
1/31 Bal.	36,000
Bal. $36,000	

Land

	Debit
1/31 Bal.	52,000
Bal. $52,000	

Liability and Owners' Equity Accounts

Notes Payable

	Credit
1/31 Bal.	30,000
Bal. $30,000	

Accounts Payable

	Credit
1/31 Bal.	7,000
2/2	470
2/4	1,400
2/28	1,600
Bal. $10,470	

Capital Stock

	Credit
1/31 Bal.	80,000
Bal. $80,000	

Dividends

	Debit
1/31 Bal.	0
2/28	3,200
Bal. $3,200	

Repair Service Revenue

	Credit
1/31 Bal.	2,200
2/15	4,980
2/28	5,400
Bal. $12,580	

Advertising Expense

	Debit
2/1	360
2/2	470
Bal. $830	

Wages Expense

	Debit
1/31 Bal.	1,200
2/28	4,900
Bal. $6,100	

Utilities Expense

	Debit
1/31 Bal.	200
2/28	1,600
Bal. $1,800	

we show in *red* the *February 28 balance* of each account (debit balances appear to the left of the account; credit balances appear to the right).

The accounts in this illustration appear in *financial statement order*—that is, balance sheet accounts first (assets, liabilities, and owners' equity), followed by the income statement accounts (revenue and expenses).

The Trial Balance

Since equal dollar amounts of debits and credits are entered in the accounts for every transaction recorded, the sum of all the debits in the ledger must be equal to the sum of all the credits. If the computation of account balances has been accurate, it follows that the total of the accounts with debit balances must be equal to the total of the accounts with credit balances.

Before using the account balances to prepare a balance sheet, it is desirable to *prove* that the total of accounts with debit balances is in fact equal to the total of accounts with credit balances. This proof of the equality of debit and credit balances is called a **trial balance.** A trial balance is a two-column schedule listing the names and balances of all the accounts *in the order in which they appear in the ledger;* the debit balances are listed in the left-hand column and the credit balances in the right-hand column. The totals of the two columns should agree. A trial balance taken from Overnight Auto's ledger accounts on page 110 is shown in Exhibit 3–9.

LO3-9

LEARNING OBJECTIVE
Prepare a trial balance and explain its uses and limitations.

OVERNIGHT AUTO SERVICE TRIAL BALANCE FEBRUARY 28, 2015		
Cash	$ 13,120	
Accounts receivable	6,600	
Shop supplies	1,400	
Tools and equipment	12,000	
Building	36,000	
Land	52,000	
Notes payable		$ 30,000
Accounts payable		10,470
Capital stock		80,000
Retained earnings		0
Dividends	3,200	
Repair service revenue		12,580
Advertising expense	830	
Wages expense	6,100	
Utilities expense	1,800	
	$133,050	$133,050

EXHIBIT 3–9
Overnight Auto Service's Trial Balance

 A trial balance proves the equality of debits and credits—but it also gives you a feel for how the business stands; but wait—there's more to consider

This trial balance proves the equality of the debit and credit entries in the company's accounting system. Notice that the trial balance contains both balance sheet and income statement accounts. Note also that the Retained Earnings balance is *zero*. It is zero because *no debit or credit entries were made to the Retained Earnings account in January or February.* Overnight, like most companies, updates its Retained Earnings balance only *once each year.* In Chapter 5, we will show how the Retained Earnings account is updated to its proper balance at year-end on December 31.[3]

---

[3] The balance of $0 in the Retained Earnings account is a highly unusual situation. Because the company is still in its first year of operations, no entries have ever been made to update the account's balance. In any trial balance prepared after the first year of business activity, the Retained Earnings account may be expected to have a balance other than $0.

USES AND LIMITATIONS OF THE TRIAL BALANCE

The trial balance provides proof that the ledger is in balance. The agreement of the debit and credit totals of the trial balance gives assurance that:

1. Equal debits and credits have been recorded for all transactions.
2. The addition of the account balances in the trial balance has been performed correctly.

Suppose that the debit and credit totals of the trial balance do not agree. This situation indicates that one or more errors have been made. Typical of such errors are (1) the posting of a debit as a credit, or vice versa; (2) arithmetic mistakes in determining account balances; (3) clerical errors in copying account balances into the trial balance; (4) listing a debit balance in the credit column of the trial balance, or vice versa; and (5) errors in addition of the trial balance.

The preparation of a trial balance does *not* prove that transactions have been correctly analyzed and recorded in the proper accounts. If, for example, a receipt of cash were erroneously recorded by debiting the Land account instead of the Cash account, the trial balance would still balance. Also, if a transaction were completely omitted from the ledger, the error would not be disclosed by the trial balance. In brief, *the trial balance proves only one aspect of the ledger, and that is the equality of debits and credits.*

Concluding Remarks

THE ACCOUNTING CYCLE IN PERSPECTIVE

LO3-10

LEARNING OBJECTIVE
Distinguish between accounting cycle procedures and the *knowledge* of accounting.

We view the accounting cycle as an efficient means of introducing basic accounting terms, concepts, processes, and reports. This is why we introduce it early in the course. As we conclude the accounting cycle in Chapters 4 and 5, please don't confuse your familiarity with this sequence of procedures with a knowledge of *accounting.* The accounting cycle is but one accounting process—and a relatively simple one at that.

Computers now free accountants to focus upon the more *analytical* aspects of their discipline. These include, for example:

- Determining the information needs of decision makers.
- Designing systems to provide the information quickly and efficiently.
- Evaluating the efficiency of operations throughout the organization.
- Assisting decision makers in interpreting accounting information.
- Auditing (confirming the reliability of accounting information).
- Forecasting the probable results of future operations.
- Tax planning.

We will emphasize such topics in later chapters of this text. But let us first repeat a very basic point from Chapter 1: The need for some familiarity with accounting concepts and processes is not limited to individuals planning careers in accounting. Today, an understanding of accounting information and of the business world go hand in hand. You cannot know much about one without understanding quite a bit about the other.

Ethics, Fraud, & Corporate Governance

As discussed in Chapter 2, the Sarbanes-Oxley Act (SOX) potentially increases the civil and criminal penalties associated with securities fraud, including fraudulent financial reporting. The increased Penalties—which can be substantial—are intended to reduce illegal behaviors. For example, in 2006, Jeffery Skilling, former Chief executive officer of **Enron**, was convicted of several fraud-related criminal charges for which he was sentenced to a prison term exceeding 24 years.

Businesspeople are sometimes told by their superiors to commit actions that are unethical and in some instances even illegal. The clear message of management is "participate in this behavior or find a job elsewhere." Management pressure and intimidation can make it difficult to resist demands to engage in unethical behavior. Employees sometimes believe that they are insulated from responsibility and liability because "they were just following orders."

As you encounter ethical dilemmas during your business career, remember that obeying orders from your superiors that are unethical, and certainly those that are illegal, may expose you to serious consequences, including criminal prosecution and incarceration.

© AP Photo/David J. Phillip

LO3-1 **Identify the steps in the accounting cycle and discuss the role of accounting records in an organization.** The accounting cycle generally consists of eight specific steps: (1) journalizing (recording) transactions, (2) posting each journal entry to the appropriate ledger accounts, (3) preparing a trial balance, (4) making end-of-period adjustments, (5) preparing an adjusted trial balance, (6) preparing financial statements, (7) journalizing and posting closing entries, and (8) preparing an after-closing trial balance.

Accounting records provide the information that is summarized in financial statements, income tax returns, and other accounting reports. In addition, these records are used by the company's management and employees for such purposes as:

- Establishing accountability for assets and transactions.
- Keeping track of routine business activities.
- Obtaining details about specific transactions.
- Evaluating the performance of units within the business.
- Maintaining a documentary record of the business's activities. (Such a record is required by tax laws and is useful for many purposes, including audits.)

LO3-2 **Describe a ledger account and a ledger.** A ledger account is a device for recording the increases or decreases in one financial statement item, such as a particular asset, a type of liability, or owners' equity. The general ledger is an accounting record that includes all the ledger accounts—that is, a separate account for each item included in the company's financial statements.

LO3-3 **Understand how balance sheet accounts are increased or decreased.** Increases in assets are recorded by debits and decreases are recorded by credits. Increases in liabilities and in owners' equity are recorded by credits and decreases are recorded by debits. Notice that the debit and credit rules are related to an account's *location in the balance sheet*. If the account appears on the *left side* of the balance sheet (asset accounts), increases in the account balance are recorded by *left-side entries* (debits). If the account appears on the *right side* of the balance sheet (liability and owners' equity accounts), increases are recorded by *right-side entries* (credits).

LO3-4 **Explain the double-entry system of accounting.** The double-entry system of accounting takes its name from the fact that every business transaction is recorded by *two types of entries:* (1) debit entries to one or more accounts and (2) credit entries to one or more accounts. In recording any transaction, the total dollar amount of the debit entries must equal the total dollar amount of the credit entries.

LO3-5 **Explain the purpose of a journal and its relationship to the ledger.** The journal is the accounting record in which business transactions are initially recorded. The entry in the journal shows which ledger accounts have increased as a result of the transaction and which have decreased. After the effects of the transaction have been recorded in the journal, the changes in the individual ledger accounts are then posted to the ledger.

LO3-6 **Explain the nature of *net income, revenue, and expenses.*** Net income is an increase in owners' equity that results from the profitable operation of a business during an accounting period. Net income also may be defined as revenue minus expenses. Revenue is the price of goods sold and services rendered to customers during the period, and expenses are the costs of the goods and services used up in the process of earning revenue.

LO3-7 **Apply the *realization* and *matching* principles in recording revenue and expenses.** The realization principle indicates that revenue should be recorded in the accounting records when it is *earned*—that is, when goods are sold or services are rendered to customers. The matching principle indicates that expenses should be offset against revenue on the basis of *cause and effect.* Thus, an expense should be recorded in the period in which the related good or service is consumed in the process of earning revenue.

LO3-8 **Understand how revenue and expense transactions are recorded in an accounting system.** The debit and credit rules for recording revenue and expenses are based on the rules for recording *changes in owners' equity.* Earning revenue *increases* owners' equity; therefore, revenue is recorded with a credit entry. Expenses *reduce* owners' equity and are recorded with debit entries.

LO3-9 **Prepare a trial balance and explain its uses and limitations.** In a trial balance, separate debit and credit columns are used to list the balances of the individual ledger accounts. The two columns are then totaled to prove the equality of the debit and credit balances. This process provides assurance that (1) the total of the debits posted to the ledger was equal to the total of the credits and (2) the balances of the individual ledger accounts were correctly computed. While a trial balance proves the equality of debit and credit entries in the ledger, it does *not* detect such errors as failure to record a business transaction, improper analysis of the accounts affected by the transaction, or the posting of debit or credit entries to the wrong accounts.

LO3-10 **Distinguish between accounting cycle procedures and the *knowledge* of accounting.** Accounting procedures involve the steps and processes necessary to *prepare* accounting information. A knowledge of the discipline enables one to *use* accounting information in evaluating performance, forecasting operations, and making complex business decisions.

Key Terms Introduced or Emphasized in Chapter 3

account (p. 88) A record used to summarize all increases and decreases in a particular asset, such as cash, or any other type of asset, liability, owners' equity, revenue, or expense.

accountability (p. 88) The condition of being held responsible for one's actions by the existence of an independent record of those actions. Establishing accountability is a major goal of accounting records and of internal control procedures.

accounting cycle (p. 88) The sequence of accounting procedures used to record, classify, and summarize accounting information. The cycle begins with the initial recording of business transactions and concludes with the preparation of formal financial statements.

accounting period (p. 99) The span of time covered by an income statement. One year is the accounting period for much financial reporting, but financial statements are also prepared by companies for each quarter of the year and for each month.

accrual basis of accounting (p. 102) Calls for recording revenue in the period in which it is earned and recording expenses in the period in which they are incurred. The effect of events on the business is recognized as services are rendered or consumed rather than when cash is received or paid.

conservatism (p. 101) The traditional accounting practice of resolving uncertainty by choosing the solution that leads to the lower (more conservative) amount of income being recognized in the current accounting period. This concept is designed to avoid overstatement of financial strength or earnings.

credit (p. 89) An amount entered on the right side of a ledger account. A credit is used to record a decrease in an asset or an increase in a liability or in owners' equity.

debit (p. 89) An amount entered on the left side of a ledger account. A debit is used to record an increase in an asset or a decrease in a liability or in owners' equity.

dividends (p. 98) A distribution of resources by a corporation to its stockholders. The resource most often distributed is cash.

double-entry accounting (p. 91) A system of recording every business transaction with equal dollar amounts of both debit and credit entries. As a result of this system, the accounting equation always remains in balance; in addition, the system makes possible the measurement of net income and also the use of error-detecting devices such as a trial balance.

expenses (p. 98) The costs of the goods and services used up in the process of obtaining revenue.

fiscal year (p. 100) Any 12-month accounting period adopted by a business.

general journal (p. 91) The simplest type of journal, it has only two money columns—one for credits and one for debits. This journal may be used for all types of transactions, which are later posted to the appropriate ledger accounts.

income statement (p. 98) A financial statement summarizing the results of operations of a business by matching its revenue and related expenses for a particular accounting period. Shows the net income or net loss.

journal (p. 91) A chronological record of transactions, showing for each transaction the debits and credits to be entered in specific ledger accounts. The simplest type of journal is called a general journal.

ledger (p. 88) An accounting system includes a separate record for each item that appears in the financial statements. Collectively, these records are referred to as a company's ledger. Individually, these records are often referred to as ledger accounts.

matching principle (p. 101) The generally accepted accounting principle that determines when expenses should be recorded in the accounting records. The revenue earned during an accounting period is matched (offset) with the expenses incurred in generating that revenue.

net income (p. 98) An increase in owners' equity resulting from profitable operations. Also, the excess of revenue earned over the related expenses for a given period.

net loss (p. 98) A decrease in owners' equity resulting from unprofitable operations.

objectivity (p. 101) Accountants' preference for using dollar amounts that are relatively factual—as opposed to merely matters of personal opinion. Objective measurements can be verified.

posting (p. 92) The process of transferring information from the journal to individual accounts in the ledger.

realization principle (p. 100) The generally accepted accounting principle that determines when revenue should be recorded in the accounting records. Revenue is realized when services are rendered to customers or when goods sold are delivered to customers.

retained earnings (p. 98) That portion of stockholders' (owners') equity resulting from profits earned and retained in the business.

revenue (p. 98) The price of goods and services charged to customers for goods and services rendered by a business.

time period principle (p. 99) To provide the users of financial statements with timely information, net income is measured for relatively short accounting periods of equal length. The period of time covered by an income statement is termed the company's accounting period.

trial balance (p. 111) A two-column schedule listing the names and the debit or credit balances of all accounts in the ledger.

Demonstration Problem

Epler Consulting Services, Inc., opened for business on January 25, 2015. The company maintains the following ledger accounts:

Cash	Capital Stock
Accounts Receivable	Retained Earnings
Office Supplies	Consulting Revenue
Office Equipment	Rent Expense
Accounts Payable	Utilities Expense

The company engaged in the following business activity in January:

Jan. 20   Issued 5,000 shares of capital stock for $50,000.

Jan. 20   Paid $400 office rent for the remainder of January.

Jan. 21   Purchased office supplies for $200. The supplies will last for several months, and payment is not due until February 15.

Jan. 22   Purchased office equipment for $15,000 cash.

Jan. 26   Performed consulting services and billed clients $2,000. The entire amount will not be collected until February.

Jan. 31   Recorded $100 utilities expense. Payment is not due until February 20.

Instructions

a. Record each of the above transactions in general journal form.

b. Post each entry to the appropriate ledger accounts.

c. Prepare a trial balance dated January 31, 2015.

d. Explain why the Retained Earnings account has a zero balance in the trial balance.

Solution to the Demonstration Problem

a.

	EPLER CONSULTING SERVICES, INC. GENERAL JOURNAL		
Date	**Account Titles and Explanation**	**Debit**	**Credit**
2015			
Jan. 20	Cash	50,000	
	Capital Stock		50,000
	To record the issue of 5,000 shares of capital stock at $10 per share.		
20	Rent Expense	400	
	Cash		400
	To record payment of January rent expense.		
21	Office Supplies	200	
	Accounts Payable		200
	To record purchase of office supplies on account.		
22	Office Equipment	15,000	
	Cash		15,000
	To record the purchase of office equipment.		
26	Accounts Receivable	2,000	
	Consulting Revenue		2,000
	Billed clients for consulting services rendered.		
31	Utilities Expense	100	
	Accounts Payable		100
	To record January utilities expense due in February.		

b.

EPLER CONSULTING SERVICES, INC.
THE LEDGER
JANUARY 20–31, 2015

Asset Accounts

Cash

1/20	50,000	1/20	400	
1/22	15,000			
				Bal. $34,600

Accounts Receivable

1/26	2,000		
			Bal. $2,000

Office Supplies

1/21	200		
			Bal. $200

Office Equipment

1/22	15,000		
			Bal. $15,000

Liability and Owners' Equity Accounts

Accounts Payable

	1/21	200	
	1/31	100	
			Bal. $300

Capital Stock

	1/20	50,000	
			Bal. $50,000

Retained Earnings

	Bal. $0

Consulting Revenue

	1/26	2,000	
			Bal. $2,000

Rent Expense

1/20	400		
			Bal. $400

Utilities Expense

1/31	100		
			Bal. $100

c.

EPLER CONSULTING SERVICES, INC. TRIAL BALANCE JANUARY 31, 2015		
Cash..	$34,600	
Accounts receivable	2,000	
Office supplies	200	
Office equipment	15,000	
Accounts payable		$ 300
Capital stock		50,000
Retained earnings		0
Consulting revenue		2,000
Rent expense...	400	
Utilities expense	100	
	$52,300	$52,300

d. Epler's Retained Earnings account balance is zero because the company has been in business for only one week and has not yet updated the Retained Earnings account for *any* revenue or expense activities. The periodic adjustment needed to update the Retained Earnings account is discussed in Chapter 5.

Self-Test Questions

The answers to these questions appear on page 139.

1. According to the rules of debit and credit for balance sheet accounts:

   a. Increases in asset, liability, and owners' equity accounts are recorded by debits.

   b. Decreases in asset and liability accounts are recorded by credits.

   c. Increases in asset and owners' equity accounts are recorded by debits.

   d. Decreases in liability and owners' equity accounts are recorded by debits.

2. Sunset Tours has a $3,500 account receivable from the Del Mar Rotary. On January 20, the Rotary makes a partial payment of $2,100 to Sunset Tours. The journal entry made on January 20 by Sunset Tours to record this transaction includes:

   a. A debit to the Cash Received account of $2,100.

   b. A credit to the Accounts Receivable account of $2,100.

   c. A debit to the Cash account of $1,400.

   d. A debit to the Accounts Receivable account of $1,400.

3. Indicate all of the following statements that correctly describe net income. Net income:

   a. Is equal to revenue minus expenses.

   b. Is equal to revenue minus the sum of expenses and dividends.

   c. Increases owners' equity.

   d. Is reported by a company for a specific period of time.

4. Which of the following is provided by a trial balance in which total debits equal total credits?

   a. Proof that no transaction was completely omitted from the ledger during the posting process.

   b. Proof that the correct debit or credit balance has been computed for each account.

   c. Proof that the ledger is in balance.

   d. Proof that transactions have been correctly analyzed and recorded in the proper accounts.

5. Which of the following explains the debit and credit rules relating to the recording of revenue and expenses?

   a. Expenses appear on the left side of the balance sheet and are recorded by debits; revenue appears on the right side of the balance sheet and is recorded by credits.

   b. Expenses appear on the left side of the income statement and are recorded by debits; revenue appears on the right side of the income statement and is recorded by credits.

   c. The effects of revenue and expenses on owners' equity.

   d. The realization principle and the matching principle.

6. Which of the following is *not* considered an analytical aspect of the accounting profession?

   a. Evaluating an organization's operational efficiency.

   b. Forecasting the probable results of future operations.

   c. Designing systems that provide information to decision makers.

   d. Journalizing and posting business transactions.

7. Indicate all correct answers. In the accounting cycle:

   a. Transactions are posted before they are journalized.

   b. A trial balance is prepared after journal entries have been posted.

   c. The Retained Earnings account is not shown as an up-to-date figure in the trial balance.

   d. Journal entries are posted to appropriate ledger accounts.

8. Indicate all correct answers. Dividends:

   a. Decrease owners' equity.

   b. Decrease net income.

   c. Are recorded by debiting the Dividend account.

   d. Are a business expense.

ASSIGNMENT MATERIAL   Discussion Questions

1. Baker Construction is a small corporation owned and managed by Tom Baker. The corporation has 21 employees, few creditors, and no investor other than Tom Baker. Thus, like many small businesses, it has no obligation to issue financial statements to creditors or investors. Under these circumstances, is there any reason for this corporation to maintain accounting records?

2. What relationship exists between the position of an account in the balance sheet equation and the rules for recording increases in that account?

3. State briefly the rules of debit and credit as applied to asset accounts and as applied to liability and owners' equity accounts.

4. Does the term *debit* mean increase and the term *credit* mean decrease? Explain.

5. What requirement is imposed by the double-entry system in the recording of any business transaction?

6. Explain the effect of operating profitably on the balance sheet of a business entity.

7. Does net income represent a supply of cash that could be distributed to stockholders in the form of dividends? Explain.

8. What is the meaning of the term *revenue?* Does the receipt of cash by a business indicate that revenue has been earned? Explain.

9. What is the meaning of the term *expenses?* Does the payment of cash by a business indicate that an expense has been incurred? Explain.

10. When do accountants consider revenue to be realized? What basic question about recording revenue in accounting records is answered by the *realization principle?*

11. In what accounting period does the *matching principle* indicate that an expense should be recognized?

12. Explain the rules of debit and credit with respect to transactions recorded in revenue and expense accounts.

13. What are some of the limitations of a trial balance?

14. How do dividends affect owners' equity? Are they treated as a business expense? Explain.

15. List some of the more *analytical* functions performed by professional accountants.

Brief Exercises

LO3-1, LO3-2, LO3-5,
LO3-9, LO3-10

BRIEF EXERCISE 3.1

The Accounting Cycle

Listed below in *random order* are the eight steps comprising a complete accounting cycle:

   Prepare a trial balance.

   Journalize and post the closing entries.

   Prepare financial statements.

   Post transaction data to the ledger.

   Prepare an adjusted trial balance.

   Make end-of-period adjustments.

   Journalize transactions.

   Prepare an after-closing trial balance.

   a. List these steps in the sequence in which they would normally be performed. (A detailed understanding of these eight steps is not required until Chapters 4 and 5.)

   b. Describe ways in which the information produced through the accounting cycle is used by a company's management and employees.

LO3-3 through LO3-5

BRIEF EXERCISE 3.2

Recording Transactions in a Journal

Record the following selected transactions in general journal form for Quantum Clinic, Inc. Include a brief explanation of the transaction as part of each journal entry.

Oct. 1 The clinic issued 5,000 additional shares of capital stock to Doctor Soges at $60 per share.

Oct. 4 The clinic purchased diagnostic equipment. The equipment cost $250,000, of which $100,000 was paid in cash; a note payable was issued for the balance.

Oct. 12   Issued a check for $6,000 in full payment of an account payable to Zeller Laboratories.

Oct. 19   Purchased surgical supplies for $4,000. Payment is not due until November 28.

Oct. 25   Collected a $80,000 account receivable from Health One Insurance Company.

Oct. 30   Declared and paid a $500,000 cash dividend to stockholders.

LO3-7, LO3-8

BRIEF EXERCISE 3.3

Recording Transactions

Wagner Excavating organized as a corporation on January 18 and engaged in the following transactions during its first two weeks of operation:

Jan. 18   Issued capital stock in exchange for $400,000 cash.

Jan. 22   Borrowed $100,000 from its bank by issuing a note payable.

Jan. 23   Paid $200 for a radio advertisement aired on January 24.

Jan. 25   Provided $5,000 of services to clients for cash.

Jan. 26   Provided $18,000 of services to clients on account.

Jan. 31   Collected $4,200 cash from clients for the services provided on January 26.

    a.   Record each of these transactions.

    b.   Determine the balance in the Cash account on January 31. Be certain to state whether the balance is debit or credit.

LO3-3, LO3-8

BRIEF EXERCISE 3.4

Debit and Credit Rules

Five account classifications are shown as column headings in the table below. For each account classification, indicate the manner in which increases and decreases are recorded (i.e., by debits or by credits).

	Revenue	Expenses	Assets	Liabilities	Owners' Equity
Increases recorded by:					
Decreases recorded by:					

LO3-3, LO3-6

BRIEF EXERCISE 3.5

Changes in Retained Earnings

Hewitt Corporation's Retained Earnings account balance was $90,000 on January 1. During January, the company recorded revenue of $500,000, expenses of $260,000, and dividends of $15,000. The company also paid a $35,000 account payable during the period.

Determine the company's Retained Earnings account balance on January 31.

LO3-6, LO3-7

BRIEF EXERCISE 3.6

Realization and Matching Principles

On May 26, Breeze Camp Ground paid KPRM Radio $500 cash for ten 30-second advertisements. Three of the ads were aired in May, five in June, and two in July.

    a.   Apply the realization principle to determine how much advertising revenue KPRM Radio earned from Breeze Camp Ground in May, June, and July.

    b.   Apply the matching principle to determine how much advertising expense Breeze Camp Ground incurred in May, June, and July.

LO3-6, LO3-7

BRIEF EXERCISE 3.7

When Is Revenue Realized?

The following transactions were carried out during the month of May by Hagen and Associates, a firm of design architects. For each of the five transactions, you are to state whether the transaction represented revenue to the firm during the month of May. Give reasons for your decision in each case.

    a.   The firm received $300,000 cash by issuing additional shares of capital stock.

    b.   Collected cash of $25,000 from an account receivable. The receivable originated in April from services rendered to a client.

    c.   Borrowed $60,000 from Century Bank to be repaid in three months.

    d.   Earned $250 interest on a company savings account during the month of May. No withdrawals were made from this account in May.

    e.   Completed plans for guesthouse, pool, and spa for a client. The $7,000 fee for this project was billed to the client in May, but will not be collected until June 25.

LO3-6, LO3-7
BRIEF EXERCISE 3.8
When Are Expenses
Incurred?

During March, the activities of Evergreen Landscaping included the following transactions and events, among others. Which of these items represented expenses in March? Explain.

a.   Purchased a copying machine for $2,750 cash.

b.   Paid $192 for gasoline purchases for a delivery truck during March.

c.   Paid $2,280 salary to an employee for time worked during March.

d.   Paid an attorney $560 for legal services rendered in January.

e.   Declared and paid an $1,800 dividend to shareholders.

LO3-6, LO3-7
BRIEF EXERCISE 3.9
Realization Principle

Sky Bound Airlines has provided the following information regarding cash received for ticket sales in September and October:

Cash received in September for October flights	$1,700,000
Cash received in October for October flights	1,300,000
Cash received in October for November flights	1,800,000

Apply the realization principle to determine how much revenue Sky Bound Airlines should report in its October income statement.

LO3-6, LO3-7
BRIEF EXERCISE 3.10
Matching Principle

Harley Consulting has provided the following information regarding cash payments to its employees in May and June:

Salary payments in May for work performed by employees in April	$25,000
Salary payments in May for work performed by employees in May	30,000
Salary payments in June for work performed by employees in May	10,000

Apply the matching principle to determine how much salary expense Harley Consulting should report in its May income statement.

Exercises

LO3-1 through LO3-10
EXERCISE 3.1
Accounting Terminology

Listed below are eight technical accounting terms introduced in this chapter:

Realization principle	Credit
Time period principle	Accounting period
Matching principle	Expenses
Net income	Accounting cycle

Each of the following statements may (or may not) describe one of these technical terms. For each statement, indicate the term described, or answer "None" if the statement does not correctly describe any of the terms.

a.   The span of time covered by an income statement.

b.   The sequence of accounting procedures used to record, classify, and summarize accounting information.

c.   The traditional accounting practice of resolving uncertainty by choosing the solution that leads to the lowest amount of income being recognized.

d.   An increase in owners' equity resulting from profitable operations.

e.   The underlying accounting principle that determines when revenue should be recorded in the accounting records.

f.   The type of entry used to decrease an asset or increase a liability or owners' equity account.

g.   The underlying accounting principle of offsetting revenue earned during an accounting period with the expenses incurred in generating that revenue.

h.   The costs of the goods and services used up in the process of generating revenue.

LO3-6, LO3-7
EXERCISE 3.2
The Matching Principle:
You as a Driver

The purpose of this exercise is to demonstrate the *matching principle* in a familiar setting. Assume that you own a car that you drive about 15,000 miles each year.

a.   List the various costs to you associated with owning and operating this car. Make an estimate of the total annual cost of owning and operating the car, as well as the average cost-per-mile that you drive.

b. Assume also that you have a part-time job. You usually do not use your car in this job, but today your employer asks you to drive 100 miles (round-trip) to deliver some important documents. Your employer offers to "reimburse you for your driving expenses."

You already have a full tank of gas, so you are able to drive the whole 100 miles without stopping and you don't actually spend any money during the trip. Does this mean that you have incurred no "expenses" for which you should be reimbursed? Explain.

LO3-2 through LO3-5

EXERCISE 3.3

Relationship between Journal and Ledger Accounts

Transactions are *first* journalized and *then* posted to ledger accounts. In this exercise, however, your understanding of the relationship between the journal and the ledger is tested by asking you to study some ledger accounts and determine the journal entries that probably were made to produce these ledger entries. The following accounts show the first six transactions of Avenson Insurance Company. Prepare a journal entry (including a written explanation) for each transaction.

Cash				Vehicles			
Nov. 1	120,000	Nov. 8	33,600	Nov. 30	9,400		
		Nov. 25	12,000				
		Nov. 30	1,400				

Land				Notes Payable			
Nov. 8	70,000			Nov. 25	12,000	Nov. 8	95,000
						Nov. 30	8,000

Building				Accounts Payable			
Nov. 8	58,600			Nov. 21	480	Nov. 15	3,200

Office Equipment				Capital Stock			
Nov. 15	3,200	Nov. 21	480			Nov. 1	120,000

LO3-9

EXERCISE 3.4

Preparing a Trial Balance

Using the information in the ledger accounts presented in Exercise 3.3, prepare a trial balance for Avenson Insurance Company dated November 30.

LO3-6, LO3-8

EXERCISE 3.5

Relationship between Net Income and Equity

The following information came from a recent balance sheet of **Apple Computer, Inc.:**

	End of Year	Beginning of Year
Assets.	$176.0 billion	$116.4 billion
Liabilities.	$ 57.9 billion	?
Owners' Equity	?	$ 76.6 billion

a. Determine the amount of total liabilities reported in **Apple Computer**'s balance sheet at the beginning of the year.

b. Determine the amount of total owners' equity reported in **Apple Computer**'s balance sheet at the end of the year.

c. Retained earnings was reported in **Apple Computer**'s year-end balance sheet at $101.3 billion. If retained earnings was $62.8 billion at the beginning of the year, determine net income for the year if a $2.5 billion dividend was declared during the year.

LO3-2 through LO3-6

EXERCISE 3.6

Effects of Transactions on the Accounting Equation

Satka Fishing Expeditions, Inc., recorded the following transactions in July:

1. Provided an ocean fishing expedition for a credit customer; payment is due August 10.

2. Paid Marine Service Center for repairs to boats performed in June. (In June, Satka Fishing Expeditions, Inc., had received and properly recorded the invoice for these repairs.)

3. Collected the full amount due from a credit customer for a fishing expedition provided in June.

4. Received a bill from Baldy's Bait Shop for bait purchased and used in July. Payment is due August 3.

5. Purchased a new fishing boat on July 28, paying part cash and issuing a note payable for the balance. The new boat is first scheduled for use on August 5.

6. Declared and paid a cash dividend on July 31.

Indicate the effects that each of these transactions will have upon the following six *total amounts* in the company's financial statements for the month of July. Organize your answer in tabular form, using the column headings shown, and use the code letters **I** for increase, **D** for decrease, and **NE** for no effect. The answer to transaction **1** is provided as an example.

	Income Statement			Balance Sheet		
Transaction	Revenue −	Expenses =	Net Income	Assets =	Liabilities +	Owners' Equity
1	I	NE	I	I	NE	I

LO3-2 through LO3-6

EXERCISE 3.7

Effect of Transactions on the Accounting Equation

A number of transactions of Claypool Construction are described below in terms of accounts debited and credited:

1. Debit Wages Expense; credit Wages Payable.

2. Debit Accounts Receivable; credit Construction Revenue.

3. Debit Dividends; credit Cash.

4. Debit Office Supplies; credit Accounts Payable.

5. Debit Repairs Expense; credit Cash.

6. Debit Cash; credit Accounts Receivable.

7. Debit Tools and Equipment; credit Cash and Notes Payable.

8. Debit Accounts Payable; credit Cash.

a. Indicate the effects of each transaction upon the elements of the income statement and the balance sheet. Use the code letters **I** for increase, **D** for decrease, and **NE** for no effect. Organize your answer in tabular form using the column headings shown below. The answer for transaction **1** is provided as an example.

	Income Statement			Balance Sheet		
Transaction	Revenue −	Expenses =	Net Income	Assets =	Liabilities +	Owners' Equity
1	NE	I	D	NE	I	D

b. Write a one-sentence description of each transaction.

LO3-4, LO3-6 through LO3-8

EXERCISE 3.8

Preparing Journal Entries for Revenue, Expenses, and Dividends

Shown below are selected transactions of the architectural firm of Baxter, Claxter, and Stone, Inc.

April 5   Prepared building plans for Spangler Construction Company. Sent Spangler an invoice for $11,000 requesting payment within 30 days. (The appropriate revenue account is entitled Drafting Fees Earned.)

May 17   Declared a cash dividend of $2,000. The dividend will not be paid until June 25.

May 29   Received a $4,500 bill from Bob Needham, CPA, for accounting services performed during May. Payment is due by June 10. (The appropriate expense account is entitled Professional Expenses.)

June 4   Received full payment from Spangler Construction Company for the invoice sent on April 5.

June 10   Paid Bob Needham, CPA, for the bill received on May 29.

June 25   Paid the cash dividend declared on May 17.

a. Prepare journal entries to record the transactions in the firm's accounting records.

b. Identify any of the above transactions that *will not* result in a change in the company's net income.

LO3-3, LO3-6, LO3-7

EXERCISE 3.9

Effects of Transactions on the Financial Statements

Listed below are eight transactions the Foster Corporation made during November:

a. Issued stock in exchange for cash.

b. Purchased land. Made partial payment with cash and issued a note payable for the remaining balance.

c. Recorded utilities expense for November. Payment is due in mid-December.

d. Purchased office supplies with cash.

e. Paid outstanding salaries payable owed to employees for wages earned in October.

f. Declared a cash dividend that will not be paid until late December.

g. Sold land for cash at an amount equal to the land's historical cost.

h. Collected cash on account from customers for services provided in September and October.

Indicate the *effects of the above transactions* on each of the financial statement elements shown in the column headings below. Use the following symbols: **I** = Increase, **D** = Decrease, and **NE** = no effect.

Transaction	Net Income	Assets	Liabilities	Equity
a.				
b.				
c.				
d.				
e.				
f.				
g.				
h.				

LO3-3, LO3-5, LO3-8, LO3-9

EXERCISE 3.10

Journalizing, Posting, and Preparing a Trial Balance

Janet Enterprises incorporated on May 3, 2015. The company engaged in the following transactions during its first month of operations:

May 3	Issued capital stock in exchange for $950,000 cash.
May 4	Paid May office rent expense of $1,800.
May 5	Purchased office supplies for $600 cash. The supplies will last for several months.
May 15	Purchased office equipment for $12,400 on account. The entire amount is due June 15.
May 18	Purchased a company car for $45,000. Paid $15,000 cash and issued a note payable for the remaining amount owed.
May 20	Billed clients $120,000 on account.
May 26	Declared a $8,000 dividend. The entire amount will be distributed to shareholders on June 26.
May 29	Paid May utilities of $500.
May 30	Received $90,000 from clients billed on May 20.
May 31	Recorded and paid salary expense of $32,000.

A partial list of the account titles used by the company includes:

Cash	Dividends Payable
Accounts Receivable	Dividends
Office Supplies	Capital Stock
Office Equipment	Client Revenue
Vehicles	Office Rent Expense
Notes Payable	Salary Expense
Accounts Payable	Utilities Expense

a. Prepare journal entries, including explanations, for the above transactions.

b. Post each entry to the appropriate ledger accounts (use the T account format illustrated in Exhibit 3–8 on page 110).

c. Prepare a trial balance dated May 31, 2015. Assume accounts with zero balances are not included in the trial balance.

LO3-3, LO3-5, LO3-8, LO3-9

EXERCISE 3.11

Journalizing, Posting, and Preparing a Trial Balance

Georgia Corporation incorporated on September 2, 2015. The company engaged in the following transactions during its first month of operations:

Sept. 2	Issued capital stock in exchange for $975,000 cash.
Sept. 4	Purchased land and a building for $900,000. The value of the land was $200,000, and the value of the building was $700,000. The company paid $100,000 cash and issued a note payable for the balance.
Sept. 12	Purchased office supplies for $500 on account. The supplies will last for several months.
Sept. 19	Billed clients $180,000 on account.
Sept. 29	Recorded and paid salary expense of $60,000.
Sept. 30	Received $110,000 from clients billed on September 19.

A partial list of the account titles used by the company includes:

Cash	Notes Payable
Accounts Receivable	Accounts Payable
Office Supplies	Capital Stock
Land	Client Revenue
Building	Salary Expense

a. Prepare journal entries, including explanations, for the above transactions.

b. Post each entry to the appropriate ledger accounts (use the T account format illustrated in Exhibit 3–8 on page 110).

c. Prepare a trial balance dated September 30, 2015. Assume accounts with zero balances are not included in the trial balance.

LO3-3, LO3-5, LO3-8, LO3-9

EXERCISE 3.12

Journalizing, Posting, and Preparing a Trial Balance

Elaine Consulting incorporated on February 1, 2015. The company engaged in the following transactions during its first month of operations:

Feb. 1	Issued capital stock in exchange for $800,000 cash.
Feb. 5	Borrowed $100,000 from the bank by issuing a note payable.
Feb. 8	Purchased land, building, and office equipment for $750,000. The value of the land was $150,000, the value of the building was $540,000, and the value of the office equipment was $60,000. The company paid $200,000 cash and issued a note payable for the balance.
Feb. 11	Purchased office supplies for $800 on account. The supplies will last for several months.
Feb. 14	Paid the local newspaper $500 for a full-page advertisement. The ad will appear in print on February 18.
Feb. 20	Several of the inkjet printer cartridges that Herrold purchased on February 11 were defective. The cartridges were returned and the office supply store reduced Herrold's outstanding balance by $200.
Feb. 22	Performed consulting services for $14,000 cash.
Feb. 24	Billed clients $16,000.
Feb. 25	Paid salaries of $12,000.
Feb. 28	Paid the entire outstanding balance owed for office supplies purchased on February 11.

A partial list of the account titles used by the company includes:

Cash	Notes Payable
Accounts Receivable	Accounts Payable
Office Supplies	Capital Stock
Land	Client Service Revenue
Building	Advertising Expense
Office Equipment	Salaries Expense

a. Prepare journal entries, including explanations, for the above transactions.

b. Post each entry to the appropriate ledger accounts (use the T account format as illustrated in Exhibit 3–8 on page 110).

c. Prepare a trial balance dated February 28, 2015. Assume accounts with zero balances are not included in the trial balance.

LO3-3, LO3-6, LO3-8

EXERCISE 3.13

Analyzing Transactions

Listed below are descriptions of six transactions, followed by a table listing six unique combinations of financial statement effects (**I** is for increase, **D** is for decrease, and **NE** is for no effect). In the blank space to the left of each transaction description, place the appropriate letter from the table that indicates the effects of that transaction on the various elements of the financial statements.

1. _____ Purchased machinery for $5,000, paying $1,000 cash and issuing a $4,000 note payable for the balance.

2. _____ Billed clients $16,000 on account.

3. _____ Recorded a $500 maintenance expense of which $100 was paid in cash and the remaining amount was due in 30 days.

4. _____ Paid an outstanding account payable of $400.

5. _____ Recorded monthly utilities costs of $300. The entire amount is due in 20 days.

6. _____ Declared a $40,000 dividend to be distributed in 60 days.

Transaction	Revenue	Expenses	Assets	Liabilities	Owners' Equity
a.	NE	NE	D	D	NE
b.	NE	I	D	I	D
c.	NE	NE	NE	I	D
d.	NE	I	NE	I	D
e.	NE	NE	I	I	N
f.	I	NE	I	NE	I

LO3-3, LO3-6, LO3-8

EXERCISE 3.14

Analyzing Transactions

Listed below are descriptions of six transactions, followed by a table listing six unique combinations of financial statement effects (**I** is for increase, **D** is for decrease, and **NE** is for no effect). In the blank space to the left of each transaction description, place the appropriate letter from the table that indicates the effects of that transaction on the various elements of the financial statements.

1. _____ Issued capital stock in exchange for $50,000 cash.

2. _____ Billed clients $20,000 on account.

3. _____ Placed a $300 advertisement in the local newspaper. The entire amount is due in 30 days.

4. _____ Collected $100 on account from clients.

5. _____ Recorded and paid a $12,000 dividend.

6. _____ Recorded and paid salaries of $15,000.

Transaction	Revenue	Expenses	Assets	Liabilities	Owners' Equity
a.	NE	I	NE	I	D
b.	NE	I	D	NE	D
c.	NE	NE	D	NE	D
d.	NE	NE	I	NE	I
e.	I	NE	I	NE	I
f.	NE	NE	NE	NE	NE

LO3-1 through LO3-3, LO3-7, LO3-10

EXERCISE 3.15

Using the Financial Statements of Home Depot, Inc.

Throughout this text, we have many assignments based on the financial statements of **Home Depot, Inc.**, in Appendix A. Refer to the financial statements to respond to the following items:

a. Does the company's fiscal year end on December 31? How can you tell?

b. State the company's most recent balance sheet in terms of A = L + E.

c. Did the company post more debits to the Cash account during the year than credits? How can you tell?

Problem Set A

LO3-3 through LO3-5

PROBLEM 3.1A

Journalizing Transactions

Glenn Grimes is the founder and president of Heartland Construction, a real estate development venture. The business transactions during February while the company was being organized are listed below.

Feb. 1   Grimes and several others invested $500,000 cash in the business in exchange for 25,000 shares of capital stock.

Feb. 10   The company purchased office facilities for $300,000, of which $100,000 was applicable to the land and $200,000 to the building. A cash payment of $60,000 was made and a note payable was issued for the balance of the purchase price.

Feb. 16   Computer equipment was purchased from PCWorld for $12,000 cash.

Feb. 18   Office furnishings were purchased from Hi-Way Furnishings at a cost of $9,000. A $1,000 cash payment was made at the time of purchase, and an agreement was made to pay the remaining balance in two equal installments due March 1 and April 1. Hi-Way Furnishings did not require that Heartland sign a promissory note.

Feb. 22   Office supplies were purchased from Office World for $300 cash.

Feb. 23   Heartland discovered that it paid too much for a computer printer purchased on February 16. The unit should have cost only $359, but Heartland was charged $395. PCWorld promised to refund the difference within seven days.

Feb. 27   Mailed Hi-Way Furnishings the first installment due on the account payable for office furnishings purchased on February 18.

Feb. 28   Received $36 from PCWorld in full settlement of the account receivable created on February 23.

Instructions

a. Prepare journal entries to record the above transactions. Select the appropriate account titles from the following chart of accounts:

Cash	Land
Accounts Receivable	Office Building
Office Supplies	Notes Payable
Office Furnishings	Accounts Payable
Computer Systems	Capital Stock

b. Indicate the effects of each transaction on the company's assets, liabilities, and owners' equity for the month of February. Organize your analysis in tabular form as shown for the February 1

Transaction	Assets	=	Liabilities	+	Owners' Equity
Feb. 1	+$500,000 (Cash)		$0		+$500,000 (Capital Stock)

LO3-3 through LO3-8

PROBLEM 3.2A

Analyzing and Journalizing Transactions

Environmental Services, Inc., performs various tests on wells and septic systems. A few of the company's business transactions occurring during August are described below:

1. On August 1, the company billed customers $2,500 on account for services rendered. Customers are required to make full payment within 30 days. (Environmental Services uses an account entitled Testing Service Revenue when billing customers.)

2. On August 3, the company purchased testing supplies costing $3,800, paying $800 cash and charging the remainder on the company's 30-day account at Penn Chemicals. The testing supplies are expected to last several months.

3. On August 5, the company returned to Penn Chemicals $100 of testing supplies that were not needed. The return of these supplies reduced by $100 the amount owed to Penn Chemicals.

4. On August 17, the company issued an additional 2,500 shares of capital stock at $8 per share. The cash raised will be used to purchase new testing equipment in September.

5. On August 22, the company received $600 cash from customers it had billed on August 1.

6. On August 29, the company paid its outstanding account payable to Penn Chemicals.

7. On August 30, a cash dividend totaling $6,800 was declared and paid to the company's stockholders.

Instructions

a. Prepare an analysis of each of the above transactions. Transaction 1 serves as an example of the form of analysis to be used.

1. **(a)** The asset Accounts Receivable was increased. Increases in assets are recorded by debits. Debit Accounts Receivable $2,500.

   (b) Revenue has been earned. Revenue increases owners' equity. Increases in owners' equity are recorded by credits. Credit Testing Service Revenue $2,500.

b. Prepare journal entries, including explanations, for the above transactions.

c. How does the *realization principle* influence the manner in which the August 1 billing to customers is recorded in the accounting records?

d. How does the *matching principle* influence the manner in which the August 3 purchase of testing supplies is recorded in the accounting records?

LO3-3 through LO3-8

PROBLEM 3.3A

Analyzing and Journalizing Transactions

Weida Surveying, Inc., provides land surveying services. During September, its transactions included the following:

Sept. 1	Paid rent for the month of September, $4,400.
Sept. 3	Billed Fine Line Homes $5,620 for surveying services. The entire amount is due on or before September 28. (Weida uses an account entitled Surveying Revenue when billing clients.)
Sept. 9	Provided surveying services to Sunset Ridge Developments for $2,830. The entire amount was collected on this date.
Sept. 14	Placed a newspaper advertisement in the *Daily Item* to be published in the September 20 issue. The cost of the advertisement was $165. Payment is due in 30 days.
Sept. 25	Received a check for $5,620 from Fine Line Homes for the amount billed on September 3.
Sept. 26	Provided surveying services to Thompson Excavating Company for $1,890. Weida collected $400 cash, with the balance due in 30 days.
Sept. 29	Sent a check to the *Daily Item* in full payment of the liability incurred on September 14.
Sept. 30	Declared and paid a $7,600 cash dividend to the company's stockholders.

Instructions

a. Analyze the effects that each of these transactions will have on the following six components of the company's financial statements for the month of September. Organize your answer in tabular form, using the column headings shown. Use **I** for increase, **D** for decrease, and **NE** for no effect. The September 1 transaction is provided for you:

	Income Statement			Balance Sheet		
Transaction	Revenue	− Expenses	= Net Income	Assets	= Liabilities	+ Owners' Equity
Sept. 1	NE	I	D	D	NE	D

b. Prepare a journal entry (including explanation) for each of the above transactions.

c. Three of September's transactions involve cash payments, yet only one of these transactions is recorded as an expense. Describe three situations in which a cash payment would *not* involve recognition of an expense.

In June 2015, Wendy Winger organized a corporation to provide aerial photography services. The company, called Aerial Views, began operations immediately. Transactions during the month of June were as follows:

LO3-1 through LO3-10
PROBLEM 3.4A
The Accounting Cycle: Journalizing, Posting, and Preparing a Trial Balance

June 1	The corporation issued 60,000 shares of capital stock to Wendy Winger in exchange for $60,000 cash.
June 2	Purchased a plane from Utility Aircraft for $220,000. Made a $40,000 cash down payment and issued a note payable for the remaining balance.
June 4	Paid Woodrow Airport $2,500 to rent office and hangar space for the month.
June 15	Billed customers $8,320 for aerial photographs taken during the first half of June.
June 15	Paid $5,880 in salaries earned by employees during the first half of June.
June 18	Paid Hannigan's Hangar $1,890 for maintenance and repair services on the company plane.
June 25	Collected $4,910 of the amounts billed to customers on June 15.
June 30	Billed customers $16,450 for aerial photographs taken during the second half of the month.
June 30	Paid $6,000 in salaries earned by employees during the second half of the month.
June 30	Received a $2,510 bill from Peatree Petroleum for aircraft fuel purchased in June. The entire amount is due July 10.
June 30	Declared a $2,000 dividend payable on July 15.

The account titles used by Aerial Views are:

Cash	Retained Earnings
Accounts Receivable	Dividends
Aircraft	Aerial Photography Revenue
Notes Payable	Maintenance Expense
Accounts Payable	Fuel Expense
Dividends Payable	Salaries Expense
Capital Stock	Rent Expense

Instructions

a. Analyze the effects that each of these transactions will have on the following six components of the company's financial statements for the month of June. Organize your answer in tabular form, using the column headings shown. Use **I** for increase, **D** for decrease, and **NE** for no effect. The June 1 transaction is provided for you:

	Income Statement			Balance Sheet		
Transaction	Revenue	− Expenses	= Net Income	Assets	= Liabilities	+ Owners' Equity
June 1	NE	NE	NE	I	NE	I

b. Prepare journal entries (including explanations) for each transaction.

c. Post each transaction to the appropriate ledger accounts (use a running balance format as illustrated in Exhibit 3–4 on page 97).

d. Prepare a trial balance dated June 30, 2015.

e. Using figures from the trial balance prepared in part **d**, compute total assets, total liabilities, and owners' equity. Are these the figures that the company will report in its June 30 balance sheet? Explain your answer briefly.

LO3-1 through LO3-10

PROBLEM 3.5A

The Accounting Cycle: Journalizing, Posting, and Preparing a Trial Balance

Dr. Schekter, DVM, opened a veterinary clinic on May 1, 2015. The business transactions for May are shown below:

May 1   Dr. Schekter invested $400,000 cash in the business in exchange for 5,000 shares of capital stock.

May 4   Land and a building were purchased for $250,000. Of this amount, $70,000 applied to the land, and $180,000 to the building. A cash payment of $100,000 was made at the time of the purchase, and a note payable was issued for the remaining balance.

May 9   Medical instruments were purchased for $130,000 cash.

May 16   Office fixtures and equipment were purchased for $50,000. Dr. Schekter paid $20,000 at the time of purchase and agreed to pay the entire remaining balance in 15 days.

May 21   Office supplies expected to last several months were purchased for $5,000 cash.

May 24   Dr. Schekter billed clients $2,200 for services rendered. Of this amount, $1,900 was received in cash, and $300 was billed on account (due in 30 days).

May 27   A $400 invoice was received for several radio advertisements aired in May. The entire amount is due on June 5.

May 28   Received a $100 payment on the $300 account receivable recorded May 24.

May 31   Paid employees $2,800 for salaries earned in May.

A partial list of account titles used by Dr. Schekter includes:

Cash	Notes Payable
Accounts Receivable	Accounts Payable
Office Supplies	Capital Stock
Medical Instruments	Veterinary Service Revenue
Office Fixtures and Equipment	Advertising Expense
Land	Salary Expense
Building	

Instructions

a. Analyze the effects that each of these transactions will have on the following six components of the company's financial statements for the month of May. Organize your answer in tabular form, using the column headings shown below. Use **I** for increase, **D** for decrease, and **NE** for no effect. The May 1 transaction is provided for you:

	Income Statement			Balance Sheet		
Transaction	Revenue	− Expenses	= Net Income	Assets	= Liabilities	+ Owners' Equity
May 1	NE	NE	NE	I	NE	I

b. Prepare journal entries (including explanations) for each transaction.

c. Post each transaction to the appropriate ledger accounts (use the T account format illustrated in Exhibit 3–8 on page 110).

d. Prepare a trial balance dated May 31, 2015.

e. Using figures from the trial balance prepared in part **d**, compute total assets, total liabilities, and owners' equity. Did May appear to be a profitable month?

LO3-7 through LO3-9

PROBLEM 3.6A

Short Comprehensive
Problem

Donegan's Lawn Care Service began operations in July 2015. The company uses the following general ledger accounts:

Cash	Capital Stock
Accounts Receivable	Retained Earnings
Office Supplies	Mowing Revenue
Mowing Equipment	Salaries Expense
Accounts Payable	Fuel Expense
Notes Payable	

The company engaged in the following transactions during its first month of operations:

July 18 Issued 500 shares of capital stock to Patrick Donegan for $1,500.

July 22 Purchased office supplies on account for $100.

July 23 Purchased mowing equipment for $2,000, paying $400 cash and issuing a 60-day note payable for the remaining balance.

July 24 Paid $25 cash for gasoline. All of this fuel will be used in July.

July 25 Billed Lost Creek Cemetery $150 for mowing services. The entire amount is due July 30.

July 26 Billed Golf View Condominiums $200 for mowing services. The entire amount is due August 1.

July 30 Collected $150 from Lost Creek Cemetery for mowing services provided on July 25.

July 31 Paid $80 salary to employee Teddy Grimm for work performed in July.

a. Record each of the above transactions in general journal form. Include a brief explanation of the transaction as part of each journal entry.

b. Post each entry to the appropriate ledger accounts (use the T account format illustrated in Exhibit 3–8 on page 110).

c. Prepare a trial balance dated July 31, 2015.

d. Explain why the Retained Earnings account has a zero balance in the trial balance.

LO3-3 through LO3-9

PROBLEM 3.7A

Short Comprehensive
Problem

Sanlucas, Inc., provides home inspection services to its clients. The company's trial balance dated *June 1, 2015,* is shown below:

SANLUCAS, INC.
TRIAL BALANCE
JUNE 1, 2015

Cash	$ 5,100	
Accounts receivable	2,600	
Inspection supplies	800	
Accounts payable		$ 850
Notes payable		2,000
Dividends	600	
Capital stock		3,000
Retained earnings		1,800
Inspection revenue		8,350
Salaries expense	4,900	
Advertising expense	300	
Testing expense	1,700	
	$16,000	$16,000

Sanlucas engaged in the following transactions in June:

June 4 Borrowed cash from Community Bank by issuing a $1,500 note payable.

June 9 Collected a $1,600 account receivable from Nina Lesher.

June 10	Purchased $150 of inspection supplies on account.
June 17	Billed home owners $1,650 for inspection services. The entire amount is due on July 17.
June 25	Paid WLIR Radio $200 for ads to be aired on June 27.
June 28	Recorded and paid $1,300 for testing expenses incurred in June.
June 30	Recorded and paid June salaries of $1,100.

Instructions

a. Record the company's June transactions in general journal form. Include a brief explanation of the transaction as part of each journal entry.

b. Post each entry to the appropriate ledger accounts (use the T account format illustrated in Exhibit 3–8 on page 110).

c. Prepare a trial balance dated June 30, 2015. (Hint: Retained Earnings will be reported at the same amount as on June 1. Accounting for changes in the Retained Earnings account resulting from revenue, expense, and dividend activities is discussed in Chapter 5.)

d. Has the company paid all of the dividends that it has declared? Explain.

LO3-3, LO3-8
PROBLEM 3.8A
Analyzing the Effects of Accounting Errors

Home Team Corporation recently hired Steve Willits as its bookkeeper. Mr. Willits is somewhat inexperienced and has made numerous errors recording daily business transactions.

   Indicate the *effects of the errors* described below on each of the financial statement elements shown in the column headings. Use the following symbols: **O** for overstated; **U** for understated, and **NE** for no effect.

Error	Net Income	Total Assets	Total Liabilities	Owners' Equity
Recorded the issuance of capital stock by debiting Capital Stock and crediting Cash.				
Recorded the declaration and payment of a dividend by debiting Interest Expense and crediting Cash.				
Recorded the payment of an account payable by debiting Cash and crediting Service Revenue.				
Recorded the collection of an outstanding account receivable by debiting Cash and crediting Accounts Payable.				
Recorded client billings on account by debiting Service Revenue and crediting Cash.				
Recorded the cash purchase of land by debiting Cash and crediting Land.				
Recorded the purchase of a building on account by debiting Rent Expense and crediting Capital Stock.				

Problem Set B

LO3-3 through LO3-5
PROBLEM 3.1B
Journalizing Transactions

Chris North is the founder and president of North Enterprises, a real estate development venture. The business transactions during April while the company was being organized are listed below.

Apr. 1	North and several others invested $650,000 cash in the business in exchange for 10,000 shares of capital stock.
Apr. 6	The company purchased office facilities for $300,000, of which $60,000 was applicable to the land and $240,000 to the building. A cash payment of $100,000 was made and a note payable was issued for the balance of the purchase price.
Apr. 10	Computer equipment was purchased from Comp Central for $6,000 cash.

Apr. 12 Office furnishings were purchased from Sam's Furniture at a cost of $12,000. A $1,000 cash payment was made at the time of purchase, and an agreement was made to pay the remaining balance in two equal installments due May 1 and June 1. Sam's Furniture did not require that North sign a promissory note.

Apr. 20 Office supplies were purchased from Office Space for $750 cash.

Apr. 25 North discovered that it paid too much for a computer printer purchased on April 10. The unit should have cost only $600, but North was charged $800. Comp Central promised to refund the difference within seven days.

Apr. 28 Mailed Sam's Furniture the first installment due on the account payable for office furnishings purchased on April 12.

Apr. 29 Received $200 from Comp Central in settlement of the account receivable created on April 25.

Instructions

a. Prepare journal entries to record the above transactions. Select the appropriate account titles from the following chart of accounts:

Cash	Land
Accounts Receivable	Office Building
Office Supplies	Notes Payable
Office Furnishings	Accounts Payable
Computer Systems	Capital Stock

b. Indicate the effects of each transaction on the company's assets, liabilities, and owners' equity for the month of April. Organize your analysis in tabular form as shown below for the April 1 transaction:

Transaction	Assets	=	Liabilities	+	Owners' Equity
Apr. 1	+$650,000 (Cash)	=	$0		+$650,000 (Capital Stock)

LO3-3 through LO3-8

PROBLEM 3.2B

Analyzing and Journalizing Transactions

Lyons, Inc., provides consulting services. A few of the company's business transactions occurring during June are described below:

1. On June 1, the company billed customers $5,000 on account for consulting services rendered. Customers are required to make full payment within 30 days. (Lyons, Inc., uses an account entitled Consulting Revenue when billing customers.)

2. On June 3, the company purchased office supplies costing $3,200, paying $800 cash and charging the remainder on the company's 30-day account at Office Warehouse. The supplies are expected to last several months.

3. On June 5, the company returned to Office Warehouse $100 of supplies that were not needed. The return of these supplies reduced by $100 the amount owed to Office Warehouse.

4. On June 17, the company issued an additional 1,000 shares of capital stock at $5 per share. The cash raised will be used to purchase new equipment in September.

5. On June 22, the company received $1,200 cash from customers it had billed on June 1.

6. On June 29, the company paid its outstanding account payable to Office Warehouse.

7. On June 30, a cash dividend totaling $1,800 was declared and paid to the company's stockholders.

Instructions

a. Prepare an analysis of each of the above transactions. Transaction 1 serves as an example of the form of analysis to be used.

    1. **(a)** The asset Accounts Receivable was increased. Increases in assets are recorded by debits. Debit Accounts Receivable $5,000.

        (b) Revenue has been earned. Revenue increases owners' equity. Increases in owners' equity are recorded by credits. Credit Consulting Revenue $5,000.

b. Prepare journal entries, including explanations, for the above transactions.

c. How does the *realization principle* influence the manner in which the June 1 billings to customers are recorded in the accounting records?

d. How does the *matching principle* influence the manner in which the June 3 purchase of supplies is recorded in the accounting records?

LO3-3 through LO3-8
PROBLEM 3.3B
Analyzing and Journalizing Transactions

Dana, Inc., provides civil engineering services. During October, its transactions included the following:

Oct. 1 Paid rent for the month of October, $4,000.

Oct. 4 Billed Milton Hotels $8,500 for services. The entire amount is due on or before October 28. (Dana uses an account entitled Service Revenue when billing clients.)

Oct. 8 Provided services to Dirt Valley Development for $4,700. The entire amount was collected on this date.

Oct. 12 Placed a newspaper advertisement in the *Daily Reporter* to be published in the October 25 issue. The cost of the advertisement was $320. Payment is due in 30 days.

Oct. 20 Received a check for $8,500 from Milton Hotels for the amount billed on October 4.

Oct. 24 Provided services to Dudley Company for $3,600. Dana collected $300 cash, with the balance due in 30 days.

Oct. 25 Sent a check to the *Daily Reporter* in full payment of the liability incurred on October 12.

Oct. 29 Declared and paid a $2,600 cash dividend to the company's stockholders.

Instructions

a. Analyze the effects that each of these transactions will have on the following six components of the company's financial statements for the month of October. Organize your answer in tabular form, using the column headings shown below. Use **I** for increase, **D** for decrease, and **NE** for no effect. The October 1 transaction is provided for you:

	Income Statement			Balance Sheet		
Transaction	Revenue	− Expenses	= Net Income	Assets	= Liabilities	+ Owners' Equity
Oct. 1	NE	I	D	D	NE	D

b. Prepare a journal entry (including explanation) for each of the above transactions.

c. Three of October's transactions involve cash payments, yet only one of these transactions is recorded as an expense. Describe three situations in which a cash payment would *not* involve recognition of an expense.

LO3-1 through LO3-10
PROBLEM 3.4B
The Accounting Cycle: Journalizing, Posting, and Preparing a Trial Balance

In March 2015, Mary Tone organized a corporation to provide package delivery services. The company, called Tone Deliveries, Inc., began operations immediately. Transactions during the month of March were as follows:

Mar. 2 The corporation issued 40,000 shares of capital stock to Mary Tone in exchange for $80,000 cash.

Mar. 4 Purchased a truck for $45,000. Made a $15,000 cash down payment and issued a note payable for the remaining balance.

Mar. 5 Paid Sloan Properties $2,500 to rent office space for the month.

Mar. 9 Billed customers $11,300 for services for the first half of March.

Mar. 15 Paid $7,100 in salaries earned by employees during the first half of March.

Mar. 19 Paid Bill's Auto $900 for maintenance and repair services on the company truck.

Mar. 20 Collected $3,800 of the amounts billed to customers on March 9.

Mar. 28 Billed customers $14,400 for services performed during the second half of the month.

Mar. 30 Paid $7,500 in salaries earned by employees during the second half of the month.

Mar. 30 Received an $830 bill from SY Petroleum for fuel purchased in March. The entire amount is due by April 15.

Mar. 30 Declared a $1,200 dividend payable on April 30.

The account titles used by Tone Deliveries are:

Cash	Retained Earnings
Accounts Receivable	Dividends
Truck	Service Revenue
Notes Payable	Maintenance Expense
Accounts Payable	Fuel Expense
Dividends Payable	Salaries Expense
Capital Stock	Rent Expense

Instructions

a. Analyze the effects that each of these transactions will have on the following six components of the company's financial statements for the month of March. Organize your answer in tabular form, using the column headings shown below. Use **I** for increase, **D** for decrease, and **NE** for no effect. The March 2 transaction is provided for you:

	Income Statement			Balance Sheet		
Transaction	Revenue	− Expenses	= Net Income	Assets	= Liabilities	+ Owners' Equity
Mar. 2	NE	NE	NE	I	NE	I

b. Prepare journal entries (including explanations) for each transaction.

c. Post each transaction to the appropriate ledger accounts (use a running balance format as shown in Exhibit 3–4, page 97).

d. Prepare a trial balance dated March 31, 2015.

e. Using figures from the trial balance prepared in part **d,** compute total assets, total liabilities, and owners' equity. Are these the figures that the company will report in its March 31 balance sheet? Explain your answer briefly.

LO3-1 through LO3-10

PROBLEM 3.5B

The Accounting Cycle: Journalizing, Posting, and Preparing a Trial Balance

Dr. Cravati, DMD., opened a dental clinic on August 1, 2015. The business transactions for August are shown below:

Aug. 1   Dr. Cravati invested $280,000 cash in the business in exchange for 1,000 shares of capital stock.

Aug. 4   Land and a building were purchased for $400,000. Of this amount, $60,000 applied to the land and $340,000 to the building. A cash payment of $80,000 was made at the time of the purchase, and a note payable was issued for the remaining balance.

Aug. 9   Medical instruments were purchased for $75,000 cash.

Aug. 16   Office fixtures and equipment were purchased for $25,000. Dr. Cravati paid $10,000 at the time of purchase and agreed to pay the entire remaining balance in 15 days.

Aug. 21   Office supplies expected to last several months were purchased for $4,200 cash.

Aug. 24   Dr. Cravati billed patients $13,000 for services rendered. Of this amount, $1,000 was received in cash, and $12,000 was billed on account (due in 30 days).

Aug. 27   A $450 invoice was received for several newspaper advertisements placed in August. The entire amount is due on September 8.

Aug. 28   Received a $500 payment on the $12,000 account receivable recorded August 24.

Aug. 31   Paid employees $2,200 for salaries earned in August.

A partial list of account titles used by Dr. Cravati includes:

Cash	Office Fixtures and Equipment
Accounts Receivable	Land
Office Supplies	Building
Notes Payable	Service Revenue
Accounts Payable	Advertising Expense
Capital Stock	Salary Expense
Medical Instruments	

Instructions

a. Analyze the effects that each of these transactions will have on the following six components of the company's financial statements for the month of August. Organize your answer in tabular form, using the column headings shown below. Use **I** for increase, **D** for decrease, and **NE** for no effect. The August 1 transaction is provided for you:

	Income Statement			Balance Sheet		
Transaction	Revenue −	Expenses =	Net Income	Assets =	Liabilities +	Owners' Equity
Aug. 1	**NE**	**NE**	**NE**	**I**	**NE**	**I**

b. Prepare journal entries (including explanations) for each transaction.

c. Post each transaction to the appropriate ledger accounts (use the T account format as illustrated in Exhibit 3–8 on page 110).

d. Prepare a trial balance dated August 31, 2015.

e. Using figures from the trial balance prepared in part d, compute total assets, total liabilities, and owners' equity. Did August appear to be a profitable month?

LO3-7 through LO3-9
PROBLEM 3.6B
Short Comprehensive
Problem

Clown Around, Inc., provides party entertainment for children of all ages. The company's trial balance dated *February 1, 2015,* is shown below.

CLOWN AROUND, INC.
TRIAL BALANCE
FEBRUARY 1, 2015

Cash	$2,850	
Accounts receivable	900	
Accounts payable		$ 800
Capital stock		2,000
Retained earnings		750
Dividends	—	
Party revenue		1,350
Salaries expense	830	
Party food expense	240	
Travel expense	80	
	$4,900	$4,900

Clown Around engaged in the following transactions in February:

Feb. 2   Paid $750 in partial settlement of the outstanding account payable reported in the trial balance dated February 1.

Feb. 6   Collected $900 in full settlement of the outstanding accounts receivable reported in the trial balance dated February 1.

Feb. 18 Billed Sunflower Child Care $175 for clown services. The entire amount is due March 15.

Feb. 26 Billed and collected $480 for performing at several birthday parties.

Feb. 28 Paid clown salaries of $260 for work done in February.

Feb. 28 Recorded and paid $40 for travel expenses incurred in February.

Feb. 28 Declared and paid a $100 dividend to Ralph Jaschob, the company's only shareholder.

a. Record the company's February transactions in general journal form. Include a brief explanation of the transaction as part of each journal entry.

b. Post each entry to the appropriate ledger accounts (use the T account format as illustrated in Exhibit 3–8 on page 110).

c. Prepare a trial balance dated February 28, 2015. (Hint: Retained Earnings will be reported at the same amount as it was on February 1. Accounting for changes in the Retained Earnings account resulting from revenue, expense, and dividend activities is discussed in Chapter 5.)

d. Will the $100 dividend paid on February 28 decrease the company's income? Explain.

LO3-3 through LO3-9
PROBLEM 3.7B
Short Comprehensive
Problem

Ahuna, Inc., provides in-home cooking lessons to its clients. The company's trial balance dated *March 1, 2015,* is shown below:

AHUNA, INC.
TRIAL BALANCE
MARCH 1, 2015

Cash	$ 5,700	
Accounts receivable	1,800	
Cooking supplies	800	
Accounts payable		$ 300
Dividends payable		500
Dividends	500	
Capital stock		6,000
Retained earnings		1,400
Client revenue		5,800
Salaries expense	3,100	
Travel expense	1,500	
Printing expense	600	
	$14,000	$14,000

Ahuna engaged in the following transactions in March:

Mar. 3   Collected a $1,200 account receivable from Kim Mitchell.
Mar. 11   Purchased cooking supplies for $700 cash.
Mar. 15   Paid $200 of outstanding accounts payable.
Mar. 20   Issued additional shares of capital stock for $4,000 cash.
Mar. 24   Recorded $6,200 of client revenue on account.
Mar. 27   Paid March salaries of $900.
Mar. 30   Recorded and paid March travel expenses of $400.
Mar. 31   Recorded $300 in printing expenses for recipe books. Payment is due April 12.

Instructions

a. Record the company's March transactions in general journal form. Include a brief explanation of the transaction as part of each journal entry.

b. Post each entry to the appropriate ledger accounts (use the T account format illustrated in Exhibit 3–8 on page 110).

c. Prepare a trial balance dated March 31, 2015. (Hint: Retained Earnings will be reported at the same amount as it was on March 1. Accounting for changes in the Retained Earnings account resulting from revenue, expense, and dividend activities is discussed in Chapter 5.)

d. Has the company paid all of the dividends that it has declared? Explain.

LO3-3, LO3-8
PROBLEM 3.8B
Analyzing the Effects of
Accounting Errors

Blind River, Inc., recently hired Neil Young as its bookkeeper. Mr. Young is somewhat inexperienced and has made numerous errors recording daily business transactions.

Indicate the *effects of the errors* described below on each of the financial statement elements shown in the column headings. Use the following symbols: **O** for overstated; **U** for understated; and **NE** for no effect.

Error	Net Income	Total Assets	Total Liabilities	Owners' Equity
Recorded the issuance of capital stock by debiting Capital Stock and crediting Cash.				
Recorded the payment of an account payable by debiting Cash and crediting Accounts Payable.				
Recorded the collection of an outstanding account receivable by debiting Service Revenue and crediting Accounts Receivable.				
Recorded client billings on account by debiting Service Revenue and crediting Accounts Payable.				
Recorded the payment of an outstanding Accounts Payable by debiting Cash and crediting Service Revenue.				
Recorded the payment of salaries payable by debiting Salaries Expense and crediting Cash.				
Recorded the purchase of office supplies on account by debiting Accounts Receivable and crediting Office Supplies.				

Critical Thinking Cases

LO3-7, LO3-10

CASE 3.1

Revenue Recognition

The realization principle determines when a business should recognize revenue. Listed next are three common business situations involving revenue. After each situation, we give two alternatives as to the accounting period (or periods) in which the business might recognize this revenue. Select the appropriate alternative by applying the realization principle, and explain your reasoning.

a. Airline ticket revenue: Most airlines sell tickets well before the scheduled date of the flight. (Period ticket sold; period of flight)

b. Sales on account: In June 2015, a San Diego–based furniture store had a big sale, featuring "No payments until 2016." (Period furniture sold; periods that payments are received from customers)

c. Magazine subscriptions revenue: Most magazine publishers sell subscriptions for future delivery of the magazine. (Period subscription sold; periods that magazines are mailed to customers)

LO3-6, LO3-7, LO3-10

CASE 3.2

Measuring Income Fairly

Kim Morris purchased Print Shop, Inc., a printing business, from Chris Stanley. Morris made a cash down payment and agreed to make annual payments equal to 40 percent of the company's net income in each of the next three years. (Such "earn-outs" are a common means of financing the purchase of a small business.) Stanley was disappointed, however, when Morris reported a first year's net income far below Stanley's expectations.

The agreement between Morris and Stanley did not state precisely how "net income" was to be measured. Neither Morris nor Stanley was familiar with accounting concepts. Their agreement stated only that the net income of the corporation should be measured in a "fair and reasonable manner."

In measuring net income, Morris applied the following policies:

1. Revenue was recognized when cash was received from customers. Most customers paid in cash, but a few were allowed 30-day credit terms.

2. Expenditures for ink and paper, which are purchased weekly, were charged directly to Supplies Expense, as were the Morris family's weekly grocery and dry cleaning bills.

3. Morris set her annual salary at $60,000, which Stanley had agreed was reasonable. She also paid salaries of $30,000 per year to her husband and to each of her two teenage children. These family members did not work in the business on a regular basis, but they did help out when things got busy.

4. Income taxes expense included the amount paid by the corporation (which was computed correctly), as well as the personal income taxes paid by various members of the Morris family on the salaries they earned working for the business.

5. The business had state-of-the-art printing equipment valued at $150,000 at the time Morris purchased it. The first-year income statement included a $150,000 equipment expense related to these assets.

Instructions

a. Discuss the fairness and reasonableness of these income-measurement policies. (Remember, these policies do *not* have to conform to generally accepted accounting principles. But they should be *fair* and *reasonable*.)

b. Do you think that the net *cash flow* generated by this business (cash receipts less cash outlays) is higher or lower than the net income as measured by Morris? Explain.

LO3-6, LO3-7, LO3-10
CASE 3.3
Whistle-Blowing

Happy Trails, Inc., is a popular family resort just outside Yellowstone National Park. Summer is the resort's busy season, but guests typically pay a deposit at least six months in advance to guarantee their reservations.

The resort is currently seeking new investment capital in order to expand operations. The more profitable Happy Trails appears to be, the more interest it will generate from potential investors. Ed Grimm, an accountant employed by the resort, has been asked by his boss to include $2 million of unearned guest deposits in the computation of income for the current year. Ed explained to his boss that because these deposits had not yet been earned they should be reported in the balance sheet as liabilities, not in the income statement as revenue. Ed argued that reporting guest deposits as revenue would inflate the current year's income and may mislead investors.

Ed's boss then *demanded* that he include $2 million of unearned guest deposits in the computation of income or be fired. He then told Ed in an assuring tone, "Ed, you will never be held responsible for misleading potential investors because you are just following my orders."

Instructions

Should Ed Grimm be forced to knowingly overstate the resort's income in order to retain his job? Is Ed's boss correct in saying that Ed cannot be held responsible for misleading potential investors? Discuss.

LO3-6
INTERNET CASE 3.4
Revenue from Various Sources

Visit the home page of **PC Connection** at the following Internet location: **www.pcconnection.com**.

Follow the "Investor Relations" link at the bottom of the company's home page and access its most recent 10-K by following the link to "SEC Filings."

Locate the company's most recent annual report. What percent of the company's total revenue is generated by sales to public sector customers (e.g., governmental agencies, educational institutions, etc.)? Have sales to public sector customers increased or decreased during the past three years? What are the company's other business segments?

Internet sites are time and date sensitive. It is the purpose of these exercises to have you explore the Internet. You may need to use the Yahoo! search engine www.yahoo.com (or another favorite search engine) to find a company's current web address.

Answers to Self-Test Questions

1. d   2. b   3. a, c, and d   4. c   5. c   6. d   7. b, c, and d
8. a and c

CHAPTER 4

The Accounting Cycle
Accruals and Deferrals

AFTER STUDYING THIS CHAPTER, YOU SHOULD BE ABLE TO:

Learning Objectives

LO4-1   Explain the purpose of adjusting entries.

LO4-2   Describe and prepare the four basic types of adjusting entries.

LO4-3   Prepare adjusting entries to convert assets to expenses.

LO4-4   Prepare adjusting entries to convert liabilities to revenue.

LO4-5   Prepare adjusting entries to accrue unpaid expenses.

LO4-6   Prepare adjusting entries to accrue uncollected revenue.

LO4-7   Explain how the principles of *realization* and *matching* relate to adjusting entries.

LO4-8   Explain the concept of *materiality*.

LO4-9   Prepare an adjusted trial balance and describe its purpose.

ROYAL CARIBBEAN CRUISES, LTD.

When is revenue actually *earned* by a company? In many cases, revenue is earned when cash is received at the point of sale. For instance, when a taxicab driver takes someone to the airport, revenue is earned when the passenger is dropped off at the appropriate terminal and the fare is collected.

Suppose the same passenger boards a Royal Caribbean cruise ship to the Bahamas using a ticket that was purchased six months in advance. At what point should the cruise line recognize that ticket revenue has been earned? A recent Royal Caribbean balance sheet provides the answer to this question.

In its balance sheet, Royal Caribbean reports a $1.5 billion liability account called Customer Deposits.

As passengers purchase tickets in advance, Royal Caribbean credits the Customer Deposits account for an amount equal to the cash it receives. It is not until passengers actually *use* their tickets that the company reduces this liability account and records Passenger Revenue in its income statement.

In many industries—such as airlines, insurance companies, and newspaper publishers—customer deposits and other forms of advance payments are the primary sources of cash flow from operating activities. For Royal Caribbean, over 80 percent of its ticket revenue is collected from travelers in advance. ■

For most companies, revenue is *not* always earned as cash is received, nor is an expense necessarily incurred as cash is disbursed. Timing differences between cash flows and the recognition of revenue and expenses are referred to as *accruals* and *deferrals*. In this chapter, we examine how accounting information must be adjusted for accruals and deferrals prior to the preparation of financial statements.

The first three steps of the accounting cycle were discussed in Chapter 3. They included (1) recording transactions, (2) posting transactions, and (3) preparing a trial balance. In this chapter, we focus solely upon the fourth step of the accounting cycle: performing the end-of-period adjustments required to measure business income. The remaining steps of the cycle are covered in Chapter 5.

Adjusting Entries

There is more to the measurement of business income than merely recording simple revenue and expense transactions that affect only a single accounting period. Certain transactions affect the revenue or expenses of *two* or *more* accounting periods. The purpose of adjusting entries is to assign to each accounting period appropriate amounts of revenue and expense. For example, Overnight Auto Service purchased shop supplies that will be used for several months. Thus, an adjusting entry is required to record the expense associated with the shop supplies that Overnight *uses* each month.

THE NEED FOR ADJUSTING ENTRIES

LO4-1

LEARNING OBJECTIVE
Explain the purpose of adjusting entries.

For purposes of measuring income and preparing financial statements, the life of a business is divided into a series of *accounting periods*. This practice enables decision makers to compare the financial statements of successive periods and to identify significant trends.

But measuring net income for a relatively short accounting period—such as a month or even a year—poses a problem because, as mentioned above, some business activities affect the revenue and expenses of *multiple accounting periods*. Therefore, **adjusting entries** are needed at the end of each accounting period to make certain that appropriate amounts of revenue and expense are reported in the company's income statement.

For example, magazine publishers often sell two- or three-year subscriptions to their publications. At the end of each accounting period, these publishers make adjusting entries recognizing the portion of their advance receipts that have been earned during the current period. Most companies also purchase insurance policies that benefit more than one period. Therefore, an adjusting entry is needed to make certain that an appropriate portion of each policy's total cost is reported in the income statement as insurance expense for the period. In short, adjusting entries are needed whenever transactions affect the revenue or expenses of more than one accounting period. These entries assign revenues to the period in which they are *earned,* and expenses to the periods in which related goods or services are *used.*

In theory, a business could make adjusting entries on a daily basis. But as a practical matter, these entries are made *only at the end of each accounting period.* For most companies, adjusting entries are made on a monthly basis.

TYPES OF ADJUSTING ENTRIES

LO4-2

LEARNING OBJECTIVE
Describe and prepare the four basic types of adjusting entries.

The number of adjustments needed at the end of each accounting period depends entirely upon the nature of the company's business activities. However, most adjusting entries fall into one of four general categories:[1]

1. *Converting assets to expenses.* A cash expenditure (or cost) that will benefit more than one accounting period usually is recorded by debiting an asset account (for example, Supplies, Unexpired Insurance, and so on) and by crediting Cash. The asset account created actually represents the *deferral* (or the postponement) of an expense. In each future period

---

[1]A fifth category of adjusting entries consists of adjustments related to the valuation of certain assets, such as marketable securities and accounts receivable. These valuation adjustments are explained and illustrated in Chapter 7.

that benefits from the use of this asset, an adjusting entry is made to allocate a portion of the asset's cost from the balance sheet to the income statement as an expense. This adjusting entry is recorded by debiting the appropriate expense account (for example, Supplies Expense or Insurance Expense) and crediting the related asset account (for example, Supplies or Unexpired Insurance).

2. *Converting liabilities to revenue.* A business may collect cash in advance for services to be rendered in future accounting periods. Transactions of this nature are usually recorded by debiting Cash and by crediting a liability account (typically called Unearned Revenue or Customer Deposits). Here, the liability account created represents the *deferral* (or the postponement) of a revenue. In the period that services are actually rendered (or that goods are sold), an adjusting entry is made to allocate a portion of the liability from the balance sheet to the income statement to recognize the revenue earned during the period. The adjusting entry is recorded by debiting the liability (Unearned Revenue or Customer Deposits) and by crediting *Revenue Earned* (or a similar account) for the value of the services.

3. *Accruing unpaid expenses.* An expense may be incurred in the current accounting period even though no cash payment will occur until a future period. These *accrued* expenses are recorded by an adjusting entry made at the end of each accounting period. The adjusting entry is recorded by debiting the appropriate expense account (for example, Interest Expense or Salary Expense) and by crediting the related liability (for example, Interest Payable or Salaries Payable).

4. *Accruing uncollected revenue.* Revenue may be earned (or *accrued*) during the current period, even though the collection of cash will not occur until a future period. Unrecorded earned revenue, for which no cash has been received, requires an adjusting entry at the end of the accounting period. The adjusting entry is recorded by debiting the appropriate asset (for example, Accounts Receivable or Interest Receivable) and by crediting the appropriate revenue account (for example, Service Revenue Earned or Interest Earned).

ADJUSTING ENTRIES AND TIMING DIFFERENCES

In an accrual accounting system, there are often *timing differences* between cash flows and the recognition of expenses or revenue. A company can pay cash in advance of incurring certain expenses or receive cash before revenue has been earned. Likewise, it can incur certain expenses before paying any cash or it can earn revenue before any cash is received. These timing differences, and the adjusting entries that result from them, are summarized below.

- Adjusting entries to convert assets to expenses result from cash being paid prior to an expense being incurred.
- Adjusting entries to convert liabilities to revenue result from cash being received prior to revenue being earned.
- Adjusting entries to accrue unpaid expenses result from expenses being incurred before cash is paid.
- Adjusting entries to accrue uncollected revenue result from revenue being earned before cash is received.

As illustrated in Exhibit 4–1, adjusting entries provide important linkages between accounting periods related to these timing differences. Specifically, they link: (1) *prior* period cash outflows to *current* period expenses, (2) *prior* period cash inflows to *current* period revenue, (3) *current* period expenses to *future* cash outflows, and (4) *current* period revenue to *future* period cash inflows.

CHARACTERISTICS OF ADJUSTING ENTRIES

Keep in mind two important characteristics of all adjusting entries: First, every adjusting entry *involves the recognition of either revenue or expenses.* Revenue and expenses represent changes in owners' equity. However, owners' equity cannot change by itself; *there also must be a corresponding change in either assets or liabilities.* Thus every adjusting entry affects both an income statement account (revenue or expense) and a balance sheet account (asset or

EXHIBIT 4–1 Adjusting Entries Provide Links Between Accounting Periods

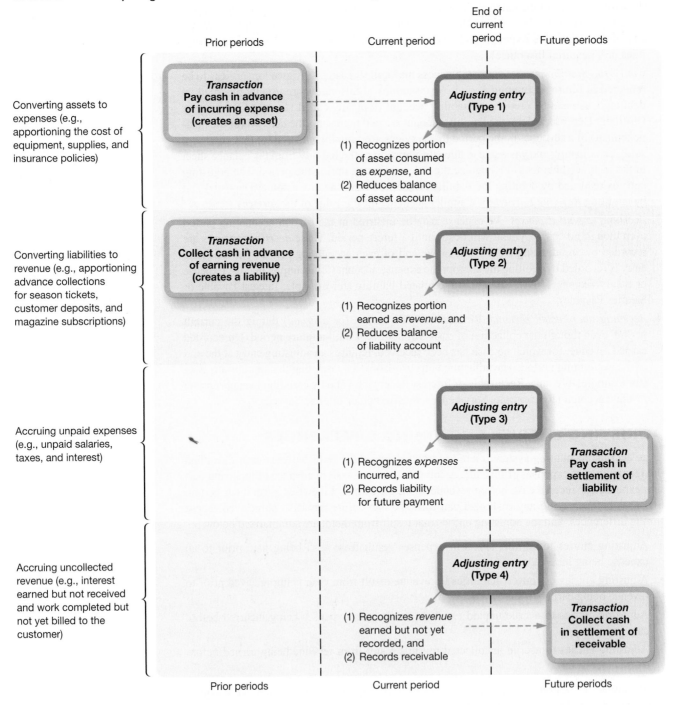

liability). Rarely do adjusting entries include an entry to Cash. It is important to recognize that none of the adjustments discussed in this chapter require a debit or a credit to Cash.

Second, adjusting entries are based on the concepts of accrual accounting, *not upon monthly bills or month-end transactions.* No one sends Overnight Auto Service a bill saying, "Shop Supply Expense for the month is $500." Yet Overnight must be aware of the need to record the estimated cost of shop supplies consumed if it is to measure income properly for the period. Making adjusting entries requires a greater understanding of accrual accounting concepts than does the recording of routine business transactions. In many businesses, the adjusting process is performed by the controller or by a professional accountant, rather than by the regular accounting staff.

YEAR-END AT OVERNIGHT AUTO SERVICE

To illustrate the various types of adjusting entries, we will again use our example involving Overnight Auto Service. Chapter 3 concluded with Overnight's trial balance dated February 28, 2015 (the end of the company's second month of operations). We will now skip ahead to *December 31, 2015*—the end of Overnight's first *year* of operations. This will enable us to illustrate the preparation of *annual* financial statements, rather than statements that cover only a single month.

Most companies make adjusting entries every *month*. We will assume that Overnight has been following this approach throughout 2015. The company's *unadjusted* trial balance dated December 31, 2015, appears in Exhibit 4–2. It is referred to as an unadjusted trial balance because Overnight last made adjusting entries on *November 30;* therefore, it is still necessary to make adjusting entries for the month of December.

In the next few pages we illustrate several transactions, as well as the related adjusting entries. Both are shown in the format of general journal entries. To help distinguish between transactions and adjusting entries, *transactions* are printed in *blue* and *adjusting entries* in *red*.

CONVERTING ASSETS TO EXPENSES

When a business makes an expenditure that will benefit more than one accounting period, the amount usually is debited to an asset account. At the end of each period benefiting from this expenditure, an adjusting entry is made to transfer an appropriate portion of the cost from the

L04-3

LEARNING OBJECTIVE
Prepare adjusting entries to convert assets to expenses.

OVERNIGHT AUTO SERVICE TRIAL BALANCE DECEMBER 31, 2015		
Cash	$ 18,592	
Accounts receivable	6,500	
Shop supplies	1,800	
Unexpired insurance	4,500	
Tools and equipment	12,000	
Accumulated depreciation: tools and equipment		2,000
Building	36,000	
Accumulated depreciation: building		$ 1,500
Land	52,000	
Notes payable		4,000
Accounts payable		2,690
Income taxes payable		1,560
Unearned rent revenue		9,000
Capital stock		80,000
Retained earnings		0
Dividends	14,000	
Repair service revenue		171,250
Advertising expense	3,900	
Wages expense	56,800	
Supplies expense	6,900	
Depreciation expense: building	1,500	
Depreciation expense: tools and equipment	2,000	
Utilities expense	19,400	
Insurance expense	13,500	
Income taxes expense	22,608	
	$272,000	$272,000

EXHIBIT 4–2
Unadjusted Trial Balance

asset account to an expense account. This adjusting entry reflects the fact that part of the asset has been used up—or become an expense—during the current accounting period.

An adjusting entry to convert an asset to an expense consists of a debit to an expense account and a credit to an asset account (or contra-asset account). Examples of these adjustments include the entries to apportion the costs of **prepaid expenses** and entries to record depreciation expense.

Prepaid Expenses   Payments in advance often are made for such items as insurance, rent, and office supplies. If the advance payment (or prepayment) will benefit more than just the current accounting period, the cost *represents an asset* rather than an expense. The cost of this asset will be allocated to expense in the accounting periods in which the services or the supplies are used. In summary, *prepaid expenses are assets;* they become expenses only as the goods or services are used up.

Shop Supplies   To illustrate, consider Overnight's accounting policies for shop supplies. As supplies are purchased, their cost is debited to the asset account Shop Supplies. It is not practical to make journal entries every few minutes as supplies are used. Instead, an estimate is made of the supplies remaining on hand at the end of each month; the supplies that are "missing" are assumed to have been used.

Prior to making adjusting entries at December 31, the balance in Overnight's Shop Supplies account is $1,800. The balance of this asset account represents shop supplies on hand on November 30. The Supplies Expense account shows a balance of $6,900, which represents the cost of supplies used through November 30. Assume that approximately $1,200 of shop supplies remain on hand at December 31. This suggests that supplies costing about $600 have been *used in December;* thus, the following *adjusting entry* is made:

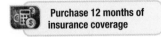
The adjusting entry required to convert the cost of supplies used from an asset account to an expense

Dec. 31	Supplies Expense	600	
	Shop Supplies		600
	December Shop Supplies adjusting entry.		

This adjusting entry serves two purposes: (1) It charges to expense the cost of supplies used in December, and (2) it reduces the balance of the Shop Supplies account to $1,200—the amount of supplies estimated to be on hand at December 31.

Insurance Policies   Insurance policies also are a prepaid expense. These policies provide a benefit, insurance protection, over a specific period of time. As the time passes, the insurance policy *expires*—that is, it is used up in business operations.

To illustrate, assume that on March 1, Overnight purchased for $18,000 a one-year insurance policy providing comprehensive liability insurance and insurance against fire and damage to customers' vehicles while in Overnight's facilities. This expenditure (a *transaction*) was debited to an asset account, as follows (again, this is a transaction, *not* an adjusting entry):

Purchase 12 months of insurance coverage

Mar. 1	Unexpired Insurance	18,000	
	Cash		18,000
	Purchased an insurance policy providing coverage for the next 12 months.		

This $18,000 expenditure provides insurance coverage for a period of one full year. Therefore, 1/12 of this cost, or $1,500, is recognized as insurance expense every month. The $13,500 insurance expense reported in Overnight's trial balance represents the portion of the insurance policy that has expired between March 1 and November 30 ($1,500/mo. × 9 months). The $4,500 amount of unexpired insurance shown in the trial balance is the remaining cost of the 12-month policy still in effect as of November 30 ($1,500/mo. × 3 months). By December 31, another full month of the policy has expired. Thus, the insurance expense for December is recorded by the following *adjusting entry* at month-end:

Dec. 31	Insurance Expense	1,500	
	Unexpired Insurance		1,500
	December Insurance Expense adjusting entry.		

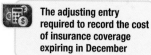

The adjusting entry required to record the cost of insurance coverage expiring in December

Notice the similarities between the *effects* of this adjusting entry and the one that we made previously for shop supplies. In both cases, the entries transfer to expense that portion of an asset used up during the period. This flow of costs from the balance sheet to the income statement is illustrated in Exhibit 4–3.

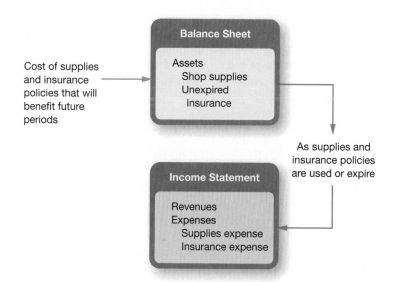

EXHIBIT 4–3

An Expired Asset Becomes An Expense

YOUR TURN You as a Car Owner

Car owners typically pay insurance premiums six months in advance. Assume that you recently paid your six-month premium of $600 on February 1 (for coverage through July 31). On March 31, you decide to switch insurance companies. You call your existing agent and ask that your policy be canceled. Are you entitled to a refund? If so, why, and how much will it be?

(See our comments on the Online Learning Center website.)

Recording Prepayments Directly in the Expense Accounts

In our illustration, payments for shop supplies and for insurance covering more than one period were debited to asset accounts. However, some companies follow an alternative policy of debiting such prepayments directly to an expense account, such as Supplies Expense. At the end of the period, the adjusting entry then would be to debit Shop Supplies and credit Supplies Expense for the cost of supplies that had *not* been used.

This alternative method leads to the *same results* as does the procedure used by Overnight. Under either approach, the cost of supplies used during the current period is treated as an *expense,* and the cost of supplies still on hand is carried forward in the balance sheet as an *asset.*

In this text, we will follow Overnight's practice of recording prepayments in asset accounts and then making adjustments to transfer these costs to expense accounts as the assets expire. This approach correctly describes the *conceptual flow of costs* through the elements of financial statements. That is, a prepayment *is* an asset that later becomes an expense. The alternative approach is used widely in practice only because it is an efficient "shortcut," which standardizes the recording of transactions and may reduce the number of adjusting entries needed at the end of the period. Remember, our goal in this course is to develop your ability to understand and use accounting information, not to train you in alternative bookkeeping procedures.

The idea of shop supplies and insurance policies being used up over several months is easy to understand. But the same concept also applies to assets such as buildings and equipment. These assets are converted to expenses through the process of *depreciation.*

THE CONCEPT OF DEPRECIATION

Depreciable assets are *physical objects* that retain their size and shape but that eventually wear out or become obsolete. They are not physically consumed, as are assets such as supplies, but nonetheless their economic usefulness diminishes over time. Examples of depreciable assets include buildings and all types of equipment, fixtures, furnishings—and even railroad tracks. Land, however, is *not* viewed as a depreciable asset, as it has an *unlimited* useful life.

Each period, a portion of a depreciable asset's usefulness *expires.* Therefore, a corresponding portion of its cost is recognized as *depreciation expense.*

What Is Depreciation?

In accounting, the term **depreciation** means the *systematic allocation of the cost of a depreciable asset to expense* over the asset's useful life. This process is illustrated in Exhibit 4–4. Notice the similarities between Exhibit 4–4 and Exhibit 4–3.

Depreciation *is not* an attempt to record changes in the asset's market value. In the short run, the market value of some depreciable assets may even increase, but the process of depreciation continues anyway. The rationale for depreciation lies in the *matching principle.* Our goal is to offset a reasonable portion of the asset's cost against revenue in each period of the asset's **useful life.**

EXHIBIT 4–4

The Depreciation Process

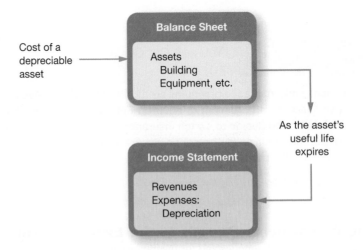

Depreciation expense occurs continuously over the life of the asset, but there are no daily "depreciation transactions." In effect, depreciation expense is paid in advance when the asset is originally purchased. Therefore, *adjusting entries* are needed at the end of each accounting period to transfer an appropriate amount of the asset's cost to depreciation expense.

Depreciation Is Only an Estimate

The appropriate amount of depreciation expense is *only an estimate.* After all, we cannot look at a building or a piece of equipment and determine precisely how much of its economic usefulness has expired during the current period.

The most widely used means of estimating periodic depreciation expense is the **straight-line method of depreciation.** Under the straight-line approach, an *equal portion* of the asset's cost is allocated to depreciation expense in every period of the asset's estimated useful life. The formula for computing depreciation expense by the straight-line method is:[2]

$$\text{Depreciation expense (per period)} = \frac{\text{Cost of the asset}}{\text{Estimated useful life}}$$

The use of an *estimated useful life* is the major reason that depreciation expense is *only an estimate.* In most cases, management does not know in advance exactly how long the asset will remain in use.

CASE IN POINT

© Digital Vision/Alamy

How long does a building last? For purposes of computing depreciation expense, most companies estimate about 30 or 40 years. Yet the Empire State Building was built in 1931, and it's not likely to be torn down anytime soon. As you might guess, it often is difficult to estimate in advance just how long depreciable assets may remain in use.

Depreciation of Overnight's Building   Overnight purchased its building for $36,000 on January 22. Because the building was old, its estimated remaining useful life is only 20 years. Therefore, the building's monthly depreciation expense is $150 ($36,000 cost ÷ 240 months). We will assume that Overnight did *not* record any depreciation expense in January because it operated for only a small part of the month. Thus, the building's $1,500 depreciation expense reported in Overnight's trial balance illustrated in Exhibit 4–2 on page 145 represents 10 *full months* of depreciation recorded in 2015, from February 1 through November 30 ($150/mo. × 10 months). An additional $150 of depreciation expense is still needed on the building for December (bringing the total to be reported in the income statement for the year to $1,650).

The *adjusting entry* to record depreciation expense on Overnight's building for the month of December is:

Dec. 31	Depreciation Expense: Building	150	
	Accumulated Depreciation: Building		150
	December building depreciation adjusting entry ($36,000 ÷ 240 mo.).		

The adjusting entry required to record monthly depreciation on the building

The *Depreciation Expense: Building* account will appear in Overnight's income statement along with other expenses for the year ended December 31, 2015. The balance in the

---

[2]At this point in our discussion, we are ignoring any possible *residual value* that might be recovered upon disposal of the asset. Residual values are discussed in Chapter 9. We will assume that Overnight Auto Service depreciates its assets using the straight-line method computed without any residual values.

Accumulated Depreciation: Building account will be reported in the December 31 balance sheet as a *deduction* from the Building Account, as shown below.

How accumulated depreciation appears in the balance sheet

Building	$36,000
Less: Accumulated Depreciation: Building	(1,650)
Book Value	$34,350

Accumulated Depreciation: Building is an example of a **contra-asset account** because (1) it has a credit balance, and (2) it is offset against an asset account (Building) to produce the book value for the asset. Accountants often use the term **book value** (or *carrying value*) to describe the net valuation of an asset in a company's accounting records. For depreciable assets, such as buildings and equipment, book value is equal to the cost of the asset, less the related amount of accumulated depreciation. The end result of crediting the Accumulated Depreciation: Building account is much the same as if the credit had been made directly to the Building account; that is, the book value reported in the balance sheet for the building is reduced from $36,000 to $34,350.

Book value is of significance primarily for accounting purposes. It represents costs that will be offset against the revenue of future periods. It also gives users of financial statements an indication of the age of a company's depreciable assets (older assets tend to have larger amounts of accumulated depreciation associated with them than newer assets). It is important to realize that the computation of book value is based upon an asset's *historical* cost. Thus, book value is *not* intended to represent an asset's current *market value.*

Depreciation of Tools and Equipment   Overnight depreciates its tools and equipment over a period of five years (60 months) using the straight-line method. The December 31 trial balance shows that the company owns tools and equipment that cost $12,000. Therefore, the *adjusting entry* to record December's depreciation expense is:

The adjusting entry required to record the monthly depreciation on tools and equipment

Dec. 31	Depreciation Expense: Tools and Equipment	200	
	Accumulated Depreciation: Tools and Equipment		200
	December tools and equipment adjusting entry		
	($12,000 ÷ 60 months = $200/mo.).		

Again, we assume that Overnight did *not* record depreciation expense for tools and equipment in January because it operated for only a small part of the month. Thus, the related $2,000 depreciation expense reported in Overnight's trial balance in Exhibit 4–2 on page 145 represents 10 *full months* of depreciation, from February 1 through November 30 ($200/mo. × 10 months). The tools and equipment still require an additional $200 of depreciation for December (bringing the total to be reported in the income statement for the year to $2,200).

What is the book value of Overnight's tools and equipment at December 31, 2015? If you said *$9,800,* you're right.[3]

Depreciation—A Noncash Expense   Depreciation is a *noncash* expense. We have made the point that net income does not represent an inflow of cash or any other asset. Rather, it is a *computation* of the overall effect of certain business transactions on owners' equity. The recognition of depreciation expense illustrates this point. As depreciable assets expire, depreciation expense is recorded, net income is reduced, and owners' equity declines, but there is no corresponding cash outlay in the current period. For this reason, depreciation is called a noncash expense. Often it represents the largest difference between net income and the cash flow from business operations.

---

[3]Cost, $12,000, less accumulated depreciation, which amounts to $2,200 after the December 31 adjusting entry.

CONVERTING LIABILITIES TO REVENUE

LO4-4

LEARNING OBJECTIVE
Prepare adjusting entries to
convert liabilities to revenue.

In some instances, customers may *pay in advance* for services to be rendered in later account-ing periods. For example, a football team collects much of its revenue in advance through the sale of season tickets. Health clubs collect in advance by selling long-term membership contracts. Airlines sell many of their tickets well in advance of scheduled flights.

For accounting purposes, amounts collected in advance *do not represent revenue,* because these amounts have *not yet been earned.* Amounts collected from customers in advance are recorded by debiting the Cash account and crediting an *unearned revenue* account. **Unearned revenue** sometimes is referred to as *deferred revenue.*

When a company collects money in advance from its customers, it has an *obligation* to render services in the future. Therefore, the balance of an unearned revenue account is consid-ered to be a liability; *it appears in the liability section of the balance sheet, not in the income statement.* Unearned revenue differs from other liabilities because it usually will be settled by rendering services, rather than by making payment in cash. In short, it will be *worked off* rather than *paid off.* Of course, if the business is unable to render the service, it must discharge this liability by refunding money to its customers.

When a company renders the services for which customers have paid in advance, it is work-ing off its liability to these customers and is earning the revenue. At the end of the account-ing period, an adjusting entry is made to transfer an appropriate amount from the unearned revenue account to a revenue account. This adjusting entry consists of a debit to a liability account (unearned revenue) and a credit to a revenue account. For instance, **The New York Times Company** reports a $67 million current liability in its balance sheet called Unexpired Subscriptions. This account represents unearned revenue from selling subscriptions for future newspaper deliveries. The liability is converted to Circulation Revenue and reported in the company's income statement as the actual deliveries occur.

To illustrate these concepts, assume that on December 1, Harbor Cab Co. agreed to rent space in Overnight's building to provide indoor storage for some of its cabs. The agreed-upon rent is $3,000 per month, and Harbor Cab paid for the first three months in advance. The journal entry to record this *transaction* on December 1 was (again, this is a transaction, *not* an adjusting entry):

Dec. 1	Cash	9,000	
	Unearned Rent Revenue		9,000
	Collected in advance from Harbor Cab for rental of storage space for three months.		

Remember that Unearned Rent Revenue is a *liability* account, *not a revenue account.* Overnight will earn rental revenue *gradually* over a three-month period as it provides storage facilities for Harbor Cab. At the end of each of these three months, Overnight will make an *adjusting entry,* transferring $3,000 from the Unearned Rent Revenue account to an earned revenue account, Rent Revenue Earned, which will appear in Overnight's income statement. The first in this series of monthly transfers will be made at December 31 with the following *adjusting entry:*

An "advance"—it's not
revenue; it's a liability

Dec. 31	Unearned Rent Revenue	3,000	
	Rent Revenue Earned		3,000
	December adjusting entry to convert Unearned Rent Revenue to Rent Revenue Earned ($9,000 ÷ 3 mo.).		

An adjusting entry
showing that some
unearned revenue was
earned in December

After this adjusting entry has been posted, the Unearned Rent Revenue account will have a $6,000 credit balance. This balance represents Overnight's obligation to render $6,000 worth of service over the next two months and will appear in the liability section of the company's balance sheet. The Rent Revenue Earned account will appear in Overnight's income statement.

The conversion of unearned revenue to recognize earned revenue is illustrated in Exhibit 4–5.

EXHIBIT 4–5

Unearned Revenue Becomes Earned Revenue

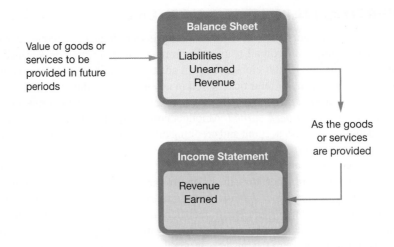

Recording Advance Collections Directly in the Revenue Accounts

We have stressed that amounts collected from customers in advance represent liabilities, not revenue. However, some companies follow an accounting policy of crediting these advance collections directly to revenue accounts. The adjusting entry then should consist of a debit to the revenue account and a credit to the unearned revenue account for the portion of the advance payments *not yet earned*. This alternative accounting practice leads to the same results as does the method used in our illustration.

In this text, we will follow the originally described practice of crediting advance payments from customers to an unearned revenue account.

ACCRUING UNPAID EXPENSES

LO4-5

LEARNING OBJECTIVE
Prepare adjusting entries to accrue unpaid expenses.

This type of adjusting entry recognizes expenses that will be paid in *future* transactions; therefore, no cost has yet been recorded in the accounting records. Salaries of employees and interest on borrowed money are common examples of expenses that accumulate from day to day but that usually are not recorded until they are paid. These expenses are said to **accrue** over time, that is, to grow or to accumulate. At the end of the accounting period, an adjusting entry should be made to record any expenses that have accrued but that have not yet been recorded. Since these expenses will be paid at a future date, the adjusting entry consists of a debit to an expense account and a credit to a liability account. We shall now use the example of Overnight Auto Service to illustrate this type of adjusting entry.

Accrual of Wages (or Salaries) Expense

Overnight, like many businesses, pays its employees every other Friday. This month, however, ends on a Tuesday—three days before the next scheduled payday. Thus Overnight's employees have worked for more than a week in December *for which they have not yet been paid.*

Time cards indicate that since the last payroll date, Overnight's employees have worked a total of 130 hours. Including payroll taxes, Overnight's wage expense averages about $15 per hour. Therefore, at December 31, the company owes its employees approximately *$1,950* for work performed in December.[4] The following *adjusting entry* should be made to record this amount both as wages expense of the current period and as a liability:

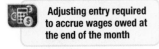

Adjusting entry required to accrue wages owed at the end of the month

Dec. 31	Wages Expense	1,950	
	Wages Payable		1,950
	Adjusting entry to accrue wages owed but unpaid as of December 31.		

---

[4]In the preparation of a formal payroll, wages and payroll taxes must be computed "down to the last cent." But this is not a payroll; it is an amount to be used in the company's financial statements. Therefore, a reasonable estimate will suffice. The accounting principle of *materiality* is discussed later in this chapter.

This adjusting entry increases Overnight's wages expense for 2015 and also creates a liability—wages payable—that will appear in the December 31 balance sheet.

On Friday, January 3, 2016, Overnight will pay its regular biweekly payroll. Let us assume that this payroll amounts to $2,397. In this case, the *transaction* to record payment is as follows (again, this is a transaction, *not* an adjusting entry):[5]

2016			
Jan. 3	Wages Expense (for January)	447	
	Wages Payable (accrued in December)	1,950	
	Cash		2,397
	Biweekly payroll, $1,950 of which had been accrued at December 31, 2015.		

Payment of wages earned in two accounting periods

Accrual of Interest Expense

On January 22, 2015, Overnight purchased its building, an old bus garage, from the Metropolitan Transit Authority for $36,000. Overnight paid $6,000 cash, and issued a $30,000 90-day note payable for the balance owed. Overnight paid the $30,000 obligation in April. There was no interest expense to accrue because this note payable was *non-interest-bearing.*

On November 30, 2015, Overnight borrowed $4,000 from American National Bank by issuing an *interest-bearing* note payable. This loan is to be repaid in three months (on February 28, 2016), along with interest computed at an annual rate of 9 percent. The entry made on November 30 to record this borrowing *transaction* is (again, this is a transaction, *not* an adjusting entry):

Nov. 30	Cash..	4,000	
	Notes Payable		4,000
	Borrowed cash from American National Bank, issuing a 9%, $4,000 note payable, due in three months.		

On February 28, Overnight must pay the bank $4,090. This represents the $4,000 amount borrowed, *plus $90 interest* ($4,000 $\times$ .09 $\times$ 3/12). The $90 interest charge covers a period of *three months*. Although no payment is made until February 28, 2016, interest expense is *incurred* (or accrued) at a rate of $30 per month, as shown in Exhibit 4–6.

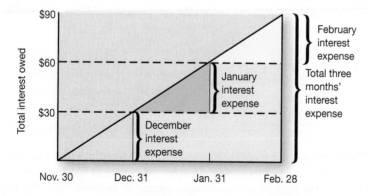

EXHIBIT 4–6

Accrual of Interest

The following *adjusting entry* is made at December 31 to accrue one month's interest expense and to record the amount of unpaid interest owed to the bank at December 31, 2015:

Dec. 31	Interest Expense...	30	
	Interest Payable		30
	Adjusting entry to accrue December Interest Expense ($4,000 $\times$ .09 $\times$ 1/12).		

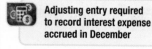
Adjusting entry required to record interest expense accrued in December

---

[5]In this illustration, we do not address the details associated with payroll taxes and amounts withheld. These topics are discussed in Chapter 10.

The $30 interest expense that accrued in December will appear in Overnight's 2015 income statement. Both the $30 interest payable and the $4,000 note payable to American National Bank will appear as *liabilities* in the December 31, 2015, balance sheet.

Overnight will make a *second* adjusting entry recognizing another $30 in interest expense on January 31, 2016. The *transaction* on February 28 to record the repayment of this loan, including $90 in interest charges, is (again, this is a transaction, *not* an adjusting entry):

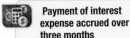
Payment of interest expense accrued over three months

2016			
Feb. 28	Notes Payable	4,000	
	Interest Payable (from December and January)	60	
	Interest Expense (February only)	30	
	Cash		4,090
	Repaid $4,000 note payable to American National Bank, including $90 in interest charges.		

LO4-6

LEARNING OBJECTIVE
Prepare adjusting entries to accrue uncollected revenue.

ACCRUING UNCOLLECTED REVENUE

A business may earn revenue during the current accounting period but not bill the customer until a future accounting period. This situation is likely to occur if additional services are being performed for the same customer, in which case the bill might not be prepared until all services are completed. Any revenue that has been *earned but not recorded* during the current accounting period should be recorded at the end of the period by means of an adjusting entry. This adjusting entry consists of a debit to an account receivable and a credit to the appropriate revenue account. The term *accrued revenue* often is used to describe revenue that has been earned during the period but that has not been recorded prior to the closing date.

To illustrate this type of adjusting entry, assume that in December, Overnight entered into an agreement to perform routine maintenance on several vans owned by Airport Shuttle Service. Overnight agreed to maintain these vans for a flat fee of $1,500 per month, payable on the fifteenth of each month.

No entry was made to record the signing of this agreement, because no services had yet been rendered. Overnight began rendering services on *December 15,* but the first monthly payment will not be received until January 15. Therefore, Overnight should make the following *adjusting entry* at December 31 to record the revenue *earned* from Airport Shuttle during the month:

Adjusting entry required to accrue revenue earned but not yet billed or collected

Dec. 31	Accounts Receivable	750	
	Repair Service Revenue		750
	Adjusting entry to record accrued Repair Service Revenue earned in December.		

The collection of the first monthly fee from Airport Shuttle will occur on January 15, 2016. Of this $1,500 cash receipt, half represents collection of the receivable recorded on December 31; the other half represents revenue earned in January. Thus, the *transaction* to record the receipt of $1,500 from Airport Shuttle on January 15 will be (again, this is a transaction, *not* an adjusting entry):

Entry to record collection of accrued revenue

2016			
Jan. 15	Cash	1,500	
	Accounts Receivable		750
	Repair Service Revenue		750
	Cash collected from Airport Shuttle for van maintenance provided December 15 through January 15.		

The net result of the December 31 adjusting entry has been to divide the revenue from maintenance of Airport Shuttle's vans between December and January in proportion to the services rendered during each month.

ACCRUING INCOME TAXES EXPENSE: THE FINAL ADJUSTING ENTRY

As a corporation earns taxable income, it incurs income taxes expense, and also a liability to governmental tax authorities. This liability is paid in four installments called *estimated quarterly payments.* The first three payments normally are made on April 15, June 15, and September 15. The final installment actually is due on *December 15;* but for purposes of our illustration and assignment materials, we will assume the final payment is not due until *January 15* of the following year.[6]

In its unadjusted trial balance (Exhibit 4–2 on page 145), Overnight shows income taxes expense of $22,608. This is the income taxes expense recognized from January 20, 2015, (the date Overnight opened for business) through November 30, 2015. Income taxes accrued through September 30 have already been paid. Thus, the $1,560 liability for income taxes payable represents only the income taxes accrued in *October* and *November.*

The amount of income taxes expense accrued for any given month is only an *estimate.* The actual amount of income taxes cannot be determined until the company prepares its annual income tax return. In our illustrations and assignment materials, we estimate income taxes expense at *40 percent of taxable income.* We also assume that taxable income is equal to *income before income taxes,* a subtotal often shown in an income statement. This subtotal is total revenue less all expenses *other than* income taxes.

INTERNATIONAL CASE IN POINT

Corporate income tax rates vary around the world. A recent survey shows that rates range from 9 percent in Montenegro to 55 percent in the United Arab Emirates. Worldwide, the average tax rate is 24 percent. The average rate in the United States is 40 percent.* In addition to corporate income taxes, some countries also (1) withhold taxes on dividends, interest, and royalties, (2) charge value-added taxes at specified production and distribution points, and (3) impose border taxes such as customs and import duties. A few countries, including the Bahanas have no corporate taxes.

*KPMG Corporate Tax Rate Survey (2013).

In 2015, Overnight earned income before income taxes of $66,570 (see the income statement in Exhibit 5–2, page 196, in Chapter 5). Therefore, income taxes expense *for the entire year* is estimated at $26,628 ($66,570 × 40 percent). Given that income taxes expense recognized through November 30 amounts to $22,608 (see the unadjusted trial balance in Exhibit 4–2), an additional $4,020 in income taxes expense must have accrued during *December* ($26,628 − $22,608). The *adjusting entry* to record this expense is:

Dec. 31	Income Taxes Expense	4,020	
	Income Taxes Payable		4,020
	Adjusting entry to record income taxes accrued in December.		

Adjusting entry required to record income taxes accrued in December

---

[6]This assumption enables us to accrue income taxes in December in the same manner as in other months. Otherwise, income taxes for this month would be recorded as a mid-month transaction, rather than in an end-of-month adjusting entry. The adjusting entry for income taxes is an example of an accrued, but unpaid, expense.

This entry increases the balance in the Income Taxes Expense account to the $26,628 amount required for the year ended December 31, 2015. It also increases the liability for income taxes payable to $5,580 ($1,560 + $4,020). The *transaction* to record the payment of this liability on January 15, 2016, will be (again, this is a transaction, *not* an adjusting entry):

2016			
Jan. 15	Income Taxes Payable	5,580	
	Cash		5,580
	Payment of the remaining 2015 income tax liability.		

Income Taxes in Unprofitable Periods

What happens to income taxes expense when *losses* are incurred? In these situations, the company recognizes a "negative amount" of income taxes expense. The adjusting entry to record income taxes at the end of an *unprofitable* accounting period consists of a *debit* to Income Taxes Payable and a *credit* to Income Taxes Expense.

"Negative" income taxes expense means that the company may be able to recover from the government some of the income taxes recognized as expense in prior periods.[7] If the Income Taxes Payable account has a *debit* balance at year-end, it is reclassified as an *asset,* called "Income Tax Refund Receivable." A credit balance in the Income Taxes Expense account is offset against the amount of the before-tax loss, as shown in Exhibit 4–7.

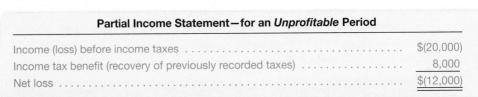

Income tax benefit can reduce a pretax loss

EXHIBIT 4–7
Partial Income Statement

Partial Income Statement—for an *Unprofitable* Period	
Income (loss) before income taxes	$(20,000)
Income tax benefit (recovery of previously recorded taxes)	8,000
Net loss	$(12,000)

We have already seen that income taxes *expense* reduces the amount of before-tax *profits.* Notice now that income tax *benefits*—in the form of tax refunds—can reduce the amount of a pretax *loss.* Thus, income taxes reduce the size of *both* profits and losses. The detailed reporting of profits and losses in the income statement is illustrated in Chapter 5.

Adjusting Entries and Accounting Principles

LO4-7

LEARNING OBJECTIVE
Explain how the principles of *realization* and *matching* relate to adjusting entries.

Adjusting entries are the means by which accountants apply the **realization** and **matching** principles. Through these entries, revenues are recognized as they are *earned,* and expenses are recognized as resources are *used* or consumed in producing the related revenue.

In most cases, the realization principle indicates that revenue should be recognized *at the time goods are sold or services are rendered.* At this point the business has essentially completed the earning process and the sales value of the goods or services can be measured objectively. At any time prior to sale, the ultimate sales value of the goods or services sold can only be estimated. After the sale, the only step that remains is to collect from the customer, and this is usually a relatively certain event.

The matching principle underlies such accounting practices as depreciating plant assets, measuring the cost of supplies used, and amortizing the cost of unexpired insurance policies. All end-of-the-period adjusting entries involving expense recognition are applications of the matching principle.

Costs are matched with revenue in one of two ways:

1. *Direct association of costs with specific revenue transactions.* The ideal method of matching revenue with expenses is to determine the actual amount of expense associated with

---

[7]Tax refunds may be limited to tax payments in recent years. In this introductory discussion, we assume the company has paid sufficient taxes in prior years to permit a full recovery of any "negative tax expense" relating to the loss in the current period.

specific revenue transactions. However, this approach works only for those costs and expenses that can be directly associated with specific revenue transactions. Commissions paid to salespeople are an example of costs that can be *directly associated* with the revenue of a specific accounting period.

2. *Systematic allocation of costs over the useful life of the expenditure.* Many expenditures contribute to the earning of revenue for a number of accounting periods but cannot be directly associated with specific revenue transactions. Examples include the costs of insurance policies and depreciable assets. In these cases, accountants attempt to match revenue and expenses by *systematically allocating the cost to expense* over its useful life. Straight-line depreciation is an example of a systematic technique used to match the cost of an asset with the related revenue that it helps to earn over its useful life.

THE CONCEPT OF MATERIALITY

LO4-8

LEARNING OBJECTIVE
Explain the concept of *materiality.*

Another underlying accounting principle also plays a major role in the making of adjusting entries—the concept of **materiality.** The term *materiality* refers to the *relative importance* of an item or an event. An item is considered material if knowledge of the item might reasonably *influence the decisions* of users of financial statements. Accountants must be sure that all material items are properly reported in financial statements.

However, the financial reporting process should be *cost-effective*—that is, the value of the information should exceed the cost of its preparation. By definition, the accounting treatment accorded to **immaterial** items is of *little or no consequence to decision makers.* Therefore, immaterial items may be handled in the *easiest and most convenient manner.*

Materiality and Adjusting Entries   The concept of materiality enables accountants to shorten and simplify the process of making adjusting entries in several ways. For example:

1. Businesses purchase many assets that have a very low cost or that will be consumed quickly in business operations. Examples include wastebaskets, lightbulbs, and janitorial supplies. The materiality concept permits charging such purchases *directly to expense accounts,* rather than to asset accounts. This treatment conveniently eliminates the need to prepare adjusting entries to depreciate these items.

2. Some expenses, such as telephone bills and utility bills, may be charged to expenses as the bills are *paid,* rather than as the services are used. Technically this treatment violates the *matching principle.* However, accounting for utility bills on a cash basis is very convenient, as the monthly cost of utility service is not even known until the utility bill is received. Under this cash basis approach, the amount of utility expense recorded each month is actually based on the *prior* month's bill.

3. Adjusting entries to accrue unrecorded expenses or unrecorded revenue may actually be *ignored* if the dollar amounts are immaterial.

Materiality Is a Matter of Professional Judgment   Whether a specific item or event is material is a matter of *professional judgment.* In making these judgments, accountants consider several factors.

First, what constitutes a material amount varies with the size of the organization. For example, a $1,000 expenditure may be material in relation to the financial statements of a small business but not to the statements of a large corporation such as **General Electric**.[8] There are no official rules as to what constitutes a material amount, but most accountants would consider amounts of less than 2 percent or 3 percent of net income to be immaterial, unless there were other factors to consider. One such other factor is the *cumulative effect* of numerous immaterial events. Each of a dozen items may be immaterial when considered by itself. When viewed together, however, the combined effect of all 12 items may be material.

---

[8]This point is emphasized by the fact that **General Electric** rounds the dollar amounts shown in its financial statements to the nearest $1 million. This rounding of financial statement amounts is, in itself, an application of the materiality concept.

Finally, materiality depends on the *nature* of the item, as well as its dollar amount. Assume, for example, that several managers systematically have been stealing money from the company that they manage. Stockholders probably would consider this fact important even if the dollar amounts were small in relation to the company's total resources.

| YOUR TURN | You as Overnight Auto's Service Department Manager |

You just found out that Betty, one of the best mechanics that you supervise for Overnight Auto, has taken home small items from the company's supplies, such as a screwdriver and a couple of cans of oil. When you talk to Betty, she suggests that these items are immaterial to Overnight Auto because they are not recorded in the inventory and they are expensed when they are purchased. How should you respond to Betty?

(See our comments on the Online Learning Center website.)

Note to students: In the assignment material accompanying this textbook, you are to consider all dollar amounts to be material, unless the problem specifically raises the question of materiality.

EFFECTS OF THE ADJUSTING ENTRIES

On pages 142 and 143, we identified four types of adjusting entries, each of which involve one income statement account and one balance sheet account. The effects of these adjustment types on the income statement and balance sheet are summarized in Exhibit 4–8.

EXHIBIT 4–8

The Effects of Adjusting Entries on The Financial Statements

	Income Statement			Balance Sheet		
Adjustment	**Revenue**	**Expenses**	**Net Income**	**Assets**	**Liabilities**	**Owners' Equity**
Type I Converting Assets to Expenses	No effect	Increase	Decrease	Decrease	No effect	Decrease
Type II Converting Liabilities to Revenue	Increase	No effect	Increase	No effect	Decrease	Increase
Type III Accruing Unpaid Expenses	No effect	Increase	Decrease	No effect	Increase	Decrease
Type IV Accruing Uncollected Revenue	Increase	No effect	Increase	Increase	No effect	Increase

The four adjustment types were illustrated and discussed in nine separate *adjusting entries* made by Overnight on December 31. These adjustments appear in the format of general journal entries in Exhibit 4–9. (Overnight also recorded many *transactions* throughout the month of December. These transactions are not illustrated here but were accounted for in the manner described in Chapter 3.)

EXHIBIT 4–9

Adjusting Entries

OVERNIGHT AUTO SERVICE GENERAL JOURNAL DECEMBER 31, 2015			
Date	**Account Titles and Explanation**	**Debit**	**Credit**
2015			
Dec. 31	Supplies Expense	600	
	Shop Supplies		600
	December shop supplies adjustment.		
31	Insurance Expense	1,500	
	Unexpired Insurance		1,500
	December Insurance adjustment.		
31	Depreciation Expense: Building	150	
	Accumulated Depreciation: Building		150
	December depreciation adjustment on buildings ($36,000 ÷ 240 mo.).		
31	Depreciation Expense: Tools and Equipment	200	
	Accumulated Depreciation: Tools and Equipment		200
	December depreciation adjustment on tools and equipment ($12,000 ÷ 60 mo.).		
31	Unearned Rent Revenue	3,000	
	Rent Revenue Earned		3,000
	December unearned revenue adjustment ($9,000 ÷ 3 mo.).		
31	Wages Expense	1,950	
	Wages Payable		1,950
	December adjustment to accrue wages payable.		
31	Interest Expense	30	
	Interest Payable		30
	December adjustment to accrue interest payable ($4,000 × .09 × 1/12).		
31	Accounts Receivable	750	
	Repair Service Revenue		750
	December adjustment to accrue repair service revenue.		
31	Income Taxes Expense	4,020	
	Income Taxes Payable		4,020
	December adjustment to accrue income taxes payable.		

 Adjusting entries are recorded only at the end of the period

After these adjustments are posted to the ledger, Overnight's ledger accounts will be up-to-date (except for the balance in the Retained Earnings account).[9] The company's **adjusted trial balance** at December 31, 2015, appears in Exhibit 4–10. (For emphasis, those accounts affected by the month-end *adjusting entries* are shown in red.)

Overnight's financial statements are prepared directly from the adjusted trial balance. Note the order of the accounts: All balance sheet accounts are followed by the statement of retained earnings accounts and then the income statement accounts. In Chapter 5, we illustrate exactly how these three financial statements are prepared.

---

[9]The balance in the Retained Earnings account will be brought up-to-date during the closing process, discussed in Chapter 5.

EXHIBIT 4–10
Adjusted Trial Balance

**OVERNIGHT AUTO SERVICE
ADJUSTED TRIAL BALANCE
DECEMBER 31, 2015**

Balance sheet accounts

Cash	$ 18,592	
Accounts receivable	7,250	
Shop supplies	1,200	
Unexpired insurance	3,000	
Tools and equipment	12,000	
Accumulated depreciation: tools and equipment		$ 2,200
Building	36,000	
Accumulated depreciation: building		1,650
Land	52,000	
Notes payable		4,000
Accounts payable		2,690
Wages payable		1,950
Income taxes payable		5,580
Interest payable		30
Unearned rent revenue		6,000
Capital stock		80,000

Statement of retained earnings accounts

Retained earnings (**Note:** still must be updated for transactions recorded in the accounts listed below. Closing entries serve this purpose.)		0
Dividends	14,000	

Income statement accounts

Repair service revenue		172,000
Rent revenue earned		3,000
Advertising expense	3,900	
Wages expense	58,750	
Supplies expense	7,500	
Depreciation expense: building	1,650	
Depreciation expense: tools and equipment	2,200	
Utilities expense	19,400	
Insurance expense	15,000	
Interest expense	30	
Income taxes expense	26,628	
	$279,100	$279,100

LO4-9

LEARNING OBJECTIVE
Prepare an adjusted trial balance and describe its purpose.

Concluding Remarks

Throughout this chapter, we illustrated end-of-period adjusting entries arising from *timing differences* between cash flows and revenue or expense recognition. In short, the adjusting process helps to ensure that appropriate amounts of revenue and expense are measured and reported in a company's income statement.

In Chapter 5, we continue with our illustration of Overnight Auto Service and demonstrate how adjusting entries are reflected throughout a company's financial statements.

Later chapters explain why accurate income measurement is of critical importance to investors and creditors in estimating the timing and amounts of a company's future cash flows. We also illustrate how understanding certain timing differences enables managers to budget and to plan for future operations.

Ethics, Fraud, & Corporate Governance

Improper accounting for operating costs has often resulted in the SEC bringing action against companies for fraudulent financial reporting. Expenditures that are expected only to benefit the year in which they are made should be expensed (deducted from revenue in the determination of net income for the current period). Companies that engage in fraud will often defer these expenditures by capitalizing them (they debit an asset account reported in the balance sheet instead of an expense account reported in the income statement).

Prior to **Enron** and **WorldCom**, one of the largest financial scandals in U.S. history occurred at **Waste Management**. **Waste Management** was the world's largest waste services company. The improper accounting at **Waste Management** lasted for approximately five years and resulted in an overstatement of earnings during this time period of $1.7 billion. Investors lost over $6 billion when **Waste Management**'s improper accounting was revealed.

Waste Management's scheme for overstating earnings was simple. The company deferred recognizing normal operating expenditures as expenses until future periods. These improper deferrals were accomplished in a number of different ways, many of which involved improper accounting for long-term assets. For example, **Waste Management** incurred costs in buying and developing land to be used as landfills (i.e., garbage dumps). Capitalizing these costs—treating them as long-term assets—was proper accounting. However, in certain cases, the company was not able to secure the necessary governmental permits and approvals to use the purchased land as intended. In these cases, the costs that had been capitalized and reported as landfills in the balance sheet should have been expensed immediately, thereby reducing net income for the year in which the company's failure to obtain government permits and approvals occurred.

END-OF-CHAPTER REVIEW

LO4-1 **Explain the purpose of adjusting entries.** The purpose of adjusting entries is to allocate revenue and expenses among accounting periods in accordance with the realization and matching principles. These end-of-period entries are necessary because revenue may be earned and expenses may be incurred in periods other than the period in which related cash flows are recorded.

LO4-2 **Describe and prepare the four basic types of adjusting entries.** The four basic types of adjusting entries are made to (1) convert assets to expenses, (2) convert liabilities to revenue, (3) accrue unpaid expenses, and (4) accrue uncollected revenue. Often a transaction affects the revenue or expenses of *two or more* accounting periods. The related cash inflow or outflow does not always coincide with the period in which these revenue or expense items are recorded. Thus, the need for adjusting entries results from *timing differences* between the receipt or disbursement of cash and the recording of revenue or expenses.

LO4-3 **Prepare adjusting entries to convert assets to expenses.** When an expenditure is made that will benefit more than one accounting period, an asset account is debited and cash is credited. The asset account is used to *defer* (or postpone) expense recognition until a later date. At the end of each period benefiting from this expenditure, an adjusting entry is made to transfer an appropriate amount from the asset account to an *expense* account. This adjustment reflects the fact that part of the asset's cost has been *matched* against revenue in the measurement of income for the current period.

LO4-4 **Prepare adjusting entries to convert liabilities to revenue.** Customers sometimes pay in advance for services to be rendered in later accounting periods. For accounting purposes, the cash received does *not* represent revenue until it has been *earned.* Thus, the recognition of revenue must be *deferred* until it is earned. Advance collections from customers are recorded by debiting Cash and by crediting a *liability* account for *unearned* revenue. This liability is sometimes called Customer Deposits, Advance Sales, or Deferred Revenue. As unearned revenue becomes earned, an adjusting entry is made at the end of each period to transfer an appropriate amount from the liability account to a *revenue* account. This adjustment reflects the fact that all or part of the company's obligation to its customers has been fulfilled and that revenue has been realized.

LO4-5 **Prepare adjusting entries to accrue unpaid expenses.** Some expenses accumulate (or *accrue*) in the current period but are not *paid* until a future period. These accrued expenses are recorded as part of the adjusting process at the end of each period by debiting the appropriate expense

(e.g., Salary Expense, Interest Expense, or Income Taxes Expense), and by crediting a liability account (e.g., Salaries Payable, Interest Payable, or Income Taxes Payable). In future periods, as cash is disbursed in settlement of these liabilities, the appropriate liability account is debited and Cash is credited. *Note:* Recording the accrued expense in the current period is the adjusting entry. Recording the disbursement of cash in a future period is *not* considered an adjusting entry.

LO4-6 **Prepare adjusting entries to accrue uncollected revenue.** Some revenues are earned (or *accrued*) in the current period but are not *collected* until a future period. These revenues are normally recorded as part of the adjusting process at the end of each period by debiting an asset account called Accounts Receivable, and by crediting the appropriate revenue account. In future periods, as cash is collected in settlement of outstanding receivables, Cash is debited and Accounts Receivable is credited. *Note:* Recording the accrued revenue in the current period is the adjusting entry. Recording the receipt of cash in a future period is *not* considered an adjusting entry.

LO4-7 **Explain how the principles of *realization* and *matching* relate to adjusting entries.** Adjusting entries are the *tools* by which accountants apply the realization and matching principles. Through these entries, revenues are recognized as they are *earned,* and expenses are recognized as resources are *used* or consumed in producing the related revenue.

LO4-8 **Explain the concept of *materiality*.** The concept of materiality allows accountants to use estimated amounts and to ignore certain accounting principles if these actions will not have a material effect on the financial statements. A material effect is one that might reasonably be expected to influence the decisions made by the users of financial statements. Thus, accountants may account for immaterial items and events in the easiest and most convenient manner.

LO4-9 **Prepare an adjusted trial balance and describe its purpose.** The adjusted trial balance reports all of the balances in the general ledger *after* the end-of-period adjusting entries have been made and posted. Generally, all of a company's balance sheet accounts are listed, followed by the statement of retained earnings accounts and, finally, the income statement accounts. The amounts shown in the adjusted trial balance are carried forward directly to the financial statements. The adjusted trial balance is *not* considered one of the four general-purpose financial statements introduced in Chapter 2. Rather, it is simply a *schedule* (or worksheet) used in preparing the financial statements.

> ## Key Terms Introduced or Emphasized in Chapter 4

accrue (p. 152)   To grow or accumulate over time: for example, interest expense.

accumulated depreciation (p. 150)   A contra-asset account shown as a deduction from the related asset account in the balance sheet. Depreciation taken throughout the useful life of an asset is accumulated in this account.

adjusted trial balance (p. 159)   A schedule indicating the balances in ledger accounts *after* end-of-period adjusting entries have been posted. The amounts shown in the adjusted trial balance are carried directly into financial statements.

adjusting entries (p. 142)   Entries made at the end of the accounting period for the purpose of recognizing revenue and expenses that are not properly measured as a result of journalizing transactions as they occur.

book value (p. 150)   The net amount at which an asset appears in financial statements. For depreciable assets, book value represents cost minus accumulated depreciation. Also called *carrying value*.

contra-asset account (p. 150)   An account with a credit balance that is offset against or deducted from an asset account to produce the proper balance sheet amount for the asset.

depreciable assets (p. 148)   Physical objects with a limited life. The cost of these assets is gradually recognized as depreciation expense.

depreciation (p. 148)   The systematic allocation of the cost of an asset to expense during the periods of its useful life.

immaterial (p. 157)   Something of little or no consequence. Immaterial items may be accounted for in the most convenient manner, without regard to other theoretical concepts.

matching (principle) (p. 156)   The accounting principle of offsetting revenue with the expenses incurred in producing that revenue. Requires recognition of expenses in the periods that the goods and services are used in the effort to produce revenue.

materiality (p. 157)   The relative importance of an item or amount. Items significant enough to influence decisions are said to be *material*. Items lacking this importance are considered *immaterial*. The accounting treatment accorded to immaterial items may be guided by convenience rather than by theoretical principles.

prepaid expenses (p. 146)   Assets representing advance payment of the expenses of future accounting periods. As time passes, adjusting entries are made to transfer the related costs from the asset account to an expense account.

realization (principle) (p. 156)   The accounting principle that governs the timing of revenue recognition. Basically, the principle indicates that revenue should be recognized in the period in which it is earned.

straight-line method of depreciation (p. 149)   The widely used approach of recognizing an equal amount of depreciation expense in each period of a depreciable asset's useful life.

unearned revenue (p. 151)   An obligation to deliver goods or render services in the future, stemming from the receipt of advance payment.

useful life (p. 148)   The period of time that a depreciable asset is expected to be useful to the business. This is the period over which the cost of the asset is allocated to depreciation expense.

Demonstration Problem

Internet Consulting Service, Inc., adjusts its accounts every month. On the following page is the company's year-end *unadjusted* trial balance dated December 31, 2015. (Bear in mind that adjusting entries already have been made for the first 11 months of 2015, but have *not* been made for December.)

Other Data

1. On December 1, the company signed a new rental agreement and paid three months' rent in advance at a rate of $2,100 per month. This advance payment was debited to the Prepaid Office Rent account.
2. Dues and subscriptions expiring during December amounted to $50.
3. An estimate of supplies on hand was made at December 31; the estimated cost of the unused supplies was $450.
4. The useful life of the equipment has been estimated at five years (60 months) from date of acquisition.
5. Accrued interest on notes payable amounted to $100 at year-end. (Set up accounts for Interest Expense and for Interest Payable.)
6. Consulting services valued at $2,850 were rendered during December to clients who had made payment in advance.

INTERNET CONSULTING SERVICE, INC. UNADJUSTED TRIAL BALANCE DECEMBER 31, 2015		
Cash	$ 49,100	
Consulting fees receivable	23,400	
Prepaid office rent	6,300	
Prepaid dues and subscriptions	300	
Supplies	600	
Equipment	36,000	
Accumulated depreciation: equipment		$ 10,200
Notes payable		5,000
Income taxes payable		12,000
Unearned consulting fees		5,950
Capital stock		30,000
Retained earnings		32,700
Dividends	60,000	
Consulting fees earned		257,180
Salaries expense	88,820	
Telephone expense	2,550	
Rent expense	22,000	
Income taxes expense	51,000	
Dues and subscriptions expense	560	
Supplies expense	1,600	
Depreciation expense: equipment	6,600	
Miscellaneous expenses	4,200	
	$353,030	$353,030

7. It is the custom of the firm to bill clients only when consulting work is completed or, in the case of prolonged engagements, at monthly intervals. At December 31, consulting services valued at $11,000 had been rendered to clients but not yet billed. No advance payments had been received from these clients.

8. Salaries earned by employees but not paid as of December 31 amount to $1,700.

9. Income taxes expense for the year is estimated at $56,000. Of this amount, $51,000 has been recognized as expense in prior months, and $39,000 has been paid to tax authorities. The company plans to pay the $17,000 remainder of its income tax liability on January 15.

Instructions

a. Prepare the necessary adjusting journal entries on December 31, 2015.

b. Determine the amounts to be reported in the company's year-end adjusted trial balance for each of the following accounts:

Consulting Fees Earned   Dues and Subscriptions Expense

Salaries Expense   Depreciation Expense: Equipment

Telephone Expense   Miscellaneous Expenses

Rent Expense   Interest Expense

Supplies Expense   Income Taxes Expense

c. Determine the company's net income for the year ended December 31, 2015. (Hint: Use the amounts determined in part **b** above.)

Solution to the Demonstration Problem

a.

INTERNET CONSULTING SERVICE, INC.
GENERAL JOURNAL
DECEMBER 31, 2015

Date	Account Titles and Explanation	Debit	Credit
Dec. 31 2015			
1.	Rent Expense	2,100	
	Prepaid Office Rent		2,100
	December rent adjustment.		
2.	Dues and Subscriptions Expense	50	
	Prepaid Dues and Subscriptions		50
	December dues and subscriptions adjustment.		
3.	Supplies Expense	150	
	Supplies		150
	December supplies adjustment.		
4.	Depreciation Expense: Equipment	600	
	Accumulated Depreciation: Equipment		600
	December depreciation adjustment ($36,000 ÷ 60 mos.).		
5.	Interest Expense	100	
	Interest Payable		100
	December interest adjustment.		
6.	Unearned Consulting Fees	2,850	
	Consulting Fees Earned		2,850
	December unearned revenue adjustment.		
7.	Consulting Fees Receivable	11,000	
	Consulting Fees Earned		11,000
	December accrued revenue adjustment.		
8.	Salaries Expense	1,700	
	Salaries Payable		1,700
	December salaries adjustment.		
9.	Income Taxes Expense	5,000	
	Income Taxes Payable		5,000
	December income tax expense adjustment.		

b.

INTERNET CONSULTING SERVICE, INC. ADJUSTED TRIAL BALANCE DECEMBER 31, 2015			
	Unadjusted Trial Balance Amount	+ Adjustment =	Adjusted Trial Balance Amount
Consulting Fees Earned	$257,180	(6) $ 2,850	
		(7) $11,000	$271,030
Salaries Expense	$ 88,820	(8) $ 1,700	$ 90,520
Telephone Expense	$ 2,550	None	$ 2,550
Rent Expense	$ 22,000	(1) $ 2,100	$ 24,100
Supplies Expense	$ 1,600	(3) $ 150	$ 1,750
Dues and Subscriptions Expense	$ 560	(2) $ 50	$ 610
Depreciation Expense: Equipment	$ 6,600	(4) $ 600	$ 7,200
Miscellaneous Expenses	$ 4,200	None	$ 4,200
Interest Expense	None	(5) $ 100	$ 100
Income Taxes Expense	$ 51,000	(9) $ 5,000	$ 56,000

c. Using the figures computed in part **b,** net income for the year is computed as follows:

Consulting Fees Earned		$271,030
Salaries Expense	$90,520	
Telephone Expense	2,550	
Rent Expense	24,100	
Supplies Expense	1,750	
Dues and Subscriptions Expense	610	
Depreciation Expense: Equipment	7,200	
Miscellaneous Expenses	4,200	
Interest Expense	100	
Income Taxes Expense	56,000	(187,030)
Net Income		$ 84,000

Self-Test Questions

The answers to these questions appear on page 191.

1. The purpose of adjusting entries is to:

   a. Adjust the Retained Earnings account for the revenue, expense, and dividends recorded during the accounting period.

   b. Adjust daily the balances in asset, liability, revenue, and expense accounts for the effects of business transactions.

   c. Apply the realization principle and the matching principle to transactions affecting two or more accounting periods.

   d. Prepare revenue and expense accounts for recording the transactions of the next accounting period.

2. Before month-end adjustments are made, the January 31 trial balance of Rover Excursions contains revenue of $27,900 and expenses of $17,340. Adjustments are necessary for the following items:

   Portion of prepaid rent applicable to January, $2,700

   Depreciation for January, $1,440

   Portion of fees collected in advance earned in January, $3,300

Fees earned in January, not yet billed to customers, $1,950

Net income for January is:

a. $10,560.

b. $17,070.

c. $7,770.

d. Some other amount.

3. The CPA firm auditing Mason Street Recording Studios found that total stockholders' equity was understated and liabilities were overstated. Which of the following errors could have been the cause?

a. Making the adjustment entry for depreciation expense twice.

b. Failure to record interest accrued on a note payable.

c. Failure to make the adjusting entry to record revenue that had been earned but not yet billed to clients.

d. Failure to record the earned portion of fees received in advance.

4. Assume Fisher Corporation usually earns taxable income, but sustains a *loss* in the current period. The entry to record income taxes expense in the current period will most likely (indicate all correct answers):

a. Increase the amount of that loss.

b. Include a credit to the Income Taxes Expense account.

c. Be an adjusting entry, rather than an entry to record a transaction completed during the period.

d. Include a credit to Income Taxes Payable.

5. The concept of *materiality* (indicate all correct answers):

a. Requires that financial statements be accurate to the nearest dollar, but need not show cents.

b. Is based upon what users of financial statements are thought to consider important.

c. Permits accountants to ignore generally accepted accounting principles in certain situations.

d. Permits accountants to use the easiest and most convenient means of accounting for events that are *immaterial*.

ASSIGNMENT MATERIAL   ## Discussion Questions

1. What is the purpose of making adjusting entries? Your answer should relate adjusting entries to the goals of accrual accounting.

2. Do adjusting entries affect income statement accounts, balance sheet accounts, or both? Explain.

3. Why does the recording of adjusting entries require a better understanding of the concepts of accrual accounting than does the recording of routine revenue and expense transactions occurring throughout the period?

4. Why does the purchase of a one-year insurance policy four months ago give rise to insurance expense in the current month?

5. If services have been rendered to customers during the current accounting period but no revenue has been recorded and no bill has been sent to the customers, why is an adjusting entry needed? What types of accounts should be debited and credited by this entry?

6. What is meant by the term *unearned revenue?* Where should an unearned revenue account appear in the financial statements? As the work is done, what happens to the balance of an unearned revenue account?

7. Briefly explain the concept of *materiality.* If an item is not material, how is the item treated for financial reporting purposes?

8. Discuss the realization principle and how it is applied in the recognition of revenue. Does the receipt of cash for customers necessarily coincide with the recognition of revenue? Explain.

9. Discuss the matching principle and how it is applied in the recognition of expenses. Does the payment of cash necessarily coincide with the recognition of an expense? Explain.

10. Would a $1,000 expenditure be considered material to all businesses? Explain.

11. List various accounts in the balance sheet that represent *deferred expenses.*

12. How is *deferred revenue* reported in the balance sheet?

13. How do accrued but unpaid expenses affect the balance sheet?

14. How does accrued but uncollected revenue affect the balance sheet?

15. Explain how Royal Caribbean accounts for customer deposits as passengers purchase cruise tickets in advance.

Brief Exercises

LO4-3, LO4-4
BRIEF EXERCISE 4.1
Prepaid Expenses and
Unearned Revenue

On November 1, Girtz Corporation purchased a six-month insurance policy from The Tomptee Agency for $4,500.

a. Prepare the necessary adjusting entry for Girtz Corporation on November 30, assuming it recorded the November 1 expenditure as Unexpired Insurance.

b. Prepare the necessary adjusting entry for The Tomptee Agency on November 30, assuming it recorded Girtz's payment as Unearned Insurance Premiums.

LO4-3, LO4-4
BRIEF EXERCISE 4.2
Prepaid Expenses and
Unearned Revenue

On February 1, Watson Storage agreed to rent Hillbourne Manufacturing warehouse space for $300 per month. Hillbourne Manufacturing paid the first three months' rent in advance.

a. Prepare the necessary adjusting entry for Hillbourne Manufacturing on February 28, assuming it recorded the expenditure on February 1 as Prepaid Rent.

b. Prepare the necessary adjusting entry for Watson Storage on February 28, assuming it recorded Hillbourne Manufacturing's payment as Unearned Rent Revenue.

LO4-3
BRIEF EXERCISE 4.3
Accounting for Supplies

On March 1, Phonic Corporation had office supplies on hand of $1,000. During the month, Phonic purchased additional supplies costing $500. Approximately $200 of unused office supplies remain on hand at the end of the month.

Prepare the necessary adjusting entry on March 31 to account for office supplies.

LO4-3
BRIEF EXERCISE 4.4
Accounting for Depreciation

On January 2, 2010, Hagen Corporation purchased equipment costing $144,000. Hagen performs adjusting entries monthly.

a. Record this equipment's depreciation expense on December 31, 2015, assuming its estimated life was eight years on January 2, 2010.

b. Determine the amount of the equipment's accumulated depreciation reported in the balance sheet dated December 31, 2015.

LO4-6
BRIEF EXERCISE 4.5
Accruing Uncollected
Revenue

Ted's Tax Service had earned—but not yet recorded—the following client service revenue at the end of the current accounting period:

Account Number	Hours Billable	Hourly Billing Rate
Account #4067	8	$80
Account #3940	15	$60
Account #1852	18	$95

Prepare the necessary adjusting entry to record Ted's unbilled client service revenue.

LO4-4
BRIEF EXERCISE 4.6
Unearned Revenue

Jasper's unadjusted trial balance reports Unearned Client Revenue of $4,000 and Client Revenue Earned of $30,000. An examination of client records reveals that $2,500 of previously unearned revenue has now been earned.

a. Prepare the necessary adjusting entry pertaining to these accounts.

b. At what amount will Client Revenue Earned be reported in Jasper's income statement?

LO4-5
BRIEF EXERCISE 4.7
Accruing Unpaid Salaries

Milford Corporation pays its employees on the fifteenth of each month. Accrued, but unpaid, salaries on December 31, 2015, totaled $175,000. Salaries earned by Milford's employees from January 1 through January 15, 2016, totaled $180,000.

a. Prepare the necessary adjusting entry for salaries expense on December 31, 2015.

b. Record the company's payment of salaries on January 15, 2016.

LO4-5
BRIEF EXERCISE 4.8
Accruing Unpaid Interest

Jump Corporation borrowed $60,000 on December 1, 2015, by issuing a two-month, 4 percent note payable to Service One Credit Union. The entire amount of the loan, plus interest, is due February 1, 2016.

a. Prepare the necessary adjusting entry for interest expense on December 31, 2015.

b. Record the repayment of the loan plus interest on February 1, 2016.

LO4-5
BRIEF EXERCISE 4.9
Accruing Unpaid Income
Taxes

Hunter's unadjusted trial balance dated December 31, 2015, reports Income Taxes Expense of $70,000, and Income Taxes Payable of $20,000. The company's accountant estimates that income taxes expense for the *entire year* ended December 31, 2015, is $85,000.

a. Prepare the necessary adjusting entry for income taxes expense on December 31, 2015.

b. Determine the amount of income taxes payable reported in the balance sheet dated December 31, 2015.

LO4-8
BRIEF EXERCISE 4.10
Concept of Materiality

The concept of materiality is an underlying principle of financial reporting.

a. Briefly explain the concept of materiality.

b. Is $2,500 a "material" dollar amount? Explain.

c. Describe two ways in which the concept of materiality may save accountants' time and effort in making adjusting entries.

Exercises

■ connect
|ACCOUNTING

LO4-1 through LO4-9

EXERCISE 4.1

Accounting Terminology

Listed below are nine technical accounting terms used in this chapter:

Unrecorded revenue	Adjusting entries	Accrued expenses
Book value	Matching principle	Accumulated depreciation
Unearned revenue	Materiality	Prepaid expenses

Each of the following statements may (or may not) describe one of these technical terms. For each statement, indicate the accounting term described, or answer "None" if the statement does not correctly describe any of the terms.

a. The net amount at which an asset is carried in the accounting records as distinguished from its market value.

b. An accounting concept that may justify departure from other accounting principles for purposes of convenience and economy.

c. The offsetting of revenue with expenses incurred in generating that revenue.

d. Revenue earned during the current accounting period but not yet recorded or billed, which requires an adjusting entry at the end of the period.

e. Entries made at the end of the period to achieve the goals of accrual accounting by recording revenue when it is earned and by recording expenses when the related goods and services are used.

f. A type of account credited when customers pay in advance for services to be rendered in the future.

g. A balance sheet category used for reporting advance payments of such items as insurance, rent, and office supplies.

h. An expense representing the systematic allocation of an asset's cost over its useful life.

LO4-1 through LO4-6, LO4-9

EXERCISE 4.2

Effects of Adjusting Entries

Security Service Company adjusts its accounts at the end of the month. On November 30, adjusting entries are prepared to record:

a. Depreciation expense for November.

b. Interest expense that has accrued during November.

c. Revenue earned during November that has not yet been billed to customers.

d. Salaries, payable to company employees, that have accrued since the last payday in November.

e. The portion of the company's prepaid insurance that has expired during November.

f. Earning a portion of the amount collected in advance from a customer, Harbor Restaurant.

Indicate the effect of each of these adjusting entries on the major elements of the company's income statement and balance sheet—that is, on revenue, expenses, net income, assets, liabilities, and owners' equity. Organize your answer in tabular form, using the column headings shown and the symbols **I** for increase, **D** for decrease, and **NE** for no effect. The answer for adjusting entry **a** is provided as an example.

	Income Statement			Balance Sheet		
Adjusting Entry	Revenue −	Expenses =	Net Income	Assets =	Liabilities +	Owners' Equity
a	NE	I	D	D	NE	D

LO4-1 through LO4-7

EXERCISE 4.3

Preparing Adjusting Entries to Convert an Asset to an Expense and to Convert a Liability to Revenue

The Freemont Flyers, a professional soccer team, prepares financial statements on a monthly basis. The soccer season begins in May, but in April the team engaged in the following transactions:

1. Paid $1,500,000 to the municipal stadium as advance rent for use of the facilities for the six-month period from May 1 through October 31. This payment was initially recorded as Prepaid Rent.

2. Collected $6,000,000 cash from the sale of season tickets for the team's home games. The entire amount was initially recorded as Unearned Ticket Revenue. During the month of May, the team played several home games at which $750,000 of the season tickets sold in April were used by fans.

Prepare the two adjusting entries required on May 31.

LO4-1 through LO4-7

EXERCISE 4.4

Preparing Adjusting Entries to Convert an Asset to an Expense and to Convert a Liability to Revenue

Royal Caribbean is one of the world's largest cruise line companies. Its printing costs for brochures are initially recorded as Prepaid Advertising and are later charged to Advertising Expense when they are mailed. Passenger deposits for upcoming cruises are considered unearned revenue and are recorded as Customer Deposits as cash is received. Deposited amounts are later converted to Cruise Revenue as voyages are completed.

a. Where in its financial statements does **Royal Caribbean** report Prepaid Advertising? Where in its financial statements does it report Customer Deposits?

b. Prepare the adjusting entry necessary when brochures costing $2 million are mailed.

c. In its most recent annual report, **Royal Caribbean** reported Customer Deposits of $1.5 billion. Prepare the adjusting entry necessary in the following year as $40 million of this amount is earned.

d. Consider the entire adjusting process at **Royal Caribbean**. Which adjusting entry do you think results in the most significant expense reported in the company's income statement?

LO4-1 through LO4-7

EXERCISE 4.5

Preparing Adjusting Entries to Accrue Revenue and Expenses for Which No Cash Has Been Received

The geological consulting firm of Gilbert, Marsh, & Kester prepares adjusting entries on a monthly basis. Among the items requiring adjustment on December 31, 2015, are the following:

1. The company has outstanding a $50,000, 9 percent, two-year note payable issued on July 1, 2014. Payment of the $50,000 note, *plus* all accrued interest for the two-year loan period, is due in full on June 30, 2016.

2. The firm is providing consulting services to Texas Oil Company at an agreed-upon rate of $1,000 per day. At December 31, 10 days of unbilled consulting services have been provided.

a. Prepare the two adjusting entries required on December 31 to record the accrued interest expense and the accrued consulting revenue earned.

b. Assume that the $50,000 note payable plus all accrued interest are paid in full on June 30, 2016. What portion of the total interest expense associated with this note will be reported in the firm's *2016* income statement?

c. Assume that on January 30, 2016, Gilbert, Marsh, & Kester receive $25,000 from Texas Oil Company in full payment of the consulting services provided in December and January. What portion of this amount constitutes revenue earned in *January?*

LO4-1, LO4-2, LO4-4

EXERCISE 4.6

Deferred Revenue

When **American Airlines** sells tickets for future flights, it debits Cash and credits an account entitled Air Traffic Liability (as opposed to crediting Passenger Revenue Earned). This account, reported recently at nearly $4.5 billion, is among the largest liabilities appearing in the company's balance sheet.

a. Explain why this liability is often referred to as a deferred revenue account.

b. What activity normally *reduces* this liability? Can you think of any *other* transaction that would also reduce this account?

c. Assume that, in a recent flight, passengers of the airline used tickets that they had purchased in advance for $87,500. Record the entry **American Airlines** would make upon completion of this flight.

LO4-1 through LO4-6, LO4-9

EXERCISE 4.7

Preparing Various Adjusting Entries

Sweeney & Allen, a large marketing firm, adjusts its accounts at the end of each month. The following information is available for the year ending December 31, 2015:

1. A bank loan had been obtained on December 1. Accrued interest on the loan at December 31 amounts to $1,500. No interest expense has yet been recorded.

2. Depreciation of the firm's office building is based on an estimated life of 30 years. The building was purchased in 2011 for $450,000.

3. Accrued, but unbilled, revenue during December amounts to $75,000.

4. On March 1, the firm paid $2,400 to renew a 12-month insurance policy. The entire amount was recorded as Prepaid Insurance.

5. The firm received $15,000 from King Biscuit Company in advance of developing a six-month marketing campaign. The entire amount was initially recorded as Unearned Revenue. At December 31, $9,000 had actually been *earned* by the firm.

6. The company's policy is to pay its employees every Friday. Since December 31 fell on a Wednesday, there was an accrued liability for salaries amounting to $1,900.

a. Record the necessary adjusting journal entries on December 31, 2015.

b. By how much did Sweeney & Allen's net income increase or decrease as a result of the adjusting entries performed in part **a?** (Ignore income taxes.)

LO4-1, LO4-2, LO4-5
EXERCISE 4.8
Notes Payable and Interest

Jesse Company adjusts its accounts *monthly* and closes its accounts on December 31. On October 31, 2015, Jesse Company signed a note payable and borrowed $150,000 from a bank for a period of six months at an annual interest rate of 6 percent.

a. How much is the total interest expense over the life of the note? How much is the monthly interest expense? (Assume equal amounts of interest expense each month.)

b. In the company's annual balance sheet at December 31, 2015, what is the amount of the liability to the bank?

c. Prepare the journal entry to record issuance of the note payable on October 31, 2015.

d. Prepare the adjusting entry to accrue interest on the note at December 31, 2015.

e. Assume the company prepared a balance sheet at March 31, 2016. State the amount of the liability to the bank at this date.

LO4-1 through LO4-7,
LO4-9
EXERCISE 4.9
Relationship of Adjusting
Entries to Business
Transactions

Among the ledger accounts used by Rapid Speedway are the following: Prepaid Rent, Rent Expense, Unearned Admissions Revenue, Admissions Revenue, Prepaid Printing, Printing Expense, Concessions Receivable, and Concessions Revenue. For each of the following items, provide the journal entry (if one is needed) to record the initial transaction and provide the adjusting entry, if any, required on May 31, assuming the company makes adjusting entries monthly.

a. On May 1, borrowed $500,000 cash from National Bank by issuing a 9 percent note payable due in three months.

b. On May 1, paid rent for six months beginning May 1 at $12,000 per month.

c. On May 2, sold season tickets for a total of $600,000 cash. The season includes 60 racing days: 15 in May, 20 in June, and 25 in July.

d. On May 4, an agreement was reached with Snack-Bars, Inc., allowing that company to sell refreshments at the track in return for 10 percent of the gross receipts from refreshment sales.

LO4-1, LO4-3, LO4-4,
LO4-5, LO4-7
EXERCISE 4.10
Adjusting Entries and the
Balance Sheet

The following information was reported in a recent balance sheet issued by **Microsoft Corporation**:

1. The book value of property and equipment is listed at $90 billion (net of depreciation). Related notes to the financial statements reveal that accumulated depreciation on property and equipment totals $12 billion.

2. Accrued compensation of $2.9 billion is listed as a liability.

3. Short-term unearned revenue is reported at $18 billion, whereas long-term unearned revenue is reported at $1.5 billion. The short-term figure will be converted to revenue within a year. The long-term figure will be converted to revenue over several years. Related notes to the financial statements reveal that the company engages in multiyear leasing of its software products.

a. Determine the original historical cost of the property and equipment reported in **Microsoft Corporation**'s balance sheet.

b. Four types of adjusting entries are illustrated in Exhibit 4–1 (page 144). Explain which type of adjusting entry resulted in the company's accrued compensation figure.

c. Explain why **Microsoft Corporation** reports unearned revenue in its balance sheet. Why might the company report short-term unearned revenue separately from long-term unearned revenue?

LO4-1, LO4-4, LO4-7
EXERCISE 4.11
Reporting of Unearned
Revenue

Listed below are seven corporations that receive cash from customers prior to earning revenue:

America West Corporation (airline)
The New York Times Company (newspaper)
Royal Caribbean (cruise company)
Devry, Inc. (for-profit technical college)
Clear Channel Communications, Inc. (radio broadcasting)
AFLAC Incorporated (health insurance)
Bally Total Fitness Corporation (fitness club)

a. Listed below are the accounts used by these corporations to report unearned revenue:

Deferred Advertising Income	Unearned Premiums
Air Traffic Liability	Unexpired Subscriptions
Deferred Member Revenues	Deferred Tuition Revenue
Customer Deposits	

Match each corporation with the account title it uses to report unearned revenue.

b. Apply the *realization* principle to explain when each of these corporations converts unearned revenue to earned revenue.

LO4-1 through LO4-7,
LO4-9

EXERCISE 4.12

Preparing Adjusting Entries from a Trial Balance

The *unadjusted* and *adjusted* trial balances for Tinker Corporation on December 31, 2015, are shown below:

TINKER CORPORATION
TRIAL BALANCES
DECEMBER 31, 2015

	Unadjusted Debit	Unadjusted Credit	Adjusted Debit	Adjusted Credit
Cash	$ 35,200		$ 35,200	
Accounts receivable	29,120		34,120	
Unexpired insurance	1,200		600	
Prepaid rent	5,400		3,600	
Office supplies	680		380	
Equipment	60,000		60,000	
Accumulated depreciation: equipment		$ 49,000		$ 50,000
Accounts payable		900		900
Notes payable		5,000		5,000
Interest payable		200		250
Salaries payable		—		2,100
Income taxes payable		1,570		2,170
Unearned revenue		6,800		3,800
Capital stock		25,000		25,000
Retained earnings		30,000		30,000
Fees earned		91,530		99,530
Advertising expense	1,500		1,500	
Insurance expense	6,600		7,200	
Rent expense	19,800		21,600	
Office supplies expense	1,200		1,500	
Repairs expense	4,800		4,800	
Depreciation expense: equipment	11,000		12,000	
Salaries expense	26,300		28,400	
Interest expense	200		250	
Income taxes expense	7,000		7,600	
	$210,000	$210,000	$218,750	$218,750

Journalize the nine adjusting entries that the company made on December 31, 2015.

LO4-1 through LO4-6

EXERCISE 4.13

Effects of Adjusting Entries

Four types of adjusting entries were identified in this chapter:

Type I	Converting Assets to Expenses
Type II	Converting Liabilities to Revenue
Type III	Accruing Unpaid Expenses
Type IV	Accruing Uncollected Revenue

Complete the following table by indicating the effect of each adjusting entry type on the major elements of the income statement and balance sheet. Use the symbols **I** for increase, **D** for decrease, and **NE** for no effect.

Adjustment Type	Income Statement			Balance Sheet		
	Revenue	Expenses	Net Income	Assets	Liabilities	Owners' Equity
Type I						
Type II						
Type III						
Type IV						

LO4-1 through LO4-8

EXERCISE 4.14

Accounting Principles

For each of the situations described below, indicate the underlying accounting principle that is being *violated*. Choose from the following principles:

Matching Materiality
Cost Realization
Objectivity

If you do not believe that the practice violates any of these principles, answer "None" and explain.

a. The bookkeeper of a large metropolitan auto dealership depreciates the $7.20 cost of metal wastebaskets over a period of 10 years.

b. A small commuter airline recognizes no depreciation expense on its aircraft because the planes are maintained in "as good as new" condition.

c. Palm Beach Hotel recognizes room rental revenue on the date that a reservation is received. For the winter season, many guests make reservations as much as a year in advance.

LO4-1, LO4-2

EXERCISE 4.15

Using the Financial Statements of Home Depot, Inc.

The financial statements of **Home Depot, Inc.,** appear in Appendix A at the end of this textbook. Examine the company's consolidated balance sheet and identify specific accounts that may have required adjusting entries at the end of the year.

Problem Set A

LO4-1 through LO4-7

PROBLEM 4.1A

Preparing Adjusting Entries

Florida Palms Country Club adjusts its accounts *monthly*. Club members pay their annual dues in advance by January 4. The entire amount is initially credited to Unearned Membership Dues. At the end of each month, an appropriate portion of this amount is credited to Membership Dues Earned. Guests of the club normally pay green fees before being allowed on the course. The amounts collected are credited to Green Fee Revenue at the time of receipt. Certain guests, however, are billed for green fees at the end of the month. The following information is available as a source for preparing adjusting entries at December 31:

1. Salaries earned by golf course employees that have not yet been recorded or paid amount to $9,600.

2. The Tampa University golf team used Florida Palms for a tournament played on December 30 of the current year. At December 31, the $1,800 owed by the team for green fees had not yet been recorded or billed.

3. Membership dues earned in December, for collections received in January, amount to $106,000.

4. Depreciation of the country club's golf carts is based on an estimated life of 15 years. The carts had originally been purchased for $180,000. The straight-line method is used.

   (*Note:* The clubhouse building was constructed in 1925 and is fully depreciated.)

5. A 12-month bank loan in the amount of $45,000 had been obtained by the country club on November 1. Interest is computed at an annual rate of 8 percent. The entire $45,000, plus all of the interest accrued over the 12-month life of the loan, is due in full on October 31 of the upcoming year. The necessary adjusting entry was made on November 30 to record the first month of accrued interest expense. However, no adjustment has been made to record interest expense accrued in December.

6. A one-year property insurance policy had been purchased on March 1. The entire premium of $7,800 was initially recorded as Unexpired Insurance.

7. In December, Florida Palms Country Club entered into an agreement to host the annual tournament of the Florida Seniors Golf Association. The country club expects to generate green fees of $4,500 from this event.

8. Unrecorded Income Taxes Expense accrued in December amounts to $19,000. This amount will not be paid until January 15.

Instructions

a. For each of the above numbered paragraphs, prepare the necessary adjusting entry (including an explanation). If no adjusting entry is required, explain why.

b. Four types of adjusting entries are described at the beginning of the chapter. Using these descriptions, identify the type of each adjusting entry prepared in part **a** above.

c. Although Florida Palms's clubhouse building is fully depreciated, it is in excellent physical condition. Explain how this can be.

LO4-1 through LO4-6, LO4-9

PROBLEM 4.2A

Preparing and Analyzing the Effects of Adjusting Entries

Enchanted Forest, a large campground in South Carolina, adjusts its accounts *monthly*. Most guests of the campground pay at the time they check out, and the amounts collected are credited to Camper Revenue. The following information is available as a source for preparing the adjusting entries at December 31:

1. Enchanted Forest invests some of its excess cash in certificates of deposit (CDs) with its local bank. Accrued interest revenue on its CDs at December 31 is $400. None of the interest has yet been received. (Debit Interest Receivable.)

2. A six-month bank loan in the amount of $12,000 had been obtained on September 1. Interest is to be computed at an annual rate of 8.5 percent and is payable when the loan becomes due.

3. Depreciation on buildings owned by the campground is based on a 25-year life. The original cost of the buildings was $600,000. The Accumulated Depreciation: Buildings account has a credit balance of $310,000 at December 31, prior to the adjusting entry process. The straight-line method of depreciation is used.

4. Management signed an agreement to let Boy Scout Troop 538 of Lewisburg, Pennsylvania, use the campground in June of next year. The agreement specifies that the Boy Scouts will pay a daily rate of $15 per campsite, with a clause providing a minimum total charge of $1,475.

5. Salaries earned by campground employees that have not yet been paid amount to $1,250.

6. As of December 31, Enchanted Forest has earned $2,400 of revenue from current campers who will not be billed until they check out. (Debit Camper Revenue Receivable.)

7. Several lakefront campsites are currently being leased on a long-term basis by a group of senior citizens. Six months' rent of $5,400 was collected in advance and credited to Unearned Camper Revenue on October 1 of the current year.

8. A bus to carry campers to and from town and the airport had been rented the first week of December at a daily rate of $40. At December 31, no rental payment has been made, although the campground has had use of the bus for 25 days.

9. Unrecorded Income Taxes Expense accrued in December amounts to $8,400. This amount will not be paid until January 15.

Instructions

a. For each of the above numbered paragraphs, prepare the necessary adjusting entry (including an explanation). If no adjusting entry is required, explain why.

b. Four types of adjusting entries are described at the beginning of the chapter. Using these descriptions, identify the type of each adjusting entry prepared in part **a** above.

c. Indicate the effects that each of the adjustments in part **a** will have on the following six *total amounts* in the campground's financial statements for the month of *December*. Organize your answer in tabular form, using the column headings shown below. Use the letters **I** for increase, **D** for decrease, and **NE** for no effect. Adjusting entry **1** is provided as an example.

	Income Statement				Balance Sheet		
Adjusting	Revenue	− Expenses	Net = Income		Assets =	Liabilities +	Owners' Equity
1	I	NE	I		I	NE	I

d. What is the amount of interest expense recognized for the *entire current year* on the $12,000 bank loan obtained September 1?

e. Compute the *book value* of the campground's buildings to be reported in the current year's December 31 balance sheet. (Refer to paragraph **3.**)

LO4-1 through LO4-7, LO4-9

PROBLEM 4.3A

Analysis of Adjusted Data

Gunflint Adventures operates an airplane service that takes fishing parties to a remote lake resort in northern Manitoba, Canada. Individuals *must* purchase their tickets at least one month in advance during the busy summer season. The company adjusts its accounts only once each month. Selected balances appearing in the company's June 30 *adjusted* trial balance appear as follows:

	Debit	Credit
Prepaid airport rent	$ 9,000	
Unexpired insurance	4,200	
Airplane	288,000	
Accumulated depreciation: airplane		$80,000
Unearned passenger revenue		75,000

Other Information

1. The airplane is being depreciated over a 15-year life with no residual value.
2. Unearned passenger revenue represents advance ticket sales for bookings in July and August at $300 per ticket.
3. Six months' airport rent had been prepaid on May 1.
4. The unexpired insurance is what remains of a 12-month policy purchased on February 1.
5. Passenger revenue earned in June totaled $40,000.

Instructions

a. Determine the following:
   1. The age of the airplane in months.
   2. The monthly airport rent expense.
   3. The amount paid for the 12-month insurance policy on February 1.

b. Prepare the adjusting entries made on June 30 involving the following accounts:
   1. Depreciation Expense: Airplane
   2. Airport Rent Expense
   3. Insurance Expense
   4. Passenger Revenue Earned

LO4-1 through LO4-7, LO4-9

PROBLEM 4.4A

Preparing Adjusting Entries from a Trial Balance

Campus Theater adjusts its accounts every *month*. The company's *unadjusted* trial balance dated August 31, 2015, is on page 176. Additional information is provided for use in preparing the company's adjusting entries for the month of August. (Bear in mind that adjusting entries *have* already been made for the first seven months of 2015, but *not* for August.)

CAMPUS THEATER
UNADJUSTED TRIAL BALANCE
AUGUST 31, 2015

Cash	$ 20,000	
Prepaid film rental	31,200	
Land	120,000	
Building	168,000	
Accumulated depreciation: building		$ 14,000
Fixtures and equipment	36,000	
Accumulated depreciation: fixtures and equipment		12,000
Notes payable		180,000
Accounts payable		4,400
Unearned admissions revenue (YMCA)		1,000
Income taxes payable		4,740
Capital stock		40,000
Retained earnings		46,610
Dividends	15,000	
Admissions revenue		305,200
Concessions revenue		14,350
Salaries expense	68,500	
Film rental expense	94,500	
Utilities expense	9,500	
Depreciation expense: building	4,900	
Depreciation expense: fixtures and equipment	4,200	
Interest expense	10,500	
Income taxes expense	40,000	
	$622,300	$622,300

Other Data

1. Film rental expense for the month is $15,200. However, the film rental expense for several months has been paid in advance.

2. The building is being depreciated over a period of 20 years (240 months).

3. The fixtures and equipment are being depreciated over a period of five years (60 months).

4. On the first of each month, the theater pays the interest that accrued in the prior month on its note payable. At August 31, accrued interest payable on this note amounts to $1,500.

5. The theater allows the local YMCA to bring children attending summer camp to the movies on any weekday afternoon for a fixed fee of $500 per month. On June 28, the YMCA made a $1,500 advance payment covering the months of July, August, and September.

6. The theater receives a percentage of the revenue earned by Tastie Corporation, the concessionaire operating the snack bar. For snack bar sales in August, Tastie owes Campus Theater $2,250, payable on September 10. No entry has yet been made to record this revenue. (Credit Concessions Revenue.)

7. Salaries earned by employees, but not recorded or paid as of August 31, amount to $1,700. No entry has yet been made to record this liability and expense.

8. Income taxes expense for August is estimated at $4,200. This amount will be paid in the September 15 installment payment.

9. Utilities expense is recorded as monthly bills are received. No adjusting entries for utilities expense are made at month-end.

Instructions

a. For each of the numbered paragraphs, prepare the necessary adjusting entry (including an explanation).

b. Refer to the balances shown in the *unadjusted* trial balance at August 31. How many *months* of expense are included in each of the following account balances? (Remember, Campus Theater adjusts its accounts *monthly*. Thus, the accounts shown were last adjusted on July 31, 2015.)

    1. Utilities Expense

    2. Depreciation Expense

    3. Accumulated Depreciation: Building

c. Assume the theater has been operating profitably all year. Although the August 31 trial balance shows substantial income taxes *expense,* income taxes *payable* is a much smaller amount. This relationship is quite normal throughout much of the year. Explain.

LO4-1 through LO4-7, LO4-9

PROBLEM 4.5A

Preparing Adjusting Entries and Determining Account Balances

Terrific Temps fills temporary employment positions for local businesses. Some businesses pay in advance for services; others are billed after services have been performed. Advanced payments are credited to an account entitled Unearned Fees. Adjusting entries are performed on a *monthly* basis. An unadjusted trial balance dated December 31, 2015, follows. (Bear in mind that adjusting entries have already been made for the first 11 months of 2015, but *not* for December.)

TERRIFIC TEMPS UNADJUSTED TRIAL BALANCE DECEMBER 31, 2015		
Cash	$ 27,020	
Accounts receivable	59,200	
Unexpired insurance	900	
Prepaid rent	3,000	
Office supplies	600	
Equipment	60,000	
Accumulated depreciation: equipment		$ 29,500
Accounts payable		4,180
Notes payable		12,000
Interest payable		320
Unearned fees		6,000
Income taxes payable		4,000
Unearned revenue		20,000
Retained earnings		49,000
Capital stock		25,000
Dividends	3,000	
Fees earned		75,000
Travel expense	5,000	
Insurance expense	2,980	
Rent expense	9,900	
Office supplies expense	780	
Utilities expense	4,800	
Depreciation expense: equipment	5,500	
Salaries expense	30,000	
Interest expense	320	
Income taxes expense	12,000	
	$225,000	$225,000

Other Data

1. Accrued but unrecorded fees earned as of December 31, 2015, amount to $1,500.

2. Records show that $2,500 of cash receipts originally recorded as unearned fees had been earned as of December 31.

3. The company purchased a six-month insurance policy on September 1, 2015, for $1,800.

4. On December 1, 2015, the company paid its rent through February 28, 2016.

5. Office supplies on hand at December 31 amount to $400.

6. All equipment was purchased when the business first formed. The estimated life of the equipment at that time was 10 years (or 120 months).

7. On August 1, 2015, the company borrowed $12,000 by signing a six-month, 8 percent note payable. The entire note, plus six months' accrued interest, is due on February 1, 2016.

8. Accrued but unrecorded salaries at December 31 amount to $2,700.

9. Estimated income taxes expense for the *entire year* totals $15,000. Taxes are due in the first quarter of 2016.

Instructions

a. For each of the numbered paragraphs, prepare the necessary adjusting entry (including an explanation).

b. Determine that amount at which each of the following accounts will be reported in the company's 2015 income statement:

    1. Fees Earned

    2. Travel Expense

    3. Insurance Expense

    4. Rent Expense

    5. Office Supplies Expense

    6. Utilities Expense

    7. Depreciation Expense: Equipment

    8. Interest Expense

    9. Salaries Expense

    10. Income Taxes Expense

c. The unadjusted trial balance reports dividends of $3,000. As of December 31, 2015, have these dividends been paid? Explain.

LO4-1 through LO4-7, LO4-9

PROBLEM 4.6A
Preparing Adjusting Entries and Determining Account Balances

Alpine Expeditions operates a mountain climbing school in Colorado. Some clients pay in advance for services; others are billed after services have been performed. Advance payments are credited to an account entitled Unearned Client Revenue. Adjusting entries are performed on a *monthly* basis. An unadjusted trial balance dated December 31, 2015, follows. (Bear in mind that adjusting entries have already been made for the first 11 months of 2015, but *not* for December.)

ALPINE EXPEDITIONS
UNADJUSTED TRIAL BALANCE
DECEMBER 31, 2015

Cash	$ 13,900	
Accounts receivable	78,000	
Unexpired insurance	18,000	
Prepaid advertising	2,200	
Climbing supplies	4,900	
Climbing equipment	57,600	
Accumulated depreciation: climbing equipment		$ 38,400
Accounts payable		1,250
Notes payable		10,000
Interest payable		150
Income taxes payable		1,200
Unearned client revenue		9,600
Capital stock		17,000
Retained earnings		62,400
Client revenue earned		188,000
Advertising expense	7,400	
Insurance expense	33,000	
Rent expense	16,500	
Climbing supplies expense	8,400	
Repairs expense	4,800	
Depreciation expense: climbing equipment	13,200	
Salaries expense	57,200	
Interest expense	150	
Income taxes expense	12,750	
	$328,000	$328,000

Other Data

1. Accrued but unrecorded fees earned as of December 31 amount to $6,400.

2. Records show that $6,600 of cash receipts originally recorded as unearned client revenue had been earned as of December 31.

3. The company purchased a 12-month insurance policy on June 1, 2015, for $36,000.

4. On December 1, 2015, the company paid $2,200 for numerous advertisements in several climbing magazines. Half of these advertisements have appeared in print as of December 31.

5. Climbing supplies on hand at December 31 amount to $2,000.

6. All climbing equipment was purchased when the business first formed. The estimated life of the equipment at that time was four years (or 48 months).

7. On October 1, 2015, the company borrowed $10,000 by signing an eight-month, 9 percent note payable. The entire note, plus eight months' accrued interest, is due on June 1, 2016.

8. Accrued but unrecorded salaries at December 31 amount to $3,100.

9. Estimated income taxes expense for the *entire year* totals $14,000. Taxes are due in the first quarter of 2016.

Instructions

a. For each of the numbered paragraphs, prepare the necessary adjusting entry (including an explanation).

b. Determine that amount at which each of the following accounts will be reported in the company's balance sheet dated December 31, 2015:

1. Cash
2. Accounts Receivable
3. Unexpired Insurance
4. Prepaid Advertising
5. Climbing Supplies
6. Climbing Equipment

7. Accumulated Depreciation: Climbing Equipment
8. Salaries Payable
9. Notes Payable
10. Interest Payable
11. Income Taxes Payable
12. Unearned Client Revenue

c. Which of the accounts listed in part **b** represent *deferred expenses?* Explain.

LO4-1 through LO4-7, LO4-9

PROBLEM 4.7A

Preparing Adjusting Entries from a Trial Balance

Ken Hensley Enterprises, Inc., is a small recording studio in St. Louis. Rock bands use the studio to mix high-quality demo recordings distributed to talent agents. New clients are required to pay in advance for studio services. Bands with established credit are billed for studio services at the end of each month. Adjusting entries are performed on a *monthly* basis. An *unadjusted* trial balance dated December 31, 2015, follows. (Bear in mind that adjusting entries already have been made for the first 11 months of 2015, but *not* for December.)

KEN HENSLEY ENTERPRISES, INC.
UNADJUSTED TRIAL BALANCE
DECEMBER 31, 2015

Cash	$ 43,170	
Accounts receivable	81,400	
Studio supplies	7,600	
Unexpired insurance	500	
Prepaid studio rent	4,000	
Recording equipment	90,000	
Accumulated depreciation: recording equipment		$ 52,500
Notes payable		16,000
Interest payable		840
Income taxes payable		3,200
Unearned studio revenue		9,600
Capital stock		80,000
Retained earnings		38,000
Studio revenue earned		107,000
Salaries expense	18,000	
Supplies expense	1,200	
Insurance expense	2,680	
Depreciation expense: recording equipment	16,500	
Studio rent expense	21,000	
Interest expense	840	
Utilities expense	2,350	
Income taxes expense	17,900	
	$307,140	$307,140

Other Data

1. Records show that $4,400 in studio revenue had not yet been billed or recorded as of December 31.

2. Studio supplies on hand at December 31 amount to $6,900.

3. On August 1, 2015, the studio purchased a six-month insurance policy for $1,500. The entire premium was initially debited to Unexpired Insurance.

4. The studio is located in a rented building. On November 1, 2015, the studio paid $6,000 rent in advance for November, December, and January. The entire amount was debited to Prepaid Studio Rent.

5. The useful life of the studio's recording equipment is estimated to be five years (or 60 months). The straight-line method of depreciation is used.

6. On May 1, 2015, the studio borrowed $16,000 by signing a 12-month, 9 percent note payable to First Federal Bank of St. Louis. The entire $16,000 plus 12 months' interest is due in full on April 30, 2016.

7. Records show that $3,600 of cash receipts originally recorded as Unearned Studio Revenue had been earned as of December 31.

8. Salaries earned by recording technicians that remain unpaid at December 31 amount to $540.

9. The studio's accountant estimates that income taxes expense for the *entire year* ended December 31, 2015, is $19,600. (Note that $17,900 of this amount has already been recorded.)

Instructions

a. For each of the above numbered paragraphs, prepare the necessary adjusting entry (including an explanation).

b. Using figures from the company's unadjusted trial balance in conjunction with the adjusting entries made in part **a,** compute net income for the year ended December 31, 2015.

c. Was the studio's monthly rent for the last 2 months of 2015 more or less than during the first 10 months of the year? Explain your answer.

d. Was the studio's monthly insurance expense for the last five months of 2015 more or less than the average monthly expense for the first seven months of the year? Explain your answer.

e. If the studio purchased all of its equipment when it first began operations, for how many months has it been in business? Explain your answer.

f. Indicate the effect of each adjusting entry prepared in part **a** on the major elements of the company's income statement and balance sheet. Organize your answer in tabular form using the column headings shown. Use the symbols **I** for increase, **D** for decrease, and **NE** for no effect. The answer for the adjusting entry number **1** is provided as an example.

	Income Statement			Balance Sheet		
Adjusting Entry	Revenue	− Expenses	= Net Income	Assets	= Liabilities	+ Owners' Equity
1	I	NE	I	I	NE	I

LO4-1 through LO4-7, LO4-9

PROBLEM 4.8A

Understanding the Effects of Various Errors

Coyne Corporation recently hired Elaine Herrold as its new bookkeeper. Herrold was not very experienced and made seven recording errors during the last accounting period. The nature of each error is described in the following table.

Instructions

Indicate the effect of the following errors on each of the financial statement elements described in the column headings in the table on page 182. Use the following symbols: **O** = overstated, **U** = understated, and **NE** = no effect.

Error	Total Revenue	Total Expenses	Net Income	Total Assets	Total Liabilities	Owners' Equity
a. Recorded a dividend as an expense reported in the income statement.						
b. Recorded the payment of an account payable as a debit to accounts payable and a credit to an expense account.						
c. Failed to record depreciation expense.						
d. Recorded the sale of capital stock as a debit to cash and a credit to retained earnings.						
e. Recorded the receipt of a customer deposit as a debit to cash and a credit to fees earned.						
f. Failed to record expired portion of an insurance policy.						
g. Failed to record accrued interest earned on an outstanding note receivable.						

Problem Set B

LO4-1 throught LO4-7

PROBLEM 4.1B

Preparing Adjusting Entries

The Georgia Gun Club adjusts its accounts *monthly* and closes its accounts annually. Club members pay their annual dues in advance by January 4. The entire amount is initially credited to Unearned Membership Dues. At the end of each month, an appropriate portion of this amount is credited to Membership Dues Earned. Guests of the club normally pay their fees before being allowed to use the facilities. The amounts collected are credited to Guest Fee Revenue at the time of receipt. Certain guests, however, are billed at the end of the month. The following information is available as a source for preparing adjusting entries at December 31:

1. Salaries earned by the club's employees that have not yet been recorded or paid amount to $13,600.
2. The Georgia State Police used the club's facilities for target practice on December 30 of the current year. At December 31, the $3,200 owed by the state police for guest fees had not yet been recorded or billed.
3. Membership dues earned in December, for collections received at the beginning of the year, amount to $140,000.
4. Depreciation of the furniture and fixtures in the clubhouse is based on an estimated life of eight years. These items had originally been purchased for $120,000. The straight-line method is used. (*Note:* The clubhouse building was constructed in 1956 and is fully depreciated.)
5. A 12-month bank loan in the amount of $60,000 had been obtained by the club on October 4. Interest is computed at an annual rate of 8 percent. The entire $60,000, plus all of the interest accrued over the 12-month life of the loan, is due in full on September 30 of the upcoming year. The necessary adjusting entry was made on November 30 to record the first two months of accrued interest expense. However, no adjustment has been made to record interest expense accrued in December.
6. A one-year property insurance policy had been purchased on April 30. The entire premium of $10,800 was initially recorded as Unexpired Insurance.
7. In December, the club entered into an agreement to host the annual tournament of the Georgia Junior Rifle Association. The club expects to generate guest fees of $7,200 from this event.
8. Unrecorded Income Taxes Expense accrued in December amounts to $12,600. This amount will not be paid until January 22.

Instructions

a. For each of the above numbered paragraphs, prepare the necessary adjusting entry (including an explanation). If no adjusting entry is required, explain why.

b. Four types of adjusting entries are described at the beginning of the chapter. Using these descriptions, identify the type of each adjusting entry prepared in part **a** above.

c. Although the clubhouse building is fully depreciated, it is in excellent physical condition. Explain how this can be.

LO4-1 through LO4-6, LO4-9

PROBLEM 4.2B

Preparing and Analyzing the Effects of Adjusting Entries

Big Oaks, a large campground in Vermont, adjusts its accounts *monthly* and closes its accounts annually on December 31. Most guests of the campground pay at the time they check out, and the amounts collected are credited to Camper Revenue. The following information is available as a source for preparing the adjusting entries at December 31:

1. Big Oaks invests some of its excess cash in certificates of deposit (CDs) with its local bank. Accrued interest revenue on its CDs at December 31 is $425. None of the interest has yet been received. (Debit Interest Receivable.)

2. An eight-month bank loan in the amount of $12,000 had been obtained on October 1. Interest is to be computed at an annual rate of 8 percent and is payable when the loan becomes due.

3. Depreciation on buildings owned by the campground is based on a 20-year life. The original cost of the buildings was $720,000. The Accumulated Depreciation: Buildings account has a credit balance of $160,000 at December 31, prior to the adjusting entry process. The straight-line method of depreciation is used.

4. Management signed an agreement to let Girl Scouts from Easton, Connecticut, use the campground in June of next year. The agreement specifies that the Girl Scouts will pay a daily rate of $15 per campsite, with a clause providing a minimum total charge of $1,200.

5. Salaries earned by campground employees that have not yet been paid amount to $1,515.

6. As of December 31, Big Oaks has earned $2,700 of revenue from current campers who will not be billed until they check out. (Debit Camper Revenue Receivable.)

7. Several lakefront campsites are currently being leased on a long-term basis by a group of senior citizens. Five months' rent of $7,500 was collected in advance and credited to Unearned Camper Revenue on November 1 of the current year.

8. A bus to carry campers to and from town and the airport had been rented the first week of December at a daily rate of $45. At December 31, no rental payment has been made, although the campground has had use of the bus for 18 days.

9. Unrecorded Income Taxes Expense accrued in December amounts to $6,600. This amount will not be paid until January 15.

Instructions

a. For each of the above numbered paragraphs, prepare the necessary adjusting entry (including an explanation). If no adjusting entry is required, explain why.

b. Four types of adjusting entries are described at the beginning of the chapter. Using these descriptions, identify the type of each adjusting entry prepared in part **a** above.

c. Indicate the effects that each of the adjustments in part **a** will have on the following six *total amounts* in the campground's financial statements for the month of *December*. Organize your answer in tabular form, using the column headings shown below. Use the letters **I** for increase, **D** for decrease, and **NE** for no effect. Adjusting entry **1** is provided as an example.

	Income Statement			Balance Sheet		
Adjusting			Net			Owners'
Entry	Revenue −	Expenses =	Income	Assets =	Liabilities +	Equity
1	I	NE	I	I	NE	I

d. What is the amount of interest expense recognized for the *entire current year* on the $12,000 bank loan obtained October 1?

e. Compute the *book value* of the campground's buildings to be reported in the current year's December 31 balance sheet. (Refer to paragraph **3**.)

LO4-1 through LO4-7, LO4-9

PROBLEM 4.3B

Analysis of Adjusted Data

River Rat, Inc., operates a ferry that takes travelers across the Wild River. The company adjusts its accounts at the end of each month. Selected account balances appearing in the April 30 *adjusted* trial balance are as follows:

	Debit	Credit
Prepaid rent	$18,000	
Unexpired insurance	3,800	
Ferry	93,600	
Accumulated depreciation: ferry		$16,900
Unearned passenger revenue		1,000

Other Data

1. The ferry is being depreciated over an 12-year estimated useful life.
2. The unearned passenger revenue represents tickets good for future rides sold to a resort hotel for $5 per ticket on April 1. During April, 150 of the tickets were used.
3. Six months' rent had been prepaid on April 1.
4. The unexpired insurance is a 12-month fire insurance policy purchased on March 1.

Instructions

a. Determine the following:
   1. The age of the ferry in months.
   2. How many $5 tickets for future rides were sold to the resort hotel on April 1.
   3. The monthly rent expense.
   4. The original cost of the 12-month fire insurance policy.

b. Prepare the adjusting entries that were made on April 30.

LO4-1 through LO4-7, LO4-9

PROBLEM 4.4B
Preparing Adjusting Entries from a Trial Balance

The Off-Campus Playhouse adjusts its accounts every *month*. Below is the company's *unadjusted* trial balance dated September 30, 2015. Additional information is provided for use in preparing the company's adjusting entries for the month of September. (Bear in mind that adjusting entries *have already* been made for the first eight months of 2015, but *not* for September.)

OFF-CAMPUS PLAYHOUSE
UNADJUSTED TRIAL BALANCE
SEPTEMBER 30, 2015

Cash	$ 8,200	
Prepaid costume rental	1,800	
Land	80,000	
Building	150,000	
Accumulated depreciation: building		$ 18,500
Fixtures and equipment	18,000	
Accumulated depreciation: fixtures and equipment		4,500
Notes payable		100,000
Accounts payable		5,700
Unearned admissions revenue (nursing homes)		1,500
Income taxes payable		4,700
Capital stock		9,000
Retained earnings		26,400
Dividends	9,000	
Admissions revenue		180,200
Concessions revenue		19,600
Salaries expense	57,400	
Costume rental expense	2,700	
Utilities expense	7,100	
Depreciation expense: building	4,000	
Depreciation expense: fixtures and equipment	2,400	
Interest expense	8,500	
Income taxes expense	21,000	
	$370,100	$370,100

Other Data

1. Costume rental expense for the month is $600. However, the costume rental expense for several months has been paid in advance.

2. The building is being depreciated over a period of 25 years (300 months).

3. The fixtures and equipment are being depreciated over a period of five years (60 months).

4. On the first of each month, the theater pays the interest which accrued in the prior month on its note payable. At September 30, accrued interest payable on this note amounts to $1,062.

5. The playhouse allows local nursing homes to bring seniors to the plays on any weekday performance for a fixed price of $500 per month. On August 31, a nursing home made a $1,500 advance payment covering the months of September, October, and November.

6. The theater receives a percentage of the revenue earned by Sweet Corporation, the concessionaire operating the snack bar. For snack bar sales in September, Sweet owes Off-Campus Playhouse $4,600, payable on October 14. No entry has yet been made to record this revenue. (Credit Concessions Revenue.)

7. Salaries earned by employees, but not recorded or paid as of September 30, amount to $2,200. No entry has yet been made to record this liability and expense.

8. Income taxes expense for September is estimated at $3,600. This amount will be paid in the October 15 installment payment.

9. Utilities expense is recorded as monthly bills are received. No adjusting entries for utilities expense are made at month-end.

Instructions

a. For each of the numbered paragraphs, prepare the necessary adjusting entry (including an explanation).

b. Refer to the balances shown in the *unadjusted* trial balance at September 30. How many *months* of expense are included in each of the following balances? (Remember, Off-Campus Playhouse adjusts its accounts *monthly*. Thus, the accounts shown were last adjusted on August 31, 2015.)

    1. Utilities expense

    2. Depreciation expense

    3. Accumulated depreciation: building

c. Assume the playhouse has been operating profitably all year. Although the September 30 trial balance shows substantial income taxes *expense*, income taxes *payable* is a much smaller amount. This relationship is quite normal throughout much of the year. Explain.

LO4-1 through LO4-7, LO4-9

PROBLEM 4.5B
Preparing Adjusting Entries and Determining Account Balances

Marvelous Music provides music lessons to student musicians. Some students pay in advance for lessons; others are billed after lessons have been provided. Advance payments are credited to an account entitled Unearned Lesson Revenue. Adjusting entries are performed on a *monthly* basis. An unadjusted trial balance dated December 31, 2015, follows. (Bear in mind that adjusting entries have already been made for the first 11 months of 2015, but *not* for December.)

MARVELOUS MUSIC
UNADJUSTED TRIAL BALANCE
DECEMBER 31, 2015

Cash	$ 15,800	
Accounts receivable	2,100	
Unexpired insurance	3,200	
Prepaid rent	6,000	
Sheet music supplies	450	
Music equipment	180,000	
Accumulated depreciation: music equipment		$ 72,000
Accounts payable		3,500
Notes payable		5,000
Dividends payable		1,000
Interest payable		25
Income taxes payable		3,400
Unearned lesson revenue		1,100
Capital stock		20,000
Retained earnings		56,600
Dividends	1,000	
Lesson revenue earned		154,375
Advertising expense	7,400	
Insurance expense	4,400	
Rent expense	16,500	
Sheet music supplies expense	780	
Utilities expense	5,000	
Depreciation expense: music equipment	33,000	
Salaries expense	27,500	
Interest expense	25	
Income taxes expense	13,845	
	$317,000	$317,000

Other Data

1. Accrued but unrecorded lesson revenue earned as of December 31, 2015, amounts to $3,200.

2. Records show that $800 of cash receipts originally recorded as unearned lesson revenue had been earned as of December 31.

3. The company purchased a 12-month insurance policy on August 1, 2015, for $4,800.

4. On October 1, 2015, the company paid $9,000 for rent through March 31, 2016.

5. Sheet music supplies on hand at December 31 amount to $200.

6. All music equipment was purchased when the business was first formed. Its estimated life at that time was five years (or 60 months).

7. On November 1, 2015, the company borrowed $5,000 by signing a three-month, 6 percent note payable. The entire note, plus three months' accrued interest, is due on February 1, 2016.

8. Accrued but unrecorded salaries at December 31 amount to $3,500.

9. Estimated income taxes expense for the *entire year* totals $22,000. Taxes are due in the first quarter of 2016.

Instructions

a. For each of the numbered paragraphs, prepare the necessary adjusting entry (including an explanation).

b. Determine that amount at which each of the following accounts will be reported in the company's 2015 income statement:

1. Lesson Revenue Earned
2. Advertising Expense
3. Insurance Expense
4. Rent Expense
5. Sheet Music Supplies Expense
6. Utilities Expense
7. Depreciation Expense: Music Equipment
8. Interest Expense
9. Salaries Expense
10. Income Taxes Expense

c. The unadjusted trial balance reports dividends of $1,000. As of December 31, 2015, have these dividends been paid? Explain.

LO4-1 through LO4-7, LO4-9
PROBLEM 4.6B
Preparing Adjusting Entries and Determining Account Balances

Mate Ease is an Internet dating service. All members pay in advance to be listed in the database. Advance payments are credited to an account entitled Unearned Member Dues. Adjusting entries are performed on a *monthly* basis. An unadjusted trial balance dated December 31, 2015, follows. (Bear in mind that adjusting entries have already been made for the first 11 months of 2015, but *not* for December.)

MATE EASE UNADJUSTED TRIAL BALANCE DECEMBER 31, 2015		
Cash	$169,500	
Unexpired insurance	12,800	
Prepaid rent	14,600	
Office supplies	2,160	
Computer equipment	108,000	
Accumulated depreciation: computer equipment		$ 54,000
Accounts payable		4,300
Notes payable		90,000
Interest payable		6,750
Income taxes payable		7,500
Unearned member dues		36,000
Capital stock		40,000
Retained earnings		28,000
Client fees earned		508,450
Advertising expense	17,290	
Insurance expense	35,200	
Rent expense	80,300	
Office supplies expense	18,400	
Internet connection expense	24,000	
Depreciation expense: computer equipment	33,000	
Salaries expense	239,000	
Interest expense	6,750	
Income taxes expense	14,000	
	$775,000	$775,000

Other Data

1. Records show that $21,000 of cash receipts originally recorded as unearned member dues had been earned as of December 31, 2015.

2. The company purchased a six-month insurance policy on October 1, 2015, for $19,200.

3. On November 1, 2015, the company paid $21,900 for rent through January 31, 2016.

4. Office supplies on hand at December 31 amount to $440.

5. All computer equipment was purchased when the business first formed. The estimated life of the equipment at that time was three years (or 36 months).

6. On March 1, 2015, the company borrowed $90,000 by signing a 12-month, 10 percent note payable. The entire note, plus 12 months' accrued interest, is due on March 1, 2016.

7. Accrued but unrecorded salaries at December 31 amount to $10,500.

8. Estimated income taxes expense for the *entire year* totals $16,000. Taxes are due in the first quarter of 2016.

Instructions

a. For each of the numbered paragraphs, prepare the necessary adjusting entry (including an explanation).

b. Determine that amount at which each of the following accounts will be reported in the company's balance sheet dated December 31, 2015:

1.	Cash	7.	Accounts Payable
2.	Unexpired Insurance	8.	Notes Payable
3.	Prepaid Rent	9.	Salaries Payable
4.	Office Supplies	10.	Interest Payable
5.	Computer Equipment	11.	Income Taxes Payable
6.	Accumulated Depreciation: Computer Equipment	12.	Unearned Member Dues

c. Why doesn't the company immediately record advance payments from customers as *revenue?*

LO4-1 through LO4-7, LO4-9

PROBLEM 4.7B

Preparing Adjusting Entries from a Trial Balance

Clint Stillmore operates a private investigating agency called Stillmore Investigations. Some clients pay in advance for services; others are billed after services have been performed. Advance payments are credited to an account entitled Unearned Retainer Fees. Adjusting entries are performed on a *monthly* basis. An *unadjusted* trial balance dated December 31, 2015, follows. (Bear in mind that adjusting entries have already been made for the first 11 months of 2015, but *not* for December.)

Other Data

1. Accrued but unrecorded client fees earned at December 31 amount to $1,500.

2. Records show that $2,500 of cash receipts originally recorded as Unearned Retainer Fees had been earned as of December 31.

3. Office supplies on hand at December 31 amount to $110.

4. The company purchased all of its office equipment when it first began business. At that time, the equipment's estimated useful life was six years (or 72 months).

5. On October 1, 2015, the company renewed its rental agreement paying $1,800 cash for six months' rent in advance.

6. On March 1 of the current year, the company paid $1,080 cash to renew its 12-month insurance policy.

7. Accrued but unrecorded salaries at December 31 amount to $1,900.

8. On June 1, 2015, the company borrowed money from the bank by signing a $9,000, 8 percent, 12-month note payable. The entire note, plus 12 months' accrued interest, is due on May 31, 2016.

9. The company's CPA estimates that income taxes expense for the *entire year* is $7,500.

STILLMORE INVESTIGATIONS
UNADJUSTED TRIAL BALANCE
DECEMBER 31, 2015

Cash	$ 40,585	
Accounts receivable	2,000	
Office supplies	205	
Prepaid rent	1,200	
Unexpired insurance	270	
Office equipment	54,000	
Accumulated depreciation: office equipment		$ 35,250
Accounts payable		1,400
Interest payable		360
Income taxes payable		1,750
Note payable		9,000
Unearned retainer fees		3,500
Capital stock		30,000
Retained earnings		8,000
Dividends	1,000	
Client fees earned		60,000
Office supplies expense	605	
Depreciation expense: office equipment	8,250	
Rent expense	5,775	
Insurance expense	1,010	
Salaries expense	27,100	
Interest expense	360	
Income taxes expense	6,900	
Totals	$149,260	$149,260

Instructions

a. For each of the above numbered paragraphs, prepare the necessary adjusting entry (including an explanation).

b. Prepare the company's adjusted trial balance dated December 31, 2015.

c. Using figures from the adjusted trial balance prepared in b, compute net income for the year ended December 31, 2015.

d. How much was the company's average monthly rent expense in January through September of 2015? Explain your answer.

e. How much was the company's average monthly insurance expense in January and February of 2015? Explain your answer.

f. If the company purchased all of its office equipment when it first began operations, for how many months has it been in business? Explain your answer.

g. Indicate the effect of each adjusting entry prepared in part **a** on the major elements of the company's income statement and balance sheet. Organize your answer in tabular form using the column headings shown. Use the symbols **I** for increase, **D** for decrease, and **NE** for no effect. The answer for adjusting entry number **1** is provided as an example.

	Income Statement			Balance Sheet		
Adjusting Entry	Revenue	− Expenses	= Net Income	Assets	= Liabilities +	Owners' Equity
1	I	NE	I	I	NE	I

**LO4-1 through LO4-7,
LO4-9**

PROBLEM 4.8B

Understanding the Effects
of Various Errors

Stephen Corporation recently hired Tom Waters as its new bookkeeper. Waters is very inexperienced and has made seven recording errors during the last accounting period. The nature of each
error is described in the following table.

Instructions

Indicate the effect of the following errors on each of the financial statement elements described
in the column headings in the table. Use the following symbols: O = overstated, **U** = understated,
and **NE** = no effect

Error	Total Revenue	Total Expenses	Net Income	Total Assets	Total Liabilities	Owners' Equity
a. Recorded a declared but unpaid dividend by debiting dividends and crediting cash.						
b. Recorded a receipt of an account receivable as a debit to cash and a credit to fees earned.						
c. Recorded depreciation expense twice.						
d. Recorded the sale of capital stock as a debit to cash and a credit to revenue.						
e. Purchased equipment and debited supplies expense and credited cash.						
f. Failed to record expired portion of prepaid advertising.						
g. Failed to record accrued and unpaid interest expense.						

Critical Thinking Cases

LO4-1 through LO4-7

CASE 4.1

Should This Be Adjusted?

Property Management Professionals provides building management services to owners of office
buildings and shopping centers. The company closes its accounts at the *end of the calendar year.*
The manner in which the company has recorded several transactions occurring during 2015 is
described as follows:

a. On September 1, received advance payment from a shopping center for property management services to be performed over the three-month period beginning September 1. The entire
amount received was credited directly to a *revenue* account.

b. On December 1, received advance payment from the same customer described in part a for services to be rendered over the three-month period beginning December 1. This time, the entire
amount received was credited to an *unearned* revenue account.

c. Rendered management services for many customers in December. Normal procedure is to
record revenue on the date the customer is billed, which is early in the month after the services
have been rendered.

d. On December 15, made full payment for a one-year insurance policy that goes into effect on
January 2, 2016. The cost of the policy was debited to Unexpired Insurance.

e. Numerous purchases of equipment were debited to asset accounts, rather than to expense
accounts.

f. Payroll expense is recorded when employees are paid. Payday for the last two weeks of
December falls on January 2, 2016.

Instructions

For each item above, explain whether an adjusting entry is needed at *December 31, 2015,* and
state the reasons for your answer. If you recommend an adjusting entry, explain the effects this
entry would have on assets, liabilities, owners' equity, revenue, and expenses in the 2015 financial
statements.

LO4-8

CASE 4.2

The Concept of Materiality

The concept of materiality is one of the most basic principles underlying financial accounting.

a.   Answer the following questions:

   1.   Why is the materiality of a transaction or an event a matter of professional judgment?

   2.   What criteria should accountants consider in determining whether a transaction or an event is material?

   3.   Does the concept of materiality mean that financial statements are not precise, down to the last dollar? Does this concept make financial statements less useful to most users?

b.   **Avis Rent-a-Car** purchases a large number of cars each year for its rental fleet. The cost of any individual automobile is immaterial to **Avis**, which is a very large corporation. Would it be acceptable for **Avis** to charge the purchase of automobiles for its rental fleet directly to expense, rather than to an asset account? Explain.

LO4-3, LO4-7, LO4-8

CASE 4.3

Hold the Expenses!

Slippery Slope, Inc., is a downhill ski area in northern New England. In an attempt to attract more ski enthusiasts, Slippery Slope's management recently engaged in an aggressive preseason advertising campaign in which it spent $9,000 to distribute brochures, $17,000 to air broadcast media spots, and $14,000 to run magazine and newspaper ads.

   Slippery Slope is now planning to borrow money from a local bank to expand its snowmaking capabilities next season. In preparing financial statements to be used by the bank, Slippery Slope's management capitalized the entire $40,000 of advertising expenditures as Prepaid Advertising in the current year's balance sheet. It decided to defer converting this asset to advertising expense for three years, arguing that it will take a least that long to realize the full benefit of its promotional efforts. Management also contends that it does not matter how the $40,000 advertising expenditure is reported, because the amount is immaterial.

Instructions

a.   Does management's decision to defer converting this $40,000 prepayment to advertising expense comply with generally accepted accounting principles? Defend your answer.

b.   Could management's decision to defer reporting this expenditure as an expense for three years have any ethical implications? Explain.

LO4-I through LO4-6

INTERNET CASE 4.4

Identifying Accounts Requiring Adjusting Entries

Visit **Hershey**'s home page at:

www.hersheys.com

From **Hershey**'s home page, access its most recent annual report (follow "Corporate Information" to the "Investor Relations" link). Examine the company's balance sheet and identify the accounts most likely to have been involved in the end-of-year adjusting entry process.

Internet sites are time and date sensitive. It is the purpose of these exercises to have you explore the Internet. You may need to use the Yahoo! search engine www.yahoo.com *(or another favorite search engine) to find a company's current web address.*

Answers to Self-Test Questions

1.   c   2.   d, $11,670 ($27,900 − $17,340 − $2,700 − $1,440 + $3,300 + $1,950)

3.   d   4.   b, c   5.   b, c, d

CHAPTER 5

The Accounting Cycle

Reporting Financial Results

AFTER STUDYING THIS CHAPTER, YOU SHOULD BE ABLE TO:

Learning Objectives

LO5-1 Prepare an income statement, a statement of retained earnings, and a balance sheet.

LO5-2 Explain how the income statement and the statement of retained earnings relate to the balance sheet.

LO5-3 Explain the concept of *adequate disclosure*.

LO5-4 Explain the purposes of *closing entries;* prepare these entries.

LO5-5 Prepare an after-closing trial balance.

LO5-6 Use financial statement information to evaluate profitability and liquidity.

LO5-7 Explain how *interim* financial statements are prepared in a business that closes its accounts only at year-end.

LO5-8 Prepare a worksheet and explain its uses.*

* Supplemental Topic, "The Worksheet."

BEST BUY

Best Buy is a multinational retailer of televisions, video equipment, stereo systems, cellular phones, and an array of other consumer electronic devices and web-based services.

The company reported an impairment expense in a recent income statement of $1.2 billion—no similar charges appeared in the previous two-year period. Disclosures accompanying Best Buy's financial statements reveal that the fair value of one of the company's operating subsidiaries, Best Buy Europe, declined. Management determined that the fair value of Best Buy Europe was less than its carrying value on the books of Best Buy. On the basis of this decline in the fair value of the Best Buy Europe operating unit, management determined that the $1.2 billion of goodwill associated with the Best Buy Europe unit was fully impaired. Hence, in accordance with accounting standards, Best Buy reported the entire amount of the loss as an impairment expense in its income statement.

Disclosures such as these are absolutely essential for the proper interpretation of a company's financial statements. The Best Buy's financial statements also include disclosures about store closings, executive compensation, sources of credit, and many other important issues. ■

© Susan Van Etten/Photoedit

In this chapter, we examine how companies prepare general-purpose financial statements used by investors, creditors, and managers. In addition, we discuss how certain events are disclosed in the notes that accompany financial statements. We also illustrate several methods of evaluating liquidity and profitability using financial statement information.

In Chapter 3, we introduced the first of the eight steps in the accounting cycle by illustrating how Overnight Auto Service (1) captured (journalized) economic events, (2) posted these transactions to its general ledger, and (3) prepared an *unadjusted* trial balance from its general ledger account balances. We continued our illustration of the accounting cycle in Chapter 4 by (4) performing the adjusting entries made by Overnight and (5) presenting the company's *adjusted* trial balance at year-end.

In this chapter, we complete the accounting cycle by (6) preparing Overnight's financial statements, (7) performing year-end closing entries, and (8) presenting the company's *after-closing* trial balance.

Preparing Financial Statements

LO5-1

LEARNING OBJECTIVE
Prepare an income statement, a statement of retained earnings, and a balance sheet.

Publicly owned companies—those with shares listed on a stock exchange—have obligations to release annual and quarterly information to their stockholders and to the public. These companies don't simply prepare financial statements—they publish *annual reports.*

An annual report *includes* comparative financial statements for several years and a wealth of other information about the company's financial position, business operations, and future prospects. (For illustrative purposes, the financial statements of **Home Depot, Inc.,** appear in Appendix A.) Before an annual report is issued, the financial statements must be *audited* by a firm of certified public accountants (CPAs). Publicly owned companies must file their audited financial statements and detailed supporting schedules with the Securities and Exchange Commission (SEC), and the auditing firm must be registered with the Public Company Accounting Oversight Board (PCAOB).

The activities surrounding the preparation of an annual report become very intense as the new year approaches. Once the fiscal year has ended, it often takes several *months* before the annual report is available for distribution. Thus, many accountants refer to the months of December through March as the "busy season."[1] We cannot adequately discuss all of the activities associated with the preparation of an annual report in a single chapter. Thus, here we focus on the *preparation of financial statements.*

The adjusted trial balance prepared in Chapter 4 is reprinted in Exhibit 5–1. The income statement, statement of retained earnings, and balance sheet can be prepared *directly from the amounts shown in this adjusted trial balance.* For illustrative purposes, we have made marginal notes indicating which accounts appear in which financial statements. Overnight's financial statements for the year ended December 31, 2015, are illustrated in Exhibit 5–2 (page 196).

The income statement is prepared first because it determines the amount of net income to be reported in the statement of retained earnings. The statement of retained earnings is prepared second because it determines the amount of retained earnings to be reported in the balance sheet. Note that we have not included Overnight's statement of cash flows with the other three reports. An in-depth discussion of the statement of cash flows is the primary focus of Chapter 13.

THE INCOME STATEMENT

LO5-2

LEARNING OBJECTIVE
Explain how the income statement and the statement of retained earnings relate to the balance sheet.

Alternative titles for the income statement include *earnings statement, statement of operations,* and *profit and loss statement.* However, *income statement* is the most popular term for this important financial statement. The income statement is used to summarize the *operating*

---

[1] Some companies elect to end their fiscal year after a seasonal high point in business activity. However, most companies *do* end their fiscal year on December 31.

EXHIBIT 5–1

Adjusted Trial Balance

OVERNIGHT AUTO SERVICE ADJUSTED TRIAL BALANCE DECEMBER 31, 2015		
Cash...	$ 18,592	
Accounts receivable...........................	7,250	
Shop supplies.................................	1,200	
Unexpired insurance	3,000	
Tools and equipment	12,000	
Accumulated depreciation: tools and equipment		2,200
Building	36,000	
Accumulated depreciation: building.............		$ 1,650
Land..	52,000	
Notes payable		4,000
Accounts payable.............................		2,690
Wages payable................................		1,950
Income taxes payable		5,580
Interest payable		30
Unearned rent revenue........................		6,000
Capital stock		80,000
Retained earnings (**Note:** still must be updated for transactions recorded in the accounts listed below. Closing entries serve this purpose.)............		0
Dividends	14,000	
Repair service revenue........................		172,000
Rent revenue earned		3,000
Advertising expense...........................	3,900	
Wages expense	58,750	
Supplies expense.............................	7,500	
Depreciation expense: building	1,650	
Depreciation expense: tools and equipment	2,200	
Utilities expense..............................	19,400	
Insurance expense............................	15,000	
Interest expense..............................	30	
Income taxes expense.........................	26,628	
	$279,100	$279,100

Balance sheet accounts

Statement of retained earnings accounts

Income statement accounts

results of a business by matching the revenue earned during a given period of time with the expenses incurred in generating that revenue.

The revenue and expenses shown in Overnight's income statement are taken directly from the company's adjusted trial balance. Overnight's 2015 income statement shows that revenue exceeded expenses for the year, thus producing a net income of $39,942. Bear in mind, however, that this measurement of net income is not absolutely accurate or precise due to the *assumptions and estimates* in the accounting process.

An income statement has certain limitations. For instance, the amounts shown for depreciation expense are based upon estimates of the useful lives of the company's building and equipment. Also, the income statement includes only those events that have been evidenced by actual business transactions. Perhaps during the year, Overnight's advertising has caught the attention of many potential customers. A good "customer base" is certainly an important step toward profitable operations; however, the development of a customer base is not reflected in the income statement because its value cannot be measured *objectively* until actual

EXHIBIT 5–2

Overnight Auto Service's
Financial Statements

Amounts are taken directly from the adjusted trial balance

Net income also appears in the statement of retained earnings

The ending balance in the Retained Earnings account also appears in the balance sheet

OVERNIGHT AUTO SERVICE
INCOME STATEMENT
FOR THE YEAR ENDED DECEMBER 31, 2015

Revenue:		
Repair service revenue		$172,000
Rent revenue earned		3,000
Total revenue		$175,000
Expenses:		
Advertising	$ 3,900	
Wages expense	58,750	
Supplies expense	7,500	
Depreciation: building	1,650	
Depreciation: tools and equipment	2,200	
Utilities expense	19,400	
Insurance	15,000	
Interest	30	108,430
Income before income taxes		$ 66,570
Income taxes		26,628
Net income		$ 39,942

OVERNIGHT AUTO SERVICE
STATEMENT OF RETAINED EARNINGS
FOR THE YEAR ENDED DECEMBER 31, 2015

Retained earnings, Jan. 20, 2015		$ 0
Add: Net income		39,942
Subtotal		$ 39,942
Less: Dividends		14,000
Retained earnings, Dec. 31, 2015		$ 25,942

OVERNIGHT AUTO SERVICE
BALANCE SHEET
DECEMBER 31, 2015

Assets

Cash		$ 18,592
Accounts receivable		7,250
Shop supplies		1,200
Unexpired insurance		3,000
Tools and equipment	$12,000	
Less: Accumulated depreciation	2,200	9,800
Building	36,000	
Less: Accumulated depreciation	1,650	34,350
Land		52,000
Total assets		$126,192

Liabilities & Stockholders' Equity

Liabilities:		
Notes payable		$ 4,000
Accounts payable		2,690
Wages payable		1,950
Income taxes payable		5,580
Interest payable		30
Unearned rent revenue		6,000
Total liabilities		$ 20,250
Stockholders' equity:		
Capital stock		80,000
Retained earnings		25,942
Total stockholders' equity		$105,942
Total liabilities and stockholders' equity		$126,192

transactions take place. Despite these limitations, the income statement is of vital importance to the users of a company's financial statements.

THE STATEMENT OF RETAINED EARNINGS

Retained earnings is that portion of stockholders' (owners') equity created by earning net income and retaining the related resources in the business. The resources retained from being profitable may include, but are certainly not limited to, *cash*. The statement of retained earnings summarizes the increases and decreases in retained earnings resulting from business operations during the period. Increases in retained earnings result from earning net income; decreases result from net losses and from the declaration of dividends.

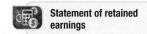
Statement of retained earnings

The format of this financial statement is based upon the following relationships:

Retained Earnings at the beginning of the period $+$ Net Income $-$ Dividends $=$ Retained Earnings at the end of the period

The amount of retained earnings at the *beginning* of the period is shown at the top of the statement. Next, the net income for the period is added (or net loss subtracted), and any dividends declared during the period are deducted. This short computation determines the amount of retained earnings at the *end* of the accounting period. The ending retained earnings ($25,942 in our example) appears at the bottom of the statement and also in the company's year-end balance sheet.

Our illustration of the statement of retained earnings for Overnight is unusual in that the beginning balance of retained earnings at the date of the company's formation (January 20, 2015) was *$0*. This occurred only because 2015 was the *first year* of Overnight's business operations. The ending retained earnings ($25,942) becomes the beginning retained earnings for the following year.

A Word about Dividends   In Chapter 3, the declaration and payment of a cash dividend were treated as a single event recorded by one journal entry. A small corporation with only a few stockholders may choose to declare and pay a dividend on the same day. In large corporations, an interval of a month or more will separate the date of declaration from the later date of payment. A liability account, Dividends Payable, comes into existence when the dividend is declared and is discharged when the dividend is paid. Because Overnight reports no dividends payable in its adjusted trial balance, we may assume that it declared and paid the entire $14,000 on December 31, 2015.[2]

Finally, it is important to realize that dividends paid to stockholders are *not* reported in the income statement as an expense. In short, dividends represent a decision by a corporation to distribute a portion of its income to stockholders. Thus, the amount of the dividend is not included in the computation of income.

THE BALANCE SHEET

The balance sheet lists the amounts of the company's assets, liabilities, and owners' equity at the *end* of the accounting period. The balances of Overnight's asset and liability accounts are taken directly from the adjusted trial balance in Exhibit 5–1. The amount of retained earnings at the end of the period, $25,942, was determined in the *statement of retainedearnings.*

Balance sheets can be presented with asset accounts appearing on the left and liabilities and owners' equity accounts appearing on the right. They may also be presented in *report form,* with liabilities and owners' equity listed *below* (rather than to the right of) the asset section. It is also common for corporations to refer to owners' equity as *stockholders'* equity.

---

[2] Details related to the declaration and payment of dividends are discussed in Chapter 12.

© The McGraw-Hill Companies, Inc./Andrew Resek, photographer

Separate Balance Sheet Subtotals Many companies group together as separate balance sheet subtotals those assets and liabilities that are considered *current*. This is referred to as peparing a **classified balance sheet.** To be classified as a **current asset,** an asset must already be cash or must be capable of *being converted into cash* within a relatively short period of time. For most companies, this period of time is usually one year or less. Those assets that get used up quickly (e.g., insurance policies and office supplies) are also classified as current assets. Of Overnight's $126,192 in total assets shown in Exhibit 5–2, the current assets include Cash, Accounts Receivable, Shop Supplies, and Unexpired Insurance. Thus, $30,042 of Overnight's total assets is considered *current.*

A **current liability** is an existing debt or obligation that a company expects to satisfy relatively soon using its current assets. Once again, this period of time is typically one year or less. While not a *debt,* unearned revenue is often considered a current liability also. *All* of Overnight's $20,250 in total liabilities shown in Exhibit 5–2 are considered current liabilities.

Computing separate subtotals for current assets and current liabilities is very useful when evaluating a company's ability to pay its debts as they come due (see this chapter's Financial Analysis discussion). The financial statements of **Home Depot, Inc.,** in Appendix A at the end of this textbook illustrate how subtotals for current assets and current liabilities are presented in the balance sheet. Coverage of several other balance sheet subtotals appears in Chapter 14.

INTERNATIONAL CASE IN POINT

International Financial Reporting Standard (IFRS) 1 identifies the international reporting requirements for the presentation of the income statement, balance sheet, cash flow statement, and statement showing changes in equity. One very significant difference between the financial reporting requirements under U.S. GAAP and IFRS requirements is that, under the latter, management and auditors are required to depart from compliance with standards when it is necessary to achieve a fair presentation. This "true and fair" override is required if, in the judgment of the management and auditors, compliance is misleading.

Relationships among the Financial Statements

A set of financial statements becomes easier to understand if we recognize that the income statement, statement of retained earnings, and balance sheet all are *related to one another.* These relationships are emphasized by the arrows in the right-hand margin of Exhibit 5–2.

DRAFTING THE NOTES THAT ACCOMPANY FINANCIAL STATEMENTS

L05-3

LEARNING OBJECTIVE
Explain the concept of
adequate disclosure.

To the users of financial statements, **adequate disclosure** is perhaps the most important accounting principle. This principle simply means that financial statements should be accompanied by any information necessary for the statements to be *interpreted properly.*

Most disclosures appear within the numerous pages of **notes** that accompany the financial statements. Drafting these notes can be one of the most challenging tasks confronting accountants at the end of the period. The content of these disclosures often cannot be drawn directly from the accounting records. Rather, they require an *in-depth understanding* of the company and its operations, of accounting principles, and of how accounting information is interpreted by users of financial statements.

Two items always disclosed in the notes to financial statements are the accounting methods in use and the due dates of major liabilities. Thus Overnight's 2015 financial statements should at least include the following notes:

Note 1: Depreciation policies
Depreciation expense in the financial statements is computed by the straight-line method. Estimated useful lives are 20 years for the building and 5 years for tools and equipment.

Note 2: Maturity dates of liabilities
The Company's notes payable consist of a single obligation that matures on February 28 of the coming year. The maturity value of this note, including interest charges, will amount to $4,090.

Note 1 above can be used to help ascertain whether the company may need to replace its depreciable assets in the near future. For instance, given that the estimated useful life of Overnight's building is 20 years, and only $1,650 of its $36,000 initial cost has been depreciated, it is reasonable for one to assume that it will not need to be replaced in the foreseeable future.

The maturity dates reported in Note 2 above should be of particular importance to American National Bank. Specifically, the bank will want to know if Overnight will have enough cash to pay this $4,090 liability in just two months. The company's balance sheet currently reports cash of $18,592; however, several other liabilities will require an outlay of cash in excess of $10,000 in the near future. Furthermore, the company has an $18,000 insurance policy to renew on March 1. Thus, even though Overnight's income statement reports net income of $39,942, the company's balance sheet suggests that the company may not have adequate liquid assets to satisfy all of its upcoming obligations.

WHAT TYPES OF INFORMATION MUST BE DISCLOSED?

There is no comprehensive list of all information that should be disclosed in financial statements. The adequacy of disclosure is based on a combination of official rules, tradition, and accountants' professional judgment. The importance of adequate disclosure is so important that the Financial Accounting Standards Board (FASB), the body that promulgates U.S. accounting standards, has added a project to its agenda to develop a disclosure framework. The FASB's goal in seeking to develop a disclosure framework is to improve the effectiveness of disclosures in notes to the financial statements. The importance of effective disclosure is of concern to accounting standard setters globally—an accounting advisory group to the European Commission is working on a similar project.

As a general rule, a company should disclose any facts that an informed user would consider necessary for the statements to be *interpreted properly*. Thus, businesses often disclose such things as:

- Lawsuits pending against the business.
- Scheduled plant closings.
- Significant events occurring *after* the balance sheet date but before the financial statements are actually issued.
- Customers that account for 10 percent or more of the company's revenues.
- Unusual transactions or conflicts of interest between the company and its key officers.

In some cases, companies must disclose information that could have a *damaging effect* on the business. For example, a manufacturer may need to disclose that it is being sued by customers who have been injured by its products. The fact that a disclosure might prove embarrassing—or even damaging to the business—is *not* a valid reason for not disclosing the

YOUR TURN   **You as Overnight Auto's Independent Auditor**

Assume that Overnight Auto Service is being sued by a former employee who was injured while on the job. The person claims that Overnight has been negligent in providing a safe work environment. If the plaintiff prevails, Overnight may have to pay damages well in excess of what is covered by its insurance policies. As Overnight's independent auditor, you have asked that the company disclose information about this lawsuit in the notes that accompany the financial statements. Overnight's management disagrees with your suggestion because, in its opinion, the likelihood of the plaintiff prevailing is extremely remote. How should you respond?

(See our comments on the Online Learning Center website.)

information. The concept of adequate disclosure demands a *good faith effort* by management to keep the users of financial statements informed about the company's operations. For a look at the types of disclosure made by publicly owned corporations, see the **Home Depot, Inc.**, financial statements, which appear in Appendix A.

Closing the Temporary Accounts

LO5-4

LEARNING OBJECTIVE
Explain the purposes of *closing entries;* prepare these entries.

As previously stated, revenue increases retained earnings, and expenses and dividends decrease retained earnings. If the only financial statement that we needed was a balance sheet, these changes in retained earnings could be recorded directly in the Retained Earnings account. However, owners, managers, investors, and others need to know amounts of specific revenues and expenses and the amount of net income earned in the period. Therefore, *separate ledger accounts* must be maintained to measure each type of revenue and expense, and to account for dividends declared.

Revenue, expense, and dividends accounts are called *temporary,* or *nominal,* accounts, because they accumulate the transactions of *only one accounting period.* At the end of an accounting period, the changes in retained earnings accumulated in these temporary accounts are transferred into the Retained Earnings account. This process serves two purposes. First, it *updates the balance of the Retained Earnings account* for changes occurring during the accounting period. Second, it *returns the balances of the temporary accounts to zero,* so that they are ready for measuring the revenue, expenses, and dividends of the next accounting period.

Retained Earnings and other balance sheet accounts are called *permanent,* or *real,* accounts, because their balances continue to exist beyond the current accounting period. Transferring the balances of the temporary accounts into the Retained Earnings account is called *the closing process.* The journal entries made for the purpose of closing the temporary accounts are called **closing entries.**

Revenue and expense accounts are closed at the end of each accounting period by *transferring their balances* to an account called the **Income Summary.** After the credit balances of the revenue accounts and the debit balances of the expense accounts have all been transferred to the Income Summary account, its balance will be the *net income* or *net loss* for the period. If revenues (credit balances) exceed expenses (debit balances), the Income Summary account will have a credit balance representing net income. Conversely, if expenses exceed revenues, the Income Summary account will have a debit balance representing a net loss. This is consistent with the rule that increases in owners' equity are recorded by credits and decreases are recorded by debits.

While adjusting entries are usually made on a monthly basis, it is common practice to close accounts only *once each year.* Thus, we will demonstrate the closing of the temporary accounts of Overnight Auto Service at December 31, 2015, the end of its first year of operations.

On the following pages, Overnight's temporary accounts are illustrated in T account form. We have eliminated the detail of every transaction posted to each account throughout the year. Therefore, each account shows only its December 31, 2015, balance as reported in the adjusted trial balance in Exhibit 5–1. The closing process is relatively straightforward and involves just four steps:

- Closing all revenue accounts to the Income Summary.
- Closing all expense accounts to the Income Summary.
- Closing the Income Summary to Retained Earnings.
- Closing the dividends account to Retained Earnings.

The first two items on the bulleted list need to be completed before the third item. The entry to close the dividends account to Retained Earnings can be made before or after closing the revenue and expense accounts.

CLOSING ENTRIES FOR REVENUE ACCOUNTS

Revenue accounts have credit balances. Therefore, closing a revenue account means transferring its credit balance to the Income Summary account. This transfer is accomplished by a journal entry debiting the revenue account in an amount equal to its credit balance, with an offsetting credit to the Income Summary account. Note that the process of closing a revenue account, debiting the account, is the opposite of credit entries that are normally made to revenue accounts. The debit portion of this closing entry returns the balance of the revenue account to zero; the credit portion transfers the former balance of the revenue account into the Income Summary account.

Overnight uses two revenue accounts: (1) Repair Service Revenue, which had a credit balance of $172,000 at December 31, 2015, and (2) Rent Revenue Earned, which had a credit balance of $3,000 at December 31, 2015. Two separate journal entries could be made to close these accounts, but the use of one *compound journal entry* is an easier, time-saving method of closing more than one account. The compound closing entry for Overnight's revenue accounts is displayed in Exhibit 5–3.

EXHIBIT 5–3

Closing of Revenue Accounts

OVERNIGHT AUTO SERVICE
GENERAL JOURNAL
DECEMBER 31, 2015

Date	Account Titles and Explanation	Debit	Credit
2015			
Dec. 31	Repair Service Revenue.	172,000	
	Rent Revenue Earned	3,000	
	Income Summary		175,000
	To close the Repair Service Revenue and Rent Revenue Earned accounts.		

After this closing entry has been posted, the two revenue accounts each have *zero* balances, whereas Income Summary has a credit balance of $175,000, as illustrated in Exhibit 5–4.

EXHIBIT 5–4

Transferring Revenue Account Balances to the Income Summary

CLOSING ENTRIES FOR EXPENSE ACCOUNTS

Expense accounts have debit balances. Closing an expense account means transferring its debit balance to the Income Summary account. The journal entry to close an expense, therefore, consists of a credit to the expense account in an amount equal to its debit balance, with an offsetting debit to the Income Summary account. Again, note that the process of closing an expense account, crediting the account, is the opposite of debt entries that are normally made to expense accounts.

There are nine expense accounts in Overnight's ledger (see the adjusted trial balance in Exhibit 5–1). Again, a compound journal entry is used to close each of these accounts. The required closing entry is displayed in Exhibit 5–5.

EXHIBIT 5–5

Closing of Expense Accounts

OVERNIGHT AUTO SERVICE
GENERAL JOURNAL
DECEMBER 31, 2015

Date	Account Titles and Explanation	Debit	Credit
2015			
Dec. 31	Income Summary	135,058	
	Advertising Expense		3,900
	Wages Expense.		58,750
	Supplies Expense		7,500
	Depreciation Expense: Building		1,650
	Depreciation Expense: Tools and Equipment		2,200
	Utilities Expense		19,400
	Insurance Expense		15,000
	Interest Expense		30
	Income Taxes Expense		26,628
	To close the expense accounts.		

After this closing entry has been posted, the Income Summary account has a *credit balance* of *$39,942* ($175,000 credit posted minus the $135,058 debit posted), and the nine expense accounts each have *zero balances* as shown in Exhibit 5–6. This $39,942 credit balance equals the *net income* reported in Overnight's income statement. Had the company's income statement reported a *net loss* for the year, the Income Summary account would have a *debit balance* equal to the amount of the loss reported.

EXHIBIT 5–6

Transferring Expense Account Balances to the Income Summary

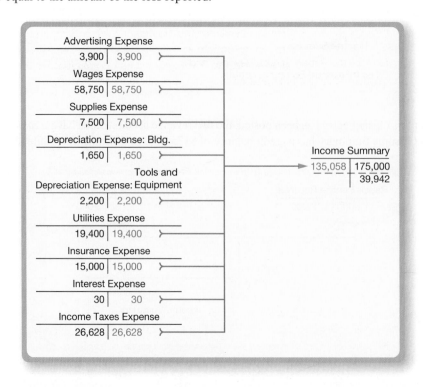

CLOSING THE INCOME SUMMARY ACCOUNT

The net income of $39,942 earned during the year causes an increase in Overnight's owners' equity. Thus, the $39,942 credit balance of the Income Summary account is transferred to the Retained Earnings account by the closing entry in Exhibit 5–7.

	OVERNIGHT AUTO SERVICE GENERAL JOURNAL DECEMBER 31, 2015		
Date	**Account Titles and Explanation**	**Debit**	**Credit**
2015			
Dec. 31	Income Summary.	39,942	
	Retained Earnings.		39,942
	Transferring net income earned in 2015 to the Retained Earnings account.		

EXHIBIT 5–7

Closing the Income Summary Account

After this closing entry has been posted, the Income Summary account has a zero balance, and the net income for the year ended December 31, 2015, appears as an increase (or credit entry) in the Retained Earnings account as shown in Exhibit 5–8.

EXHIBIT 5–8 Income Increases Retained Earnings

CLOSING THE DIVIDENDS ACCOUNT

As explained earlier in the chapter, dividends to stockholders are *not* considered an expense of the business; therefore, they are *not* taken into account in determining net income for the period. Since dividends are not an expense, the Dividends account is *not* closed to the Income Summary account. Instead, it is closed directly to the Retained Earnings account, as shown in Exhibit 5–9.

	OVERNIGHT AUTO SERVICE GENERAL JOURNAL DECEMBER 31, 2015		
Date	**Account Titles and Explanation**	**Debit**	**Credit**
2015			
Dec. 31	Retained Earnings	14,000	
	Dividends		14,000
	To transfer dividends declared in 2015 to the Retained Earnings account.		

EXHIBIT 5–9

Closing the Dividends Account

After this closing entry has been posted, the Dividends account will have a zero balance, and the Retained Earnings account will have an ending credit balance of $25,942, as shown in Exhibit 5–10.

EXHIBIT 5–10 Dividends Decrease Retained Earnings

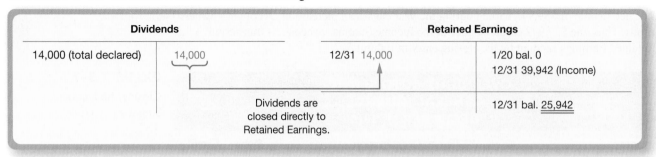

Dividends				Retained Earnings
14,000 (total declared)	14,000	12/31 14,000		1/20 bal. 0
				12/31 39,942 (Income)
	Dividends are closed directly to Retained Earnings.			12/31 bal. 25,942

Summary of the Closing Process

As illustrated, the closing process involves four simple steps:

1. Closing the various *revenue* accounts and transferring their balances to the Income Summary account.
2. Closing the various *expense* accounts and transferring their balances to the Income Summary account.
3. Closing the *Income Summary* account and transferring its balance to the Retained Earnings account. It is important to emphasize that the balance in the Income Summary account, after the revenue and expense accounts have been closed, will equal the company's net income or net loss for the period. In this example, the $39,942 credit balance indicates that revenues exceed expenses and corresponds with the net income amount reported in Exhibit 5-2.
4. Closing the *Dividends* account and transferring its balance to the Retained Earnings account.

The entire closing process is illustrated in Exhibit 5–11 using T accounts.

EXHIBIT 5–11

Flowchart of the Closing Process

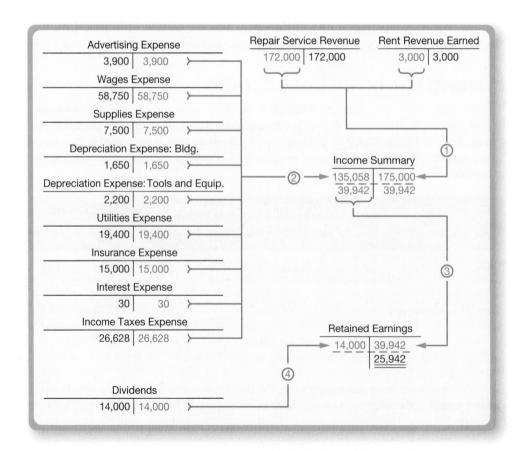

After-Closing Trial Balance

LO5-5

LEARNING OBJECTIVE
Prepare an after-closing trial balance.

After the revenue and expense accounts have been closed, it is desirable to prepare an **after-closing trial balance** that consists solely of balance sheet accounts. There is always the possibility that an error in posting the closing entries may have upset the equality of debits and credits in the ledger. The after-closing trial balance, or *post-closing trial balance* as it is often called, is prepared from the ledger. It gives assurance that the accounts are in balance and ready for recording transactions in the new accounting period. The after-closing trial balance of Overnight Auto Service is shown in Exhibit 5–12.

EXHIBIT 5–12
After-Closing Trial Balance

OVERNIGHT AUTO SERVICE AFTER-CLOSING TRIAL BALANCE DECEMBER 31, 2015		
Cash	$ 18,592	
Accounts receivable	7,250	
Shop supplies	1,200	
Unexpired insurance	3,000	
Tools and equipment	12,000	
Accumulated depreciation: tools and equipment		$ 2,200
Building	36,000	
Accumulated depreciation: building		1,650
Land	52,000	
Notes payable		4,000
Accounts payable		2,690
Wages payable		1,950
Income taxes payable		5,580
Interest payable		30
Unearned rent revenue		6,000
Capital stock		80,000
Retained earnings, Dec. 31		25,942
	$ 130,042	$130,042

In comparison with the adjusted trial balance in Exhibit 5–1, an after-closing trial balance contains only *balance sheet* accounts. Also, the Retained Earnings account no longer has a zero balance. Through the closing of the revenue, expense, and dividends accounts, the Retained Earnings account has been brought *up-to-date.*

A LAST LOOK AT OVERNIGHT: WAS 2015 A GOOD YEAR?

LO5-6

LEARNING OBJECTIVE
Use financial statement information to evaluate profitability and liquidity.

Let us now consider the financial results of Overnight's first fiscal year.

Evaluating Profitability In 2015, Overnight earned a net income of nearly *$40,000.* Thus, net income for the first year of operations amounts to 50 percent of the stockholders' $80,000 investment. This is a very impressive rate of return for the first year of operations. Of course, Overnight's stockholders (members of the McBryan family) have taken a certain amount of risk by investing their financial resources in this business. Does a 50 percent *return on investment* adequately compensate the stockholders for their risk? Stated differently, could they invest their $80,000 in a less risky venture and still generate a 50 percent rate of return? Probably not.

But in evaluating profitability, the real question is not how the business *did,* but how it is *likely to do in the future.* To generate a substantial return on investment in the first year of operations indicates good profit potential. Overnight's rental contract with Harbor Cab Company is also promising. In 2015, only $3,000 in revenue was earned by renting storage space to the company for its cabs (December's rent). In 2016, Overnight will earn 12 full months of rent revenue from Harbor Cab ($33,000 more than it earned in 2015). In addition, if Harbor Cab stores its cabs in Overnight's garage, Overnight becomes the likely candidate to perform any necessary maintenance and repairs.

Evaluating Liquidity   *Liquidity* refers to a company's ability to meet its cash obligations as they become due. Liquidity, at least in the short term, may be independent of profitability. And in the short term, Overnight appears to have *potential* cash flow problems. In the very near future, Overnight must make cash expenditures for the following items:

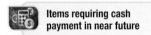
Items requiring cash payment in near future

Note and interest payable	$ 4,090
Accounts payable	2,690
Wages payable	1,950
Income taxes payable	5,580
Insurance policy renewal	18,000
Total expenditures coming due	$32,310

These outlays exceed the company's liquid assets (cash and accounts receivable) reported in its December 31, 2015, balance sheet.

It is important to note that the cash and accounts receivable amounts reported in Overnight's balance sheet represent the balances of those accounts at a *point in time*. Thus, while these liquid assets are currently insufficient to cover the cash expenditures coming due, this may not be the case for long. On the basis of its past performance, Overnight is likely to generate revenue in excess of $40,000 during the next several months. If a substantial amount of this revenue is received in cash, and expenses are kept under control, the company may actually become more liquid than it appears to be now.

FINANCIAL ANALYSIS and Decision Making

MEASURES OF PROFITABILITY

The $39,942 net income figure reported in Overnight's income statement is more meaningful when examined in the context of management's ability to control costs or when measured relative to the company's shareholders' equity.

Two commonly used measures of *profitability* that address these issues are the *net income percentage* and *return on equity*. Using data from Overnight's financial statements, these measures are computed as follows:

$$\textit{Net Income Percentage} = \textbf{Net Income} \div \textbf{Total Revenue}$$
$$= \$39,942 \div \$175,000 = \underline{\underline{22.8\%}}$$

$$\textit{Return on Equity} = \textbf{Net Income} \div \textbf{Average}$$
$$\textbf{Stockholders' Equity}$$
$$= \$39,942 \div \$92,971 = \underline{\underline{43\%}}$$

All companies must incur costs in order to generate revenue. The *net income percentage* is simply a measure of

management's ability to control these costs. In 2015, Overnight was able to convert 22.8 percent of its revenue into net income; thus, it incurred approximately 78 cents in costs for every dollar of revenue it generated.

Return on equity is a measure of net income relative to *average* stockholders' equity throughout the year. In 2015, Overnight's average stockholders' equity was $92,971 (i.e., the average of its beginning stockholders' equity of $80,000, and its ending stockholders' equity of $105,942). Thus, the company earned income of approximately 43 cents on every dollar of equity capital.

MEASURES OF LIQUIDITY

At the end of 2015, Overnight's balance sheet reports liabilities of $20,250, most of which will require payment early in 2016. However, the balance sheet reports cash of only $18,592, which may be an indication of potential liquidity problems.

Two common measures of *liquidity* are a company's *working capital* and its *current ratio*. Using data from Overnight's financial statements, these measures are computed as follows:

Working Capital = Current Assets − Current Liabilities

= $30,042 − $20,250 = **$9,792**

Current Ratio = Current Assets ÷ Current Liabilities

= $30,042 ÷ $20,250 = **1.48:1**

Working capital is a measure of short-term debt-paying ability expressed in dollars. Current assets represent a company's potential cash *inflows* in the near future, whereas current liabilities represent cash *outlays* coming due soon. Overnight's current assets exceed its current liabilities by $9,792; however, shop supplies and unexpired insurance policies are not truly *liquid* assets. Likewise, unearned rent revenue does not actually represent a future cash *obligation*.

The *current ratio* is simply working capital expressed as a ratio. Thus, Overnight has approximately $1.48 of potential cash inflow for every dollar of current obligations coming due. Again, this figure does not take into account shop supplies and insurance policies will not actually convert into cash, or that unearned revenue will not actually require a future outlay of cash.

Throughout the remainder of this textbook additional measures of performance will be discussed. Chapter 14 is devoted entirely to financial analysis.

PREPARING FINANCIAL STATEMENTS COVERING DIFFERENT PERIODS OF TIME

L05-7

LEARNING OBJECTIVE
Explain how *interim* financial statements are prepared in a business that closes its accounts only at year-end.

Many businesses prepare financial statements every quarter, as well as at year-end. In addition, they may prepare financial statements covering other time periods, such as one month or the year-to-date.

When a business closes its accounts only at year-end, the revenue, expense, and dividends accounts have balances representing the activities of the *year-to-date*. Thus, at *June 30*, these account balances represent the activities recorded over the past six months. Year-to-date financial statements can be prepared directly from an adjusted trial balance. But how might this business prepare **interim financial statements** covering only the month of June? Or the quarter (three months) ended June 30?

The answer is by doing a little *subtraction*. As an example, assume that the adjusted balance in Overnight's Repair Service Revenue account at the ends of the following months was as shown:

March 31 (end of the first quarter)	$38,000
May 31	67,000
June 30	80,000

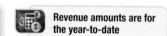
Revenue amounts are for the year-to-date

At each date, the account balance represents the revenue earned since January 1. Thus the March 31 balance represents three months' revenue; the May 31 balance, five months' revenue; and the June 30 balance, the revenue earned over a period of six months.

To prepare an income statement for the *six months* ended June 30, we simply use the June 30 balance in the revenue account—*$80,000*. But to prepare an income statement for the *month* ended June 30, we would have to subtract from the June 30 balance of this account its balance as of May 31. The remainder, *$13,000*, represents the amount of revenue recorded in the account during June ($80,000 − $67,000 = $13,000).

To prepare an income statement for the *quarter* ended June 30, we would subtract from the June 30 balance in this revenue account its balance as of March 31. Thus the revenue earned during the second quarter (April 1 through June 30) amounts to *$42,000* ($80,000 − $38,000 = $42,000).

Computations like these are not required for the balance sheet accounts. A balance sheet always is based on the account balances *at the balance sheet date*. Therefore, a June 30 balance sheet looks exactly the same *regardless* of the time period covered by the other financial statements.

Ethics, Fraud, & Corporate Governance

As stated previously in this chapter, a company should disclose any facts that an intelligent person would consider necessary for the statements to be *interpreted properly.* Public companies are required to file annual reports with the Securities and Exchange Commission (SEC). These annual reports include a section labeled, "Management Discussion and Analysis" (MD&A). The SEC requires that companies include an MD&A in their annual reports because the financial statements and related notes may be inadequate for assessing the quality and sustainability of a company's earnings.

As an example of the importance of the MD&A, the SEC brought an enforcement action against **Sony Corporation** alleging inadequate disclosure in its MD&A. Although a Japanese corporation, **Sony** lists its stock on the New York Stock Exchange and is therefore subject to SEC oversight. **Sony** had reported only two industry segments in its annual report (electronics and entertainment). The entertainment segment included two separate units, Sony Music Entertainment and Sony Pictures Entertainment. The music group was profitable, whereas the pictures group was losing significant amounts of money. By combining its music and picture units as a single entertainment segment, **Sony** was able to conceal significant losses incurred by Sony Pictures. This decision was at odds with both **Sony**'s external auditor and with its U.S.–based financial staff.

Although **Sony** chose to report only two segments, it could have elaborated on the entertainment segment's performance in its MD&A by separately discussing the results of Sony Music and Sony Pictures. **Sony** did discuss Sony Pictures separately, but not in a manner necessary for an intelligent person to properly interpret the results of Sony Pictures. **Sony**'s MD&A did not discuss the nature and extent of the losses incurred by Sony Pictures. Conversely, **Sony**'s MD&A highlighted certain positive developments at Sony Pictures, including box office receipts, box office market share, and Academy Award nominations.

The SEC concluded that **Sony**'s MD&A disclosures were inadequate. **Sony** consented to an SEC cease-and-desist order without either admitting or denying guilt. In essence, **Sony** did not agree that it did anything wrong, but it promised to never do what it did again. As part of its settlement, **Sony** also agreed to have its external auditor examine the MD&A for the following year and to publicly report the findings. This penalty was meaningful because an examination of the MD&A normally does not fall within the scope of an external audit.

Concluding Remarks

We have now completed the *entire accounting cycle,* the eight steps of which include:

1. *Journalize (record) transactions.* Enter all transactions in the journal, thus creating a chronological record of events.
2. *Post to ledger accounts.* Post debits and credits from the journal to the proper ledger accounts, thus creating a record classified by accounts.
3. *Prepare a trial balance.* Prove the equality of debits and credits in the ledger.
4. *Make end-of-period adjustments.* Make adjusting entries in the general journal and post to ledger accounts.
5. *Prepare an adjusted trial balance.* Prove again the equality of debits and credits in the ledger. (***Note:*** These are the amounts used in the preparation of financial statements.)
6. *Prepare financial statements and appropriate disclosures.* An income statement shows the results of operation for the period. A statement of retained earnings shows changes in retained earnings during the period. A balance sheet shows the financial position of the business at the end of the period. Financial statements should be accompanied by *notes* disclosing facts necessary for the proper interpretation of those statements.
7. *Journalize and post the closing entries.* The closing entries "zero" the revenue, expense, and dividends accounts, making them ready for recording the events of the next accounting period. These entries also bring the balance in the Retained Earnings account up-to-date.
8. *Prepare an after-closing trial balance.* This step ensures that the ledger remains in balance after the posting of the closing entries.

SUPPLEMENTAL TOPIC

The Worksheet

A **worksheet** illustrates in one place the relationships among the unadjusted trial balance, proposed adjusting entries, and financial statements. A worksheet is prepared at the end of the period, but *before* the adjusting entries are formally recorded in the accounting records. It is not a formal step in the accounting cycle. Rather, it is a *tool* used by accountants to work out the details of the proposed end-of-period adjustments. It also provides them with a preview of how the financial statements will look.

LO5-8

LEARNING OBJECTIVE
Prepare a worksheet and explain its uses.

You can see a worksheet for Overnight Auto Service at December 31, 2015, in Exhibit 5–13 on page 211.

ISN'T THIS REALLY A SPREADSHEET?

Yes. The term *worksheet* is a holdover from the days when these schedules were prepared manually on large sheets of columnar paper. Today, most worksheets are prepared using a spreadsheet software or with **general ledger software.**

Since the worksheet is simply a tool used by accountants, it often isn't printed out in hard copy—it may exist only on a computer screen. But the concept remains the same; the worksheet displays *in one place* the unadjusted account balances, proposed adjusting entries, and financial statements as they will appear if the proposed adjustments are made.

HOW IS A WORKSHEET USED?

A worksheet serves several purposes. It allows accountants to *see the effects* of adjusting entries without actually entering these adjustments in the accounting records. This makes it relatively easy for them to correct errors or make changes in estimated amounts. It also enables accountants and management to preview the financial statements before the final drafts are developed. Once the worksheet is complete, it serves as the source for recording adjusting and closing entries in the accounting records and for preparing financial statements.

Another important use of the worksheet is in the preparation of *interim financial statements*. Interim statements are financial statements developed at various points *during* the fiscal year. Most companies close their accounts only once each year. Yet they often need to develop quarterly or monthly financial statements. Through the use of a worksheet, they can develop these interim statements *without* having to formally adjust and close their accounts.

THE MECHANICS: HOW IT'S DONE

Whether done manually or on a computer, the preparation of a worksheet involves five basic steps. We begin by describing these steps as if the worksheet were being prepared manually. Afterward, we explain how virtually all of the mechanical steps can be performed automatically by a computer.

1. *Enter the ledger account balances in the Trial Balance columns.* The worksheet begins with an *unadjusted trial balance.* A few lines should be left blank immediately below the last balance sheet account. It is often necessary to add a few more accounts during the adjusting process. Additional income statement accounts also may be necessary. In our illustration, the unadjusted trial balance appears in *blue.*

2. *Enter the adjustments in the Adjustments columns.* This step is the most important: Enter the appropriate end-of-period adjustments in the Adjustments columns. In our illustration, these adjustments appear in *red.*

Notice that each adjustment includes both debit and credit entries, which are linked together by the small key letters appearing to the left of the dollar amount. Thus, adjusting entry *a* consists of a $600 debit to Supplies Expense and a $600 credit to Shop Supplies. Because the individual adjusting entries include equal debit and credit amounts, the totals of the debit and credit Adjustments columns should be equal.

Sometimes the adjustments require adding accounts to the original trial balance. (The four ledger account titles printed in *red* were added during the adjusting process.)

3. *Prepare an adjusted trial balance.* The balances in the original trial balance (*blue*) are adjusted for the debit or credit amounts in the Adjustments columns (*red*). The adjusted trial balance is totaled to determine that the accounts remain in balance.

   At this point, the worksheet is almost complete. We have emphasized that financial statements are prepared *directly from the adjusted trial balance.* Thus we have only to arrange these accounts into the format of financial statements.

4. *Extend the adjusted trial balance amounts into the appropriate financial statement columns.* The balance sheet accounts—assets, liabilities, and owners' equity—are extended into the Balance Sheet columns; income statement amounts, into the Income Statement columns. (The "Balance Sheet" and "Income Statement" captions in the original trial balance should simplify this procedure. Notice each amount is extended to only one column. Also, the account retains the same debit or credit balance as shown in the adjusted trial balance.)

5. *Total the financial statement columns; determine and record net income or net loss.* The final step in preparing the worksheet consists of totaling the Income Statement and Balance Sheet columns and then bringing each set of columns into balance. These tasks are performed on the bottom three lines of the worksheet. In our illustration, the amounts involved in this final step are shown in *black.*

When the Income Statement and Balance Sheet columns are first totaled, their respective debit and credit columns will *not* be equal. But each set of columns should be out of balance by the *same amount*—and that amount should be the amount of net income or net loss for the period.

Let us briefly explain *why* both sets of columns initially are out of balance by this amount. First consider the Income Statement columns. The Credit column contains the revenue accounts, and the Debit column, the expense accounts. The difference, therefore, represents the net income (net loss) for the period.

Now consider the Balance Sheet columns. All of the balance sheet amounts are shown at up-to-date amounts *except* for the Retained Earnings account, which still contains the balance from the *beginning* of the period. To bring the Retained Earnings account up-to-date, we must add net income and subtract any dividends. The dividends already appear in the Balance Sheet Debit column. So what's the only thing missing? The net income (or net loss) for the period.

To bring both sets of columns into balance, we enter the net income (or net loss) on the next line. The same amount will appear in both the Income Statement columns and the Balance Sheet columns. But in one set of columns it appears as a debit, and in the other, it appears as a credit.[3] After this amount is entered, each set of columns should balance.

Computers Do the Pencil-Pushing   When a worksheet is prepared by computer, accountants perform only *one* of the steps listed above—*entering the adjustments.* The computer automatically lists the ledger accounts in the form of a trial balance. After the accountant has entered the adjustments, it automatically computes the adjusted account balances and completes the worksheet. (Once the adjusted balances are determined, completing the worksheet involves nothing more than putting these amounts in the appropriate column and determining the column totals.)

---

[3] To bring the Income Statement columns into balance, net *income* is entered in the *Debit column.* This is because the Credit column (revenue) exceeds the Debit column (expenses). But in the balance sheet, net income is an element of owners' equity, which is represented by a credit. In the event of a net *loss,* this situation reverses.

EXHIBIT 5–13 The Worksheet

OVERNIGHT AUTO SERVICE
WORKSHEET
FOR THE YEAR ENDED DECEMBER 31, 2015

	Trial Balance		Adjustments*		Adjusted Trial Balance		Income Statement		Balance Sheet	
	Dr	Cr	Dr	Cr	Dr	Cr	Dr	Cr	Dr	Cr
Balance sheet accounts:										
Cash	18,592				18,592				18,592	
Accounts Receivable	6,500		(h) 750		7,250				7,250	
Shop Supplies	1,800			(a) 600	1,200				1,200	
Unexpired Insurance	4,500			(b) 1,500	3,000				3,000	
Tools and Equipment	12,000				12,000				12,000	
Accumulated Depreciation: Tools and Equipment		2,000		(d) 200		2,200				2,200
Building	36,000				36,000				36,000	
Accumulated Depreciation: Building		1,500		(c) 150		1,650				1,650
Land	52,000				52,000				52,000	
Notes Payable		4,000				4,000				4,000
Accounts Payable		2,690				2,690				2,690
Income Taxes Payable		1,560		(i) 4,020		5,580				5,580
Unearned Rent Revenue		9,000	(e) 3,000			6,000				6,000
Capital Stock		80,000				80,000				80,000
Retained Earnings		0				0				0
Dividends	14,000				14,000				14,000	
Wages Payable				(f) 1,950		1,950				1,950
Interest Payable				(g) 30		30				30
Income statement accounts:										
Repair Service Revenue		171,250		(h) 750		172,000		172,000		
Advertising Expense	3,900				3,900		3,900			
Wages Expense	56,800		(f) 1,950		58,750		58,750			
Supplies Expense	6,900		(a) 600		7,500		7,500			
Depreciation Expense: Building	1,500		(c) 150		1,650		1,650			
Depreciation Expense: Tools and Equipment	2,000		(d) 200		2,200		2,200			
Utilities Expense	19,400				19,400		19,400			
Insurance Expense	13,500		(b) 1,500		15,000		15,000			
Income Taxes Expense	22,608		(i) 4,020		26,628		26,628			
Rent Revenue Earned				(e) 3,000		3,000		3,000		
Interest Expense			(g) 30		30		30			
	272,000	272,000	12,200	12,200	279,100	279,100	135,058	175,000	144,042	104,100
Net income							39,942			39,942
Totals							175,000	175,000	144,042	144,042

*Adjustments:
(a) Shop supplies used in December.
(b) Portion of insurance cost expiring in December.
(c) Depreciation on building for December.
(d) Depreciation of tools and equipment for December.
(e) Earned one-third of rent revenue collected in advance from Harbor Cab.

(f) Unpaid wages owed to employees at December 31.
(g) Interest payable accrued during December.
(h) Repair service revenue earned in December but not yet billed.
(i) Income taxes expense for December.

WHAT IF: A SPECIAL APPLICATION OF WORKSHEET SOFTWARE

We have discussed a relatively simple application of the worksheet concept—illustrating the effects of proposed *adjusting entries* on account balances. But the same concept can be applied to proposed *future transactions*. The effects of the proposed transactions simply are entered in the "Adjustments" columns. Thus, without disrupting the accounting records, accountants can prepare schedules showing how the company's financial statements might be affected by such events as a merger with another company, a 15 percent increase in sales volume, or the closure of a plant.

There is a tendency to view worksheets as mechanical and old-fashioned. This is not at all the case. Today, the mechanical aspects are handled entirely by computer. The real purpose of a worksheet is to show quickly and efficiently how specific events or transactions will affect the financial statements. This isn't bookkeeping—it's *planning*.

END-OF-CHAPTER REVIEW

LO5-1   Prepare an income statement, a statement of retained earnings, and a balance sheet. The financial statements are prepared directly from the adjusted trial balance. The income statement is prepared by reporting all revenue earned during the period, less all expenses incurred in generating the related revenue. The retained earnings statement reports any increase to Retained Earnings resulting from net income earned for the period, as well as any decreases to Retained Earnings resulting from dividends declared or a net loss incurred for the period. The balance sheet reveals the company's financial position by reporting its economic resources (assets) and the claims against those resources (liabilities and owners' equity).

LO5-2   Explain how the income statement and the statement of retained earnings relate to the balance sheet. An income statement shows the revenue and expenses of a business for a specified accounting period. In the statement of retained earnings, the net income figure from the income statement is added to the beginning Retained Earnings balance, while dividends declared during the period are subtracted, in arriving at the ending Retained Earnings balance. The ending Retained Earnings balance is then reported in the balance sheet as a component of owners' equity.

LO5-3   Explain the concept of *adequate disclosure*. Adequate disclosure is the generally accepted accounting principle that financial statements should include any information that an informed user needs to interpret the statements properly. The appropriate disclosures usually are contained in several pages of notes that accompany the statements.

LO5-4   Explain the purposes of *closing entries*; prepare these entries. Closing entries serve two basic purposes. The first is to return the balances of the temporary owners' equity accounts (revenue, expense, and dividends accounts) to zero so that these accounts may be used to measure the activities of the next reporting period. The second purpose of closing entries is to update the balance of the Retained Earnings account. Four closing entries generally are needed: (1) Close the revenue accounts to the Income Summary account, (2) close the expense accounts to the Income Summary account, (3) close the balance of the Income Summary account to the Retained Earnings account, and (4) close the Dividends account to the Retained Earnings account.

LO5-5   Prepare an after-closing trial balance. After the revenue and expense accounts have been closed, it is desirable to prepare an after-closing trial balance consisting solely of balance sheet accounts. The after-closing trial balance, or post-closing trial balance, gives assurance that the accounts of the general ledger are in balance and ready for recording transactions for the new accounting period.

LO5-6   Use financial statement information to evaluate profitability and liquidity. Profitability is an increase in stockholders' equity resulting from revenue exceeding expenses, whereas liquidity refers to a company's ability to meet its cash obligations as they come due. Liquidity, at least in the short term, may be *independent* of profitability. Financial statements are useful tools for evaluating both profitability and liquidity. In the Financial Analysis feature, we illustrated several measures of profitability and liquidity computed using financial statement information. throughout the remainder of this text we introduce and discuss many additional measures.

LO5-7   Explain how *interim* financial statements are prepared in a business that closes its accounts only at year-end. When a business closes its accounts only at year-end, the revenue, expense, and dividends accounts have balances representing the activities of the year-to-date. To prepare an income statement for any period shorter than the year-to-date, we subtract from the current balance in the revenue or expense account the balance in the account as of the beginning of the desired period. This process of subtracting prior balances from the current balance is repeated for each revenue and expense account and for the dividends account. No computations of this type are required for the balance sheet accounts, as a balance sheet is based on the account balances at the balance sheet date.

LO5-8   Prepare a worksheet and explain its uses. A worksheet is a "testing ground" on which the ledger accounts are adjusted, balanced, and arranged in the format of financial statements. A worksheet consists of a trial balance, the end-of-period adjusting entries, an adjusted trial balance, and columns showing the ledger accounts arranged as an income statement and as a balance sheet. The completed worksheet is used as the basis for preparing financial statements and for recording adjusting and closing entries in the formal accounting records.

---

*Supplemental Topic, "The Worksheet."

> ## Key Terms Introduced or Emphasized in Chapter 5

adequate disclosure (p. 198)   The generally accepted accounting principle of providing with financial statements any information that users need to interpret those statements properly.

after-closing trial balance (p. 205)   A trial balance prepared after all closing entries have been made. Consists only of accounts for assets, liabilities, and owners' equity.

classified balance sheet (p. 198)   A balance sheet where current assets and current liabilities are listed separately from noncurrent assets and noncurrent liabilities.

closing entries (p. 200)   Journal entries made at the end of the period for the purpose of closing temporary accounts (revenue, expense, and dividends accounts) and transferring balances to the Retained Earnings account.

current assets (p. 198)   Cash and other assets that can be converted into cash or used up within a relatively short period of time without interfering with normal business operations.

current liabilities (p. 198)   Existing obligations that are expected to be satisfied with a company's current assets within a relatively short period of time.

general ledger software (p. 209)   Computer software used for recording transactions, maintaining journals and ledgers, and preparing financial statements. Also includes spreadsheet capabilities for showing the effects of proposed adjusting entries or transactions on the financial statements without actually recording these entries in the accounting records.

Income Summary (p. 200)   The summary account in the ledger to which revenue and expense accounts are closed at the end of the period. The balance (credit balance for a net income, debit balance for a net loss) is transferred to the Retained Earnings account.

interim financial statements (p. 207)   Financial statements prepared for periods of less than one year (includes monthly and quarterly statements).

notes (accompanying financial statements) (p. 199)   Supplemental disclosures that accompany financial statements. These notes provide users with various types of information considered necessary for the proper interpretation of the statements.

worksheet (p. 209)   A multicolumn schedule showing the relationships among the current account balances (a trial balance), proposed or actual adjusting entries or transactions, and the financial statements that would result if these adjusting entries or transactions were recorded. Used both at the end of the accounting period as an aid to preparing financial statements and for planning purposes.

Demonstration Problem

Jan's Dance Studio, Inc., performs adjusting entries every month, but closes its accounts only at year-end. The studio's year-end *adjusted trial balance* dated December 31, 2015, appears below. (Bear in mind, the balance shown for Retained Earnings was last updated on December 31, *2014*.)

JAN'S DANCE STUDIO, INC.
ADJUSTED TRIAL BALANCE
DECEMBER 31, 2015

Cash	$171,100	
Accounts receivable	9,400	
Prepaid studio rent	3,000	
Unexpired insurance	7,200	
Supplies	500	
Equipment	18,000	
Accumulated depreciation: equipment		$ 7,200
Notes payable		10,000
Accounts payable		3,200
Salaries payable		4,000
Income taxes payable		6,000
Unearned studio revenue		8,800
Capital stock		100,000
Retained earnings		40,000
Dividends	6,000	
Studio revenue earned		165,000
Salary expense	85,000	
Supply expense	3,900	
Rent expense	12,000	
Insurance expense	1,900	
Advertising expense	500	
Depreciation expense: equipment	1,800	
Interest expense	900	
Income taxes expense	23,000	
	$344,200	$344,200

Instructions

a.   Prepare an income statement and statement of retained earnings for the year ended December 31, 2015. Also prepare the studio's balance sheet dated December 31, 2015.

b.   Prepare the necessary closing entries at December 31, 2015.

c.   Prepare an after-closing trial balance dated December 31, 2015.

Solution to the Demonstration Problem

a.

JAN'S DANCE STUDIO, INC.
INCOME STATEMENT
FOR THE YEAR ENDED DECEMBER 31, 2015

Revenue:

Studio revenue earned		$165,000

Expenses:

Salary expense	$85,000	
Supply expense	3,900	
Rent expense	12,000	
Insurance expense	1,900	
Advertising expense	500	
Depreciation expense: equipment	1,800	
Interest expense	900	106,000
Income before income taxes		$ 59,000
Income taxes expense		23,000
Net income		$ 36,000

JAN'S DANCE STUDIO, INC.
STATEMENT OF RETAINED EARNINGS
FOR THE YEAR ENDED DECEMBER 31, 2015

Retained earnings, January 1, 2015	$40,000
Add: Net income earned in 2015	36,000
Subtotal	$76,000
Less: Dividends declared in 2015	6,000
Retained earnings, December 31, 2015	$70,000

JAN'S DANCE STUDIO, INC.
BALANCE SHEET
DECEMBER 31, 2015

Assets

Cash		$171,100
Accounts receivable		9,400
Prepaid studio rent		3,000
Unexpired insurance		7,200
Supplies		500
Equipment	$18,000	
Less: Accumulated depreciation: equipment	7,200	10,800
Total assets		$202,000

Liabilities & Stockholders' Equity

Liabilities:

Notes payable		$ 10,000
Accounts payable		3,200
Salaries payable		4,000
Income taxes payable		6,000
Unearned studio revenue		8,800
Total liabilities		$ 32,000

Stockholders' equity:

Capital stock		$100,000
Retained earnings		70,000
Total stockholders' equity		$170,000
Total liabilities and stockholders' equity		$202,000

b.

JAN'S DANCE STUDIO, INC. GENERAL JOURNAL DECEMBER 31, 2015			
Date	**Account Titles and Explanations**	**Debit**	**Credit**
Dec. 31 2015			
1.	Studio Revenue Earned	165,000	
	Income Summary		165,000
	To close Studio Revenue Earned.		
2.	Income Summary	129,000	
	Salary Expense		85,000
	Supply Expense		3,900
	Rent Expense		12,000
	Insurance Expense		1,900
	Advertising Expense		500
	Depreciation Expense: Equipment		1,800
	Interest Expense		900
	Income Taxes Expense		23,000
	To close all expense accounts.		
3.	Income Summary	36,000	
	Retained Earnings		36,000
	To transfer net income earned in 2015 to the Retained Earnings account ($165,000 − $129,000 = $36,000).		
4.	Retained Earnings	6,000	
	Dividends		6,000
	To transfer dividends declared in 2015 to the Retained Earnings account.		

c.

JAN'S DANCE STUDIO, INC. AFTER-CLOSING TRIAL BALANCE DECEMBER 31, 2015		
Cash	$171,100	
Accounts receivable	9,400	
Prepaid studio rent	3,000	
Unexpired insurance	7,200	
Supplies	500	
Equipment	18,000	
Accumulated depreciation: equipment		$ 7,200
Notes payable . . , ...		10,000
Accounts payable.		3,200
Salaries payable		4,000
Income taxes payable		6,000
Unearned studio revenue		8,800
Capital stock		100,000
Retained earnings, December 31		70,000
	$209,200	$209,200

Self-Test Questions

The answers to these questions appear on page 242.

1. For a publicly owned company, indicate which of the following accounting activities are likely to occur at or shortly after year-end. (More than one answer may be correct.)

   a. Preparation of income tax returns.

   b. Adjusting and closing of the accounts.

   c. Drafting of disclosures that accompany the financial statements.

   d. An audit of the financial statements by an independent CPA firm.

2. Which of the following financial statements is generally prepared first?

   a. Income statement.

   b. Balance sheet.

   c. Statement of retained earnings.

   d. Statement of cash flows.

3. Which of the following accounts would *never* be reported in the income statement as an expense?

   a. Depreciation expense.

   b. Income taxes expense.

   c. Interest expense.

   d. Dividends expense.

4. Which of the following accounts would *never* appear in the after-closing trial balance? (More than one answer may be correct.)

   a. Unearned revenue.

   b. Dividends.

   c. Accumulated depreciation.

   d. Income taxes expense.

5. Which of the following journal entries is required to close the Income Summary account of a profitable company?

   a. Debit Income Summary, credit Retained Earnings.

   b. Credit Income Summary, debit Retained Earnings.

   c. Debit Income Summary, credit Capital Stock.

   d. Credit Income Summary, debit Capital Stock.

6. Indicate those items for which generally accepted accounting principles *require* disclosure in notes accompanying the financial statements. (More than one answer may be correct.)

   a. A large lawsuit was filed against the company two days *after* the balance sheet date.

   b. The depreciation method in use, given that several different methods are acceptable under generally accepted accounting principles.

   c. Whether small but long-lived items—such as electric pencil sharpeners and handheld calculators—are charged to asset accounts or to expense accounts.

   d. As of year-end, the chief executive officer had been hospitalized because of chest pains.

7. Ski West adjusts its accounts at the end of each month but closes them only at the end of the calendar year (December 31). The ending balances in the Equipment Rental Revenue account and the Cash account in February and March appear below.

	Feb. 28	Mar. 31
Cash.	$14,200	$26,500
Equipment rental revenue	12,100	18,400

Ski West prepares financial statements showing separately the operating results of each month. In the financial statements prepared for the *month* ended March 31, Equipment Rental Revenue and Cash should appear as follows:

   a. Equipment Rental Revenue, $18,400; Cash, $26,500.

   b. Equipment Rental Revenue, $18,400; Cash, $12,300.

   c. Equipment Rental Revenue, $6,300; Cash, $26,500.

   d. Equipment Rental Revenue, $6,300; Cash, $12,300.

8. Which of the following accounts is *not* closed to the Income Summary account at the end of the accounting period? (More than one answer may be correct.)

   a. Rent Expense.

   b. Accumulated Depreciation.

   c. Unearned Revenue.

   d. Supplies Expense.

ASSIGNMENT MATERIAL   Discussion Questions

1. Explain briefly the items generally included in a company's annual report. (You may use the financial statements appearing in Appendix A to support your answer.)

2. Some people think that a company's retained earnings represent *cash* reserved for the payment of dividends. Are they correct? Explain.

3. Discuss the relationship among the income statement, the statement of retained earnings, and the balance sheet.

4. Identify several items that may require disclosure in the notes that accompany financial statements.

5. What type of accounts are referred to as *temporary* or *nominal* accounts? What is meant by these terms?

6. What type of accounts are referred to as *permanent* or *real* accounts? What is meant by these terms?

7. Explain *why* the Dividends account is closed directly to the Retained Earnings account.

8. Which accounts appear in a company's after-closing trial balance? How do these accounts differ from those reported in an adjusted trial balance?

9. Can a company be profitable but not liquid? Explain.

10. What are interim financial statements? Do accounts that appear in a company's interim balance sheet require any special computations to be reported correctly? Explain.

11. Explain the accounting principle of *adequate disclosure*.

12. How does depreciation expense differ from other operating expenses?

13. Explain the need for closing entries and describe the process by which temporary owners' equity accounts are closed at year-end.

14. Explain the significance of measuring a company's *return on equity*.

15. Explain several purposes that may be served by preparing a worksheet (or using computer software that achieves the goals of a worksheet).

———————

Supplemental Topic, "The Worksheet."

Brief Exercises

LO5-1, LO5-2

BRIEF EXERCISE 5.1

Balancing the Accounting Equation

During the current year, the total assets of Mifflinburg Corporation decreased by $60,000 and total liabilities decreased by $300,000. The company issued $100,000 of new stock, and its net income for the year was $250,000. No other changes to stockholders' equity occurred during the year. Determine the dollar amount of dividends declared by the company during the year.

LO5-1, LO5-2

BRIEF EXERCISE 5.2

Income Statement and Balance Sheet Relationships

On November 1, 2015, RockCreek Corporation invested $50,000 in a new delivery truck. The truck is being depreciated at a monthly rate of $750. During 2015, the company issued stock for $80,000 and declared dividends of $10,000. Its net income in 2015 was $90,000. RockCreek's *ending* Retained Earnings balance as reported in its December 31, 2015, balance sheet was $100,000. Its beginning Capital Stock balance on January 1, 2015, was $150,000. Given this information, determine the total stockholders' equity reported in the company's balance sheet dated December 31, 2015.

LO5-1, LO5-2

BRIEF EXERCISE 5.3

Classifying Balance Sheet Accounts

Indicate in which section of the balance sheet each of the following accounts is *classified*. Use the symbols **CA** for current assets, **NCA** for noncurrent assets, **CL** for current liabilities, **LTL** for long-term liabilities, and **SHE** for stockholders' equity.

a. Prepaid Rent
b. Dividends Payable
c. Salaries Payable
d. Accumulated Depreciation: Equipment
e. Retained Earnings

f. Mortgage Payable (due in 15 years)
g. Unearned Service Revenue
h. Accounts Receivable
i. Land
j. Office Supplies

LO5-4

BRIEF EXERCISE 5.4

Identifying and Closing Temporary Accounts

Indicate whether a debit or credit is required to *close* each of the following accounts. Use the symbols **D** if a debit is required, **C** if a credit is required, and **N** if the account is *not* closed at the end of the period.

a. Salary Expense
b. Unexpired Insurance
c. Consulting Fees Earned
d. Depreciation Expense
e. Dividends
f. Retained Earnings
g. Interest Revenue
h. Accumulated Depreciation
i. Income Taxes Expense
j. Unearned Revenue
k. Income Summary (of a *profitable* company)
l. Income Summary (of an *unprofitable* company)

LO5-4

BRIEF EXERCISE 5.5

Closing Entries of a
Profitable Company

The following account balances were taken from Harris Corporation's year-end *adjusted* trial balance (assume these are the company's only *temporary* accounts):

Dividends	$ 800
Service revenue	25,600
Supplies expense	730
Rent expense	4,900
Depreciation expense: equipment	1,500
Salaries expense	15,300
Income taxes expense	910

Prepare the company's necessary closing entries.

LO5-4

BRIEF EXERCISE 5.6

Closing Entries of an
Unprofitable Company

The following account balances were taken from Jachobson Consulting's year-end *adjusted* trial balance (assume these are the company's only *temporary* accounts):

Consulting fees earned	$26,000
Interest revenue	300
Insurance expense	1,900
Rent expense	10,800
Depreciation expense: office equipment	5,600
Salaries expense	16,400
Dividends	400

Prepare the company's necessary closing entries.

Indicate whether each of the following accounts appears in the debit column or in the credit column of an *after-closing* trial balance. Use the symbols **D** for debit column, **C** for credit column, and **N** if the account does *not* appear in an after-closing trial balance.

a. Unearned Service Revenue

b. Accumulated Depreciation: Office Equipment

c. Land

d. Consulting Fees Earned

e. Capital Stock

LO5-5

BRIEF EXERCISE 5.7

After-Closing Trial Balance

f. Income Summary (of a *profitable* company)

g. Depreciation Expense: Office Equipment

h. Income Taxes Payable

i. Unexpired Insurance

j. Dividends

k. Retained Earnings

l. Dividends Payable

LO5-6

BRIEF EXERCISE 5.8

Profitability and Liquidity
Measures

Cat Fancy, Inc., has provided the following information from its most current financial statements:

Total revenue	$125,000
Total expenses	80,000
Total current assets	32,000
Total current liabilities	8,000
Total stockholders' equity, January 1, 2015	74,000
Total stockholders' equity, December 31, 2015	76,000

a. Compute the company's net income percentage in 2015.

b. Compute the company's return on equity in 2015.

c. Compute the company's current ratio at December 31, 2015.

LO5-7

BRIEF EXERCISE 5.9

Measuring Interim Revenue

The following revenue figures were taken from Rosemont Corporation's adjusted trial balance at the end of the following months (adjusting entries are performed *monthly* whereas closing entries are performed *annually,* on December 31):

March 31 (end of the first quarter)	$140,000
September 30 (end of the third quarter)	450,000
December 31 (end of the fourth quarter)	680,000

Compute how much revenue the company earned from:

a. April 1 through September 30.

b. October 1 through December 31 (the fourth quarter).

c. April 1 through December 31.

LO5-8

*BRIEF EXERCISE 5.10

The Worksheet

Accountants at Warner Co. use worksheets similar to the one shown in Exhibit 5–13, on page 211. In the company's most current year-end worksheet, the amounts transferred *from* the adjusted trial balance columns *to* the balance sheet and income statement columns are as follows:

Total amount transferred to the credit column of the balance sheet	$410,000
Total amount transferred to the debit column of the balance sheet	540,000
Total amount transferred to the credit column of the income statement	380,000

a. What was the company's net income for the year?

b. What was the total amount transferred from the adjusted trial balance columns to the debit column of the income statement?

Exercises

LO5-1 through LO5-7

EXERCISE 5.1

Accounting Terminology

Listed below are nine technical terms used in this chapter:

Liquidity	Nominal accounts	Real accounts
Adequate disclosure	After-closing trial balance	Closing entries
Income summary	Interim financial statements	Dividends

Each of the following statements may (or may not) describe one of these technical terms. For each statement, indicate the accounting term described, or answer "None" if the statement does not describe any of the items.

a. The accounting principle intended to assist users in *interpreting* financial statements.

b. A term used to describe a company's ability to pay its obligations as they come due.

c. A term used in reference to accounts that are closed at year-end.

d. A term used in reference to accounts that are not closed at year-end.

e. A document prepared to assist management in detecting whether any errors occurred in posting the closing entries.

f. A policy decision by a corporation to distribute a portion of its income to stockholders.

g. The process by which the Retained Earnings account is updated at year-end.

h. Entries made during the accounting period to correct errors in the original recording of complex transactions.

LO5-1, LO5-2, LO5-6

EXERCISE 5.2

Financial Statement Preparation

Green Lawns, Inc., performs adjusting entries every month, but closes its accounts *only at year-end.* The company's year-end *adjusted trial balance* dated December 31, 2015, was:

---

* *Supplemental Topic,* "The Worksheet."

GREEN LAWNS, INC.
ADJUSTED TRIAL BALANCE
DECEMBER 31, 2015

Cash	$ 182,200	
Accounts receivable	9,000	
Supplies	600	
Equipment	24,000	
Accumulated depreciation: equipment		$ 10,000
Accounts payable		3,000
Income taxes payable		7,000
Capital stock		50,000
Retained earnings		90,000
Dividends	4,000	
Lawn care revenue earned		192,000
Salary expense	104,000	
Supply expense	2,400	
Advertising expense	600	
Depreciation expense: equipment	2,000	
Income taxes expense	23,200	
	$ 352,000	$352,000

a. Prepare an income statement and statement of retained earnings for the year ended December 31, 2015. Also prepare the company's balance sheet dated December 31, 2015.

b. Does the company appear to be liquid? Defend your answer.

c. Has the company been profitable in the past? Explain.

LO5-1, LO5-2, LO5-6
EXERCISE 5.3
Financial Statement
Preparation

Wilderness Guide Services, Inc., performs adjusting entries every month, but closes its accounts *only at year-end.* The company's year-end *adjusted trial balance* dated December 31, 2015, follows:

WILDERNESS GUIDE SERVICES, INC.
ADJUSTED TRIAL BALANCE
DECEMBER 31, 2015

Cash	$ 12,200	
Accounts receivable	31,000	
Camping supplies	7,900	
Unexpired insurance policies	2,400	
Equipment	70,000	
Accumulated depreciation: equipment		$ 60,000
Notes payable (due 4/1/16)		18,000
Accounts payable		9,500
Capital stock		25,000
Retained earnings		15,000
Dividends	1,000	
Guide revenue earned		102,000
Salary expense	87,500	
Camping supply expense	1,200	
Insurance expense	9,600	
Depreciation expense: equipment	5,000	
Interest expense	1,700	
	$229,500	$229,500

a. Prepare an income statement and statement of retained earnings for the year ended December 31, 2015. Also prepare the company's balance sheet dated December 31, 2015. (Hint: Unprofitable companies have no income taxes expense.)

b. Does the company appear to be liquid? Defend your answer.

c. Has the company been profitable in the past? Explain.

LO5-2, LO5-4, LO5-5
EXERCISE 5.4
Preparing Closing Entries
and an After-Closing Trial
Balance

Refer to the adjusted trial balance of Green Lawns, Inc., illustrated in Exercise 5.2 to respond to the following items:

a. Prepare all necessary closing entries at December 31, 2015.

b. Prepare an after-closing trial balance dated December 31, 2015.

c. Compare the Retained Earnings balance reported in the after-closing trial balance prepared in part **b** to the balance reported in the adjusted trial balance. Explain *why* the two balances are different. (Include in your explanation why the balance reported in the after-closing trial balance has increased or decreased subsequent to the closing process.)

LO5-2, LO5-4, LO5-5
EXERCISE 5.5
Preparing Closing Entries
and an After-Closing Trial
Balance

Refer to the adjusted trial balance of Wilderness Guide Services, Inc., illustrated in Exercise 5.3 to respond to the following items:

a. Prepare all necessary closing entries at December 31, 2015.

b. Prepare an after-closing trial balance dated December 31, 2015.

c. Compare the Retained Earnings balance reported in the after-closing trial balance prepared in part **b** to the balance reported in the adjusted trial balance. Explain *why* the two balances are different. (Include in your explanation why the balance reported in the after-closing trial balance has increased or decreased subsequent to the closing process.)

LO5-3
EXERCISE 5.6
Adequate Disclosure

The following information was taken directly from the footnotes to the financial statements of **Best Buy**:

1. "We recognize revenue at the time the customer takes possession of the merchandise."

2. "We sell gift cards to customers and initially establish an Unredeemed Gift Card Liability for the cash value of the gift card."

3. "Advertising costs are recorded as expenses the first time the advertisement runs."

4. "We compute depreciation using the straight-line method."

a. Discuss what is meant by each of the above footnote items.

b. As noted, **Best Buy** uses a Unredeemed Gift Card Liability account to record the sale of gift cards. Assume that you purchase a $500 gift card from **Best Buy** as a birthday present for a friend. Prepare the journal entries made by **Best Buy** to record (1) your purchase of the gift card and (2) the *use* of the gift card by your friend to purchase a $500 television.

c. Discuss how the *matching principle* relates to **Best Buy**'s treatment of advertising expenditures.

LO5-2, LO5-4
EXERCISE 5.7
Closing Entries of a
Profitable Company

Gerdes Psychological Services, Inc., closes its temporary accounts once each year on December 31. The company recently issued the following income statement as part of its annual report:

GERDES PSYCHOLOGICAL SERVICES, INC.
INCOME STATEMENT
FOR THE YEAR ENDED DECEMBER 31, 2015

Revenue:		
Counseling revenue		$225,000
Expenses:		
Advertising expense	$ 1,800	
Salaries expense	94,000	
Office supplies expense	1,200	
Utilities expense	850	
Malpractice insurance expense	6,000	
Office rent expense	24,000	
Continuing education expense	2,650	
Depreciation expense: fixtures	4,500	
Miscellaneous expense	6,000	
Income taxes expense	29,400	170,400
Net income		$ 54,600

The firm's statement of retained earnings indicates that a $6,000 cash dividend was declared and paid during 2015.

a. Prepare the necessary closing entries on December 31, 2015.

b. If the firm's Retained Earnings account had a $92,000 balance on January 1, 2015, at what amount should Retained Earnings be reported in the firm's balance sheet dated December 31, 2015?

LO5-2, LO5-4
EXERCISE 5.8
Closing Entries of an
Unprofitable Company

Hammerstone Consulting provides risk management services to individuals and to corporate clients. The company closes its temporary accounts once each year on December 31. The company recently issued the following income statement as part of its annual report:

HAMMERSTONE CONSULTING
INCOME STATEMENT
FOR THE YEAR ENDED DECEMBER 31, 2015

Revenue:		
Consulting revenue—individual clients.		$ 60,000
Consulting revenue—corporate clients		240,000
		$ 300,000
Expenses:		
Advertising expense	$ 24,000	
Depreciation expense: computers	36,000	
Rent expense	14,400	
Office supplies expense	6,600	
Travel expense	86,700	
Utilities expense	4,950	
Telephone and Internet expense.	2,850	
Salaries expense.	233,250	
Interest expense	3,750	412,500
Net loss		$(112,500)

The firm's statement of retained earnings indicates that a $37,500 cash dividend was declared and paid in 2015.

a. Prepare the necessary closing entries on December 31, 2015.

b. If the firm's Retained Earnings account had a $450,000 balance on January 1, 2015, at what amount should Retained Earnings be reported in the firm's balance sheet dated December 31, 2015?

LO5-2, LO5-4
EXERCISE 5.9
Distinction between the
Adjusting and the Closing
Process

When Torretti Company began business on August 1, it purchased a one-year fire insurance policy and debited the entire cost of $7,200 to Unexpired Insurance. Torretti *adjusts* its accounts at the end of each month and *closes* its books at the end of the year.

a. Give the *adjusting entry* required at December 31 with respect to this insurance policy.

b. Give the *closing entry* required at December 31 with respect to insurance expense. Assume that this policy is the only insurance policy Torretti had during the year.

c. Compare the dollar amount appearing in the December 31 adjusting entry (part **a**) with that in the closing entry (part **b**). Are the dollar amounts the same? Why or why not? Explain.

LO5-6
EXERCISE 5.10
Measuring and Evaluating
Profitability and Liquidity

A recent balance sheet of Save-A-Lot Supplies is provided below:

SAVE-A-LOT SUPPLIES
BALANCE SHEET
DECEMBER 31, 2015

Assets		
Cash.		$13,600
Accounts receivable.		14,400
Office supplies		600
Prepaid rent		3,400
Equipment	$24,000	
Accumulated depreciation: equipment	(9,600)	$14,400
Total assets.		$46,400
Liabilities		
Accounts payable.		$ 4,400
Income taxes payable		3,600
Total liabilities		$ 8,000
Stockholders' Equity		
Capital stock		$20,000
Retained earnings		18,400
Total stockholders' equity		$38,400
Total liabilities and stockholders' equity.		$46,400

Other information provided by the company is as follows:

Total revenue for the year ended December 31, 2015.....................	$51,000
Total expenses for the year ended December 31, 2015	38,250
Total stockholders' equity, January 1, 2015.............................	29,600

Compute and discuss briefly the significance of the following measures as they relate to Save-A-Lot Supplies:

a. Net income percentage in 2015.
b. Return on equity in 2015.
c. Working capital on December 31, 2015.
d. Current ratio on December 31, 2015.

LO5-6

EXERCISE 5.11

Measuring and Evaluating Profitability and Liquidity

A recent balance sheet of Denver Tours is provided below:

DENVER TOURS
BALANCE SHEET
DECEMBER 31, 2015

Assets

Cash......		$ 75,100
Accounts receivable.....		14,000
Office supplies		1,500
Prepaid rent		3,400
Buses	$ 240,000	
Accumulated depreciation: buses	(18,000)	$222,000
Total assets......		$316,000

Liabilities

Accounts payable	$140,200
Unearned revenue	94,800
Total liabilities......	$235,000

Stockholders' Equity

Capital stock......	$ 80,000
Retained earnings	1,000
Total stockholders' equity	$ 81,000
Total liabilities and stockholders' equity	$316,000

Other information provided by the company is as follows:

Total revenue for the year ended December 31, 2015.....................	$152,000
Total expenses for the year ended December 31, 2015	148,960
Total stockholders' equity, January 1, 2015.............................	79,000

Compute and discuss briefly the significance of the following measures as they relate to Denver Tours:

a. Net income percentage in 2015.
b. Return on equity in 2015.
c. Working capital on December 31, 2015.
d. Current ratio on December 31, 2015.

LO5-1, LO5-2, LO5-7		
EXERCISE 5.12		
Interim Results		

Ski Powder Resort ends its fiscal year on April 30. The business adjusts its accounts monthly, but *closes them only at year-end* (April 30). The resort's busy season is from December 1 through March 31.

Adrian Pride, the resort's chief financial officer, keeps a close watch on Lift Ticket Revenue and Cash. The balances of these accounts at the end of each of the last five months are as follows:

	Lift Ticket Revenue	Cash
November 30	$ 30,000	$ 9,000
December 31	200,000	59,000
January 31	640,000	94,000
February 28	850,000	116,000
March 31	990,000	138,000

Mr. Pride prepares income statements and balance sheets for the resort. Indicate what amounts will be shown in these statements for (1) Lift Ticket Revenue and (2) Cash, assuming they are prepared for:

a. The *month* ended February 28.

b. The entire "busy season to date"—that is, December 1 through March 31.

c. In terms of Lift Ticket Revenue and increases in Cash, which has been the resort's best month? (Indicate the dollar amounts.)

LO5-1, LO5-2, LO5-7
EXERCISE 5.13
Interim Results

Custodian Commandos, Inc., provides janitorial services to public school systems. The business adjusts its accounts monthly, but *closes them only at year-end*. Its fiscal year ends on December 31.

A summary of the company's total revenue and expenses at the end of five selected months is as follows:

	Total Revenue	Total Expenses
March 31	$ 69,000	$ 48,000
June 30	129,000	90,000
August 31	134,000	115,000
September 30	159,000	130,000
December 31	249,000	175,000

a. Rank the company's fiscal quarters from most profitable to least profitable.

b. Compute the company's income for the month of September.

c. Compute the company's net income (or loss) for the first two months of the *third quarter*. Provide a possible explanation why profitability for the first two months of the third quarter differs significantly from profitability achieved in the third month of the quarter (as computed in part **b**).

LO5-2, LO5-3
EXERCISE 5.14
Understanding the Effects of Errors on the Financial Statements

Indicate the effect of the following errors on each of the financial statement elements described in the column headings in the table below. Use the following symbols: **O** = overstated, **U** = understated, and **NE** = no effect.

Error	Net Income	Total Assets	Total Liabilities	Retained Earnings
a. Recorded a dividend as an *expense* in the income statement.				
b. Recorded unearned revenue as *earned* revenue in the income statement.				
c. Failed to record accrued wages payable at the end of the accounting period.				
d. Recorded a declared but unpaid dividend by debiting Dividends and crediting Cash.				
e. Failed to disclose a pending lawsuit in the notes accompanying the financial statements.				

LO5-3, LO5-6

EXERCISE 5.15

Examining Home Depot, Inc., Financial Statements

The **Home Depot, Inc.**, financial statements appear in Appendix A at the end of this textbook.

a. Does the company use straight-line depreciation? How can you tell?

b. At what point does the company recognize and record revenue from its customers?

c. Using information from the consolidated financial statements, evaluate briefly the company's profitability and liquidity.

Problem Set A

LO5-1, LO5-2, LO5-4, LO5-6

PROBLEM 5.1A

Correcting Classification Errors

Party Wagon, Inc., provides musical entertainment at weddings, dances, and various other functions. The company performs adjusting entries *monthly,* but prepares closing entries *annually* on December 31. The company recently hired Jack Armstrong as its new accountant. Jack's first assignment was to prepare an income statement, a statement of retained earnings, and a balance sheet using an *adjusted* trial balance given to him by his predecessor, dated December 31, 2015.

From the adjusted trial balance, Jack prepared the following set of financial statements:

PARTY WAGON, INC.
INCOME STATEMENT
FOR THE YEAR ENDED DECEMBER 31, 2015

Revenue:

Party revenue earned		$130,000
Unearned party revenue		1,800
Accounts receivable		9,000
Total revenue.		$140,800
Expenses:		
Insurance expense	$ 1,800	
Office rent expense.	12,000	
Supplies expense	1,200	
Dividends	1,000	
Salary expense	75,000	
Accumulated depreciation: van	16,000	
Accumulated depreciation: equipment and music.	14,000	
Repair and maintenance expense	2,000	
Travel expense	6,000	
Miscellaneous expense	3,600	
Interest expense	4,400	137,000
Income before income taxes		$ 3,800
Income taxes payable		400
Net income.		$ 3,400

PARTY WAGON, INC.
STATEMENT OF RETAINED EARNINGS
FOR THE YEAR ENDED DECEMBER 31, 2015

Retained earnings (per adjusted trial balance)............................	$15,000
Add: Income..	3,400
Less: Income taxes expense	2,000
Retained earnings Dec. 31, 2015.....................................	$16,400

PARTY WAGON, INC.
BALANCE SHEET
DECEMBER 31, 2015

Assets

Cash...		$15,000
Supplies		500
Van	$40,000	
Less: Depreciation expense: van	8,000	32,000
Equipment and music	$35,000	
Less: Depreciation expense: music and equipment	7,000	28,000
Total assets...		$75,500

Liabilities & Stockholders' Equity

Liabilities:

Accounts payable......................................	$ 7,000
Notes payable...	39,000
Salaries payable	1,600
Prepaid rent	2,000
Unexpired insurance...................................	4,500
Total liabilities	$54,100

Stockholders' Equity:

Capital stock...	5,000
Retained earnings.....................................	16,400
Total stockholders' equity.............................	$21,400
Total liabilities and stockholders' equity................	$75,500

Instructions

a. Prepare a corrected set of financial statements dated December 31, 2015. (You may assume that all of the figures in the company's adjusted trial balance were reported correctly except for Interest Payable of $200, which was mistakenly omitted in the financial statements prepared by Jack.)

b. Prepare the necessary year-end closing entries.

c. Using the financial statements prepared in part **a,** briefly evaluate the company's profitability and liquidity.

**LO5-1, LO5-2, LO5-4
through LO5-6**

PROBLEM 5.2A

Preparing Financial
Statements and Closing
Entries of a Profitable
Company

Affordable Lawn Care, Inc., provides lawn-mowing services to both commercial and residential customers. The company performs adjusting entries on a *monthly* basis, whereas closing entries are prepared *annually* at December 31. An *adjusted* trial balance dated December 31, 2015, follows.

AFFORDABLE LAWN CARE, INC.
ADJUSTED TRIAL BALANCE
DECEMBER 31, 2015

	Debits	Credits
Cash	$117,050	
Accounts receivable	9,600	
Unexpired insurance	16,000	
Prepaid rent	6,000	
Supplies	2,150	
Trucks	300,000	
Accumulated depreciation: trucks		$240,000
Mowing equipment	40,000	
Accumulated depreciation: mowing equipment		24,000
Accounts payable		3,000
Notes payable		100,000
Salaries payable		1,800
Interest payable		300
Income taxes payable		2,100
Unearned mowing revenue		1,800
Capital stock		40,000
Retained earnings		60,000
Dividends	10,000	
Mowing revenue earned		340,000
Insurance expense	4,800	
Office rent expense	72,000	
Supplies expense	10,400	
Salary expense	120,000	
Depreciation expense: trucks	60,000	
Depreciation expense: mowing equipment	8,000	
Repair and maintenance expense	6,000	
Fuel expense	3,000	
Miscellaneous expense	10,000	
Interest expense	6,000	
Income taxes expense	12,000	
	$813,000	$813,000

Instructions

a. Prepare an income statement and statement of retained earnings for the year ended December 31, 2015. Also prepare the company's balance sheet dated December 31, 2015.

b. Prepare the necessary year-end closing entries.

c. Prepare an after-closing trial balance.

d. Using the financial statements prepared in part **a,** briefly evaluate the company's profitability and liquidity.

LO5-1 through LO5-4,
LO5-6

PROBLEM 5.3A

Preparing Financial
Statements and Closing
Entries of an Unprofitable
Company

Mystic Masters, Inc., provides fortune-telling services over the Internet. In recent years the company has experienced severe financial difficulty. Its accountant prepares adjusting entries on a *monthly* basis, and closing entries on an *annual* basis, at December 31. An *adjusted* trial balance dated December 31, 2015, follows.

MYSTIC MASTERS, INC. ADJUSTED TRIAL BALANCE DECEMBER 31, 2015		
	Debits	Credits
Cash	$ 960	
Accounts receivable.	300	
Unexpired insurance	2,000	
Prepaid rent	1,500	
Supplies	200	
Furniture and fixtures	8,400	
Accumulated depreciation: furniture and fixtures		$ 5,200
Accounts payable.		6,540
Notes payable		24,000
Salaries payable.		1,700
Interest payable		360
Unearned client revenue		200
Capital stock		4,000
Retained earnings		2,600
Client revenue earned		52,000
Insurance expense.	6,000	
Office rent expense	9,000	
Supplies expense.	440	
Salary expense.	48,000	
Depreciation expense: furniture and fixtures	1,400	
Office and telephone expense	3,000	
Internet service expense	4,900	
Legal expense	1,500	
Interest expense.	4,000	
Miscellaneous expense	5,000	
	$96,600	$96,600

Instructions

a. Prepare an income statement and statement of retained earnings for the year ended December 31, 2015. Also prepare the company's balance sheet dated December 31, 2015. (Hint: The company incurred no income taxes expense in 2015.)

b. Prepare the necessary year-end closing entries.

c. Prepare an after-closing trial balance.

d. Using the financial statements prepared in part **a,** briefly evaluate the company's performance.

e. Identify information that the company is apt to disclose in the notes that accompany the financial statements prepared in part **a.**

LO5-1, LO5-2, LO5-7
PROBLEM 5.4A
Interim Financial
Statements

Guardian Insurance Agency adjusts its accounts monthly but closes them only at the end of the calendar year. Below are the adjusted balances of the revenue and expense accounts at September 30 of the current year and at the ends of two earlier months:

	Sept. 30	Aug. 31	June 30
Commissions earned	$144,000	$128,000	$90,000
Advertising expense.	28,000	23,000	15,000
Salaries expense	36,000	32,000	24,000
Rent expense.	22,500	20,000	15,000
Depreciation expense.	2,700	2,400	1,800

Instructions

a. Prepare a three-column income statement, showing net income for three separate time periods, all of which end on September 30. Use the format illustrated below. Show supporting computations for the amounts of revenue reported in the first two columns.

GUARDIAN INSURANCE AGENCY
INCOME STATEMENT
FOR THE FOLLOWING TIME PERIODS

	Month Ended Sept. 30	Quarter Ended Sept. 30	9 Months Ended Sept. 30
Revenue:			
Commissions earned	$ ____	$ ____	$ ____
Expenses:			

b. Briefly explain how you determined the dollar amounts for each of the three time periods. Would you apply the same process to the balances in Guardian's balance sheet accounts? Explain.

c. Assume that Guardian adjusts *and closes* its accounts at the end of *each month*. Briefly explain how you then would determine the revenue and expenses that would appear in each of the three columns of the income statement prepared in part **a**.

LO5-1 through LO5-4,
LO5-6

PROBLEM 5.5A
Short Comprehensive
Problem Including Both
Adjusting and Closing
Entries

Silver Lining, Inc., provides investment advisory services. The company adjusts its accounts *monthly,* but performs closing entries *annually* on December 31. The firm's *unadjusted* trial balance dated December 31, 2015, is shown on the following page.

SILVER LINING, INC.
UNADJUSTED TRIAL BALANCE
DECEMBER 31, 2015

	Debit	Credit
Cash	$ 42,835	
Accounts receivable.	2,000	
Office supplies	205	
Prepaid rent	1,200	
Unexpired insurance	270	
Office equipment	54,000	
Accumulated depreciation: office equipment		$ 35,250
Accounts payable.		1,400
Interest payable		360
Income taxes payable		1,750
Notes payable		9,000
Unearned consulting services revenue		3,500
Capital stock		30,000
Retained earnings		8,000
Dividends	1,000	
Consulting services revenue		60,000
Office supplies expense.	605	
Depreciation expense: office equipment	8,250	
Rent expense	3,525	
Insurance expense.	1,010	
Salaries expense	27,100	
Interest expense.	360	
Income taxes expense	6,900	
Totals	$149,260	$149,260

Other Data

1. Accrued but *unrecorded* and uncollected consulting services revenue totals $1,500 at December 31, 2015.
2. The company determined that $2,500 of previously unearned consulting services revenue had been earned at December 31, 2015.
3. Office supplies on hand at December 31 total $110.
4. The company purchased all of its equipment when it first began business. At that time, the estimated useful life of the equipment was six years (72 months).
5. The company prepaid its six-month rent agreement on October 1, 2015.
6. The company prepaid its 12-month insurance policy on March 1, 2015.
7. Accrued but *unpaid* salaries total $1,900 at December 31, 2015.
8. On June 1, 2015, the company borrowed $9,000 by signing a nine-month, 8 percent note payable. The entire amount, plus interest, is due on March 1, 2016.
9. The company's CPA estimates that income taxes expense for the *entire year* is $7,500. The unpaid portion of this amount is due early in 2016.

Instructions

a. Prepare the necessary adjusting journal entries on December 31, 2015. Prepare also an *adjusted trial balance* dated December 31, 2015.

b.   From the adjusted trial balance prepared in part **a,** prepare an income statement and statement of retained earnings for the year ended December 31, 2015. Also prepare the company's balance sheet dated December 31, 2015.

c.   Prepare the necessary year-end closing entries.

d.   Prepare an after-closing trial balance.

e.   Compute the company's average *monthly* insurance expense for January and February of 2015.

f.   Compute the company's average *monthly* rent expense for January through September of 2015.

g.   If the company purchased all of its office equipment when it first incorporated, for how long has it been in business as of December 31, 2015?

LO5-1 through LO5-4, LO5-6

PROBLEM 5.6A
Short Comprehensive Problem Including Both Adjusting and Closing Entries

Brushstroke Art Studio, Inc., provides quality instruction to aspiring artists. The business adjusts its accounts *monthly,* but performs closing entries *annually* on December 31. This is the studio's *unadjusted* trial balance dated December 31, 2015.

BRUSHSTROKE ART STUDIO, INC.
UNADJUSTED TRIAL BALANCE
DECEMBER 31, 2015

	Debits	Credits
Cash.	$ 22,380	
Client fees receivable.	71,250	
Supplies	6,000	
Prepaid studio rent.	2,500	
Studio equipment.	96,000	
Accumulated depreciation: studio equipment		$ 52,000
Accounts payable.		6,420
Note payable		24,000
Interest payable		480
Unearned client fees		8,000
Income taxes payable		5,000
Capital stock		50,000
Retained earnings		20,000
Client fees earned		82,310
Supplies expense.	4,000	
Salary expense.	17,250	
Interest expense.	480	
Studio rent expense	11,250	
Utilities expense.	3,300	
Depreciation expense: studio equipment.	8,800	
Income taxes expense	5,000	
	$248,210	$248,210

Other Data

1.   Supplies on hand at December 31, 2015, total $1,000.

2.   The studio pays rent quarterly (every three months). The last payment was made November 1, 2015. The next payment will be made early in February 2016.

3.   Studio equipment is being depreciated over 120 months (10 years).

4.   On October 1, 2015, the studio borrowed $24,000 by signing a 12-month, 12 percent note payable. The entire amount, plus interest, is due on September 30, 2016.

5. At December 31, 2015, $3,000 of previously unearned client fees had been *earned.*

6. Accrued, but *unrecorded* and uncollected client fees earned total $690 at December 31, 2015.

7. Accrued, but *unrecorded* and unpaid salary expense totals $750 at December 31, 2015.

8. Accrued income taxes expense for the *entire year* ending December 31, 2015, *total* $7,000. The full amount is due early in 2016.

Instructions

a. Prepare the necessary adjusting journal entries on December 31, 2015. Prepare also an *adjusted trial balance* dated December 31, 2015.

b. From the adjusted trial balance prepared in part **a,** prepare an income statement and statement of retained earnings for the year ended December 31, 2015. Also prepare the company's balance sheet dated December 31, 2015.

c. Prepare the necessary year-end closing entries.

d. Prepare an after-closing trial balance.

e. Has the studio's monthly rent remained the same throughout the year? If not, has it gone up or down? Explain.

LO5-8

*PROBLEM 5.7A

Short Comprehensive
Problem Including Adjusting
Entries, Closing Entries,
and Worksheet Preparation

Refer to the Demonstration Problem illustrated in the previous chapter on pages 163–166. Prepare a 10-column worksheet for Internet Consulting Service, Inc., dated December 31, 2015. At the bottom of your worksheet, prepare a brief explanation keyed to each adjusting entry.

LO5-6

PROBLEM 5.8A

Evaluating Profitability and
Liquidity

A recent annual report issued by hhgregg revealed the following data:

	End of Year	Beginning of Year
Current assets	$330.2 million	$404.7 million
Current liabilities.	$165.3 million	$215.5 million
Stockholders' equity	$316.6 million	$253.4 million

The company's income statement reported total annual revenue of $2,077.7 million and net income for the year of $48.2 million.

Instructions

a. Evaluate hhgregg's profitability by computing its net income percentage and its return on equity for the year.

b. Evaluate hhgregg's liquidity by computing its working capital and its current ratio at the beginning of the year and at the end of the year.

c. Does hhgregg appear to be both profitable and liquid? Explain.

---

* *Supplemental Topic,* "The Worksheet."

Problem Set B

Strong Knot, Inc., a service company, performs adjusting entries *monthly,* but prepares closing entries *annually* on December 31. The company recently hired Sally Addsup as its new accountant. Sally's first assignment was to prepare an income statement, a statement of retained earnings, and a balance sheet using an *adjusted* trial balance given to her by her predecessor, dated December 31, 2015. The statements Sally prepared are as follows:

STRONG KNOT, INC.
INCOME STATEMENT
FOR THE YEAR ENDED DECEMBER 31, 2015

Revenue:

Service revenue earned		$160,000
Unearned revenue		3,500
Accounts receivable		8,200
Total revenue		$171,700
Expenses:		
Insurance expense	$ 1,800	
Office rent expense	18,000	
Supplies expense	1,200	
Dividends	3,000	
Salary expense	96,000	
Accumulated depreciation: auto	12,000	
Accumulated depreciation: equipment	13,000	
Repair and maintenance expense	1,700	
Travel expense	6,600	
Miscellaneous expense	2,100	
Interest expense	2,800	158,200
Income before income taxes		$ 13,500
Income taxes payable		400
Net income		$ 13,100

STRONG KNOT, INC.
STATEMENT OF RETAINED EARNINGS
FOR THE YEAR ENDED DECEMBER 31, 2015

Retained earnings (per adjusted trial balance)	$17,500
Add: Income	13,100
Less: Income taxes expense	4,000
Retained earnings, Dec. 31, 2015	$26,600

STRONG KNOT, INC.
BALANCE SHEET
DECEMBER 31, 2015

Assets

Cash		$15,400
Supplies		900
Automobile	$37,000	
Less: Depreciation expense: automobile	4,000	33,000
Equipment and music	$39,000	
Less: Depreciation expense: equipment	3,000	36,000
Total assets.		$85,300

Liabilities & Stockholders' Equity

Liabilities:

Accounts payable	$ 5,200
Notes payable	45,800
Salaries payable	900
Prepaid rent	800
Unexpired insurance	3,000
Total liabilities	$55,700

Stockholders' Equity:

Capital stock	3,000
Retained earnings	26,600
Total stockholders' equity	$29,600
Total liabilities and stockholders' equity	$85,300

Instructions

a. Prepare a corrected set of financial statements dated December 31, 2015. (You may assume that all of the figures in the company's adjusted trial balance were reported correctly except for Notes Payable, which is some amount other than $45,800.)

b. Prepare the necessary year-end closing entries.

c. Using the financial statements prepared in part **a,** briefly evaluate the company's profitability and liquidity.

LO5-1, LO5-2, LO5-4 through LO5-6

PROBLEM 5.2B

Preparing Financial Statements and Closing Entries of a Profitable Company

Garden Wizards provides gardening services to both commercial and residential customers. The company performs adjusting entries on a *monthly* basis, whereas closing entries are prepared *annually* at December 31. An adjusted trial balance dated December 31, 2015, follows.

GARDEN WIZARDS
ADJUSTED TRIAL BALANCE
DECEMBER 31, 2015

	Debits	Credits
Cash	$ 27,800	
Accounts receivable	4,300	
Unexpired insurance	8,700	
Prepaid rent	3,200	
Supplies	1,400	
Trucks	140,000	
Accumulated depreciation: trucks		$ 75,000
Equipment	28,000	
Accumulated depreciation: equipment		14,000
Accounts payable		2,200
Notes payable		38,000
Salaries payable		900
Interest payable		300
Income taxes payable		1,700
Unearned service revenue		2,000
Capital stock		18,000
Retained earnings		21,000
Dividends	3,300	
Service revenue earned		194,000
Insurance expense	1,800	
Office rent expense	28,000	
Supplies expense	5,600	
Salary expense	72,000	
Depreciation expense: trucks	16,000	
Depreciation expense: equipment	4,000	
Repair and maintenance expense	5,300	
Fuel expense	2,200	
Miscellaneous expense	2,700	
Interest expense	3,800	
Income taxes expense	9,000	
	$367,100	$367,100

Instructions

a. Prepare an income statement and statement of retained earnings for the year ended December 31, 2015. Also prepare the company's balance sheet dated December 31, 2015.

b. Prepare the necessary year-end closing entries.

c. Prepare an after-closing trial balance.

d. Using the financial statements prepared in part **a,** briefly evaluate the company's profitability and liquidity.

LO5-1, LO5-4 through
LO5-6

PROBLEM 5.3B

Preparing Financial
Statements and Closing
Entries of an Unprofitable
Company

Debit Doctors, Inc., provides accounting advice over the Internet. In recent years the company has experienced severe financial difficulty. Its accountant prepares adjusting entries on a *monthly* basis and closing entries on an *annual* basis at December 31. An *adjusted* trial balance dated December 31, 2015, follows.

DEBIT DOCTORS, INC. ADJUSTED TRIAL BALANCE DECEMBER 31, 2015	Debits	Credits
Cash	$ 450	
Accounts receivable	220	
Unexpired insurance	1,600	
Prepaid rent	1,800	
Supplies	900	
Furniture and fixtures	10,000	
Accumulated depreciation: furniture and fixtures		$ 6,600
Accounts payable		7,100
Notes payable		24,000
Salaries payable		2,100
Interest payable		170
Unearned client revenue		600
Capital stock		4,000
Retained earnings		2,000
Client revenue earned		56,700
Insurance expense	6,200	
Office rent expense	12,000	
Supplies expense	300	
Salary expense	48,000	
Depreciation expense: furniture and fixtures	1,200	
Office and telephone expense	4,600	
Internet service expense	7,200	
Legal expense	1,800	
Interest expense	2,700	
Miscellaneous expense	4,300	
	$103,270	$103,270

Instructions

a. Prepare an income statement and statement of retained earnings for the year ended December 31, 2015. Also prepare the company's balance sheet dated December 31, 2015. (Hint: The company incurred no income taxes expense in 2015.)

b. Prepare the necessary year-end closing entries.

c. Prepare an after-closing trial balance.

d. Using the financial statements prepared in part **a**, briefly evaluate the company's performance.

e. Identify information that the company is apt to disclose in the notes that accompany the financial statements prepared in part **a**.

Howard Realty adjusts its accounts monthly but closes them only at the end of the calendar year. Below are the adjusted balances of the revenue and expense accounts at September 30 of the current year and at the ends of two earlier months:

	Sept. 30	Aug. 31	June 30
Commissions earned	$320,000	$290,000	$200,000
Advertising expense	66,000	56,000	36,000
Salaries expense	76,000	70,000	56,000
Rent expense	40,000	36,000	28,000
Depreciation expense	4,400	4,200	3,000

Instructions

a. Prepare a three-column income statement, showing net income for three separate time periods, all of which end on September 30. Use the format illustrated below. Show supporting computations for the amounts of revenue in the first two columns.

HOWARD REALTY
INCOME STATEMENT
FOR THE FOLLOWING TIME PERIODS

	Month Ended Sept. 30	Quarter Ended Sept. 30	Nine Months Ended Sept. 30
Revenue:			
Commissions earned	$	$	$
Expenses:			

b. Briefly explain how you determined the dollar amounts for each of the three time periods. Would you apply the same process to the balances in Howard's balance sheet accounts? Explain.

c. Assume that Howard adjusts *and closes* its accounts at the end of *each month*. Briefly explain how you then would determine the revenue and expenses that would appear in each of the three columns of the income statement prepared in part **a**.

LO5-1 through LO5-4, LO5-6

PROBLEM 5.5B
Short Comprehensive
Problem Including Both
Adjusting and Closing
Entries

Next Job, Inc., provides employment consulting services. The company adjusts its accounts *monthly* but performs closing entries *annually* on December 31. The firm's *unadjusted* trial balance dated December 31, 2015, is shown on the following page.

Other Data

1. Accrued but *unrecorded* and uncollected consulting fees earned total $25,000 at December 31, 2015.
2. The company determined that $15,000 of previously unearned consulting services fees had been earned at December 31, 2015.
3. Office supplies on hand at December 31 total $300.
4. The company purchased all of its equipment when it first began business. At that time, the estimated useful life of the equipment was six years (72 months).
5. The company prepaid its nine-month rent agreement on June 1, 2015.
6. The company prepaid its six-month insurance policy on December 1, 2015.
7. Accrued but *unpaid* salaries total $12,000 at December 31, 2015.
8. On September 1, 2015, the company borrowed $60,000 by signing an eight-month, 4 percent note payable. The entire amount, plus interest, is due on March 1, 2016.
9. The company's accounting firm estimates that income taxes expense for the *entire year* is $50,000. The unpaid portion of this amount is due early in 2016.

NEXT JOB, INC.
UNADJUSTED TRIAL BALANCE
DECEMBER 31, 2015

Cash.	$276,500	
Accounts receivable.	90,000	
Office supplies	800	
Prepaid rent	3,600	
Unexpired insurance	1,500	
Office equipment	72,000	
Accumulated depreciation: office equipment		$ 24,000
Accounts payable.		4,000
Notes payable (due 3/1/16)		60,000
Interest payable		600
Income taxes payable		9,000
Dividends payable		3,000
Unearned consulting fees		22,000
Capital stock		200,000
Retained earnings		40,000
Dividends.	3,000	
Consulting fees earned		500,000
Rent expense	14,700	
Insurance expense.	2,200	
Office supplies expense.	4,500	
Depreciation expense: office equipment	11,000	
Salaries expense	330,000	
Utilities expense.	4,800	
Interest expense.	3,000	
Income taxes expense	45,000	
Totals	$862,600	$862,600

Instructions

a. Prepare the necessary adjusting journal entries on December 31, 2015. Also prepare an *adjusted trial balance* dated December 31, 2015.

b. From the adjusted trial balance prepared in part **a,** prepare an income statement and statement of retained earnings for the year ended December 31, 2015. Also prepare the company's balance sheet dated December 31, 2015.

c. Prepare the necessary year-end closing entries.

d. Prepare an after-closing trial balance.

e. Compute the company's average *monthly* insurance expense for January through November of 2015.

f. Compute the company's average *monthly* rent expense for January through May of 2015.

g. If the company purchased all of its office equipment when it first incorporated, for how long has it been in business as of December 31, 2015?

h. Assume that the company had a note payable outstanding on January 1, 2015, that it paid off on April 1, 2015. How much interest expense accrued on this note in 2015?

**LO5-1 through LO5-4,
LO5-6**

PROBLEM 5.6B

Short Comprehensive
Problem Including Both
Adjusting and Closing
Entries

Tammy Touchtone operates a talent agency called Touchtone Talent Agency. Some clients pay in advance for services; others are billed after services have been performed. Advance payments are credited to an account entitled Unearned Agency Fees. Adjusting entries are performed on a *monthly* basis. Closing entries are performed *annually* on December 31. An *unadjusted* trial balance dated December 31, 2015, follows. (Bear in mind that adjusting entries have already been made for the first 11 months of 2015, but *not* for December.)

TOUCHTONE TALENT AGENCY
UNADJUSTED TRIAL BALANCE
DECEMBER 31, 2015

Cash	$ 14,950	
Fees receivable	35,300	
Prepaid rent	1,200	
Unexpired insurance policies	375	
Office supplies	900	
Office equipment	15,000	
Accumulated depreciation: office equipment		$ 12,000
Accounts payable		1,500
Note payable (due 3/1/16)		6,000
Income taxes payable		3,200
Unearned agency fees		8,000
Capital stock		20,000
Retained earnings		10,800
Dividends	800	
Agency fees earned		46,500
Telephone expense	480	
Office supply expense	1,130	
Depreciation expense: office equipment	2,750	
Rent expense	6,100	
Insurance expense	1,175	
Salaries expense	24,640	
Income taxes expense	3,200	
	$108,000	$108,000

Other Data

1. Office equipment is being depreciated over 60 months (five years).
2. At December 31, 2015, $2,500 of previously unearned agency fees had been earned.
3. Accrued but *unrecorded* and unpaid salary expense totals $1,360 at December 31, 2015.
4. The agency pays rent quarterly (every three months). The most recent advance payment of $1,800 was made November 1, 2015. The next payment of $1,800 will be made on February 1, 2016.
5. Accrued but *unrecorded* and uncollected agency fees earned total $3,000 at December 31, 2015.
6. Office supplies on hand at December 31, 2015, total $530.
7. On September 1, 2015, the agency purchased a six-month insurance policy for $750.
8. On December 1, 2015, the agency borrowed $6,000 by signing a three-month, 9 percent note payable. The entire amount borrowed, plus interest, is due March 1, 2016.
9. Accrued income taxes payable for the *entire year* ending December 31, 2015, *total* $3,900. The full amount is due early in 2016.

Instructions

a. Prepare the necessary adjusting journal entries on December 31, 2015. Also prepare an *adjusted trial balance* dated December 31, 2015.

b. From the adjusted trial balance prepared in part **a,** prepare an income statement and statement of retained earnings for the year ended December 31, 2015. Also prepare the company's balance sheet dated December 31, 2015.

c. Prepare the necessary year-end closing entries.

d. Prepare an after-closing trial balance.

e. Assume that the agency purchased all of its office equipment when it first began business activities. For how many months has the agency been in operation?

f. Has the agency's monthly office rent remained the same throughout the year? If not, has it gone up or down? Explain.

g. Has the agency's monthly insurance expense remained the same throughout the year? If not, has it gone up or down? Explain.

LO5-8

*PROBLEM 5.7B

Short Comprehensive Problem Including Adjusting Entries, Closing Entries, and Worksheet Preparation

Refer to Problem 4.4A on pages 175–177 in the previous chapter. Prepare a 10-column work-sheet for Campus Theater dated August 31, 2015. At the bottom of your worksheet, prepare a brief explanation keyed to each adjusting entry.

LO5-6

PROBLEM 5.8B

Evaluating Profitability and Liquidity

A recent annual report issued by **The Gap, Inc.**, revealed the following data:

	End of Year	Beginning of Year
Current assets	$4.3 billion	$3.9 billion
Current liabilities	$2.1 billion	$2.1 billion
Stockholders' equity	$2.8 billion	$4.1 billion

The company's income statement reported total annual revenue of $14.5 billion and net income for the year of $833 million.

Instructions

a. Evaluate **The Gap's** profitability by computing its net income percentage and its return on equity for the year.

b. Evaluate **The Gap's** liquidity by computing its working capital and its current ratio at the beginning of the year and at the end of the year.

c. Does **The Gap, Inc.,** appear to be both profitable and liquid? Explain.

_____
* *Supplemental Topic, "The Worksheet."*

Critical Thinking Cases

LO5-3

CASE 5.1

Adequate Disclosure

Listed below are five items that may—or may not—require disclosure in the notes that accompany financial statements.

a. Mandella Construction Co. uses the percentage-of-completion method to recognize revenue on long-term construction contracts. This is one of two acceptable methods of accounting for such projects. Over the life of the project, both methods produce the same overall results, but the annual results may differ substantially.

b. One of the most popular artists at Spectacular Comics is leaving the company and going to work for a competitor.

c. Shortly after the balance sheet date, but before the financial statements are issued, one of Coast Foods's two processing plants was damaged by a tornado. The plant will be out of service for at least three months.

d. The management of Soft Systems believes that the company has developed systems software that will make Windows® virtually obsolete. If they are correct, the company's profits could increase by 10-fold or more.

e. College Property Management (CPM) withheld a $500 security deposit from students who, in violation of their lease, kept a dog in their apartment. The students have sued CPM for this amount in small claims court.

Instructions

For each case, explain what, if any, disclosure is required under generally accepted accounting principles. Explain your reasoning.

LO5-1

CASE 5.2

Working for the Competition

This problem focuses on the following question: *Is it ethical for a CPA (or CPA firm) to provide similar services to companies that compete directly with one another?* These services may include assistance in the preparation of financial statements, income tax services, consulting engagements, and audit work.

Instructions

a. *Before* doing any research, discuss this question as a group. Identify potential arguments on *each side* of the issue.

b. Arrange an interview with a practicing (or retired) public accountant. Learn the accounting profession's position on this issue, and discuss the various arguments developed in part **a.**

c. Develop your group's position on this issue and be prepared to explain it in class. Explain why you have chosen to overlook the conflicting arguments developed in part **a.** (If your group is not in agreement, dissenting members may draft a dissenting opinion.)

LO5-3

CASE 5.3

Certifications by CEOs and CFOs

The Sarbanes-Oxley Act requires that the CEO (chief executive officer) and CFO (chief financial officer) of publicly traded corporations include statements of *personal certification* in the disclosures accompanying the financial reports filed with the SEC. In essence, these statements hold the CEO and CFO personally liable for their company's annual report content. The personal certifications must be signed by both the CEO and the CFO. Each certification requires that the CEO and CFO commit to the following statements:

1. I have reviewed this annual report.

2. On the basis of my knowledge, this report does not contain any untrue statements of material facts or omissions of material facts.

3. On the basis of my knowledge, the financial statements, and other financial information included in this report, fairly present in all material respects the financial condition, results of operations, and cash flows of the business.

4. I am responsible for establishing and maintaining disclosure controls and procedures.

5. I have disclosed any fraud, whether or not material, and have disclosed all significant control deficiencies and material weaknesses involving the company's financial reporting.

Instructions

As a group, discuss the meaning and purpose of the personal certification requirement. How might this requirement contribute to improved investor confidence?

LO5-3

INTERNET CASE 5.4

Annual Report Disclosures

Visit the home page of the **Ford Motor Company** at:

www.ford.com

From **Ford**'s home page, access the company's most recent annual report (select the "Investors" menu item). Locate the notes to the financial statements and identify the information topics disclosed in these footnotes.

Internet sites are time and date sensitive. It is the purpose of these exercises to have you explore the Internet. You may need to use the Yahoo! search engine **www.yahoo.com** *(or another favorite search engine) to find a company's current web address.*

Answers to Self-Test Questions

1. a, b, c, d   2. a   3. d   4. b, d   5. a   6. a, b   7. c   8. b, c

COMPREHENSIVE PROBLEM

Susquehanna Equipment Rentals

A COMPREHENSIVE ACCOUNTING CYCLE PROBLEM

On December 1, 2015, John and Patty Driver formed a corporation called Susquehanna Equipment Rentals. The new corporation was able to begin operations immediately by purchasing the assets and taking over the location of Rent-It, an equipment rental company that was going out of business. The newly formed company uses the following accounts:

Cash	Income Taxes Payable
Accounts Receivable	Capital Stock
Prepaid Rent	Retained Earnings
Unexpired Insurance	Dividends
Office Supplies	Income Summary
Rental Equipment	Rental Fees Earned
Accumulated Depreciation:	Salaries Expense
Rental Equipment	Maintenance Expense
Notes Payable	Utilities Expense
Accounts Payable	Rent Expense
Interest Payable	Office Supplies Expense
Salaries Payable	Depreciation Expense
Dividends Payable	Interest Expense
Unearned Rental Fees	Income Taxes Expense

The corporation performs adjusting entries monthly. Closing entries are performed annually on December 31. During December, the corporation entered into the following transactions:

Dec. 1 Issued to John and Patty Driver 20,000 shares of capital stock in exchange for a total of $200,000 cash.

Dec. 1 Purchased for $240,000 all of the equipment formerly owned by Rent-It. Paid $140,000 cash and issued a one-year note payable for $100,000. The note, plus all 12-months of accrued interest, are due November 30, 2016.

Dec. 1 Paid $12,000 to Shapiro Realty as three months' advance rent on the rental yard and office formerly occupied by Rent-It.

Dec. 4 Purchased office supplies on account from Modern Office Co., $1,000. Payment due in 30 days. (These supplies are expected to last for several months; debit the Office Supplies asset account.)

Dec. 8 Received $8,000 cash as advance payment on equipment rental from McNamer Construction Company. (Credit Unearned Rental Fees.)

Dec. 12 Paid salaries for the first two weeks in December, $5,200.

Dec. 15 Excluding the McNamer advance, equipment rental fees earned during the first 15 days of December amounted to $18,000, of which $12,000 was received in cash.

Dec. 17 Purchased on account from Earth Movers, Inc., $600 in parts needed to repair a rental tractor. (Debit an expense account.) Payment is due in 10 days.

Dec. 23 Collected $2,000 of the accounts receivable recorded on December 15.

Dec. 26 Rented a backhoe to Mission Landscaping at a price of $250 per day, to be paid when the backhoe is returned. Mission Landscaping expects to keep the backhoe for about two or three weeks.

Dec. 26 Paid biweekly salaries, $5,200.

Dec. 27 Paid the account payable to Earth Movers, Inc., $600.

Dec. 28 Declared a dividend of 10 cents per share, payable on January 15, 2016.

Dec. 29 Susquehanna Equipment Rentals was named, along with Mission Landscaping and Collier Construction, as a co-defendant in a $25,000 lawsuit filed on behalf of Kevin Davenport. Mission Landscaping had left the rented backhoe in a fenced construction site owned by Collier Construction. After working hours on December 26, Davenport had climbed the fence to play on parked construction equipment. While playing on the backhoe, he fell and broke his arm. The extent of the company's legal and financial responsibility for this accident, if any, cannot be determined at this time. (*Note:* This event does not require a journal entry at this time, but may require disclosure in notes accompanying the statements.)

Dec. 29 Purchased a 12-month public-liability insurance policy for $9,600. This policy protects the company against liability for injuries and property damage caused by its equipment. However, the policy goes into effect on January 1, 2016, and affords no coverage for the injuries sustained by Kevin Davenport on December 26.

Dec. 31 Received a bill from Universal Utilities for the month of December, $700. Payment is due in 30 days.

Dec. 31 Equipment rental fees earned during the second half of December amounted to $20,000, of which $15,600 was received in cash.

Data for Adjusting Entries

a. The advance payment of rent on December 1 covered a period of three months.

b. The annual interest rate on the note payable to Rent-It is 6 percent.

c. The rental equipment is being depreciated by the straight-line method over a period of eight years.

d. Office supplies on hand at December 31 are estimated at $600.

e. During December, the company earned $3,700 of the rental fees paid in advance by McNamer Construction Company on December 8.

f. As of December 31, six days' rent on the backhoe rented to Mission Landscaping on December 26 has been earned.

g. Salaries earned by employees since the last payroll date (December 26) amounted to $1,400 at month-end.

h. It is estimated that the company is subject to a combined federal and state income tax rate of 40 percent of income before income taxes (total revenue minus all expenses *other than* income taxes). These taxes will be payable in 2016.

Instructions

a. Perform the following steps of the accounting cycle for the month of December:

   1. Journalize the December transactions. Do *not* record adjusting entries at this point.

   2. Post the December transactions to the appropriate ledger accounts.

   3. Prepare the *unadjusted* trial balance columns of a 10-column worksheet for the year ended December 31.

   4. Prepare the necessary adjusting entries for December.

   5. Post the December adjusting entries to the appropriate ledger accounts.

   6. Complete the 10-column worksheet for the year ended December 31.

b. Prepare an income statement and statement of retained earnings for the year ended December 31, and a balance sheet (in report form) as of December 31.

c. Prepare required disclosures to accompany the December 31 financial statements. Your solution should include a separate note addressing each of the following areas: (1) depreciation policy, (2) maturity dates of major liabilities, and (3) potential liability due to pending litigation.

d. Prepare closing entries and post to ledger accounts.

e. Prepare an after-closing trial balance as of December 31.

f. During December, this company's cash balance has fallen from $200,000 to $65,000. Does it appear headed for insolvency in the near future? Explain your reasoning.

g. Would it be ethical for Patty Driver to maintain the accounting records for this company, or must they be maintained by someone who is *independent* of the organization?

CHAPTER 6

Merchandising Activities

AFTER STUDYING THIS CHAPTER, YOU SHOULD BE ABLE TO:

Learning Objectives

LO6-1 Describe the *operating cycle* of a merchandising company.

LO6-2 Understand the components of a merchandising company's income statement.

LO6-3 Account for purchases and sales of merchandise in a *perpetual* inventory system.

LO6-4 Explain how a *periodic* inventory system operates.

LO6-5 Discuss the factors to be considered in selecting an inventory system.

LO6-6 Account for additional merchandising transactions related to purchases and sales.

LO6-7 Define *special journals* and explain their usefulness.

LO6-8 Measure the performance of a merchandising business.

© AP Photo/Chitose Suzuki

SAKS INC.

Saks Inc. is a retailer of a wide variety of distinctive fashion apparel, shoes, accessories, jewelry, cosmetics, and gifts. The company operates 106 stores in 28 states, including 46 Saks Fifth Avenue stores and 60 Saks Fifth Avenue Off 5th stores. Saks Fifth Avenue stores are located in exclusive shopping destinations or as anchor stores in upscale regional malls. Saks Fifth Avenue Off 5th aims to be the premier luxury off-price retailer in the United States.

Saks Inc. tailors the merchandise in each store location to the tastes and lifestyle needs of its local customers. The company has invested in online information technology to provide detailed information about its customers and their purchasing patterns and preferences. In addition, Saks has vendor relationships with leading American and European fashion houses, including Giorgio Armani, Chanel, Gucci, Prada, Louis Vuitton, St. John, Zegna, Cartier, Hugo Boss, Ralph Lauren, Burberry, among many others. Although Saks carries merchandise for both men and women, sales to its female customer base comprise more than 75 percent of total sales.

Saks Inc.'s financial statements are similar to those of the service organizations illustrated in previous chapters. They differ, however, because Saks sells *merchandise* to its customers. Companies that sell merchandise must report information about inventory costs in their financial statements. ■

In this chapter we examine accounting issues related to merchandising businesses, such as clothing retailers and grocery stores. In addition to discussing the unique features of a merchandising company's financial statements, we illustrate ways to use financial information to evaluate the performance of these companies.

Saks Inc.'s retail stores are good examples of merchandising outlets. Managing **inventory** (goods that are purchased for the purpose of resale to customers) is of utmost importance to merchandising businesses. For a luxury chain like **Saks** to be successful, its stores must acquire hundreds of inventory items and sell them quickly at competitive prices.

In most merchandising companies, inventory is a relatively liquid asset—that is, it usually is sold within a few days or weeks. For this reason, inventory appears near the top of the balance sheet, immediately below accounts receivable.

Merchandising Companies

THE OPERATING CYCLE OF A MERCHANDISING COMPANY

LO6-1

LEARNING OBJECTIVE
Describe the *operating cycle* of a merchandising company.

The series of transactions through which a business generates its revenue and its cash receipts from customers is called the **operating cycle.** The operating cycle of a merchandising company consists of the following basic transactions: (1) purchases of merchandise; (2) sales of the merchandise, often on account; and (3) collection of the accounts receivable from customers. As the word *cycle* suggests, this sequence of transactions repeats continuously. Some of the cash collected from the customers is used to purchase more merchandise, and the cycle begins anew. This continuous sequence of merchandising transactions is illustrated in Exhibit 6–1.

EXHIBIT 6–1

The Operating Cycle

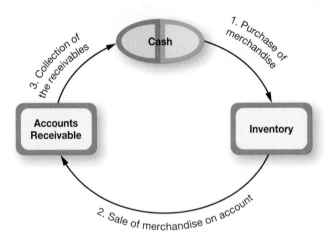

Comparing Merchandising Activities with Manufacturing Activities

Most merchandising companies purchase their inventories from other business organizations in a *ready-to-sell* condition. Companies that manufacture their inventories, such as **General Motors**, **IBM**, and **Boeing Aircraft**, are called *manufacturers,* rather than merchandisers. The operating cycle of a manufacturing company is longer and more complex than that of a merchandising company, because the first transaction—purchasing merchandise—is replaced by the many activities involved in manufacturing the merchandise.

Our examples and illustrations in this chapter are limited to companies that purchase their inventory in a ready-to-sell condition. The basic concepts, however, also apply to manufacturers.

Retailers and Wholesalers   Merchandising companies include both retailers and wholesalers. A *retailer* is a business that sells merchandise directly to the public. Retailers may be large or small; they vary in size from national store chains, such as **Saks**, **The Gap,**

and **Walmart,** to small neighborhood businesses, such as gas stations and convenience stores. In fact, more businesses engage in retail sales than in any other type of business activity.

The other major type of merchandising company is the *wholesaler.* Wholesalers buy large quantities of merchandise from several different manufacturers and then resell this merchandise to many different retailers. Because wholesalers do not sell directly to the public, even the largest wholesalers are not well known to most consumers. Nonetheless, wholesaling is a major type of merchandising activity.

The concepts discussed in the remainder of this chapter apply equally to retailers and to wholesalers.

INCOME STATEMENT OF A MERCHANDISING COMPANY

The income statement of a merchandising company differs somewhat from that of a service organization illustrated in previous chapters. Exhibit 6–2 compares the income statement structure of a service company to that of a merchandising company.

L06-2

LEARNING OBJECTIVE
Understand the components of a merchandising company's income statement.

EXHIBIT 6–2

A Comparison of Income Statements used by a Service Company and a Merchandising Company

The income statement of Computer City is shown in Exhibit 6–3. The following discussion of its structure and components will illustrate the unique characteristics of income statements prepared by merchandising companies.

Computer City's $900,000 in sales represents the *selling price* of merchandise it sold to customers during the period. Selling merchandise introduces a new and major cost of doing business: the *cost* incurred by Computer City *to acquire* the inventory it sold to customers. As items are sold from inventory, their costs must be removed from the balance sheet and transferred to the income statement to offset sales revenue. This $540,000 cost subtracted from sales revenue in Computer City's income statement is referred to as the **cost of goods sold.** In essence, the cost of goods sold is an *expense;* however, this item is of such importance to a merchandising company that it is shown separately from other expenses in the company's income statement.

EXHIBIT 6–3

A Merchandising Company's
Income Statement

COMPUTER CITY INCOME STATEMENT FOR THE YEAR ENDED DECEMBER 31, 2015		
Sales		$900,000
Less: Cost of goods sold		540,000
Gross profit		$360,000
Operating expenses:		
Wages expense	$150,900	
Advertising expense	6,800	
Insurance expense	9,600	
Utilities expense	6,400	
Office supplies expense	1,700	
Depreciation expense	58,600	234,000
Income before taxes		$126,000
Income taxes expense		36,000
Net income		$ 90,000

The $360,000 difference between sales and the cost of goods sold is Computer City's **gross profit** (or gross margin). Gross profit is a useful means of measuring the profitability of sales transactions, but it does *not* represent the overall profitability of the business. A merchandising company has many expenses in addition to the cost of goods sold. Computer City's $270,000 in other expenses includes wages expense, advertising expense, insurance expense, utilities expense, office supplies expense, depreciation expense, and income taxes expense.[1] A company earns net income only if its gross profit exceeds the sum of its other expenses.

ACCOUNTING SYSTEM REQUIREMENTS FOR MERCHANDISING COMPANIES

In previous chapters, we recorded economic events using only *general ledger* accounts. These accounts, often referred to as **control accounts,** are used to prepare financial statements that *summarize* the financial position of a business and the results of its operations. Although general ledger accounts provide a useful *overview* of a company's financial activities, they do not provide the *detailed information* needed to effectively manage most business enterprises. This detailed information is found in accounting records called *subsidiary ledgers.*

Subsidiary ledgers contain information about specific control accounts in the company's general ledger. Merchandising companies always maintain accounts receivable and accounts payable subsidiary ledgers. Thus, if a company has 500 credit customers, there are 500 individual customer accounts in the *accounts receivable subsidiary ledger* that, in total, add up to the Accounts Receivable general ledger balance reported in the balance sheet. Likewise, if a company has 20 creditors, there are 20 individual records in the *accounts payable subsidiary ledger* that contain detailed information about the amount owed to each creditor. The individual balances of these accounts add up to the Accounts Payable control balance in the general ledger.

Many merchandising companies also maintain an *inventory subsidiary ledger* by creating a separate inventory account for each item that they sell. The inventory subsidiary ledger for a large department store contains thousands of accounts. Each of these accounts tracks information for *one type of product,* showing the quantities and costs of all units purchased, sold, and currently in stock.

---

[1] The income statement presented in Exhibit 6–3 is somewhat condensed. For instance, it is a common practice for companies to subdivide operating expenses into *selling expenses and general and administrative expenses.* A more detailed income statement presentation is developed in Chapter 12.

It may seem that maintaining records for thousands of separate accounts would involve an incredible amount of work. And it would, in a *manual* accounting system. However, in a *computerized* accounting system, subsidiary ledger accounts and general ledger control accounts are posted *automatically* as transactions are recorded. Thus, no significant amount of effort is required.

Throughout the remainder of this chapter we will record various merchandise transactions directly in the general ledger control accounts. To avoid excessive detail, we will *assume* that the specific account information underlying these transactions has been posted to the necessary subsidiary accounts.

TWO APPROACHES USED IN ACCOUNTING FOR MERCHANDISE INVENTORIES

Either of two approaches may be used in accounting for merchandise inventories: (1) a *perpetual inventory system,* or (2) a *periodic inventory system.* In the past, both systems were in widespread use. Today, however, the growing use of computerized accounting systems has made the perpetual approach easy and cost-effective to implement. Thus, the periodic approach is used primarily by very small businesses with manual accounting systems.

Before we examine perpetual and periodic inventory systems, it is important to realize that accounting for inventory is similar to accounting for the *prepaid expenses* we discussed in Chapter 4 (for example, office supplies, unexpired insurance policies, prepaid rent, etc.). As inventory is purchased, it is initially reported as an *asset* in the balance sheet. As it is sold to customers, this asset is converted to an *expense,* specifically, the cost of goods sold.

Both perpetual and periodic inventory systems account for the flow of inventory costs from the balance sheet to the income statement as illustrated in Exhibit 6–4.

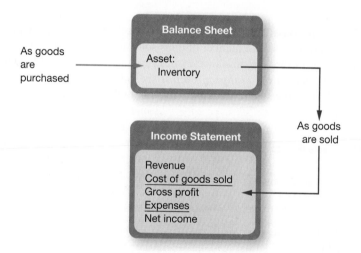

EXHIBIT 6–4
The Flow of Inventory Costs

Perpetual Inventory Systems

In a **perpetual inventory system,** all transactions involving costs of merchandise are recorded immediately *as they occur.* The system draws its name from the fact that the accounting records are kept perpetually up-to-date. Purchases of merchandise are recorded by debiting an asset account entitled Inventory. When merchandise is sold, two entries are necessary: one to recognize the *revenue earned* and the second to recognize the related *cost of goods sold.* This second entry also reduces the balance of the Inventory account to reflect the sale of some of the company's inventory.

A perpetual inventory system uses an *inventory subsidiary ledger.* This ledger provides company personnel with up-to-date information about each type of product that the company buys and sells, including the per-unit cost and the number of units purchased, sold, and currently on hand.

LO6-3

LEARNING OBJECTIVE
Account for purchases and sales of merchandise in a *perpetual* inventory system.

To illustrate the perpetual inventory system, we follow specific items of merchandise through the operating cycle of Computer City, a retail store. The transactions comprising this illustration are as follows:

Sept. 1   Purchased 10 Regent 21-inch computer monitors on account from Okawa Wholesale Co. The monitors cost $600 each, for a total of $6,000; payment is due in 30 days.

Sept. 7   Sold two monitors on account to RJ Travel Agency at a retail sales price of $1,000 each, for a total of $2,000. Payment is due in 30 days.

Oct. 1   Paid the $6,000 account payable to Okawa Wholesale Co.

Oct. 7   Collected the $2,000 account receivable from RJ Travel Agency.

Purchases of Merchandise   Purchases of inventory are recorded at cost. Thus Computer City records its purchase of the 10 computer monitors on September 1 as follows:

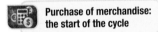
Purchase of merchandise: the start of the cycle

Inventory.	6,000	
Accounts Payable (Okawa Wholesale Co.).		6,000
Purchased 10 Regent 21-inch computer monitors for $600 each; payment due in 30 days.		

This entry is posted both to the general ledger control accounts and to the *subsidiary ledgers*. Thus, the debit to Inventory is also posted to the Regent 21-Inch Monitors account in the inventory subsidiary ledger. Information regarding the quantity of monitors purchased and their unit cost is also recorded in this subsidiary ledger. Likewise, the credit to Accounts Payable is posted to the account for Okawa Wholesale Co. in Computer City's accounts payable subsidiary ledger.

Sales of Merchandise   The revenue earned in a sales transaction is equal to the *sales price* of the merchandise times the number of units sold, and is credited to a revenue account entitled Sales. Except in rare circumstances, sales revenue is considered realized when the merchandise is *delivered to the customer,* even if the sale is made on account. Therefore, Computer City will recognize the revenue from the sale to RJ Travel Agency on September 7, as follows:

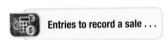
Entries to record a sale . . .

Accounts Receivable (RJ Travel Agency).	2,000	
Sales		2,000
Sold two Regent 21-inch monitors for $1,000 each; payment due in 30 days.		

The *matching principle* requires that revenue be matched (offset) with all of the costs and expenses incurred in producing that revenue. Therefore, a *second journal entry* is required at the date of sale to record the cost of goods sold.

and the related cost of goods sold

Cost of Goods Sold	1,200	
Inventory		1,200
To transfer the cost of two Regent 21-inch monitors ($600 each) from Inventory to the Cost of Goods Sold account.		

Notice that this second entry is based on the *cost* of the merchandise to Computer City, not on its retail sales price.[2]

Both of the journal entries relating to this sales transaction are posted to Computer City's general ledger. In addition, the $2,000 debit to Accounts Receivable (first entry) is posted to the

---

[2] In our illustration, all of the Regent monitors were purchased on the same date and have the same unit cost. Often a company's inventory of a given product includes units acquired at several *different* per-unit costs. This situation is addressed in Chapter 8.

account for RJ Travel Agency in the accounts receivable ledger. The credit to Inventory (second entry) also is posted to the Regent 21-Inch Monitors account in the inventory subsidiary ledger.

Payment of Accounts Payable to Suppliers   The payment to Okawa Wholesale Co. on October 1 is recorded as follows:

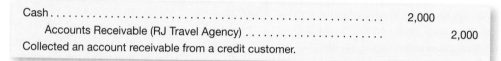

Accounts Payable (Okawa Wholesale Co.)	6,000	
Cash		6,000
Paid account payable.		

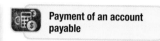

Payment of an account payable

Both portions of this entry are posted to the general ledger. In addition, payment of the account payable is entered in the Okawa Wholesale Co. account in Computer City's accounts payable subsidiary ledger.

Collection of Accounts Receivable from Customers   On October 7, collection of the account receivable from RJ Travel Agency is recorded as follows:

Cash	2,000	
Accounts Receivable (RJ Travel Agency)		2,000
Collected an account receivable from a credit customer.		

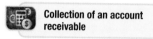

Collection of an account receivable

Both portions of this entry are posted to the general ledger; the credit to Accounts Receivable also is posted to the RJ Travel Agency account in the accounts receivable ledger.

Collection of the cash from RJ Travel Agency completes Computer City's operating cycle with respect to these two units of merchandise.

TAKING A PHYSICAL INVENTORY

The basic characteristic of the perpetual inventory system is that the Inventory account is *continuously updated* for all purchases and sales of merchandise. When a *physical inventory* is taken, management uses the inventory ledger to determine on a product-by-product basis whether a physical count of the inventory on hand corresponds to the amount indicated in the inventory subsidiary ledger. Over time normal inventory shrinkage may cause some discrepancies between the quantities of merchandise shown in the inventory records and the quantities actually on hand. **Inventory shrinkage** refers to unrecorded decreases in inventory resulting from such factors as breakage, spoilage, employee theft, and shoplifting.

In order to ensure the accuracy of their perpetual inventory records, most corporations are required to take a *complete physical count* of the merchandise on hand at least once a year. This procedure is called **taking a physical inventory,** and it usually is performed near year-end.

Once the quantity of merchandise on hand has been determined by a physical count, the per-unit costs in the inventory ledger accounts are used to determine the total cost of the inventory. The Inventory control account and the accounts in the inventory subsidiary ledger then are *adjusted* to the quantities and dollar amounts indicated by the physical inventory.

To illustrate, assume that at year-end both the Inventory control account and inventory subsidiary ledger of Computer City show an inventory with a cost of $72,200. A physical count, however, reveals that some of the merchandise listed in the accounting records is missing; the items actually on hand have a total cost of $70,000. Computer City would make the following adjusting entry to correct its Inventory control account:

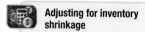

Cost of Goods Sold	2,200	
Inventory		2,200
To adjust the perpetual inventory records to reflect the results of the year-end physical count.		

Adjusting for inventory shrinkage

Computer City also will adjust the appropriate accounts in its inventory subsidiary ledger to reflect the quantities indicated by the physical count.

Reasonable amounts of inventory shrinkage are viewed as a normal cost of doing business and simply are debited to the Cost of Goods Sold account, as illustrated above.[3]

INTERNATIONAL CASE IN POINT

International Financial Reporting Standards (IFRSs) for valuing inventory differ in some respects from U.S. GAAP rules. For example, U.S. GAAP does not allow reversals of inventory write-downs, but international standards allow such reversals if certain criteria are met. Thus, the inventory values on the balance sheet and the cost of goods sold on the income statement of a firm could differ depending on whether their financial statements are prepared under GAAP or under IFRSs.

CLOSING ENTRIES IN A PERPETUAL INVENTORY SYSTEM

As explained and illustrated in the previous chapters, revenue and expense accounts are *closed* at the end of each accounting period. A merchandising business with a perpetual inventory system makes closing entries that parallel those of a service-type business. The Sales account is a revenue account and is closed into the Income Summary account along with other revenue accounts. The Cost of Goods Sold account is closed into the Income Summary account in the same manner as the other expense accounts.

YOUR TURN   You as the Inventory Manager for Computer City

Assume you are the inventory manager for the largest store owned by Computer City. You are very busy one day when Fran Mally, an auditor from the accounting firm employed by Computer City, arrives and asks for assistance in determining the store's physical inventory on hand. You are overwhelmed with work and tell Fran that you do not have the time or the personnel needed to assist her in this task. You are also annoyed because you were not told that she was coming today to complete the physical inventory count. What should you do?

(See our comments on the Online Learning Center website.)

Periodic Inventory Systems

A **periodic inventory system** is an *alternative* to a perpetual inventory system. In a periodic inventory system, no effort is made to keep up-to-date records of either the inventory or the cost of goods sold. Instead, these amounts are determined only periodically—usually at the end of each year.

OPERATION OF A PERIODIC INVENTORY SYSTEM

A traditional periodic inventory system operates as follows. When merchandise is purchased, its cost is debited to an account entitled *Purchases,* rather than to the Inventory account. When merchandise is sold, an entry is made to recognize the sales revenue, but *no entry* is made to record the cost of goods sold or to reduce the balance of the Inventory account. As the inventory records are not updated as transactions occur, there is no inventory subsidiary ledger.

The foundation of the periodic inventory system is the taking of a *complete physical inventory* at year-end. This physical count determines the amount of inventory appearing in the balance sheet. The cost of goods sold for the entire year then is determined by a short computation.

L06-4

LEARNING OBJECTIVE
Explain how a *periodic*
inventory system operates.

---

[3] If a large inventory shortage is caused by an event such as a fire or theft, the cost of the missing or damaged merchandise may be debited to a special loss account, such as Fire Loss. In the income statement, a loss is deducted from revenue in the same manner as an expense.

Data for an Illustration   To illustrate, assume that one of Computer City's suppliers, Wagner Office Products, has a periodic inventory system. At December 31, 2015, the following information is available:

1. The inventory on hand at the end of *2014* cost $14,000.
2. During *2015* purchases of merchandise for resale to customers totaled $130,000.
3. Inventory on hand at the end of *2015* cost $12,000.

The inventories at the end of 2014 and at the end of 2015 were determined by taking a complete physical inventory at (or very near) each year-end. (Because the Inventory account was not updated as transactions occurred during 2015, it still shows a balance of $14,000—the inventory on hand at the *beginning* of the year.)

The $130,000 cost of merchandise purchased during 2015 was recorded in the Purchases account.

Recording Purchases of Merchandise   Wagner Office Products made many purchases of merchandise totaling $130,000 during 2015. The entry to record the first of these purchases is as follows:

Jan. 6 Purchases......................................	2,000	
Accounts Payable (Ink Jet Solutions)		2,000
Purchased inventory on account; payment due in 30 days.		

This entry was posted to the Purchases and Accounts Payable accounts in the general ledger. The credit portion also was posted to the account for Ink Jet Solutions in Wagner's accounts payable subsidiary ledger. The debit to Purchases was *not* "double-posted," as there is *no inventory subsidiary ledger* in a periodic system.

Computing the Cost of Goods Sold   The year-end inventory is determined by taking a complete physical count of the merchandise on hand. Once the ending inventory is known, the cost of goods sold for the entire year can be determined by a short computation. The following computation uses the three information items for Wagner Office Products just presented:

Inventory (beginning of the year) (1).....................................	$ 14,000
Add: Purchases (2)...	130,000
Cost of goods available for sale	$144,000
Less: Inventory (end of the year) (3)....................................	12,000
Cost of goods sold	$132,000

Computation of the cost of goods sold

The $132,000 cost of goods sold is made up of two elements: the $130,000 cost of merchandise purchased during the year and the *decrease* in inventory of $2,000 ($14,000 beginning inventory − $12,000 ending inventory).

Recording Inventory and the Cost of Goods Sold   Wagner has now determined its inventory at the end of 2015 and its cost of goods sold for the year. But neither of these amounts has yet been recorded in the company's accounting records.

In a periodic system, the ending inventory and the cost of goods sold are recorded during the company's year-end *closing procedures* (The term *closing procedures* refers to the end-of-period adjusting and closing entries.)

CLOSING PROCESS IN A PERIODIC INVENTORY SYSTEM

There are several different ways of recording the ending inventory and cost of goods sold in a periodic system, but they all produce the same results. One approach is to *create* a Cost of Goods Sold account with the proper balance as part of the closing process. Once this account has been created, the company can complete its closing procedures in the same manner as if a perpetual inventory system had been in use.

Creating a Cost of Goods Sold Account

A Cost of Goods Sold account is created with two special closing entries. The first entry creates the new account by bringing together the costs contributing toward the cost of goods sold. The second entry adjusts the Cost of Goods Sold account to its proper balance and records the ending inventory in the Inventory account.

The costs contributing to the cost of goods sold include (1) beginning inventory and (2) purchases made during the year. These costs are brought together by closing both the Inventory account (which contains its beginning-of-the-year balance) and the Purchases account into a new account entitled Cost of Goods Sold. This year-end closing entry is:

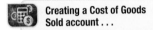

Dec. 31	Cost of Goods Sold	144,000	
	Inventory (beginning balance)		14,000
	Purchases.		130,000
	To close the accounts contributing to the cost of goods sold for the year.		

Wagner's Cost of Goods Sold account now includes the cost of all goods *available for sale* during the year. Of course, not all of these goods were sold; the physical inventory taken at the end of 2015 shows that merchandise costing $12,000 is still on hand. Therefore, a second closing entry is made transferring the cost of merchandise still on hand *out* of the Cost of Goods Sold account and *into* the Inventory account. For Wagner, this second closing entry is:

Dec. 31	Inventory (year-end balance)	12,000	
	Cost of Goods Sold		12,000
	To reduce the balance of the Cost of Goods Sold account by the cost of merchandise still on hand at year-end.		

With these two entries, Wagner has created a Cost of Goods Sold account with a balance of $132,000 ($144,000 − $12,000) and has brought its Inventory account up-to-date. Exhibit 6–5 provides a T account presentation of these entries.

EXHIBIT 6–5
Creating the Cost of Goods Sold Account

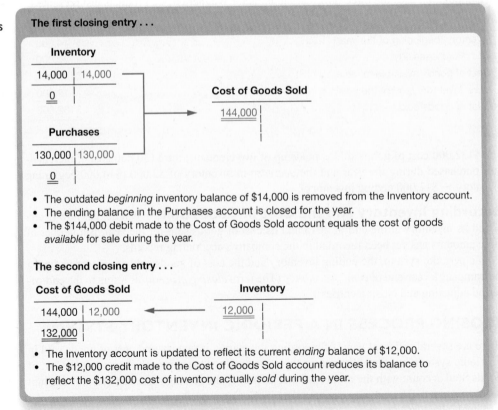

Completing the Closing Process   Wagner may now complete its closing process in the same manner as a company using a perpetual inventory system. The company will make the usual four closing entries, closing the (1) revenue accounts, (2) expense accounts (including Cost of Goods Sold), (3) Income Summary account, and (4) Dividends account.

COMPARISON OF PERPETUAL AND PERIODIC INVENTORY SYSTEMS

Exhibit 6–6 provides a comparison of the way in which various events are recorded in perpetual and periodic systems. Perpetual systems are used when management needs information throughout the year about inventory levels and gross profit. Periodic systems are used when the primary goals are to develop annual data and to minimize record-keeping requirements. A single business may use *different inventory systems* to account for *different types of merchandise.*

Who Uses Perpetual Systems?   When management or employees *need up-to-date information about inventory levels,* there is no substitute for a perpetual inventory system. Almost all manufacturing companies use perpetual systems. These businesses need current

EXHIBIT 6–6   Summary of the Journal Entries Made in Perpetual and Periodic Inventory Systems

Event	Perpetual System	Periodic System

Acquiring merchandise inventory	Inventory xxx
	    Accounts Payable (or Cash) xxx
	To record the purchase of
	   merchandise inventory.
		Purchases xxx
		    Accounts Payable (or Cash) xxx
		To record the purchase of
		   merchandise inventory.

Sale of merchandise inventory	Accounts Receivable (or Cash) xxx
	    Sales xxx
	To record the sale of
	   merchandise inventory.
	
	Cost of Goods Sold xxx
	    Inventory xxx
	To update the Cost of Goods Sold
	   and Inventory accounts.
		Accounts Receivable (or Cash) xxx
		    Sales xxx
		To record the sale of
		   merchandise inventory.
		
		In a periodic system, no entry at the time of
		sale is made to update the Cost of
		Goods Sold and Inventory accounts.

Settlement of Accounts Payable to suppliers	Accounts Payable xxx
	    Cash xxx
	To record payment for
	   merchandise inventory
	   purchased on account.
		Accounts Payable xxx
		    Cash xxx
		To record payment for
		   merchandise inventory
		   purchased on account.

Collections from credit customers	Cash xxx
	    Accounts Receivable xxx
	To record cash collections from
	   credit customers.
		Cash xxx
		    Accounts Receivable xxx
		To record cash collections from
		   credit customers.

Creating year-end balances for Cost of Goods Sold and Inventory accounts	No entry necessary. Cost of Goods Sold and Inventory accounts should both reflect year-end balances in a perpetual system. If a year-end physical count reveals less inventory on hand than reported in the Inventory account, the following entry is needed to record inventory shrinkage:
	
	Cost of Goods Sold xxx
	    Inventory (shrinkage amount) xxx
	To reduce year-end inventory balance
	   for shrinkage.
		Cost of Goods Sold xxx
		    Inventory (beginning bal.) xxx
		    Purchases xxx
		To close the Purchases and Inventory balances
		   to the Cost of Goods Sold account.
		
		Inventory (ending balance) xxx
		    Cost of Goods Sold xxx
		To create the year-end balance in the
		   Inventory account.

Note: In a periodic inventory system, the Cost of Goods Sold account is both debited and credited to create its year-end balance.

information to coordinate their inventories of raw materials with their production schedules. Most large merchandising companies—and many small ones—also use perpetual systems.

In the days when all accounting records were maintained by hand, businesses that sold many types of low-cost products had no choice but to use periodic inventory systems. A **Walmart** store, for example, may sell several thousand items *per hour.* Imagine the difficulty of keeping a perpetual inventory system up-to-date if the records were maintained by hand. But with today's *computerized terminals* and *bar-coded merchandise,* many high-volume retailers now use perpetual inventory systems. In fact, **Walmart** has been a leader among retailers in developing perpetual inventory systems.

INTERNATIONAL CASE IN POINT

Walmart, referred to as the company Sam Walton built, is the world's largest retailer. By diversifying from its original discount stores to include **Sam's Club** and its super stores, **Walmart** has fueled its retail engine. International expansion includes 333 stores in Canada, 2,088 in Mexico, 541 in the United Kingdom, 622 stores in Central America, 512 stores in Brazil, 370 Chinese stores, 88 stores in Argentina, 419 Japanese stores, and 316 stores in Chile. According to a recent annual report, 28 percent of total sales came from international locations. **Walmart** employs approximately 1,400,000 associates in the United States and approximately 800,000 internationally.

Source: Walmart stores Inc., 10-K, January 31, 2012.

Perpetual inventory systems are not limited to businesses with computerized inventory systems. Many small businesses with manual systems also use perpetual inventory systems. However, these businesses may update their inventory records on a weekly or a monthly basis, rather than at the time of each sales transaction.

Whether accounting records are maintained manually or by computer, most businesses use perpetual inventory systems in accounting for products with a *high per-unit cost.* Examples include automobiles, heavy machinery, electronic equipment, home appliances, and jewelry. Management has a greater interest in keeping track of inventory when the merchandise is expensive. Also, sales volume usually is low enough that a perpetual system can be used, even if accounting records are maintained by hand.

Who Uses Periodic Systems?
Periodic systems are used when the need for current information about inventories and sales *does not justify the cost* of maintaining a perpetual system. In a small retail store, for example, the owner may be so familiar with the inventory that formal perpetual inventory records are unnecessary. Most businesses—large and small—use periodic systems for inventories that are *immaterial* in dollar amount, or when management has little interest in the quantities on hand. As stated previously, businesses that sell many low-cost items and have manual accounting systems sometimes have no choice but to use the periodic method.

SELECTING AN INVENTORY SYSTEM

LO6-5

LEARNING OBJECTIVE
Discuss the factors to be considered in selecting an inventory system.

Accountants—and business managers—often must select an inventory system appropriate for a particular situation. Some of the factors usually considered in these decisions are listed in Exhibit 6–7.

The Trend in Today's Business World
Advances in technology are quickly extending the use of perpetual inventory systems to more businesses and more types of inventory. This trend is certain to continue. Throughout this textbook, you may assume that a *perpetual inventory system* is in use unless we specifically state otherwise.

Factors Suggesting a Perpetual Inventory System	Factors Suggesting a Periodic Inventory System
Large company with professional management.	Small company, run by owner.
Management and employees wanting information about items in inventory and the quantities of specific products that are selling.	Accounting records of inventories and specific product sales not needed in daily operations; such information developed primarily for use in annual income tax returns.
Items in inventory with a high per-unit cost.	Inventory with many different kinds of low-cost items.
Low volume of sales transactions or a computerized accounting system.	High volume of sales transactions and a manual accounting system.
Merchandise stored at multiple locations or in warehouses separate from the sales sites.	All merchandise stored at the sales site (for example, in the store).

EXHIBIT 6–7

Factors Influencing Choice of Inventory System

 YOUR TURN You as a Buyer for a Retail Business

Assume you are in charge of purchasing merchandise for Ace Hardware Stores You are currently making a decision about the purchase of barbecue grills for sale during the upcoming summer season. You must decide how many of each brand and type of grill to order. Describe the types of accounting information that would be useful in making this decision and where this information might be found.

(See our comments on the Online Learning Center website.)

© The McGraw-Hill Companies, Inc./Jill Braaten, photographer

Transactions Relating to Purchases

In addition to the basic transactions illustrated and explained in this chapter, merchandising companies must account for a variety of additional transactions relating to purchases of merchandise. Examples include discounts offered for prompt payment, merchandise returns, and transportation costs. In our discussion of these transactions, we continue to assume the use of a *perpetual* inventory system.

CREDIT TERMS AND CASH DISCOUNTS

Manufacturers and wholesalers normally sell their products to merchandisers *on account*. The credit terms are stated in the seller's bill, or *invoice*. One common example of credit terms is "net 30 days," or "n/30," meaning full payment is due in 30 days. Another common form of credit terms is "10 eom," meaning payment is due 10 days after the end of the month in which the purchase occurred.

Manufacturers and wholesalers usually allow their customers 30 or 60 days in which to pay for credit purchases. Frequently, however, sellers offer their customers a small discount to encourage earlier payment.

Perhaps the most common credit terms offered by manufacturers and wholesalers are *2/10, n/30*. This expression is read "2, 10, net 30," and means that full payment is due in 30 days, but that the buyer may take a *2 percent discount* if payment is made within 10 days. The period during which the discount is available is termed the *discount period*. Because the discount

LO6-6

LEARNING OBJECTIVE
Account for additional merchandising transactions related to purchases and sales.

provides an incentive for the customer to make an early cash payment, it is called a *cash discount.* Buyers, however, often refer to these discounts as *purchase discounts,* while sellers frequently call them *sales discounts.*

Most well-managed companies have a policy of taking advantage of all cash discounts available on purchases of merchandise.[4] These companies initially record purchases of merchandise at the *net cost*—that is, the invoice price *minus* any available discount. After all, this is the amount that the company expects to pay.

To illustrate, assume that on November 3 Computer City purchases 100 spreadsheet programs from PC Products. The cost of these programs is $100 each, for a total of $10,000. However, PC Products offers credit terms of 2/10, n/30. If Computer City pays for this purchase within the discount period, it will have to pay only *$9,800,* or 98 percent of the full invoice price. Therefore, Computer City will record this purchase as follows:

Purchase recorded at net cost

Inventory.	9,800	
Accounts Payable (PC Products).		9,800
To record purchase of 100 spreadsheet programs at net cost ($100 × 98% × 100 units).		

If the invoice is paid within the discount period, Computer City simply records payment of a $9,800 account payable.

Through oversight or carelessness, Computer City might fail to make payment within the discount period. In this event, Computer City must pay PC Products the entire invoice price of *$10,000,* rather than the recorded liability of $9,800. The journal entry to record payment *after the discount period*—on, say, December 3—is:

Recording the loss of a cash discount

Accounts Payable (PC Products).	9,800	
Purchase Discounts Lost	200	
Cash		10,000
To record payment of invoice after expiration of the discount period.		

Notice that the $200 paid above the $9,800 recorded amount is debited to an account entitled Purchase Discounts Lost. Purchase Discounts Lost is an *expense account.* The only benefit to Computer City from this $200 expenditure was a *20-day delay* in paying an account payable. Thus the lost purchase discount is basically a *finance charge,* similar to interest expense. In an income statement, finance charges usually are classified as nonoperating expenses.

The fact that purchase discounts *not taken* are recorded in a separate expense account is the primary reason why a company should record purchases of merchandise at *net cost.* The use of a Purchase Discounts Lost account immediately brings to management's attention any failure to take advantage of the cash discounts offered by suppliers.

Recording Purchases at Gross Invoice Price

As an alternative to recording purchases at net cost, some companies record merchandise purchases at the gross (total) invoice price. If payment is made within the discount period, these companies must record the amount of the purchase discount *taken.*

To illustrate, assume that Computer City followed a policy of recording purchases at gross invoice price. The entry on November 3 to record the purchase from PC Products would have been:

Purchases recorded at gross price

Inventory.	10,000	
Accounts Payable (PC Products).		10,000
To record purchase of 100 spreadsheet programs at gross invoice price ($100 × 100 units).		

---

[4] The terms 2/10, n/30 offer the buyer a 2 percent discount for paying 20 days prior to when the full amount is due. Saving 2 percent over only 20 days is equivalent to earning an annual rate of return of more than 36 percent (2% × 365/20 = 36.5%). Thus, taking cash discounts represents an excellent investment opportunity. Most companies take advantage of all cash discounts, even if they must borrow the necessary cash from a bank to make payment within the discount period.

If payment is made within the discount period, Computer City will discharge this $10,000 account payable by paying only $9,800. The entry will be:

Accounts Payable (PC Products).	10,000	
Cash.		9,800
Purchase Discounts Taken.		200
To record payment of $10,000 invoice within the discount period; 2% purchase discount taken.		

Buyer records discounts taken

Purchase Discounts Taken is treated as a reduction in the cost of goods sold.

Both the net cost and gross price methods are widely used and produce substantially the same results in financial statements.[5] A shortcoming of the gross price method as compared to the net cost method for valuing inventory is that it does not direct management's attention to discounts lost. Instead, these discounts are buried in the costs assigned to inventory. Management can use financial reporting policies to motivate the purchasing staff to take advantage of purchase discounts when possible. By recording inventory with the net cost method, management can highlight the success of their purchasing efforts to obtain the lowest possible costs for purchased inventory. Because of the advantage of the net cost method, it is the approach recommended by the authors of this textbook.

RETURNS OF UNSATISFACTORY MERCHANDISE

On occasion, a buyer may find the purchased merchandise unsatisfactory and want to return it to the seller for a refund. Most sellers permit such returns.

To illustrate, assume that on November 9 Computer City returns to PC Products five of the spreadsheet programs purchased on November 3, because these programs were not properly labeled. As Computer City has not yet paid for this merchandise, the return will reduce the amount that Computer City owes PC Products. The gross invoice price of the returned merchandise was $500 ($100 per program). Assume that Computer City records purchases at *net cost.* Therefore, these spreadsheet programs are carried in Computer City's inventory subsidiary ledger at a per-unit cost of *$98,* or $490 for the five programs being returned. The entry to record this purchase return is:

Accounts Payable (PC Products).	490	
Inventory		490
Returned five mislabeled spreadsheet programs to supplier. Net cost of the returned items, $490 ($100 × 98% × 5 units).		

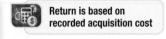
Return is based on recorded acquisition cost

The reduction in inventory must also be recorded in the subsidiary ledger accounts.

TRANSPORTATION COSTS ON PURCHASES

The purchaser sometimes may pay the costs of having the purchased merchandise delivered to its premises. Transportation costs relating to the *acquisition* of inventory, or any other asset, are *not expenses* of the current period; rather, these charges are *part of the cost of the asset* being acquired. If the purchaser is able to associate transportation costs with specific products, these costs should be debited directly to the Inventory account as part of the cost of the merchandise.

Often, many different products arrive in a single shipment. In such cases, it may be impractical for the purchaser to determine the amount of the total transportation cost applicable to each product. For this reason, many companies follow the convenient policy of debiting all transportation costs on inbound shipments of merchandise to an account entitled *Transportation-in.* The dollar amount of transportation-in usually is too small to show separately in the financial statements. Therefore, it is often simply added to the amount reported in the income statement as cost of goods sold.

---

[5] The net cost method values the ending inventory at net cost, whereas the gross cost method shows this inventory at gross invoice price. This difference, however, is usually *immaterial.*

This treatment of transportation costs is not entirely consistent with the *matching principle*. Some of the transportation costs apply to merchandise still in inventory rather than to goods sold during the current period. We have mentioned, however, that transportation costs are relatively small in dollar amount. The accounting principle of *materiality*, therefore, usually justifies accounting for these costs in the most convenient manner.

Transactions Relating to Sales

Credit terms and merchandise returns also affect the amount of sales revenue earned by the seller. To the extent that credit customers take advantage of cash discounts or return merchandise for a refund, the seller's revenue is reduced. Thus revenue shown in the income statement of a merchandising concern is often called *net sales*.

The term **net sales** means total sales revenue *minus* sales returns and allowances and *minus* sales discounts. The partial income statement in Exhibit 6–8 illustrates this relationship.

EXHIBIT 6–8

Partial Income Statement

COMPUTER CITY PARTIAL INCOME STATEMENT FOR THE YEAR ENDED DECEMBER 31, 2015		
Revenue:		
Sales.		$912,000
Less: Sales returns and allowances.	$8,000	
Sales discounts	4,000	12,000
Net sales		$900,000

The details of this computation seldom are shown in an actual income statement. The normal practice is to begin the income statement with the amount of net sales.

SALES RETURNS AND ALLOWANCES

Most merchandising companies allow customers to obtain a refund by returning any merchandise considered to be unsatisfactory. If the merchandise has only minor defects, customers sometimes agree to keep the merchandise if an *allowance* (reduction) is made in the sales price.

Under the perpetual inventory system, two entries are needed to record the sale of merchandise: one to recognize the revenue earned and the other to transfer the cost of the merchandise from the Inventory account to Cost of Goods Sold. If some of the merchandise is returned, both of these entries are partially reversed.

First, let us consider the effects on revenue of granting either a refund or an allowance. Both refunds and allowances have the effect of nullifying previously recorded sales and reducing the amount of revenue earned by the business. This journal entry reduces sales revenue as the result of a sales return (or allowance):

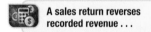
A sales return reverses recorded revenue . . .

Sales Returns and Allowances.	1,000	
Accounts Receivable (or Cash).		1,000
Customer returned merchandise purchased on account for $1,000. Allowed customer full credit for returned merchandise.		

Sales Returns and Allowances is a **contra-revenue account**—that is, it is deducted from gross sales revenue as a step in determining net sales.

Why use a separate Sales Returns and Allowances account rather than merely debiting the Sales account? The answer is that using a separate contra-revenue account enables management to see both the total amount of sales *and* the amount of sales returns. The relationship between these amounts gives management an indication of *customer satisfaction* with the merchandise.

If merchandise is returned by the customer, a second entry is made to remove the cost of this merchandise from the Cost of Goods Sold account and restore it to the inventory records. This entry is:

Inventory...	600	
Cost of Goods Sold......................................		600
To restore in the Inventory account the cost of merchandise returned by a customer.		

 and the recorded cost of goods sold

Notice that this entry is based on the *cost* of the returned merchandise to the seller, *not on its sales price*. (This entry is not necessary when a sales *allowance* is granted to a customer who keeps the merchandise.)

SALES DISCOUNTS

We have explained that sellers frequently offer cash discounts, such as 2/10, n/30, to encourage customers to make early payments for purchases on account.

Sellers and buyers account for cash discounts quite differently. To the seller, the cost associated with cash discounts is not the discounts *lost* when payments are delayed, but rather the discounts *taken* by customers who do pay within the discount period. Therefore, sellers design their accounting systems to measure the sales discounts *taken* by their customers. To achieve this goal, the seller records the sale and the related account receivable at the *gross* (full) invoice price.

To illustrate, assume that Computer City sells merchandise to the Highlander Pub for $1,000, offering terms of 2/10, n/30. The sales revenue is recorded at the full invoice price, as follows:

Accounts Receivable (Highlander Pub)	1,000	
Sales		1,000
Sold merchandise on account. Invoice price, $1,000; terms, 2/10, n/30.		

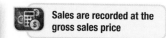 Sales are recorded at the gross sales price

If the Highlander Pub makes payment after the discount period has expired, Computer City records the receipt of $1,000 cash in full payment of this account receivable. If it pays *within* the discount period, however, the pub will pay only *$980* to settle its account. In this case, Computer City will record the receipt of the pub's payment as follows:

Cash...	980	
Sales Discounts	20	
Accounts Receivable (Highlander Pub).......................		1,000
Collected a $1,000 account receivable from a customer who took a 2% discount for early payment.		

 Seller records discounts taken by customers

Sales Discounts is another contra-revenue account. In the computing of net sales, sales discounts are deducted from gross sales along with any sales returns and allowances. (If the customer has returned part of the merchandise, a discount may be taken only on the gross amount owed *after* the return.)

Contra-revenue accounts have much in common with expense accounts; both are deducted from gross revenue in determining net income, and both have debit balances. Thus contra-revenue accounts (Sales Returns and Allowances and Sales Discounts) are closed to the Income Summary account *in the same manner as expense accounts.*

DELIVERY EXPENSES

If the seller incurs any costs in delivering merchandise to the customer, these costs are debited to an expense account entitled Delivery Expense. In an income statement, delivery expense is classified as a regular operating expense, not as part of the cost of goods sold.

ACCOUNTING FOR SALES TAXES

Sales taxes are levied by many states and cities on retail sales.[6] Sales taxes actually are imposed on the consumer, not on the seller. However, the seller must collect the tax, file tax returns at times specified by law, and remit to governmental agencies the taxes collected.

For cash sales, sales tax is collected from the customer at the time of the sales transaction. For credit sales, the sales tax is included in the amount charged to the customer's account. In a computerized accounting system, the liability to the governmental unit for sales taxes is recorded automatically at the time the sale is made, as shown in the following journal entry:

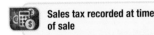 Sales tax recorded at time of sale

Cash (or Accounts Receivable)	1,070	
Sales Tax Payable		70
Sales		1,000
To record sales of $1,000, subject to 7% sales tax.		

Modifying an Accounting System

LO6-7

LEARNING OBJECTIVE
Define *special journals* and explain their usefulness.

Throughout this textbook we illustrate the effects of many transactions using the format of a two-column *general journal*. This format is ideal for textbook illustrations, as it allows us to concisely show the effects of *any type* of business transaction.

But while general journal entries are useful for our purposes, they are not the most efficient way for a business to record routine transactions. A supermarket, for example, may sell 10,000 to 15,000 items *per hour*. Clearly, it would not be practical to make a general journal entry to record each of these sales transactions. Therefore, most businesses use *special journals,* rather than a general journal, to record *routine transactions that occur frequently.*

SPECIAL JOURNALS PROVIDE SPEED AND EFFICIENCY

A **special journal** is an accounting record or device designed to record *a specific type of routine transaction quickly and efficiently.*

Some special journals are maintained by hand. An example is the *check register* in your personal checkbook. If properly maintained, this special journal provides an efficient record of all cash disbursements made by check.

But many special journals are highly automated. Consider the **point-of-sale (POS) terminals** that you see in supermarkets and large retail stores. These devices record sales transactions and the related cost of goods sold as quickly as the bar-coded merchandise can be passed over the scanner.

Relative to the general journal, special journals offer the following advantages:

- Transactions are recorded faster and more efficiently.
- Many special journals may be in operation at one time, further increasing the company's ability to handle a large volume of transactions.
- Automation may reduce the risk of errors.
- Employees maintaining special journals generally do not need expertise in accounting.
- The recording of transactions may be an automatic side effect of other basic business activities, such as collecting cash from customers.

Most businesses use separate special journals to record repetitive transactions such as sales of merchandise, cash receipts, cash payments, purchases of merchandise on account, and payrolls. There are no rules for the design or content of special journals. Rather, they are tailored to suit the needs, activities, and resources of the particular business organization.

Let us stress that the *accounting principles* used in special journals are the *same* as those used for transactions recorded in a general journal. The differences lie in the *recording techniques,* not in the information that is recorded.

---

[6] Sales taxes are applicable only when merchandise is sold to the *final consumer;* thus no sales taxes are normally levied when manufacturers or wholesalers sell merchandise to retailers.

Remember also that special journals are *highly specialized* in terms of the transactions they can record. Thus every business still needs a general journal to record transactions that do not fit into any of its special journals, including, for example, adjusting entries, closing entries, and unusual events such as a loss sustained from a fire.

Management uses information about departments and products for many purposes. These include setting prices, deciding which products to carry and to advertise, and evaluating the performance of departmental managers. By concentrating sales efforts on the products and departments with the *highest margins,* management usually can increase the company's overall gross profit rate.

FINANCIAL ANALYSIS and Decision Making

In evaluating the performance of a merchandising business, managers and investors look at more than just net income. Two key measures of past performance and future prospects are trends in the company's *net sales* and *gross profit.*

NET SALES

LO6-8

LEARNING OBJECTIVE
Measure the performance of a merchandising business.

Most investors and business managers consider the *trend* in net sales to be a key indicator of both past performance and future prospects. Increasing sales suggest the probability of larger profits in future periods. Declining sales, on the other hand, may provide advance warning of financial difficulties.

As a measure of performance, the trend in net sales has some limitations, especially when the company is adding new stores. For these companies, an increase in overall net sales in comparison to the prior year may have resulted solely from sales at the new stores. Sales at existing stores may even be declining. Business managers and investors often focus on measures that adjust for changes in the number of stores from period to period, and on measures of space utilization. These measures include:

1. **Comparable store sales.** Net sales at established stores, excluding new stores opened during the period. Indicates whether customer demand is rising or falling at established locations. (Also called *same-store sales.*)
2. **Sales per square foot of selling space.** A measure of how effectively the company is using its physical facilities (such as floor space or, in supermarkets, shelf space).

GROSS PROFIT MARGINS

Increasing net sales is *not enough* to ensure increasing profitability. Some products are more profitable than others. In evaluating the profitability of sales transactions, managers and investors keep a close eye on the company's **gross profit margin** (also called *gross profit rate*).

Gross profit margin is the dollar amount of gross profit, expressed as a *percentage* of net sales revenue. Gross profit margins can be computed for the business as a whole, for specific sales departments, and for individual products.

To illustrate the computation of gross profit margin, consider selected income statement data for **Home Depot**, **Saks**, and **Walmart**. The sales, cost of sales, and gross profit for these companies are as follows (in thousands of dollars):

The Overall Gross Profit Margin The average gross profit margin (gross profit rate) is a measure of relative profitability. The gross profit rate is calculated by dividing gross profit (in dollars) by net sales. The gross profit rates for **Home Depot**, **Saks**, and **Walmart** are:

- **Home Depot**: 34.60 percent ($25,842/$74,754)
- **Saks**: 40.75 percent ($1,228,174/$3,013,593)
- **Walmart**: 24.50 percent ($108,727/$443,854)

Using Information about Gross Profit Margins
Investors usually compute companies' overall gross profit rates from one period to the next. High—or increasing—margins generally indicate popular products and successful marketing strategies. A substandard or declining profit margin, on the other hand, often indicates weak customer demand or intense price competition.[7]

	Home Depot	Saks	Walmart
Net sales	$74,754,000	$3,013,593	$443,854,000
Cost of sales	48,912,000	1,785,419	335,127,000
Gross profit	$25,842,000	$1,228,174	$108,727,000

---

[7] We discuss the interpretation of gross profit in greater depth in Chapter 14.

Ethics, Fraud, & Corporate Governance

As discussed previously in this chapter, sales discounts and allowances are contra-revenue accounts. Sales discounts and allowances reduce gross sales. As such, net income will be incorrect if discounts and allowances are not properly recorded. The Securities and Exchange Commission (SEC) brought an enforcement action against **Pepsi-Cola Puerto Rico (Pepsi PR)** alleging that **Pepsi PR** understated its sales discounts and allowances. **Pepsi PR** produces, distributes, and markets **Pepsi Co** beverages throughout Puerto Rico. **Pepsi PR** is a separate company and its stock was listed on the New York Stock Exchange at the time of the SEC enforcement action.

The **Coca-Cola** bottler in Puerto Rico attempted to gain market share by cutting prices. **Pepsi PR** responded by offering more generous sales discounts and allowances. However, offering these additional discounts and allowances would have reduced **Pepsi PR**'s net income. The **Pepsi PR** general manager instructed the company's finance staff not to record some of the sales discounts and allowances given to customers. **Pepsi PR**'s failure to record discounts and allowances resulted in net income for the first quarter being overstated by $3.3 million and net income for the second quarter being overstated by $5.7 million. **Pepsi PR** consented to an SEC cease-and-desist order without either admitting or denying guilt.

Although **Pepsi PR**'s general manager initiated the scheme that led to the misstatement of **Pepsi PR**'s financial statements, the failure to record sales discounts and allowances was carried out by the company's director of finance and other finance department staffers. The individuals who carried out this scheme knew that **Pepsi PR**'s financial results would be misstated if sales discounts and allowances were not recorded correctly. However, these individuals were unwilling to defy their superior, even when their superior was asking them to engage in unethical and illegal behavior. In cases of fraudulent

financial reporting, subordinates being pressured by superiors to implement the fraud scheme is relatively common.

The pressure brought to bear on subordinates to implement fraudulent schemes developed by top management can often be intense. Top management can threaten employees with termination if they fail to participate in the fraud. Unfortunately, employees who acquiesce to such pressure face tremendous legal risks. Unlike their superiors, the fingerprints of lower-level employees who actually implement the fraudulent scheme are all over the incriminating documents. For example, a midlevel tax manager who was convicted of participating in a scheme to misstate **Dynergy**'s financial statements was sentenced to 24 years in federal prison (although this sentence was substantially reduced on appeal). This individual's bosses, who were equally complicit in the scheme, pled guilty and testified against their former employee. They received less than five years in prison.

The Sarbanes-Oxley Act provides some protection for lower-level employees who are pressured to participate in an accounting fraud. Public company audit committees must establish procedures (typically company "hotlines") that can be used by employees reporting concerns related to questionable accounting or auditing matters. In addition, Sarbanes-Oxley includes certain "whistleblower" protections. No public company may discharge, demote, suspend, threaten, harass, or in any other manner discriminate against an employee if the employee provides information or assistance in an investigation involving securities fraud. In addition, under the Dodd-Frank Act of 2010, Congress authorized the Securities and Exchange Commission to pay monetary awards to whistleblowers who provide original information that leads to an SEC action where penalties of $1 million or more are assessed. The whistleblower is entitled to a reward of between 10 and 30 percent of the SEC penalty. Dodd-Frank also strengthened the whitstlerblower protections in SOX.

Concluding Remarks

The Overnight Auto Service illustration presented in Chapter 2 through Chapter 5 addressed measurement and reporting issues pertaining to a service-type business. Throughout this chapter, we have had an opportunity to see how merchandising companies measure and report the results for their operations. Many of the illustrations and assignments throughout the remainder of this textbook are based upon merchandising enterprises.

In Chapter 7, we examine accounts receivable and other liquid assets common to merchandisers. In Chapter 8, we focus upon issues related to merchandise inventories. Measurement and reporting issues that pertain primarily to manufacturing companies are generally covered in a subsequent course.

END-OF-CHAPTER REVIEW

LO6-1 **Describe the *operating cycle* of a merchandising company.** The operating cycle is the repeating sequence of transactions by which a company generates revenue and cash receipts from customers. In a merchandising company, the operating cycle consists of the following transactions: (1) purchases of merchandise, (2) sale of the merchandise—often on account—and (3) collection of accounts receivable from customers.

LO6-2 **Understand the components of a merchandising company's income statement.** In a merchandising company's income statement, *sales* (or *net sales*) represent the total revenue generated by selling merchandise to its customers. As items are sold from inventory, their costs are transferred from the balance sheet to the income statement, where they appear as the *cost of goods sold*. The cost of goods sold is subtracted from sales to determine the company's *gross profit*. *Other expenses* (such as wages, advertising, utilities, and depreciation) are subtracted from gross profit in the determination of *net income*. Only if a company's gross profit exceeds the sum of its other expenses will it be profitable.

LO6-3 **Account for purchases and sales of merchandise in a *perpetual* inventory system.** In a perpetual inventory system, purchases of merchandise are recorded by debiting the Inventory account. Two entries are required to record each sale: one to recognize sales revenue and the second to record the cost of goods sold. This second entry consists of a debit to Cost of Goods Sold and a credit to Inventory.

LO6-4 **Explain how a *periodic* inventory system operates.** In a periodic system, up-to-date records are *not* maintained for inventory or the cost of goods sold. Thus less record keeping is required than in a perpetual system.

The beginning and ending inventories are determined by taking a complete physical count at each year-end. Purchases are recorded in a Purchases account, and no entries are made to record the cost of individual sales transactions. Instead, the cost of goods sold is determined at year-end by a computation such as the following (dollar amounts are provided only for purposes of example):

Beginning inventory	$ 30,000
Add: Purchases	180,000
Cost of goods available for sale.	$210,000
Less: Ending inventory.	40,000
Cost of goods sold.	$170,000

The amounts of inventory and the cost of goods sold are recorded in the accounting records during the year-end closing procedures.

LO6-5 **Discuss the factors to be considered in selecting an inventory system.** In general terms, a perpetual system should be used when (1) management and employees need timely information about inventory levels and product sales, and (2) the company has the resources to develop this information at a reasonable cost. A periodic system should be used when the usefulness of current information about inventories does not justify the cost of maintaining a perpetual system.

Perpetual systems are most widely used in companies with computerized accounting systems and in businesses that sell high-cost merchandise. Periodic systems are most often used in small businesses that have manual accounting systems and that sell many types of low-cost merchandise.

LO6-6 **Account for additional merchandising transactions related to purchases and sales.** Buyers should record purchases at the net cost and record any cash discounts lost in an expense account. Sellers record sales at the gross sales price and record in a contra-revenue account all cash discounts taken by customers.

Assuming a perpetual inventory system, the buyer records a purchase return by crediting the Inventory account for the net cost of the returned merchandise. In recording a sales return, the seller makes two entries: one to record Sales Returns and Allowances (a contra-revenue account) for the amount of the refund and the other to transfer the cost of the returned merchandise from the Cost of Goods Sold account back into the Inventory account.

Buyers record transportation charges on purchased merchandise either as part of the cost of the merchandise or directly as part of the cost of goods sold. Sellers view the cost of delivering merchandise to customers as an operating expense.

Sales taxes are collected by retailers from their customers and paid to state and city governments. Thus collecting sales taxes increases the retailer's assets and liabilities. Paying the sales tax to the government is payment of the liability, not an expense.

LO6-7 **Define *special journals* and explain their usefulness.** Special journals are accounting records or devices designed to record a specific type of transaction in a highly efficient manner. Because a special journal is used only to record a specific type of transaction, the journal may be located at the transaction site and maintained by employees other than accounting personnel. Thus special journals reduce the time, effort, and cost of recording routine business transactions.

LO6-8 **Measure the performance of a merchandising business.** There are numerous measures used to evaluate the performance of merchandising businesses. In this chapter, we introduced three of these measures: (1) comparable store sales, which helps determine whether customer demand is rising or falling at established locations, (2) sales per square foot of selling space, which is a measure of how effectively a merchandising business is using its facilities to generate revenue, and (3) gross profit percentages, which help users of financial statements gain insight about a company's pricing policies and the demand for its products.

Key Terms Introduced or Emphasized in Chapter 6

comparable store sales (p. 265)   A comparison of sales figures at established stores with existing "track records." (Also called *same-store sales.*)

contra-revenue account (p. 262)   A debit balance account that is offset against revenue in the income statement. Examples include Sales Discounts and Sales Returns and Allowances.

control account (p. 250)   A general ledger account that summarizes the content of a specific subsidiary ledger.

cost of goods sold (p. 249)   The cost to a merchandising company of the goods it has sold to its customers during the period.

gross profit (p. 250)   Net sales revenue minus the cost of goods sold.

gross profit margin (p. 265)   Gross profit expressed as a percentage of net sales. Also called *gross profit rate.*

inventory (p. 248)   Merchandise intended for resale to customers.

inventory shrinkage (p. 253)   The loss of merchandise through such causes as shoplifting, breakage, and spoilage.

net sales (p. 262)   Gross sales revenue less sales returns and allowances and sales discounts. The most widely used measure of dollar sales volume; usually the first figure shown in an income statement.

operating cycle (p. 248)   The repeating sequence of transactions by which a business generates its revenue and cash receipts from customers.

periodic inventory system (p. 254)   An alternative to the perpetual inventory system. It eliminates the need for recording the cost of goods sold as sales occur. However, the amounts of inventory and the cost of goods sold are not known until a complete physical inventory is taken at year-end.

perpetual inventory system (p. 251)   A system of accounting for merchandising transactions in which the Inventory and Cost of Goods Sold accounts are kept perpetually up-to-date.

point-of-sale (POS) terminals (p. 264)   Electronic cash registers used for computer-based processing of sales transactions. The POS terminal identifies each item of merchandise from its bar code and then automatically records the sale and updates the computer-based inventory records. These terminals permit the use of perpetual inventory systems in many businesses that sell a high volume of low-cost merchandise.

sales per square foot of selling space (p. 265)   A measure of efficient use of available space.

special journal (p. 264)   An accounting record or device designed for recording large numbers of a particular type of transaction quickly and efficiently. A business may use many different kinds of special journals.

subsidiary ledger (p. 250)   A ledger containing separate accounts for each of the items making up the balance of a control account in the general ledger. The total of the account balances in a subsidiary ledger are equal to the balance in the general ledger control account.

taking a physical inventory (p. 253)   The procedure of counting all merchandise on hand and determining its cost.

Demonstration Problem

STAR-TRACK sells satellite tracking systems for receiving television broadcasts from communications satellites in space. At December 31, 2015, the company's inventory amounted to $44,000. During the first week in January 2016, STAR-TRACK made only one purchase and one sale. These transactions were as follows:

Jan. 3   Sold a tracking system to Mystery Mountain Resort for $20,000 cash. The system consisted of seven different devices, which had a total cost to STAR-TRACK of $11,200.

Jan. 7   Purchased two Model 400 and four Model 800 satellite dishes from Yamaha Corp. The total cost of this purchase amounted to $10,000; terms 2/10, n/30.

STAR-TRACK records purchases of merchandise at net cost. The company has full-time accounting personnel and uses a manual accounting system.

Instructions

a.   Briefly describe the operating cycle of a merchandising company.

b.   Prepare journal entries to record these transactions, assuming that STAR-TRACK uses a perpetual inventory system.

c.   Explain what information in part **b** should be posted to subsidiary ledger accounts.

d.   Compute the balance in the Inventory control account at January 7.

e.   Prepare journal entries to record the two transactions, assuming that STAR-TRACK uses a *periodic* inventory system.

f.   Compute the cost of goods sold for the first week of January, assuming use of the periodic system. As the amount of ending inventory, use your answer to part **d.**

g.   Which type of inventory system do you think STAR-TRACK should use? Explain your reasoning.

h.   Determine the gross profit margin on the January 3 sales transaction.

Solution to the Demonstration Problem

a. The operating cycle of a merchandising company consists of purchasing merchandise, selling that merchandise to customers (often on account), and collecting the sales proceeds from these customers. In the process, the business converts cash into inventory, the inventory into accounts receivable, and the accounts receivable into cash.

b. Journal entries assuming use of a *perpetual* inventory system:

GENERAL JOURNAL			
Date	**Account Titles and Explanation**	**Debit**	**Credit**
2016			
Jan. 3	Cash..	20,000	
	Sales		20,000
	Sold tracking system to Mystery Mountain Resort.		
3	Cost of Goods Sold	11,200	
	Inventory......................................		11,200
	To record cost of merchandise sold.		
7	Inventory......................................	9,800	
	Accounts Payable (Yamaha Corp.)		9,800
	Purchased merchandise. Terms, 2/10, n/30; net cost, $9,800 ($10,000, less 2%).		

c. The debits and credits to the Inventory account should be posted to the appropriate accounts in the inventory subsidiary ledger. The information posted would be the costs and quantities of the types of merchandise purchased or sold. The account payable to Yamaha also should be posted to the Yamaha account in STAR-TRACK's accounts payable ledger. No postings are required to the accounts receivable ledger, as this was a cash sale. If STAR-TRACK maintains more than one bank account, however, the debit to cash should be posted to the proper account in the cash subsidiary ledger.

d. $42,600 ($44,000 beginning balance, less $11,200, plus $9,800).

e. Journal entries assuming use of a *periodic* inventory system:

GENERAL JOURNAL			
Date	**Account Titles and Explanation**	**Debit**	**Credit**
2016			
Jan. 3	Cash..	20,000	
	Sales		20,000
	Sold tracking system to Mystery Mountain Resort.		
7	Purchases	9,800	
	Accounts Payable (Yamaha Corp.)		9,800
	Purchased merchandise. Terms, 2/10, n/30; net cost, $9,800 ($10,000, less 2%).		

f. Computation of the cost of goods sold:

Inventory, January 1..	$44,000
Add: Purchases	9,800
Cost of goods available for sale.................................	$53,800
Less: Inventory, January 7 (per part **d**)...........................	42,600
Cost of goods sold..	$11,200

g. STAR-TRACK should use a *perpetual* inventory system. The items in its inventory have a high per-unit cost. Therefore, management will want to know the costs of the individual products included in specific sales transactions and will want to keep track of the items in stock. Although the company has a manual accounting system, its volume of sales transactions is low enough that maintaining a perpetual inventory record will not be difficult.

h. Gross profit = Sales revenue − Cost of goods sold
$$= \$20,000 - \$11,200$$
$$= \$8,800$$

Gross profit margin = Gross profit ÷ Sales revenue
$$= \$8,800 \div 20,000$$
$$= 44\%$$

Self-Test Questions

The answers to these questions appear on page 286.

1. Mark and Amanda Carter own an appliance store and a restaurant. The appliance store sells merchandise on a 12-month installment plan; the restaurant sells only for cash. Which of the following statements are true? (More than one answer may be correct.)

   a. The appliance store has a longer operating cycle than the restaurant.

   b. The appliance store probably uses a perpetual inventory system, whereas the restaurant probably uses a periodic system.

   c. Both businesses require subsidiary ledgers for accounts receivable and inventory.

   d. Both businesses probably have subsidiary ledgers for accounts payable.

2. Which of the following statements about merchandising activities is true? (More than one answer may be correct.)

   a. As inventory is purchased, the Inventory Expense account is debited and Cash (or Accounts Payable) is credited.

   b. Inventory is recorded as an asset when it is first purchased.

   c. As inventory is sold, its cost is transferred from the balance sheet to the income statement.

   d. As inventory is sold, its cost is transferred from the income statement to the balance sheet.

3. Marietta Corporation uses a *perpetual* inventory system. All of its sales are made on account. The company sells merchandise costing $3,000 at a sales price of $4,300. In recording this transaction, Marietta will make all of the following entries *except:*

   a. Credit Sales, $4,300.

   b. Credit Inventory, $4,300.

   c. Debit Cost of Goods Sold, $3,000.

   d. Debit Accounts Receivable, $4,300.

4. Fashion House uses a *perpetual* inventory system. At the beginning of the year, inventory amounted to $50,000. During the year, the company purchased merchandise for $230,000 and sold merchandise costing $245,000. A physical inventory taken at year-end indicated shrinkage losses of $4,000. *Prior* to recording these shrinkage losses, the year-end balance in the company's Inventory account was:

   a. $31,000.

   b. $35,000.

   c. $50,000.

   d. Some other amount.

5. Best Hardware uses a *periodic* inventory system. Its inventory was $38,000 at the beginning of the year and $40,000 at the end. During the year, Best made purchases of merchandise totaling $107,000. Identify all of the correct answers:

   a. To use this system, Best must take a complete physical inventory twice each year.

   b. Prior to making adjusting and closing entries at year-end, the balance in Best's Inventory account is $38,000.

   c. The cost of goods sold for the year is $109,000.

   d. As sales transactions occur, Best makes no entries to update its inventory records or to record the cost of goods sold.

6. The two basic approaches to accounting for inventory and the cost of goods sold are the *perpetual* inventory system and the *periodic* inventory system. Indicate which of the following statements are correct. (More than one answer may be correct.)

   a. Most large merchandising companies and manufacturing businesses use periodic inventory systems.

   b. As a practical matter, a grocery store or a large department store could not maintain a perpetual inventory system without the use of point-of-sale terminals.

   c. In a periodic inventory system, the cost of goods sold is not determined until a complete physical inventory is taken.

   d. In a perpetual inventory system, the Cost of Goods Sold account is debited promptly for the cost of merchandise sold.

7. Big Brother, a retail store, purchased 100 television sets from Krueger Electronics on account at a cost of $200 each. Krueger offers credit terms of 2/10, n/30. Big Brother uses a perpetual inventory system and records purchases at *net cost*.

Big Brother determines that 10 of these television sets are defective and returns them to Krueger for full credit. In recording this return, Big Brother will:

a. Debit Sales Returns and Allowances, $1,960.

b. Debit Accounts Payable, $1,960.

c. Debit Cost of Goods Sold, $1,960.

d. Credit Inventory, $2,000.

8. Two of the lawn mowers sold by Garden Products Co. are the LawnMaster and the Mark 5. LawnMasters sell for $250 apiece, which results in a 35 percent gross profit margin.

Each Mark 5 costs Garden Products $300 and sells for $400. Indicate all correct answers.

a. The dollar amount of gross profit is greater on the sale of a Mark 5 than a LawnMaster.

b. The gross profit margin is higher on Mark 5s than on LawnMasters.

c. Garden profits relatively more by selling one Mark 5 than by selling one LawnMaster.

d. Garden profits more by selling $2,000 worth of Mark 5s than $2,000 worth of LawnMasters.

ASSIGNMENT MATERIAL **Discussion Questions**

1. The income statement of a merchandising company includes a major type of cost that does not appear in the income statement of a service-type business. Identify this cost and explain what it represents.

2. During the current year, Green Bay Company earned a gross profit of $350,000, whereas New England Company earned a gross profit of only $280,000. Both companies had net sales of $900,000. Does this mean that Green Bay is more profitable than New England? Explain.

3. Explain the need for subsidiary ledgers in accounting for merchandising activities.

4. Define the term *inventory shrinkage*. How is the amount of inventory shrinkage determined in a business using a perpetual inventory system, and how is this shrinkage recorded in the accounting records?

5. Briefly contrast the accounting procedures in *perpetual* and *periodic* inventory systems.

6. Evaluate the following statement: "Without electronic point-of-sale terminals, it simply would not be possible to use perpetual inventory systems in businesses that sell large quantities of many different products."

7. Explain the distinguishing characteristics of (a) a general journal and (b) a special journal.

8. How does a balance arise in the Purchase Discounts Lost account? Why does management pay careful attention to the balance (if any) in this account?

9. European Imports pays substantial freight charges to obtain inbound shipments of purchased merchandise. Should

these freight charges be debited to the company's Delivery Expense account? Explain.

10. Outback Sporting Goods purchases merchandise on terms of 4/10, n/60. The company has a line of credit that enables it to borrow money as needed from Northern Bank at an annual interest rate of 13 percent. Should Outback pay its suppliers within the 10-day discount period if it must draw on its line of credit (borrow from Northern Bank) to make these early payments? Explain.

11. TireCo is a retail store in a state that imposes a 6 percent sales tax. Would you expect to find sales tax expense and sales tax payable in TireCo's financial statements? Explain.

12. A seller generally records sales at the full invoice price, but the buyer often records purchases at *net cost*. Explain the logic of the buyer and seller recording the transaction at different amounts.

13. Define the term *gross profit margin*. Explain several ways in which management might improve a company's overall profit margin.

14. Under a perpetual inventory system, a company should know the quantity and price of its inventory at any moment in time. Given this, why do companies that use a perpetual inventory system still take a physical count of their merchandise inventory at least once a year?

15. Under which type of inventory system is an inventory subsidiary ledger maintained?

Brief Exercises

LO6-2, LO6-8

BRIEF EXERCISE 6.1

Computation of Gross Profit

Office Today is an office supply store. Office Today's revenue in the current year is $800 million and its cost of goods sold is $640 million. Compute Office Today's gross profit and its gross profit percentage.

LO6-7

BRIEF EXERCISE 6.2

Accounts Receivable Subsidiary Ledger

The accounts receivable subsidiary ledger for Ranalli's Lawn Care has the following customer accounts and balances at the end of the current year. What should be the Accounts Receivable balance in the general ledger? [Hint: Customer accounts with a credit balance are not considered in determining the total balance in the Accounts Receivable account; rather these amounts are reclassified as Accounts Payable.]

Customer Name	Balance	Debit or Credit
Peter Gurney	$200	Dr
Robert King	150	Dr
Bruce Landis	50	Cr
Robert McNeil	100	Dr
Mark Noakes	50	Dr
Frank Rimshaw	300	Dr
Michael Sangster	50	Dr
Lawrence Williams	100	Cr

LO6-2, LO6-3, LO6-8

BRIEF EXERCISE 6.3

Perpetual Inventory System—Computation of Income

Alberto & Sons, Inc., a retailer of antique figurines, engages in the following transactions during October of the current year:

Oct. 1 Purchases 100 Hummels at $50 each.

Oct. 5 Sells 50 of the Hummels at $80 each.

Compute Alberto & Sons's gross profit for October.

LO6-2, LO6-4, LO6-8

BRIEF EXERCISE 6.4

Periodic Inventory System—Inventory Balance during Year

Home Sweet Home Inc. is a retailer of home accessories. The company's inventory balance at the beginning of the year was $600,000; Home Sweet Home purchased $500,000 of goods during January, and sales during January were $800,000. What is the balance that would appear in Home Sweet Home's inventory account on February 1 assuming use of a periodic inventory system?

LO6-2, LO6-4, LO6-8

BRIEF EXERCISE 6.5

Periodic Inventory System—Determine Cost of Goods Sold

Murphy Co. is a high-end retailer of fine fashions for men. Murphy's inventory balance at the beginning of the year is $300,000, and Murphy purchases $600,000 of goods during the year. Its inventory balance at the end of the year is $250,000. What is the cost of goods sold for the year?

LO6-2, LO6-4, LO6-8

BRIEF EXERCISE 6.6

Periodic Inventory System—Working Backward through the COGS Section

Yang & Min Inc. is a retailer of contemporary furniture. You are told that Yang & Min's ending inventory is $200,000 and its cost of goods sold is $500,000. Yang & Min had $100,000 of inventory at the beginning of the year. What was the dollar amount of goods purchased by Yang & Min during the year?

LO6-2, LO6-4

BRIEF EXERCISE 6.7

Periodic Inventory System—Closing Process

FunLand Inc. is a retailer of toys and games. FunLand's beginning inventory is $160,000 and its purchases during the year are $500,000. Its ending inventory is $60,000. Make the closing entries necessary given that FunLand uses a periodic inventory system.

LO6-6

BRIEF EXERCISE 6.8

Benefit of Taking a Purchase Discount

Pag Inc. is a clothing retailer and it has terms from one of its vendors of *1/10, n/30*. Compute the equivalent annual rate of return that Pag earns by always paying its bills within the discount period.

LO6-6

BRIEF EXERCISE 6.9

Sales Returns and Allowances

Smith & Sons Inc. is a sporting goods manufacturer. The firm uses a periodic inventory system. Smith & Sons shipped $30,000 of defective goods to a retailer. The retailer and Smith & Sons agreed that the retailer would keep the goods in exchange for a $3,000 allowance. The cost of the goods was $1,500. What journal entry (or entries) would Smith & Sons record?

LO6-7

BRIEF EXERCISE 6.10

Special Journals

List three special journals often used in accounting to facilitate the recording of repetitive transactions.

LO6-8
BRIEF EXERCISE 6.11
Ethics, Fraud, and
Corporate Governance

You are the assistant controller for a public company. Wall Street stock analysts are projecting an earnings per share figure of $0.25 for your company. On December 29, a large customer returns a very large shipment of your goods that were defective. You tell the controller about the customer return and that the debit to sales returns and allowances will have the effect of reducing earnings per share from $0.25 to $0.24. The controller indicates that failing to meet the consensus earnings expectations of the analyst community will result in a large stock price decline. The controller suggests waiting until January 2 (your company operates on a calendar year-end basis) to record the customer return. What should you do?

Exercises

LO6-1, LO6-6
EXERCISE 6.1
You as a Student

As a fund-raiser, the pep band at Melrose University sells T-shirts fans can wear when attending the school's 12 home basketball games. As the band's business manager, you must choose among several options for ordering and selling the T-shirts.

1. Place a single order in October large enough to last the entire season. The band must pay for the shirts in full when the order is placed. A 5 percent quantity discount applies to this option.

2. Place a series of small orders, as needed, throughout the season. Again, payment in full is due when the order is submitted. No discount applies to this option.

3. Have band members sell shirts directly to members of the student body. Cash is collected immediately as sales are made.

4. Sell all of the T-shirts through the university bookstore. The bookstore would receive a 6 percent commission on total sales and would remit to the band its share of the proceeds in a lump-sum payment at the end of the season.

a. Describe which combination of options would give the pep band the shortest operating cycle.

b. Describe which combination of options would give the pep band the longest operating cycle.

c. Discuss briefly the advantages and disadvantages of each option.

LO6-1
EXERCISE 6.2
Effects of Basic
Merchandising Transactions

Shown below are selected transactions of Konshock's, a retail store that uses a perpetual inventory system.

a. Purchased merchandise on account.

b. Recognized the revenue from a sale of merchandise on account. (Ignore the related cost of goods sold.)

c. Recognized the cost of goods sold relating to the sale in transaction **b**.

d. Collected in cash the account receivable from the customer in transaction **b**.

e. Following the taking of a physical inventory at year-end, made an adjusting entry to record a normal amount of inventory shrinkage.

Indicate the effects of each of these transactions on the elements of the company's financial statements shown below. Organize your answer in tabular form, using the column headings shown below. (Notice that the cost of goods sold is shown separately from all other expenses.) Use the code letters **I** for increase, **D** for decrease, and **NE** for no effect.

	Income Statement				Balance Sheet		
Transaction	Net Sales	− Cost of Goods Sold	− All Other Expenses	= Net Income	Assets	= Liabilities	+ Owners' Equity
a	___	___	___	___	___	___	___

LO6-2, LO6-5, LO6-8
EXERCISE 6.3
Understanding Inventory
Cost Flows

PC Connection is a leading mail order retailer of personal computers. A recent financial report issued by the company revealed the following information:

Merchandise inventory (beginning of the year)	$77 million
Merchandise inventory (end of the year)	$70 million
Net sales for the year	$2.15 billion
Gross profit margin	13%

   a.   Compute the company's cost of goods sold for the year.

   b.   Approximately how much inventory did **PC Connection** *purchase* during the year?

   c.   What factors might contribute to the company's low gross profit margin?

   d.   Discuss reasons why **PC Connection** uses a perpetual inventory system.

LO6-3, LO6-8

EXERCISE 6.4

Perpetual Inventory
Systems

Ranns Supply uses a perpetual inventory system. On January 1, its inventory account had a beginning balance of $6,450,000. Ranns engaged in the following transactions during the year:

   1.   Purchased merchandise inventory for $9,500,000.

   2.   Generated net sales of $26,000,000.

   3.   Recorded inventory shrinkage of $10,000 after taking a physical inventory at year-end.

   4.   Reported gross profit for the year of $15,000,000 in its income statement.

   a.   At what amount was Cost of Goods Sold reported in the company's year-end income statement?

   b.   At what amount was Merchandise Inventory reported in the company's year-end balance sheet?

   c.   Immediately prior to recording inventory shrinkage at the end of the year, what was the balance of the Cost of Goods Sold account? What was the balance of the Merchandise Inventory account?

LO6-6, LO6-8

EXERCISE 6.5

Evaluating Performance

These selected statistics are from recent annual reports of two well-known retailers:

	Walmart	Target
Percentage increase (decrease) in net sales	5.9%	4.1%
Percentage increase (decrease) in gross profit rate	−1.2%	−1.3%
Percentage increase (decrease) in comparable store net sales	1.6%	3.0%

   a.   Explain the significance of each of these three measures.

   b.   Evaluate briefly the performance of each company on the basis of these three measures.

LO6-3

EXERCISE 6.6

Taking a Physical Inventory

Frisbee Hardware uses a perpetual inventory system. At year-end, the Inventory account has a balance of $250,000, but a physical count shows that the merchandise on hand has a cost of only $246,000.

   a.   Explain the probable reason(s) for this discrepancy.

   b.   Prepare the journal entry required in this situation.

   c.   Indicate all the accounting records to which your journal entry in part **b** should be posted.

LO6-4

EXERCISE 6.7

Periodic Inventory Systems

Boston Bait Shop uses a periodic inventory system. At December 31, Year 2, the accounting records include the following information:

Inventory (as of December 31, Year 1)	$ 2,800
Net sales	79,600
Purchases	30,200

   A complete physical inventory taken at December 31, Year 2, indicates merchandise costing $3,000 remains in stock.

   a.   How were the amounts of beginning and ending inventory determined?

   b.   Compute the amount of the cost of goods sold in Year 2.

   c.   Prepare two closing entries at December 31, Year 2: the first to create a Cost of Goods Sold account with the appropriate balance and the second to bring the Inventory account up-to-date.

   d.   Prepare a partial income statement showing the shop's gross profit for the year.

   e.   Describe why a company such as Boston Bait Shop would use a periodic inventory system rather than a perpetual inventory system.

LO6-4

EXERCISE 6.8

Relationships within
Periodic Inventory Systems

This exercise stresses the relationships between the information recorded in a periodic inventory system and the basic elements of an income statement. Each of the five lines represents a separate set of information. You are to fill in the missing amounts. A net loss in the right-hand column is to be indicated by placing brackets around the amount, as for example in line **e** <15,000 >.

Net Sales	Begin-ing Inventory	Net Pur-chases	Ending Inventory	Cost of Goods Sold	Gross Profit	Expenses	Net Income or (Loss)
a. 240,000	76,000	104,000	35,200	?	95,200	72,000	?
b. 480,000	72,000	272,000	?	264,000	?	?	20,000
c. 630,000	207,000	?	166,500	441,000	189,000	148,500	?
d. 810,000	?	450,000	135,000	?	234,000	270,000	?
e. ?	156,000	?	153,000	396,000	135,000	?	<15,000>

LO6-5, LO6-8

EXERCISE 6.9

Selecting an Inventory
System

Year after year two huge supermarket chains—**Publix Super Markets, Inc.**, and **Safeway, Inc.**—consistently report gross profit rates between 26 percent and 29 percent. Each uses a sophisticated perpetual inventory system to account for billions of dollars in inventory transactions.

a. Discuss reasons why these firms consistently report such similar and stable gross profit rates.

b. What technologies make it possible for these retailing giants to use perpetual inventory systems?

LO6-6

EXERCISE 6.10

Cash Discounts

Golf World sold merchandise to Mulligans for $10,000, offering terms of 1/15, n/30. Mulligans paid for the merchandise within the discount period. Both companies use perpetual inventory systems.

a. Prepare journal entries in the accounting records of Golf World to account for this sale and the subsequent collection. Assume the original cost of the merchandise to Golf World had been $6,500.

b. Prepare journal entries in the accounting records of Mulligans to account for the purchase and subsequent payment. Mulligans records purchases of merchandise at *net cost.*

c. Assume that, because of a change in personnel, Mulligans failed to pay for this merchandise within the discount period. Prepare the journal entry in the accounting records of Mulligans to record payment *after* the discount period.

LO6-8

EXERCISE 6.11

Evaluating Performance

This selected information is from recent annual reports of the two largest retail pharmaceutical companies in the United States. (Dollar amounts are stated in billions.)

	Walgreen Company	Rite Aid Corporation
Net sales	$71.6	$26.1
Cost of goods sold.	?	19.3
Gross profit	?	?
Gross profit margin (or rate)	28.4%	?%
Total square feet of selling space.	87 million	47 million
Sales per square foot of selling space.	?	?

a. Fill in the missing amounts and percentages. (Round all amounts to one decimal place.)

b. On the basis of the information provided above, do you expect Walgreen or Rite Aid to be more profitable and why?

LO6-3, LO6-5

EXERCISE 6.12

Comparison of Inventory
Systems

Sky Probe sells state-of-the-art telescopes to individuals and organizations interested in studying the solar system. At December 31 last year, the company's inventory amounted to $250,000. During the first week of January this year, the company made only one purchase and one sale. These transactions were as follows:

Jan. 2 Sold one telescope costing $90,000 to Central State University for cash, $117,000.

Jan. 5 Purchased merchandise on account from Lunar Optics, $50,000. Terms, net 30 days.

a. Prepare journal entries to record these transactions assuming that Sky Probe uses the perpetual inventory system. Use separate entries to record the sales revenue and the cost of goods sold for the sale on January 2.

b. Compute the balance of the Inventory account on January 7.

c. Prepare journal entries to record the two transactions, assuming that Sky Probe uses the periodic inventory system.

d. Compute the cost of goods sold for the first week of January assuming use of a periodic inventory system. Use your answer to part **b** as the ending inventory.

e. Which inventory system do you believe that a company such as Sky Probe would probably use? Explain your reasoning.

LO6-4, LO6-5

EXERCISE 6.13

The Periodic Inventory System

Mountain Mabel's is a small general store located just outside of Yellowstone National Park. The store uses a periodic inventory system. Every January 1, Mabel and her husband close the store and take a complete physical inventory while watching the Rose Bowl Parade on television. The inventory balance on January 1 of the prior year was $6,240, and the inventory balance on December 31 was $4,560. Sales were $150,000 during the prior year, and purchases were $74,400.

a. Compute the cost of goods sold for the prior year.

b. Explain why a small business such as this might use the periodic inventory system.

c. Explain some of the *disadvantages* of the periodic system to a larger business, such as a Sears store.

LO6-8

EXERCISE 6.14

Difference between Income and Cash Flow

State College Technology Store (SCTS) is a retail computer store in the university center of a large midwestern university. SCTS engaged in the following transactions during November of the current year:

Nov. 1 Purchased 20 Nopxe laptop computers on account from Led Inc. The laptop computers cost $800 each, for a total of $16,000. Payment is due in 30 days.

Nov. 6 Sold four Nopxe laptop computers on account to the Department of Microbiology at State College at a retail sales price of $1,200 each, for a total of $4,800. Payment is due in 30 days.

Dec. 1 Paid the $16,000 account payable to Led Inc.

Dec. 6 Collected the $4,800 account receivable from State College's Department of Microbiology.

Assume that the other expenses incurred by SCTS during November and December were $1,000, and assume that all of these expenses were paid in cash. SCTS is not subject to income tax because it is a wholly owned unit of a nonprofit organization. Compute the net income of SCTS during November and December using accrual accounting principles. Also, compute what SCTS's net income would have been had it used the cash basis of accounting. Explain the difference.

LO6-8

EXERCISE 6.15

Using Home Depot, Inc., Financial Statements

The Home Depot, Inc., financial statements appear in Appendix A at the end of this textbook. Use the statements to complete the following requirements:

a. Calculate the gross profit percentage of Home Depot, Inc., for each of the years shown in the company's income statements.

b. Evaluate the company's trend in sales and gross profit.

Problem Set A

LO6-1, LO6-3, LO6-8

PROBLEM 6.1A

Evaluating Profitability

Claypool Hardware is the only hardware store in a remote area of northern Minnesota. Some of Claypool's transactions during the current year are as follows:

Nov. 5 Sold lumber on account to Bemidji Construction, $13,390. The inventory subsidiary ledger shows the cost of this merchandise was $9,105.

Nov. 9 Purchased tools on account from Owatonna Tool Company, $3,800.

Dec. 5 Collected in cash the $13,390 account receivable from Bemidji Construction.

Dec. 9 Paid the $3,800 owed to Owatonna Tool Company.

Dec. 31 Claypool's personnel counted the inventory on hand and determined its cost to be $182,080. The accounting records, however, indicate inventory of $183,790 and a cost of goods sold of $695,222. The physical count of the inventory was observed by the company's auditors and is considered correct.

Instructions

a. Prepare journal entries to record these transactions and events in the accounting records of Claypool Hardware. (The company uses a perpetual inventory system.)

b. Prepare a partial income statement showing the company's gross profit for the year. (Net sales for the year amount to $1,024,900.)

c. Claypool purchases merchandise inventory at the same wholesale prices as other hardware stores. Due to its remote location, however, the company must pay between $18,000 and $20,000 per year in extra transportation charges to receive delivery of merchandise. (These additional charges are included in the amount shown as cost of goods sold.)

Assume that an index of key business ratios in your library shows hardware stores of Claypool's approximate size (in total assets) average net sales of $1 million per year and a gross profit margin of 25 percent.

Is Claypool able to pass its extra transportation costs on to its customers? Does the business appear to suffer or benefit financially from its remote location? Explain your reasoning and support your conclusions with specific accounting data comparing the operations of Claypool Hardware with the industry averages.

LO6-1 through LO6-3, LO6-6, LO6-8

PROBLEM 6.2A

Preparation and Interpretation of a Merchandising Company's Income Statement

Hendry's Boutique is a retail clothing store for women. The store operates out of a rented building in Storm Lake, Iowa. Shown below is the store's *adjusted* year-end trial balance dated December 31, 2015.

HENDRY'S BOUTIQUE
ADJUSTED TRIAL BALANCE
DECEMBER 31, 2015

Cash	$ 15,200	
Accounts receivable	2,600	
Merchandise inventory	17,500	
Prepaid rent	1,800	
Office supplies	900	
Office equipment	41,000	
Accumulated depreciation: office equipment		$ 12,000
Accounts payable		12,750
Sales taxes payable		3,200
Capital stock		18,000
Retained earnings		21,050
Sales		226,000
Sales returns and allowances	2,500	
Cost of goods sold	100,575	
Purchase discounts lost	250	
Utilities expense	4,120	
Office supply expense	520	
Depreciation expense: office equipment	2,750	
Rent expense	6,100	
Insurance expense	900	
Salaries expense	88,095	
Income taxes expense	8,190	
	$293,000	$293,000

Instructions

a. Prepare an income statement for Hendry's Boutique dated December 31, 2015.

b. Compute the store's gross profit margin as a percentage of *net sales.*

c. Do the store's customers seem to be satisfied with their purchases? Defend your answer.

d. Explain how you can tell that the business records inventory purchases *net* of any purchase discounts.

e. The store reports sales taxes payable of $3,200 in its adjusted trial balance. Explain why it does not report any *sales taxes expense*.

f. Which accounts appearing in the store's adjusted trial balance comprise its *operating cycle?*

LO6-8

PROBLEM 6.3A

Trend Analysis

Shown below is information from the financial reports of Knauss Supermarkets for the past few years.

	2016	2015	2014
Net sales (in millions)	$5,495	$5,184	$4,800
Number of stores	448	445	430
Square feet of selling space (in millions)	11.9	11.1	10.0
Average net sales of comparable stores (in millions)	$ 10.8	$ 11.0	$ 11.4

Instructions

a. Calculate the following statistics for Knauss Supermarkets (round your answers to one decimal place):

   1. The percentage change in net sales from 2014 to 2015 and 2015 to 2016. Hint: The percentage change is computed by dividing the dollar amount of the change between years by the amount of the base year. For example, the percentage change in net sales from 2014 to 2015 is computed by dividing the difference between 2014 to 2015 net sales by the amount of 2014 net sales, or ($5,184 − $4,800) ÷ $4,800 = 8% increase.

   2. The percentage change in net sales per square foot of selling space from 2014 to 2015 and 2015 to 2016.

   3. The percentage change in comparable store sales from 2014 to 2015 and 2015 to 2016.

b. Evaluate the sales performance of Knauss Supermarkets.

LO6-3, LO6-6

PROBLEM 6.4A

Comparison of Net Cost and Gross Price Methods

Kitchen Electrics uses a perpetual inventory system. The following are three recent merchandising transactions:

Apr. 10 Purchased 10 refrigerators from Polar Co. on account. Invoice price, $600 per unit, for a total of $6,000. The terms of purchase were 2/10, n/30.

Apr. 15 Sold one of these refrigerators for $900 cash.

Apr. 20 Paid the account payable to Polar Co. within the discount period.

Instructions

a. Prepare journal entries to record these transactions assuming that Kitchen Electrics records purchases of merchandise at:

   1. Net cost

   2. Gross invoice price

b. Assume that Kitchen Electrics did *not* pay Polar Co. within the discount period but instead paid the full invoice price on May 10. Prepare journal entries to record this payment assuming that the original liability had been recorded at:

   1. Net cost

   2. Gross invoice price

c. Assume that you are evaluating the efficiency of Kitchen Electric's bill-paying procedures. Which accounting method—net cost or gross invoice price—provides you with the most *useful* information? Explain.

LO6-3, LO6-6

PROBLEM 6.5A

Merchandising Transactions

The following is a series of related transactions between Siogo Shoes, a shoe wholesaler, and Sole Mates, a chain of retail shoe stores:

Feb. 9 Siogo Shoes sold Sole Mates 100 pairs of hiking boots on account, terms 1/10, n/30. The cost of these boots to Siogo Shoes was $60 per pair, and the sales price was $100 per pair.

Feb. 12 United Express charged $80 for delivering this merchandise to Sole Mates. These charges were split evenly between the buyer and seller and were paid immediately in cash.

Feb. 13 Sole Mates returned 10 pairs of boots to Siogo Shoes because they were the wrong size. Siogo Shoes allowed Sole Mates full credit for this return.

Feb. 19 Sole Mates paid the remaining balance due to Siogo Shoes within the discount period.

Both companies use a perpetual inventory system.

Instructions

a. Record this series of transactions in the general journal of Siogo Shoes. (The company records sales at gross sales price.)

b. Record this series of transactions in the general journal of Sole Mates. (The company records purchases of merchandise at *net cost* and uses a Transportation-in account to record transportation charges on inbound shipments.)

c. Sole Mates does not always have enough cash on hand to pay for purchases within the discount period. However, it has a line of credit with its bank, which enables Sole Mates to easily borrow money for short periods of time at an annual interest rate of 11 percent. (The bank charges interest only for the number of days until Sole Mates repays the loan.) As a matter of general policy, should Sole Mates take advantage of 1/10, n/30 cash discounts even if it must borrow the money to do so at an annual rate of 11 percent? Explain fully—and illustrate any supporting computations.

LO6-2, LO6-3, LO6-6

PROBLEM 6.6A

Correcting Errors—Recording of Merchandising Transactions

King Enterprises is a book wholesaler. King hired a new accounting clerk on January 1 of the current year. The new clerk does not understand accrual accounting and recorded the transactions below based on when cash receipts and disbursements changed hands rather than when the transaction occurred. King uses a perpetual inventory system, and its accounting policy calls for inventory purchases to be recorded net of any discounts offered.

Jan. 10 Paid Aztec Enterprises $9,800 for books that it received on December 15. (This purchase was recorded as a debit to Inventory and a credit to Accounts Payable on December 15 of last year, but the accounting clerk ignores that fact.)

Dec. 27 Received books from McSaw Inc. for $20,000; terms 2/10, n/30.

Dec. 30 Sold books to Booksellers Unlimited for $30,000; terms 1/10, n/30. The cost of these books to King was $24,500.

Instructions

a. As a result of the accounting clerk's errors, compute the amount by which the following accounts are overstated or understated.

   1. Accounts Receivable

   2. Inventory

   3. Accounts Payable

   4. Sales

   5. Cost of Goods Sold

b. Compute the amount by which net income is overstated or understated.

c. Prepare a single journal entry to correct the errors that the accounting clerk has made. (Assume that King has yet to close its books for the current year.)

d. Assume that King has already closed its books for the current year. Make a single journal entry to correct the errors that the accounting clerk has made.

e. Assume that the ending inventory balance is correctly stated based on adjustments resulting from a physical inventory count. (Cost of Goods Sold was debited or credited based on the inventory adjustment.) Assume that King has already closed its books for the current year, and make a single journal entry to correct the errors that the accounting clerk has made.

LO6-1, LO6-3, LO6-6
PROBLEM 6.7A
Accrual Accounting, Cash
Flow, and Fair Value

Thompson Plumbing Inc. is a wholesaler of plumbing accessories. Thompson Plumbing began operations in September of the current year and engaged in the following transactions during September and October of this year. Thompson Plumbing uses a perpetual inventory system.

Sept. 3   Purchased $200,000 of plumbing accessories, terms n/30.

Sept. 15   Sold $150,000 of plumbing accessories, terms n/60. The cost of the accessories sold is $100,000.

Sept. 28   Purchased $300,000 of plumbing accessories, terms n/45.

Oct. 3   Settled the $200,000 purchase of September 3.

Oct. 15   Sold $375,000 of plumbing accessories, terms n/60. The cost of the accessories sold is $250,000.

Oct. 27   Purchased $450,000 of plumbing accessories, terms n/30.

Instructions

a. Compute the gross profit on Thompson Plumbing's transactions during September and October.

b. Compute the gross profit on Thompson Plumbing's transactions during September and October if a cash-basis accounting system was used.

c. Explain the difference between the results in **a** and **b**.

d. Assume that the fair value of Thompson Plumbing's inventory at October 31 is $750,000. A potential lender asks Thompson Plumbing to prepare a fair-value–based balance sheet. Prepare the journal entry to reflect inventory at fair value. Comment on how a wholesaler might determine fair value for inventory items. [Hint: Increase the Inventory account by the difference between fair value and book value with the offset to an account titled Revaluation of Inventory to Market Value.]

LO6-1 through LO6-8
PROBLEM 6.8A
A Comprehensive Problem

CPI sells computer peripherals. At December 31, 2015, CPI's inventory amounted to $500,000. During the first week in January 2016, the company made only one purchase and one sale. These transactions were as follows:

Jan. 2   Purchased 20 modems and 80 printers from Sharp. The total cost of these machines was $25,000, terms 3/10, n/60.

Jan. 6   Sold 30 different types of products on account to Pace Corporation. The total sales price was $10,000, terms 5/10, n/90. The total cost of these 30 units to CPI was $6,100 (net of the purchase discount).

CPI has a full-time accountant and a computer-based accounting system. It records sales at the gross sales price and purchases at net cost and maintains subsidiary ledgers for accounts receivable, inventory, and accounts payable.

Instructions

a. Briefly describe the operating cycle of a merchandising company. Identify the assets and liabilities directly affected by this cycle.

b. Prepare journal entries to record these transactions, assuming that CPI uses a *perpetual* inventory system.

c. Compute the balance in the Inventory account at the close of business on January 6.

d. Prepare journal entries to record the two transactions, assuming that CPI uses a *periodic* inventory system.

e. Compute the cost of goods sold for the first week of January assuming use of the periodic system. (Use your answer to part **c** as the ending inventory.)

f. Which type of inventory system do you think CPI most likely would use? Explain your reasoning.

g. Compute the gross profit margin on the January 6 sales transaction.

Problem Set B

LO6-1, LO6-3, LO6-8
PROBLEM 6.1B
Evaluating Profitability

Big Oak Lumber is a lumber yard on Angel Island. Some of Big Oak's transactions during the current year are as follows:

Apr. 15 Sold lumber on account to Hard Hat Construction, $19,700. The inventory subsidiary ledger shows the cost of this merchandise was $10,300.

Apr. 19 Purchased lumber on account from LHP Company, $3,700.

May 10 Collected in cash the $19,700 account receivable from Hard Hat Construction.

May 19 Paid the $3,700 owed to LHP Company.

Dec. 31 Big Oak's personnel counted the inventory on hand and determined its cost to be $114,000. The accounting records, however, indicate inventory of $116,500 and a cost of goods sold of $721,000. The physical count of the inventory was observed by the company's auditors and is considered correct.

Instructions

a. Prepare journal entries to record these transactions and events in the accounting records of Big Oak Lumber. (The company uses a perpetual inventory system.)

b. Prepare a partial income statement showing the company's gross profit for the year. (Net sales for the year amount to $1,422,000.)

c. Big Oak purchases merchandise inventory at the same wholesale prices as other lumber yards. Because of its remote location the company must pay between $8,000 and $18,000 per year in extra transportation charges to receive delivery of merchandise. (These additional charges are included in the amount shown as cost of goods sold.)

Assume that an index of key business ratios in your library shows lumber yards of Big Oak's approximate size (in total assets) average net sales of $1 million per year and a gross profit rate of 22 percent.

Is Big Oak able to pass its extra transportation costs on to its customers? Does the business appear to suffer or benefit financially from its remote location? Explain your reasoning and support your conclusions with specific accounting data comparing the operations of Big Oak Lumber with the industry averages.

LO6-1 through LO6-3, LO6-6, LO6-8

PROBLEM 6.2B

Preparation and Interpretation of a Merchandising Company's Income Statement

Harry's Haberdashery is a retail clothing store for men. The store operates out of a rented building in Albertsville, Virginia. Shown below is the store's *adjusted* year-end trial balance dated December 31, 2015.

HARRY'S HABERDASHERY ADJUSTED TRIAL BALANCE DECEMBER 31, 2015		
Cash	$ 39,270	
Accounts receivable	4,400	
Merchandise inventory	29,700	
Prepaid rent	3,100	
Office supplies	1,500	
Office equipment	70,000	
Accumulated depreciation: office equipment		$ 20,000
Accounts payable		22,000
Sales taxes payable		5,000
Capital stock		31,000
Retained earnings		36,000
Sales		384,000
Sales returns and allowances	4,000	
Cost of goods sold	157,630	
Purchase discounts lost	400	
Utilities expense	7,000	
Office supply expense	900	
Depreciation expense: office equipment	4,700	
Rent expense	10,000	
Insurance expense	1,500	
Salaries expense	150,000	
Income tax expense	13,900	
	$498,000	$498,000

Instructions

a. Prepare an income statement for Harry's Haberdashery dated December 31, 2015.

b. Compute the store's gross profit margin as a percentage of *net sales*.

c. Do the store's customers seem to be satisfied with their purchases? Defend your answer.

d. Explain how you can tell that the business records inventory purchases *net* of any purchase discounts.

e. The store reports sales taxes payable of $5,000 in its adjusted trial balance. Explain why it does not report any *sales taxes expense*.

f. What is meant by the term "operating cycle" and which accounts in the trial balance comprise Harry's Haberdashery's operating cycle?

LO6-8

PROBLEM 6.3B

Trend Analysis

Shown below is information from the financial reports of Pete's Auto Parts for the past few years.

	2016	2015	2014
Net sales (in millions)	$18,480	$17,800	$16,560
Number of stores	266	244	230
Square feet of selling space (in millions)	12.0	11.4	10.2
Average net sales of comparable stores (in millions)	$ 71.15	$ 72.25	$ 73.50

Instructions

a. Calculate the following statistics for Pete's Auto Parts (round all computations to one decimal place):

1. The percentage change in net sales from 2014 to 2015 and 2015 to 2016. Hint: The percentage change is computed by dividing the dollar amount of the change between years by the amount of the base year. For example, the percentage change in net sales from 2014 to 2015 is computed by dividing the difference between 2015 and 2014 net sales by the amount of 2014 net sales, or ($17,800 − $16,560) ÷ $16,560 = 7.5% increase.

2. The percentage change in net sales per square foot of selling space from 2014 to 2015 and 2015 to 2016.

3. The percentage change in comparable store sales from 2014 to 2015 and 2015 to 2016.

b. Evaluate the sales performance of Pete's Auto Parts.

LO6-3, LO6-6

PROBLEM 6.4B

Comparison of Net Cost and Gross Price Methods

Mary's TV uses a perpetual inventory system. The following are three recent merchandising transactions:

Mar. 6 Purchased eight TVs from Whosa Industries on account. Invoice price, $350 per unit, for a total of $2,800. The terms of purchase were 2/10, n/30.

Mar. 11 Sold two of these televisions for $600 cash.

Mar. 16 Paid the account payable to Whosa Industries within the discount period.

Instructions

a. Prepare journal entries to record these transactions assuming that Mary's records purchases of merchandise at:

1. Net cost

2. Gross invoice price

b. Assume that Mary's did *not* pay Whosa Industries within the discount period but instead paid the full invoice price on April 6. Prepare journal entries to record this payment assuming that the original liability had been recorded at:

1. Net cost

2. Gross invoice price

c. Assume that you are evaluating the efficiency of Mary's bill-paying procedures. Which accounting method—net cost or gross invoice price—provides you with the most *useful* information? Explain.

LO6-3, LO6-6
PROBLEM 6.5B
Merchandising Transactions

The following is a series of related transactions between Hip Pants and Sleek, a chain of retail clothing stores:

Oct. 12 Hip Pants sold Sleek 300 pairs of pants on account, terms 1/10, n/30. The cost of these pants to Hip Pants was $20 per pair, and the sales price was $60 per pair.

Oct. 15 Wings Express charged $50 for delivering this merchandise to Sleek. These charges were split evenly between the buyer and the seller and were paid immediately in cash.

Oct. 16 Sleek returned four pairs of pants to Hip Pants because they were the wrong size. Hip Pants allowed Sleek full credit for this return.

Oct. 22 Sleek paid the remaining balance due to Hip Pants within the discount period.

Both companies use a perpetual inventory system.

Instructions

a. Record this series of transactions in the general journal of Hip Pants. (The company records sales at gross sales price.)

b. Record this series of transactions in the general journal of Sleek. (The company records purchases of merchandise at *net cost* and uses a Transportation-in account to record transportation charges on inbound shipments.)

c. Sleek does not always have enough cash on hand to pay for purchases within the discount period. However, it has a line of credit with its bank, which enables Sleek to easily borrow money for short periods of time at an annual interest rate of 12 percent. (The bank charges interest only for the number of days until Sleek repays the loan.) As a matter of general policy, should Sleek take advantage of 1/10, n/30 cash discounts even if it must borrow the money to do so at an annual rate of 12 percent? Explain fully—and illustrate any supporting computations.

LO6-2, LO6-3, LO6-6
PROBLEM 6.6B
Correcting Errors—
Recording of Merchandising
Transactions

Queen Enterprises is a furniture wholesaler. Queen hired a new accounting clerk on January 1 of the current year. The new clerk does not understand accrual accounting and recorded the transactions below based on when cash receipts and disbursements changed hands rather than when the transaction occurred. Queen uses a perpetual inventory system, and its accounting policy calls for inventory purchases to be recorded net of any discounts offered.

Jan. 7 Paid Hardwoods Forever Inc. $4,900 for furniture that it received on December 20. (This purchase was recorded as a debit to Inventory and a credit to Accounts Payable on December 20 of last year, but the accounting clerk ignores that fact.)

Dec. 23 Received furniture from Koos Hoffwan Co. for $10,000; terms 2/10, n/30.

Dec. 26 Sold furniture to Beige Chipmunk Inc. for $15,000; terms 1/10, n/30. The cost of the furniture to Queen was $12,250.

Instructions

a. As a result of the accounting clerk's errors, compute the amount by which the following accounts are overstated or understated:
   1. Accounts Receivable
   2. Inventory
   3. Accounts Payable
   4. Sales
   5. Cost of Goods Sold

b. Compute the amount by which net income is overstated or understated.

c. Prepare a single journal entry to correct the errors that the accounting clerk has made. (Assume that Queen has yet to close its books for the current year.)

d. Assume that Queen has already closed its books for the current year. Make a single journal entry to correct the errors that the accounting clerk has made.

e. Assume that the ending inventory balance is correctly stated based on adjustments resulting from a physical inventory count. (Cost of Goods Sold was debited or credited based on the inventory adjustment.) Assume that Queen has already closed its books for the current year, and make a single journal entry to correct the errors that the accounting clerk has made.

LO6-1, LO6-3, LO6-6
PROBLEM 6.7B
Accrual Accounting, Cash Flow, and Fair Value

Computer Resources Inc. is a computer retailer. Computer Resources began operations in December of the current year and engaged in the following transactions during that month. Computer Resources uses a perpetual inventory system.

Dec. 5   Purchased $100,000 of computer equipment, terms n/30.

Dec. 12   Sold $100,000 of computer equipment, terms n/30. The cost of the equipment sold is $50,000.

Dec. 26   Purchased $200,000 of computer equipment, terms n/30.

Instructions

a. Compute the gross profit on Computer Resources's transactions during December.

b. Compute the gross profit on Computer Resources's transactions during December if a cash-basis accounting system was used.

c. Explain the difference between the results in **a** and **b**.

d. Assume that the fair value of Computer Resources's inventory at December 31 is $375,000. A potential lender asks Computer Resources to prepare a fair-value–based balance sheet. Prepare the journal entry to reflect inventory at fair value. Comment on how a retailer might determine fair value for inventory items. [Hint: Increase the Inventory account by the difference between fair value and book value with the offset to an account titled Revaluation of Inventory to Market Value.]

LO6-1 through LO6-8
PROBLEM 6.8B
A Comprehensive Problem

Hearthstone sells commercial kitchen equipment. At December 31, 2015, Hearthstone's inventory amounted to $750,000. During the first week of January 2016, the company made only one purchase and one sale. These transactions were as follows:

Jan. 5   Purchased 90 machines from Rock Creek Corporation. The total cost of these machines was $60,000, terms 3/10, n/60.

Jan. 10   Sold 45 different types of products on account to Harolds, Inc. The total sales price was $42,000, terms 5/10, n/90. The total cost of these 45 units to Hearthstone was $15,000 (net of the purchase discount).

Hearthstone has a full-time accountant and a computer-based accounting system. It records sales at the gross sales price and purchases at net cost and maintains subsidiary ledgers for accounts receivable, inventory, and accounts payable.

Instructions

a. Briefly describe the operating cycle of a merchandising company. Identify the assets and liabilities directly affected by this cycle.

b. Prepare journal entries to record these transactions, assuming Hearthstone uses a *perpetual* inventory system.

c. Explain the information in part **b** that should be posted to subsidiary ledger accounts.

d. Compute the balance in the Inventory control account at the close of business on January 10.

e. Prepare journal entries to record the two transactions, assuming that Hearthstone uses a *periodic* inventory system.

f. Compute the cost of goods sold for the two weeks of January assuming use of the periodic system. (Use your answer to part **d** as the ending inventory.)

g. Which type of inventory system do you think Hearthstone most likely would use? Explain your reasoning.

h. Compute the gross profit margin on the January 10 sales transaction. [Round your answer to one decimal place.]

Critical Thinking Cases

LO6-5
CASE 6.1
Selecting an Inventory System

In each of the following situations, indicate whether you would expect the business to use a periodic inventory system or a perpetual inventory system. Explain the reasons for your answer.

a. The Frontier Shop is a small retail store that sells boots and Western clothing. The store is operated by the owner, who works full-time in the business, and by one part-time sales-clerk. Sales transactions are recorded on an antique cash register. The business uses a manual accounting system, which is maintained by ACE Bookkeeping Service. At the end of each month, an employee of ACE visits The Frontier Shop to update its accounting records, prepare sales tax returns, and perform other necessary accounting services.

b. Allister's Corner is an art gallery in the Soho district of New York. All accounting records are maintained manually by the owner, who works in the store on a full-time basis. The store sells three or four paintings each week, at sales prices ranging from about $5,000 to $50,000 per painting.

c. A publicly owned corporation publishes about 200 titles of college-level textbooks. The books are sold to college bookstores throughout the country. Books are distributed to these bookstores from four central warehouses located in California, Texas, Ohio, and Virginia.

d. Toys-4-You operates a national chain of 86 retail toy stores. The company has a state-of-the-art computerized accounting system. All sales transactions are recorded on electronic point-of-sale terminals. These terminals are tied into a central computer system that provides the national headquarters with information about the profitability of each store on a weekly basis.

e. Mr. Jingles is an independently owned and operated ice cream truck.

f. TransComm is a small company that sells very large quantities of a single product. The product is a low-cost spindle of recordable compact disks (CDRs) manufactured by a large Japanese company. Sales are made only in large quantities, primarily to chains of computer stores and large discount stores. This year, the average sales transaction amounted to $14,206 of merchandise. All accounting records are maintained by a full-time employee using commercial accounting software and a personal computer.

LO6-4, LO6-8

CASE 6.2

A Cost-Benefit Analysis

Village Hardware is a retail store selling hardware, small appliances, and sporting goods. The business follows a policy of selling all merchandise at exactly twice the amount of its cost to the store and uses a *periodic* inventory system.

At year-end, the following information is taken from the accounting records:

Net sales	$580,000
Inventory, January 1	58,000
Purchases	$297,250

A physical count indicates merchandise costing $49,300 is on hand at December 31.

Instructions

a. Prepare a partial income statement showing computation of the gross profit for the year.

b. On seeing your income statement, the owner of the store makes the following comment: "Inventory shrinkage losses are really costing me. If it weren't for shrinkage losses, the store's gross profit would be 50 percent of net sales. I'm going to hire a security guard and put an end to shoplifting once and for all."

   Determine the amount of loss from inventory shrinkage stated (1) at cost and (2) at retail sales value. (Hint: Without any shrinkage losses, the cost of goods sold and the amount of gross profit would each amount to 50 percent of net sales.)

c. Assume that Village Hardware could virtually eliminate shoplifting by hiring a security guard at a cost of $1,800 per month. Would this strategy be profitable? Explain your reasoning.

LO6-3 through LO6-5, LO6-7

CASE 6.3

Group Assignment— Evaluating an Inventory System

Identify one local business that uses a perpetual inventory system and another that uses a periodic system. Interview an individual in each organization who is familiar with the inventory system and the recording of sales transactions.

Instructions

Separately for each business organization:

a. Describe the procedures used in accounting for sales transactions, keeping track of inventory levels, and determining the cost of goods sold.

b. Explain the reasons offered by the person interviewed as to *why* the business uses this type of system.

c. Indicate whether your group considers the system in use appropriate under the circumstances. If not, recommend specific changes. *Explain your reasoning.*

LO6-8

CASE 6.4

Manipulating Income

You have recently taken a position with Albers, Inc., a wholesale company that relies heavily on sales outside the United States. In order to facilitate sales worldwide, the company has warehouses at several non–U.S. locations from which it services important markets in different parts of the world.

You are in the midst of year-end closings, and your supervisor approaches you about what can be done to improve the appearance of the company's performance for the current year. His idea is to intentionally overstate year-end inventory at locations outside the United States, thereby reducing cost of goods sold and improving gross profit and net income. Because of the remote locations where much of the inventory is housed, he reasons that it is unlikely that the overstatement will be discovered. You are aware that his compensation includes a bonus based, in part, on reported income. He has also indicated that he will "take care of you" in the future if you are supportive in taking steps to improve the company's reported financial performance, such as the inventory overstatement he currently proposes.

Instructions

a. Once you get over the shock of being asked to engage in this activity, how will you deal with this situation? What are the implications to you of going along with your supervisor's plan? If you are not inclined to cooperate, how will you deal with this situation?

b. Besides being unethical, what other implications does your supervisor's plan have for your company's reported performance in future years?

LO6-8

INTERNET CASE 6.5

Exploring the Annual Report of **Gap, Inc.**

You can find a large amount of information on the Internet to evaluate the performance of companies. Many firms provide links to this information on their home pages.

Access the home page of **The Gap, Inc.**, at the following Internet location:

www.gapinc.com

Instructions

a. What links to financial information are available on the company's home page? (Click on the link for "investors.")

b. Download the company's most recent annual report and use it to answer the following questions:

1. By what percentage amounts did net sales increase or decrease in each of the three years reported?

2. What was the company's gross profit rate for each of the three years reported?

3. What were the company's sales per square foot of selling space for each of the three years reported?

4. For the most recent year reported, how many new stores were opened? How many existing stores, if any, were closed?

5. By what percentage amounts did comparable store sales increase or decrease in each of the three years reported?

6. What dollar amount of inventory does the company report in its most recent balance sheet?

Internet sites are time and date sensitive. It is the purpose of these exercises to have you explore the Internet. You may need to use the Yahoo! search engine **www.yahoo.com** *(or another favorite search engine) to find a company's current web address.*

Answers to Self-Test Questions

1. a, b, d   **2.** b, c   **3.** b   **4.** b   **5.** b, d   **6.** b, c, d   **7.** b   **8.** a, c

CHAPTER 7

Financial Assets

AFTER STUDYING THIS CHAPTER, YOU SHOULD BE ABLE TO:

Learning Objectives

LO7-1 Define financial assets and explain their valuation in the balance sheet.

LO7-2 Describe the objectives of cash management and internal controls over cash.

LO7-3 Prepare a bank reconciliation and explain its purpose.

LO7-4 Describe how short-term investments are reported in the balance sheet and account for transactions involving marketable securities.

LO7-5 Describe internal controls over accounts receivable.

LO7-6 Account for uncollectible receivables using the allowance and direct write-off methods.

LO7-7 Explain, compute, and account for notes receivable and interest revenue.

LO7-8 Evaluate the liquidity of a company's accounts receivable.

© The McGraw-Hill Companies, Inc./Christopher Kerrigan, photographer

APPLE INC.

Apple Inc. is a company that designs, manufactures, and markets mobile communication and media devices, personal computers, and portable digital music players and sells a variety of related software, services, and peripherals. The company has operations worldwide, and its reportable operating segments are the Americas, Europe, Japan, Asia-Pacific, and Retail, which operates retail stores in 13 countries.

You might assume that the company has most of its resources tied up in plant assets and, in fact, the company's balance sheet recently reported $15.5 billion in property, plant, and equipment. However, the same balance sheet reported total assets of $176 billion. Therefore, property and equipment make up only 8.8 percent of Apple's total assets.

Financial assets, including non-trade receivables, of $140 billion comprise 80 percent of Apple's total assets. Financial assets are a company's most liquid resources. They include cash, cash equivalents, certain investments in marketable securities, accounts receivable, and notes receivable.

Apple is fortunate to have an abundance of liquid resources. In challenging economic times, when the ability to generate or borrow money may be difficult, companies can use their financial assets that are easily and directly convertible into known amounts of cash to continue operations and purchase inventory, pay bills, and honor commitments to employees.

Our coverage of financial assets throughout this chapter directly relates to the recent instability in financial markets. We address topics including commercial paper and other cash equivalents, the volatility of investment portfolios, and the inability of companies to collect outstanding accounts receivable. ■

Financial assets are a company's most liquid (or cashlike) resources. The ability of a company to service its debt, purchase inventory, pay taxes, and cover payroll obligations hinges on the availability of these highly liquid assets. In this chapter, we will examine how companies determine and report the *current values* of financial assets, and how effective companies quickly convert certain financial assets into cash.

HOW MUCH CASH SHOULD A BUSINESS HAVE?

In response to this question, most businesspeople would say, "As little as necessary." In a well-managed company, daily cash receipts are deposited promptly in the bank. Often, a principal source of these daily receipts is the collection of accounts receivable. If the daily receipts exceed routine cash outlays, the company can meet its obligations while maintaining relatively low balances in its bank accounts.

Cash that will not be needed in the immediate future often is invested in highly liquid short-term securities. These investments are more productive than cash because they earn revenue in the forms of interest and dividends. If the business should need more cash than it has in its bank accounts, it can easily convert some of its investments back into cash.

The term **financial assets** describes not just cash but also those assets easily and directly *convertible into known amounts of cash.* These assets include cash, short-term investments (also called **marketable securities**), and receivables. We address these three types of financial assets in a single chapter because they are so closely related. All of these assets represent *forms of money;* financial resources flow quickly among these asset categories.

In summary, businesses "store" money in three basic forms: cash, short-term investments, and receivables. The flow of cash among these types of financial assets is illustrated in Exhibit 7–1.

L07-1

LEARNING OBJECTIVE
Define financial assets and explain their valuation in the balance sheet.

EXHIBIT 7–I

Money Flows Among the Financial Assets

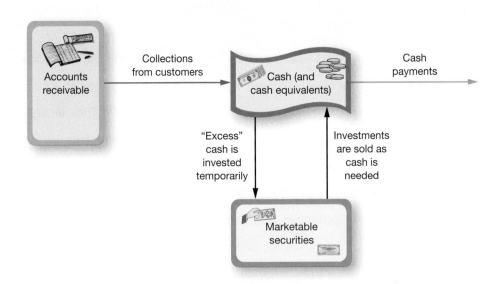

THE VALUATION OF FINANCIAL ASSETS

In the balance sheet, financial assets are shown at their *current values,* meaning the amounts of cash that these assets represent. Interestingly, current value is measured differently for each type of financial asset.

The current value of cash is simply its face amount. But the current value of marketable securities may change daily, based on fluctuations in stock prices, interest rates, and other factors. Therefore, most short-term investments appear in the balance sheet at their current *market values.* (Notice that the valuation of these investments represents an exception to the cost principle.)

Accounts receivable, like cash, have stated face amounts. But large companies usually do not expect to collect every dollar of their accounts receivable. Some customers simply will be unable to make full payment. Therefore, receivables appear in the balance sheet at the estimated *collectible* amount—called **net realizable value.**

The three methods of measuring the current value of financial assets are summarized in Exhibit 7–2.

Type of Financial Asset	Basis for Valuation in the Balance Sheet
Cash (and cash equivalents)	Face amount
Short-term investments (marketable securities)	Fair market value
Receivables	Net realizable value

EXHIBIT 7–2

Methods of Measuring the Current Value of Financial Assets

Cash

Accountants define *cash* as money on deposit in banks and any items that banks will accept for deposit. These items include not only coins and paper money, but also checks, money orders, and travelers' checks. Banks also accept drafts signed by customers using bank credit cards, such as **Visa** and **MasterCard.** Thus sales to customers using bank cards are considered *cash sales,* not credit sales, to the enterprise that makes the sale.

Most companies maintain several bank accounts as well as keep a small amount of cash on hand. Therefore, the Cash account in the general ledger is often a *control account.* A cash subsidiary ledger includes separate accounts corresponding to each bank account and each supply of cash on hand within the organization.

REPORTING CASH IN THE BALANCE SHEET

Cash is listed first in the balance sheet because it is the most liquid of all assets. For purposes of balance sheet presentation, the balance in the Cash control account is combined with that of the control account for **cash equivalents.**

Cash Equivalents   Some short-term investments are so liquid that they are termed *cash equivalents.* Examples include money market funds, U.S. Treasury bills, and high-grade commercial paper (very short-term notes payable that are issued by large, creditworthy corporations). These assets are considered so similar to cash that they are combined with the amount of cash in the balance sheet. Therefore, the first asset listed in the balance sheet often is called Cash and Cash Equivalents.

To qualify as a cash equivalent, an investment must be very safe, have a very stable market value, and mature within 90 days of the date of acquisition. Investments in even the highest quality stocks and bonds of large corporations are *not* viewed as meeting these criteria. Short-term investments that do not qualify as cash equivalents are listed in the balance sheet as Marketable Securities.

Restricted Cash   Some bank accounts are restricted as to their use, so they are not available to meet the normal operating needs of the company. For example, a bank account may contain cash specifically earmarked for the repayment of a noncurrent liability, such as a bond payable. Restricted cash should be presented in the balance sheet as part of the section entitled "Investments and Restricted Funds."

As a condition for granting a loan, banks often require the borrower to maintain a **compensating balance** (minimum average balance) on deposit in a non-interest-bearing checking account. This agreement does not actually prevent the borrower from using the cash, but it does mean the company must quickly replenish this bank account. Compensating balances are included in the amount of cash listed in the balance sheet, but these balances should be disclosed in the notes accompanying the financial statements.

Lines of Credit   Many businesses arrange **lines of credit** with their banks. A line of credit means that the bank has agreed *in advance* to lend the company any amount of money up to a specified limit. The company can borrow this money at any time simply by drawing checks on a special bank account. A liability to the bank arises as soon as a portion of the credit line is used.

The *unused* portion of a line of credit is neither an asset nor a liability; it represents only the *ability* to borrow money quickly and easily. Although an unused line of credit does not appear as an asset or a liability in the balance sheet, it increases the company's liquidity. Thus unused lines of credit usually are *disclosed* in notes accompanying the financial statements. For example, Wet Seal, Inc., recently included the following information in the footnotes accompanying its financial statements:

> We maintain a $35 million line of credit that can be increased up to $50 million in absence of any defaults. To date, $5.2 million of this amount has been used for the purchase of inventory.

CASH MANAGEMENT

L07-2

LEARNING OBJECTIVE
Describe the objectives
of cash management and
internal controls over cash.

The term **cash management** refers to planning, controlling, and accounting for cash transactions and cash balances. Because cash moves so readily between bank accounts and other financial assets, cash management really means the management of *all financial resources.* Efficient management of these resources is essential to the success—even to the survival—of every business organization. The basic objectives of cash management are as follows:

- Provide accurate accounting for cash receipts, cash disbursements, and cash balances.
- Prevent or minimize losses from theft or fraud.
- Anticipate the need for borrowing and assure the availability of adequate amounts of cash for conducting business operations.
- Prevent unnecessarily large amounts of cash from sitting idle in bank accounts that produce no revenue.

INTERNAL CONTROL OVER CASH

Internal control over cash is sometimes regarded merely as a means of preventing fraud and theft. A good system of internal control, however, will also aid in achieving the other objectives of efficient cash management, including accurate accounting for cash transactions, anticipating the need for borrowing, and the maintenance of adequate but not excessive cash balances.

The major steps in achieving internal control over cash transactions and cash balances include the following:

- Separate the function of handling cash from the maintenance of accounting records. Employees who handle cash *should not have access to the accounting records,* and accounting personnel should not have access to cash.
- Prepare *cash budgets* (or forecasts) of planned cash receipts, cash payments, and cash balances, scheduled month-by-month for the coming year.
- Prepare a *control listing* of cash receipts at the time and place the money is received.
- Require that all cash receipts be *deposited daily* in the bank.
- Make all payments *by check.* The only exception should be for small payments to be made in cash from a *petty cash fund.*

- Require that every expenditure be verified *before* a check is issued in payment. Separate the function of approving expenditures from the function of signing checks.
- Promptly reconcile bank statements with the accounting records. The person who reconciles the bank statements should not have any opportunities to physically handle cash. (Bank statement reconciliations are discussed later in this chapter.)

Cash Over and Short   In the handling of daily cash transactions, a few minor errors inevitably will occur. These errors may cause a cash shortage or overage at the end of the day when the cash is counted and compared with the reading on the cash registers.

For example, assume that total cash sales recorded during the day amount to $4,500. However, the cash receipts in the register drawers total only $4,485. The following entry would be made to adjust the accounting records for this $15 shortage in the cash receipts:

Cash Over and Short	15	
Cash		15
To record a shortage in cash receipts for the day.		

The account entitled Cash Over and Short is debited for shortages and credited with overages. If the account has a debit balance, it appears in the income statement as a miscellaneous expense; if it has a credit balance, it is shown as a miscellaneous revenue.

BANK STATEMENTS

Each month the bank provides the depositor with a statement of the depositor's account.[1] As illustrated in Exhibit 7–3, a bank statement shows the account balance at the beginning of the month, the deposits, the checks paid, any other additions and subtractions during the month, and the new balance at the end of the month. (To keep the illustration short, we have shown a limited number of deposits rather than one for each business day in the month.)

RECONCILING THE BANK STATEMENT

A **bank reconciliation** is a schedule *explaining any differences* between the balance shown in the bank statement and the balance shown in the depositor's accounting records. The bank and the depositor maintain independent records of the deposits, the checks, and the current balance of the bank account. Each month, the depositor should prepare a bank reconciliation to verify that these independent sets of records are in agreement. This reconciliation may disclose internal control failures, such as unauthorized cash disbursements or failures to deposit cash receipts, as well as errors in either the bank statement or the depositor's accounting records. In addition, the reconciliation identifies certain transactions that must be recorded in the depositor's accounting records and helps to determine the actual amount of cash on deposit.

L07-3

LEARNING OBJECTIVE
Prepare a bank reconciliation and explain its purpose.

Normal Differences between Bank Records and Accounting Records

The balance shown in a monthly bank statement seldom equals the balance appearing in the depositor's accounting records. Certain transactions recorded by the depositor may not have been recorded by the bank. The most common examples are:

- *Outstanding checks.* Checks issued and recorded by the company but not yet presented to the bank for payment.
- *Deposits in transit.* Cash receipts recorded by the depositor that reached the bank too late to be included in the bank statement for the current month.

---

[1] Large businesses may receive bank statements on a weekly basis.

EXHIBIT 7–3

A Bank Statement

Western National Bank **100 Olympic Boulevard** **Los Angeles, CA**		**Customer Account No. 501390** **Parkview Company** **109 Parkview Road** **Los Angeles, CA**	

Bank Statement for the Month Ended July 31, 2015

Date			Amount
June 30	Previous statement balance		$ 5,029.30
	Deposits and Other Increases (Credits)		
July 1	300.00		
July 2	1,250.00		
July 8	993.60		
July 12	1,023.77		
July 18	1,300.00		
July 22	500.00	CM	
July 24	1,083.25		
July 30	711.55		
July 31	24.74	INT	
	Total deposits and other increases (credits)		7,186.91
	Checks Written and Other Decreases (Debits)		
July 2	Ck. 882	1,100.00	
July 3	Ck. 883	415.20	
July 3	Ck. 884	10.00	
July 10	Ck. 885	96.00	
July 10	Ck. 886	400.00	
July 12	Ck. 887	1,376.57	
July 15	Ck. 889	425.00	
July 18	Ck. 892	2,095.75	
July 22	Ck. 893	85.00	
July 22		5.00 DM	
July 24	Ck. 894	1,145.27	
July 30		50.25 NSF	
July 31		12.00 SC	
	Total checks written and other decreases (debits)		(7,216.04)
July 31	Balance this statement		$5,000.17

Explanation of Symbols

CM	Credit Memoranda
DM	Debit Memoranda
INT	Interest Earned on Average Balance
NSF	Not Sufficient Funds
SC	Service Charge

In addition, certain transactions appearing in the bank statement may not have been recorded by the depositor. For example:

- *Service charges.* Banks often charge a fee for handling small accounts. The amount of this charge usually depends on both the average balance of the account and the number of checks paid during the month.

- *Charges for depositing NSF checks.* **NSF** stands for "Not Sufficient Funds." When checks from customers are deposited, the bank generally gives the depositor immediate credit. On occasion, one of these checks may prove to be uncollectible, because the customer who wrote the check did not have sufficient funds in his or her account. In such cases, the bank will reduce the depositor's account by the amount of this uncollectible item and return the check to the depositor marked "NSF." The depositor should view an NSF check as an account receivable from the customer, not as cash.

- *Credits for interest earned.* Checking accounts may earn interest. At month-end, this interest is credited to the depositor's account and reported in the bank statement.

- *Miscellaneous bank charges and credits.* Banks charge for services—such as printing checks, handling collections of notes receivable, and processing NSF checks. The bank *deducts* these charges from the depositor's account and notifies the depositor by including a debit memorandum in the monthly bank statement. If the bank collects a note receivable on behalf of the depositor, it credits the depositor's account and issues a credit memorandum.[2]

In a bank reconciliation, the balances shown in the bank statement and in the accounting records are both *adjusted for any unrecorded transactions.* Additional adjustments may be required to correct any errors discovered in the bank statement or in the accounting records.

Steps in Preparing a Bank Reconciliation
The specific steps in preparing a bank reconciliation are as follows:

1. Compare deposits listed in the bank statement with the deposits shown in the accounting records. Any deposits not yet recorded by the bank are deposits in transit and should be added to the balance shown in the bank statement.
2. Compare checks paid by the bank with the corresponding entries in the accounting records. Any checks issued but not yet paid by the bank should be listed as outstanding checks to be deducted from the balance reported in the bank statement.
3. Add to the balance per the depositor's accounting records any credit memoranda issued by the bank that have not been recorded by the depositor.
4. Deduct from the balance per the depositor's records any debit memoranda issued by the bank that have not been recorded by the depositor.
5. Make appropriate adjustments to correct any errors in either the bank statement or the depositor's accounting records.
6. Determine that the adjusted balance of the bank statement is equal to the adjusted balance in the depositor's records.
7. Prepare journal entries to record any items in the bank reconciliation listed as adjustments to the balance per the depositor's records.

Illustration of a Bank Reconciliation
The July bank statement sent by the bank to Parkview Company was illustrated in Exhibit 7–3. This statement shows a balance of cash on deposit at July 31 of $5,000.17. Assume that on July 31, Parkview's ledger shows a bank balance of $4,262.83. The employee preparing the bank reconciliation has identified the following reconciling items:

1. A deposit of $410.90 made after banking hours on July 31 does not appear in the bank statement.
2. Four checks issued in July have not yet cleared the bank. These checks are:

Check No.	Date	Amount
881	July 1	$100.00
888	July 14	10.25
890	July 16	402.50
891	July 17	205.00

3. Two credit memoranda were included in the bank statement:

Date	Amount	Explanation
July 22	$500.00	Proceeds from collection of a non-interest-bearing note receivable from J. David. The bank's collection department collected this note for Parkview Company.
July 31	24.74	Interest earned on average account balance during July.

---

[2] Banks view each depositor's account as a *liability.* Debit memoranda are issued for transactions that reduce this liability, such as bank service charges. Credit memoranda are issued to recognize an increase in this liability, as results, for example, from interest earned by the depositor.

4. Three debit memoranda accompanied the bank statement:

Date	Amount	Explanation
July 22	$ 5.00	Fee charged by bank for handling collection of note receivable.
July 30	50.25	Check from customer J. B. Ball deposited by Parkview Company charged back as NSF.
July 31	12.00	Service charge by bank for the month of July.

5. Check no. 893 was issued to the telephone company in the amount of $85 but was errone-
ously recorded in the cash payments journal as $58. The check, in payment of telephone
expense, was paid by the bank and correctly listed at $85 in the bank statement. In Parkview's
ledger, the Cash account is *overstated* by $27 because of this error ($85 − $58 = $27).

The July 31 bank reconciliation for Parkview Company is shown in Exhibit 7–4. (The numbered arrows coincide both with the steps in preparing a bank reconciliation and with the
reconciling items just listed.)

EXHIBIT 7–4

The Bank Reconciliation

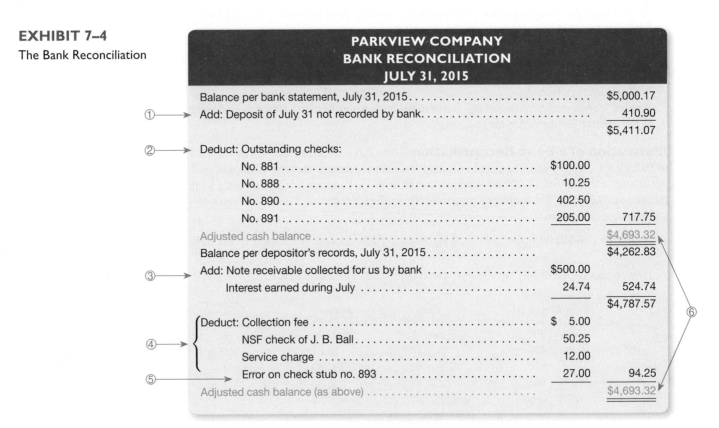

PARKVIEW COMPANY
BANK RECONCILIATION
JULY 31, 2015

Balance per bank statement, July 31, 2015		$5,000.17
① Add: Deposit of July 31 not recorded by bank		410.90
		$5,411.07
② Deduct: Outstanding checks:		
No. 881	$100.00	
No. 888	10.25	
No. 890	402.50	
No. 891	205.00	717.75
Adjusted cash balance		$4,693.32
Balance per depositor's records, July 31, 2015		$4,262.83
③ Add: Note receivable collected for us by bank	$500.00	
Interest earned during July	24.74	524.74
		$4,787.57
④ Deduct: Collection fee	$ 5.00	
NSF check of J. B. Ball	50.25	
Service charge	12.00	
⑤ Error on check stub no. 893	27.00	94.25
Adjusted cash balance (as above)		$4,693.32

⑥

Updating the Accounting Records   The last step in reconciling a bank statement is to update the depositor's accounting records for any unrecorded cash transactions
brought to light. In the bank reconciliation, every adjustment to the *balance per depositor's
records* is a cash receipt or a cash payment that has not been recorded in the depositor's
accounts. Therefore, *each of these items should be recorded.*

In this illustration and in our assignment material, we follow a policy of making one journal entry to record the unrecorded cash receipts and another to record the unrecorded cash
reductions. (Acceptable alternatives would be to make separate journal entries for each item
or to make one compound entry for all items.) On the basis of our recording policy, the entries
to update the accounting records of Parkview Company are:

Cash		524.74
Notes Receivable		500.00
Interest Revenue		24.74

To record collection of note receivable from J. David collected by bank and interest earned on bank account in July.

Bank Service Charges		17.00
Accounts Receivable (J. B. Ball)		50.25
Telephone Expense		27.00
Cash		94.25

To record bank charges (service charge, $12; collection fee, $5); to reclassify NSF check from customer J. B. Ball as an account receivable; and to correct understatement of cash payment for telephone expense.

 Per bank credit memoranda

 Per bank debit memoranda (and correction of an error)

Short-Term Investments

L07-4

LEARNING OBJECTIVE
Describe how short-term investments are reported in the balance sheet and account for transactions involving marketable securities.

Companies with large amounts of liquid resources often hold most of these resources in the form of marketable securities rather than cash.

Marketable securities consist primarily of investments in bonds and in the capital stocks of publicly owned corporations. These marketable securities are traded (bought and sold) daily on organized securities exchanges, such as the **New York Stock Exchange**, the **Tokyo Stock Exchange**, and **Mexico's Bolsa.** A basic characteristic of all marketable securities is that they are *readily marketable*—meaning that they can be purchased or sold quickly and easily *at quoted market prices*.

Investments in marketable securities earn a return for the investor in the form of interest, dividends, and—if all goes well—an increase in market value. Meanwhile, these investments are *almost as liquid as cash itself.* They can be sold immediately over the telephone, simply by placing a "sell order" with a brokerage firm such as **Merrill Lynch** or **Morgan Stanley**, or on the Internet, by using an online brokerage firm such as **E*TRADE Financial**.

Due to their liquidity, investments in marketable securities often are listed immediately after Cash in the balance sheet and are most often classified as *available for sale* securities.[3] However, if the company plans to hold a marketable security for more than one year, then the security would be classified as a noncurrent asset.

© Digital Vision/Getty Images

CASE IN POINT

It is common for enterprises to invest a portion of their excess cash in marketable securities in anticipation of earning higher returns than they would by keeping these funds in the form of cash and cash equivalents. The following sample taken from recently issued balance sheets illustrates the willingness of companies to invest millions, even billions, of dollars in short-term marketable securities:

	Amount Invested
IBM	$ 717 million
The Coca-Cola Company	$ 3.0 billion
Ford Motor Company	$ 20.3 billion
Pfizer, Inc.	$ 22.3 billion
Microsoft Corporation	$ 56.1 billion

---

[3] Other investment classifications include *trading* securities and *held-to-maturity* securities. These classifications are discussed in more advanced courses.

Accounting for Marketable Securities

There are four basic events relating to investments in marketable securities: (1) the purchase of investments, (2) the receipt of dividends or interest revenue, (3) the sale of investments, and (4) end-of-period adjustments.

PURCHASE OF MARKETABLE SECURITIES

Investments in marketable securities are originally recorded at cost, which includes any brokerage commissions. To illustrate, assume that Foster Corporation purchases as a short-term investment 4,000 shares of **The Coca-Cola Company** on December 1. Foster paid *$48.98 per share,* plus a brokerage commission of $80. The entry to record the purchase of these shares is:

Marketable Securities	196,000	
Cash		196,000
Purchased 4,000 shares of **Coca-Cola** capital stock. Total cost $196,000 ($48.98 × 4,000 shares + $80); cost per share, $49 ($196,000 ÷ 4,000 shares).		

Marketable Securities is a control account used to report *all* of a company's short-term investments. If Foster Corporation invests in other companies, it will make an entry similar to the one shown above; however, it will also create a marketable securities *subsidiary ledger* to maintain a separate record of each security owned.

Notice that the $49 cost per share computed in the explanation of the above journal entry includes a portion of the total brokerage commission. The $49 per share *cost basis* will be used in computing any gains or losses when Foster Corporation sells these securities.

RECOGNITION OF INVESTMENT REVENUE

Entries to recognize interest and dividend revenue typically involve a debit to Cash and a credit to either Interest Revenue or Dividend Revenue. To illustrate, assume that on December 15, Foster Corporation receives a $0.30 per share dividend on its 4,000 shares of **Coca-Cola.** The entry to record this receipt is:

Cash	1,200	
Dividend Revenue		1,200
Received a quarterly dividend on shares of **Coca-Cola** capital stock ($0.30 per share × 4,000 shares).		

Dividend and interest revenue is reported in the income statement as a component of a company's net income. It most often appears near the bottom of the income statement in the computation of income before taxes. The reporting of investment revenue is discussed further in Chapter 11.

SALE OF INVESTMENTS

When an investment is sold, a gain or a loss often results. If an investment is sold for more than its cost basis a **gain** is recorded, whereas selling an investment for an amount less than its cost basis results in a **loss.** These items appear in the "Other Income/Expense" section of the income statement.

Investments Sold at a Gain   To illustrate, assume that Foster Corporation sells 500 shares of its **Coca-Cola** stock on December 18 for $50.04 per share, less a $20 brokerage commission. Recall that Foster's cost basis, as computed on December 1, is $49 per share. Thus, the entry to record the sale and the $500 gain is as follows:

Cash	25,000	
Marketable Securities		24,500
Gain on Sale of Investments		500
Sold 500 shares of **Coca-Cola** stock at a gain:		
Sale proceeds ($50.04 × 500 shares − $20 commission)	$25,000	
Cost basis ($49 × 500 shares)	24,500	
Gain on sale	$ 500	

This transaction results in a gain because Foster Corporation sold the shares at an amount above their cost basis. The gain on the sale increases the company's net income for the period and is reported in the income statement in similar fashion to interest and dividend revenue. At the end of the period, the credit balance in the Gain on Sale of Investments account is closed to the Income Summary account, along with the credit balances of the other revenue accounts.

Investments Sold at a Loss   Assume that Foster Corporation sells an additional 2,500 shares of its **Coca-Cola** stock on December 27 for $48.01 per share, less a $25 brokerage commission. The entry to record the sale and the $2,500 loss is recorded as follows:

Cash	120,000	
Loss on Sale of Investments	2,500	
Marketable Securities		122,500
Sold 2,500 shares of **Coca-Cola** stock at a loss:		
Cost basis ($49 × 2,500 shares)	$122,500	
Sale proceeds ($48.01 × 2,500 shares − $25 commission)	120,000	
Loss on sale	$ 2,500	

This loss reduces Foster Corporation's net income and is reported near the bottom of the income statement. The debit balance in the Loss on Sale of Investments account is closed to the Income Summary account at the end of the period, along with the debit balances of the other expense accounts.

ADJUSTING MARKETABLE SECURITIES TO MARKET VALUE

Securities classified as available for sale are presented in the balance sheet at their *current market value* as of the balance sheet date. Hence, this valuation principle is often called **fair value accounting.** The adjustment of marketable securities to their current market value requires the use of an account entitled **Unrealized Holding Gain (or Loss) on Investments.** This account appears as a stockholders' equity item in the balance sheet.[4]

To illustrate, let us assume that Foster Corporation's 1,000 remaining shares of **Coca-Cola** capital stock have a current market value of $47,000 on December 31 (1,000 shares at a market price of $47 per share). Prior to any adjustment, the company's Marketable Securities account has a balance of $49,000 (1,000 shares at $49 per share). Thus, Foster Corporation must make the following fair value adjustment on December 31:

Unrealized Holding Loss on Investments	2,000	
Marketable Securities		2,000
To adjust the balance sheet valuation of marketable securities from $49,000 (1,000 shares × $49) to the December 31 market value of $47,000 (1,000 shares × $47).		

---

[4] Unrealized holding gains and losses are often combined with other activities and reported in a stockholders' equity account entitled Accumulated Other Comprehensive Income. Comprehensive income is discussed in Chapter 12.

Exhibit 7–5 illustrates Foster Corporation's condensed balance sheet following its marketable securities valuation adjustment.

EXHIBIT 7–5

Presentation of Marketable Securities in the Balance Sheet

FOSTER CORPORATION BALANCE SHEET AS OF DECEMBER 31 OF THE CURRENT YEAR			
Assets		**Liabilities & Stockholders' Equity**	
Current assets:		**Liabilities:**	
Cash	$ 50,000	(Detail not shown)	$350,000
Marketable securities (cost, $49,000; market value, $47,000)	47,000	**Stockholders' equity:**	
Accounts receivable	23,000	Capital stock	$400,000
Total current assets	$120,000	Retained earnings	152,000
		Unrealized holding loss on investments	(2,000)
Other assets:		Total stockholders' equity	$550,000
(Detail not shown)	$780,000		
Total	$900,000	Total	$900,000

Although the $49,000 cost of Foster Corporation's marketable securities is *disclosed* in the balance sheet, the $47,000 market value is used in the computation of total assets. The difference between the cost and market value also appears as an *element of stockholders' equity,* entitled Unrealized Holding Loss on Investments. When the market value of investment falls *below* cost, as in the case just presented, this special equity account is a *subtraction* from equity, representing a holding *loss.* But if the market value is *above* cost, this account is an *addition* to equity, representing a holding *gain.* Thus, if Foster's 1,000 shares of **Coca-Cola** had a market value on December 31 of $51 per share, the investment would have been reported in the asset section of the balance sheet at $51,000, and the stockholders' equity section of the balance sheet would have included the addition of a $2,000 unrealized holding *gain* on investments.

Unrealized holding gains and losses are *not* subject to income taxes. Income taxes are levied only upon *realized* gains and losses recognized when investments are sold. Nonetheless, unrealized holding gains and losses are actually reported in the balance sheet net of expected *future* income tax effects. The computation of future tax effects is beyond the scope of our introductory discussion and is addressed in more advanced accounting courses. In the assignment material at the end of this chapter, unrealized holding gains and losses simply represent the difference between the cost and the current market value of the securities owned.

 INTERNATIONAL CASE IN POINT

The ability to treat marketable securities as available-for-sale is more limited under *International Financial Reporting Standards* (IFRS No. 9) than under U.S. GAAP. Under IFRS, marketable debt securities are not eligible to be classified as available-for-sale. Marketable equity securities can be classified as available-for-sale, but once that election is made it is irrevocable.

Accounts Receivable

One of the key factors underlying the growth of the American economy is the trend toward selling goods and services on credit. Accounts receivable comprise the largest financial asset of many merchandising companies.

Accounts receivable are relatively liquid assets, usually converting into cash within a period of 30 to 60 days. Therefore, accounts receivable from customers usually appear in the balance sheet immediately after cash and short-term investments in marketable securities.

In Chapter 5, we explained that assets capable of being converted quickly into cash are classified in the balance sheet as current assets. The period used to define current assets is typically one year or the company's operating cycle, whichever is longer. The operating cycle was defined in Chapter 6 as the normal period of time required to convert cash into inventory, inventory into accounts receivable, and accounts receivable back into cash. Some companies sell merchandise on long-term installment plans that require accounts receivable be outstanding for 12, 24, or even 48 months before being collected. These receivables are part of the company's normal operating cycle. Therefore, *all* accounts receivable arising from normal sales activity are generally classified as current assets, even if the credit terms extend beyond one year.

INTERNAL CONTROL OVER RECEIVABLES

L07-5

LEARNING OBJECTIVE
Describe internal controls over accounts receivable.

Internal control over receivables is designed to ensure that only valid (legitimate) customer orders are recorded as both a receivable and revenue, and that all shipments of goods during the period are recorded. In addition, internal control over receivables should ensure that the sale transaction is recorded for the correct dollar amount, in the correct general ledger account, and in the correct period (i.e., that transactions near period-end are recorded in the accounting period in which the goods are shipped). Moreover, effective internal control ensures that credit is only extended to customers that meet the company's credit standards, that goods shipped match those that were ordered, and that the customer is billed correctly. Finally, internal control over receivables is designed to ensure that cash collections from customers are promptly deposited, that the payment is applied to the correct customer account, and that the cash collection is recorded in the accounting records.

The major steps in achieving internal control over accounts receivable and the resulting cash collections include the following:

- The Customer Order department prepares a sales order upon receipt of an order. The sales order describes the goods ordered (e.g., inventory number, units ordered, unit prices, and payment terms).
- The Credit department reviews the sales order and the customer's credit file and decides whether and how much credit should be extended.
- The Shipping department ensures that the goods shipped match those ordered by the customer.
- The Billing department compares what was shipped with what was ordered and prepares and mails a sales invoice.
- The Accounting department records the sale by debiting Accounts Receivable and crediting Sales, and by debiting Cost of Goods Sold and crediting Inventory (assuming a perpetual inventory system is used). In addition, an entry is made to reflect the credit sale in the Accounts Receivable subsidiary ledger.
- If customer payments are received by mail, checks are restrictively endorsed for deposit to the company's bank account and a daily listing of checks received is prepared (check number, party issuing the check, and check amount).
- The Cash Receipts department receives the checks and the mailroom listing of checks received and prepares the daily bank deposit.
- The Accounting department records the cash collection by debiting Cash and crediting Accounts Receivable. In addition, an entry is made to reflect the cash collection in the Accounts Receivable subsidiary ledger.[5]

UNCOLLECTIBLE ACCOUNTS

L07-6

LEARNING OBJECTIVE
Account for uncollectible receivables using the allowance and direct write-off methods.

We have stated that accounts receivable are shown in the balance sheet at the estimated collectible amount—called *net realizable value*. No business wants to sell merchandise on account to customers who will be unable to pay. Nonetheless, if a company makes credit sales to hundreds—perhaps thousands—of customers, some accounts inevitably will turn out to be uncollectible.

A limited amount of uncollectible accounts is not only expected—it is evidence of a sound credit policy. If the credit department is overly cautious, the business may lose many sales opportunities by rejecting customers who should have been considered acceptable credit risks.

---

[5] The above description of internal control over sales, receivables, and cash collections is a high-level summary. More specificity is provided in future courses, particularly Accounting Information Systems and Auditing.

Reflecting Uncollectible Accounts in the Financial Statements

An account receivable that has been determined to be uncollectible is no longer an asset. The loss of this asset represents an *expense,* termed Uncollectible Accounts Expense.

In measuring business income, one of the most fundamental principles of accounting is that revenue should be *matched* with (offset by) the expenses incurred in generating that revenue. Uncollectible accounts expense is *caused by selling goods on credit* to customers who fail to pay their bills. Therefore, this expense is estimated and recorded in the time period in which the *related sales* are made, even though specific accounts receivable may not be determined to be uncollectible until a later accounting period. Thus an account receivable that originates from a credit sale in January and is determined to be uncollectible in June represents an expense in *January.* Exhibit 7–6 illustrates how uncollectible accounts expense is matched to revenue in the period in which the credit sale is made.

EXHIBIT 7–6

Matching Uncollectible Accounts Expense to the Period in Which the Credit Sale is Made

January	February	March	April	May	June

A credit sale is made.

An expense associated with future uncollectible accounts must offset January sales.

The account receivable is determined to be uncollectible.

To illustrate the matching process, assume that World Famous Toy Co. begins business on January 1, 2015, and makes most of its sales on account. At January 31, accounts receivable amount to $250,000. On this date, the credit manager reviews the accounts receivable and *estimates* that approximately $10,000 of these accounts will prove to be uncollectible. The following adjusting entry should be made at January 31:

Provision for uncollectible accounts

Uncollectible Accounts Expense	10,000	
Allowance for Doubtful Accounts		10,000
To record the portion of total accounts receivable estimated to be uncollectible.		

The Uncollectible Accounts Expense account created by the debit part of this entry is closed into the Income Summary account in the same manner as any other expense account. The Allowance for Doubtful Accounts that was credited in the above journal entry appears in the balance sheet as a deduction from the face amount of the accounts receivable. It reduces the accounts receivable to their *net realizable value* in the balance sheet, as shown in Exhibit 7–7.

EXHIBIT 7–7

Reporting Accounts Receivable at Estimated Net Realizable Value

WORLD FAMOUS TOY CO. PARTIAL BALANCE SHEET JANUARY 31, 2015		
Current assets:		
Cash and cash equivalents		$ 75,000
Marketable securities		25,000
Accounts receivable	$250,000	
Less: Allowance for doubtful accounts	10,000	240,000
Inventory		300,000
Total current assets		$640,000

THE ALLOWANCE FOR DOUBTFUL ACCOUNTS

There is no way of telling in advance *which* accounts receivable will prove to be uncollectible. It is therefore not possible to credit the accounts of specific customers for our estimate of probable uncollectible accounts. A practical solution, therefore, is to credit a separate account called **Allowance for Doubtful Accounts** with the amount estimated to be uncollectible.

The Allowance for Doubtful Accounts often is described as a *contra-asset* account or a *valuation* account. The Allowance for Doubtful Accounts has a credit balance which offsets the Accounts Receivable control account to produce a more useful and reliable measure of a company's liquidity. Because the Allowance for Doubtful Accounts is merely an estimate and not a precise calculation, *professional judgment* plays a considerable role in determining the size of this valuation account.

Monthly Adjustments of the Allowance Account In the adjusting entry made by World Famous Toy Co. at January 31, the amount of the adjustment ($10,000) was equal to the estimated amount of uncollectible accounts. This is true only because January was the first month of operations and this was the company's first estimate of its uncollectible accounts. In future months, the amount of the adjusting entry will depend on two factors: (1) the *estimate* of uncollectible accounts and (2) the *current balance* in the Allowance for Doubtful Accounts. Before we illustrate the adjusting entry for a future month, let us see why the balance in the allowance account may change during the accounting period.

WRITING OFF AN UNCOLLECTIBLE ACCOUNT RECEIVABLE

Whenever an account receivable from a specific customer is determined to be uncollectible, it no longer qualifies as an asset and should be written off. To *write off* an account receivable is to reduce the balance of the customer's account to zero. The journal entry to accomplish this consists of a credit to the Accounts Receivable control account in the general ledger (and to the customer's account in the subsidiary ledger) and an offsetting debit to the Allowance for Doubtful Accounts.

To illustrate, assume that, early in February, World Famous Toy Co. learns that Discount Stores has gone out of business and that the $4,000 account receivable from this customer is now worthless. The entry to write off this uncollectible account receivable is:

Writing off a receivable "against the allowance"

Allowance for Doubtful Accounts	4,000	
Accounts Receivable (Discount Stores)		4,000
To write off the account receivable from Discount Stores as uncollectible.		

The important thing to note in this entry is that the debit is made to the Allowance for Doubtful Accounts and *not* to the Uncollectible Accounts Expense account. The estimated expense of credit losses is charged to the Uncollectible Accounts Expense account at the end of each accounting period. When a specific account receivable is later determined to be worthless and is written off, this action does not represent an additional expense but merely confirms our previous estimate of the expense.

Notice also that the entry to write off an uncollectible account receivable reduces both the asset account and the contra-asset account by the same amount. Thus writing off an uncollectible account *does not change* the net realizable value of accounts receivable in the balance sheet. The net realizable value of World Famous Toy Co.'s accounts receivable before and after the write-off of the account receivable from Discount Stores is:

What happens to net realizable value?

Before the Write-off		After the Write-off	
Accounts receivable	$250,000	Accounts receivable	$246,000
Less: Allowance for doubtful		Less: Allowance for doubtful	
accounts	10,000	accounts	6,000
Net realizable value	$240,000	Net realizable value	$240,000

Let us repeat the point that underlies the allowance approach. Credit losses are recognized as an expense in the period in which the *sale occurs,* not the period in which the account is determined to be uncollectible. The reasoning for this position is based on the *matching principle.*

Write-offs Seldom Agree with Previous Estimates

The total amount of accounts receivable actually written off will seldom, if ever, be exactly equal to the estimated amount previously credited to the Allowance for Doubtful Accounts.

If the amounts written off as uncollectible turn out to be less than the estimated amount, the Allowance for Doubtful Accounts will continue to show a credit balance. If the amounts written off as uncollectible are greater than the estimated amount, the Allowance for Doubtful Accounts will acquire a *temporary debit balance,* which will be eliminated by the adjustment at the end of the period.

MONTHLY ESTIMATES OF CREDIT LOSSES

At the end of each month, management should again estimate the probable amount of uncollectible accounts and adjust the Allowance for Doubtful Accounts to this new estimate.

To illustrate, assume that at the end of February the credit manager of World Famous Toy Co. analyzes the accounts receivable and estimates that approximately *$11,000* of these accounts will prove uncollectible. Currently, the Allowance for Doubtful Accounts has a credit balance of only *$6,000,* determined as follows:

Current balance in the allowance account

Balance at January 31 (credit)	$10,000
Less: Write-off of account considered worthless (Discount Stores)	4,000
Credit balance at February 28 (prior to adjustment)	$ 6,000

To increase the balance in the allowance account to $11,000 at February 28, the month-end adjusting entry must add $5,000 to the allowance. The entry will be:

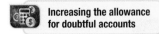
Increasing the allowance for doubtful accounts

Uncollectible Accounts Expense	5,000	
Allowance for Doubtful Accounts		5,000
To increase the Allowance for Doubtful Accounts to $11,000, computed as follows:		
Required allowance at Feb. 28	$11,000	
Credit balance prior to adjustment	6,000	
Required adjustment	$ 5,000	

In the World Famous Toy illustration, estimates of the required allowance for doubtful accounts at January 31 and February 28 were simply given. There are actually two general approaches to estimating credit losses: (1) a *balance sheet approach,* and (2) an *income statement approach.*

Estimating Credit Losses—The Balance Sheet Approach

The most widely used method of estimating the probable amount of uncollectible accounts is based on **aging the accounts receivable.** This method is sometimes called the *balance sheet* approach because the method emphasizes the proper balance sheet valuation of accounts receivable.

"Aging" accounts receivable means classifying each receivable according to its age. An aging schedule for the accounts receivable of Valley Ranch Supply is illustrated in Exhibit 7–8.

An aging schedule is useful to management in reviewing the status of individual accounts receivable and in evaluating the overall effectiveness of credit and collection policies. In addition, the schedule is used as the basis for estimating the amount of uncollectible accounts.

The longer an account is past due, the greater the likelihood that it will not be collected in full. On the basis of past experience, the credit manager estimates the percentage of credit losses likely to occur in each age group of accounts receivable. This percentage, when applied

EXHIBIT 7-8

Accounts Receivable Aging Schedule

VALLEY RANCH SUPPLY
ANALYSIS OF ACCOUNTS RECEIVABLE BY AGE
DECEMBER 31, 2015

	Total	Not Yet Due	1–30 Days Past Due	31–60 Days Past Due	61–90 Days Past Due	Over 90 Days Past Due
Animal Care Center	$ 9,000	$ 9,000				
Butterfield, John D.	2,400			$ 2,400		
Citrus Groves, Inc.	4,000	3,000	$ 1,000			
Dairy Fresh Farms	1,600				$ 600	$1,000
Eastlake Stables	13,000	7,000	6,000			
(Other customers)	70,000	32,000	22,000	9,600	2,400	4,000
Totals	$100,000	$51,000	$29,000	$12,000	$3,000	$5,000

to the total dollar amount in the age group, gives the estimated uncollectible portion for that group. By adding together the estimated uncollectible portions for all age groups, the *required balance* in the Allowance for Doubtful Accounts is determined. Exhibit 7–9 provides a schedule listing the group totals from the aging schedule and shows how the estimated total amount of uncollectible accounts is computed.

EXHIBIT 7-9

Estimated Dollar Amount of Uncollectible Accounts

VALLEY RANCH SUPPLY
ESTIMATED UNCOLLECTIBLE ACCOUNTS RECEIVABLE
DECEMBER 31, 2015

	Age Group Total		Percentage Considered Uncollectible*		Estimated Uncollectible Accounts
Not yet due	$ 51,000	×	1%	=	$ 510
1–30 days past due	29,000	×	3	=	870
31–60 days past due	12,000	×	10	=	1,200
61–90 days past due	3,000	×	20	=	600
Over 90 days past due	5,000	×	50	=	2,500
Totals	$100,000				$5,680

* These percentages are estimated each month by the credit manager, based on recent experience and current economic conditions.

At December 31, Valley Ranch Supply has total accounts receivable of $100,000, of which $5,680 are estimated to be uncollectible. Thus, an adjusting entry is needed to increase the Allowance for Doubtful Accounts from its present level to $5,680. If the allowance account currently has a credit balance of *$4,000,* the month-end adjusting entry should be in the amount of *$1,680,* determined as follows:[6]

---

[6] If accounts receivable written off during the period *exceed* the Allowance for Doubtful Accounts at the last adjustment date, the allowance account temporarily acquires a *debit balance.* This situation seldom occurs if the allowance is adjusted each month but often occurs if adjusting entries are made only at year-end.

If Valley Ranch Supply makes only an annual adjustment for uncollectible accounts, the allowance account might have a debit balance of $10,000. In this case, the year-end adjusting entry should be for *$15,680* in order to offset the $10,000 debit balance and to bring the allowance up to the required credit balance of $5,680.

Regardless of how often adjusting entries are made, the balance in the allowance account of Valley Ranch Supply should be *$5,680 at year-end.*

Determine the difference between the current balance and the required balance

Credit balance at December 31 (prior to adjustment)	$4,000
Credit adjustment required	1,680
Credit balance required at December 31 (per aging schedule)	$5,680

Thus, the following adjusting entry is made at December 31:

The difference between the current balance and the required balance is the Uncollectible Accounts Expense matched to the period

Uncollectible Accounts Expense	1,680	
Allowance for Doubtful Accounts		1,680
To increase the Allowance for Doubtful Accounts to its required		
balance of $5,680.		

Estimating Credit Losses—The Income Statement Approach

An alternative method of estimating and recording credit losses is called the *income statement* approach. This method focuses on estimating the uncollectible accounts *expense* to be reported in the income statement for the period. On the basis of past experience, the uncollectible accounts expense is estimated at some percentage of net credit sales. The adjusting entry is made in the *full amount of the estimated expense,* without regard for the current balance in the Allowance for Doubtful Accounts.

To illustrate, assume that a company's past experience indicates that about 2 percent of its credit sales will prove to be uncollectible. If credit sales for September amount to $150,000, the month-end adjusting entry to record uncollectible accounts expense is:

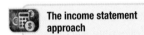

The income statement approach

Uncollectible Accounts Expense	3,000	
Allowance for Doubtful Accounts		3,000
To record uncollectible accounts expense, estimated at 2%		
of credit sales ($150,000 × 2% = $3,000).		

This approach is fast and simple—no aging schedule is required and no consideration is given to the existing balance in the Allowance for Doubtful Accounts. The aging of accounts receivable, however, provides a more reliable estimate of uncollectible accounts because of the consideration given to the age and collectibility of specific accounts receivable at the balance sheet date.

In past years, many small companies used the income statement approach in preparing monthly financial statements but used the balance sheet method in annual financial statements. Most businesses today have computer software that quickly and easily prepares monthly aging schedules of accounts receivable. Thus most businesses now use the *balance sheet approach* in both their monthly and annual financial statements.

RECOVERY OF AN ACCOUNT RECEIVABLE PREVIOUSLY WRITTEN OFF

Occasionally a receivable that has been written off as worthless will later be collected in full or in part. Such collections are often referred to as *recoveries* of bad debts. Collection of an account receivable previously written off is evidence that the write-off was an error; the receivable should therefore be reinstated as an asset.

Let us assume, for example, that a company wrote off a $500 account receivable from Brad Wilson on February 16. The write-off of this account was recorded as follows:

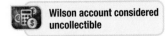

Wilson account considered uncollectible

Allowance for Doubtful Accounts	500	
Accounts Receivable (Brad Wilson)		500
To write off the account receivable from Brad Wilson as uncollectible.		

If the customer, Brad Wilson, pays the account in full on February 27, the entry to reverse the previous write-off is as follows:

Accounts Receivable (Brad Wilson)	500	
Allowance for Doubtful Accounts		500
To reinstate as an asset an account receivable previously written off.		

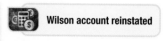 Wilson account reinstated

Notice that this entry is *exactly the opposite* of the entry made when the account was written off as uncollectible. A separate entry will be made to record the cash collected from Brad Wilson and to remove his reinstated account from the system.

Cash	500	
Accounts Receivable (Brad Wilson)		500
To record the collection of account receivable from Brad Wilson.		

 Wilson account previously reinstated is finally collected

DIRECT WRITE-OFF METHOD

Some companies do not use any valuation allowance for accounts receivable. Instead of making end-of-period adjusting entries to record uncollectible accounts expense on the basis of estimates, these companies recognize no uncollectible accounts expense until specific receivables are determined to be worthless. This method makes no attempt to match revenue with the expense of uncollectible accounts.

When a particular customer's account is determined to be uncollectible, it is written off directly to Uncollectible Accounts Expense, as follows:

Uncollectible Accounts Expense	250	
Accounts Receivable (Bell Products)		250
To write off the account receivable from Bell Products as uncollectible.		

When the **direct write-off method** is used, the accounts receivable will be listed in the balance sheet at their gross amount, and *no valuation allowance* will be used. The receivables, therefore, are not stated at estimated net realizable value.

The allowance method is preferable to the direct write-off method because the allowance method does a better job of matching revenues and expenses. In some situations, however, use of the direct write-off method is acceptable. If a company makes most of its sales for cash, the amount of its accounts receivable will be small in relation to other assets. The expense from uncollectible accounts should also be small. Consequently, the direct write-off method is acceptable because its use does not have a *material* effect on the reported net income.

It is important to note that current income tax regulations *require* taxpayers to use the direct write-off method in determining the uncollectible accounts expense used in computing *taxable income*. From the standpoint of accounting theory, the allowance method is better because it enables expenses to be *matched* with the related revenue and thus provides a more logical measurement of net income. Therefore, most companies use the allowance method in their financial statements.[7]

FACTORING ACCOUNTS RECEIVABLE

The term **factoring** describes transactions in which a business sells its accounts receivable to a financial institution (often called a *factor*). These arrangements enable a business to obtain cash immediately instead of having to wait until the receivables can be collected.

---

[7] An annual survey of the accounting practices of 600 publicly owned corporations consistently shows more than 500 of these companies use the allowance method in their financial statements. All of these companies, however, use the direct write-off method in their income tax returns.

Factoring accounts receivable is a popular practice among small business organizations that do not have well-established credit. Large and liquid organizations often can borrow money using unsecured lines of credit.

YOUR TURN You as a Used Car Purchaser

Assume you purchased a car from John's Used Cars for $500 down and 24 payments of $150 per month. After making three months of payments to John's Used Cars, you are notified that John's plans to factor your account receivable to the Barb Smith Collection Agency. You are concerned about owing money to this particular collection agency because you have heard it uses very aggressive tactics to collect overdue payments. You call the car lot and speak directly with John. You question the legality and ethics of factoring accounts receivable. You state that you entered into a contract with him and not a collection agency. You state that you did not give permission to sell your receivable and that selling the receivable to another organization eliminates your obligation to pay it. John says factoring accounts receivable is legal and suggests that you consult the Uniform Commercial Code. What would you do?

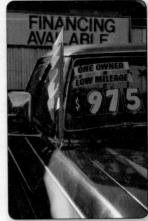

© Photodisc Green/Getty Images

(See our comments on the Online Learning Center website.)

CREDIT CARD SALES

By making sales through credit card companies, merchants receive cash more quickly from credit sales and avoid uncollectible accounts expense. They also avoid the expenses of investigating customers' credit, maintaining an accounts receivable subsidiary ledger, and making collections from customers.

Bank Credit Cards   Some widely used credit cards (such as **Visa** and **MasterCard**) are issued by banks. When the credit card company is a bank, the retailing business may deposit the signed credit card drafts directly in its bank account. Because banks accept these credit card drafts for immediate deposit, sales to customers using bank credit cards are recorded as *cash sales*.

In exchange for handling the credit card drafts, the bank imposes a monthly service charge that usually runs between 1¼ percent and 3½ percent of the amount of the drafts. This monthly service charge is deducted from the merchant's bank account and appears with other bank service charges in the merchant's monthly bank statement.

Other Credit Cards   When customers use nonbank credit cards (such as **American Express**), the retailing business cannot deposit the credit card drafts directly in its bank account. Instead of debiting Cash, the merchant records an account receivable from the credit card company. Periodically, the credit card company reimburses the merchant. Businesses, however, are not reimbursed for the full amount of the outstanding receivable. The agreement between the credit card company and merchants usually allows the credit card company to discount the amount reimbursed by 3½ percent to 5 percent.

To illustrate, assume that Bradshaw Camera Shop sells a camera for $1,200 to a customer who uses a Quick Charge credit card. The entry would be:

Accounts Receivable (Quick Charge Co.)	1,200	
Sales		1,200
To record sale to customer using Quick Charge credit card.		

This receivable is from the credit card company

At the end of the week, Bradshaw Camera Shop mails the $1,200 credit card draft to Quick Charge Company, which redeems the draft after deducting a 5 percent discount. When payment is received by Bradshaw, the entry is:

Cash..	1,140	
Credit Card Discount Expense................................	60	
Accounts Receivable (Quick Charge Co.)......................		1,200
To record collection of account receivable from Quick Charge Co., less 5% discount.		

The expense account, Credit Card Discount Expense, is included among the selling expenses in the income statement of Bradshaw Camera Shop.

Notes Receivable and Interest Revenue

L07-7

LEARNING OBJECTIVE
Explain, compute, and account for notes receivable and interest revenue.

Accounts receivable usually do not bear interest. When interest will be charged, creditors usually require the debtor to sign a formal promissory note. A promissory note is an unconditional promise in writing to pay on demand or at a future date a definite sum of money.

The person who signs the note and thereby promises to pay is called the *maker* of the note. The person to whom payment is to be made is called the *payee* of the note. In Exhibit 7–10, Pacific Rim Corp. is the maker of the note and First National Bank is the payee.

EXHIBIT 7–10
Simplified Form of Promissory Note

$200,000	Los Angeles, California	July 10, 2015

One year   AFTER DATE   Pacific Rim Corp.   PROMISES TO PAY

TO THE ORDER OF   First National Bank

---Two hundred thousand and no/100---   DOLLARS

PLUS INTEREST COMPUTED AT THE RATE OF   6% per annum

SIGNED   G. L. Smith

TITLE   Treasurer

From the viewpoint of the maker, Pacific Rim, the illustrated note is a liability and is recorded by crediting the Notes Payable account. However, from the viewpoint of the payee, First National Bank, this same note is an asset and is recorded by debiting the Notes Receivable account. The maker of a note expects to pay cash at the *maturity date* (or due date); the payee expects to receive cash at that date.

NATURE OF INTEREST

Interest is a charge made for the use of money. A borrower incurs interest expense. A lender earns interest revenue. When you see notes payable in a company's financial statements, you know that the company has borrowed money, so you should expect to find interest expense in its income statement. If you see notes receivable, you know that the company has loaned money, so you should expect its income statement to report interest revenue.

Computing Interest   In Chapter 4, we introduced the following formula to compute interest:

$$\text{Interest} = \text{Principal} \times \text{Rate of Interest} \times \text{Time}$$

(This formula is often expressed as $I = P \times R \times T$.)

Interest rates usually are stated on an *annual basis*. For example, the total interest charge on a $200,000, one-year, 6 percent note receivable is computed as follows:

$$P \times R \times T = \$200,000 \times .06 \times 1 = \$12,000$$

If the term of the note were only *four months* instead of one year, the total interest revenue earned in the life of the note would be $4,000, computed as follows:

$$P \times R \times T = \$200,000 \times .06 \times {}^{4}\!/_{12} = \$4,000$$

It should be noted that these computations illustrate *simple* interest, meaning no interest accrues on the unpaid interest amounts each month. We will introduce *compound* interest in Chapter 10.

ACCOUNTING FOR NOTES RECEIVABLE

In some fields of business, notes receivable are seldom encountered; in other fields they occur frequently and may constitute an important part of total assets. In banks and financial institutions, for example, notes receivable often represent the company's largest asset category and generate most of the company's revenue.

All notes receivable are usually posted to a single account in the general ledger. The amount debited to Notes Receivable is always the *face amount* of the note, regardless of whether the note bears interest. When an interest-bearing note is collected, the amount of cash received may be larger than the face amount of the note. The interest collected is credited to an Interest Revenue account, and only the face amount of the note is credited to the Notes Receivable account.

Illustrative Entries   Assume that on December 1, a three-month, 6 percent note receivable is acquired from a customer, Marvin White, in settlement of an existing account receivable of $60,000. The entry for acquisition of the note is as follows:

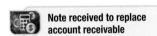
Note received to replace account receivable

Notes Receivable	60,000	
Accounts Receivable (Marvin White).		60,000
Accepted 3-month, 6% note in settlement of account receivable.		

At December 31, the end of the company's fiscal year, the interest earned to date on notes receivable should be accrued by an adjusting entry as follows:

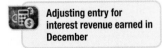
Adjusting entry for interest revenue earned in December

Interest Receivable.	300	
Interest Revenue		300
To accrue interest for the month of December on Marvin White note ($60,000 × 6% × $^{1}\!/_{12}$ = $300).		

To simplify this illustration, we will assume our company makes adjusting entries *only at year-end*. Therefore, no entries are made to recognize the interest revenue accruing during January and February.

On March 1 (three months after the date of the note), the note matures. The entry to record collection of the note will be:

Cash..	60,900	
Notes Receivable		60,000
Interest Receivable		300
Interest Revenue		600
Collected 90-day, 6% note from Marvin White ($60,000 × 6% × 3/12 = $900 interest, of which $600 was earned in current year).		

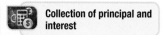 Collection of principal and interest

The preceding three entries show that interest is being earned throughout the term of the note and that the interest should be apportioned between years on a time basis. The revenue of each year will then include the interest actually earned in that year.

If the Maker of a Note Defaults A note receivable that cannot be collected at maturity is said to have been **defaulted** by the maker. Immediately after the default of a note, an entry should be made by the holder to transfer the amount due from the Notes Receivable account to an account receivable from the debtor.

To illustrate, assume that on March 1, our customer, Marvin White, had defaulted on the note used in the preceding example. In this case, the entry on March 1 would have been:

Accounts Receivable (Marvin White)	60,900	
Notes Receivable		60,000
Interest Receivable		300
Interest Revenue		600
To record default by Marvin White on 3-month, 6% note.		

Notice that the interest earned on the note is recorded through the maturity date and is included in the account receivable from the maker. The interest receivable on a defaulted note is just as valid a claim against the maker as is the principal amount of the note.

LO7-8

LEARNING OBJECTIVE
Evaluate the liquidity of a company's accounts receivable.

FINANCIAL ANALYSIS and Decision Making

Collecting accounts receivable *on time* is important; it spells the success or failure of a company's credit and collection policies. A past-due receivable is a candidate for write-off as a credit loss. To help us judge how good a job a company is doing in granting credit and collecting its receivables, we compute the ratio of net sales to average receivables. This **accounts receivable turnover rate** tells us how many times the company's average investment in receivables was converted into cash during the year. The ratio is computed by dividing annual net sales by average accounts receivable. The higher the turnover rate, the more liquid the company's receivables. Dividing 365 days by the turnover rate provides an estimate of the average number of *days* an account receivable remains outstanding before it is collected. High turnover rates result in shorter collection periods than low turnover rates.

In some companies, such as restaurants, hotels, and public utilities, turnover rates are relatively high. For other enterprises, such as large manufacturing firms, turnover rates are relatively low, making the average time it takes to collect an outstanding receivable much longer.

To illustrate, Exhibit 7–11 contains information taken from recent financial statements issued by **Allete, Inc.** (an electric utility company), and **3M (Minnesota Mining and Manufacturing Company).**

EXHIBIT 7–11

Accounts Receivable
Collection Performance

	Allete, Inc.	3M
a. Net sales	$961.2 million	$29.9 billion
Accounts receivable (beginning of year)	79.7 million	3.9 billion
Accounts receivable (end of year)	89.0 million	4.1 billion
	$168.7 million	$ 8.0 billion
	÷ 2	÷ 2
b. Average accounts receivable	$ 84.35 million	$ 4.0 billion
c. Accounts receivable turnover rate (a ÷ b)	11.4 times	7.5 times
Average days outstanding (**365 days** ÷ **c**)	32 days	49 days

As shown in Exhibit 7–11, **Allete**'s accounts receivable turnover rate is *11.4 times* compared to **3M**'s turnover rate of only *7.5 times*. Thus, **Allete**'s accounts receivable remain outstanding an average of *32 days* before being collected, whereas **3M**'s accounts receivable remain outstanding an average of *49 days* prior to collection.

YOUR TURN   You as a Credit Manager

Assume that you were hired by Regis Department Stores in 2012 to develop and implement a new credit policy. At the time of your hire, the average collection period for an outstanding receivable was in excess of 90 days (far greater than the industry average). Thus the primary purpose of the new policy was to better screen credit applicants in an attempt to improve the quality of the company's accounts receivable.

Shown below are sales and accounts receivable data for the past four years (in thousands):

	2015	2014	2013	2012
Sales	$17,000	$14,580	$9,600	$9,000
Average accounts receivable	1,700	1,620	1,600	1,800

Based on the above data, was the credit policy you developed successful? Explain.

(See our comments on the Online Learning Center website.)

Ethics, Fraud, & Corporate Governance

As discussed previously in this chapter, determining the balance in the allowance for doubtful accounts depends on management's judgments. Therefore, it is important to disclose material facts as to how management determines the allowance for doubtful accounts including changes in management's approach.

When such disclosures are deficient, securities laws are violated and the U.S. Securities and Exchange Commission (SEC) can bring an enforcement action against the company and/or against senior management. The SEC recently brought an enforcement action against the chief accounting officer of Integrated Electrical Services, Inc. (IES), for improper disclosure related to IES's allowance for doubtful accounts.

IES was headquartered in Houston, Texas, and during the relevant time period IES was a leading provider of electrical contracting services. IES changed the percentage basis for estimating the allowance for doubtful accounts from approximately 1 percent to 0.25 percent. This resulted in IES reducing the allowance account by up to $1.1 million in a quarterly filing with the SEC, and increasing its pretax income by a like amount. This amount was material to IES's financial statements. Notwithstanding the material effect of this change on IES's financial statements, the change in the percentage used to compute the allowance for doubtful accounts was not disclosed.

A public company's chief accounting officer signs the Form 10-K and is responsible for ensuring that the financial statements are fairly presented in accordance with GAAP. Inadequate disclosure, if material, prevents financial statements from being fairly presented in accordance with GAAP.

Concluding Remarks

This is the first of three chapters in which we explore the issues involved in accounting for assets. The central theme in these chapters is the *valuation* of assets. In Exhibit 7–2 (page 291), we have summarized how a company's financial assets are reported in the balance sheet.

We have illustrated numerous transactions involving the financial assets throughout this chapter. In addition to addressing balance sheet valuation issues, we have also determined whether these transactions are reported in the income statement and the statement of cash flows.

In the next two chapters, we explore the valuation of inventories and of plant assets. For each of these assets, you will see that several *alternative* valuation methods are acceptable. These different methods, however, may produce *significantly different results.* An understanding of these alternative accounting methods is essential to the proper use and interpretation of financial statements and in the preparation of income tax returns.

END-OF-CHAPTER REVIEW

SUMMARY OF LEARNING OBJECTIVES

LO7-1 **Define financial assets and explain their valuation in the balance sheet.** Financial assets are cash and other assets that convert directly into *known amounts* of cash. The three basic categories are cash, marketable securities, and receivables. In the balance sheet, financial assets are listed at their *current value*. For cash, this means the face amount; for marketable securities, current market value; and for receivables, net realizable value.

LO7-2 **Describe the objectives of cash management and internal controls over cash.** The objectives of cash management are accurate accounting for cash transactions, the prevention of losses through theft or fraud, and maintaining adequate—but not excessive—cash balances. The major steps in achieving internal control over cash transactions are as follows: (1) separate cash handling from the accounting function, (2) prepare departmental cash budgets, (3) prepare a control listing of all cash received through the mail and from over-the-counter cash sales, (4) deposit all cash receipts in the bank daily, (5) make all payments by check, (6) verify every expenditure before issuing a check in payment, and (7) promptly reconcile bank statements.

LO7-3 **Prepare a bank reconciliation and explain its purpose.** The cash balance shown in the month-end bank statement usually will differ from the amount of cash shown in the depositor's ledger. The difference is caused by items that have been recorded by either the depositor or the bank, but not recorded by both. Examples are outstanding checks and deposits in transit. The bank reconciliation adjusts the cash balance per the books and the cash balance per the bank statement for any unrecorded items and thus produces the correct amount of cash to be included in the balance sheet at the end of the month.

The purpose of a bank reconciliation is to achieve the control inherent in the maintenance of two independent records of cash transactions: one record maintained by the depositor and the other by the bank. When these two records are reconciled (brought into agreement), we gain assurance of a correct accounting for cash transactions.

LO7-4 **Describe how short-term investments are reported in the balance sheet and account for transactions involving marketable securities.**

Short-term investments (marketable securities) are adjusted to their *market value* at each balance sheet date (a valuation principle often referred to as *fair value accounting*). If the value of a company's marketable securities has increased above their original cost, an *unrealized holding gain* is reported as a component of stockholders' equity. If the value of its marketable securities has fallen below their original cost, an *unrealized holding loss* is reported as a component of stockholders' equity.

Interest and dividends generally are recognized as revenue when they are received. When securities are sold, the cost is compared to the sales price, and the difference is recorded as a gain or a loss in the income statement.

LO7-5 **Describe internal controls over accounts receivable.** The objectives of internal control over receivables are designed to ensure that only valid (legitimate) customer orders are recorded as both a receivable and revenue, and that all shipments of goods during the period are recorded. The major steps in achieving internal control over receivables are as follows: (1) Prepare a sales order when a customer wants to buy product; (2) review and approve the customer's credit application; (3) ensure that goods ordered match those shipped; (4) bill, via a sales invoice, the customer for goods shipped; (5) record the sale and the receivable in the accounting records, including in the Accounts Receivable subsidiary ledger; (6) prepare a daily listing of customer payments and restrictively endorse checks received; (7) deposit checks received daily; and (8) record the cash collection in the accounting records, including in the Accounts Receivable subsidiary ledger.

LO7-6 **Account for uncollectible receivables using the allowance and direct write-off methods.** Under the allowance method, the portion of each period's credit sales expected to prove uncollectible is *estimated*. This estimated amount is recorded by a debit to the Uncollectible Accounts Expense account and a credit to the contra-asset account Allowance for Doubtful Accounts. When specific accounts are determined to be uncollectible, they are written off by debiting Allowance for Doubtful Accounts and crediting Accounts Receivable.

Under the direct write-off method, uncollectible accounts are charged to expense in the period that they are determined to be worthless.

The allowance method is theoretically preferable because it is based on the matching principle. However, only the direct write-off method may be used in income tax returns.

LO7-7 **Explain, compute, and account for notes receivable and interest revenue.** Accounts receivable usually do not bear interest. When interest will be charged, creditors usually require the debtor to sign a formal, legally binding promissory note. Promissory notes appear in the balance sheet as assets designated as notes receivable.

Interest on a note receivable is a contractual amount that accumulates (accrues) over time. The amount of interest accruing over a time period may be computed by the formula **Principal $\times$ Rate $\times$ Time.**

LO7-8 **Evaluate the liquidity of a company's accounts receivable.** The most liquid financial asset is cash, followed by cash equivalents, marketable securities, and receivables. The liquidity of receivables varies depending on their collectibility and maturity dates.

The Allowance for Doubtful Accounts should provide for those receivables that may prove to be uncollectible. However, users of financial statements may also want to evaluate the concentrations-of-credit-risk disclosure and, perhaps, the credit ratings of major debtors. The accounts receivable turnover rate provides insight as to how quickly receivables are being collected.

Key Terms Introduced or Emphasized in Chapter 7

accounts receivable turnover rate (p. 311)   A ratio used to measure the liquidity of accounts receivable and the reasonableness of the accounts receivable balance. Computed by dividing net sales by average receivables.

aging the accounts receivable (p. 304)   The process of classifying accounts receivable by age groups such as current, 1–30 days past due, 31–60 days past due, etc. A step in estimating the uncollectible portion of the accounts receivable.

Allowance for Doubtful Accounts (p. 303)   A valuation account or contra-asset account relating to accounts receivable and showing the portion of the receivables estimated to be uncollectible.

bank reconciliation (p. 293)   An analysis that explains the difference between the balance of cash shown in the bank statement and the balance of cash shown in the depositor's records.

cash equivalents (p. 291)   Very short-term investments that are so liquid that they are considered equivalent to cash. Examples include money market funds, U.S. Treasury bills, certificates of deposit, and commercial paper. These investments must mature within 90 days of acquisition.

cash management (p. 292)   Planning, controlling, and accounting for cash transactions and cash balances.

compensating balance (p. 292)   A minimum average balance that a bank may require a borrower to leave on deposit in a non-interest-bearing account.

default (p. 311)   Failure to pay interest or principal of a promissory note at the due date.

direct write-off method (p. 307)   A method of accounting for uncollectible receivables in which no expense is recognized until individual accounts are determined to be worthless. At that point the account receivable is written off, with an offsetting debit to uncollectible accounts expense. Fails to match revenue and related expenses and is used primarily for tax accounting.

factoring (p. 307)   Transactions in which a business either sells its accounts receivable to a financial institution (often called a

factor) or borrows money by pledging its accounts receivable as collateral.

fair value accounting (p. 299)   The balance sheet valuation standard applied to investments in marketable securities. Involves adjusting the securities to market value at each balance sheet date. (Represents an exception to the cost principle.)

financial assets (p. 290)   Cash and assets convertible directly into known amounts of cash (such as marketable securities and receivables).

gain (p. 298)   An increase in owners' equity resulting from a transaction other than earning revenue or investment by the owners. The most common example is the sale of an asset at a price above book value.

line of credit (p. 292)   A prearranged borrowing agreement in which a bank stands ready to advance the borrower without delay any amount up to a specified credit limit. Once used, a line of credit becomes a liability. The unused portion of the line represents the ability to borrow cash without delay.

loss (p. 298)   A decrease in owners' equity resulting from any transaction other than an expense or a distribution to the owners. The most common example is the sale of an asset at a price below book value.

marketable securities (p. 290)   Highly liquid investments, primarily in stocks and bonds, that can be sold at quoted market prices on organized securities exchanges.

net realizable value (p. 291)   The balance sheet valuation standard applied to receivables. Equal to the gross amount of accounts and notes receivable, less an estimate of the portion that may prove to be uncollectible.

NSF check (p. 294)   A customer's check that was deposited but returned because of a lack of funds (Not Sufficient Funds) in the account on which the check was drawn.

Unrealized Holding Gain (or Loss) on Investments (p. 299)   A stockholders' equity account representing the difference between the cost of investments owned and their market value at the balance sheet date. In short, gains or losses on these investments that have not been "realized" through the sale of the securities.

Demonstration Problem

Shown below are selected transactions of Gulf Corp. during the month of December 2015.

Dec. 1   Accepted a one-year, 8 percent note receivable from a customer, Glenn Holler. The note is in settlement of an existing $1,500 account receivable. The note, plus interest, is due in full on November 30, 2016.

Dec. 8   An account receivable from S. Willis in the amount of $700 is determined to be uncollectible and is written off against the Allowance for Doubtful Accounts.

Dec. 15   Unexpectedly received $200 from F. Hill in full payment of her account. The $200 account receivable from Hill previously had been written off as uncollectible.

Dec. 31   The month-end bank reconciliation includes the following items: outstanding checks, $12,320; deposit in transit, $3,150; check from customer T. Jones returned "NSF," $358; bank service charges, $10; bank collected $20,000 in maturing U.S. Treasury bills (a cash equivalent) on the company's behalf. (These Treasury bills had cost $19,670, so the amount collected includes $330 interest revenue.)

Data for Adjusting Entries

1. An aging of accounts receivable indicates probable uncollectible accounts totaling $9,000. Prior to the month-end adjustment, the Allowance for Doubtful Accounts had a credit balance of $5,210.

2. Prior to any year-end adjustment, the balance in the Marketable Securities account was $213,800. At year-end, marketable securities owned had a cost of $198,000 and a market value of $210,000.

3. Accrued interest revenue on the note receivable from Glenn Holler dated December 1.

Instructions

a. Prepare entries in general journal entry form for the December transactions. In adjusting the accounting records from the bank reconciliation, make one entry to record any increases in the Cash account and a separate entry to record any decreases.

b. Prepare the month-end adjustments indicated by the data for adjusting entries given above.

c. What is the adjusted balance in the Unrealized Holding Gain (or Loss) on Investments account at December 31? Where in the financial statements does this account appear?

Solution to the Demonstration Problem

a.

Date	Account Titles and Explanation	Debit	Credit
GENERAL JOURNAL			
Dec. 1	Notes Receivable	1,500	
	Accounts Receivable (Glenn Holler)		1,500
	Accepted a one-year, 8% note in settlement of a $1,500 account receivable.		
8	Allowance for Doubtful Accounts.	700	
	Accounts Receivable (S. Willis).		700
	To write off receivable from S. Willis as uncollectible.		
15	Accounts Receivable (F. Hill)	200	
	Allowance for Doubtful Accounts		200
	To reinstate account receivable previously written off as uncollectible.		
15	Cash.	200	
	Accounts Receivable (F. Hill).		200
	To record collection of account receivable.		
31	Cash.	20,000	
	Cash Equivalents		19,670
	Interest Revenue		330
	To record collection of maturing T-bills by bank.		
31	Accounts Receivable (T. Jones)	358	
	Bank Service Charges	10	
	Cash		368
	To record bank service charge and to reclassify NSF check from T. Jones as an account receivable.		

```
                    GENERAL JOURNAL
b.                      Adjusting Entries

Dec. 31    Uncollectible Accounts Expense . . . . . . . . . . . . . . . . . . . . . . . .    3,790
              Allowance for Doubtful Accounts . . . . . . . . . . . . . . . . . . . .              3,790
           To increase Allowance for Doubtful Accounts to
              $9,000 ($9,000 – $5,210 = $3,790).
      31   Unrealized Holding Gain (or Loss) on Investments . . . . . . . . . . .    3,800
              Marketable Securities . . . . . . . . . . . . . . . . . . . . . . . . . . . .           3,800
           To reduce the balance in the Marketable Securities
              account to a market value of $210,000.
      31   Interest Receivable. . . . . . . . . . . . . . . . . . . . . . . . . . . . . . . . . .        10
              Interest Revenue . . . . . . . . . . . . . . . . . . . . . . . . . . . . . . . . .                10
           Accrued one-month interest revenue
              on note receivable: $1,500 × 8% × 1/12 = $10.
```

c. The Unrealized Holding Gain (or Loss) on Investments account has a *$12,000 credit balance,* representing the unrealized gain on securities owned as of December 31. (The unrealized gain is equal to the $210,000 market value of these securities, less their $198,000 cost.) The account appears in the stockholders' equity section of Gulf Corp.'s balance sheet.

Self-Test Questions

The answers to these questions appear on page 339.

1. In general terms, financial assets appear in the balance sheet at:
   a. Face value.
   b. Current value.
   c. Cost.
   d. Estimated future sales value.

2. Which of the following practices contributes to efficient cash management?
   a. Never borrow money—maintain a cash balance sufficient to make all necessary payments.
   b. Record all cash receipts and cash payments at the end of the month when reconciling the bank statements.
   c. Prepare monthly forecasts of planned cash receipts, payments, and anticipated cash balances up to a year in advance.
   d. Pay each bill as soon as the invoice arrives.

3. Each of the following measures strengthens internal control over cash receipts *except:*
   a. Factoring accounts receivable.
   b. Preparation of a daily listing of all checks received through the mail.
   c. The deposit of cash receipts in the bank on a daily basis.
   d. The use of cash registers.

Use the following data for questions 4 and 5:
Quinn Company's bank statement at January 31 shows a balance of $13,360, while the ledger account for Cash in Quinn's ledger shows a balance of $12,890 at the same date. The only reconciling items are the following:
- Deposit in transit, $890.
- Bank service charge, $24.
- NSF check from customer Greg Denton in the amount of $426.
- Error in recording check no. 389 for rent: check was written in the amount of $1,320, but was recorded improperly in the accounting records as $1,230.
- Outstanding checks, $?

4. What is the total amount of outstanding checks at January 31?
   a. $1,048.   b. $868.   c. $1,900.   d. $1,720.

5. Assuming a single journal entry is made to adjust Quinn Company's accounting records at January 31, the journal entry includes:
   a. A debit to Rent Expense for $90.
   b. A credit to Accounts Receivable, G. Denton, for $426.
   c. A credit to Cash for $450.
   d. A credit to Cash for $1,720.

6. Which of the following best describes the application of generally accepted accounting principles to the valuation of accounts receivable?
   a. Realization principle—Accounts receivable are shown at their net realizable value in the balance sheet.
   b. Matching principle—The loss due to an uncollectible account is recognized in the period in which the sale is

made, not in the period in which the account receivable is determined to be worthless.

c. Cost principle—Accounts receivable are shown at the initial cost of the merchandise to customers, less the cost the seller must pay to cover uncollectible accounts.

d. Principle of conservatism—Accountants favor using the lowest reasonable estimate for the amount of uncollectible accounts.

7. On January 1, Dillon Company had a $3,100 credit balance in the Allowance for Doubtful Accounts. During the year, sales totaled $780,000, and $6,900 of accounts receivable were written off as uncollectible. A December 31 aging of accounts receivable indicated the amount probably uncollectible to be $5,300. (No recoveries of accounts previously written off were made during the year.) Dillon's financial statements for the current year should include:

a. Uncollectible accounts expense of $9,100.

b. Uncollectible accounts expense of $5,300.

c. Allowance for Doubtful Accounts with a credit balance of $1,500.

d. Allowance for Doubtful Accounts with a credit balance of $8,400.

8. Under the *direct write-off* method of accounting for uncollectible accounts:

a. The current year uncollectible accounts expense is less than the expense would be under the allowance approach.

b. The relationship between the current period net sales and current period uncollectible accounts expense illustrates the matching principle.

c. The Allowance for Doubtful Accounts is debited when specific accounts receivable are determined to be worthless.

d. Accounts receivable are not stated in the balance sheet at net realizable value, but at the balance of the Accounts Receivable control account.

9. Which of the following actions is *least* likely to increase a company's accounts receivable turnover?

a. Encouraging customers to use bank credit cards, such as Visa and MasterCard, rather than other national credit cards, such as American Express.

b. Offer customers larger cash discounts for making early payments.

c. Reduce the interest rate charged to credit customers.

d. Sell accounts receivable to a factor.

10. On October 1, *2015,* Coast Financial loaned Barr Corporation $300,000, receiving in exchange a nine-month, 12 percent note receivable. Coast ends its fiscal year on December 31 and makes adjusting entries to accrue interest earned on all notes receivable. The interest earned on the note receivable from Barr Corporation during *2016* will amount to:

a. $9,000 **b.** $18,000.

c. $27,000 **d.** $36,000.

11. Puget Sound Co. sold marketable securities costing $80,000 for $92,000 cash. In the company's income statement and statement of cash flows, respectively, this will appear as:

a. A $12,000 gain and a $92,000 cash receipt.

b. A $92,000 gain and an $8,000 cash receipt.

c. A $12,000 gain and an $80,000 cash receipt.

d. A $92,000 sale and a $92,000 cash receipt.

ASSIGNMENT MATERIAL | ## Discussion Questions

1. Briefly describe the flow of cash among receivables, cash, and marketable securities.

2. Different categories of financial assets are valued differently in the balance sheet. These different valuation methods have one common goal. Explain.

3. What are *cash equivalents?* Provide two examples. Why are these items often combined with cash for the purpose of balance sheet presentation?

4. What are lines of credit? From the viewpoint of a short-term creditor, why do lines of credit increase a company's liquidity? How are the unused portions of these lines presented in financial statements?

5. Why are cash balances in *excess* of those needed to finance business operations viewed as relatively nonproductive assets? Suggest several ways in which these excess cash balances may be utilized effectively.

6. List two items often encountered in reconciling a bank statement that may cause cash per the bank statement to be *larger* than the balance of cash shown in the depositor's accounting records.

7. Why are investments in marketable securities shown separately from cash equivalents in the balance sheet?

8. Explain the *fair value adjustment procedure* for short-term investments classified as available-for-sale securities.

9. What does the account Unrealized Holding Gain (or Loss) on Investment represent? How is this account presented in the financial statements for short-term investments classified as available-for-sale securities?

10. Explain the relationship between the *matching principle* and the need to estimate uncollectible accounts receivable.

11. In making the annual adjusting entry for uncollectible accounts, a company may utilize a *balance sheet approach* to make the estimate, or it may use an *income statement approach*. Explain these two alternative approaches.

12. Must companies use the same method of accounting for uncollectible accounts receivable in their financial statements and in their income tax returns? Explain.

13. What are the advantages to a retailer of making credit sales only to customers who use nationally recognized credit cards?

14. Explain how each of the following is presented in (1) a multiple-step income statement and (2) a statement of cash flows.

    a. Sale of marketable securities at a loss.

    b. Adjusting entry to create (or increase) the allowance for doubtful accounts.

    c. Entry to write off an uncollectible account against the allowance.

    d. Adjusting entry to increase the balance in the Marketable Securities account to a higher market value (assume these investments are classified as available-for-sale securities).

15. What is the formula for computing interest on a note receivable, and what does each term mean?

Brief Exercises

LO7-1, LO7-2

BRIEF EXERCISE 7.1

Cash and Cash Equivalents

The following footnote appeared in a recent financial statement of Oakwood Corporation:

> The Corporation considers all investment securities with a maturity of three months or less when acquired to be cash equivalents. All cash and temporary investments are placed with high-credit-quality financial institutions, and the amount of credit exposure to any one financial institution is limited. At December 31, cash and cash equivalents include restricted funds of $36 million.

a. Are the company's cash equivalents debt or equity securities? How do you know?

b. Explain what is meant by the statement that "the credit exposure to any one financial institution is limited."

c. Explain what is meant by the term *restricted funds* used in the footnote.

LO7-2, LO7-3

BRIEF EXERCISE 7.2

Bank Reconciliation and Cash Equivalents

The Cash account in the general ledger of Lyco Corporation showed a balance of $21,749 at December 31 (but prior to performing a bank reconciliation). The company's bank statement showed a balance of $22,000 at the same date. The only reconciling items consisted of: (1) a $5,000 deposit in transit, (2) a bank service charge of $200, (3) outstanding checks totaling $9,000, (4) a $3,000 check marked "NSF" from Susque Company, one of Lyco's customers, and (5) a check written for office supplies in the amount of $1,832, recorded by the company's bookkeeper as a debit to Office Supplies of $1,283, and a credit to Cash of $1,283.

In addition to the above information, Lyco owned the following financial assets at December 31: (1) a money market account of $60,000, (2) $3,000 of high-grade, 120-day commercial paper, and (3) $5,000 of highly liquid stock investments.

a. Prepare the company's December 31 bank reconciliation.

b. Determine the amount at which cash and cash equivalents will be reported in the company's balance sheet dated December 31.

c. Prepare the necessary journal entry to update the accounting records.

LO7-1, LO7-4

BRIEF EXERCISE 7.3

Fair Value Adjustment

Apple Inc. accumulates large amounts of excess cash throughout the year. It typically invests these funds in marketable securities until they are needed. The company's most recent financial statements revealed a nearly $160 million unrealized gain on short-term investments. Footnotes to the financial statements disclosed that Apple Inc. reports its short-term investments at fair value.

a. Explain the meaning of the company's unrealized gain on short-term investments.

b. How does the unrealized gain impact the company's financial statements?

c. Is the unrealized gain included in the computation of the company's taxable income? Explain.

d. Evaluate fair value accounting from the perspective of the company's creditors.

LO7-1, LO7-4

BRIEF EXERCISE 7.4

Accounting for Marketable Securities

Mumford Corporation invested $30,000 in marketable securities on December 4. On December 9, it sold some of these investments for $10,000, and on December 18, it sold more of these investments for $5,000. The securities sold on December 9 had cost the company $7,000, whereas the securities sold on December 18 had cost the company $6,000.

a. Record the purchase of marketable securities on December 4.

b. Record the sale of marketable securities on December 9.

c. Record the sale of marketable securities on December 18.

d. Record the necessary fair value adjustment on December 31, assuming that the market value of the company's remaining unsold securities was $20,000.

LO7-5

BRIEF EXERCISE 7.5

Internal Control Over
Receivables

Match the department on the left to the task that the department performs on the right, all of which relate to accounts receivable and cash collections. Each department should be used only once.

Department	Task Description
_____ Customer Order department	a. Ensures that the goods shipped match those ordered by the customer.
_____ Credit department	b. Makes journal entries to record sales and cash collection transactions.
_____ Shipping department	c. Receives checks and prepares the daily bank deposit.
_____ Billing department	d. Prepares the sales order upon receipt of a customer order.
_____ Accounting department	e. Compares goods shipped to goods ordered and prepares a sales invoice.
_____ Mailroom	f. Reviews the customer's file and decides whether, and how much, credit should be extended.
_____ Cash Receipts department	g. Restrictively endorses checks and prepares a daily listing of checks received.

LO7-1, LO7-6

BRIEF EXERCISE 7.6

Accounting for
Uncollectible Accounts: A
Balance Sheet Approach

Pachel Corporation reports the following information pertaining to its accounts receivable:

	Days Past Due			
Current	**1–30**	**31–60**	**61–90**	**Over 90**
$60,000	$40,000	$25,000	$12,000	$2,000

The company's credit department provided the following estimates regarding the percent of accounts expected to eventually be written off from each category listed above:

Current receivables outstanding	2%
Receivables 1–30 days past due	4
Receivables 31–60 days past due	16
Receivables 61–90 days past due	40
Receivables over 90 days past due	90

The company uses a *balance sheet* approach to estimate credit losses.

a. Record the company's uncollectible accounts expense, assuming it has a *$1,400 credit balance* in its Allowance for Doubtful Accounts *prior* to making the necessary adjustment.

b. Record the company's uncollectible accounts expense, assuming it has a *$1,600 debit balance* in its Allowance for Doubtful Accounts *prior* to making the necessary adjustment.

LO7-1, LO7-6

BRIEF EXERCISE 7.7

Accounting for
Uncollectible Accounts:
An Income Statement
Approach

Wilson Corporation uses an *income statement* approach to estimate credit losses. Its *gross* Accounts Receivable of $5,000,000 at the *beginning* of the period had a *net realizable value* of $4,925,000. During the period, the company *wrote off* actual accounts receivable of $100,000 and collected $7,835,000 from credit customers. Credit sales for the year amounted to $9,000,000. Of its credit sales, 1 percent was estimated to eventually be uncollectible.

Determine the *net realizable value* of the company's accounts receivable at the *end* of the period.

LO7-1, LO7-6, LO7-8

BRIEF EXERCISE 7.8

Analyzing Accounts
Receivable

Following are the average accounts receivable and net sales reported recently by two large beverage companies (dollar amounts are stated in millions):

	Average Accounts Receivable	Net Sales
Molson Coors Brewing Co.	$517	$ 5,170
Anheuser-Busch InBev	2,606	39,046

a. Compute the accounts receivable turnover rate for each company (round your results to one decimal place).

b. Compute the average number of days that it takes for each company to collect its accounts receivable (round your results to the nearest whole day).

c. Based upon your computations in **a** and **b,** which company's accounts receivable appear to be most liquid? Defend your answer.

LO7-7

BRIEF EXERCISE 7.9

Notes Receivable and Interest

On September 1, 2015, Health Wise International acquired a 12 percent, nine-month note receivable from Herbal Innovations, a credit customer, in settlement of a $22,000 account receivable. Prepare journal entries to record the following:

a. The receipt of the note on September 1, 2015, in settlement of the account receivable.

b. The adjustment to record accrued interest revenue on December 31, 2015.

c. The collection of the principal and interest on May 31, 2016.

LO7-6, LO7-8

BRIEF EXERCISE 7.10

Industry Characteristics and Allowances for Doubtful Accounts

The following percentages were computed using figures from recent annual reports of **Weis Markets,** a large grocery store chain, and **Sprint Nextel Corporation,** a provider of telecommunication services:

	Weis	Sprint
Allowance for doubtful accounts as a percentage of net sales	0.06%	0.52%
Accounts receivable as a percentage of net sales.	2.0	10.3

LO7-8

BRIEF EXERCISE 7.11

Analyzing Accounts Receivable

Explain why **Sprint**'s percentages are so much larger than **Weis Markets**' percentages.

Cromley Corporation reports annual sales of $1,500,000. Its accounts receivable throughout the year averaged $125,000.

a. Compute the company's accounts receivable turnover rate.

b. Compute the average days outstanding of the company's accounts receivable.

Exercises

≣ connect
|ACCOUNTING

LO7-3

EXERCISE 7.1

You as a Student

Assume that the following information relates to your most recent bank statement dated September 30:

Balance per bank statement at September 30	$3,400

Checks written that had not cleared the bank as of September 30:

#203	University tuition	$1,500
#205	University bookstore	350
#208	Rocco's Pizza	25
#210	Stereo purchase	425
#211	October apartment rent	500

Interest amounting to $4 was credited to your account by the bank in September. The bank's service charge for the month was $5. In addition to your bank statement, you received a letter from your parents informing you that they had made a $2,400 electronic funds transfer directly into your account on October 2. After reading your parents' letter, you looked in your checkbook and discovered its balance was $601. Adding your parents' deposit brought that total to $3,001.

Prepare a bank reconciliation to determine your correct checking account balance. Explain why neither your bank statement nor your checkbook shows this amount.

LO7-1, LO7-2

EXERCISE 7.2

Financial Assets

The following financial assets appeared in a recent balance sheet of **Apple, Inc.** (dollar amounts are stated in millions):

Cash and cash equivalents	$ 10,746
Marketable securities (short-term investments)	18,383
Accounts receivable (net of allowance for doubtful accounts of $98)	10,930

a. Define *financial assets*.

b. A different approach is used in determining the balance sheet value for each category of **Apple Inc.**'s financial assets, although each approach serves a common goal. Explain.

c. Why do companies like **Apple Inc.** hold so much of their financial assets in the form of marketable securities and receivables?

d. What types of investments might **Apple Inc.** own that are considered cash equivalents?

e. Explain what is meant by the balance sheet presentation of **Apple Inc.**'s Accounts Receivable as shown in the table.

LO7-2

EXERCISE 7.3

Grandmother's Secret

The former bookkeeper of **White Electric Supply** is serving time in prison for embezzling nearly $416,000 in less than five years. She describes herself as "an ordinary mother of three kids and a proud grandmother of four." Like so many other "ordinary" employees, she started out by taking only small amounts. By the time she was caught, she was stealing lump sums of $5,000 and $10,000.

Her method was crude and simple. She would write a check for the correct amount payable to a supplier for, say, $15,000. However, she would record in the company's check register an amount significantly greater, say, $20,000. She would then write a check payable to herself for the $5,000 difference. In the check register, next to the number of each check she had deposited in her personal bank account, she would write the word "void," making it appear as though the check had been destroyed. This process went undetected for nearly five years.

a. What controls must have been lacking at **White Electric Supply** to enable the bookkeeper to steal nearly $416,000 before being caught?

b. What the bookkeeper did was definitely unethical. But *what if* one of her grandchildren had been ill and needed an expensive operation? If this had been the case, would it have been ethical for her to take company funds to pay for the operation if she intended to pay the company back in full? Defend your answer.

LO7-2

EXERCISE 7.4

Embezzlement Issues

D. J. Fletcher, a trusted employee of Bluestem Products, found himself in personal financial difficulties and decided to "borrow" $3,000 from the company and to conceal his theft.

As a first step, Fletcher removed $3,000 in currency from the cash register. This amount represented the bulk of the cash received in over-the-counter sales during the three business days since the last bank deposit. Fletcher then removed a $3,000 check from the day's incoming mail; this check had been mailed in by a customer, Michael Adams, in full payment of his account. Fletcher made no journal entry to record the $3,000 collection from Adams, but deposited the check in Bluestem Products's bank account in place of the $3,000 over-the-counter cash receipts he had stolen.

In order to keep Adams from protesting when his month-end statement reached him, Fletcher made a journal entry debiting Sales Returns and Allowances and crediting Accounts Receivable—Michael Adams. Fletcher posted this entry to the two general ledger accounts affected and to Adams's account in the subsidiary ledger for accounts receivable.

a. Did these actions by Fletcher cause the general ledger to be out of balance or the subsidiary ledger to disagree with the control account? Explain.

b. Assume that Bluestem Products prepares financial statements at the end of the month without discovering the theft. Would any items in the balance sheet or the income statement be in error? Explain.

c. Several weaknesses in internal control apparently exist in Bluestem Products. Indicate three specific changes needed to strengthen internal control over cash receipts.

LO7-3

EXERCISE 7.5

Bank Reconciliation

Shown below is the information needed to prepare a bank reconciliation for Warren Electric at December 31:

1. At December 31, cash per the bank statement was $15,200; cash per the company's records was $17,500.

2. Two debit memoranda accompanied the bank statement: service charges for December of $25, and a $775 check drawn by Jane Jones marked "NSF."

3. Cash receipts of $10,000 on December 31 were not deposited until January 4.

4. The following checks had been issued in December but were not included among the paid checks returned by the bank: no. 620 for $1,000, no. 630 for $3,000, and no. 641 for $4,500.

a. Prepare a bank reconciliation at December 31.

b. Prepare the necessary journal entry or entries to update the accounting records.

c. Assume that the company normally is *not* required to pay a bank service charge if it maintains a minimum average daily balance of $1,000 throughout the month. If the company's average daily balance for December had been $8,000, why did it have to pay a $25 service charge?

LO7-1, LO7-2
EXERCISE 7.6
Evaluating Cash Equivalents

Tyson Furniture has $100,000 in excess cash that it wants to invest in one or more cash equivalents. The treasurer has researched two money market accounts and two certificates of deposit (CDs) offered by four major banks. This is the information she gathered:

Investment Institution	Investment Type	Minimum Investment	Interest Rate	Penalty for Early Withdrawal?	Financial Risk
Fidelity Bank	Money market account	$ 2,500	0.05%	No	Very low
Bank of America	Money market account	10,000	0.08	No	Very low
Discover Bank	90-day CD	2,500	0.90	Yes	Very low
Commerce Bank	90-day CD	2,500	0.15	Yes	Very low

All of these accounts are FDIC insured for up to $250,000.

Suggest how Tyson Furniture might allocate its $100,000 cash among these four opportunities. Discuss the trade-offs that management must consider.

LO7-1, LO7-4
EXERCISE 7.7
The Nature of Marketable Securities

Many companies hold a significant portion of their financial assets in the form of marketable securities. For example, **Microsoft Corporation** recently reported investments in marketable securities totaling $56.1 billion, an amount equal to 71 percent of its total financial assets. In contrast, only 20 percent of its financial assets were in the form of accounts receivable.

a. Define *marketable securities* (also referred to as short-term investments). What characteristics of these securities justify classifying them as financial assets?

b. What is the basic advantage of **Microsoft Corporation** keeping financial assets in the form of marketable securities instead of cash? Is there any disadvantage?

c. Explain how **Microsoft Corporation** values these investments in its balance sheet.

d. Discuss whether the valuation of marketable securities represents a departure from (1) the cost principle and (2) the objectivity principle.

e. Explain how *fair value accounting* benefits the *users* of **Microsoft Corporation**'s financial statements.

LO7-1, LO7-6
EXERCISE 7.8
Reporting Uncollectible Accounts

The credit manager of Montour Fuel has gathered the following information about the company's accounts receivable and credit losses during the current year:

Net credit sales for the year		$8,000,000
Accounts receivable at year-end		1,750,000
Uncollectible accounts receivable:		
Actually written off during the year	$96,000	
Estimated portion of year-end receivables expected to prove uncollectible (per aging schedule)	84,000	180,000

Prepare one journal entry summarizing the recognition of uncollectible accounts expense for the entire year under each of the following independent assumptions:

a. Uncollectible accounts expense is estimated at an amount equal to 2.5 percent of net credit sales.

b. Uncollectible accounts expense is recognized by adjusting the balance in the Allowance for Doubtful Accounts to the amount indicated in the year-end aging schedule. The balance in the allowance account at the *beginning* of the current year was $25,000. (Consider the effect of the write-offs during the year on the balance in the Allowance for Doubtful Accounts.)

c. The company uses the direct write-off method of accounting for uncollectible accounts.

d. Which of the three methods gives investors and creditors the most accurate assessment of a company's liquidity? Defend your answer.

LO7-8

EXERCISE 7.9

Industry Characteristics and Collection Performance

The following information was taken from recent annual reports of Goodyear Tire & Rubber and PPL Corp., a public utility:

	Goodyear	PPL
Net sales.	$21.0 billion	$ 12.2 billion
Average accounts receivable	2.7 billion	824 million

a. Compute for each company the accounts receivable turnover rate for the year.

b. Compute for each company the average number of days required to collect outstanding receivables (round answers to nearest whole day).

c. Explain why the figures computed for Goodyear in parts **a** and **b** are so different from those computed for PPL.

LO7-1 through LO7-6

EXERCISE 7.10

Analyzing the Effects of Transactions

Six events pertaining to financial assets are described as follows:

a. Invested idle cash in marketable securities and classified them as available for sale.

b. Collected an account receivable.

c. Sold marketable securities at a loss (proceeds from the sale were equal to the market value reflected in the last balance sheet).

d. Determined a particular account receivable to be uncollectible and wrote it off against the Allowance for Doubtful Accounts.

e. Received interest earned on an investment in marketable securities (company policy is to recognize interest as revenue *when received*).

f. Made a fair value adjustment increasing the balance in the Marketable Securities account to reflect a rise in the market value of securities owned.

Indicate the effects of each transaction or adjusting entry upon the financial measurements in the four column headings listed below. Use the code letters **I** for increase, **D** for decrease, and **NE** for no effect. Cash flow classifications were discussed in Chapter 2.

Transaction	Total Assets	Net Income	Operating Cash Flow	Nonoperating Cash Flow
a				

LO7-1

EXERCISE 7.11

Reporting Financial Assets

Explain how each of the following items is reported in a complete set of financial statements, including the accompanying notes. (In one or more cases, the item may not appear in the financial statements.) The answer to the first item is provided as an example.

a. Cash equivalents.

b. Cash in a special fund being accumulated as legally required for the purpose of retiring a specific long-term liability.

c. Compensating balances.

d. The amount by which the current market value of securities classified as available for sale exceeds their cost.

e. The Allowance for Doubtful Accounts.

f. The accounts receivable turnover rate.

g. Realized gains and losses on investments sold during the period.

h. Proceeds from converting cash equivalents into cash.

i. Proceeds from converting investments in marketable securities into cash.

Example: a. Cash equivalents normally are *not* shown separately in financial statements. Rather, they are combined with other types of cash and reported under the caption "Cash and Cash Equivalents." A note to the statements often shows the breakdown of this asset category.

LO7-I, LO7-6, LO7-8
EXERCISE 7.12
Effects of Accounting Errors

Indicate the effects of *the following errors* on each of the items listed in the column headings below. Use the following symbols: **O** = overstated, **U** = understated, and **NE** = no effect. Assume that the company does *not* use the direct write-off method to account for uncollectible accounts.

Transaction	Gross Profit	Current Ratio	Receivables Turnover Rate	Net Income	Retained Earnings	Working Capital
a. Recorded uncollectible accounts expense by debiting Sales and crediting Accounts Receivable.						
b. Wrote off an account receivable deemed uncollectible by debiting Uncollectible Accounts Expense and crediting Accounts Receivable.						
c. Collected cash from credit customers in settlement of outstanding accounts receivable by debiting Cash and crediting Sales.						

- Gross Profit = Sales − Cost of Goods Sold
- Current Ratio = Current Assets ÷ Current Liabilities
- Receivables Turnover Rate = Sales ÷ Average Accounts Receivable (net)
- Working Capital = Current Assets − Current Liabilities

LO7-I, LO7-4

EXERCISE 7.13

Accounting for Marketable Securities

Wharton, Inc. pays income taxes on capital gains at a rate of 30 percent. At December 31, *2015,* the company owns marketable securities that cost $180,000 but have a current market value of $520,000.

a. How will users of Wharton's financial statements be made aware of this substantial increase in the market value of the company's investments?

b. As of December 31, 2015, what income taxes has Wharton paid on the increase in value of these investments? Explain.

c. Prepare a journal entry at January 4, 2016, to record the cash sale of these investments at $520,000.

d. What effect will the sale recorded in part **c** have on Wharton's tax obligation for 2016?

LO7-7
EXERCISE 7.14
Notes and Interest

On August 1, 2015, Hampton Construction received a 9 percent, six-month note receivable from Dusty Roads, one of Hampton Construction's problem credit customers. Roads had owed $36,000 on an outstanding account receivable. The note receivable was taken in settlement of this amount. Assume that Hampton Construction makes adjusting entries for accrued interest revenue *once each year* on December 31.

a. Journalize the following four events on the books of Hampton Construction.

1. Record the receipt of the note on August 1 in settlement of the account receivable.

2. Record accrued interest at December 31, 2015.

3. Assume that Dusty Roads pays the note plus accrued interest in full. Record the collection of the principal and interest on January 31, 2016.

4. Assume that Dusty Roads did *not* make the necessary principal and interest payment on January 31, 2016. Rather, assume that he defaulted on his obligation. Record the default on January 31, 2016.

b. Indicate the effects of each of the four transactions journalized in part **a** on the elements of the financial statement shown below. Use the code letters **I** for increase, **D** for decrease, and **NE** for no effect.

Transaction	Revenue	−	Expenses	=	Net Income	Assets	=	Liabilities	+	Equity
1										

LO7-1, LO7-4, LO7-6, LO7-8

EXERCISE 7.15

Using the Financial Statements of Home Depot, Inc.

The Home Depot, Inc., financial statements appear in Appendix A at the end of this textbook. Use these statements to answer the following questions:

a. What is the total dollar value of the company's current financial assets for the most current year reported?

b. Does the company report any investments in marketable securities? If so, how does it report unrealized gains and losses?

c. What is the company's allowance for uncollectible accounts for the most current year reported? (Hint: Examine the footnotes to the financial statements.)

d. On average, for how many days do the company's accounts receivable remain outstanding before collection?

Problem Set A

LO7-1, LO7-3

PROBLEM 7.1A

Bank Reconciliation

The cash transactions and cash balances of Banner, Inc., for July were as follows:

1. The ledger account for Cash showed a balance at July 31 of $125,568.

2. The July bank statement showed a closing balance of $114,828.

3. The cash received on July 31 amounted to $16,000. It was left at the bank in the night depository chute after banking hours on July 31 and therefore was not recorded by the bank on the July statement.

4. Also included with the July bank statement was a debit memorandum from the bank for $50 representing service charges for July.

5. A credit memorandum enclosed with the July bank statement indicated that a non-interest-bearing note receivable for $4,000 from Rene Manes, left with the bank for collection, had been collected and the proceeds credited to the account of Banner, Inc.

6. Comparison of the paid checks returned by the bank with the entries in the accounting records revealed that check no. 821 for $519, issued July 15 in payment for office equipment, had been erroneously entered in Banner's records as $915.

7. Examination of the paid checks also revealed that three checks, all issued in July, had not yet been paid by the bank: no. 811 for $314; no. 814 for $625; no. 823 for $175.

8. Included with the July bank statement was a $200 check drawn by Howard Williams, a customer of Banner, Inc. This check was marked "NSF." It had been included in the deposit of July 27 but had been charged back against the company's account on July 31.

Instructions

a. Prepare a bank reconciliation for Banner, Inc., at July 31.

b. Prepare journal entries (in general journal form) to adjust the accounts at July 31. Assume that the accounts have not been closed.

c. State the amount of cash that should be included in the balance sheet at July 31.

d. Explain why the balance per the company's bank statement is often larger than the balance shown in its accounting records.

LO7-2, LO7-3

PROBLEM 7.2A

Protecting Cash

Osage Farm Supply had poor internal control over its cash transactions. Facts about the company's cash position at November 30 are described below.

The accounting records showed a cash balance of $35,400, which included a deposit in transit of $1,245. The balance indicated in the bank statement was $20,600. Included in the bank statement were the following debit and credit memoranda:

Debit Memoranda:	
Check from customer G. Davis, deposited by Osage Farm Supply, but charged back as NSF.	$ 130
Bank service charges for November	15
Credit Memorandum:	
Proceeds from collection of a note receivable from Regal Farms, which Osage Farm Supply had left with the bank's collection department	$6,255

Outstanding checks were as follows:

Check No.	Amount
8231	$ 400
8263	524
8288	176
8294	5,000

Bev Escola, the company's cashier, has been taking portions of the company's cash receipts for several months. Each month, Escola prepares the company's bank reconciliation in a manner that conceals her thefts. Her bank reconciliation for November was as follows:

Balance per bank statement, Nov. 30		$20,600
Add: Deposits in transit	$2,145	
Collection of note from Regal Farms.	6,255	8,400
Subtotal		$30,000
Less: Outstanding checks:		
No. 8231	$ 400	
8263	524	
8288	176	1,000
Adjusted cash balance per bank statement.		$29,000
Balance per accounting records, Nov. 30		$35,400
Add: Credit memorandum from bank		6,255
Subtotal		$29,145
Less: Debit memoranda from bank:		
NSF check of G. Davis	$ 130	
Bank service charges	15	145
Adjusted cash balance per accounting records.		$29,000

Instructions

a. Determine the amount of the cash shortage that has been concealed by Escola in her bank reconciliation. (As a format, we suggest that you prepare the bank reconciliation correctly. The amount of the shortage then will be the difference between the adjusted balances per the bank statement and per the accounting records. You can then list this unrecorded cash shortage as the final adjustment necessary to complete your reconciliation.)

b. Carefully review Escola's bank reconciliation and explain in detail how she concealed the amount of the shortage. Include a listing of the dollar amounts that were concealed in various ways. This listing should total the amount of the shortage determined in part **a.**

c. Suggest some specific internal control measures that appear to be necessary for Osage Farm Supply.

LO7-1, LO7-6

PROBLEM 7.3A

Aging Accounts Receivable; Write-offs

Putnam & Putnam, a legal firm, uses the balance sheet approach to estimate uncollectible accounts expense. At year-end, an aging of the accounts receivable produced the following five groupings:

a.	Not yet due	$250,000
b.	1–30 days past due..................................	105,000
c.	31–60 days past due................................	40,000
d.	61–90 days past due................................	7,500
e.	Over 90 days past due	15,000
	Total	$417,500

On the basis of past experience, the company estimated the percentages probably uncollectible for the above five age groups to be as follows: Group a, 1 percent; Group b, 3 percent; Group c, 10 percent; Group d, 20 percent; and Group e, 50 percent.

The Allowance for Doubtful Accounts before adjustment at December 31 showed a credit balance of $5,900.

Instructions

a. Compute the estimated amount of uncollectible accounts based on the above classification by age groups.

b. Prepare the adjusting entry needed to bring the Allowance for Doubtful Accounts to the proper amount.

c. Assume that on January 10 of the following year, Putnam & Putnam learned that an account receivable that had originated on September 1 in the amount of $4,300 was worthless because of the bankruptcy of the client, Safeland Co. Prepare the journal entry required on January 10 to write off this account.

d. The firm is considering the adoption of a policy whereby clients whose outstanding accounts become more than 60 days past due will be required to sign an interest-bearing note for the full amount of their outstanding balance. What advantages would such a policy offer?

LO7-1, LO7-6

PROBLEM 7.4A

Accounting for Uncollectible Accounts

Wilcox Mills is a manufacturer that makes all sales on 30-day credit terms. Annual sales are approximately $30 million. At the end of *2014,* accounts receivable were presented in the company's balance sheet as follows:

Accounts receivable from clients	$3,100,000
Less: Allowance for doubtful accounts	80,000

During *2015,* $165,000 of specific accounts receivable were written off as uncollectible. Of these accounts written off, receivables totaling $15,000 were subsequently collected. At the end of 2015, an aging of accounts receivable indicated a need for a $90,000 allowance to cover possible failure to collect the accounts currently outstanding.

Wilcox Mills makes adjusting entries for uncollectible accounts *only at year-end.*

Instructions

a. Prepare the following general journal entries:

1. One entry to summarize all accounts written off against the Allowance for Doubtful Accounts during 2015.

2. Entries to record the $15,000 in accounts receivable that were subsequently collected.

3. The adjusting entry required at December 31, 2015, to increase the Allowance for Doubtful Accounts to $90,000.

b. Notice that the Allowance for Doubtful Accounts was only $80,000 at the end of 2014, but uncollectible accounts during 2015 totaled $150,000 ($165,000 less the $15,000 reinstated). Do these relationships appear reasonable, or was the Allowance for Doubtful Accounts greatly understated at the end of 2014? Explain.

LO7-1, LO7-4

PROBLEM 7.5A

Accounting for Marketable Securities

At December 31, *2014,* Charter Holding Co. owned the following investments in capital stock of publicly traded companies (classified as available-for-sale securities):

	Cost	Current Market Value
Limited Brands, Inc. (5,000 shares: cost, $40 per share; market value, $44)	$ 200,000	$220,000
The Gap, Inc. (4,000 shares: cost, $40 per share; market value, $36)	160,000	144,000
	$ 360,000	$364,000

In *2015,* Charter engaged in the following two transactions:

Apr. 10 Sold 1,000 shares of its investment in Limited Brands, Inc., at a price of $45 per share, less a brokerage commission of $100.

Aug. 7 Sold 2,000 shares of its investment in The Gap, Inc., at a price of $35 per share, less a brokerage commission of $150.

At December 31, 2015, the market values of these stocks were: Limited Brands, Inc., $42 per share; and The Gap, Inc., $37 per share.

Instructions

a. Illustrate the presentation of marketable securities and the unrealized holding gain or loss in Charter's balance sheet at December 31, *2014.* Include a caption indicating the section of the balance sheet in which each of these accounts appears.

b. Prepare journal entries to record the transactions on April 10 and August 7.

c. Prior to making a fair value adjustment at the end of 2015, determine the unadjusted balance in the Marketable Securities control account and the Unrealized Holding Gain (or Loss) on Investments account. (Assume that no unrealized gains or losses have been recognized since last year.)

d. Prepare a schedule showing the cost and the market values of securities owned at the end of 2015. (Use the same format as the schedule illustrated above.)

e. Prepare the fair value adjusting entry required at December 31, 2015.

f. Illustrate the presentation of the marketable securities and unrealized holding gain (or loss) in the balance sheet at December 31, *2015.* (Follow the same format as in part a.)

g. Illustrate the presentation of the net *realized* gains (or losses) in the 2015 income statement. Assume a multiple-step income statement and show the caption identifying the section in which this amount would appear.

h. Explain how both the realized and unrealized gains and losses will affect the company's 2015 income tax return.

LO7-7
PROBLEM 7.6A
Notes Receivable

Eastern Supply sells a variety of merchandise to retail stores on account, but it insists that any customer who fails to pay an invoice when due must replace their account receivable with an interest--bearing note. The company adjusts and closes its accounts at December 31. Among the transactions relating to notes receivable were the following:

Sept. 1   Received from a customer (Party Plus) a nine-month, 10 percent note for $75,000 in settlement of an account receivable due today.

June 1   Collected in full the nine-month, 10 percent note receivable from Party Plus, including interest.

Instructions

a. Prepare journal entries (in general journal form) to record: (1) the receipt of the note on September 1; (2) the adjustment for interest on December 31; and (3) collection of principal and interest on June 1. (To better illustrate the allocation of interest revenue between accounting periods, we will assume Eastern Supply makes adjusting entries *only at year-end.*)

b. Assume that instead of paying the note on June 1, the customer (Party Plus) had defaulted. Give the journal entry by Eastern Supply to record the default. Assume that Party Plus has sufficient resources that the note eventually will be collected.

c. Explain why the company insists that any customer who fails to pay an invoice when due must replace it with an interest-bearing note.

LO7-1, LO7-3 through
LO7-8
PROBLEM 7.7A
Short Comprehensive
Problem

The Ski Factory provided the following information at December 31, 2015:

Bank Reconciliation

General ledger cash balance, 12/31/15	$35,132		Bank statement balance, 12/31/15		$32,612
Bank service charge	(50)		Deposits in transit		4,900
Returned customer checks marked NSF	(750)		Outstanding checks		(2,712)
Error in recording of office supplies	468				
Adjusted cash balance, 12/31/15	$34,800		Adjusted cash balance, 12/31/15		$34,800

Marketable Securities

The company invested $52,000 in a portfolio of marketable securities on December 22, 2015. The portfolio's market value on December 31, 2015, had increased in value to $57,000.

Notes Receivable

On November 1, 2015, The Ski Factory sold 250 pairs of skis to Arctic Lodge for $130,000. The lodge paid $10,000 at the point of sale and issued a one-year, $120,000, 5 percent note for the remaining balance. The note, plus accrued interest, is due in full on October 31, 2016. The Ski Factory adjusts for accrued interest revenue monthly.

Accounts Receivable

The Ski Factory uses a *balance sheet* approach to account for uncollectible accounts expense. Outstanding accounts receivable on December 31, 2015, total $900,000. After aging these accounts, the company estimates that their *net realizable value* is $870,000. Prior to making any adjustment to record uncollectible accounts expense, The Ski Factory's Allowance for Doubtful Accounts has a *credit balance* of $8,000.

Instructions

a. Prepare the journal entry necessary to update the company's accounts immediately after performing its bank reconciliation on December 31, 2015.

b. Prepare the journal entry necessary to adjust the company's marketable securities to market value at December 31, 2015.

c. Prepare the journal entry necessary to accrue interest in December 2015.

d. Prepare the journal entry necessary to report the company's accounts receivable at their net realizable value at December 31, 2015.

e. Discuss briefly how the entry performed in part **d** affects the accounts receivable turnover rate. Does the *write-off* of an account receivable affect the accounts receivable turnover rate differently than the entry performed in part **d**? Explain.

LO7-1, LO7-3 through LO7-8

PROBLEM 7.8A

Short Comprehensive Problem

The Cash account in the general ledger of Hendry Corporation shows a balance of $96,990 at December 31, 2015 (prior to performing a bank reconciliation). The company's bank statement shows a balance of $100,560 at the same date. An examination of the bank statement reveals the following:

1. Deposits in transit amount to $24,600.

2. Bank service charges total $200.

3. Outstanding checks total $31,700.

4. A $3,600 check marked "NSF" from Kent Company (one of Hendry Corporation's customers) was returned to Hendry Corporation by the bank. This was the only NSF check that Hendry Corporation received during 2015.

5. A canceled check (no. 244) written by Hendry Corporation in the amount of $1,250 for office equipment was incorrectly recorded in the general ledger as a debit to Office Equipment of $1,520, and a credit to Cash of $1,520.

In addition to the above information, Hendry Corporation owns the following assets at December 31, 2015: (1) money market accounts totaling $75,000, (2) $3,000 of high-grade, 90-day, commercial paper, and (3) highly liquid stock investments valued at $86,000 at December 31, 2015 (these investments originally cost Hendry Corporation $116,000).

On December 1, 2015, Hendry Corporation sold an unused warehouse to Moran Industries for $100,000. Hendry accepted a six-month, $100,000, 6 percent note receivable from Moran. The note, plus accrued interest, is due in full on May 31, 2016. Hendry Corporation adjusts for accrued interest revenue *monthly.*

Hendry Corporation uses the *income statement approach* to compute its uncollectible accounts expense. The general ledger had reported Accounts Receivable of $2,150,000 at *January 1, 2015.* At that time, the Allowance for Doubtful Accounts had a credit balance of $40,000. Throughout 2015, the company *wrote off* actual accounts receivable of $140,000 and collected $21,213,600 on account from credit customers (this amount includes the $3,600 NSF check received from Kent Company). Credit sales for the year ended December 31, 2015, totaled $20,000,000. Of these credit sales, 2 percent were estimated to eventually become uncollectible.

Instructions

a. Prepare Hendry Corporation's bank reconciliation dated December 31, 2015, and provide the journal entry necessary to update the company's general ledger balances.

b. Compute cash and cash equivalents to be reported in Hendry Corporation's balance sheet dated December 31, 2015.

c. Prepare the adjusting entry necessary to account for the note receivable from Moran Industries at December 31, 2015.

d. Determine the net realizable value of Hendry Corporation's accounts receivable at December 31, 2015.

e. Determine the total dollar amount of financial assets to be reported in Hendry Corporation's balance sheet dated December 31, 2015.

f. Assume that it is normal for firms similar to Hendry Corporation to take an average of 45 days to collect an outstanding receivable. Is Hendry Corporation's collection performance above or below this average?

Problem Set B

LO7-1, LO7-3

PROBLEM 7.1B

Bank Reconciliation

The cash transactions and cash balances of Dodge, Inc., for November were as follows:

1. The ledger account for Cash showed a balance at November 30 of $6,750.
2. The November bank statement showed a closing balance of $4,710.
3. The cash received on November 30 amounted to $3,850. It was left at the bank in the night depository chute after banking hours on November 30 and therefore was not recorded by the bank on the November statement.
4. Also included with the November bank statement was a debit memorandum from the bank for $15 representing service charges for November.
5. A credit memorandum enclosed with the November bank statement indicated that a non-interest-bearing note receivable for $4,000 from Wright Sisters, left with the bank for collection, had been collected and the proceeds credited to the account of Dodge, Inc.
6. Comparison of the paid checks returned by the bank with the entries in the accounting records revealed that check no. 810 for $430, issued November 15 in payment for computer equipment, had been erroneously entered in Dodge's records as $340.
7. Examination of the paid checks also revealed that three checks, all issued in November, had not yet been paid by the bank: no. 814 for $115; no. 816 for $170; no. 830 for $530.
8. Included with the November bank statement was a $2,900 check drawn by Steve Dial, a customer of Dodge, Inc. This check was marked "NSF." It had been included in the deposit of November 27 but had been charged back against the company's account on November 30.

Instructions

a. Prepare a bank reconciliation for Dodge, Inc., at November 30.

b. Prepare journal entries (in general journal form) to adjust the accounts at November 30. Assume that the accounts have not been closed.

c. State the amount of cash that should be included in the balance sheet at November 30.

LO7-2, LO7-3

PROBLEM 7.2B

Protecting Cash

Jason Chain Saws, Inc., had poor internal control over its cash transactions. Facts about the company's cash position at April 30 are described below.

The accounting records showed a cash balance of $20,325, which included a deposit in transit of $5,000. The balance indicated in the bank statement was $14,300. Included in the bank statement were the following debit and credit memoranda:

Debit Memoranda:	
Check from customer, deposited but charged back as NSF	$ 125
Bank service charges for April	50
Credit Memorandum:	
Proceeds from collection of a note receivable on company's behalf.	$6,200

Outstanding checks as of April 30 were as follows:

Check No.	Amount
836	$ 500
842	440
855	330
859	1,300

Tom Crook, the company's cashier, has been taking portions of the company's cash receipts for several months. Each month, Crook prepares the company's bank reconciliation in a manner that conceals his thefts. His bank reconciliation for April is illustrated as follows:

Balance per bank statement, April 30		$14,300
Add: Deposits in transit	$7,120	
Collection of note......................................	6,200	13,320
Subtotal		$27,620
Less: Outstanding checks:		
No. 836..	$ 500	
No. 842..	440	
No. 855..	330	1,270
Adjusted cash balance per bank statement		$26,350
Balance per accounting records, April 30		20,325
Add: Credit memorandum from bank		6,200
Subtotal		$26,525
Less: Debit memoranda from bank:		
NSF check	$ 125	
Bank service charges.................................	50	175
Adjusted cash balance per accounting records		$26,350

Instructions

a. Determine the amount of cash shortage that has been concealed by Crook in his bank reconciliation. (As a format, we suggest that you prepare the bank reconciliation correctly. The amount of the shortage then will be the difference between the adjusted balances per the bank statement and per the accounting records. You can then list this unrecorded cash shortage as the final adjustment necessary to complete your reconciliation.)

b. Carefully review Crook's bank reconciliation and explain in detail how he concealed the amount of the shortage. Include a listing of the dollar amounts that were concealed in various ways. This listing should total the amount of shortage determined in part **a.**

c. Suggest some specific internal control measures that appear to be necessary for Jason Chain Saws, Inc.

LO7-1, LO7-6

PROBLEM 7.3B

Aging Accounts Receivable; Write-offs

Starlight, a Broadway media firm, uses the balance sheet approach to estimate uncollectible accounts expense. At year-end an aging of the accounts receivable produced the following five groupings:

a. Not yet due	$500,000
b. 1–30 days past due..	110,000
c. 31–60 days past due..	50,000
d. 61–90 days past due..	30,000
e. Over 90 days past due	60,000
Total	$750,000

On the basis of past experience, the company estimated the percentages probably uncollectible for the above five age groups to be as follows: Group a, 1 percent; Group b, 3 percent; Group c, 10 percent; Group d, 20 percent; and Group e, 50 percent.

The Allowance for Doubtful Accounts before adjustments at December 31 showed a credit balance of $4,700.

Instructions

a. Compute the estimated amount of uncollectible accounts based on the above classification by age groups.

b. Prepare the adjusting entry needed to bring the Allowance for Doubtful Accounts to the proper amount.

c. Assume that on January 18 of the following year, Starlight learned that an account receivable that had originated on August 1 in the amount of $1,600 was worthless because of the bankruptcy of the client, May Flowers. Prepare the journal entry required on January 18 to write off this account.

d. The firm is considering the adoption of a policy whereby clients whose outstanding accounts become more than 60 days past due will be required to sign an interest-bearing note for the full amount of their outstanding balance. What advantages would such a policy offer?

LO7-1, LO7-6

PROBLEM 7.4B

Accounting for
Uncollectible Accounts

Redstone Mill is a manufacturer that makes all sales on 30-day credit terms. Annual sales are approximately $40 million. At the end of *2014,* accounts receivable were presented in the company's balance sheet as follows:

Accounts receivable from clients	$3,600,000
Less: Allowance for doubtful accounts	80,000

During 2015, $230,000 of specific accounts receivable were written off as uncollectible. Of these accounts written off, receivables totaling $18,000 were subsequently collected. At the end of 2015, an aging of accounts receivable indicated a need for a $150,000 allowance to cover possible failure to collect the accounts currently outstanding.

Redstone Mill makes adjusting entries for uncollectible accounts *only at year-end.*

Instructions

a. Prepare the following general journal entries:

1. One entry to summarize all accounts written off against the Allowance for Doubtful Accounts during 2015.

2. Entries to record the $18,000 in accounts receivable that were subsequently collected.

3. The adjusting entry required at December 31, 2015, to increase the Allowance for Doubtful Accounts to $150,000.

b. Notice that the Allowance for Doubtful Accounts was only $80,000 at the end of 2014, but uncollectible accounts during 2015 totaled $212,000 ($230,000 less the $18,000 reinstated). Do these relationships appear reasonable, or was the Allowance for Doubtful Accounts greatly understated at the end of 2014? Explain.

LO7-1, LO7-4

PROBLEM 7.5B

Accounting for Marketable
Securities

At December 31, *2014,* Westport Manufacturing Co. owned the following investments in the capital stock of publicly owned companies (all classified as available-for-sale securities):

	Cost	Current Market Value
Lamb Computer, Inc. (1,000 shares: cost, $30 per share; market value, $50)	$30,000	$50,000
Dry Foods (5,000 shares: cost, $9 per share; market value, $8)	45,000	40,000
Totals	$75,000	$90,000

In *2015,* Westport engaged in the following two transactions:

Apr. 6   Sold 100 shares of its investment in Lamb Computer at a price of $55 per share, less a brokerage commission of $20.

Apr. 20   Sold 2,500 shares of its Dry Foods stock at a price of $7 per share, less a brokerage commission of $20.

At December 31, 2015, the market values of these stocks were: Lamb Computer, $40 per share; Dry Foods, $7.

Instructions

a. Illustrate the presentation of marketable securities and the unrealized holding gain or loss in Westport's balance sheet at December 31, *2014*. Include a caption indicating the section of the balance sheet in which each of these accounts appears.

b. Prepare journal entries to record the transactions on April 6 and April 20.

c. Prior to making a fair value adjustment at the end of 2015, determine the unadjusted balance in the Marketable Securities controlling account and the Unrealized Holding Gain (or Loss) on Investments account. (Assume that no unrealized gains or losses have been recognized since last year.)

d. Prepare a schedule showing the cost and market values of securities owned at the end of 2015. (Use the same format as the schedule illustrated above.)

e. Prepare the fair value adjusting entry required at December 31, 2015.

f. Illustrate the presentation of the marketable securities and unrealized holding gain (or loss) in the balance sheet at December 31, *2015*. (Follow the same format as in part **a.**)

g. Illustrate the presentation of the net *realized* gains (or losses) in the 2015 income statement. Assume a multiple-step income statement and show the caption identifying the section in which this amount would appear.

h. Explain how both the realized and the unrealized gains and losses will affect the company's 2015 income tax return.

LO7-7
PROBLEM 7.6B
Notes Receivable

Midtown Distribution sells a variety of merchandise to retail stores on account, but it insists that any customer who fails to pay an invoice when due must replace their account receivable with an interest-bearing note. The company adjusts and closes its accounts at December 31. Among the transactions relating to notes receivable were the following:

Nov. 1 Received from a customer (Sampson Co.) a nine-month, 12 percent note for $30,000 in settlement of an account receivable due today.

Aug. 1 Collected in full the nine-month, 12 percent note receivable from Sampson Co., including interest.

Instructions

a. Prepare journal entries (in general journal form) to record: (1) the receipt of the note on November 1; (2) the adjustment for interest on December 31; and (3) the collection of principal and interest on August 1. (To better illustrate the allocation of interest revenue between accounting periods, we will assume Midtown makes adjusting entries *only at year-end.*)

b. Assume that instead of paying the note on August 1, the customer (Sampson Co.) had defaulted. Give the journal entry by Midtown to record the default. Assume that Sampson Co. has sufficient resources that the note eventually will be collected.

c. Explain why the company insists that any customer who fails to pay an invoice when due must replace it with an interest-bearing note.

LO7-1, LO7-3 through
LO7-8
PROBLEM 7.7B
Short Comprehensive
Problem

Data Management, Inc., provided the following information at December 31, 2015:

Bank Reconciliation

General ledger cash balance, 12/31/15	$44,637	Bank statement balance, 12/31/15	$37,960
Bank service charge.	(125)	Deposits in transit.	18,800
Returned customer checks marked NSF	(2,350)	Outstanding checks	(15,560)
Error in recording of office supplies.	(962)		
Adjusted cash balance, 12/31/15	$41,200	Adjusted cash balance, 12/31/15	$41,200

Marketable Securities

The company invested $75,000 in a portfolio of marketable securities on December 9, 2015. The portfolio's market value on December 31, 2015, had decreased in value to $68,000.

Notes Receivable

On October 1, 2015, Data Management sold 50 laptop computers to the Mifflinburg School District for $74,500. The school district paid $2,500 at the point of sale and issued a one-year, $72,000, 6 percent note for the remaining balance. The note, plus accrued interest, is due in full on September 30, 2016. Data Management adjusts for accrued interest revenue monthly.

Accounts Receivable

Data Management uses a *balance sheet* approach to account for uncollectible accounts expense. Outstanding accounts receivable on December 31, 2015, total $900,000. After aging these accounts, the company estimates that their *net realizable value* is $860,000. Prior to making any adjustment to record uncollectible accounts expense, Data Management's Allowance for Doubtful Accounts has a *debit balance* of $9,000.

Instructions

a. Prepare the journal entry necessary to update the company's accounts immediately after performing its bank reconciliation on December 31, 2015.

b. Prepare the journal entry necessary to adjust the company's marketable securities to market value at December 31, 2015.

c. Prepare the journal entry necessary to accrue interest revenue in December 2015.

d. Prepare the journal entry necessary to report the company's accounts receivable at their net realizable value at December 31, 2015.

e. Discuss briefly why the company's Allowance for Doubtful Accounts had a *debit balance* prior to the adjustment made in part **d.** How might the company change the percentages it applies to the accounts receivable aging categories to avoid future debit balances in its Allowance for Doubtful Accounts?

LO7-1, LO7-3 through LO7-8

PROBLEM 7.8B

Short Comprehensive Problem

The Cash account in the general ledger of Ciavarella Corporation shows a balance of $112,000 at December 31, 2015 (prior to performing a bank reconciliation). The company's bank statement shows a balance of $104,100 at the same date. An examination of the bank statement reveals the following:

1. Deposits in transit amount to $16,800.
2. Bank service charges total $100.
3. Outstanding checks total $12,400.
4. A $2,500 check marked "NSF" from Needham Company (one of Ciavarella's customers) was returned to Ciavarella Corporation by the bank. This was the only NSF check that Ciavarella received during 2015.
5. Check no. 550 was actually written by Ciavarella in the amount of $3,200 for computer equipment but was incorrectly recorded in the general ledger as a debit to Computer Equipment of $2,300, and a credit to Cash of $2,300.

In addition to the above information, Ciavarella owns the following assets at December 31, 2015: (1) money market accounts totaling $150,000, (2) $5,000 of high-grade, 60-day commercial paper, and (3) highly liquid stock investments valued at $245,000 at December 31, 2015 (these investments originally cost Ciavarella $225,000).

On December 1, 2015, Ciavarella sold a used truck to Ritter Industries for $18,000. Ciavarella accepted a three-month, $18,000, 9 percent note receivable from Ritter. The note, plus accrued interest, is due in full on March 1, 2016. Ciavarella adjusts for accrued interest revenue monthly.

Ciavarella uses the *income statement approach* to compute uncollectible accounts expense. The general ledger had reported Accounts Receivable of $540,000 at *January 1, 2015*. At that time, the Allowance for Doubtful Accounts had a credit balance of $12,000. Throughout 2015, the company *wrote off* actual accounts receivable of $14,000 and collected $5,252,500 on account from credit customers (this amount includes the $2,500 NSF check received from Needham Company). Credit sales for the year ended December 31, 2015, totaled $6,480,000. Of these credit sales, 1 percent were estimated to eventually become uncollectible.

Instructions

a. Prepare Ciavarella's bank reconciliation dated December 31, 2015, and provide the journal entry necessary to update the company's general ledger balances.

b. Compute cash and cash equivalents to be reported in Ciavarella's balance sheet dated December 31, 2015.

c. Prepare the adjusting entry necessary to account for the note receivable from Ritter Industries at December 31, 2015.

d. Determine the net realizable value of Ciavarella's accounts receivable at December 31, 2015.

e. Determine the total dollar amount of financial assets to be reported in Ciavarella's balance sheet dated December 31, 2015.

f. Assume that it is normal for firms similar to Ciavarella to take an average of 60 days to collect an outstanding receivable. Is Ciavarella Corporation's collection performance above or below this average?

Critical Thinking Cases

LO7-1, LO7-6, LO7-7
CASE 7.1
Accounting Principles

In each of the situations described below, indicate the accounting principles or concepts, if any, that have been violated and explain briefly the nature of the violation. If you believe the practice is *in accord* with generally accepted accounting principles, state this as your position and defend it.

a. A small business in which credit sales fluctuate greatly from year to year uses the direct write-off method both for income tax purposes and in its financial statements.

b. Computer Systems often sells merchandise in exchange for interest-bearing notes receivable, maturing in 6, 12, or 24 months. The company records these sales transactions by debiting Notes Receivable for the maturity value of the notes, crediting Sales for the sales price of the merchandise, and crediting Interest Revenue for the balance of the maturity value of the note. The cost of goods sold also is recorded.

c. A company has $400,000 in unrestricted cash, $1 million in a bank account specifically earmarked for the construction of a new factory, and $2 million in cash equivalents. In the balance sheet, these amounts are combined and shown as "Cash and cash equivalents . . . $3.4 million."

LO7-2, LO7-6, LO7-8
CASE 7.2
If Things Get Any Better, We'll Be Broke

Rock, Inc., sells stereo equipment. Traditionally, the company's sales have been in the following categories: cash sales, 25 percent; customers using national credit cards, 35 percent; sales on account (due in 30 days), 40 percent. With these policies, the company earned a modest profit, and monthly cash receipts exceeded monthly cash payments by a comfortable margin. Uncollectible accounts expense was approximately 1 percent of net sales. (The company uses the direct write-off method in accounting for uncollectible accounts receivable.)

Two months ago, the company initiated a new credit policy, which it calls "Double Zero." Customers may purchase merchandise on account, with no down payment and no interest charges. The accounts are collected in 12 monthly installments of equal amounts.

The plan has proven quite popular with customers, and monthly sales have increased dramatically. Despite the increase in sales, however, Rock is experiencing cash flow problems—it hasn't been generating enough cash to pay its suppliers, most of which require payment within 30 days.

The company's bookkeeper has prepared the following analysis of monthly operating results:

Sales	Before Double Zero	Last Month
Cash	$12,500	$ 5,000
National credit card	17,500	10,000
30-day accounts	20,000	–0–
Double Zero accounts	–0–	75,000
Total monthly sales	$50,000	$ 90,000
Cost of goods sold and expenses	40,000	65,000
Net income	$10,000	$ 25,000
Cash receipts		
Cash sales	$12,500	$ 5,000
National credit card companies	17,500	10,000
30-day accounts	19,500	–0–
Double Zero accounts	–0–	11,250
Total monthly cash receipts	$49,500	$ 26,250
Accounts written off as uncollectible	$ 500	$ –0–
Accounts receivable at month-end	$20,000	$135,000

The bookkeeper offered the following assessment: "Double Zero is killing us. Since we started that plan, our accounts receivable have increased nearly sevenfold, and they're still growing. We can't afford to carry such a large nonproductive asset on our books. Our cash receipts are down to nearly half of what they used to be. If we don't go back to more cash sales and receivables that can be collected more quickly, we'll become insolvent."

In reply Maxwell "Rock" Swartz, founder and chief executive officer, shouted out: "Why do you say that our accounts receivable are nonproductive? They're the most productive asset we have! Since we started Double Zero, our sales have nearly doubled, our profits have more than doubled, and our bad debt expense has dropped to nothing!"

Instructions

a.   Is it logical that the Double Zero plan is causing sales and profits to increase while also causing a decline in cash receipts? Explain.

b.   Why has the uncollectible accounts expense dropped to zero? What would you expect to happen to the company's uncollectible accounts expense in the future—say, next year? Why?

c.   Do you think that the reduction in monthly cash receipts is permanent or temporary? Explain.

d.   In what sense are the company's accounts receivable a "nonproductive" asset?

e.   Suggest several ways that Rock may be able to generate the cash it needs to pay its bills without terminating the Double Zero plan.

f.   Would you recommend that the company continue offering Double Zero financing, or should it return to the use of 30-day accounts? Explain the reasons for your answer, and identify any unresolved factors that might cause you to change this opinion in the future.

LO7-1 through LO7-6, LO7-8

CASE 7.3

"Improving" the Balance Sheet

Affections manufactures candy and sells only to retailers. It is not a publicly owned company and its financial statements are not audited. But the company frequently must borrow money. Its creditors insist that the company provide them with unaudited financial statements at the end of each quarter.

In October, management met to discuss the fiscal year ending next December 31. Due to a sluggish economy, Affections was having difficulty collecting its accounts receivable, and its cash position was unusually low. Management knew that if the December 31 balance sheet did not look good, the company would have difficulty borrowing the money it would need to boost production for Valentine's Day.

Thus the purpose of the meeting was to explore ways in which Affections might improve its December 31 balance sheet. Some of the ideas discussed are as follows:

1. Offer customers purchasing Christmas candy a 10 percent discount if they make payment within 30 days.

2. Allow a 30-day grace period on all accounts receivable overdue at the end of the year. As these accounts will no longer be overdue, the company will not need an allowance for overdue accounts.

3. For purposes of balance sheet presentation, combine all forms of cash, including cash equivalents, compensating balances, and unused lines of credit.

4. Require officers who have borrowed money from the company to repay the amounts owed at December 31. This would convert into cash the "notes receivable from officers," which now appear in the balance sheet as noncurrent assets. The loans could be renewed immediately after year-end.

5. Present investments in marketable securities at their market value, rather than at cost.

6. Treat inventory as a financial asset and show it at current sales value.

7. On December 31, draw a large check against one of the company's bank accounts and deposit it in another of the company's accounts in a different bank. The check won't clear the first bank until after year-end. This will substantially increase the amount of cash in bank accounts at year-end.

Instructions

a. Separately evaluate each of these proposals. Consider ethical issues as well as accounting issues.

b. Do you consider it ethical for management to hold this meeting in the first place? That is, should management plan in advance how to improve financial statements that will be distributed to creditors and investors?

LO7-1, LO7-2

INTERNET CASE 7.4

Returns on Idle Cash from Various Cash Equivalents

Prudent cash management is an important function in any business. Large amounts of cash sitting idle in non-interest-bearing checking accounts can cost a company thousands—even millions—of dollars annually in foregone revenue. Thus, many businesses invest large amounts of idle cash in Treasury bills, certificates of deposit (CDs), and money market accounts.

Visit the **Bankrate.com** home page at the following address:

www.bankrate.com

Search the site for information on CDs, money market accounts, and other interest-bearing products. Look for links under the "Compare Rates" menu.

Instructions

a. Prepare a table showing the current interest rates on Treasury bills, various CDs, and money market accounts.

b. If you were in charge of investing $1 million among the cash equivalents identified in part **a,** how would you make your allocation? Defend your answer.

Internet sites are time and date sensitive. It is the purpose of these exercises to have you explore the Internet. You may need to use the Yahoo! search engine www.yahoo.com (or another favorite search engine) to find a company's current web address.

Answers to Self-Test Questions

1. b 2. c 3. a 4. c 5. a 6. b 7. a 8. d
9. c 10. b ($300,000 $\times$ 12% $\times$ $^{6}/_{12}$) 11. a

CHAPTER 8

Inventories and the Cost of Goods Sold

AFTER STUDYING THIS CHAPTER, YOU SHOULD BE ABLE TO:

Learning Objectives

LO8-1 In a perpetual inventory system, determine the cost of goods sold using (a) specific identification, (b) average cost, (c) FIFO, and (d) LIFO. Discuss the advantages and shortcomings of each method.

LO8-2 Explain the need for taking a physical inventory.

LO8-3 Record shrinkage losses and other year-end adjustments to inventory.

LO8-4 In a periodic inventory system, determine the ending inventory and the cost of goods sold using (a) specific identification, (b) average cost, (c) FIFO, and (d) LIFO.

LO8-5 Explain the effects on the income statement of errors in inventory valuation.

LO8-6 Estimate the cost of goods sold and ending inventory by the gross profit method and by the retail method.

LO8-7 Compute inventory turnover and explain its uses.

© Royce DeGrie/Getty Images

BELK, INC.

Having the right merchandise available at the right time, in the right places, and in the needed quantities is critically important for all companies that sell products to their customers. These businesses include chain stores, such as grocery stores, drug stores, and department stores.

Consider the case of Belk, Inc. Belk is the largest privately owned mainline department store business in the United States with 303 stores in 16 states, primarily in the southern United States. The company and its successors have been in the department store business since 1888.

Merchandise inventory represents those items available for sale to customers of companies like Belk. To be successful, the company must carefully manage its inventory to have available the items customers want,

in the right quantities, sizes, and other characteristics. Managing and accounting for inventory is of great importance, and merchandise inventory is often one of the largest assets in the statement of financial position of merchandising companies.

Over a recent five-year period, to support sales of between $3.0 and 4.0 billion, Belk consistently held between $800 million and $950 million in merchandise inventory in its various stores, warehouses, and other sites. Accounting for the movement of inventory into and out of a company like Belk represents a significant challenge. Not only is inventory one of the largest assets on the balance sheet, as goods are sold and inventory moves into the income statement as cost of goods sold, several significant accounting and financial reporting issues emerge that we learn about in this chapter. ∎

Buying, storing, displaying, selling, and accounting for merchandise inventory presents one of the greatest challenges for companies that sell products. These companies must maintain not only a record of inventory items for sale but also the prices at which these items are purchased and sold, both of which change over time. This adds a significant complication to accounting for inventory and the expense included in the income statement when inventory is sold to customers. You learn how to account for inventory and its cost in this chapter.

INVENTORY DEFINED

In a merchandising company, inventory consists of all goods owned and held for sale to customers. Inventory is expected to be converted into cash within the company's *operating cycle*.[1] In the balance sheet, inventory is listed immediately after accounts receivable, because it is just one step farther removed from conversion into cash than customer receivables.

The Flow of Inventory Costs

Inventory is a nonfinancial asset and usually is shown in the balance sheet at its cost.[2] As items are sold from inventory, their costs are removed from the balance sheet and transferred to the cost of goods sold, which is offset against sales revenue in the income statement. This flow of costs is illustrated in Exhibit 8–1.

EXHIBIT 8–1 The Flow of Costs Through Financial Statements

In a perpetual inventory system, entries in the accounting records parallel this flow of costs. When merchandise is purchased, its cost (net of allowable cash discounts) is added to the asset account Inventory. As the merchandise is sold, its cost is removed from the Inventory account and transferred to the Cost of Goods Sold account.

The valuation of inventory and cost of goods sold is of critical importance to managers and to external users of financial statements. In many cases, inventory is a company's largest asset, and the cost of goods sold is its largest expense. These two accounts have a significant effect on the financial statement subtotals and ratios used in evaluating the liquidity and profitability of the business.

Several different methods of pricing inventory and of measuring the cost of goods sold are acceptable under generally accepted accounting principles. These different methods may produce significantly different results, both in a company's financial statements and in its income tax returns. Therefore, managers and investors should understand the effects of the different inventory valuation methods.

---

[1] As explained in Chapter 6, the *operating cycle* of a merchandising business is the period of time required to convert cash into inventory, inventory into accounts receivable, and accounts receivable into cash. Assets expected to be converted into cash within one year or the operating cycle, whichever is longer, are regarded as current assets.

[2] Some companies deal in inventories that can be sold in a worldwide market at quoted market prices. Examples include mutual funds, stock brokerages, and companies that deal in commodities such as agricultural crops or precious metals. Often these companies value their inventories at market price rather than at cost. Our discussions in this chapter are directed to the more common situation in which inventories are valued at cost.

WHICH UNIT DID WE SELL?

Purchases of merchandise are recorded in the same manner under all of the inventory valuation methods. The differences in these methods lie in determining *which costs* are removed from the Inventory account when merchandise is sold.

We illustrated the basic entries relating to purchases and sales of merchandise in Chapter 6. In that introductory discussion, however, we made a simplifying assumption: All of the units in inventory had been acquired at the same unit cost. In practice, a company often has in its inventory identical units of a given product that were acquired at *different costs.* Acquisition costs may vary because the units were purchased at different dates, from different suppliers, or in different quantities.

When identical units of inventory have different unit costs, a question arises as to *which of these costs* should be used in measuring the cost of goods sold.

DATA FOR AN ILLUSTRATION

To illustrate the alternative methods of measuring the cost of goods sold, assume that Mead Electric Company sells electrical equipment and supplies. Included in the company's inventory are five Elco AC-40 generators. These generators are identical; however, two were purchased on January 5 at a per-unit cost of *$1,000,* and the other three were purchased a month later, shortly after Elco had announced a price increase, at a per-unit cost of *$1,200.* These purchases are reflected in Mead's inventory subsidiary ledger in Exhibit 8–2.

EXHIBIT 8–2
Inventory Subsidiary Ledger

Item Elco AC-40   **Primary supplier** Elco Manufacturing
Description Portable generator   **Secondary supplier** Vegas Wholesale Co.
Location Daily St. warehouse   **Inventory level: Min:** 2   **Max:** 5

	Purchased			Sold			Balance		
Date	Units	Unit Cost	Total	Units	Unit Cost	Cost of Goods Sold	Units	Unit Cost	Total
Jan. 5	2	$1,000	$2,000				2	$1,000	$2,000
Feb. 5	3	1,200	3,600				{ 2	1,000 }	
							{ 3	1,200 }	5,600

Notice that, on February 5, the Balance columns contain two "layers" of unit cost information, representing the units purchased at the two different unit costs. A new **cost layer** is created whenever units are acquired at a different per-unit cost. (As all units comprising a cost layer are sold, the layer is eliminated from the inventory. Therefore, a business is unlikely to have more than three or four cost layers in its inventory at any given time.)

Now assume that, on March 1, Mead sells one of these Elco generators to Boulder Construction Company for $1,800 cash. What cost should be removed from the Inventory account and recognized as the cost of goods sold—$1,000 or $1,200?

In answering such questions, accountants may use an approach called **specific identification**, or they may adopt a **cost flow assumption**. Either of these approaches is acceptable. Once an approach has been selected, however, it should be *applied consistently* in accounting for all sales of this particular type of merchandise.

L08-1

LEARNING OBJECTIVE
In a perpetual inventory system, determine the cost of goods sold using (a) specific identification, (b) average cost, (c) FIFO, and (d) LIFO. Discuss the advantages and shortcomings of each method.

SPECIFIC IDENTIFICATION

The specific identification method is acceptable only when the actual costs of individual units of merchandise can be determined from the accounting records. For example, each of the generators in Mead's inventory may have an identification number, and these numbers may appear on the purchase invoices. With this identification number, Mead's accounting department can determine whether the generator sold to Boulder Construction cost $1,000 or $1,200. The *actual cost* of this particular unit then is used in recording the cost of goods sold.

COST FLOW ASSUMPTIONS

If the items in inventory are *homogeneous* in nature (identical, except for insignificant differences), it is *not necessary* for the seller to use the specific identification method. Rather, the seller may follow the more convenient practice of using a *cost flow assumption.* Using a cost flow assumption, often referred to as simply a flow assumption, is particularly common where the company has a large number of identical inventory items that were purchased at different prices.

When a cost flow assumption is in use, the seller makes an *assumption* as to the sequence in which units are withdrawn from inventory. For example, the seller might assume that the oldest merchandise always is sold first or that the most recently purchased items are the first to be sold.

Three cost flow assumptions are in widespread use:

1. *Average cost.* This assumption values all merchandise—units sold and units remaining in inventory—at the *average* per-unit cost. (In effect, the average-cost method assumes that units are withdrawn from the inventory in random order.)

2. *First-in, first-out (FIFO).* As the name implies, FIFO involves the assumption that goods sold are the *first* units that were purchased—that is, the *oldest* goods on hand. Thus the remaining inventory is comprised of the most recent purchases.

3. *Last-in, first-out (LIFO).* Under LIFO, the units sold are assumed to be those *most recently* acquired. The remaining inventory, therefore, is assumed to consist of the earliest purchases.

The cost flow assumption selected by a company *need not* correspond to the actual physical movement of the company's merchandise. When the units of merchandise are identical (or nearly identical), it *does not matter* which units are delivered to the customer in a particular sales transaction. Therefore, in measuring the income of a business that sells units of identical merchandise, accountants consider the flow of *costs* to be more important than the physical flow of the merchandise.

The use of a cost flow assumption *eliminates the need for separately identifying each unit sold and looking up its actual cost.* Experience has shown that these cost flow assumptions provide useful and reliable measurements of the cost of goods sold, as long as they are applied consistently to all sales of the particular type of merchandise.

AVERAGE-COST METHOD

When the **average-cost method** is in use, the *average cost* of all units in inventory is computed after every purchase. This average cost is computed by dividing the total cost of goods available for sale by the number of units in inventory. Because the average cost may change following each purchase, this method also is called the **moving average method** when a perpetual inventory system is used.

As of January 5, Mead had only two Elco generators in its inventory, each acquired at a purchase cost of $1,000. Therefore, the average cost is $1,000 per unit. After the purchase on February 5, Mead had five Elco generators in inventory, acquired at a total cost of $5,600 (2 units @ $1,000, plus 3 units @ $1,200 = $5,600). Therefore, the *average* per-unit cost now is *$1,120* ($5,600 ÷ 5 units = $1,120).

On March 1, two entries are made to record the sale of one of these generators to Boulder Construction Company. The first recognizes the revenue from this sale, and the second recognizes the cost of the goods sold. These entries follow, with the cost of goods sold measured by the average-cost method:

Cash	1,800	
Sales		1,800
To record the sale of one Elco AC-40 generator.		
Cost of Goods Sold	1,120	
Inventory		1,120
To record the cost of one Elco AC-40 generator sold to Boulder		
Construction Co. Cost determined by the average-cost method.		

(The entry to recognize the $1,800 in sales revenue is the same, regardless of the inventory method in use. Therefore, we will not repeat this entry in our illustrations of the other cost flow assumptions.)

When the average-cost method is in use, the inventory subsidiary ledger is modified slightly from the format in Exhibit 8–2. Following the sale on March 1, Mead's subsidiary ledger for Elco generators would be modified to show the average unit cost as in Exhibit 8–3.

	Purchased			Sold			Balance		
Date	Units	Unit Cost	Total	Units	Unit Cost	Cost of Goods Sold	Units	Unit Cost	Total
Jan. 5	2	$1,000	$2,000				2	$1,000*	$2,000
Feb. 5	3	1,200	3,600				5	$1,120**	5,600
Mar. 1				1	$1,120	$1,120	4	$1,120	4,480

EXHIBIT 8–3

Inventory Subsidiary Ledger—Average-Cost Basis

*$2,000 total cost ÷ 2 units = $1,000.
**$5,600 total cost ÷ 5 units = $1,120.

Notice that the Unit Cost column for purchases still shows actual unit costs—$1,000 and $1,200. The Unit Cost columns relating to sales and to the remaining inventory, however, show the *average unit cost* ($5,600 total ÷ 5 units = $1,120).

Under the average-cost assumption, all items in inventory are assigned the *same* per-unit cost (the average cost). Hence, it does not matter which units are sold; the cost of goods sold always is based on the current average unit cost. When one generator is sold on March 1, the cost of goods sold is $1,120; if three generators had been sold on this date, the cost of goods sold would have been $3,360 (3 units × $1,120 per unit).

FIRST-IN, FIRST-OUT METHOD First in goes out first

The **first-in, first-out method**, often called *FIFO,* is based on the assumption that the *first merchandise purchased is the first merchandise sold.* Thus, the accountant for Mead Electric would assume that the generator sold on March 1 was one of those purchased on *January 5.* The entry to record the cost of goods sold would be:

Cost of Goods Sold	1,000	
Inventory		1,000
To record the cost of one Elco AC-40 generator sold to Boulder		
Construction Co. Cost determined by the FIFO flow assumption.		

Following this sale, Mead's inventory ledger would appear as shown in Exhibit 8–4.

EXHIBIT 8–4

Inventory Subsidiary
Ledger—Fifo Basis

	Purchased			Sold			Balance		
Date	Units	Unit Cost	Total	Units	Unit Cost	Cost of Goods Sold	Units	Unit Cost	Total
Jan. 5	2	$1,000	$2,000				2	$1,000	$2,000
Feb. 5	3	1,200	3,600				{2	1,000}	
							{3	1,200}	5,600
Mar. 1				1	$1,000	$1,000	{1	1,000}	
							{3	1,200}	4,600

Notice that FIFO uses actual purchase costs, rather than an average cost. Thus, if merchandise has been purchased at several different costs, the inventory will include several different cost layers. The cost of goods sold for a given sales transaction also may involve several different cost layers. To illustrate, assume that Mead had sold *four* generators to Boulder Construction, instead of only one. Under the FIFO flow assumption, Mead would assume that it first sold the two generators purchased on January 5 and then two of those purchased on February 5. Thus the total cost of goods sold ($4,400) would include items at *two different unit costs,* as shown here:

2 generators from Jan. 5 purchase @ $1,000	$2,000
2 generators from Feb. 5 purchase @ $1,200	$2,400
Total cost of goods sold (4 units)	$4,400

In the FIFO Method, the cost of goods sold always is recorded at the oldest available purchase costs, the units remaining in inventory are valued at the more recent acquisition costs.

LAST-IN, FIRST-OUT METHOD Last in goes out first

The **last-in, first-out method**, commonly known as *LIFO,* is among the most widely used methods of determining the cost of goods sold and valuing inventory. As the name suggests, the *most recently* purchased merchandise (the last in) is assumed to be sold first. If Mead were using the LIFO method, it would assume that the generator sold on March 1 was one of those acquired on *February 5,* the most recent purchase date. Thus, the cost transferred from inventory to the cost of goods sold would be *$1,200.*

The journal entry to record the cost of goods sold is shown below. The inventory subsidiary ledger record after this entry has been posted is shown in Exhibit 8–5.

Cost of Goods Sold	1,200	
Inventory		1,200
To record the cost of one Elco AC-40 generator sold to Boulder		
Construction Co. Cost determined by the LIFO flow assumption.		

	Purchased			Sold			Balance		
Date	Units	Unit Cost	Total	Units	Unit Cost	Cost of Goods Sold	Units	Unit Cost	Total
Jan. 5	2	$1,000	$2,000				2	$1,000	$2,000
Feb. 5	3	1,200	3,600				{2	1,000	
							{3	1,200	5,600
Mar. 1				1	$1,200	$1,200	{2	1,000	
							{2	1,200	4,400

EXHIBIT 8–5

Inventory Subsidiary Ledger—Lifo Basis

Like FIFO, the LIFO method uses actual purchase costs, rather than an average cost. Thus, the inventory may have several different cost layers. If a sale includes more units than are included in the most recent cost layer, some of the goods sold are assumed to come from the next most recent layer. For example, if Mead had sold four generators (instead of one) on March 1, the cost of goods sold determined under the LIFO assumption would be $4,600:

3 generators from Feb. 5 purchase @ $1,200	$3,600
1 generator from Jan. 5 purchase @ $1,000	$1,000
Total cost of goods sold (4 units)	$4,600

Because LIFO transfers the most recent purchase costs to the cost of goods sold, the goods remaining in inventory are valued at the oldest acquisition costs.

EVALUATION OF THE METHODS

All three of the cost flow assumptions just described are acceptable for use in financial statements and in income tax returns. As we have explained, it is not necessary that the physical flow of merchandise correspond to the cost flow assumption. Different flow assumptions may be used for different types of inventory or for inventories in different geographical locations.

The only requirement for using a flow assumption is that the units to which the assumption is applied should be *homogeneous* in nature—that is, virtually identical to one another. If each unit is unique, such as the sale of portraits by an art studio, only the specific identification method can properly match sales revenue with the cost of goods sold.

Each inventory valuation method has certain advantages and shortcomings. In the final analysis, the selection of inventory valuation methods is a managerial decision. However, the method (or methods) used in financial statements always should be disclosed in notes accompanying the statements.

Specific Identification The specific identification method is best suited to inventories of high-priced, low-volume items. This is the only method that exactly parallels the physical flow of the merchandise. If each item in the inventory is unique, as in the case of valuable paintings, custom jewelry, and most real estate, specific identification is clearly the logical choice.

The specific identification method has an intuitive appeal, because it assigns actual purchase costs to the specific units of merchandise sold or in inventory. However, when the units in inventory are identical (or nearly identical), the specific identification method may produce *misleading results* by implying differences in value that—under current market conditions—do not exist. There is also the potential to manipulate the company's financial statement numbers by selecting which items (and as a result which costs) are sold.

As an example, assume that a coal dealer has purchased 100 tons of coal at a cost of $90 per ton. A short time later, the company purchases another 100 tons of the *same grade* of coal— but this time the cost is $120 per ton. The two purchases are in separate piles; thus it would be possible for the company to use the specific identification method in accounting for sales.

Assume now that the company has an opportunity to sell 10 tons of coal at a retail price of $180 per ton. Does it really matter from which pile this coal is removed? The answer is *no;* the coal is a homogeneous product. Under current market conditions, the coal in each pile is equally valuable. To imply that it is more profitable to sell coal from one pile rather than the other is an argument of questionable logic.

Average Cost   Identical items will have the same accounting values only under the average-cost method. Assume, for example, that a hardware store sells a given size nail for 65 cents per pound. The hardware store buys the nails in 100-pound quantities at different times at prices ranging from 40 to 50 cents per pound. Several hundred pounds of nails are always on hand, stored in a large bin. The average-cost method properly recognizes that when a customer buys a pound of nails it is not necessary to know exactly which nails the customer selected from the bin in order to measure the cost of goods sold. Therefore, the average-cost method avoids the shortcomings of the specific identification method. It is not necessary to keep track of the specific items sold and of those still in inventory. Also, it is not possible to manipulate income merely by selecting the specific items to be delivered to customers.

A shortcoming of the average-cost method is that changes in current replacement costs of inventory are concealed because these costs are averaged with older costs. Thus neither the valuation of ending inventory nor the cost of goods sold will quickly reflect changes in the current replacement cost of merchandise.

First-In, First-Out   The distinguishing characteristic of the FIFO method is that the oldest purchase costs are transferred to the cost of goods sold, while the most recent costs remain in inventory.

Over the past 50 years, we have lived in an inflationary economy, which means that most prices rise over time. When purchase costs are rising, the FIFO method assigns *lower* (older) costs to the cost of goods sold and the higher (more recent) costs to the goods remaining in inventory.

By assigning lower costs to the cost of goods sold, FIFO usually causes a business to report *higher profits* than would be reported under the other inventory valuation methods. Some companies favor the FIFO method for financial reporting purposes, because their goal is to report the highest net income possible. For income tax purposes, however, reporting more income than necessary results in paying more income taxes than necessary.

Some accountants and decision makers believe that FIFO tends to *overstate* a company's profitability in periods of rising prices. Revenue is based on current market conditions. By offsetting this revenue with a cost of goods sold based on older (and lower) prices, gross profits may be overstated consistently.

A conceptual advantage of the FIFO method is that in the balance sheet inventory is valued at recent purchase costs. Therefore, this asset appears in the balance sheet at an amount more closely approximating its current replacement cost.

Last-In, First-Out   The LIFO method is one of the most interesting and controversial flow assumptions. The basic assumption in the LIFO method is that the most recently purchased units are sold first and that the older units remain in inventory. This assumption is *not* in accord with the physical flow of merchandise in many businesses. Yet there are strong logical arguments in support of the LIFO method, in addition to income tax considerations.

For the purpose of measuring income, most accountants consider the *flow of costs* more important than the physical flow of merchandise. Supporters of the LIFO method contend that the measurement of income should be based on *current market conditions*. Therefore, current sales revenue should be offset by the *current* cost of the merchandise sold. By the LIFO method, the costs assigned to the cost of goods sold are relatively current because they reflect the most recent purchases.

There is one significant shortcoming to the LIFO method. The valuation of the asset inventory is based on the company's oldest inventory acquisition costs. After the company has been in business for many years, these oldest costs may greatly understate the current replacement cost of the inventory. Thus, when an inventory is valued by the LIFO method, the company also should disclose the current replacement cost of the inventory in a note to the financial statements.

During periods of rising inventory replacement costs, the LIFO method results in the lowest valuation of inventory and measurement of net income. Therefore, LIFO is regarded as the most *conservative* of the inventory pricing methods. FIFO, on the other hand, is the least conservative method.[3]

Income tax considerations are the principal strategic reason for the popularity of the LIFO method. Remember that the LIFO method assigns the most recent inventory purchase costs to the cost of goods sold. In the common situation of rising prices, these most recent costs are also the highest costs. By reporting a higher cost of goods sold than results from other inventory valuation methods, the LIFO method usually results in *lower taxable income*. In short, if inventory costs are rising, a company can reduce the amount of its income tax obligation by using the LIFO method in its income tax return.

It may seem reasonable that a company would use the LIFO method in its tax return to reduce taxable income and use the FIFO method in its financial statements to increase the amount of net income reported to investors and creditors. However, income tax regulations allow a corporation to use LIFO in its income tax return *only* if the company also uses LIFO in its financial statements. This is referred to as the LIFO conformity requirement. Thus, income tax considerations often provide the overriding strategic reason for selecting the LIFO method.

DO INVENTORY METHODS REALLY AFFECT PERFORMANCE?

Except for their effects on income taxes, the answer to this question is *no.*

During a period of rising prices, a company might *report* higher profits by using FIFO instead of LIFO. But the company would not really *be* any more profitable. An inventory valuation method affects only the *allocation of costs* between the Inventory account and the Cost of Goods Sold account. It has *no effect* on the total costs actually *incurred* in purchasing or manufacturing inventory. Except for the amount of income taxes paid, differences in the profitability reported under different inventory methods exist only on paper.

The inventory method in use *does* affect the amount of income taxes owed. To the extent that an inventory method reduces these taxes, it *does* increase profitability. In Exhibit 8–6 we summarize characteristics of the basic inventory valuation methods.

THE PRINCIPLE OF CONSISTENCY

The principle of **consistency** is one of the basic concepts underlying reliable financial statements. This principle means that, once a company has adopted a particular accounting method, it must *follow that method consistently,* rather than switch methods from one year to the next. Thus, once a company has adopted a particular inventory flow assumption (or the specific identification method), it should continue to apply that assumption to all sales of that type of merchandise.

The principle of consistency does *not* prohibit a company from *ever* changing its accounting methods. If a change is made, however, the reasons for the change must be explained, and the effects of the change on the company's net income must be fully disclosed.

JUST-IN-TIME (JIT) INVENTORY SYSTEMS

In recent years, much attention has been paid to the **just-in-time (JIT) inventory system** in manufacturing operations. The phrase "just-in-time" usually means that purchases of raw materials and component parts arrive just in time for use in the manufacturing process—often within a few hours of the time they are scheduled for use. A second application of the just-in-time concept is completing the manufacturing process just in time to ship the finished goods to customers.

---

[3] During a prolonged period of *declining* inventory replacement costs, this situation reverses: FIFO becomes the most conservative method, and LIFO the least conservative.

EXHIBIT 8–6 Summary of Inventory Valuation Methods

	Costs Allocated to:		
Valuation Method	**Cost of Goods Sold**	**Inventory**	**Comments**
Specific identification	Actual costs of the units sold	Actual cost of units remaining	• Parallels physical flow • Logical method when units are unique • May be misleading when the units are identical
Flow assumptions (accep-table only for an inventory of *homogeneous units*):			
Average cost	Number of units sold times the *average unit cost*	Number of units on hand times the *average unit cost*	• Assigns all units the same *average unit cost* • Current costs are aver-aged in with older costs
First-in, first-out (FIFO)	Costs of *earliest purchases* on hand at the time of the sale (first-in, first-out)	Cost of *most recently* purchased units	• Cost of goods sold is based on older costs • Inventory valued at most recent costs • May overstate income during periods of rising prices; may increase income taxes due
Last-in, first-out (LIFO)	Cost of *most recently* purchased units (last-in, first-out)	Costs of *earliest* purchases (assumed *still* to be in inventory)	• Cost of goods sold shown at most recent prices • Inventory shown at old (and perhaps out-of-date) costs • Most conservative method during periods of rising prices; often results in lower income taxes due

Although a just-in-time system reduces the size of a company's inventories, it does not elimi-nate them entirely. The February 1, 2008, balance sheet of **Dell Computer Corporation**, for exam-ple, shows inventories of *almost $1.2 billion* (**Dell** reports its inventories by the FIFO method).

CASE IN POINT

© The McGraw-Hill Companies, Inc./Jill Braaten, photographer

Dell Computer Corporation generates millions in revenue each day by selling computers on the Internet. The company has long been a model of just-in-time manufacturing. **Dell** doesn't start order-ing components or assembling comput-ers until an order has been booked. To have computer components available on a timely basis, many of **Dell**'s suppliers keep components warehoused in close proximity to **Dell**'s factories. The JIT phi-losophy applies to suppliers, assemblers, and distributors. A customer order placed Monday morning can be on a delivery truck by Tuesday evening.

The concept of minimizing inventories applies more to manufacturing operations than to retailers. Ideally, manufacturers have buyers lined up for their merchandise even before the goods are produced. Many retailers, in contrast, want to offer their customers a large selection of in-stock merchandise—which means a big inventory.

The just-in-time concept actually involves much more than minimizing the size of inventories. It has been described as the philosophy of constantly working to increase efficiency throughout the organization. One basic goal of an accounting system is to provide management with useful information about the efficiency—or inefficiency—of operations.

Taking a Physical Inventory

In Chapter 6 we explained the need for businesses to make a complete physical count of the merchandise on hand at least once a year. The primary reason for this procedure of taking inventory is to adjust the perpetual inventory records for unrecorded **shrinkage losses**, such as theft, spoilage, or breakage.

The **physical inventory** usually is taken at (or near) the end of the company's fiscal year.[4] Often a business selects a fiscal year ending after a period of high activity. For example, many large retailers use a fiscal year that starts February 1 and ends January 31.

L08-2

LEARNING OBJECTIVE
Explain the need for taking
a physical inventory.

RECORDING SHRINKAGE LOSSES

In most cases, the year-end physical count of the inventory reveals some shortages or damaged merchandise. The costs of missing or damaged units are removed from the inventory records using the same flow assumption as is used in recording the costs of goods sold.

To illustrate, assume that a company's inventory subsidiary ledger shows the following 158 units of a particular product in inventory at year-end:

L08-3

LEARNING OBJECTIVE
Record shrinkage losses
and other year-end
adjustments to inventory.

8 units purchased Nov. 2 @ $100.	$ 800
150 units purchased Dec. 10 @ $115.	17,250
Total (158 units)	$18,050

A year-end physical count, however, discloses that only *148* of these units actually are on hand. On the basis of this physical count, the company should adjust its inventory records to reflect the loss of 10 units.

The inventory flow assumption in use affects the measurement of shrinkage losses in the same way it affects the cost of goods sold. If the company uses *FIFO,* for example, the missing units are valued at the oldest purchase costs shown in the inventory records. Eight of the missing units are assumed to have cost $100 per unit and the other 2, $115 per unit. Under FIFO, the shrinkage loss amounts to *$1,030* (8 units @ $100 + 2 units @ $115). But if this company uses *LIFO,* the missing units all are assumed to have come from the most recent purchase (on December 10). Therefore, the shrinkage loss amounts to *$1,150* (10 units @ $115).

If shrinkage losses are small, the costs removed from inventory may be charged (debited) directly to the Cost of Goods Sold account. If these losses are *material* in amount, the offsetting debit should be entered in a special loss account, such as Inventory Shrinkage Losses. In the income statement, a loss account is deducted from revenue in the same manner as an expense account.

LCM AND OTHER WRITE-DOWNS OF INVENTORY ✗ not going to use for class purposes or test purposes

In addition to shrinkage losses, the value of inventory may decline because the merchandise has become obsolete or is unable to be sold for other reasons. If inventory has become obsolete or is otherwise unsalable, its carrying amount in the accounting records should be *written down* to zero (or to its "scrap value," if any). A **write-down** of inventory reduces both

---

[4] The reason for taking a physical inventory near year-end is to ensure that any shrinkage losses are reflected in the annual financial statements. The stronger the company's system of internal control over inventories, the farther away this procedure may be moved from the balance sheet date.

the carrying amount of the inventory in the balance sheet and the net income of the current period. The reduction in income is handled in the same manner as a shrinkage loss. If the write-down is relatively small, the loss is changed or debited directly to the Cost of Goods Sold account. If the write-down is *material in amount,* however, it is charged to a special loss account, perhaps entitled Loss from Write-Down of Inventory.

The Lower-of-Cost-or-Market (LCM) Rule An asset is an economic resource. It may be argued that no economic resource is worth more than it would cost to *replace* that resource in the open market. For this reason, accountants traditionally have valued inventory in the balance sheet at the lower of its (1) cost or (2) market value. In this context, "market value" usually means *current replacement cost.* Thus the inventory is valued at the lower of its historical cost or its current replacement cost. This accounting convention is referred to as the **lower-of-cost-or-market (LCM) rule**.

The LCM rule can be used in conjunction with any cost flow assumption. It may also be applied on the basis of individual inventory items, major inventory categories, or the entire inventory. To illustrate, assume that Joel's Ski Shop uses the FIFO cost flow assumption. The store sells various lines of merchandise with costs and market values shown in Exhibit 8–7.

EXHIBIT 8–7

Applying the LCM Rule by Individual Item, by Category, and by Total Inventory

	FIFO Cost	Market Value	LCM Applied on the Basis of . . .		
			Individual Items	Inventory Category	Total Inventory
Ski equipment					
Downhill skis	$16,000	$18,000	$16,000		
Cross-country skis	4,000	3,000	3,000		
Total ski equipment	$20,000	$21,000		$20,000	
Ski accessories					
Ski boots	$ 2,400	$ 1,500	1,500		
Ski jackets	6,600	6,000	6,000		
Total ski accessories	$ 9,000	$ 7,500		7,500	
Total inventory	$29,000	$28,500	$26,500	$27,500	$28,500

Measured at its FIFO cost, the inventory of Joel's Ski Shop is currently recorded at $29,000 in the general ledger. If management applies the LCM rule on the basis of *individual items,* the inventory must be written down to its market value of $26,500. This is accomplished by reducing or crediting the Merchandise Inventory account for $2,500 ($29,000 − $26,500). The offsetting debit is charged to either the Cost of Goods Sold or to the Loss from Write-Down of Inventory account, depending on the materiality of the dollar amount.

If management applies the LCM rule on the basis of *inventory category,* it would write down the $29,000 FIFO cost by $1,500 ($29,000 − $27,500). Likewise, if the LCM rule is applied on the basis of *total inventory,* a write-down of only $500 is required ($29,000 − $28,500).

In their financial statements, most companies state that inventory is valued at the lower-of-cost-or-market. In an inflationary economy, however, the lower of these two amounts is usually cost, especially for companies using LIFO.[5]

THE YEAR-END CUTOFF OF TRANSACTIONS

Making a proper *cutoff* of transactions is an essential step in the preparation of reliable financial statements. A proper cutoff simply means that the transactions occurring near year-end are *recorded in the correct accounting period.*

---

[5] A notable exception is the petroleum industry, in which the replacement cost of inventory can fluctuate very quickly and in either direction. Large oil companies occasionally report LCM adjustments of several hundred million dollars in a single year.

One aspect of a proper cutoff is determining that all purchases of merchandise through the end of the period are recorded in the inventory records and included in the physical count of merchandise on hand at year-end. Of equal importance is determining that the cost of all merchandise sold through the end of the period has been removed from the inventory accounts and charged to the Cost of Goods Sold. This merchandise should *not* be included in the year-end physical count.

If some sales transactions have not been recorded as of year-end, the quantities of merchandise shown in the inventory records will exceed the quantities actually on hand. When the results of the physical count are compared with the inventory records, these unrecorded sales easily could be mistaken for inventory shortages.

Making a proper cutoff may be difficult if sales transactions are occurring while the merchandise is being counted. For this reason, many businesses count their physical inventory during nonbusiness hours, even if they must shut down their sales operations for a day.

Matching Revenue and the Cost of Goods Sold   Accountants must determine that both the sales revenue and the cost of goods sold relating to sales transactions occurring near year-end are recorded in the *same* accounting period. Otherwise, the revenues and expenses from these transactions will not be properly matched in the company's income statements.

Goods in Transit   A sale should be recorded *when title to the merchandise passes to the buyer.* In making a year-end cutoff of transactions, questions may arise when goods are in transit between the seller and the buyer as to which company owns the merchandise. The answer to such questions lies in the terms of shipment. If these terms are **F.O.B.** (free on board) **shipping point**, title passes at the point of shipment and the goods are the property of the buyer while in transit. If the terms of the shipment are **F.O.B. destination**, title does not pass until the shipment reaches its destination and the goods belong to the seller while in transit.

Many companies ignore these distinctions, because goods in transit usually arrive within a day or two. In such cases, the amount of merchandise in transit usually is *not material* in dollar amount, and the company may follow the *most convenient* accounting procedures. It usually is most convenient to record all purchases when the inbound shipments arrive and all sales when the merchandise is shipped to the customer.

In some industries, however, goods in transit may be very material. Oil companies, for example, often have millions of dollars of inventory in transit in pipelines and supertankers. In these situations, the company must consider the terms of each shipment in recording its purchases and sales.

 YOUR TURN   You as a Sales Manager

As sales manager for Tempto Co., a producer of fine home furnishings, you have responsibility for the northeast region of the country. Assume you have just returned from the company's annual sales managers' conference in New Orleans. At the conference, in casual conversation with some of the regional managers, you became aware that several managers report sales that are scheduled for shipment in early January as if they were shipped in late December. What should you do?

(See our comments on the Online Learning Center website.)

L08-4

PERIODIC INVENTORY SYSTEMS

In our preceding discussions, we have emphasized the perpetual inventory system—that is, inventory records that are kept continuously up-to-date. With the extensive use of technology, today most large business organizations use perpetual inventory systems.

Some small businesses, however, use *periodic* inventory systems. In a periodic inventory system, the cost of merchandise purchased during the year is debited to a *Purchases* account,

LEARNING OBJECTIVE
In a periodic inventory system, determine the ending inventory and the cost of goods sold using (a) specific identification, (b) average cost, (c) FIFO, and (d) LIFO.

rather than to the Inventory account. When merchandise is sold to a customer, an entry is made recognizing the sales revenue, but no entry is made to reduce the inventory account or to recognize the cost of goods sold.

The inventory on hand and the cost of goods sold for the year are not determined until year-end. At the end of the year, all goods on hand are counted and priced at cost. The cost assigned to this ending inventory is then used to compute the cost of goods sold. (The dollar amounts are assumed for the purpose of completing this illustration.)

Inventory at the beginning of the year	$10,000
Add: Purchases during the year.	80,000
Cost of goods available for sale during the year	$90,000
Less: Inventory based on year-end count	7,000
Cost of goods sold.	$83,000

The only item in this computation that is kept continuously up-to-date in the accounting records is the Purchases account. The amounts of inventory at the beginning and end of the year are determined by annual physical observation.

Determining the cost of the year-end inventory involves two distinct steps: counting the merchandise and pricing the inventory—that is, determining the cost of the units on hand. Together, these procedures determine the proper valuation of inventory and the cost of goods sold.

Applying Flow Assumptions in a Periodic System
In our discussion of perpetual inventory systems, we have emphasized the costs that are transferred from inventory *to the cost of goods sold* as the sales occur. In a periodic system, the emphasis shifts to determining the costs that should be assigned *to inventory* at the end of the period.

To illustrate, assume that The Kitchen Counter, a retail store, uses a periodic inventory system. The year-end physical inventory indicates that 12 units of a particular model food processor are on hand. Purchases of these food processors during the year are listed in Exhibit 8–8.

EXHIBIT 8–8

Summary of Inventory Purchases

	Number of Units	Cost per Unit	Total Cost
Beginning inventory	10	$ 80	$ 800
First purchase (Mar. 1)	5	90	450
Second purchase (July 1).	5	100	500
Third purchase (Oct. 1).	5	120	600
Fourth purchase (Dec. 1)	5	130	650
Available for sale.	30		$3,000
Units in ending inventory	12		
Units sold	18		

In Exhibit 8–8, note that of the 30 food processors available for sale in the course of the year, 12 are still on hand. Thus, 18 of these food processors apparently were sold.[6] We will now use these data to determine the cost of the year-end inventory and the cost of goods sold using the specific identification method and the average-cost, FIFO, and LIFO flow assumptions.

Specific Identification
If specific identification is used, the company must identify the 12 food processors on hand at year-end and determine their actual costs from purchase invoices. Assume that these 12 units have an actual total cost of $1,240. The cost of goods

---

[6] The periodic inventory method does not distinguish between merchandise sold and shrinkage losses. Shrinkage losses are included automatically in the cost of goods sold.

sold then is determined by subtracting this ending inventory from the cost of goods available for sale as shown below:

Cost of goods available for sale.	$3,000
Less: Ending inventory (specific identification)	1,240
Cost of goods sold.	$1,760

Average Cost   The average cost is determined by dividing the total cost of goods available for sale during the year by the total number of units available for sale. Thus the average per-unit cost is *$100* ($3,000 ÷ 30 units). Under the average-cost method, the ending inventory would be priced at $1,200 (12 units × $100 per unit), and the cost of goods sold would be *$1,800* ($3,000 cost of goods available for sale, less $1,200 in costs assigned to the ending inventory).

FIFO   Under the FIFO flow assumption, the oldest units are assumed to be the first sold. The ending inventory, therefore, is assumed to consist of the *most recently* acquired goods. (Remember, we are now talking about the goods *remaining in inventory,* not the goods sold.) Thus the inventory of 12 food processors would be valued at the following costs:
The cost of goods sold would be *$1,550* ($3,000 − $1,450).

5 units from the Dec. 1 purchase @ $130	$ 650
5 units from the Oct. 1 purchase @ $120.	600
2 units from the July 1 purchase @ $100.	200
Ending inventory, 12 units at FIFO cost.	$1,450

Notice that the FIFO method results in an inventory valued at relatively recent purchase costs. The cost of goods sold, however, is based on the older acquisition costs.

LIFO   Under LIFO, the last units purchased are considered to be the first goods sold. Therefore, the ending inventory is assumed to contain the *earliest* purchases. The 12 food processors in inventory would be valued as:
The cost of goods sold under the LIFO method is *$2,020* ($3,000 − $980).

Only China + Russica uses this.

10 units from the beginning inventory @ $80.	$800
2 units from the Mar. 1 purchase @ $90.	180
Ending inventory, 12 units at LIFO cost.	$980

Notice that the cost of goods sold under LIFO is *higher* than that determined by the FIFO method ($2,020 under LIFO, as compared with $1,550 under FIFO). LIFO always results in a higher cost of goods sold when purchase costs are rising. Thus LIFO tends to minimize reported net income and income taxes during periods of rising prices in both perpetual and periodic systems.

Notice also that the LIFO method may result in an ending inventory that is priced *well below* its current replacement cost. In this illustration, ending inventory is determined at $80 and $90 per unit, but the most recent purchase price is $130 per unit.

INTERNATIONAL CASE IN POINT

Although FIFO techniques are allowed for financial reporting in nearly all countries, LIFO is more controversial in international settings. International accounting standards prohibit LIFO because it leads to outdated inventory numbers in the balance sheet. Thus, to make inventory amounts between U.S. companies using LIFO and non–U.S. companies using FIFO (or weighted-average methods) comparable, a financial analyst must revalue inventory numbers.

Receiving the Maximum Tax Benefit from the LIFO Method   Many companies that use LIFO in a perpetual inventory system *restate* their year-end inventory at the costs indicated by the *periodic* LIFO costing procedures illustrated above. This restatement is accomplished by either debiting or crediting the Inventory account and making an offsetting entry to the Cost of Goods Sold account.

Often, restating ending inventory using periodic costing procedures results in older (and lower) unit costs than those shown in the perpetual inventory records. When less cost is assigned to the ending inventory, it follows that more of these costs will be assigned to the cost of goods sold. A higher cost of goods sold, in turn, means lower taxable income.

Why would applying LIFO on a periodic basis at year-end result in a lower valuation of inventory than does applying LIFO on a perpetual basis? Consider the last purchase in our example. This purchase of five food processors was made on December 1, at the relatively high unit cost of $130. Assuming that no additional units were sold in December, they would be included in the year-end inventory in perpetual inventory records, even if these records were maintained on a LIFO basis. When the ending inventory is priced using "periodic LIFO," however, a last-minute purchase is *not* included in inventory, but rather is transferred to the income statement as part of cost of goods sold.

Both the LIFO and average-cost methods produce different valuations of inventory under perpetual and periodic costing procedures. Only companies using LIFO, however, usually adjust their perpetual records to indicate the unit costs determined by periodic costing procedures. When FIFO is in use, the perpetual and periodic costing procedures result in the same valuation of inventory.

Pricing the Year-End Inventory by Computer   If purchase records are maintained by computer, as is now the case for most companies, the value of the ending inventory can be computed automatically using any of the flow assumptions that have been discussed. Only the number of units must be entered at year-end. A computer also can apply the specific identification method, but the system requires an identification number for each unit in the ending inventory. This is one reason why the specific identification method usually is not used for inventories consisting of a large number of low-cost items.

INTERNATIONAL FINANCIAL REPORTING STANDARDS

To introduce this chapter we covered the importance of establishing the cost of inventory and the movement of that cost to the income statement as cost of goods sold. The general principles upon which this important feature of financial reporting are based are essentially the same in U.S. generally accepted accounting principles and in international financial reporting standards. There are differences, however, in how those principles are applied.

One major difference is that international standards do not recognize the LIFO method of accounting for the cost of inventory. Only the first-in, first-out (FIFO) or weighted average cost methods are acceptable under international standards. This is a major difference because of the widespread use of LIFO in the United States due to its income tax benefits. Remember that the conformity requirement in U.S. tax law requires a company that uses LIFO for tax purposes to also use that method in its financial statements.

An effort is currently under way to bring U.S. generally accepted accounting principles and international financial reporting standards closer together. This effort is often referred to as "convergence" of the two. The facts that international standards do not permit the use of LIFO and LIFO is the most popular inventory method for companies reporting under U.S. generally accepted accounting principles are difficult to reconcile. In the authors' opinion, either to change U.S. standards to preclude the use of LIFO or to include LIFO as an acceptable method in international standards is unlikely. The most logical approach appears to be to eliminate the conformity requirement, thereby allowing companies accounting by U.S. standards to use LIFO in their income tax filings, but not require that LIFO be used in its financial statements. LIFO would, in effect, become a tax method that is not used in a company's financial statements. The current conformity requirement has been in place for many years and any change in it would require a significant change in the U.S. tax law. The political process that would be required for such a change is unlikely to happen quickly, but may eventually be the outcome as we seek conformity between U.S. and *International Financial Reporting Standards.*

There are other areas where accounting for inventories differs between U.S. and international standards. One of those is accounting for the lower-of-cost-or-market. Under U.S. generally accepted accounting standards, once an inventory is written down to a lower market value, recovery of that value before the inventory is sold is not permitted. Under international standards, however, the subsequent recovery of market value is treated as a reduction in cost of goods sold in the period of the recovery.

IMPORTANCE OF AN ACCURATE VALUATION OF INVENTORY

The most important liquid assets in the balance sheets of most companies are cash, accounts receivable, and inventory. Of these assets, inventory often is the largest. It also is the only one of these assets for which alternative valuation methods are acceptable.

Because of the relatively large size of inventory, and because many different products may be stored in different locations, an error in inventory valuation may not be readily apparent. Even a small error in the valuation of inventory may have a material effect on net income. Therefore, care must be taken in counting and pricing the inventory at year-end.

An error in the valuation of inventory will affect several balance sheet measurements, including assets and total owners' equity. It also will affect key figures in the *income statement,* including the cost of goods sold, gross profit, and net income. And remember that the ending inventory of one year is the beginning inventory of the next. Thus an error in inventory valuation will *carry over* into the financial statements of the following year.

Effects of an Error in Valuing Ending Inventory

To illustrate, assume that some items of merchandise in a company's inventory are overlooked during the year-end physical count. As a result of this error, the ending inventory is *understated.* The costs of the uncounted merchandise erroneously are transferred out of the Inventory account and included in the cost of goods sold. This overstatement of the cost of goods sold, in turn, results in an understatement of gross profit and net income.[7]

Inventory Errors Affect Two Years

An error in the valuation of ending inventory affects not only the financial statements of the current year but also the income statement for the *following* year.

Assume that the ending inventory in 2015 is *understated* by $10,000. As we have described above, the cost of goods sold in 2015 is overstated by this amount, and both gross profit and net income are *understated.*

The ending inventory in 2015, however, becomes the *beginning inventory* in 2016. An understatement of the beginning inventory results in an understatement of the cost of goods sold and, therefore, an *overstatement* of gross profit and net income in 2016.

Notice that the original error has exactly the *opposite effects* on the net incomes of the two successive years. Net income was *understated* by the amount of the error in 2015 and *overstated* by the same amount in 2016. For this reason, inventory errors are said to be "counterbalancing" or "self-correcting" over a two-year period.

The fact that offsetting errors occur in the financial statements of two successive years does not lessen the consequences of errors in inventory valuation. Rather, it *exaggerates* the misleading effects of the error on *trends* in the company's performance from one year to the next.

Effects of Errors in Inventory Valuation: A Summary

In Exhibit 8–9 we summarize the effects of an error in the valuation of ending inventory over two successive years. In this exhibit we indicate the effects of the error on various financial statement measurements using the code letters **U** (understated), **O** (overstated), and **NE** (no effect). The effects of errors in the valuation of inventory are the same regardless of whether the company uses a perpetual or a periodic inventory system. The **NE** for owners' equity at year-end in the Following Year column results from the offsetting of the first-year error in the second year.

L08-5

LEARNING OBJECTIVE
Explain the effects on the income statement of errors in inventory valuation.

---

[7] If income tax effects are ignored, the amount of the error is exactly the same in inventory, gross profit, and net income. If tax effects are considered, the amount of the error may be lessened in the net income figure.

EXHIBIT 8–9

Effects of Inventory Errors

Original Error: Ending Inventory Understated	Year of the Error	Following Year
Beginning inventory	NE	U
Cost of goods available for sale.	NE	U
Ending inventory.	U	NE
Cost of goods sold.	O	U
Gross profit.	U	O
Net income.	U	O
Owners' equity at year-end	U	NE

Original Error: Ending Inventory Overstated	Year of the Error	Following Year
Beginning inventory	NE	O
Cost of goods available for sale.	NE	O
Ending inventory.	O	NE
Cost of goods sold.	U	O
Gross profit.	O	U
Net income.	O	U
Owners' equity at year-end	O	NE

TECHNIQUES FOR ESTIMATING THE COST OF GOODS SOLD AND THE ENDING INVENTORY

Taking a physical inventory several times during a year would be expensive and time-consuming. Therefore, if a business using a periodic inventory system prepares monthly or quarterly financial statements, it may *estimate* the amounts of its inventory and cost of goods sold except at the end of its annual period. One approach to making these estimates is called the gross profit method; another—used primarily by retail stores—is the retail method.

THE GROSS PROFIT METHOD

LO8-6

LEARNING OBJECTIVE
Estimate the cost of goods sold and ending inventory by the gross profit method and by the retail method.

The **gross profit method** is a quick and simple technique for estimating the cost of goods sold and the amount of inventory on hand. Using this method assumes that the rate of gross profit earned in the preceding year (or several years) will remain the same for the current year. When we know the rate of gross profit, we can divide the dollar amount of net sales into two elements: (1) the gross profit and (2) the cost of goods sold. We view net sales as 100 percent. If the gross profit rate, for example, is 40 percent of net sales, the cost of goods sold must be 60 percent. The cost of goods sold percentage (or **cost ratio**) is determined by deducting the gross profit rate from 100 percent.

When the gross profit rate is known, the ending inventory can be estimated by the following procedures:

1. Determine the *cost of goods available for sale* from the general ledger records of beginning inventory and net purchases.
2. Estimate the *cost of goods sold* by multiplying the net sales by the cost ratio.
3. Deduct the estimated *cost of goods sold* from the *cost of goods available for sale* to find the estimated ending inventory.

To illustrate, assume that Metro Hardware has a beginning inventory of $50,000 on January 1. During the month of January, net purchases amount to $20,000 and net sales total $30,000. Assume that the company's normal gross profit rate is 40 percent of net sales; it follows that the cost ratio is *60 percent*. Using these facts, the inventory on January 31 may be estimated as indicated at the top of the following page.

The gross profit method of estimating inventory has several uses apart from the preparation of interim financial statements. For example, if an inventory is destroyed by fire, the company must estimate the amount of the inventory on hand at the date of the fire to file an insurance claim. A convenient way to determine this inventory amount may be the gross profit method.

The gross profit method is also used at year-end after the taking of a physical inventory to confirm the overall reasonableness of the amount determined by the counting and pricing

Goods available for sale:		
Beginning inventory, Jan. 1		$50,000
Purchases		20,000
Cost of goods available for sale		$70,000
Deduct: Estimated cost of goods sold:		
Net sales	$30,000	
Cost ratio (100% − 40%)	60%	
Estimated cost of goods sold ($30,000 × 60%)		18,000
Estimated ending inventory, Jan. 31		$52,000

When gross profit rate is known:

Step 1 Determine cost of goods available for sale (COGAS);

Step 2 Estimate the cost of goods sold (COGS) (multiply net sales by cost ratio); and

Step 3 Deduct estimated COGS from the COGAS to find estimated ending inventory.

process. The gross profit method is not, however, a satisfactory substitute for periodically taking an actual physical inventory.

THE RETAIL METHOD

The **retail method** of estimating inventory and the cost of goods sold is similar to the gross profit method. The basic difference is that the retail method requires that management determine the value of ending inventory at *retail* prices. The retail value of ending inventory is then converted to its approximate cost using a cost ratio.

To determine the cost ratio, a business must keep track of goods available for sale at both cost and at retail prices. To illustrate, assume that Ski Valley has merchandise available for sale costing $450,000 for the year, and that management offers this merchandise for sale to customers at *retail* prices totaling $1,000,000. Thus Ski Valley's cost ratio for the year is 45 percent ($450,000 ÷ $1,000,000). Ski Valley can use this ratio to convert the retail value of its ending merchandise inventory to its estimated *cost*.

Assume that Ski Valley's employees determine that inventory on hand at the end of the year has a total *retail* value of $300,000. This amount is converted to *cost* using the 45 percent cost ratio as follows:

a	Goods available for sale at *cost*	$ 450,000
b	Goods available for sale at *retail*	1,000,000
c	Cost ratio [**a** ÷ **b**]	45%
d	Physical count of ending inventory priced at *retail*	300,000
e	Estimated ending inventory at cost [**c** × **d**]	$ 135,000

This application of the retail method approximates a valuation of ending inventory at its average cost. A widely used variation of this method enables management to estimate a LIFO valuation of ending inventory.

"TEXTBOOK" INVENTORY SYSTEMS CAN BE MODIFIED . . . AND THEY OFTEN ARE

In this chapter we have described the basic characteristics of the most common inventory systems. In practice, businesses often modify these systems to suit their particular needs. Some businesses also use *different inventory systems for different purposes.*

We described one modification in Chapter 6—a company that maintains only a small inventory may simply charge (debit) all purchases directly to the cost of goods sold. Another common modification is to maintain perpetual inventory records showing only the *quantities* of merchandise bought and sold, with no dollar amounts. Such systems require less record keeping than a full-blown perpetual system, and they still provide management with useful information about sales and inventories. To generate the dollar amounts needed in financial statements and tax returns, these companies might use the gross profit method, the retail method, or a periodic inventory system.

Businesses such as restaurants often update their inventory records by physically counting products on a daily or weekly basis. In effect, they use frequent periodic counts as the basis for maintaining a perpetual inventory system.

In summary, real-world inventory systems often differ from the illustrations in a textbook. But the underlying principles remain the same.

FINANCIAL ANALYSIS and Decision Making

Inventory often is the largest of a company's current assets. But how liquid is this asset? How quickly will it be converted into cash? As a step toward answering these questions, short-term creditors often compute the **inventory turnover.**

INVENTORY TURNOVER

The inventory turnover is equal to the cost of goods sold divided by the average amount of inventory (beginning inventory plus ending inventory, divided by 2). This ratio indicates how many *times* in the course of a year the company is able to sell the amount of its average inventory.

L08-7

LEARNING OBJECTIVE
Compute the inventory turnover and explain its uses.

© AP Photo/The Canadian Press, Dave Chidley

The higher this rate, the more quickly the company sells its inventory.

To illustrate, a recent annual report of Target shows a cost of goods sold of $50,568 million and average inventory of $7,911 million. The inventory turnover rate for Target, therefore, is 6.39 ($50,568 million ÷ $7,911 million). We

may compute the number of *days* required for the company to sell its inventory by dividing 365 days by the turnover rate. Thus Target requires *57 days* to turn over (sell) the amount of its average inventory. The computation of Target's inventory turnover and the average number of days required to sell its inventory is summarized as follows:

Inventory Turnover

$$\frac{\text{Cost of Goods Sold}}{\text{Average Inventory*}} = \frac{\$50,568}{\$7,911} = \underline{6.39 \text{ times}}$$

Average Number of Days to Sell Inventory

$$\frac{\text{Days in the Year}}{\text{Inventory Turnover}} = \frac{365 \text{ days}}{6.39 \text{ times}} = \underline{57 \text{ days}}$$

*Average Inventory = (Beginning Inventory + Ending Inventory) + 2

Users of financial statements find the inventory turnover useful in evaluating the liquidity of the company's inventory. Managers and independent auditors may use this computation to help identify inventory that is not selling well and that may have become obsolete. A declining turnover indicates that merchandise is not selling as quickly as in the past. Comparing a company's inventory turnover with that of competitors is particularly useful in evaluating how effective a company is at managing its inventory, often one of its largest assets.

RECEIVABLES TURNOVER

Many businesses sell merchandise on account. Therefore, the sale of inventory often does not provide an immediate source of cash. To determine how quickly inventory is converted into cash, the number of days required to *sell the inventory* must be combined with the number of days required to *collect the accounts receivable that result from the sale.*

The number of days required to collect accounts receivable depends on a company's *accounts receivable turnover.* This figure is computed by dividing net sales by the average

YOUR TURN   You as a Credit Analyst

Assume that you are employed by GE Capital as a credit analyst, and that Target is seeking to borrow money using its merchandise inventory as collateral. You have determined that the company's inventory turnover is 3.46 times, and that the average time to sell its inventory is 100 days (see previous computations). Assume that Target's inventory reported at *cost* is currently $3.2 billion, and that its gross profit as a percentage of sales is approximately 37 percent. Estimate the *market value* of the company's inventory for use as collateral.

(See our comments on the Online Learning Center website.)

accounts receivable. The number of days required to collect these receivables then is determined by dividing 365 days by the turnover rate. Data for the Target annual report indicate that the company needed approximately *12 days* (on average) for credit card receivables to convert to cash.

Length of the Operating Cycle The *operating cycle* of a merchandising company is the average time period between the purchase of merchandise and the conversion of this merchandise back into cash. In other words, the merchandise acquired as inventory gradually is converted into accounts receivable by sale of the goods on account, and these receivables are later converted into cash through the process of collection.

The operating cycle of Target was approximately *69 days,* computed by adding the average *57 days* required to sell its inventory and the *12 days* required to collect cash from customers. From the viewpoint of short-term creditors, the shorter the operating cycle, the higher the quality of the company's liquid assets because they will be converted into cash more quickly.

In calculating the inventory turnover and the receivables turnover, we used the average inventory and average receivables for the year. If these amounts do not vary greatly during the year, using the year-end amounts may be an acceptable alternative.

Ethics, Fraud, & Corporate Governance

As discussed previously in this chapter, the valuation of inventory and the cost of goods sold is of critical importance to managers and to users of the company's financial statements. The two primary issues with regard to inventory valuation are existence and valuation.

In a well-known case of inventory fraud, the Securities and Exchange Commission (SEC) brought an enforcement action against an officer of MiniScribe Corporation related to his involvement in overstating inventory reported in the company's balance sheet. The overstatement of inventory resulted in an understatement of cost of goods sold and an overstatement of profits reported in the company's income statement (MiniScribe's net income was actually inflated by $22 million, or *244 percent*).

Prior to being acquired by Maxtor Corporation, Mini-Scribe manufactured computer disk drives and its stock was quoted on NASDAQ. The company had discovered a material shortfall in its inventory balance. Reporting this shortfall would have increased the cost of goods sold and reduced the company's net income significantly. So MiniScribe concealed the shortfall from its independent auditors by taking a number of actions to inappropriately overstate its actual inventory balance. First, it recorded a fictitious transfer of nonexistent inventory from its headquarters to an overseas subsidiary. Second, it repackaged scrap items and obsolete inventory as if they were "good" inventory items. Third, it packed *bricks* into computer disk drive boxes and shipped them to its distributors (these shipments were still counted as inventory by MiniScribe until the distributors sold the boxes).

Concluding Remarks

Throughout this chapter we have learned about different inventory valuation methods. Each method is based upon a particular assumption about cost flows and does not necessarily parallel the physical movement of merchandise. Moreover, the choice of valuation by management can have significant effects on a company's income statement, balance sheet, and tax returns.

In the following chapter, we will see that a similar situation exists with respect to alternative methods used to account for plant and equipment.

END-OF-CHAPTER REVIEW

SUMMARY OF LEARNING OBJECTIVES

LO8-1 **In a perpetual inventory system, determine the cost of goods sold using (a) specific identification, (b) average cost, (c) FIFO, and (d) LIFO.** Discuss the advantages and shortcomings of each method. By the *specific identification method,* the actual costs of the specific units sold are transferred from inventory to the cost of goods sold. (Debit Cost of Goods Sold: credit Inventory.) This method achieves the proper matching of sales revenue and cost of goods sold when the individual units in the inventory are unique. However, the method becomes cumbersome and may produce misleading results if the inventory consists of homogeneous items.

The remaining three methods are flow assumptions, which should be applied only to an inventory of homogeneous items.

By the *average-cost method,* the average cost of all units in the inventory is computed and used in recording the cost of goods sold. This is the only method in which all units are assigned the same (average) per-unit cost.

FIFO (first-in, first-out) is based on the assumption that the first units purchased are the first units sold. Thus, inventory is assumed to consist of the most recently purchased units. FIFO assigns current costs to inventory but older (and often lower) costs to the cost of goods sold.

LIFO (last-in, first-out) is based on the assumption that the most recently acquired goods are sold first. This method matches sales revenue with relatively current costs. In a period of inflation, LIFO usually results in lower reported profits and lower income taxes than the other methods. However, the oldest purchase costs are assigned to inventory, which may result in inventory becoming grossly understated in the statement of financial position in terms of current replacement costs.

LO8-2 **Explain the need for taking a physical inventory.** In a perpetual inventory system, a physical inventory is taken to adjust the inventory records for shrinkage losses. In a periodic inventory system, the physical inventory is the basis for determining the cost of the ending inventory and for computing the cost of goods sold.

LO8-3 **Record shrinkage losses and other year-end adjustments to inventory.** Shrinkage losses are recorded by removing from the Inventory account the cost of the missing or damaged units. The offsetting debit may be to Cost of Goods Sold, if the shrinkage is normal in amount, or to a special loss account. If inventory is found to be obsolete and unlikely to be sold, it is written down to zero (or its scrap value, if any). If inventory is valued at the lower-of-cost-or-market, it is written down to its current replacement cost, if at year-end this amount is substantially below the cost shown in the inventory records.

LO8-4 **In a periodic inventory system, determine the ending inventory and the cost of goods sold using (a) specific identification, (b) average cost, (c) FIFO, and (d) LIFO.** The cost of goods sold is determined by combining the beginning inventory with the purchases during the period and subtracting the cost of the ending inventory. Thus, the cost assigned to ending inventory also determines the cost of goods sold.

By the specific identification method, the ending inventory is determined by the specific costs associated with the units on hand. By the average-cost method, the ending inventory is determined by multiplying the number of units on hand by the average cost of the units available for sale during the year. By FIFO, the units in inventory are priced using the unit costs from the most recent cost layers. By the LIFO method, inventory is priced using the unit costs in the oldest cost layers.

LO8-5 **Explain the effects on the income statement of errors in inventory valuation.** In the current year, an error in the costs assigned to ending inventory will cause an opposite error in the cost of goods sold and, therefore, a repetition of the original error in the amount of gross profit. For example, understating ending inventory results in an overstatement of the cost of goods sold and an understatement of gross profit.

The error has the opposite effect on the cost of goods sold and the gross profit of the following year, because the error is now in the cost assigned to *beginning* inventory.

LO8-6 **Estimate the cost of goods sold and ending inventory by the gross profit method and by the retail method.** Both the gross profit and retail methods use a cost ratio to estimate the cost of goods sold and ending inventory. The cost of goods sold is estimated by multiplying net sales by this cost ratio; ending inventory then is estimated by subtracting this cost of goods sold from the cost of goods available for sale.

In the gross profit method, the cost ratio is 100 percent minus the company's historical gross profit rate. In the retail method, the cost ratio is the percentage of cost to the retail prices of merchandise available for sale.

LO8-7 **Compute inventory turnover and explain its uses.** A company's inventory turnover rate is equal to the cost of goods sold divided by the average inventory. Users of financial statements find the inventory turnover rate useful in evaluating the liquidity of the company's inventory. In addition, managers and independent auditors use this computation to help identify inventory that is not selling well and that may have become obsolete.

Key Terms Introduced or Emphasized in Chapter 8

average-cost method (p. 344)   A method of valuing all units in inventory at the same average per-unit cost, which is recomputed after every purchase.

consistency (in inventory valuation) (p. 349)   An accounting principle that calls for the use of the same method of inventory pricing from year to year, with full disclosure of the effects of any change in method. Intended to make financial statements comparable.

cost flow assumption (p. 343)   Assumption as to the sequence in which units are removed from inventory for the purpose of sale. Is not required to parallel the physical movement of merchandise if the units are homogeneous.

cost layer (p. 343)   Units of merchandise acquired at the same unit cost. An inventory comprised of several cost layers is characteristic of all inventory valuation methods except *average cost.*

cost ratio (p. 358)   The cost of merchandise expressed as a percentage of its retail selling price. Used in inventory estimating techniques, such as the gross profit method and the retail method.

first-in, first-out (FIFO) method (p. 345)   A method of computing the cost of inventory and the cost of goods sold based on the assumption that the first merchandise acquired is the first merchandise sold and that the ending inventory consists of the most recently acquired goods.

F.O.B. destination (p. 353)   A term meaning the seller bears the cost of shipping goods to the buyer's location. Title to the goods remains with the seller while the goods are in transit.

F.O.B. shipping point (p. 353)   The buyer of goods bears the cost of transportation from the seller's location to the buyer's location. Title to the goods passes at the point of shipment, and the goods are the property of the buyer while in transit.

gross profit method (p. 358)   A method of estimating the cost of the ending inventory based on the assumption that the rate of gross profit remains approximately the same from year to year. Used for interim valuations and for estimating losses.

inventory turnover (p. 360)   The cost of goods sold divided by the average amount of inventory. Indicates how many times the average inventory is sold during the course of the year.

just-in-time (JIT) inventory system (p. 349)   A technique designed to minimize a company's investment in inventory. In a manufacturing company, this means receiving purchases of raw materials just in time for use in the manufacturing process and completing the manufacture of finished goods just in time to fill sales orders. Just-in-time also may be described as the philosophy of constantly striving to become more efficient by purchasing and storing less inventory.

last-in, first-out (LIFO) method (p. 346)   A method of computing the cost of goods sold by using the prices paid for the most recently acquired units. Ending inventory is valued on the basis of prices paid for the units first acquired.

lower-of-cost-or-market (LCM) rule (p. 352)   A method of inventory pricing in which goods are valued at the lower of original cost or replacement cost (market).

moving average method (p. 344)   A method of valuing all units of inventory at the same average per-unit cost, recalculating this cost after each purchase. This method is used in a perpetual inventory system.

physical inventory (p. 351)   A systematic count of all goods on hand, followed by the application of unit prices to the quantities counted and development of a dollar valuation of the ending inventory.

retail method (p. 359)   A method of estimating the cost of goods sold and ending inventory. Similar to the gross profit method, except that the cost ratio is based on the current cost-to-retail price relationships rather than on those of the prior year.

shrinkage losses (p. 351)   Losses of inventory resulting from theft, spoilage, or breakage.

specific identification (p. 343)   Recording as the cost of goods sold the actual costs of the specific units sold. Necessary if each unit in inventory is unique, but not if the inventory consists of homogeneous products.

write-down (of an asset) (p. 351)   A reduction in the carrying amount of an asset because it has become obsolete or its usefulness has otherwise been impaired. Involves a credit to the appropriate asset account, with an offsetting debit to a loss account.

Demonstration Problem

Audio World sells high-performance stereo equipment. Simmons Acoustic recently introduced the Carnegie-440, a state-of-the-art speaker system. During the current year, Audio World purchased nine of these speaker systems from Simmons Acoustic at the following dates and acquisition costs:

Date	Units Purchased	Unit Cost	Total Cost
Oct. 1	2	$3,000	$ 6,000
Nov. 17	3	3,200	9,600
Dec. 1	4	3,250	13,000
Available for sale during the year	9		$28,600

On *November 21,* Audio World sold four of these speaker systems to the Denver Symphony. The other five Carnegie-440s remained in Audio World's inventory at December 31.

Instructions

Assume that Audio World uses a *perpetual inventory system.* Compute (1) the cost of goods sold relating to the sale of Carnegie-440 speakers to the Denver Symphony and (2) the ending inventory of these speakers at December 31, using each of the following flow assumptions:

a. Average cost.

b. First-in, first-out (FIFO).

c. Last-in, first-out (LIFO).

Show the number of units and the unit costs of the cost layers comprising the cost of goods sold and the ending inventory.

Solution to the Demonstration Problem

a. 1. Cost of goods sold (at average cost):
    Average unit cost at Nov. 21 [($6,000 + $9,600) ÷ 5 units] .... $ 3,120
    Cost of goods sold (4 units × $3,120 per unit). $12,480

   2. Inventory at Dec. 31 (at average cost):
    Units remaining after sale of Nov. 21 (1 unit @ $3,120) . . . . $ 3,120
    Units purchased on Dec. 1 (4 units @ $3,250) 13,000
    Total cost of 5 units in inventory. $16,120
    Average unit cost at Dec. 31 ($16,120 ÷ 5 units). . . . . $ 3,224
    Inventory at Dec. 31 (5 units × $3,224 per unit). $16,120

b. 1. Cost of goods sold (FIFO basis):
    (2 units @ $3,000 + 2 units @ $3,200) $12,400
   2. Inventory at Dec. 31 (4 units @ $3,250 + 1 unit @ $3,200) $16,200

c. 1. Cost of goods sold (LIFO basis):
    (3 units @ $3,200 + 1 unit @ $3,000) $12,600
   2. Inventory at Dec. 31 (4 units @ $3,250 + 1 unit @ $3,000) $16,000

Self-Test Questions

The answers to these questions appear on page 382.

1. The primary purpose for using an inventory cost flow *assumption* is to:

a. Parallel the physical flow of units of merchandise.

b. Offset against revenue an appropriate cost of goods sold.

c. Minimize income taxes.

d. Maximize the reported amount of net income.

2. Ace Auto Supply uses a perpetual inventory system. On March 10, the company sells two Shelby four-barrel carburetors. Immediately prior to this sale, the perpetual inventory records indicate three of these carburetors on hand, as follows:

Date	Quantity Purchased	Unit Cost	Units on Hand	Total Cost
Feb. 4	1	$220	1	$220
Mar. 2	2	235	3	690

With respect to the sale on March 10: (More than one of the following answers may be correct.)

a. If the average-cost method is used, the cost of goods sold is $460.

b. If these carburetors have identification numbers, Ace must use the specific identification method to determine the cost of goods sold.

c. If the company uses LIFO, the cost of goods sold will be $15 higher than if it were using FIFO.

d. If the company uses LIFO, the carburetor *remaining* in inventory after the sales will be assumed to have cost $220.

3. T-Shirt City uses a *periodic* inventory system. During the first year of operations, the company made four purchases of a particular product. Each purchase was for 500 units and the prices paid were $9 per unit in the first purchase, $10 per unit in the second purchase, $12 per unit in the third purchase, and $13 per unit in the fourth purchase. At year-end,

650 of these units remained unsold. Compute the cost of goods sold under the FIFO method and LIFO method, respectively.

   a. $13,700 (FIFO) and $16,000 (LIFO).

   b. $8,300 (FIFO) and $6,000 (LIFO).

   c. $16,000 (FIFO) and $13,700 (LIFO).

   d. $6,000 (FIFO) and $8,300 (LIFO).

4. Trendy Department Store uses a perpetual inventory system but adjusts its inventory records at year-end to reflect the results of a complete physical inventory. In the physical inventory taken at the ends of 2014 and 2015, Trendy's employees failed to count the merchandise in the store's window displays. The cost of this merchandise amounted to $13,000 at the end of 2014 and $19,000 at the end of 2015. As a result of these errors, the cost of goods sold for 2015 will be:

   a. Understated by $19,000.

   b. Overstated by $6,000.

   c. Understated by $6,000.

   d. None of the above.

5. In July 2015, the accountant for Bradford Imports is in the process of preparing financial statements for the quarter ended June 30, 2015. The physical inventory, however, was last taken on June 5, and the accountant must establish the approximate cost at June 30 from the following data:

Physical inventory, June 5, 2015	$900,000
Transactions for the period June 5–June 30:	
Sales	700,000
Purchases	400,000

The gross profit on sales has consistently averaged 40 percent of sales. Using the gross profit method, compute the approximate inventory cost at June 30, 2015.

   a. $420,000.

   b. $880,000.

   c. $480,000.

   d. $1,360,000.

6. Allied Products maintains a large inventory. The company has used the LIFO inventory method for many years, during which the purchase costs of its products have risen substantially. (More than one of the following answers may be correct.)

   a. Allied would have reported a *higher* net income in past years if it had been using the average-cost method.

   b. Allied's financial statements imply a *lower* inventory turnover rate than they would if the company were using FIFO.

   c. Allied would have paid more income taxes in past years if it had been using the FIFO method.

   d. If Allied were to let its inventory fall far below normal levels, the company's gross profit rate would *decline*.

ASSIGNMENT MATERIAL   Discussion Questions

1. Briefly describe the rationale for using a cost flow assumption, rather than the specific identification method, to value an inventory.

2. Under what circumstances do generally accepted accounting principles permit the use of an inventory cost flow assumption? Must a cost flow assumption closely parallel the physical movement of the company's merchandise?

3. A large art gallery has in inventory more than 100 paintings. No two are alike. The least expensive is priced at more than $1,000 and the higher-priced items carry prices of $100,000 and more. Which of the four methods of inventory valuation discussed in this chapter would you consider to be most appropriate for this business? Give reasons for your answer.

4. During a period of steadily increasing purchase costs, which inventory flow assumption results in the highest reported profits? The lowest taxable income? The valuation of inventory that is closest to current replacement cost? Briefly explain your answers.

5. What are the characteristics of a *just-in-time* inventory system? Briefly explain some advantages and risks of this type of system.

6. Why do companies that use perpetual inventory systems also take an annual *physical inventory?* When is this physical inventory usually taken? Why?

7. Under what circumstances might a company write down its inventory to carrying value below cost?

8. What is meant by the year-end *cutoff* of transactions? If merchandise in transit at year-end is material in dollar amount, what determines whether these goods should be included in the inventory of the buyer or the seller? Explain.

9. Explain why errors in the valuation of inventory at the end of the year are sometimes called "counterbalancing" or "self-correcting."

10. Briefly explain the *gross profit method* of estimating inventories. In what types of situations is this technique likely to be useful?

11. A store using the *retail inventory method* takes its physical inventory by applying current retail prices as marked on the merchandise to the quantities counted. Does this procedure mean that the inventory will appear in the financial statements at retail selling price? Explain.

12. How is the *inventory turnover* computed? Why is this measurement of interest to short-term creditors?

13. Baxter Corporation has been using FIFO during a period of rising costs. Explain whether you would expect each of the following measurements to be higher or lower if the company had been using LIFO.

    a. Net income.

    b. Inventory turnover rate.

    c. Income taxes expense.

14. In anticipation of *declining* inventory replacement costs, the management of Computer Products Co. elects to use the *FIFO* inventory method rather than LIFO. Explain how this decision should affect the company's future:

    a. Rate of gross profit.

    b. Net cash flow from operating activities.

15. Notes to the financial statements of two clothing manufacturers follow:

Inventories: The inventories are stated at the lower of cost, determined principally by the LIFO method, or market.

Inventories: Inventories are stated at the lower of cost (first-in, first-out method) or market value, assuming a period of rising prices.

    a. Which company is using the more conservative method of pricing its inventories? Explain.

    b. On the basis of the inventory methods in use in their financial statements, which company is in the better position to minimize the amount of income taxes that it must pay? Explain.

    c. Could either company increase its cash collections from customers or reduce its cash payments to suppliers of merchandise by switching from FIFO to LIFO, or from LIFO to FIFO? Explain.

Brief Exercises

LO8-1, LO8-4

BRIEF EXERCISE 8.1

FIFO Inventory

Smalley, Inc., purchased items of inventory as follows:

Jan. 4   100 units @ $2.10

Jan. 23 120 units @ $2.25

Smalley sold 50 units on January 28. Compute the cost of goods sold for the month under the FIFO inventory method.

LO8-1, LO8-4

BRIEF EXERCISE 8.2

LIFO Inventory

Mason Company purchased items of inventory as follows:

Dec. 2   50 units @ $20

Dec. 12 12 units @ $21

Mason sold 15 units on December 20. Determine the cost of goods sold for the month under the LIFO inventory method.

LO8-4

BRIEF EXERCISE 8.3

Average-Cost Inventory

Fox Company purchased items of inventory as follows:

May 3   100 units @ $3.05

May 10 150 units @ $3.10

May 15 120 units @ $3.15

By the end of the month of May, Fox had sold 125 units. If the company uses the average-cost method of accounting for inventory, what is the amount of the ending inventory?

LO8-4

BRIEF EXERCISE 8.4

FIFO and LIFO Inventory

Murphy, Inc., purchased a new inventory item two times during the month of April, as follows:

Apr. 5   100 units @ $5.00

Apr. 15 100 units @ $5.05

    a. What is the amount of the ending inventory of this item on April 30 if the company has sold 75 units and uses the LIFO inventory method?

    b. How would this amount differ if the company used the FIFO inventory method?

LO8-4

BRIEF EXERCISE 8.5

FIFO and Average-Cost Inventory

Franklin Co. had 10 units of an inventory item on hand at the beginning of the current year, each of which had a per-unit cost of $10. During the year, 20 additional units were purchased at $11, and 25 units were sold. What is the amount of the ending inventory under the LIFO and the average-cost methods of accounting for inventory?

LO8-3

BRIEF EXERCISE 8.6

Inventory Shrinkage

Bruing Company's inventory is subject to shrinkage via evaporation. At the end of the current financial reporting period, the company's inventory had a cost of $100,000. Management estimates that evaporation has resulted in a 6 percent inventory loss. Assuming that loss is recorded in a separate inventory loss account, prepare the general journal entry to record the inventory shrinkage for the year.

LO8-5

BRIEF EXERCISE 8.7

Inventory Error

Pixy, Inc., overlooked $125,000 of inventory at the end of the current year because it was stored temporarily in a warehouse owned by another company. Before discovering this error, the company's income statement showed the following:

Sales	$990,000
Cost of goods sold	(560,000)
Gross profit.	$430,000

Restate these figures to reflect the inclusion of the overlooked inventory.

LO8-5

BRIEF EXERCISE 8.8

Inventory Error

Due to ineffective controls while counting its inventory, Walker & Comer, Inc., double-counted $50,000 of inventory at the end of the current year. Before discovering this error, the company's ending inventory was $670,000. How will correction of this error affect the company's inventory and cost of goods sold figures?

LO8-7

BRIEF EXERCISE 8.9

Inventory Turnover

Alamo Company has sales, cost of goods sold, and average ending inventory for the current year in the following amounts: $650,000, $500,000, and $128,000, respectively. Calculate the amount of the company's inventory turnover for the year. What is the company's average number of days to sell inventory?

LO8-7

BRIEF EXERCISE 8.10

Inventory Turnover

Rouse Incorporated reported sales, cost of sales, and inventory figures for 2014 and 2015 as follows (all dollars in thousands):

	Sales	Cost of Goods Sold	Average Inventory
2014	$100	$85	$27
2015	110	90	35

What is the amount of inventory turnover for each year, and in which year did Rouse manage its inventory most efficiently?

Exualt Exercises

LO8-1 through LO8-7

EXERCISE 8.1

Accounting Terminology

Listed below are eight technical accounting terms introduced in this chapter.

Retail method	FIFO method	Lower-of-cost-or-market
Gross profit method	LIFO method	Specific identification
Cost flow assumption	Average-cost method	

Each of the following statements may (or may not) describe one of these technical terms. For each statement, indicate the term described, or answer "None" if the statement does not correctly describe any of the terms.

a. A pattern of transferring unit costs from the Inventory account to the Cost of Goods Sold that may (or may not) parallel the physical flow of merchandise.

b. The only flow assumption in which all units of merchandise are assigned the same per-unit cost.

c. The method used to record the cost of goods sold when each unit in the inventory is unique.

d. The most conservative of the flow assumptions during a period of sustained rising prices.

e. The flow assumption that provides the most current valuation of inventory in the balance sheet.

f. A technique for estimating the cost of goods sold and the ending inventory that is based on the relationship between cost and sales price during the *current* accounting period.

LO8-1

EXERCISE 8.2

Cost Flow Assumptions

On May 10, Hudson Computing sold 90 Millennium laptop computers to Apex Publishers. At the date of this sale, Hudson's perpetual inventory records included the following cost layers for the Millennium laptops:

Purchase Date	Quantity	Unit Cost	Total Cost
Apr. 9	70	$1,500	$105,000
May 1	30	$1,600	48,000
Total on hand	100		$153,000

Prepare journal entries to record the cost of the 90 Millennium laptops sold on May 10, assuming that Hudson Computing uses the:

a. Specific identification method (62 of the units sold were purchased on April 9, and the remaining units were purchased on May 1).

b. Average-cost method.

c. FIFO method.

d. LIFO method.

e. Discuss briefly the financial reporting differences that may arise from choosing the FIFO method over the LIFO method.

LO8-4

EXERCISE 8.3

Physical Flow versus Cost Flow Assumptions

The Comfort Store sells heating oil, coal, and kerosene fuel to residential customers. Heating oil is kept in large storage tanks that supply the company's fleet of delivery trucks. Coal is kept in huge bins that are loaded and emptied from the top by giant scooping machines. Kerosene is sold "off the shelf" in five-gallon containers at the company's retail outlet. Separate inventory records are maintained for each fuel type.

a. Which of the cost flow assumptions (average-cost, FIFO, or LIFO) best describes the *physical flow* of:

    1. The heating oil inventory? Explain.

    2. The coal inventory? Explain.

    3. The kerosene inventory? Explain.

b. Which of these cost flow assumptions is likely to result in the *lowest* income tax liability for the company? Explain.

c. Explain why management keeps separate inventory records for its heating oil, coal, and kerosene inventories.

LO8-4

EXERCISE 8.4

Effects of Different Cost Flow Assumptions

Gable, Inc., is a provider of home furnishings. The company uses the FIFO inventory method. The following information was taken from the company's recent financial statements (dollar amounts are in thousands):

Cost of goods sold.	$1,850,000
Income before taxes.	125,000
Income taxes expense (and payments)	52,500
Net income.	72,500
Net cash provided by operating activities	123,250

The financial statements also revealed that had Gable been using *LIFO,* its cost of goods sold would have been $1,865,000. The company's income taxes and payments amount to approximately 40 percent of income before taxes.

a. Explain how LIFO can result in a higher cost of goods sold. Would you expect LIFO to result in a greater or lesser valuation of the company's ending inventories? Defend your answer.

b. Assuming that Lollar had been using *LIFO,* compute the following amounts for the current year. Show your supporting computations, with dollar amounts in thousands.

1. Income before taxes

2. Income taxes expense (which are assumed equal to income taxes actually paid)

3. Net income

4. Net cash provided by operating activities

LO8-2

EXERCISE 8.5

Transfer of Title

Jensen Tire had two large shipments in transit at December 31. One was a $130,000 inbound shipment of merchandise (shipped December 28, F.O.B. shipping point), which arrived at Jensen's receiving dock on January 2. The other shipment was a $95,000 outbound shipment of merchandise to a customer, which was shipped and billed by Jensen on December 30 (terms F.O.B. shipping point) and reached the customer on January 3.

In taking a physical inventory on December 31, Jensen counted all goods on hand and priced the inventory on the basis of average cost. The total inventory amount was $600,000. No goods in transit were included in this figure.

What amount should appear as inventory on the company's balance sheet at December 31? Explain. If you indicate an amount other than $600,000, state which asset or liability other than inventory also would be changed in amount, assuming that all inventory purchases are made on credit.

LO8-3

EXERCISE 8.6

Inventory Write-Downs

Late in the year, Software City began carrying WordCrafter, a new word processing software program. At December 31, Software City's perpetual inventory records included the following cost layers in its inventory of WordCrafter programs:

Purchase Date	Quantity	Unit Cost	Total Cost
Nov. 14.	8	$400	$3,200
Dec. 12.	20	310	6,200
Total available for sale at Dec. 31.	28		$9,400

a. At December 31, Software City takes a physical inventory and finds that all 28 units of WordCrafter are on hand. However, the current replacement cost (wholesale price) of this product is only $250 per unit. Prepare the entries to record:

1. This write-down of the inventory to the lower-of-cost-or-market at December 31. (Company policy is to charge LCM adjustments of less than $2,000 to Cost of Goods Sold and larger amounts to a separate loss account.)

2. The cash sale of 15 WordCrafter programs on January 9, at a retail price of $350 each. Assume that Software City uses the FIFO flow assumption.

b. Now assume that the current replacement cost of the WordCrafter programs is $405 each. A physical inventory finds only 25 of these programs on hand at December 31. (For this part, return to the original information and ignore what you did in part **a.**)

1. Prepare the journal entry to record the shrinkage loss assuming that Software City uses the FIFO flow assumption.

2. Prepare the journal entry to record the shrinkage loss assuming that Software City uses the LIFO flow assumption.

3. Which cost flow assumption (FIFO or LIFO) results in the lowest net income for the period? Would using this assumption really mean that the company's operations are less efficient? Explain.

LO8-4

EXERCISE 8.7

Costing Inventory in a
Periodic System

Rogers Products uses a *periodic* inventory system. The company's records show the beginning inventory of PH4 oil filters on January 1 and the purchases of this item during the current year to be as follows:

Jan. 1	Beginning inventory	90 units @ $3.00	$ 270.00
Feb. 23	Purchase	120 units @ $3.50	420.00
Apr. 20	Purchase	300 units @ $3.80	1,140.00
May 4	Purchase	400 units @ $4.00	1,600.00
Nov. 30	Purchase	190 units @ $5.00	950.00
	Totals	1,100 units	$4,380.00

A physical count indicates 200 units in inventory at year-end.

Determine the cost of the ending inventory on the basis of each of the following methods of inventory valuation. (Remember to use *periodic* inventory costing procedures.)

a. Average cost.

b. FIFO.

c. LIFO.

d. Which of the above methods (if any) results in the same ending inventory valuation under *both* periodic and perpetual costing procedures? Explain.

LO8-5

EXERCISE 8.8

Effects of Errors in
Inventory Valuation

Branson Electric prepared the following condensed income statements for two successive years:

	2015	2014
Sales	$2,000,000	$1,500,000
Cost of goods sold	1,250,000	900,000
Gross profit on sales	$ 750,000	$ 600,000
Operating expenses	400,000	350,000
Net income	$ 350,000	$ 250,000

At the end of 2014 (right-hand column above), the inventory was understated by $40,000, but the error was not discovered until after the accounts had been closed and financial statements prepared at the end of 2015. The balance sheets for the two years showed owner's equity of $500,000 at the end of 2014 and $580,000 at the end of 2015. (Branson is organized as a sole proprietorship and does not incur income taxes expense.)

a. Compute the corrected net income figures for 2014 and 2015.

b. Compute the gross profit amounts and the gross profit percentages for each year on the basis of corrected data.

c. What correction, if any, should be made in the amounts of the company's owner's equity at the end of 2014 and at the end of 2015?

LO8-6

EXERCISE 8.9

Estimating Inventory by the
Gross Profit Method

When Mary Potts arrived at her store on the morning of January 29, she found empty shelves and display racks; thieves had broken in during the night and stolen the entire inventory. Accounting records showed that inventory costing $50,000 on January 1. From January 1 to January 29, Potts had made net sales of $70,000 and net purchases of $80,000. The gross profit during the past several years had consistently averaged 42 percent of net sales. Potts plans to file an insurance claim for the theft loss.

a. Using the gross profit method, estimate the cost of inventory at the time of the theft.

b. Does Potts use the periodic inventory method or does she account for inventory using the perpetual method? Defend your answer.

LO8-6

EXERCISE 8.10

Estimating Inventory by the
Retail Method

Phillips Supply uses a periodic inventory system but needs to determine the approximate amount of inventory at the end of each month without taking a physical inventory. Phillips has provided the following inventory data:

	Cost Price	Retail Selling Price
Inventory of merchandise, June 30	$300,000	$500,000
Purchases during July	222,000	400,000
Goods available for sale during July	$522,000	$900,000
Net sales during July		$600,000

a. Estimate the cost of goods sold and the cost of the July 31 ending inventory using the retail method of evaluation.

b. Was the cost of Phillips's inventory, as a percentage of retail selling prices, higher or lower in July than it was in June? Explain.

LO8-1

EXERCISE 8.11

Evaluating Cost Flow
Assumptions

A recent annual report of Chrysler indicates that the cost of a substantial portion of the company's inventory is determined by the specific identification method. The cost of other inventory is determined by FIFO. These include direct costs of materials, labor, inbound transportation, and indirect manufacturing costs.

Does the company's use of more than one inventory method violate the accounting principle of consistency? Defend your answer.

LO8-1, LO8-7

EXERCISE 8.12

FIFO versus LIFO: A
Challenging Analysis

Ford Motor Company uses FIFO and LIFO to account for different segments of its inventories. A note to the company's most recent financial statements indicated that if FIFO had been used for the entire inventory, the total amount of inventory would have been almost $1 billion higher ($8.3 million vs. $7.3 billion).

a. Indicate whether each of the following financial measurements would have been *higher, lower,* or *unaffected* had **Ford Motor Company** used FIFO for its entire inventory. Explain the reasoning behind your answers.

  1. Gross profit rate.

  2. Reported net income.

  3. Current ratio (**Ford**'s current ratio is greater than 1 to 1).

  4. Inventory turnover rate.

  5. Accounts receivable turnover rate.

  6. Cash payments made to suppliers.

  7. Net cash flow from operations (**Ford**'s operating cash flows are positive).

b. Provide *your own* assessment of whether using LIFO has made **Ford Motor Company** more or less (1) liquid and (2) well-off. Defend your answers.

LO8-7

EXERCISE 8.13

Inventory Turnover

A recent annual report of **Kraft Foods Group, Inc.**, reveals the following information (dollar amounts are stated in millions):

Cost of goods sold	$12,499
Inventory (beginning of year)	1,943
Inventory (end of year)	1,928
Average time required to collect accounts receivable	18 days

a. Compute Kraft Food Group, Inc.'s inventory turnover for the year (round to nearest tenth).

b. Compute the number of days required to sell its average inventory (round to the nearest day).

c. What is the length of Kraft's *operating cycle?*

d. What comparative information would you want to be able to evaluate Kraft's operating cycle figure?

LO8-7

EXERCISE 8.14

Inventory Analysis

A recent income statement of Walmart reports net sales of $466,114 million and cost of goods sold of $352,488 million for the year ended January 31, 2013. The comparable sales and cost of goods sold figures for the year ended one year earlier were $443,854 million and $335,127 million, respectively. As you would expect, to be able to achieve this high level of sales, a great deal of inventory must be maintained so that customers will find what they want to buy when they shop in Walmart stores. In fact, in the January 31, 2013, balance sheet, inventory is presented at $43,803 million and the comparable figure for a year earlier is $40,714 million.

a. Using the year-end inventory figures, compute the inventory turnover for Walmart for both years.

b. Compute the average number of days required by Walmart to sell its inventory for the same years.

c. In which year was the company more efficient in its management of inventory? Explain your answer.

LO8-7

EXERCISE 8.15

Using the Financial Statements of Home Depot, Inc.

The Home Depot, Inc., financial statements appear in Appendix A at the end of this textbook. Using figures from the income statement and balance sheet, answer the following questions:

a. What was the company's inventory turnover for the most recent year reported?

b. Using your answer from part **a**, what was the average number of days that merchandise remained in inventory before it was sold?

c. Is the company's operating cycle influenced significantly by its accounts receivable turnover rate? Explain.

Problem Set A

LO8-1

PROBLEM 8.1A

Four Methods of Inventory Valuation

On January 15, 2015, Sports World sold 1,000 Ace-5 fishing reels to Angler's Warehouse. Immediately prior to this sale, Sports World perpetual inventory records for Ace-5 reels included the following cost layers:

Purchase Date	Quantity	Unit Cost	Total Cost
Dec. 12, 2014	600	$29	$17,400
Jan. 9, 2015	900	32	28,800
Total on hand	1,500		$46,200

Instructions

Note: We present this problem in the normal sequence of the accounting cycle—that is, journal entries before ledger entries. However, you may find it helpful to work part **b** first.

a. Prepare a separate journal entry to record the cost of goods sold relating to the January 15 sale of 1,000 Ace-5 reels, assuming that Sports World uses:

1. Specific identification (500 of the units sold were purchased on December 12, and the remaining 500 were purchased on January 9).

2. Average cost.

3. FIFO.

4. LIFO.

b. Complete a subsidiary ledger record for Ace-5 reels using each of the four inventory valuation methods listed above. Your inventory records should show both purchases of this product, the sale on January 15, and the balance on hand at December 12, January 9, and January 15. Use the formats for inventory subsidiary records illustrated on pages 345–347 of this chapter.

c. Refer to the cost of goods sold figures computed in part **a.** For financial reporting purposes, can the company use the valuation method that resulted in the *lowest* cost of goods sold if, for tax purposes, it used the method that resulted in the *highest* cost of goods sold? Explain.

Problems 8.2A and 8.3A are based on the following data:

Speed World Cycles sells high-performance motorcycles and motocross racers. One of Speed World's most popular models is the Kazomma 900 dirt bike. During the current year, Speed World Cycles purchased eight of these bikes at the following costs:

Purchase Date	Units Purchased	Unit Cost	Total Cost
July 1	2	$4,950	$ 9,900
July 22	3	5,000	15,000
Aug. 3	3	5,100	15,300
	8		$40,200

On *July 28,* Speed World Cycles sold four Kazomma 900 dirt bikes to the Vince Wilson racing team. The remaining four bikes remained in inventory at September 30, the end of Speed World's fiscal year.

Assume that Speed World Cycles uses a *perpetual inventory system.* (See the data given above.)

LO8-I

PROBLEM 8.2A

Alternative Cost Flow Assumptions in a Perpetual System

Instructions

a. Compute the cost of goods sold relating to the sale on July 28 and the ending inventory of Kazomma 900 dirt bikes at September 30, using the following cost flow assumptions:

  1. Average cost.

  2. FIFO.

  3. LIFO.

Show the number of units and the unit costs of each layer comprising the cost of goods sold and ending inventory.

b. Using the cost figures computed in part **a,** answer the following questions:

  1. Which of the three cost flow assumptions will result in Speed World Cycles reporting the *highest net income* for the current year? Would this always be the case? Explain.

  2. Which of the three cost flow assumptions *minimizes the income taxes owed* by Speed World Cycles for the year? Would you expect this usually to be the case? Explain.

  3. May Speed World Cycles use the cost flow assumption that results in the highest net income for the current year in its financial statements, but use the cost flow assumption that minimizes taxable income for the current year in its income tax return? Explain.

Assume that Speed World uses a *periodic inventory system.* (See the data given before Problem 8.2A.)

LO8-4

PROBLEM 8.3A

Alternative Cost Flow Assumptions in a Periodic System

Instructions

a. Compute the cost of goods sold relating to the sale on July 28 and the ending inventory of Kazomma 900 dirt bikes at September 30, using the following cost flow assumptions:

  1. Average cost.

  2. FIFO.

  3. LIFO.

Show the number of units and unit costs in each cost layer of the *ending inventory*. You may determine the cost of goods sold by deducting ending inventory from the cost of goods available for sale.

b.   If Speed World Cycles uses the LIFO cost flow assumption for financial reporting purposes, can it use the FIFO method for income tax purposes? Explain.

LO8-I through LO8-3

PROBLEM 8.4A

Year-End Adjustments; Shrinkage Losses and LCM

Mary's Nursery uses a perpetual inventory system. At December 31, the perpetual inventory records indicate the following quantities of a particular blue spruce tree:

	Quantity	Unit Cost	Total Cost
First purchase (oldest)	130	$25.00	$ 3,250
Second purchase	120	28.50	3,420
Third purchase	100	39.00	3,900
Total	350		$10,570

A year-end physical inventory, however, shows only 310 of these trees on hand.

In its financial statements, Mary's Nursery values its inventories at the lower-of-cost-or-market. At year-end, the per-unit replacement cost of this tree is $40. (Use $3,500 as the "level of materiality" in deciding whether to debit losses to Cost of Goods Sold or to a separate loss account.)

Instructions

Prepare the journal entries required to adjust the inventory records at year-end, assuming that:

a.   Mary's Nursery uses:

   1.   Average cost.

   2.   Last-in, first-out.

b.   Mary's Nursery uses the first-in, first-out method. However, the replacement cost of the trees at year-end is $20 apiece, rather than the $40 stated originally. [Make separate journal entries to record (1) the shrinkage losses and (2) the restatement of the inventory at a market value lower than cost. Record the shrinkage losses first.]

c.   Assume that the company had been experiencing monthly inventory shrinkage of 30 to 60 trees for several months. In response, management placed several hidden security cameras throughout the premises. Within days, an employee was caught on film loading potted trees into his pickup truck. The employee's attorney asked that the case be dropped because the company had "unethically used a hidden camera to entrap his client." Do you agree with the attorney? Defend your answer.

LO8-4

PROBLEM 8.5A

Periodic Inventory Costing Procedures

Clear Sound Audio uses a periodic inventory system. One of the store's most popular products is an MP8 car stereo system. The inventory quantities, purchases, and sales of this product for the most recent year are as follows:

	Number of Units	Cost per Unit	Total Cost
Inventory, Jan. 1	12	$299	$ 3,588
First purchase (May 12)	15	306	4,590
Second purchase (July 9)	21	308	6,468
Third purchase (Oct. 4)	8	315	2,520
Fourth purchase (Dec. 18)	17	320	5,440
Goods available for sale	73		$22,606
Units sold during the year	51		
Inventory, Dec. 31	22		

Instructions

a. Using *periodic* costing procedures, compute the cost of the December 31 inventory and the cost of goods sold for the MP8 systems during the year under each of the following cost flow assumptions:

  1. First-in, first-out.

  2. Last-in, first-out.

  3. Average cost (round to nearest dollar, except unit cost).

b. Which of the three inventory pricing methods provides the most realistic balance sheet valuation of inventory in light of the current replacement cost of the MP8 units? Does this same method also produce the most realistic measure of income in light of the costs being incurred by Clear Sound Audio to replace the MP8 systems when they are sold? Explain.

LO8-5
PROBLEM 8.6A
Effects of Inventory Errors on Earnings

The owners of Health Foods are offering the business for sale. The partial income statements of the business for the three years of its existence are summarized below.

	2015	2014	2013
Net sales	$875,000	$840,000	$820,000
Cost of goods sold	481,250	487,200	480,000
Gross profit on sales	$393,750	$352,800	$340,000
Gross profit percentage	45%	42%	41%

In negotiations with prospective buyers of the business, the owners of Health Foods are calling attention to the rising trends of the gross profit and the gross profit percentage as favorable elements.

Assume that you are retained by a prospective purchaser of the business to make an investigation of the fairness and reliability of the enterprise's accounting records and financial statements. You find everything in order except for the following: (1) An arithmetic error in the computation of inventory at the end of 2013 had caused a $40,000 understatement in that inventory, and (2) a duplication of figures in the computation of inventory at the end of 2015 had caused an overstatement of $81,750 in that inventory. The company uses the periodic inventory system, and these errors had not been brought to light prior to your investigation.

Instructions

a. Prepare a revised three-year abbreviated income statement summary.

b. Comment on the trends of gross profit and gross profit percentage before and after the revision.

LO8-2, LO8-3, LO8-6
PROBLEM 8.7A
Retail Method

Between The Ears (BTE.com) is a popular Internet music store. During the current year, the company's cost of goods available for sale amounted to $462,000. The retail sales value of this merchandise amounted to $840,000. Sales for the year were $744,000.

Instructions

a. Using the retail method, estimate (1) the cost of goods sold during the year and (2) the inventory at the end of the year.

b. At year-end, BTE.com takes a physical inventory. The general manager walks through the warehouse counting each type of product and reading its retail price into a recorder. From the recorded information, another employee prepares a schedule listing the entire ending inventory at retail sales prices. The schedule prepared for the current year reports ending inventory at $84,480 at retail sales prices.

  1. Use the cost ratio computed in part **a** to reduce the inventory counted by the general manager from its retail value to an estimate of its cost.

2. Determine the estimated shrinkage losses (measured at cost) incurred by BTE.com during the year.

3. Compute BTE.com's gross profit for the year. (Include inventory shrinkage losses in the cost of goods sold.)

c. What controls might BTE.com implement to reduce inventory shrinkage?

LO8-1, LO8-7

PROBLEM 8.8A

FIFO versus LIFO Comparisons

Walmart uses LIFO to account for its inventories. Recent financial statements were used to compile the following information (dollar figures are in millions):

Average inventory (throughout the year)	$42,259
Current assets (at year-end)	59,940
Current liabilities (at year-end)	71,818
Sales	469,162
Cost of goods sold	352,488
Gross profit	116,674
Average time required to collect outstanding receivables (approximate)	10 days

Instructions

a. Using the information provided, compute the following measures based upon the *LIFO* method:

  1. Inventory turnover.

  2. Current ratio (see Chapter 5 for a discussion of this ratio).

  3. Gross profit rate (see Chapter 6 for a discussion of this statistic).

b. Assuming cost of goods sold would be lower under FIFO, what circumstances must the company have encountered to cause this situation? (Were replacement costs, on average, rising or falling?)

c. How would you expect these ratios to differ (i.e., what direction) had the company used FIFO instead of LIFO?

d. Explain why the average number of days required by **Walmart** to collect its accounts receivable is so low. (See Chapter 7 for a discussion of the accounts receivable turnover rate.)

Problem Set B

LO8-1

PROBLEM 8.1B

Four Methods of Inventory Valuation

On January 22, 2015, Dobbins Supply, Inc., sold 700 toner cartridges to Foster Office Fitters. Immediately prior to this sale, Dobbins Supply's perpetual inventory records for these units included the following cost layers:

Purchase Date	Quantity	Unit Cost	Total Cost
Dec. 12, 2014	400	$20	$ 8,000
Jan. 16, 2015	1,200	22	26,400
Total on hand	1,600		$34,400

Instructions

Note: We present this problem in the normal sequence of the accounting cycle—that is, journal entries before ledger entries. However, you may find it helpful to work part **b** first.

a. Prepare a separate journal entry to record the cost of goods sold relating to the January 22 sale of 700 toner cartridges, assuming that Dobbins supply uses:

  1. Specific identification (300 of the units sold had been purchased on December 12, and the remaining 400 had been purchased on January 16).

2. Average cost.

3. FIFO.

4. LIFO.

b. Complete a subsidiary ledger record for the toner cartridges using each of the four inventory valuation methods listed above. Your inventory records should show both purchases of this product, the sale on January 22, and the balance on hand at December 12, January 16, and January 22. Use the formats for inventory subsidiary records illustrated on pages 345–347 of this chapter.

c. Refer to the cost of goods sold figures computed in part **a.** For financial reporting purposes, can Dobbins Supply, Inc. use the valuation method that resulted in the *highest* cost of goods sold if, for tax purposes, it used the method that resulted in the *lowest* cost of goods sold? Explain.

Problems 8.2B and 8.3B are based on the following data:

Sea Travel sells motor boats. One of Sea Travel's most popular models is the Wing. During the current year, Sea Travel purchased 12 Wings at the following costs:

Purchase Date	Units Purchased	Unit Cost	Total Cost
Apr. 1	4	$8,000	$ 32,000
Apr. 19	5	8,200	41,000
May 8	3	8,500	25,500
	12		$98,500

On *April 28,* Sea Travel sold five Wings to the Jack Sport racing team. The remaining seven boats remained in inventory at June 30, the end of Sea Travel's fiscal year.

LO8-1

PROBLEM 8.2B

Alternative Cost Flow Assumptions in a Perpetual System

Assume that Sea Travel uses a *perpetual inventory system.* (See the data given above.)

Instructions

a. Compute (a) the cost of goods sold relating to the sale on April 28 and (b) the ending inventory of Wing boats at June 30, using the following cost flow assumptions:

1. Average cost (round cost to nearest whole dollar).

2. FIFO.

3. LIFO.

Show the number of units and the unit costs of each layer comprising the cost of goods sold and ending inventory.

b. Using the cost figures computed in part **a,** answer the following questions:

1. Which of the three cost flow assumptions will result in Sea Travel reporting the *lowest net income* for the current year? Would this always be the case? Explain.

2. Which of the three cost flow assumptions will result in the *highest* income tax expense for the year? Would you expect this usually to be the case? Explain.

3. May Sea Travel use the cost flow assumption that results in the *lowest* net income for the current year in its financial statements, but use the cost flow assumption that *maximizes* taxable income for the current year in its income tax return? Explain.

LO8-4

PROBLEM 8.3B

Alternative Cost Flow Assumptions in a Periodic System

Assume that Sea Travel uses a *periodic inventory system.* (Refer to the data that precede Problem 8.2B.)

Instructions

a. Compute the cost of goods sold relating to the sale on April 28 and the ending inventory of Wing boats at June 30, using the following cost flow assumptions:

1. Average cost (round cost to nearest whole dollar).

2. FIFO.

3. LIFO.

Show the number of units and the unit costs of each layer comprising the *ending inventory*. You may determine the cost of goods sold by deducting ending inventory from the cost of goods available for sale.

b. If Sea Travel uses the LIFO cost flow assumption for income tax purposes, can it use the FIFO method for financial reporting purposes? Explain.

LO8-1 through LO8-3

PROBLEM 8.4B

Year-End Adjustments;
Shrinkage Losses and LCM

Sam's Lawn Maintenance uses a perpetual inventory system. At December 31, the perpetual inventory records indicate the following quantities of a particular mower.

	Quantity	Unit Cost	Total Cost
First purchase (oldest)	80	$100	$ 8,000
Second purchase	100	110	11,000
Third purchase	20	120	2,400
Total	200		$21,400

A year-end physical inventory, however, shows only 199 of these lawn mowers on hand.

In its financial statements, Sam's values its inventories at the lower-of-cost-or-market. At year-end, the per-unit replacement cost of this particular model is $125.

Instructions

Prepare the journal entries required to adjust the inventory records at year-end assuming that:

a. Sam's uses:

1. Average cost.

2. Last-in, first-out.

b. Sam's uses the first-in, first-out method. However, the replacement cost of the lawn mowers at year-end is $90 apiece, rather than the $125 stated originally. Make separate journal entries to record (1) the shrinkage loss and (2) the restatement of the inventory at a market value lower than cost. Record the shrinkage loss first.

c. Assume that the company had been experiencing monthly inventory shrinkage of one to four lawn mowers for several months. In response, management placed several hidden security cameras throughout the premises. Within days, an employee was caught on film loading lawn mowers into his pickup truck. The employee's attorney asked that the case be dropped because the company had "unethically used a hidden camera to entrap his client." Do you agree with the attorney? Defend your answer.

LO8-4

PROBLEM 8.5B

Periodic Inventory Costing
Procedures

Ryan Sound uses a periodic inventory system. One of the store's products is a wireless headphone. The inventory quantities, purchases, and sales of this product for the most recent year are as follows:

	Number of Units	Cost per Unit	Total Cost
Inventory, Jan. 1	15	$100	$ 1,500
First purchase	32	101	3,232
Second purchase	40	103	4,120
Third purchase	5	106	530
Fourth purchase	16	108	1,728
Goods available for sale	108		$11,110
Units sold during the year	82		
Inventory, Dec. 31	26		

Instructions

a. Using *periodic* costing procedures, compute the cost of the December 31 inventory and the cost of goods sold for the year under each of the following cost assumptions:

1. First-in, first-out.

2. Last-in, first-out.

3. Average cost (round to the nearest dollar, except unit cost).

b. Which of the three inventory pricing methods provides the most realistic balance sheet valuation of inventory in light of the current replacement cost of these headphones? Does this same method also produce the most realistic measure of income in light of the costs being incurred by Roman Sound to replace these units when they are sold? Explain.

LO8-5

PROBLEM 8.6B

Effects of Inventory Errors on Earnings

The owners of City Software are offering the business for sale. The income statements of the business for the three years of its existence are summarized below.

	2015	2014	2013
Net sales	$1,000,000	$920,000	$840,000
Cost of goods sold	600,000	570,400	546,000
Gross profit on sales	$ 400,000	$349,600	$294,000
Gross profit percentage	40%	38%	35%

In negotiations with prospective buyers of the business, the owners are calling attention to the rising trends of the gross profit and the gross profit percentage as very favorable elements.

Assume that you are retained by a prospective purchaser of the business to make an investigation of the fairness and reliability of the enterprise's accounting records and financial statements. You find everything in order except for the following: (1) An arithmetic error in the computation of inventory at the end of 2013 caused a $20,000 understatement in that inventory, and (2) an error in the computation of inventory at the end of 2015 caused an overstatement of $80,000 in that inventory. The company uses the periodic inventory system, and these errors have not been brought to light prior to your investigation.

Instructions

a. Prepare a revised three-year abbreviated income statement summary.

b. Comment on the trends of gross profit and gross profit percentage before and after the revision.

LO8-2, LO8-3, LO8-6

PROBLEM 8.7B

Retail Method

Song Meister is a popular music store. During the current year, the company's cost of goods available for sale amounted to $330,000. The retail sales value of this merchandise amounted to $600,000. Sales for the year were $520,000.

Instructions

a. Using the retail method, estimate (1) the cost of goods sold during the year and (2) the inventory at the end of the year.

b. At year-end, Song Meister takes a physical inventory. The general manager walks through the store counting each type of product and reading its retail price into a tape recorder. From the recorded information, another employee prepares a schedule listing the entire ending inventory at retail sales prices. The schedule prepared for the current year reports ending inventory of $75,000 at retail sales prices.

1. Use the cost ratio computed in part **a** to reduce the inventory counted by the general manager from its retail value to an estimate of its cost.

2. Determine the estimated shrinkage losses (measured at cost) incurred by Sing Along during the year.

3. Compute Song Meister's gross profit for the year. (Include inventory shrinkage losses in the cost of goods sold.)

LO8-1, LO8-7

PROBLEM 8.8B

FIFO versus LIFO Comparisons

c. What controls might Song Meister implement to reduce inventory shrinkage?

JC Penney Company uses LIFO in applying the lower-of-cost-or-market. Recent financial statements were used to compile the following information (dollar figures in millions):

Average inventory (throughout the year)	$ 2,629
Current assets (at year-end)	3,683
Current liabilities (at year-end)	2,583
Net sales	12,985
Cost of goods sold	8,919
Gross profit (Margin)	4,066
Average time required to collect outstanding receivables (approximate)	5 days

Instructions

a. Using the information provided, compute the following measures based on the *LIFO* method:

    1. Inventory turnover.

    2. Current ratio (see Chapter 5 for a discussion of this ratio).

    3. Gross profit rate (see Chapter 6 for a discussion of this statistic).

b. Assuming the cost of goods sold would be lower under FIFO, what circumstances must the company have encountered to cause this situation? (Were replacement costs, on average, rising or falling?)

c. How would you expect these ratios to differ (i.e., what direction) had the company used FIFO instead of LIFO?

d. Explain why the average number of days required by **JC Penney** to collect its accounts receivable is so low. (See Chapter 7 for a discussion of the accounts receivable turnover.)

Critical Thinking Cases

LO8-5

CASE 8.1

It's Not Right, but at Least It's Consistent

Our Little Secret is a small manufacturer of swimsuits and other beach apparel. The company is closely held and has no external reporting obligations, other than payroll reports and income tax returns. The company's accounting system is grossly inadequate. Accounting records are maintained by clerical employees with little knowledge of accounting and with many other job responsibilities. Management has decided that the company must hire a competent controller, who can establish and oversee an adequate accounting system.

    Amy Lee, CPA, has applied for this position. During a recent interview, Dean Frost, the company's director of personnel, said, "Amy, the job is yours. But you should know that we have a big inventory problem here.

    "For some time now, it appears that we have been understating our ending inventory in income tax returns. No one knows when this all got started, or who was responsible. We never even counted our inventory until a few months ago. But the problem is pretty big. In our latest tax return—that's for 2010—we listed inventory at only about half its actual cost. That's an understatement of, maybe, $400,000.

    "We don't know what to do. We sure don't want a big scandal—tax evasion, and all that. Maybe the best thing is to continue understating inventory by the same amount as we did in 2014. That way, taxable income will be correctly stated in future years. Anyway, this is just something I thought you should know about."

Instructions

a. Briefly identify the ethical issues raised for Lee by Frost's disclosure.

b. From Lee's perspective, evaluate the possible solution proposed by Frost.

c. Identify and discuss the alternative ethical courses of action that are open to Lee.

LO8-4

CASE 8.2

LIFO Liquidation

Jackson Specialties has been in business for more than 50 years. The company maintains a perpetual inventory system, uses a LIFO flow assumption, and ends its fiscal year at December 31. At year-end, the cost of goods sold and inventory are adjusted to reflect periodic LIFO costing procedures.

A railroad strike has delayed the arrival of purchases ordered during the past several months of 2015, and Jackson Specialties has not been able to replenish its inventories as merchandise is sold. At December 22, one product appears in the company's perpetual inventory records at the following unit costs:

Purchase Date	Quantity	Unit Cost	Total Cost
Nov. 14, 1962	3,000	$6	$18,000
Apr. 12, 1963	2,000	8	16,000
Available for sale at Dec. 22, 2015	5,000		$34,000

Jackson Specialties has another 8,000 units of this product on order at the current wholesale cost of $30 per unit. Because of the railroad strike, however, these units have not yet arrived (the terms of purchase are F.O.B. destination). Jackson Specialties also has an order from a customer who wants to purchase 4,000 units of this product at the retail sales price of $47 per unit. Jackson Specialties intends to make this sale on December 30, regardless of whether the 8,000 units on order arrive by this date. (The 4,000-unit sale will be shipped by truck, F.O.B. shipping point.)

Instructions

a. Are the units in inventory really more than 50 years old? Explain.

b. Prepare a schedule showing the sales revenue, cost of goods sold, and gross profit that will result from this sale on December 30, assuming that the 8,000 units currently on order (1) arrive before year-end and (2) do not arrive until some time in the following year. (In each computation, show the number of units comprising the cost of goods sold and their related per-unit costs.)

c. Comment on these results.

d. Might management be wise to delay this sale by a few days? Explain.

LO8-3

CASE 8.3

Dealing with the Bank

Millinium Frozen Foods owes the bank $50,000 on a line of credit. Terms of the agreement specify that Millinium must maintain a minimum current ratio of 1.2 to 1, or the entire outstanding balance becomes immediately due in full. To date, the company has complied with the minimum requirement. However, management has just learned that a failed warehouse freezer has ruined thousands of dollars of frozen foods inventory. If the company records this loss, its current ratio will drop to approximately 0.8 to 1.

Whether any or all of this loss may be covered by insurance currently is in dispute and will not be known for at least 90 days—perhaps much longer. There are several reasons why the insurance company may have no liability.

In trying to decide how to deal with the bank, management is considering the following options: (1) postpone recording the inventory loss until the dispute with the insurance company is resolved, (2) increase the current ratio to 1.2 to 1 by making a large purchase of inventory on account, (3) explain to the bank what has happened, and request that it be flexible until things get back to normal.

Instructions

a. Given that the Millinium's management expects at least partial reimbursement from the insurance company, is it really unethical for management to postpone recording the inventory loss in the financial statements it submits to the bank?

b. Is it possible to increase the Millinium's current ratio from 0.8 to 1 to 1.2 to 1 by purchasing more inventory on account? Explain.

c. What approach do you think Millinium management should follow in dealing with the bank?

LO8-7

INTERNET CASE 8.4

Inventory Turnover

A company's inventory turnover is one measure of its potential to convert inventory into cash. But what is considered a good inventory turnover? The answer to that question depends on a variety of industry and company characteristics.

Access the EDGAR database at the following Internet address:

www.sec.gov

Locate the most recent 10-K reports of **Safeway, Inc.**, and **Staples, Inc.** Compute the inventory turnover of each company. Does the higher turnover computed for **Safeway** mean that the company manages its inventory more effectively than **Staples**? Explain.

Internet sites are time and date sensitive. It is the purpose of these exercises to have you explore the Internet. You may need to use the Yahoo! search engine www.yahoo.com *(or another favorite search engine) to find a company's current web address.*

Answers to Self-Test Questions

1. b   **2.** a, c, d   **3.** a   **4.** b   **5.** b   **6.** a, c

Music-Is-Us, Inc.

Music-Is-Us, Inc., is a supplier of musical instruments for professional and amateur musicians. The company's accountants make adjusting entries *monthly*, and they make all closing entries *annually*. The company is growing rapidly and prides itself on having no long-term liabilities.

The company has provided the following *trial balance* dated *December 31, 2015:*

MUSIC-IS-US, INC. TRIAL BALANCE DECEMBER 31, 2015		
Cash	$ 45,000	
Marketable securities	25,000	
Accounts receivable	125,000	
Allowance for doubtful accounts		$ 5,000
Merchandise inventory	250,000	
Office supplies	1,200	
Prepaid insurance	6,600	
Building and fixtures	1,791,000	
Accumulated depreciation		800,000
Land	64,800	
Accounts payable		70,000
Unearned customer deposits		8,000
Income taxes payable		75,000
Capital stock		1,000,000
Retained earnings		240,200
Unrealized holding gain on investments		6,000
Sales		1,600,000
Cost of goods sold	958,000	
Bank service charges	200	
Uncollectible accounts expense	9,000	
Salary and wages expense	395,000	
Office supplies expense	400	
Insurance expense	6,400	
Utilities expense	3,600	
Depreciation expense	48,000	
Income tax expense	75,000	
	$3,804,200	$3,804,200

Other information pertaining to the company's trial balance is shown below:

1. The most recent bank statement reports a balance of $46,975. Included with the bank statement was a $2,500 check from Iggy Smarts, a professional musician, charged back to Music-Is-Us as NSF. The bank's monthly service charge was $25. Three checks written by Music-Is-Us to suppliers of merchandise inventory had not yet cleared the bank for payment as of the statement date. These checks included: no. 508, $5,500; no. 511, $7,500; and no. 521, $8,000. Deposits of $16,500 reached the bank too late for inclusion in the current bank statement. The company prepares a bank reconciliation at the end of each month.

2. Music-Is-Us has a portfolio of marketable securities that originally cost $19,000. As of December 31, the market value of these securities was $27,500. All short-term investments are classified as "available for sale."

3. During December, $6,400 of accounts receivable were written off as uncollectible. A recent aging of the company's accounts receivable led management to conclude that an allowance for doubtful accounts of $8,500 is needed at December 31, 2015.

4. The company uses a perpetual inventory system. A year-end physical count revealed that several guitars reported in the inventory records were missing. The cost of the missing units amounted to $1,350. This amount is not considered significant relative to the total cost of inventory on hand.

5. At December 31, approximately $900 in office supplies remained on hand.

6. The company pays for its insurance policies 12 months in advance. Its most recent payment was made on November 1, 2015. The cost of this policy was slightly higher than the cost of coverage for the previous 12 months.

7. Depreciation expense related to the company's building and fixtures is $5,000 for the month ending December 31, 2015.

8. Although Music-Is-Us carries an extensive inventory, it is not uncommon for experienced musicians to order custom guitars made to their exact specifications. Manufacturers do not allow any sales returns of custom-made guitars. The entire sales amount is collected at the time a custom order is placed, and is credited to an account entitled "Unearned Customer Deposits." As of December 31, $4,800 of these deposits remained unfilled because the special-order guitars have not been received from the manufacturer. The cost of goods sold and the reduction in inventory associated with all custom orders is recorded when the custom merchandise is delivered to customers. At that time, the adjusting entry requires only a decrease to unearned customer deposits and an increase in sales.

9. Accrued income taxes payable for the *entire year ending* December 31, 2015, total $81,000. No income tax payments are due until early in 2016.

Instructions

a. Prepare a bank reconciliation and make the journal entries to update the accounting records of Music-Is-Us as of December 31, 2015.

b. Prepare the adjusting entry to update the company's marketable securities portfolio to its mark-to-market value.

c. Prepare the adjusting entry at December 31, 2015, to report the company's accounts receivable at their net realizable value.

d. Prepare the entry to account for the guitars missing from the company's inventory at the end of the year.

e. Prepare the adjusting entry to account for the office supplies used during December.

f. Prepare the adjusting entry to account for the expiration of the company's insurance policies during December.

g. Prepare the adjusting entry to account for the depreciation of the company's building and fixtures during December.

h. Prepare the adjusting entry to report the portion of unearned customer deposits that were earned during December.

i. Prepare the adjusting entry to account for income tax expense that accrued during December.

j. On the basis of the adjustments made to the accounting records in parts **a** through **i** above, prepare the company's adjusted trial balance at December 31, 2015.

k. Using the adjusted trial balance prepared in part **j** above, prepare an *annual* income statement, statement of retained earnings, and a balance sheet dated December 31, 2015.

l. Using the financial statements prepared in part **k** above, determine approximately how many days on average an account receivable remains outstanding before it is collected. You may assume that the company's ending accounts receivable balance on December 31 is a close approximation of its average accounts receivable balance throughout the year.

m. Using the financial statements prepared in part **k,** determine approximately how many days on average an item of merchandise remains in stock before it is sold. You may assume that the company's ending merchandise inventory balance on December 31 is a close approximation of its average merchandise inventory balance throughout the year.

n. Using the financial statements prepared in part **k,** determine approximately how many days it takes to convert the company's inventory into cash. In other words, what is the length of the company's operating cycle?

o. Comment briefly upon the company's financial condition from the perspective of a short-term creditor.

CHAPTER 9

Plant and Intangible Assets

AFTER STUDYING THIS CHAPTER, YOU SHOULD BE ABLE TO:

Learning Objectives

LO9-1 Determine the cost of plant assets.

LO9-2 Distinguish between capital expenditures and revenue expenditures.

LO9-3 Compute depreciation by the straight-line and declining-balance methods.

LO9-4 Account for depreciation using methods other than straight-line or declining-balance.

LO9-5 Account for the disposal of plant assets.

LO9-6 Explain the nature of intangible assets, including goodwill.

LO9-7 Account for the depletion of natural resources.

LO9-8 Explain the cash effects of transactions involving plant assets.

© Ken James/Bloomberg via Getty Images

UNITED PARCEL SERVICE

What kind of plant and intangible assets would you expect United Parcel Service to have? Probably the first thing you would think of is vehicles, primarily trucks, because you frequently see UPS trucks on the streets and highways virtually every day. In addition, UPS has a very large investment in aircraft. In fact, property, plant, and equipment make up over 46 percent of UPS's total assets ($17,894 of $38,863 million), according to the company's 2012 consolidated balance sheet. Of the $17,894 million, aircraft and vehicles are the largest types of asset.

How do the amount of plant assets and percentage of plant assets to total assets for UPS compare with other companies? These amounts vary considerably from company to company as evidenced by the following examples:

Ford Motor Company—$24,942 million or 13 percent of total assets; Kimberly-Clark—$8,095 million or 41 percent of total assets; Carnival Corporation—$32,137 million or 82 percent of total assets.

Plant assets are important for companies such as United Parcel Service, Ford Motor Company, Kimberly-Clark, and Carnival Corporation to be successful in their daily operations. The exact types and amount of plant assets used by a particular company depend on the nature of the company and its operations. Virtually all companies need some types of plant assets to operate efficiently and be successful. In addition, some companies require certain intangible assets to do business. Intangibles are rights and privileges that have been developed or acquired, such as trade names and patents; these may be as important to a business as its equipment, buildings, and land. ■

In earlier chapters, we introduced the idea of plant assets and depreciation and stressed the importance of such assets to the successful functioning of any business. In this chapter, we explore in greater depth the accounting issues surrounding plant assets and discuss intangible assets. Together, plant and intangible assets make up significant elements of corporate balance sheets because they represent major investments of resources. The future of many business enterprises depends on their investment in plant and intangible assets.

PLANT ASSETS AS A "STREAM OF FUTURE SERVICES"

Plant assets represent a bundle of future services and, thus, can be thought of as long-term prepaid expenses. Ownership of a delivery truck, for example, may provide 100,000 miles of transportation. The cost of the truck is entered in an asset account, which in essence represents the *advance purchase* of these transportation services. Similarly, a building represents the advance purchase of many years of housing services. As the years go by, these services are utilized by the business, and the cost of the plant asset gradually is transferred to depreciation expense to reflect the cost of using the asset to generate revenue.

MAJOR CATEGORIES OF PLANT ASSETS

Plant and equipment items may be classified into the following groups:

1. **Tangible plant assets.** The term *tangible* refers to an asset's physical characteristics, as exemplified by land, a building, or a machine. This category may be further separated into two distinct classifications:

   a. *Property subject to depreciation.* Included are plant assets of limited useful life such as buildings and office equipment.

   b. *Land.* Generally, the only plant asset not subject to depreciation is land, which has an unlimited term of existence and whose usefulness does not decline over time.

2. **Intangible assets.** The term *intangible assets* is used to describe assets that are used in the operation of the business but have no physical characteristics and are noncurrent. Examples include patents, copyrights, trademarks, franchises, and goodwill. Current assets such as accounts receivable or prepaid rent are not included in the intangible classification, even though they also have value and are lacking in physical substance.

3. **Natural resources.** A site acquired for the purpose of extracting or removing some valuable resource such as oil, minerals, or timber is classified as a *natural resource,* not as land. This type of plant asset is gradually converted into *inventory* as the natural resource is extracted from the site.

ACCOUNTABLE EVENTS IN THE LIVES OF PLANT ASSETS

For all categories of plant assets, there are three primary *accountable events:* (1) acquisition, (2) with the exception of land, allocation of the acquisition cost to expense over the asset's useful life (depreciation), and (3) sale or disposal.

Acquisitions of Plant Assets

LO9-1

LEARNING OBJECTIVE
Determine the cost of plant assets.

The cost of a **plant asset** includes all expenditures that are *reasonable* and *necessary* for getting the asset to the desired location and *ready for use.* In addition to the basic cost of the asset, other incidental costs may be included in the cost assigned to a plant asset. These include, for example, sales taxes on the purchase price, delivery costs, and installation costs.

Only reasonable and necessary costs should be included. Assume, for example, that a machine is dropped and damaged while it is being unloaded. The cost of repairing this damage should be recognized as an expense of the current period, *not* added to the cost of the machine. Although it is necessary to repair the machine, it was not necessary to drop it—and that's what brought about the need for the repairs.

Companies often purchase plant assets on an installment plan or by issuing a note payable. Interest charges after the asset is ready for use are recorded as interest expense, not as part of the cost of the asset. But if a company constructs a plant asset for its own use, the interest charges *during the construction period* are viewed as part of the asset's cost.

DETERMINING COST: AN EXAMPLE

The concept of including in the cost of a plant asset the incidental charges necessary to put the asset in use is illustrated by the following example. A factory in Mississippi orders a machine from a Colorado tool manufacturer at a list price of $10,000. Payment will be made in 48 monthly installments of $250, which include $2,000 in interest charges. Sales taxes of $600 must be paid, as well as freight charges of $1,350. Installation and other set-up costs amount to $500. The cost of this machine to be established in the Machinery account of the purchasing company is computed as follows:

List price*	$10,000
Sales taxes	600
Transportation charges	1,350
Cost of installation and set-up	500
Total	$12,450

 All reasonable and necessary costs are capitalized

*The $2,000 in interest charges on the installment purchase will be recognized as interest expense over the next 48 months. (Accounting for installment notes payable is discussed in the next chapter.)

SOME SPECIAL CONSIDERATIONS

Land   When land is purchased, various incidental costs may be incurred in addition to the purchase price. These additional costs may include commissions to real estate brokers, escrow fees, legal fees for examining and insuring the title, delinquent taxes paid by the purchaser, and fees for surveying, draining, clearing, and grading the property. All these expenditures become part of the cost of the land.

Sometimes land purchased as a building site has on it an old building that is not suitable for the buyer's use. In this case, the only useful asset being acquired is the land. Therefore, the entire purchase price is charged to the Land account, as well as the costs of tearing down and removing the unusable building.

Land Improvements   Improvements to real estate such as driveways, fences, parking lots, landscaping, and sprinkler systems have limited lives separate from the land and are therefore subject to depreciation. For this reason, they should be recorded in a separate account entitled Land Improvements.

Buildings   Buildings are sometimes purchased with the intention of remodeling them prior to placing them in use. Costs incurred under these circumstances are charged to the Buildings account. After the building has been placed in use, however, ordinary repairs are considered to be maintenance expense when incurred.

Equipment   When equipment is purchased, all of the sales taxes, delivery costs, and costs of getting the equipment in good operating order are treated as part of the cost of the equipment. Once the equipment has been placed in operation, maintenance costs (including interest, insurance, and property taxes) are treated as expenses of the current period.

Allocation of a Lump-Sum Purchase   Several different types of plant assets may be purchased at one time. Separate asset accounts are maintained for each type of plant asset, such as land, buildings, and equipment.[1]

When land and buildings (and perhaps other assets) are purchased for a lump sum, the purchase price must be *allocated* among the types of assets acquired. An appraisal may be

---

[1] Each control account is supported by a subsidiary ledger providing information about the cost, annual depreciation, and book value of each asset (or group of similar assets).

needed for this purpose. Assume, for example, that Exercise-for-Health, Inc., purchases a complete fitness center from Golden Health Spas. Exercise-for-Health purchases the entire facility at a bargain price of $800,000. The allocation of this cost on the basis of an appraisal is illustrated as follows:

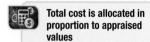

Total cost is allocated in proportion to appraised values

	Value per Appraisal	Percentage of Total Appraised Value	Allocation of $800,000 Cost
Land	$ 250,000	25%	$200,000
Land improvements	50,000	5	40,000
Building	300,000	30	240,000
Equipment	400,000	40	320,000
Total	$1,000,000	100%	$800,000

Assuming that Exercise-for-Health purchased this facility for cash, the journal entry to record this acquisition would be:

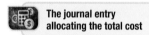

The journal entry allocating the total cost

Land	200,000	
Land Improvements	40,000	
Building	240,000	
Equipment	320,000	
Cash		800,000

To record purchase of fitness center from Golden Health Spas for cash.

YOUR TURN — You as the New Facility Manager for Exercise-for-Health

Assume you have been hired as manager of the new Golden Health Spas facility that was recently purchased by Exercise-for-Health. One of your responsibilities as manager is to show that the facility is profitable. In fact, your contract specifies a bonus for you if the profits are at least 10 percent above the budgeted amount each year. In a recent conversation with the appraiser, it becomes clear to you that some of the items classified as land in the appraisal were really building improvements. No one at Exercise-for-Health is aware of this misclassification. As a result, the appraised value for the building asset account should be $350,000 instead of $300,000. When budgeted profits for the Golden Health Spas facility are computed each year, a charge for depreciation on the building is deducted in determining the amount of profit. What impact does the improper appraisal have on your ability to achieve the bonus? What should you do?

(See our comments on the Online Learning Center website.)

LO9-2

LEARNING OBJECTIVE
Distinguish between capital expenditures and revenue expenditures.

CAPITAL EXPENDITURES AND REVENUE EXPENDITURES

Expenditures for the purchase or expansion of plant assets are called **capital expenditures** and are recorded in asset accounts. Accountants often use the verb **capitalize** to mean charging an expenditure to an asset account rather than to an expense account. Expenditures for ordinary repairs, maintenance, fuel, and other items necessary to the ownership and use of plant and equipment are called **revenue expenditures** and are recorded in expense accounts. The charge to an expense account is based on the assumption that the benefits from the expenditure will be used up in the current period, and therefore the cost should be deducted from the revenue of the period in determining the net income. Charging an expenditure directly to an expense account is often called "expensing" the item.

A business may purchase many small items that will benefit several accounting periods but that have a relatively low cost. Examples of such items include auto batteries, hand tools, wastebaskets, and pencil sharpeners. Such items are theoretically capital expenditures, but if they are recorded as assets in the accounting records, it will be necessary to compute and record the related depreciation expense in future periods. We have previously mentioned the idea that the extra work involved in developing more precise accounting information should be weighed against the benefits that result. Thus, for reasons of convenience and economy, expenditures that are *not material* in dollar amount are treated in the accounting records as expenses of the current period.

In brief, any material expenditure that will benefit several accounting periods is considered a *capital expenditure.* Any expenditure that will benefit only the current period or that is not material in amount is treated as a *revenue expenditure.*

Many companies develop formal policies defining capital and revenue expenditures as a guide toward consistent accounting practice from year to year. These policy statements often set a minimum dollar amount (such as $500) for expenditures that are to be capitalized, regardless of the expected useful life of the asset.

Depreciation

We first introduced the concept of depreciation in Chapter 4. Now we expand that discussion to address such topics as residual values and alternative depreciation methods.

ALLOCATING THE COST OF PLANT AND EQUIPMENT OVER THE YEARS OF USE

Tangible plant assets, with the exception of land, are of use to a company for only a limited number of years. **Depreciation,** as the term is used in accounting, is the *allocation of the cost of a tangible plant asset to expense in the periods in which services are received from the asset.* The basic purpose of depreciation is to offset the revenue of an accounting period with the costs of the goods and services being consumed in the effort to generate that revenue. (See Exhibit 9–1.)

Earlier in this chapter, we described a delivery truck as a stream of transportation services to be received over the years that the truck is owned and used. The cost of the truck initially is added to an asset account, because the purchase of these transportation services will benefit several future accounting periods. As these services are received, however, the cost of the truck gradually is removed from the balance sheet and becomes an expense, through the process of depreciation.

Depreciation: a process of allocating the cost of an asset to expense over the asset's useful life

The journal entry to record depreciation expense consists of a debit to Depreciation Expense and a credit to Accumulated Depreciation. The credit portion of the entry removes

EXHIBIT 9–1 The Depreciation Process

from the balance sheet that portion of the asset's cost estimated to have been used up during the current period. The debit portion of the entry allocates this expired cost to expense.

Separate Depreciation Expense and Accumulated Depreciation accounts are maintained for different types of depreciable assets, such as factory buildings, delivery equipment, and office equipment. These separate accounts help accountants to measure separately the costs of different business activities, such as manufacturing, sales, and administration.

Depreciation Is Not a Process of Valuation   Depreciation is a process of *cost allocation,* not a process of asset valuation. Accounting records do not attempt to show the current market values of plant assets. The market value of a building, for example, may increase during some accounting periods within the building's useful life. The recognition of depreciation expense continues, however, without regard to such temporary increases in market value. Accountants recognize that the building will render useful services only for a limited number of years and that the full cost of the building should be *systematically allocated to expense* during these years.

Depreciation differs from most other expenses in that it does not depend on cash payments at or near the time the expense is recorded. For this reason, depreciation often is called a "non-cash" expense. Bear in mind, however, that large cash payments usually are required at the time depreciable assets are purchased.

Book Value   Plant assets are shown in the balance sheet at their book values (or *carrying values*). The **book value** of a plant asset is its *cost minus the related accumulated depreciation.* Accumulated depreciation is a contra-asset account, representing that portion of the asset's cost that has *already* been allocated to expense. Thus, book value represents the portion of the asset's cost that remains to be allocated to expense in future periods.

CAUSES OF DEPRECIATION

The need to systematically allocate plant asset costs over multiple accounting periods arises from two major causes: (1) physical deterioration and (2) obsolescence.

Physical Deterioration   Physical deterioration of a plant asset results from use, as well as from exposure to sun, wind, and other climatic factors. When a plant asset has been carefully maintained, it is not uncommon for the owner to claim that the asset is as "good as new." Such statements are not literally true. Although a good repair policy may lengthen the useful life of a machine, every machine eventually reaches the point at which it must be discarded. Making repairs does not eliminate the need for recognition of depreciation.

Obsolescence   The term *obsolescence* refers to the process of an asset's becoming out of date as a result of improved, more efficient assets becoming available. An airplane, for example, may become obsolete even though it is in excellent physical condition; it becomes obsolete because better planes of superior design and performance become available.

METHODS OF COMPUTING DEPRECIATION

LO9-3

LEARNING OBJECTIVE
Compute depreciation by the straight-line and declining-balance methods.

In Chapter 4, we computed depreciation only by the **straight-line depreciation** method. Companies actually may use several depreciation methods. Generally accepted accounting principles require only that a depreciation method result in a *rational and systematic* allocation of cost over the asset's useful life. The straight-line method is by far the most commonly used depreciation method for financial reporting purposes.

The straight-line method allocates an *equal portion* of depreciation expense to each period of the asset's expected useful life. Most of the other depreciation methods are various forms of accelerated depreciation. The term **accelerated depreciation** means that larger amounts of depreciation are recognized in the early years of the asset's life, and the amount of depreciation gradually diminishes during the useful life of the asset. Over the entire life of the asset, however, both the straight-line method and accelerated methods recognize the same *total* amount of depreciation.

The differences between the straight-line method and accelerated methods are illustrated in Exhibit 9–2.

STRAIGHT-LINE METHOD

Annual depreciation expense

1 2 3 4 5
Years

AN ACCELERATED METHOD

Annual depreciation expense

1 2 3 4 5
Years

EXHIBIT 9–2

Straight-Line And Accelerated Depreciation Methods

 Both methods recognize the same total depreciation

There are several accelerated methods, each producing slightly different results. Different depreciation methods may be used for different assets. The depreciation methods in use should be disclosed in notes accompanying the financial statements.

In this section, we illustrate and explain straight-line depreciation and one variation of the most widely used accelerated method, which is called *fixed-percentage-of-declining-balance,* or simply the *declining-balance* method. Other depreciation methods are discussed briefly in the section that follows.

© The McGraw-Hill Companies, Inc./Ken Karp, photographer

Data for Our Illustrations   Our illustrations of depreciation methods are based on the following data: On January 2, S&G Wholesale Grocery acquires a new delivery truck. The data and estimates needed for the computation of the annual depreciation expense are:

Cost	$17,000
Estimated residual value	$ 2,000
Estimated useful life	5 years

THE STRAIGHT-LINE METHOD

Under the straight-line method, an *equal portion* of the asset's cost is recognized as depreciation expense in each year of the asset's useful life. Annual depreciation expense is computed by deducting the estimated **residual value** (or **salvage value**) from the cost of the asset and dividing the remaining *depreciable cost* by the years of estimated useful life. Using the data in our example, the annual straight-line depreciation is computed as follows:

$$\frac{\textbf{Cost} - \textbf{Residual Value}}{\textbf{Years of Useful Life}} = \frac{\$17,000 - \$2,000}{5 \textbf{ years}} = \$3,000 \textbf{ per year}$$

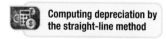 **Computing depreciation by the straight-line method**

In Exhibit 9–3, the schedule summarizes the effects of straight-line depreciation over the entire life of the asset.

(We present several depreciation schedules in this chapter. In each schedule we highlight in red those features that we want to emphasize.)

The term "book value" in Exhibit 9–3 is the amount of the depreciable cost of the asset that has not yet been recognized as depreciation expense at a point in time. For example, book value at the end of the third year after depreciation for that year has been recognized is $8,000, computed as follows:

Cost	$17,000
Accumulated depreciation at end of third year ($3,000 × 3 years)	(9,000)
Book value	$ 8,000

EXHIBIT 9–3

Straight-Line Depreciation
Schedule

Constant annual
depreciation expense

Depreciation Schedule: Straight-Line Method				
Year	Computation	Depreciation Expense	Accumulated Depreciation	Book Value
				$17,000
First	$15,000 × ⅕	$ 3,000	$ 3,000	14,000
Second.................	15,000 × ⅕	3,000	6,000	11,000
Third	15,000 × ⅕	3,000	9,000	8,000
Fourth..................	15,000 × ⅕	3,000	12,000	5,000
Fifth	15,000 × ⅕	3,000	15,000	2,000
Total		$15,000		

This amount is presented as an asset in the statement of financial position (balance sheet).

Notice that the depreciation expense over the life of the truck totals *$15,000*—the cost of the truck *minus the estimated residual value.* The residual value is *not* part of the cost "used up" in business operations. Instead, the residual value is expected to be recovered in cash upon disposal of the asset.

In practice, residual values may be ignored if they are not expected to be *material* in amount. Office equipment, furniture, fixtures, and special-purpose equipment seldom are considered to have significant residual values. Assets such as vehicles, aircraft, and construction equipment, in contrast, often do have residual values that are material in amount.

It often is convenient to state the portion of an asset's depreciable cost that will be written off during the year as a percentage, called the *depreciation rate.* When straight-line depreciation is in use, the depreciation rate is simply *1* divided by the *life* (in years) of the asset. The delivery truck in our example has an estimated life of five years, so the depreciation expense each year is ⅕, or 20 percent, of the depreciable amount. Similarly, an asset with a 10-year life has a depreciation rate of $\frac{1}{10}$ or 10 percent; and an asset with an eight-year life, a depreciation rate of ⅛, or 12½ percent.

Depreciation for Fractional Periods

When an asset is acquired during an accounting period, it is not necessary to compute depreciation expense to the nearest day or week. In fact, such a computation would give a misleading impression of great precision. Since depreciation is based on an estimated useful life of many years, the depreciation applicable to any one year is *only an approximation.*

One widely used method of computing depreciation for part of a year is to round the calculation to the nearest whole month. In our example, S&G acquired the delivery truck on January 2. Therefore, we computed a full year's depreciation for the year of acquisition. Assume, however, that the truck had been acquired later in the year on *October 1.* Thus the truck would have been in use for only three months (or $\frac{3}{12}$) of the first year. In this case, depreciation expense for the first year would be only *$750,* or $\frac{3}{12}$ of a full year's depreciation ($3,000 × $\frac{3}{12}$ = $750).

Another widely used approach, called the **half-year convention,** is to record one-half year's depreciation on all assets acquired during the year. This approach is based on the assumption that the actual purchase dates will average out to approximately midyear. The half-year convention is widely used for assets such as office equipment, automobiles, and machinery. To complete the depreciation process for an asset by the half-year convention, a one-half-year's depreciation is also taken in the last year of the asset's life.

Assume that S&G Wholesale Grocery uses straight-line depreciation with the half-year convention. In Exhibit 9–4, we summarize depreciation on the $17,000 delivery truck with the five-year life.

When the half-year convention is in use, we ignore the date on which the asset was actually purchased. We simply recognize *one-half year's depreciation* in both the first year and the last year of the depreciation schedule. Notice that our depreciation schedule now includes depreciation expense in the sixth year. Taking only a partial year's depreciation in the first year always extends the recognition of depreciation into one additional year.

EXHIBIT 9–4

Straight-Line Depreciation
Schedule

Depreciation Schedule
Straight-Line Method with Half-Year Convention

Year	Computation	Depreciation Expense	Accumulated Depreciation	Book Value
				$17,000
First	$15,000 × ⅕ × ½	$ 1,500	$ 1,500	15,500
Second	15,000 × ⅕	3,000	4,500	12,500
Third	15,000 × ⅕	3,000	7,500	9,500
Fourth	15,000 × ⅕	3,000	10,500	6,500
Fifth	15,000 × ⅕	3,000	13,500	3,500
Sixth	15,000 × ⅕ × ½	1,500	15,000	2,000
Total		$15,000		

The half-year convention enables us to treat similar assets acquired at different dates during the year as a single group. For example, assume that an insurance company purchases hundreds of desktop computers throughout the current year at a total cost of $600,000. The company depreciates these computers by the straight-line method, assuming a five-year life and no residual value. Using the half-year convention, the depreciation expense on all of the computers purchased during the year may be computed as follows: $600,000 ÷ 5 years × ⁶⁄₁₂ = $60,000. If we did not use the half-year convention, depreciation would have to be computed separately for computers purchased in different months.

THE DECLINING-BALANCE METHOD

The most widely used accelerated depreciation method is called **fixed-percentage-of-declining-balance depreciation.** However, the method is used primarily in *income tax returns,* rather than financial statements.[2]

Under the declining-balance method, an accelerated *depreciation rate* is computed as a specified percentage of the straight-line depreciation rate. Annual depreciation expense then is computed by applying this accelerated depreciation rate to the undepreciated cost (book value) of the asset. This computation may be summarized as follows:

$$\text{Depreciation Expense} = \text{Remaining Book Value} \times \text{Accelerated Depreciation Rate}$$

The accelerated depreciation rate *remains constant* throughout the life of the asset. Hence, the rate represents the "fixed-percentage" described in the name of this depreciation method. The book value (cost minus accumulated depreciation) *decreases every year* and represents the "declining-balance."

Thus far, we have described the accelerated depreciation rate as a "specified percentage" of the straight-line rate. Most often, this specified percentage is 200 percent, meaning that the accelerated rate is exactly twice the straight-line rate. As a result, the declining-balance method of depreciation often is called *double-declining-balance* (or 200 percent declining-balance). Tax rules, however, often specify a *lower* percentage, such as 150 percent of the straight-line rate. This version of the declining-balance method may be described as "150 percent declining-balance."[3]

---

[2] In 1986, Congress adopted an accelerated method of depreciation called the *Modified Accelerated Cost Recovery System* (or MACRS). Companies may use straight-line depreciation for federal income tax purposes, but most prefer to use MACRS because of its favorable income tax consequences. MACRS is the *only* accelerated depreciation method that may be used in federal income tax returns.

[3] The higher the specified percentage of the straight-line rate, the more accelerated this depreciation becomes. Experience and tradition have established 200 percent of the straight-line rate as the maximum level. For federal income tax purposes, MACRS (see footnote 2) is based upon a 200 percent declining-balance for some assets, and a 150 percent declining-balance for others. The 150 percent declining-balance slows down the rates at which taxpayers may depreciate specific types of assets in their income tax returns.

Double-Declining-Balance To illustrate the double-declining-balance method, consider our example of the $17,000 delivery truck. The estimated useful life is five years; therefore, the straight-line depreciation rate is 20 percent (1 ÷ 5 years). Doubling this straight-line rate indicates an accelerated depreciation rate of 40 percent. Each year, we will recognize as depreciation expense 40 percent of the truck's book value, as we show in Exhibit 9–5.

EXHIBIT 9–5

200% Declining-Balance Depreciation Schedule

Depreciation Schedule: 200% Declining-Balance Method				
Year	Computation	Depreciation Expense	Accumulated Depreciation	Book Value
				$17,000
First	$17,000 × 40%	$ 6,800	$ 6,800	10,200
Second...............	10,200 × 40%	4,080	10,880	6,120
Third	6,120 × 40%	2,448	13,328	3,672
Fourth...............	3,672 × 40%	1,469	14,797	2,203
Fifth	2,203 − $2,000	203	15,000	2,000
Total		$15,000		

As with the straight-line method illustrated earlier, the asset's book value is computed by subtracting depreciation recognized to date from the asset's cost. For example, from Exhibit 9–5, the book value of the asset at the end of the third year is computed as follows:

Cost	$ 17,000
Accumulated depreciation at end of third year ($6,800 + $4,080 + $2,448)	(13,328)
Book value	$ 3,672

Recall that book value at the end of the third year by the straight-line method was $8,000. The difference between that figure and the $3,672 computed above is due to the more rapid depreciation recognized by the declining-balance method compared with the straight-line method.

Notice that the estimated residual value of the delivery truck *does not* enter into the computation of depreciation expense until the end. This is because the declining-balance method provides an *"automatic"* residual value. As long as each year's depreciation expense is equal to only a portion of the undepreciated cost of the asset, the asset *will never be entirely written off.* However, if the asset has a significant residual value, depreciation should *stop at this point.* Since our delivery truck has an estimated residual value of *$2,000,* the depreciation expense for the fifth year is *limited to $203,* rather than the $881 indicated by taking 40 percent of the remaining book value (40% × $2,203 = $881). With the last year's depreciation expense limited in this manner, the book value of the truck at the end of the fifth year is exactly equal to its $2,000 estimated residual value.

In Exhibit 9–5 we computed a full year's depreciation in the first year because the asset was acquired on January 2. But if the half-year convention were in use, depreciation in the first year would be *reduced by half,* to $3,400. The depreciation in the second year would be ($17,000 − $3,400) × 40%, or *$5,440.*

150 Percent Declining-Balance Now assume that we wanted to depreciate this truck using 150 percent of the straight-line rate. In this case, the depreciation rate will be 30 percent, instead of 40 percent (a 20% straight-line rate × 150% = 30%). This depreciation schedule is in Exhibit 9–6.

Notice that we switched to straight-line depreciation in the last two years. The undepreciated cost of the truck at the end of Year 3 was *$5,831.* To depreciate the truck to an estimated residual value of $2,000 at the end of Year 5, $3,831 in depreciation expense must be recognized over the next two years. At this point, *larger depreciation charges* can be recognized if we simply allocate this $3,831 by the straight-line method, rather than continuing to compute 30 percent of the remaining book value. (In our table, we round the allocation of this amount to the nearest dollar.)

Depreciation Schedule: 150% Declining-Balance Method				
Year	Computation	Depreciation Expense	Accumulated Depreciation	Book Value
				$17,000
First	$17,000 × 30%	$ 5,100	$ 5,100	11,900
Second	11,900 × 30%	3,570	8,670	8,330
Third	8,330 × 30%	2,499	11,169	5,831
Fourth	(5,831 − 2,000) ÷ 2	1,916*	13,085	3,915*
Fifth	3,915 − 2,000	1,915*	15,000	2,000*
Total		$15,000		

EXHIBIT 9–6

150% Declining-Balance Depreciation Schedule

*Switched to the straight-line method for Years 4 and 5.

Allocating the remaining book value over the remaining life by the straight-line method does *not* represent a change in depreciation methods. Rather, a switch to straight-line when this will result in larger depreciation is *an accepted part of the declining-balance method.* This is the way in which we arrive at the desired residual value.

WHICH DEPRECIATION METHODS DO MOST BUSINESSES USE?

Many businesses use the straight-line method of depreciation in their financial statements and accelerated methods in their income tax returns. The reasons for these choices are easy to understand.

Accelerated depreciation methods result in higher charges to depreciation expense early in the asset's life and, therefore, lower reported net income than straight-line depreciation. Most publicly owned companies want to appear as profitable as possible—certainly as profitable as their competitors. Therefore, the majority of publicly owned companies use straight-line depreciation in their financial statements.

For income tax purposes, it's a different story. Management wants to report the *lowest* possible taxable income in the company's income tax returns. Accelerated depreciation methods can substantially reduce both taxable income and tax payments for a period of years.[4]

Accounting principles and income tax laws both permit companies to use *different depreciation methods* in their financial statements and their income tax returns. Therefore, many companies use straight-line depreciation in their financial statements and accelerated methods (variations of the declining-balance method) in their income tax returns.

The Differences in Depreciation Methods: Are They "Real"?   Using the straight-line depreciation method will cause a company to *report* higher profits than would be reported if an accelerated method were in use in the early years of the asset's life. But *is* the company better off than if it had used an accelerated method? The answer is *no!* Depreciation—no matter how it is computed—*is only an estimate*. The amount of this estimate has *no effect* on the actual financial strength of the business. Thus, a business that uses an accelerated depreciation method in its financial statements is simply measuring its net income *more conservatively* than a business that uses straight-line. However, the benefits of using an accelerated method for income tax purposes *are* real because the amount of depreciation claimed affects the amount of taxes owed. Lower income taxes translate directly into increased cash availability in the early years of the asset's life.

In the preceding chapter, we made the point that if a company wants to use LIFO in its income tax return, it *must* use LIFO in its financial statements. *No similar requirement exists for depreciation methods.* A company may use an accelerated method in its income tax returns and the straight-line method in its financial statements—and most companies do.

---

[4] For a *growing* business, the use of accelerated depreciation in income tax returns may reduce taxable income *every* year. This is because a growing business may always have more assets in the early years of its recovery periods than in the later years.

FINANCIAL STATEMENT DISCLOSURES

A company must *disclose* in the accounting policy note to its financial statements the methods used to depreciate plant assets. Readers of the statements should recognize that accelerated depreciation methods transfer the costs of plant assets to expense more quickly than the straight-line method. Accelerated methods result in more *conservative* (lower) balance sheet amounts of plant assets and lower amounts of net income in the early years of an asset's life. These differences eventually reverse as assets more through their life cycles.

Estimates of Useful Life and Residual Value

Estimating the useful lives and residual values of plant assets is the *responsibility of management.* These estimates usually are based on the company's past experience with similar assets, but they also reflect the company's current circumstances and management's future plans. The estimated lives of similar assets may vary from one company to another.

The estimated lives of plant assets affect the amount of net income reported each period. The longer the estimated useful life, the smaller the amount of cost transferred each period to depreciation expense and the larger the amount of reported net income. Bear in mind, however, that all large corporations are *audited* annually by a firm of independent public accountants. One of the responsibilities of these auditors is to determine that management's estimates of the useful lives of plant assets are reasonable under the circumstances.

Automobiles typically are depreciated over relatively short estimated lives—say, from three to five years. Other types of equipment are generally depreciated over a period of 5 to 15 years. Buildings are usually depreciated over longer lives—perhaps 30 to 50 years for a new building and 15 years or more for a building acquired used.

The Principle of Consistency

The *consistent* application of accounting methods is a fundamental concept underlying generally accepted accounting principles. With respect to depreciation methods, this means that a company *does not change* from year to year the method used in computing the depreciation expense for a given plant asset. However, management *may* use different methods in computing depreciation for different assets. For example, a common practice is to depreciate vehicles and equipment by an accelerated method and buildings by the straight-line method. Also, as we have stressed repeatedly, a company may—and often *must*— use different depreciation methods in its financial statements and income tax returns.

Revision of Estimated Useful Lives

What should be done if, after a few years of using a plant asset, management decides that the asset actually is going to last for a longer or shorter period than was originally estimated? When this situation arises, a *revised estimate* of useful life should be made and the periodic depreciation expense decreased or increased accordingly.

The procedure for changing the depreciation schedule is to spread the remaining undepreciated cost of the asset *over the years of remaining useful life.* This change affects only the amount of depreciation expense that will be recorded in the current and future periods. The financial statements of past periods are *not* revised to reflect changes in the estimated useful lives of depreciable assets.

To illustrate, assume that a company acquires a $10,000 asset estimated to have a five-year useful life and no residual value. Under the straight-line method, the annual depreciation expense is $2,000. At the end of the third year, accumulated depreciation is $6,000, and the asset has an undepreciated cost (or book value) of $4,000.

At the beginning of the fourth year, management decides that the asset will last for five *more* years. The revised estimate of useful life is, therefore, a total of eight years. The depreciation expense to be recognized for the fourth year and for each of the remaining years is $800, computed as follows:

Undepreciated cost at end of third year ($10,000 − $6,000).....................	$4,000
Revised estimate of remaining years of useful life............................	5 years
Revised amount of annual depreciation expense ($4,000 ÷ 5).................	$ 800

THE IMPAIRMENT OF PLANT ASSETS

A company may determine that if cannot reasonably expect to recover the carrying amount of certain plant assets, either through use or through sale. For example, a computer manufacturer may have paid a high price to acquire specialized production equipment. If new technology renders the equipment obsolete, however, it may become apparent that it is worth less than the amount at which the equipment is carried in the accounting records.

If the carrying amount of an asset cannot be recovered through future use or sale, the asset should be *written down* to its fair value. The offsetting debit is to an **impairment loss** account.

CASE IN POINT

The 2012 balance sheet of JCPenney includes $5,353 million of property and equipment. This represents approximately 55 percent of the company's reported assets. A note to the financial statements indicates that the company evaluates long-lived assets, such as store property and equipment and other corporate assets, for impairment whenever events or changes in circumstances indicate that the carrying amount of those assets may not be recoverable. Factors that may trigger an impairment review include significant underperformance relative to historical or projected operating results, significant changes in the manner of use of the assets, and changes in the company's overall business strategies. The amount of the impairment loss represents the excess of the carrying value (i.e., book value) of the asset over its fair value.

Other Depreciation Methods

Most companies that prepare financial statements in conformity with generally accepted accounting principles use the straight-line method of depreciation. However, any rational and systematic method is acceptable, as long as costs are allocated to expense in a reasonable manner. Several such methods are discussed here.

LO9-4

LEARNING OBJECTIVE
Account for depreciation using methods other than straight-line or declining-balance.

THE UNITS-OF-OUTPUT METHOD

Under the **units-of-output** method, depreciation is based on some measure of output *rather than* on the passage of time. When depreciation is based on units of output, more depreciation is recognized in the periods in which the assets are most heavily used.

To illustrate this method, consider S&G's delivery truck, which cost $17,000 and has an estimated salvage value of $2,000. Assume that S&G plans to retire this truck after it has been driven 100,000 miles. The depreciation rate *per mile of operation is 15 cents,* computed as follows:

$$\frac{\text{Cost} - \text{Residual Value}}{\text{Estimated Units of Output (Miles)}} = \frac{\text{Cost per}}{\text{Unit of Output (Mile)}}$$

$$\frac{\$17,000 - \$2,000}{100,000 \text{ miles}} = \$0.15 \text{ Depreciation per Mile}$$

At the end of each year, the amount of depreciation to be recorded is determined by multiplying the 15-cent rate by the number of miles the truck was actually driven during the year. After the truck has gone 100,000 miles, it is fully depreciated, and the depreciation process is stopped.

This method provides an excellent matching of expense with revenue. However, the method should be used only when the total units of output can be estimated with reasonable accuracy. Also, this method is used only for assets such as vehicles and certain types of machinery. Assets such as buildings, computers, and furniture do not have well-defined "units of output" and ordinarily do not use this method.

In many cases, units-of-output becomes an *accelerated method.* Often assets are used more extensively in the earlier years of their useful lives than in the later years.

MACRS

Most businesses use **MACRS** (Modified Accelerated Cost Recovery System) in their federal income tax returns. Some small businesses also use this method in their financial statements, so they do not have to compute depreciation in several different ways. MACRS is based on the declining-balance method, but should be considered for use in financial statements only if the *designated "recovery periods"* and the *assumption of no salvage value* are reasonable. For publicly traded companies, the use of MACRS in financial statements is usually not considered to be in conformity with generally accepted accounting principles.

SUM-OF-THE-YEARS' DIGITS

Sum-of-the-years' digits, or **SYD,** is a form of accelerated depreciation. It generally produces results that lie between the double-declining-balance and 150 percent-declining-balance methods.

SYD is a traditional topic that is included in many accounting textbooks. But it is the most complex of the accelerated methods—especially when partial years are involved. SYD is rarely used in today's business world. Because of its complexity, it is even less frequently used in small businesses. SYD is seldom used for income tax purposes, because tax laws usually define allowable depreciation rates in terms of the declining-balance method. For these reasons, we defer coverage of the mechanics of this method to later accounting courses.

DECELERATED DEPRECIATION METHODS

Depreciation methods exist that recognize *less* depreciation expense in the early years of an asset's useful life and *more in the later years.* Such methods may achieve a reasonable matching of depreciation expense and revenue when the plant asset is expected to become *increasingly productive* over time. Utility companies, for example, may use these methods for new power plants that will be more fully utilized as the population of the area increases.

These depreciation methods are rarely used; thus we defer coverage to later accounting courses.

DEPRECIATION METHODS IN USE: A SURVEY

For many years, the American Institute of Certified Public Accountants (AICPA) has conducted a survey of 600 publicly owned companies to determine the accounting methods most widely used in financial statements. The number of methods in use exceeds 600 because some companies use different depreciation methods for different types of assets.

For many consecutive years, the straight-line method has consistently been by far the most widely used method of depreciation in financial statements. In fact, in most years the straight-line method accounts for approximately 90 percent of the depreciation methods used by these companies. Other methods covered in this chapter—units-of-output and various accelerated methods—are used relatively infrequently in the financial statements of these companies.

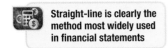 **Straight-line is clearly the method most widely used in financial statements**

Bear in mind this survey indicates only the depreciation methods used in financial statements. In income tax returns, most companies use accelerated depreciation methods such as MACRS.

Disposal of Plant and Equipment

L09-5

LEARNING OBJECTIVE
Account for the disposal of plant assets.

When depreciable assets are disposed of at any date other than the end of the year, an entry should be made to update depreciation to the date of disposal. If the half-year convention is in use, six months' depreciation should be recorded on all assets disposed of during the year. In the following illustrations of the disposal of items of plant and equipment, it is assumed that any necessary entries for fractional-period depreciation already have been recorded.

As units of plant and equipment wear out or become obsolete, they must be scrapped, sold, or traded in on new equipment. Upon the disposal or retirement of a depreciable asset, the cost of the property is removed from the asset account, and the accumulated depreciation is removed from the related contra-asset account. Assume, for example, that office equipment purchased 10 years ago at a cost of $20,000 has been fully depreciated and is no longer useful. The entry to record the scrapping of the worthless equipment is as follows:

Accumulated Depreciation: Office Equipment.......................	20,000	
Office Equipment		20,000

To remove from the accounts the cost and the accumulated depreciation on fully depreciated office equipment now being scrapped. No salvage value.

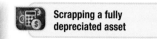

Scrapping a fully depreciated asset

Once an asset has been fully depreciated, no more depreciation should be recorded on it, even though the property may still be in use. The objective of depreciation is to spread the *cost* of an asset over the periods of its usefulness; in no case can depreciation expense be greater than the cost of the asset. When a fully depreciated asset remains in use beyond the original estimate of useful life, the asset account and the Accumulated Depreciation account should remain in the accounting records without further entries until the asset is retired.

GAINS AND LOSSES ON THE DISPOSAL OF PLANT AND EQUIPMENT

Since the residual values and useful lives of plant assets are only estimates, it is not uncommon for a plant asset to be disposed of at an amount that differs from its book value at the date of disposal. When plant assets are sold, any gain or loss on the disposal is computed by comparing the *book value with the amount received from the sale*. A sales price in excess of the book value produces a gain; a sales price below the book value produces a loss. These gains or losses, if material in amount, are shown separately in the income statement following the computation of income from operations, usually in a section titled "other income."

Disposal at a Price above Book Value Assume that a machine costing $10,000 had accumulated depreciation of $8,000 and a book value of $2,000 at the time it was sold for $3,000 cash. The journal entry to record this disposal is as follows:

Cash..	3,000	
Accumulated Depreciation: Machinery	8,000	
Machinery		10,000
Gain on Disposal of Plant Assets		1,000

To record sale of machinery at a price above book value.

Gain on disposal of plant asset

In this situation, the gain on the disposal is calculated as follows:

Cost	$10,000
Accumulated depreciation at time of disposal	(8,000)
Book value at time of disposal...................................	$ 2,000
Cash received	3,000
Gain on disposal	$ 1,000

Disposal at a Price below Book Value Now assume instead that the same machine is sold for $500. The journal entry in this case would be as follows:

Cash..	500	
Accumulated Depreciation: Machinery	8,000	
Loss on Disposal of Plant Assets...............................	1,500	
Machinery.......................................		10,000

To record sale of machinery at a price below book value.

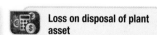

Loss on disposal of plant asset

In this situation, the loss on the disposal is calculated as follows:

Cost	$10,000
Accumulated depreciation at time of disposal	(8,000)
Book value at time of disposal	$ 2,000
Cash received	500
Loss on disposal	$ 1,500

The disposal of a depreciable asset at a price *equal to* book value results in neither a gain nor a loss. The entry for such a transaction consists of a debit to Cash for the amount received, a debit to Accumulated Depreciation for the balance accumulated, and a credit to the asset account for the original cost.

TRADING IN USED ASSETS FOR NEW ONES

Certain types of depreciable assets, such as automobiles and trucks, sometimes are traded in for new assets of the same type. In most instances, a trade-in is viewed as both a *sale* of the old asset and a purchase of a new one. Transactions of this type are usually considered to have "commercial substance," and give rise to the recognition of a gain or loss.

To illustrate, assume that Rancho Landscape has an old pickup truck that originally cost $10,000 but that now has a book value (and tax basis) of $2,000. Rancho trades in this old truck for a new one with a fair market value of $25,000. The truck dealership grants Rancho a trade-in allowance of $3,500 for the old truck, and Rancho pays the remaining $21,500 cost of the new truck in cash. Rancho Landscape will record this transaction as follows:

 Entry to record a typical trade-in

Vehicles (new truck)	25,000	
Accumulated Depreciation: Trucks (old truck)	8,000	
Vehicles (old truck)		10,000
Cash		21,500
Gain on Disposal of Plant Assets		1,500
Traded in old truck for a new one costing $25,000. Received $3,500 trade-in allowance on the old truck, which had a book value of $2,000.		

Notice that Rancho treats the $3,500 trade-in allowance granted by the truck dealership as the *sales price* of the old truck. Thus Rancho recognizes a *$1,500 gain* on the disposal (trade-in) of this asset ($3,500 trade-in allowance − $2,000 book value = $1,500 gain).

For financial reporting purposes, gains and losses on routine trade-ins are recorded in the accounting records whenever the transaction also involves the payment of a significant amount of cash (or the creation of debt). Income tax rules do *not* permit recognition of gains or losses on exchanges of assets that are used for similar purposes. Thus, the $1,500 gain recorded in our example is not regarded as taxable income.[5]

INTERNATIONAL FINANCIAL REPORTING STANDARDS

In discussing plant assets and depreciation, we have emphasized the use of historical cost and that depreciation is a process of allocating or spreading that cost over the useful life of the asset. Under U.S. generally accepted accounting principles, this emphasis on cost and depreciation is due primarily to the importance of including as an expense a portion of the cost of the plant assets which contributed to the earning of a company's income. Cost reduced by accumulated depreciation is the amount shown in the statement of financial position (balance sheet) and generally does not reflect the current value of the asset other than situations where an impairment in value is recorded as described earlier.

---

[5] Had the trade-in allowance been less than book value, the resulting loss would *not be deductible* in the determination of taxable income.

Under international accounting standards, companies have an option to follow a revaluation process rather than continuing to use historical cost throughout the asset's useful life. This revaluation alternative requires that an asset's fair value can be reliably measured and it must be applied to an entire class of plant assets. Revaluation is not required every financial reporting period, but must be frequent enough to ensure that the carrying amount of the asset (i.e., its revalued amount less accumulated depreciation) does not differ materially from what it would be if determined by fair value at the end of the financial reporting period.

If an asset's carrying amount is increased as a result of a revaluation, the increase is recorded in other comprehensive income and accumulated equity. This subject is covered in greater depth in Chapter 12 of this textbook.

Intangible Assets

CHARACTERISTICS

As the word *intangible* suggests, assets in this classification have no physical characteristics. Common examples are patents, trademarks, and goodwill. Intangible assets are classified in the balance sheet as a subgroup of plant assets. However, not all assets that lack physical substance are regarded as intangible assets. An account receivable, for example, has no physical attributes but is classified as a current asset and is not regarded as an intangible. In brief, *intangible assets are assets that are used in the operation of the business but that have no physical substance and are noncurrent.*

L09-6

LEARNING OBJECTIVE
Explain the nature of intangible assets, including goodwill.

The basis of valuation for intangible assets is cost. In some companies, however, certain intangible assets such as trademarks may be of great importance but may have been acquired without incurring any significant cost. These intangible assets appear in the balance sheet at their *cost,* regardless of their value to the company. Intangible assets are listed only if significant costs are incurred in their acquisition or development. If these costs are *insignificant,* they are treated as revenue expenditures (ordinary expenses).

OPERATING EXPENSES VERSUS INTANGIBLE ASSETS

For an expenditure to qualify as an intangible asset, there must be reasonable evidence of future benefits. Many expenditures offer some prospects of yielding benefits in subsequent years, but the existence and life span of these benefits are so uncertain that most companies treat these expenditures as operating expenses. Examples are the expenditures required to reorganize a business and the expense of training employees to work with new types of machinery or office equipment. There is little doubt that some benefits from these outlays continue beyond the current period, but because of the uncertain duration of the benefits, it is almost universal practice to treat expenditures of this nature as an expense of the current period.

AMORTIZATION

The term **amortization** describes the systematic write-off to expense of the cost of an intangible asset over its useful life. Amortization of an intangible asset is essentially the same as depreciation for a tangible asset. The usual accounting entry for amortization consists of a debit to Amortization Expense and a credit to the intangible asset account. There is no theoretical objection to crediting an accumulated amortization account rather than the intangible asset account, but this method is seldom encountered in practice.

Although it is difficult to estimate the useful life of an intangible such as a trademark, it is probable that such an asset will not contribute to future earnings on a permanent basis. The cost of the intangible asset should, therefore, be deducted from revenue during the years in which it may be expected to aid in producing revenue. The straight-line method normally is used for amortizing intangible assets.

GOODWILL

The intangible asset **goodwill** is often found in corporate balance sheets. While this word has a variety of meanings in our general vocabulary, it has a specific and specialized meaning in financial reporting. Goodwill represents an amount that a company has paid to acquire certain favorable intangible attributes as part of an acquisition of another company. For example, assume a company purchases another company that has a favorable reputation for high-quality customer service. The purchasing company might be willing to pay a premium price to acquire this favorable attribute because of the positive impact this customer service is expected to have on future profitability. Even though an intangible asset such as a favorable reputation for customer service lacks the physical qualities of land, buildings, and equipment, such service may be just as important for the future success of a company.

Goodwill is a general term that encompasses a wide variety of favorable attributes expected to permit the acquiring company to operate at a greater-than-normal level of profitability. Positive attributes often included in goodwill are:

- Favorable reputation.
- Positive market share.
- Positive advertising image.
- Reputation for high quality and loyal employees.
- Superior management.
- Manufacturing and other operating efficiency.

All of these attributes can be expected to contribute to positive future cash flows of the acquiring company. The **present value** of future cash flows is the amount that a knowledgeable investor would pay today for the right to receive those future cash flows. (The present value concept is discussed further in later chapters and in Appendix B.)

Goodwill is sometimes described and measured as the price paid to receive an *above-normal return* on the purchase of another company's net identifiable assets. *Net assets* refers to assets minus liabilities, or owners' equity. Goodwill is not a separately identifiable asset, however, and the existence of goodwill is implied by the ability of a business to earn an above-average return. The term **net identifiable assets** is used to mean all assets except goodwill, minus liabilities.

A *normal return* on net identifiable assets is the rate of return that investors demand in a particular industry to justify purchasing a business at the fair value of its net identifiable assets. A business has goodwill when investors will pay an even *higher* price because the business earns *more* than the normal rate of return.

Assume that two similar restaurants are offered for sale and that the normal return on the fair market value of the net identifiable assets of restaurants of this type is 15 percent a year. The relative earning power of the two restaurants during the past five years is as follows:

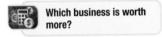
Which business is worth more?

	Mandarin Coast	Golden Dragon
Fair market value of net identifiable assets	$1,000,000	$1,000,000
Normal rate of return on net assets	15%	15%
Normal earnings, computed as 15% of net identifiable assets ...	$ 150,000	$ 150,000
Average actual net income for past five years	150,000	200,000
Earnings in excess of normal	$ –0–	$ 50,000

An investor presumably would be willing to pay $1,000,000 to buy Mandarin Coast, because this restaurant earns the expected 15 percent return that justifies the fair market value of its net identifiable assets. Although Golden Dragon has the same amount of net identifiable assets, an investor should be willing to pay *more* for Golden Dragon than for Mandarin Coast, because Golden Dragon has a record of superior earnings. The *extra amount* that a buyer pays to purchase Golden Dragon represents the value of this business's *goodwill.*

Estimating Goodwill   How much will an investor pay for goodwill? Above-average earnings in past years are of significance to prospective purchasers only if they believe that these earnings *will continue* after they acquire the business. Investors' appraisals of goodwill, therefore, will vary with their estimates of the *future earning power* of the business. Few businesses, however, are able to maintain above-average earnings indefinitely. Consequently, the purchaser of a business will usually limit any amount paid for goodwill to not more than four or five times the amount by which annual earnings exceed normal earnings.

Estimating an amount for goodwill in the purchase of a business is a difficult and speculative process. In attempting to make such an estimate, you are essentially trying to look into the future and predict the extent to which purchasing another business will add enough value to your current business that you are willing to pay a price greater than the value of the identifiable net assets of the business you are acquiring. For example, in the previous example, how much more than $1,000,000 would you be willing to pay for Golden Dragon in comparison with Mandarin Coast? History indicates that Golden Dragon is more profitable, and thus worth more, than Mandarin Coast, but whether that extra profitability will continue in the future requires considerable judgment.

Several methods are used to place a monetary value on the amount of goodwill in the purchase of a business. One widely used method that is consistent with the description of goodwill is to value the business as a whole and then subtract the current value of the net identifiable assets to estimate the amount of goodwill. For example, assume that successful restaurants sell at about 6½ times annual earnings.[6] This suggests that Golden Dragon is worth about $1,300,000, which is the company's $200,000 average net income times 6.5. Because the company's net identifiable assets have a fair value of only $1,000,000, using this method a reasonable estimate of the positive attributes of Golden Dragon, such as positive reputation or market share, is $300,000, determined as follows:

Estimated value of the business as a whole ($200,000 × 6.5)	$1,300,000
Fair market value of net identifiable assets	1,000,000
Estimated value of goodwill.......................................	$ 300,000

If a buyer of Golden Dragon pays $1,300,000 to purchase the business, $300,000 of goodwill would be recorded. On the other hand, if the buyer is able to purchase Golden Dragon for less than $1,300,000, say, $1,250,000, only $250,000 of goodwill would be recorded ($1,250,000 − $1,000,000 = $250,000), even though the estimated value of goodwill is more than the amount paid.

Recording Goodwill in the Accounts
Because of the difficulties in objectively estimating the value of goodwill, this asset is recorded only when it is purchased. Goodwill is purchased when one company buys another. The purchaser records the identifiable assets it has purchased at their fair values and then establishes any additional amount paid to an asset account entitled Goodwill.

Many businesses never purchase goodwill but develop goodwill attributes like good customer relations, superior management, or other factors that result in above-average earnings. Because there is no objective way of determining the value of these qualities unless the business is sold, internally generated goodwill is *not recorded* in the accounting records. The absence of internally generated goodwill and other intangible assets is one of the reasons why a balance sheet does not indicate a company's current market value.

For many years, generally accepted accounting principles required that purchased goodwill be amortized over a period not exceeding 40 years. Goodwill is no longer required to be amortized, but is now subject to assessment for impairment in value, similar to that for plant assets as explained earlier in this chapter. When the recorded amount of goodwill is no longer recoverable, an impairment loss must be recorded by reducing the asset amount and including a loss in the income statement of the same accounting period.

---

[6] Investments in small businesses involve more risk and less liquidity than investments in publicly owned companies. For these reasons, the price-earnings ratios of small businesses tend to be substantially lower than those of publicly owned corporations.

INTERNATIONAL CASE IN POINT

Goodwill was identified as a topic for harmonization efforts when the FASB and the International Accounting Standards Board (IASB) agreed to work toward convergence of reporting requirements in 2002, an effort that continues today and will undoubtedly continue for years to come. U.S. GAAP requires capitalization of goodwill but no amortization. Instead, goodwill is reviewed annually and its value is adjusted if subject to impairment. Until March 2004, international standards required goodwill to be capitalized and amortized over its estimated useful life (20 years or less). In 2004, the IASB changed international standards for goodwill to be consistent with the U.S. GAAP approach by requiring an impairment test rather than amortization for goodwill.

PATENTS

A patent is an exclusive right granted by the federal government for manufacture, use, and sale of a particular product. The purpose of this exclusive grant is to encourage the invention of new products and processes. When a company acquires a patent by purchase from the inventor or other holder, the purchase price is recorded in an intangible asset account Patents.

Patents are granted for 20 years, and the period of amortization should not exceed that period. However, if the patent is likely to lose its usefulness in less than 20 years, amortization is based on the shorter estimated useful life. Assume that a patent is purchased from the inventor at a cost of $100,000 after five years of the legal life have expired. The remaining *legal* life is, therefore, 15 years. But if the estimated *useful* life is only eight years, amortization is based on this shorter period. The entry to record the annual amortization expense would be:

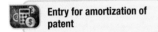

Entry for amortization of patent

Amortization Expense: Patents	12,500	
Patents		12,500
To amortize cost of patent on a straight-line basis over an estimated useful life of 8 years.		

TRADEMARKS AND TRADE NAMES

Coca-Cola's famous name, usually printed in a distinctive typeface, is a classic example of a trademark known around the world. A trademark is a name, symbol, or design that identifies a product or group of products. A permanent exclusive right to use a trademark, brand name, or commercial symbol may be obtained by registering it with the federal government.

The costs of developing a trademark or brand name often consist of advertising campaigns, which should be treated as expenses when incurred. If a trademark or brand name is *purchased,* however, the cost may be substantial. Such cost is capitalized and amortized to expense over the time period the trademark or brand name is expected to be used. If the use of the trademark is discontinued or its contribution to earnings becomes doubtful, any unamortized cost is written off immediately.

FRANCHISES

A franchise is a right granted by a company or a governmental unit to conduct a certain type of business in a specific geographical area. An example of a franchise is the right to operate a **McDonald's** restaurant in a specific geographic region. The cost of franchises varies greatly and often is quite substantial. When the cost of a franchise is small, it may be charged immediately to expense or amortized over a short period such as five years. When the cost is material, amortization is based on the life of the franchise (if defined by the franchise agreement);

the amortization period, however, should not exceed the period the franchise is expected to generate revenue.

COPYRIGHTS

A copyright is an exclusive right granted by the federal government to protect the production and sale of literary or artistic materials for the life of the creator plus 70 years. The cost of obtaining a copyright may be minor and therefore is chargeable to expense when paid. Only when a copyright is *purchased* from an existing owner will the expenditure be *material enough* to warrant its being capitalized and spread over the useful life. The revenue from copyrights is usually limited to only a few years, and the purchase cost is amortized over the years in which the revenue is expected.

OTHER INTANGIBLES AND DEFERRED CHARGES

Among the other intangibles found in the published balance sheets of large corporations are moving costs, plant rearrangement costs, formulas, processes, name lists, and film rights. Some companies group items of this type under the title of Deferred Charges, meaning expenditures that will provide benefits beyond the current year and that will be written off to expense over their useful economic lives. It is also common practice to combine these items under the heading of Other Assets, which is listed at the bottom of the asset section of the balance sheet.

RESEARCH AND DEVELOPMENT (R&D) COSTS

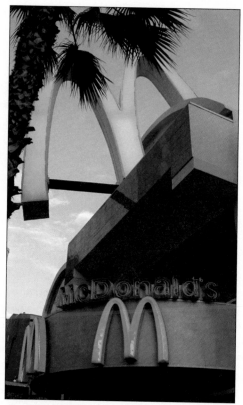

© The McGraw-Hill Companies, Inc./John Flournoy, photographer

Companies spend billions of dollars each year on research and development of new products. In fact, expenditures for R&D are a striking characteristic of U.S. industry. The annual research and development expenditures of some companies often exceed $1 billion and account for a substantial percentage of their total costs and expenses.

In the past, some companies treated all research and development costs as expenses in the year incurred; other companies recorded these costs as intangible assets and amortized them over future years. This diversity of practice prevented financial statements of different companies from being comparable.

The Financial Accounting Standards Board standardized accounting for R&D when it ruled that as a general rule research and development expenditures are required to be charged to expense *when incurred*. This action by the FASB had the beneficial effect of reducing the number of alternative accounting practices and helping to make financial statements of different companies more comparable.

FINANCIAL ANALYSIS and Decision Making

The success of many businesses depends on research and development activities (R&D). To better understand a company's commitment to funding R&D, users of financial statements often examine the level of, and trends in, a company's R&D expenditures as a percentage of revenue.

R&D to Sales = R&D Costs ÷ Net Sales

R&D expenditures as a percentage of revenue are naturally higher in some industries than in others. To illustrate this point, see the R&D figures in the following exhibit for a recent year for well-known companies from three industries that rely heavily on research and development.

EXHIBIT 9–7

Comparative R&D
Expenditures

	R&D Costs (in millions)	Revenue (in millions)	R&D (%)
Chemical Products			
DuPont	2,067	35,310	5.9
Dow Chemical	1,708	56,789	3.0
Pharmaceuticals			
Eli Lilly & Co.	5,278	22,603	23.4
Pfizer	7,870	58,986	13.3
Computer Software			
Oracle	4,523	37,121	12.2
Microsoft	9,811	73,723	13.3

YOUR TURN   You as a Financial Analyst

You are working as an equity analyst on Wall Street and a college intern asks you to explain why companies can differ greatly in the R&D expense to net sales ratio. How do you respond?

(See our comments on the Online Learning Center website.)

Natural Resources

ACCOUNTING FOR NATURAL RESOURCES

L09-7

LEARNING OBJECTIVE
Account for the depletion of natural resources.

Mining properties, oil and gas reserves, and tracts of standing timber are examples of natural resources. The distinguishing characteristic of these assets is that they are physically removed from their natural environment and are converted into inventory. Theoretically, a coal mine might be regarded as an underground inventory of coal; however, such an inventory is certainly not a current asset. In the balance sheet, mining property and other natural resources are classified as property, plant, and equipment. Once the coal is removed from the ground, however, this coal *does* represent inventory.

We have explained that plant assets such as buildings and equipment depreciate because of physical deterioration or obsolescence. A mine or an oil reserve does not depreciate for these reasons, but it is gradually *depleted* as the natural resource is removed from the ground. Once all of the coal has been removed from a coal mine, for example, the mine is "fully depleted" and will be abandoned or sold for its residual value.

To illustrate the **depletion** of a natural resource, assume that Rainbow Minerals pays $45 million to acquire the Red Valley Mine, which is believed to contain 10 million tons of coal. The residual value of the mine after all of the coal is removed is estimated to be $5 million. The depletion that will occur over the life of the mine is the original cost minus the residual value, or $40 million. This depletion will occur at the rate of *$4 per ton* ($40 million ÷ 10 million tons) as the coal is removed from the mine. If we assume that 2 million tons are mined during the first year of operations, the entry to record the depletion of the mine would be as follows:

 Recording depletion

Inventory	8,000,000	
Accumulated Depletion: Red Valley Mine		8,000,000
To record depletion of the Red Valley Mine for the year; 2,000,000 tons mined @ $4 per ton.		

Once removed from the mine, coal becomes available for sale. Therefore, the estimated cost of this coal is added to the Inventory account. As the coal is sold, this cost is transferred from the Inventory account to the Cost of Goods Sold account.

Accumulated Depletion is a *contra-asset account* similar to the Accumulated Depreciation account; it represents the portion of the mine that has been used up (depleted) to date. In Rainbow Minerals's balance sheet, the Red Valley Mine now appears as follows:

Property, Plant, & Equipment:		
Mining properties: Red Valley Mine	$45,000,000	
Less: Accumulated depletion	8,000,000	$37,000,000

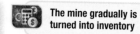
The mine gradually is turned into inventory

Depreciation of Buildings and Equipment Closely Related to Natural Resources

Buildings and equipment installed at a mine or drilling site may be useful only at that particular location. Consequently, such assets should be depreciated over their normal useful lives or over the life of the natural resource, *whichever is shorter.* Often depreciation on such assets is computed using the units-of-output method, which was discussed earlier in the chapter, based on the quantity of the natural resource removed.

DEPRECIATION, AMORTIZATION, AND DEPLETION— A COMMON GOAL

The processes of depreciation, amortization, and depletion discussed in this chapter all have a common goal. That goal is to *allocate the acquisition cost of long-lived assets to expense over the years in which the asset contributes to revenue.* Allocating the acquisition cost of long-lived assets over the years that benefit from the use of these assets is an important application of the *matching principle.* The determination of income requires matching revenue with the expenses incurred to produce that revenue.

Plant Transactions and the Statement of Cash Flows

The cash effects of plant and equipment transactions are different from the effects reported in the income statement. Cash payments for plant assets occur when those assets are *purchased*—or, more precisely, when payment is made. Cash receipts often occur when assets are sold. (These receipts are equal to the *total proceeds* received from the sale, not just the amount of any gain.) Cash flows relating to acquisitions and disposals of plant assets appear in the statement of cash flows, classified as *investing activities.*

Depreciation and amortization expense both *reduce net income,* but they have *no effect on cash flows.* As a result, both tend to make net income *less* than the net cash flows from operating activities. Likewise, the write-down of impaired assets is another example of a **noncash charge or expense** against income having no immediate effect on cash flows.

LO9-8

LEARNING OBJECTIVE
Explain the cash effects of transactions involving plant assets.

Noncash Investing Activities

Not all purchases and sales of plant assets result in cash payments or cash receipts during the current accounting period. For example, a company may finance the purchase of plant assets by issuing notes payable, or it may sell plant assets in exchange for notes receivable. The noncash aspects of investing and financing activities are summarized in a special schedule that accompanies a statement of cash flows. This schedule is illustrated and explained in Chapter 13.

Ethics, Fraud, & Corporate Governance

A learning objective for this chapter is to distinguish between capital expenditures and revenue expenditures (a revenue expenditure is an operating expense). A capital expenditure is charged to an asset account rather than to an expense account. The largest instance of fraudulent financial reporting in U.S. history was primarily due to improper capitalization of operating expenditures. **WorldCom Inc. (WorldCom)** from as early as 1999 through the first quarter of 2002 overstated its reported income by approximately $11 billion, including approximately $7 billion of ordinary operating expenses that were improperly capitalized. The revelation of the fraud led to **WorldCom**'s filing for protection from its creditors under the provisions of the U.S. Bankruptcy Code. Although the fraud at **Enron** had prompted congressional interest in auditing, financial reporting, and corporate governance, by the spring of 2002 congressional efforts to draft a law in response to the **Enron** fraud had stalled due to disagreements between the two houses of Congress. The fraud at **WorldCom** broke this congressional logjam and resulted in the passage of the Sarbanes-Oxley Act less than two months after the revelation of the **WorldCom** fraud.

Almost immediately after the revelation of the **WorldCom** fraud—in June 2002—the Securities and Exchange Commission (SEC) brought an enforcement action against **WorldCom**. **WorldCom** is a major global telecommunications provider, providing services in more than 65 countries. At the time of the fraud, **WorldCom** was traded on NASDAQ.

As the economy began to cool in 1999, demand for **WorldCom**'s telecommunications services was reduced, leading to a decline in profits. The slowing economy made it difficult for **WorldCom** to continue to meet the expectations of Wall Street analysts for reported profitability.

WorldCom's senior management directed subordinates to take steps to hide the deterioration in **WorldCom**'s profitability from analysts and other external parties. A primary means of carrying out the fraud was to transfer ordinary operating expenses, line costs, to a capital asset account, fixed assets. This accounting treatment resulted in the overstatement of assets, the understatement of operating expenses, and an increase in income.

The fraud at **WorldCom** has numerous ethical and corporate governance implications. Although the fraud at **WorldCom** was directed by top management, much of the implementation was carried out by midlevel finance and accounting personnel.

WorldCom did not have a code of ethics. Attempts to develop such a code were met by the CEO's description of a code of ethics as a "colossal waste of time." The Sarbanes-Oxley Act and related SEC interpretations now require public companies to disclose whether they have a code of ethics that applies to the CEO, CFO, and chief accounting officer and, if not, why not. Moreover, the NYSE and NASDAQ now require companies listed on these exchanges to have a code of ethics. Although these requirements are a step in the right direction, they will fail to have their intended effect if senior management doesn't fully embrace the written code.

Concluding Remarks

This chapter completes our discussion of accounting for various types of assets. To briefly review, we have seen that cash is reported in the financial statements at its face value, marketable securities at their market value, accounts receivable at their net realizable value (i.e., net amount of cash expected to be collected), inventories at the lower-of-cost-or-market, and plant assets at cost less accumulated depreciation.

Two ideas that have been consistently reflected in each of these valuation bases are the matching principle and conservatism. A major determinant of the amount at which many assets are accounted for in the balance sheet is the future amount to be released as an expense into the income statement. Closely related to this is the objective of not overstating the current and future expectations of a company's financial activities by overstating assets and understating current expenses.

In the next chapter, we turn our attention to the measurement and presentation of liabilities.

END-OF-CHAPTER REVIEW

LO9-1 Determine the cost of plant assets. Plant assets are long-lived assets acquired for use in the business and not for resale to customers. The matching principle requires that we include in the plant and equipment accounts those costs that will provide services over a period of years. During these years, the use of the plant assets contributes to the earning of revenue. The cost of a plant asset includes all expenditures reasonable and necessary in acquiring the asset and placing it in a position and condition for use in the operations of the business.

LO9-2 Distinguish between capital expenditures and revenue expenditures. Capital expenditures include all material expenditures that will benefit several accounting periods. These expenditures are charged to asset accounts (capitalized) and are recognized as expense in future periods.

Revenue expenditures are charged directly to expense accounts because either (1) there is no objective evidence of future benefits or (2) the amounts are immaterial.

LO9-3 Compute depreciation by the straight-line and declining-balance methods. Straight-line depreciation assigns an equal portion of an asset's cost to expense in each period of the asset's life. Declining-balance depreciation is an accelerated method. Each year, a fixed (and relatively high) depreciation rate is applied to the remaining book value of the asset. There are several variations of declining-balance depreciation.

LO9-4 Account for depreciation using methods other than straight-line or declining-balance. Most companies that prepare financial statements in conformity with generally accepted accounting principles use the straight-line method of depreciation. Other accepted methods include the units-of-output method, sum-of-the-years' digits, and, in rare circumstances, decelerated depreciation methods.

LO9-5 Account for the disposal of plant assets. When plant assets are disposed of, depreciation is recorded to the date of disposal. The cost is then removed from the asset account and the total recorded depreciation is removed

from the Accumulated Depreciation account. The sale of a plant asset at a price above or below book value results in a gain or loss that is reported in the income statement.

Because different depreciation methods are used for income tax purposes, the gain or loss reported in income tax returns may differ from that shown in the income statement. The gain or loss shown in the financial statement is recorded in the company's general ledger accounts.

LO9-6 Explain the nature of intangible assets, including goodwill. Intangible assets are assets owned by the business that have no physical substance, are noncurrent, and are used in business operations. Examples include trademarks and patents.

Among the most interesting intangible assets is goodwill. Goodwill is the expected future earnings in excess of a normal return on net identifiable assets. It stems from such factors as a good reputation, loyal customers, and superior management. Any business that earns significantly more than a normal rate of return actually has goodwill. But goodwill is recorded in the accounts only if it is purchased by acquiring another business at a price higher than the fair market value of its net identifiable assets.

LO9-7 Account for the depletion of natural resources. Natural resources (or wasting assets) include mines, oil fields, and standing timber. Their cost is converted into inventory as the resource is mined, pumped, or cut. This allocation of the cost of a natural resource to inventories is called depletion. The depletion rate per unit extracted equals the cost of the resource (less residual value) divided by the estimated number of units it contains.

LO9-8 Explain the cash effects of transactions involving plant assets. Depreciation is a noncash expense; cash expenditures for the acquisition of plant assets are independent of the amount of depreciation for the period. Cash payments to acquire plant assets (and cash receipts from disposals) appear in the statement of cash flows, classified as investing activities.

Write-downs of plant assets also are noncash charges, which do not involve cash payments.

Key Terms Introduced or Emphasized in Chapter

accelerated depreciation (p. 392) Methods of depreciation that call for recognition of relatively large amounts of depreciation in the early years of an asset's useful life and relatively small amounts in the later years.

amortization (p. 403) The systematic write-off to expense of the cost of an intangible asset over the periods of its economic usefulness.

book value (p. 392) The cost of a plant asset minus the total recorded depreciation, as shown by the Accumulated Depreciation account. The remaining undepreciated cost is also known as *carrying value*.

capital expenditures (p. 390)   Costs incurred to acquire a long-lived asset. Expenditures that will benefit several accounting periods.

capitalize (p. 390)   A verb with two different meanings in accounting. The first is to debit an expenditure to an asset account, rather than directly to expense. The second is to estimate the value of an investment by dividing the annual return by the investor's required rate of return.

depletion (p. 408)   Allocating the cost of a natural resource to the units removed as the resource is mined, pumped, cut, or otherwise consumed.

depreciation (p. 391)   The systematic allocation of the cost of an asset to expense over the years of its estimated useful life.

fixed-percentage-of-declining-balance depreciation (p. 395) An accelerated method of depreciation in which the rate is a multiple of the straight-line rate and is applied each year to the undepreciated cost of the asset. The most commonly used rate is double the straight-line rate.

goodwill (p. 403)   The amount of expected future earnings of a business in excess of the earnings normally realized in the industry. Recorded when a business entity is purchased at a price in excess of the fair value of its net identifiable assets less liabilities.

half-year convention (p. 394)   The practice of taking six months' depreciation in the year of acquisition and in the year of disposition, rather than computing depreciation for partial periods to the nearest month. This method is widely used and is acceptable for both income tax reporting and financial reports, as long as it is applied to all assets of a particular type acquired during the year.

impairment loss (p. 399)   The write-down of a long-lived asset for the difference between its carrying amount less its fair value.

intangible assets (p. 388)   Those assets that are used in the operation of a business but that have no physical substance and are noncurrent.

MACRS (p. 400) The Modified Accelerated Cost Recovery System. The accelerated depreciation method permitted in federal income tax returns for assets acquired after December 31, 1986. Depreciation is based on prescribed recovery periods and depreciation rates.

natural resources (p. 388)   Mines, oil fields, standing timber, and similar assets that are physically consumed and converted into inventory.

net identifiable assets (p. 404)   The total of all assets minus liabilities.

noncash charge or expense (p. 409)   A charge against earnings—either an expense or a loss—that does not require a cash expenditure at or near the time of recognition. The charge reduces net income but does not affect cash flows (except, perhaps, for income tax payments). Examples are depreciation and the write-off of asset values because an asset has become impaired.

plant assets (p. 388)   Long-lived assets that are acquired for use in business operations rather than for resale to customers.

present value (p. 404)   The amount that a knowledgeable investor would pay today for the right to receive future cash flows. The present value is always less than the sum of the future cash flows because the investor requires a return on the investment.

residual (salvage) value (p. 393)   The portion of an asset's cost expected to be recovered through sale or trade-in of the asset at the end of its useful life.

revenue expenditures (p. 391)   Expenditures that will benefit only the current accounting period.

straight-line depreciation (p. 392)   A method of depreciation that allocates the cost of an asset (minus any residual value) equally to each year of its useful life.

sum-of-the-years' digits (SYD) depreciation (p. 400)   A seldom-used method of accelerated depreciation. Usually produces results that lie in between the 200 percent- and 150 percent-declining-balance methods.

tangible plant assets (p. 388)   Plant assets that have physical substance but that are not natural resources. Examples include land, buildings, and all types of equipment.

units-of-output (p. 399)   A depreciation method in which cost (minus residual value) is divided by the estimated units of lifetime output. The unit depreciation cost is multiplied by the actual units of output each year to compute the annual depreciation expense.

Demonstration Problem

On April 1, 2015, Jones Industries purchased new equipment at a cost of $325,000. The useful life of this equipment was estimated at five years, with a residual value of $25,000.

Instructions

Compute the annual depreciation expense for each year until this equipment becomes fully depreciated under each depreciation method listed below. Because you will record depreciation for only a fraction of a year in 2015, depreciation will extend into 2020 for both methods. Show supporting computations.

a.   Straight-line, with depreciation for fractional years rounded to the nearest whole month.

b.   200 percent declining-balance, with the half-year convention. Limit depreciation in 2020 to an amount that reduces the undepreciated cost to the estimated residual value.

c.   Assume that the equipment is sold at the end of December 2017 for $178,700 cash. Record the necessary gain or loss resulting from the sale under the straight-line method.

Solution to the Demonstration Problem

		a.	b.
		Expense under Each Method of Depreciation	
Year		**Straight-Line**	**200% Declining-Balance**
2015		$ 45,000	$ 65,000
2016		60,000	104,000
2017		60,000	62,400
2018		60,000	37,440
2019		60,000	22,464
2020		15,000	8,696
Totals		$300,000	$300,000

c. Entry to record sale of equipment in 2017:

Cash	$178,700	
Accumulated Depreciation: Equipment	165,000	
Equipment		$325,000
Gain on Sale of Equipment		18,700

Supporting computations:

a. 2015: ($325,000 − $25,000) × $\frac{1}{5}$ × $\frac{9}{12}$ = $45,000

2016–2015: $300,000 × $\frac{1}{5}$ = $60,000

2020: $300,000 × $\frac{1}{5}$ × $\frac{3}{12}$ = $15,000

b.

	Undepreciated Cost	**Rate**	**Depreciation Expense**
2015	$325,000	× 40% × ½ =	$ 65,000
2016	260,000	× 40% =	104,000
2017	156,000	× 40% =	62,400
2018	93,600	× 40% =	37,440
2019	56,160	× 40% =	22,464
2020	33,696	− $25,000 =	8,696

c. Accumulated depreciation at the end of 2017:

Depreciation expense, 2015	$ 45,000
Depreciation expense, 2016	60,000
Depreciation expense, 2017	60,000
Accumulated depreciation at the end of 2017	$165,000
Original cost of equipment in 2015	$325,000
Less: Accumulated depreciation at the end of 2017	(165,000)
Book value of equipment at time of disposal	$160,000
Cash proceeds from sale	$178,700
Less: Book value of equipment at time of disposal	(160,000)
Gain on sale of disposal	$ 18,700

Self-Test Questions

The answers to these questions appear on page 428.

1. In which of the following situations should the named company *not* record any depreciation expense on the asset described?

   a. Commuter Airline is required by law to maintain its aircraft in "as good as new" condition.

   b. Metro Advertising owns an office building that has been increasing in value each year since it was purchased.

   c. Computer Sales Company has in inventory a new type of computer, designed "never to become obsolete."

   d. None of the above answers is correct—in each case, the named company should record depreciation on the asset described.

2. Which of the following statements is (are) correct?

   a. Accumulated depreciation represents a cash fund being accumulated for the replacement of plant assets.

   b. The cost of a machine includes the cost of repairing damage to the machine during the installation process.

   c. A company may use different depreciation methods in its financial statements and its income tax return.

   d. The use of an accelerated depreciation method causes an asset to wear out more quickly than does use of the straight-line method.

3. On April 1, 2014, Sanders Construction paid $10,000 for equipment with an estimated useful life of 10 years and a residual value of $2,000. The company uses the double-declining-balance method of depreciation and applies the half-year convention to fractional periods. In 2015, the amount of depreciation expense to be recognized on this equipment is:

   a. $1,600.

   b. $1,440.

   c. $1,280.

   d. Some other amount.

4. Evergreen Mfg. is a rapidly growing company that acquires equipment every year. Evergreen uses straight-line depreciation in its financial statements and an accelerated method in its tax returns. Identify all correct statements:

   a. Using straight-line depreciation in the financial statements instead of an accelerated method reduces Evergreen's reported net income.

   b. Using straight-line depreciation in the financial statements instead of an accelerated method increases Evergreen's annual net cash flow.

   c. Using an accelerated method instead of straight-line depreciation in income tax returns increases Evergreen's cash flow from operating activities.

   d. As long as Evergreen keeps growing, it will probably report more depreciation in its income tax returns *each year* than it does in its financial statements.

5. Ladd Company sold a plant asset that originally cost $50,000 for $22,000 cash. If Ladd correctly reports a $5,000 gain on this sale, the *accumulated depreciation* on the asset at the date of sale must have been:

   a. $33,000.

   b. $28,000.

   c. $23,000.

   d. Some other amount.

6. In which of the following situations would Daniel Industries include goodwill in its balance sheet?

   a. The fair market value of Daniel's net identifiable assets amounts to $2,000,000. Normal earnings for this industry are 15 percent of net identifiable assets. Net income for the past five years has averaged $390,000.

   b. Daniel Industries acquired Baxter Electronics at a price in excess of the fair market value of Baxter's net identifiable assets.

   c. Daniel Industries spent $800,000 during the current year for research and development for a new product that promises to generate substantial revenue for at least 10 years.

   d. A buyer wishing to purchase Daniel's entire operation has offered a price in excess of the fair market value of the company's net identifiable assets.

| ASSIGNMENT MATERIAL | # Discussion Questions |

1. Coca-Cola's distinctive trademark is more valuable to the company than its bottling plants. But the company's bottling plants are listed in the balance sheet, and the famous trademark isn't. Explain.

2. Identify the basic "accountable events" in the life of a depreciable plant asset. Which of these events directly affect the net income of the current period? Which directly affect cash flows (other than income tax payments)?

3. The following expenditures were incurred in connection with a new machine acquired by a metals manufacturing company. Identify those that should be included in the cost of the asset. (a) Freight charges, (b) sales tax on the machine, (c) payment to a passing motorist whose car was damaged by the equipment used in unloading the machine, (d) wages of employees for time spent in installing and testing the machine before it was placed in service, (e) wages of employees assigned to lubricate and make minor adjustments to the machine one year after it was placed in service.

4. What is the distinction between a *capital expenditure* and a *revenue expenditure?*

5. If a capital expenditure is erroneously treated as a revenue expenditure, will the net income of the current year be over-stated or understated? Will this error have any effect on the net income reported in future years? Explain.

6. Shoppers' Market purchased for $265,000 a site on which it planned to build a new store. The site consisted of three acres of land and included an old house and two barns. County property tax records showed the following appraised values for this property: land, $160,000; buildings, $40,000. Indicate what Shoppers' should do with this $265,000 cost in its financial statements, and explain your reasoning.

7. Should depreciation continue to be recorded on a building when ample evidence exists that the current market value is greater than original cost and that the rising trend of market values is continuing? Explain.

8. Explain what is meant by an *accelerated* depreciation method. Are accelerated methods more widely used in financial statements or in income tax returns? Explain.

9. One accelerated depreciation method is called *fixed-per-centage-of-declining-balance.* Explain what is meant by the terms "fixed-percentage" and "declining-balance." For what purpose is this method most widely used?

10. Evaluate the following quotation: "We shall have no difficulty in paying for new plant assets needed during the coming year because our estimated outlays for new equipment amount to only $80,000, and we have more than twice that amount in our accumulated depreciation account at present."

11. Explain two approaches to computing depreciation for a fractional period in the year in which an asset is purchased. (Neither of your approaches should require the computation of depreciation to the nearest day or week.)

12. Over what period of time should the cost of various types of intangible assets be amortized by regular charges against revenue? (Your answer should be in the form of a principle or guideline rather than a specific number of years.) What method of amortization is generally used?

13. Mineral World recognizes $20 depletion for each ton of ore mined. During the current year the company mined 600,000 tons but sold only 500,000 tons, as it was attempting to build up inventories in anticipation of a possible strike by employees. How much depletion should be deducted from revenue of the current year?

14. Explain the meaning of an *impairment* of an asset. Provide several examples. What accounting event should occur when an asset has become substantially impaired?

15. Several years ago Bennet Security purchased for $150,000 a well-known trademark for padlocks and other security products. After using the trademark for three years, Bennet Security discontinued it altogether when the company withdrew from the lock business and concentrated on the manufacture of aircraft parts. Amortization of the trademark at the rate of $7,500 a year is being continued on the basis of a 20-year life, which the owner says is consistent with accounting standards. Do you agree? Explain.

Brief Exercises

LO9-1, LO9-2

BRIEF EXERCISE 9.1

Cost of Plant Asset

Amigos, Inc., purchased a used piece of heavy equipment for $30,000. Delivery of the equipment to Amigos' business site cost $750. Expenditures to recondition the equipment and prepare it for use totaled $2,230. The maintenance for the first year Amijo owned the equipment was $1,370. Determine the cost that is the basis for calculating annual depreciation on the equipment.

LO9-3

BRIEF EXERCISE 9.2

Straight-Line Depreciation

Twin-Cities, Inc., purchased a building for $600,000. Straight-line depreciation was used for each of the first two years using the following assumptions: 25-year estimated useful life, with a residual value of $100,000.

a. Calculate the annual depreciation for the first two years that Twin-Cities owned the building.

b. Calculate the book value of the building at the end of the second year.

LO9-3

BRIEF EXERCISE 9.3

Straight-Line and Declining-Balance Depreciation

Messer Company purchased equipment for $24,000. The company is considering whether to determine annual depreciation using the straight-line method or the declining-balance method at 150 percent of the straight-line rate. Waller expects to use the equipment for 10 years, at the end of which it will have an estimated salvage value of $4,000. Prepare a comparison of these two alternatives for the first two years Messer will own the equipment.

LO9-3

BRIEF EXERCISE 9.4

Declining-Balance Depreciation

Equipment costing $86,000 was purchased by Spence, Inc., at the beginning of the current year. The company will depreciate the equipment by the declining-balance method, but it has not determined whether the rate will be at 150 percent or 200 percent of the straight-line rate. The estimated useful life of the equipment is eight years. Prepare a comparison of the two alternative rates for management for the first two years Spence owns the equipment.

LO9-3, LO9-4

BRIEF EXERCISE 9.5

Straight-Line and Units-of-
Output Depreciation

Finx, Inc., purchased a truck for $40,000. The truck is expected to be driven 15,000 miles per year over a five-year period and then sold for approximately $5,000. Determine depreciation for the first year of the truck's useful life by the straight-line and units-of-output methods if the truck is actually driven 16,000 miles. (Round depreciation per mile for the units-of-output method to the nearest whole cent.)

LO9-3, LO9-5

BRIEF EXERCISE 9.6

Disposal of Plant Asset

Alexander Company purchased a piece of equipment for $14,000 and depreciated it for three years over a five-year estimated life with an expected residual value at the end of five years of $2,000. At the end of the third year, Alex decided to upgrade to equipment with increased capacity and sold the original piece of equipment for $7,500. Calculate the gain or loss on the disposal at the end of the third year.

LO9-3, LO9-5

BRIEF EXERCISE 9.7

Disposal of Plant Asset

Taylor Company purchased equipment for $27,500. It depreciated the equipment over a five-year life by the double-declining-balance method until the end of the second year, at which time the asset was sold for $8,300. Calculate the gain or loss on the sale at the end of the second year.

LO9-6

BRIEF EXERCISE 9.8

Goodwill

Hunt Company is considering purchasing a competing company in order to expand its market share. Estimates of the excess of the value of the individual assets, less liabilities to be assumed, range from $50,000 to $60,000, depending on the manner in which that excess is calculated. Hunt believes it can purchase the competitor for a direct cash outlay of $700,000, which is only $25,000 more than the value of the individual assets less the liabilities that Hunt will assume. Assuming Hunt makes the purchase for $700,000, at what amount should goodwill be recorded? Briefly explain your answer.

LO9-7

BRIEF EXERCISE 9.9

Natural Resources

Miller Mining acquired rights to a tract of land with the intent of extracting from the land a valuable mineral. The cost of the rights was $2,500,000 and an estimated 10,000 tons of the mineral are expected to be extracted. Assuming that 1,600 tons of the mineral are actually extracted in the first year, determine the amount of depletion expense that should be recognized for that year.

LO9-4

BRIEF EXERCISE 9.10

Alternative Depreciation
Methods

M. C. Jones purchased a truck for $30,500 to be used in his business. He is considering depreciating the truck by two methods: units-of-output (assuming total miles driven of 80,000) and double-declining balance (assuming a five-year useful life). The truck is expected to be sold for approximately $6,500 at the end of its useful life. Prepare a comparison of the first year's depreciation expense that would be recognized by Jones under these methods, assuming the truck was actually driven 10,000 miles in the first year. Briefly state why the difference between the two is so great.

Exercises

LO9-2, LO9-3

EXERCISE 9.1

Depreciation

Assume that you recently applied for a student loan to go to graduate school. As part of the application process, your bank requested a list of your assets. Aside from an extensive CD collection, your only other asset is a pickup truck. You purchased the truck six years ago for $15,000. Its current fair value is approximately $5,000.

a. What factors caused your pickup truck to decline $10,000 in value?

b. Assume that the bank is willing to lend you money for graduate school. Even with the loan, however, you still need to raise an additional $5,000. Do you think that the bank will lend you $5,000 more for graduate school if you agree to use your truck as collateral? Explain.

c. Assume that the truck has been used solely in a delivery service business that you operate while in college. Would your balance sheet necessarily show $10,000 in accumulated depreciation related to the truck? Explain.

LO9-1, LO9-2

EXERCISE 9.2

Distinguishing Capital Expenditures from Revenue Expenditures

Identify the following expenditures as capital expenditures or revenue expenditures:

a. Immediately after acquiring a new delivery truck, paid $260 to have the name of the store and other advertising material painted on the vehicle.

b. Painted delivery truck at a cost of $450 after two years of use.

c. Purchased new battery at a cost of $40 for two-year-old delivery truck.

d. Installed an escalator at a cost of $17,500 in a three-story building that had been used for some years without elevators or escalators.

e. Purchased a pencil sharpener at a cost of $15.00.

f. Original life of the delivery truck had been estimated at four years, and straight-line depreciation of 25 percent yearly had been recognized. After three years' use, however, it was decided to recondition the truck thoroughly, including replacing the engine.

LO9-3

EXERCISE 9.3

Depreciation for Partial Years

On August 3, Cinco Construction purchased special-purpose equipment at a cost of $1,000,000. The useful life of the equipment was estimated to be eight years, with an estimated residual value of $50,000.

a. Compute the depreciation expense to be recognized each calendar year for financial reporting purposes under the straight-line depreciation method (half-year convention).

b. Compute the depreciation expense to be recognized each calendar year for financial reporting purposes under the 200 percent declining-balance method (half-year convention) with a switch to straight-line when it will maximize depreciation expense.

c. Which of these two depreciation methods (straight-line or double-declining-balance) results in the highest net income for financial reporting purposes during the first two years of the equipment's use? Explain.

LO9-3

EXERCISE 9.4

Depreciation Methods

Next Class

Switch to at 50%

On January 2, 2015, Jatson Corporation acquired a new machine with an estimated useful life of five years. The cost of the equipment was $40,000 with an estimated residual value of $5,000.

a. Prepare a complete depreciation table under the three depreciation methods listed below. Use a format similar to the illustrations in Exhibits 9–4, 9–5, and 9–6. In each case, assume that a full year of depreciation was taken in 2015.

  1. Straight-line.

  2. 200 percent declining-balance.

  3. 150 percent declining-balance with a switch to straight-line when it will maximize depreciation expense.

b. Comment on significant differences or similarities that you observe among the patterns of depreciation expense recognized under each of these methods.

LO9-3

EXERCISE 9.5

Evaluation of Disclosures in Annual Reports

A recent annual report of **H. J. Heinz Company** includes the following note:

Depreciation: For financial reporting purposes, depreciation is provided on the straight-line method over the estimated useful lives of the assets, which generally have the following ranges: buildings—40 years or less; machinery and equipment—15 years or less; computer software—3–7 years; and lease hold improvements—over the life of the lease, not to exceed 15 years. Accelerated depreciation methods are generally used for income tax purposes.

a. Is the company violating the accounting principle of consistency by using different depreciation methods in its financial statements than in its income tax returns? Explain.

b. *Why* do you think that the company uses accelerated depreciation methods in its income tax returns?

c. Would the use of accelerated depreciation in the financial statements be more conservative or less conservative than the current practice of using the straight-line method? Explain.

LO9-3

EXERCISE 9.6

Revision of Depreciation Estimates

Swindall Industries uses straight-line depreciation on all of its depreciable assets. The company records annual depreciation expense at the end of each calendar year. On January 11, 2011, the company purchased a machine costing $90,000. The machine's useful life was estimated to be 12 years with an estimated residual value of $18,000. Depreciation for partial years is recorded to the nearest full month.

In 2015, after almost five years of experience with the machine, management decided to revise its estimated life from 12 years to 20 years. No change was made in the estimated residual value. The revised estimate of the useful life was decided *prior* to recording annual depreciation expense for the year ended December 31, 2015.

a. Prepare journal entries in chronological order for the above events, beginning with the purchase of the machinery on January 11, 2011. Show separately the recording of depreciation expense in 2011 through 2015.

b. What factors may have caused the company to revise its estimate of the machine's useful life?

LO9-5

EXERCISE 9.7

Accounting for Trade-ins

Willis Bus Service traded in a used bus for a new one. The original cost of the old bus was $52,000. Accumulated depreciation at the time of the trade-in amounted to $34,000. The new bus cost $67,000, but Mathews was given a trade-in allowance of $10,000.

a. What amount of cash did Mathews have to pay to acquire the new bus?

b. Compute the gain or loss on the disposal for financial reporting purposes.

c. Explain how the gain or loss would be reported in the company's income statement.

LO9-6

EXERCISE 9.8

Estimating Goodwill

During the past several years the annual net income of Avery Company has averaged $540,000. At the present time the company is being offered for sale. Its accounting records show the book value of net assets (total assets minus all liabilities) to be $2,800,000. The fair value of Avery's net identifiable assets, however, is $3,000,000.

An investor negotiating to buy the company offers to pay an amount equal to the fair value for the net identifiable assets and to assume all liabilities. In addition, the investor is willing to pay for goodwill an amount equal to the above-average earnings for three years.

On the basis of this agreement, what price should the investor offer? A normal return on the fair value of net assets in this industry is 15 percent.

LO9-5, LO9-8

EXERCISE 9.9

The Write-Down of Impaired Assets

For several years, a number of **Food Lion, Inc.**, grocery stores were unprofitable. The company closed some of these locations. It was apparent that the company would not be able to recover the cost of the assets associated with the closed stores. Thus, the current value of these impaired assets had to be written down.

A note in the financial statements indicated that the company tests assets for impairment when circumstances indicate that an impairment may exist. For impairment testing, each store is considered a cash-generating unit. Stores with potential impairments are tested by comparing their carrying value with their recoverable amounts.

a. Explain why **Food Lion** wrote down the current carrying value of its unprofitable stores.

b. Explain why the write-down of impaired assets is considered a noncash expense.

LO9-1, LO9-6

EXERCISE 9.10

Ethics: "Let the Buyer Beware"

Bill Gladstone has owned and operated Gladstone's Service Station for over 30 years. The business, which is currently the town's only service station, has always been extremely profitable. Gladstone recently decided that he wanted to sell the business and retire. His asking price exceeds the fair market value of its net identifiable assets by nearly $100,000. Gladstone attributes this premium to the above-normal returns that the service station has always generated.

Gladstone recently found out about two issues that could have a profound effect upon the future of the business: (1) A well-known service station franchise will be built across the street from his station in approximately 18 months, and (2) one of his underground fuel tanks *may* have developed a very slow leak.

a. How might these issues affect the $100,000 in goodwill that Gladstone included in his selling price?

b. Assume that Gladstone is *not* disclosing this information to potential buyers. Does he have an ethical obligation to do so? Defend your answer.

LO9-7

EXERCISE 9.11

Depletion of Natural Resources

Salter Mining Company purchased the Northern Tier Mine for $21 million cash. The mine was estimated to contain 2.5 million tons of ore and to have a residual value of $1 million.

During the first year of mining operations at the Northern Tier Mine, 50,000 tons of ore were mined, of which 40,000 tons were sold.

a. Prepare a journal entry to record depletion during the year.

b. Show how the Northern Tier Mine, and its accumulated depletion, would appear in Salter Mining Company's balance sheet after the first year of operations.

c. Will the entire amount of depletion computed in part **a** be deducted from revenue in the determination of income for the year? Explain.

d. Indicate how the journal entry in part **a** affects the company's current ratio (its current assets divided by its current liabilities). Do you believe that the activities summarized in this entry do, in fact, make the company any more or less liquid? Explain.

LO9-6, LO9-8

EXERCISE 9.12

Researching a Real Company

Locate an annual report in your library (or some other source) that includes a large gain or loss on the disposal of fixed assets. Report to the class the amount of the gain or loss and where in the company's income statement it is reported. Describe how the gain or loss is reported in the company's statement of cash flows. Summarize any discussion in the footnotes concerning the cause of the disposal.

LO9-4

EXERCISE 9.13

Units-of-Output Method

During the current year, Central Auto Rentals purchased 60 new automobiles at a cost of $14,000 per car. The cars will be sold to a wholesaler at an estimated $5,000 each as soon as they have been driven 50,000 miles. Central Auto Rentals computes depreciation expense on its automobiles by the units-of-output method, based on mileage.

a. Compute the amount of depreciation to be recognized for each mile that a rental automobile is driven.

b. Assuming that the 60 rental cars are driven a total of 1,570,000 miles during the current year, compute the total amount of depreciation expense that Central Auto Rentals should recognize on this fleet of cars for the year.

c. In this particular situation, do you believe the units-of-output depreciation method achieves a better matching of expenses with revenue than would the straight-line method? Explain.

LO9-4

EXERCISE 9.14

Units-of-Output Depreciation Method

Sexton Company acquired a truck for use in its business for $26,500 in a cash transaction. The truck is expected to be used over a five-year period, will be driven approximately 18,000 miles per year, and is expected to have a value at the end of the five years of $4,800.

a. Compute the amount of depreciation that will be taken in the first two years of the truck's useful life if the actual miles driven are 16,000 and 18,200, respectively. Round the depreciation per mile to the nearest whole cent.

b. How does the amount of accumulated depreciation at the end of the second year compare with what it would have been had the company chosen the straight-line depreciation method?

LO9-1, LO9-3

EXERCISE 9.15

Using the **Home Depot**, Inc., Financial Statements to Determine Depreciation Methods Used

The **Home Depot** financial statements and related material appear in Appendix A at the end of this textbook. Use this to answer the following questions and indicate where in the financial statements you found the information.

a. What depreciation method does **Home Depot** use for buildings, furniture, fixtures, and equipment? What are the useful lives over which these assets are depreciated?

b. From the notes to **Home Depot**'s financial statements, what can you learn about the company's policy regarding impairment of plant assets?

c. Locate **Home Depot**'s balance sheet and find the section entitled "Property and Equipment, at cost." As of February 3, 2013, determine the amount of the company's investment in property and equipment and the amount of depreciation taken to date on those assets. Are these assets, as a whole, near the beginning or end of their estimated useful lives? Explain your answer.

Problem Set A

LO9-1 through LO9-3

PROBLEM 9.1A

Determining the Cost of Plant Assets and Depreciation

Hamlet College recently purchased new computing equipment for its library. The following information refers to the purchase and installation of this equipment:

1. The list price of the equipment was $285,000; however, Hamlet College qualified for an "education discount" of $25,000. It paid $50,000 cash for the equipment, and issued a three-month, 9 percent note payable for the remaining balance. The note, plus accrued interest charges of $4,500, was paid promptly at the note's maturity date.

2. In addition to the amounts described in **1**, Hamlet paid sales taxes of $15,000 at the date of purchase.

3. Freight charges for delivery of the equipment totaled $1,000.

4. Installation costs related to the equipment amounted to $5,000.

5. During installation, one of the computer terminals was accidentally damaged by a library employee. It cost the college $500 to repair this damage.

6. As soon as the computers were installed, the college paid $4,000 to print admissions brochures featuring the library's new, state-of-the-art computing facilities.

Instructions

a. In one sentence, make a general statement summarizing the nature of expenditures that qualify for inclusion in the cost of plant assets such as computing equipment.

b. For each of the six numbered paragraphs, indicate which items should be included by Hamlet College in the total cost added to its Computing Equipment account. Also briefly indicate the proper accounting treatment of those items that *are not* included in the cost of the equipment.

c. Compute the total cost added to the college's Computing Equipment account.

d. Prepare a journal entry at the end of the current year to record depreciation on the computing equipment. Hamlet College intends to depreciate this equipment by the straight-line method (half-year convention) over an estimated useful life of five years. Assume a zero residual value.

LO9-3, LO9-5

PROBLEM 9.2A

Comparison of Straight-Line and Accelerated Methods

Swanson & Hiller, Inc., purchased a new machine on September 1, 2012 at a cost of $108,000. The machine's estimated useful life at the time of the purchase was five years, and its residual value was $8,000.

Instructions

a. Prepare a complete depreciation schedule, beginning with calendar year 2012, under each of the methods listed below (assume that the half-year convention is used):

1. Straight-line.

2. 200 percent declining-balance.

3. 150 percent declining-balance, switching to straight-line when that maximizes the expense.

b. Which of the three methods computed in part **a** is most common for financial reporting purposes? Explain.

c. Assume that Swanson & Hiller sells the machine on December 31, 2015, for $29,000 cash. Compute the resulting gain or loss from this sale under each of the depreciation methods used in part **a**. Does the gain or loss reported in the company's income statement have any direct cash effects? Explain.

LO9-1 through LO9-3, LO9-5

PROBLEM 9.3A

Issues Involving Alternative Depreciation Methods

Hills Hardware purchased new shelving for its store on April 1, 2015. The shelving is expected to have a 20-year life and no residual value. The following expenditures were associated with the purchase:

Cost of the shelving	$12,000
Freight charges	520
Sales taxes.	780
Installation of shelving	2,700
Cost to repair shelf damaged during installation	400

Instructions

a. Compute depreciation expense for the years 2015 through 2018 under each depreciation method listed below:

1. Straight-line, with fractional years rounded to the nearest whole month.

2. 200 percent declining-balance, using the half-year convention.

3. 150 percent declining-balance, using the half-year convention.

b. Hills Hardware has two conflicting objectives. Management wants to report the highest possible earnings in its financial statements, yet it also wants to minimize its taxable income reported to the IRS. Explain how both of these objectives can be met.

c. Which of the depreciation methods applied in part **a** will result in the lowest reported book value at the end of 2018? Is book value an estimate of an asset's fair value? Explain.

d. Assume that Hills Hardware sold the old shelving that was being replaced. The old shelving had originally cost $9,000. Its book value at the time of the sale was $400. Record the sale of the old shelving under the following conditions:

1. The shelving was sold for $1,100 cash.

2. The shelving was sold for $175 cash.

LO9-5

PROBLEM 9.4A

Disposal of Plant Assets

During the current year, Hitchcock Developers disposed of plant assets in the following transactions:

Feb. 10 Office equipment costing $24,000 was given to a scrap dealer at no charge. At the date of disposal, accumulated depreciation on the office equipment amounted to $21,800.

Apr. 1 Hitchcock sold land and a building to Claypool Associates for $900,000, receiving $100,000 cash and a five-year, 9 percent note receivable for the remaining balance. Hitchcock's records showed the following amounts: Land, $50,000; Building, $550,000; Accumulated Depreciation: Building (at the date of disposal), $250,000.

Aug. 15 Hitchcock traded in an old truck for a new one. The old truck had cost $26,000, and its accumulated depreciation amounted to $18,000. The list price of the new truck was $39,000, but Hitchcock received a $10,000 trade-in allowance for the old truck and paid $28,000 in cash. Hitchcock includes trucks in its Vehicles account.

Oct. 1 Hitchcock traded in its old computer system as part of the purchase of a new system. The old system had cost $15,000, and its accumulated depreciation amounted to $11,000. The new computer's list price was $8,000. Hitchcock accepted a trade-in allowance of $500 for the old computer system, paying $1,500 down in cash and issuing a one-year, 8 percent note payable for the $6,000 balance owed.

Instructions

a. Prepare journal entries to record each of the disposal transactions. Assume that depreciation expense on each asset has been recorded up to the date of disposal. Thus, you need not update the accumulated depreciation figures stated in the problem.

b. Will the gains and losses recorded in part **a** above affect the *gross profit* reported in Hitchcock's income statement? Explain.

c. Explain how the financial reporting of gains and losses on plant assets differs from the financial reporting of *unrealized* gains and losses on marketable securities discussed in Chapter 7.

LO9-6

PROBLEM 9.5A

Accounting for Intangible Assets

During the current year, Reddick Corporation incurred the following expenditures which must be recorded either as operating expenses or as intangible assets:

a. Expenditures were made for the training of new employees. The average employee remains with the company for five years, but is trained for a new position every two years.

b. Reddick purchased a controlling interest in a vinyl flooring company. The expenditure resulted in the recording of a significant amount of goodwill. Reddick expects to earn above-average returns on this investment indefinitely.

c. Reddick incurred large amounts of research and development costs in developing a dirt-resistant carpet fiber. The company expects that the fiber will be patented and that sales of the resulting products will contribute to revenue for at least 25 years. The legal life of the patent, however, will be only 20 years.

d. Reddick made an expenditure to acquire the patent on a popular carpet cleaner. The patent had a remaining legal life of 14 years, but Reddick expects to produce and sell the product for only six more years.

e. Reddick spent a large amount to sponsor the televising of the Olympic Games. Reddick's intent was to make television viewers more aware of the company's name and its product lines.

Instructions

Explain whether each of the above expenditures should be recorded as an operating expense or an intangible asset. If you view the expenditure as an intangible asset, indicate the number of years over which the asset should be amortized, if any. Explain your reasoning.

LO9-6

PROBLEM 9.6A

Accounting for Goodwill

Kivi Service Stations is considering expanding its operations to include the greater Dubuque area. Rather than build new service stations in the Dubuque area, management plans to acquire existing service stations and convert them into Kivi outlets.

Kivi is evaluating two similar acquisition opportunities. Information relating to each of these service stations is presented below:

	Joe's Garage	Gas N' Go
Estimated normal rate of return on net assets	20%	20%
Fair value of net identifiable assets	$950,000	$980,000
Actual average net income for past five years	220,000	275,000

Instructions

a. Compute an estimated fair value for any goodwill associated with Kivi purchasing Joe's Garage. Base your computation upon an assumption that successful service stations typically sell at about 9.25 times their annual earnings.

b. Compute an estimated fair value for any goodwill associated with Kivi purchasing Gas N' Go. Base your computation upon an assumption that Kivi's management expects excess earnings to continue for four years.

c. Many of Kivi's existing service stations are extremely profitable. If Kivi acquires Joe's Garage or Gas N' Go, should it also record the goodwill associated with its existing locations? Explain.

LO9-4

PROBLEM 9.7A

Alternative Depreciation Methods

Thaxton, Inc., purchased a truck to use for deliveries and is attempting to determine how much depreciation expense would be recognized under three different methods. The truck cost $20,000 and is expected to have a value of $4,000 at the end of its five-year life. The truck is expected to be used at the rate of 10,000 miles in the first year, 20,000 miles in the second and third years, and 15,000 miles in each of the fourth and fifth years.

Instructions

a. Determine the amount of depreciation expense that Thaxton should expect to recognize under each of the following depreciation methods in the first and second years of the truck's useful life. A full year's depreciation will be recognized in the first year the truck is used.

   1. Straight-line.

   2. Double-declining-balance.

   3. Units-of-output (based on miles).

b. Prepare the plant assets section of the balance sheet at the end of the second year of the asset's useful life under the straight-line method, assuming the truck is the only plant asset owned by Thaxton, Inc.

c. By which of the three methods is it *not* possible to determine the actual amount of depreciation expense prior to the end of each year? What uncertainty causes this to be true?

LO9-2, LO9-3, LO9-5

PROBLEM 9.8A

Depreciation and Disposal of Plant and Intangible Assets

During the current year, Rothchild, Inc., purchased two assets that are described as follows:

Heavy Equipment

Purchase price, $275,000.

Expected to be used for 10 years, with a residual value at the end of that time of $50,000.

Expenditures required to recondition the equipment and prepare it for use, $75,000.

Patent

Purchase price, $75,000.

Expected to be used for five years, with no value at the end of that time.

Rothchild depreciates heavy equipment by the declining-balance method at 150 percent of the straight-line rate. It amortizes intangible assets by the straight-line method. At the end of two years, because of changes in Rothchild's core business, it sold the patent to a competitor for $30,000.

Instructions

a. Compute the amount of depreciation expense on the heavy equipment for each of the first three years of the asset's life.

b. Compute the amount of amortization on the patent for each of the two years it was owned by Rothchild.

c. Prepare the plant and intangible assets section of Rothchild's balance sheet at the end of the first and second years. Also, calculate the amount of the gain or loss on the patent that would be included in the second year's income statement.

Problem Set B

LO9-1 through LO9-3
PROBLEM 9.1B
Determining the Cost of Plant Assets and Depreciation

Smithfield Hotel recently purchased new exercise equipment for its exercise room. The following information refers to the purchase and installation of this equipment:

1. The list price of the equipment was $42,000; however, Smithfield qualified for a "special discount" of $5,000. It paid $10,000 cash, and issued a three-month, 12 percent note payable for the remaining balance. The note, plus accrued interest charges of $750, was paid promptly at the maturity date.

2. In addition to the amounts described in **1**, Smithfield paid sales taxes of $2,100 at the date of purchase.

3. Freight charges for delivery of the equipment totaled $600.

4. Installation and training costs related to the equipment amounted to $900.

5. During installation, one of the pieces of equipment was accidentally damaged by an employee. Smithfield paid $400 to repair this damage.

6. As soon as the equipment was installed, the hotel paid $3,200 to print brochures featuring the exercise room's new, state-of-the-art exercise facilities.

Instructions

a. In one sentence, make a general statement summarizing the nature of expenditures that qualify for inclusion in the cost of plant assets such as exercise equipment.

b. For each of the six numbered paragraphs, indicate which items should be included by Smithfield Hotel in the total cost added to its Equipment account. Also briefly indicate the proper accounting treatment of those items that *are not* included in the cost of the equipment.

c. Compute the total cost added to the hotel's Equipment account.

d. Prepare a journal entry at the end of the current year to record depreciation on the exercise equipment. Smithfield Hotel plans to depreciate this equipment by the straight-line method (half-year convention) over an estimated useful life of five years. Assume a zero residual value.

LO9-3, LO9-5
PROBLEM 9.2B
Comparison of Straight-Line and Accelerated Methods

R&R, Inc., purchased a new machine on September 1, 2013, at a cost of $180,000. The machine's estimated useful life at the time of the purchase was five years, and its expected residual value was $10,000.

Instructions

a. Prepare a complete depreciation schedule, beginning with calendar year 2013, under each of the methods listed below (assume that the half-year convention is used):

1. Straight-line.
2. 200 percent declining-balance.
3. 150 percent declining-balance (not switching to straight-line).

b. Which of the three methods computed in part **a** is most common for financial reporting purposes? Explain.

c. Assume that R&R sells the machine on December 31, 2016, for $58,000 cash. Compute the resulting gain or loss from this sale under each of the depreciation methods used in part **a**. Does the gain or loss reported in the company's income statement have any direct cash effects? Explain.

LO9-1 through LO9-3, LO9-5

PROBLEM 9.3B

Issues Involving Alternative Depreciation Methods

Davidson, DDS, purchased new furniture for its store on May 1, 2015. The furniture is expected to have a 10-year life and no residual value. The following expenditures were associated with the purchase:

Cost of the furniture	$11,000
Freight charges	375
Sales taxes	550
Installation of furniture	75
Cost to repair furniture damaged during installation	400

Instructions

a. Compute depreciation expense for the years 2015 through 2018 under each depreciation method listed below:

1. Straight-line, with fractional years rounded to the nearest whole month.

2. 200 percent declining-balance, using the half-year convention.

3. 150 percent declining-balance, using the half-year convention.

b. Davidson, DDS, has two conflicting objectives. Management wants to report the highest possible earnings in its financial statements, yet it also wants to minimize its taxable income reported to the IRS. Explain how both of these objectives can be met.

c. Which of the depreciation methods applied in part **a** resulted in the lowest reported book value at the end of 2018? Is book value an estimate of an asset's fair value? Explain.

d. Assume that Davidson, DDS, sold the old furniture that was being replaced. The old furniture had originally cost $3,000. Its book value at the time of the sale was $400. Record the sale of the old furniture under the following conditions:

1. The furniture was sold for $780 cash.

2. The furniture was sold for $250 cash.

LO9-5

PROBLEM 9.4B

Disposal of Plant Assets

During the current year, Blake Construction disposed of plant assets in the following transactions:

Jan. 6   Equipment costing $18,000 was given to a scrap dealer at no charge. At the date of disposal, accumulated depreciation on the office equipment amounted to $16,800.

Mar. 3   Blake sold land and a building for $800,000, receiving $100,000 cash and a five-year, 12 percent note receivable for the remaining balance. Blake's records showed the following amounts: Land, $50,000; Buildings, $680,000; Accumulated Depreciation: Building (at the date of disposal), $250,000.

Jul. 10   Blake traded in an old truck for a new one. The old truck had cost $26,000, and its accumulated depreciation amounted to $22,000. The list price of the new truck was $37,000, but Blake received a $12,000 trade-in allowance for the old truck and paid $25,000 in cash. Blake includes trucks in its Vehicles account.

Sept. 3   Blake traded in its old computer system as part of the purchase of a new system. The old system had cost $12,000, and its accumulated depreciation amounted to $9,000. The new computer's list price was $10,000. Blake accepted a trade-in allowance of $400 for the old computer system, paying $1,000 down in cash and issuing a one-year, 10 percent note payable for the $8,600 balance owed.

Instructions

a. Prepare journal entries to record each of the disposal transactions. Assume that depreciation expense on each asset has been recorded up to the date of disposal. Thus you need not update the accumulated depreciation figures stated in the problem.

b. Will the gains and losses recorded in part **a** above affect the *gross profit* reported in Blake's income statement? Explain.

c. Explain how the financial reporting of gains and losses on plant assets differs from the financial reporting of *unrealized* gains and losses on marketable securities discussed in Chapter 7.

LO9-6
PROBLEM 9.5B

Accounting for Intangible
Assets

During the current year, Delta Products Corporation incurred the following expenditures which should be recorded either as operating expenses or as intangible assets:

a. Expenditures were made for the training of new employees. The average employee remains with the company for five years, but is trained for a new position every two years.

b. Delta purchased a controlling interest in a wallpaper company. The expenditure resulted in recording a significant amount of goodwill. Management expects to earn above-average returns on this investment indefinitely.

c. Delta incurred large amounts of research and development costs in developing a superior product. The company expects that it will be patented and that sales of the resulting products will contribute to revenue for at least 40 years. The legal life of the patent, however, will be only 20 years.

d. Delta made an expenditure to acquire the patent on a product identified as a "whatsa." The patent had a remaining legal life of 10 years, but Delta expects to produce and sell the product for only four more years.

e. Delta spent a large amount to sponsor the televising of the World Series. Management's intent was to make television viewers more aware of the company's name and product lines.

Instructions

Explain whether each of the above expenditures should be recorded as an operating expense or an intangible asset. If you view the expenditure as an intangible asset, indicate the number of years over which the asset should be amortized. Explain your reasoning.

LO9-6
PROBLEM 9.6B

Accounting for Goodwill

Jell Stores is considering expanding its operations to include the greater Portsmouth area. Rather than build new stores in Portsmouth, management plans to acquire existing stores and convert them into Jell outlets.

Jell is evaluating two similar acquisition opportunities. Information relating to each of these stores is presented below:

	Missy's	Mell's
Estimated normal rate of return on net assets..................	20%	20%
Fair market value of net identifiable assets	$900,000	$980,000
Actual average net income for past five years..................	250,000	280,000

Instructions

a. Compute an estimated fair value for any goodwill associated with Jell purchasing Missy's. Base your computation upon an assumption that successful stores of this type typically sell at about 10 times their annual earnings.

b. Compute an estimated fair value for any goodwill associated with Jell purchasing Mell's. Base your computation upon an assumption that Jell's management wants to generate a target return on investment of 35 percent.

c. Many of Jell's existing stores are extremely profitable. If Jell acquires Missy's or Mell's, should it also record the goodwill associated with its existing locations? Explain.

LO9-4
PROBLEM 9.7B

Alternative Depreciation
Methods

Haywood, Inc., purchased a truck to use for deliveries and is attempting to determine how much depreciation expense would be recognized under three different methods. The truck cost $24,000 and is expected to have a value of $6,000 at the end of its six-year life. The truck is expected to be used at the rate of 15,000 miles in the first year, 20,000 miles in the second and third years, and 12,000 miles in each of the fourth, fifth, and sixth years.

Instructions

a. Determine the amount of depreciation expense that would be recognized under each of the following depreciation methods in the first and second years of the truck's useful life. A full year's depreciation will be recognized in the first year the truck is used.

   1. Straight-line.

   2. Double-declining-balance.

   3. Units-of-output (based on miles).

b. Prepare the plant assets section of the balance sheet at the end of the second year in the asset's useful life under the units-of-output method, assuming the truck is the only plant asset owned by Haywood, Inc.

c. By which of the three methods is it *not* possible to determine the actual amount of depreciation expense prior to the end of each year? What uncertainty causes this to be true?

LO9-2, LO9-3, LO9-5
PROBLEM 9.8B
Depreciation and Disposal of Plant and Intangible Assets

During the current year, Rodgers Company purchased two assets that are described as follows:

Heavy Equipment

Purchase price, $550,000.

Expected to be used for 10 years, with a residual value at the end of that time of $70,000.

Expenditures required to recondition the equipment and prepare it for use, $120,000.

Patent

Purchase price, $80,000.

Expected to be used for six years, with no value at the end of that time.

Rodgers depreciates heavy equipment by the declining-balance method at 200 percent of the straight-line rate. It amortizes intangible assets by the straight-line method. At the end of two years, because of changes in Rodgers's core business, it sold the patent to a competitor for $38,000.

Instructions

a. Compute the amount of depreciation expense on the heavy equipment for each of the first three years of the asset's life.

b. Compute the amount of amortization on the patent for each of the two years it was owned by Rodgers.

c. Prepare the plant and intangible assets section of Rodgers's balance sheet at the end of the first and second years. Also, calculate the amount of the gain or loss on the patent that would be included in the second year's income statement.

Critical Thinking Cases

LO9-3
CASE 9.1
Are Useful Lives "Flexible"?

Mickey Gillespie is the controller of Print Technologies, a publicly owned company. The company is experiencing financial difficulties and is aggressively looking for ways to cut costs.
Suzanne Bedell, the CEO, instructs Gillespie to lengthen from 5 to 10 years the useful life used in computing depreciation on certain special-purpose machinery. Bedell believes that this change represents a substantial cost savings, as it will reduce the depreciation expense on these assets by nearly one-half.

Note: The proposed change affects only the depreciation expense recognized in financial statements. Depreciation deductions in income tax returns will not be affected.

Instructions

a. Discuss the extent to which Bedell's idea will, in fact, achieve a cost savings. Consider the effects on both net income and cash flows.

b. Who is responsible for estimating the useful lives of plant assets?

c. Discuss any ethical issues that Gillespie should consider with respect to Bedell's instructions.

LO9-1
CASE 9.2
Departures from GAAP— Are They Ethical?

Maggie Miller owns Miller Construction Co. The company maintains accounting records for the purposes of exercising control over its construction activities and meeting its reporting obligations regarding payrolls and income tax returns. As it has no other financial reporting obligations, Miller does not prepare formal financial statements.

The company owns land and several other assets with current market values well in excess of their historical costs. Maggie Miller directs the company's accountant, Max O'Shaughnessey, to prepare a balance sheet in which assets are shown at estimated market values. Miller says this type of balance sheet will give her a better understanding of where the business stands. She also thinks it will be useful in obtaining bank loans, as loan applications always ask for the estimated market values of real estate owned.

Instructions

a. Would the financial statements requested by Maggie Miller be in conformity with generally accepted accounting principles?

b. Is Miller Construction under any legal or ethical obligation to prepare financial statements that *do* conform to generally accepted accounting principles?

c. Discuss any ethical issues that O'Shaughnessey should consider with respect to Miller's request.

LO9-3, LO9-4

CASE 9.3

Depreciation Policies in Annual Reports

The following is a note accompanying a recent financial statement of **International Paper Company**:

Plants, Properties, and Equipment

Plants, properties, and equipment are stated at cost, less accumulated depreciation. Expenditures for betterments are capitalized, whereas normal repairs and maintenance are expensed as incurred. The units-of-production method of depreciation is used for major pulp and paper mills, and the straight-line method is used for other plants and equipment. Annual straight-line depreciation rates are, for buildings—2.50 percent to 8.50 percent, and for machinery and equipment—5 percent to 33 percent.

Instructions

a. Are the depreciation methods used in the company's financial statements determined by current income tax laws? If not, who is responsible for selecting these methods? Explain.

b. Does the company violate the consistency principle by using different depreciation methods for its paper mills and wood products facilities than it uses for its other plants and equipment? If not, what does the principle of consistency mean? Explain.

c. What is the estimated useful life of the machinery and equipment being depreciated with a straight-line depreciation rate of:

1. 5 percent.

2. 33 percent (round to the nearest year).

Who determines the useful lives over which specific assets are to be depreciated?

d. Why do you think a company would use accelerated depreciation methods for income tax purposes, rather than using the straight-line method?

LO9-2

CASE 9.4

Capitalization vs. Expense

One of your responsibilities as division manager of an important component of Paramount Industries is to oversee accounting for the division. One of the issues you grapple with on an almost continuous basis is whether particular costs should be expensed immediately or whether they should be capitalized. The company has an accounting policy manual that includes a section on this topic, but it is rather vague in this regard. It simply says that if a cost benefits multiple accounting periods, the cost should be capitalized; otherwise, that cost should be expensed immediately. It also makes a brief reference to *materiality* by stating that, if a cost is sufficiently small, it should be immediately expensed despite the fact that it may benefit multiple accounting periods. No additional guidance is provided with regard to how these general concepts should be applied.

Over several years you have noticed a tendency of your staff to capitalize rather than expense more costs. While you and your coworkers in the division do not receive a bonus or other direct compensation that is tied to your division's performance, you know that upper management monitors carefully the financial performance of divisions. From time to time in various meetings and in written correspondence, comments are made praising individuals and divisions of the company for their positive financial performance. In fact, within your division you have done the same when you meet with your employees and either compliment them for strong financial performance or express concern about weak financial performance.

Paramount Industries has a code of professional conduct that is discussed with employees when they are hired. Within that code are references to personal integrity and the responsibility of employees to carry out company policy and not engage in activities that benefit themselves at the expense of the company. Like the accounting policies referred to above, there is no guidance on how this general principle might be carried out.

Instructions

a. What behavior may your comments in meetings with your employees, or the comments made to you from upper management, be motivating in terms of the continuous decisions that are being made about capitalizing and expensing costs?

b. What steps might you take to ensure that you and the employees in your division are taking actions that are consistent with the company's accounting policies and code of professional conduct?

LO9-2

INTERNET CASE 9.5

R&D in the Pharmaceutical Industry

The pharmaceutical industry spends billions of dollars each year on research and development. Rather than capitalize these R&D expenditures as intangible assets, companies are required to charge them to expense in the year incurred.

Perform a keyword search of Pharmaceutical Companies using the search engine of your choice (e.g., Yahoo, Google).

Your search will result in a list of companies that research and develop pharmaceutical products. Select three of these companies and obtain their 10-K reports using the SEC's EDGAR system or going directly to the websites of the companies you choose.

Instructions

a. For each of the companies you selected, determine:

1. Total R&D expense for the most current year.

2. Total R&D expense as a percentage of total operating costs and expenses.

3. Total R&D expense as a percentage of net sales.

4. The percentage by which operating income would have increased had the entire R&D expenditure been recorded as an intangible asset instead of being charged to expense.

b. Using information from the 10-K reports, summarize briefly the kinds of drugs being researched and developed by each of these companies. To a potential investor, which company appears to be the most innovative and promising? Explain.

Internet sites are time and date sensitive. It is the purpose of these exercises to have you explore the Internet. You may need to use the Yahoo! search engine www.yahoo.com (or another favorite search engine) to find a company's current web address.

Answers to Self-Test Questions

1. c (Depreciation is not recorded on inventory.)   **2.** c   **3.** d, $1,800 [2014 depreciation = $10,000 × 20% × ½ = $1,000; 2015 depreciation = ($10,000 − $1,000) × 20% = $1,800]
4. c, d   **5.** a ($22,000 selling price − $17,000 book value = $5,000 gain; $50,000 cost − $17,000 book value = $33,000 accumulated depreciation)   **6.** b

CHAPTER 10

Liabilities

AFTER STUDYING THIS CHAPTER, YOU SHOULD BE ABLE TO:

Learning Objectives

LO10-1 Define *liabilities* and distinguish between current and long-term liabilities.

LO10-2 Account for notes payable and interest expense.

LO10-3 Describe the costs and the basic accounting activities relating to payrolls.

LO10-4 Prepare an amortization table allocating payments between interest and principal.

LO10-5 Describe corporate bonds and explain the tax advantage of debt financing.

LO10-6 Account for bonds issued at a discount or premium.

LO10-7 Explain the concept of present value as it relates to bond prices.

LO10-8 Explain how estimated liabilities, loss contingencies, and commitments are disclosed in financial statements.

LO10-9 Evaluate the safety of creditors' claims.

LO10-10 Describe reporting issues related to leases, postretirement benefits, and deferred taxes.

© AP Photo/Wilfredo Lee

PROCTER & GAMBLE

Buying items on credit is a characteristic of modern business. Each day, large retailers and credit card companies encourage consumers to go deeper and deeper into debt. Add to credit card and other consumer debt various long-term obligations—such as home mortgages and automobile loans—and it's no wonder that payments on total household debt make up a high percentage of total disposable income in the United States.

Large corporations also borrow large amounts of capital issuing by debt to finance expansion, acquisitions, and for a wide variety of other purposes. The tremendous debt service costs associated with corporate borrowing can require a significant portion of a company's operating cash flows.

Consider the case of corporate giant Procter & Gamble. In the company's 2012 balance sheet, total liabilities are over $68 billion, which represents slightly over 50 percent of the company's assets. Included in this amount are noncurrent liabilities of over $43 billion, including various long-term debt issues of approximately $21 billion. This includes 25 different issues of bonds and other forms of debt instruments whose repayment dates range from 2012 to 2037.

From this illustration, you can see that long-term debt financing is a major source of capital for large companies like Procter & Gamble. Debt has a significant impact on all of P&G's financial statements. It also places significant responsibility on management in terms of having available the necessary cash to service the debt each year, as well as being in the financial position required to repay the debt as it matures. Debt financing is one of the major financial resources of companies. ∎

Creditors and investors evaluate carefully the liabilities appearing in financial reports. Understanding short-term versus long-term debt is important for managers choosing how to finance their businesses. This chapter provides a basic understanding of concepts related to liabilities and describes how liabilities are recorded and later presented in the financial statements. In addition, the impact of debt on various financial ratios is illustrated.

THE NATURE OF LIABILITIES

LO10-1

LEARNING OBJECTIVE
Define *liabilities* and distinguish between current and long-term liabilities.

Liabilities may be defined as *debts or obligations arising from past transactions or events* that require settlement at a future date. All liabilities have certain characteristics in common; however, the specific terms of different liabilities and the rights of the creditors vary greatly.

Distinction between Debt and Equity
Businesses have two basic sources of financing: liabilities and owners' equity. Liabilities differ from owners' equity in several respects. The feature that most clearly distinguishes the claims of creditors from owners' equity is that all liabilities eventually *mature*—that is, they come due. Owners' equity does not mature. The date on which a liability comes due is called the **maturity date.**[1]

Although liabilities eventually mature, their maturity dates vary. Some liabilities are so short in term that they are paid before the financial statements are prepared. Long-term liabilities, in contrast, may not mature for many years. The maturity dates of key liabilities may be a critical factor in the solvency of a business.

The providers of borrowed capital are *creditors* of the business, not owners. As creditors, they have financial claims against the business but usually do *not* have the right to control business operations. The traditional roles of owners, managers, and creditors may be modified, however, in an *indenture contract.* Creditors sometimes insist on being granted some control over business operations as a condition of making a loan, particularly if the business is in weak financial condition. Indenture contracts may impose such restrictions as limits on management salaries and on dividends, and may require the creditor's approval for additional borrowing or for large capital expenditures.

The claims of creditors have *legal priority* over the claims of owners. If a business ceases operations and liquidates, creditors must be *paid in full* before any distributions can be made to the owners. The relative security of creditors' claims, however, can vary among the creditors. Sometimes the borrower pledges title to specific assets as **collateral** for a loan. If the borrower defaults on a secured loan, the creditor may foreclose on the pledged assets. Assets that have been pledged as security for loans should be identified in notes accompanying the borrower's financial statements.

Liabilities that are not secured by specific assets are termed *general credit obligations.* The priorities of general credit obligations vary with the nature of the liability and the terms of indenture contracts.

Many Liabilities Bear Interest
Many long-term liabilities, and some short-term ones, require the borrower to pay interest. Only interest accrued *as of the balance sheet date* appears as a liability in the borrower's balance sheet. The borrower's obligation to pay interest in *future* periods may be disclosed in the notes to the financial statements, but it is not an existing liability.

Estimated Liabilities
Many liabilities are for a definite dollar amount, clearly stated by contract. Examples include notes payable, accounts payable, and accrued expenses, such as interest payable and salaries payable. In some cases, however, the dollar amount of a liability must be *estimated* at the balance sheet date.

---

[1] Some liabilities are *due on demand,* which means that the liability is payable upon the creditor's request. Liabilities due on demand may come due at any time and are generally classified as current liabilities.

Estimated liabilities have two basic characteristics: The liability is *known to exist,* but the precise dollar amount cannot be determined until a later date. For instance, the automobiles sold by most automakers are accompanied by a warranty obligating the automaker to replace defective parts for a period of several years. As each car is sold, the automaker *incurs a liability* to perform any work that may be required under the warranty. The dollar amount of this liability, however, can only be estimated.

Current Liabilities

Current liabilities are obligations that are expected to be paid within one year or within the operating cycle, whichever is longer. Another requirement for classification as a current liability is the expectation that the debt will be paid from current assets (or through the rendering of services). Liabilities that do not meet these conditions are classified as long-term or noncurrent liabilities.

The time period used in defining current liabilities parallels that used in defining current assets. The amount of *working capital* (current assets less current liabilities) and the *current ratio* (current assets divided by current liabilities) are valuable indicators of a company's ability to pay its debts in the near future.

Among the most common examples of current liabilities are accounts payable, short-term notes payable, the current portion of long-term debt, accrued liabilities (such as interest payable, income taxes payable, and payroll liabilities), and unearned revenue.

ACCOUNTS PAYABLE

Accounts payable often are subdivided into the categories of *trade* accounts payable and *other* accounts payable. Trade accounts payable are short-term obligations to suppliers for purchases of merchandise. Other accounts payable include liabilities for any goods and services other than merchandise.

Technically, the date at which a trade account payable comes into existence depends on whether goods are purchased F.O.B. (free on board) shipping point or F.O.B. destination. Under F.O.B. shipping point, a liability arises and title to the goods transfers when the merchandise is *shipped* by the supplier. Under F.O.B. destination, a liability does not arise and title of ownership does not transfer until the goods are *received* by the buyer. However, unless *material* amounts of merchandise are purchased on terms F.O.B. shipping point, most companies follow the convenient practice of recording trade accounts payable when merchandise is received.

NOTES PAYABLE

Notes payable usually are issued when bank loans are obtained. Other transactions that may give rise to notes payable include the purchase of real estate or costly equipment, the purchase of merchandise, and the substitution of a note for a past-due account payable.

Notes payable usually require the borrower to pay an interest charge. Normally, the interest rate is stated separately from the **principal amount** of the note.[2]

To illustrate, assume that on November 1, Porter Company borrows $10,000 from its bank for a period of six months at an annual interest rate of 9 percent. Six months later on May 1, Porter Company will have to pay the bank the principal amount of $10,000, plus $450 interest ($10,000 × .09 × 6/12) As evidence of this loan, the bank will require Porter Company to issue a note payable similar to the one in Exhibit 10–1.

LO10-2

LEARNING OBJECTIVE
Account for notes payable and interest expense.

---

[2] An alternative is to include the interest charges in the face amount of the note. This form of note is seldom used today, largely because of the disclosure requirements under "truth-in-lending" laws.

EXHIBIT 10–1

A Note Payable

San Antonio, Texas	November 1, 20__
Six months **AFTER THIS DATE**	Porter Company

PROMISES TO PAY TO SECURITY NATIONAL BANK THE SUM OF $ ___$10,000___

WITH INTEREST AT THE RATE OF ___9%___ **PER ANNUM.**

SIGNED ___John Caldwell___

TITLE ___Treasurer___

The journal entry in Porter Company's accounting records for this November 1 borrowing is:

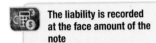

The liability is recorded at the face amount of the note

Cash	10,000	
Notes Payable		10,000
Borrowed $10,000 for 6 months at 9% interest per year.		

Notice that no liability is recorded for the interest charges when the note is issued. At the date the $10,000 is borrowed, the borrower has a liability *only for the principal amount of the loan;* the liability for interest accrues gradually over the life of the loan. At December 31, two months' interest expense has accrued, and the following year-end adjusting entry is made:

A liability for interest accrues day by day

Interest Expense	150	
Interest Payable		150
To record interest expense incurred through year-end on 9%, 6-month note dated Nov. 1 ($10,000 × 9% × 2/12 = $150).		

For simplicity, we assume that Porter Company makes adjusting entries *only at year-end.* The entry on May 1 to record payment of the note will be:

Payment of principal and interest

Notes Payable	10,000	
Interest Payable	150	
Interest Expense	300	
Cash		10,450
To record payment of 9%, 6-month note on maturity date and to recognize interest expense accrued since Dec. 31 ($10,000 × 9% × 4/12 = $300).		

If Porter Company paid this note *prior* to May 1, interest charges usually would be computed only through the date of early payment.[3]

THE CURRENT PORTION OF LONG-TERM DEBT

Some long-term debts, such as mortgage loans, are payable in a series of monthly or quarterly installments. In these cases, the *principal* amount due within one year (or the operating cycle)

---

[3] Computing interest charges only through the date of payment is the normal business practice. However, some notes are written in a manner requiring the borrower to pay interest for the full term of the note even if payment is made early. Borrowers should look carefully at these terms.

is regarded as a current liability, and the remainder of the obligation is classified as a long-term liability.

As the maturity date of a long-term liability approaches, the entire obligation eventually becomes due within the current period. Long-term liabilities that become payable within one year of the balance sheet date are *reclassified* in the balance sheet as current liabilities.[4] Changing the classification of a liability does not require a journal entry; the obligation is simply shown in a different section of the balance sheet.

ACCRUED LIABILITIES

Accrued liabilities arise from the recognition of expenses for which payment will be made in a future period. For this reason, accrued liabilities are sometimes referred to as *accrued expenses*. Examples of accrued liabilities include interest payable, income taxes payable, and a number of liabilities relating to payrolls. As accrued liabilities stem from the recording of expenses, the *matching* principle governs the timing of their recognition.

All companies incur accrued liabilities. In most cases, however, these liabilities are paid at frequent intervals. Therefore, they usually do not accumulate to large amounts. In a balance sheet, small amounts of various types of accrued liabilities are sometimes combined and presented as a single accrued liabilities amount or even combined with other current liabilities, such as accounts payable.

PAYROLL LIABILITIES

The preparation of a payroll is a specialized accounting function beyond the scope of this text. But we believe that every student should have some understanding of the various costs associated with payrolls. Employers must compute, record, and pay a number of costs in addition to the wages and salaries owed to employees. In fact, the total wages and salaries expense (or gross pay) represents only the starting point of payroll computations.

To illustrate, assume that Fulbright Medical Lab employs 20 highly skilled employees. If monthly wages for this workforce in January were $100,000, the *total* payroll costs incurred by this employer would actually be much higher, as shown in Exhibit 10–2.

Gross pay (wages expense)	$100,000
Social Security and Medicare taxes	7,650
Federal and state unemployment taxes	6,200
Workers' Compensation Insurance	4,000
Group health and life insurance benefits	6,000
Employee pension plan benefits	9,500
Total payroll costs for January	$133,350

> **LO10-3**
>
> **LEARNING OBJECTIVE**
> Describe the costs and the basic accounting activities relating to payrolls.

EXHIBIT 10–2

The Computation of Total Payroll Costs

The amounts in Exhibit 10–2 shown in red are **payroll taxes** and insurance premiums required by law. Costs shown in green currently are not required by law but often are included in the total compensation package provided to employees at the discretion of the employer.

In our example, total payroll-related costs exceed wages expense *by more than 30 percent*. This relationship will vary from one employer to another, but our illustration is typical of many payrolls.

Payroll Taxes and Mandated Costs
All employers must pay Social Security and Medicare taxes on the wages or salary paid to each employee. The percentages of the employee's earnings subject to these taxes vary from year to year. Federal unemployment taxes apply only to the *first* set dollar amount earned by each employee during the year (state unemployment taxes may vary). As a result, these taxes tend to decline dramatically as the year progresses.

---

[4] Exceptions are made to this rule if the liability will be *refinanced* (that is, extended or renewed) on a long-term basis and certain specific conditions are met or if a special *sinking fund* has been accumulated for the purpose of repaying this obligation. In these cases, the debt remains classified as a long-term liability, even though it will mature within the current period.

Workers' Compensation Insurance is a state-mandated program that provides insurance to employees against job-related injury. Like most other insurance policies, the premiums are generally paid *in advance* by debiting a current asset account, Prepaid Workers' Compensation Insurance, and by crediting Cash. The premiums vary greatly by state and by occupational classification. In some high-risk industries (for example, roofers), workers' compensation premiums may exceed 50 percent of the employees' wages.

Other Payroll-Related Costs   Many employers pay some or all of the costs of health and life insurance for their employees and their family members, as well as make contributions to employee pension plans. Contributions to employee pension plans, if any, vary greatly among employers.

Amounts Withheld from Employees' Pay   Thus far, our illustration has specified only those taxes and other mandated costs levied on the *employer*. Employees, too, incur taxes on their earnings. In addition to federal and state income taxes, employees share in paying Social Security and Medicare taxes.[5] Employers must withhold these amounts from their employees' pay and forward them directly to the appropriate tax authorities.[6] (The net amount of cash actually paid to employees after all required withholdings have been made is often referred to as the employees' *take-home pay*.)

In our illustration, Fulbright Medical Lab's 20 employees earned gross wages of $100,000 in January. Their take-home pay will be significantly less than the gross amount, as shown in Exhibit 10–3, using assumed numbers for state and federal income tax withholdings.

EXHIBIT 10–3

Computation of Employee Take-Home Pay

Gross pay (wages expense)	$100,000
Less:	
State income tax withholdings	(2,350)
Federal income tax withholdings	(22,500)
Social Security and Medicare tax withholdings	(7,650)
Employee take-home pay for January	$ 67,500

Employers act as tax collectors by withholding taxes from their employees

An important distinction is that amounts withheld from employees' pay do *not* represent taxes on the *employer*. The amounts withheld are simply a portion of the gross wages and salaries expense that must be sent directly by the employer to the tax authorities, rather than paid to the employees. In essence, the employer is required by law to act as the tax *collector*. In the employer's balance sheet, these withholdings represent current liabilities until they are forwarded to the proper tax authorities, but they do not represent payroll taxes of the employer.

Recording Payroll Activities   We conclude our illustration of Fulbright Medical Lab by making the necessary entries to record its payroll activities. In Exhibit 10–2, the lab's *total* payroll costs for January were computed as $133,350. Of this amount, $100,000 represented gross wages earned by employees, $17,850 represented employer payroll taxes and other mandated costs (shown in red), and $15,500 represented other employee benefits paid by the employer (shown in green). The accounting for these three amounts by Fulbright Medical Lab is summarized in Exhibit 10–4.

---

[5] Social Security and Medicare taxes are levied on *employees* at the same percentage rate as levied upon *employers*. Thus, total Social Security and Medicare taxes amount to more than 15 percent of gross wages and salaries. There is a cap on the portion of an employee's earnings that is subject to Social Security taxes. There is no cap on employee wages or salaries subject to Medicare taxes.

[6] In many companies, employers make additional withholdings when their employees share in paying for the cost of health insurance, life insurance, retirement contributions, and other fringe benefits.

EXHIBIT 10–4

Payroll Activities Recorded
by the Employer

A. Record gross wages, employee withholdings, and employee take-home pay (withholdings and take-home pay figures taken from Exhibit 10–3).

Wages Expense	100,000	
State Income Tax Payable		2,350
Federal Income Tax Payable		22,500
Social Security and Medicare Taxes Payable		7,650
Cash (or Wages Payable)		67,500

To record gross wages, employee withholdings, and employee take-home pay.

B. Record employer's payroll tax expense (red figures taken from Exhibit 10–2).

Payroll Tax Expense	17,850	
Social Security and Medicare Taxes Payable		7,650
Federal and State Unemployment Taxes Payable		6,200
Prepaid Workers' Compensation Insurance		4,000

To record employer payroll tax expense, $4,000 of which is the expiration of prepaid workers' compensation insurance premiums.

C. Record employee benefit expenses (green figures taken from Exhibit 10–2).

Employee Health and Life Insurance Expense	6,000	
Pension Fund Expense	9,500	
Prepaid Employee Health and Life Insurance		6,000
Cash (or Pension Benefits Payable)		9,500

To record employee benefit expenses, $6,000 of which is the expiration of prepaid employee health and life insurance premiums.

UNEARNED REVENUE

A liability for unearned revenue arises when a customer pays in advance. Upon receipt of an advance payment from a customer, the company debits Cash and credits a liability account such as Unearned Revenue or Customers' Deposits. As the services are rendered to the customer, an entry is made debiting the liability account and crediting a revenue account. Notice that the liability for unearned revenue normally is satisfied by rendering services to the creditor, rather than by making cash payments.

Unearned revenue ordinarily is classified as a current liability because activities involved in earning revenue are part of the business's normal operating cycle.

Long-Term Liabilities

Long-term obligations usually arise from major financial requirements, such as funding a start-up company, expanding an existing company, aquiring, plant assets, purchasing another company, or refinancing an existing long-term obligation that is about to mature. Transactions involving long-term liabilities are relatively few in number but usually involve large dollar amounts. In contrast, current liabilities usually arise from routine operating transactions.

Many businesses regard long-term liabilities as an alternative to owners' equity as a source of permanent financing. Although long-term liabilities eventually mature, they often are *refinanced*—that is, the maturing obligation simply is replaced with a new long-term liability. As a result, long-term debt financing becomes a permanent part of the financial structure of the business.

MATURING OBLIGATIONS INTENDED TO BE REFINANCED

One special type of long-term liability is an obligation that will mature in the current period but that is expected to be refinanced on a long-term basis. For example, a company may have a bank loan that comes due each year but is routinely extended for the following year. Both the company and the bank may intend for this arrangement to continue on a long-term basis.

If management has both the *intent* and the *ability* to refinance soon-to-mature obligations on a long-term basis, these obligations are classified as long-term liabilities. In this situation, the accountant looks to the *economic substance* of the situation rather than to its legal form.

When the economic substance of a transaction differs from its legal form or its outward appearance, financial statements should reflect the *economic substance.* Accountants summarize this concept with the phrase *"Substance takes precedence over form."* Today's business world is characterized by transactions of ever-increasing complexity. Recognizing those situations in which the substance of a transaction differs from its form is an important challenge confronting the accounting profession.

INTERNATIONAL CASE IN POINT

It is typical in Japan for short-term debt to have lower interest rates than long-term debt. As a result, Japanese managers find short-term debt more attractive than long-term debt. In addition, banks are willing to renew these loans because this allows them to adjust the interest rates to changing market conditions. The outcome is that, short-term debt in Japan works like long-term debt elsewhere. In fact, the use of short-term debt to finance long-term assets appears to be the rule, not the exception, in Japan.

INSTALLMENT NOTES PAYABLE

Purchases of real estate and certain types of equipment often are financed by the issuance of long-term notes that call for a series of installment payments. These payments (often called **debt service**) may be due monthly, quarterly, semiannually, or at any other interval. If these installments continue until the debt is completely repaid, the loan is said to be "fully amortizing." Often, however, installment notes contain a due date at which the remaining unpaid balance is to be repaid in a single "balloon" payment.

Some installment notes call for installment payments equal to the periodic interest charges (an "interest only" note). Under these terms, the principal amount of the loan is payable at a specified maturity date. More often, however, the installment payments are *greater* than the amount of interest accruing during the period. In this case, a portion of each installment payment represents interest expense, and the remainder of the payment reduces the principal amount of the liability. As the amount owed is reduced by each payment, the portion of each successive payment representing interest expense *decreases,* and the portion going toward repayment of principal *increases.*

Allocating Installment Payments between Interest and Principal In accounting for an installment note, the accountant must determine the portion of each payment that represents interest expense and the portion that reduces the principal amount of the liability. This distinction is made by preparing an **amortization table.**

To illustrate, assume that on October 15, Year 1, King's Inn purchases furnishings at a total cost of $16,398. In payment, the company issues an installment note payable for this amount, plus interest at 12 percent per annum (or 1 percent per month). This note will be paid in 18 monthly installments of $1,000 each, beginning on November 15. An amortization table for this installment note payable is shown in Exhibit 10–5 (amounts of interest expense are *rounded to the nearest dollar*).

Preparing an Amortization Table Let us explore the content of Exhibit 10–5. First, notice that the payments are made on a *monthly* basis. Therefore, the amounts of the payments (column A), interest expense (column B), and reduction in the unpaid balance (column C) are all *monthly amounts.*

LO10-4

LEARNING OBJECTIVE
Prepare an amortization table allocating payments between interest and principal.

		(A)	(B) Interest Expense (1% of the Last	(C) Reduction in	(D)
Interest Period	Payment Date	Monthly Payment	Unpaid Balance)	Unpaid Balance (A) – (B)	Unpaid Balance
Issue date	Oct. 15, Year 1	—	—	—	$16,398
1	Nov. 15	$1,000	$164	$836	15,562
2	Dec. 15	1,000	156	844	14,718
3	Jan. 15, Year 2	1,000	147	853	13,865
4	Feb. 15	1,000	139	861	13,004
5	Mar. 15	1,000	130	870	12,134
6	Apr. 15	1,000	121	879	11,255
7	May 15	1,000	113	887	10,368
8	June 15	1,000	104	896	9,472
9	July 15	1,000	95	905	8,567
10	Aug. 15	1,000	86	914	7,653
11	Sept. 15	1,000	77	923	6,730
12	Oct. 15	1,000	67	933	5,797
13	Nov. 15	1,000	58	942	4,855
14	Dec. 15	1,000	49	951	3,904
15	Jan. 15, Year 3	1,000	39	961	2,943
16	Feb. 15	1,000	29	971	1,972
17	Mar. 15	1,000	20	980	992
18	Apr. 15	1,000	8*	992	–0–

AMORTIZATION TABLE (12% NOTE PAYABLE FOR $16,398; PAYABLE IN 18 MONTHLY INSTALLMENTS OF $1,000)

EXHIBIT 10–5

Amortization Table for a Note Payable

*In the last period, interest expense is equal to the amount of the final payment minus the remaining unpaid balance. This compensates for the cumulative effect of rounding interest amounts to the nearest dollar.

The interest rate used in the table is of special importance; this rate must coincide with the period of time *between payment dates*—in this case, one month. Thus, if payments are made monthly, column B must be based on the *monthly* rate of interest. If payments were made quarterly, this column would use the quarterly rate of interest.

An amortization table begins with the original amount of the liability ($16,398) listed at the top of the Unpaid Balance column. The amounts of the monthly payments, shown in column A, are specified by the installment contract. The monthly interest expense, shown in column B, is computed for each month by applying the monthly interest rate to the unpaid balance at the *beginning of that month.* The portion of each payment that reduces the amount of the liability (column C) is simply the remainder of the payment (column A minus column B). Finally, the unpaid balance of the liability (column D) is reduced each month by the amount indicated in column C.

Rather than continuing to make monthly payments, King's Inn could settle this liability at any time by paying the amount currently shown as the unpaid balance.

Notice that the amount of interest expense listed in column B decreases each month, because the unpaid balance is continually decreasing.[7]

Preparing each horizontal line in an amortization table involves making the same computations, based on a new unpaid balance. An amortization table of any length can be easily

---

[7] If the monthly payments were *less* than the amount of the monthly interest expense, the unpaid balance of the note would *increase* each month. This, in turn, would cause the interest expense to increase each month. This pattern, termed *negative amortization,* occurs temporarily in some "adjustable-rate" home mortgages.

and quickly prepared by computer software. (Most "money management" software includes a program for preparing amortization tables.) Only three items of data need to be entered into such a program: (1) the original amount of the liability, (2) the amount of periodic payments, and (3) the interest rate (per payment period).

Using an Amortization Table   Once an amortization table has been prepared, the entries to record each payment are taken directly from the amounts shown in the table. For example, the entry to record the first monthly payment (November 15, Year 1) is:

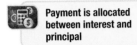

Payment is allocated between interest and principal

Interest Expense	164	
Installment Note Payable	836	
Cash		1,000
Made Nov. payment on installment note payable.		

Similarly, the entry to record the *second* payment, made on *December 15, Year 1,* is:

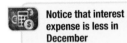

Notice that interest expense is less in December

Interest Expense	156	
Installment Note Payable	844	
Cash		1,000
Made Dec. payment on installment note payable.		

If December 31, Year 1, is the end of the King's Inn's financial reporting period, the company must make an adjusting entry to record one-half month's accrued interest on this liability. The amount of this adjusting entry is based on the unpaid balance shown in the amortization table as of the last payment (December 15). This entry is:

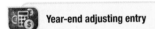

Year-end adjusting entry

Interest Expense	74	
Interest Payable		74
Adjusting entry to record interest expense on installment note for the last half of Dec.: $14,718 $\times$ 1% $\times$ ½ = $74.		

The Current Portion of Long-Term Debt   Notice that as of December 31, Year 1, the unpaid balance of this note is $14,718. As of December 31, *Year 2,* however, the unpaid balance will be $3,904. The principal amount of this note will be reduced by *$10,814* during Year 2 ($14,718 − $3,904 = $10,814). In the balance sheet prepared at December 31, Year 1, the $10,814 portion of this debt that is scheduled for repayment within the *next 12 months* is classified as a *current liability.* The remaining $3,904 is classified as a long-term liability.

BONDS PAYABLE

L010-5

LEARNING OBJECTIVE
Describe corporate bonds and explain the tax advantage of debt financing.

Financially sound corporations may arrange limited amounts of long-term financing by issuing notes payable to banks or to insurance companies. But to finance a large project, such as developing an oil field or purchasing a controlling interest in the capital stock of another company, a corporation may need more capital than any single lender can supply. When a corporation needs to raise particularly large amounts of long-term capital—perhaps 50, 100, or 500 million dollars (or more)—it generally sells additional shares of capital stock or issues **bonds payable.**

WHAT ARE BONDS?

The issuance of bonds payable is a technique for splitting a very large loan into many transferable units, called bonds. Each bond represents a *long-term, interest-bearing note payable,* usually in the face amount (or par value) of $1,000 or some multiple of $1,000. The bonds are sold to the investing public, enabling many different investors (bondholders) to participate in the loan.

Bonds usually are very long-term notes, maturing in as many as 15 or 30 years. Bonds are transferable, however, so individual bondholders may sell their bonds to other investors at any time. Most bonds call for quarterly or semiannual interest payments to the bondholders, with interest computed at a specified *contract rate* throughout the life of the bond. Investors often describe bonds as "fixed income" investments.

An example of a corporate bond issue is the 8½ percent bonds of **Pacific Bell** (a Pacific Telesis company, known as **PacBell**), due August 15, 2031. Interest on these bonds is payable semiannually on February 15 and August 15. With this bond issue, **PacBell** borrowed $225 million by issuing 225,000 bonds of $1,000 each.

PacBell did not actually print and issue 225,000 separate notes payable. Each bondholder is issued a single *bond certificate* indicating the number of bonds purchased. Each certificate is in the face amount of $25,000 and, therefore, represents ownership of 25 bonds. Investors such as mutual funds, banks, and insurance companies often buy thousands of bonds at one time.

The Issuance of Bonds Payable   When bonds are issued, the corporation usually utilizes the services of an investment banking firm, called an **underwriter.** The underwriter guarantees the issuing corporation a specific price for the entire bond issue and makes a profit by selling the bonds to the investing public at a higher price. The corporation records the issuance of the bonds at the net amount received from the underwriter. The use of an underwriter assures the corporation that the entire bond issue will be sold without delay and that the entire amount of the proceeds will be available at a specific date.

Transferability of Bonds   Corporate bonds, like capital stocks, are traded daily on organized securities exchanges, such as the *New York Bond Exchange.* The holders of a 25-year bond issue need not wait 25 years to convert their investments into cash. By placing a telephone call to a broker, an investor may sell bonds almost immediately at the going market price. This *liquidity* is one of the most attractive features of an investment in corporate bonds.

© Digital Vision/Getty Images

Quoted Market Prices   Bond prices are quoted as a *percentage* of their face value or *maturity* value, which is usually $1,000. The maturity value is the amount the issuing company must pay to redeem the bond at the date it matures (becomes due). A $1,000 bond quoted at *102* has a market price of $1,020 (102 percent of $1,000). Similarly, a $1,000 bond quoted at 98 has a market price of $980 (98 percent of $1,000). The following line for a hypothetical company illustrates the type of information available in print or on the Internet summarizing the previous day's trading in bonds.

Bonds	Sales	High	Low	Close	Net Change
Alvaro, Inc. 8½ 17	175	97½	95½	97	+1

This line of condensed information indicates that 175 of Alvaro's 8½ percent, $1,000 bonds maturing in 2017 were traded during the day. The highest price is reported as 97½, or $975 for a bond of $1,000 face value. The lowest price was 95½, or $955 for a $1,000 bond. The closing price (last sale of the day) was 97, or $970. This was one point above the closing price of the previous day, an increase of $10 in the price of a $1,000 bond.

Types of Bonds   Bonds secured by the pledge of specific assets are called *mortgage bonds.* An unsecured bond is called a *debenture bond*; its value rests on the general credit of the corporation rather than the value of a specific asset. A debenture bond issued by a large and strong corporation may have a higher investment rating than a secured bond issued by a corporation in less satisfactory financial condition.

Bond interest is paid semiannually by transferring to each bondholder six months' interest on the bonds he or she owns.[8] Some bonds are *callable,* which means that the corporation has the right to redeem the bonds *in advance* of the maturity date by paying a specified *call price.* To compensate bondholders for being forced to give up their investments, the call price usually is somewhat higher than the face value of the bonds.

Traditionally, bonds have appealed to conservative investors, interested primarily in a reliable income stream from their investments. To make a bond issue more attractive to these investors, some corporations create a bond **sinking fund,** designated for repaying the bonds at maturity. At regular intervals, the corporation deposits cash into this sinking fund. Even though a bond sinking fund is essentially a cash fund, it is not classified as a current asset, because it is not available for the payment of current liabilities. Such funds are shown in the balance sheet under the caption "Long-Term Investments," which appears after the current asset section.

As an additional attraction to investors, corporations sometimes include a conversion privilege in the bond indenture. A **convertible bond** is one that may be exchanged at the option of the bondholder for a specified number of shares of capital stock. The market value of a convertible bond tends to fluctuate with the market value of an equivalent number of shares of capital stock.

Junk Bonds   Some corporations have issued securities that have come to be known as **junk bonds.** This term describes a bond issue that involves a substantially greater risk of default than normal. A company issuing junk bonds usually has so much long-term debt that its ability to meet interest and principal repayment obligations is questionable. To compensate bondholders for this unusual level of risk, junk bonds promise a substantially higher rate of interest than do "investment quality" bonds.

TAX ADVANTAGE OF BOND FINANCING

A principal advantage of raising money by issuing bonds instead of stock is that interest payments are *deductible* in determining income subject to corporate income taxes. Dividends paid to stockholders, however, are *not deductible* in computing taxable income.

To illustrate, assume that a corporation pays income taxes at a rate of *30 percent* on its taxable income. If this corporation issues $10 million of 6 percent bonds payable, it will incur interest expense of $600,000 per year. This interest expense, however, will reduce taxable income by $600,000, thus reducing the corporation's annual income taxes by $180,000. As a result, the *after-tax* cost of borrowing the $10 million is only *$420,000:*

Interest expense ($10,000,000 × 6%)	$600,000
Less: Income tax savings ($600,000 deduction × 30%)	180,000
After-tax cost of borrowing	$420,000

This effectively reduces the cost of borrowing to 4.2 percent ($420,000/$10,000,000).

A shortcut approach to computing the after-tax cost of borrowing is simply multiplying the interest expense by *1 minus the company's tax rate,* as follows: $600,000 × (1 − .30) = $420,000.

ACCOUNTING FOR BONDS PAYABLE

Accounting for bonds payable closely parallels accounting for notes payable. The accountable events for a bond issue usually are (1) issuance of the bonds, (2) semiannual interest

---

[8] In recent years, corporations have issued only *registered* bonds, for which interest is paid by transferring cash by check or electronically to the registered owners of the bonds. In the past, some companies issued *coupon bonds* or *bearer bonds,* which had a series of redeemable coupons attached. At each interest date, the bondholder had to "clip" the coupon and present it to a bank to collect the interest. These bonds posed a considerable hazard to investors—if the investor lost the coupon, or forgot about an interest date, he or she received no interest. In many states, issuing coupon bonds now is illegal.

payments, (3) accrual of interest payable at the end of each accounting period, and (4) retirement of the bonds at maturity.[9]

To illustrate these events, assume that on March 1, 2015, Wells Corporation issues $1 million of 6 percent, 20-year bonds payable.[10] These bonds are dated March 1, 2015, and interest is computed from this date. Interest on the bonds is payable semiannually, each September 1 and March 1. If all of the bonds are sold at par value (also referred to as face value), the issuance of the bonds on March 1 will be recorded by the following entry:

Cash	1,000,000	
Bonds Payable		1,000,000
Issued 6%, 20-year bonds payable at a price of 100.		

Entry at the issuance date

Every September 1 during the term of the bond issue, Wells Corporation must pay $60,000 to the bondholders ($1,000,000 × .6 × ½ = $30,000). This semiannual interest payment will be recorded as shown below:

Bond Interest Expense	30,000	
Cash		30,000
Semiannual payment of bond interest.		

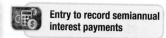
Entry to record semiannual interest payments

Every December 31, Wells Corporation must make an adjusting entry to record the four months' interest that has accrued since September 1:

Bond Interest Expense	20,000	
Bond Interest Payable		20,000
To accrue bond interest payable for four months ended Dec. 31 ($1,000,000 × .06 × 4/12 = $20,000).		

Adjusting entry at year-end

The accrued liability for bond interest payable will be paid within a few months and, therefore, is classified as a current liability.

Two months later, on March 1, a semiannual interest payment is made to bondholders. This transaction represents payment of the four months' interest accrued at December 31 and the two months' interest that has accrued since year-end. Thus the entry to record the semiannual interest payments every March 1 will be:

Bond Interest Expense	10,000	
Bond Interest Payable	20,000	
Cash		30,000
To record semiannual interest payment to bondholders, and to recognize two months' interest expense accrued since Dec. 31 ($1,000,000 × .06 × 2/12 = $10,000).		

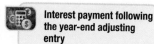
Interest payment following the year-end adjusting entry

---

[9] To simplify our illustrations, we assume in all of our examples and assignment material that adjusting entries for accrued bond interest payable are made *only at year-end*. In practice, these adjustments usually are made on a monthly basis.

[10] The amount of $1 million is used only for purposes of illustration. As explained earlier, actual bond issues are for many millions of dollars.

When the bonds mature 20 years later on March 1, 2035, two entries are required: one to record the regular semiannual interest payment and a second to record the retirement of the bonds. The entry to record the retirement of the bond issue is:

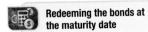
Redeeming the bonds at the maturity date

Bonds Payable	1,000,000	
Cash		1,000,000
Paid face amount of bonds at maturity.		

Bonds Issued between Interest Dates

The semiannual interest dates (such as January 1 and July 1, or April 1 and October 1) are printed on the bond certificates. However, bonds are often issued between the specified interest dates. The *investor* is then required to pay the interest accrued to the date of issuance *in addition* to the stated price of the bond. This practice enables the corporation to pay a full six months' interest on all bonds outstanding at the semiannual interest payment date. The accrued interest collected from investors who purchase bonds between interest payment dates is returned to them on the next interest payment date.

To illustrate, let us modify our illustration to assume that Wells Corporation issues $1 million of 6 percent bonds at par value on *May 1*—two months *after* the March interest date printed on the bonds. The amount received from the bond purchasers now will include two months' accrued interest, as follows:

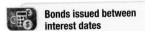
Bonds issued between interest dates

Cash	1,010,000	
Bonds Payable		1,000,000
Bond Interest Payable		10,000
Issued $1,000,000 of 6%, 20-year bonds at face value plus accrued interest for two months ($1,000,000 × 6% × $2/12$ = $10,000).		

Four months later on the regular September 1 semiannual interest payment date, a full six months' interest ($60 per $1,000 bond) will be paid to all bondholders, *regardless of when they purchased their bonds*. The entry for the semiannual interest payment is illustrated below:

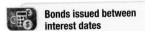
Notice only part of the interest payment is charged to expense

Bond Interest Payable	10,000	
Bond Interest Expense	20,000	
Cash		30,000
Paid semiannual interest on $1,000,000 face value of 6% bonds.		

Now consider these interest transactions from the standpoint of the *investors*. They paid for two months' accrued interest ($10,000) at the time of purchasing the bonds and then received six months' interest ($30,000) after holding the bonds for only four months.

When bonds are subsequently sold by one investor to another investor, they sell at the quoted market price *plus accrued interest* since the last interest payment date. This practice enables the issuing corporation to pay all the interest for an interest period to the investor owning the bond at the interest date. Otherwise, the corporation would have to make partial payments to every investor who bought or sold the bond during the interest period.

The amount that investors pay for bonds is the *present value* of the principal and interest payments they will receive. The concept of present value is discussed on pages 450–451. A more in-depth coverage of present value appears in Appendix B at the end of this textbook.

BONDS ISSUED AT A DISCOUNT OR A PREMIUM

L010-6

LEARNING OBJECTIVE
Account for bonds issued at a discount or premium.

Underwriters normally sell corporate bonds to investors either at face value or at a price very close to face value. Therefore, the underwriter usually purchases these bonds from the issuing corporation at a discount—that is, at a price below face value. The discount percentage generally is quite small—perhaps 1 percent or 2 percent of the face amount of the bonds.

When bonds are issued, the borrower records a liability equal to the *amount received.* If the bonds are issued at a small discount—which is the normal case—this liability is smaller than the face value of the bond issue. At the maturity date, of course, the issuing corporation must redeem the bonds at full face value. As a result of this process, over the term of the bond issue, the borrower's liability gradually *increases* from the original issue price to the maturity value.

ACCOUNTING FOR A BOND DISCOUNT: AN ILLUSTRATION

To illustrate, assume that on March 1, 2015, Wells Corporation sells $1 million of 6 percent, 20-year bonds payable to an underwriter at a price of *97* (meaning that the bonds were sold to the underwriter at 97 percent of their face value). On March 1, 2015, Wells Corporation receives $970,000 cash from the underwriter and records a *net* liability of this amount ($1,000,000 × .97 = $970,000). When these bonds mature in 20 years, however, Wells will owe its bondholders the *full* $1 million face value of the bond issue. Over the 20-year term of the bonds, the company's liability must be *increased* by $30,000 ($1,000,000 − $970,000 = $30,000).

The gradual growth in the company's liability is illustrated in Exhibit 10–6. Notice that the liability increases at an average rate of $1,500 per year ($30,000 total increase ÷ 20-year life of the bond issue).

EXHIBIT 10–6

The Carrying Value of a Bond Discount

Bond Discount: Part of the Cost of Borrowing
As illustrated above, when bonds are issued at a discount, the borrower must repay more than the amount originally borrowed. Any discount in the issuance price becomes an additional cost of the overall borrowing transaction.

In terms of cash outlays, the additional cost represented by the discount is not paid until the bonds mature. But the *matching principle* generally requires the borrower to recognize this cost gradually over the life of the bond issue.[11]

When the bonds are issued, the amount of any discount is debited to an account entitled *Discount on Bonds Payable.* Wells Corporation will record the March 1 issuance as follows:

Cash	970,000	
Discount on Bonds Payable	30,000	
Bonds Payable		1,000,000
Issued 20-year bonds with $1,000,000 face value to an underwriter at a price of 97.		

---

[11] If the amount of the discount is immaterial, it may be charged directly to expense as a matter of convenience. In this text, the straight-line method of amortizing bond discounts and premiums is used. The effective interest method is more common and conceptually correct and is covered in more advanced accounting textbooks.

Wells Corporation's liability at the date of issuance appears in the balance sheet as follows:

Long-Term Liabilities	
Bonds payable	$1,000,000
Less: Discount on bonds payable	30,000
Net carrying value of bonds payable	$ 970,000

The Discount on Bonds Payable account is treated as a *contra-liability account.* As illustrated, it is shown in the balance sheet as a *reduction* in the face or par value of bonds payable. The net carrying value of the bonds payable on the date of issuance is equal to the *amount borrowed.*

Amortization of the Discount   On March 1, 2015, Wells Corporation received $970,000 from the underwriter. When the bonds mature 20 years later on March 1, 2035, the company must pay its bondholders the *full* $1 million face value of the bond issue. This additional $30,000 represents *interest expense* that is spread (i.e., amortized) over the 20-year life of the bond. At each interest payment date, an adjusting entry is made to transfer a portion of the Discount on Bonds Payable account into interest expense. Thus, over time, the discount declines and the carrying value of the bonds—the face amount less the remaining discount balance—rises toward the $1 million maturity value of the bond issue.

Each September 1, the company records the following interest expense of *$30,750:*

Semiannual interest *payment* ($1,000,000 $\times$ 6% $\times$ ½)	$30,000
Add: Semiannual amortization of bond discount	
[($30,000 discount ÷ 20 years) $\times$ ½]	750
Semiannual interest expense	$30,750

The entry to record interest expense on September 1 throughout the life of the bond issue is:

Bond Interest Expense	30,750	
Cash		30,000
Discount on Bonds Payable		750
To record semiannual interest at 3% plus six months'		
amortization of the $30,000 discount on 20-year bonds payable.		

Notice that the amortization of the discount increases Wells Corporation's semiannual interest expense by $750. It does not, however, require any immediate cash outlay. The interest expense represented by the *entire* amortized discount will not be paid until the bonds mature on March 1, 2035.

Every December 31, Wells Corporation makes an adjusting entry to record four months' interest expense that has accrued since September 1. The computation of this $20,500 accrual is computed as follows:

Four months' accrued interest *payable* ($1,000,000 $\times$ 6% $\times$ ⁴⁄₁₂)	$20,000
Add: Four months' amortization of bond discount	
[($30,000 discount ÷ 20 years) $\times$ ⁴⁄₁₂]	500
Interest accrued from September 1 through December 31	$20,500

The adjusting entry required each December 31 throughout the life of the bond issue is as follows:

Bond Interest Expense	20,500	
Bond Interest Payable		20,000
Discount on Bonds Payable		500
To record four months' interest expense and to recognize four months' amortization of the discount on 20-year bonds payable.		

Two months later, on every March 1, a *full* semiannual interest payment is made to the company's bondholders, and an additional two months' amortization of the discount is recognized. The $10,250 interest expense recorded on this date is computed as:

Two months' accrued interest *payable* ($1,000,000 × 6% × 2/12)	$10,000
Add: Two months' amortization of bond discount [($30,000 discount ÷ 20 years) × 2/12]	250
Interest accrued from January 1 through March 1	$10,250

The semiannual interest payment recorded on March 1 throughout the life of the bond issue is:

Bond Interest Expense	10,250	
Bond Interest Payable	20,000	
Cash		30,000
Discount on Bonds Payable		250
To record two months' interest expense, to recognize two months' amortization of the discount on 20-year bonds payable, and to record semiannual interest payment to bondholders.		

When the bonds mature 20 years later on March 1, 2035, two entries are required: one to record the regular semiannual interest payment, and a second to record the retirement of the bonds. At this date, the original $30,000 discount will be *fully amortized* (that is, the Discount on Bonds Payable account will have a zero balance). The carrying amount of the bond issue will be $1 million, and the entry required to record the retirement of the bond issue will be:

Bonds Payable	1,000,000	
Cash		1,000,000
Paid the face amount of bonds at maturity.		

It is important to realize that over the life of this bond issue, Wells Corporation recognized *total* interest expense of $1,230,000 (40 semiannual interest payments of $30,000, plus the additional $30,000 discount).

ACCOUNTING FOR A BOND PREMIUM: AN ILLUSTRATION

As noted previously, underwriters normally purchase bonds from the issuing corporation at a discount. Under some circumstances, however, an underwriter may actually pay a slight premium to the issuer—that is, a price above par.

To illustrate, assume that on March 1, 2015, Wells Corporation sells $1 million of 6 percent, 20-year bonds payable to an underwriter at a price of *103* (meaning that the bonds were sold to the underwriter at 103 percent of their face value). On March 1, 2015, Wells

Corporation receives $1,030,000 cash from the underwriter ($1,000,000 × 1.03) and records a liability equal to this amount. When these bonds mature in 20 years, however, Wells will owe its bondholders only the $1 million *face value* of the bond issue. The company's initial liability must be *reduced* by $30,000 over the 20 years that the bonds are outstanding.

The gradual decrease in the company's liability is illustrated in Exhibit 10–7. Notice that the liability decreases at an average rate of $1,500 per year ($30,000 total increase ÷ 20-year life of the bond issue).

EXHIBIT 10–7

The Carrying Value of a Bond Premium

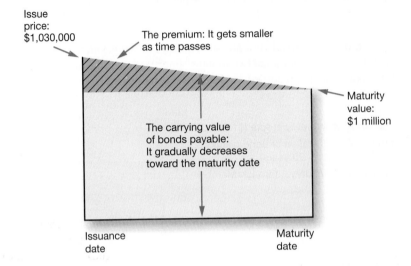

Bond Premium: A Reduction in the Cost of Borrowing   When bonds are issued at a premium, the borrower repays less than the amount originally received at the date of issuance. The premium represents a reduction in the overall cost of borrowing. Unlike bonds issued at a discount, the interest expense associated with bonds issued at a premium will be *less* than the semiannual cash payment made to bondholders.

When the bonds are issued, the amount of any premium is credited to an account entitled *Premium on Bonds Payable*. Thus, Wells Corporation will record the March 1 issuance as follows:

Cash	1,030,000	
Premium on Bonds Payable		30,000
Bonds Payable		1,000,000
Issued 20-year bonds with $1,000,000 face value to an underwriter at a price of 103.		

Wells Corporation's liability at the date of issuance will appear in the balance sheet as follows:

Long-Term Liabilities	
Bonds payable	$1,000,000
Add: Premium on bonds payable	30,000
Carrying value of bonds payable	$1,030,000

Note that, because the Premium on Bonds Payable account has a credit balance, it is shown in the balance sheet as an *increase* in the face or par value of bonds payable.

Amortization of the Premium   On March 1, 2015, Wells Corporation received $1,030,000 from the underwriter. When the bonds mature 20 years later on March 1, 2035, the company must pay back its bondholders only the $1 million *face value* of the bond issue. This $30,000 reduction in the amount owed represents *interest savings* that is amortized over the 20-year life of the bond. Over the 20-year term of the bond, the premium declines, and the carrying value of the bonds—the face amount plus the remaining premium balance—also declines toward the $1 million maturity value of the bond issue.

Each September 1, the company records interest expense of *$29,250,* computed as:

Semiannual interest *payment* ($1,000,000 × 6% × ½)	$30,000
Less: Semiannual amortization of bond premium	
[($30,000 premium ÷ 20 years) × ½]	750
Semiannual interest expense	$29,250

The entry to record interest expense on September 1 throughout the life of the bond issue is:

Bond Interest Expense	29,250	
Premium on Bonds Payable	750	
Cash		30,000
To record semiannual interest expense and to recognize six months' amortization of the $30,000 premium on 20-year bonds payable.		

Notice that the $30,000 semiannual interest payment is the same regardless of whether the bonds are issued at face value, at a discount, or at a premium. The amortization of the premium does, however, reduce the amount of interest expense recognized by the company over the life of the bond issue.

Every December 31, Wells Corporation must make an adjusting entry to record four months' interest expense that has accrued since September 1. The $19,500 accrual is computed as follows:

Four months' accrued interest *payable* ($1,000,000 × 6% × 4/12)	$20,000
Less: Four months' amortization of bond premium	
[($30,000 premium ÷ 20 years) × 4/12]	500
Interest accrued from September 1 through December 31	$19,500

Thus, the following adjusting entry is required on December 31 throughout the life of the bond issue:

Bond Interest Expense	19,500	
Premium on Bonds Payable	500	
Bond Interest Payable		20,000
To record four months' interest expense and to recognize four months' amortization of the premium on 20-year bonds payable.		

Two months later, on every March 1, a *full* semiannual interest payment is made to the company's bondholders, and an additional two months' amortization of the premium is recognized. The $9,750 interest expense recorded on this date is computed as:

Two months' accrued interest *payable* ($1,000,000 × 6% × 2/12)	$10,000
Less: Two months' amortization of bond premium	
[($30,000 premium ÷ 20 years) × 2/12]	250
Interest accrued from January 1 through March 1	$ 9,750

The semiannual interest payment recorded on March 1 throughout the life of the bond issue is:

Bond Interest Expense	9,750	
Bond Interest Payable	20,000	
Premium on Bonds Payable	250	
Cash		30,000

To record two months' interest expense, to recognize two months' amortization of the premium on 20-year bonds payable, and to record semiannual interest payment to bondholders.

When the bonds mature 20 years later on March 1, 2035, two entries are required: one to record the regular semiannual interest payment, and a second to record the retirement of the bonds. At this date, the original $30,000 premium will be *fully amortized* (that is, the Premium on Bonds Payable account will have a zero balance). The carrying value of the bond issue have been reduced to $1 million, and the entry required to record the retirement of the bond issue will be as follows:

Bonds Payable	1,000,000	
Cash		1,000,000

Paid the face amount of bonds at maturity.

In the previous illustration involving a bond discount, Wells Corporation recognized total interest expense of $1,230,000 over the life of the bonds. Had these same bonds been issued at a premium of 103, however, we see that the company would have incurred total interest expense of $1,170,000 (40 semiannual interest payments of $30,000, less the $30,000 premium).

BOND DISCOUNT AND PREMIUM IN PERSPECTIVE

From a conceptual point of view, investors might pay a premium price to purchase bonds that pay an *above-market* rate of interest. If the bonds pay a *below-market* rate, investors will buy them only at a discount.

But these concepts seldom come into play when bonds are first issued. Most bonds are issued *at* the market rate of interest. Corporate bonds are rarely issued at a premium. Bonds often are issued at a small discount, but this discount represents only the underwriter's profit margin, not investors' response to a below-market interest rate.[12] The annual effects of amortizing bond discounts or premiums are diluted further because these amounts are amortized over the entire life of the bond issue—usually 20 years or more. We defer further discussion of this topic to more advanced accounting courses.[13]

THE CONCEPT OF PRESENT VALUE

LO10-7

LEARNING OBJECTIVE Explain the concept of present value as it relates to bond prices.

The concept of present value is based on the time value of money—the idea that receiving money today is preferable to receiving money at some future date. Assume, for example, that an investment promises to pay $1,000 five years from today and will pay no interest in the meantime. Investors would not pay $1,000 for this opportunity today, because they would receive no return on their investment over the next five years. There is a price less than $1,000, however, at which investors would be interested. For example, if the investment could be purchased for $600, the investor could expect a return (interest) of $400 over the five-year period ($1,000 − $600 = $400).

[12] A study of 685 bond issues indicates that none were issued at a premium, and over 95 percent were issued at par or at a discount of less than 2 percent of face value.

[13] Some companies issue *zero-coupon* bonds, which pay *no* interest but are issued at huge discounts. In these situations, amortization of the discount *is* material and may comprise much of the company's total interest expense. Zero-coupon bonds are a specialized form of financing that will be discussed in later accounting courses and courses in corporate finance.

The **present value** of a future cash receipt is the amount that a knowledgeable investor will pay *today* for the right to receive that future payment. The exact amount of the present value depends on (1) the amount of the future payment, (2) the length of time until the payment will be received, and (3) the rate of return required by the investor. However, the present value will always be *less* than the future amount. This is because money received today can be invested to earn interest and grow to a larger amount in the future.

The rate of interest that will cause a given present value to grow to a given future amount is called the *discount rate* or *effective rate*. The effective interest rate required by investors at any given time is regarded as the going *market rate* of interest. (The procedures for computing the present value of a future amount are illustrated in Appendix B at the end of this textbook. The concept of present value is very useful in managing your personal financial affairs. We suggest that you read Appendix B for your own personal development—even if it has not been assigned.)

The Present Value Concept and Bond Prices   The price at which bonds sell is the present value to investors of the future principal and interest payments. If the bonds sell at face value, the market rate is equal to the *contract interest rate* (also referred to as the stated or nominal rate) printed on the bonds. The *higher* the effective interest rate that investors require, the *less* they will pay underwriters for bonds with a given contract rate of interest. For example, if investors insist on a 10 percent return, they will pay less than $1,000 for a 9 percent, $1,000 bond. In other words, if investors require an effective interest rate *greater* than the contract rate of interest, the bonds will be sold by underwriters at a *discount* (a price less than their face value). On the other hand, if market conditions support an effective interest rate of *less* than the contract rate, the bonds will sell at a *premium* (a price above their face value). Since market rates of interest fluctuate constantly, it is reasonable to expect that the contract rate of interest will sometimes vary from the market rate at the date the bonds are issued.

BOND PRICES AFTER ISSUANCE

As stated earlier, many corporate bonds are traded daily on organized securities exchanges at quoted market prices. After bonds are issued, their market prices vary *inversely* with changes in market interest rates. As interest rates rise, investors will be willing to pay less money to own a bond that pays a given contract rate of interest. Conversely, as interest rates decline, the market prices of bonds rise.

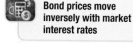
Bond prices move inversely with market interest rates

CASE IN POINT

This is a historical case on the impact of interest rates on the price of bonds. IBM sold to underwriters $500 million of 9⅜ percent, 25-year debenture bonds. The underwriters planned to sell the bonds to the public at a price of 99⅝. Just as the bonds were offered for sale, however, a change in Federal Reserve credit policy started an upward surge in interest rates. The underwriters encountered great difficulty selling the bonds. Within one week, the market price of the bonds had fallen to 94½. The underwriters dumped their unsold inventory at this price and sustained one of the largest underwriting losses in Wall Street history.

During the months that followed, interest rates soared to record levels. Within five months, the price of the bonds had fallen to 76⅜. Thus nearly one-fourth of the market value of these bonds evaporated in less than half a year. At this time, the financial strength of IBM was never in question; this dramatic loss in market value was caused entirely by rising interest rates.

Changes in the current level of interest rates are not the only factors influencing the market prices of bonds. The length of time remaining until the bonds mature is another major force. As a bond nears its maturity date, its market price normally moves closer and closer to the maturity value. This trend is dependable because the bonds are redeemed at face value on the maturity date.

Volatility of Short-Term and Long-Term Bond Prices   When interest rates fluctuate, the market prices of long-term bonds are affected to a far greater extent than the market prices of bonds due to mature in the near future. To illustrate, assume that market interest rates suddenly soar from 6 percent to 9 percent. A 6 percent bond scheduled to mature in a few days will still have a market value of approximately $1,000—the amount to be collected in a few days from the issuing corporation. However, the market price of a 6 percent bond maturing in 10 years will drop significantly. Investors who must accept these below-market interest payments for many years will buy the bonds only at a discounted price.

In summary, fluctuations in interest rates have a far greater effect on the market prices of long-term bonds than on the prices of short-term bonds.

Remember that, after bonds have been issued, they belong to the bondholder, *not to the issuing corporation.* Therefore, changes in the market price of bonds subsequent to their issuance *do not* affect the amounts shown in the financial statements of the issuing corporation, and these changes are not recorded in the company's accounting records.

YOUR TURN   You as a Financial Advisor

Assume that you are the financial advisor for a recently retired investor. Your client wants to invest her savings in such a way as to receive a stable stream of cash flow every year throughout her retirement. She has expressed concern to you regarding the volatility of long-term bond prices when interest rates fluctuate.

If your client invests her savings in a variety of long-term bonds and holds these bonds until maturity, will interest rate fluctuations affect her annual cash flow during her retirement years?

(See our comments on the Online Learning Center website.)

EARLY RETIREMENT OF BONDS PAYABLE

Bonds are sometimes retired before the maturity date. The principal reason for retiring bonds early is to relieve the issuing corporation of the obligation to make future interest payments. If interest rates decline to the point that a corporation can borrow at an interest rate below that being paid on an outstanding bond issue, the corporation may benefit from retiring those bonds early and issuing new bonds at a lower interest rate.

Most bond issues contain a call provision, permitting the corporation to redeem the bonds by paying a specified price, usually a few points above face value. Even without a call provision, the corporation may retire its bonds before maturity by purchasing them in the open market. If the bonds can be purchased by the issuing corporation at less than their carrying value, a *gain* is realized on the retirement of the debt. If the bonds are reacquired by the issuing corporation at a price in excess of their carrying value, a *loss* must be recognized.

For example, assume that Briggs Corporation has outstanding a 6 percent, $10 million bond issue, callable on any interest date at a price of 102. Assume also that the bonds were issued at par and will not mature for nine years. Recently, however, market interest rates have declined to less than 5 percent, and the market price of Briggs's bonds has increased to 106.[14]

Regardless of the market price, by prior agreement Briggs can call these bonds at 102. If the company exercises this call provision for 10 percent of the bonds ($1,000,000 face value), the entry will be:

Bonds Payable	1,000,000	
Loss on Early Retirement of Bonds	20,000	
Cash		1,020,000
To record the call of $1 million in bonds payable at a call price of 102.		

---

[14] Falling interest rates cause bond prices to rise. On the other hand, falling interest rates also provide the issuing company with an incentive to call the bonds and, perhaps, replace them with bonds bearing a lower rate of interest. For this reason, call prices often serve as an approximate "ceiling" on market prices.

Notice that Briggs *called* these bonds, rather than repurchasing them at market prices. Therefore, Briggs is able to retire these bonds at their call price of 102. (Had the market price of the bonds been *below* 102, Briggs might have been able to retire the bonds at less cost by purchasing them in the open market.)

Estimated Liabilities, Loss Contingencies, and Commitments

ESTIMATED LIABILITIES

The term *estimated liabilities* refers to *liabilities that appear in financial statements at estimated dollar amounts.* Let us consider the example of the automaker's liability to honor its new car warranties. A manufacturer's liability for warranty work is recorded by recording both Warranty Expense and a Liability for Warranty Claims. The *matching principle* requires that the expense of performing warranty work be recognized in the period in which the products are *sold,* in order to offset this expense against the related sales revenue. As the warranty may extend several years into the future, the dollar amount of this liability (and expense) must be estimated. Because of the uncertainty regarding when warranty work will be performed, accountants traditionally have classified the liability for warranty claims as a current liability.

By definition, estimated liabilities involve some degree of uncertainty. However, (1) the liabilities are known to exist, and (2) the uncertainty as to dollar amount is *not so great* as to prevent the company from making a reasonable estimate and recording the liability.

LOSS CONTINGENCIES

Loss contingencies are similar to estimated liabilities but may involve even more uncertainty. A loss contingency is a *possible loss,* stemming from *past events,* that is expected to be resolved in the future.

Central to the definition of a loss contingency is the element of *uncertainty*—uncertainty as to the amount of loss and, in some cases, uncertainty as to *whether or not any loss actually has been incurred.* A common example of a loss contingency is a lawsuit pending against a company. The lawsuit is based on past events, but until the suit is resolved, uncertainty exists as to whether the company has sustained a loss and, if it has, how much was that loss.

Loss contingencies differ from estimated liabilities in two ways. First, a loss contingency may involve a *greater degree of uncertainty.* Often the uncertainty extends to whether any loss or expense actually has been incurred. In contrast, the loss or expense relating to an estimated liability is *known to exist.*

Second, the concept of a loss contingency extends not only to possible liabilities but also to possible *impairments of assets.* Assume, for example, that a bank has made large loans to a foreign country now experiencing political instability. Uncertainty exists as to the amount of loss, if any, associated with this loan. From the bank's point of view, this loan is an asset that may be impaired, not a liability.

Loss Contingencies in Financial Statements　The manner in which loss contingencies are presented in financial statements depends on the *degree of uncertainty involved.*

Loss contingencies are *recorded* in the accounting records only when both of the following criteria are met: (1) It is *probable* that a loss has been incurred, and (2) the amount of loss can be *reasonably estimated.* An example of a loss contingency that usually meets these criteria and is recorded in the accounts is the obligation a company has for product warranties and defects.

When these criteria are *not* met, loss contingencies are *disclosed* in notes to the financial statements if there is a *reasonable possibility* that a material loss has been incurred. Pending lawsuits, for example, usually are disclosed in notes accompanying the financial statements, but the loss, if any, is not recorded in the accounting records until the lawsuit is settled. Companies are not required to disclose loss contingencies if the risk of a material loss having occurred is considered *remote.*

LO10-8

LEARNING OBJECTIVE
Explain how estimated liabilities, loss contingencies, and commitments are disclosed in financial statements.

Notice the *judgmental nature* of the criteria used in accounting for loss contingencies. These criteria involve assessments as to whether the risk of material loss is "probable," "reasonably possible," or "remote." The collective *professional judgment* of the company's management, accountants, legal counsel, and auditors is the deciding factor in accounting for loss contingencies. Loss contingencies relate only to possible losses from *past events*. The risk that losses may result from *future* events is *not* a loss contingency.

When loss contingencies are disclosed in notes to the financial statements, the note should describe the nature of the contingency and, if possible, provide an estimate of the amount of possible loss. If a reasonable estimate of the amount of possible loss cannot be made, the disclosure should include the range of possible loss or a statement that an estimate cannot be made. The following note is typical of the disclosure of the loss contingency arising from pending litigation:

Note 8: Contingencies

Note disclosure of a loss contingency

In October of 2014, the Company was named as defendant in a $250 million patent infringement lawsuit. The Company denies all charges and is preparing its defense against them. It is not possible at this time to determine the ultimate legal or financial responsibility that may arise as a result of this litigation.

Sometimes a *portion* of a loss contingency qualifies for immediate recognition, whereas the remainder only meets the criteria for disclosure. Assume, for example, that a company is required by the Superfund Act to clean up an environmental hazard over a 10-year period. The company cannot predict the total cost of the project but considers it probable that it will cost at least $1 million. The company should recognize a $1 million expected loss and record it as a liability. In addition, it should disclose in the notes to the financial statements that the actual cost ultimately may exceed the recorded amount.

COMMITMENTS

Contracts for future transactions are called **commitments.** They are not liabilities, but, if material, they are disclosed in notes to the financial statements. For example, a professional baseball club may issue a three-year contract to a player at an annual salary of, $8 million. This is a commitment to pay for services to be rendered in the future. There is no obligation to make payment until the services are received. As liabilities stem only from *past transactions,* this commitment has not yet created a liability.

Other examples of commitments include a corporation's long-term employment contract with a key officer, a contract for construction of a new plant, and a contract to buy or sell inventory at future dates. The common quality of all these commitments is an intent to enter into transactions *in the future.* Commitments that are material in amount should be disclosed in notes to the financial statements.

Evaluating the Safety of Creditors' Claims

LO10-9

LEARNING OBJECTIVE
Evaluate the safety of creditors' claims.

Creditors, of course, want to be sure that their claims are safe—that is, that they will be paid on time. Actually, *everyone* associated with a business—management, owners, employees—should be concerned with the company's ability to pay its debts. If a business becomes *illiquid* (unable to pay its obligations), it may be forced into **bankruptcy.**[15]

Not only does management want the business to remain liquid, but it also wants the company to maintain a high *credit rating* with agencies such as **Moody's** and **Standard & Poor's.** A high credit rating helps a company borrow money more easily and at lower interest rates.

In evaluating debt-paying ability, short-term creditors and long-term creditors look at different relationships. Short-term creditors are interested in the company's *immediate* liquidity. Long-term creditors, in contrast, are interested in the company's ability to meet its interest

---

[15] Bankruptcy is a legal status under which the company's fate is determined largely by the U.S. Bankruptcy Court. Sometimes the company is reorganized and allowed to continue its operations. In other cases, the business is closed and its assets are sold. Often managers and other employees lose their jobs. In almost all bankruptcies, the company's creditors and owners incur legal costs and sustain financial losses.

obligations over a *period of years,* as well as its ability to repay or refinance large obligations as they come due.

In previous chapters we introduced several measures of short-term liquidity and long-term credit risk. These measures are summarized in Exhibit 10–8—along with the *interest coverage ratio,* which is discussed below.

METHODS OF DETERMINING CREDITWORTHINESS

Interest Coverage Ratio   Creditors, investors, and managers all feel more comfortable when a company has enough income to cover its interest payments by a wide margin. One widely used measure of the relationship between earnings and interest expense is the **interest coverage ratio,** which is sometimes referred to as times interest earned.

The interest coverage ratio is computed by dividing *operating income* by the annual interest expense. From a creditor's point of view, the higher this ratio, the better. In past years, most companies with good credit ratings had interest coverage ratios of, perhaps, 4 to 1 or more.

Less Formal Means of Determining Creditworthiness   Not all decisions to extend credit involve formal analysis of the borrower's financial statements. Most suppliers of goods or services, for example, will sell on account to almost any long-established business—unless they know the customer is in severe financial difficulty. If the customer is not a well-established business, these suppliers may investigate the customer's credit history by contacting a credit-rating agency.

In lending to small businesses organized as corporations, lenders may require key stockholders to *personally guarantee* repayment of the loan.

HOW MUCH DEBT SHOULD A BUSINESS HAVE?

All businesses incur some debts as a result of normal business operations. These include, for example, accounts payable and accrued liabilities. But many businesses aggressively use long-term debt, such as mortgages and bonds payable, to finance growth and expansion. Is this wise? Does it benefit the stockholders? The answer hinges on another question: *Can the borrowed funds be invested to earn a return higher than the rate of interest paid to creditors?*

Using borrowed money to finance business operations is called applying **leverage.** Extensive use of leverage—that is, a great deal of debt—sometimes benefits a business dramatically. But if things don't work out, it can "wipe out" the borrower.

If borrowed money can be invested to earn a rate of return *higher* than the interest rates paid to the lenders, net income and the return on stockholders' equity will *increase.*[16] For example, if you borrow money at an interest rate of 6 percent and invest it to earn 10 percent, you will benefit from "the spread."

But leverage is a double-edged sword—the effects may be favorable *or unfavorable.* If the rate of return earned on the borrowed money falls *below* the rate of interest being paid, the use of borrowed money *reduces* net income and the return on equity. Companies with large amounts of debt sometimes become victims of their own debt-service requirements.

The effects of leverage may be summarized as follows:

Relationship of Return on Assets to Interest Rate on Borrowed Funds	Effect on Net Income and Return on Equity
Return on Assets > Interest Rates Being Paid	Increase
Return on Assets < Interest Rates Being Paid	Decrease

The more leverage a company applies, the greater the effects on net income and the return on equity. Using more leverage simply means having more debt. Therefore, the *debt ratio* is a basic measure of the amount of leverage being applied.

---

[16] The rate of return earned on invested capital usually is viewed as the overall *return on assets*—that is, operating income divided by average total assets. *Return on equity* is net income expressed as a percentage of average stockholders' equity. Both of these return on investment measures are discussed in Chapter 14.

FINANCIAL ANALYSIS and Decision Making

Exhibit 10–8 provides a summary of common measures used by creditors and investors to evaluate a company's *short-term and long-term debt-paying ability.*

EXHIBIT 10–8

Measures of Debt-Paying Ability

Short-Term	Long-Term
Quick ratio—Most liquid assets divided by current liabilities; a stringent measure of liquidity.	Debt ratio—Total liabilities divided by total assets. Measures percentage of capital structure financed by creditors.
Current ratio—Current assets divided by current liabilities; the most common measure of liquidity, but less stringent than the quick ratio.	Interest coverage ratio—Operating income divided by interest expense. Shows how many times the company earns its annual interest obligations.
Working capital—Current assets less current liabilities; the "uncommitted" liquid resources.	
Turnover rates—Measures of how quickly receivables are collected or inventory is sold. (Computed separately for receivables and inventory.)	Trend in net cash flows from operating activities—Indicates trend in cash generating ability. Determined from comparative statements of cash flows.
Operating cycle—The period of time required to convert inventory into cash.	Trend in net income—Less related to debt-paying ability than cash flow, but still an excellent measure of long-term financial health.
Net cash flows from operating activities— Measures a company's ability to generate cash. (Shown in the statement of cash flows.)	
Lines of credit—Indicates ready access to additional cash should the need arise.	

YOUR TURN   You as a Credit Analyst

Assume that you are a credit analyst at a bank. Dell Inc. wants to borrow from your bank on a short-term basis. You assign the task of reviewing Dell's short-term creditworthiness to a college intern working for your bank. The intern remembers that working capital (current assets minus current liabilities) and the current ratio (current assets divided by current liabilities) are useful tools for evaluating short-term liquidity. Selected financial information for Dell is as follows (all items are in millions):

	Recent Year	Prior Year
Cash and cash equivalents	$12,569	$13,852
Short-term investments	208	966
Accounts receivable (net)	6,629	6,476
Financing Receivables	3,213	3,327
Inventories	1,382	1,404
Other Current assets	3,967	3,423
Total current liabilities	23,439	22,001
Cash provided by operations	3,283	5,527
Net income	2,372	3,492

The intern is concerned about lending Dell money because working capital for the most recent year is $4,529 million.

As a result, Dell's current ratio is only 1.19. Do you agree with the intern's assessment?

(See our comments on the Online Learning Center Web site.)

Ethics, Fraud, & Corporate Governance

The most infamous financial fraud in U.S. history occurred at **Enron** and was revealed in the fall of 2001. A major part of the **Enron** fraud involved the understatement of debt. **Enron** understated its debt by at least $550 million each year from 1997 to 2000. **Enron**'s management was motivated to understate debt in order to maintain a high credit rating from **Moody's** and **Standard & Poor's.**

Enron was engaged in the energy business and was also a trader of contracts to buy and sell commodities. At the time of the fraud, **Enron** was traded on the New York Stock Exchange. The revelation of the financial improprieties at **Enron** in October 2001 ultimately led to a collapse in **Enron**'s credit rating. Without access to ongoing financing, **Enron** was forced to file for bankruptcy in December 2001. At the time of **Enron**'s bankruptcy filing, it was the seventh-largest corporation in the United States.

Enron understated its liabilities by transferring debt to **special purpose entities (SPEs)**. SPEs are separate entities established by corporations to accomplish specific purposes. Often, the economic objective of an SPE is to borrow money and then transfer it to the sponsoring corporation without the sponsoring corporation having to report the SPE's debt in its balance sheet.

These SPEs were organized as partnerships, and **Enron**'s chief financial officer, Andrew Fastow, was the managing general partner of a number of them. Fastow and other **Enron** employees were among the parties providing equity capital to the SPEs. **Enron** guaranteed these investors that they would not only get back what they had invested, but that they would also receive substantial returns.

The fraud at **Enron** has numerous ethical and corporate governance implications. Given the complexity of **Enron**'s fraudulent activity, it could not have been accomplished without the cooperation of outside professionals (e.g., attorneys, auditors, credit rating agencies, and investment bankers). The external auditor, **Arthur Andersen**, issued unqualified audit opinions on **Enron**'s financial statements despite severe doubt that **Enron**'s filings conformed with GAAP. Credit rating agencies maintained investment grade credit ratings on **Enron**'s debt throughout the entire period of the fraud and did not downgrade **Enron**'s debt until a few weeks before the bankruptcy filing. Finally, major Wall Street investment banks created the SPE structures, including numerous transactions that resulted in debt being transferred from **Enron**'s books to the SPEs.

The unethical conduct of **Enron**'s outside professionals has not been without severe consequences. **Arthur Andersen** was convicted of a felony for its role in shredding its working papers related to the **Enron** audit. The felony indictment and conviction led to the dissolution of this former large, international accounting firm. A number of major Wall Street investment banks have paid the U.S. government multimillion-dollar settlements stemming from their **Enron** involvement. Private litigation related to the **Enron** debacle is ongoing and is likely to remain active for a number of years.

Special Types of Liabilities

LO10-10

LEARNING OBJECTIVE
Describe reporting issues related to leases, postretirement benefits, and deferred taxes.

The types of liabilities discussed up to this point have been those short-term and long-term obligations encountered by most organizations. Here we examine three special types of liabilities most common to large organizations: (1) leases, (2) postretirement benefits, and (3) deferred taxes.

LEASE PAYMENT OBLIGATIONS

A company may purchase the assets needed in its business operations or, as an alternative, it may lease them. A *lease* is a contract in which the lessor gives the lessee the right to use an asset for a specified period of time in exchange for periodic rental payments. The **lessor** is the owner of the property; the **lessee** is a tenant or renter. Examples of assets frequently acquired by lease include automobiles, building space, computers, and equipment.

OPERATING LEASES

When the lessor gives the lessee the right to use leased property for a limited period of time but retains the usual risks and rewards of ownership, the contract is known as an **operating lease.** An example of an operating lease is a contract leasing office space in an office building.

If the building increases in value, the *lessor* can receive the benefits of this increase by either selling the building or increasing the rental rate once the initial lease term has expired. Likewise, if the building declines in value, the lessor bears the loss.

In accounting for an operating lease, the lessor accounts for the monthly lease payments received as rental revenue, and the lessee regards these payments as rental expense. No asset or liability (other than a short-term liability for accrued rent payable) relating to the lease appears in the lessee's balance sheet. Thus, operating leases are sometimes termed **off-balance sheet financing** and disclosure is required of the amounts due in each of the next five years, plus the balance thereafter.

CAPITAL LEASES

Some lease contracts are intended to provide financing to the lessee for the eventual purchase of the property or to provide the lessee with use of the property over most of its useful life. These lease contracts are called **capital leases** (or financing leases). In contrast to an operating lease, a capital lease transfers most of the risks and rewards of ownership from the lessor to the *lessee.*

From an accounting viewpoint, capital leases are regarded as *equivalent to a sale* of the property by the lessor to the lessee, even though title to the leased property has not been transferred. A capital lease should be recorded by the *lessor as a sale* of property and by the *lessee as a purchase.*

When equipment is acquired through a capital lease, the lessee *debits an asset account,* Leased Equipment, and *credits a liability account,* Lease Payment Obligation, for the present value of the future lease payments. Lease payments made by the lessee are allocated between Interest Expense and a reduction in the liability Lease Payment Obligation. The portion of the lease payment obligation that will be repaid within the next year is classified as a current liability, and the remainder is classified as long-term.

No rent expense is recorded by the lessee in a capital lease. The asset account Leased Equipment is usually depreciated by the lessee over the life of the equipment rather than the term of the lease. Disclosure of future payments on the lease is also required. Accounting for capital leases is illustrated in Appendix B at the end of this textbook.

Distinguishing between Capital Leases and Operating Leases The Financial Accounting Standards Board (FASB) has identified certain criteria that qualify a lease as a capital lease. For example, if the lease transfers ownership of the property to the lessee at the end of the lease term, the lease is a capital lease. Similarly, if the lease term is equal to 75 percent or more of the estimated economic life of the leased property, the lease is a capital lease. Leases that do not meet any of specified criteria are accounted for as operating leases.

LIABILITIES FOR PENSIONS AND OTHER POSTRETIREMENT BENEFITS

Many employers agree to pay their employees a pension: that is, monthly cash payments for life, beginning at retirement. Pensions are not an expense of the years in which cash payments are made to retired workers. Employees earn the right to receive the pension *while they are working for their employer.* Therefore, the employer's cost of future pension payments *accrues* over the years that each employee is on the payroll.

The amounts of the retirement benefits that will be paid to today's workers after they retire are not known with certainty. Among other things, these amounts depend on how long retired employees live. Therefore, the employer's obligation for future pension payments arising during the current year *must be estimated.*

Employers do not usually pay retirement pensions directly to retired employees. Most employers meet their pension obligations by making periodic payments to a **pension fund** (or pension plan) throughout the years of each worker's employment. That fund then pays retirement benefits directly to retirees.

A pension fund is an *independent entity* managed by a trustee (usually a bank or an insurance company). As the employer makes payments to the pension fund, the trustee invests the money in securities such as stocks and bonds. Over time, the pension fund earns investment income and normally accumulates to a balance far in excess of the employer's deposits. The *pension fund*—not the employer—disburses monthly pension benefits to retired workers.

If the employer meets *all* of its estimated pension obligations by promptly paying cash in a pension fund, the pension fund is said to be *fully funded.* If a pension plan is fully funded, *no liability* for pension payments appears in the employer's balance sheet. The employer's obligation is discharged in the *current period* through the payments made to the pension fund. The employer records each payment to this fund by debiting Pension Expense and crediting Cash.

Determining Pension Expense

From a conceptual point of view, the pension expense of a given period is the *present value* of the future pension rights granted to employees as a result of their services during the period. The computation of annual pension expense is complex and involves many assumptions. The amount of this expense is computed not by accountants, but rather by an **actuary,** who considers factors like the following:

- Average age, retirement age, and life expectancy of employees
- Employee turnover rates
- Compensation levels and estimated rate of pay increases
- Expected rate of return to be earned on pension fund assets

For example, assume that the actuarial firm of Gibson & Holt computes a pension expense for Cramer Cable Company of $450,000 for the current year. This amount represents the present value of pension rights granted to Cramer's employees for the work they performed during the year. To fully fund this obligation, Cramer transfers $450,000 to National Trust Co., the trustee of the company's pension plan.

The following entry summarizes Cramer's fully funded pension expense for the year:

Pension Expense	450,000	
Cash		450,000
Pension expense for the year as determined by actuarial firm of Gibson & Holt; fully funded by payments to National Trust Co.		

Postretirement Benefits Other Than Pensions

In addition to pension plans, many companies have promised their employees other types of **postretirement benefits,** such as continuing health insurance. In most respects, these nonpension postretirement benefits are accounted for in the same manner as are pension benefits. Many companies, however, do not fully fund their obligations for nonpension postretirement benefits. Recognition of the annual expense often includes a credit to an unfunded liability for part of the cost.

Continuing with our illustration of Cramer Cable Company, assume that Gibson & Holt computes for the company a $185,000 nonpension postretirement benefits expense for the current year. Unlike its pension expense, however, Cramer does *not* fully fund its nonpension obligations.

If only $125,000 of the total amount was paid in cash, the entry to summarize this expense for the year is:

Postretirement Benefits Expense	185,000	
Cash		125,000
Unfunded Liability for Postretirement Benefits		60,000
To record nonpension postretirement benefits expense per report of Gibson & Holt, actuaries; expense funded to the extent of $125,000.		

The portion of the unfunded liability that the company expects to fund during the next year is classified as a *current liability;* the remainder is classified as a *long-term liability.*

Unfunded Postretirement Costs Are Noncash Expenses

Postretirement costs are recognized as expenses as workers earn the right to receive these benefits. If these costs are fully funded, the company makes cash payments to a trustee within the current period equal to this expense. But if these benefits are *not* funded, the cash payments are not made until after the employees retire.

Unfunded retirement benefits often are called a noncash expense. That is, the expense is charged against current earnings, but there are no corresponding cash payments in the period. In the previous illustration, notice that the expense exceeds the cash outlays by $60,000 ($185,000 − $125,000). This amount corresponds to the growth in the unfunded liability.

Unfunded Liabilities for Postretirement Costs: Are They Significant Amounts?

Many of America's largest and best-known corporations have obligations for unfunded postretirement benefits that are large relative to their total assets and other liabilities. Let us suggest several things to consider in evaluating a company's ability to pay its unfunded liability for postretirement costs. First, this liability represents only the *present value* of the estimated future payments. The future payments are expected to be *substantially more* than the amount shown in the balance sheet. Next, this liability may *continue to grow,* especially if the company has more employees today than in the past. On the other hand, this liability does *not* have to be paid all at once. It will be paid over a *great many years*—the life span of today's workforce.

In evaluating a company's ability to meet its postretirement obligations, we suggest looking to the *statement of cash flows* in addition to the balance sheet and income statement. In the statement of cash flows, payments of postretirement costs are classified as operating activities. If a company has a steadily increasing net cash flow from operating activities, it is in a stronger position to handle retirement costs as they come due. But if the net cash flow from operating activities starts to decline, the company may have no choice but to reduce the benefits it provides to retired employees. Often these benefits are *not* contractual and can be reduced at management's discretion.

DEFERRED INCOME TAXES

We have learned in earlier chapters that certain differences exist between the way some revenues or expenses are recognized in financial statements and the way these same items are reported in income tax returns. For example, most companies use the straight-line method of depreciation in their financial reports but use an accelerated method in their income tax returns. Because of such differences between accounting principles and tax rules, income appearing in the income statement today may not be subject to income taxes until future years. However, the *matching principle* requires that the income shown in an income statement be offset by all related income taxes expense, regardless of when these taxes will be paid. The entry to record a corporation's income tax expense might appear as follows, assuming that $200,000 of the current-year income tax expense is deferred to future years:

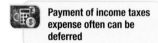
Payment of income taxes expense often can be deferred

Income Tax Expense	1,000,000	
Income Tax Payable		800,000
Deferred Income Taxes		200,000
To record corporate income taxes applicable to the income of the current year.		

Income Tax Payable is a current liability representing the portion of the income taxes expense that must be paid when the company files its income tax return for the current year. The portion of income taxes expense that is deferred to future tax returns is credited to a liability account entitled **Deferred Income Taxes,** which is usually treated as a noncurrent liability.

Deferred Income Taxes in Financial Statements   How deferred income taxes are classified in the balance sheet depends on the classification of the assets and liabilities that *caused* the tax deferrals. Although deferred taxes often appear as liabilities, certain conditions may require that they be classified as assets. Accounting for deferred taxes involves a number of complex issues that are addressed in more advanced accounting courses.

Concluding Remarks

Businesses have two basic sources of financing their assets: liabilities and owners' equity. Throughout this chapter, we have studied current liabilities, long-term liabilities, and estimated liabilities common to most large businesses. We have learned that liabilities differ from owners' equity in several respects. The feature that most clearly distinguishes the claims of creditors from those of owners is that virtually all liabilities eventually mature and become due. We have also learned that the claims of creditors have legal priority over the claims of owners.

In the next two chapters, we turn our attention to owners' equity. We examine many important topics including treasury stock transactions, cash dividends, stock dividends, stock splits, and the differences between common and preferred stockholders.

END-OF-CHAPTER REVIEW

SUMMARY OF LEARNING OBJECTIVES

LO10-1 Define *liabilities* and distinguish between current and long-term liabilities. Liabilities are obligations arising from past transactions or events that require payment (or the rendering of services) at some future date. Current liabilities are those maturing within one year or the company's operating cycle (whichever is longer) and that are expected to be paid from current assets. Liabilities classified as long-term include obligations maturing more than one year in the future and shorter-term obligations that will be refinanced or paid from noncurrent assets.

LO10-2 Account for notes payable and interest expense. Initially, a liability is recorded only for the principal amount of a note—that is, the amount owed *before* including any interest charges. Interest expense accrues over time. Any accrued interest expense is recognized at the end of an accounting period by an adjusting entry that records both the expense and a short-term liability for accrued interest payable.

LO10-3 Describe the costs and the basic accounting activities relating to payrolls. The basic cost of payrolls is, of course, the salaries and wages earned by employees. However, all employers also incur costs for various payroll taxes, such as the employer's share of Social Security and Medicare, workers' compensation premiums, and unemployment insurance. Many employers also incur costs for various employee benefits, such as health insurance and postretirement benefits. (These additional payroll-related costs often amount to 30 percent to 40 percent of the basic wages and salaries expense.)

LO10-4 Prepare an amortization table allocating payments between interest and principal. An amortization table includes four money columns, showing (1) the amount of each payment, (2) the portion of the payment representing interest expense, (3) the portion of the payment that reduces the principal amount of the loan, and (4) the remaining unpaid balance (or principal amount). The table begins with the original amount of the loan listed in the unpaid balance column. A separate line then is completed showing the allocation of each payment between interest and principal reduction and indicating the new unpaid balance subsequent to the payment.

LO10-5 Describe corporate bonds and explain the tax advantage of debt financing. Corporate bonds are transferable long-term notes payable. Each bond usually has a face value of $1,000 (or a multiple of $1,000), calls for interest payments at a contractual rate, and has a stated maturity date. By issuing thousands of bonds to the investing public at one time, the corporation divides a very large and long-term loan into many transferable units.

The principal advantage of issuing bonds instead of capital stock is that interest payments to bondholders are deductible in determining taxable income, whereas dividend payments to stockholders are not.

LO10-6 Account for bonds issued at a discount or premium. When bonds are issued at a discount, the borrower must repay more than the amount originally borrowed. Any discount in the issuance price represents additional cost in the overall borrowing transaction. The matching principle requires that the borrower recognize this cost gradually over the life of the bond issue as interest expense.

If bonds are issued at a premium, the borrower will repay an amount less than the amount originally borrowed. The premium serves to reduce the overall cost of the borrowing transaction. Again, the matching principle requires that this reduction in interest expense be recognized gradually over the life of the bond issue.

LO10-7 Explain the concept of present value as it relates to bond prices. The basic concept of present value is that an amount of money that will not be paid or received until some future date is equivalent to a smaller amount of money today. This is because the smaller amount available today could be invested to earn interest and thereby accumulate over time to the larger future amount.

The amount today considered equivalent to the future amount is termed the present value of that future amount. The concept of present value is used in the valuation of most long-term liabilities. It also is widely used in investment decisions. Readers who are not familiar with this concept are encouraged to read Appendix B at the end of this textbook.

LO10-8 Explain how estimated liabilities, loss contingencies, and commitments are disclosed in financial statements. Estimated liabilities, such as an automobile manufacturer's responsibility to honor new car warranties, appear in the financial statements at their estimated dollar amounts. Loss contingencies appear as liabilities *only* when it is probable that a loss has been incurred *and* the amount can be reasonably estimated. Unless both these conditions are met, loss contingencies are simply disclosed in the notes to the financial statements. Commitments are contracts for future transactions; they are *not* liabilities. However, if considered material, they are often disclosed in the notes to the financial statements.

LO10-9 Evaluate the safety of creditors' claims. Short-term creditors may evaluate the safety of their claims using such measures of liquidity as the current ratio, the quick ratio, the available lines of credit, and the debtor's credit rating. Long-term creditors look more to signs of stability and long-term financial health, including the debt ratio, interest coverage ratio, and trends in net income and net cash flow from operating activities.

LO10-10 **Describe reporting issues related to leases, post-retirement benefits, and deferred taxes.** Leases that are essentially equivalent to a sale of property by the lessor to the lessee are regarded as capital leases. Under a capital lease arrangement, the lessee reports in its balance sheet the present values of both an asset (for example, leased equipment) and a liability (lease payment obligations). Lease arrangements that do not qualify as capital leases are treated as operating leases, requiring that lease payments be treated as expenses when paid.

Unfunded postretirement costs are reported in the balance sheet at their discounted present values as long-term liabilities. Unfunded postretirement benefits are often called a noncash expense. That is, the expense is charged against current earnings without a corresponding outlay of cash.

Deferred income taxes result because timing differences exist between financial accounting principles and tax rules. Income appearing in the income statement today may not be subject to income taxes until future years. Likewise, income subject to income taxes today may not appear in the company's income statement until future periods. Depending on the circumstances, deferred taxes may appear in the balance sheet as liabilities and/or assets (both current and long-term).

Key Terms Introduced or Emphasized in Chapter 10

accrued liabilities (p. 435)   The liability to pay an expense that has accrued during the period. Also called *accrued expenses.*

actuary (p. 459)   A statistician who performs computations involving assumptions as to human life spans. One function is computing companies' liabilities for pensions and postretirement benefits.

amortization table (p. 438)   A schedule that indicates how installment payments are allocated between interest expense and repayments of principal.

bankruptcy (p. 454)   A legal status in which the financial affairs of an illiquid business (or individual) are managed, in large part, by the U.S. Bankruptcy Court.

bonds payable (p. 440)   Long-term debt securities that subdivide a very large and long-term corporate debt into transferable increments of $1,000 or multiples thereof.

capital lease (p. 458)   A lease contract that finances the eventual purchase by the lessee of leased property. The lessor accounts for a capital lease as a sale of property; the lessee records an asset and a liability equal to the present value of the future lease payments. Also called a *financing lease.*

collateral (p. 432)   Assets that have been pledged to secure specific liabilities. Creditors with secured claims can foreclose on (seize title to) these assets if the borrower defaults.

commitments (p. 454)   Agreements to carry out future transactions. Although they are not a liability (because the transaction has not yet been performed), they may be disclosed in notes to the financial statements.

convertible bond (p. 442)   A bond that may be exchanged (at the bondholder's option) for a specified number of shares of the company's capital stock.

debt service (p. 438)   The combined cash outlays required for repayment of principal amounts borrowed and for payments of interest expense during the period.

Deferred Income Taxes (p. 460)   A liability account to pay income taxes that have been postponed to a future year's income tax return. In some cases, this account can also be an asset account representing income taxes to be saved in a future year's income tax return.

estimated liabilities (p. 433)   Liabilities known to exist, but that must be recorded in the accounting records at estimated dollar amounts.

interest coverage ratio (p. 455)   Operating income divided by interest expense. Indicates the number of times that the company was able to earn the amount of its interest charges.

junk bonds (p. 442)   Bonds payable that involve a greater than normal risk of default and, therefore, must pay higher than normal rates of interest in order to be attractive to investors.

lessee (p. 457)   The tenant, user, or renter of leased property.

lessor (p. 457)   The owner of property leased to a lessee.

leverage (p. 455)   The use of borrowed money to finance business operations.

loss contingencies (p. 453)   Situations involving uncertainty as to whether a loss has occurred. The uncertainty will be resolved by a future event. An example of a loss contingency is the possible loss relating to a lawsuit pending against a company. Although loss contingencies are sometimes recorded in the accounts, they are more frequently disclosed only in notes to the financial statements.

maturity date (p. 432)   The date on which a liability becomes due.

off-balance sheet financing (p. 458)   An arrangement in which the use of resources is financed without the obligation for future payments appearing as a liability in the balance sheet. An operating lease is a common example of off-balance sheet financing.

operating lease (p. 457)   A lease contract which is in essence a rental agreement. The lessee has the use of the leased property, but the lessor retains the usual risks and rewards of ownership. The periodic lease payments are accounted for as rent expense by the lessee and as rental revenue by the lessor.

payroll taxes (p. 435)   Taxes levied on an employer based on the amount of wages and salaries being paid to employees during the period. They include the employer's share of Social Security and Medicare taxes, unemployment taxes, and (though not called a "tax") workers' compensation premiums.

pension fund (p. 458)   A fund managed by an independent trustee into which an employer-company makes periodic payments. The fund is used to make pension payments to retired employees.

postretirement benefits (p. 459)   Benefits that will be paid to retired workers. The present value of the future benefits earned by workers during the current period is an expense of the period. If not fully funded, this expense results in a liability for unfunded postretirement benefits. (For many companies, these liabilities have become very large.)

present value (of a future amount) (p. 451)   The amount of money that an informed investor would pay today for the right to receive the future amount, based on a specific rate of return required by the investor.

principal amount (p. 433)   The unpaid balance of an obligation, exclusive of any interest charges for the current period.

sinking fund (p. 442)   Cash set aside by a corporation at regular intervals (usually with a trustee) for the purpose of repaying a bond issue at its maturity date.

special purpose entities (p. 457)   SPEs are separate entities established by corporations to accomplish specific purposes. SPEs are often used to borrow money and then transfer it to the sponsoring corporation as an off-balance sheet financing arrangement.

underwriter (p. 441)   An investment banking firm that handles the sale of a corporation's stocks or bonds to the public.

Workers' Compensation Insurance (p. 436)   A state-mandated insurance program insuring workers against job-related injuries. Premiums are charged to employers as a percentage of the employees' wages and salaries. The amounts vary by state and by the employees' occupations but, in some cases, can be very substantial.

Demonstration Problem

Listed below are selected items from the financial statements of Bachman Manufacturing Company for the year ended December 31, 2015.

Note payable to Williamsburg Bank	$ 99,000
Income taxes payable	63,000
Loss contingency relating to lawsuit	175,000
Accounts payable and accrued expenses	174,675
Mortgage note payable	240,864
Bonds payable	2,200,000
Premium on bonds payable	10,400
Accrued bond interest payable	110,000
Pension expense	61,400
Unearned revenue	25,300

Other Information

1. The note payable owed to Williamsburg Bank is due in 30 days. Bachman has arranged with this bank to renew the note for an additional two years.

2. Bachman has been sued for $175,000 by someone claiming the company's pumps are excessively noisy. It is reasonably possible, but not probable, that a loss has been sustained.

3. The mortgage note is payable at $8,000 per month over the next three years. During the next 12 months, the principal amount of this note will be reduced to $169,994.

4. The bonds payable mature in seven months. A sinking fund has been accumulated to repay the full maturity of this bond issue.

Instructions

a. Using this information, prepare the current liabilities and long-term liabilities sections of Bachman's classified balance sheet at December 31, 2015.

b. Explain briefly how the information in each of the four numbered paragraphs affected your presentation of the company's liabilities.

Solution to the Demonstration Problem

a.

BACHMAN MANUFACTURING COMPANY
PARTIAL BALANCE SHEET
DECEMBER 31, 2015

Liabilities:

Current liabilities:

Accounts payable and accrued expenses		$ 174,675
Income taxes payable		63,000
Accrued bond interest payable		110,000
Unearned revenue		25,300
Current portion of long-term debt		70,870
Total current liabilities		$ 443,845

Long-term liabilities:

Note payable to Williamsburg Bank		$ 99,000
Mortgage note payable		169,994
Bonds payable	$2,200,000	
Add: Premium on bonds payable	10,400	2,210,400
Total long-term liabilities		$2,479,394
Total liabilities		$2,923,239

b. **1.** Although the note payable to Williamsburg Bank is due in 30 days, it is classified as a long-term liability as it will be refinanced on a long-term basis.

2. The pending lawsuit is a loss contingency requiring disclosure, but it is not included in the liability section of the balance sheet.

3. The $70,870 of the mortgage note that will be repaid within the next 12 months ($240,864 − $169,994) is a current liability; the remaining balance, due after December 31, 2016, is long-term debt.

4. Although the bonds payable mature in seven months, they will be repaid from a sinking fund, rather than from current assets. Therefore, these bonds retain their long-term classification.

Self-Test Questions

The answers to these questions appear on page 483.

1. Which of the following is characteristic of liabilities rather than of equity? (More than one answer may be correct.)

   a. The obligation matures.

   b. Interest paid to the provider of the capital is deductible in the determination of taxable income.

   c. The capital providers' claims are *residual* in the event of liquidation of the business.

   d. The capital providers normally have the right to exercise control over business operations.

2. On October 1, Dalton Corp. borrows $100,000 from National Bank, signing a six-month note payable for that amount, plus interest to be computed at a rate of 9 percent per annum. Indicate all correct answers.

   a. Dalton's liability at October 1 is only $100,000.

   b. The maturity value of this note is $104,500.

   c. At December 31, Dalton will have a liability for accrued interest payable in the amount of $4,500.

   d. Dalton's total liability for this loan at November 30 is $101,500.

3. Identify all correct statements concerning payrolls and related payroll costs.

   a. Both employers and employees pay Social Security and Medicare taxes.

b. Workers' compensation premiums are withheld from employees' wages.

c. An employer's total payroll costs usually exceed total wages expense by about 7½ percent.

d. Under current law, employers are required to pay Social Security taxes on employees' earnings, but they are not required to pay for health insurance.

4. Identify the types of information that can readily be determined from an amortization table for an installment loan. (More than one answer may be correct.)

a. Interest expense on this liability for the current year.

b. The present value of the future payments under changing market conditions.

c. The unpaid balance remaining after each payment.

d. The portion of the unpaid balance that is a current liability.

5. Which of the following statements is (are) correct? (More than one statement may be correct.)

a. A bond issue is a technique for subdividing a very large loan into many small, transferable units.

b. Bond interest payments are contractual obligations, whereas the board of directors determines whether or not dividends will be paid.

c. Bond interest payments are deductible in determining income subject to income taxes, whereas dividends paid to stockholders are not deductible.

d. As interest rates rise, the market prices of bonds fall; as interest rates fall, bond prices tend to rise.

6. Identify all statements that are *consistent* with the concept of present value. (More than one answer may be correct.)

a. The present value of a future amount always is *less* than that future amount.

b. An amount of money available today is considered *more* valuable than the *same sum* that will not become available until a future date.

c. A bond's issue price is equal to the present value of its future cash flows.

d. The liability for an installment note payable is recorded at only the *principal* amount, rather than the sum of the scheduled future payments.

7. Identify those trends that are *unfavorable* from the viewpoint of a bondholder. (More than one answer may be correct.)

a. Market interest rates are steadily rising.

b. The issuing company's interest coverage ratio is steadily rising.

c. The issuing company's net cash flow from operating activities is steadily declining.

d. The issuing company's debt ratio is steadily declining.

8. A basic difference between *loss contingencies* and "real" liabilities is:

a. Liabilities stem from past transactions; loss contingencies stem from future events.

b. The extent of uncertainty involved.

c. Liabilities always are recorded in the accounting records, whereas loss contingencies never are.

d. Liabilities can be large in amount, whereas loss contingencies are immaterial.

9. Which of the following situations require recording a liability in 2015? (More than one answer may be correct.)

a. In 2015, a company manufactures and sells stereo equipment that carries a three-year warranty.

b. A company is a defendant in a legal action. At the end of 2015, the company's attorney feels it is possible the company will lose and that the amount of the loss might be material.

c. In 2015, a theater group receives payments in advance from season ticket holders for productions to be performed in 2016.

d. During 2015, a Midwest agricultural cooperative is concerned about the risk of loss if inclement weather destroys the crops.

10. Silverado maintains a fully funded pension plan. During 2015, $1 million was paid to retired workers, and workers currently employed by the company earned a portion of the right to receive pension payments expected to total $6 million *over their lifetimes*. Silverado's pension *expense* for 2015 amounts to:

a. $1 million.

b. $6 million.

c. $7 million.

d. Some other amount.

11. Deferred income taxes result from:

a. Differences between certain revenue and expense items recognized in financial statements but not in income tax returns.

b. The fact that bond interest is deductible in the computation of taxable income.

c. Depositing income taxes due in future years in a special fund managed by an independent trustee.

d. The inability of a bankrupt company to pay its income tax liability on schedule.

ASSIGNMENT MATERIAL | # Discussion Questions

1. Define *liabilities*. Identify several characteristics that distinguish liabilities from owners' equity.

2. Explain the relative priority of the claims of owners and of creditors to the assets of a business. Do all creditors have equal priority? Explain.

3. Define *current liabilities* and *long-term liabilities*. Under what circumstances might a 10-year bond issue be classified as a current liability? Under what circumstances might a note payable maturing 30 days after the balance sheet date be classified as a long-term liability?

4. Explain why an employer's "total cost" of a payroll may exceed by a substantial amount the total wages and salaries earned by employees.

5. A friend of yours has just purchased a house and has taken out a $50,000, 11 percent mortgage, payable at $476.17 per month. After making the first monthly payment, he received a receipt from the bank stating that only $17.84 of the $476.17 had been applied to reducing the principal amount of the loan. Your friend computes that, at the rate of $17.84 per month, it will take over 233 years to pay off the $50,000 mortgage. Do you agree with your friend's analysis? Explain.

6. Briefly explain the income tax advantage of raising capital by issuing bonds rather than by selling capital stock.

7. Seattle Boat Company pays federal income taxes at a rate of 35 percent on taxable income. Compute the company's annual *after-tax* cost of borrowing on an 8 percent, $5 million bond issue. Express this after-tax cost as a percentage of the borrowed $5 million.

8. Why do bond prices vary inversely with interest rates?

9. Some bonds now being bought and sold by investors on organized securities exchanges were issued when interest rates were much higher than they are today. Would you expect these bonds to be trading at prices above or below their face values? Explain.

10. There is a business saying that "You shouldn't *be* in business if your company doesn't earn higher than bank rates." This means that if a company is to succeed, its return on assets should be *significantly higher* than its cost of borrowing. Why is this so important?

11. Identify two characteristics of *estimated liabilities*. Provide at least two examples of estimated liabilities.

12. What is the meaning of the term *loss contingency*? Give several examples. How are loss contingencies presented in financial statements? Explain.

13. Explain how the lessee accounts for operating leases and capital leases. Why is an operating lease sometimes called *off-balance sheet financing?*

14. When are the costs of postretirement benefits recognized as an expense? When are the related cash payments made?

15. What are *deferred income tax liabilities?* How are these items presented in financial statements?

Brief Exercises

LO10-2

BRIEF EXERCISE 10.1

Cash Effects of Borrowing

Jansen Company borrowed $12,000 on a one-year, 8 percent note payable from the local bank on April 1. Interest was paid quarterly, and the note was repaid one year from the time the money was borrowed. Calculate the amount of cash payments Jansen was required to make in each of the two calendar years that were affected by the note payable.

LO10-5

BRIEF EXERCISE 10.2

Effective Interest Rate

One of the advantages of borrowing is that interest is deductible for income tax purposes.

a. If a company pays 8 percent interest to borrow $500,000, but is in an income tax bracket that requires it to pay 40 percent income tax, what is the actual net-of-tax interest cost that the company incurs?

b. What is the effective interest rate that is paid by the company?

LO10-6

BRIEF EXERCISE 10.3

Bonds Issued at a Discount

Crosby, Inc., sells $1,000,000 general obligation bonds for 98. The interest rate on the bonds, paid quarterly, is 6 percent. Calculate (a) the amount that the company will actually receive from the sale of the bonds, and (b) the amount of both the quarterly and the total annual cash interest that the company will be required to pay.

LO10-6

BRIEF EXERCISE 10.4

Bonds Issued at a Premium

Presley Company sells $1,000,000 general obligation bonds for 102. The interest rate on the bonds, paid quarterly, is 5 percent. Calculate (a) the amount that the company will actually receive from the sale of the bonds, and (b) the amount of both the quarterly and the total annual cash interest that the company will be required to pay.

LO10-6

BRIEF EXERCISE 10.5

Recording Bonds Issued at a Discount

Lewis Company sold $500,000 of bonds at 97 on an interest payment date. Assuming the bonds will be retired in 10 years and interest is paid annually, calculate the amount of cash that will be received and paid by Lewis in the first year, as well as the interest expense that will be recognized in that year. The bonds carry a stated interest rate of 5 percent.

LO10-6

BRIEF EXERCISE 10.6

Recording Bonds Issued at a Premium

Purple & Orange, Inc., sold $800,000 of bonds on an interest payment date at 102. Assuming the bonds will be retired in 10 years and interest is paid annually, calculate the amount of cash that will be received and paid by Purple & Orange in the first full year, as well as the amount of interest expense that will be recognized in that year. The bonds carry a stated interest rate of 6.5 percent.

LO10-9

BRIEF EXERCISE 10.7

Debt Ratio

Wolfe Company has debt totaling $2,000,000 and total stockholders' equity of $4,200,000. Tiger Company has debt totaling $3,100,000 and stockholders' equity of $5,000,000.

a. Calculate the debt ratio for each company. (Hint: You will find an explanation of the debt ratio and how it is computed in Exhibit 10–8.)

b. Briefly explain the meaning of the debt ratio.

LO10-7

BRIEF EXERCISE 10.8

Early Retirement of Bonds

Joseph Max, Inc., sold 10-year, 7 percent bonds for $1,000,000 at 98. On the interest payment date at the end of the 5th year the bonds were outstanding, 50 percent of the bonds were retired by Max at 102 under an early retirement option that was included in the bond agreement. Determine the gain or loss that Max will incur as a result of retiring the bonds.

LO10-10

BRIEF EXERCISE 10.9

Deferred Income Taxes

Alberto Company determines its annual income tax expense to be $459,000. Of that amount, $300,000 has already been paid during the year (on a quarterly basis) and charged to the Income Taxes Expense account. The company has determined that, of the amount that has not yet been paid or recorded, $75,000 will be deferred into future years under certain favorable income tax provisions available to the company. Prepare the end-of-year general journal entry to recognize income taxes accrued.

LO10-10

BRIEF EXERCISE 10.10

Pension and Other Postretirement Benefit Costs

Grammar, Inc., offers its full-time employees pension and other postretirement benefits, primarily health insurance. During the current year, pension benefits for the employees totaled $250,000. Other postretirement benefits totaled $140,000. The pension benefits are fully funded by the company by transferring cash to a trustee that administers the plan. The other postretirement benefits are similarly funded, but only at the 50 percent level. Prepare journal entries to record the two expenses, and determine the total amount that Grammar will need to transfer to its trustee for both benefit plans during the current year.

Exercises

LO10-4

EXERCISE 10.1

You as a Student

Assume that you will have a 10-year, $10,000 loan to repay when you graduate from college next month. The loan, plus 8 percent annual interest on the unpaid balance, is to be repaid in 10 annual installments of $1,490 each, beginning one year after you graduate. You have accepted a well-paying job and are considering an early settlement of the entire unpaid balance in just three years (immediately after making the third annual payment of $1,490).

Prepare an amortization schedule showing how much money you will need to save to pay the entire unpaid balance of your loan three years after your graduation. (Round amounts to the nearest dollar.)

LO10-1 through LO10-6

EXERCISE 10.2

Effects of Transactions on the Accounting Equation

Listed below are eight events or transactions of Lone Star Corporation.

a. Made an adjusting entry to record interest on a short-term note payable.

b. Made a monthly installment payment of a fully amortizing, six-month, interest-bearing installment note payable.

c. Recorded a regular biweekly payroll, including the amounts withheld from employees, the issuance of paychecks, and payroll taxes on the employer.

d. Came within 12 months of the maturity date of a note payable originally issued for a period of 24 months.

e. Deposited employee tax withholdings with proper tax authorities.

f. Issued bonds payable at face value.

g. Recognized semiannual interest expense on bonds payable described in part **f** and paid bond-holders the full interest amount.

h. Recorded the necessary adjusting entry on December 31, 2015, to accrue three months' interest on bonds payable that had been issued at a discount several years prior. The next semiannual interest payment will occur March 31, 2016.

Indicate the effects of each of these transactions on the following financial statement categories. Organize your answer in tabular form, using the illustrated column headings. Use the following code letters to indicate the effects of each transaction on the accounting element listed in the column heading: **I** for increase, **D** for decrease, and **NE** for no effect.

	Income Statement			Balance Sheet			
Transaction	Revenue −	Expenses =	Net Income	Assets =	Current + Liab.	Long-Term Liab. +	Owners' Equity
a							

LO10-1, LO10-2, LO10-4 through LO10-6, LO10-8

EXERCISE 10.3

Effects of Transactions on Various Financial Measurements

Six events relating to liabilities follow:

a. Paid the liability for interest payable accrued at the end of the last accounting period.

b. Made the current monthly payment on a 12-month installment note payable, including interest and a partial repayment of principal.

c. Issued bonds payable at 98 on March 1, 2015. The bonds pay interest March 1 and September 1.

d. Recorded September 1, 2015, interest expense and made semiannual interest payment on bonds referred to in part **c.**

e. Recorded necessary adjusting entry on December 31, 2015, for bonds referred to in part **c.**

f. Recorded estimated six-month warranty expense on December 31, 2015.

Indicate the effects of each transaction or adjusting entry on the financial measurements in the five column headings listed below. Use the code letters **I** for increase, **D** for decrease, and **NE** for no effect.

Transaction	Current Liabilities	Long-Term Liabilities	Net Income	Net Cash Flow from Operating Activities	Net Cash Flow (from All Sources)
a					

LO10-3

EXERCISE 10.4

Employees—What Do They Really Cost?

Big Game, Inc., is a manufacturer of hunting supplies. The following is a summary of the company's annual payroll-related costs:

Wages and salaries expense (of which $2,200,000 was withheld from employees' pay and forwarded directly to tax authorities)	$7,200,000
Payroll taxes	580,000
Workers' compensation premiums	250,000
Group health insurance premiums	725,000
Contributions to employees' pension plan	450,000

a. Compute Big Game's total payroll-related costs for the year.

b. Compute the net amount of cash actually paid to employees (their take-home pay).

c. Express total payroll-related costs as a percentage of (1) total wages and salaries expense, and (2) employees' take-home pay. (Round computations to the nearest 1 percent.)

LO10-3

EXERCISE 10.5

Accounting for Payroll
Activities

Spirit Corporation reported the following payroll-related costs for the month of February:

Gross pay (wages expense)	$250,000
Social Security and Medicare taxes	19,125
Federal and state unemployment taxes	15,500
Workers' compensation insurance	8,500
Group health and life insurance benefits	10,000
Employee pension plan benefits	22,875
Total payroll costs for February	$326,000

Spirit's insurance premiums for workers' compensation and group health and life insurance were paid for in a prior period and recorded initially as prepaid insurance expense. Withholdings from employee wages in February were as follows:

State income tax withholdings	$ 5,875
Federal income tax withholdings	56,000
Social Security and Medicare tax withholdings	19,125

a.   Record Spirit's gross wages, employee withholdings, and employee take-home pay for February.

b.   Record Spirit's payroll tax expense for February.

c.   Record Spirit's employee benefit expenses for February.

d.   Do the amounts withheld from spirit's employees represent taxes levied on spirit Corporation? Explain.

LO10-4

EXERCISE 10.6

Use of an Amortization
Table

Glen Pool Club, Inc., has a $150,000 mortgage liability. The mortgage is payable in monthly installments of $1,543, which include interest computed at an annual rate of 12 percent (1 percent monthly).

a.   Prepare a partial amortization table showing (1) the original balance of this loan, and (2) the allocation of the first two monthly payments between interest expense and the reduction in the mortgage's unpaid balance. (Round to the nearest dollar.)

b.   Prepare the journal entry to record the second monthly payment.

c.   Will monthly interest increase, decrease, or stay the same over the life of the loan? Explain your answer, including why in this case the amount of principal included in the first two payments is the same.

LO10-5

EXERCISE 10.7

After-Tax Cost of Borrowing

DuPont reports in a recent balance sheet $1,383 million of 6.00 percent notes payable due in 2018. The company's income tax rate is approximately 20 percent.

a.   Compute the company's after-tax cost of borrowing on this bond issue stated as a total dollar amount.

b.   Compute the company's after-tax cost of borrowing on this bond issue stated as a percentage of the amount borrowed.

c.   Describe briefly the advantage of raising funds by issuing bonds as opposed to stocks.

LO10-5

EXERCISE 10.8

Bond Interest on Bonds
Issued at Face Value

On March 31, 2015, Gardner Corporation received authorization to issue $50,000 of 9 percent, 30-year bonds payable. The bonds pay interest on March 31 and September 30. The entire issue was dated March 31, 2015, but the bonds were not issued until April 30, 2015. They were issued at face value.

a.   Prepare the journal entry at April 30, 2015, to record the sale of the bonds.

b.   Prepare the journal entry at September 30, 2015, to record the semiannual bond interest payment.

c. Prepare the adjusting entry at December 31, 2015, to record bond interest expense accrued since September 30, 2015. (Assume that no monthly adjusting entries to accrue interest expense had been made prior to December 31, 2015.)

d. Explain why the issuing corporation charged its bond investors for interest accrued in April 2015, prior to the issuance date (see part **b** above).

LO10-5, LO10-6

EXERCISE 10.9

Accounting for Bonds Issued at a Premium: Issuance, Interest Payments, and Retirement

Xonic Corporation issued $8 million of 20-year, 8 percent bonds on April 1, 2015, at 102. Interest is due on March 31 and September 30 of each year, and all of the bonds in the issue mature on March 31, 2035. Xonic's fiscal year ends on December 31. Prepare the following journal entries:

a. April 1, 2015, to record the issuance of the bonds.

b. September 30, 2015, to pay interest and to amortize the bond premium.

c. March 31, 2035, to pay interest, amortize the bond premium, and retire the bonds at maturity (make two separate entries).

d. Briefly explain the effect of amortizing the bond premium on (1) annual net income and (2) annual net cash flow from operating activities. (Ignore possible income tax effects.)

LO10-5, LO10-6

EXERCISE 10.10

Accounting for Bonds Issued at a Discount: Issuance, Interest Payments, and Retirement

Mellilo Corporation issued $5 million of 20-year, 9.5 percent bonds on July 1, 2015, at 98. Interest is due on June 30 and December 31 of each year, and all of the bonds in the issue mature on June 30, 2035. Mellilo's fiscal year ends on December 31. Prepare the following journal entries:

a. July 1, 2015, to record the issuance of the bonds.

b. December 31, 2015, to pay interest and amortize the bond discount.

c. June 30, 2035, to pay interest, amortize the bond discount, and retire the bonds at maturity (make two separate entries).

d. Briefly explain the effect of amortizing the bond discount upon (1) annual net income and (2) annual net cash flow from operating activities. (Ignore possible income tax effects.)

LO10-9

EXERCISE 10.11

Safety of Creditors' Claims

Shown below are data from recent reports of two toy makers. Dollar amounts are stated in thousands.

	Toyco	Pemco
Total assets	$615,132	$2,780,500
Total liabilities	349,792	1,105,735
Interest expense	28,026	39,588
Operating income	13,028	304,672

a. Compute for each company (1) the debt ratio and (2) the interest coverage ratio. (Round the debt ratio to the nearest percent and the interest coverage ratio to two decimal places.)

b. In your opinion, which of these companies would a long-term creditor probably view as the safer investment? Explain.

LO10-10

EXERCISE 10.12

Accounting for Leases

On July 1, Pine Region Dairy leased equipment from Farm America for a period of three years. The lease calls for monthly payments of $2,500 payable in advance on the first day of each month, beginning July 1.

Prepare the journal entry needed to record this lease in the accounting records of Pine Region Dairy on July 1 under each of the following independent assumptions:

a. The lease represents a simple rental arrangement.

b. At the end of three years, title to this equipment will be transferred to Pine Region Dairy at no additional cost. The present value of the 36 monthly lease payments is $76,021, of which $2,500 is paid in cash on July 1. None of the initial $2,500 is allocated to interest expense.

c. Why is situation **a,** the operating lease, sometimes called off-balance sheet financing?

d. Would it be acceptable for a company to account for a capital lease as an operating lease to report rent expense rather than a long-term liability?

LO10-10

EXERCISE 10.13

Pension Plans

At the end of the current year, Eastern Electric received the following information from its actuarial firm:

Pension expense	$2,300,000
Postretirement benefits expense	750,000

The pension plan is fully funded. Eastern Electric has funded only 40% of the nonpension postretirement benefits this year.

a. Prepare the journal entry to summarize pension expense for the entire year.

b. Prepare the journal entry to summarize the nonpension postretirement benefits expense for the entire year.

c. If the company becomes illiquid in future years, what prospects, if any, do today's employees have of receiving the pension benefits that they have earned to date?

d. Does the company have an ethical responsibility to fully fund its nonpension postretirement benefits?

LO10-10

EXERCISE 10.14

Deferred Income Taxes

The following journal entry summarizes for the current year the income tax expense of Sophie's Software Warehouse:

Income Tax Expense	1,500,000	
Cash		960,000
Income Tax Payable		330,000
Deferred Income Tax		210,000
To record income tax expense for the current year.		

Of the deferred income taxes, only $30,000 is classified as a current liability.

a. Define the term *deferred income tax*.

b. What is the amount of income tax that the company has paid or expects to pay in conjunction with its income tax return for the current year?

c. Illustrate the allocation of the liabilities shown in the above journal entry between the classifications of current liabilities and long-term liabilities.

LO10-8

EXERCISE 10.15

Examining Home Depot's Capital Structure

To answer the following questions use the financial statements for **Home Depot, Inc.**, in Appendix A at the end of the textbook:

a. Compute the company's current ratio and quick ratio for the most recent year reported. Do these ratios provide support that **Home Depot** is able to repay its current liabilities as they come due? Explain.

b. Compute the company's debt ratio. Does **Home Depot** appear to have excessive debt? Explain.

c. Examine the company's statement of cash flows. Does **Home Depot**'s cash flow from operating activities appear adequate to cover its current liabilities as they come due? Explain.

Problem Set A

LO10-1 through LO10-6, LO10-8

PROBLEM 10.1A

Effects of Transactions on Financial Statements

Fifteen transactions or events affecting Technology Specialists, Inc., are as follows:

a. Made a year-end adjusting entry to accrue interest on a note payable.

b. A liability classified for several years as long-term becomes due within the next 12 months.

c. Recorded the regular biweekly payroll, including payroll taxes, amounts withheld from employees, and the issuance of paychecks.

d. Earned an amount previously recorded as unearned revenue.

e. Made arrangements to extend a bank loan due in 60 days for another 18 months.

f. Made a monthly payment on a fully amortizing installment note payable. (Assume this note is classified as a current liability.)

g. Called bonds payable due in seven years at a price above the carrying value of the liability in the accounting records.

h. Issued bonds payable at 97 on May 1, 2015. The bonds pay interest May 1 and November 1.

i. Recorded November 1, 2015, interest expense and made semiannual interest payment on bonds referred to in part **h.**

j. Recorded necessary adjusting entry on December 31, 2015, for bonds referred to in part **h.**

k. Issued bonds payable at 102 on July 31, 2015. The bonds pay interest July 31 and January 31.

l. Recorded necessary adjusting entry on December 31, 2015, for bonds referred to in part **k.**

m. Recorded an estimated liability for warranty claims.

n. Entered into a two-year commitment to buy all hard drives from a particular supplier at a price 10 percent below market.

o. Received notice that a lawsuit has been filed against the company for $7 million. The amount of the company's liability, if any, cannot be reasonably estimated at this time.

Instructions

Indicate the effects of each of these transactions upon the following elements of the Technology Specialists, Inc.'s financial statements. Organize your answer in tabular form, using the column headings shown below. Use the following code letters to indicate the effects of each transaction on the accounting element listed in the column headings: **I** for increase, **D** for decrease, and **NE** for no effect.

	Income Statement			Balance Sheet			
Transaction	Revenue −	Expenses =	Net Income	Assets =	Current + Liab.	Long-Term Liab.	+ Owners' Equity
a							

LO10-1, LO10-2, LO10-4, LO10-8

PROBLEM 10.2A

Balance Sheet Presentation of Liabilities

The following are selected items from the accounting records of Denver Chocolates for the year ended December 31, 2015:

Note payable to Northwest Bank	$500,000
Income taxes payable	40,000
Accrued expenses and payroll taxes	60,000
Mortgage note payable	750,000
Accrued interest on mortgage note payable	5,000
Trade accounts payable	250,000
Unearned revenue	15,000
Potential liability in pending lawsuit	100,000

Other Information

1. The note payable to Northwest Bank is due in 60 days. Arrangements have been made to renew this note for an additional 12 months.

2. The mortgage requires payments of $6,000 per month. An amortization table shows that its balance will be paid down to $739,000 by December 31, 2016.

3. Accrued interest on the mortgage note payable is paid monthly. The next payment is due near the end of the first week in January 2016.

4. Denver Chocolates has been sued for $160,000 in a contract dispute. It is not possible at this time, however, to make a reasonable estimate of the possible loss, if any, that the company may have sustained.

Instructions

a. Using the information provided, prepare the current and long-term liability sections of the Denver Chocolates balance sheet dated December 31, 2015. (Within each classification, items may be listed in any order.)

b. Explain briefly how the information in each of the four numbered paragraphs above influenced your presentation of the company's liabilities.

LO10-2
PROBLEM 10.3A
Notes Payable: Accruing Interest

During the fiscal year ended December 31, Swanson Corporation engaged in the following transactions involving notes payable:

Aug. 6 Borrowed $12,000 from Maple Grove Bank, signing a 45-day, 12 percent note payable.

Sept. 16 Purchased office equipment from Seawald Equipment. The invoice amount was $18,000, and Seawald agreed to accept, as full payment, a 10 percent, three-month note for the invoice amount.

Sept. 20 Paid Maple Grove Bank the note plus accrued interest.

Nov. 1 Borrowed $250,000 from Mike Swanson, a major corporate stockholder. The corporation issued Swanson a $250,000, 15 percent, 90-day note payable.

Dec. 1 Purchased merchandise inventory in the amount of $5,000 from Gathman Corporation. Gathman accepted a 90-day, 14 percent note as full settlement of the purchase. Swanson Corporation uses a perpetual inventory system.

Dec. 16 The $18,000 note payable to Seawald Equipment matured today. Swanson paid the accrued interest on this note and issued a new 30-day, 16 percent note payable in the amount of $18,000 to replace the note that matured.

Instructions

a. Prepare journal entries (in general journal form) to record the above transactions. Use a 360-day year in making the interest calculations.

b. Prepare the adjusting entry needed at December 31, prior to closing the accounts. Use one entry for all three notes (round to the nearest dollar).

c. Provide a possible explanation why the new 30-day note payable to Seawald Equipment pays 16 percent interest instead of the 10 percent rate charged on the September 16 note.

LO10-4
PROBLEM 10.4A
Preparation and Use of an Amortization Table

On September 1, 2015, Speedy Lube signed a 30-year, $1,080,000 mortgage note payable to Jonstown Bank and Trust in conjunction with the purchase of a building and land. The mortgage note calls for interest at an annual rate of 12 percent (1 percent per month). The note is fully amortizing over a period of 360 months.

The bank sent Speedy Lube an amortization table showing the allocation of monthly payments between interest and principal over the life of the loan. A small part of this amortization table is illustrated below. (For convenience, amounts have been rounded to the nearest dollar.)

AMORTIZATION TABLE (12%, 30-YEAR MORTGAGE NOTE PAYABLE FOR $1,080,000; PAYABLE IN 360 MONTHLY INSTALLMENTS OF $11,110)					
Interest Period	Payment Date	Monthly Payment	Interest Expense	Principal Reduction	Unpaid Balance
Issue date	Sept. 1, 2011	—	—	—	$1,080,000
1	Oct. 1	$11,110	$10,800	$310	1,079,690
2	Nov. 1	11,110	10,797	313	1,079,377

Instructions

a. Explain whether the amounts of interest expense and the reductions in the unpaid principal are likely to change in any predictable pattern from month to month.

b. Prepare journal entries to record the first two monthly payments on this mortgage.

c. Complete this amortization table for two more monthly installments—those due on December 1, 2015, and January 1, 2016. (Round amounts to the nearest dollar.)

d. Will any amounts relating to this 30-year mortgage be classified as current liabilities in Speedy Lube's December 31, 2015, balance sheet? Explain, but you need not compute any additional dollar amounts.

LO10-5

PROBLEM 10.5A

Bond Interest (Bonds Issued at Face Value)

Green Mountain Power Company obtained authorization to issue 20-year bonds with a face value of $10 million. The bonds are dated May 1, 2015, and have a contract rate of interest of 10 percent. They pay interest on November 1 and May 1. The bonds were issued on August 1, 2015, at 100 plus three months' accrued interest.

Instructions

Prepare the necessary journal entries in general journal form on:

a. August 1, 2015, to record the issuance of the bonds.

b. November 1, 2015, to record the first semiannual interest payment on the bond issue.

c. December 31, 2015, to record interest expense accrued through year-end. (Round to the nearest dollar.)

d. May 1, 2016, to record the second semiannual interest payment. (Round to the nearest dollar.)

e. What was the prevailing market rate of interest on the date that the bonds were issued? Explain.

LO10-5, LO10-6

PROBLEM 10.6A

Amortization of a Bond Discount and Premium

On September 1, 2015, Evansville Lumber Company issued $80 million in 20-year, 10 percent bonds payable. Interest is payable semiannually on March 1 and September 1. Bond discounts and premiums are amortized at each interest payment date and at year-end. The company's fiscal year ends at December 31.

Instructions

a. Make the necessary adjusting entries at December 31, 2015, and the journal entry to record the payment of bond interest on March 1, 2016, under each of the following assumptions:

1. The bonds were issued at 98. (Round to the nearest dollar.)

2. The bonds were issued at 101. (Round to the nearest dollar.)

b. Compute the net bond liability at December 31, 2016, under assumptions **1** and **2** above. (Round to the nearest dollar.)

c. Under which of the above assumptions, **1** or **2**, would the investor's effective rate of interest be higher? Explain.

LO10-1, LO10-5, LO10-6, LO10-10

PROBLEM 10.7A

Reporting Liabilities in a Balance Sheet

The following items were taken from the accounting records of Murfreesboro Telephone Corporation (MTC) for the year ended December 31, 2015 (dollar amounts are in thousands):

Accounts payable	$ 65,600
Accrued expenses payable (other than interest)	11,347
6¾% Bonds payable, due Feb. 1, 2016	100,000
8½% Bonds payable, due June 1, 2016	250,000
Discount on bonds payable (8½% bonds of 2016)	260
11% Bonds payable, due June 1, 2025	300,000
Premium on bonds payable (11% bonds of 2025)	1,700
Accrued interest payable	7,333
Bond interest expense	61,000
Other interest expense	17,000
Notes payable (short-term)	110,000
Lease obligations—capital leases	23,600
Pension obligation	410,000
Unfunded obligations for postretirement benefits other than pensions	72,000
Deferred income taxes	130,000
Income tax expense	66,900
Income tax payable	17,300
Operating income	280,800
Net income	134,700
Total assets	2,093,500

Other Information

1. The 6¾ percent bonds due in February 2016 will be refinanced in January 2016 through the issuance of $150,000 in 9 percent, 20-year bonds payable.
2. The 8½ percent bonds due June 1, 2016, will be repaid entirely from a bond sinking fund.
3. MTC is committed to total lease payments of $14,400 in 2016. Of this amount, $7,479 is applicable to operating leases, and $6,921 to capital leases. Payments on capital leases will be applied as follows: $2,300 to interest expense and $4,621 to reduction in the capitalized lease payment obligation.
4. MTC's pension plan is fully funded with an independent trustee.
5. The obligation for postretirement benefits other than pensions consists of a commitment to maintain health insurance for retired workers. During 2016, MTC will fund $18,000 of this obligation.
6. The $17,300 in income tax payable relates to income taxes levied in 2015 and must be paid on or before March 15, 2016. No portion of the deferred tax liability is regarded as a current liability.

Instructions

a. Using this information, prepare the current liabilities and long-term liabilities sections of MTC's classified balance sheet as of December 31, 2015. (Within each classification, items may be listed in any order.)
b. Explain briefly how the information in each of the six numbered paragraphs affected your presentation of the company's liabilities.
c. Compute as of December 31, 2015, MTC's (1) debt ratio and (2) interest coverage ratio.
d. Solely on the basis of information stated in this problem, indicate whether this company appears to be an outstanding, medium, or poor long-term credit risk. State specific reasons for your conclusion.

LO10-1, LO10-5, LO10-6, LO10-8, LO10-10

PROBLEM 10.8A

Financial Statement Presentation of Liabilities

As of December 31 of the current year, Petersen Corporation has prepared the following information regarding its liabilities and other obligations:

Notes payable, of which $12,000 will be repaid within the next 12 months	$ 80,000
Interest expense that will result from existing liabilities over the next 12 months	125,000
Lawsuit pending against Petersen, in which $600,000 is claimed in damages. Legal counsel can make no reasonable estimate of the company's ultimate liability at this time	600,000
20-year bond issue that matures in two years. The entire amount will be repaid from a bond sinking fund	900,000
Accrued interest on the 20-year bond issue as of the balance sheet date	36,000
Three-year commitment to John Hoskins as chief financial officer at a salary of $275,000 per year	825,000
Note payable due within 90 days (but that is approved to be extended for an additional 18 months)	75,000
Cash deposits from customers for goods and services to be delivered over the next nine months	300,000
Income taxes, of which $100,000 are currently payable and the remainder deferred indefinitely	185,000

Instructions

a. Prepare a listing of the Petersen Corporation's current and long-term liabilities as they should be presented in the company's December 31 balance sheet.
b. Briefly explain why you have excluded any of the listed items in your listing of current and long-term liabilities.

Problem Set B

LO10-1 through LO10-6,
LO10-8

PROBLEM 10.1B

Effects of Transactions on
Financial Statements

Fifteen transactions or events affecting Philmar, Inc., are as follows:

a. Made a year-end adjusting entry to accrue interest on a note payable that has the interest rate stated separately from the principal amount.

b. A liability classified for several years as long-term becomes due within the next 12 months.

c. Recorded the regular weekly payroll, including payroll taxes, amounts withheld from employees, and the issuance of paychecks.

d. Earned an amount previously recorded as unearned revenue.

e. Made arrangements to extend a bank loan due in 60 days for another 36 months.

f. Made a monthly payment on a fully amortizing installment note payable. (Assume this note is classified as a current liability.)

g. Called bonds payable due in 10 years at a price below the carrying value of the liability in the accounting records.

h. Issued bonds payable at 101 on January 31, 2015. The bonds pay interest on January 31 and July 31.

i. Recorded July 31, 2015, interest expense and made semiannual interest payment on bonds referred to in part **h.**

j. Recorded necessary adjusting entry on December 31, 2015, for bonds referred to in part **h.**

k. Issued bonds payable at 98 on August 31, 2015. The bonds pay interest August 31 and February 28.

l. Recorded the necessary adjusting entry on December 31, 2015, for bonds referred to in part **k.**

m. Recorded an estimated liability for warranty claims.

n. Entered into a five-year commitment to buy all supplies from a particular supplier at a price 20 percent below market.

o. Received notice that a lawsuit has been filed against the company for $8 million. The amount of the company's liability, if any, cannot be reasonably estimated at this time.

Instructions

Indicate the effects of each of these transactions upon the following elements of the company's financial statements. Organize your answer in tabular form, using the column headings shown below. Use the following code letters to indicate the effects of each transaction on the accounting elements listed in the column headings: **I** for increase, **D** for decrease, and **NE** for no effect.

	Income Statement			Balance Sheet			
Transaction	Revenue −	Expenses =	Net Income	Assets =	Current Liabilities +	Long-Term Liabilities +	Owner's Equity
a							

LO10-1, LO10-2, LO10-4,
LO10-8

PROBLEM 10.2B

Balance Sheet
Presentation of Liabilities

The following are selected items from the accounting records of Georgia Peach for the year ended December 31, 2015:

Note payable to SmithField Bank	$ 140,000
Income taxes payable	15,000
Accrued expenses and payroll taxes	26,000
Mortgage note payable	750,000
Accrued interest on mortgage note payable	15,000
Trade accounts payable	275,000
Unearned revenue	33,000
Potential liability in pending lawsuit	2,000,000

Other Information

1. The note payable to Smithfield Bank is due in 60 days. Arrangements have been previously approved to renew this note for an additional 24 months.

2. The mortgage requires payments of $10,000 per month. An amortization table shows that its balance will be paid down to $733,000 by December 31, 2016.

3. Accrued interest on the mortgage note payable is paid monthly. The next payment is due near the end of the first week in January 2016.

4. Georgia Peach has been sued for $2,000,000 in a product liability case. It is not possible at this time, however, to make a reasonable estimate of the possible loss, if any, that the company may have sustained.

Instructions

a. Using the information provided, prepare the current and long-term liability sections of Georgia Peach's balance sheet dated December 31, 2015. (Within each classification, items may be listed in any order.)

b. Explain briefly how the information in each of the four numbered paragraphs above influenced your presentation of the company's liabilities.

LO10-2

PROBLEM 10.3B

Notes Payable: Accruing Interest

During the fiscal year ended December 31, Swanlee Corporation engaged in the following transactions involving notes payable:

July	1	Borrowed $20,000 from Weston Bank, signing a 90-day, 12 percent note payable.
Sept.	16	Purchased office equipment from Moontime Equipment. The invoice amount was $30,000, and Moontime agreed to accept, as full payment, a 10 percent, three-month note for the invoice amount.
Oct.	1	Paid Weston Bank the note plus accrued interest.
Dec.	1	Borrowed $170,000 from Jean Jones, a major corporate stockholder. The corporation issued a $170,000, 5 percent, 120-day note payable.
Dec.	1	Purchased merchandise inventory in the amount of $10,000 from Listen Corporation. Listen accepted a 90-day, 12 percent note as a full settlement of the purchase. Swanlee Corporation uses a perpetual inventory system.
Dec.	16	The $30,000 note payable to Moontime Equipment matured today. Swanlee paid the accrued interest on this note and issued a new 60-day, 12 percent note payable in the amount of $30,000 to replace the note that matured.

Instructions

a. Prepare journal entries (in general journal form) to record the above transactions. Use a 360-day year in making the interest calculations.

b. Prepare the adjusting entry needed at December 31, prior to closing the accounts. Use one entry for all three notes (round to the nearest dollar).

c. Provide a possible explanation why the new 60-day note payable to Moontime Equipment pays 16 percent interest instead of the 10 percent rate charged on the September 16 note.

LO10-4

PROBLEM 10.4B

Preparation and Use of an Amortization Table

On October 1, 2015, Jenco signed a four-year, $100,000 note payable to Vicksburg State Bank in conjunction with the purchase of equipment. The note calls for interest at an annual rate of 12 percent (1 percent per month). The note is fully amortizing over a period of 48 months.

The bank sent Jenco an amortization table showing the allocation of monthly payments between interest and principal over the life of the loan. A small part of this amortization table is illustrated below. (For convenience, amounts have been rounded to the nearest dollar.)

| AMORTIZATION TABLE
(12%, 4-YEAR NOTE PAYABLE FOR $100,000;
PAYABLE IN 48 MONTHLY INSTALLMENTS OF $2,633) | | | | | |
Interest Period	Payment Date	Monthly Payment	Interest Expense	Principal Reduction	Unpaid Balance
Issue date	Oct. 1, 2015	—	—	—	$100,000
1	Nov. 1	$2,633	$1,000	$1,633	98,367
2	Dec. 1	2,633	984	1,649	96,718

Instructions

a. Explain whether the amounts of interest expense and the reductions in the unpaid principal are likely to change in any predictable pattern from month to month.

b. Prepare journal entries to record the first two monthly payments on this note.

c. Complete this amortization table for two more monthly installments.

d. Will any amounts relating to this four-year note be classified as current liabilities in Jenco's December 31, 2015, balance sheet? Explain, but you need not compute any additional dollar amounts.

LO10-5
PROBLEM 10.5B

Bond Interest (Bonds Issued at Face Value)

Stevens Manufacturing Company obtained authorization to issue 10-year bonds with a face value of $5 million. The bonds are dated June 1, 2015, and have a contract rate of interest of 6 percent. They pay interest on December 1 and June 1. The bonds are issued on September 1, 2015, at 100 plus three months' accrued interest.

Instructions

Prepare the necessary journal entries in general journal form on:

a. September 1, 2015, to record the issuance of the bonds.

b. December 1, 2015, to record the first semiannual interest payment on the bond issue.

c. December 31, 2015, to record interest expense accrued through year-end.

d. June 1, 2016, to record the second semiannual interest payment.

e. What was the prevailing market rate of interest on the date that the bonds were issued? Explain.

LO10-5, LO10-6
PROBLEM 10.6B

Amortization of a Bond Discount and Premium

On September 1, 2011, Rodriguez Plumbing Company issued $5 million in 10-year, 12 percent bonds payable. Interest is payable semiannually on March 1 and September 1. Bond discounts and premiums are amortized at each interest payment date and at year-end. The company's fiscal year ends at December 31.

Instructions

a. Make the necessary adjusting entries at December 31, 2015, and the journal entry to record the payment of bond interest on March 1, 2016, under each of the following assumptions:

1. The bonds were issued at 98. (Round to the nearest dollar.)

2. The bonds were issued at 104. (Round to the nearest dollar.)

b. Compute the net bond liability at December 31, 2016, under assumptions 1 and 2 above. (Round to the nearest dollar.)

c. Under which of the above assumptions, 1 or 2, would the investor's effective rate of interest be higher? Explain.

LO10-1, LO10-5, LO10-6, LO10-10

PROBLEM 10.7B

Reporting Liabilities in a Balance Sheet

The following items were taken from the accounting records of Nevada Utility Company for the year ended December 31, 2015 (dollar amounts are in thousands):

Accounts payable	$ 48,000
Accrued expenses payable (other than interest)	7,200
10% Bonds payable, due April 1, 2016	100,000
8% Bonds payable, due October 1, 2016	150,000
Unamortized bond discount (8% bonds of 2016)	270
12% Bonds payable, due April 1, 2030	300,000
Unamortized bond premium (12% bonds of 2030)	2,000
Accrued interest payable	3,650
Bond interest expense	57,000
Other interest expense	8,000
Notes payable (short-term)	75,000
Lease obligations—capital leases	18,000
Pension obligation	410,000
Unfunded obligations for postretirement benefits other than pensions	60,000
Deferred income taxes	110,000
Income tax expense	42,000
Income tax payable	8,000
Operating income	341,250
Net income	210,000
Total assets	2,203,950

Other Information

1. The 10 percent bonds due in April 2016 will be refinanced in March 2016 through the issuance of $125,000 in 9 percent, 20-year bonds payable.

2. The 8 percent bonds due October 1, 2016, will be repaid entirely from a bond sinking fund.

3. Nevada Utility is committed to total lease payments of $11,000 in 2016. Of this amount, $6,000 is applicable to operating leases, and $5,000 to capital leases. Payments on capital leases will be applied as follows: $2,000 to interest expense and $3,000 to reduction in the capitalized lease payment obligation.

4. Nevada Utility's pension plan is fully funded with an independent trustee.

5. The obligation for postretirement benefits other than pensions consists of a commitment to maintain health insurance for retired workers. During 2016, Nevada Utility will fund $16,000 of this obligation.

6. The $8,000 in income taxes payable relates to income taxes levied in 2015 and must be paid on or before March 15, 2016. No portion of the deferred tax liability is regarded as a current liability.

Instructions

a. Using this information, prepare the current liabilities and long-term liabilities sections of Nevada Utility Company's classified balance sheet as of December 31, 2015. (Within each classification, items may be listed in any order.)

b. Explain briefly how the information in each of the six numbered paragraphs affected your presentation of the company's liabilities.

c. Compute as of December 31, 2015, the company's (1) debt ratio and (2) interest coverage ratio.

d. Solely on the basis of information stated in this problem, indicate whether this company appears to be an outstanding, medium, or poor long-term credit risk. State specific reasons for your conclusion.

LO10-1, LO10-5, LO10-6,
LO10-8, LO10-10

PROBLEM 10.8B

Financial Statement
Presentation of Liabilities

As of December 31 of the current year, Alexander Company has prepared the following information regarding its liabilities and other obligations:

Notes payable, of which $27,000 will be repaid within the next 12 months	$150,000
Interest expense that will result from existing liabilities over the next 12 months	175,000
Lawsuit pending against Alexander, in which $525,000 is claimed in damages. Legal counsel can make no reasonable estimate of the company's ultimate liability at this time	525,000
20-year bond issue that matures in two years. The entire amount will be repaid from a bond sinking fund	750,000
Accrued interest on the 20-year bond issue as of the balance sheet date	22,500
Three-year commitment to Fred Money as chief financial officer at a salary of $150,000 per year	450,000
Note payable due within 90 days (but that is approved for extension for an additional 18 months)	90,000
Cash deposits from customers for goods and services to be delivered over the next nine months	268,000
Income taxes, of which $145,000 are currently payable and the remainder deferred indefinitely	260,000

Instructions

a. Prepare a listing of Alexander's current and long-term liabilities as they should be presented in the company's December 31 balance sheet.

b. Briefly explain why you have excluded any of the listed items in your listing of current and long-term liabilities.

Critical Thinking Cases

LO10-1, LO10-10
CASE 10.1

The Nature of Liabilities

Listed below are seven publicly owned corporations and a liability that regularly appears in each corporation's balance sheet:

a. **Wells Fargo & Company** (banking): Deposits: interest bearing

b. **The New York Times Company** (news paper publisher): Unexpired subscriptions

c. **The Hollywood Park Companies** (horse racing): Outstanding mutuel tickets

d. **American Greetings** (greeting cards and gift wrap products manufacturer): Sales returns

e. **Wausau Paper Mills Company** (paper manufacturer): Current maturities of long-term debt

f. **Club Med., Inc.** (resorts): Amounts received for future vacations

g. **Apple Computer, Inc.** (computer manufacturer): Accrued marketing and distribution

h. **General Motors Corporation** (automobile manufacturer): obligation for postretirement benefits

Instructions

Briefly explain what you believe to be the nature of each of these liabilities, including how the liability arose and the manner in which it is likely to be discharged.

LO10-5 through LO10-7
CASE 10.2

Factors Affecting Bond
Prices

In the past, **Abbott Labs** had two bond issues outstanding with the following characteristics:

Issue	Interest Rate	Maturity	Current Price
A	6%	2008	115
B	6%	2012	118

Instructions

Answer the following questions regarding these bond issues:

a. Which issue, A or B, has the higher effective rate of interest? How can you tell?

b. Assume that the bonds of both issues had face values of $1,000 each. How much cash did each bond from *issue A* provide investors in *12 months?* How much cash did each bond from *issue B* provide investors in *12 months?*

c. Note that both issues are by the same company, have the same contract rate of interest, and have identical credit ratings. In view of these facts, explain the current price difference of each issue.

LO10-8

CASE 10.3

Loss Contingencies

Discuss each of the following situations, indicating whether the situation is a loss contingency that should be recorded or disclosed in the financial statements of Freedom Airlines. If the situation is not a loss contingency, explain how (if at all) it should be reported in the company's financial statements. (Assume that all dollar amounts are material.)

Instructions

a. 1. Freedom estimates that $700,000 of its accounts receivable will prove to be uncollectible.

2. The company's president is in poor health and has previously suffered two heart attacks.

3. As with any airline, Freedom faces the risk that a future airplane crash could cause considerable loss.

4. Freedom is being sued for $2 million for failing to adequately provide alternative service for passengers whose reservations were canceled as a result of the airline's overbooking certain flights. This suit will not be resolved for a year or more.

b. Make a general statement that summarizes management's ethical responsibility regarding reporting loss contingencies in its financial statements.

LO10-1, LO10-10

CASE 10.4

Off-Balance Sheet Financing

Airlines AMR (American Airlines) leases most of its commercial aircraft and is currently committed to pay almost $10 billion in future lease obligations. However, the company's 2012 financial statement reported only $431 million of these commitments as long-term capital lease obligations in the liability section of its balance sheet. The remaining commitments are structured as operating leases. Obligations to pay future operating lease obligations are not reported in the balance sheet as liabilities. Instead, cash outlays for operating leases appear only in the income statement as expenses as the obligations come due.

American's recent balance sheet reports assets totaling $23,264 million. The company's long-term debt, including its capital lease obligations, total approximately $8,471 million, and the stockholders' equity section of its balance sheet reveals a deficit (negative) balance in retained earnings.

Instructions

a. If **American Airlines** had structured its aircraft commitments as capital leases instead of operating leases, how would the appearance and potential interpretation of its balance sheet have changed?

b. Is it ethical for **American Airlines** to structure less than $1 billion of its aircraft commitments as capital leases and the remaining as off-balance sheet financing? Defend your answer.

c. With regard to **American Airlines**'s lease obligations, why is it important for investors and creditors to read and understand the footnotes accompanying the airline's financial statements?

LO10-5, LO10-6, LO10-9

INTERNET CASE 10.5

Credit Ratings on Bonds

The Internet provides a wealth of information concerning long-term liabilities, bond ratings, and credit markets. Visit the home page of **BondsOnline** at the following Internet address:

www.BondsOnline.com

Instructions

a. Go to the "Chart Center" section of the website. Define in your own words the term "yield curve." Why is the yield curve relevant to you as a bond investor?

b. Return to the home page. On the left side of the screen, locate the heading that provides current market information. Summarize two things you learned about the current financial markets by studying this information.

c. Again return to the home page. Select the option "Financial Career Center" and select the job classification that interests you the most. Browse the jobs listed under that classification and select a specific job you would apply for were you currently qualified. Write a brief description why this job interests you.

Internet sites are time and date sensitive. It is the purpose of these exercises to have you explore the Internet. You may need to use the Yahoo! search engine www.yahoo.com (or another favorite search engine) to find a company's current web address.

Answers to Self-Test Questions

1. a, b   **2.** a, b, d   **3.** a, d   **4.** a, c, d   **5.** a, b, c, d   **6.** a, b, c, d
7. a, c   **8.** b   **9.** a, c   **10.** d   **11.** a

CHAPTER II

Stockholders' Equity: Paid-In Capital

AFTER STUDYING THIS CHAPTER, YOU SHOULD BE ABLE TO:

Learning Objectives

LO11-1	Explain the advantages and disadvantages of organizing a business as a corporation.
LO11-2	Distinguish between publicly owned and closely held corporations.
LO11-3	Explain the rights of stockholders and the roles of corporate directors and officers.
LO11-4	Account for paid-in capital and prepare the equity section of a corporate balance sheet.
LO11-5	Contrast the features of common stock with those of preferred stock.
LO11-6	Discuss the factors affecting the market price of preferred stock and common stock.
LO11-7	Explain the significance of book value and market value of capital stock.
LO11-8	Explain the purpose and effects of a stock split.
LO11-9	Account for treasury stock transactions.

© Rick Friedman/Corbis

TARGET CORPORATION

Stockholders' equity is a major source of resources for corporations. As we learn in Chapter 11, stockholders' equity comes from two primary sources: the original contributions of stockholders when they purchase shares of common or preferred stock directly from the company. The second source is the company's accumulated earnings, less dividends and other adjustments, that have been achieved since the company's inception.

How important is stockholders' equity as a source of funds for a company like Target Corporation? The answer is "very important." In Target's 2012 statement of financial position (balance sheet), stockholders' equity totals $16,558 million, which represents more than 34 percent of total assets. Of the total stockholders' equity of $16,558 million, only $3,979 million came from the original investments of stockholders. The remainder came from profitable operations. Clearly the original investment of owners in Target has been enhanced via profitable operations of the company.

Companies like Target carefully manage their relationship of debt to stockholders' equity. Unlike debt, equity has no maturity date. If a stockholder in a company like Target wants to sell his or her investment, the shares owned are offered for sale on a stock exchange or over-the-counter market in which sellers and buyers come together in exchange transactions. The numbers you often see in the business news about stock prices usually represent transactions between willing buyers and sellers, not between buyers and the issuing corporation. ■

In this chapter we explore issues related to stockholders' equity, including treasury stock transactions, preferred stock, and stock splits. We also discuss why businesses incorporate and describe the factors that influence the price of their stock in the open market.

Corporations

The corporate form is the organization of choice for many businesses—large and small. The owners of a corporation are called **stockholders.** In many small corporations, there are only one or two stockholders. But in large corporations, such as **IBM** and **AT&T**, there are literally millions of stockholders.

A **corporation** is a form of business organization that is recognized under the law as a *separate legal entity,* with rights and responsibilities *apart from those of its owners.* The assets of a corporation belong to the corporation *itself,* not to the stockholders. The corporation is responsible for its own debts and must pay income taxes on its earnings. As a separate legal entity, a corporation has status in court; it may enter into contracts, and it may sue and be sued as if it were a person. The major advantages and disadvantages of this form of business organization are summarized in Exhibit 11–1.

EXHIBIT 11–1

Advantages and Disadvantages of the Corporate Form

LO11-1

LEARNING OBJECTIVE
Explain the advantages and disadvantages of organizing a business as a corporation.

Advantages	Disadvantages
1. *Stockholders are not personally liable for the debts of a corporation.* This concept is called *limited personal liability* and often is cited as the greatest advantage of the corporate form of organization.	1. *Heavy taxation.* Corporate earnings are subject to **double taxation**. First, the corporation must pay *corporate income taxes* on its earnings. Second, stockholders must pay *personal income taxes* on any portion of these earnings that they receive as *dividends*.
2. *Transferability of ownership.* Ownership of a corporation is evidenced by *transferable shares of stock,* which may be sold by one investor to another.	2. *Greater regulation.* Corporations are affected by state and federal laws to a far greater extent than are unincorporated businesses.
3. *Professional management.* The stockholders own a corporation, but they do not manage it on a daily basis. To administer the affairs of the corporation, the stockholders elect a *board of directors.* The directors, in turn, hire professional managers to run the business.	3. *Cost of formation.* An unincorporated business can be formed at little or no cost. Forming a corporation, however, normally requires the services of an attorney.
4. *Continuity of existence.* Changes in the names and identities of stockholders do not directly affect the corporation. Therefore, the corporation may continue its operations *without disruption,* despite the retirement or death of individual stockholders.	4. *Separation of ownership and management.* If stockholders do not approve of the manner in which management runs the business, they may find it difficult to take the united action necessary to remove that management group.

What types of businesses choose the corporate form of organization? The answer, basically, is *all kinds.* When we think of corporations, we often think of large, well-known companies such as **ExxonMobil, General Motors**, and **Procter & Gamble.** Indeed, almost all large businesses are organized as corporations. Limited shareholder liability, transferability of ownership, professional management, and continuity of existence make the corporation the best form of organization for pooling the resources of a great many equity investors. Not all corporations, however, are large and publicly owned. Many small businesses are organized as corporations.

WHY BUSINESSES INCORPORATE

Businesses incorporate for many reasons, but the two of greatest importance are (1) limited shareholder liability and (2) transferability of ownership.

We have previously discussed the concept of **limited personal liability.** This simply means that shareholders are not personally responsible for the debts of the corporation. Thus, if the corporation has financial problems, the most that a stockholder usually can lose is the amount of his or her equity investment.

Another special feature of the corporation is the *transferability of ownership*—that is, ownership is represented by shares of **capital stock** that can be bought and sold. For a small, family-owned business, this provides a convenient means of gradually transferring ownership and control of the business from one generation to the next. For a large company, it makes ownership of the business a *highly liquid investment,* which can be purchased and sold in organized securities exchanges.[1]

YOUR TURN   You as a Loan Officer

GOTCHA! is a small business that manufactures board games. It is one of the many business ventures of Gayle Woods, who is very wealthy and one of your bank's most valued customers. She has done business with your bank for more than 20 years, and the balance in her personal checking, savings, and money market accounts normally exceeds $500,000. GOTCHA! is organized as a corporation, and Woods is the only stockholder.

GOTCHA! has applied for a $200,000 line of credit, which it intends to use to purchase copyrights to additional board games. Although the company is profitable, its most recent balance sheet shows total assets of only $52,000, including $47,000 in copyrights. The corporation has just under $3,000 in liabilities and over $49,000 in stockholders' equity.

Do you consider GOTCHA! a good credit risk? Would you make the loan? Under what conditions?

(See our comments on the Online Learning Center website.)

PUBLICLY OWNED CORPORATIONS

The capital stock of many large corporations is bought and sold (traded) through organized securities exchanges. As these shares are available for purchase by the general public, these large corporations are said to be **publicly owned.**

Far more people have a financial interest in the shares of publicly owned companies than one might expect. If you purchase the stock of such a corporation, you become a stockholder with a *direct* ownership interest—that is, *you* are a stockholder. But mutual funds and pension funds invest heavily in the stocks of many publicly owned corporations. If you invest in a mutual fund or you are covered by a pension plan, you have an *indirect* financial interest in the stocks of many publicly owned corporations.

Corporations whose shares are *not* traded on any organized stock exchanges are said to be **closely held.** Because there is no organized market for buying and selling their shares, these corporations usually have relatively few stockholders. Often, a closely held corporation is owned by one individual or by the members of one family.

Publicly Owned Corporations Face Different Rules   The government seeks to protect the interests of the public. Therefore, publicly owned corporations are subject to more regulation than those that are closely held. For example, publicly owned corporations are *required by law* to:

- Prepare and issue quarterly and annual financial statements in conformity with generally accepted accounting principles. (These statements are **public information.**)
- Have their annual financial statements audited by an independent firm of certified public accountants.
- Comply with federal securities laws, which include both criminal penalties and civil liability for deliberately or carelessly distributing misleading information to the public.
- Submit much of their financial information to the Securities and Exchange Commission for review.

L011-2

LEARNING OBJECTIVE
Distinguish between publicly owned and closely held corporations.

---

[1] These securities exchanges include, among others, the New York Stock Exchange, the National Association of Securities Dealers' Automated Quotations (NASDAQ), the Tokyo Stock Exchange, and Mexico's Bolsa. Collectively, stock exchanges often are described simply as *the stock market.*

Closely held corporations normally are exempt from these requirements. Our discussions will focus primarily on the accounting and reporting issues confronting *publicly owned companies.*

Formation of a Corporation

In the United States, a corporation is brought into existence under the laws of a particular state. The state in which the corporation is formed is called the **state of incorporation.**

The state of incorporation is not necessarily where the corporation does business. Rather, a state often is selected because of the leniency of its laws regulating corporate activities. Indeed, many corporations conduct most—sometimes all—of their business activities *outside* the state in which they are incorporated.

The first step in forming a corporation is to obtain a *corporate charter* from the state of incorporation. To obtain this charter, the organizers of the corporation submit an application called the *articles of incorporation.* Once the charter is obtained, the stockholders in the new corporation hold a meeting to elect a *board of directors* and to pass *bylaws* that will govern the corporation's activities. The directors in turn hold a meeting at which the top corporate officers and managers are appointed.

Organization Costs   Forming a corporation is more costly than starting a sole proprietorship. The costs may include, for example, attorneys' fees, incorporation fees paid to the state, and other outlays necessary to bring the corporation into existence. Conceptually, organization costs are an *intangible asset* that will benefit the corporation over its entire life. As a practical matter, however, most corporations expense those costs immediately, even though they are often spread over a five-year period for income tax purposes.

Thus you will seldom see organization costs in the balance sheet of a publicly owned corporation. They have long since been recognized as an expense.

LO11-3

LEARNING OBJECTIVE
Explain the rights of stockholders and the roles of corporate directors and officers.

Rights of Stockholders   A corporation is owned collectively by its stockholders. Each stockholder's ownership interest is determined by the number of *shares* that he or she owns. Assume that a corporation issues 10,000 shares of capital stock. If you own 1,000 of these shares, you own *10 percent* of the corporation. If you acquire another 500 shares from another stockholder, you will own *15 percent.*

Each stockholder, or the stockholder's brokerage firm, receives from the corporation a **stock certificate** indicating the number of shares he or she owns.

The ownership of capital stock in a corporation usually carries the following basic rights:

1. *To vote for directors and on certain other key issues.* A stockholder has one vote for each share owned. The issues on which stockholders may vote are specified in the corporation's bylaws. Any stockholder—or group of stockholders—that owns *more than 50 percent* of the capital stock has the power to elect the board of directors and to set basic corporate policies. Therefore, these stockholders control the corporation.

2. *To participate in dividends declared by the board of directors.* Stockholders in a corporation *may not* make withdrawals of company assets, as may the owners of unincorporated businesses. However, the directors may elect to distribute some or all of the earnings of a profitable corporation to its stockholders in the form of cash *dividends.* Dividends can be distributed only after they have been formally *declared* (authorized) by the board of directors. Dividends are paid to all shareholders in proportion to the number of shares owned.

3. *To share in the distribution of assets if the corporation is liquidated.* When a corporation ends its existence, the creditors must first be paid in full. The shareholders have a residual interest, and any remaining assets are divided among the shareholders in proportion to the number of shares owned.

Stockholders' meetings usually are held once each year. At these meetings, stockholders may ask questions of management and vote on certain issues. In large corporations, these meetings usually are attended by relatively few people—often less than 1 percent of the company's stockholders. Prior to these meetings, however, the management group requests that stockholders who do not plan to attend send in *proxy statements,* granting management the voting rights associated with their shares.

Functions of the Board of Directors

The primary functions of the **board of directors** are to set corporate policies and to protect the interests of the stockholders. Specific duties of the directors include hiring corporate officers and setting those officers' salaries, declaring dividends, and reviewing the findings of both internal auditors and independent auditors.

The board of a large corporation always includes several members of top management. In recent years, increasing importance has been attached to the inclusion of "outside" directors. The term *outside directors* refers to individuals who are *not* officers of the corporation and, therefore, bring an *independent perspective* to the board.

Functions of the Corporate Officers

The top management of a corporation is appointed (hired) by the board of directors. These individuals are called the *corporate officers*. Individual stockholders *do not* have the right to transact corporate business *unless they have been properly appointed to a managerial position.*

The top level of management usually includes a chief executive officer (CEO) or president, a chief financial officer (CFO) or controller, a treasurer, and a secretary. In addition, a vice president usually oversees each functional area, such as sales, personnel, and production.

The responsibilities of the CFO (controller), treasurer, and secretary are most directly related to the accounting phase of business operation. The CFO is responsible for the maintenance of adequate internal control and for the preparation of accounting records and financial statements. Such specialized activities as budgeting, tax planning, and preparation of tax returns are usually placed under the CFO's jurisdiction. The *treasurer* has custody of the company's funds and is generally responsible for planning and controlling the company's cash position. The treasurer's department also has responsibility for relations with the company's financial institutions and major creditors.

The *secretary* represents the corporation in many contractual and legal matters and maintains minutes of the meetings of directors and stockholders. Other responsibilities of the secretary are to coordinate the preparation of the annual report and to manage the investor relations department. In small corporations, one officer frequently acts as both secretary and treasurer.

The organization chart in Exhibit 11–2 indicates lines of authority extending from stockholders to the directors to the CEO and other officers.

EXHIBIT 11–2 Corporate Organization Chart

STOCKHOLDER RECORDS IN A CORPORATION

Many corporations with shares listed on the New York Stock Exchange have millions of shares outstanding and hundreds of thousands of stockholders. Each day many stockholders sell their shares; the buyers of these shares become new members of the company's family of stockholders.

A corporation must have an up-to-date record of the names and addresses of this constantly changing group of stockholders so that it can send dividend checks, financial statements, and voting forms to the right people.

Stockholders Subsidiary Ledger When there are numerous stockholders, it is not practical to include a separate account for each stockholder in the general ledger. Instead, a single controlling account entitled Capital Stock appears in the general ledger, and a **stockholders subsidiary ledger** is maintained. This ledger contains an account for each individual stockholder. Entries in the stockholders subsidiary ledger are made in *number of shares,* rather than in dollars. Thus each stockholder's account shows the number of shares owned and the dates of acquisitions and sales. This record enables the corporation to send each stockholder a single dividend check, even though the stockholder may have acquired shares on different dates.

Stock Transfer Agent and Stock Registrar Many large publicly owned corporations use an independent **stock transfer agent** and a **stock registrar** to maintain their stockholder records and to establish strong internal control over the issuance of stock certificates. These transfer agents and registrars are usually banks or trust companies. When stock certificates are transferred from one owner to another, the old certificates are sent to the transfer agent, who cancels them, makes the necessary entries in the stockholders subsidiary ledger, and prepares a new certificate for the new owner of the shares. This new certificate then must be registered with the stock registrar before it represents valid and transferable ownership of stock in the corporation.

Small closely held corporations generally do not use the services of independent registrars and transfer agents. In these companies, the stockholder records usually are maintained by a corporate officer. To prevent the accidental or fraudulent issuance of an excessive number of stock certificates, the corporation should require that each certificate be signed by at least two designated corporate officers.

Paid-In Capital of a Corporation

LO11-4

LEARNING OBJECTIVE
Account for paid-in capital and prepare the equity section of a corporate balance sheet.

Stockholders' equity of a corporation is normally increased in one of two ways: (1) from contributions by investors in exchange for capital stock—called **paid-in capital** or **contributed capital**—and (2) from the retention of profits earned by the corporation over time—called **retained earnings.** As previously noted, our focus in this chapter is primarily on issues related to paid-in capital. In Chapter 12, we shift our attention to issues concerning retained earnings.

AUTHORIZATION AND ISSUANCE OF CAPITAL STOCK

The articles of incorporation specify the number of shares that a corporation is *authorized* to issue by the state of incorporation. Issues of capital stock that will be sold to the general public must be approved by the federal Securities and Exchange Commission, as well as by state officials.

Corporations normally obtain authorization for more shares than they initially plan to issue. This way, if more capital is needed later, the corporation already has the authorization to issue additional shares.

Shares that have been *issued* and are in the hands of stockholders are called the *outstanding* shares. At any time, these outstanding shares represent 100 percent of the stockholders' investment in the corporation.

When a large amount of stock is to be issued, most corporations use the services of an investment banking firm, frequently referred to as an **underwriter.** The underwriter guarantees the issuing corporation a specific price for the stock and earns a profit by selling the shares to the investing public at a slightly higher price. The corporation records the issuance of the stock at the net amount received from the underwriter. The use of an underwriter assures the corporation that the entire stock issue will be sold without delay and that the entire amount of funds to be raised will be available on a specific date.

The price that a corporation will seek for a new issue of stock is based on such factors as (1) expected future earnings and dividends, (2) the financial strength of the company, and (3) the current state of the investment markets. If the corporation asks too high a price, it will not find an underwriter or other buyers willing to purchase the shares.

State Laws Affect the Balance Sheet Presentation of Stockholders' Equity

The number of different accounts that a corporation must use in the stockholders' equity section of its balance sheet is determined largely by state laws. We have seen that corporations use separate stockholders' equity accounts to represent (1) contributed capital, or paid-in capital, and (2) earned capital, or retained earnings. Up to this point, we have assumed that all paid-in capital is presented in a single account entitled Capital Stock. But this often is not the case.

Some corporations issue several *different types* (or classes) of capital stock. In these situations, a separate account is used to indicate each type of stock outstanding. A legal concept called *par value* also affects the balance sheet presentation of paid-in capital.

Par Value Par value (or stated value) represents the **legal capital** per share—the amount below which stockholders' equity cannot be reduced, except by losses from business operations (or by special legal action). Par value, therefore, may be regarded as a minimum cushion of equity capital existing for the protection of creditors.

Because of the legal restrictions associated with par value, most state laws require corporations to show separately in the stockholders' equity section of the balance sheet the par value of shares issued. This special balance sheet presentation has led some people to believe that par value has some special significance. In many corporations, however, the par value of the shares issued is a small portion of total stockholders' equity.

A corporation may set the par value of its stock at $1 per share, $5 per share, or any other amount that it chooses. Most large corporations set the par value of their common stocks at nominal amounts, such as 1 cent per share or $1 per share. The par value of the stock is *not an indication of its market value;* the par value merely indicates the amount per share to be entered in the Capital Stock account. The common stock of Ford has a par value of $.01 and Target's common stock has a par value of $1. The market values of each of these securities are far above their par values.

Issuance of Par Value Stock Authorization of a stock issue does not create an asset for the corporation, nor does it give the corporation any capital. The obtaining of authorization from the state for a stock issue merely affords a legal opportunity to obtain assets through the sale of stock. Additional capital is created for the company only when that stock is sold to stockholders.

When par value stock is *issued,* the Capital Stock account is credited with the par value of the shares issued, regardless of whether the issuance price is more or less than par. Assuming that 50,000 shares of $2 par value stock have been authorized and that 10,000 of these authorized shares are sold at a price of $2 each, Cash is debited and Capital Stock is credited for $20,000. When stock is sold for more than par value, the Capital Stock account is credited with the par value of the shares issued, and a separate account, **Additional Paid-in Capital,** is credited for the excess of selling price over par. If, for example, our 10,000 shares were issued at a price of $8 per share, the entry would be:

Cash..	80,000	
Capital Stock		20,000
Additional Paid-in Capital		60,000
Issued 10,000 shares of $2 par value stock at a price of		
$8 per share.		

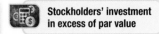
Stockholders' investment in excess of par value

The additional paid-in capital does not represent a profit to the corporation. It is part of the *invested capital,* and it is added to the capital stock in the balance sheet to show the total paid-in capital. The stockholders' equity section of the balance sheet follows. (The $150,000 in retained earnings is assumed in order to have a complete illustration.)

Stockholders' equity:	
Capital stock, $2 par value; authorized, 50,000 shares; issued and outstanding, 10,000 shares	$ 20,000
Additional paid-in capital	60,000
Total paid-in capital	$ 80,000
Retained earnings	150,000
Total stockholders' equity	$230,000

If stock is issued by a corporation for *less* than par, the account Discount on Capital Stock should be debited for the difference between the issuance price and the par value. A discount on capital stock reduces, rather than increases, the amount of stockholders' equity in the balance sheet. The issuance of stock at a discount is seldom encountered.

In some cases, stock is issued in exchange for assets other than cash. When this occurs, the appropriate asset account is debited (for example, Inventory or Land) and the stock accounts are credited as if the stock had been sold for cash. Establishing a value for recording a transaction of this type is sometimes difficult, but should be based on either the fair value of the assets received or the stock issued, whichever can be more objectively determined.

No-Par Stock   Some states allow corporations to issue stock without designating a par or stated value. When this "no-par" stock is issued, the *entire issue price* is credited to the Capital Stock account and is viewed as legal capital not subject to withdrawal.

COMMON STOCK AND PREFERRED STOCK

The account title Capital Stock is widely used when a corporation has issued only *one type* of stock. In order to appeal to as many investors as possible, however, some corporations issue several types (or classes) of capital stock, each providing investors with different rights and opportunities.

The basic type of capital stock issued by every corporation often is called **common stock.** Common stock possesses the traditional rights of ownership—voting rights, participation in dividends, and a residual claim to assets in the event of liquidation. When the rights of stockholders are modified, the term **preferred stock** is often used to describe the resulting type of capital stock. Some corporations issue two or more classes of preferred stock, with each class having distinctive features designed to appeal to a particular type of investor.

The following stockholders' equity section illustrates the balance sheet presentation for a corporation having both preferred and common stock. As before, a retained earnings amount is assumed so we can provide a complete example.

L011-5

LEARNING OBJECTIVE
Contrast the features of common stock with those of preferred stock.

Balance sheet presentation of common stock and preferred stock

Stockholders' equity:	
9% cumulative preferred stock, $100 par value, authorized 100,000 shares, issued and outstanding 50,000 shares	$ 5,000,000
Common stock, $5 par value, authorized 3 million shares, issued and outstanding 2 million shares	10,000,000
Additional paid-in capital:	
Preferred stock	500,000
Common stock	20,000,000
Total paid-in capital	$35,500,000
Retained earnings	17,500,000
Total stockholders' equity	$53,000,000

CHARACTERISTICS OF PREFERRED STOCK

Preferred stocks typically have some combination of the following distinctive features:

1. Preference over common stock as to dividends.
2. Cumulative dividend rights.
3. Preference over common stock as to assets in event of the liquidation of the company.
4. Callable at the option of the corporation.
5. No voting power.

Another important but less common feature of some preferred stocks is a clause permitting the *conversion* of preferred stock into common stock at the option of the holder. Preferred stocks vary widely with respect to the special rights and privileges granted. Careful study of the terms of the individual preferred stock contract is a necessary step in the evaluation of any preferred stock.

 ## INTERNATIONAL CASE IN POINT

Specific preferred stock characteristics can affect the reporting location on the balance sheet. For example, preferred stock that is mandatorily redeemable by the issuing company is required by international accounting standards to be classified as a liability (rather than an equity) on the balance sheet. In 2003, the FASB changed U.S. GAAP reporting requirements from allowing redeemable preferred stock to be reported in the equity section to requiring it to be reported in the liability section, consistent with international standards.

Stock Preferred as to Dividends   Corporations often make periodic cash payments, called **dividends,** to stockholders.[2] Dividends normally involve a distribution of cash that represents accumulated earnings and therefore cannot exceed the amount of a corporation's retained earnings.

Preferred stock is said to have dividend preference because preferred stock investors are entitled to receive a specified amount each year before any dividend is paid to common stock investors. The specified dividend may be stated as a dollar amount, such as $5 per share. Some preferred stocks, however, state the specified dividend as a *percentage of par value.* For example, a share of preferred stock with a par value of $100 and a dividend preference of *7 percent* must provide a $7 dividend ($100 × 7%) each year to each share of preferred stock before any dividends can be paid on the common shares.

The holders of preferred stock have no guarantee that they will always receive the indicated dividend. A corporation is obligated to pay dividends to stockholders only when cash is available and the board of directors declares a dividend. However, dividends must be paid on preferred stock before anything is paid to the common stockholders, but if the corporation is not prospering, it may decide not to pay any dividends at all. For a corporation to pay dividends, profits must be earned and cash must be available.

Cumulative Preferred Stock   The dividend preference carried by most preferred stocks is *cumulative.* If all or any part of the regular dividend on the preferred stock is omitted in a given year, the amount omitted is said to be *in arrears* and must be paid in a subsequent year before any dividend can be paid on the common stock.

Assume that a corporation is organized on January 1, 2013, with 10,000 shares of $8 preferred stock and 50,000 shares of common stock. If the preferred stock is *noncumulative,* the

---

[2] In Chapter 12, we will discuss specific accounting issues related to cash dividends and other forms of distributions to stockholders. For the purposes of this chapter, dividends may be viewed simply as the distribution to stockholders of accumulated profits that reduce both cash and retained earnings.

$8 per share dividend does not carry forward if it is not paid each year. On the other hand, if the preferred stock is *cumulative,* the $8 per share dividend carries forward to future years if it is not paid and the accumulated amount must be paid before any dividend can be paid on common stock. Assume that the $8 preferred dividend is paid in 2013, a partial dividend of $2 per share is paid on preferred stock in 2014, and no preferred dividend is paid in 2015. Following is an analysis of the status of the preferred dividend at the end of 2015.

	2013	2014	2015
If preferred stock is noncumulative			
Dividend paid	$80,000	$20,000	—
Dividend in arrears		Not applicable	
If preferred stock is cumulative			
Dividend paid	$80,000	$20,000	—
Dividends in arrears	—	$60,000	$140,000

In the case of noncumulative preferred stock, the unpaid dividend does *not* carry forward to future years and has no effect on the company's ability to pay dividends on common stock in the future. In the case of cumulative preferred stock, however, any unpaid dividend on preferred stock carries forward and must be paid before dividends can be paid on common stock. In 2014, the partial unpaid dividend of $60,000 would have to have been paid before any dividend could have been paid on common stock. At the end of 2015, this amount has grown to $140,000 (the $60,000 carried forward from 2014, plus the $80,000 that was not paid in 2015). Before a dividend could have been paid on common stock in 2015, the $60,000 preferred dividend *in arrears* from 2014 and the current preferred dividend of $80,000 for 2015 would have to have been paid.

Dividends in arrears are not included among the liabilities of a corporation, because no liability exists until a dividend is declared by the board of directors. The amount of any dividends in arrears on preferred stock is an important factor to investors, however, and should always be *disclosed.* This disclosure is usually made by a note accompanying the balance sheet such as the following:

Footnote disclosure of dividends in arrears

Note 6: Dividends in arrears
As of December 31, 2015, dividends on the $8 cumulative preferred stock were in arrears to the extent of $14 per share and amounted in total to $140,000.

In 2016, we shall assume that the company earned large profits, has available cash, and wished to pay dividends on both the preferred and common stocks. Before paying a dividend on the common stock, the corporation must pay the $140,000 in arrears on the cumulative preferred stock *plus* the regular $8 per share applicable to the current year. The preferred stockholders would, therefore, receive a total of $220,000 ($140,000 + $80,000) in dividends in 2016 ($22 per share); the board of directors would then be free to declare dividends on the common stock.

Other Features of Preferred Stock   To add to the attractiveness of preferred stock as an investment, corporations sometimes offer a *conversion privilege* that entitles the preferred stockholders to exchange their shares for common stock at a stipulated ratio. If the corporation prospers, its common stock will probably rise in market value, and dividends on the common stock will probably increase. The investor who buys a convertible preferred stock rather than common stock has greater assurance of regular dividends. In addition, through the conversion privilege, the investor is assured of an opportunity to share in any substantial increase in value of the company's common stock.

The three primary elements of stockholders' equity for most companies are common stock, preferred stock, and retained earnings. While important, other elements that we learn about later in this chapter, as well as in Chapter 12, are typically smaller in amount than these three

EXHIBIT 11–3
Primary Sources of
Corporate Equity

primary elements. The relationship of common stock, preferred stock, and retained earnings is depicted in Exhibit 11–3.

BOOK VALUE PER SHARE OF COMMON STOCK

Because the equity of each stockholder in a corporation is determined by the number of shares he or she owns, an accounting measurement of interest to some stockholders is book value per share of common stock. **Book value per share** is the amount of net assets represented by each share of stock. The term *net assets* means total assets minus total liabilities; in other words, net assets are equal to *total stockholders' equity*. For a corporation that has issued common stock only, the book value per share is computed by dividing total stockholders' equity by the number of shares outstanding.

For example, assume that a corporation has 4,000 shares of common stock outstanding and the stockholders' equity section of the balance sheet is as follows:

Stockholders' equity:	
Common stock, $1 par value (4,000 shares issued and outstanding)	$ 4,000
Additional paid-in capital	50,000
Retained earnings	76,000
Total stockholders' equity	$130,000

The book value per share is *$32.50;* it is computed by dividing the stockholders' equity of $130,000 by the 4,000 shares of outstanding stock.

Book Value When a Company Has Both Preferred and Common Stock
Book value is usually computed only for common stock. If a company has both preferred and common stock outstanding, the computation of book value per share of common stock requires two steps. First, the amount assigned to preferred stock and any *dividends in arrears* are deducted from total stockholders' equity. Second, the remaining amount of stockholders' equity is divided by the number of common shares outstanding to determine book value per common share. This procedure reflects the fact that the common stockholders are the *residual owners* of the corporate entity.

How much is book value per share?

To illustrate the computation of book value per share when preferred stock is outstanding, assume that the stockholders' equity of Hart Company at December 31 is as follows:

 Two classes of stock

Stockholders' equity:

8% preferred stock, $100 par value, 10,000 shares authorized, issued, and outstanding	$1,000,000
Common stock, $10 stated value, authorized 100,000 shares, issued and outstanding 50,000 shares	500,000
Additional paid-in capital: common stock	750,000
Total paid-in capital	$2,250,000
Retained earnings	130,000
Total stockholders' equity	$2,380,000

Because of a weak cash position, Hart Company has paid no dividends during the current year. As of December 31, dividends in arrears on the cumulative preferred stock total *$80,000* (10,000 shares × 100 par value × 8%).

All the equity belongs to the common stockholders, except the $1,000,000 par value applicable to the preferred stock plus the $80,000 of dividends in arrears on preferred stock. The calculation of book value per share of common stock is as follows:

Total stockholders' equity		$2,380,000
Less: Equity of preferred stockholders:		
Par value of preferred stock	$1,000,000	
Dividends in arrears	80,000	1,080,000
Equity of common stockholders		$1,300,000
Number of common shares outstanding		50,000
Book value per share of common stock ($1,300,000 ÷ 50,000 shares)		$26

In a statement of cash flows, transactions with the stockholders of a corporation are classified as *financing activities.* For example, the issuance of capital stock for cash represents a *receipt* from financing activities. Distributions of cash to stockholders—including the payment of cash dividends—represent a cash *outlay,* which is also classified under financing activities.

Transactions with owners do not always have an immediate effect on cash flows. Consider an exchange of the corporation's capital stock for a noncash asset, such as land. Cash is not increased or decreased by this event. These types of noncash transactions are described in a special schedule that accompanies the statement of cash flows.

Market Value

After shares of stock have been issued, they may be sold by one investor to another. The price at which these shares change hands between investors represents the *market price* of the stock. This market price may differ substantially from such amounts as par value, the original issue price, and the current book value. Which is the most relevant amount? That depends on your point of view.

After shares are issued, they belong to the stockholder, not to the issuing corporation. Changes in the market price of these shares directly affect the financial position of the stockholder, but not that of the issuing company. This concept explains why the issuing company and stockholders apply different accounting principles to the same outstanding shares.

Accounting by the Issuer   From the viewpoint of the issuing company, outstanding stock represents an amount invested in the company by its owners at a particular date. This amount represents capital available to the company from the original sale of the stock. While the market value of the stockholders' investment may change, the amount of resources that they originally invested in the company does not change.

The company issuing stock records the issue price—that is, the proceeds received from issuing the stock—in its paid-in capital accounts. The balances in these accounts remain unchanged unless (1) more shares are issued or (2) outstanding shares are permanently retired (for example, preferred stock is called or stock is purchased on the open market and then retired).

Accounting by the Investor   From the investor's point of view, shares owned in a publicly owned company are an asset, usually called Marketable Securities.

To the investor, the current market value of securities owned is more relevant than the original issue price—or than the securities' par values or book values. The market value indicates what the securities are worth today. Changes in market value directly affect the investor's liquidity and financial position. For these reasons, investors show investments in marketable securities at current market value in their balance sheets.

CASE IN POINT

In a single day, the market price of IBM's capital stock dropped over $31 per share, falling from $135 to $103.25. Of course, this was not a typical day. The date, October 19, 1987, will long be remembered as "Black Monday." On this day, stock prices around the world suffered the greatest one-day decline in history.

Stocks listed on the New York Stock Exchange lost about 20 percent of their value in less than six hours. Given that the annual dividends on these stocks averaged about 2 percent of their market value, this one-day market loss was approximately equal to the loss by investors of all dividend revenue for about 10 years.

© Royalty-Free/Corbis

How did this disastrous decline in IBM's stock price directly affect the balance sheet of IBM on October 19, 1987? Actually, it didn't. IBM's stock isn't owned by IBM—it is owned by the company's stockholders.

Because market prices are of such importance to investors, we will briefly discuss the factors that most affect the market prices of preferred and common stocks.

MARKET PRICE OF PREFERRED STOCK

Investors buy preferred stocks primarily to receive the dividends that these shares pay. This means that the dividend rate is one important factor in determining the market price of a preferred stock. A second important factor is *risk*. In the long run, a company must be profitable enough to pay dividends. If there is a distinct possibility that the company will *not* operate profitably and pay dividends, the price of its preferred stock will probably decline.

A third factor greatly affecting the value of preferred stocks is the level of *interest rates*. What happens to the market price of an 8 percent preferred stock, originally issued at a par value of $100, if government policies and other factors cause long-term interest rates to rise to, say, 10 percent or 12 percent? If investments offering a return of 12 percent with the same level of risk are readily available, investors will no longer pay $100 for a share of preferred stock that provides a dividend of only 8 percent per year. The market price of the preferred stock will fall to about two-thirds of its original issue price, or about $67 per share. At this market price, the stock offers a competitive return of about 12 percent ($8 ÷ $67) (called the **dividend yield**) to an investor purchasing the stock.

However, if the prevailing long-term interest rates should again decline to the 8 percent range, the market price of an 8 percent preferred stock should rise to approximately par

L011-6

LEARNING OBJECTIVE
Discuss the factors affecting the market price of preferred stock and common stock.

value. In summary, the market price of preferred stock *varies inversely with interest rates*. As interest rates rise, preferred stock prices decline; as interest rates fall, preferred stock prices rise.

MARKET PRICE OF COMMON STOCK

Prevailing interest rates also affect the market price of common stock. However, dividends paid to common stockholders are not fixed in amount. Both the amount of the dividend and the market price of the stock may increase dramatically if the corporation is successful. Alternatively, if the company is unsuccessful, the common stockholders may not even recover their original investment. Therefore, the most important factors in the market price of common stock are *investors' expectations* as to the future profitability of the business and the *risk* that this level of profitability may not be achieved.

BOOK VALUE AND MARKET PRICE

LO11-7

LEARNING OBJECTIVE
Explain the significance of book value and market value of capital stock.

To some extent, *book value* is used in evaluating the reasonableness of the market price of a stock. However, it must be used with caution; the fact that a stock is selling at less than book value does not necessarily indicate a bargain.

Book value is a historical concept, representing the amounts invested by stockholders plus the amounts earned and retained by the corporation. If a stock is selling at a price *above* book value, investors believe that management has created a business worth more than the historical cost of the resources entrusted to its care. This, in essence, is the sign of a successful corporation.

On the other hand, if the market price of a stock is *less than* book value, investors believe that the company's resources are worth less than their cost while under the control of current management. The relationship between book value and market price is one measure of investors' *confidence in a company's management*.

STOCK SPLITS

LO11-8

LEARNING OBJECTIVE
Explain the purpose and effects of a stock split.

Over time, the market price of a corporation's common stock may increase in value so much that it becomes too expensive for many investors. When this happens, a corporation may *split* its stock by increasing the number of its common shares outstanding. The purpose of a **stock split** is to reduce substantially the market price of the company's common stock, with the intent of making it more affordable to investors.

For example, assume that Felix Corporation has outstanding 1 million shares of $10 par value common stock. The market price is currently $90 per share. To make the stock more affordable, the corporation decides to increase the number of outstanding shares from 1 million to 2 million. This action is called a *2-for-1 stock split*. A stockholder who owned 100 shares of the stock before the split will own 200 shares after the split. Since the number of outstanding shares has doubled without any change in total assets or total stockholders' equity, the market price of the stock should drop from $90 to approximately $45 per share. In splitting its stock, a corporation is required to reduce the par value per share in proportion to the size of the split. As this was a 2-for-1 split, the company must reduce the par value of the stock from $10 to $5 per share. Had it been a 4-for-1 split, the par value would have been reduced from $10 to $2.50 per share and the stock price would have declined to approximately 25 percent of its former amount.

A stock split does not change the balance of any accounts in the balance sheet; consequently, the transaction is recorded merely by a *memorandum entry*. For Felix Corporation, this memorandum entry might read as follows:

Sept. 30　Memorandum: Issued additional 1 million shares of common stock in a 2-for-1 stock split. Par value reduced from $10 per share to $5 per share.

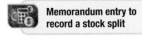

Memorandum entry to record a stock split

The description of common stock also is changed in the balance sheet to reflect the lower par value and the greater number of shares outstanding.

Another form of stock distribution to current stockholders is a stock dividend. While stock dividends are similar to stock splits in some respects, they are much smaller in size and have a different intent. Because they are important considerations in a company's dividend policy, we defer the detailed coverage of stock dividends to Chapter 12.

Treasury Stock

Treasury stock is defined as shares of a corporation's own capital stock that have been issued and later *reacquired by the issuing company* but that have not been canceled or permanently retired. Treasury shares may be held indefinitely or may be issued again at any time. Shares of capital stock held in the treasury ordinarily are not entitled to receive dividends, to vote, or to share in assets upon dissolution of the company.

L011-9

LEARNING OBJECTIVE
Account for treasury stock transactions.

Stock option plans are an important part of employee compensation for many companies. They permit employees to purchase stock in the company, often at advantageous prices, and are a means of creating employee loyalty to the company. Treasury stock purchases are one means by which the company can have available the shares of stock needed to satisfy the requirement of stock option plans to issue shares of stock to employees. Rather than increasing the total number of outstanding shares, thereby reducing or diluting the ownership of each share, the company purchases shares of stock from the current owners and then sells the same shares a second time to its employees.

RECORDING PURCHASES OF TREASURY STOCK

Purchases of treasury stock are usually recorded by debiting the Treasury Stock account with the cost of the stock. For example, if Riley Corporation reacquires 1,600 shares of its own $5 par stock at a price of $90 per share, the entry is as follows:

Treasury Stock	144,000	
Cash		144,000
Purchased 1,600 shares of $5 par treasury stock at $90 per share.		

Note that the Treasury Stock account is debited for the *cost* of the shares purchased, not their par value. Treasury stock is a *contra-equity* account. When treasury stock is purchased, the corporation is eliminating part of its stockholders' equity by a payment to one or more stockholders. The purchase of treasury stock should be regarded as a *reduction of stockholders' equity,* not as the acquisition of an asset. For this reason, the Treasury Stock account appears in the balance sheet as a deduction in the stockholders' equity section. Treasury shares are both authorized and issued, but while they are held by the issuing company, they are *not* outstanding.

The presentation of treasury stock in Riley Corporation's balance sheet appears as follows, based on assumed numbers (except for treasury stock):

Stockholders' equity:	
Common stock, $5 par value, authorized 250,000 shares, issued 100,000 shares (of which 1,600 are held in treasury)	$ 500,000
Additional paid-in capital: common stock	800,000
Total paid-in capital	$1,300,000
Retained earnings	600,000
Subtotal	$1,900,000
Less: Treasury stock (1,600 shares of common, at $90 cost)	144,000
Total stockholders' equity	$1,756,000

REISSUANCE OF TREASURY STOCK

When treasury shares are reissued, the Treasury Stock account is credited for the cost of the shares reissued and Additional Paid-in Capital from Treasury Stock Transactions is debited or credited for any *difference* between cost and the reissue price. To illustrate, assume that 1,000 of the treasury shares acquired by Riley Corporation at a cost of $90 per share are now reissued at a price of $115 per share. The entry to record the reissuance of these shares at a price above cost is:

Treasury stock reissued at a price above cost

Cash..	115,000	
Treasury Stock		90,000
Additional Paid-in Capital: Treasury Stock		25,000
Sold 1,000 shares of treasury stock, which cost $90,000, at a price of $115 per share.		

The $25,000 of additional paid-in capital resulting from the reissuance of Riley's treasury stock is reported in the stockholders' equity section of the company's balance sheet. It appears immediately after additional paid-in capital from common stock, as shown below. For purposes of illustration, we assume that retained earnings increased by $50,000 while the original purchase of treasury stock was held.

Stockholders' equity:	
Common stock, $5 par value, authorized 250,000 shares, issued 100,000 shares (of which 600 are held in treasury)	$ 500,000
Additional paid-in capital:	
Common stock.....................................	800,000
Treasury stock	25,000
Total paid-in capital	$1,325,000
Retained earnings	650,000
Subtotal	$1,975,000
Less: Treasury stock (600 shares of common, at $90 cost)...............	54,000
Total stockholders' equity...........................	$1,921,000

If treasury stock is reissued at a price below cost, additional paid-in capital from previous treasury stock transactions is reduced (debited) by the excess of cost over the reissue price. To illustrate, assume that Riley Corporation later reissues its remaining 600 shares of treasury stock (acquired at a cost of $90 per share) at a price of $75 per share. The entry is:

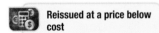
Reissued at a price below cost

Cash..	45,000	
Additional Paid-in Capital: Treasury Stock	9,000	
Treasury Stock		54,000
Sold 600 shares of treasury stock, which cost $54,000, at a price of $75 each.		

If there is no additional paid-in capital from previous treasury stock transactions, the excess of the cost of the treasury shares over the reissue price is recorded as a reduction in Additional Paid-in Capital: Common Stock account. If that account is not sufficient, Retained Earnings is reduced.

Notice that *no gain or loss is recognized on treasury stock transactions,* even when the shares are reissued at a price above or below cost. A corporation earns profits by selling goods and services to outsiders, not by issuing or reissuing shares of its own capital stock. When treasury shares are reissued at a price above cost, the corporation receives from the new stockholder an amount of paid-in capital that is larger than the reduction in stockholders' equity that occurred when the corporation acquired the treasury shares. Conversely, if treasury shares are reissued at a price below cost, the corporation has less paid-in capital as a result of the purchase and reissuance of the shares.

STOCK BUYBACK PROGRAMS

Historically, most treasury stock transactions involved relatively small dollar amounts. Some corporations have buyback programs, in which they repurchase large amounts of their own common stock. As a result of these programs, treasury stock may become a material item in the balance sheets of these corporations.

Transactions between the corporation and its stockholders are classified in the statement of cash flows as *financing activities.* When treasury stock is purchased, a financing cash *outflow* is reported in the statement of cash flows. When treasury stock is reissued, the amount of cash received is reported as a financing cash *inflow* in the statement of cash flows.

Because treasury stock transactions do not give rise to gains or losses, they have no direct effect on the corporation's net income. Any difference between the purchase price of the treasury stock and the cash received when it is reissued is reported as an increase or decrease in the corporation's paid-in capital.

FINANCIAL ANALYSIS and Decision Making

The following information was taken from a recent annual report of **Verizon Communications** (in millions):

Net income...	$ 10,557
Average total assets..	$227,842
Average stockholders' equity...............................	$ 85,721

Several frequently used measures of profitability that are based, in part, on capital stock concepts covered in this chapter can be derived from the above figures:

Profitability Measure	Computation	Significance
Return on total assets	$\dfrac{\text{Net Income}}{\text{Average Total Assets}}$	The rate of return on the total asset investment used to earn that return
Return on stockholders' equity	$\dfrac{\text{Net Income}}{\text{Average Stockholders' Equity}}$	The rate of return earned on the stockholders' equity when the company has only common stock

Using the figures provided, **Verizon**'s profitability measures would be:

Return on total assets:	$10,557 ÷ $227,842 = 4.6%
Return on common shareholders' equity:	$10,557 ÷ $ 85,721 = 12.3%

YOUR TURN You as a Financial Analyst

You are working for a stock market research firm and your boss has asked you to assess **Verizon**'s return on assets and on common shareholders' equity. How might you proceed?

(See our comments on the Online Learning Center website.)

Ethics, Fraud, & Corporate Governance

A learning objective for this chapter is to understand the advantages of organizing a business as a corporation. Corporations often choose to go public in order to raise equity capital from many investors.

Unfortunately, the process of going public can be abused and can result in the defrauding of investors. A common scheme is the use of "shell companies" in a "pump-and-dump scheme." The Securities and Exchange Commission (SEC) defines a shell company as a company with little or no operating activities, little or no assets, or assets consisting solely of cash and cash equivalents. Most commonly, a private operating business is combined with the public shell company in a reverse merger. In a reverse merger, the public shell company is the surviving entity but it is controlled by the shareholders of the previously private business. The rest of the "pump-and-dump scheme" works as follows: (1) The owners (promoters) of the company claim that the previously private business has high growth potential, (2) limited financial and other information on the combined company is filed with the SEC, (3) the owners (promoters) "pump" the stock through unduly positive press releases and other manipulative devices, (4) high-pressure sales tactics are often employed to get individuals to buy the stock, and (5) the owners (promoters) "dump" their stock at artificially high prices.

An example of a stock manipulation scheme using a shell company occurred in the case of **2DoTrade, Inc.** 2DoTrade was a public shell company when a group of promoters secretly acquired over 99 percent of its shares. The promoters

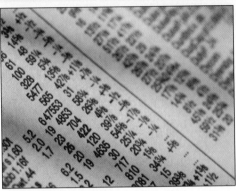

© Royalty-Free/Corbis

merged **2DoTrade** with a private company controlled by a convicted felon. The promoters "pumped" the stock by claiming that the company had import/export contracts worth more than $300 million and that the company was developing an antianthrax compound. In reality, the contracts were worthless because no antianthrax compound was in development, and one was never seriously contemplated. At one point during the "pump" campaign the market value of the company exceeded $46 million, yet the company had no assets and no revenue. The promoters then "dumped" their shares, reaping almost $2 million in profits.

The SEC has brought civil enforcement actions against the promoters of **2DoTrade**, and the FBI has arrested a number of the promoters as criminal charges have also been filed by the U.S. Justice Department.

Concluding Remarks

In this chapter, we covered the aspects of stockholders' equity that result primarily from various transactions between the company and its stockholders, including the sale and repurchase of capital stock. We explored different characteristics of stock, including the unique features of preferred stock.

Another major source of stockholders' equity is the accumulated earnings of previous years that have been retained for purposes of expansion and meeting other business objectives. This is the subject of Chapter 12, which follows. While paid-in capital and retained earnings are two distinct aspects of stockholders' equity, they are closely related and, therefore, are virtually impossible to discuss totally independently of each other. For that reason, in this chapter there were occasional references to retained earnings. Similarly, in Chapter 12 you will find references to common and preferred stock, additional paid-in capital, treasury stock, and other aspects of stockholders' equity that we covered primarily in this chapter. Combining the content of Chapters 11 and 12, you will have a good working knowledge of stockholders' equity and how it fits together with assets and liabilities to form the basis for a company's balance sheet.

END-OF-CHAPTER REVIEW

LO11-1 **Explain the advantages and disadvantages of organizing a business as a corporation.** The primary advantages are no personal liability of stockholders for the debts of the business, the transferability of ownership shares, continuity of existence, the ability to hire professional management, and the relative ease of accumulating large amounts of capital. The primary disadvantages are double taxation of earnings and greater governmental regulation.

LO11-2 **Distinguish between publicly owned and closely held corporations.** The stock of publicly owned corporations is available for purchase by the general public, usually on an organized stock exchange. Stock in a closely held corporation, in contrast, is not available to the public.

Publicly owned corporations tend to be so large that individual stockholders seldom control the corporation; in essence, most stockholders in publicly owned companies are investors, rather than owners in the traditional sense. Closely held corporations usually are quite small, and one or two stockholders often do exercise control. Publicly owned corporations are subject to more government regulation than are closely held companies, and they must disclose to the public much information about their business operations.

LO11-3 **Explain the rights of stockholders and the roles of corporate directors and officers.** Stockholders in a corporation normally have the right to elect the board of directors, to share in dividends declared by the directors, and to share in the distribution of assets if the corporation is liquidated.

The directors formulate company policies, review the actions of the corporate officers, and protect the interests of the company's stockholders. Corporate officers are professional managers appointed by the board of directors to manage the business on a daily basis.

LO11-4 **Account for paid-in capital and prepare the equity section of a corporate balance sheet.** When capital stock is issued, appropriate asset accounts are increased for cash or the market value of the goods or services received in exchange for the stock. A capital stock account (which indicates the type of stock issued) is established or increased for the par value of the issued shares. Any excess of the market value received over the par value of the issued shares is added to an Additional Paid-in Capital account.

The equity section of a corporate balance sheet shows for each class of capital stock outstanding (1) the total par value (legal capital) and (2) any additional paid-in capital. Together, these amounts represent the corporation's total paid-in capital. In addition, the equity section shows separately any earned capital— that is, retained earnings.

LO11-5 **Contrast the features of common stock with those of preferred stock.** Common stock represents the residual ownership of a corporation. These shares have voting rights and cannot be called. Also, the common stock dividend is not fixed in dollar amount—it may increase or decrease based on the company's performance.

Preferred stock has preference over common stock with respect to dividends and to distributions in the event of liquidation. This preference means that preferred stockholders must be paid in full before any dividend payments can be made to holders of common stock. The dividends on preferred stock usually are fixed in amount. In addition, the stock often has no voting rights. Preferred stocks sometimes have special features, such as being convertible into shares of common stock.

LO11-6 **Discuss the factors affecting the market price of preferred stock and common stock.** The market price of preferred stock varies inversely with interest rates. As interest rates rise, preferred stock prices decline; as interest rates fall, preferred stock prices rise. If a company's ability to continue the preferred dividend is in doubt, this may affect preferred stock prices.

Interest rates also affect the market price of common stock. However, common stock dividends are not fixed in amount. Both the amount of the dividend and the market value of the stock may fluctuate, based on the prosperity of the company. Therefore, the principal factor in the market price of common stock is investors' expectations as to the future profitability of the company.

LO11-7 **Explain the significance of book value and market value of capital stock.** Par value has the least significance. It is a legal concept, representing the amount by which stockholders' equity cannot be reduced except by losses. Intended as a buffer for the protection of creditors, it usually is so low as to be of little significance.

Book value per share is the net assets per share of common stock. This value is based on amounts invested by stockholders, plus retained earnings. It often provides insight into the reasonableness of market price.

To investors, market price is the most relevant of the three values. This is the price at which they can buy or sell the stock today. Changes in market price directly affect the financial position of the stockholder, but not of the issuing company. Therefore, market values do not appear in the equity section of the issuing company's balance sheet—but they are readily available in the daily newspaper and on the Internet.

LO11-8 **Explain the purpose and effects of a stock split.** When the market price of a corporation's common stock appreciates in value significantly, it may become too expensive for many investors. When this happens, the corporation may split its stock by increasing the number of its common shares outstanding. The purpose of a stock split is to reduce the market price of the company's common stock, with the intent of making it more affordable to investors. A stock split does not change the balance of any ledger account; consequently, the transaction is recorded merely by a memorandum entry.

LO11-9   Account for treasury stock transactions.
Purchases of treasury stock are recorded by establishing a contra-equity account, Treasury Stock. No profit or loss is recorded when the treasury shares are reissued at a price above or below cost. Rather, any difference between the reissuance price and the cost of the shares is debited or credited to a paid-in capital account. While treasury stock transactions may affect cash flow, they have no effect on the net income of the corporation.

Key Terms Introduced or Emphasized in Chapter 11

Additional Paid-in Capital (p. 491)   An account showing the amounts invested in a corporation by stockholders in excess of par value or stated value. In short, this account shows paid-in capital in excess of legal capital.

board of directors (p. 489)   Persons elected by common stockholders to direct the affairs of a corporation.

book value per share (p. 495)   The stockholders' equity represented by each share of common stock, computed by dividing common stockholders' equity by the number of common shares outstanding.

capital stock (p. 487)   Transferable units of ownership in a corporation. A broad term that can refer to common stock, preferred stock, or both.

closely held corporation (p. 487)   A corporation owned by a small group of stockholders. Not publicly owned.

common stock (p. 492)   A type of capital stock that possesses the basic rights of ownership, including the right to vote. Represents the residual element of ownership in a corporation.

contributed capital (p. 490)   The stockholders' equity that results from capital contributions by investors in exchange for shares of common or preferred stock. Also referred to as paid-in capital.

corporation (p. 486)   A business organized as a legal entity separate from its owners. Chartered by the state with ownership divided into shares of transferable stock. Stockholders are not liable for debts of the corporation.

dividend yield (p. 497)   The annual dividend paid to a share of stock, expressed as a percentage of the stock's market value. Indicates the rate of return represented by the dividend.

dividends (p. 493)   Distribution of assets (usually cash) by a corporation to its stockholders. Normally viewed as a distribution of profits, dividends cannot exceed the amount of retained earnings. Must be formally declared by the board of directors and distributed on a per-share basis. *Note:* Stockholders *cannot* simply withdraw assets from a corporation at will.

double taxation (p. 486)   The fact that corporate income is taxed to the corporation when earned and then again taxed to the stockholders when distributed as dividends.

legal capital (p. 491)   Equal to the par value or stated value of capital stock issued. This amount represents a permanent commitment of capital by the owners of a corporation and cannot be removed without special legal action. Of course, it may be eroded by losses.

limited personal liability (p. 486)   The concept that the owners of a corporation are not personally liable for the debts of the business. Thus stockholders' potential financial losses are limited to the amount of their equity investment.

paid-in capital (p. 490)   The amounts invested in a corporation by its stockholders.

par value (or stated value) (p. 491)   The legal capital of a corporation. Represents the minimum amount per share invested in the corporation by its owners and cannot be withdrawn except by special legal action.

preferred stock (p. 492)   A class of capital stock usually having preferences as to dividends and in the distribution of assets in the event of liquidation.

public information (p. 487)   Information that, by law, must be made available to the general public. Includes the quarterly and annual financial statements—and other financial information—about publicly owned corporations.

publicly owned corporation (p. 487)   Any corporation whose shares are offered for sale to the general public.

retained earnings (p. 490)   The element of owners' equity in a corporation that has accumulated through profitable business operations. Net income increases retained earnings; net losses and dividends reduce retained earnings.

state of incorporation (p. 488)   The state in which the corporation is legally formed. This may or may not be the state in which the corporation conducts most or any of its business.

stock certificate (p. 488)   A document issued by a corporation (or its transfer agent) as evidence of the ownership of the number of shares stated on the certificate.

stock registrar (p. 490)   An independent fiscal agent, such as a bank, retained by a corporation to provide assurance against overissuance of stock certificates.

stock split (p. 498)   An increase in the number of shares outstanding with a corresponding decrease in par value per share. The additional shares are distributed proportionately to all common shareholders. The purpose of a stock split is to reduce market price per share and encourage wider public ownership of the company's stock. For example, 2-for-1 stock split will give each stockholder twice as many shares as previously owned.

stock transfer agent (p. 490)   A bank or trust company retained by a corporation to maintain its records of capital stock ownership and make transfers from one investor to another.

stockholders (p. 486)   The owners of a corporation. The name reflects the fact that their ownership is evidenced by transferable shares of capital stock.

stockholders subsidiary ledger (p. 490)   A record showing the number of shares owned by each stockholder.

treasury stock (p. 499)   Shares of a corporation's stock that have been issued and then reacquired, but not canceled.

underwriter (p. 490)   An investment banking firm that handles the sale of a corporation's stock to the public.

Demonstration Problem

The stockholders' equity section of Elmwood Corporation's balance sheet appears as follows:

Stockholders' equity:

8% preferred stock, $100 par value, 200,000 shares authorized		$12,000,000
Common stock, $5 par value, 5,000,000 shares authorized		14,000,000
Additional paid-in capital:		
Preferred stock	$ 360,000	
Common stock	30,800,000	31,160,000
Retained earnings		3,680,000
Total stockholders' equity.		$60,840,000

Instructions

On the basis of this information, answer the following questions and show any necessary supporting computations:

a. How many shares of preferred stock have been issued?

b. What is the total annual dividend requirement on the outstanding preferred stock?

c. How many shares of common stock have been issued?

d. What was the average price per share received by the corporation for its common stock?

e. What is the total amount of legal capital?

f. What is the total paid-in capital?

g. What is the book value per share of common stock? (Assume no dividends in arrears and round to the nearest cent.)

Solution to the Demonstration Problem

a. 120,000 shares ($12,000,000 total par value, divided by $100 par value per share)

b. $960,000 (120,000 shares outstanding × $8 per share)

c. 2,800,000 shares ($14,000,000 total par value, divided by $5 par value per share)

d.

Par value of common shares issued	$14,000,000
Additional paid-in capital on common shares	30,800,000
Total issue price of common shares	$44,800,000
Number of common shares issued (part **c**)	2,800,000
Average issue price per share ($44,800,000 ÷ 2,800,000 shares)	$ 16

e. $26,000,000 ($12,000,000 preferred, $14,000,000 common)

f. $57,160,000 ($26,000,000 legal capital, plus $31,160,000 additional paid-in capital)

g.

Total stockholders' equity	$60,840,000
Less: Claims of preferred stockholders (120,000 shares × $100).	12,000,000
Equity of common stockholders	$48,840,000
Number of common shares outstanding (part **c**)	2,800,000
Book value per share ($47,840,000 ÷ 2,800,000 shares)	$ 17.44

Self-Test Questions

The answers to these questions appear on page 520.

1. When a business is organized as a corporation, which of the following statements is true?

   a. Stockholders are liable for the debts of the business in proportion to their percentage ownership of capital stock.

   b. Fluctuations in the market value of outstanding shares of capital stock do *not* directly affect the amount of stockholders' equity shown in the balance sheet.

   c. Stockholders do *not* have to pay personal income taxes on dividends received, because the corporation is subject to income taxes on its earnings.

   d. Each stockholder has the right to bind the corporation to contracts and to make other managerial decisions.

2. Morgan Moving Corporation was organized with authorization to issue 100,000 shares of $1 par value common stock. Forty thousand shares were issued to Tom Morgan, the company's founder, at a price of $5 per share. No other shares have yet been issued. Which of the following statements is true?

   a. Morgan owns *40 percent* of the stockholders' equity of the corporation.

   b. The corporation should recognize a $160,000 gain on the issuance of these shares.

   c. If the balance sheet includes retained earnings of $50,000, total *paid-in* capital amounts to $250,000.

   d. In the balance sheet, the Additional Paid-in Capital account will have a $160,000 balance, regardless of the profits earned or losses incurred since the corporation was organized.

3. Which of the following is *not* a characteristic of the *common stock* of a large, publicly owned corporation?

   a. A cumulative right to receive dividends.

   b. The shares may be transferred from one investor to another without disrupting the continuity of business operations.

   c. Voting rights in the election of the board of directors.

   d. After issuance, the market value of the stock is unrelated to its par value.

4. Tri-State Electric is a profitable utility company that has increased its dividend to *common* stockholders every year for 42 consecutive years. Which of the following is *least* likely to affect the market price of the company's *preferred* stock by a significant amount?

   a. A decrease in long-term interest rates.

   b. An increase in long-term interest rates.

   c. The board of directors announces its intention to increase common stock dividends in the current year.

   d. Whether or not the preferred stock carries a conversion privilege.

5. The following information is taken from the balance sheet and related disclosures of Filsor, Inc.:

Total paid-in capital	$5,400,000
Outstanding shares:	
Common stock, $5 par value	100,000 shares
6% preferred stock, $100 par value	10,000 shares
Preferred dividends in arrears	2 years
Total stockholders' equity	$4,700,000

   Which of the following statements is (are) true? (For this question, more than one answer may be correct.)

   a. The preferred dividends in arrears amount to $120,000 and should appear as a liability in the corporate balance sheet.

   b. The book value per share of common stock is $35.

   c. The stockholders' equity section of the balance sheet should indicate a deficit (negative amount in retained earnings) of $700,000.

   d. The company has paid no dividend on its *common* stock during the past two years.

6. On December 10, 2014, Smitty Corporation reacquired 2,000 shares of its own $5 par value common stock at a price of $60 per share. In 2015, 500 of the treasury shares are reissued at a price of $70 per share. Which of the following statements is correct?

   a. The treasury stock purchased is recorded at cost and is shown in Smitty's December 31, 2014, balance sheet as an asset.

   b. The two treasury stock transactions result in an overall net reduction in Smitty's stockholders' equity of $85,000.

   c. Smitty's stockholders' equity was increased by $110,000 when the treasury stock was acquired.

   d. Smitty recognizes a gain of $10 per share on the reissuance of the 500 treasury shares in 2015.

ASSIGNMENT MATERIAL | # Discussion Questions

1. Why are large corporations often described as *publicly owned?*

2. Distinguish between corporations and sole proprietorships in terms of the following characteristics:

   a. Owners' liability for debts of the business.

   b. Transferability of ownership interest.

   c. Continuity of existence.

   d. Federal taxation on income.

3. Distinguish between *paid-in capital* and *retained earnings* of a corporation. Why is such a distinction useful?

4. Explain the significance of *par value*. Does par value indicate the reasonable market price for a share of stock? Explain.

5. Describe the usual nature of the following features as they apply to a share of preferred stock: (a) cumulative, and (b) convertible.

6. Why is noncumulative preferred stock often considered an unattractive form of investment?

7. State the balance sheet or income statement classification (asset, liability, stockholders' equity, revenue, or expense) of each of the following accounts:

   a. Cash (received from the issuance of capital stock).

   b. Organization Costs.

   c. Preferred Stock.

   d. Retained Earnings.

   e. Additional Paid-in Capital.

   f. Income Taxes Payable.

8. What does *book value per share* of common stock represent? Does it represent the amount common stockholders would receive in the event of liquidation of the corporation? Explain briefly.

9. What would be the effect, if any, on book value per share of common stock as a result of each of the following independent events: (**a**) A corporation obtains a bank loan; (**b**) a dividend is declared (to be paid in the next accounting period)?

10. In the stock market crash of October 19, 1987, the market price of **IBM**'s capital stock fell by over $31 per share. Explain the effects, if any, of this decline in share price on **IBM**'s balance sheet.

11. What is the purpose of a *stock split?*

12. What is *treasury stock?* Why do corporations purchase their own shares? Is treasury stock an asset? How should it be reported in the balance sheet?

13. In many states, corporation law requires that retained earnings be restricted for dividend purposes to the extent of the cost of treasury shares. What is the reason for this legal rule?

14. The basic accounting equation for a corporation is **Assets = Liabilities + Stockholders' Equity.** Stockholders' equity is further divided into two categories: paid-in capital and retained earnings. What are the major transactions and other financial activities that impact the amount of paid-in capital of a corporation? Identify for each major type of transaction or activity whether it increases or decreases the amount of paid-in capital.

15. If you were going to start a corporation and expected to need to raise capital from several investors, would you include preferred stock in your capital structure? Why or why not? If your answer is that you would include preferred stock, what features would you incorporate into this class of stock?

Brief Exercises

LO11-4

BRIEF EXERCISE 11.1

Stockholders' Equity

Omega Co. sold 10,000 shares of common stock, which has a par value of $8, for $13 per share. The company's balance in retained earnings is $75,000. Prepare the stockholders' equity section of the company's balance sheet.

LO11-4

BRIEF EXERCISE 11.2

Stockholders' Equity

Beta Co. sold 10,000 shares of common stock, which has a par value of $25, for $28 per share. The company also sold 1,000 shares of $100 par value preferred stock for $110. Assume the balance in retained earnings is $80,000. Prepare the stockholders' equity section of Beta's balance sheet.

LO11-5

BRIEF EXERCISE 11.3

Dividends on Preferred Stock

Zeta Co. has outstanding 100,000 shares of $100 par value cumulative preferred stock which has a dividend rate of 7 percent. The company has not declared any cash dividends on the preferred stock for the last three years. Calculate the amount of dividends in arrears for the last three years on Zeta's preferred stock and briefly explain how this amount will be known to investors and creditors who may use the company's financial statements.

LO11-5

BRIEF EXERCISE 11.4

Dividends on Common and Preferred Stock

Mega, Inc., has common and 6 percent preferred stock outstanding as follows:

   Preferred stock: 10,000 shares, $100 par value, cumulative
   Common stock: 50,000 shares, $50 par value

The company declares a total dividend of $225,000. If the dividends on preferred stock are one year in arrears (in addition to the current year), how will the total dividend be divided between the common and preferred stock?

LO11-5

BRIEF EXERCISE 11.5

Dividends on Common and Preferred Stock

Baker Company has common and preferred stock outstanding as follows:

   Common stock: 100,000 shares, $30 par value
   8 percent preferred stock: 10,000 shares, $100 par value

Dividends on preferred stock have not been paid for the last three years (in addition to the current year). If the company pays a total of $120,000 in dividends, how much will the common stockholders receive per share if the preferred stock is not cumulative? How will your answer differ if the preferred stock is cumulative?

LO11-7
BRIEF EXERCISE 11.6
Book Value

Menza Company has stockholders' equity accounts as follows:

Common stock (100,000 shares @ $10 par value)......................	$1,000,000
Additional paid-in capital on common stock..........................	750,000
Retained earnings	800,000

Calculate the amount of book value per share for common stock and summarize briefly what that figure means in relation to the current market value of the stock.

LO11-7
BRIEF EXERCISE 11.7
Book Value

Franks, Inc., has preferred and common stock outstanding as follows:

$5 preferred stock, 40,000 shares @ $100 par value....................	$4,000,000
Common stock, 500,000 shares at $10 par value	5,000,000
Additional paid-in capital on common stock..........................	800,000
Retained earnings	1,750,000

Calculate the book value on common stock, assuming preferred dividends are cumulative and are currently one year in arrears.

LO11-8
BRIEF EXERCISE 11.8
Stock Split

Smelling Company declared a 2-for-1 stock split on its common stock in order to intentionally reduce the market value of its stock so that it would be an attractive investment for a larger set of investors. The company's common stock is described as follows:

Common stock: 100,000 shares outstanding, $10 par value, originally sold at $12.50, current market price $50.

Describe the likely impact, if any, that the 2-for-1 stock split will have on **(a)** the number of shares outstanding, **(b)** the market price of the stock, and **(c)** the total stockholders' equity attributable to common stock.

LO11-4, LO11-9
BRIEF EXERCISE 11.9
Treasury Stock

Melcher, Inc., originally sold 100,000 shares of its $10 par value common stock at $25 per share. Several years later the company repurchased 10,000 of these shares at $57 per share. Melcher currently holds those shares in treasury. Prepare the company's stockholders' equity section of the balance sheet to reflect this information.

LO11-4, LO11-9
BRIEF EXERCISE 11.10
Treasury Stock

Weller, Inc., sold 1,000,000 shares of $25 par value common stock at $32. It subsequently repurchased 100,000 of those shares at $50 per share and then sold 70,000 of those shares at $55. Calculate the total amount of stockholders' equity given the above transactions.

Exercises

LO11-1 through LO11-3
EXERCISE 11.1
Form of Organization

Assume that you have recently obtained your scuba instructor's certification and have decided to start a scuba diving school.

a. Describe the advantages and disadvantages of organizing your scuba diving school as a:
   1. Sole proprietorship
   2. Corporation
b. State your opinion about which form of organization would be best and explain the basis for your opinion.

LO11-1 through LO11-9
EXERCISE 11.2
Accounting Terminology

Listed below are 12 technical accounting terms discussed in this chapter:

Par value	Board of directors	Double taxation
Book value	Paid-in capital	Dividends in arrears

Market value	Preferred stock	Closely held corporation
Retained earnings	Common stock	Publicly owned corporation

Each of the following statements may (or may not) describe one of these technical terms. For each statement, indicate the term described, or answer "None" if the statement does not correctly describe any of the terms.

a. A major *disadvantage* of the corporate form of organization.

b. From investors' point of view, the most important value associated with capital stock.

c. Cash available for distribution to the stockholders.

d. The class of capital stock that normally has the most voting power.

e. A distribution of assets that may be made in future years to the holders of common stock.

f. A corporation whose shares are traded on an organized stock exchange.

g. Equity arising from investments by owners.

h. The element of stockholders' equity that is increased by net income.

i. Total assets divided by the number of common shares outstanding.

j. The class of stock for which market price normally rises as interest rates increase.

LO11-4, LO11-5

EXERCISE 11.3

Stockholders' Equity Section of a Balance Sheet

When Resisto Systems, Inc., was formed, the company was authorized to issue 5,000 shares of $100 par value, 8 percent cumulative preferred stock, and 100,000 shares of $2 stated value common stock.

Half of the preferred stock was issued at a price of $103 per share, and 70,000 shares of the common stock were sold for $13 per share. At the end of the current year, Resisto has retained earnings of $475,000.

a. Prepare the stockholders' equity section of the company's balance sheet at the end of the current year.

b. Assume Resisto Systems's common stock is trading at $24 per share and its preferred stock is trading at $107 per share at the end of the current year. Would the stockholders' equity section prepared in part **a** be affected by this additional information?

LO11-4, LO11-5

EXERCISE 11.4

Dividends: Preferred and Common

A portion of the stockholders' equity section from the balance sheet of Walland Corporation appears as follows:

Stockholders' equity:

Preferred stock, 9% cumulative, $50 par, 40,000 shares authorized, issued, and outstanding	$2,000,000
Preferred stock, 12% noncumulative, $100 par, 8,000 shares authorized, issued, and outstanding	800,000
Common stock, $5 par, 400,000 shares authorized, issued, and outstanding	2,000,000
Total paid-in capital	$4,800,000

Assume that all the stock was issued on January 1 and that no dividends were paid during the first two years of operation. During the third year, Walland Corporation paid total cash dividends of $736,000.

a. Compute the amount of cash dividends paid during the third year to each of the three classes of stock.

b. Compute the dividends paid *per share* during the third year for each of the three classes of stock.

LO11-4 through LO11-7

EXERCISE 11.5

Analyzing Stockholders' Equity

c. What was the average issue price of each type of preferred stock?

The year-end balance sheet of Columbus Products, Inc., includes the following stockholders' equity section (with certain details omitted):

Stockholders' equity:

Capital stock:

7% cumulative preferred stock, $100 par value	$ 15,000,000
Common stock, $5 par value, 5,000,000 shares authorized, 4,000,000 shares issued and outstanding..............	20,000,000
Additional paid-in capital:	
Common stock...	44,000,000
Retained earnings	64,450,000
Total stockholders' equity..................................	$143,450,000

From this information, compute answers to the following questions:

a. How many shares of preferred stock have been issued?

b. What is the total amount of the annual dividends to which preferred stockholders are entitled?

c. What was the average issuance price per share of common stock?

d. What is the amount of legal capital and the amount of total paid-in capital?

e. What is the book value per share of common stock, assuming no dividends in arrears?

f. Is it possible to determine the fair market value per share of common stock from the stockholders' equity section above? Explain.

LO11-5, LO11-6

EXERCISE 11.6

Preferred Stock Alternatives

Easy Moncy, Inc., has the following capital structure:

Preferred stock—$25 par value, 10,000 shares authorized, 7,000 shares issued and outstanding	$ 175,000
Common stock—$10 par value, 100,000 shares authorized, 80,000 shares issued and outstanding	800,000
Total paid-in capital	$ 975,000
Retained earnings	550,000
Total stockholders' equity	$1,525,000

The number of issued and outstanding shares of both preferred and common stock have been the same for the last two years. Dividends on preferred stock are 8 percent of par value and have been paid each year the stock was outstanding except for the immediate past year. In the current year, management declares a total dividend of $60,000. Indicate the amount that will be paid to both preferred and common stockholders assuming (**a**) the preferred stock is not cumulative and (**b**) the preferred stock is cumulative.

LO11-4, LO11-7

EXERCISE 11.7

Reporting the Effects of Transactions

Three events pertaining to Lean Machine Co. are described below.

a. Issued common stock for cash.

b. The market value of the corporation's stock increased.

c. Declared and paid a cash dividend to stockholders.

Indicate the immediate effects of the events on the financial measurements in the four columnar headings listed below. Use the code letters **I** for increase, **D** for decrease, and **NE** for no effect.

Event	Current Assets	Stockholders' Equity	Net Income	Net Cash Flow (from any source)
a				

LO11-4 through LO11-7

EXERCISE 11.8

Computing Book Value

The following information is necessary to compute the net assets (stockholders' equity) and book value per share of common stock for Rothchild Corporation:

8% cumulative preferred stock, $100 par	$200,000
Common stock, $5 par, authorized 100,000 shares, issued 60,000 shares	300,000
Additional paid-in capital	452,800
Deficit (negative amount in retained earnings)	146,800
Dividends in arrears on preferred stock, 1 full year	16,000

a. Compute the amount of net assets (stockholders' equity).

b. Compute the book value per share of common stock.

c. Is book value per share (answer to part **b**) the amount common stockholders should expect to receive if Rothchild Corporation were to cease operations and liquidate? Explain.

LO11-9

EXERCISE 11.9

Recording Treasury Stock Transactions

Johnston, Inc., engaged in the following transactions involving treasury stock:

Feb. 10 Purchased for cash 17,000 shares of treasury stock at a price of $25 per share.

June 4 Reissued 6,000 shares of treasury stock at a price of $33 per share.

Dec. 22 Reissued 4,000 shares of treasury stock at a price of $22 per share.

a. Prepare general journal entries to record these transactions.

b. Compute the amount of retained earnings that should be restricted because of the treasury stock still owned at December 31.

c. Does a restriction on retained earnings affect the dollar amount of retained earnings reported in the balance sheet? Explain briefly.

LO11-8

EXERCISE 11.10

Effects of a Stock Split

The common stock of Fido Corporation was trading at $45 per share on October 15, 2014. A year later, on October 15, 2015, it was trading at $80 per share. On this date, Fido's board of directors decided to split the company's common stock.

a. If the company decides on a 2-for-1 split, at what price would you expect the stock to trade immediately after the split goes into effect?

b. If the company decides on a 4-for-1 split, at what price would you expect the stock to trade immediately after the split goes into effect?

c. Why do you think Fido's board of directors decided to split the company's stock?

LO11-9

EXERCISE 11.11

Treasury Stock Presentation

Ashton Company was experiencing financial difficulty late in the current year. The company's income was sluggish, and the market price of its common stock was tumbling. On December 21, the company began to buy back shares of its own stock in an attempt to boost its market price per share and to improve its earnings per share.

a. Is it unethical for a company to purchase shares of its own stock to improve measures of financial performance? Defend your answer.

b. Assume that the company classified the shares of treasury stock as short-term investments in the current asset section of its balance sheet. Is this appropriate? Explain.

LO11-4

EXERCISE 11.12

Authorized Stock

The 2012 balance sheet for Kimberly-Clark Corporation indicates that the company has 1.2 billion shares of common stock authorized, of which approximately 428.6 million have been issued. In addition, the company holds 39.3 million shares in treasury.

a. How many additional shares of common stock could Kimberly-Clark sell?

b. How are the shares that have not yet been issued included in the company's balance sheet? Do they represent an asset of the company?

LO11-4, LO11-9

EXERCISE 11.13

Accounting Terminology

Minor Company, is authorized to sell 1,200,000 shares of $10 par value common stock and 60,000 shares of $100 par value 6 percent preferred stock. As of the end of the current year, the company has actually sold 550,000 shares of common stock at $12 per share and 40,000 shares of preferred stock at $110 per share. In addition, of the 550,000 shares of common that have been sold, 25,000 shares have been repurchased at $23 per share and are currently being held in treasury to be used to meet the future requirements of a stock option plan that the company intends to implement.

a. Prepare the general journal entries required to record all of the above transactions.

b. Prepare the stockholders' equity section of Minor's balance sheet to reflect the transactions you have recorded.

LOII-8, LOII-9
EXERCISE 11.14
Treasury Stock and Stock Split

Twin Towns, Inc., was authorized to issue 300,000 shares of common stock and originally issued 100,000 shares of $10 par value stock at $18 per share. Subsequently, 25,000 shares were repurchased at $20, of which 10,000 were subsequently resold at $23.

Assume the company's retained earnings balance is $120,000.

a. Prepare the stockholders' equity section of Twin Towns's balance sheet, including all appropriate disclosures.

b. Briefly explain how the declaration and distribution of a 2-for-1 stock split subsequent to the above transactions would affect the stockholders' equity section you have prepared.

LOII-4, LOII-7
EXERCISE 11.15
Using the **Home Depot, Inc.,** Financial Statements

The financial statements of **Home Depot, Inc.,** appear in Appendix A of this text. These statements contain information describing the details of the company's stockholders' equity.

a. What is the par value of the company's common stock? Did the common stock originally sell at, above, or below par value? How do you know this?

b. For the most current year shown, how many shares of common stock are authorized? What is the meaning of "authorized shares"?

c. What is the total stockholders' equity amount for **Home Depot** for the most recent year reported? Does this figure mean that the total outstanding stock is actually worth this amount? Explain your answer.

Problem Set A

LOII-4 through LOII-6
PROBLEM 11.1A
Stockholders' Equity in a Balance Sheet

Early in 2012, Robbinsville Press was organized with authorization to issue 100,000 shares of $100 par value preferred stock and 500,000 shares of $1 par value common stock. Ten thousand shares of the preferred stock were issued at par, and 170,000 shares of common stock were sold for $15 per share. The preferred stock pays an 8 percent cumulative dividend.

During the first four years of operations (2012 through 2015), the corporation earned a total of $1,385,000 and paid dividends of 75 cents per share in each year on its outstanding common stock.

Instructions

a. Prepare the stockholders' equity section of the balance sheet at December 31, 2015. Include a supporting schedule showing your computation of the amount of retained earnings reported. (Hint: Income increases retained earnings, whereas dividends decrease retained earnings.)

b. Are there any dividends in arrears on the company's preferred stock at December 31, 2015? Explain your answer.

LOII-4 through LOII-6
PROBLEM 11.2A
Stockholders' Equity Section

McMinn Publications was organized early in 2010 with authorization to issue 20,000 shares of $100 par value preferred stock and 1 million shares of $1 par value common stock. All of the preferred stock was issued at par, and 300,000 shares of common stock were sold for $20 per share. The preferred stock pays a 10 percent cumulative dividend.

During the first five years of operations (2010 through 2014) the corporation earned a total of $4,560,000 and paid dividends of $1 per share each year on the common stock. In 2015, however, the corporation reported a net loss of $1,825,000 and paid no dividends.

Instructions

a. Prepare the stockholders' equity section of the balance sheet at December 31, 2015. Include a supporting schedule showing your computation of retained earnings at the balance sheet date. (Hint: Income increases retained earnings, whereas dividends and net losses decrease retained earnings.)

b. Draft a note to accompany the financial statements disclosing any dividends in arrears at the end of 2015.

LOII-4 through LOII-6
PROBLEM 11.3A
Stockholders' Equity in a Balance Sheet

c. Do the dividends in arrears appear as a liability of the corporation as of the end of 2015? Explain.

Maria Martinez organized Manhattan Transport Company in January 2012. The corporation immediately issued at $8 per share one-half of its 200,000 authorized shares of $2 par value common stock. On January 2, 2013, the corporation sold at par value the entire 5,000 authorized shares of 8 percent, $100 par value cumulative preferred stock. On January 2, 2014, the company again needed capital and issued 5,000 shares of an authorized 10,000 shares of no-par cumulative preferred stock for a total of $512,000. The no-par shares have a stated dividend of $9 per share.

The company declared no dividends in 2012 and 2013. At the end of 2013, its retained earnings were $170,000. During 2014 and 2015 combined, the company earned a total of $890,000. Dividends of 50 cents per share in 2014 and $1.60 per share in 2015 were paid on the common stock.

Instructions

a. Prepare the stockholders' equity section of the balance sheet at December 31, 2015. Include a supporting schedule showing your computation of retained earnings at the balance sheet date. (Hint: Income increases retained earnings, whereas dividends decrease retained earnings.)

b. Assume that on January 2, 2013, the corporation could have borrowed $500,000 at 8 percent interest on a long-term basis instead of issuing the 5,000 shares of the $100 par value cumulative preferred stock. Identify two reasons a corporation may choose to issue cumulative preferred stock rather than finance operations with long-term debt.

LOII-4, LOII-5
PROBLEM 11.4A
Stockholders' Equity: A Short Comprehensive Problem

Early in the year Bill Sharnes and several friends organized a corporation called Sharnes Communications, Inc. The corporation was authorized to issue 50,000 shares of $100 par value, 10 percent cumulative preferred stock and 400,000 shares of $2 par value common stock. The following transactions (among others) occurred during the year:

Jan. 6	Issued for cash 20,000 shares of common stock at $14 per share. The shares were issued to Sharnes and 10 other investors.
Jan. 7	Issued an additional 500 shares of common stock to Sharnes in exchange for his services in organizing the corporation. The stockholders agreed that these services were worth $7,000.
Jan. 12	Issued 2,500 shares of preferred stock for cash of $250,000.
June 4	Acquired land as a building site in exchange for 15,000 shares of common stock. In view of the appraised value of the land and the progress of the company, the directors agreed that the common stock was to be valued for purposes of this transaction at $15 per share.
Nov. 15	The first annual dividend of $10 per share was declared on the preferred stock to be paid December 20.
Dec. 20	Paid the cash dividend declared on November 15.
Dec. 31	After the revenue and expenses were closed into the Income Summary account, that account indicated a net income of $147,200.

Instructions

a. Prepare journal entries in general journal form to record the above transactions. Include entries at December 31 to close the Income Summary account and the Dividends account.

b. Prepare the stockholders' equity section of the Sharnes Communications, Inc., balance sheet at December 31.

LOII-4, LOII-5
PROBLEM 11.5A
Analysis of an Equity Section of a Balance Sheet

The year-end balance sheet of Ft. Smith Products includes the following stockholders' equity section (with certain details omitted):

Stockholders' equity:	
7½% cumulative preferred stock, $100 par value, 100,000 shares authorized	$ 2,400,000
Common stock, $2 par value, 900,000 shares authorized	900,000
Additional paid-in capital: common stock	8,325,000
Retained earnings	2,595,000
Total stockholders' equity	$14,220,000

Instructions

From this information, compute answers to the following questions:

a. How many shares of preferred stock have been issued?

b. What is the total amount of the annual dividends paid to preferred stockholders?

   c. How many shares of common stock are outstanding?

   d. What was the average issuance price per share of common stock?

   e. What is the amount of legal capital?

   f. What is the total amount of paid-in capital?

   g. What is the book value per share of common stock? (There are no dividends in arrears.)

   h. Assume that retained earnings at the beginning of the year amounted to $717,500 and that net income for the year was $3,970,000. What was the dividend declared during the year on *each share* of common stock? (Hint: Net income increases retained earnings, whereas dividends decrease retained earnings.)

LO11-1 through LO11-7

PROBLEM 11.6A

Analysis of an Equity Section—More Comprehensive

Parsons, Inc., is a publicly owned company. The following information is excerpted from a recent balance sheet. Dollar amounts (except for per share amounts) are stated in thousands.

Stockholders' equity:	
Convertible $17.20 preferred stock, $250 par value, 1,000,000 shares authorized; 345,000 shares issued and outstanding	$ 86,250
Common stock, par value $0.50; 25,000,000 shares authorized.	6,819
Additional paid-in capital	87,260
Retained earnings	57,263
Total stockholders' equity.	$237,592

Instructions

From this information, answer the following questions:

   a. How many shares of common stock have been issued?

   b. What is the total amount of the annual dividends paid to preferred stockholders?

   c. What is the total amount of paid-in capital?

   d. What is the book value per share of common stock, assuming no dividends in arrears?

   e. Briefly explain the advantages and disadvantages to Parsons of being publicly owned rather than operating as a closely held corporation.

   f. What is meant by the term *convertible* used in the caption of the preferred stock? Is there any more information that investors need to know to evaluate this conversion feature?

   g. Assume that the preferred stock currently is selling at *$248* per share. Does this provide a higher or lower dividend yield than an 8 percent, $50 par value preferred with a market price of $57 per share? Show computations (round to the nearest tenth of 1 percent). Explain why one preferred stock might yield less than another.

LO11-4, LO11-7

PROBLEM 11.7A

Par, Book, and Market Values

Techno Corporation is the producer of popular business software. Recently, an investment service published the following per-share amounts relating to the company's only class of stock:

Par value	$ 0.001
Book value (estimated)	6.50
Market value	$ 65.00

Instructions

   a. Without reference to dollar amounts, explain the nature and significance of *par value, book value,* and *market value.*

   b. Comment on the *relationships,* if any, among the per-share amounts shown for the company. What do these amounts imply about Techno Corporation and its operations? Comment on what these amounts imply about the security of *creditors'* claims against the company.

LO11-4, LO11-5, LO11-7,
LO11-9
PROBLEM 11.8A
Reporting Stockholders'
Equity with Treasury Stock

Early in 2013, Feller Corporation was formed with authorization to issue 50,000 shares of $1 par value common stock. All shares were issued at a price of $8 per share. The corporation reported net income of $95,000 in 2013, $27,500 in 2014, and $75,700 in 2015. No dividends were declared in any of these three years.

In 2014, the company purchased its own shares for $35,000 in the open market. In 2015, it reissued all of its treasury stock for $40,000.

Instructions

a. Prepare the stockholders' equity section of the balance sheet at December 31, 2015. Include a supporting schedule showing your computation of retained earnings at the balance sheet date. (Hint: Income increases retained earnings.)

b. As of December 31, compute the company's book value per share of common stock.

c. Explain how the treasury stock transactions in 2014 and 2015 were reported in the company's statement of cash flows.

LO11-4, LO11-5, LO11-7
through LO11-9
PROBLEM 11.9A
Reporting Stockholders'
Equity with Treasury Stock
and Stock Splits

Early in 2011, Herndon Industries was formed with authorization to issue 250,000 shares of $10 par value common stock and 30,000 shares of $100 par value cumulative preferred stock. During 2011, all the preferred stock was issued at par, and 120,000 shares of common stock were sold for $16 per share. The preferred stock is entitled to a dividend equal to 10 percent of its par value before any dividends are paid on the common stock.

During its first five years of business (2011 through 2015), the company earned income totaling $3,700,000 and paid dividends of 50 cents per share each year on the common stock outstanding.

On January 2, 2013, the company purchased 20,000 shares of its own common stock in the open market for $400,000. On January 2, 2015, it reissued 10,000 shares of this treasury stock for $250,000. The remaining 10,000 were still held in treasury at December 31, 2015.

Instructions

a. Prepare the stockholders' equity section of the balance sheet for Herndon Industries at December 31, 2015. Include supporting schedules showing (1) your computation of any paid-in capital on treasury stock and (2) retained earnings at the balance sheet date. (Hint: Income increases retained earnings, whereas dividends reduce retained earnings. Dividends are not paid on shares of stock held in treasury.)

b. As of December 31, compute Herndon's book value per share of common stock. (Hint: Book value per share is computed only on the shares of stock outstanding.)

c. At December 31, 2015, shares of the company's common stock were trading at $30. Explain what would have happened to the market price per share had the company split its stock 3-for-1 at this date. Also explain what would have happened to the par value of the common stock and to the number of common shares outstanding.

Problem Set B

LO11-4 through LO11-6
PROBLEM 11.1B
Stockholders' Equity in a
Balance Sheet

Early in 2012, Searfoss, Inc., was organized with authorization to issue 2,000 shares of $100 par value preferred stock and 300,000 shares of $1 par value common stock. Five hundred shares of the preferred stock were issued at par, and 80,000 shares of common stock were sold at $15 per share. The preferred stock pays a 10 percent cumulative dividend.

During the first four years of operations (2012 through 2015), the corporation earned a total of $1,950,000 and paid dividends of 40 cents per share in each year on its outstanding common stock.

Instructions

a. Prepare the stockholders' equity section of the balance sheet at December 31, 2015. Include a supporting schedule showing your computation of the amount of retained earnings reported. Assume the call price of preferred stock is $110 per share as of December 31, 2015. (Hint: Income increases retained earnings, whereas dividends decrease retained earnings.)

b. Are there any dividends in arrears on the company's preferred stock at December 31, 2015? Explain your answer.

c. Assume that interest rates increase steadily from 2012 through 2015. Would you expect the market price of the company's preferred stock to be higher or lower than its call price of $110 at December 21, 2015? (The call price is the amount the company must pay to repurchase the shares from the stockholders.)

LO11-4 through LO11-6
PROBLEM 11.2B
Stockholders' Equity
Section

Banner Publications was organized early in 2012 with authorization to issue 10,000 shares of $100 par value preferred stock and 1 million shares of $1 par value common stock. All of the preferred stock was issued at par, and 400,000 shares of common stock were sold for $15 per share. The preferred stock pays a 10 percent cumulative dividend.

During the first five years of operations (2010 through 2014) the corporation earned a total of $4,100,000 and paid dividends of $.80 per share each year on the common stock. In 2015, however, the corporation reported a net loss of $1,250,000 and paid no dividends.

Instructions

a. Prepare the stockholders' equity section of the balance sheet at December 31, 2015. Include a supporting schedule showing your computation of retained earnings at the balance sheet date. (Hint: Income increases retained earnings, whereas dividends and net losses decrease retained earnings.)

b. Draft a note to accompany the financial statements disclosing any dividends in arrears at the end of 2015.

c. Do the dividends in arrears appear as a liability of the corporation as of the end of 2015? Explain.

LO11-4 through LO11-6
PROBLEM 11.3B
Stockholders' Equity in a
Balance Sheet

Joy Sun organized Ray Beam, Inc., in January 2012. The corporation immediately issued at $15 per share one-half of its 260,000 authorized shares of $1 par value common stock. On January 2, 2013, the corporation sold at par value the entire 10,000 authorized shares of 10 percent, $100 par value cumulative preferred stock. On January 2, 2014, the company again needed capital and issued 5,000 shares of an authorized 8,000 shares of no-par cumulative preferred stock for a total of $320,000. The no-par shares have a stated dividend of $6 per share.

The company declared no dividends in 2012 and 2013. At the end of 2013, its retained earnings were $530,000. During 2014 and 2015 combined, the company earned a total of $1,400,000. Dividends of 90 cents per share in 2014 and $2 per share in 2015 were paid on the common stock.

Instructions

a. Prepare the stockholders' equity section of the balance sheet at December 31, 2015. Include a supporting schedule showing your computation of retained earnings at the balance sheet date. (Hint: Income increases retained earnings, whereas dividends decrease retained earnings.)

b. Assume that on January 2, 2013, the corporation could have borrowed $1,000,000 at 10 percent interest on a long-term basis instead of issuing the 10,000 shares of the $100 par value cumulative preferred stock. Identify two reasons a corporation may choose to issue cumulative preferred stock rather than finance operations with long-term debt.

LO11-4, LO11-5
PROBLEM 11.4B
Stockholders' Equity: A
Short Comprehensive
Problem

Early in the year Debra Deal and several friends organized a corporation called Markup, Inc. The corporation was authorized to issue 100,000 shares of $100 par value, 5 percent cumulative preferred stock and 100,000 shares of $1 par value common stock. The following transactions (among others) occurred during the year:

Jan. 7   Issued for cash 30,000 shares of common stock at $10 per share. The shares were issued to Deal and four other investors.

Jan. 12   Issued an additional 1,000 shares of common stock to Deal in exchange for her services in organizing the corporation. The stockholders agreed that these services were worth $12,000.

Jan. 18   Issued 4,000 shares of preferred stock for cash of $400,000.

July 5   Acquired land as a building site in exchange for 10,000 shares of common stock. In view of the appraised value of the land and the progress of the company, the directors agreed that the common stock was to be valued for purposes of this transaction at $12 per share.

Nov. 25   The first annual dividend of $5 per share was declared on the preferred stock to be paid December 11.

Dec. 11   Paid the cash dividend declared on November 25.

Dec. 31   After the revenue and expenses were closed into the Income Summary account, that amount indicated a net income of $810,000.

Instructions

a. Prepare journal entries in general journal form to record the above transactions. Include entries at December 31 to close the Income Summary account and the Dividends account.

b. Prepare the stockholders' equity section of the Markup, Inc., balance sheet at December 31.

LO11-4, LO11-5
PROBLEM 11.5B
Analysis of an Equity
Section of a Balance Sheet

The year-end balance sheet of Mirror, Inc., includes the following stockholders' equity section (with certain details omitted):

Stockholders' equity:	
10% cumulative preferred stock, $100 par value, authorized 100,000 shares	$ 4,400,000
Common stock, $2 par value, authorized 2,000,000 shares	3,400,000
Additional paid-in capital: common stock	6,800,000
Donated capital	400,000
Retained earnings	3,160,000
Total stockholders' equity.	$18,160,000

Instructions

From this information, compute answers to the following questions:

a. How many shares of preferred stock have been issued?

b. What is the total amount of the annual dividends paid to preferred stockholders?

c. How many shares of common stock are outstanding?

d. What was the average issuance price per share of common stock?

e. What is the amount of legal capital?

f. What is the total amount of paid-in capital?

g. What is the book value per share of common stock? (There are no dividends in arrears.)

h. Assume that retained earnings at the beginning of the year amounted to $1,200,000 and the net income for the year was $4,800,000. What was the dividend declared during the year on *each share* of common stock? (Hint: Net income increases retained earnings, whereas dividends decrease retained earnings.)

LO11-1 through LO11-7
PROBLEM 11.6B
Analysis of an Equity
Section—More
Comprehensive

Timberlake Corporation is a publicly owned company. The following information is taken from a recent balance sheet. Dollar amounts (except for per-share amounts) are stated in thousands.

Stockholders' equity:	
Convertible $10 preferred stock, no par value, 1,000,000 shares authorized, 250,000 shares issued and outstanding, $200 per share liquidation preference.	$ 50,000
Common stock, $3 par value, 40,000,000 shares authorized.	9,600
Additional paid-in capital	76,800
Retained earnings	50,600
Total stockholders' equity.	$187,000

Instructions

From this information, compute answers to the following questions:

a. How many shares of common stock have been issued?

b. What is the total amount of the annual dividends paid to preferred stockholders?

c. What is the total amount of paid-in capital?

d. What is the book value per share of common stock, assuming no dividends and arrears?

e. Briefly explain the advantages and disadvantages to Toasty of being publicly owned rather than operating as a closely held corporation.

f. What is meant by the term *convertible* used in the caption of the preferred stock? Is there any more information that investors need to know to evaluate this conversion feature?

g. Assume that the preferred stock currently is selling at *$190* per share. Does this provide a higher or lower dividend yield than a 6 percent, $50 par value preferred with a market price of $52 per share? Show computations. Explain why one preferred stock might yield less than another.

LOII-4, LOII-7
PROBLEM 11.7B
Par, Book, and Market
Values

Whitaker Video is the producer of popular video games. Recently, an investment service published the following per-share amounts relating to the company's only class of stock:

Par value	$ 0.05
Book value (estimated)...	10.00
Market value..	96.00

Instructions

a. Without reference to dollar amounts, explain the nature and significance of *par value, book value,* and *market value.*

b. Comment on the *relationships,* if any, among the per-share accounts shown for the company. What do these amounts imply about Brain and its operations? Comment on what these amounts imply about the security of *creditors'* claims against the company.

LOII-4, LOII-5, LOII-7,
LOII-9
PROBLEM 11.8B
Reporting Stockholders'
Equity with Treasury Stock

Early in 2013, Teek Corporation was formed with authorization to issue 50,000 shares of $3 par value common stock. All shares were issued at a price of $10 per share. The corporation reported net income of $160,000 in 2013, $89,200 in 2014, and $97,000 in 2015. No dividends were declared in any of these three years.

In 2014, the company purchased its own shares for $30,000 in the open market. In 2015, it reissued all of its treasury stock for $40,000.

Instructions

a. Prepare the stockholders' equity section of the balance sheet at December 31, 2015. Include a supporting schedule showing your computation of retained earnings at the balance sheet date. (Hint: Income increases retained earnings.)

b. As of December 31, compute the company's book value per share of common stock.

c. Explain how the treasury stock transactions in 2014 and 2015 were reported in the company's statement of cash flows.

LOII-4, LOII-5, LOII-7
through LOII-9
PROBLEM 11.9B
Reporting Stockholders'
Equity with Treasury Stock
and Stock Splits

Early in 2011, Laird Industries was formed with authorization to issue 150,000 shares of $20 par value common stock and 10,000 shares of $100 par value cumulative preferred stock. During 2011, all the preferred stock was issued at par, and 80,000 shares of common stock were sold for $35 per share. The preferred stock is entitled to a dividend equal to 6 percent of its par value before any dividends are paid on the common stock.

During its first five years of business (2011 through 2015), the company earned income totaling $3,800,000 and paid dividends of 60 cents per share each year on the common stock outstanding.

On January 2, 2013, the company purchased 1,000 shares of its own common stock in the open market for $40,000. On January 2, 2015, it reissued 600 shares of this treasury stock for $30,000. The remaining 400 shares were still held in treasury at December 31, 2015.

Instructions

a. Prepare the stockholders' equity section of the balance sheet at December 31, 2015. Include a supporting schedule showing (1) your computation of any paid-in capital on treasury stock and (2) retained earnings at the balance sheet date. (Hint: Income increases retained earnings, whereas dividends reduce retained earnings. Dividends are not paid on shares of stock held in treasury.)

b. As of December 31, 2015, compute the company's book value per share of common stock. (Hint: Book value per share is computed only on the shares of stock outstanding.)

c. At December 31, 2015, shares of the company's common stock were trading at $56. Explain what would have happened to the market price per share had the company split its stock 2-for-1 at this date. Also explain what would have happened to the par value of the common stock and to the number of common shares outstanding.

Critical Thinking Cases

LO11-5, LO11-7

CASE 11.1

Factors Affecting the Market Prices of Preferred and Common Stocks

SciFi Labs is a publicly owned company with several issues of capital stock outstanding. Over the past decade, the company has consistently earned modest profits and has increased its common stock dividend annually by 5 or 10 cents per share. Recently the company has had several important research successes and has introduced several new products that you believe will motivate future sales and profits to increase dramatically. You also expect a gradual increase in long-term interest rates from their present level of about 8 percent to, perhaps, 9 percent or 10 percent.

Instructions

On the basis of these forecasts, explain whether you would expect to see the market prices of the following issues of SciFi capital stock increase or decrease. Explain your reasoning in each answer.

a. 10 percent, $100 par value preferred stock (currently selling at $80 per share).

b. $5 par value common stock (currently paying an annual dividend of $2.50 and selling at $40 per share).

c. 7 percent, $100 par value convertible preferred stock (currently selling at $95 per share).

LO11-7

CASE 11.2

Factors Affecting the Market Prices of Common Stocks

Each of the following situations describes an event that affected the stock market price of a particular company.

a. The price of a common share of **McDonnell Douglas, Inc.**, increased by over $5 per share in the several days after it was announced that Saudia Airlines would order $6 billion of commercial airliners from **Boeing** and **McDonnell Douglas**.

b. **Citicorp**'s common stock price fell by over $3.50 per share shortly after the Federal Reserve Board increased the discount rate by ¼ percent. The discount rate is the rate charged to banks for short-term loans they need to meet their reserve requirements.

c. The price of a common share of **Ventitex, Inc.**, a manufacturer of medical devices, fell over $10 (27.7 percent) after it was announced that representatives of the Federal Drug Administration paid a visit to the company.

Instructions

For each of the independent situations described, explain the likely underlying rationale for the change in market price of the stock.

LO11-1 through LO11-3

CASE 11.3

Selecting a Form of Business Organization

Interview the owners of two local small businesses. One business should be organized as a corporation and the other as either a sole proprietorship or a partnership. Inquire as to:

- *Why* this form of entity was selected.
- Have there been any unforeseen complications with this form of entity?
- Is the form of entity likely to be changed in the foreseeable future? And if so, why?

LO11-1 through LO11-3

CASE 11.4

SEC Enforcement Division

The Enforcement Division of the Securities and Exchange Commission (SEC) is an important aspect of the corporate governance structure in the United States that is intended to protect investors. Locate the home page of the SEC by doing a general search on the title "Securities and Exchange Commission," and answer the following.

Instructions

a. Identify the divisions of the SEC.

b. Access the category "Enforcement Division," and write a one-sentence description of the purpose of this division.

c. Explore the website and locate the SEC information that deals with pump-and-dump schemes on the Internet.

d. Write a concise description of a pump-and-dump scheme, and list the suggestions of the SEC to investors to avoid these schemes.

LOII-4, LOII-5, LOII-7, LOII-9

INTERNET CASE 11.5

Stockholders' Equity Items

Visit the home page of **Staples, Inc.**, at the following Internet address:

www.staples.com

Locate the company's most current balance sheet by selecting "Investor Information."

Instructions

Answer the following questions:

a. Does the company report preferred stock in its balance sheet? If so, how many shares are currently outstanding?

b. How much common stock does the company report in its most recent balance sheet? What is the par value of each share?

c. Does the company report any treasury stock? Has this amount changed since the previous year?

Internet sites are time and date sensitive. It is the purpose of these exercises to have you explore the Internet. You may need to use the Yahoo! search engine www.yahoo.com (or another favorite search engine) to find a company's current web address.

Answers to Self-Test Questions

1. b   **2.** d   **3.** a   **4.** c   **5.** c, d   **6.** b [(2,000 × $60) − (500 × $70)]

COMPREHENSIVE PROBLEM 3

Springdale Retail, Inc.

Springdale Retail, Inc., is a retailer that has engaged you to assist in the preparation of its financial statements at December 31, 2015. Following are the correct adjusted account balances, in alphabetical order, as of that date. Each balance is the "normal" balance for that account. (Hint: The "normal" balance is the same as the debit or credit side that increases the account.)

Accounts payable	$ 12,750
Accounts receivable	2,600
Accumulated depreciation: office equipment	12,000
Additional paid-in capital (common stock)	7,000
Bonds payable (due December 31, 2018)	22,500
Cash	15,200
Common stock (1,800 shares, $10 par value)	18,000
Cost of goods sold	100,575
Deferred income taxes	5,750
Depreciation expense: office equipment	2,750
Dividends declared	5,000
Income tax expense	8,190
Insurance expense	900
Land	37,500
Merchandise inventory	17,500
Notes payable (due December 31, 2016)	2,500
Office equipment	41,000
Office supplies	900
Office supplies expense	520
Preferred stock (250 shares, $20 par value)	5,000
Premium on bonds payable	1,750
Prepaid rent	1,800
Rent expense	6,100
Retained earnings (January 2016)	21,050
Salaries expense	88,095
Sales	226,000
Sales returns and allowances	2,500
Sales taxes payable	3,200
Treasury stock (200 common shares at cost)	2,250
Utilities expense	4,120

Instructions

a. Prepare an income statement for the year ended December 31, 2015, which includes amounts for gross profit, income before income taxes, and net income. List expenses (other than cost of goods sold and income tax expense) in order, from the largest to the smallest dollar balance. You may ignore earnings per share.

b. Prepare a statement of retained earnings for the year ending December 31, 2015.

c. Prepare a statement of financial position (balance sheet) as of December 31, 2015, following these guidelines:

- Include separate asset and liability categories for those assets which are "current."

- Include and label amounts for total assets, total liabilities, total stockholders' equity, and total liabilities and stockholders' equity.

- Present deferred income taxes as a noncurrent liability.

- To the extent information is available that should be disclosed, include that information in your statement.

CHAPTER 12

Income and Changes in Retained Earnings

AFTER STUDYING THIS CHAPTER, YOU SHOULD BE ABLE TO:

Learning Objectives

LO12-1 Describe how irregular income items, such as discontinued operations and extraordinary items, are presented in the income statement.

LO12-2 Compute earnings per share.

LO12-3 Distinguish between basic and diluted earnings per share.

LO12-4 Account for cash dividends and stock dividends, and explain the effects of these transactions on a company's financial statements.

LO12-5 Describe and prepare a statement of retained earnings.

LO12-6 Define *prior period adjustments,* and explain how they are presented in financial statements.

LO12-7 Define *comprehensive income,* and explain how it differs from net income.

LO12-8 Describe and prepare a statement of stockholders' equity and the stockholders' equity section of the balance sheet.

LO12-9 Illustrate steps management might take to improve the appearance of the company's net income.

© AP Photo/Amy Sancetta

COLGATE-PALMOLIVE COMPANY

A company's pattern of sales and net income are important factors in evaluating its financial success. Consider Colgate-Palmolive Company, for example. Colgate-Palmolive products are marketed in over 200 countries around the world. The company has a strong portfolio of recognizable brands, including Colgate, Palmolive, Softsoap, Irish Spring, Speed Stick, Ajax, Murphy's Oil Soap, and Hill's Science Diet.

One of the attributes of financially successful companies like Colgate-Palmolive is their consistent strength over time in terms of primary measures of financial performance, such as net sales and net earnings. Net sales, measuring the value of merchandise sold less returns, increased from $15,564 million in 2010 to $16,734 in 2011 and to $17,085 million in 2012.

This represents an approximate 7.5 percent increase in 2011 and a modest 2 percent increase in 2012, for a combined increase for the two years of approximately 10 percent. Net income, which starts with sales and is reduced by various expenses required to generate those sales, increased from $2,203 million in 2010 to $2,431 million in 2011 (an approximate 10 percent increase) and to $2,472 million in 2012 (an approximate 2 percent increase), or a combined increase for the two years of approximately 12 percent. These figures represent impressive financial performance in terms of the company's ability to provide goods to its customers and to operate in a manner that results in a profit that benefits the company's stockholders. ■

For investors seeking companies in which to place their funds, a pattern of increases in key performance figures such as sales and net income is very attractive. In this chapter, we look more closely at the income statement and learn about the useful information available in that financial statement for making important investment and credit decisions. In addition to learning more about how an income statement is prepared, you will learn about earnings per share, dividends, and other key factors that indicate the financial success of a company.

Reporting the Results of Operations

The most important aspect of corporate financial reporting, in the view of many investors, is periodic income. Both the market price of common stock and the amount of cash dividends per share depend on the current and future earnings of the corporation.

DEVELOPING PREDICTIVE INFORMATION

Revenue is a measure of the value of products and services that have been sold to customers. Revenue represents the increases in the company's assets that result from its profit-directed activities. Generally, revenue increases cash either at the time it is included in the income statement or at an earlier or later date. Expenses are measures of the cost of producing and distributing the products and services that are sold to customers. They represent decreases in the company's assets that result from its profit-directed activities. Expenses decrease cash at the time they are incurred, or at an earlier or later date. An income statement presents a company's revenue and expenses for a stated period of time, such as a quarter or year.

As this brief description of revenue and expenses indicates, the income statement provides important information for investors and creditors as they attempt to make estimates of future cash flows. Because of the importance of income reporting in making assessments about the future, events and transactions that are irregular require careful attention in the preparation and interpretation of an income statement.

For information about financial performance to be of maximum usefulness to investors, creditors, and other financial statement users, the results of items that are unusual and not likely to recur should be presented separately from the results of the company's normal, recurring activities. Two categories of unusual, nonrecurring events that require special treatment are (1) the results of *discontinued operations* and (2) the impact of *extraordinary items*. One of the challenges that has faced the accounting profession is to define these terms with sufficient clarity that users of financial statements can reliably compare the information provided by different companies and by the same company over time.

REPORTING IRREGULAR ITEMS: AN ILLUSTRATION

To illustrate the presentation of irregular items in an income statement, assume that Farmer Corporation operates both a small chain of retail stores and two motels. Near the end of the current year, the company sells both motels to a national hotel chain. In addition, Farmer Corporation reports two "extraordinary items." An income statement illustrating the correct format for reporting these events appears in Exhibit 12–1.

CONTINUING OPERATIONS

The first section of the Farmer Corporation income statement contains only the results of *continuing business activities*—that is, the retail stores. Notice that the income tax expense shown in this section ($300,000) relates *only to continuing operations*. The income taxes relating to the irregular items are shown separately in the income statement as adjustments to the amounts of these items.

Income from Continuing Operations The subtotal *income from continuing operations* measures the profitability of the ongoing operations. This subtotal should be helpful in making predictions of the company's future earnings. For example, if we predict no

FARMER CORPORATION INCOME STATEMENT FOR THE YEAR ENDED DECEMBER 31, 2015		
Net sales		$8,000,000
Cost and expenses:		
Cost of goods sold	$4,500,000	
Selling expenses	1,500,000	
General and administrative expenses	920,000	
Loss on settlement of lawsuit	80,000	
Income tax (on continuing operations)	300,000	7,300,000
Income from continuing operations		$ 700,000
Discontinued operations:		
Operating loss on motels (net of $90,000 income tax benefit)	$ (210,000)	
Gain on sale of motels (net of $195,000 income tax)	455,000	245,000
Income before extraordinary items		$ 945,000
Extraordinary items:		
Gain on condemnation of land by State Highway Department (net of $45,000 income tax)	$ 105,000	
Loss from earthquake damage to New York store (net of $75,000 income tax benefit)	(175,000)	(70,000)
Net income		$ 875,000

EXHIBIT 12–1

Income Statement with Nonrecurring Items

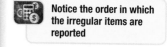 **Notice the order in which the irregular items are reported**

significant change in the profitability of its retail stores, we would expect Farmer Corporation to earn a net income of approximately $700,000 next year.

DISCONTINUED OPERATIONS

When management enters into a formal plan to sell or discontinue a **segment of the business,** the results of that segment's operations are shown separately in the income statement. Excluding that part of the business that will no longer be part of the company's operations enables users of the financial statements to better evaluate the performance of the company's ongoing (continuing) operations.

Two items are included in the **discontinued operations** section of the income statement: (1) the income or loss from *operating* the segment prior to its disposal and (2) the gain or loss on *disposal* of the segment. The income taxes relating to the discontinued operations are *shown separately* from the income tax expense relating to continuing business operations.

EXTRAORDINARY ITEMS

The second category of irregular events requiring disclosure in a separate section of the income statement is extraordinary items. An **extraordinary item** is a gain or loss that is (1) *unusual in nature* and (2) *not expected to recur in the foreseeable future.* An example of an extraordinary item is the loss of a company's plant due to an earthquake in a geographic location where earthquakes rarely occur.

When a gain or loss qualifies as an extraordinary item, it appears after the section on discontinued operations (if any), following the subtotal *income before extraordinary items.* This subtotal is necessary to show investors what the net income *would have been* if the extraordinary gain or loss *had not occurred.* Extraordinary items are shown net of any related income tax effects.

LO12-1

LEARNING OBJECTIVE
Describe how irregular income items, such as discontinued operations and extraordinary items, are presented in the income statement.

Over the years, the Financial Accounting Standards Board has continued to refine the definition of extraordinary items in a manner that restricts the transactions companies can classify in this manner. As a result, today few extraordinary items are found in the financial statements of publicly held companies.

Other Unusual Gains and Losses

Some transactions are not typical of normal operations but also do not meet the stringent criteria for separate presentation as extraordinary items. Among such events are losses incurred because of labor strikes and the gains or losses resulting from sales of plant assets. Such items, if material, should be individually listed as items of revenue or expense, rather than being combined with other items in broad categories such as sales revenue or general and administrative expenses.

In the income statement of Farmer Corporation (Exhibit 12–1), the $80,000 loss resulting from the settlement of a lawsuit is listed separately in the income statement but is *not* shown as an extraordinary item. This loss is important enough to bring to the attention of readers of the income statement by presenting it as a separate item, but it is not considered sufficiently unusual or infrequent to be an extraordinary item.

Restructuring Charges

One important type of unusual loss relates to the restructuring of operations. The restructuring of operations has become a common aspect of the American economy. As companies struggle to meet the competitive challenges of a global economy, they incur significant costs to close plants, reduce workforces, and consolidate operating facilities.

Restructuring charges consist of items such as losses from write-downs or sales of plant assets, severance pay for terminated workers, and expenses related to the relocation of operations and remaining personnel. In determining operating income, they are presented in the company's income statement as a single item like the loss incurred in the settlement of a lawsuit in the Farmer Corporation income statement in Exhibit 12–1. If the restructuring involves discontinuing a segment of the business, the expenses related to that aspect of the restructuring are presented as discontinued operations.

Distinguishing between the Unusual and the Extraordinary

In the past, some corporate managements had a tendency to classify many *losses* as extraordinary, while classifying many *gains* as a part of normal recurring operations. This resulted in reporting higher income before extraordinary items, but the final net income figure was not affected.

YOUR TURN   You as an Investor

One of the most important determinants of a company's stock price is expected future earnings. Assume that you are considering investing in Worsham Corporation and are evaluating the company's profitability in the current year. The net income of the corporation, which amounted to $4,000,000, includes the following items:

Loss on a discontinued segment of the business (net of income tax benefit)	$750,000
Extraordinary gain (net of income tax paid)	300,000

Adjust net income to develop a number that represents a good starting point for predicting the future net income of Worsham Corporation. Explain the reason for each of the adjustments. Explain how this adjusted number may help you predict future earnings for the company.

(See our comments on the Online Learning Center website.)

To counter this potentially misleading practice, the accounting profession now strictly defines extraordinary items and intends for them to be quite rare. There is no comprehensive list of extraordinary items. Thus the classification of a specific event is a matter of *judgment.*

EARNINGS PER SHARE (EPS)

One of the most widely used accounting statistics is **earnings per share** on common stock. Investors who buy or sell stock in a corporation need to know the annual earnings per share. Stock market prices are quoted on a per-share basis. If you are considering investing in a company's stock at a price of $50 per share, you need to know the earnings per share and the annual dividend per share to decide whether this price is reasonable.

To compute earnings per share, the common stockholders' share of the company's net income is divided by the average number of common shares outstanding. Earnings per share applies only to *common stock;* preferred stockholders have no claim to earnings beyond the stipulated preferred stock dividends.

Computing earnings per share is easiest when the corporation has issued only common stock and the number of outstanding shares has not changed during the year. In this case, earnings per share is equal to net income divided by the number of shares outstanding.

In many companies, the number of shares of stock outstanding changes during the year. If additional shares are sold, or if shares of common stock are retired (repurchased from the shareholders), the computation of earnings per share is based on the *weighted-average* number of shares outstanding.[1]

The weighted-average number of shares for the year is determined by multiplying the number of shares outstanding by the fraction of the year that number of shares outstanding remained unchanged. For example, assume that 80,000 shares of common stock were outstanding during the first nine months of 2015 and 140,000 shares were outstanding during the last three months. The increase in shares outstanding resulted from the sale of 60,000 shares for cash. The weighted-average number of shares outstanding during 2015 is *95,000,* determined as follows:

80,000 shares × $9/12$ of a year	60,000
140,000 shares × $3/12$ of a year	35,000
Weighted-average number of common shares outstanding	95,000

By using the weighted-average number of shares in calculating earnings per share, we recognize that the cash received from the sale of the 60,000 additional shares was available to generate earnings only during the last three months of the year.

Preferred Dividends and Earnings per Share   When a company has preferred stock outstanding, the preferred stockholders participate in net income only to the extent of the preferred stock dividends. To determine the earnings *applicable to the common stock,* we first deduct from net income the amount of current year preferred dividends. The annual dividend on *cumulative* preferred stock is *always* deducted, even if not declared by the board of directors for the current year. When there are preferred dividends in arrears, only the *current year's* cumulative preferred stock dividend is deducted in the earnings per share computation. Noncumulative preferred dividends are deducted only if they have been declared.

L012-2

LEARNING OBJECTIVE
Compute earnings per share.

---

[1] When the number of shares outstanding changes as a result of a stock split or a stock dividend (discussed later in this chapter), the computation of the weighted-average number of shares outstanding should be adjusted *retroactively* rather than weighted for the period the new shares were outstanding. This makes earnings per share data for prior years consistent in terms of the current capital structure.

To illustrate, let us assume that Perry Corporation has 200,000 shares of common stock and 12,000 shares of $6 cumulative preferred stock outstanding throughout the year. Net income for the year totals $595,000. Earnings per share of common stock would be computed as follows:

Net income	$595,000
Less: Dividends on preferred stock (12,000 shares × $6)	72,000
Earnings applicable to common stock	$523,000
Weighted-average number of common shares outstanding	200,000
Earnings per share of common stock ($523,000 ÷ 200,000 shares)	$2.62

Earnings per share figures are required in the income statements of publicly owned companies

Presentation of Earnings per Share in the Income Statement

All publicly owned corporations are *required* to present earnings per share figures in their income statements.[2] If an income statement includes subtotals for income from continuing operations, or for income before extraordinary items, per-share figures are shown for these amounts as well as for net income. These additional per-share amounts are computed by substituting the amount of the appropriate subtotal for the net income figure in the preceding calculation.

To illustrate all of the potential per-share computations, we will expand our Perry Corporation example to include income from continuing operations and income before extraordinary items. We should point out, however, that all of these figures seldom appear in the same income statement. The condensed income statement shown in Exhibit 12–2 is intended to illustrate the proper format for presenting earnings per share figures and to provide a review of the calculations.

EXHIBIT 12–2

Earnings Per Share Presentation

PERRY CORPORATION CONDENSED INCOME STATEMENT FOR THE YEAR ENDED DECEMBER 31, 2015	
Net sales	$ 9,115,000
Costs and expenses (including tax on continuing operations)	8,310,000
Income from continuing operations	$ 805,000
Loss from discontinued operations (net of income tax benefits)	(90,000)
Income before extraordinary items	$ 715,000
Extraordinary loss (net of income tax benefit)	$ (120,000)
Net income	$ 595,000
Earnings per share of common stock:	
Earnings from continuing operations	$3.67[a]
Loss from discontinued operations	(0.45)
Earnings before extraordinary items	$3.22[b]
Extraordinary loss	(0.60)
Net earnings	$2.62[c]

[a]($805,000 − $72,000 preferred dividends) ÷ 200,000 shares
[b]($715,000 − $72,000) ÷ 200,000 shares
[c]($595,000 − $72,000) ÷ 200,000 shares

---

[2]The FASB has exempted closely held corporations (those not publicly owned) from the requirement of computing and reporting earnings per share, although some do it voluntarily.

FINANCIAL ANALYSIS and Decision Making

The relationship between earnings per share and stock price is expressed by the **price-earnings (p/e) ratio.** This ratio is simply the current stock price divided by the earnings per share for the year. Price-earnings ratios are of such interest to investors that they are published daily in the financial pages of major newspapers. Price-earnings ratios and other measures useful for evaluating financial performance are covered in Chapter 14.

Stock prices actually reflect investors' expectations of *future* earnings. The p/e ratio, however, is based on the earnings over the *past* year. Thus, if investors expect earnings to *increase* substantially from current levels, the p/e ratio may be quite high—perhaps 20, 30, or even more. But if investors expect earnings to *decline* from current levels, the p/e ratio may be quite low, say, 8 or less. A mature company with stable earnings usually sells between 10 and 20 times earnings, depending on current market conditions and investor sentiment. Thus the p/e ratio reflects *investors' expectations* of the company's future prospects.[3]

When using per-share information, it is important to know exactly *which* per-share statistic is being presented. For example, the price-earnings ratios (market price divided by earnings per share) for common stocks listed on major stock exchanges are reported daily in *The Wall Street Journal* and other financial publications. Which earnings per share figures are used in computing these ratios? If a company reports an extraordinary gain or loss, the price-earnings ratio is computed using the per-share *earnings before the extraordinary item.* Otherwise, the ratio is based on *net earnings.*

INTERNATIONAL CASE IN POINT

Valuation multiples such as price-earnings ratios are often used to estimate a firm's value. The use of price multiples to compare firms from different countries is challenging for many reasons. One important reason is that national differences in accounting principles are a source of cross-country differences. For example, research has shown that such differences in accounting principles cause p/e ratios in Japan to be generally lower than in the United States for comparable companies with similar financial results.

YOUR TURN   You as a Financial Analyst

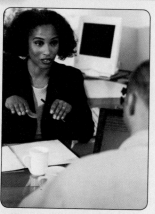

© Ryan McVay/Getty Images

You are working for a stock market research firm and your boss asks you to present an analysis of Foster, Inc.'s performance, focusing primarily on earnings per share. Her primary purpose for having you do this analysis is to consider whether Foster, Inc., is a good investment in terms of the company's expectations for future profitability. In analyzing Foster, Inc.'s income statement you determine the following:

---

[3] A word of caution—if current earnings are *very low,* the p/e ratio tends to be quite high *regardless* of whether future earnings are expected to rise or fall. In such situations, the p/e ratio is not a meaningful measurement.

	2016	2015	2014
Basic earnings per share on:			
Income from continuing operations	$3.02	$2.56	$1.75
Discontinued operations	(1.90)	(1.05)	(0.15)
Net income	$1.12	$1.51	$1.60

On the basis of only the limited information presented above, what is your recommendation to your boss regarding Foster, Inc.'s prospects for future profitability? Justify your conclusion.

(See our comments on the Online Learning Center website.)

BASIC AND DILUTED EARNINGS PER SHARE

LEARNING OBJECTIVE
Distinguish between basic and diluted earnings per share.

Let us assume that a company has an outstanding issue of preferred stock that is convertible into shares of common stock at a rate of two shares of common stock for each share of preferred stock. The conversion of this preferred stock would increase the number of common shares outstanding and might *dilute* (reduce) earnings per share. Any common stockholder interested in the trend of earnings per share needs to know what effect the conversion of the preferred stock would have on earnings per share of common stock. Keep in mind that the decision to convert the preferred shares into common shares is made by the stockholders, not the corporation.

To inform investors of the potential dilution that might occur, two figures are presented for each income number from the income statement. The first figure, called **basic earnings per share,** is based on the weighted-average number of common shares *actually outstanding* during the year. This figure excludes the potential dilution represented by the convertible preferred stock. The second figure, called **diluted earnings per share,** incorporates the *impact that conversion* of the preferred stock would have on basic earnings per share.[4]

Convertible preferred stock is not the only potential diluter of earnings per share. Convertible debt instruments (e.g., convertible bonds) are another type of financial instrument that may reduce earnings per share if the holders choose to redeem them. Similarly, stock options may reduce earnings per share if the holders choose to exercise them and purchase additional shares of stock.

---

[4] If the preferred stock had been issued during the current year, we would assume that it was converted into common stock on the date it was issued.

To informed users of financial statements, each of these figures has a different significance. Earnings per share from continuing operations represents the results of continuing and ordinary business activity. This figure is the most useful one for predicting future operating results. *Net earnings* per share, on the other hand, shows the overall operating results of the current year, including any discontinued operations and extraordinary items.

Other Transactions Affecting Retained Earnings

CASH DIVIDENDS

LEARNING OBJECTIVE
Account for cash dividends and stock dividends, and explain the effects of these transactions on a company's financial statements.

Investors buy stock in a corporation with the expectation of getting their original investment back as well as earning a reasonable return on that investment. The return on a stock investment is a combination of two forms: (1) the increase in value of the stock (stock appreciation) and (2) **cash dividends.**

Some profitable corporations do not pay dividends. Generally, these corporations are in an early stage of development and must conserve cash for the purchase of plant and equipment or for other needs of the company. These so-called growth companies cannot obtain sufficient financing at reasonable interest rates to finance their operations, so they must rely on their earnings. Often only after a significant number of years of profitable operations does the board of directors decide that paying cash dividends is appropriate.

The preceding discussion suggests three requirements for the payment of a cash dividend. These are:

1. *Retained earnings.* Since dividends are a distribution of assets that represent earnings to stockholders, the theoretical maximum for dividends is the total undistributed net income of the company, represented by the credit balance of the Retained Earnings account. As a practical matter, many corporations limit dividends to amounts significantly less than annual net income, on the basis that a major portion of the net income must be retained in the business if the company is to grow and keep pace with its competitors.

2. *An adequate cash position.* The fact that the company reports earnings does not necessarily mean that it has a large amount of cash on hand. Cash generated from earnings may have been invested in new plant and equipment, or it may have already been used to pay off debts or to acquire a larger inventory. There is no necessary relationship between the balance in the Retained Earnings account and the balance in the Cash account. The common expression of "paying dividends out of retained earnings" is misleading. Cash dividends can be paid only out of cash.

3. *Dividend action by the board of directors.* Even though a company's net income is substantial and its cash position seemingly satisfactory, dividends are not paid automatically. A formal action by the board of directors is necessary to declare a dividend.

DIVIDEND DATES

Four significant dates are involved in the distribution of a dividend. These are:

1. *Date of declaration.* On the day on which the dividend is declared by the board of directors, a liability to make the payment comes into existence.

2. *Ex-dividend date.* The **ex-dividend date** is significant for investors in companies whose stocks trade on stock exchanges. To permit the compilation of the list of stockholders as of the record date, it is customary for the stock to go *ex-dividend* three business days before the date of record (see following discussion). A person who buys the stock before the ex-dividend date is entitled to receive the dividend that has already been declared; conversely, a stockholder who sells shares before the ex-dividend date does not receive the dividend. A stock is said to be selling ex-dividend on the day that it *loses* the right to receive the latest declared dividend.

3. *Date of record.* The **date of record** follows the date of declaration, usually by two or three weeks, and is always stated in the dividend declaration. To be eligible to receive the dividend, a person must be listed in the corporation's records as the owner of the stock on this date.

4. *Date of payment.* The declaration of a dividend always includes announcement of the date of payment as well as the date of record. Usually the date of payment comes two to four weeks after the date of record.

Journal entries are required only on the dates of declaration and of payment, as these are the only transactions affecting the corporation declaring the dividend. These entries are illustrated below:

Dec. 15	Dividends	125,000	
	Dividends Payable		125,000
	To record declaration of a cash dividend of $1 per share on the 125,000 shares of common stock outstanding. Payable Jan. 25 to stockholders of record on Jan. 10.		

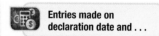

Entries made on declaration date and . . .

Jan. 25	Dividends Payable	125,000	
	Cash		125,000
	To record payment of $1 per share dividend declared Dec. 15 to stockholders of record on Jan. 10.		

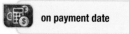

on payment date

No entries are made on either the ex-dividend date or the date of record. These dates are of importance only in determining *to whom* the dividend checks will be sent. From the stockholders' point of view, it is the *ex-dividend date* that determines who receives the dividend. The date of record is of significance primarily to the stock transfer agent and the stock registrar.

At the end of the accounting period, a closing entry is required to transfer the debit balance of the Dividends account into the Retained Earnings account. (Some companies follow the alternative practice of debiting Retained Earnings when the dividend is declared instead of using a Dividends account. Under either method, the balance of the Retained Earnings account ultimately is reduced by all dividends declared during the period.)

LIQUIDATING DIVIDENDS

A *liquidating dividend* occurs when a corporation pays a dividend that *exceeds the balance in the Retained Earnings account.* Thus the dividend returns to stockholders all or part of their paid-in capital investment. Liquidating dividends usually are paid only when a corporation is going out of existence or is making a permanent reduction in the size of its operations. Stockholders may assume that a dividend represents a distribution of profits unless they are notified by the corporation that the dividend is a return of invested capital.

STOCK DIVIDENDS

Stock dividend is a term used to describe a distribution of *additional shares of stock* to a company's stockholders in proportion to their present holdings. In other words, the dividend is payable in additional shares of stock rather than in cash. Most stock dividends consist of additional shares of common stock distributed to holders of common stock. Therefore, our discussion focuses on this type of stock dividend.

An important distinction exists between a cash dividend and a stock dividend. A *cash dividend* is a distribution of cash by a corporation to its stockholders. A cash dividend reduces both assets and stockholders' equity. In a *stock dividend,* however, *no assets are distributed.* Thus a stock dividend causes *no change* in assets, liabilities, or in total stockholders' equity. Each stockholder receives additional shares, but his or her percentage ownership in the corporation is *no larger than before,* and the company receives no assets in the transaction.

To illustrate this point, assume that a corporation with 2,000 shares of stock is owned equally by James Davis and Susan Miller, each owning 1,000 shares of stock. The corporation declares a stock dividend of 10 percent and distributes 200 additional shares (10 percent of 2,000 shares), with 100 shares going to each of the two stockholders. Davis and Miller now hold 1,100 shares apiece, but each *still owns one-half of the business.* Furthermore, the corporation has not changed in size; its assets and liabilities and its total stockholders' equity are exactly the same as before the dividend.

Now let us consider the logical effect of this stock dividend on the *market price* of the company's stock. Assume that, before the stock dividend, the outstanding 2,000 shares in our example had a market price of $110 per share. This price indicates a total market value for the corporation of $220,000 (2,000 shares × $110 per share). Because the stock dividend does not change total assets or total stockholders' equity, the total market value of the corporation *should remain $220,000* after the stock dividend. As 2,200 shares are now outstanding, the market price of each share *should fall* to $100 ($220,000 ÷ 2,200 shares). In other words, the market value of the stock *should fall in proportion* to the number of new shares issued. Whether the market price per share *will* fall in proportion to a small increase in the number of outstanding shares is another matter.

Entries to Record a Stock Dividend
In accounting for relatively *small* stock dividends (say, less than 20 percent), the *market value* of the new shares is transferred from the Retained Earnings account to the paid-in capital accounts. This process sometimes is called *capitalizing* retained earnings. The overall effect is the same as if the dividend had been paid in cash, and the stockholders had immediately reinvested the cash in the business in exchange for additional shares of stock. Of course, no cash actually changes hands—the new shares of stock are simply sent directly to the stockholders.

To illustrate, assume that on June 1, Aspen Corporation has outstanding 100,000 shares of $5 par value common stock with a market value of $25 per share. On this date, the company declares a 10 percent stock dividend, distributable on July 15 to stockholders of record on June 20. The entry at June 1 to record the *declaration* of this dividend is:

Retained Earnings	250,000	
Stock Dividend to Be Distributed		50,000
Additional Paid-in Capital: Stock Dividends		200,000
Declared a 10% stock dividend consisting of 10,000 shares (100,000 shares × 10%) of $5 par value common stock, market price $25 per share. Distributable July 15 to stockholders of record on June 20.		

Stock dividend declared; use market price of stock

The Stock Dividend to Be Distributed account is *not a liability* because there is no obligation to distribute cash or any other asset. If a balance sheet is prepared between the date of declaration of a stock dividend and the date of distribution of the shares, this account, as well as the Additional Paid-in Capital: Stock Dividends account, should be presented in the stockholders' equity section of the balance sheet.

Notice that the Retained Earnings account was reduced by the *market value* of the shares to be issued (10,000 shares × $25 per share = $250,000). Notice also that *no change* occurs in the total amount of stockholders' equity. The amount removed from the Retained Earnings account was simply transferred into two other stockholders' equity accounts.

On July 15, the entry to record the *distribution* of the dividend shares is:

Stock Dividend to Be Distributed	50,000	
Common Stock		50,000
Distributed 10,000-share stock dividend declared on June 1.		

Stock dividend distributed

Reasons for Stock Dividends

Although stock dividends cause *no change* in total assets, liabilities, or stockholders' equity, they are popular both with management and with stockholders. Management often finds stock dividends appealing because they allow management to distribute something of perceived value to stockholders while conserving cash which may be needed for other purposes like expanding facilities and introducing new product lines.

Stockholders like stock dividends because they receive more shares, often the stock price does *not* fall proportionately, and the dividend is not subject to income taxes (until the shares received are sold). Also, *large* stock dividends tend to keep the stock price down in a trading range that appeals to most investors.

CASE IN POINT

An investor who purchased 100 shares of Home Depot, Inc., in 1985 would have paid about $1,700. Fifteen years later, that stock was worth about $273,000!

Does this mean that each share increased in value from $17 to more than $2,730? No— in fact, this probably couldn't happen. Investors like to buy stock in lots of 100 shares. At $2,730 per share, who could afford 100 shares? Certainly not the average small investor.

Home Depot's board of directors *wanted* to attract small investors. These investors help create more demand for the company's stock—and in many cases, they also become loyal customers.

So as the price of Home Depot's stock rose, the board declared several stock splits and stock dividends. An investor who had purchased 100 shares in 1985 owned over *3,900* shares 15 years later without ever having had to purchase additional shares. Each share had a market value of $70, a price considered affordable to the average investor.

Distinction between Stock Splits and Stock Dividends

What is the difference between a stock dividend and a stock split (discussed in Chapter 11)? In some respects the two are similar. Both involve the distribution of shares of a company's own stock to its present stockholders without payment by those stockholders to the company. Both stock dividends and stock splits increase the number of outstanding shares of stock in the company's stockholders' equity. The difference between a stock dividend and a stock split lies in the intent of management and the size of the distribution. A stock dividend usually is intended to substitute for a cash dividend and is small enough that the market price of the stock is relatively unaffected. Stock dividends typically increase the number of outstanding shares by 2, 5, or 10 percent. Stock splits, on the other hand, are intended to reduce the market price of the stock to bring it down to a desired trading range. Stock splits typically represent much larger increases in the number of outstanding shares, such as 100 percent (2:1 split) or 200 percent (3:1 split).

The previous discussion focuses on the purposes and management intent of stock dividends and stock splits. Accounting for the two also varies. Stock dividends do not result in a change in the par value of the stock, and usually an amount equal to the market value of the shares issued is transferred from retained earnings to the par value and additional paid-in capital accounts. Stock splits, on the other hand, result in a pro rata reduction in the par value of the stock and no change in the actual dollar balances of the stockholders' equity accounts. Both stock dividends and stock splits are integral parts of management strategy with regard to the company's ownership, and the accounting differences parallel these differences in management intent.

STATEMENT OF RETAINED EARNINGS

LO12-5

LEARNING OBJECTIVE
Describe and prepare a statement of retained earnings.

The term *retained earnings* refers to the portion of stockholders' equity derived from profitable operations. Retained earnings is increased by earning net income and is reduced by incurring net losses and by the declaration of dividends. Prior period adjustments, discussed later in this chapter, may increase or decrease retained earnings.

In addition to a balance sheet, an income statement, and a statement of cash flows, some companies present a **statement of retained earnings,** as in Exhibit 12–3.

EXHIBIT 12–3

Statement of Retained Earnings for Salt Lake Corporation

SALT LAKE CORPORATION STATEMENT OF RETAINED EARNINGS FOR THE YEAR ENDED DECEMBER 31, 2015		
Retained earnings, Dec. 31, 2014		$ 750,000
Net income for 2015		280,000
Subtotal		$1,030,000
Less dividends:		
Cash dividends on preferred stock ($5 per share)	$ 15,000	
Cash dividends on common stock ($2 per share)	59,600	
10% stock dividend	140,000	214,600
Retained earnings, Dec. 31, 2015		$ 815,400

Notice that the 2015 net income is added to the beginning balance of retained earnings. Earlier in this text when we studied the accounting cycle, we learned that, as part of the end-of-period process of closing the books and preparing financial statements, the revenue and expense accounts are brought to a zero balance, and the net amount of these items (either net income or net loss) is added to or subtracted from owners' equity. For a corporation, net income or loss is added to or subtracted from retained earnings. The addition of net income in the statement of retained earnings is a reflection of this closing process. Notice, also, that in the statement of retained earnings the balance is reduced by the amounts of cash dividends declared during the year, as well as the amount of the stock dividend that was declared.

PRIOR PERIOD ADJUSTMENTS

LO12-6

LEARNING OBJECTIVE
Define *prior period adjustments*, and explain how they are presented in financial statements.

On occasion, a company may discover that a *material error* was made in the measurement of net income in a prior year. Because net income is closed into the Retained Earnings account, an error in reported net income will cause an error in the amount of retained earnings shown in all subsequent balance sheets. When such errors are discovered, they should be corrected. The correction, called a **prior period adjustment,** is shown in the *statement of retained earnings* as an adjustment to the balance of retained earnings at the beginning of the current year. The amount of the adjustment is shown net of any related income tax effects.

To illustrate, assume that late in 2015 Salt Lake Corporation discovers that it failed to record depreciation on certain assets in 2014. After considering the income tax effects of this error, the company finds that the net income reported in 2014 was overstated by $35,000. Thus, the beginning 2015 balance of the Retained Earnings account ($750,000 at December 31, 2014) also is *overstated by $35,000*. The statement of retained earnings in *2015* must include a *correction* of the retained earnings at the beginning of the year. (See the illustration in Exhibit 12–4.)

SALT LAKE CORPORATION
STATEMENT OF RETAINED EARNINGS
FOR THE YEAR ENDED DECEMBER 31, 2015

Retained earnings, Dec. 31, 2014		
As originally reported		$750,000
Less: Prior period adjustment for error in recording 2014 depreciation expense (net of $15,000 income taxes)		35,000
As restated		$715,000
Net income for 2015		280,000
Subtotal		$995,000
Less dividends:		
Cash dividends on preferred stock ($5 per share)	$ 15,000	
Cash dividends on common stock ($2 per share)	59,600	
10% stock dividend	140,000	214,600
Retained earnings, Dec. 31, 2015		$780,400

EXHIBIT 12–4

Statement of Retained Earnings with Prior Period Adjustment

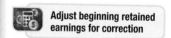

Adjust beginning retained earnings for correction

Prior period adjustments rarely appear in the financial statements of large publicly owned corporations. The financial statements of these corporations are audited annually by certified public accountants and are not likely to contain material errors that subsequently will require correction by prior period adjustments. Such adjustments are much more likely to appear in the financial statements of closely held corporations that are not audited on an annual basis.

Restrictions of Retained Earnings
Some portion of retained earnings may be restricted because of various contractual agreements. A restriction of retained earnings prevents a company from declaring a dividend that would cause retained earnings to fall below a designated level. Most companies disclose restrictions of retained earnings in notes accompanying the financial statements. For example, a company with total retained earnings of $10 million might include the following note in its financial statements:

Note disclosure of restrictions placed on retained earnings

Note 7: Restriction of retained earnings

As of December 31, 2015, certain long-term debt agreements prohibited the declaration of cash dividends that would reduce the amount of retained earnings below $5,200,000. Retained earnings in excess of this restriction total $4,800,000.

COMPREHENSIVE INCOME

LO12-7

LEARNING OBJECTIVE
Define *comprehensive income*, and explain how it differs from net income.

The Financial Accounting Standards Board (FASB) has identified certain changes in financial position that should be recorded but should not enter into the determination of net income. One way to describe these events is that they are *recognized* (that is, recorded and incorporated in the financial statements) but not *realized* (that is, not included in the determination of the company's net income). We have studied one of these items earlier in this text—the change in market value of available-for-sale debt and equity investments.

Recall from Chapter 7 the way changes in value for various types of investments are recorded. Those investments identified as available for sale are revalued to their current market value at the end of each accounting period. These changes in value are accumulated and reported in a separate stockholders' equity account. The change in value does *not* enter into the determination of net income as it would had investments been sold. The change in market value of available-for-sale investments adds to the amount of stockholders' equity if the value has gone up; it reduces the amount of stockholders' equity if the value has gone down. This adjustment is described as an element of *other comprehensive income.*

Comprehensive income is a term that identifies the total of net income plus or minus the elements of other comprehensive income. Comprehensive income may be displayed to users of financial statements in one of two ways:

- *As a second income statement.* One income statement displays the components of net income and the other displays the components of comprehensive income, one element of which is net income. If this option is selected, the Statement of Comprehensive Income must immediately follow the Income Statement in the company's annual report.

- *As a single income statement* that includes both the components of net income and the components of other comprehensive income.

In addition to the presentation of each year's changes in the elements of other comprehensive income, the accumulated amount of these changes is an element in the stockholders' equity section of the balance sheet. The components of comprehensive income are presented net of income tax, much like an extraordinary item.

Home Depot, Inc., whose financial statements for the year ended February 3, 2013, are included in Appendix A of this text, follows the first of these alternatives and presents Consolidated Statements of Earnings followed immediately by Consolidated Statements of Comprehensive Income. For each of the three years presented, the primary adjustments to Comprehensive Income, other than the company's annual net earnings, relate to the company's foreign operations. These are considered part of the company's overall income history, but are not part of its net income that is presented in the income statement.

STATEMENT OF STOCKHOLDERS' EQUITY

LO12-8

LEARNING OBJECTIVE
Describe and prepare a statement of stockholders' equity and the stockholders' equity section of the balance sheet.

Many corporations expand their statement of retained earnings to show the changes during the year in *all* of the stockholders' equity accounts. This expanded statement, called a **statement of stockholders' equity,** is illustrated in Exhibit 12–5 for Salt Lake Corporation.

The top line of the statement includes the beginning balance of each major category of stockholders' equity. Notice that the fourth column, Retained Earnings, includes the same information as the statement of retained earnings for Salt Lake Corporation that was presented in Exhibit 12–4. We have added several other stock transactions to illustrate the full range of information you will typically find in a statement of stockholders' equity:

- Issuance of common stock for $260,000 (resulting in an increase in both common stock and additional paid-in capital).

- Conversion of shares of preferred stock into common stock at $100,000, resulting in a decrease in 5 percent convertible preferred stock and an increase in common stock and additional paid-in capital.

- Purchase of $47,000 of treasury stock, increasing the amount of treasury stock and decreasing the total of stockholders' equity (as discussed in Chapter 11).

STOCKHOLDERS' EQUITY SECTION OF THE BALANCE SHEET

The stockholders' equity section of Salt Lake Corporation's balance sheet for the year ended December 31, 2015, is shown in Exhibit 12–6. Note that these figures are taken directly from the last line of the statement of stockholders' equity as illustrated in Exhibit 12–5. You should be able to explain the nature and origin of each account and disclosure printed in red as a result of having studied this chapter.

The published financial statements of leading corporations indicate that there is no one standard arrangement for the various items making up the stockholders' equity section. Variations occur in the selection of titles, in the sequence of items, and in the extent of detailed classification. Many companies, in an effort to avoid excessive detail in the balance sheet, combine several related ledger accounts into a single balance sheet item.

EXHIBIT 12–5 Statement of Stockholders' Equity

SALT LAKE CORPORATION STATEMENT OF STOCKHOLDERS' EQUITY FOR THE YEAR ENDED DECEMBER 31, 2015						
	5% Convertible Preferred Stock ($100 par value)	Common Stock ($10 par value)	Additional Paid-in Capital	Retained Earnings	Treasury Stock	Total Stockholders' Equity
Balances, Dec. 31, 2014	$400,000	$200,000	$300,000	$750,000	$ –0–	$1,650,000
Prior period adjustment (net of $15,000 taxes)				(35,000)		(35,000)
Issued 5,000 common shares @ $52		50,000	210,000			260,000
Conversion of 1,000 preferred into 3,000 common shares	(100,000)	30,000	70,000			
Distributed 10% stock dividend (2,800 shares at $50; market price)		28,000	112,000	(140,000)		
Purchased 1,000 shares of common stock held in treasury at $47 a share					(47,000)	(47,000)
Net income				280,000		280,000
Cash dividends:						
Preferred ($5 a share)				(15,000)		(15,000)
Common ($2 a share)				(59,600)		(59,600)
Balances, Dec. 31, 2015	$300,000	$308,000	$692,000	$780,400	$(47,000)	$2,033,400

Note: The numbers that are not bracketed represent positive stockholders' equity amounts. The bracketed numbers represent negative stockholders' equity amounts.

EXHIBIT 12–6

Stockholders' Equity Section of Balance Sheet

Stockholders' Equity

Capital stock:

5% convertible preferred, $100 par value, 3,000 shares authorized and issued		$ 300,000
Common stock, $10 par value, 100,000 shares authorized, issued 30,800 (of which 1,000 are held in treasury)		308,000
Additional paid-in capital:		
From issuance of common stock	$580,000	
From stock dividends	112,000	692,000
Total paid-in capital		$1,300,000
Retained earnings		780,400
Subtotal		$2,080,400
Less: Treasury stock (1,000 shares at $47 per share)		47,000
Total stockholders' equity		$2,033,400

Ethics, Fraud, & Corporate Governance

As discussed in this chapter, the most important aspect of periodic reporting for many investors is the reporting of net income. Investors often are attracted to companies that report increasing income each year. As a result, overstating net income is the most common practice for engaging in inappropriate financial reporting.

The Securities and Exchange Commission (SEC) brought a series of enforcement actions against **Just for Feet, Inc.,** its former employees, and employees of former vendors related to the overstatement of **Just for Feet's** reported income. Although **Just for Feet** overstated its income through a number of different techniques, two prominent techniques used to overstate income related to fictitious co-op revenue and fictitious "booth" income.

Just for Feet was a national retailer of athletic and outdoor footwear and apparel. **Just for Feet** filed for bankruptcy protection, and it began the process of liquidating its assets and settling its liabilities.

Just for Feet incurred large amounts of advertising expenses. A vendor (e.g., **Adidas, Fila, Nike**) would often reduce the amount that **Just for Feet** owed for merchandise purchases if a particular advertisement featured the vendor's products. These reductions in amounts owed were referred to as "advertising co-op" or "vendor allowances." These vendor allowances were unwritten and not guaranteed. **Just for Feet** sent vendors copies of advertisements placed, and the vendor determined whether to grant an advertising allowance.

In one fiscal year, **Just for Feet** recorded $19.4 million in co-op receivables (and recognized revenue as a result of

L012-9

LEARNING OBJECTIVE
Illustrate steps management might take to improve the appearance of the company's net income.

© Blend Images/Getty Images

recording the receivables) that was not earned. The fictitious revenue of over $19 million was a substantial percentage of **Just for Feet's** reported income of $43 million.

One important facet of the **Just for Feet** fraud is that the SEC brought enforcement actions against a number of vendor representatives for providing false confirmations to **Just for Feet's** auditor. When fraud exists, management at the company committing the fraud often tries to convince customers to falsely confirm to the auditors that they owe amounts that are in fact not owed. Such behavior represents a crime. It is worth noting that the criminal penalties for lying to external auditors have been substantially increased under the Sarbanes-Oxley Act, and that the SEC and the U.S. Justice Department are more likely to prosecute individuals for this type of behavior than was true in the past. Individuals in sales and marketing positions are often targets for requests to falsely confirm facts to external auditors (i.e., to lie). They should be aware of the substantial civil and criminal penalties that can result from lying to auditors.

Concluding Remarks

We discussed various aspects of stockholders' equity, focusing first on paid-in capital in Chapter 11 and then on earned capital in Chapter 12. These discussions complete our detailed coverage of assets, liabilities, and stockholders' equity, which began in Chapter 7 and included financial assets, inventories, plant and intangible assets, liabilities, and, finally, stockholders' equity. While these chapters generally follow a balance sheet organization, in Chapter 12 we also covered the income statement, including the presentation of irregular income items and earnings per share.

In the next chapter, we turn our attention to the statement of cash flows. Companies present four primary financial statements to their stockholders, creditors, and other interested parties—a statement of financial position or balance sheet, an income statement, a statement of comprehensive income, and a statement of cash flows. We delayed the detailed coverage of the statement of cash flows to this point in this textbook because of the importance of the material we have now covered, particularly in Chapters 7 to 12, for a full understanding of that financial statement.

END-OF-CHAPTER REVIEW

SUMMARY OF LEARNING OBJECTIVES

LO12-1 **Describe how irregular income items, such as discontinued operations and ~~extraordinary items,~~ are presented in the income statement.** Each of these irregular items is shown in a separate section of the income statement, following income or loss from ordinary and continuing operations. Each special item is shown net of any related income tax effects.

LO12-2 **Compute earnings per share.** Earnings per share is computed by dividing the income applicable to the common stock by the weighted-average number of common shares outstanding. If the income statement includes subtotals for income from continuing operations, or for income before extraordinary items, per-share figures are shown for these amounts, as well as for net income.

LO12-3 **Distinguish between basic and diluted earnings per share.** Diluted earnings per share is computed for companies that have outstanding securities convertible into shares of common stock. In such situations, the computation of basic earnings per share is based on the number of common shares actually outstanding during the year. The computation of diluted earnings per share, however, is based on the potential number of common shares outstanding if the various securities were converted into common shares. The purpose of showing diluted earnings is to alert investors to the extent to which conversions of securities could reduce basic earnings per share.

LO12-4 **Account for cash dividends and stock dividends, and explain the effects of these transactions on a company's financial statements.** Cash dividends reduce retained earnings at the time the company's board of directors declares the dividends. At that time, the dividends become a liability for the company. Stock dividends generally are recorded by transferring the market value of the additional shares to be issued from retained earnings to the appropriate paid-in capital accounts. Stock dividends increase the number of shares outstanding but do not change total stockholders' equity, nor do they change the relative amount of the company owned by each individual stockholder.

LO12-5 **Describe and prepare a statement of retained earnings.** A statement of retained earnings shows the changes in the balance of the Retained Earnings account during the period. In its simplest form, this financial statement shows the beginning balance of retained earnings, adds the net income for the period, subtracts any dividends declared, and thus computes the ending balance of retained earnings.

LO12-6 **Define *prior period adjustments*, and explain how they are presented in financial statements.** A prior period adjustment corrects errors in the amount of net income reported in a *prior* year. Because the income of the prior year has already been closed into retained earnings, the error is corrected by increasing or decreasing the Retained Earnings account. Prior period adjustments appear in the statement of retained earnings as adjustments to beginning retained earnings. They are *not* reported in the income statement for the current period.

LO12-7 **Define *comprehensive income*, and explain how it differs from net income.** Net income is a component of comprehensive income. Comprehensive income is broad and includes the effect of certain transactions that are recognized in the financial statements but that are not included in net income because they have not yet been realized. An example is the change in market value of available-for-sale investments. Net income is presented in the income statement. Comprehensive income may be presented in a combined statement with net income or in a separate statement of comprehensive income that immediately follows the income statement in the company's annual report.

LO12-8 **Describe and prepare a statement of stockholders' equity and the stockholders' equity section of the balance sheet.** This expanded version of the statement of retained earnings explains the changes during the year in each stockholders' equity account. It is not a required financial statement but is often prepared instead of disclosing the changes in the stockholders' equity accounts in the financial statement notes. The statement lists the beginning balance in each stockholders' equity account, explains the nature and the amount of each change, and computes the ending balance in each equity account.

LO12-9 **Illustrate steps management might take to improve the appearance of the company's net income.** Companies may take certain steps that are intended to improve the appearance of the company's financial performance in its financial statements. The Securities and Exchange Commission brought a series of enforcement actions against **Just for Feet** for taking steps to artificially enhance the appearance of the company's performance.

Key Terms Introduced or Emphasized in Chapter 12

basic earnings per share (p. 530) Net income applicable to the common stock divided by the weighted-average number of common shares outstanding during the year.

cash dividend (p. 530) A distribution of cash by a corporation to its stockholders.

comprehensive income (p. 536) Net income plus or minus certain changes in financial position that are recorded as direct adjustments to stockholders' equity (for example, changes in the value of available-for-sale investments) rather than as elements in the determination of net income.

date of record (p. 531)   The date on which a person must be listed as a shareholder to be eligible to receive a dividend. Follows the date of declaration of a dividend by two or three weeks.

diluted earnings per share (p. 530)   Earnings per share computed under the assumption that all convertible securities were converted into additional common shares at the beginning of the current year. The purpose of this pro forma computation is to alert common stockholders to the risk that future earnings per share might be reduced by the conversion of other securities into common stock.

discontinued operations (p. 525)   The net operating results (revenue and expenses) of a segment of a company that has been or is being sold, as well as the gain or loss on disposal.

earnings per share (p. 527)   Net income applicable to the common stock divided by the weighted-average number of common shares outstanding during the year.

ex-dividend date (p. 531)   A date three days prior to the date of record specified in a dividend declaration. A person buying a stock prior to the ex-dividend date also acquires the right to receive the dividend. The three-day interval permits the compilation of a list of stockholders as of the date of record.

extraordinary items (p. 525)   Transactions and events that are unusual in nature and occur infrequently—for example, most large earthquake losses. Such items are shown separately in the income statement after the determination of income before extraordinary items.

price-earnings (p/e) ratio (p. 529)   Market price of a share of common stock divided by annual earnings per share.

prior period adjustment (p. 535)   A correction of a material error in the earnings reported in the financial statements of a prior year. Prior period adjustments are recorded directly in the Retained Earnings account and are not included in the income statement of the current period.

restructuring charges (p. 526)   Costs related to reorganizing and downsizing the company to make the company more efficient. These costs are presented in the income statement as a single line item in determining operating income.

segment of the business (p. 525)   Those elements of a business that represent a separate and distinct line of business activity or that service a distinct category of customers.

statement of retained earnings (p. 534)   A financial statement explaining the change during the year in the amount of retained earnings. May be expanded into a statement of stockholders' equity.

statement of stockholders' equity (p. 536)   An expanded version of a statement of retained earnings. Summarizes the changes during the year in all stockholders' equity accounts. Not a required financial statement, but widely used as a substitute for disclosing the changes in the stockholders' equity accounts in the financial statement notes.

stock dividend (p. 532)   A distribution of additional shares to common stockholders in proportion to their holdings.

Demonstration Problem

The stockholders' equity of Embassy Corporation at December 31, 2014, is shown below.

Stockholders' equity:	
Common stock, $10 par, 100,000 shares authorized, 40,000 shares issued and outstanding	$ 400,000
Additional paid-in capital: common stock	200,000
Total paid-in capital	$ 600,000
Retained earnings	1,700,000
Total stockholders' equity	$2,300,000

Transactions affecting stockholders' equity during 2015 are as follows:

Mar. 31   A 5-for-4 stock split proposed by the board of directors was approved by vote of the stockholders. The 10,000 new shares were distributed to stockholders.

Apr. 1   The company purchased 2,000 shares of its common stock on the open market at $37 per share.

July 1   The company reissued 1,000 shares of treasury stock at $48 per share.

July 1   The company issued for cash 20,000 shares of previously unissued $8 par value common stock at a price of $47 per share.

Dec. 1   A cash dividend of $1 per share was declared, payable on December 30, to stockholders of record at December 14.

Dec. 22   A 10 percent stock dividend was declared; the dividend shares are to be distributed on January 15 of the following year. The market price of the stock on December 22 was $48 per share.

The net income for the year ended December 31, 2015, amounted to $173,000, after an extraordinary loss of $47,400 (net of related income tax benefits).

Instructions

a. Prepare journal entries (in general journal form) to record the transactions affecting stockholders' equity that took place during the year.

b. Prepare the lower section of the income statement for 2015, beginning with *income before extraordinary items* and showing the extraordinary loss and the net income. Also illustrate the presentation of earnings per share in the income statement, assuming that earnings per share is determined on the basis of the *weighted-average* number of shares outstanding during the year.

c. Prepare a statement of retained earnings for the year ending December 31, 2015.

Solution to the Demonstration Problem

a.

	GENERAL JOURNAL		Page 1
Date	**Account Titles and Explanations**	**Debit**	**Credit**
Mar. 31	Memorandum: A 5-for-4 stock split increased the number of shares of common stock outstanding from 40,000 to 50,000 and reduced the par value from $10 to $8 per share. The 10,000 new shares were distributed.		
Apr. 1	Treasury Stock	74,000	
	Cash		74,000
	Acquired 2,000 shares of treasury stock at $37.		
July 1	Cash	48,000	
	Treasury Stock		37,000
	Additional Paid-in Capital: Treasury Stock Transactions		11,000
	Sold 1,000 shares of treasury stock at $48 per share.		
July 1	Cash	940,000	
	Common Stock, $8 par		160,000
	Additional Paid-in Capital: Common Stock		780,000
	Issued 20,000 shares at $47.		
Dec. 1	Dividends	69,000	
	Dividends Payable		69,000
	To record declaration of cash dividend of $1 per share on 69,000 shares of common stock outstanding (1,000 shares in treasury are not entitled to receive dividends).		
	Note: Entry to record the payment of the cash dividend is not shown here because the action does not affect the stockholders' equity.		
Dec. 22	Retained Earnings	331,200	
	Stock Dividends to Be Distributed		55,200
	Additional Paid-in Capital: Stock Dividends		276,000
	To record declaration of 10% stock dividend (10% × 69,000 shares outstanding): 6,900 shares of $8 par value common stock to be distributed on Jan. 15 of next year. Market price at date of issuance, $48.		
Dec. 31	Income Summary	173,000	
	Retained Earnings		173,000
	To close Income Summary account.		
Dec. 31	Retained Earnings	69,000	
	Dividends		69,000
	To close Dividends account.		

b.

EMBASSY CORPORATION
PARTIAL INCOME STATEMENT
FOR THE YEAR ENDED DECEMBER 31, 2015

Income before extraordinary items	$220,400
Extraordinary loss (net of income tax benefit)	(47,400)
Net income	$173,000
Earnings per share:*	
Income before extraordinary items	$3.73
Extraordinary loss	(0.80)
Net income	$2.93

*The 59,000 weighted-average number of shares of common stock outstanding during 2015 determined as follows:

Jan. 1–Mar. 31: (40,000 + 10,000 shares issued pursuant to a 5-for-4 split) × ¼ of year	12,500
Apr. 1–June 30: (50,000 − 2,000 shares of treasury stock) × ¼ of year	12,000
July 1–Dec. 31: (50,000 + 20,000 shares of new stock − 1,000 shares of treasury stock) × ½ of year	34,500
Weighted-average number of shares outstanding	59,000

c.

EMBASSY CORPORATION
STATEMENT OF RETAINED EARNINGS
FOR THE YEAR ENDED DECEMBER 31, 2015

Retained earnings, Dec. 31, 2014		$1,700,000
Net income for 2015		173,000
Subtotal		$1,873,000
Less: Cash dividends ($1 per share)	$ 69,000	
10% stock dividend	331,200	400,200
Retained earnings, Dec. 31, 2015		$1,472,800

Self-Test Questions

The answers to these questions appear on page 563.

1. The primary purpose of showing special types of events separately in the income statement is to:

   a. Increase earnings per share.

   b. Assist users of the income statement in evaluating the profitability of normal, ongoing operations.

   c. Minimize the income taxes paid on the results of ongoing operations.

   d. Prevent unusual losses from recurring.

2. Which of the following situations would *not* be presented in a separate section of the current year's income statement of Hamilton Corporation? During the current year:

   a. Hamilton's Los Angeles headquarters are destroyed by a tornado.

   b. Hamilton sells its entire juvenile furniture operations and concentrates on its remaining children's clothing segment.

   c. Hamilton's accountant discovers that the entire price paid several years ago to purchase company offices in Texas had been charged to a Land account; consequently, no depreciation has ever been taken on these buildings.

   d. As a result of labor union contract changes, Hamilton paid increased compensation expense during the year.

3. When a corporation has outstanding both common and preferred stock:

   a. Basic and diluted earnings per share are reported only if the preferred stock is cumulative.

   b. Earnings per share is reported for each type of stock outstanding.

   c. Earnings per share is computed without regard to the amount of the annual preferred dividends.

   d. Earnings per share is computed without regard to the amount of dividends declared on common stock.

4. Which of the following is (are) *not* true about a stock dividend?

   a. Total stockholders' equity does not change when a stock dividend is declared but does change when it is distributed.

   b. Between the time a stock dividend is declared and when it is distributed, the company's commitment is presented in the balance sheet as a current liability.

   c. Stock dividends do not change the relative portion of the company owned by individual stockholders.

   d. Stock dividends have no impact on the amount of the company's assets.

5. The statement of retained earnings:

   a. Includes prior period adjustments, cash dividends, and stock dividends.

   b. Indicates the amount of cash available for the payment of dividends.

   c. Is not a required financial statement.

   d. Shows revenue, expenses, and dividends for the accounting period.

ASSIGNMENT MATERIAL **Discussion Questions**

1. What is the purpose of arranging an income statement to show subtotals for *income from continuing operations* and *income before extraordinary items?*

2. Frank's Fun Company owns 30 pizza parlors and a minor league baseball team. During the current year, the company sold three of its pizza parlors and closed another when the lease on the building expired. Should any of these events be classified as discontinued operations in the company's income statement? Explain.

3. Define *extraordinary items.* How are extraordinary items distinguished from items that are presented as separate line items in an income statement, but are not extraordinary?

4. In an effort to make the company more competitive, Fast-Guard, Inc., incurred significant expenses related to a reduction in the number of employees, consolidation of offices and facilities, and disposition of assets that are no longer productive. Explain how these costs should be presented in the financial statements of the company, and describe how an investor should view these costs in predicting future earnings of the company.

5. A *prior period adjustment* relates to the income of past accounting periods. Explain how such an item is shown in the financial statements.

6. In evaluating the potential future profitability of a company, how would you consider irregular income items, such as extraordinary items, discontinued operations, and prior period adjustments?

7. Explain how each of the following is computed:

   a. Price-earnings ratio.

   b. Basic earnings per share.

   c. Diluted earnings per share.

8. Throughout the year, Baker Construction Company had 3 million shares of common stock and 150,000 shares of convertible preferred stock outstanding. Each share of preferred is convertible into two shares of common. What number of shares should be used in the computation of (**a**) basic earnings per share and (**b**) diluted earnings per share?

9. A financial analyst notes that Collier Corporation's earnings per share have been rising steadily for the past five years. The analyst expects the company's net income to continue to increase at the same rate as in the past. In forecasting future basic earnings per share, what special risk should the analyst consider if Collier's basic earnings are significantly larger than its diluted earnings?

10. Distinguish between a *stock split* and a *stock dividend.* Is there any reason for the difference in accounting treatment of these two events?

11. What are *restructuring charges?* How are they presented in financial statements?

12. If a company's total stockholders' equity is unchanged by the distribution of a stock dividend, how is it possible for a stockholder who received shares in the distribution of the dividend to benefit?

13. What is a liquidating dividend, and how does it relate to a regular (nonliquidating) dividend?

14. In discussing stock dividends and stock splits in an investments class you are taking, one of the students says, "Stock splits and stock dividends are exactly the same—both are distributions of a company's stock to existing owners without payment to the company." Do you agree? Why or why not?

15. A *statement of stockholders' equity* sometimes is described as an "expanded" statement of retained earnings. Why?

Brief Exercises

LO12-1	Fellups, Inc., had net income for the year just ended of $75,000, without considering the following

LO12-1

BRIEF EXERCISE 12.1

Extraordinary Loss

Fellups, Inc., had net income for the year just ended of $75,000, without considering the following item or its tax effects. During the year, a tornado damaged one of the company's warehouses and its contents. Tornado damage is quite rare in Fellups's location. The estimated amount of the loss from the tornado is $100,000 and the related tax effect is 40 percent. Prepare the final section of Fellups's income statement, beginning with income before extraordinary items.

LO12-1

BRIEF EXERCISE 12.2

Extraordinary Gain

Hudson Company had total revenue and expense numbers of $750,000 and $600,000, respectively, in the current year. In addition, the company had a gain of $115,000 that resulted from the passage of new legislation, which is considered unusual and infrequent for financial reporting purposes. The gain is expected to be subject to a 35 percent income tax rate. Prepare an abbreviated income statement for Hudson for the year.

LO12-1

BRIEF EXERCISE 12.3

Discontinued Operations

Wabash, Inc., had revenue and expenses from ongoing business operations for the current year of $480,000 and $430,000, respectively. During the year, the company sold a division which had revenue and expenses (not included in the previous figures) of $100,000 and $75,000, respectively. The division was sold at a loss of $55,000. All items are subject to an income tax rate of 40 percent. Prepare an abbreviated income statement for Wabash for the year.

LO12-4

BRIEF EXERCISE 12.4

Cash and Stock Dividends

Gannon, Inc., had 100,000 shares of common stock outstanding. During the current year, the company distributed a 10 percent stock dividend and subsequently paid a $0.50 per share cash dividend. Calculate the number of shares outstanding at the time of the cash dividend and the amount of cash required to fund the cash dividend.

LO12-5

BRIEF EXERCISE 12.5

Statement of Retained Earnings

Messer Company had retained earnings at the beginning of the current year of $590,000. During the year, the following activities occurred:

- Net income of $88,000 was earned.

- A cash dividend of $1.20 per share was declared and distributed on the 50,000 shares of common stock outstanding.

Prepare a statement of retained earnings for the year.

LO12-5, LO12-6

BRIEF EXERCISE 12.6

Statement of Retained Earnings

Salt & Pepper, Inc., had retained earnings at the beginning of the current year of $460,000. During the year the company earned net income of $250,000 and declared dividends as follows:

- $1 per share for the current-year dividend on the 10,000 shares of preferred stock outstanding.

- $1 per share for the dividend in arrears for one year on the 10,000 shares of preferred stock outstanding.

- $0.50 per share for the current-year dividend on the 200,000 shares of common stock outstanding.

In addition, the company discovered an overstatement in the prior year's net income of $65,000 and corrected that error in the current year. Prepare a statement of retained earnings for the year.

LO12-4

BRIEF EXERCISE 12.7

Cash Dividend Journal Entries

Gannon, Inc., declared dividends during the current year as follows:

- The current year's cash dividend on the 6 percent, $100 par value preferred stock. 100,000 shares were outstanding at the time of the declaration.

- A cash dividend of $0.75 per share on the $10 par value common stock. 750,000 shares were outstanding at the time of the declaration.

Prepare the general journal entries to record the declaration and payment of these dividends, assuming the declaration is recorded directly to retained earnings.

LO12-4

BRIEF EXERCISE 12.8

Stock Dividend Journal Entries

Fossil, Inc., declared a 4 percent stock dividend on its 750,000 shares of common stock. The $10 par value common stock was originally sold for $14 and was selling at $17 at the time the stock dividend was declared. Prepare the general journal entries to record and distribute the stock dividend.

LO12-4, LO12-8

BRIEF EXERCISE 12.9

Stockholders' Equity Section of Balance Sheet

Alexander, Inc., declared and distributed a 10 percent stock dividend on its 700,000 shares of outstanding $5 par value common stock when the stock was selling for $12 per share. The outstanding shares had originally been sold at $8 per share. The balance in retained earnings before the declaration of the stock dividend, but after the addition of the current year's net income, was $995,000. Prepare the stockholders' section of Alexander's balance sheet to reflect these facts.

LO12-7

BRIEF EXERCISE 12.10

Comprehensive Income

Crasher Company had net income in the current year of $500,000. In addition, the company had an unrealized gain on its portfolio of available-for-sale investments of $20,000, net of related income taxes. Assuming the company uses the two-income statement approach for presenting elements of other comprehensive income to its investors and creditors, prepare the statement of comprehensive income for the current year.

Exercises

LO12-4

EXERCISE 12.1

Stock Dividends and Stock Splits

Assume that when you were in high school you saved $1,000 to invest for your college education. You purchased 200 shares of Smiley Incorporated, a small but growing company. Over the three years that you have owned the stock, the corporation's board of directors has taken the following actions:

1. Declared a 2-for-1 stock split.

2. Declared a 20 percent stock dividend.

3. Declared a 3-for-1 stock split.

The current price of the stock is $12 per share.

  a. Calculate the current number of shares and the market value of your investment.

  b. Explain the likely reason the board of directors of the company has not declared a cash dividend.

  c. State your opinion as to whether or not you would have been better off if the board of directors had declared a cash dividend instead of the stock dividend and stock splits.

LO12-1 through LO12-4, LO12-6, LO12-7

EXERCISE 12.2

Accounting Terminology

The following are 10 technical accounting terms introduced or emphasized in Chapters 11 and 12:

P/e ratio	Treasury stock	Discontinued operations
Stock dividend	Extraordinary item	Prior period adjustment
Basic earnings per share	Additional paid-in capital	Diluted earnings per share
Comprehensive income		

Each of the following statements may (or may not) describe one of these technical terms. For each statement, indicate the term described, or answer "None" if the statement does not correctly describe any of the terms.

  a. A gain or loss that is unusual in nature and not expected to recur in the foreseeable future.

  b. The asset represented by shares of capital stock that have not yet been issued.

  c. A distribution of additional shares of stock that reduces retained earnings but causes no change in total stockholders' equity.

  d. The amount received when stock is sold in excess of par value.

  e. An adjustment to the beginning balance of retained earnings to correct an error previously made in the measurement of net income.

  f. A statistic expressing a relationship between the current market value of a share of common stock and the underlying earnings per share.

  g. A separate section sometimes included in an income statement as a way to help investors evaluate the profitability of ongoing business activities.

h. A pro forma figure indicating what earnings per share would have been if all securities convertible into common stock had been converted at the beginning of the current year.

i. A broadly defined measure of financial performance that includes, but is not limited to, net income.

LO12-1, LO12-2

EXERCISE 12.3

Discontinued Operations

During the current year, Sports +, Inc., operated two business segments: a chain of surf and dive shops and a small chain of tennis shops. The tennis shops were not profitable and were sold near year-end to another corporation. Sports + operations for the current year are summarized below. The first two captions, "Net sales" and "Costs and expenses," relate only to the company's continuing operations.

Net sales	$12,500,000
Costs and expenses (including applicable income tax)	8,600,000
Operating loss from tennis shops (net of income tax benefit)	192,000
Loss on sale of tennis shops (net of income tax benefit)	348,000

The company had 182,000 shares of a single class of capital stock outstanding throughout the year.

a. Prepare a condensed income statement for the year. At the bottom of the statement, show any appropriate earnings per share figures. (A condensed income statement is illustrated in Exhibit 12–2.)

b. Which earnings per share figure in part **a** do you consider most useful in predicting future operating results for Sports +, Inc.? Why?

LO12-1, LO12-2

EXERCISE 12.4

Reporting an Extraordinary Item

For the year ended December 31, Southern Supply had net sales of $3,875,000, costs and other expenses (including income tax) of $3,100,000, and an extraordinary gain (net of income tax) of $210,000.

a. Prepare a condensed income statement (including earnings per share), assuming that 620,000 shares of common stock were outstanding throughout the year. (A condensed income statement is illustrated in Exhibit 12–2.)

b. Which earnings per share figure is used in computing the price-earnings ratio for Southern Supply reported in financial publications such as *The Wall Street Journal?* Explain briefly.

LO12-2

EXERCISE 12.5

Computing Earnings per Share: Effect of Preferred Stock

The net income of Foster Furniture, Inc., amounted to $1,920,000 for the current year.

a. Compute the amount of earnings per share assuming that the shares of capital stock outstanding throughout the year consisted of:

1. 400,000 shares of $1 par value common stock and no preferred stock.

2. 100,000 shares of 8 percent, $100 par value preferred stock and 300,000 shares of $5 par value common stock.

b. Is the earnings per share figure computed in part **a(2)** considered to be basic or diluted? Explain.

LO12-2, LO12-4

EXERCISE 12.6

Restating Earnings per Share after a Stock Dividend

The 2015 annual report of Software City, Inc., included the following comparative summary of earnings per share over the last three years:

	2015	2014	2013
Earnings per share	$3.15	$2.40	$1.64

In 2016, Software City, Inc., declared and distributed a 100 percent stock dividend. Following this stock dividend, the company reported earnings per share of $1.88 for 2016.

a. Prepare a three-year schedule similar to the one above, but compare earnings per share during the years 2016, 2015, and 2014. (Hint: All per-share amounts in your schedule should be based on the number of shares outstanding *after* the stock dividend.)

b. In preparing your schedule, which figure (or figures) did you have to restate? Why? Explain the logic behind your computation.

LO12-4

EXERCISE 12.7

Cash Dividends, Stock Dividends, and Stock Splits

HiTech Manufacturing Company has 1,000,000 shares of $1 par value capital stock outstanding on January 1. The following equity transactions occurred during the current year:

Apr. 30	Distributed additional shares of capital stock in a 2-for-1 stock split. Market price of stock was $35 per share.
June 1	Declared a cash dividend of $0.60 per share.
July 1	Paid the $0.60 cash dividend to stockholders.
Aug. 1	Declared a 5 percent stock dividend. Market price of stock was $19 per share.
Sept. 10	Issued shares resulting from the 5 percent stock dividend declared on August 1.

a. Prepare journal entries to record the above transactions.

b. Compute the number of shares of capital stock outstanding at year-end.

c. What is the par value per share of HiTech Manufacturing stock at the end of the year?

d. Determine the effect of each of the following on *total* stockholders' equity: stock split, declaration and payment of a cash dividend, declaration and distribution of a stock dividend. (Your answers should be either *increase, decrease,* or *no effect.*)

LO12-4

EXERCISE 12.8

Effect of Stock Dividends on Stock Price

Inland Co., has a total of 40,000 shares of common stock outstanding and no preferred stock. Total stockholders' equity at the end of the current year amounts to $2.5 million and the market value of the stock is $33 per share. At year-end, the company declares a 10 percent stock dividend—one share for each 10 shares held. If all parties concerned clearly recognize the nature of the stock dividend, what should you expect the market price per share of the common stock to be on the ex-dividend date?

LO12-8

EXERCISE 12.9

Reporting the Effects of Transactions

Five events pertaining to Lubbock Manufacturing Co. are described below.

a. Declared and paid a cash dividend.

b. Issued a 10 percent stock dividend.

c. Issued a 2-for-1 stock split.

d. Purchased treasury stock.

e. Reissued the treasury stock at a price greater than the purchase price.

Indicate the immediate effects of the events on the financial measurements in the four columnar headings listed below. Use the code letters **I** for increase, **D** for decrease, and **NE** for no effect.

Event	Current Assets	Stockholders' Equity	Net Income	Net Cash Flow (from any source)

LO12-2, LO12-4

EXERCISE 12.10

Effects of Various Transactions on Earnings per Share

Explain the immediate effects, if any, of each of the following transactions on a company's earnings per share:

a. Split the common stock 3-for-1.

b. Realized a gain from the sale of a discontinued operation.

c. Declared and paid a cash dividend on common stock.

d. Declared and distributed a stock dividend on common stock.

e. Acquired several thousand shares of treasury stock.

LOI2-1, LOI2-5, LOI2-8
EXERCISE 12.11
Where to Find Financial
Information

You have now learned about the following financial statements issued by corporations: balance sheet, income statement, statement of retained earnings, statement of stockholders' equity, statement of comprehensive income, and statement of cash flows. Listed below are various items frequently of interest to a corporation's owners, potential investors, and creditors, among others. You are to specify which of the above corporate financial statements, if any, reports the desired information. If the listed item is not reported in any formal financial statement issued by a corporation, indicate an appropriate source for the desired information.

a. Number of shares of stock outstanding as of year-end.

b. Total dollar amount of cash dividends declared during the current year.

c. Market value per share at balance sheet date.

d. Cumulative dollar effect of an accounting error made in a previous year.

e. Detailed disclosure of why the number of shares of stock outstanding at the end of the current year is greater than the number of shares of stock outstanding at the end of the prior year.

f. Earnings per share of common stock.

g. Book value per share.

h. Price-earnings (p/e) ratio.

i. The total amount the corporation paid to buy back shares of its own stock, which it now holds.

j. Change in the fair market value of available-for-sale investments.

LOI2-7
EXERCISE 12.12
Comprehensive Income

Minor, Inc., had revenue of $572,000 and expenses (other than income taxes) of $282,000 for the current year. The company is subject to a 35 percent income tax rate. In addition, available-for-sale investments, which were purchased for $17,500 early in the year, had a market value at the end of the year of $19,200.

a. Determine the amount of Minor's net income for the year.

b. Determine the amount of Minor's comprehensive income for the year.

c. How would your answers to parts **a** and **b** differ if the market value of Minor's investments at the end of the year had been $14,200?

LOI2-4
EXERCISE 12.13
Cash and Stock Dividends

Kosmier Company has outstanding 500,000 shares of $50 par value common stock that originally sold for $60 per share. During the three most recent years, the company carried out the following activities in the order presented: declared and distributed a 10 percent stock dividend, declared and paid a cash dividend of $1 per share, declared and distributed a 2-for-1 stock split, and declared and paid a $0.60 per share cash dividend.

a. Determine the number of shares of stock outstanding after the four transactions described above.

b. Determine the amount of cash that the company paid in the four transactions described above.

c. If you were a stockholder who held 100 shares of stock that you purchased four years ago when the market value of the shares was $65, how many shares would you own after the four transactions described above? If the market value of the stock was $40 after the four transactions, would you be better or worse off than before the four transactions?

LOI2-3, LOI2-5
EXERCISE 12.14
EPS and Dividends
Using **Home Depot, Inc.,**
Financial Statements

Home Depot, Inc.'s income statements for 2011, 2012, and 2013 show basic earnings per share of $2.03, $2.49, and $3.03, respectively. Diluted earnings per share figures are slightly lower than these numbers, indicating the impact of potential capital stock activity that could reduce earnings per share for current stockholders.
The company paid cash dividends of $0.945 per share in 2011, $1.04 per share in 2012, and $1.16 per share in 2013.

a. Why do you think **Home Depot** is paying out only about 38 percent to 47 percent of its net income to stockholders in the form of cash dividends?

b. If you were an investor in **Home Depot**'s stock, would you be unhappy because your dividends represented such a small percentage of the company's net income?

LOI2-I, LOI2-8
EXERCISE 12.15
Analysis of Stock
Information using Home
Depot, Inc., Financial
Statements

Use the financial statements of **Home Depot, Inc.**, in Appendix A of this text to answer these questions:

a. Study the income statements of **Home Depot, Inc.**, for the three years ending on or about February 1, 2013, 2012, and 2011. Do these statements include any irregular items that might affect your use of the information to project future earnings?

b. Review the stockholders' equity section of the company's balance sheet at February 3, 2013. What type of capital stock is in the capital structure, and how many shares are authorized, issued, and outstanding, and held in treasury on that date?

c. Locate the statement of stockholders' equity and comprehensive income. What treasury stock transactions has **Home Depot** engaged in during the three-year period presented? Has any additional stock (other than treasury stock) been issued during the period reported? If so, what were the circumstances in which that stock was issued? What was the amount of Other Comprehensive Income in each year?

Problem Set A

LOI2-I, LOI2-2
PROBLEM 12.1A
Reporting Unusual Events;
Using Predictive Subtotals

Eastern Aviation operated both an airline and several restaurants located near airports. During the year just ended, all restaurant operations were discontinued and the following operating results were reported:

Continuing operations (airline):	
Net sales	$27,560,000
Costs and expenses (including income taxes on continuing operations)	21,660,000
Other data:	
Operating income from restaurants (net of income tax)	432,000
Gain on sale of restaurants (net of income tax)	2,478,000
Extraordinary loss (net of income tax benefit)	1,680,000

The extraordinary loss resulted from the destruction of an airliner by a hurricane. Eastern Aviation had 1,000,000 shares of capital stock outstanding throughout the year.

Instructions

a. Prepare a condensed income statement, including proper presentation of the discontinued restaurant operations and the extraordinary loss. Include all appropriate earnings per share figures.

b. Assume that you expect the profitability of Eastern Aviation operations to *decline by 5 percent* next year, and the profitability of the restaurants to decline by 10 percent. What is your estimate of the company's net earnings per share next year?

LOI2-I, LOI2-2, LOI2-5,
LOI2-6
PROBLEM 12.2A
Format of an Income
Statement and a Statement
of Retained Earnings

The following data relate to the operations of Slick Software, Inc., during 2015.

Continuing operations:	
Net sales	$19,850,000
Costs and expenses (including applicable income tax)	16,900,000
Other data:	
Operating income during 2015 on segment of the business discontinued near year-end (net of income tax)	140,000
Loss on disposal of discontinued segment (net of income tax benefit)	550,000
Extraordinary loss (net of income tax benefit)	900,000
Prior period adjustment (increase in 2014 depreciation expense, net of income tax benefit)	350,000
Cash dividends declared	950,000

Instructions

a. Prepare a condensed income statement for 2015, including earnings per share figures. Slick Software, Inc., had 200,000 shares of $1 par value common stock and 80,000 shares of $6.25, $100 par value preferred stock outstanding throughout the year.

b. Prepare a statement of retained earnings for the year ended December 31, 2015. As originally reported, retained earnings at December 31, 2014, amounted to $7,285,000.

c. Compute the amount of cash dividend *per share of common stock* declared by the board of directors for 2015. Assume no dividends in arrears on the preferred stock.

d. Assume that 2016 earnings per share is a single figure and amounts to $8.00. Assume also that there are no changes in outstanding common or preferred stock in 2016. Do you consider the $8.00 earnings per share figure in 2016 to be a favorable or unfavorable statistic in comparison with 2015 performance? Explain.

LO12-1, LO12-2, LO12-5, LO12-8

PROBLEM 12.3A
Reporting Unusual Events:
A Comprehensive Problem

The income statement below was prepared by a new and inexperienced employee in the accounting department of Phoenix, Inc., a business organized as a corporation.

PHOENIX, INC.
INCOME STATEMENT
FOR THE YEAR ENDED DECEMBER 31, 2015

Net sales		$10,800,000
Gain on sale of treasury stock		62,000
Excess of issuance price over par value of capital stock		510,000
Prior period adjustment (net of income tax)		60,000
Extraordinary gain (net of income tax)		36,000
Total revenue		$11,468,000
Less:		
Cost of goods sold	$6,000,000	
Selling expenses	1,104,000	
General and administrative expenses	1,896,000	
Loss from settlement of litigation	24,000	
Income tax on continuing operations	720,000	
Operating loss on discontinued operations (net of income tax benefit)	252,000	
Loss on disposal of discontinued operations (net of income tax benefit)	420,000	
Dividends declared on common stock	350,000	
Total costs and expenses		10,766,000
Net income		$ 702,000

Instructions

a. Prepare a corrected income statement for the year ended December 31, 2015, using the format illustrated in Exhibit 12–2. Include at the bottom of your income statement all appropriate earnings-per-share figures. Assume that throughout the year the company had outstanding a weighted average of 180,000 shares of a single class of capital stock.

b. Prepare a statement of retained earnings for 2015. (As originally reported, retained earnings at December 31, 2014, amounted to $2,175,000.)

c. What does the $62,000 "gain on sale of treasury stock" represent? How would you report this item in Phoenix's financial statements at December 31, 2015?

At the beginning of the year, Albers, Inc., has total stockholders' equity of $840,000 and 40,000 outstanding shares of a single class of capital stock. During the year, the corporation completes the following transactions affecting its stockholders' equity accounts:

Jan. 10   A 5 percent stock dividend is declared and distributed. (Market price, $20 per share.)

Mar. 15   The corporation acquires 2,000 shares of its own capital stock at a cost of $21.00 per share.

May 30   All 2,000 shares of the treasury stock are reissued at a price of $31.50 per share.

July 31   The capital stock is split 2-for-1.

Dec. 15   The board of directors declares a cash dividend of $1.10 per share, payable on January 15.

Dec. 31   Net income of $525,000 is reported for the year ended December 31.

Instructions

Compute the amount of total stockholders' equity, the number of shares of capital stock outstanding, and the book value per share following each successive transaction. Organize your solution as a three-column schedule with these separate column headings: (1) Total Stockholders' Equity, (2) Number of Shares Outstanding, and (3) Book Value per Share.

A summary of the transactions affecting the stockholders' equity of Riverton Corporation during the current year follows:

Prior period adjustment (net of income tax benefit)	$ (160,000)
Issuance of common stock: 10,000 shares of $10 par value capital stock at $68 per share	680,000
Declaration and distribution of 5% stock dividend (11,500 shares, market price $40 per share)	(460,000)
Purchased 1,000 shares of treasury stock at $70	(70,000)
Reissued 500 shares of treasury stock at a price of $72 per share	36,000
Net income	1,690,000
Cash dividends declared	(285,400)

Note: Parentheses (   ) indicate a reduction in stockholders' equity.

Instructions

a.   Prepare a statement of stockholders' equity for the year. Use these column headings and beginning balances. (Notice that all additional paid-in capital accounts are combined into a single column.)

	Capital Stock ($10 par value)	Additional Paid-in Capital	Retained Earnings	Treasury Stock	Total Stock-holders' Equity
Balances, Jan. 1	$2,200,000	$3,530,000	$1,900,000	$ –0–	$7,630,000

b.   What was the overall effect on total stockholders' equity of the 5 percent stock dividend of 11,500 shares? What was the overall effect on total stockholders' equity of the cash dividends declared? Do these two events have the same impact on stockholders' equity? Why or why not?

LOI2-4, LOI2-8

PROBLEM 12.6A

Recording Stock Dividends
and Treasury Stock
Transactions

At the beginning of 2015, Thompson Service, Inc., showed the following amounts in the stockholders' equity section of its balance sheet:

Stockholders' equity:

Capital stock, $1 par value, 500,000 shares authorized, 382,000 issued and outstanding	$ 382,000
Additional paid-in capital: capital stock	4,202,000
Total paid-in capital	$4,584,000
Retained earnings	2,704,600
Total stockholders' equity	$7,288,600

The transactions relating to stockholders' equity during the year are as follows:

Jan. 3 Declared a dividend of $1 per share to stockholders of record on January 31, payable on February 15.

Feb. 15 Paid the cash dividend declared on January 3.

Apr. 12 The corporation purchased 6,000 shares of its own capital stock at a price of $40 per share.

May 9 Reissued 4,000 shares of the treasury stock at a price of $44 per share.

June 1 Declared a 5 percent stock dividend to stockholders of record at June 15, to be distributed on June 30. The market price of the stock at June 1 was $42 per share. (The 2,000 shares remaining in the treasury do not participate in the stock dividend.)

June 30 Distributed the stock dividend declared on June 1.

Aug. 4 Reissued 600 of the 2,000 remaining shares of treasury stock at a price of $37 per share.

Dec. 31 The Income Summary account, showing net income for the year of $1,928,000, was closed into the Retained Earnings account.

Dec. 31 The $382,000 balance in the Dividends account was closed into the Retained Earnings account.

Instructions

a. Prepare in general journal form the entries to record the above transactions.

b. Prepare the stockholders' equity section of the balance sheet at December 31, 2015. Use the format illustrated in Exhibit 12–6. Include a supporting schedule showing your computation of retained earnings at that date.

c. Compute the maximum cash dividend per share that legally could be declared at December 31, 2015, without impairing the paid-in capital of Thompson Service. (Hint: The availability of retained earnings for dividends is restricted by the cost of treasury stock owned.)

LOI2-8

PROBLEM 12.7A

Effects of Transactions

Tech Process, Inc., manufactures a variety of computer peripherals, such as tape drives and printers. Listed below are five events that occurred during the current year.

1. Declared a $1.00 per share cash dividend.

2. Paid the cash dividend.

3. Purchased 1,000 shares of treasury stock for $20.00 per share.

4. Reissued 500 shares of the treasury stock at a price of $18.00 per share.

5. Declared a 15 percent stock dividend.

Instructions

a. Indicate the effects of each of these events on the financial measurements listed in the four columnar headings listed below. Use the following code letters: **I** for increase, **D** for decrease, and **NE** for no effect

Event	Current Assets	Stockholders' Equity	Net Income	Net Cash Flow (from any source)

b. For each event, *explain* the reasoning behind your answers. Be prepared to explain this reasoning in class.

LO12-4, LO12-8

PROBLEM 12.8A

Preparing the Stockholders' Equity Section: A Challenging Case

The Mandella family decided early in 2015 to incorporate their family-owned vineyards under the name Mandella Corporation. The corporation was authorized to issue 500,000 shares of a single class of $10 par value capital stock. Presented below is the information necessary to prepare the stockholders' equity section of the company's balance sheet at the end of 2015 and at the end of 2016.

2015. In January the corporation issued to members of the Mandella family 150,000 shares of capital stock in exchange for cash and other assets used in the operation of the vineyards. The fair market value of these assets indicated an issue price of $30 per share. In December, Joe Mandella died, and the corporation purchased 10,000 shares of its own capital stock from his estate at $34 per share. Because of the large cash outlay to acquire this treasury stock, the directors decided not to declare cash dividends in 2015 and instead declared a 10 percent stock dividend to be distributed in January 2016. The stock price at the declaration date was $35 per share. (The treasury shares do not participate in the stock dividend.) Net income for 2015 was $940,000.

2016. In January the corporation distributed the stock dividend declared in 2015, and in February, the 10,000 treasury shares were sold to Maria Mandella at $39 per share. In June, the capital stock was split 2-for-1. (Approval was obtained to increase the authorized number of shares to 1 million.) On December 15, the directors declared a cash dividend of $2 per share, payable in January 2017. Net income for 2016 was $1,080,000.

Instructions

Using the format illustrated in Exhibit 12–6, prepare the stockholders' equity section of the balance sheet at:

a. December 31, 2015.

b. December 31, 2016.

Show any necessary computations in supporting schedules.

LO12-1, LO12-2

PROBLEM 12.9A

Format of an Income Statement; EPS

The following information is excerpted from the financial statements in a recent annual report of Esper Corporation. (Dollar figures and shares of stock are in thousands.)

Extraordinary loss due to hurricane	$ (8,490)
Loss from continuing operations	$ (16,026)
Income from discontinued operations	$ 6,215
Preferred stock dividend requirements	$ (2,778)
Weighted-average number of shares of common stock outstanding	39,739

Instructions

a. Rearrange the items to present in good form the last portion of the income statement for Esper Corporation, beginning with "Loss from continuing operations."

b. Calculate the amount of *net loss* per share for the period. (Do *not* calculate per-share amounts for subtotals, such as income from continuing operations, loss before extraordinary items, etc. You are required to compute only a single earnings per share amount.)

Problem Set B

LOI2-I, LOI2-2

PROBLEM 12.1B

Reporting Unusual Events:
Using Predictive Subtotals

Pacific Airlines operated both an airline and several rental car operations located near airports. During the year just ended, all rental car operations were discontinued and the following operating results were reported:

Continuing operations (airline):	
Net sales	$61,440,000
Costs and expenses (including income taxes on continuing operations)	53,980,000
Other data:	
Operating income from car rentals (net of income tax)	670,000
Gain on sale of rental car business (net of income tax)	4,330,000
Extraordinary loss (net of income tax benefit)	3,120,000

The extraordinary loss resulted from the destruction of an airliner by terrorists. Pacific Airlines had 4,000,000 shares of capital stock outstanding throughout the year.

Instructions

a. Prepare a condensed income statement, including proper presentation of the discontinued rental car operations and the extraordinary loss. Include all appropriate earnings per share figures.

b. Assume that you expect the profitability of Pacific's airline operations to *decline by 10 percent* next year and the profitability of the rental car operation to decline by 10 percent. What is your estimate of the company's net earnings per share next year?

LOI2-I, LOI2-2, LOI2-5,
LOI2-8

PROBLEM 12.2B

Format of an Income
Statement and a Statement
of Retained Earnings

Shown below are data relating to the operations of Beach, Inc., during 2015.

Continuing operations:	
Net sales	$37,400,000
Costs and expenses (including applicable income taxes)	21,500,000
Other data:	
Operating income during 2015 on segment of the business	
discontinued near year-end (net of income taxes)	205,000
Loss on disposal of discontinued segment (net of income	
tax benefit)	510,000
Extraordinary loss (net of income tax benefit)	930,000
Prior period adjustment (increase in 2014 amortization	
expense, net of income tax benefit)	310,000
Cash dividends declared	2,000,000

Instructions

a. Prepare a condensed income statement for 2015, including earnings per share statistics. Beach, Inc., had 200,000 shares of $1 par value common stock and 100,000 shares of $6, $100 par value preferred stock outstanding throughout the year.

b. Prepare a statement of retained earnings for the year ended December 31, 2015. As originally reported, retained earnings at December 31, 2014, amounted to $10,700,000.

c. Compute the amount of cash dividend *per share of common stock* declared by the board of directors for 2015. Assume no dividends in arrears on the preferred stock.

d. Assume that 2016 earnings per share is a single figure and amounts to $75. Assume also that there are no changes in outstanding common or preferred stock in 2016. Do you consider the $75 earnings per share figure in 2016 to be a favorable or unfavorable statistic in comparison with 2015 performance? Explain.

LO12-1, LO12-2, LO12-5, LO12-6

PROBLEM 12.3B

Reporting Unusual Events: A Comprehensive Problem

The income statement below was prepared by a new and inexperienced employee in the accounting department of Dexter, Inc., a business organized as a corporation:

DEXTER, INC.
INCOME STATEMENT
FOR THE YEAR ENDED DECEMBER 31, 2015

Net sales		$10,200,000
Gain on sale of treasury stock		56,000
Excess of issuance price over par value of capital stock		710,000
Prior period adjustment (net of income tax)		80,000
Extraordinary gain (net of income tax)		110,000
Total revenue		$11,156,000
Less:		
Cost of goods sold	$4,000,000	
Selling expenses	1,050,000	
General and administrative expenses	840,000	
Loss from settlement of litigation	10,000	
Income tax on continuing operations	612,000	
Operating loss on discontinued operations (net of income tax benefit)	180,000	
Loss on disposal of discontinued operations (net of income tax benefit)	240,000	
Dividends declared on common stock	300,000	
Total costs and expenses.		7,232,000
Net income		$ 3,924,000

Instructions

a. Prepare a corrected income statement for the year ended December 31, 2015, using the format illustrated in Exhibit 12–2. Include at the bottom of your income statement all appropriate earnings per share figures. Assume that throughout the year the company had outstanding a weighted average of 500,000 shares of a single class of capital stock.

b. Prepare a statement of retained earnings for 2015. (As originally reported, retained earnings at December 31, 2014, amount to $3,200,000.)

c. What does the $56,000 "Gain on sale of treasury stock" represent? How would you report this item in Dexter's financial statements at December 31, 2015?

LO12-4

PROBLEM 12.4B

Effects of Stock Dividends, Stock Splits, and Treasury Stock Transactions

At the beginning of the year, Sunstone, Inc., has total stockholders' equity of $1,200,000 and 20,000 outstanding shares of a single class of capital stock. During the year, the corporation completes the following transactions affecting its stockholders' equity accounts:

Jan. 16 A 5 percent stock dividend is declared and distributed. (Market price, $100 per share.)

Feb. 9 The corporation acquires 300 shares of its own capital stock at a cost of $110 per share.

Mar. 3 All 300 shares of the treasury stock are reissued at a price of $130 per share.

Jul. 5 The capital stock is split 2-for-1.

Nov. 22 The board of directors declares a cash dividend of $12 per share, payable on January 22.

Dec. 31 Net income of $174,000 is reported for the year ended December 31.

Instructions

Compute the amount of total stockholders' equity, the number of shares of capital stock outstanding, and the book value per share following each successive transaction. Organize your solution as a three-column schedule with these separate column headings: (1) "Total Stockholders' Equity," (2) "Number of Shares Outstanding," and (3) "Book Value per Share."

LO12-4, LO12-8

PROBLEM 12.5B

Preparing a Statement of Stockholders' Equity

The following is a summary of the transactions affecting the stockholders' equity of Dry Wall, Inc., during the current year:

Prior period adjustment (net of income tax benefit)	$ (47,000)
Issuance of common stock: 20,000 shares of $1 par value capital stock at $15 per share	300,000
Declaration and distribution of 10% stock dividend (15,000 shares, market price $17 per share)	255,000*
Purchased 3,000 shares of treasury stock at $16	(48,000)
Reissued 1,000 shares of treasury stock at a price of $18 per share	18,000
Net income	1,200,000
Cash dividends declared ($1 per share)	(163,000)

Note: Parentheses ( ) indicate a reduction in stockholders' equity. Asterisk * indicates no change in total shareholders' equity.

Instructions

a. Prepare a statement of stockholders' equity for the year. Use the column headings and beginning balances shown below. (Notice that all additional paid-in capital accounts are combined into a single column.)

	Capital Stock ($1 par value)	Additional Paid-in Capital	Retained Earnings	Treasury Stock	Total Stockholders' Equity
Balances, Jan. 1	$130,000	$1,170,000	$1,400,000	–0–	$2,700,000

b. What was the overall effect on total stockholders' equity of the 10 percent stock dividend of 15,000 shares? What was the overall effect on total stockholders' equity of the cash dividends declared? Do these two events have the same impact on stockholders' equity? Why or why not?

LO12-4, LO12-8

PROBLEM 12.6B

Recording Stock Dividends and Treasury Stock Transactions

At the beginning of 2015, Greene, Inc., showed the following amounts in the stockholders' equity section of its balance sheet:

Stockholders' equity:	
Capital stock, $1 par value, 1,000,000 shares authorized, 560,000 issued and outstanding	$ 560,000
Additional paid-in capital: capital stock	4,480,000
Total paid-in capital	5,040,000
Retained earnings	3,000,000
Total stockholders' equity	$8,040,000

The transactions relating to stockholders' equity during the year are as follows:

Jan. 5   Declared a dividend of $1 per share to stockholders of record on January 31, payable on February 18.

Feb. 18   Paid the cash dividend declared on January 5.

Apr. 20   The corporation purchased 1,000 shares of its own capital stock at a price of $10 per share.

May 25   Reissued 500 shares of the treasury stock at a price of $12 per share.

June 15   Declared a 5 percent stock dividend to stockholders of record at June 22, to be distributed on June 30. The market price of the stock at June 15 was $11 per share. (The 500 shares remaining in the treasury do not participate in the stock dividend.)

June 30   Distributed the stock dividend declared on June 15.

Aug. 12   Reissued 300 of the 500 remaining shares of treasury stock at a price of $9.75 per share.

Dec. 31   The Income Summary account, showing net income for the year of $1,750,000, was closed into the Retained Earnings account.

Dec. 31   The $560,000 balance in the Dividends account was closed into the Retained Earnings account.

Instructions

a. Prepare in general journal form the entries to record the above transactions.

b. Prepare the stockholders' equity section of the balance sheet at December 31, 2015. Use the format illustrated in Exhibit 12–6. Include a supporting schedule showing your computation of retained earnings at that date.

c. Compute the maximum cash dividend per share that legally could be declared at December 31, 2015, without impairing the paid-in capital of Greene, Inc. (Hint: The availability of retained earnings for dividends is restricted by the cost of treasury stock owned.)

LO12-8

PROBLEM 12.7B

Effects of Transactions

Hot Water, Inc., manufactures a variety of dry cleaning equipment. Listed below are five events that occurred during the current year:

1. Declared a $5 per share cash dividend.
2. Paid the cash dividend.
3. Purchased 1,000 shares of treasury stock for $37 per share.
4. Reissued 600 shares of the treasury stock at a price of $36 per share.
5. Declared a 5 percent stock dividend.

Instructions

a. Indicate the effects of each of these events on the financial measurements listed in the four column headings listed below. Use the following code letters: **I** for increase, **D** for decrease, and **NE** for no effect.

Event	Current Assets	Stockholders' Equity	Net Income	Net Cash Flow (from any source)

b. For each event, *explain* the reasoning behind your answers. Be prepared to explain this reasoning in class.

LO12-4, LO12-8

PROBLEM 12.8B

Preparing the Stockholders' Equity Section: A Challenging Case

The Adams family decided early in 2015 to incorporate their family-owned farm under the name Adams Corporation. The corporation was authorized to issue 100,000 shares of a single class of $1 par value capital stock. Presented below is the information necessary to prepare the stockholders' equity section of the company's balance sheet at the end of 2015 and at the end of 2016.

2015. In January the corporation issued to members of the Adams family 20,000 shares of capital stock in exchange for cash and other assets used in the operation of the farm. The fair market value of these assets indicated an issue price of $25 per share. In December, George Adams died and the corporation purchased 4,000 shares of its own capital stock from his estate at $30 per share. Because of the large cash outlay to acquire this treasury stock, the directors decided not to declare cash dividends in 2015 and instead declared a 10 percent stock dividend to be distributed in January 2016. The stock price at the declaration date was $31 per share. (The treasury shares do not participate in the stock dividend.) Net income for 2015 was $850,000.

2016. In January the corporation distributed the stock dividend declared in 2015, and in February, the 4,000 treasury shares were sold to Joan Adams at $35 per share. In June, the capital stock was split 2-for-1. (Approval was obtained to increase the authorized number of shares to 200,000.) On December 11, the directors declared a cash dividend of $1 per share, payable in January 2017. Net income for 2016 was $810,000.

Instructions

Using the format illustrated in Exhibit 12–6, prepare the stockholders' equity section of the balance sheet at:

a. December 31, 2015.

b. December 31, 2016.

Show any necessary computations in supporting schedules.

LO12-1, LO12-2

PROBLEM 12.9B

Format of an Income Statement EPS

The following information is excerpted from the financial statements in a recent annual report of Cardinal Manufacturing Corporation. (Dollar figures and shares of stock are in thousands.)

Extraordinary loss on expropriation of foreign subsidiary	$ (17,500)
Loss from continuing operations	(38,940)
Income from discontinued operations	24,000
Preferred stock dividend requirements	(6,200)
Weighted-average number of shares of common stock outstanding	10,000

Instructions

a. Rearrange the items to present in good form the last portion of the income statement for Cardinal Manufacturing Corporation, beginning with "Loss from continuing operations."

b. Calculate the amount of *net loss* per share for the period. (Do *not* calculate per-share amounts for subtotals, such as income from continuing operations, loss before extraordinary items, and so forth. You are required to compute only a single earnings per share amount.)

Critical Thinking Cases

LO12-1

CASE 12.1

What's This?

The following events were reported in the financial statements of large, publicly owned corporations:

a. **Atlantic Richfield Company (ARCO)**, previously a separate company that is now owned by BP America, sold or abandoned the entire noncoal minerals segment of its operations. In the year of disposal, this segment had an operating loss. ARCO also incurred a loss of $514 million on disposal of its noncoal minerals segment of the business.

b. **American Airlines** increased the estimated useful life used in computing depreciation on its aircraft. If the new estimated life had always been in use, the net income reported in prior years would have been substantially higher.

c. **Union Carbide Corp.**, previously a separate company that is now a wholly owned subsidiary of The Dow Chemical Company, sustained a large loss as a result of the explosion of a chemical plant.

d. **Georgia-Pacific Corporation** realized a $10 million gain as a result of condemnation proceedings in which a governmental agency purchased assets from the company in a "forced sale."

Instructions

Indicate whether each event should be classified as a discontinued operation, or an extraordinary item, or included among the revenue and expenses of normal and recurring business operations. Briefly explain your reasons for each answer.

LO12-1

CASE 12.2

Is There Life without Baseball?

Jackson Publishing, Inc. (JPI), publishes two newspapers and, until recently, owned a professional baseball team. The baseball team had been losing money for several years and was sold at the end of 2015 to a group of investors who plan to move it to a larger city. Also in 2015, JPI suffered an extraordinary loss when its Raytown printing plant was damaged by a tornado. The damage has since been repaired. A condensed income statement follows:

JACKSON PUBLISHING, INC.
INCOME STATEMENT
FOR THE YEAR ENDED DECEMBER 31, 2015

Net revenue		$41,000,000
Costs and expenses		36,500,000
Income from continuing operations		$ 4,500,000
Discontinued operations:		
Operating loss on baseball team	$(1,300,000)	
Gain on sale of baseball team	4,700,000	3,400,000
Income before extraordinary items		$ 7,900,000
Extraordinary loss:		
Tornado damage to Raytown printing plant		(600,000)
Net income		$ 7,300,000

Instructions

On the basis of this information, answer the following questions. Show any necessary computations and explain your reasoning.

a. What would JPI's net income have been for 2015 if it *had not* sold the baseball team?

b. Assume that for 2016 you expect a 7 percent increase in the profitability of JPI's newspaper business but had projected a $2,000,000 operating loss for the baseball team if JPI had continued to operate the team in 2016. What amount would you forecast as JPI's 2016 net income *if the company had continued to own and operate the baseball team?*

c. Given your assumptions in part **b,** but given that JPI *did* sell the baseball team in 2015, what would you forecast as the company's estimated net income for 2016?

d. Assume that the expenses of operating the baseball team in 2015 amounted to $32,200,000, net of any related income tax effects. What was the team's *net revenue* for the year?

LO12-1 through LO12-3

CASE 12.3

Using Earnings per Share Statistics

For many years New York Studios has produced television shows and operated several FM radio stations. Late in the current year, the radio stations were sold to Times Publishing, Inc. Also during the current year, New York Studios sustained an extraordinary loss when one of its camera trucks caused an accident in an international grand prix auto race. Throughout the current year, the company had 3 million shares of common stock and a large quantity of convertible preferred stock outstanding. Earnings per share reported for the current year were as follows:

	Basic	Diluted
Earnings from continuing operations	$8.20	$6.80
Earnings before extraordinary items	$6.90	$5.50
Net earnings	$3.60	$2.20

Instructions

a. Briefly explain why New York Studios reports diluted earnings per share amounts as well as basic earnings per share. What is the purpose of showing investors the diluted figures?

b. What was the total dollar amount of the extraordinary loss sustained by New York Studios during the current year?

c. Assume that the price-earnings ratio shown in the morning newspaper for New York Studios's common stock indicates that the stock is selling at a price equal to 10 times the reported earnings per share. What is the approximate market price of the stock?

d. Assume that you expect both the revenue and expenses involved in producing television shows to increase by 10 percent during the coming year. What would you forecast as the company's basic earnings per share for the coming year under each of the following independent assumptions? (Show your computations and explain your reasoning.)

1. *None* of the convertible preferred stock is converted into common stock during the coming year.

2. *All* of the convertible preferred stock is converted into common stock at the beginning of the coming year.

LO12-8

CASE 12.4

Interpreting a
Statement of
Stockholders' Equity

The following information has been excerpted from the statement of stockholders' equity included in a recent annual report of Thompson Supply Company. (Dollar figures are in millions.)

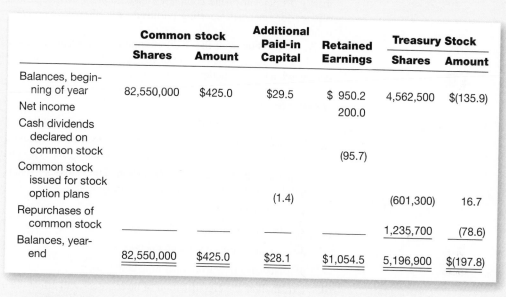

	Common stock		Additional Paid-in Capital	Retained Earnings	Treasury Stock	
	Shares	Amount			Shares	Amount
Balances, beginning of year	82,550,000	$425.0	$29.5	$ 950.2	4,562,500	$(135.9)
Net income				200.0		
Cash dividends declared on common stock				(95.7)		
Common stock issued for stock option plans			(1.4)		(601,300)	16.7
Repurchases of common stock					1,235,700	(78.6)
Balances, year-end	82,550,000	$425.0	$28.1	$1,054.5	5,196,900	$(197.8)

Instructions

Use the information about Thompson Supply to answer the following questions.

a. How many shares of common stock are outstanding at the *beginning* of the year? At the *end* of the year?

b. What was the total common stock dividend declared during the presented year? Thompson's annual report disclosed that the common stock dividend during that year was $1.23 per share. Approximately how many shares of common stock were entitled to the $1.23 per share dividend during the year? Is this answer compatible with your answers in part **a?**

c. The statement presented indicates that common stock was both issued and repurchased during the year, yet the number of common shares shown and the common stock amount (first and second columns) did not change from the beginning to the end of the year. Explain.

d. What was the average price per share Thompson paid to acquire the treasury shares held at the *beginning* of the year?

e. Was the aggregate issue price of the 601,300 treasury shares issued during the year for stock option plans higher or lower than the cost Thompson paid to acquire those treasury shares? (Hint: Analyze the impact on Additional Paid-in Capital.)

f. What was the average purchase price per share paid by Thompson to acquire treasury shares *during the current year?*

g. In its annual report, Thompson disclosed that the (weighted) average number of common shares outstanding during the year was 77,500,000. In part **a** above, you determined the number of common shares outstanding as of the end of the year. Which figure is used in computing *earnings per share?* Which is used in computing *book value per share?*

LO12-1, LO12-2, LO12-8

CASE 12.5

Classification of Unusual
Items—and the Potential
Financial Impact

Elliot-Cole is a publicly owned international corporation, with operations in over 90 countries. Net income has been growing at approximately 15 percent per year, and the stock consistently trades at about 20 times earnings.

To attract and retain key management leadership, the company has developed a compensation plan in which managers receive earnings in the form of bonuses as well as opportunities to purchase shares of the company's stock at a reduced price. In general, the higher the company's net income each year, the greater the benefit to management in terms of their personal compensation.

During the current year, political unrest and economic upheaval threatened Elliot-Cole's business operations in three foreign countries. At year-end, the company's auditors insisted that management write off the company's assets in these countries, stating that these assets were "severely impaired." Said one corporate official, "We can't argue with that. Each of these countries is a real trouble spot. We might be pulling out of these places at any time, and any assets probably would just be left behind."

Management agreed that the carrying value of Elliot-Cole's assets in these three countries should be reduced to "scrap value"—which was nothing. These write-downs amounted to approximately 18 percent of the company's income *prior* to recognition of these losses. (These write-offs are for financial reporting purposes only; they have *no effect* on the company's income tax obligations.)

At the meeting with the auditors, one of Elliot-Cole's officers states, "There's no doubt we should write these assets off. But of course, this is an extraordinary loss. A loss of this size can't be considered a routine matter."

Instructions

a. Explain the logic behind writing down the book values of assets that are still in operation.

b. Evaluate the officer's statement concerning the classification of these losses. Do you agree that they should be classified as an extraordinary item? Explain.

c. Explain the effect that the classification of these losses—that is, as ordinary or extraordinary—will have in the current period on Elliot-Cole's:

1. Net income.

2. Income before extraordinary items.

3. Income from continuing operations.

4. Net cash flow from operating activities.

d. Explain how the classification of these losses will affect the p/e ratio reported in newspapers such as *The Wall Street Journal*.

e. Does management appear to have any self-interest in the classification of these losses? Explain.

f. Explain how (if at all) these write-offs are likely to affect the earnings of *future* periods.

g. What "ethical dilemma" confronts management in this case?

LO12-9

CASE 12.6

Managing Profitability

You are a staff accountant for Pearce, Pearce, and Smith, CPAs, and have worked for several years on the audit of a major client of the firm, Flexcom, Inc. Flexcom sells its products in a highly competitive market and relies heavily on the careful management of inventory because of the unique nature of the products sold and the importance of minimizing the company's investment in inventory. Flexcom sells cellular phones, personal handheld computers, and other communications devices that are particularly sensitive to changes in consumer demands and changes in technology, which are both frequent and significant in terms of their impact on the attractiveness of Flexcom's products to buyers.

In the course of your work, you have noticed several trends related to inventory that interest you and that have caused you to explore further the underlying details. Specifically, you have determined the following:

• Despite sluggish sales volume, the company's net income has steadily increased for each of the last three years.

• Inventory has been increasing at a higher-than-normal rate.

• The allowance to reduce inventory for obsolescence has dramatically declined during the last three years, going from nearly 10 percent of inventory three years ago to approximately 2 percent at the end of the most recent year.

You are aware that, within Flexcom, profitability is a major factor in the evaluation of management and has been cited in at least two recent situations as the basis for replacing individuals in leadership positions.

Instructions

Prepare a brief report to your supervisor explaining why you are bothered by these trends and offer one or more explanations that may underlie what is actually going on within Flexcom.

LO12-2

INTERNET CASE 12.7

Analyzing Stockholders' Equity and EPS

Important information concerning a company's operating performance can be found in its income statement and statement of financial position (balance sheet). Using the search mechanism of your choice, locate the most recent annual report of **Martin Marietta Materials, Inc.** and respond to the following.

Instructions

a. For the most recent day indicated, what were the highest and lowest prices at which the company's common stock sold?

b. Find the company's balance sheet and determine the following: the number of outstanding shares of common stock and the average price at which those shares were originally sold.

c. What is the relationship between the current market price and the amount you have calculated in part b as the average price at which the stock originally sold?

d. Find the company's income statement and identify the trend in basic earnings per share, including discontinued operations. Did discontinued operations have a significant impact on EPS?

e. For the most recent year, what is the average number of shares of common stock that was used to compute basic earnings per share? Why is that number different from the number outstanding in the company's balance sheet?

Internet sites are time and date sensitive. It is the purpose of these exercises to have you explore the Internet. You may need to use the Yahoo! search engine www.yahoo.com (or another favorite search engine) to find a company's current web address.

Answers to Self-Test Questions

1. b   **2.** c, d   **3.** d   **4.** a, b   **5.** a, c

CHAPTER 13

Statement of Cash Flows

AFTER STUDYING THIS CHAPTER, YOU SHOULD BE ABLE TO:

Learning Objectives

LO13-1 Explain the purposes and uses of a statement of cash flows.

LO13-2 Describe how cash transactions are classified in a statement of cash flows.

LO13-3 Compute the major cash flows relating to operating activities.

LO13-4 Compute the cash flows relating to investing and financing activities.

LO13-5 Distinguish between the direct and indirect methods of reporting operating cash flows.

LO13-6 Explain why net income differs from net cash flows from operating activities.

LO13-7 Compute net cash flows from operating activities using the *indirect* method.

LO13-8 Discuss the likely effects of various business strategies on cash flows.

LO13-9 Explain how a worksheet may be helpful in preparing a statement of cash flows.

© Tim Clayton/Corbis

PEPSI

Cash is sometimes referred to as the "lifeblood" of a company, implying that companies require cash to be successful and to even continue to exist. Cash is required on a daily basis to meet current obligations and to position the company for future success. Cash requirements include activities as broad ranging as meeting payroll requirements for employees, purchasing inventory to meet the shopping needs of customers, repaying debt when it is due, paying dividends to stockholders, and from time to time expanding the business by acquiring plant assets or even entire other businesses.

Cash flow is particularly important for large companies like PepsiCo, Inc. as it continuously seeks to expand its markets. Pepsi's 2012 annual report includes three-year comparative statements of cash flows for 2012, 2011, and 2010. These statements are presented in three major categories: operating activities, investing activities, and financing activities. Pepsi's statements show $8 billion and $9 billion positive operating cash flows each year. This cash was used for many purposes, including capital spending, repayment of debt, repurchasing the company's common stock, and paying dividends to stockholders.

Efficiently managing cash flows of this magnitude is an important responsibility of the company's leadership and is critical for the company's continued success. ■

Cash flow information about a company is helpful to investors and creditors in judging future cash flows. If the company itself does not have strong cash flow, it is unlikely that the company will be in a cash position to provide strong cash flows to its investors and creditors. We introduced in Chapter 2 the idea of a financial statement that describes cash flows, and in Chapter 13 we go into greater depth regarding this important financial statement. The statement of cash flows shows how the company's cash changed during the period and explains how the company managed its cash in terms of its operating, investing, and financing activities.

Statement of Cash Flows

PURPOSES OF THE STATEMENT

L013-1

LEARNING OBJECTIVE
Explain the purposes and uses of a statement of cash flows.

The objective of a statement of cash flows is to provide information about the *cash receipts* and *cash payments* of a business entity during the accounting period. The term **cash flows** includes both cash receipts and payments. In a statement of cash flows, information about cash receipts and cash payments is classified in terms of the company's operating activities, investing activities, and financing activities. The statement of cash flows assists investors, creditors, and others in assessing such factors as:

- The company's ability to generate positive cash flows in future periods.
- The company's ability to meet its obligations and to pay dividends.
- The company's need for external financing.
- Reasons for differences between the amount of net income and the related net cash flows from operating activities.
- Both the cash and noncash aspects of the company's investment and financing transactions for the period.
- Causes of the change in the amount of cash and cash equivalents between the beginning and the end of the accounting period.

Stated simply, a statement of cash flows helps users of financial statements evaluate a company's ability to have sufficient cash—both on a short-run and on a long-run basis. For this reason, the statement of cash flows is useful to virtually everyone interested in the company's financial health: short- and long-term creditors, investors, management—and both current and prospective competitors.

EXAMPLE OF A STATEMENT OF CASH FLOWS

An example of a statement of cash flows appears in Exhibit 13–1. Cash outflows are shown in parentheses.[1]

CLASSIFICATION OF CASH FLOWS

L013-2

LEARNING OBJECTIVE
Describe how cash transactions are classified in a statement of cash flows.

The cash flows shown in the statement are presented in three major categories: (1) **operating activities**, (2) **investing activities**, and (3) **financing activities**.[2] We will now look briefly at the way cash flows are classified among these three categories.

Operating Activities   The operating activities section shows the *cash effects* of revenue and expense transactions. Stated another way, the operating activities section of the statement of cash flows includes the cash effects of those transactions reported in the continuing operations section of the income statement. To illustrate this concept, consider the effects of

---

[1] In this illustration, net cash flows from operating activities are determined by the *direct method.* An alternative approach, called the *indirect method,* is illustrated later in this chapter.

[2] To reconcile to the ending cash balance, "effects of changes in exchange rates on cash" is used in the cash flow statements of companies with foreign currency holdings. This classification, as well as other complexities, is discussed in more advanced accounting courses.

EXHIBIT 13-1

Allison Corporation
Statement of Cash Flows

ALLISON CORPORATION
STATEMENT OF CASH FLOWS
FOR THE YEAR ENDED DECEMBER 31, 2015

Cash flows from operating activities:

Cash received from customers	$ 870,000	
Interest and dividends received	10,000	
Cash provided by operating activities		$ 880,000
Cash paid to suppliers and employees	$ (764,000)	
Interest paid	(28,000)	
Income taxes paid	(38,000)	
Cash disbursed for operating activities		(830,000)
Net cash flows from operating activities		$ 50,000

Cash flows from investing activities:

Purchases of marketable securities	$ (65,000)	
Proceeds from sales of marketable securities	40,000	
Loans made to borrowers	(17,000)	
Collections on loans	12,000	
Purchases of plant assets	(160,000)	
Proceeds from sales of plant assets	75,000	
Net cash flows from investing activities		(115,000)

Cash flows from financing activities:

Proceeds from short-term borrowing	$ 45,000	
Payments to settle short-term debts	(55,000)	
Proceeds from issuing bonds payable	100,000	
Proceeds from issuing capital stock	50,000	
Dividends paid	(40,000)	
Net cash flows from financing activities		100,000
Net increase (decrease) in cash		$ 35,000
Cash and cash equivalents, Jan. 1, 2015		20,000
Cash and cash equivalents, Dec. 31, 2015		$ 55,000

credit sales. Credit sales are reported in the income statement in the period when the sales occur. But the cash effects occur later—when the receivables are collected in cash. For many credit sales, cash will be received in the same financial reporting period. If the credit sale and the cash receipt occur in different accounting periods, however, the income statement and the operating activities section of the statement of cash flows will differ. Similar differences may exist between the recognition of an expense and the related cash payment. Consider, for example, the expense of postretirement benefits earned by employees during the current period. If this expense is not funded with a trustee, the cash payments may not occur for many years—after today's employees have retired.

Cash flows from operating activities include:

Cash Receipts	Cash Payments
Collections from customers for sales of goods and services	Payments to suppliers of merchandise and services, including payments to employees
Interest and dividends received	Payments of interest
Other receipts from operations; for example, proceeds from settlement of litigation	Payments of income taxes
	Other expenditures relating to operations; for example, payments in settlement of litigation

Notice that receipts of *interest and dividends* and payments of *interest* are classified as operating activities, not as investing or financing activities.

Investing Activities
Cash flows relating to investing activities present the cash effects of transactions involving plant assets, intangible assets, and investments. They include:

Cash Receipts	Cash Payments
Cash proceeds from selling investments and plant and intangible assets	Payments to acquire investments and plant and intangible assets
Cash proceeds from collecting principal amounts on loans	Amounts advanced to borrowers

Financing Activities
Cash flows classified as financing activities include the following items that result from debt and equity financing transactions:

Cash Receipts	Cash Payments
Proceeds from both short-term and long-term borrowing	Repayment of amounts borrowed (excluding interest payments)
Cash received from owners (for example, from issuing stock)	Payments to owners, such as cash dividends

Repayment of amounts borrowed refers to repayment of *loans,* not to payments made on accounts payable or accrued liabilities. Payments of accounts payable and of accrued liabilities are payments to suppliers of merchandise and services related to revenues and expenses and are classified as cash outflows from operating activities. Also, remember that all interest payments are classified as operating activities.

Why Are Receipts and Payments of Interest Classified as Operating Activities?
A case can be made that interest and dividend receipts are related to investing activities, and that interest payments are related to financing activities. The Financial Accounting Standards Board (FASB) considered this point of view but decided instead to require companies to present interest and dividend receipts and interest payments as operating activities. The FASB position reflects the view that cash flows from operating activities should include the cash effects of the revenue and expense transactions entering into the determination of net income. Because dividend and interest revenue and interest expense enter into the determination of net income, the FASB determined that the related cash flows should be presented as operating activities in the statement of cash flows. Payments of dividends, however, *do not* enter into the determination of net income. Therefore, dividend payments are classified as financing activities.

INTERNATIONAL CASE IN POINT

Both the Financial Accounting Standards Board in the United States and the International Accounting Standards Board require companies to present a statement of cash flows organized into three categories: operating activities, investing activities, and financing activities. One difference in these two sets of financial reporting standards is the classification of interest received on investments and interest paid on debt financing. As you have learned in this chapter, the FASB requires these to be presented as part of operating cash flows. IASB standards, on the other hand, allow interest received to be classified as either operating or investing and interest paid to be classified as either operating or financing.

Cash and Cash Equivalents

For purposes of preparing a statement of cash flows, cash is defined as including *both cash and cash equivalents.* **Cash equivalents** are short-term, highly liquid investments, such as money market funds, commercial paper, and Treasury bills that will mature within 90 days from the acquisition date.

If an item is determined to not be a cash equivalent, its cash flows are presented in the investing activities section of the statement of cash flows. The amount shown as *cash and cash equivalents* in the balance sheet must be the same as the amount shown on the statement of cash flows. Transfers of money between a company's bank accounts and these cash equivalents are *not viewed as cash receipts or cash payments.* Money is considered cash regardless of whether it is held in currency, in a bank account, or in the form of cash equivalents. Interest received from holding cash equivalents is included in cash receipts from operating activities.

Marketable securities, such as investments in the stocks and bonds of other companies, *do not qualify as cash equivalents.* Therefore, purchases and sales of marketable securities *do* result in cash flows that are reported in the statement of cash flows as investing activities.

In the long run, a company must have a strategy that generates positive net cash flows from its operating activities if it is to be successful. A business with a consistent pattern of negative cash flows from operations will not be able to raise cash from other sources indefinitely. In fact, the ability of a business to raise cash through financing activities is highly dependent on its ability to generate cash from its normal business operations. Creditors and stockholders are reluctant to invest in a company that does not generate enough cash from operating activities to ensure prompt payment of maturing liabilities, interest, and dividends.

Similarly, companies cannot expect to survive indefinitely on cash provided by investing activities. At some point, plant assets, investments, and other assets available for sale will be depleted.

Cash versus Accrual Information

The items in an income statement and a balance sheet represent the balances of specific general ledger accounts. Notice, however, that the captions used in the statement of cash flows *do not* correspond to specific ledger accounts. A statement of cash flows summarizes *cash transactions* during the accounting period. The general ledger, however, is maintained on the **accrual basis** of accounting, not the cash basis. An amount such as "Cash received from customers . . . $870,000" does not appear as the balance in a specific ledger account, but it is derived from one or more such accounts.

In a small business, it may be practical to prepare a statement of cash flows directly from the special journals for cash receipts and cash payments. For most businesses, however, it is easier to prepare the statement of cash flows by examining the income statement and the *changes* during the period in all of the balance sheet accounts *except for* Cash. This approach is based on the double-entry system of accounting; any transaction affecting cash must also affect some other asset, liability, or owners' equity account.[3] The change in these *other accounts* determines the nature of the cash transaction, as we see in the example that follows.

Preparing a Statement of Cash Flows

Earlier in this chapter we illustrated the statement of cash flows of Allison Corporation. We will now show how this statement was developed from the company's accrual-basis accounting records.

Basically, a statement of cash flows can be prepared from the information contained in an income statement and *comparative* balance sheets at the beginning and end of the period. It is also necessary, however, to have some detailed information about the *changes* occurring during the period in certain balance sheet accounts. Shown in Exhibit 13–2 is Allison's income statement, and in Exhibit 13–3 the firm's comparative balance sheets for the current year are presented.

Additional Information

An analysis of changes in the balance sheet accounts of Allison Corporation provides the following information about the company's activities in the

---

[3] Revenue, expenses, and dividends represent changes in owners' equity and, therefore, may be regarded as owners' equity accounts.

EXHIBIT 13–2

Allison Corporation Income Statement

ALLISON CORPORATION INCOME STATEMENT FOR THE YEAR ENDED DECEMBER 31, 2015		
Revenue and gains:		
Net sales		$900,000
Dividend revenue		3,000
Interest revenue		6,000
Gain on sales of plant assets		31,000
Total revenue and gains		$940,000
Costs, expenses, and losses:		
Cost of goods sold	$500,000	
Operating expenses (including depreciation of $40,000)	300,000	
Interest expense	35,000	
Income tax expense	36,000	
Loss on sales of marketable securities	4,000	
Total costs, expenses, and losses		875,000
Net income		$ 65,000

current year. To assist in the preparation of a statement of cash flows, we have classified this information into the categories of operating activities, investing activities, and financing activities.

OPERATING ACTIVITIES

1. Accounts receivable increased by $30,000 during the year.
2. Dividend revenue is recognized on the cash basis, but interest revenue is recognized on the accrual basis. Accrued interest receivable decreased by $1,000 during the year.
3. Inventory increased by $10,000 and accounts payable increased by $15,000 during the year.
4. During the year, short-term prepaid expenses increased by $3,000 and accrued expenses payable (other than for interest or income taxes) decreased by $6,000. Depreciation for the year amounted to $40,000.
5. The accrued liability for interest payable increased by $7,000 during the year.
6. The accrued liability for income taxes payable decreased by $2,000 during the year.

INVESTING ACTIVITIES

7. Analysis of the Marketable Securities account shows debit entries of $65,000, representing the cost of securities purchased, and credit entries of $44,000, representing the cost of securities sold. (No marketable securities are classified as cash equivalents.)
8. Analysis of the Notes Receivable account shows $17,000 in debit entries, representing cash loaned by Allison Corporation to borrowers during the year, and $12,000 in credit entries, representing collections of notes receivable. (Collections of interest were recorded in the Interest Revenue account and are considered cash flows from operating activities.)
9. Allison's plant asset accounts increased by $116,000 during the year. An analysis of the underlying transactions indicates the following:

	Effect on Plant Asset Accounts
Purchased $200,000 in plant assets, paying $160,000 cash and issuing a long-term note payable for the $40,000 balance	$200,000
Sold for $75,000 cash plant assets with a book value of $44,000	(44,000)
Recorded depreciation expense for the period	(40,000)
Net change in plant asset controlling accounts	$116,000

ALLISON CORPORATION COMPARATIVE BALANCE SHEETS DECEMBER 31, 2015 AND 2014		
	2015	**2014**
Assets		
Current assets:		
Cash and Cash Equivalents	$ 55,000	$ 20,000
Marketable Securities	85,000	64,000
Notes Receivable	17,000	12,000
Accounts Receivable	110,000	80,000
Accrued Interest Receivable	2,000	3,000
Inventory	100,000	90,000
Prepaid Expenses	4,000	1,000
Total current assets	$373,000	$270,000
Plant and Equipment (net of accumulated depreciation)	616,000	500,000
Total assets	$989,000	$770,000
Liabilities & Stockholders' Equity		
Current liabilities:		
Notes Payable (short-term)	$ 45,000	$ 55,000
Accounts Payable	76,000	61,000
Interest Payable	22,000	15,000
Income Taxes Payable	8,000	10,000
Other Accrued Expenses Payable	3,000	9,000
Total current liabilities	$154,000	$150,000
Long-term liabilities:		
Notes Payable (long-term)	40,000	–0–
Bonds Payable	400,000	300,000
Total liabilities	$594,000	$450,000
Stockholders' equity:		
Capital Stock	$ 60,000	$ 50,000
Additional Paid-in Capital	140,000	100,000
Retained Earnings	195,000	170,000
Total stockholders' equity	$395,000	$320,000
Total liabilities & stockholders' equity	$989,000	$770,000

EXHIBIT 13–3

Allison Corporation Balance Sheets

FINANCING ACTIVITIES

10. During the year, Allison Corporation borrowed $45,000 cash by issuing short-term notes payable to banks. Also, the company repaid $55,000 in principal amounts due on these loans and other notes payable. (Interest payments are classified as operating activities.)

11. The company issued bonds payable for $100,000 cash.

12. The company issued 1,000 shares of $10 par value capital stock for cash at a price of $50 per share.

13. Cash dividends declared and paid to stockholders amounted to $40,000 during the year.

CASH AND CASH EQUIVALENTS

14. Cash and cash equivalents as shown in Allison Corporation's balance sheets amounted to $20,000 at the beginning of the year and $55,000 at year-end—a net increase of $35,000.

Using this information, we will now illustrate the steps in preparing Allison Corporation's statement of cash flows and a supporting schedule disclosing the noncash investing and financing activities. In our discussion, we often refer to these items of additional information by citing the paragraph numbers shown in the list just described.

The distinction between accrual-basis measurements and cash flows is fundamentally important in understanding financial statements and other accounting reports. To assist in making this distinction, we use two colors in our illustrated computations. We show in blue the accrual-based data from Allison Corporation's income statement and the preceding numbered paragraphs. The cash flows that we compute from these data are shown in red.

CASH FLOWS FROM OPERATING ACTIVITIES

L013-3

LEARNING OBJECTIVE
Compute the major cash flows relating to operating activities.

As shown in the statement of cash flows in Exhibit 13–1, net cash flows from operating activities are determined by combining certain cash inflows and subtracting certain cash outflows. The inflows are cash received from customers and interest and dividends received; the outflows are cash paid to suppliers and employees, interest paid, and income taxes paid.

In computing each of these cash flows, our starting point is an income statement amount, such as net sales, cost of goods sold, or interest expense. As you study each computation, be sure that you *understand why* the income statement amount must be increased or decreased to determine the related cash flows. You will find that an understanding of these computations will do more than show you how to compute cash flows; it will also strengthen your understanding of the income statement and the balance sheet.

Cash Received from Customers   To the extent that sales are made for cash, there is no difference between the amount of cash received from customers in the statement of cash flows and the amount included as sales revenue in the income statement. Differences arise, however, when sales are made on account. If accounts receivable increase during the year, credit sales will have exceeded collections of cash from accounts receivable. Therefore, we *deduct the increase* in accounts receivable from net sales to determine the amount of cash received during the year. If accounts receivable decrease, collections of these accounts will have exceeded credit sales. In that case, we *add the decrease* in accounts receivable to net sales to determine the amount of cash received during the year. The relationship between cash received from customers and net sales is summarized below:

$$\text{Cash Received from Customers} = \text{Net Sales} \begin{cases} + \text{ Decrease in Accounts Receivable} \\ \qquad\qquad\text{or} \\ - \text{ Increase in Accounts Receivable} \end{cases}$$

In our Allison Corporation example, paragraph **1** of the additional information tells us that accounts receivable *increased* by $30,000 during the year. The income statement shows net sales for the year of $900,000. Therefore, the amount of cash received from customers is computed as follows:

Net sales (accrual basis)	$900,000
Less: Increase in accounts receivable	30,000
Cash received from customers	$870,000

Interest and Dividends Received   Our next step is to determine the amounts of cash received during the year from dividends and interest on the company's investments. As explained in paragraph **2** of the additional information, dividend revenue is recorded on the cash basis. Therefore, the $3,000 shown in the income statement also represents the amount of cash received as dividends.

Interest revenue, on the other hand, is recognized on the accrual basis. We have already shown how to convert one type of revenue, net sales, from the accrual basis to the cash basis. We use the same approach to convert interest revenue from the accrual basis to the **cash basis.** Our formula for converting net sales to the cash basis may be modified to convert interest revenue to the cash basis as follows:

$$\text{Interest Received} = \text{Interest Revenue} \left\{ \begin{array}{c} + \text{ Decrease in Interest Receivable} \\ \text{or} \\ - \text{ Increase in Interest Receivable} \end{array} \right\}$$

The income statement for Allison Corporation shows interest revenue of $6,000, and paragraph **2** states that the amount of accrued interest receivable *decreased* by $1,000 during the year. Thus the amount of cash received as interest is computed as follows:

Interest revenue (accrual basis)	$6,000
Add: Decrease in accrued interest receivable	1,000
Interest received (cash basis)	$7,000

The amounts of interest and dividends received in cash are combined for presentation in the statement of cash flows:

Interest received (cash basis)	$ 7,000
Dividends received (cash basis)	3,000
Interest and dividends received	$10,000

CASH PAYMENTS FOR MERCHANDISE AND FOR EXPENSES

The next item in the statement of cash flows, "Cash paid to suppliers and employees," includes all cash payments for purchases of merchandise and for operating expenses (excluding interest and income taxes). Payments of interest and income taxes are listed as separate items in the statement. The amounts of cash paid for purchases of merchandise and for operating expenses are computed separately.

Cash Paid for Purchases of Merchandise   An accrual basis income statement reflects the *cost of goods sold* during the year, regardless of whether the merchandise was acquired or paid for in that period. The statement of cash flows, on the other hand, reports the *cash paid* for merchandise during the year, even if the merchandise was acquired in a previous period or remains unsold at year-end. The relationship between cash payments for merchandise and the cost of goods sold depends on the changes during the period in *two* related balance sheet accounts: inventory and accounts payable to suppliers of merchandise. This relationship may be stated as follows:

$$\text{Cash Payments for Purchases} = \text{Cost of Goods Sold} \left\{ \begin{array}{c} + \text{ Increase in Inventory} \\ \text{or} \\ - \text{ Decrease in Inventory} \end{array} \right\} \text{ and } \left\{ \begin{array}{c} + \text{ Decrease in Accounts Payable} \\ \text{or} \\ - \text{ Increase in Accounts Payable} \end{array} \right\}$$

Using information from the Allison Corporation income statement and paragraph **3**, the cash payments for purchases is computed as follows:

Cost of goods sold	$500,000
Add: Increase in inventory	10,000
Net purchases (accrual basis)	$510,000
Less: Increase in accounts payable to suppliers	15,000
Cash payments for purchases of merchandise	$495,000

Here is the logic behind this computation: If a company is increasing its inventory, it is *buying more merchandise than it sells* during the period. If the company is increasing its accounts payable to merchandise creditors, it is *not paying cash* for all of these purchases in the current period. Some portion of the purchases will be paid for in the next period.

Cash Payments for Expenses Expenses, as shown in the income statement, represent the cost of goods and services used up during the period. However, the amounts shown as expenses may differ from the cash payments made during the period. Consider, for example, depreciation expense. Recording depreciation expense *requires no cash payment,* but it does increase total expenses determined on the accrual basis. In converting accrual-basis expenses to the cash basis, we deduct depreciation expense and any other noncash expenses from our accrual-basis operating expenses. Other noncash expenses—expenses not requiring cash outlays—include amortization of intangible assets, any unfunded portion of postretirement benefits expense, and amortization of bond discount.

A second type of difference arises from short-term *timing differences* between the recognition of expenses and the actual cash payments. Expenses are recorded in accounting records when the related goods or services are used. However, the cash payments for these expenses might occur (1) in an earlier period, (2) in the same period, or (3) in a later period. Let us briefly consider each case.

1. If payment is made in advance, the payment creates an asset, termed a prepaid expense, or, in our formula, a "prepayment." To the extent that prepaid expenses increase over the year, cash payments *exceed* the amount recognized as expense.
2. If payment is made in the same period, the cash payment is equal to the amount of expense.
3. If payment is made in a later period, the payment reduces a liability for an accrued expense payable. To the extent that accrued expenses payable decrease during the year, cash payments exceed the amount recognized as expense.

The relationship between cash payments for expenses and accrual-basis expenses is summarized below:

$$
\begin{array}{c}
\text{Cash Payments} \\
\text{for Expenses}
\end{array}
=
\text{Expenses}
\left\{
\begin{array}{l}
\\
\text{Depreciation} \\
\text{and Other} \\
- \text{Noncash} \\
\text{Expenses} \\
\\
\end{array}
\right\}
\text{ and }
\left\{
\begin{array}{l}
\text{Increase in} \\
+ \text{Related} \\
\text{Prepayments} \\
\text{or} \\
\text{Decrease in} \\
- \text{Related} \\
\text{Prepayments}
\end{array}
\right\}
\text{ and }
\left\{
\begin{array}{l}
\text{Decrease in} \\
+ \text{Related Accrued} \\
\text{Liabilities} \\
\text{or} \\
\text{Increase in} \\
- \text{Related Accrued} \\
\text{Liabilities}
\end{array}
\right\}
$$

In a statement of cash flows, cash payments for interest and for income taxes are shown separately from cash payments for operating expenses. Using information from Allison Corporation's income statement and from paragraph **4,** we may compute the company's cash payments for operating expenses as follows:

Operating expenses (including depreciation)		$300,000
Less: Noncash expenses (depreciation)		40,000
Subtotal		$260,000
Add: Increase in short-term prepayments	$3,000	
Decrease in accrued liabilities	6,000	9,000
Cash payments for operating expenses		$269,000

Cash Paid to Suppliers and Employees The caption used in our cash flow statement, "Cash paid to suppliers and employees," includes cash payments for both purchases of merchandise and for operating expenses. This cash outflow may now be computed by combining the two previous calculations:

Cash payments for purchases of merchandise	$495,000
Cash payments for operating expenses	269,000
Cash payments to suppliers and employees	$764,000

Cash Payments for Interest and Taxes

Interest expense and income taxes expense may be converted to cash payments with the same formula we used to convert operating expenses. Allison Corporation's income statement shows interest expense of $35,000, and paragraph **5** states that the liability for interest payable increased by $7,000 during the year. The fact that the liability for unpaid interest *increased* over the year means that *not all of the interest expense shown in the income statement was paid in cash* in the current year. To determine the amount of interest actually paid, we *subtract* from total interest expense the portion that has been financed through an increase in the liability for interest payable. The computation is as follows:

Interest expense	$35,000
Less: Increase in related accrued liability	7,000
Interest paid	$28,000

Similar reasoning is used to determine the amount of income tax paid by Allison Corporation during the year. The accrual-based income tax expense reported in the income statement amounts to $36,000. However, paragraph **6** states that the company reduced its liability for income taxes payable by $2,000 during the year. Incurring income tax expense increases the tax liability; making cash payments to tax authorities reduces it. If the liability *decreased* over the year, cash payments to tax authorities *must have been greater* than the income tax expense for the current year. The amount of the cash payments is determined as follows:

Income tax expense	$36,000
Add: Decrease in related accrued liability	2,000
Income tax paid	$38,000

A Quick Review

We have now shown the computation of each cash flow relating to Allison Corporation's operating activities. In Exhibit 13–1 we illustrated a complete statement of cash flows for the company. For your convenience, we again show the operating activities section of that statement, illustrating the information developed in the preceding paragraphs.

Cash flows from operating activities:		
Cash received from customers	$ 870,000	
Interest and dividends received	10,000	
Cash provided by operating activities		$ 880,000
Cash paid to suppliers and employees	$ (764,000)	
Interest paid	(28,000)	
Income taxes paid	(38,000)	
Cash disbursed for operating activities		(830,000)
Net cash flows from operating activities		$ 50,000

CASH FLOWS FROM INVESTING ACTIVITIES

Paragraphs **7** through **9** in the additional information for our Allison Corporation example provide most of the information necessary to determine the cash flows from investing activities. In the following discussion, we illustrate the presentation of these cash flows and explain the sources of the information contained in the numbered paragraphs.

Much information about investing activities can be obtained simply by looking at the changes in the related asset accounts during the year. Debit entries in these accounts represent purchases of the assets, or cash outlays. Credit entries represent sales of the assets, or cash receipts. However, credit entries in asset accounts represent the *cost* (or *book value*) of the assets sold. To determine the cash proceeds from these transactions, we must adjust the amount of the credit entries for any gains or losses recognized on the sales.

13-3

LO13-4

LEARNING OBJECTIVE
Compute the cash flows relating to investing and financing activities.

Purchases and Sales of Securities

To illustrate, consider paragraph **7,** which summarizes the debit and credit entries to the Marketable Securities account. As explained earlier in this chapter, the $65,000 in debit entries represents purchases of marketable securities. The $44,000 in credit entries represents the *cost* of marketable securities sold during the period. However, the income statement shows that these securities were sold at a *$4,000 loss.* Thus the cash proceeds from these sales amounted to only *$40,000* ($44,000 cost, minus $4,000 loss on sale). In the statement of cash flows, these investing activities are summarized as follows:

3⁵

Purchases of marketable securities	$(65,000)
Proceeds from sales of marketable securities	40,000

Loans Made and Collected

Paragraph **8** provides all the information necessary to summarize the cash flows from making and collecting loans:

Loans made to borrowers	$(17,000)
Collections on loans	12,000

This information comes directly from the Notes Receivable account. Debit entries in the account represent new loans made during the year; credit entries indicate collections of the *principal* amount on outstanding notes (loans). (Interest received is credited to the Interest Revenue account and is included among the cash receipts from operating activities.)

 YOUR TURN   You as a Sales Manager

Assume you are a regional sales manager for Wiggins Foods, Inc., a distributor of bulk food products to schools, nursing homes, hospitals, prisons, and other institutions. Recently, the purchasing agent for Baggins Preschools, Inc., tells you the company will likely have to forgo its normal monthly order because of cash flow problems. The purchasing agent tells you other companies are helping it through the cash flow squeeze and asks if your company could loan the payment to Baggins. The purchasing agent suggests you could record the sale as revenue and increase notes receivable (rather than accounts receivable) by the same amount. Baggins is one of your largest customers. Without its order, you will not meet your sales goals for the month—so you are tempted to say yes. However, on reflection you wonder if it might be unethical for the company to lend its customer money to finance purchases. What should you do?

(See our comments on the Online Learning Center website.)

Cash Paid to Acquire Plant Assets

Paragraph **9** states that Allison Corporation purchased plant assets during the year for $200,000, paying $160,000 in cash and issuing a long-term note payable for the $40,000 balance. Notice that *only the $160,000 cash payment* appears in the statement of cash flows. However, one objective of this financial statement is to show all of the company's *investing and financing activities* during the year. Therefore, the *noncash aspects* of these transactions are shown in a supplementary schedule, as follows:

Supplementary Schedule of Noncash Investing and Financing Activities	
Purchases of plant assets	$200,000
Less: Portion financed through issuance of long-term debt	40,000
Cash paid to acquire plant assets	$160,000

This supplementary schedule accompanies the statement of cash flows.

Proceeds from Sales of Plant Assets

Proceeds from Sales of Plant Assets Assume that an analysis of the plant asset accounts shows net credit entries totaling $44,000 in the year. ("Net credit entries" means all credit entries, net of related debits to accumulated depreciation when assets were sold.) These net credit entries represent the *book value* of plant assets sold during the year. However, the income statement shows that these assets were sold at a *gain of $31,000.* Therefore, the *cash proceeds* from sales of plant assets amounted to $75,000, as follows:

Book value of plant assets sold	$44,000
Add: Gain on sales of plant assets	31,000
Proceeds from sales of plant assets	$75,000

The amount credited to the Accumulated Depreciation account during the year is not a cash flow and is not included in the statement of cash flows.

A Quick Review We have now shown the computation of each cash flow related to Allison Corporation's investing activities. In Exhibit 13–1 we illustrated a complete statement of cash flows for the company. For your convenience, we again show the investing activities section of that statement, illustrating the information developed in the preceding paragraphs.

Cash flows from investing activities:	
Purchases of marketable securities	$ (65,000)
Proceeds from sales of marketable securities	40,000
Loans made to borrowers	(17,000)
Collections on loans	12,000
Purchases of plant assets	(160,000)
Proceeds from sales of plant assets	75,000
Net cash flows from investing activities	$(115,000)

An important feature of the investing activities section of a statement of cash flows is that increases and decreases in cash from similar transactions are presented separately rather than being combined and netted against each other. For example, in this illustration the negative cash flow from purchasing marketable securities ($65,000) is shown separately from the positive cash flow from the sales of marketable securities ($40,000) rather than netting the two to a single negative figure of $25,000 ($65,000 − $40,000).

CASH FLOWS FROM FINANCING ACTIVITIES

Cash flows from financing activities are determined by analyzing the debit and credit changes recorded during the period in the related liability and stockholders' equity accounts. Cash flows from financing activities are more easily determined than those relating to investing activities, because financing activities seldom involve gains or losses.[4] The debit or credit changes in the balance sheet accounts usually are equal to the amounts of the related cash flows.

Credit changes in such accounts as Notes Payable and the accounts for long-term debt and paid-in capital usually indicate cash receipts; debit changes indicate cash payments.

Short-Term Borrowing Transactions To illustrate, consider paragraph **10,** which provides the information supporting the following cash flows:

Proceeds from short-term borrowing	$45,000
Payments to settle short-term debts	(55,000)

---

[4] An early retirement of debt is an example of a financing transaction that may result in a gain or a loss.

Both the proceeds from short-term borrowing of $45,000 (a positive cash flow) and the payments to settle short-term debts of $55,000 (a negative cash flow) are presented in the statement of cash flows. Presenting both directions of the changes in cash, rather than combining the two and presenting a net amount of $10,000 ($55,000 − $45,000), is an important feature of the statement of cash flows. Presenting both positive and negative cash flows is referred to as presenting *gross* cash flows rather than presenting *net* cash flows.

Is it possible to determine the proceeds of short-term borrowing transactions throughout the year without carefully reviewing each cash receipt? The answer is yes—the proceeds from short-term borrowing are equal to the *sum of the credit entries* in the short-term *Notes Payable* account. Payments to settle short-term debts are equal to the *sum of the debit entries* in this account.

Proceeds from Issuing Bonds Payable and Capital Stock   Paragraph **11** states that Allison Corporation received cash of $100,000 by issuing bonds payable. This amount was determined by summing the credit entries in the Bonds Payable account. The Bonds Payable account included no debit entries during the year; thus, no bonds were retired.

Paragraph **12** states that during the year Allison Corporation issued capital stock for $50,000. The proceeds from issuing stock are equal to the sum of the credit entries made in the Capital Stock and Additional Paid-in Capital accounts ($10,000 + $40,000).

Cash Dividends Paid to Stockholders   Paragraph **13** states that Allison Corporation declared and paid cash dividends of $40,000 during the year. If dividends are both declared and paid during the same year, the cash payments are equal to the related debit entries in the Retained Earnings account.

If the balance sheet includes a liability for dividends payable, the amounts debited to Retained Earnings represent dividends *declared* during the period, which may differ from the amount of dividends *paid*. To determine cash dividends paid, we adjust the amount of dividends declared by adding any decrease (or subtracting any increase) in the Dividends Payable account over the period.

A Quick Review   We have now shown the computation of each cash flow related to Allison Corporation's financing activities. In Exhibit 13–1 we illustrated a complete statement of cash flows for the company. For your convenience, we again show the financing activities section of that statement, illustrating the information developed in the preceding paragraphs.

Cash flows from financing activities:	
Proceeds from short-term borrowing	$ 45,000
Payments to settle short-term debts	(55,000)
Proceeds from issuing bonds payable	100,000
Proceeds from issuing capital stock	50,000
Dividends paid	(40,000)
Net cash flows from financing activities	$100,000

RELATIONSHIP BETWEEN THE STATEMENT OF CASH FLOWS AND THE BALANCE SHEET

The first asset appearing in the balance sheet is Cash and Cash Equivalents. The statement of cash flows explains in some detail the change in this asset from one balance sheet date to the next. The last three lines in the statement of cash flows illustrate this relationship, as shown in our Allison Corporation example:

Net increase (decrease) in cash and cash equivalents	$35,000
Cash and cash equivalents, beginning of year	20,000
Cash and cash equivalents, end of year	$55,000

This is referred to as a reconciliation of the beginning and ending cash balances.

CASE IN POINT

Successful companies sometimes experience reductions in cash. Often these reductions are intentional in order to more productively use the company's cash in different ways. For example, in the years ending June 30, 2010 and 2012 combined, Microsoft Corporation reported *decreases* in cash in excess of $3 billion! Does this mean that the company was experiencing extreme financial difficulty? Not necessarily. In these years, operations provided $24,073 million (2010) and $31,626 million (2012). The overall declines were due to very large amounts being used in investing and

© Imaginechina via AP Images

financing activities, primarily for acquiring other companies and investments, paying cash dividends to stockholders, and purchasing treasury stock.

Lessons to be learned from this example are twofold. First, a decrease in cash does not necessarily signal financial problems, and second, a company's cash position may change in ways very different from its net income.

REPORTING OPERATING CASH FLOWS BY THE INDIRECT METHOD

In determining cash flows from operating activities for Allison Corporation, we have followed what is commonly referred to as the direct method. To this point in our study of the statement of cash flows, we have emphasized the direct method because we consider it to be the more informative and more readily understood approach. The direct method is recommended by the FASB, although companies are permitted to use either the direct or indirect method. Before completing our Allison Corporation illustration of preparing a statement of cash flows, we look more carefully at the indirect method.

Exhibit 13–4 includes a comparison of the direct and indirect methods of determining net cash provided by operating activities for Allison Corporation. The direct method is the same as discussed earlier in this chapter. The two methods are more similar than it may appear at first glance. Both methods are based on the same underlying information and they result in the same net cash flow amount—in Allison Corporation's case, $50,000. Both methods convert information originally prepared on the accrual basis to information prepared on the cash basis. In Exhibit 13–4, accrual-based data appear in blue: cash flows are shown in red.

To illustrate the similarity in the computations, look briefly at the formulas for computing the cash inflows and outflows shown under the direct method (pages 572–574). Each formula begins with an income statement amount and then adds or subtracts the change during the period in related balance sheet accounts. Now look at our illustration of the indirect method in Exhibit 13–4. Notice that this computation also focuses on the net changes during the period in balance sheet accounts.

The difference between the two methods lies only in approach. However, the two approaches provide readers of the statement of cash flows with different types of information. The direct method informs these readers of the nature and dollar amounts of the *specific cash inflows and outflows* comprising the operating activities of the business. The indirect method, in contrast, *explains why* the net cash flows from operating activities differ from another measurement of performance—net income. As you can see, the indirect method starts with net income and essentially works backwards through a series of adjustments to reach the net cash provided by operating activities amount.

EXHIBIT 13–4
Comparison of Direct and
Indirect Methods

Direct Method		
Cash flows from operating activities:		
Cash received from customers	$ 870,000	
Interest and dividends received	10,000	
Cash provided by operating activities		$880,000
Cash paid to suppliers and employees	$(764,000)	
Interest paid	(28,000)	
Income taxes paid	(38,000)	
Cash disbursed for operating activities		(830,000)
Net cash provided by operating activities		$ 50,000

Indirect Method		
Net income		$ 65,000
Add: Depreciation expense		40,000
Decrease in accrued interest receivable		1,000
Increase in accounts payable		15,000
Increase in accrued interest liabilities		7,000
Nonoperating loss on sales of marketable securities		4,000
Subtotal		$132,000
Less: Increase in accounts receivable	$30,000	
Increase in inventory	10,000	
Increase in prepaid expenses	3,000	
Decrease in accrued operating expenses payable	6,000	
Decrease in accrued income taxes payable	2,000	
Nonoperating gain on sales of plant assets	31,000	82,000
Net cash provided by operating activities		$ 50,000

LO13-5

LEARNING OBJECTIVE
Distinguish between the
direct and indirect methods
of reporting operating cash
flows.

Focus on ✗

RECONCILING NET INCOME WITH NET CASH FLOWS

To further your understanding of the indirect method, we now discuss common adjustments
required to reconcile net income with net cash flows from operating activities. The nature and
dollar amounts of these adjustments are determined by an accountant using a worksheet or a
computer program; they are *not* entered in the company's accounting records.

LO13-6

LEARNING OBJECTIVE
Explain why net income differs
from net cash flows from
operating activities.

1. *Adjusting for Noncash Expenses*

   Depreciation is an example of a noncash expense—that is, depreciation expense reduces
   net income but does not require any cash outlay during the period. The cash outflow related
   to depreciation resulted when the asset was purchased and was presented as an investing
   activity at that time—before any depreciation was ever recognized. Depreciation causes
   expenses on the accrual basis to exceed cash payments, and results in net income for the
   period being less than net cash flows. To reconcile net income with net cash flows, we add
   back to net income the amount of depreciation and any other noncash expenses. (Other
   noncash expenses include unfunded pension expense, amortization of intangible assets,
   depletion of natural resources, and amortization of bond discount.)

2. *Adjusting for Timing Differences*

   Timing differences between elements of net income and net cash flows arise whenever
   revenue or expenses are recognized by debiting or crediting an account *other than* Cash.
   Changes during the period in the balances of these asset and liability accounts represent
   differences between the amount of revenues and expenses recognized in the income statement on the accrual basis and the net cash flows from operating activities. The balance
   sheet accounts that give rise to these timing differences include Accounts Receivable,
   Inventories, Prepaid Expenses, Accounts Payable, and Accrued Expenses Payable.

3. *Adjusting for Nonoperating Gains and Losses*

Nonoperating gains and losses include gains and losses from sales of investments, plant assets, and discontinued operations (which relate to investing activities); and gains and losses on early retirement of debt (which relate to financing activities).

We have learned in this chapter that cash flows are classified as operating activities, investing activities, or financing activities. Nonoperating gains and losses, by definition, do not affect *operating activities*. However, these gains and losses do enter into the determination of net income. Therefore, in converting net income to net cash flows from operating activities, we *add back any nonoperating losses* and *deduct any nonoperating gains* included in net income. The full cash effect of the underlying transaction is then presented as an investing activity (for example, sale of a building) or as a financing activity (for example, retirement of debt) in the statement of cash flows.

THE INDIRECT METHOD: A SUMMARY

The adjustments to net income explained in our preceding discussion are summarized as follows:

Net income	
Add:	Depreciation
	Decrease in accounts receivable
	Decrease in inventories
	Decrease in prepaid expenses
	Increase in accounts payable
	Increase in accrued expenses payable
	Increase in deferred income taxes payable
	Nonoperating losses deducted in computing net income
Deduct:	Increase in accounts receivable
	Increase in inventories
	Increase in prepaid expenses
	Decrease in accounts payable
	Decrease in accrued expenses payable
	Decrease in deferred income taxes payable
	Nonoperating gains added in computing net income
Net cash provided by (used in) operating activities	

LO13-7

LEARNING OBJECTIVE
Compute net cash flows from operating activities using the *indirect* method.

INDIRECT METHOD MAY BE REQUIRED IN A SUPPLEMENTARY SCHEDULE

The FASB recommends use of the *direct method* in presenting net cash flows from operating activities. The majority of companies, however, elect to use the indirect method. One reason is that the FASB requires companies using the direct method to meet an additional reporting requirement.

They are required to provide a *supplementary schedule* showing the computation of net cash flows from operating activities by the indirect method. However, no supplementary computations are required of companies that present the indirect method computations in their cash flow statements because this same information is already presented in the body of the statement.

THE STATEMENT OF CASH FLOWS: A SECOND LOOK

We have now completed our explanation of Allison Corporation's statement of cash flows. We have analyzed each type of cash flow by reconciling amounts included in the other two financial statements—the income statement and the balance sheet—to determine the amounts of individual operating, investing, and financing cash flows. In computing cash flows from operating activities, we began by using the direct method, in which major categories of both positive and negative cash flows were determined and presented.

We also illustrated the indirect method to determine the amount of operating cash flows. Rather than adjusting each individual operating cash flow category for changes in balance sheet accounts, these same adjustments were made to net income.

Exhibit 13–5 includes an expanded statement of cash flows for Allison Corporation. This statement uses the direct method for operating activities and includes two supplementary schedules.

EXHIBIT 13–5

Allison Corporation (Expanded) Statement of Cash Flows

ALLISON CORPORATION
STATEMENT OF CASH FLOWS
FOR THE YEAR ENDED DECEMBER 31, 2015

Cash flows from operating activities:		
Cash received from customers	$ 870,000	
Interest and dividends received	10,000	
Cash provided by operating activities		$ 880,000
Cash paid to suppliers and employees	$(764,000)	
Interest paid	(28,000)	
Income taxes paid	(38,000)	
Cash disbursed for operating activities		(830,000)
Net cash provided by operating activities		$ 50,000
Cash flows from investing activities:		
Purchases of marketable securities	$ (65,000)	
Proceeds from sales of marketable securities	40,000	
Loans made to borrowers	(17,000)	
Collections on loans	12,000	
Cash paid to acquire plant assets (see Supplementary Schedule B)	(160,000)	
Proceeds from sales of plant assets	75,000	
Net cash used in investing activities		(115,000)
Cash flows from financing activities:		
Proceeds from short-term borrowing	$ 45,000	
Payments to settle short-term debts	(55,000)	
Proceeds from issuing bonds payable	100,000	
Proceeds from issuing capital stock	50,000	
Dividends paid	(40,000)	
Net cash provided by financing activities		100,000
Net increase (decrease) in cash		$ 35,000
Cash and cash equivalents, Jan. 1, 2015		20,000
Cash and cash equivalents, Dec. 31, 2015		$ 55,000
Supplementary Schedule A: Net Cash Provided by Operating Activities		
Net income		$ 65,000
Add: Depreciation expense		40,000
Decrease in accrued interest receivable		1,000
Increase in accounts payable		15,000
Increase in accrued liabilities		7,000
Nonoperating loss on sales of marketable securities		4,000
Subtotal		$ 132,000
Less: Increase in accounts receivable	$ 30,000	
Increase in inventory	10,000	
Increase in prepaid expenses	3,000	
Decrease in accrued liabilities	8,000	
Nonoperating gain on sales of plant assets	31,000	82,000
Net cash provided by operating activities		$ 50,000
Supplementary Schedule B: Noncash Investing and Financing Activities		
Purchases of plant assets		$ 200,000
Less: Portion financed through issuance of long-term debt		40,000
Cash paid to acquire plant assets		$ 160,000

 Notice this supplementary schedule illustrates the indirect method of determining cash flows from operations

Supplementary Schedule A in Exhibit 13–5 illustrates the determination of net cash flows from operating activities by the *indirect method. Supplementary Schedule B* in Exhibit 13–5 discloses any noncash aspects of the company's investing and financing activities. This type of supplementary schedule is required whenever some of the company's investing and financing activities do not coincide with cash flows occurring within the current period.

How would the statement of cash flows in Exhibit 13–5 differ if the indirect method were used? The information included in Supplementary Schedule A would be substituted for the direct method information in the "Cash flows from operating activities" section of the financial statement and would no longer be required as a supplemental disclosure. In fact, this is one reason for the popularity of the indirect method. Because the indirect method calculation is required to be disclosed if the direct method is used, many companies prefer to include the reconciliation of net income to net cash from operating activities in the body of the statement of cash flows and avoid the supplemental disclosure of that same information.

FINANCIAL ANALYSIS and Decision Making

The users of a statement of cash flows are particularly interested in the *net cash flows from operating activities.* Is the amount large enough to provide for necessary replacements of plant assets and maturing liabilities? And if so, is there enough left for the current dividend to look secure—or even be increased?

Consider two competitors in the import craft supplies business, Gonzalez, Inc., and Alvarez Company. These companies have approximately the same size assets, liabilities, and sales. Selected information from their most recent statements of cash flows follows:

	Beginning Cash Balance	Net Cash Flow from (in thousands)			Ending Cash Balance
		Operating Activities	Investing Activities	Financing Activities	
Gonzalez	$150	$600	$(500)	$400	$650
Alvarez	150	50	500	(50)	650

Which company is in the stronger cash flow position? Although both have the same beginning and ending cash balances ($150,000 and $650,000, respectively), Gonzalez is in the stronger position because of its strong operating cash flows of $600,000. Gonzalez has been able to invest $500,000 in operating assets, while financing only $400,000, and still has a $650,000 ending cash balance. Alvarez, on the other hand, has generated only a small amount of cash from operations ($50,000) and has sold assets to generate cash ($500,000) to support its ending cash balance. Whether Alvarez will be able to sustain its cash position over time,

and be able to meet its recurring obligations in the future, is questionable.

Even more important than net cash flows from operating activities in any one year is the *trend* in cash flows over a period of years—and the *consistency* of that trend from year to year. The best results are net cash flows from operating activities that increase each year by a substantial—but also predictable—percentage.[5]

Free Cash Flow Many analysts compute an amount called *free cash flow*. Free cash flow represents the cash flow available to management for discretionary purposes, *after* the company has met all of its basic obligations relating to business operations. The term *free cash flow* is widely cited within the business community. Different analysts

Net cash flows from operating activities		$ 50,000
Less: Net cash used for acquiring plant assets		
($160,000 − $75,000 proceeds)	$85,000	
Dividends paid	40,000	125,000
Free cash flow		$(75,000)

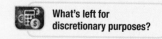

What's left for discretionary purposes?

---

[5] Percentage change is the dollar amount of change from one year to the next, expressed as a percentage of (divided by) the amount from the *earlier* of the two years. For example, if net cash provided by operating activities was $100,000 in the first year and $120,000 in the second year, the percentage increase is 20 percent, computed as follows: ($120,000 − $100,000) ÷ $100,000.

compute this measure in different ways. For example, are all expenditures for plant assets "basic obligations," or only those expenditures made to maintain the current level of productive capacity?

One common method of computing free cash flow is to deduct from the net cash flows from operating activities net cash used to purchase plant assets and any dividends paid. This computation follows, using information from the Allison Corporation statement of cash flows shown earlier.

This computation suggests that Allison Corporation *did not* generate enough cash from operations to meet its basic obligations. Thus, management had to raise cash from other sources. But, of course, an analyst always should look behind the numbers. For example, was Allison's purchase of plant assets during the year a basic obligation, or did it represent a discretionary expansion of the business?

YOUR TURN   You as a Financial Analyst

You are working for the same stock market research firm as in Chapter 12, but unlike your previous boss (who tended to focus on growth and relative value, both based on reported earnings), your new boss focuses primarily on free cash flow and dividends in choosing stocks.

Your new boss is interested in stocks where free cash flow equals at least 50 percent of cash flow from operations. He also wants dividends to be 25 percent or more of cash flow from operations. You are considering the same stocks as before: Home Depot, Intel, Coca-Cola, and Amazon. Your new boss provides you with the following information and asks you to recommend which stocks are consistent with his investment criteria.

| | In Millions | | |
Company	Cash Flow from Operations (CFO)	Net Capital Expenditures	Dividends
Home Depot	$ 6,975	$ 1,312	$1,743
Intel	18,884	11,027	4,350
Coca-Cola	10,645	2,780	4,595
Amazon	4,180	3,785	—

He also tells you that a potential new client is going to be calling you this afternoon. This potential client is an elderly widow and experienced investor who is quite wealthy. She is interested in learning why the relative levels of free cash flow and dividends are important metrics. She also doesn't understand why all firms don't pay dividends. Your boss tells you to answer this prospective client's questions.

(See our comments on the Online Learning Center website.)

Managing Cash Flows

Management can do much to influence the cash flows of a particular period. In fact, it has a responsibility to manage cash flows. No business can afford to run out of cash and default on its obligations. Even being a few days late in meeting payrolls, or paying suppliers or creditors, can severely damage important business relationships. One of management's most basic responsibilities is to ensure that the business has enough cash to meet its obligations as they come due.

BUDGETING: THE PRIMARY CASH MANAGEMENT TOOL

A primary tool used by management to anticipate and shape future cash flows is a *cash budget*. A **cash budget** is a *forecast* of future cash receipts and payments. This budget is *not* a financial statement and is not widely distributed outside the organization. To managers, however, it is among the most useful of all accounting reports.

In many ways, a cash budget is similar to a statement of cash flows. However, the budget shows the results *expected in future periods,* rather than those achieved in the past. Also, the cash budget is more *detailed,* usually showing expected cash flows month-by-month and separately for every department within the organization.

Cash budgets serve many purposes. Among the most important are:

- Encouraging managers to plan and coordinate their activities in advance.
- Providing managers with advance notice of the resources at their disposal and the results they are expected to achieve.
- Providing targets useful in evaluating performance.
- Providing advance warnings of potential cash shortages.

WHAT PRIORITY SHOULD MANAGERS GIVE TO INCREASING NET CASH FLOWS?

Creditors and investors look to a company's cash flows to protect their investment and provide future returns. Trends in key cash flows (such as from operations and free cash flow) affect a company's credit rating, stock price, and access to additional investment capital. For these reasons, management is under constant pressure to improve the key measures of cash flow. Unfortunately, the pressure to report higher cash flows in the current period may *conflict* with managers' long-run responsibilities.

LO13-8

LEARNING OBJECTIVE
Discuss the likely effects of various business strategies on cash flows.

Short-Term Results versus Long-Term Growth Often, short-term operating results can be improved at the expense of long-term growth. For example, reducing expenditures for developing new products will increase earnings and net cash flows in the current period. But over time, this strategy may lessen the company's competitiveness and long-term profitability. Many of the most successful products took many years to develop and test before they contributed positive cash flows to the company.

One-Time Boosts to Cash Flows Some strategies can increase the net cash flows of the current period, but *without having much effect* on future cash flows. Such strategies include collecting receivables more quickly and reducing the size of inventory.

Assume, for example, that a company offers 60-day terms to its credit customers. Credit sales made in January are collected in March, and credit sales made in February are collected in April. Notice that in each month, the company is collecting about *one month's amount* of credit sales, but the receipt of cash is delayed two months from the point of sale.

Now assume that on March 1 the company changes its policies to allow only *30-day* credit terms. In April, the company will collect *two months* of credit sales—those made in February (under the former 60-day terms) *and* those made in March (under the new 30-day terms).

This significantly increases the cash received from customers for the one month of April. But it does not signal higher cash flows for the months ahead. In May, the company will collect only those credit sales made in April. It quickly returns to the pattern of collecting about *one month's* credit sales in the current month. Shortening the collection period provided only a one-time boost in cash receipts.

A similar one-time boost may be achieved by reducing the size of inventory. This reduces the need for purchasing merchandise, *but only while inventory levels are falling.* Once the company stabilizes the size of its inventory at the new and lower level, its monthly purchases must return to approximately the quantity of goods sold during the period.

SOME STRATEGIES FOR PERMANENT IMPROVEMENTS IN CASH FLOW

Several strategies may improve cash flows in *both* the short and long term. These are *deferring income taxes, peak pricing,* and developing an *effective product mix.*

Deferring Income Taxes
Deferring income taxes means using accounting methods for income tax purposes that legally postpone the payment of income taxes. An example is using an *accelerated depreciation method* for income tax purposes.

Deferring taxes may benefit a growing business *every year.* As a result, it is an effective and popular cash management strategy.[6]

Peak Pricing
Some businesses have more customers than they can handle—at least at certain times of the day or year. Examples of such businesses include popular restaurants, resort hotels, telephone companies, and providers of electricity.

Peak pricing is a strategy of using sales prices both to increase revenue and to ration goods and services when total demand exceeds supply (or capacity). A higher price is charged during the peak periods of customer demand and a lower price during off-peak periods. For example, a restaurant might charge a higher price during the peak dinner hours than the rest of the day. A theater might charge a higher price in the peak week and evening hours than the rest of the week. Peak pricing has two related goals. First, it *increases the seller's revenue* during the periods of greatest demand. Second, it *shifts* some of the demand to off-peak periods, when the business is better able to service additional customers.

Peak pricing may make goods and services available to customers who otherwise could not afford them. Also, peak pricing may prevent systems, such as cellular telephones, from becoming so overloaded that they simply cannot function. Peak pricing is *not always appropriate.* For example, we would not expect hospitals or physicians to raise their prices during epidemics or natural disasters. The alternative to peak pricing is a single price all the time.

Develop an Effective Product Mix
Another tool for increasing revenue and cash receipts is the mix of products offered for sale. The dual purposes of an effective **product mix** are to (1) increase total sales and (2) increase gross margins (that is, the excess of the selling price over the cost of the product).

Some products complement one another, meaning the customer who buys one product often may purchase the other. Common examples of **complementary products** include french fries at a hamburger restaurant, snacks at a movie theater, and a car wash connected to a gas station.

Some complementary products are *essential* to satisfying the customer. (Would you be happy at a sports stadium that didn't sell food?) Others increase sales by *attracting customers* who also purchase other types of merchandise.

Some complementary products appear to be only incidental to the company's main product lines. But, in reality, these incidental items may *be* the company's most important products.

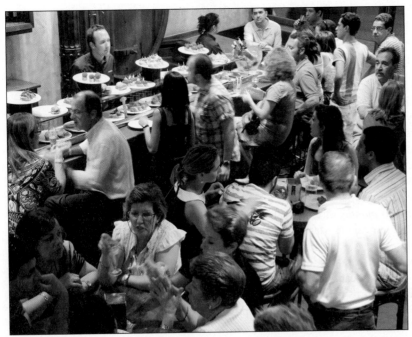

© Lonely Planet Images/Getty Images

---

[6] The Modified Accelerated Cost Recovery System (MACRS) is an accelerated method widely used for income tax purposes. Deferred income taxes were discussed briefly in Chapter 10. The reason a growing business can benefit from deferred taxes *every year* is that each year it defers a *greater amount* than comes due from the past.

Ethics, Fraud, & Corporate Governance

As discussed in this chapter, cash flow from operations is the subtotal on the statement of cash flows that is most closely scrutinized by financial statement readers. A large and growing cash flow from operations is viewed positively for at least three reasons. First, companies pay bills with cash, not with earnings. Second, a company with significant cash flows from operations is better positioned to fund future growth with its own cash flows rather than having to borrow additional monies or issue more stock. Third, the quality of a company's earnings is viewed as better if cash flow from operations closely matches reported net income.

Although it may be difficult to manipulate cash flows from operations, it is not impossible, as the Securities and Exchange Commission (SEC) enforcement action involving **Dynergy, Inc.**, illustrates. **Dynergy** produces and delivers energy, including natural gas, electricity, and coal, to customers throughout North America and Europe, and its shares are traded on the New York Stock Exchange. **Dynergy** entered into a structured transaction (hereafter referred to as Project Alpha) that resulted in **Dynergy** reporting $300 million in cash flow from operations that should have been reported as cash flow from financing activities. A primary motivation for **Dynergy**'s involvement with Project Alpha was to bring cash flow from operations closer to reported net income.

Project Alpha had a five-year term and worked as follows. **Dynergy** sponsored a special-purpose entity, **ABG Supply**, to sell **Dynergy** natural gas. In the first year of the five-year term of Project Alpha, **ABG Supply** sold **Dynergy** gas at below-market prices. **Dynergy** then sold this gas at a $300 million profit and reported the resulting cash flow in the operating activities portion of the statement of cash flows. In the remaining four years of Project Alpha's life, **Dynergy** was obligated to buy gas from **ABG Supply** at above-market prices. These purchases at above-market prices would be sufficient to pay back the $300 million, plus interest. In substance, the original sale of gas to **Dynergy** in year 1 at $300 million below market prices represented a loan, and transactions in years 2 to 5 would result in the loan being repaid with interest. As such, the $300 million cash flow in Year 1 should have been reported in the financing activities portion of the statement of cash flows—not in the operating activities portion of the statement.

Three midlevel **Dynergy** tax executives were largely responsible for Project Alpha's structure, and they participated in an active scheme to hide the details of the structure from **Dynergy**'s outside auditors. Two of these executives pled guilty to federal *criminal* charges and testified against the third executive. The third executive, Jamie Olis, was convicted of criminal charges and was sentenced to over 20 years in federal prison (although this sentence was reduced substantially on appeal). This case clearly illustrates the personal risk of violating securities laws, particularly when there is an active scheme to hide the true nature of transactions from auditors, investors, and other outside parties.

A Worksheet for Preparing a Statement of Cash Flows

A statement of cash flows is developed by *systematically analyzing all changes in the noncash balance sheet accounts.* This process can be formalized and documented through the preparation of a specially designed worksheet. The worksheet also provides the accountant with visual assurance that the changes in balance sheet accounts have been fully explained.

LO13-9

LEARNING OBJECTIVE
Explain how a worksheet may be helpful in preparing a statement of cash flows.

DATA FOR AN ILLUSTRATION

We will illustrate the worksheet approach using the 2015 financial data of Auto Supply Co.[7] Shown in Exhibit 13–6 are the balances in Auto's balance sheet accounts at the beginning and end of 2015. (Notice in this illustration that the account balances at the end of the current year appear in the *right-hand* column. This format also is used in the worksheet.)

---

[7] Our example involving Allison Corporation was quite comprehensive. Therefore, a worksheet for Allison Corporation would be too long and detailed for use as an introductory illustration of a worksheet for the statement of cash flows.

EXHIBIT 13–6

Auto Supply Co. Balance Sheets

 Changes in the noncash accounts are the key to identifying cash flows

AUTO SUPPLY CO. COMPARATIVE BALANCE SHEETS		
	December 31,	
	2014	2015
Assets		
Cash	$ 50,000	$ 45,000
Marketable Securities	40,000	25,000
Accounts Receivable	320,000	330,000
Inventory	240,000	235,000
Plant and Equipment (net of accumulated depreciation)	600,000	640,000
Totals	$1,250,000	$1,275,000
Liabilities & Stockholders' Equity		
Accounts Payable	$ 150,000	$ 160,000
Accrued Expenses Payable	60,000	45,000
Mortgage Note Payable (long-term)	–0–	70,000
Bonds Payable (due in 2020)	500,000	350,000
Capital Stock (no par value)	160,000	160,000
Retained Earnings	380,000	490,000
Totals	$1,250,000	$1,275,000

Additional Information   The following information also is used in the preparation of the worksheet. (Accrual-based measurements appear in blue, cash flows in red.)

1. Net income for the year amounted to $250,000. Cash dividends of $140,000 were declared and paid.

2. Auto's only noncash expense was depreciation, which totaled $60,000.

3. Marketable securities costing $15,000 were sold for $35,000 cash, resulting in a $20,000 nonoperating gain.

4. The company purchased plant assets for $100,000, making a $30,000 cash down payment and issuing a $70,000 mortgage note payable for the balance of the purchase price.

THE WORKSHEET

Auto Supply Co. reports cash flows from operating activities by the *indirect method*.[8] A worksheet for preparing a statement of cash flows appears in Exhibit 13–7.

To set up the worksheet, the company's balance sheet accounts are listed in the top portion of the worksheet, with the beginning balances in the first column and the year-end balances in the last (right-hand) column. (For purposes of illustration, we have shown these accounts and account balances in **black**.)

The two middle columns are used to (1) explain the changes in each balance sheet account over the year and (2) indicate how each change affected cash.

Entries in the Two Middle Columns   The entries in the *top portion of the worksheet* summarize the transactions recorded in the account over the year. (Because these entries summarize transactions recorded on the accrual basis, they are shown in blue.)

For each summary entry in the top portion of the worksheet, we make an offsetting entry (in the opposite column) in the *bottom portion* of the worksheet indicating the *cash effects* of the transactions. These cash effects are classified as operating, investing, or financing activities and are explained with a descriptive caption. (Entries representing the *cash effects* of transactions and the related descriptive captions appear in red.)

---

[8] If the worksheet utilizes the direct method, numerous subclassifications are required within the operating activities section. Such worksheets are illustrated in more advanced accounting courses.

EXHIBIT 13–7
Worksheet for a Statement
of Cash Flows

AUTO SUPPLY CO.
WORKSHEET FOR A STATEMENT OF CASH FLOWS
FOR THE YEAR ENDED DECEMBER 31, 2015

Balance sheet effects:	Beginning Balance	Debit Changes	Credit Changes	Ending Balance
Assets				
Cash and Cash Equivalents	50,000		(x) 5,000	45,000
Marketable Securities	40,000		(8) 15,000	25,000
Accounts Receivable	320,000	(4) 10,000		330,000
Inventory	240,000		(5) 5,000	235,000
Plant and Equipment (net of accumulated depreciation)	600,000	(9) 100,000	(3) 60,000	640,000
Totals	1,250,000			1,275,000
Liabilities & Stockholders' Equity				
Accounts Payable	150,000		(6) 10,000	160,000
Accrued Expenses Payable	60,000	(7) 15,000		45,000
Mortgage Note Payable	–0–		(9) 70,000	70,000
Bonds Payable	500,000	(10) 150,000		350,000
Capital Stock	160,000			160,000
Retained Earnings	380,000	(2) 140,000	(1) 250,000	490,000
Totals	1,250,000	415,000	415,000	1,275,000

"Effects of Transactions" spans Beginning Balance, Debit Changes, Credit Changes, Ending Balance.

Up here we summarize the changes in each noncash account

Cash effects:	Sources	Uses
Operating activities:		
Net income	(1) 250,000	
Depreciation expense	(3) 60,000	
Increase in accounts receivable		(4) 10,000
Decrease in inventory	(5) 5,000	
Increase in accounts payable	(6) 10,000	
Decrease in accrued expenses payable		(7) 15,000
Gain on sales of marketable securities		(8) 20,000
Investing activities:		
Proceeds from sales of marketable securities	(8) 35,000	
Cash paid to acquire plant assets		(9) 30,000
Financing activities:		
Dividends paid		(2) 140,000
Payments to retire bonds payable		(10) 150,000
Subtotals	360,000	365,000
Net decrease in cash	(x) 5,000	
Totals	365,000	365,000

Down here we identify and classify the related cash effects of these changes

Cash provided by operations—$280,000

Cash provided by investing activities—$5,000

Cash used in financing activities—$290,000

Entries in the two middle columns may be made in any sequence, but we recommend the following approach:

1. Explain the change in the Retained Earnings account.

2. Account for depreciation expense (and any other noncash expenses).

3. Account for timing differences between net income and cash flows from operating activities.

4. Explain any remaining changes in balance sheet accounts *other than Cash*. (Hint: Changes in asset accounts represent investing activities; changes in liability and equity accounts represent financing activities.)

5. Compute and record the net increase or decrease in cash.

Using this approach, we next explain the entries in our illustrated worksheet.

ENTRY

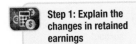

Step 1: Explain the changes in retained earnings

1. Auto's net income explains a $250,000 *credit* to the Retained Earnings account. In the bottom portion of the working paper, an offsetting entry is made in the *Sources* column and is classified as an operating activity.[9]

2. Cash dividends of $140,000 caused a *debit* to the Retained Earnings account during 2015. The offsetting entry is made in the *Uses* column; payments of dividends are classified as a financing activity.

With these first two entries, we have explained how Auto's Retained Earnings account increased during 2015 from $380,000 to $490,000.

Step 2: Account for noncash expenses

3. Auto's only noncash expense was depreciation. In the top portion of the worksheet, depreciation explains a $60,000 credit (decrease) in Plant and Equipment (which includes the Accumulated Depreciation accounts). The offsetting entry in the bottom of the worksheet is placed in the Sources column. We have explained that depreciation is not really a source of cash, but that it *is added back* to net income as a step in computing the cash flows from operating activities.

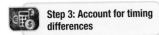

Step 3: Account for timing differences

4–7. Fluctuations in current assets and current liabilities create *timing differences* between net income and the net cash flows from operating activities. In the top portion of the worksheet, entries (4) through (7) summarize the changes in these current asset and current liability accounts. In the bottom portion, they show how these changes affect the computation of cash flows from operating activities.

8. In 2015, Auto sold marketable securities with a cost of $15,000 for $35,000 cash, resulting in a $20,000 nonoperating gain. In the top portion of the worksheet, the entry explains the $15,000 credit change in the Marketable Securities account. In the bottom portion, it reports cash proceeds of $35,000. The difference? The $20,000 nonoperating gain, which is *removed from the Operating Activities section* of the worksheet and included instead within the amount reported as "Proceeds from sales of marketable securities" in the Investing Activities category.

Step 4: Explain any remaining changes in noncash accounts

9. Auto purchased $100,000 in plant assets, paying $30,000 cash and issuing a $70,000 note payable. These events explain a $100,000 debit in Plant and Equipment and the $70,000 credit change in Mortgage Note Payable; they involved a cash outlay of $30,000, which is classified as an investing activity. (The $70,000 financed by issuance of a note payable is a *noncash* investing and financing activity.)

10. The $150,000 debit change in Auto's Bonds Payable account indicates that this amount of the liability has been repaid—that is, $150,000 in bonds has been retired. This is included in the financing activities category.

At this point, we should check to determine that our entries in the two middle columns *fully explain* the differences between the beginning and ending balance of each noncash balance sheet account. If the top portion of the worksheet explains the changes in every noncash account, the bottom section should include all of the cash flows for the year.

Step 5: Compute and record the net change in cash

(x) We now total the Sources (cash increases) and Uses (cash decreases) columns in the bottom portion of the worksheet. The difference between these column subtotals represents the *net increase or decrease* in cash. In our example, the Sources column totals $360,000, while the Uses column totals $365,000, indicating a *$5,000 decrease*

---

[9] When the *indirect method* is used, net income serves as the *starting point* for computing net cash flows from operating activities.

in cash over the period. Notice that this is exactly the amount by which Cash decreased during 2015: $50,000 − $45,000 = $5,000. Our last entry, labeled *(x)*, explains the credit change in the Cash account at the top of the worksheet and brings the bottom of the worksheet into balance.

The formal statement of cash flows, reporting the cash flows from operating activities by the indirect method, can be prepared directly from the bottom portion of this worksheet. In Exhibit 13–8, amounts appearing in accrual-based accounting records are shown in blue; cash flows appear in red.

AUTO SUPPLY CO.
STATEMENT OF CASH FLOWS
FOR THE YEAR ENDED DECEMBER 31, 2015

Cash flows from operating activities:

Net income		$ 250,000
Add: Depreciation expense		60,000
Decrease in inventory		5,000
Increase in accounts payable		10,000
Subtotal		$ 325,000
Less: Increase in accounts receivable	$ 10,000	
Decrease in accrued expenses payable	15,000	
Gain on sales of marketable securities	20,000	45,000
Net cash provided by operating activities		$ 280,000

Cash flows from investing activities:

Proceeds from sales of marketable securities	$ 35,000	
Cash paid to acquire plant assets (see supplementary schedule below)	(30,000)	
Net cash provided by investing activities		5,000

Cash flows from financing activities:

Dividends paid	$ (140,000)	
Payments to retire bonds payable	(150,000)	
Net cash used for financing activities		(290,000)
Net decrease in cash		$ (5,000)
Cash and cash equivalents, Jan. 1, 2015		50,000
Cash and cash equivalents, Dec. 31, 2015		$ 45,000

Supplementary Schedule: Noncash Investing and Financing Activities

Purchases of plant assets	$ 100,000
Less: Portion financed through issuance of long-term debt	70,000
Cash paid to acquire plant assets	$ 30,000

EXHIBIT 13–8

Auto Supply Co. Statement of Cash Flows

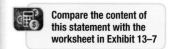 Compare the content of this statement with the worksheet in Exhibit 13–7

Concluding Remarks

In this chapter, we have discussed the importance of cash flow information for investors and creditors and how that information is arranged and presented in the statement of cash flows. We delayed in-depth coverage of this important topic to this point in this text because of the importance of understanding accounting for assets, liabilities, and stockholders' equity as a forerunner to understanding how cash flow information differs from accrual accounting information.

As stated earlier, companies have an option of presenting cash flow from operations information by either the direct or the indirect method. Although we have presented both in this chapter, our emphasis has been on the direct method despite the fact that most companies employ the indirect method in their financial reporting. We have done this for two reasons. First, we believe the direct method is more readily understood by students and others who are learning for the first time how cash-based and accrual-based information relate. Second, and perhaps more important, investors appear to generally favor the direct method, as evidenced by the following quote from the former chief accountant of the Securities and Exchange Commission, speaking to a group of certified public accountants:

> I've heard many investors express a strong preference for use of the direct method of preparing the statement of cash flows. It's widely understood and believed by many to be a more informative presentation. We are not requiring a change, but it is an action you could consider to promote transparency given the importance to investors of cash flow information.[10]

In the next chapter, we take a broader look at financial statement analysis, including how information about cash flows is combined with information from the other financial statements, to better understand a company's financial activities. Managers and investors alike must look beyond short-term changes in earnings and cash flows from one period to the next. They must consider factors that cause these changes and how they may affect future operations. Throughout this text, we have introduced analytical techniques that are useful in better understanding a company. In Chapter 14, we bring those techniques together into a comprehensive model for analyzing financial statements in a way that assists informed decision makers in understanding a company's business activities and in anticipating the long-term effects of business strategies.

---

[10] Donald T. Nicolaisen in a speech entitled, "Remarks before the 2003 Thirty-First AICPA National Conference on Current SEC Developments," December 11, 2003.

END-OF-CHAPTER REVIEW

SUMMARY OF LEARNING OBJECTIVES

LO13-1 **Explain the purposes and uses of a statement of cash flows.** The primary purpose of a statement of cash flows is to provide information about the cash receipts and cash payments of the entity and how they relate to the entity's operating, investing, and financing activities. Readers of financial statements use this information to assess the liquidity of a business and to evaluate its ability to generate positive cash flows in future periods, pay dividends, and finance growth.

LO13-2 **Describe how cash transactions are classified in a statement of cash flows.** Cash flows are classified as (1) operating activities, (2) investing activities, or (3) financing activities. Receipts and payments of interest are classified as operating activities.

LO13-3 **Compute the major cash flows relating to operating activities.** The major operating cash flows are (1) cash received from customers, (2) cash paid to suppliers and employees, (3) interest and dividends received, (4) interest paid, and (5) income taxes paid. These cash flows are computed by converting the income statement amounts for revenue, cost of goods sold, and expenses from the accrual basis to the cash basis. This is done by adjusting the income statement amounts for changes occurring over the period in related balance sheet accounts.

LO13-4 **Compute the cash flows relating to investing and financing activities.** Cash flows from investing and financing activities are determined by examining the entries in the related asset and liability accounts, along with any related gains or losses shown in the income statement. Debit entries in asset accounts represent purchases of assets (an investing activity). Credit entries in asset accounts represent the cost of assets sold. The amount of these credit entries must be adjusted by any gains or losses recognized on these sales transactions.

Debit entries to liability accounts represent repayment of debt, while credit entries represent borrowing. Both types of transactions are classified as financing activities. Other financing activities include the issuance of stock (indicated by credits to the paid-in capital accounts) and payment of dividends (indicated by a debit change in the Retained Earnings account).

LO13-5 **Distinguish between the direct and indirect methods of reporting operating cash flows.** The direct and indirect methods are alternative formats for reporting net cash flows from operating activities. The *direct* method shows the specific cash inflows and outflows comprising the operating activities of the business. By the *indirect* method, the computation begins with accrual-based net income and then makes adjustments necessary to arrive at net cash flows from operating activities. Both methods result in the same dollar amount of net cash flows from operating activities. When the direct method is used, the indirect method must also be disclosed.

LO13-6 **Explain why net income differs from net cash flows from operating activities.** Net income differs from net operating cash flows for several reasons. One reason is noncash expenses, such as depreciation and the amortization of intangible assets. These expenses, which require no cash outlays when they are recognized, reduce net income but do not require cash payments. Another reason is the many timing differences existing between the recognition of revenue and expense and the occurrence of the underlying cash flows. Finally, nonoperating gains and losses enter into the determination of net income, but the related cash flows are classified as investing or financing activities, not operating activities.

LO13-7 **Compute net cash flows from operating activities using the *indirect* method.** The indirect method uses net income (as reported in the income statement) as the starting point in the computation of net cash flows from operating activities. Adjustments to net income necessary to arrive at net cash flows from operating activities can be described in three categories: noncash expenses, timing differences, and nonoperating gains and losses. Adjustments reconcile net income (accrual basis) to net cash flows from operating activities. Specific adjustments from each category are illustrated in the summary analysis of the indirect method on page 581.

LO13-8 **Discuss the likely effects of various business strategies on cash flows.** It is difficult to predict the *extent* to which a business strategy will affect cash flows. However, an informed decision maker should understand the *direction* in which a strategy is likely to affect cash flows—both in the short term and over a longer term.

LO13-9 **Explain how a worksheet may be helpful in preparing a statement of cash flows.** A worksheet can be used to analyze the changes in balance sheet accounts other than Cash and, thereby, determine the related cash flows. In the top portion of the worksheet, entries are made summarizing the changes in each noncash account. In the bottom half, offsetting entries are made to represent the cash effects of the transactions summarized in the top portion. The entries in the bottom half of the worksheet are classified into the same categories as in a statement of cash flows—operating, investing, and financing. The statement of cash flows then is prepared from the data in the bottom portion of the worksheet.

Key Terms Introduced or Emphasized in Chapter 13

accrual basis (p. 569)   A method of summarizing operating results in terms of revenue earned and expenses incurred, rather than cash receipts or cash payments.

cash basis (p. 572)   The practice of summarizing operating results in terms of cash receipts and cash payments, rather than revenue earned or expenses incurred.

cash budget (p. 585)   A detailed forecast of expected future cash receipts, usually organized department by department and month by month for the coming year.

cash equivalents (p. 569)   Highly liquid short-term investments, such as Treasury bills, money market funds, and commercial paper. For purposes of preparing a statement of cash flows, money held in cash equivalents is considered the same as cash. Thus transfers between a bank account and cash equivalents are not considered receipts or disbursements of cash.

cash flows (p. 566)   A term describing both cash receipts (inflows) and cash payments (outflows).

complementary products (p. 586)   Products that "fit together"— that tie in with a company's other products. As a result, customers attracted to one product may also purchase others.

financing activities (p. 566)   Transactions such as borrowing, repaying borrowed amounts, raising equity capital, or making distributions to owners. The cash effects of these transactions are reported in the financing activities section of the statement of cash flows. Noncash aspects of these transactions are disclosed in a supplementary schedule.

free cash flow (p. 583)   The portion of the annual net cash flows from operating activities that remains available for discretionary purposes after the basic obligations of the business have been met. Can be computed in several different ways.

investing activities (p. 566)   Transactions involving acquisitions or sales of investments or plant assets and making or collecting loans. The cash aspects of these transactions are shown in the investing activities section of the statement of cash flows. Noncash aspects of these transactions are disclosed in a supplementary schedule to this financial statement.

operating activities (p. 566)   Transactions entering into the determination of net income, with the exception of gains and losses relating to financing or investing activities. The category includes such transactions as selling goods or services, earning investment income, and incurring costs and expenses, such as payments to suppliers and employees, interest, and income taxes. The cash effects of these transactions are reflected in the operating activities section of the statement of cash flows.

peak pricing (p. 586)   The strategy of charging a higher price during periods of high demand, and a lower price during periods of slack demand. Intended to both maximize revenue and shift excess demand to periods in which it can be more easily accommodated.

product mix (p. 586)   The variety and relative quantities of goods and services that a company offers for sale.

Demonstration Problem

You are the chief accountant for Electro Products, Inc. Your assistant has prepared an income statement for the current year and has developed the following additional information by analyzing changes in the company's balance sheet accounts.

ELECTRO PRODUCTS, INC.
INCOME STATEMENT
FOR THE YEAR ENDED DECEMBER 31, 2015

Revenue:		
Net sales		$9,500,000
Interest income		320,000
Gain on sales of marketable securities		70,000
Total revenue and gains		$9,890,000
Costs and expenses:		
Cost of goods sold	$4,860,000	
Operating expenses (including depreciation of $700,000)	3,740,000	
Interest expense	270,000	
Income tax expense	300,000	
Loss on sales of plant assets	90,000	
Total costs, expenses, and losses		9,260,000
Net income		$ 630,000

Changes in the company's balance sheet accounts over the year are summarized as follows:

1. Accounts Receivable decreased by $85,000.
2. Accrued Interest Receivable increased by $15,000.
3. Inventory decreased by $280,000, and Accounts Payable to suppliers of merchandise decreased by $240,000.
4. Short-term prepayments of operating expenses decreased by $18,000, and accrued liabilities for operating expenses increased by $35,000.
5. The liability for Accrued Interest Payable decreased by $16,000 during the year.
6. The liability for Accrued Income Taxes Payable increased by $25,000 during the year.
7. The following schedule summarizes the total debit and credit entries during the year in other balance sheet accounts:

	Debit Entries	Credit Entries
Marketable Securities	$ 120,000	$ 210,000
Notes Receivable (cash loans made to others)	250,000	190,000
Plant Assets (see paragraph **8**)	3,800,000	360,000
Notes Payable (short-term borrowing)	620,000	740,000
Bonds Payable		1,100,000
Capital Stock		50,000
Additional Paid-in Capital (from issuance of stock)		840,000
Retained Earnings (see paragraph **9**)	320,000	630,000

8. The $360,000 in credit entries to the Plant Assets account is net of any debits to accumulated depreciation when plant assets were retired. Thus, the $360,000 in credit entries represents the *book value* of all plant assets sold or retired during the year.
9. The $320,000 debit to Retained Earnings represents dividends declared and paid during the year. The $630,000 credit entry represents the net income for the year.
10. All investing and financing activities were cash transactions.
11. Cash and cash equivalents amounted to $448,000 at the beginning of the year and to $330,000 at year-end.

Instructions

You are to prepare a statement of cash flows for the current year, following the format illustrated in Exhibit 13–1. Cash flows from operating activities are to be determined by the *direct method*. Place brackets around dollar amounts representing cash outlays. Show separately your computations of the following amounts:

a. Cash received from customers.

b. Interest received.

c. Cash paid to suppliers and employees.

d. Interest paid.

e. Income taxes paid.

f. Proceeds from sales of marketable securities.

g. Proceeds from sales of plant assets.

h. Proceeds from issuing capital stock.

Solution to the Demonstration Problem

ELECTRO PRODUCTS, INC.
STATEMENT OF CASH FLOWS
FOR THE YEAR ENDED DECEMBER 31, 2015

Cash flows from operating activities:		
Cash received from customers **(a)**	$ 9,585,000	
Interest received **(b)**	305,000	
Cash provided by operating activities		$9,890,000
Cash paid to suppliers and employees **(c)**	$(7,807,000)	
Interest paid **(d)**	(286,000)	
Income taxes paid **(e)**	(275,000)	
Cash disbursed for operating activities		(8,368,000)
Net cash provided by operating activities		$1,522,000
Cash flows from investing activities:		
Purchases of marketable securities	$ (120,000)	
Proceeds from sales of marketable securities **(f)**	280,000	
Loans made to borrowers	(250,000)	
Collections on loans	190,000	
Cash paid to acquire plant assets	(3,800,000)	
Proceeds from sales of plant assets **(g)**	270,000	
Net cash used for investing activities		(3,430,000)
Cash flows from financing activities:		
Proceeds from short-term borrowing	$ 740,000	
Payments to settle short-term debts	(620,000)	
Proceeds from issuing bonds payable	1,100,000	
Proceeds from issuing capital stock **(h)**	890,000	
Dividends paid	(320,000)	
Net cash provided by financing activities		1,790,000
Net increase (decrease) in cash		$ (118,000)
Cash and cash equivalents, Jan. 1, 2015		448,000
Cash and cash equivalents, Dec. 31, 2015		$ 330,000

Supporting computations:

a. Cash received from customers:

Net sales	$9,500,000
Add: Decrease in accounts receivable	85,000
Cash received from customers	$9,585,000

b. Interest received:

Interest income	$ 320,000
Less: Increase in accrued interest receivable	15,000
Interest received	$ 305,000

c. Cash paid to suppliers and employees:

Cash paid for purchases of merchandise:

Cost of goods sold	$4,860,000
Less: Decrease in inventory	280,000
Net purchases	$4,580,000
Add: Decrease in accounts payable to suppliers	240,000
Cash paid for purchases of merchandise	$4,820,000

ELECTRO PRODUCTS, INC. (continued)
STATEMENT OF CASH FLOWS
FOR THE YEAR ENDED DECEMBER 31, 2015

Cash paid for operating expenses:		
Operating expenses		$3,740,000
Less: Depreciation (a "noncash" expense) . . . . $ 700,000		
Decrease in prepayments 18,000		
Increase in accrued liabilities for operating expenses 35,000		753,000
Cash paid for operating expenses		$2,987,000
Cash paid to suppliers and employees ($4,820,000 + $2,987,000)		$7,807,000
d. Interest paid:		
Interest expense		$ 270,000
Add: Decrease in accrued interest payable		16,000
Interest paid		$ 286,000
e. Income taxes paid:		
Income tax expense		$ 300,000
Less: Increase in accrued income taxes payable		25,000
Income taxes paid		$ 275,000
f. Proceeds from sales of marketable securities:		
Cost of marketable securities sold (credit entries to the Marketable Securities account)		$ 210,000
Add: Gain reported on sales of marketable securities . . .		70,000
Proceeds from sales of marketable securities		$ 280,000
g. Proceeds from sales of plant assets:		
Book value of plant assets sold (paragraph **8**)		$ 360,000
Less: Loss reported on sales of plant assets		90,000
Proceeds from sales of plant assets		$ 270,000
h. Proceeds from issuing capital stock:		
Amounts credited to the Capital Stock account		$ 50,000
Add: Amounts credited to Additional Paid-in Capital account		840,000
Proceeds from issuing capital stock		$ 890,000

Self-Test Questions

The answers to these questions appear on page 621.

1. The statement of cash flows is designed to assist users in assessing each of the following, *except:*

   a. The ability of a company to remain liquid.

   b. The company's profitability.

   c. The major sources of cash receipts during the period.

   d. The reasons why net cash flows from operating activities differ from net income.

2. Which of the following is *not* included in the statement of cash flows, or in a supplementary schedule accompanying the statement of cash flows?

   a. Disclosure of investing or financing activities that did not involve cash.

   b. A reconciliation of net income to net cash flows from operating activities.

   c. Disclosure of the amount of cash invested in money market funds during the accounting period.

   d. The amount of cash and cash equivalents owned by the business at the end of the accounting period.

3. Cash flows are grouped in the statement of cash flows into the following major categories:

   a. Cash receipts, cash disbursements, and noncash activities.

   b. Operating activities, investing activities, and financing activities.

   c. Direct cash flows and indirect cash flows.

   d. Operating activities, investing activities, and collecting activities.

4. The following is a list of various cash payments and cash receipts:

Cash paid to suppliers and employees	$420,000
Dividends paid	18,000
Interest paid	12,000
Purchases of plant assets	45,000
Interest and dividends received	17,000
Payments to settle short-term bank loans	29,000
Income taxes paid	23,000
Cash received from customers	601,000

Based only on the above items, net cash flows from operating activities are:

a. $138,000

b. $91,000

c. $120,000

d. $163,000

5. During the current year, two transactions were recorded in the Land account of Duke Industries. One involved a debit of $320,000 to the Land account; the second was a $210,000 credit to the Land account. Duke's income statement for the year reported a loss on sale of land in the amount of $25,000. All transactions involving the Land account were cash transactions. These transactions would be shown in the statement of cash flows as:

a. $320,000 cash provided by investing activities, and $210,000 cash disbursed for investing activities.

b. $185,000 cash provided by investing activities, and $320,000 cash disbursed for investing activities.

c. $235,000 cash provided by investing activities, and $320,000 cash disbursed for investing activities.

d. $210,000 cash provided by investing activities, and $320,000 cash disbursed for investing activities.

6. Which of the following business strategies is *most likely* to increase the net cash flows of a software developer in the short run but *reduce* them over a longer term?

a. Develop software that is more costly to create but easier to update and improve.

b. Lower the price of existing versions of products as customer demand begins to fall.

c. Reduce expenditures for the purpose of developing new products.

d. Purchase the building in which the business operates (assume the company currently rents this location).

ASSIGNMENT MATERIAL   Discussion Questions

1. Briefly state the purposes of a statement of cash flows.

2. Does a statement of cash flows or an income statement best measure the profitability of a financially sound business? Explain.

3. Give two examples of cash receipts and two examples of cash payments that fit into each of the following classifications:

   a. Operating activities.

   b. Investing activities.

   c. Financing activities.

4. Why are payments and receipts of interest classified as operating activities rather than as financing or investing activities?

5. In the long run, is it more important for a business to have positive cash flows from its operating activities, investing activities, or financing activities? Why?

6. Of the three types of business activities summarized in a statement of cash flows, which type is *least* likely to show positive net cash flows in a successful, growing business? Explain your reasoning.

7. Identify three factors that may cause net income to differ from net cash flows from operating activities.

8. Briefly explain the difference between the *direct* and *indirect methods* of computing net cash flows from operating activities. Which method results in higher net cash flows?

9. Frost, Inc., acquired land by issuing $770,000 of capital stock. No cash changed hands in this transaction. Will the transaction be disclosed in the company's statement of cash flows? Explain.

10. The only transaction recorded in the plant assets account of Pompei Company in the current year was a $263,000 credit to the Land account. Assuming that this credit resulted from a cash transaction, does this entry indicate a cash receipt or a cash payment? Should this $263,000 appear in the statement of cash flows, or is some adjustment necessary?

11. During the current year, the following credit entries were posted to the paid-in capital accounts of Crawford Shipyards:

Capital Stock	$15,000,000
Additional Paid-in Capital	27,500,000

Explain the type of cash transaction that probably caused these credit changes, and illustrate the presentation of this transaction in a statement of cash flows.

12. At the beginning of the current year, Waxler Corporation had dividends payable of $1,600,000. During the current year, the company declared cash dividends of $4,500,000, of which $970,000 appeared as a liability at year-end. Determine the amount of cash dividends *paid* during this year.

13. Define the term *free cash flow.* Explain the significance of this measurement to (1) short-term creditors, (2) long-term creditors, (3) stockholders, and (4) management.

14. Explain the concept of *peak pricing* and provide an example from your own experience.

15. Explain why speeding up the collection of accounts receivable provides only a one-time increase in cash receipts.

Brief Exercises

LO13-3

BRIEF EXERCISE 13.1

Cash Flows from
Operations (Direct)

Presley, Inc., had the following positive and negative cash flows during the current year:

Positive cash flows:	
Received from customers *operating*	$270,000
Interest and dividends *operating*	50,000
Sale of plant assets *investing*	360,000
Negative cash flows:	
Paid to suppliers and employees *OP*	$127,000
Purchase of investments *in*	45,000
Purchase of treasury stock *fina*	40,000

Determine the amount of cash provided by or used for operating activities by the direct method.

LO13-7

BRIEF EXERCISE 13.2

Cash Flows from
Operations (Indirect)

Garagiola Company had net income in the current year of $470,000. Depreciation expense for the year totaled $67,000. During the year the company experienced an increase in accounts receivable (all from sales to customers) of $35,000 and an increase in accounts payable (all to suppliers) of $56,000. Compute the amount of cash provided by or used for operating activities by the indirect method.

LO13-3

BRIEF EXERCISE 13.3

Cash Flows from
Operations (Direct)

Mississippi Products Co. had the following positive cash flows during the current year: received cash from customers of $750,000; received bank loans of $35,000; and received cash from the sale of common stock of $145,000. During the same year, cash was paid out to purchase inventory for $345,000, to employees for $230,000, and for the purchase of plant assets of $217,000. Calculate the amount of cash provided by or used for operating activities by the direct method.

LO13-7

BRIEF EXERCISE 13.4

Cash Flows from
Operations (Indirect)

Patterson Company reported net income for the current year of $722,000. During the year the company's accounts receivable increased by $50,000, inventory decreased by $23,000, accounts payable decreased by $55,000, and accrued expenses payable increased by $14,000. Determine the amount of cash provided by or used for operating activities by the indirect method.

LO13-4

BRIEF EXERCISE 13.5

Cash Flows from Investing

Old South Company purchased investments for $55,000 and plant assets for $147,000 during the current year, during which it also sold plant assets for $66,000, at a gain of $6,000. The company also purchased treasury stock for $78,000 and sold a new issue of common stock for $523,000. Determine the amount of cash provided by or used for investing activities for the year.

LO13-4

BRIEF EXERCISE 13.6

Cash Flows from Financing
Activities

Nen Mexico, Inc., sold common stock for $560,000 and preferred stock for $56,000 during the current year. In addition, the company purchased treasury stock for $47,000 and paid dividends on common and preferred stock for $24,000. Determine the amount of cash provided by or used for financing activities during the year.

LO13-3

BRIEF EXERCISE 13.7

Cash Payment for
Merchandise

Spinx, Inc., reported cost of goods sold of $100,800 during the current year. Following are the beginning and ending balances of merchandise inventory and accounts payable for the year:

	Beginning	Ending
Merchandise inventory	$35,000	$43,000
Accounts payable	23,000	32,000

Determine the amount of cash payments for purchases during the year.

LO13-2

BRIEF EXERCISE 13.8

Determining Beginning
Cash Balance

Tyler, Inc.'s cash balance at December 31, 2015, the end of its financial reporting year, was $155,000. During 2015, cash provided by operations was $145,000, cash used in investing activities was $67,000, and cash provided by financing activities was $10,000. Calculate the amount of Tyler's beginning cash balance at January 1, 2015.

LO13-6

BRIEF EXERCISE 13.9

Reconciling Net Income
to Cash from Operations

Zephre Company reported net income for the year of $68,000. Depreciation expense for the year was $15,000. During the year, accounts receivable increased by $4,000, inventory decreased by $6,000, accounts payable increased by $3,000, and accrued expenses payable decreased by $2,000. Reconcile the amount of net income to the amount of cash provided by or used for operating activities.

LO13-2

BRIEF EXERCISE 13.10

Preparing Statement
of Cash Flows

Maines, Inc., had a cash balance at the beginning of the year of $72,000. During the year, the following cash flows occurred:

From operating activities	$136,000
From investing activities	(56,000)
From financing activities	(34,000)

Prepare an abbreviated statement of cash flows, including a reconciliation of the beginning and ending cash balances for the year.

Exercises

LO13-1, LO13-2

EXERCISE 13.1

Using a Statement
of Cash Flows

Wallace Company's statement of cash flows for the current year is summarized as follows:

Cash provided by operating activities	$275,000
Cash used in investing activities	(140,000)
Cash provided by financing activities	45,000
Increase in cash during the year	$180,000
Cash balance, beginning of the year	75,000
Cash balance, end of the year	$255,000

a. Briefly explain what is included in each of the first three categories listed (i.e., the cash from operating, investing, and financing activities categories).

b. On the basis of the limited information presented above, describe the company's change in cash position during the year and your interpretation of the strength of the company's current (end-of-year) cash position.

LO13-1, LO13-2, LO13-6

EXERCISE 13.2

Using a Statement
of Cash Flows

Auto Supply Company's 2015 statement of cash flows appears in Exhibit 13–8. Study the statement and respond to the following questions:

a. What was the company's free cash flow in 2015?

b. What were the major sources and uses of cash from financing activities during 2015? Did the net effect of financing activities result in an increase or a decrease in cash during the year?

c. What happened to the total amount of cash and cash equivalents during the year? Assuming 2015 was a typical year, is the firm in a position to continue its dividend payments in the future? Explain.

d. Look at the reconciliation of net income to net cash provided by operating activities, and explain the following:

    1. Net loss (gain) from the sale of marketable securities.

    2. Increase in accounts receivable.

LO13-4

EXERCISE 13.3

Computing Cash Flows

An analysis of the Marketable Securities control account of Fancher Products, Inc., shows the following entries during the year:

Balance, Jan. 1	$ 290,000
Debit entries	125,000
Credit entries	(140,000)
Balance, Dec. 31	$ 275,000

In addition, the company's income statement includes a $25,000 loss on sales of marketable securities. None of the company's marketable securities is considered a cash equivalent.

Compute the amounts that should appear in the statement of cash flows as:

a. Purchases of marketable securities.

b. Proceeds from sales of marketable securities.

LO13-3, LO13-6

EXERCISE 13.4

Comparing Net Sales and Cash Receipts

During the current year, Tachnic, Inc., made cash sales of $289,000 and credit sales of $472,000. During the year, accounts receivable decreased by $32,000.

a. Compute for the current year the amounts of:

    1. Net sales reported as revenue in the income statement.

    2. Cash received from collecting accounts receivable.

    3. Cash received from customers.

b. Write a brief statement explaining *why* cash received from customers differs from the amount of net sales.

LO13-3

EXERCISE 13.5

Computing Cash Paid for Purchases of Merchandise

The general ledger of AXM, Inc., provides the following information relating to purchases of merchandise:

	End of Year	Beginning of Year
Inventory	$820,000	$780,000
Accounts payable to merchandise suppliers	430,000	500,000

The company's cost of goods sold during the year was $2,882,000. Compute the amount of cash payments made during the year to suppliers of merchandise.

LO13-3, LO13-6

EXERCISE 13.6

Reporting Lending Activities and Interest Revenue

During the current year, Maine Salvage Company took out new loans of $17 million. In addition, the company repaid $2 million of prior loans and paid $1.5 million of interest expense. Explain how these cash flows will appear in the company's statement of cash flows, indicating the classification and the dollar amount of each cash flow.

LO13-2

EXERCISE 13.7

Format of a Statement of Cash Flows

The accounting staff of Wyoming Outfitters, Inc., has assembled the following information for the year ended December 31, 2015:

Cash and cash equivalents, Jan. 1	$ 35,800
Cash and cash equivalents, Dec. 31	74,800
Cash paid to acquire plant assets	21,000
Proceeds from short-term borrowing	10,000
Loans made to borrowers	5,000
Collections on loans (excluding interest)	4,000
Interest and dividends received	27,000
Cash received from customers	795,000
Proceeds from sales of plant assets	9,000
Dividends paid	55,000
Cash paid to suppliers and employees	635,000
Interest paid	19,000
Income taxes paid	71,000

Using this information, prepare a statement of cash flows. Include a proper heading for the financial statement, and classify the given information into the categories of operating activities, investing activities, and financing activities. Determine net cash flows from operating activities by the direct method. Place brackets around the dollar amounts of all cash disbursements.

Indicate how you would expect the following strategies to affect the company's net cash flows from *operating activities* (1) in the near future and (2) in later periods (after the strategy's long-term effects have "taken hold"). *Fully explain your reasoning.*

LO13-8

EXERCISE 13.8

Effects of Business Strategies

a.   A successful pharmaceutical company substantially reduces its expenditures for research and development.

b.   A restaurant that previously sold only for cash adopts a policy of accepting bank credit cards, such as Visa and MasterCard.

c.   A manufacturing company reduces by 50 percent the size of its inventories of raw materials (assume no change in inventory storage costs).

d.   Through tax planning, a rapidly growing real estate developer is able to defer significant amounts of income taxes.

e.   A rapidly growing software company announces that it will stop paying cash dividends for the foreseeable future and will instead distribute stock dividends.

LO13-6, LO13-7

EXERCISE 13.9

An Analysis of Possible Reconciling Items

An analysis of the annual financial statements of O'Connell Corporation reveals the following:

a.   The company had a $5 million extraordinary loss from insurance proceeds received due to a tornado that destroyed a factory building.

b.   Depreciation for the year amounted to $9 million.

c.   During the year, $2 million in cash was transferred from the company's checking account into a money market fund.

d.   Accounts receivable from customers increased by $3.5 million over the year.

e.   Cash received from customers during the year amounted to $169 million.

f.   Prepaid expenses decreased by $1 million over the year.

g.   Dividends declared during the year amounted to $8 million; dividends paid during the year amounted to $6 million.

h.   Accounts payable (to suppliers of merchandise) increased by $2.7 million during the year.

i.   The liability for accrued income taxes payable amounted to $5 million at the beginning of the year and $3 million at year-end.

In the computation of net cash flows from operating activities by the *indirect method,* explain whether each of the above items should be *added to net income, deducted from net income,* or *omitted from the computation.* Briefly explain your reasons for each answer.

LOI3-7
EXERCISE 13.10

Computation of Net Cash
Flows from Operating
Activities—Indirect Method

The following data are taken from the income statement and balance sheet of Freeman Machinery, Inc.:

	Dec. 31, 2015	Jan. 1, 2015
Income statement:		
Net Income	$385,000	
Depreciation Expense	135,000	
Amortization of Intangible Assets	40,000	
Gain on Sale of Plant Assets	90,000	
Loss on Sale of Investments	35,000	
Balance sheet:		
Accounts Receivable	$335,000	$380,000
Inventory	503,000	575,000
Prepaid Expenses	22,000	13,000
Accounts Payable (to merchandise suppliers)	379,000	410,000
Accrued Expenses Payable	180,000	155,000

Using this information, prepare a partial statement of cash flows for the year ended December 31, 2015, showing the computation of net cash flows from operating activities by the *indirect* method.

LOI3-2
EXERCISE 13.11

Classifying Cash Flows

Among the transactions of Salem, Inc., were the following:

a. Made payments on accounts payable to merchandise suppliers.

b. Paid the principal amount of a note payable to First State Bank.

c. Paid interest charges relating to a note payable to First State Bank.

d. Issued bonds payable for cash; management plans to use this cash in the near future to expand manufacturing and warehouse capabilities.

e. Paid salaries to employees in the finance department.

f. Collected an account receivable from a customer.

g. Transferred cash from the general bank account into a money market fund.

h. Used the cash received in **d,** above, to purchase land and a building suitable for a manufacturing facility.

i. Made a year-end adjusting entry to recognize depreciation expense.

j. At year-end, purchased for cash an insurance policy covering the next 12 months.

k. Paid the quarterly dividend on preferred stock.

l. Paid the semiannual interest on bonds payable.

m. Received a quarterly dividend from an investment in the preferred stock of another corporation.

n. Sold for cash an investment in the preferred stock of another corporation.

o. Received cash upon the maturity of an investment in cash equivalents. (Ignore interest.)

Instructions

Most of the preceding transactions should be included among the activities summarized in a statement of cash flows. For each transaction that should be included in this statement, indicate whether the transaction should be classified as an operating activity, an investing activity, or a financing activity. If the transaction *should not be included* in the current year's statement of cash flows, briefly explain why not. (Assume that net cash flows from operating activities are determined by the *direct method.*)

LOI3-2
EXERCISE 13.12

Classifying Cash Flows

Among the transactions of Marvel Manufacturing were the following:

1. Made payments on accounts payable to office suppliers.

2. Paid the principal amount of a mortgage to Seventh Bank.

3. Paid interest charges relating to a mortgage to Seventh Bank.

4. Issued preferred stock for cash; management plans to use this cash in the near future to purchase another company.

5. Paid salaries to employees in the finance department.

6. Collected an account receivable from a customer.

7. Transferred cash from the general bank account into a money market fund.

8. Used the cash received in **4**, above, to purchase Moran Manufacturing Co.

9. Made a year-end adjusting entry to recognize amortization expense.

10. At year-end, purchased for cash an advertising spot on a local radio station for the next eight months.

11. Paid the annual dividend on preferred stock.

12. Paid the semiannual interest on bonds payable.

13. Received a semiannual dividend from an investment in the common stock of another corporation.

14. Sold for cash an investment in the common stock of another corporation.

15. Received cash upon the maturity of an investment in cash equivalents. (Ignore interest.)

Instructions

Most of the preceding transactions should be included among the activities summarized in a statement of cash flows. For each transaction that should be included in this statement, indicate whether the transaction should be classified as an operating activity, an investing activity, or a financing activity. If the transaction *should not be included* in the current year's statement of cash flows, briefly explain why not. (Assume that net cash flows from operating activities are determined by the *direct method*.)

LO13-4

EXERCISE 13.13

Cash Flows from Investing Activities

Sorensen Company provides the following information related to its investing and financing activities for the current year:

Cash receipts:	
Sale of common stock	$250,000
Sale of equipment (at $34,000 loss)	156,000
Sale of land (at $50,000 gain)	160,000
Cash payments:	
Purchase of equipment	$178,000
Purchase of treasury stock	45,000
Retirement of debt	36,500
Dividends on preferred and common stock	75,000

a. Calculate the net amount of cash provided by or used for investing activities for the year.

b. What impact, if any, do the following facts have on your calculation? (**1**) Equipment was sold at a $34,000 loss, and (**2**) land was sold at a $50,000 gain.

c. Briefly explain your decision to exclude any of the items listed above if they were not included in your calculation in part **a**.

LO13-4

EXERCISE 13.14

Cash Flows from Financing Activities

Shepherd Industries had the following cash flows by major categories during the current year:

Cash provided by:	
Receipts from customers	$560,000
Sale of bonds	420,000
Sale of treasury stock	52,000
Interest and dividends received	56,000
Sale of equipment (at a $56,000 loss)	236,000
Cash used for:	
Payments to employees	$145,000
Payments to purchase inventory	190,000
Dividends on common stock	60,000
Purchase of treasury stock	20,000
Interest expense	82,000

a. Calculate the net amount of cash provided by or used for financing activities for the year.

b. Briefly justify why you excluded any of the above items in your calculation in part **a.**

c. Briefly explain your treatment of interest expense in your calculation in part **a.**

LO13-1, LO13-2, LO13-4
EXERCISE 13.15

Home Depot, Inc. Using a
Statement of Cash Flows

Statements of cash flow for Home Depot, Inc., for 2012, 2011, and 2010 are included in Appendix A of this text.

a. Focus on the information for 2012 (year ending February 3, 2013). How does net earnings compare with net cash provided by or used in operations, and what accounts for the primary difference between the two amounts?

b. What are the major uses of cash, other than operations, and how have these varied over the three-year period presented?

c. Cash flows from both investing and financing activities have been negative for all three years presented. Considering Home Depot's overall cash flows, including its cash flows from operations, would you say that this leads to a negative interpretation of Home Depot's cash position at February 3, 2013? Why or why not?

d. Calculate the amount of free cash flow for each of 2010, 2011, and 2012, and comment briefly on your conclusion concerning this information.

Problem Set A

LO13-2 through LO13-4
PROBLEM 13.1A

Format of a Statement
of Cash Flows

The accounting staff of Lambert Company has assembled the following information for the year ended December 31, 2015:

Cash sales	$ 825,000
Credit sales	2,500,000
Collections on accounts receivable	2,200,000
Cash transferred from the money market fund to the general bank account	250,000
Interest and dividends received	100,000
Purchases (all on account)	1,800,000
Payments on accounts payable to merchandise suppliers	1,500,000
Cash payments for operating expenses	1,050,000
Interest paid	180,000
Income taxes paid	95,000
Loans made to borrowers	500,000
Collections on loans (excluding receipts of interest)	260,000
Cash paid to acquire plant assets	3,100,000
Book value of plant assets sold	660,000
Loss on sales of plant assets	80,000
Proceeds from issuing bonds payable	2,500,000
Dividends paid	120,000
Cash and cash equivalents, Jan. 1	512,000

Instructions

Prepare a statement of cash flows in the format illustrated in Exhibit 13–1. Place brackets around amounts representing cash outflows. Use the *direct method* of reporting cash flows from operating activities.

Some of the items above will be listed in your statement without change. However, you will have to combine certain given information to compute the amounts of (1) collections from customers, (2) cash paid to suppliers and employees, and (3) proceeds from sales of plant assets. (Hint: Not every item listed is used in preparing a statement of cash flows.)

LO13-4
PROBLEM 13.2A

Reporting Investing
Activities

An analysis of the income statement and the balance sheet accounts of Hampton, Inc., at December 31, 2015, provides the following information:

Income statement items:

Gain on Sale of Marketable Securities	$ 42,000
Loss on Sales of Plant Assets	33,000

Analysis of balance sheet accounts:

Marketable Securities account:

Debit entries	$ 75,000
Credit entries	90,000

Notes Receivable account:

Debit entries	210,000
Credit entries	162,000

Plant and Equipment accounts:

Debit entries to plant asset accounts	196,000
Credit entries to plant asset accounts	120,000
Debit entries to accumulated depreciation accounts	75,000

Additional Information

1. Except as noted in **4** below, payments and proceeds relating to investing transactions were made in cash.
2. The marketable securities are not cash equivalents.
3. All notes receivable relate to cash loans made to borrowers, not to receivables from customers.
4. Purchases of new equipment during the year ($196,000) were financed by paying $60,000 in cash and issuing a long-term note payable for $136,000.
5. Debits to the accumulated depreciation accounts are made whenever depreciable plant assets are retired. The book value of plant assets retired during the year was $45,000 ($120,000 − $75,000).

Instructions

a. Prepare the investing activities section of a statement of cash flows. Show supporting computations for the amounts of (1) proceeds from sales of marketable securities and (2) proceeds from sales of plant assets. Place brackets around numbers representing cash outflows.

b. Prepare the supporting schedule that should accompany the statement of cash flows in order to disclose the noncash aspects of the company's investing and financing activities.

c. Assume that Hampton's management expects approximately the same amount of cash to be used for investing activities next year. In general terms, explain how the company might generate cash for this purpose.

LO13-4

PROBLEM 13.3A

Reporting Investing Activities

An analysis of the income statement and the balance sheet accounts of Holmes Export Co. at December 31, 2015 provides the following information:

Income statement items:

Gain on Sale of Plant Assets	$ 12,000
Loss on Sales of Marketable Securities	16,000

Analysis of balance sheet accounts:

Marketable Securities account:

Debit entries	$ 78,000
Credit entries	62,000

Notes Receivable account:

Debit entries	55,000
Credit entries	62,000

Plant and Equipment accounts:

Debit entries to plant asset accounts	170,000
Credit entries to plant asset accounts	140,000
Debit entries to accumulated depreciation accounts	100,000

Additional Information

1. Except as noted in **4** below, payments and proceeds relating to investing transactions were made in cash.

2. The marketable securities are not cash equivalents.

3. All notes receivable relate to cash loans made to borrowers, not to receivables from customers.

4. Purchases of new equipment during the year ($170,000) were financed by paying $60,000 in cash and issuing a long-term note payable for $110,000.

5. Debits to the accumulated depreciation accounts are made whenever depreciable plant assets are sold or retired. The book value of plant assets sold or retired during the year was $40,000 ($140,000 − $100,000).

Instructions

a. Prepare the investing activities section of a statement of cash flows. Show supporting computations for the amounts of (1) proceeds from sales of marketable securities and (2) proceeds from sales of plant assets. Place brackets around amounts representing cash outflows.

b. Prepare the supplementary schedule that should accompany the statement of cash flows in order to disclose the noncash aspects of the company's investing and financing activities.

c. Does management have *more* control or *less* control over the timing and amount of cash outlays for investing activities than for operating activities? Explain.

LO13-3, LO13-8

PROBLEM 13.4A

Reporting Operating Cash Flows by the Direct Method

The following income statement and selected balance sheet account data are available for Treece, Inc., at December 31, 2015:

TREECE, INC.
INCOME STATEMENT
FOR THE YEAR ENDED DECEMBER 31, 2015

Revenue:

Net sales		$2,850,000
Dividend income		104,000
Interest income		70,000
Gain on sales of marketable securities		4,000
Total revenue and gains		$3,028,000

Costs and expenses:

Cost of goods sold	$1,550,000	
Operating expenses	980,000	
Interest expense	185,000	
Income tax expense	90,000	
Total costs and expenses		2,805,000
Net income		$ 223,000

Selected account balances:	End of Year	Beginning of Year
Accounts receivable	$ 650,000	$ 720,000
Accrued interest receivable	9,000	6,000
Inventories	800,000	765,000
Short-term prepayments	20,000	15,000
Accounts payable (merchandise suppliers)	570,000	562,000
Accrued operating expenses payable	65,000	94,000
Accrued interest payable	21,000	12,000
Accrued income taxes payable	22,000	35,000

Additional Information

1. Dividend revenue is recognized on the cash basis. All other income statement amounts are recognized on the accrual basis.
2. Operating expenses include depreciation expense of $115,000.

Instructions

a. Prepare a partial statement of cash flows, including only the *operating activities* section of the statement and using the *direct method.* Place brackets around numbers representing cash payments. Show supporting computations for the following:

1. Cash received from customers.

2. Interest and dividends received.

3. Cash paid to suppliers and employees.

4. Interest paid.

5. Income taxes paid.

b. Management of Treece, Inc., is exploring ways to increase the cash flows from operations. One way that cash flows could be increased is through more aggressive collection of receivables. Assuming that management has already taken all the steps possible to increase revenue and reduce expenses, describe two other ways that cash flows from operations could be increased.

LO13-6, LO13-7

PROBLEM 13.5A

Reporting Operating Cash Flows by the Indirect Method

Using the information presented in Problem **13.4A,** prepare a partial statement of cash flows for the current year, showing the computation of net cash flows from operating activities by the *indirect method.* Explain why the decline in accounts receivable over the year was *added* to net income in computing the cash flows from operating activities.

LO13-2 through LO13-4, LO13-6, LO13-8

PROBLEM 13.6A

Preparing a Statement of Cash Flows: A Comprehensive Problem without a Worksheet

You are the controller for 21st Century Technologies. Your staff has prepared an income statement for the current year and has developed the following additional information by analyzing changes in the company's balance sheet accounts.

21ST CENTURY TECHNOLOGIES
INCOME STATEMENT
FOR THE YEAR ENDED DECEMBER 31, 2015

Revenue:

Net sales		$3,200,000
Interest revenue		40,000
Gain on sales of marketable securities		34,000
Total revenue and gains		$3,274,000

Costs and expenses:

Cost of goods sold	$1,620,000	
Operating expenses (including depreciation of $150,000)	1,240,000	
Interest expense	42,000	
Income tax expense	100,000	
Loss on sales of plant assets	12,000	
Total costs, expenses, and losses		3,014,000
Net income		$ 260,000

Additional Information

1. Accounts receivable increased by $60,000.
2. Accrued interest receivable decreased by $2,000.

3. Inventory decreased by $60,000, and accounts payable to suppliers of merchandise decreased by $16,000.

4. Short-term prepayments of operating expenses increased by $6,000, and accrued liabilities for operating expenses decreased by $8,000.

5. The liability for accrued interest payable increased by $4,000 during the year.

6. The liability for accrued income taxes payable decreased by $14,000 during the year.

7. The following schedule summarizes the total debit and credit entries during the year in other balance sheet accounts:

	Debit Entries	Credit Entries
Marketable Securities	$ 60,000	$ 38,000
Notes Receivable (cash loans made to borrowers)	44,000	28,000
Plant Assets (see paragraph 8)	500,000	36,000
Notes Payable (short-term borrowing)	92,000	82,000
Capital Stock		20,000
Additional Paid-in Capital—Capital Stock		160,000
Retained Earnings (see paragraph 9)	120,000	260,000

8. The $36,000 in credit entries to the Plant Assets account is net of any debits to Accumulated Depreciation when plant assets were retired. Thus, the $36,000 in credit entries represents the book value of all plant assets sold or retired during the year.

9. The $120,000 debit to Retained Earnings represents dividends declared and paid during the year. The $260,000 credit entry represents the net income shown in the income statement.

10. All investing and financing activities were cash transactions.

11. Cash and cash equivalents amounted to $244,000 at the beginning of the year and to $164,000 at year-end.

Instructions

a. Prepare a statement of cash flows for the current year. Use the *direct method* of reporting cash flows from operating activities. Place brackets around dollar amounts representing cash outflows. Show separately your computations of the following amounts:

   1. Cash received from customers.

   2. Interest received.

   3. Cash paid to suppliers and employees.

   4. Interest paid.

   5. Income taxes paid.

   6. Proceeds from sales of marketable securities.

   7. Proceeds from sales of plant assets.

   8. Proceeds from issuing capital stock.

b. Explain the *primary reason* why:

   1. The amount of cash provided by operating activities was substantially greater than the company's net income.

   2. There was a net decrease in cash over the year, despite the substantial amount of cash provided by operating activities.

c. As 21st Century's controller, you think that through more efficient cash management, the company could have held the increase in accounts receivable for the year to $10,000, without affecting net income. Explain how holding down the growth in receivables affects cash. Compute the effect that limiting the growth in receivables to $10,000 would have had on the company's net increase or decrease in cash (and cash equivalents) for the year.

LO13-1 through LO13-8
PROBLEM 13.7A
Prepare and Analyze a
Statement of Cash Flows
with a Worksheet

Satellite World was founded in 2014 to apply a new technology for efficiently transmitting closed-circuit (cable) television signals without the need for an in-ground cable. The company earned a profit of $115,000 in 2014, its first year of operations, even though it was serving only a small test market. In 2015, the company began dramatically expanding its customer base. Management expects both sales and net income to more than triple in each of the next five years.

Comparative balance sheets at the end of 2014 and 2015, the company's first two years of operations, follow. (Notice that the balances at the end of the current year appear in the right-hand column.)

Additional Information

The following information regarding the company's operations in 2015 is available in either the company's income statement or its accounting records:

1. Net income for the year was $440,000. The company has never paid a dividend.

2. Depreciation for the year amounted to $147,000.

3. During the year the company purchased plant assets costing $2,200,000, for which it paid $1,850,000 in cash and financed $350,000 by issuing a long-term note payable. (Much of the cash used in these purchases was provided by short-term borrowing, as described below.)

4. In 2015, Satellite World borrowed $1,450,000 against a $5.5 million line of credit with a local bank. In its balance sheet, the resulting obligations are reported as notes payable (short-term).

5. Additional shares of capital stock (no par value) were issued to investors for $500,000 cash.

SATELLITE WORLD COMPARATIVE BALANCE SHEETS		
	December 31,	
	2014	2015
Assets		
Cash and cash equivalents	$ 80,000	$ 37,000
Accounts receivable	100,000	850,000
Plant and equipment (net of accumulated depreciation)	600,000	2,653,000
Totals	$780,000	$3,540,000
Liabilities & Stockholders' Equity		
Notes payable (short-term)	$ –0–	$1,450,000
Accounts payable	30,000	63,000
Accrued expenses payable	45,000	32,000
Notes payable (long-term)	390,000	740,000
Capital stock (no par value)	200,000	700,000
Retained earnings	115,000	555,000
Totals	$780,000	$3,540,000

Instructions

a. Prepare a worksheet for a statement of cash flows, following the general format illustrated in Exhibit 13–7. (*Note:* If this problem is completed as a group assignment, each member of the group should be prepared to explain in class all entries in the worksheet, as well as the group's conclusions in parts **c** and **d**.)

b. Prepare a formal statement of cash flows for 2015, including a supplementary schedule of noncash investing and financing activities. (Follow the format illustrated in Exhibit 13–8. Cash provided by operating activities is to be presented by the *indirect method.*)

c. Briefly explain how operating activities can be a net *use* of cash when the company is operating so profitably.

d. Because of the expected rapid growth, management forecasts that operating activities will be an even greater use of cash in the year 2016 than in 2015. If this forecast is correct, does Satellite World appear to be heading toward illiquidity? Explain.

LO13.1 through LO13-8
PROBLEM 13.8A
Prepare and Analyze a
Statement of Cash Flows;
Involves Preparation of a
Worksheet

Miracle Tool, Inc., sells a single product (a combination screwdriver, pliers, hammer, and crescent wrench) exclusively through television advertising. The comparative income statements and balance sheets are for the past two years.

Additional Information

The following information regarding the company's operations in 2015 is available from the company's accounting records:

1. Early in the year the company declared and paid a $4,000 cash dividend.
2. During the year marketable securities costing $15,000 were sold for $14,000 cash, resulting in a $1,000 nonoperating loss.
3. The company purchased plant assets for $20,000, paying $2,000 in cash and issuing a note payable for the $18,000 balance.
4. During the year the company repaid a $10,000 note payable, but incurred an additional $18,000 in long-term debt as described in 3.
5. The owners invested $15,000 cash in the business as a condition of the new loans described in paragraph 4.

MIRACLE TOOL, INC.
COMPARATIVE INCOME STATEMENT
FOR THE YEARS ENDED DECEMBER 31, 2014 AND 2015

	2014	2015
Sales	$500,000	$ 350,000
Less: Cost of goods sold	200,000	140,000
Gross profit on sales	$300,000	$ 210,000
Less: Operating expenses (including depreciation of $34,000 in 2014 and $35,000 in 2015)	260,000	243,000
Loss on sale of marketable securities	–0–	1,000
Net income (loss)	$ 40,000	($ 34,000)

MIRACLE TOOL, INC.
COMPARATIVE BALANCE SHEETS

	December 31,	
	2014	2015
Assets		
Cash and cash equivalents	$ 10,000	$ 60,000
Marketable securities	20,000	5,000
Accounts receivable	40,000	23,000
Inventory	120,000	122,000
Plant and equipment (net of accumulated depreciation)	300,000	285,000
Totals	$490,000	$495,000
Liabilities & Stockholders' Equity		
Accounts payable	$ 50,000	$ 73,000
Accrued expenses payable	17,000	14,000
Note payable	245,000	253,000
Capital stock (no par value)	120,000	135,000
Retained earnings	58,000	20,000
Totals	$490,000	$495,000

Instructions

a. Prepare a worksheet for a statement of cash flows, following the general format illustrated in Exhibit 13–7. (*Note:* If this problem is completed as a group assignment, each member of the group should be prepared to explain in class all entries in the worksheet, as well as the group's conclusions in parts **c, d,** and **e.**)

b. Prepare a formal statement of cash flows for 2015, including a supplementary schedule of noncash investing and financing activities. (Use the format illustrated in Exhibit 13–8. Cash provided by operating activities is to be presented by the *indirect method.*)

c. Explain how Miracle Tool, Inc., achieved positive cash flows from operating activities, despite incurring a net loss for the year.

d. Does the company's financial position appear to be improving or deteriorating? Explain.

e. Does Miracle Tool, Inc., appear to be a company whose operations are growing or contracting? Explain.

f. Assume that management *agrees* with your conclusions in parts **c, d,** and **e.** What decisions should be made and what actions (if any) should be taken? Explain.

Problem Set B

LO13-2 through LO13-4

PROBLEM 13.1B

Format of a Statement of Cash Flows

The accounting staff of Welch Company has assembled the following information for the year ended December 31, 2015:

Cash sales	$ 230,000
Credit sales	3,450,000
Collections on accounts receivable	2,810,000
Cash transferred from the money market fund to the general bank account	200,000
Interest and dividends received	40,000
Purchases (all on account)	1,822,000
Payments on accounts payable to merchandise suppliers	1,220,000
Cash payments for operating expenses	930,000
Interest paid	130,000
Income taxes paid	65,000
Loans made to borrowers	690,000
Collections on loans (excluding receipts of interest)	300,000
Cash paid to acquire plant assets	1,700,000
Book value of plant assets sold	520,000
Loss on sales of plant assets	30,000
Proceeds from issuing bonds payable	2,000,000
Dividends paid	250,000
Cash and cash equivalents, Jan. 1	278,000

Instructions

Prepare a statement of cash flows in the format illustrated in Exhibit 13–1. Place brackets around amounts representing cash outflows. Use the *direct method* of reporting cash flows from operating activities.

Some of the items above will be listed in your statement without change. However, you will have to combine certain given information to compute the amounts of (1) collections from customers, (2) cash paid to suppliers and employees, and (3) proceeds from sales of plant assets. (Hint: Not every item listed above is used in preparing a statement of cash flows.)

LO13-4

PROBLEM 13.2B

Reporting Investing Activities

An analysis of the income statement and the balance sheet accounts of Mary's Fashions at December 31, 2015, provides the following information:

Income statement items:

Gain on Sales of Marketable Securities	$ 15,000
Loss on Sales of Plant Assets	10,000

Analysis of balance sheet accounts:

Marketable Securities account:

Debit entries	65,000
Credit entries	74,000

Notes Receivable account:

Debit entries	175,000
Credit entries	50,000

Plant and Equipment accounts:

Debit entries to plant asset accounts	245,000
Credit entries to plant asset accounts	150,000
Debit entries to accumulated depreciation accounts	60,000

Additional Information

1. Except as noted in **4,** payments and proceeds relating to investing transactions were made in cash.
2. The marketable securities are not cash equivalents.
3. All notes receivable relate to cash loans made to borrowers, not to receivables from customers.
4. Purchases of new equipment during the year ($245,000) were financed by paying $85,000 in cash and issuing a long-term note payable for $160,000.
5. Debits to the accumulated depreciation accounts are made whenever depreciable plant assets are retired. The book value of plant assets retired during the year was $90,000 ($150,000 − $60,000).

Instructions

a. Prepare the investing activities section of a statement of cash flows. Show supporting computations for the amounts of (1) proceeds from sales and marketable securities and (2) proceeds from sales from plant assets. Place brackets around numbers representing cash outflows.

b. Prepare the supporting schedule that should accompany the statement of cash flows in order to disclose the noncash aspects of the company's investing and financing activities.

c. Assume that Mary's Fashions's management expects approximately the same amount of cash to be used for investing activities next year. In general terms, explain how the company might generate cash for this purpose.

LO13-4

PROBLEM 13.3B

Reporting Investing Activities

An analysis of the income statement and the balance sheet accounts of RPZ Imports at December 31, 2015, provides the following information:

Income statement items:

Gain on Sales of Plant Assets	$ 9,000
Loss on Sales of Marketable Securities	8,000

Analysis of balance sheet accounts:

Marketable Securities account:

Debit entries	59,000
Credit entries	60,000

Notes Receivable account:

Debit entries	40,000
Credit entries	31,000

Plant and Equipment accounts:

Debit entries to plant asset accounts	140,000
Credit entries to plant asset accounts	100,000
Debit entries to accumulated depreciation accounts	75,000

Additional Information

1. Except as noted in **4**, payments and proceeds relating to investing transactions were made in cash.

2. The marketable securities are not cash equivalents.

3. All notes receivable relate to cash loans made to borrowers, not to receivables from customers.

4. Purchases of new equipment during the year ($140,000) were financed by paying $50,000 in cash and issuing a long-term note payable for $90,000.

5. Debits to the accumulated depreciation accounts are made whenever depreciable plant assets are retired. Thus, the book value of plant assets sold or retired during the year was $25,000 ($100,000 − $75,000).

Instructions

a. Prepare the investing activities section of a statement of cash flows. Show supporting computations for the amounts of (1) proceeds from sales and marketable securities and (2) proceeds from sales from plant assets. Place brackets around numbers representing cash outflows.

b. Prepare the supplementary schedule that should accompany the statement of cash flows in order to disclose the noncash aspects of the company's investing and financing activities.

c. Does management have *more* control or *less* control over the timing and amount of cash outlays for investing activities than for operating activities? Explain.

LO13-3, LO13-8

PROBLEM 13.4B

Reporting Operating Cash Flows by the Direct Method

The following income statement and selected balance sheet account data are available for Royce Interiors, Inc., at December 31, 2015:

ROYCE INTERIORS, INC.
INCOME STATEMENT
FOR THE YEAR ENDED DECEMBER 31, 2015

Revenue:

Net sales		$2,600,000
Dividend income		55,000
Interest income		40,000
Gain on sales of marketable securities		3,000
Total revenue and gains		$2,698,000
Costs and expenses:		
Cost of goods sold	$1,300,000	
Operating expenses	300,000	
Interest expense	60,000	
Income tax expense	110,000	
Total costs and expenses		$1,770,000
Net income		$ 928,000

	End of Year	Beginning of Year
Selected account balances:		
Accounts receivable	$ 450,000	$ 440,000
Accrued interest receivable	7,000	3,000
Inventories	575,000	550,000
Short-term prepayments	9,000	8,000
Accounts payable (merchandise suppliers)	415,000	410,000
Accrued operating expenses payable	86,000	90,000
Accrued interest payable	10,000	8,000
Accrued income taxes payable	20,000	22,000

Additional Information

1. Dividend revenue is recognized on the cash basis. All other income statement amounts are recognized on the accrual basis.

2. Operating expenses include depreciation expense of $49,000.

Instructions

a. Prepare a partial statement of cash flows, including only the *operating activities* section of the statement and using the *direct method*. Place brackets around numbers representing cash payments. Show supporting computations for the following:

   1. Cash received from customers.

   2. Interest and dividends received.

   3. Cash paid to suppliers and employees.

   4. Interest paid.

   5. Income taxes paid.

b. Management of Royce Interiors, Inc., is exploring ways to increase the cash flows from operations. One way that cash flows could be increased is through more aggressive collection of receivables. Assuming that management has already taken all the steps possible to increase revenue and reduce expenses, describe two other ways that cash flows from operations could be increased.

LO13-6, LO13-7
PROBLEM 13.5B
Reporting Operating Cash Flows by the Indirect Method

Using the information presented in Problem **13.4B,** prepare a partial statement of cash flows for the current year, showing the computation of net cash flows from operating activities using the *indirect method*. Explain why the increase in accounts receivable over the year was *subtracted* from net income in computing the cash flows from operating activities.

LO13-2 through LO13-4, LO13-6, LO13-8
PROBLEM 13.6B
Preparing a Statement of Cash Flows: A Comprehensive Problem without a Worksheet

You are the controller for Foxboro Technologies. Your staff has prepared an income statement for the current year and has developed the following additional information by analyzing changes in the company's balance sheet accounts.

FOXBORO TECHNOLOGIES
INCOME STATEMENT
FOR THE YEAR ENDED DECEMBER 31, 2015

Revenue:		
Net sales		$3,400,000
Interest income		60,000
Gain on sales of marketable securities		25,000
Total revenue and gains		$3,485,000
Costs and expenses:		
Cost of goods sold	$1,500,000	
Operating expenses (including depreciation of $75,000)	900,000	
Interest expense	27,000	
Income tax expense	115,000	
Loss on sales of plant assets	8,000	
Total costs, expenses, and losses		2,550,000
Net income		$ 935,000

Additional Information

1. Accounts receivable increased by $60,000.

2. Accrued interest receivable decreased by $5,000.

3. Inventory decreased by $30,000, and accounts payable to suppliers of merchandise decreased by $22,000.

4. Short-term prepayments of operating expenses increased by $8,000, and accrued liabilities for operating expenses decreased by $9,000.

5. The liability for accrued interest payable increased by $4,000 during the year.

6. The liability for accrued income taxes payable decreased by $10,000 during the year.

7. The following schedule summarizes the total debit and credit entries during the year in other balance sheet accounts:

	Debit Entries	Credit Entries
Marketable Securities	$ 50,000	$ 40,000
Notes Receivable (cash loans made to borrowers)	30,000	27,000
Plant Assets (see paragraph **8**)	350,000	30,000
Notes Payable (short-term borrowing)	70,000	56,000
Capital Stock		60,000
Additional Paid-in Capital—Capital Stock		100,000
Retained Earnings (see paragraph **9**)	300,000	935,000

8. The $30,000 in credit entries to the Plant Assets account is net of any debits to Accumulated Depreciation when plant assets were retired. Thus the $30,000 in credit entries represents the book value of all plant assets sold or retired during the year.

9. The $300,000 debit to Retained Earnings represents dividends declared and paid during the year. The $935,000 credit entry represents the net income shown in the income statement.

10. All investing and financing activities were cash transactions.

11. Cash and cash equivalents amount to $20,000 at the beginning of the year and to $473,000 at year-end.

Instructions

a. Prepare a statement of cash flows for the current year. Use the *direct method* of reporting cash flows from operating activities. Place brackets around dollar amounts representing cash outflows. Show separately your computations of the following amounts:

    1. Cash received from customers.

    2. Interest received.

    3. Cash paid to suppliers and employees

    4. Interest paid.

    5. Income taxes paid

    6. Proceeds from sales of marketable securities.

    7. Proceeds from sales of plant assets.

    8. Proceeds from issuing capital stock

b. Explain why cash paid to suppliers is so much higher than cost of goods sold.

c. Does the fact that Foxboro's cash flows from both investing and financing activities are negative indicate that the company is in a weak cash position?

LO13-1 through LO13-9

PROBLEM 13.7B

Prepare and Analyze a Statement of Cash Flows

LGIN was founded in 2014 to apply a new technology for the Internet. The company earned a profit of $190,000 in 2014, its first year of operations. Management expects both sales and net income to more than double in each of the next four years.

Comparative balance sheets at the end of 2014 and 2015, the company's first two years of operations, appear below. (Notice that the balances at the end of the current year appear in the right-hand column.)

LGIN
COMPARATIVE BALANCE SHEETS

	December 31,	
	2014	2015
Assets		
Cash and cash equivalents	$ 45,000	$ 42,000
Accounts receivable	15,000	880,000
Plant and equipment (net of accumulated depreciation)...	680,000	3,140,000
Totals	$740,000	$4,062,000
Liabilities and Stockholders' Equity		
Notes payable (short-term)	$ 0	$1,490,000
Accounts payable	45,000	82,000
Accrued expenses payable	55,000	38,000
Notes payable (long-term)	200,000	785,000
Capital stock (no par value)	250,000	915,000
Retained earnings	190,000	752,000
Totals	$740,000	$4,062,000

Additional Information

The following information regarding the company's operations in 2015 is available in either the company's income statement or its accounting records:

1. Net income for the year was $562,000. The company has never paid a dividend.
2. Depreciation for the year amounted to $125,000.
3. During the year the company purchased plant assets costing $2,585,000, for which it paid $2,000,000 in cash and financed $585,000 by issuing a long-term note payable. (Much of the cash used in these purchases was provided by short-term borrowing, as described below.)
4. In 2015, LGIN borrowed $1,490,000 against a $4.5 million line of credit with a local bank. In its balance sheet, the resulting obligations are reported as notes payable (short-term).
5. Additional shares of capital stock (no par value) were issued to investors for $665,000 cash.

Instructions

a. Prepare a formal statement of cash flows for 2015, including a supplementary schedule of noncash investing and financing activities. (Follow the format illustrated in Exhibit 13–8. Cash provided by operating activities is to be presented by the *indirect method.*)

b. Briefly explain how operating activities can be a net *use* of cash when the company is operating so profitably.

c. Because of the expected rapid growth, management forecasts that operating activities will include an even greater use of cash in the year 2016 than in 2015. If this forecast is correct, does LGIN appear to be heading toward insolvency? Explain.

LO13-1 through LO13-9
PROBLEM 13.8B
Prepare and Analyze a
Statement of Cash Flows;
Involves Preparation of a
Worksheet

Purcells, Inc., sells a single product (Pulsa) exclusively through newspaper advertising. The comparative income statements and balance sheets are for the past two years.

PURCELLS, INC.
COMPARATIVE INCOME STATEMENT
FOR THE YEARS ENDED DECEMBER 31, 2014 AND 2015

	2014	2015
Sales	$640,000	$ 410,000
Less: Cost of goods sold	310,000	190,000
Gross profit on sales	330,000	220,000
Less: Operating expenses (including depreciation of $28,000 in 2014 and $29,000 in 2015)	260,000	250,000
Loss on sale of marketable securities	0	4,000
Net income (loss)	$ 70,000	$ (34,000)

PURCELLS, INC.
COMPARATIVE BALANCE SHEETS

	December 31,	
	2014	2015
Assets		
Cash and cash equivalents	$ 22,000	$ 60,000
Marketable securities	27,000	12,000
Accounts receivable	40,000	35,000
Inventory	120,000	128,000
Plant and equipment (net of accumulated depreciation)	250,000	241,000
Totals	$459,000	$476,000
Liabilities & Stockholders' Equity		
Accounts payable	50,000	70,000
Accrued expenses payable	16,000	14,000
Notes payable	235,000	237,000
Capital stock (no par value)	108,000	143,000
Retained earnings	50,000	12,000
Totals	$459,000	$476,000

Additional Information

The following information regarding the company's operations in 2015 is available from the company's accounting records:

1. Early in the year the company declared and paid a $4,000 cash dividend.
2. During the year marketable securities costing $15,000 were sold for $11,000 cash, resulting in a $4,000 nonoperating loss.
3. The company purchased plant assets for $20,000, paying $8,000 in cash and issuing a note payable for the $12,000 balance.
4. During the year the company repaid a $10,000 note payable, but incurred an additional $12,000 in long-term debt as described in **3,** above.
5. The owners invested $35,000 cash in the business as a condition of the new loans described in paragraphs **3** and **4,** above.

Instructions

a. Prepare a worksheet for a statement of cash flows, following the example shown in Exhibit 13–7.

b. Prepare a formal statement of cash flows for 2011, including a supplementary schedule of noncash investing and financing activities. (Use the format illustrated in Exhibit 13–8. Cash provided by operating activities is to be presented by the *indirect method.*)

c. Explain how Purcells, Inc., achieved positive cash flows from operating activities, despite incurring a net loss for the year.

   d.   Does the company's financial position appear to be improving or deteriorating? Explain.

   e.   Does Purcells, Inc., appear to be a company whose operations are growing or contracting? Explain.

   f.   Assume that management *agrees* with your conclusions in parts **c, d,** and **e.** What decisions should be made and what actions (if any) should be taken? Explain.

Critical Thinking Cases

LO13-1

CASE 13.1

Another Look at Allison Corporation

This case is based on the statement of cash flows for Allison Corporation, illustrated in Exhibit 13–1. Use this statement to evaluate the company's ability to continue paying the current level of dividends—$40,000 per year. The following information also is available:

1.   The net cash flows from operating activities shown in the statement are relatively normal for Allison Corporation. Net cash flows from operating activities have not varied by more than a few thousand dollars in any of the past three years.

2.   The net outflow for investing activities was unusually high, because the company modernized its production facilities during the year. The normal investing cash outflow is about $45,000 per year, the amount required to replace existing plant assets as they are retired. Over the long run, marketable securities transactions and lending transactions have a very small impact on Allison's net cash flows from investing activities.

3.   The net cash flows from financing activities were unusually large in the current year because of the issuance of bonds payable and capital stock. These securities were issued to finance the modernization of the production facilities. In a typical year, financing activities include only short-term borrowing transactions and payments of dividends.

Instructions

a.   Solely on the basis of the company's past performance, do you believe that the $40,000 annual dividend payments are secure? That is, does the company appear able to pay this amount in dividends every year without straining its cash position? Do you think it more likely that Allison Corporation will increase or decrease the amount of dividends that it pays? Explain fully.

b.   Should any of the unusual events appearing in the statement of cash flows for the current year affect your analysis of the company's ability to pay future dividends? Explain.

LO13-1, LO13-8

CASE 13.2

Cash Budgeting for You as a Student

Individuals generally do not prepare statements of cash flows concerning their personal activities. But they do engage in cash budgeting—if not on paper, then at least in their heads.

   Assume it is December 29—a Monday. While you are in school, you share a small apartment with another student and work part-time, both near your school to minimize expenses. In two days your rent for January, $200, will be due. You now have $140 in the bank; every Friday you receive a paycheck for $100. You probably see the problem. And it may not look too serious; you can find a way to deal with it. That's what *budgeting* is all about.

   Let's take this example a step further. In addition to the facts given above, your weekly cash payments include meals, $30; entertainment, $20; and gasoline, $10.

Instructions

a.   Using the following cash budget, compute your cash balance at the end of weeks 2, 3, and 4.

	Week			
	1	**2**	**3**	**4**
Beginning cash balance	$ 140	$(20)	$?	$?
Expected cash receipts	100	100	100	100
Less: Expected cash outlays:				
Monthly rent	(200)			
Meals	(30)			
Entertainment	(20)			
Gasoline	(10)			
Ending cash balance	$ (20)	$?	$?	$?

b.   Evaluate your financial situation.

LO13-1, LO13-4, LO13-8

CASE 13.3

Lookin' Good?

It is late summer and General Wheels, Inc., an auto manufacturer, is facing a financial crisis. A large issue of bonds payable will mature next March, and the company must issue stock or new bonds to raise the money to retire this debt. Unfortunately, profits and cash flows have been declining over recent years. Management fears that if cash flows and profits do not improve in the current year, the company will not be able to raise the capital needed to replace the maturing bonds. Therefore, members of management have made the following proposals to improve the cash flows and profitability that will be reported in the financial statements dated this coming December 31.

1. Switch from the LIFO method to the FIFO method of valuing inventories. Management estimates that the FIFO method will result in a lower cost of goods sold but in higher income taxes for the current year. However, the additional income taxes will not actually be paid until early next year.

2. Switch from the 150 percent declining-balance method of depreciation to the straight-line method and lengthen the useful lives over which assets are depreciated. (These changes would be made only for financial reporting purposes, not for income tax purposes.)

3. Pressure dealers to increase their inventories—in short, to buy more cars. (The dealerships are independently owned; dealers are the customers to whom General Wheels sells automobiles.) Management estimates that this strategy could increase sales for the current year by 5 percent. However, any additional sales in the current year would be almost entirely offset by fewer sales in the following year.

4. Require dealers to pay for purchases more quickly. Currently, dealers must pay for purchases of autos within 60 days. Management is considering reducing this period to 30 days.

5. Pass up cash discounts offered by suppliers for prompt payment (that is, 2/10, n/30), and do not pay any bills until the final due date.

6. Borrow at current short-term interest rates (about 10 percent) and use the proceeds to pay off long-term debt bearing an interest rate of 13 percent.

7. Substitute stock dividends for the cash dividends currently paid on capital stock.

Instructions

a. Prepare a schedule with four columns. The first column is to be headed "Proposals" and is to contain the paragraph numbers of the seven proposals listed above. The next three columns are to be headed with the following financial statement captions: (1) "Net Income," (2) "Net Cash Flows from Operating Activities," and (3) "Cash."

For each of the seven proposals in the left-hand column, indicate whether you expect the proposal to "Increase," "Decrease," or have "No Effect" in the current year on each of the financial statement captions listed in the next three columns. (*Note:* Only a few months remain in the current year. Therefore, you are to determine the *short-term* effects of these proposals.)

b. For each of the seven proposals, write a short paragraph explaining the reasoning behind your answers to part **a**.

LO13-8

CASE 13.4

Peak Pricing

"Peak pricing is unfair. It makes goods and services available only to the wealthy and prices the average person out of the market."

Instructions

a. Comment on the extent to which you agree or disagree with the preceding statement.

b. What is the alternative to peak pricing?

c. Explain how peak pricing might be applied by:

1. A hotel in Palm Springs, California. (Palm Springs is a winter resort in southern California with wonderful golf facilities. In the summer months, however, temperatures are well over 100 degrees and the tourist business slows dramatically.)

2. Movie theaters.

d. Both in general terms and using specific examples, describe the conditions (if any) under which you might regard peak pricing as *unethical*.

LO13-3
CASE 13.5

Improving the Statement of
Cash Flows

The Securities and Exchange Commission (SEC) is an important governmental organization that exists primarily for the protection of the interests of investors in the U.S. securities markets. The SEC provides a wealth of information through its website, www.sec.gov.

Instructions

a. Access the SEC's website at the above address. Generally review the site to become familiar with the types of information provided.

b. Enter the section of the website identified as "About the SEC;" then proceed to the section on "Commissioners." Within that section, maneuver around until you are able to access speeches made by the SEC and its staff.

c. Locate the following speech given by Scott A. Taub, former Deputy Chief Accountant, Office of the Chief Accountant of the SEC, in the second quarter of 2004: "Remarks at the University of Southern California, Leventhal School of Accounting, SEC and Financial Reporting Conference."

d. Peruse that entire speech, and then read carefully Mr. Taub's conclusion. Write a paragraph that captures what Mr. Taub had to say about how financial reporting could be improved in general, and how he specifically believes the statement of cash flows could be improved.

LO13-2 through LO13-4
INTERNET CASE 13.6

Comparing Cash Flow
Information from Two
Companies

In the long run, a company must generate positive net cash flows from operating activities to survive. A business that has negative cash flows from operations will not be able to raise cash indefinitely from other sources and will eventually cease existing. Many creditors and stockholders are reluctant to invest in companies that do not generate positive cash flows from operations. However, some investors will invest in companies with negative cash flows from operations due to an optimistic future outlook for the company. Thus, investors have invested millions of dollars in Internet companies that have negative cash flows from operations.

Instructions

a. Using the search approach of your choice, locate Coca-Cola's most recent 10K filing or annual report. View the Consolidated Statements of Cash Flows.

b. Using the search approach of your choice, locate Amazon's most recent 10K filing or annual report. View the Consolidated Statements of Cash Flows.

c. Compare the Net Cash Provided by Operating Activities for these companies. Which company has higher Net Cash Provided by Operating Activities? Speculate why one company has much higher Net Cash Provided by Operating Activities than the other.

d. What type of company may have Negative Net Cash Provided from Operating Activities?

e. What type of company may have large Positive Net Cash Provided from Operating Activities?

Internet sites are time and date sensitive. It is the purpose of these exercises to have you explore the Internet. You may need to use the Yahoo! search engine www.yahoo.com (or another favorite search engine) to find a company's current web address.

Answers to Self-Test Questions

1. b 2. c 3. b 4. d ($601,000 − $420,000 − $12,000 + $17,000 − $23,000)

5. b 6. c

CHAPTER 14

Financial Statement Analysis

AFTER STUDYING THIS CHAPTER, YOU SHOULD BE ABLE TO:

Learning Objectives

LO14-1 Explain the uses of dollar and percentage changes, trend percentages, component percentages, and ratios.

LO14-2 Discuss the quality of a company's earnings, assets, and working capital.

LO14-3 Explain the nature and purpose of classifications in financial statements.

LO14-4 Prepare a classified balance sheet and compute widely used measures of liquidity and credit risk.

LO14-5 Prepare a multiple-step and a single-step income statement and compute widely used measures of profitability.

LO14-6 Put a company's net income into perspective by relating it to sales, assets, and stockholders' equity.

LO14-7 Compute the ratios widely used in financial statement analysis and explain the significance of each.

LO14-8 Analyze financial statements from the viewpoints of common stockholders, creditors, and others.

JOHNSON & JOHNSON

Johnson & Johnson is the world's most comprehensive and broadly based manufacturer of health care products and related services. In 2012 it had over $67 billion in sales. Other measures of Johnson & Johnson's size include the facts that it has over $120 billion in assets and conducts business in virtually all countries of the world.

How does one gain an understanding of the financial performance of a huge company such as Johnson & Johnson? Financial statements, including the statement of financial position, income statement, and statement of cash flows, provide a wealth of information that is helpful in accomplishing this significant task. Financial statement analysis involves taking key items from these financial statements and gleaning as much useful information as possible from them. For example, we

can determine that the amount of Johnson & Johnson's 2012 net income ($10,514 million) represented a return of approximately 8.8 percent on the total assets used to generate that income. Is a return on assets of almost 9 percent satisfactory or unsatisfactory? This is a difficult question to answer. To make this judgment we would need more information than we have at this point. For example, we would like to know the trend in various financial measures for Johnson & Johnson over several years. We would also like to know how J & J's performance compares with that of other companies with similar operating characteristics (i.e., in the same industry). We will study all of this and more in this chapter as we look at the interesting and challenging subject of financial statement analysis. ∎

Financial measures are used often to evaluate corporate performance. As a result, the Securities and Exchange Commission, the Financial Accounting Standards Board, the financial press, and the accounting profession are committed to high-quality financial reporting. Throughout this text, we emphasize the importance of integrity in financial reporting as a means of protecting the interests of investors and creditors. This chapter explores financial statement analysis in depth, building on the introductory sections of this important subject in preceding chapters.

Our discussion of financial statement analysis is presented in three sections. First, we consider general analytical tools that emphasize comparing information about enterprises with relevant benchmarks. Second, we consider measures of liquidity and credit risk, followed by a consideration of profitability. Third, we present and discuss a comprehensive illustration in which we analyze a company's financial statements from the perspective of three important users of information—common stockholders, long-term creditors, and short-term creditors. Throughout this chapter, we draw on information that was covered in earlier chapters and we use new information that is presented here for the first time.

FINANCIAL STATEMENTS ARE DESIGNED FOR ANALYSIS

In today's global economy, investment capital is always on the move. Through organized capital markets such as the New York Stock Exchange, investors each day shift billions of investment dollars among different companies, industries, and nations. Capital flows to those areas in which investors expect to earn the greatest returns with the least risk. How do investors forecast risk and potential returns? One of the most important ways is by analyzing accounting information for a specific company in the context of its unique industry setting.

The goal of accounting information is to provide economic decision makers with useful information. The financial statements generated through the accounting process are designed to assist users in identifying key relationships and trends. The financial statements of most publicly owned companies are classified and are presented in comparative form. Often, the word *consolidated* appears in the headings of the statements. Users of financial statements should have a clear understanding of these terms.

Most business organizations prepare **classified financial statements**, meaning that items with certain characteristics are placed together in a group, or classification. The purpose of these classifications is to *develop useful subtotals* that will assist users of the statements in their analyses. These classifications and subtotals are standardized throughout most of American business, a practice that assists decision makers in comparing the financial statements of different companies. An example of a classified financial statement is a balance sheet that separates assets and liabilities into current and noncurrent categories.

In **comparative financial statements**, the financial statement amounts *for more than one accounting period* appear side by side in vertical columns. This assists investors in identifying and evaluating significant changes and trends.

Many large corporations own other companies through which they conduct some of their business activities. A corporation that owns other businesses is the **parent company**, and the owned companies are called divisions or **subsidiaries**. For example, **PepsiCo**, which produces and distributes Pepsi-Cola, also owns and operates the companies that make **Frito-Lay**, **Quaker Foods**, **Gatorade**, and **Tropicana** products. In essence, these subsidiaries are part of the organization generally known as **PepsiCo**. **Consolidated financial statements** present the financial position and operating results of the parent company and its subsidiaries *as if they were a single business organization.*

For Example . . . At this point, take a brief look at the financial statements of **Home Depot, Inc.**, which appear in Appendix A at the end of the text. These financial statements illustrate all of the concepts discussed; they are classified and presented in comparative form, and they describe a consolidated business entity. These financial statements also have been *audited* by **KPMG LLP**, an international public accounting firm.

© AP Photo/Steven Senne

Tools of Analysis

Significant changes in financial data are easier to identify when financial statement amounts for two or more years are placed side by side in adjacent columns. Such a statement is called a *comparative financial statement.* The amounts for the most recent year are usually placed in the left-hand money column, closest to the words that describe the item. The balance sheet, income statement, and statement of cash flows are often prepared in the form of comparative statements. A highly condensed comparative income statement covering three years is shown in Exhibit 14–1.

BENSON CORPORATION
COMPARATIVE INCOME STATEMENT
FOR THE YEARS ENDED DECEMBER 31, 2015, 2014, 2013
(IN THOUSANDS OF DOLLARS)

	2015	2014	2013
Net sales	$600	$500	$400
Cost of goods sold	370	300	235
Gross profit	$230	$200	$165
Expenses	194	160	115
Net income	$ 36	$ 40	$ 50

EXHIBIT 14–1

Comparative Income Statement

Comparative statements place important financial information in a context that is useful for gaining better understanding. For example, knowing that Benson Corporation had sales of $600,000 in 2015 after years in which sales were $500,000 (2014) and $400,000 (2013) is helpful in understanding Benson's sales trend.

Few figures in a financial statement are highly significant in and of themselves. It is their relationship to other quantities or the amount and direction of change that is most important. Analysis is largely a matter of establishing significant relationships and identifying changes and trends. Four widely used analytical techniques are (1) dollar and percentage changes, (2) trend percentages, (3) component percentages, and (4) ratios.

DOLLAR AND PERCENTAGE CHANGES

The dollar amount of change from year to year is significant, and expressing the change in percentage terms adds perspective. For example, if sales this year have increased by $100,000, knowing that this is an increase of 10 percent over last year's sales of $1 million puts the $100,000 increase in a different perspective than if it represented a 1 percent increase over sales of $10 million for the prior year.

The dollar amount of any change is the difference between the amount for a *comparison* year and the amount for a *base* year. The percentage change is computed by dividing the amount of the dollar change between years by the amount for the previous year. This is illustrated in the following tabulation, using data from the comparative income statement shown in Exhibit 14–1.

LO14-1

LEARNING OBJECTIVE
Explain the uses of dollar and percentage changes, trend percentages, component percentages, and ratios.

	$ In Thousands			Increase or (Decrease)			
				2015 over 2014		2014 over 2013	
	Year 2015	Year 2014	Year 2013	Amount	%	Amount	%
Net sales	$600	$500	$400	$100	20%	$100	25%
Net income	36	40	50	(4)	(10)	(10)	(20)

Dollar and percentage changes

Although net sales increased $100,000 in both 2015 and 2014, the percentage change differs because of the change in the previous period between 2013 and 2014. These calculations present no problems when the figures for the base year are positive amounts. If a negative amount or a zero amount appears in the base year, however, a percentage change cannot be computed. If Benson Corporation had incurred a net loss in 2014, the percentage change in net income from 2014 to 2015 could not have been calculated.

Evaluating Percentage Changes in Sales and Earnings   Computing the percentage changes in sales, gross profit, and net income from one year to the next provides insight into a company's rate of growth. If a company is experiencing growth in its economic activities, sales and earnings should increase at *more than the rate of inflation*. Assume, for example, that a company's sales increase by 6 percent while the general price level rises by 10 percent. The entire increase in the dollar amount of sales may be explained by inflation, rather than by an increase in sales volume (the number of units sold). In fact, the company may well have sold *fewer* goods than in the preceding year, even though its sales figure increased.

In measuring the dollar or percentage change in *quarterly* sales or earnings, it is customary to compare the results of the current quarter with those of the *same quarter in the preceding year*. Use of the same quarter of the preceding year as the base period prevents our analysis from being distorted by seasonal fluctuations in business activity.

Percentages Become Misleading When the Base Is Small   Percentage changes may create a misleading impression when the dollar amount used as a base is unusually small. Occasionally we hear a television newscaster say that a company's profits have increased by a very large percentage, such as 900 percent. The initial impression created by such a statement is that the company's profits must now be excessively large. But assume, for example, that a company had net income of $100,000 in its first year, that in the second year net income drops to $10,000, and then in the third year net income returns to the $100,000 level. In this third year, net income increased by $90,000, representing a 900 percent increase over the profits of the second year. What needs to be added to the news commentary is that this 900 percent increase in profits in the third year follows a very small profit in the second year and *exactly offsets* the 90 percent decline in profits in the second year.

TREND PERCENTAGES

The changes in financial statement items from a base year to following years are often expressed as *trend percentages* to show the extent and direction of change. Two steps are necessary to compute trend percentages. First, a base year is selected and each item in the financial statements for the base year is given a weight of 100 percent. The second step is to express each item in the financial statements for following years as a percentage of its base-year amount. This computation consists of dividing an item such as sales in the years after the base year by the amount of sales in the base year.

For example, assume that 2010 is selected as the base year and that sales in the base year amounted to $300,000, as shown in the following table. The trend percentages for sales are computed by dividing the sales amount of each following year by $300,000. Also shown in the illustration are the yearly amounts of net income. The trend percentages for net income are computed by dividing the net income amount for each following year by the base-year amount of $15,000.

These trend percentages indicate a modest growth in sales in the early years and accelerated growth in 2014 and 2015. Net income also shows an increasing growth trend with the

Dollar Amounts	2015	2014	2013	2012	2011	2010
Sales	$450,000	$360,000	$330,000	$321,000	$312,000	$300,000
Net income	22,950	14,550	21,450	19,200	15,600	15,000
Trend Percentages	**2015**	**2014**	**2013**	**2012**	**2011**	**2010**
Sales	150%	120%	110%	107%	104%	100%
Net income	153	97	143	128	104	100

exception of the year 2014, when net income declined despite a solid increase in sales. The problem was overcome in 2015 with a sharp rise in net income. Overall the trend percentages give a picture of a profitable, growing enterprise.

An important difference to note in computing comparative percentage changes and trend percentages is that, in the case of trend percentages, each year's number is computed as a percentage of the same base year. In the case of comparative percentage changes, the base of the calculation is the previous year.

COMPONENT PERCENTAGES

Component percentages indicate the *relative size* of each item included in a total. For example, each item in a balance sheet could be expressed as a percentage of total assets. This shows quickly the relative importance of each type of asset as well as the relative amount of financing obtained from current creditors, long-term creditors, and stockholders. By computing component percentages for several successive balance sheets, we can see which items are increasing in importance and which are becoming less significant.

Another application of component percentages is to express all items in an income statement as a percentage of net sales. Such a statement is called a *common size income statement.* See the condensed income statement in dollars and in common size form in Exhibit 14–2.

Income Statement				
	Dollars		Component Percentages	
	2015	2014	2015	2014
Net sales	$1,000,000	$600,000	100.0%	100.0%
Cost of goods sold	700,000	360,000	70.0	60.0
Expenses (including income taxes)	250,000	180,000	25.0	30.0
Net income	$ 50,000	$ 60,000	5.0%	10.0%

EXHIBIT 14–2

Component Percentages

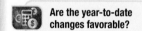 Are the year-to-date changes favorable?

Looking only at the component percentages, we see that the increase in cost of goods sold (60 percent to 70 percent) was only partially offset by the decrease in expenses as a percentage of net sales, causing net income to decrease from 10 percent of net sales in 2014 to 5 percent of net sales in 2015.

RATIOS

A ratio is a mathematical expression of the relationship of one item to another. Every percentage may be viewed as a ratio—that is, one number expressed as a percentage of another.

Ratios may be stated in several ways. To illustrate, let us consider the current ratio, which expresses the relationship between a company's most liquid assets (current) and its liabilities that require payment soon (current). If current assets are $200,000 and current liabilities are $80,000, we may say either that the current ratio is 2.5 to 1 (which is written as 2.5:1) or that current assets are 250 percent of current liabilities. Either statement correctly summarizes the relationship—that is, that current assets are 2½ times as large as current liabilities.

Ratios are particularly important in understanding financial statements because they permit us to compare information from one financial statement with information from another financial statement. For example, we might compare net income (taken from the income statement) with total assets (taken from the balance sheet) to see how effectively management is using available resources to earn a profit. For a ratio to be useful, however, the two amounts being compared must be logically related. In subsequent sections of this chapter, we make extensive use of ratios to better demonstrate important dimensions of an enterprise's financial activities.

STANDARDS OF COMPARISON

In using dollar and percentage changes, trend percentages, component percentages, and ratios, financial analysts constantly search for some standard of comparison against which to judge whether the relationships they have determined are favorable or unfavorable. Two commonly used standards are (1) the past performance of the company being analyzed and (2) the performance of other companies in the same industry. For internal management purposes, another important comparison is with expected or budgeted numbers.

Past Performance of the Company   Comparing financial information for a current period with similar information for prior years affords some basis for judging whether the condition of the business is improving or worsening. This comparison of data over time is sometimes called *horizontal analysis,* to express the idea of reviewing data for a number of consecutive periods. It is distinguished from *vertical,* or *static,* analysis, which refers to the review of the financial information within a single accounting period.

In addition to determining whether the situation is improving or becoming worse, horizontal analysis may aid in making estimates of future prospects. Because changes may reverse their direction at any time, however, projecting past trends into the future always involves some uncertainty.

A weakness of horizontal analysis is that comparison with the past does not afford any basis for evaluation in absolute terms. The fact that net income was 2 percent of sales last year and is 3 percent of sales this year indicates improvement, but if there is evidence that, based on industry standards, net income *should be* 7 percent of sales, the record for both years is unfavorable.

Industry Standards   The limitations of horizontal analysis may be overcome to some extent by finding appropriate benchmarks against which to measure a particular company's performance. The benchmarks used by most analysts are the performance of comparable companies and the average performance of several companies in the same industry.[1]

Assume, for example, that the revenue of Alpha Airlines drops by 8 percent during the current year. If the revenue for the airlines industry had dropped an average of 15 percent during this year, Alpha's 8 percent decline might be viewed as a *favorable* performance. As another example, assume that Omega Co. earns a net income equal to 3 percent of net sales. This would be substandard if Omega were a pharmaceutical company, but it may be considered satisfactory performance if it were a retail grocery chain because of the difference in earnings expected in the two industries.

When we compare a given company with its competitors or with industry averages, our conclusions are valid only if the companies in question are comparable. Because of the large number of diversified companies formed in recent years, the term *industry* is difficult to define, and even companies that fall roughly within the same industry may not be comparable in many respects. For example, one company may engage only in the marketing of oil products; another may be a fully integrated producer from the well to the gas pump; yet both are said to be in the oil industry.

QUALITY OF EARNINGS

L014-2

LEARNING OBJECTIVE
Discuss the quality of a company's earnings, assets, and working capital.

Profits are the lifeblood of a business entity. No entity can survive indefinitely and accomplish its other goals unless it is profitable. Continuous losses drain assets from the business, consume owners' equity, and leave the company at the mercy of creditors. In assessing the prospects of a company, we are interested not only in the total *amount* of earnings but also in the *rate* of earnings on sales, on total assets, and on owners' equity. In addition, we must look at the *stability* and *source* of earnings. An erratic earnings performance over a period of years, for example, is less desirable than a steady level of earnings. A history of increasing earnings is preferable to a flat earnings record.

A breakdown of sales and earnings by *major product lines* may be useful in evaluating the future performance of a company. Publicly owned companies include with their financial statements supplementary schedules showing sales and profits by product line and by geographical area. These schedules assist financial analysts in forecasting the effect on the company of changes in consumer demand for particular types of products. This type of analysis is

---

[1] Industry data are available from a number of sources. For example, Robert Morris Associates publishes *Annual Statement Studies,* which includes data from many thousands of annual reports, grouped into several hundred industry classifications. Industry classifications are subdivided further by company size. Dun & Bradstreet, Inc., annually publishes *Key Business Ratios* for more than 800 lines of business.

particularly useful for a company whose overall performance is based heavily on the performance of one or a small number of major product lines.

Financial analysts often express the opinion that the earnings of one company are of higher quality than the earnings of other similar companies. This concept of *quality of earnings* arises because each company's management can choose from a variety of accounting principles and methods, all of which are considered generally acceptable. A company's management often is under pressure to report rising earnings or to meet previously stated earnings projections, and accounting policies may be tailored toward these objectives. We have already pointed out the impact on current reported earnings of the choice between the LIFO and FIFO methods of inventory valuation and the choice of depreciation policies. In judging the quality of earnings, the financial analyst should consider whether the accounting principles and methods selected by management lead to a conservative measurement of earnings (high quality) or tend to inflate reported earnings (low quality).

QUALITY OF ASSETS AND THE RELATIVE AMOUNT OF DEBT

Although a satisfactory level of earnings may be a good indication of the company's long-run ability to pay its debts and dividends, we must also look at the composition of assets, their condition and liquidity, the timing of repayment of liabilities, and the total amount of debt outstanding. A company may be profitable and yet be unable to pay its liabilities on time; sales and earnings may appear satisfactory, but plant and equipment may be deteriorating because of poor maintenance policies; valuable patents may be expiring; substantial losses may be imminent due to slow-moving inventories and past-due receivables. Companies with large amounts of debt often are vulnerable to increases in interest rates and are particularly vulnerable to declines in profitability and operating cash flows.

Measures of Liquidity and Credit Risk

Liquidity refers to a company's ability to meet its continuing obligations as they come due. For example, a company that has borrowed money must make interest and principal payments to a financial institution. A company that has purchased its inventory and other necessities on credit may be required to pay the seller within 30 days of the purchase date. Transactions like these require a company to maintain a close watch on its liquidity.

We emphasize throughout this text the importance to investors, creditors, and other users of financial statements of information that permits them to assess the amount, timing, and uncertainty of future cash flows from the enterprise to them. As a result, analyzing an enterprise's liquidity and its credit risk is very important and is a natural place for us to start our study of analyzing financial statements.

In this section we learn about ways to assess liquidity, starting with the classified balance sheet and then looking at several ratios commonly used to glean information about liquidity from the financial statements.

A CLASSIFIED BALANCE SHEET

In a classified balance sheet, assets usually are presented in three groups: (1) current assets, (2) plant and equipment, and (3) other assets. Liabilities are classified into two categories: (1) current liabilities and (2) long-term or noncurrent liabilities. A classified balance sheet for Computer City appears in Exhibit 14–3.

The classifications *current assets* and *current liabilities* are especially useful in evaluating a company's liquidity.

LO14-3

LEARNING OBJECTIVE
Explain the nature and purpose of classifications in financial statements.

Current Assets   **Current assets** represent relatively liquid resources. These assets include cash, investments in marketable securities, receivables, inventories, and prepaid expenses. To qualify as a current asset, an asset must already be cash or must be expected to be *converted into cash* or used up within a relatively short period of time, without interfering with normal business operations.

EXHIBIT 14–3

Computer City Classified Balance Sheet

COMPUTER CITY BALANCE SHEET DECEMBER 31, 2015			
Assets			
Current assets:			
Cash			$ 30,000
Marketable securities			11,000
Notes receivable			5,000
Accounts receivable			60,000
Inventory			70,000
Prepaid expenses			4,000
Total current assets			$180,000
Plant and equipment:			
Land		$151,000	
Building	$120,000		
Less: Accumulated depreciation	9,000	111,000	
Sales Fixtures and equipment	$ 45,000		
Less: Accumulated depreciation	27,000	18,000	
Total plant and equipment			280,000
Other assets:			
Land held as a future building site			170,000
Total assets			$630,000
Liabilities & Stockholders' Equity			
Current liabilities:			
Notes payable (due in 6 months)			$ 10,000
Accounts payable			62,000
Income taxes payable			13,000
Sales taxes payable			3,000
Accrued expenses payable			8,000
Unearned revenue and customer deposits			4,000
Total current liabilities			$100,000
Long-term liabilities:			
Mortgage payable (due in 10 years)			110,000
Total liabilities			$210,000
Stockholders' equity:			
Capital stock (15,000 shares issued and outstanding)		$150,000	
Retained earnings		270,000	
Total stockholders' equity			420,000
Total liabilities & stockholders' equity			$630,000

LO14-4

LEARNING OBJECTIVE

Prepare a classified balance sheet and compute widely used measures of liquidity and credit risk.

Current assets are tied to an enterprise's **operating cycle**. Most companies have several operating cycles within a year. This means that they take cash and purchase inventory, sell the inventory, and collect the receivable in cash several times within a year. For these companies, the time period used to identify current assets is one year, so any asset that is expected to be converted into cash within one year is classified as a current asset in the enterprise's balance sheet. Some enterprises, however, have relatively long operating cycles. For example, a company that constructs very large items (for example, airplanes or ships) may have a production period that extends well beyond one year. In these cases, the length of the company's operating cycle is used to define those assets that are classified as current. While most current assets are expected to be converted into cash, we also include as current assets those that will be used up or consumed during the year or operating cycle, if longer. For example, prepaid expenses are classified as current assets on the basis that their having been paid in advance preserves cash that otherwise would have to be paid in the current period. Combining these ideas, we can define current assets as assets that are already cash, or are expected to be converted into cash or used up within the next year or operating cycle, whichever is longer.

In a balance sheet, current assets are listed in order of liquidity. (The closer an asset is to becoming cash, the greater its liquidity.) Cash is listed first among the current assets, usually followed by investments in marketable securities, receivables, inventory, and prepaid expenses, in that order.

Current Liabilities　**Current liabilities** are *existing obligations* that are expected to be paid by using the enterprise's current assets. Among the most common current liabilities are notes payable (due within one year), accounts payable, unearned revenue, and accrued expenses, such as income taxes payable, salaries payable, and interest payable. In the balance sheet, notes payable usually are listed first, followed by accounts payable; other types of current liabilities may be listed in any sequence.

The *relationship* between current assets and current liabilities is as important as the total dollar amount in either category. Current liabilities must be paid in the near future, and the cash to pay these liabilities is expected to come from current assets. Decision makers evaluating the liquidity of a business often compare the relative amounts of current assets and current liabilities, whereas an evaluation of *long-term* credit risk requires a comparison of total assets to total liabilities.

We will now use Computer City's classified balance sheet to examine some widely applied measures of short-term liquidity and long-term credit risk.

WORKING CAPITAL

Working capital is a measurement sometimes used to express the relationship between current assets and current liabilities. **Working capital** is the *excess* of current assets over current liabilities. Computer City's working capital at December 31, 2015 is *$80,000,* computed as follows:

Current assets	$180,000
Less: Current liabilities	100,000
Working capital	$ 80,000

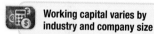 **Working capital varies by industry and company size**

Recall that current assets are expected to convert into cash (or be used up) within a relatively short period of time, and that current liabilities require a prompt cash payment. Working capital measures a company's ability to satisfy its current liabilites from existing liquid assets.

The amount of working capital that a company needs to satisfy its liabilities as they come due varies with the size of the organization and the nature of its business activities. An analyst familiar with the nature of a company's operations usually can determine from the amount of working capital whether the company is in a sound financial position or is heading for financial difficulties.

CURRENT RATIO

A widely used measure of short-term debt-paying ability is the **current ratio**. This ratio is computed by *dividing* total current assets by total current liabilities.

In the illustrated balance sheet of Computer City, current assets amount to $180,000 and current liabilities total $100,000. Therefore, Computer City's current ratio is *1.8 to 1,* computed as follows:

Current assets	$180,000
Current liabilities	$100,000
Current ratio ($180,000 ÷ $100,000)	1.8 to 1

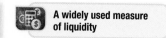 **A widely used measure of liquidity**

A current ratio of 1.8 to 1 means that the company's current assets are 1.8 times as large as its current liabilities.

The *higher* the current ratio, the more liquid the company appears to be. Historically, some bankers and other short-term creditors have believed that a company should have a current ratio of 2 to 1 or higher to qualify as a good credit risk. Such rules of thumb are questionable, however, because many successful businesses have current ratios of less than 2 to 1 because their receivables and inventory convert into cash quickly relative to the amount and timing of their payables. Likewise, it is possible for financially weak businesses to have high current ratios as a result of slow turnover in receivables and inventory. In other words, care must be taken in interpreting all ratios, including the current ratio, to ensure that inappropriate conclusions are not reached as a result of superficial analysis. Confirming the information communicated via one ratio by looking at other financial measures is often a good way to help ensure a valid interpretation. Understanding the company and its operating characteristics is always important.

QUICK RATIO

Inventory and prepaid expenses are the *least liquid* of the current assets. In a business with a long operating cycle, it may take several months to convert inventory into cash. Therefore, some short-term creditors prefer the **quick ratio** (sometimes called the acid-test ratio) to the current ratio as a measure of short-term liquidity.

The quick ratio compares only the *most liquid* current assets—called **quick assets**—with current liabilities. Quick assets include cash, marketable securities, and receivables—the current assets that can be converted most quickly into cash. Computer City's quick ratio is *1.06 to 1,* computed as follows:

Quick assets (cash, marketable securities, and receivables)	$106,000
Current liabilities	$100,000
Quick ratio ($106,000 ÷ $100,000)	1.06 to 1

 A more demanding measure of liquidity

The quick, or acid-test, ratio is especially useful in evaluating the liquidity of companies that have inventories of slow-moving merchandise (such as real estate) or inventories that have become excessive in size.

DEBT RATIO

If a business fails and must be liquidated, the claims of creditors take priority over those of the owners. But if the business has a great deal of debt, there may not be enough assets even to make full payment to all creditors.

A basic measure of the safety of creditors' claims is the **debt ratio**, which states total liabilities as a *percentage* of total assets. A company's debt ratio is computed by dividing total liabilities by total assets, as shown below for Computer City:

Total liabilities	$210,000
Total assets	$630,000
Debt ratio ($210,000 ÷ $630,000)	33⅓%

The debt ratio is not a measure of short-term liquidity. Rather, it is a measure of creditors' *long-term* risk. The smaller the portion of total assets financed by creditors, the smaller the risk that the business may become unable to pay its debts. From the creditors' point of view, the *lower* the debt ratio, the *safer* their position.

Many financially sound American companies traditionally have maintained debt ratios under 50 percent. But again, the financial analyst must be familiar with industry characteristics. Banks, for example, may have very high debt ratios—often over 90 percent.

EVALUATING FINANCIAL RATIOS

We caution users of financial statements *against* placing too much emphasis on rules of thumb, such as *a current ratio should be at least 2 to 1, a quick ratio should be at least 1 to 1,* or *a debt ratio should be under 50 percent.* To interpret any financial ratio properly, the decision maker must first understand the characteristics of the company and the industry in which it operates.

Retailers, for example, tend to have higher current ratios than do wholesalers or manufacturing companies. Service-type businesses—which have no inventory—generally have lower current ratios than merchandising or manufacturing companies. Large businesses with good credit ratings and reliable sources of cash receipts are able to operate with lower current ratios than are small companies whose continuous inflow of cash may be less predictable.

Although a high current ratio is one indication of strong debt-paying ability, an extremely high ratio—say, 4 or 5 to 1—may indicate that *too much* of the company's resources are tied up in current assets. In maintaining such a highly liquid position, the company may be using its financial resources inefficiently and not earning the return that could be earned if the assets were invested in a more productive way.

Standards for Comparison   Financial analysts generally use two criteria in evaluating the reasonableness of a financial ratio. One criterion is the *trend* in the ratio over a period of years. By reviewing this trend, analysts are able to determine whether a company's performance or financial position is improving or deteriorating. Second, analysts often compare a company's financial ratios with those of *similar companies* and with *industrywide averages*. These comparisons assist analysts in evaluating a particular ratio in light of the company's current business environment.

Annual Reports   Publicly owned corporations issue **annual reports** that provide a great deal of information about the company. For example, annual reports include comparative financial statements that have been audited by a firm of independent public accountants. They also include 5- or 10-year *summaries* of key financial data and **management's discussion and analysis** of the company's operating results, liquidity, and financial position. This is where management identifies and discusses favorable and unfavorable trends and events that may affect the company in the future.

Annual reports are mailed directly to all stockholders of the corporation. They are also available to the public either through the Internet, in libraries, or by writing or calling the stockholder relations department of the corporation.

Industry Information   Financial information about *entire industries* is available through financial publications (such as **Dun & Bradstreet, Inc.**) and through online databases (such as **Media General Financial Services**). Such information allows investors and creditors to compare the financial health of an individual company with the industry in which that company operates.

Usefulness and Limitations of Financial Ratios   A financial ratio expresses the relationship of one amount to another. Most users of financial statements find that certain ratios assist them in quickly evaluating the financial position, profitability, and future prospects of a business. A comparison of key ratios for several successive years usually indicates whether the business is becoming stronger or weaker. Ratios also provide a way to compare quickly the financial strength and profitability of different companies.

Users of financial statements should recognize, however, that ratios have several limitations. For example, management may enter into year-end transactions that temporarily improve key ratios—a process called **window dressing.**

INTERNATIONAL CASE IN POINT

Two issues confront accountants analyzing international companies. First, there is great variation in accounting measurement, disclosure, and audit quality across countries. Second, obtaining the information necessary to conduct cross-border accounting analyses is frequently difficult and sometimes not possible. Financial reporting in China is a case in point. Until recent years China did not have active stock markets requiring financial reporting. In addition, there was no external auditing in forms that would be familiar to Westerners. Dealing with these differences is one of the primary objectives of establishing international financial accounting standards.

To illustrate, the December 31, 2015, balance sheet of Computer City (Exhibit 14–3) includes current assets of $180,000 and current liabilities of $100,000, indicating a current ratio of *1.8 to 1*. What would happen if, shortly before year-end, management used $20,000 of the company's cash to pay accounts payable that are not due until January 2016? This transaction would reduce current assets to $160,000 ($180,000 − $20,000) and current liabilities to $80,000 ($100,000 − $20,000), resulting in an increase in the current ratio to a more impressive 2 to 1 ($160,000 ÷ $80,000). Is the company really better off as a result of having simply paid $20,000 of liabilities a few days early? The answer is probably no, although looking only at the current ratio one might think it is stronger after paying the $20,000 than before. Such steps to improve the company's appearance in its financial statements are common and, within reason, are a natural part of financial reporting. The astute reader of financial statements needs to be aware of this, however, and should look for instances where there is evidence that steps have been taken to artificially improve a company's appearance. Usually this can be done by looking at multiple financial measures rather than focusing on a single financial measure.

Financial statement ratios contain the same limitations as do the dollar amounts used in financial statements. For example, some assets are reported at historical cost rather than current market value. Also, financial statement ratios express only *financial* relationships. They give no indication of a company's progress in achieving nonfinancial goals, such as improving customer satisfaction or worker productivity. A thorough analysis of investment opportunities involves more than merely computing and comparing financial ratios.

LIQUIDITY, CREDIT RISK, AND THE LAW

Accountants view a business entity as separate from the other economic activities of its owners, regardless of how the business is organized. The law, however, draws an important distinction between *corporations* and *unincorporated* business organizations. Users of financial statements should understand this legal distinction, as it may affect both creditors and owners.

The owners of unincorporated businesses (sole proprietorships and partnerships) are *personally liable* for any and all debts of the business organization. Therefore, creditors of unincorporated businesses often base their lending decisions on the financial position of the *owners,* rather than the financial strength of the business entity.[2]

If a business is organized as a corporation, however, the owners (stockholders) are *not* personally responsible for the liabilities of the business. Creditors may look *only to the business entity* in seeking payment of their claims. Therefore, the liquidity of the business entity becomes much more important if the business is organized as a corporation.

Small Corporations and Loan Guarantees   Small corporations often do not have sufficient financial resources to qualify for the credit they need. In such cases, creditors may require that one or more of the company's stockholders personally guarantee (or co-sign) specific debts of the business entity. By co-signing debts of the corporation, the individual stockholders *do* become personally liable for the debt if the corporation fails to make payment.

Measures of Profitability

Measures of a company's *profitability* are of interest to equity investors and management and are drawn primarily from the income statement. The measures that we discuss in this chapter include percentage changes in key measurements, gross profit rates, operating income, net income as a percentage of sales, earnings per share, return on assets, and return on equity.

Public opinion polls show that many people believe that most businesses earn a profit equal to 30 percent or more of the sales price of their merchandise. Actually, this is far from

---

[2] In a *limited* partnership, only the *general partners* are personally responsible for the debts of the business. Every limited partnership must have one or more general partners.

true. Most successful companies earn a net income that is between 5 percent and, in unusual cases, 15 percent of sales revenue.

CLASSIFICATIONS IN THE INCOME STATEMENT

An income statement may be prepared in either the *multiple-step* or the *single-step* format. The multiple-step income statement is more useful in illustrating accounting concepts because it provides more detailed information than the single-step format. A multiple-step income statement for Computer City is shown in Exhibit 14–4.

EXHIBIT 14–4

Computer City Income Statement (Multiple-Step)

COMPUTER CITY INCOME STATEMENT FOR THE YEAR ENDED DECEMBER 31, 2015			
Net sales			$900,000
Less: Cost of goods sold (including transportation-in)			540,000
Gross profit			$360,000
Less: Operating expenses:			
Selling expenses:			
Sales salaries and commissions	$64,800		
Advertising	42,000		
Delivery service	14,200		
Depreciation: store equipment	9,000		
Other selling expenses	6,000		
Total selling expenses		$136,000	
General and administrative expenses:			
Administrative and office salaries	$93,000		
Utilities	3,100		
Depreciation: building	3,000		
Other general and administrative expenses	4,900		
Total general and administrative expenses		104,000	
Total operating expenses			240,000
Operating income			$120,000
Less (add): Nonoperating items:			
Interest expense	$12,000		
Purchase discounts lost	1,200		
Interest revenue	(3,200)		10,000
Income before income taxes			$110,000
Income tax expense			38,000
Net income			$ 72,000
Earnings per share			$4.80

A knowledge of accounting does not enable you to say what the level of corporate earnings *should be;* however, it does enable you to read audited financial statements that show what corporate earnings *actually are.* Moreover, you are aware that the information in published financial statements of corporations has been audited by CPA firms and has been periodically reviewed in detail by government agencies, such as the Securities and Exchange Commission (SEC). Consequently, you have some assurance that the profits reported in these published financial statements are reliable; they have been determined in accordance with generally accepted accounting principles and verified by independent experts.

YOUR TURN

You as a Member of the House of Representatives

Assume you are a member of the U.S. House of Representatives. Because of the financial frauds at Enron, WorldCom, and other public companies, the Congress passed, and President Bush signed, the Sarbanes-Oxley Act of 2002. The Sarbanes-Oxley Act significantly expanded the compliance burden, particularly related to financial reporting, on public companies. Certain of your business constituents argue that the compliance burden is excessive and that smaller public companies will go private, and that private businesses that need capital to expand will not go public because of the increased compliance burden. Your constituents also argue that the economy will grow more slowly, creating fewer jobs for your constituents, if companies are excluded from the capital markets because of the compliance burden imposed by the Sarbanes-Oxley Act. How would you respond?

(See our comments on the Online Learning Center website.)

MULTIPLE-STEP INCOME STATEMENTS

LO14-5

LEARNING OBJECTIVE
Prepare a multiple-step and a single-step income statement and compute widely used measures of profitability.

A multiple-step income statement draws its name from the *series of steps* in which costs and expenses are deducted from revenue and other nonoperating items are incorporated into the income statement. As a first step, the cost of goods sold is deducted from net sales to determine the subtotal *gross profit*. As a second step, operating expenses are deducted to obtain a subtotal called **operating income** (or income from operations). As a final step, income tax expense and other nonoperating items are taken into consideration to arrive at *net income*.

Notice that the income statement is divided into four major sections: (1) revenue, (2) cost of goods sold, (3) operating expenses, and (4) nonoperating items. Multiple-step income statements are noted for their numerous sections and the development of significant subtotals.

The Revenue Section In a merchandising company, the revenue section of the income statement usually contains only one line, entitled *net sales*. (Other types of revenue, if any, appear in the final section of the statement.)

Investors and managers are vitally interested in the *trend* in net sales. As one means of evaluating this trend, they often compute the percentage change in net sales from year to year. As discussed earlier in this chapter, a **percentage change** is the dollar amount of the *change* in a financial measurement, expressed as a percentage. It is computed by dividing the dollar amount of increase or decrease by the dollar amount of the measurement *before* the change occurred. (Dollar changes *cannot* be expressed as percentages if the financial statement amount in the earlier period is zero or has changed from a negative amount to a positive amount.)

In our economy, most prices increase over time. The average increase in prices during the year is called the *rate of inflation*. Because of inflation, a company's net sales may increase slightly from year to year even if the company is not selling greater amounts of merchandise. If a company's physical sales volume is increasing, net sales usually will grow faster than the rate of inflation.

If a company's sales grow faster than the *industry average,* the company increases its **market share**—that is, its share of total industry sales.

Publicly owned corporations include in their annual reports schedules summarizing operating data—such as net sales—for a period of 5 or 10 years. This information is also readily available through several online databases.

The Cost of Goods Sold Section The second section of a merchandising company's income statement shows cost of goods sold for the period. Cost of goods sold usually appears as a single dollar amount, which includes such incidental items as freight costs and normal shrinkage losses.

Gross Profit: A Key Subtotal In a multiple-step income statement, gross profit appears as a subtotal. This makes it easy for users of the income statement to compute the company's *gross profit rate* (or profit margin).

The gross profit rate is gross profit expressed as a *percentage of net sales.* In 2015, Computer City earned an average gross profit rate of *40 percent,* computed as follows:

Dollar amount of gross profit	$360,000
Net sales	$900,000
Gross profit rate ($360,000 ÷ $900,000)	40%

In evaluating the gross profit rate of a particular company, the analyst should consider the rates earned in prior periods, as well as the rates earned by *other companies* in the same industry. For most merchandising companies, gross profit rates are often between 20 percent and 50 percent, depending on the types of products they sell. These rates usually are lowest on fast-moving merchandise, such as groceries, and highest on specialty and novelty products.

Under normal circumstances, a company's gross profit rate tends to remain *reasonably stable* from one period to the next. Significant changes in this rate may provide investors with an early indication of changing consumer demand for the company's products.

The Operating Expenses Section

Operating expenses are incurred for the purpose of *producing revenue.* These expenses often are subdivided into the classifications of *selling expenses* and *general and administrative expenses.* Subdividing operating expenses into functional classifications aids management and other users of the statements in separately evaluating different aspects of the company's operations. For example, selling expenses often rise and fall in concert with changes in net sales. Administrative expenses, on the other hand, usually remain more constant from one period to the next.

Operating Income: Another Key Subtotal

Some of the revenue and expenses of a business result from activities other than the company's basic business operations. Common examples include interest earned on investments and income tax expense.

Operating income (or income from operations) shows the relationship between revenue earned from customers and expenses incurred in producing this revenue. In effect, operating income measures the profitability of a company's *basic or core business operations* and leaves out other types of revenue and expenses.

Nonoperating Items

Revenue and expenses that are not directly related to the company's primary business activities are listed in a final section of the income statement following operating income.

Two significant nonoperating items are interest expense and income tax expense. Interest expense results from the manner in which assets are *financed,* not the manner in which these assets are used in business operations. Income tax expense is not included among the operating expenses because paying income taxes *does not directly contribute to the production of revenue.* Nonoperating revenues, such as interest and dividends earned on investments, also are listed in this section of the income statement.

Net Income

Many equity investors consider net income (or net loss) to be the most important figure in a company's financial statements. This amount usually represents the overall increase (or decrease) in owners' equity resulting from all profit-directed activities during the period.

Financial analysts often compute net income as a *percentage of net sales* (net income divided by net sales). This measurement provides an indication of management's *ability to control expenses* and to retain a reasonable portion of its revenue as profit.

The normal ratio of net income to net sales varies greatly by industry. In some industries, companies may be successful by earning a net income equal to only 2 percent or 3 percent of net sales. In other industries, net income may be much higher. In 2015, Computer City's net income amounts to *8 percent* of net sales.

Net income	$ 72,000
Net sales	$900,000
Net income as a percentage of net sales ($72,000 ÷ $900,000)	8%

LO14-6

LEARNING OBJECTIVE
Put a company's net income into perspective by relating it to sales, assets, and stockholders' equity.

EARNINGS PER SHARE

Ownership of a corporation is evidenced by *shares* of capital stock. What does the net income of a corporation mean to someone who owns, say, 100 shares of a corporation's capital stock? To assist individual stockholders in relating the corporation's net income to *their ownership shares,* public companies compute **earnings per share** and show these amounts at the bottom of their income statements.[3]

In the simplest case, earnings per share is net income, expressed on a per-share basis. For example, the balance sheet in Exhibit 14–3 indicates that Computer City has 15,000 shares of capital stock outstanding.[4] Assuming these shares had been outstanding all year, earnings per share amounts to *$4.80:*

Net income	$72,000
Shares of capital stock outstanding	15,000
Earnings per share ($72,000 ÷ 15,000 shares)	$4.80

Earnings per share is one of the most widely used of all accounting ratios. The *trend* in earnings per share and the expected earnings in future periods are *major factors* affecting the market value of a company's shares.

PRICE-EARNINGS RATIO

LO14-7

LEARNING OBJECTIVE
Compute the ratios widely used in financial statement analysis and explain the significance of each.

Financial analysts express the relationship between the market price of a company's stock and the underlying earnings per share as a **price-earnings (p/e) ratio**. This ratio is computed by dividing the current market price per share of the company's stock by annual earnings per share. (A p/e ratio cannot be computed for a period in which the company incurs a net loss.)

To illustrate, assume that, at the end of 2015, Computer City's capital stock is trading among investors at a market price of *$96* per share. The p/e ratio of the company's stock is computed as follows:

Current market price per share of stock	$96
Earnings per share (for the last 12 months)	$4.80
Price-earnings ratio ($96 ÷ $4.80)	20

Technically, this ratio is 20 to 1. But it is common practice to omit the "to 1" and merely describe a p/e ratio by the first number. The p/e ratios of many publicly owned corporations are quoted daily in the financial pages of many newspapers.

The p/e ratio reflects *investors' expectations* concerning the company's *future performance.* The more optimistic these expectations, the higher the p/e ratio is likely to be.

A p/e ratio of 10 or less often indicates that investors expect earnings to *decline* from the current level. It could also mean, however, that the stock is *undervalued.* Likewise, a stock with a p/e ratio of 30 or more usually means that investors expect earnings to *increase* from the current level. However, it may also signal that the stock is *overvalued.*

One word of caution. If earnings decline to *very low levels,* the price of the stock usually does not follow the earnings all the way down. Therefore, a company with *very low earnings* may have a *high p/e ratio* even if investors are not optimistic about future earnings. From this discussion, it should be obvious that significant judgment is required in interpreting the p/e and other financial statement ratios.

---

[3] Only publicly held corporations are *required* to report earnings on a per-share basis. For small businesses, such as Computer City, the reporting of earnings per share is optional.

[4] Assume that all 15,000 shares have been outstanding throughout the year. Computation of earnings per share in more complex situations is addressed in Chapter 12.

SINGLE-STEP INCOME STATEMENTS

In their annual reports, some publicly owned corporations present their financial statements in a highly condensed format. For this reason, the *single-step* income statement is widely used in annual reports. The 2015 income statement of Computer City in Exhibit 14–5 has been revised to a single-step format.

COMPUTER CITY INCOME STATEMENT FOR THE YEAR ENDED DECEMBER 31, 2015		
Revenue:		
Net sales		$900,000
Interest earned		3,200
Total revenue		$903,200
Less: Costs and expenses:		
Cost of goods sold	$540,000	
Selling expenses	136,000	
General and administrative expenses	104,000	
Interest expense	12,000	
Purchase discounts lost	1,200	
Income tax expense	38,000	
Total costs and expenses		831,200
Net income		$ 72,000
Earnings per share		$4.80

EXHIBIT 14–5

Computer City Income Statement (Single-Step)

The single-step form of income statement takes its name from the fact that all costs and expenses are deducted from total revenue in a single step. No subtotals are shown for gross profit or for operating income, although the statement provides investors with enough information to compute these subtotals on their own. Notice that the amounts of net income and earnings per share are the same in the multiple-step and single-step income statements.

EVALUATING THE ADEQUACY OF NET INCOME

How much net income must a business earn to be considered successful? Obviously, the dollar amount of net income that investors consider adequate depends on the *size of the business.* An annual net income of $1 million might seem impressive for a local automobile dealership but would represent poor performance for a company the size of **Ford, Procter & Gamble,** or **Home Depot**.

Investors usually consider two factors in evaluating a company's profitability: (1) the trend in earnings and (2) the amount of current earnings in relation to the amount of the resources needed to produce the earnings.

Some investors regard the *trend* in earnings from year to year as important as the amount of net income in the current period. Equity investors stand to benefit from the company's performance over the long run. Years of steadily increasing earnings may increase the value of the stockholders' investment manyfold.

In evaluating the current level of earnings, many investors use *return on investment* analysis.

© Jim R. Bounds/Bloomberg/Getty Images

RETURN ON INVESTMENT (ROI)

We have emphasized throughout this text that a basic purpose of accounting is to assist decision makers in efficiently allocating and using economic resources. In deciding where to invest their money, equity investors want to know how efficiently a company utilizes its resources. A common method of evaluating the efficiency with which financial resources are employed is to compute the rate of return earned on these resources. This rate of return is called the *return on investment,* or *ROI,* and is sometimes referred to as return on assets.

Mathematically, computing return on investment is simple: The annual return (or profit) generated by the investment is stated as a *percentage* of the average amount invested throughout the year. The basic idea is illustrated by the following formula:

ROI general formula

$$\text{Return on Investment (ROI)} = \frac{\text{Return}}{\text{Average Amount Invested}}$$

The return is earned throughout the period. Therefore, it is logical to express this return as a percentage of the *average* amount invested during the period, rather than the investment at year-end. The average amount invested usually is computed by adding the amounts invested as of the beginning and end of the year, and dividing this total by 2. If the investment is relatively stable over time, the year-end balance may be used instead of an average.

The concept of ROI is applied in many different situations, such as evaluating the profitability of a business, a branch location, or a specific investment opportunity. As a result, a number of variations in the basic ROI ratio have been developed, each suited to a particular type of analysis. These ratios differ in the manner in which return and average amount invested are defined. We will discuss two common applications of the ROI concept: *return on assets* and *return on equity.*

RETURN ON ASSETS (ROA)

This ratio is used in evaluating whether management has earned a reasonable return with the assets under its control. In this computation, return usually is defined as *operating income,* since interest expense and income taxes are determined by factors other than the manner in which assets are used. The **return on assets** is computed as follows:

The return on total assets is operating income

$$\text{Return on Assets (ROA)} = \frac{\text{Operating Income}}{\text{Average Total Assets}}$$

Let us now determine the return on assets earned by the management of Computer City in 2015. Operating income, as shown in the income statement in Exhibit 14–4, amounts to *$120,000.* Assume that Computer City's assets at the beginning of 2015 totaled $570,000. The illustrated balance sheet in Exhibit 14–3 shows total assets of $630,000 at year-end. Therefore, the company's *average* total assets during the year amounted to *$600,000* [($570,000 + $630,000) ÷ 2]. The return on assets in 2015 is *20 percent,* determined as follows:

$$\frac{\text{Operating Income}}{\text{Average Total Assets}} = \frac{\$120,000}{\$600,000} = 20\%$$

Most successful businesses earn a return on average total assets of, perhaps, 15 percent or more. At this writing, businesses must pay interest rates of between 3 percent and 8 percent to borrow money. However, interest rates are at historic lows in the United States and are likely to rise in the future. If a business is well managed and has good future prospects, management should be able to earn a return on assets that is higher than the company's cost of borrowing.

RETURN ON EQUITY (ROE)

The return on assets that we calculated above measures the efficiency with which management has utilized the assets under its control, regardless of whether these assets were financed with debt or equity capital. The **return on equity** ratio, in contrast, looks only at the return earned by management on the stockholders' investment—that is, on *owners' equity.*

The return to stockholders is *net income,* which represents the return from all sources, both operating and nonoperating. Return on equity is computed as follows:

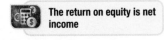
The return on equity is net income

$$\text{Return on Equity (ROE)} = \frac{\text{Net Income}}{\text{Average Total Stockholders' Equity}}$$

To illustrate, let us again turn to the 2015 financial statements of Computer City. The company earned net income of *$72,000.* The year-end balance sheet (Exhibit 14–3) shows total stockholders' equity of $420,000. To enable us to complete our computation, we will assume that the stockholders' equity at the *beginning* of the year amounted to $380,000. Therefore, the *average* stockholders' equity for the year amounts to *$400,000* [($380,000 + $420,000) ÷ 2]. The return on stockholders' equity in 2015 is *18 percent,* computed as follows:

$$\frac{\text{Net Income}}{\text{Average Total Stockholders' Equity}} = \frac{\$72{,}000}{\$400{,}000} = 18\%$$

Traditionally, stockholders have expected to earn an average annual return of 12 percent or more from equity investments in large, financially strong companies. Annual returns on equity of 30 percent or more are not uncommon, especially in rapidly growing companies with new or highly successful products.

The return on equity may be higher or lower than the overall return on assets, depending on how the company has financed its assets and on the amounts of its nonoperating revenue and expenses. A company that suffers a net loss provides its stockholders with a *negative* return on stockholders' equity.

Comprehensive Illustration: Seacliff Company

Now that we have presented several techniques that are useful in better understanding an enterprise's financial statements, we will show the comprehensive analysis of a company. This illustration draws from material presented in this chapter as well as from information presented earlier in the text. We take a comprehensive look at the analysis of financial statements from the perspectives of three important groups: common stockholders, long-term creditors, and short-term creditors.

The basic information for our analysis is contained in a set of condensed two-year comparative financial statements for Seacliff Company shown in Exhibits 14–6 through 14–10. Summarized statement data, together with computations of dollar increases and decreases, and component percentages where applicable, have been compiled. For convenience in this illustration, relatively small dollar amounts have been used in the Seacliff Company financial statements.

© Digital Vision Ltd.

EXHIBIT 14–6 Seacliff Income Statements

SEACLIFF COMPANY COMPARATIVE INCOME STATEMENT FOR THE YEARS ENDED DECEMBER 31, 2015, AND DECEMBER 31, 2014						
			Increase or (Decrease)		Percentage of Net Sales	
	2015	2014	Dollars	%	2015	2014
Net sales	$900,000	$750,000	$ 150,000	20.0	100.0	100.0
Cost of goods sold	530,000	420,000	110,000	26.2	58.9	56.0
Gross profit on sales	$370,000	$330,000	$ 40,000	12.1	41.1	44.0
Operating expenses:						
Selling expenses	$117,000	$ 75,000	$ 42,000	56.0	13.0	10.0
General and administrative expenses	126,000	95,000	31,000	32.6	14.0	12.7
Total operating expenses	$243,000	$170,000	$ 73,000	42.9	27.0	22.7
Operating income	$127,000	$160,000	$ (33,000)	(20.6)	14.1	21.3
Interest expense	24,000	30,000	(6,000)	(20.0)	2.7	4.0
Income before income tax	$103,000	$130,000	$ (27,000)	(20.8)	11.4	17.3
Income tax expense	28,000	40,000	(12,000)	(30.0)	3.1	5.3
Net income	$ 75,000	$ 90,000	$ (15,000)	(16.7)	8.3	12.0
Earnings per share of common stock	$ 13.20	$ 20.25	$ (7.05)	(34.8)		

EXHIBIT 14-7 Seacliff Statements of Retained Earnings

SEACLIFF COMPANY STATEMENT OF RETAINED EARNINGS FOR THE YEARS ENDED DECEMBER 31, 2015, AND DECEMBER 31, 2014				
			Increase or (Decrease)	
	2015	**2014**	**Dollars**	**%**
Retained earnings, beginning of year	$176,000	$115,000	$ 61,000	53.0
Net income	75,000	90,000	(15,000)	(16.7)
	$251,000	$205,000	$ 46,000	22.4
Less: Dividends on common stock ($5.00 per share in 2014, $4.80 per share in 2015)	$ 24,000	$ 20,000	$ 4,000	20.0
Dividends on preferred stock ($9 per share)	9,000	9,000		
	$ 33,000	$ 29,000	$ 4,000	13.8
Retained earnings, end of year	$218,000	$176,000	$ 42,000	23.9

EXHIBIT 14-8 Seacliff Balance Sheets

SEACLIFF COMPANY CONDENSED COMPARATIVE BALANCE SHEET* DECEMBER 31, 2015, AND DECEMBER 31, 2014						
			Increase or (Decrease)		Percentage of Total Assets	
Assets	**2015**	**2014**	**Dollars**	**%**	**2015**	**2014**
Current assets	$390,000	$288,000	$ 102,000	35.4	41.1	33.5
Plant and equipment (net)	500,000	467,000	33,000	7.1	52.6	54.3
Other assets (loans to officers)	60,000	105,000	(45,000)	(42.9)	6.3	12.2
Total assets	$950,000	$860,000	$ 90,000	10.5	100.0	100.0
Liabilities & Stockholders' Equity						
Liabilities:						
Current liabilities	$112,000	$ 94,000	$ 18,000	19.1	11.8	10.9
12% long-term note payable (due in 7 years)	200,000	250,000	(50,000)	(20.0)	21.1	29.1
Total liabilities	$312,000	$344,000	$ (32,000)	(9.3)	32.9	40.0
Stockholders' equity:						
9% preferred stock, $100 par	$100,000	$100,000	—	—	10.5	11.6
Common stock, $50 par	250,000	200,000	$ 50,000	25.0	26.3	23.2
Additional paid-in capital	70,000	40,000	30,000	75.0	7.4	4.7
Retained earnings	218,000	176,000	42,000	23.9	22.9	20.5
Total stockholders' equity	$638,000	$516,000	$ 122,000	23.6	67.1	60.0
Total liabilities & stockholders' equity	$950,000	$860,000	$ 90,000	10.5	100.0	100.0

*In order to focus attention on important subtotals, this statement is highly condensed and does not show individual asset and liability items. These details will be introduced as needed in the text discussion. For example, a list of Seacliff Company's current assets and current liabilities appears in Exhibit 14–18.

EXHIBIT 14–9 Seacliff Statement Of Cash Flows

SEACLIFF COMPANY CONDENSED COMPARATIVE STATEMENT OF CASH FLOWS FOR THE YEARS ENDED DECEMBER 31, 2015, AND DECEMBER 31, 2014				
			Increase or (Decrease)	
	2015	2014	Dollars	%
Cash flows from operating activities:				
Net cash flows from operating activities	$ 19,000	$ 95,000	$ (76,000)	(80.0)
Cash flows from investing activities:				
Purchases of plant assets	(63,000)	(28,000)	(35,000)	125.0
Collections of loans from officers	45,000	(35,000)	80,000	N/A*
Net cash used by investing activities	$ (18,000)	$(63,000)	$ 45,000	(71.4)
Cash flows from financing activities:				
Dividends paid	$ (33,000)	$(29,000)	$ (4,000)	13.8
Repayment of long-term debt	(50,000)	–0–	(50,000)	N/A*
Proceeds from issuing capital stock	80,000	–0–	80,000	N/A*
Net cash used by financing activities	$ (3,000)	$(29,000)	$ 26,000	(89.7)
Net increase (decrease) in cash and cash equivalents	$ (2,000)	$ 3,000	$ (5,000)	N/A*
Cash and cash equivalents, January 1, 2015	40,000	37,000	3,000	8.1
Cash and cash equivalents, December 31, 2015	$ 38,000	$ 40,000	$ (2,000)	(5.0)

*N/A indicates that computation of the percentage change is not appropriate. Percentage changes cannot be determined if the base year is zero or if a negative amount (cash outflow) changes to a positive amount (cash inflow).

SEACLIFF COMPANY NOTES TO FINANCIAL STATEMENTS FOR THE YEARS ENDED DECEMBER 31, 2015, AND DECEMBER 31, 2014

EXHIBIT 14–10

Seacliff Notes to Financial Statements

Note 1—Accounting Policies

Inventories   Inventories are determined by the LIFO method.

Depreciation   Depreciation is computed by the straight-line method. Buildings are depreciated over 40 years, and equipment and fixtures over periods of 5 or 10 years.

Note 2—Unused Lines of Credit

The company has a confirmed line of credit in the amount of $35,000. None was in use at December 31, 2015.

Note 3—Contingencies and Commitments

As of December 31, 2015, the company has no material commitments or noncancellable obligations. There currently are no loss contingencies known to management.

Note 4—Current Values of Financial Instruments

All financial instruments appear in the financial statements at dollar amounts that closely approximate their current values.

Note 5—Concentrations of Credit Risk

The company engages in retail sales to the general public from a single location in Seattle, Washington. No individual customer accounts for more than 2% of the company's total sales or accounts receivable. Accounts receivable are unsecured.

LO14-8

LEARNING OBJECTIVE
Analyze financial statements from the viewpoints of common stockholders, creditors, and others.

ANALYSIS BY COMMON STOCKHOLDERS

Common stockholders and potential investors in common stock look first at a company's earnings record. Their investment is in shares of stock, so *earnings per share* and *dividends per share* are of particular interest.

Earnings per Share of Common Stock   As indicated in Chapter 12, earnings per share of common stock are computed by dividing the income applicable to the common stock by the weighted-average number of shares of common stock outstanding during the year. Any preferred dividend requirements are subtracted from net income to determine income applicable to common stock, as shown in the computations for Seacliff Company in Exhibit 14–11.

EXHIBIT 14–11

Earnings Per Share of Common Stock

Earnings related to number of common shares outstanding

	2015	2014
Net income	$75,000	$90,000
Less: Preferred dividend requirements	9,000	9,000
Income applicable to common stock	(a) $66,000	$81,000
Shares of common stock outstanding, during the year	(b) 5,000	4,000
Earnings per share of common stock (a ÷ b)	$ 13.20	$ 20.25

Notice that earnings per share have decreased by *$7.05* in 2015, representing a decline of nearly *35 percent* from their level in 2014 ($7.05 ÷ $20.25 = 34.8%). Common stockholders consider a decline in earnings per share to be an unfavorable development. A decline in earnings per share generally represents a decline in the profitability of the company and creates uncertainty as to the company's prospects for future growth.

With such a significant decline in earnings per share, we should expect to see a decline in the market value of Seacliff's common stock during 2015. [For purposes of our illustration, we assume the common stock had a market value of *$160* at December 31, 2014, and of *$132* at the end of 2015. This drop of $28 per share represents a *17½ percent* decline in the market value of every common stockholder's investment ($28 decline ÷ $160 = 17.5%).]

Price-Earnings Ratio   As we mentioned earlier in this chapter, the relationship between the market price of common stock and earnings per share is widely recognized and is expressed as a ratio, called the *price-earnings ratio* (or *p/e ratio*). The p/e ratio is determined by dividing the market price per share by the annual earnings per share.

The outlook for future earnings is the major factor influencing a company's p/e ratio. Companies with track records of rapid growth may sell at p/e ratios of perhaps 30 to 1, or even higher. Companies with "flat" earnings or earnings expected to decline in future years often sell at price-earnings ratios below 10 to 1.

At the end of 2014, Seacliff's p/e ratio was approximately *8 to 1* ($160 ÷ $20.25 = 7.9), suggesting that investors *were expecting* earnings to decline in 2015. At December 31, 2015, the price-earnings ratio was *10 to 1* ($132 ÷ $13.20 = 10.0). A p/e ratio in this range suggests that investors expect future earnings to stabilize around the current level.

Dividend Yield   Dividends are of prime importance to some stockholders, but a secondary factor to others. Some stockholders invest primarily to receive regular cash income, while others invest in stocks principally with the expectation of rising market prices. If a corporation is profitable and retains its earnings for expansion of the business, the expanded operations should produce an increase in the net income of the company and thus tend to make each share of stock more valuable.

In comparing the merits of alternative investment opportunities, we should relate earnings and dividends per share to the *market value* of the stock at a particular date. Dividends per share divided by market price per share determine the *yield* rate of a company's stock. Dividend yield is especially important to those investors whose objective is to maximize the dividend revenue from their investments. For Seacliff, the dividend yield on its common stock was 3.1 percent in 2014 ($5 ÷ $160) and 3.6 percent in 2015 ($4.80 ÷ $132).

Summary of Earnings and Dividend Data for Seacliff   The relationships
of Seacliff's per-share earnings and dividends to its year-end stock prices are summarized in
Exhibit 14–12.

Date	Market Value per Share	Earnings per Share	Price-Earnings Ratio	Dividends per Share	Dividend Yield, %
Dec. 31, 2014	$160	$20.25	8	$5.00	3.1
Dec. 31, 2015	132	13.20	10	4.80	3.6

EXHIBIT 14–12

Earnings and Dividends Per Share of Common Stock

Earnings and dividends related to market price of common stock

The decline in market value during 2015 presumably reflects the decreases in both earnings
and dividends per share. Investors appraising this stock at December 31, 2014, should consider
whether a price-earnings ratio of 10 and a dividend yield of 3.6 percent meet their expectations in light of alternative investment opportunities. These investors will also place considerable weight on estimates of the company's prospective future earnings and the probable effect
of such estimated earnings on the market price of the stock and on dividend payments.

Revenue and Expense Analysis   The trend of earnings of Seacliff Company is
unfavorable, and stockholders will want to know the reasons for the decline in net income.
The comparative income statements in Exhibit 14–6 show that despite a 20 percent increase in
net sales, net income fell from $90,000 in 2014 to $75,000 in 2015, a decline of 16.7 percent.
As a percentage of net sales, net income fell from 12 percent to only 8.3 percent. The primary causes of this decline were the increases in selling expenses (56.0 percent), general and
administrative expenses (32.6 percent), and the cost of goods sold (26.2 percent), all of which
exceeded the 20 percent increase in net sales.

Let us assume that further investigation reveals Seacliff Company decided in 2015 to
reduce its sales prices in an effort to generate greater sales volume. This would explain the
decrease in the gross profit rate from 44 percent to 41.1 percent of net sales. Since the dollar amount of gross profit increased $40,000 in 2015, the strategy of reducing sales prices to
increase volume would have been successful if there had been little or no increase in operating
expenses. However, operating expenses rose by $73,000, resulting in a $33,000 decrease in
operating income.

The next step is to find which expenses increased and why. An investor may be limited here,
because detailed operating expenses are not usually shown in published financial statements.
Some conclusions, however, can be reached on the basis of even the condensed information
available in the comparative income statements for Seacliff Company shown in Exhibit 14–6.

The substantial increase in selling expenses presumably reflects greater selling effort during
2015 in an attempt to improve sales volume. However, the fact that selling expenses increased
$42,000 while gross profit increased only $40,000 indicates that the cost of this increased sales
effort was not justified in terms of results. Even more bothersome is the increase in general and
administrative expenses. Some growth in administrative expenses might be expected to accompany increased sales volume, but because some of the expenses are fixed, the growth generally
should be *less than proportional* to any increase in sales. The increase in general and administrative expenses from 12.7 percent to 14 percent of sales should be of concern to informed investors.

Management generally has greater control over operating expenses than over revenue. The
operating expense ratio is often used as a measure of management's ability to control its operating expenses. We show the unfavorable trend in this ratio for Seacliff Company in Exhibit 14–13.

	2015	2014
Operating expenses	(a) $243,000	$170,000
Net sales	(b) $900,000	$750,000
Operating expense ratio (a ÷ b)	27.0%	22.7%

EXHIBIT 14–13

Operating Expense Ratio

Does a higher operating expense ratio indicate higher net income?

If management were able to increase the sales volume while at the same time increasing the gross profit rate and decreasing the operating expense ratio, the effect on net income could be dramatic. For example, if in the year 2016 Seacliff Company can increase its sales by approximately 11 percent, to $1,000,000, increase its gross profit rate from 41.1 to 44 percent, and reduce the operating expense ratio from 27 to 24 percent, its operating income would increase from $127,000 to $200,000 ($1,000,000 − $560,000 − $240,000), an increase of over 57 percent.

RETURN ON INVESTMENT (ROI)

The rate of return on investment (often called ROI) is a measure of management's efficiency in using available resources. Regardless of the size of the organization, capital is a scarce resource and must be used efficiently. In judging the performance of branch managers or of companywide management, it is reasonable to raise the question: What rate of return have you earned on the resources under your control?

Return on Assets   An important test of management's ability to earn a return on funds supplied from all sources is the rate of return on total assets.

As noted previously, the income figure used in computing this ratio should be *operating income,* since interest expense and income taxes are determined by factors other than the efficient use of resources. Operating income is earned throughout the year and therefore should be related to the *average* investment in assets during the year. In Exhibit 14–14, the computation of this ratio of Seacliff Company assumes total assets at the beginning of 2014 were $820,000.

EXHIBIT 14–14

Percentage Return on Assets

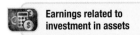
Earnings related to investment in assets

		2015	2014
Operating income	(a)	$127,000	$160,000
Total assets, beginning of year	(b)	$860,000	$820,000
Total assets, end of year	(c)	$950,000	$860,000
Average investment in assets [(b + c) ÷ 2]	(d)	$905,000	$840,000
Return on assets (a ÷ d)		14%	19%

This ratio shows that the rate of return earned on the company's assets fell in 2015. Before drawing conclusions as to the effectiveness of Seacliff's management, however, we should consider the trend in the return on assets earned by other companies of similar kind and size.

Return on Common Stockholders' Equity   We introduced the concept of return on equity using a company that had only one class of capital stock. Therefore, the return on equity was simply net income divided by average stockholders' equity. But Seacliff has issued both preferred stock *and* common stock. The preferred stock does not participate fully in the company's earnings; rather, the return to preferred stockholders is limited to their dividend. We must adjust the return on equity computation to reflect the return on *common* stockholders' equity.

The return to common stockholders is equal to net income *less* any preferred dividends. The return on common stockholders' equity, assuming common stockholders' equity at the beginning of 2014 was $355,000, is computed in Exhibit 14–15.

EXHIBIT 14–15

Return on Common Stockholders' Equity

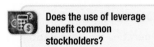
Does the use of leverage benefit common stockholders?

		2015	2014
Net income		$ 75,000	$ 90,000
Less: Preferred dividend requirements		9,000	9,000
Net income applicable to common stock	(a)	$ 66,000	$ 81,000
Common stockholders' equity, beginning of year	(b)	$416,000	$355,000
Common stockholders' equity, end of year	(c)	$538,000	$416,000
Average common stockholders' equity [(b + c) ÷ 2]	(d)	$477,000	$385,500
Return on common stockholders' equity (a ÷ d)		13.8%	21.0%

In both years, the rate of return on common stockholders' equity was higher than the 12 percent rate of interest paid to long-term creditors or the 9 percent dividend rate paid to preferred stockholders. This result was achieved through the favorable use of leverage.

LEVERAGE

Leverage refers to using borrowed money to earn a return *greater* than the cost of borrowing, increasing net income and the return on common stockholders' equity. For example, if you can borrow money at 12 percent and use it to earn 20 percent, you will benefit by doing so. However, leverage can act as a double-edged sword; the effects may be favorable or unfavorable to the holders of common stock.

If the rate of return on total assets should fall *below* the average rate of interest on borrowed capital, leverage will *reduce* the return on common stockholders' equity. In this situation, paying off the loans that carry high interest rates would appear to be a logical move. However, many companies do not have enough cash to retire long-term debt on short notice. Therefore, the common stockholders may become locked in to the unfavorable effects of leverage.

In deciding how much leverage is appropriate, the common stockholders should consider the *stability* of the company's return on assets as well as the relationship of this return to the average cost of borrowed capital. If a business incurs so much debt that it becomes unable to meet the required interest and principal payments, the creditors may force liquidation or reorganization of the business.

Debt Ratio   One indicator of the amount of leverage used by a business is the debt ratio. This ratio measures the proportion of the total assets financed by creditors, as distinguished from stockholders. It is computed by dividing total liabilities by total assets. A *high* debt ratio indicates an extensive use of leverage, that is, a large proportion of financing provided by creditors. A low debt ratio, on the other hand, indicates that the business is making little use of leverage.

The debt ratio at year-end for Seacliff is determined as shown in Exhibit 14–16.

	2015	2014
Total liabilities	(a) $312,000	$344,000
Total assets (or total liabilities & stockholders' equity)	(b) $950,000	$860,000
Debt ratio (a ÷ b)...	32.8%	40.0%

EXHIBIT 14–16

Debt Ratio

 Proportion of assets financed by creditors

Seacliff Company has a lower debt ratio in 2015 than in 2014. Is this favorable or unfavorable?

From the viewpoint of the common stockholder, a high debt ratio produces maximum benefits if management is able to earn a rate of return on assets greater than the rate of interest paid to creditors. However, a high debt ratio can be *unfavorable* if the return on assets falls *below* the rate of interest paid to creditors. Since the return on total assets earned by Seacliff Company has declined from 19 percent in 2014 to a relatively low 14 percent in 2015, the common stockholders probably would *not* want to risk a high debt ratio. The action by management in 2015 of retiring $50,000 in long-term liabilities will help to protect the common stockholders from the unfavorable effects of leverage if the rate of return on assets continues to decline.

CASE IN POINT

A historical example from **Dell Inc.** provides an interesting case study in how financial leverage can be used to greatly increase the return earned by common stockholders without appreciably increasing the company's risk profile. **Dell**'s 2004 return on assets was an impressive 20 percent, and its return on common equity was an eye-popping 47 percent. Clearly **Dell** benefited from favorable financial leverage.

Moreover, **Dell** benefited from favorable financial leverage without increasing its risk profile. That is, most of **Dell**'s leverage was in the form of *non-interest*-bearing liabilities. Although liabilities comprised 67.5 percent of **Dell**'s assets, *interest-bearing* liabilities represented only 2.6 percent of assets. Approximately 84 percent of **Dell**'s liabilities were current, representing either trade credit (accounts payable) or accrued liabilities (e.g., unpaid salaries and benefits). In essence, much of **Dell**'s financing was being provided by its trade creditors and employees, which are essentially free sources of financing.

ANALYSIS BY LONG-TERM CREDITORS

Bondholders and other long-term creditors are primarily interested in three factors: (1) the rate of return on their investment, (2) the firm's ability to meet its interest requirements, and (3) the firm's ability to repay the principal of the debt when it falls due.

Yield Rate on Bonds   The yield rate on bonds or other long-term indebtedness cannot be computed in the same manner as the yield rate on shares of stock, because bonds, unlike stocks, have a definite maturity date and amount. The ownership of a 12 percent, 10-year, $1,000 bond represents the right to receive $120 each year for 10 years plus the right to receive $1,000 at the end of 10 years. If the market price of this bond is $950, the yield rate on an investment in the bond is the rate of interest that will make the *present value* of these two contractual rights equal to the $950 market price.

When bonds sell at maturity value, the yield rate is equal to the bond interest rate. *The yield rate varies inversely with changes in the market price of the bond.* If interest rates rise, the market price of existing bonds will fall; if interest rates decline, the price of bonds will rise. If the price of a bond is above maturity value, the yield rate is less than the bond interest rate; if the price of a bond is below maturity value, the yield rate is higher than the bond interest rate.

Interest Coverage Ratio   Bondholders feel that their investments are relatively safe if the issuing company earns enough income to cover its annual interest obligations by a comfortable margin.

A common measure of creditors' safety is the ratio of operating income available for the payment of interest to the annual interest expense, called the *interest coverage ratio* or *times interest earned.* See this computation for Seacliff Company in Exhibit 14–17.

EXHIBIT 14–17

Interest Coverage Ratio

Long-term creditors watch this ratio

	2015	2014
Operating income (before interest and income taxes) . . . . (a)	$127,000	$160,000
Annual interest expense . . . . (b)	$ 24,000	$ 30,000
Interest coverage (a ÷ b)	5.3 times	5.3 times

The ratio remained unchanged at a satisfactory level during 2015. Generally an interest coverage ratio above 2.0 is considered strong.

Debt Ratio   Long-term creditors are interested in the percentage of total assets financed by debt, as distinguished from the percentage financed by stockholders. The percentage of total assets financed by debt is measured by the debt ratio, which was computed in Exhibit 14–16.

From a creditor's viewpoint, the lower the debt ratio, the better, since this means that stockholders have contributed a higher percentage of the funds to the business, and therefore the margin of protection to creditors against a shrinkage of the assets is high.

As shown in Exhibit 14–16, the debt ratio, or the percentage of assets financed by debt, decreased from 2014 to 2015 from 40 percent to 32.8 percent. This would generally be considered by long-term creditors to be a favorable change because the debt burden, including required interest payments, is less in 2015 than in 2014, thereby making the claim of each creditor more secure.

Secured Claims   Sometimes the claims of long-term creditors are secured with specific collateral, such as the land and buildings owned by the borrower. In these situations, the secured creditors may look primarily to the *value of the collateral* in assessing the safety of their claims.

Assets pledged as collateral to secure specific liabilities are disclosed in notes to the financial statements. As Seacliff makes no such disclosures, we may assume that none of its assets have been pledged as collateral to secure specific liabilities.

ANALYSIS BY SHORT-TERM CREDITORS

Bankers and other short-term creditors share the interest of stockholders and bondholders in the profitability and long-run stability of a business. Their primary interest, however, is in the current position of the company—its ability to generate sufficient funds (working capital) to meet current operating needs and to pay current debts promptly. The analysis of financial statements by a banker considering a short-term loan, or by a trade creditor investigating the credit status of a customer, is likely to center on the working capital position of the prospective debtor.

Amount of Working Capital Working capital is the excess of current assets over current liabilities. It represents the cash and near-cash assets that provide a "cushion" of liquidity over the amount expected to be needed in the near future to satisfy maturing obligations. The details of the working capital of Seacliff Company are shown in Exhibit 14–18.

EXHIBIT 14–18 Seacliff Schedule of Working Capital

SEACLIFF COMPANY COMPARATIVE SCHEDULE OF WORKING CAPITAL AS OF DECEMBER 31, 2015, AND DECEMBER 31, 2014						
			Increase or (Decrease)		Percentage of Total Current Items	
	2015	**2014**	**Dollars**	**%**	**2015**	**2014**
Current assets:						
Cash	$ 38,000	$ 40,000	$ (2,000)	(5.0)	9.7	13.9
Accounts receivable (net)	117,000	86,000	31,000	36.0	30.0	29.9
Inventories	180,000	120,000	60,000	50.0	46.2	41.6*
Prepaid expenses	55,000	42,000	13,000	31.0	14.1	14.6
Total current assets	$390,000	$288,000	$102,000	35.4	100.0	100.0
Current liabilities:						
Notes payable to creditors	$ 14,600	$ 10,000	$ 4,600	46.0	13.1*	10.7*
Accounts payable	66,000	30,000	36,000	120.0	58.9	31.9
Accrued liabilities	31,400	54,000	(22,600)	(41.9)	28.0	57.4
Total current liabilities	$112,000	$ 94,000	$ 18,000	19.1	100.0	100.0
Working capital	$278,000	$194,000	$ 84,000	43.3		

*Amounts adjusted so that totals equal 100.0.

This schedule shows that current assets increased $102,000, while current liabilities rose by only $18,000. As a result, working capital increased $84,000.

Quality of Working Capital In evaluating the debt-paying ability of a business, short-term creditors should consider the quality of working capital as well as the total dollar amount. The principal factors affecting the quality of working capital are (1) the nature of the current assets and (2) the length of time required to convert those assets into cash.

The schedule in Exhibit 14–18 shows an unfavorable shift in the composition of Seacliff Company's working capital during 2015: cash decreased from 13.9 percent to 9.7 percent of current assets, while inventory rose from 41.6 percent to 46.2 percent. Inventory is a less liquid resource than cash. Therefore, the quality of working capital is not as liquid as in 2014. *Turnover rates* (or *ratios*) may be used to assist short-term creditors in estimating the time required to turn assets such as receivables and inventory into cash.

Accounts Receivable Turnover Rate As explained in Chapter 7, the accounts receivable turnover rate indicates how quickly a company converts its accounts receivable into cash. The accounts receivable turnover *rate* is determined by dividing net sales by the average balance of accounts receivable.[5] The number of *days* required (on average) to collect accounts receivable then may be determined by dividing the number of days in a year (365)

---

[5] Ideally, the accounts receivable turnover is computed by dividing net *credit* sales by the *monthly* average of receivables. Such detailed information, however, generally is not provided in annual financial statements.

by the turnover rate. The computations in Exhibit 14–19 use the data in our Seacliff example, assuming accounts receivable at the beginning of 2014 were $80,000.

EXHIBIT 14–19

Accounts Receivable Turnover

 Are customers paying promptly?

	2015	2014
Net sales .... (a)	$900,000	$750,000
Accounts receivable, beginning of year	$ 86,000	$ 80,000
Accounts receivable, end of year	$117,000	$ 86,000
Average accounts receivable .... (b)	$101,500	$ 83,000
Accounts receivable turnover per year (a ÷ b)	8.9 times	9.0 times
Average number of days to collect accounts receivable (divide 365 days by accounts receivable turnover)	41 days	41 days

There has been no change in the average time required to collect receivables. The interpretation of the average age of receivables depends upon the company's credit terms and the seasonal activity immediately before year-end. For example, if the company grants 30-day credit terms to its customers, the analysis in Exhibit 14–19 indicates that accounts receivable collections are lagging. If the terms are for 60 days, however, collections are being made ahead of schedule.

Inventory Turnover Rate   The inventory turnover rate indicates how many times during the year the company is able to sell a quantity of goods equal to its average inventory. Mechanically, this rate is determined by dividing the cost of goods sold for the year by the average amount of inventory on hand during the year. The number of days required to sell this amount of inventory may be determined by dividing 365 days by the turnover rate. These computations were explained in Chapter 8 and are demonstrated in Exhibit 14–20 using the information for Seacliff Company, assuming inventory at the beginning of 2014 was $100,000. The trend indicated by this analysis is unfavorable, since the length of time required for Seacliff to turn over (sell) its inventory is increasing.

EXHIBIT 14–20

Inventory Turnover

	2015	2014
Cost of goods sold .... (a)	$530,000	$420,000
Inventory, beginning of year	$120,000	$100,000
Inventory, end of year	$180,000	$120,000
Average inventory .... (b)	$150,000	$110,000
Average inventory turnover per year (a ÷ b)	3.5 times	3.8 times
Average number of days to sell inventory (divide 365 days by inventory turnover)	104 days	96 days

Companies that have low gross profit rates often need high inventory turnover rates in order to operate profitably. This is another way of saying that if the gross profit rate is low, a high volume of transactions is necessary to produce a satisfactory amount of profits. Companies that sell high markup items, such as jewelry stores and art galleries, can operate successfully with much lower inventory turnover rates.

Operating Cycle   The inventory turnover rate indicates how quickly inventory *sells,* but not how quickly this asset converts into *cash.* Short-term creditors, of course, are interested primarily in the company's ability to generate cash.

The period of time required for a merchandising company to convert its inventory into cash is called the *operating cycle.* The illustration appeared in Chapter 6 and is repeated in Exhibit 14–21 for your convenience.

Seacliff's operating cycle in 2015 was approximately 145 days, computed by adding the 104 days required to turn over inventory and the average 41 days required to collect

EXHIBIT 14–21

Operating Cycle

The operating cycle repeats continuously

receivables. This compares with an operating cycle of only 137 days in 2014, computed as 96 days to dispose of the inventory plus 41 days to collect the resulting receivables. From the viewpoint of short-term creditors, the *shorter* the operating cycle, the *higher the quality* of the borrower's working capital. Therefore, these creditors would regard the lengthening of Seacliff Company's operating cycle as an unfavorable trend.

Current Ratio   The current ratio expresses the relationship between current assets and current liabilities. A strong current ratio provides considerable evidence that a company will be able to meet its obligations coming due in the near future. The current ratio for Seacliff Company is computed in Exhibit 14–22.

	2015	2014
Total current assets	(a) $390,000	$288,000
Total current liabilities	(b) $112,000	$ 94,000
Current ratio (a ÷ b)	3.5	3.1

EXHIBIT 14–22

Current Ratio

Does this indicate satisfactory debt-paying ability?

Quick Ratio   Because inventories and prepaid expenses are further removed from conversion into cash than other current assets, the *quick ratio* is sometimes computed as a supplement to the current ratio. The quick ratio compares the most liquid current assets (cash, marketable securities, and receivables) with current liabilities. Seacliff Company has no marketable securities; its quick ratio is computed in Exhibit 14–23.

	2015	2014
Quick assets (cash and accounts receivable)	(a) $155,000	$126,000
Current liabilities	(b) $112,000	$ 94,000
Quick ratio (a ÷ b)	1.4	1.3

EXHIBIT 14–23

Quick Ratio

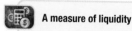   A measure of liquidity

Here again the analysis reveals a favorable trend and a strong position. If the credit periods extended to customers and granted by creditors are roughly equal, a quick ratio of 1.0 or better is considered satisfactory.

Unused Lines of Credit   From the viewpoint of a short-term creditor, a company's unused lines of credit represent a resource almost as liquid as cash. An unused line of credit means that a bank has agreed in advance to lend the company any amount, up to the specified limit. As long as this line of credit remains available, creditors know that the business can borrow cash quickly and easily for any purpose, including payments of creditors' claims.

Existing unused lines of credit are *disclosed* in notes accompanying the financial statements. See Note 2 to the financial statements in Exhibit 14–10. Short-term creditors would view Seacliff's $35,000 line of credit as enhancing the company's liquidity.

CASH FLOW ANALYSIS

We often have stressed the importance of a company's being able to generate sufficient cash flows from its operations. In 2014, Seacliff generated net cash flows of $95,000 from its operating activities—a relatively "normal" amount, considering that net income for the year was $90,000. This $95,000 remained *after* payment of interest to creditors and amounted to more than three times the dividends paid to stockholders. In 2014 the net cash flows from operating activities appeared quite sufficient to ensure that Seacliff could pay its interest obligations and also pay dividends.

In 2015, however, net cash flows from operating activities declined to $19,000, an amount far below the company's $75,000 net income and only approximately 58 percent of the amount of dividends paid. Stockholders and creditors would view this dramatic decline in cash flows as a negative and potentially dangerous development.

A reconciliation of Seacliff's net income in 2015 with its net cash flows from operating activities is shown in Exhibit 14–24. For purposes of this analysis, we assume that the notes payable to creditors resulted from purchases from suppliers rather than loans from a financial institution. Therefore, the increase in notes payable is treated in the same way as the increase in accounts payable as part of the reconciliation of net income to net cash from operating activities. Had the notes payable resulted from borrowing activities, the change would be classified as a financing activity and not as an adjustment to net income in determining net cash from operating activities.

EXHIBIT 14–24

Seacliff Reconciliation of Net Income to Net Cash from Operating Activities

Net income		$ 75,000
Add:		
Depreciation expense	$30,000	
Increase in notes payable to creditors	4,600	
Increase in accounts payable	36,000	70,600
		$145,600
Less:		
Increase in accounts receivable	$31,000	
Increase in inventories	60,000	
Increase in prepaid expenses	13,000	
Decrease in accrued liabilities	22,600	126,600
Net cash flows from operating activities		$ 19,000

As explained in Chapter 13, the FASB requires companies to provide this reconciliation either in the body of the statement of cash flows or in a supplemental schedule.

The primary reasons for Seacliff's low net operating cash flows appear to be the growth in uncollected accounts receivable and inventories, combined with the substantial reduction in accrued liabilities. Given the significant increase in sales during 2015, the increase in accounts receivable is to be expected. The large reduction in accrued liabilities may be a one-time event that will not necessarily recur next year. The large increase in inventory, however, may have reduced Seacliff's liquidity unnecessarily.

Seacliff's financial position, particularly its short-term liquidity, would appear considerably stronger if its increased sales volume were supported by a higher *inventory turnover rate,* instead of a larger inventory.

Cash Flows from Operations to Current Liabilities
An additional measure of liquidity that is sometimes computed, based in part on information from the statement of cash flows, is the ratio of cash flows from operations to current liabilities. This measure provides evidence of the company's ability to cover its currently maturing liabilities from normal operations. For 2010 and 2011, the ratio is computed for Seacliff Corporation in Exhibit 14–25.

	2015	2014
Cash flows from operations	(a) $ 19,000	$95,000
Current liabilities	(b) $112,000	$94,000
Cash flows from operations to current liabilities (a ÷ b)	0.17	1.01

EXHIBIT 14–25
Cash Flows from Operations to Current Liabilities

As you can see from this measure, Seacliff was much stronger in 2014 than in 2015. In 2014, operating cash flows were slightly more than current liabilities at year-end, indicating an ability to cover current obligations from normal operations without regard to the amount of existing current assets. In 2015, however, operations provided only 17 percent as much cash as needed to meet current obligations, implying a need to rely more heavily on existing current assets than in 2014. Some analysts consider a ratio of cash flows from operations to current liabilities of 0.40 or higher to be strong.

USEFULNESS OF NOTES TO FINANCIAL STATEMENTS

A set of financial statements normally is accompanied by several *notes,* disclosing information useful in *interpreting* the statements. Users should view these notes as an *integral part* of the financial statements.

In preceding chapters we have identified many items that are disclosed in notes accompanying the financial statements. Among the most useful are the following:

- Accounting policies and methods.
- Unused lines of credit.
- Significant commitments and loss contingencies.
- Current values of financial instruments (if different from the carrying values shown in the statements).
- Dividends in arrears.
- Concentrations of credit risk.
- Assets pledged to secure specific liabilities.

In Exhibit 14–10 the notes accompanying Seacliff's financial statements are quite clean—that is, they contain no surprises or cause for concern. Of course, the unused line of credit disclosed in Note 2 would be of interest to anyone evaluating the company's short-term debt-paying ability.

 YOUR TURN   You as a Financial Analyst

Assume that you are a financial analyst and that two of your clients are requesting your advice on certain companies as potential investments. Both clients are interested in purchasing common stock. One is primarily interested in the dividends to be received from the investment. The second is primarily interested in the growth of the market value of the stock. What information would you advise your clients to focus on in their respective analyses?

(See our comments on the Online Learning Center website.)

INTERNATIONAL FINANCIAL REPORTING STANDARDS

As you have learned throughout this text, an effort is currently under way to standardize financial reporting practices worldwide. During this period of transition, which is expected to require several years, analyzing financial statements that originate in different countries poses a significant challenge due to differences in reporting practices. There exist many different local standards, as in the United States, and there are emerging international standards which are rapidly being accepted in various countries.

Two areas of particular interest in analyzing financial statements are consolidated statements and segment reporting. Earlier in this chapter, we briefly covered consolidated financial statements; where there are strong financial connections (e.g., overlapping ownership) between or among two or more companies, those companies typically present consolidated financial statements. This means that they report as a single entity rather than as separate entities, although legally they may be recognized as separate entities. At the present time, there is no single agreed-upon criterion for when consolidated financial statements should be prepared. This makes comparisons difficult because of the significant impact preparing consolidated statements has on the information provided when compared with presenting information about each separate entity.

Segment reporting refers to the presentation of information about parts of a business, usually along industry or product lines and geographic areas. Because risks that companies take vary considerably by industry and location, accounting standards require companies to provide supplemental information that informs investors and creditors of the extent of contribution a company's operations in different industries and in different geographic areas to the totals found in the primary financial statements. Some of the differences that exist around the world among individual country standards and between those standards and international standards deal with the definitions used in presenting segment information, the criteria used to identify segments for which disclosure is required, and the specific information that must be presented when disclosure is required.

Policies regarding consolidated financial statements and segment reporting are only two of the many areas the financial statement analyst must be aware of in approaching financial statements from different parts of the world. The authors are confident that, over time, we will move toward greater standardization for these and other aspects of financial reporting so that, in the future, we will be able to place even greater reliance than today on the comparability of financial statements worldwide.

SUMMARY OF ANALYTICAL MEASUREMENTS

The financial ratios and other measurements introduced in this textbook thus far, including this chapter—and their significance—are summarized in Exhibit 14–26.

EXHIBIT 14–26 Summary of Analytical Measures

Ratios or Other Measurements	Method of Computation	Significance
Measures of short-term liquidity		
Current ratio	$\dfrac{\text{Current Assets}}{\text{Current Liabilities}}$	A measure of short-term debt-paying ability
Quick ratio	$\dfrac{\text{Quick Assets}}{\text{Current Liabilities}}$	A measure of short-term debt-paying ability
Working capital	Current Assets − Current Liabilities	A measure of short-term debt-paying ability
Net cash provided by operating activities	Appears in the statement of cash flows	Indicates the cash generated by operations after allowing for cash payment of expenses and operating liabilities
Cash flow from operations to current liabilities	$\dfrac{\text{Cash Flows from Operating Activities}}{\text{Current Liabilities}}$	Indicates ability to cover currently maturing obligations from recurring operations
Accounts receivable turnover rate	$\dfrac{\text{Net Sales}}{\text{Average Accounts Receivable}}$	Indicates how quickly receivables are collected
Days to collect average accounts receivable	$\dfrac{\text{365 Days}}{\text{Accounts Receivable Turnover Rate}}$	Indicates in days how quickly receivables are collected
Inventory turnover rate	$\dfrac{\text{Cost of Goods Sold}}{\text{Average Inventory}}$	Indicates how quickly inventory sells

Ratios or Other Measurements	Method of Computation	Significance
Days to sell the average inventory	$\dfrac{\text{365 Days}}{\text{Inventory Turnover Rate}}$	Indicates in days how quickly inventory sells
Operating cycle	Days to Sell Inventory + Days to Collect Receivables	Indicates in days how quickly cash invested in inventory converts back into cash
Free cash flow	Net Cash from Operating Activities − Cash Used for Investing Activities and Dividends	Excess of operating cash flow over basic needs
Measures of long-term credit risk		
Debt ratio	$\dfrac{\text{Total Liabilities}}{\text{Total Assets}}$	Percentage of assets financed by creditors; indicates relative size of the equity position
Trend in net cash provided by operating activities	Appears in comparative statements of cash flows	Indicator of a company's ability to generate the cash necessary to meet its obligations
Interest coverage ratio	$\dfrac{\text{Income before Interest and Taxes}}{\text{Annual Interest Expense}}$	Indicator of a company's ability to meet its interest payment obligations
Measures of profitability		
Percentage changes; that is, in net sales and net income	$\dfrac{\text{Dollar Amount of Change}}{\text{Financial Statement Amount in the Earlier Year}}$	The rate at which a key measure is increasing or decreasing; the "growth rate"
Gross profit rate	$\dfrac{\text{Gross Profit}}{\text{Net Sales}}$	A measure of the profitability of the company's products
Operating expense ratio	$\dfrac{\text{Operating Expenses}}{\text{Net Sales}}$	A measure of management's ability to control expenses
Operating income	Gross Profit − Operating Expenses	The profitability of a company's basic business activities
Net income as a percentage of net sales	$\dfrac{\text{Net Income}}{\text{Net Sales}}$	An indicator of management's ability to control costs
Earnings per share	$\dfrac{\text{Net Income − Preferred Dividends}}{\text{Average Number of Common Shares Outstanding}}$	Net income applicable to each share of common stock
Return on assets	$\dfrac{\text{Operating Income}}{\text{Average Total Assets}}$	A measure of the productivity of assets, regardless of how the assets are financed
Return on equity	$\dfrac{\text{Net Income}}{\text{Average Total Equity}}$	The rate of return earned on the stockholders' equity in the business
Return on common stockholders' equity	$\dfrac{\text{Net Income − Preferred Dividends}}{\text{Average Common Stockholders' Equity}}$	The rate of return earned on the common stockholders' equity; appropriate when company has both common and preferred stock
Measures for evaluating the current market price of common stock		
Market value of financial instruments	Quoted in financial press or disclosed in financial statements	Reflects both investors' expectations and current market conditions
Price-earnings ratio	$\dfrac{\text{Current Stock Price}}{\text{Earnings per Share}}$	A measure of investors' expectations about the company's future prospects
Dividend yield	$\dfrac{\text{Annual Dividend}}{\text{Current Stock Price}}$	Dividends expressed as a rate of return on the market price of the stock
Book value per share	$\dfrac{\text{Common Stockholders' Equity}}{\text{Shares of Common Stock Outstanding}}$	The recorded value of net assets underlying each share of common stock

Ethics, Fraud, & Corporate Governance

The tools discussed in this chapter involve using financial statement information to help make investment and credit decisions. Given the high-profile accounting frauds of the early 2000s and the resulting focus on corporate governance, a new type of tool has arisen to help investors and creditors make investment decisions. This new tool involves ratings of the quality of a company's corporate governance. Many investors and creditors believe that better-governed firms are better managed, and that these firms will either offer superior performance (returns) over time and/or will offer returns comparable to less well governed firms but with less risk.

A number of organizations provide ratings of corporate governance quality for public companies. Two of the most prominent of these organizations are **ISS Governance Services**, a unit of **Risk Metrics Group**, and **The Corporate Library (TCL)** (Portland, Maine).

ISS Governance Services describes itself as "a leader in proxy voting and corporate governance matters." **ISS** provides coverage of a large number of shareholder meetings across many markets, serving institutional and corporate clients. These clients hire **ISS** to analyze corporate proxy statements and to make recommendations on the manner in which these institutional and corporate clients should vote on matters subject to shareholder ratification.

ISS rates the quality of a company's corporate governance by computing a Corporate Governance Quotient (CGQ). **ISS** computes CGQs for more than 7,500 companies worldwide. A company's CGQ is based on its ratings in these eight core categories: (1) board structure and composition, (2) audit issues, (3) charter and bylaw provisions, (4) laws of the state of incorporation, (5) executive and director compensation, (6) progressive practices, (7) D&O stock ownership, and (8) director education.

The Corporate Library (TCL) is a more recent entrant into the market for rating governance effectiveness. Unlike **ISS**, **TCL** claims that its proprietary dynamic indicators go beyond conventional benchmarks for good corporate governance. Many rating systems are based on a company's compliance with governance practices perceived as best practices; **TCL** attempts to differentiate its rating system by focusing only on those board characteristics that its proprietary research has found to be associated with preserving and enhancing shareholder wealth. **TCL** considers a company's governance in four key areas: (1) board composition and succession planning, (2) CEO compensation practices, (3) takeover defenses, and (4) board level accounting concerns.

Concluding Remarks

For the most part, our discussion in this chapter has been limited to the kinds of analysis that can be performed by external users who do not have access to the company's accounting records. Investors and creditors must rely to a considerable extent on the financial statements published in annual and quarterly reports. In the case of publicly owned corporations, additional information is filed with the Securities and Exchange Commission (SEC) and is available to the public in hard copy, as well as on the Internet. In fact, the Internet is the fastest growing source of *free* information available to decision makers in this information age.

Many financial analysts who evaluate the financial statements and future prospects of publicly owned companies sell their conclusions and investment advice for a fee. For example, detailed financial analyses of most large companies are available from **Standard & Poor's**, **Moody's Investors Service**, and **The Value Line Investment Survey**. Anyone may subscribe to these investment services.

Bankers and major creditors usually are able to obtain detailed financial information from borrowers simply by requesting it as a condition for granting a loan. Suppliers and other trade creditors may obtain some financial information about almost any business from credit-rating agencies, such as **Dun & Bradstreet**.

Stock prices, like p/e ratios, are a *measure of investors' expectations*. A company may be highly profitable and growing fast. But if investors had expected even better performance, the market price of its stock may decline. Similarly, if a troubled company's losses are smaller than expected, the price of its stock may rise.

In financial circles, evaluating stock price by looking at the underlying profitability of the company is termed **fundamental analysis**. This approach to investing works better in the long run than in the short run. In the short run, stock prices can be significantly affected by many factors, including short-term interest rates, current events, political events, fads, and rumors. But in the long run, good companies increase in value.

END-OF-CHAPTER REVIEW

LO14-1 **Explain the uses of dollar and percentage changes, trend percentages, component percentages, and ratios.** An important aspect of financial statement analysis is determining relevant relationships among specific items of information. Companies typically present financial information for more than one time period, which permits users of the information to make comparisons that help them understand changes over time. Dollar and percentage changes and trend percentages are tools for comparing information from successive time periods. Component percentages and ratios, on the other hand, are tools for establishing relationships and making comparisons within an accounting period. Both types of comparisons are important in understanding an enterprise's financial position, results of operations, and cash flows.

LO14-2 **Discuss the quality of a company's earnings, assets, and working capital. Assessing the quality of** information is an important aspect of financial statement analysis. Enterprises have significant latitude in the selection of financial reporting methods within generally accepted accounting principles. Assessing the quality of a company's earnings, assets, and working capital is done by evaluating the accounting methods selected for use in preparing financial statements. Management's choice of accounting principles and methods that are in the best long-term interests of the company, even though they may currently result in lower net income, reported total assets, or working capital, leads to a conclusion of high quality in reported accounting information.

LO14-3 **Explain the nature and purpose of classifications in financial statements.** In classified financial statements, items with certain common characteristics are placed together in a group, or classification. The purpose of these classifications is to develop subtotals that will assist users in analyzing the financial statements.

LO14-4 **Prepare a classified balance sheet and compute widely used measures of liquidity and credit risk.** In a classified balance sheet, assets are subdivided into the categories of current assets, plant and equipment, and other assets. Liabilities are classified either as current or long-term.

The liquidity measures derived from the balance sheet are as follows:

Working capital. Current assets minus current liabilities.

Current ratio. Current assets divided by current liabilities.

Quick ratio. Quick assets divided by current liabilities.

A measure of long-term credit risk is the debt ratio, which is total liabilities expressed as a percentage of (divided by) total assets.

LO14-5 **Prepare a multiple-step and a single-step income statement and compute widely used measures of profitability.** In a multiple-step income statement, cost of goods sold is deducted from net sales to provide the subtotal, gross profit. Operating expenses then are deducted to arrive at income from operations. As a final step, nonoperating items are added together and subtracted from income from operations to arrive at net income. In a single-step income statement, all revenue items are listed first, and then all expenses are combined and deducted from total revenue.

The profitability measures discussed in this chapter are as follows:

Percentage change. The dollar amount of change in a financial statement item from one period to the next, expressed as a percentage of (divided by) the item value in the earlier of the two periods being compared.

Gross profit rate. Dollar amount of gross profit divided by net sales. A measure of the profitability of a company's products.

Net income as a percentage of sales. Net income divided by net sales. A measure of management's ability to control expenses.

Earnings per share. In the simplest case, net income divided by shares of capital stock outstanding. Indicates the earnings applicable to each share of stock.

Price-earnings ratio. Market price of the stock divided by earnings per share. A measure of investors' expectations regarding future profitability.

Return on assets. Operating income divided by average total assets. Measures the return generated by assets, regardless of how the assets are financed.

Return on equity. Net income divided by average total equity. Indicates the rate of return earned on owners' equity.

LO14-6 **Put a company's net income into perspective by relating it to sales, assets, and stockholders' equity.** Financial accounting information is most useful if viewed in comparison with other relevant information. Net income is an important measure of the financial success of an enterprise. To make the amount of net income even more useful than if it were viewed simply in isolation, it is often compared with the sales from which net income results, the assets used to generate the income, and the amount of stockholders' equity invested by owners to earn the net income.

LO14-7 **Compute the ratios widely used in financial statement analysis and explain the significance of each. Ratios are mathematical calculations that** compare one financial statement item with another financial statement item. The two items may come from the same financial statement, such as the current ratio, which compares the amount of current assets with the amount of current liabilities, both of which appear in the statement of financial position (balance sheet). On the other hand, the elements of some ratios come from different financial statements, such as the return on stockholders' equity, which compares net income from the income statement with the amount of stockholders' equity from the statement of financial position (balance sheet). Accountants and financial analysts have developed many ratios that place information from a company's financial statements in a context to permit better understanding to support decision making.

LO14-8 **Analyze financial statements from the viewpoints of common stockholders, creditors, and others.** Different groups of users of financial statements are interested in different aspects of a company's financial activities. Short-term creditors are interested primarily in the

company's ability to make cash payments in the short term; they focus their attention on operating cash flows and current assets and liabilities. Long-term creditors, on the other hand, are more interested in the company's long-term ability to pay interest and principal and would not limit their analysis to the company's ability to make cash payments in the immediate future. The focus of common stockholders can vary from one investor to another, but generally stockholders are interested in the company's ability to pay dividends and increase the market value of the stock of the company. Each group may focus on different information in the financial statements to meet its unique objectives.

Key Terms Introduced or Emphasized In Chapter 14

annual report (p. 633)   A document issued annually by publicly owned companies to their stockholders. Includes audited comparative financial statements, management's discussion and analysis of performance and liquidity, and other information about the company.

classified financial statements (p. 624)   Financial statements in which similar items are arranged in groups, and subtotals are shown to assist users in analyzing the statements.

comparative financial statements (p. 624)   Financial statements of one company for two or more years presented in a side-by-side format to facilitate comparison.

consolidated financial statements (p. 624)   Financial statements that show the combined activities of a parent company and its subsidiaries.

current assets (p. 629)   Cash and other assets that can be converted into cash or used up within one year or the operating cycle (whichever is longer) without interfering with normal business operations.

current liabilities (p. 631)   Existing liabilities that are expected to be satisfied by using the enterprise's current assets.

current ratio (p. 631)   Current assets divided by current liabilities. A measure of short-term debt-paying ability.

debt ratio (p. 632)   Total liabilities divided by total assets. Represents the portion of total assets financed by debt, rather than by equity capital.

earnings per share (p. 638)   Net income expressed on a per-share basis.

fundamental analysis (p. 657)   Evaluating the reasonableness of a company's stock price by evaluating the performance and financial strength of the company.

management's discussion and analysis (p. 633)   A discussion by management of the company's performance during the current year and its financial position at year-end. These discussions are included in the annual reports of publicly owned companies.

market share (p. 636)   A company's percentage share of total dollar sales within its industry.

operating cycle (p. 630)   The time required to invest cash in inventory, sell the inventory, and collect the receivable, resulting in an increase in cash.

operating income (p. 636)   A subtotal in a multiple-step income statement representing the income resulting from the company's principal business activities.

parent company (p. 624)   A corporation that does portions of its business through other companies that it owns (termed *subsidiaries*).

percentage change (p. 636)   The change in a dollar amount between two accounting periods, expressed as a percentage of the amount in an earlier period. Used in evaluating rates of growth (or decline).

price-earnings (p/e) ratio (p. 638)   The current market price of a company's capital stock, expressed as a multiple of earnings per share. Reflects investors' expectations regarding future earnings.

quick assets (p. 632)   The most liquid current assets, which include only cash, marketable securities, and receivables.

quick ratio (p. 632)   Quick assets (cash, marketable securities, and receivables) divided by current liabilities. A measure of short-term debt-paying ability. (Sometimes referred to as the acid-test ratio.)

return on assets (p. 640)   Operating income expressed as a percentage of average total assets. A measure of the efficiency with which management utilizes the assets of a business.

return on equity (p. 640)   Net income expressed as a percentage of average total stockholders' equity. A measure of the rate of return earned on the stockholders' equity in the business.

subsidiary (p. 624)   A company that is owned and operated by a parent company. In essence, the subsidiary is a part of the parent organization.

window dressing (p. 633)   Measures taken by management to make a business look as strong as possible at the balance sheet date.

working capital (p. 631)   Current assets less current liabilities. A measure of short-term debt-paying ability.

Demonstration Problem

The following data are adapted from a recent annual report of Walgreen Drug Stores (dollar amounts are stated in millions):

	2012	2011
Balance sheet data:		
Quick assets	$ 3,464	$ 4,053
Current assets	10,760	12,322
Current liabilities	8,722	8,083
Stockholders' equity	18,236	14,847
Total assets	33,462	27,454
Income statement data:		
Net sales	$71,633	$72,184
Gross profit	20,342	20,492
Operating income	3,464	4,365
Net earnings	2,127	2,714

Instructions

a. Compute the following for 2012 and 2011. (Round to one decimal place.)

1. Working capital
2. Current ratio
3. Quick ratio

b. Comment on the trends in the liquidity measures and state whether Walgreen appears to be able to satisfy its liabilities at the end of 2012.

c. Compute the percentage changes for 2012 in the amounts of net sales and net income. (Round to one-tenth of 1 percent.)

d. Compute the following for 2012 and 2011. (Round to one-tenth of 1 percent. For items **3** and **4,** use the year-end amounts stated above as substitutes for average assets and average stockholders' equity.)

1. Gross profit rate
2. Net income as a percentage of sales
3. Return on assets
4. Return on stockholders' equity

e. Comment on the trends in the profitability measures computed in parts **c** and **d.**

Solution to the Demonstration Problem

a.

		2012	2011
1.	**Working capital:**		
	$10,760 − $8,722	$2,038	
	$12,322 − $8,083		$4,239
2.	**Current ratio:**		
	$10,760 ÷ $8,722	1.23 to 1	
	$12,322 ÷ $8,083		1.52 to 1
3.	**Quick ratio:**		
	$3,464 ÷ $8,722	0.40 to 1	
	$4,053 ÷ $8,083		0.50 to 1

b. Working capital during 2012 decreased $2,201 million, from $4,239 million to $2,038 million. The current ratio decreased from 1.52 to 1.23. The quick ratio decreased from 0.50 to 0.40. The relatively low quick ratio may be of some concern in terms of the company's ability to satisfy its future obligations.

c. Percentage change from 2011:

	2012
Net sales: [($71,633 − $72,184) ÷ $72,184]	−.8%
Net income: [($2,127 − $2,714) ÷ $2,714]	−21.6%

d.

		2012	2011
1.	**Gross profit rate:**		
	$20,342 ÷ $71,633	28.4%	
	$20,492 ÷ $72,184		28.4%
2.	**Net income as a percentage of sales:**		
	$2,127 ÷ $71,633	3.0%	
	$2,714 ÷ $72,184		3.8%
3.	**Return on assets:**		
	$3,464 ÷ $33,462	10.4%	
	$4,365 ÷ $27,454		15.9%
4.	**Return on equity:**		
	$2,172 ÷ $18,236	11.9%	
	$2,714 ÷ $14,847		18.3%

e. Profitability indicators are generally negative.

- Both net sales and net earnings decreased.
- The gross profit rate was unchanged (28.4%).
- Net income as a percentage of sales decreased by 0.8% (3.8% to 3.0%).
- Return on assets decreased by 5.5% (15.9% to 10.4%).
- Return on equity decreased by 6.4% (18.3% to 11.9%).

While some of the percentage changes are relatively small, they are applied to very large dollar amounts, resulting in relatively large dollar changes. Small percentage improvements in these key financial statement numbers can render significant improvements in the company's financial performance. Perhaps the most concerning is the significant decline in net income on only a modest decline in net sales.

Self-Test Questions

The answers to these questions appear on page 681.

1. Which of the following usually is *least* important as a measure of short-term liquidity?
   a. Quick ratio.
   b. Current ratio.
   c. Debt ratio.
   d. Cash flows from operating activities.

2. In each of the past five years, the net sales of Plaza Co. have increased at about half the rate of inflation, but net income has increased at approximately *twice* the rate of inflation. During this period, the company's total assets, liabilities, and equity have remained almost unchanged; dividends are approximately equal to net income. These relationships suggest (indicate all correct answers):
   a. Management is successfully controlling costs and expenses.
   b. The company is selling more merchandise every year.
   c. The annual return on assets has been increasing.
   d. Financing activities are likely to result in a net use of cash.

3. From the viewpoint of a stockholder, which of the following relationships do you consider of *least* significance?

   a. Net income is greater than the amount of working capital.

   b. The return on assets consistently is higher than the industry average.

   c. The return on equity has increased in each of the past five years.

   d. The return on assets is greater than the rate of interest being paid to creditors.

4. The following information is available from the annual report of Frixell, Inc.:

Current assets	$ 480,000	Current liabilities	$300,000
Average total assets	2,000,000	Operating income	240,000
Average total equity	800,000	Net income	80,000

   Which of the following statements are correct? (More than one statement may be correct.)

   a. The return on equity exceeds the return on assets.

   b. The current ratio is 0.625 to 1.

   c. Working capital is $1,200,000.

   d. None of the above answers is correct.

5. Evans Corporation's net income was $400,000 in 2014 and $160,000 in 2015. What percentage increase in net income must Evans achieve in 2016 to offset the decline in profits in 2015?

   a. 60%.

   b. 150%.

   c. 600%.

   d. 67%.

6. If a company's current ratio declined in a year during which its quick ratio improved, which of the following is the most likely explanation?

   a. Inventory is increasing.

   b. Receivables are being collected more slowly than in the past.

   c. Receivables are being collected more rapidly than in the past.

   d. Inventory is declining.

7. In financial statement analysis, the most difficult of the following items to predict is whether:

   a. The company will be liquid in six months.

   b. The company's market share is increasing or declining.

   c. The market price of capital stock will rise or fall over the next two months.

   d. Profits have increased since the previous year.

ASSIGNMENT MATERIAL   Discussion Questions

1. In financial statement analysis, what is the basic objective of observing trends in data and ratios? Suggest some standards of comparison.

2. In financial statement analysis, what information is produced by computing a ratio that is not available in a simple observation of the underlying data?

3. Distinguish between *trend percentages* and *component percentages*. Which would be better suited for analyzing the change in sales over several years?

4. Differentiate between *horizontal* and *vertical* analysis.

5. What is the basic purpose of *classifications* in financial statements? Identify the classifications widely used in a balance sheet, a multiple-step income statement, and a statement of cash flows.

6. Distinguish between the terms *classified, comparative,* and *consolidated* as they apply to financial statements. May a given set of financial statements have more than one of these characteristics?

7. What is the characteristic common to all *current assets?* Many retail stores regularly sell merchandise on installment plans, calling for payments over a period of 24 or 36 months. Do such receivables qualify as current assets? Explain.

8. Identify four ratios or other analytical tools used to evaluate profitability. Explain briefly how each is computed.

9. Distinguish between *operating income* and *net income.*

10. Why might earnings per share be more significant to a stockholder in a large corporation than the total amount of net income?

11. Assume that Congress announces its intention to limit the prices and profits of pharmaceutical companies as part of an effort to control health care costs. What effect would you expect this announcement to have on the p/e ratios and stock prices of pharmaceutical companies such as Merck and Bristol-Myers Squibb? Explain.

12. Under what circumstances might a company have a high p/e ratio even when investors are *not* optimistic about the company's future prospects?

13. Moffett Company earned a 16 percent return on its total assets. Current liabilities are 10 percent of total assets. Long-term bonds carrying an 11 percent coupon rate are equal to

30 percent of total assets. There is no preferred stock. Is this application of leverage favorable or unfavorable from the viewpoint of Moffett's stockholders?

14. Mei Co. has a current ratio of 3 to 1. Ono Corp. has a current ratio of 2 to 1. Does this mean that Mei's operating cycle is longer than Ono's? Why?

15. An investor states, "I bought this stock for $50 several years ago and it now sells for $100. It paid $5 per share in dividends last year so I'm earning 10 percent on my investment." Evaluate this statement.

Brief Exercises

LO14-1

BRIEF EXERCISE 14.1

Dollar and Percentage Change

Galaxy Company had net sales of $150,000 in its first year and $189,500 in its second year. Calculate the amount of change in terms of both dollars and percentage.

LO14-1

BRIEF EXERCISE 14.2

Trend Percentages

Star, Inc., had depreciation expenses on its plant assets as follows for 2013, 2014, and 2015, respectively: $267,000, $289,000, and $368,000. Compute the trend percentages for these years, assuming 2013 is the base year.

LO14-1

BRIEF EXERCISE 14.3

Component Percentages

Moon, Inc., had the following income statement figures:

Sales	$560,000
Cost of sales	(340,000)
Gross margin	$220,000
Operating expenses	(160,000)
Net income	$ 60,000

Calculate component percentages for this information.

LO14-4

BRIEF EXERCISE 14.4

Working Capital and Current Ratio

Harrisonburg Company had current and total assets of $470,000 and $1,000,000, respectively. The company's current and total liabilities were $267,000 and $600,000, respectively. Calculate the amount of working capital and the current ratio using this information.

LO14-4

BRIEF EXERCISE 14.5

Current and Quick Ratio

Foster Company had current assets and current liabilities as follows:

Current assets:	
Cash	$ 50,000
Accounts receivable	80,000
Inventory	125,000
Current liabilities:	
Accrued expenses	$ 25,000
Accounts payable	110,000
Current portion of long-term debt	56,000

Calculate the current and quick ratios using the information provided.

LO14-4
BRIEF EXERCISE 14.6
Debt Ratio

Jarman Company had current and noncurrent liabilities of $50,000 and $160,000, respectively. The company's current assets were $76,000, out of a total asset figure of $457,000. Calculate the company's debt ratio.

LO14-6
BRIEF EXERCISE 14.7
Net Income as Percentage of Sales

Lone Star, Inc., reported sales of $560,000, cost of sales of $255,000, and operating expenses of $130,000 for the current year. Using this information, calculate the amount of net income and net income as a percentage of sales.

LO14-6
BRIEF EXERCISE 14.8
Earnings Per Share

Multi-Star, Inc., had sales of $890,000, cost of sales and operating expenses of $450,000 and $225,000, respectively, and 10,000 shares of common stock outstanding. Calculate the amount of earnings per share.

LO14-7
BRIEF EXERCISE 14.9
Return on Assets

Flanders Company's operating income for the current year was $475,000. The company's average total assets for the same period were $3,500,000, and its total liabilities were $1,000,000. Calculate the company's return on assets.

LO14-7
BRIEF EXERCISE 14.10
Return on Equity

Prince Company had net income of $45,500 in a year when its stockholders' equity averaged $450,000 and its total assets averaged $2,500,000. Calculate the company's return on equity for the period.

Exercises

LO14-1
EXERCISE 14.1
Percentages Changes

Selected information taken from the financial statements of Wiley Company for two successive years follows. You are to compute the percentage change from 2014 to 2015 whenever possible. Round all calculations to the nearest whole percentage.

		2015	2014
a.	Accounts receivable	$126,000	$160,000
b.	Marketable securities	–0–	250,000
c.	Retained earnings	80,000	(80,000)
d.	Notes receivable	120,000	–0–
e.	Notes payable	890,000	800,000
f.	Cash	84,000	80,000
g.	Sales	970,000	910,000

LO14-1
EXERCISE 14.2
Trend Percentages

Compute *trend percentages* for the following items taken from the financial statements of Lopez Plumbing over a five-year period. Treat 2011 as the base year. State whether the trends are favorable or unfavorable. (Dollar amounts are stated in thousands.)

	2015	2014	2013	2012	2011
Sales	$81,400	$74,000	$61,500	$59,000	$50,000
Cost of goods sold	58,500	48,000	40,500	37,000	30,000

LO14-1
EXERCISE 14.3
Common Size Income Statements

Prepare *common size* income statements for Price Company, a sole proprietorship, for the two years shown below by converting the dollar amounts into percentages. For each year, sales will appear as 100 percent and other items will be expressed as a percentage of sales. (Income taxes are not involved as the business is not incorporated.) Comment on whether the changes from 2014 to 2015 are favorable or unfavorable.

	2015	2014
Sales	$ 500,000	$400,000
Cost of goods sold	330,000	268,000
Gross profit	$ 170,000	$132,000
Operating expenses	125,000	116,000
Net income	$ 45,000	$ 16,000

LOI4-4

EXERCISE 14.4

Measures of Liquidity

Roy's Toys is a manufacturer of toys and children's products. The following are selected items appearing in a recent balance sheet (dollar amounts are in millions):

Cash and short-term investments	$ 47.3
Receivables	159.7
Inventories	72.3
Prepaid expenses and other current assets	32.0
Total current liabilities	130.1
Total liabilities	279.4
Total stockholders' equity	344.0

a. Using the information above, compute the amounts of Roy's Toys (1) quick assets and (2) total current assets.

b. Compute for Roy's Toys the (1) quick ratio, (2) current ratio, and (3) dollar amount of working capital. (Round ratios to one decimal place.)

c. Discuss whether Roy's Toys appears liquid from the viewpoint of a short-term creditor.

LOI4-5

EXERCISE 14.5

Multiple-Step Income Statements

SPINX, INC.
STATEMENT OF EARNINGS
FOR THE YEAR ENDED DECEMBER 31, 2015

Net sales	$4,395,253
Costs and expenses:	
Cost of goods sold	(2,821,455)
Operating expenses	(1,004,396)
Interest revenue	15,797
Earnings before income tax	$ 585,199
Income tax expense	(204,820)
Net earnings	$ 380,379
Earnings per share	$1.70

Comparative balance sheets report average total assets for the year of *$2,575,000* and average total equity of *$1,917,000* (dollar amounts in thousands, except earnings per share).

a. Prepare an income statement for the year in a multiple-step format.

b. Compute the (1) gross profit rate, (2) net income as a percentage of net sales, (3) return on assets, and (4) return on equity for the year. (Round computations to the nearest one-tenth of 1 percent.)

c. Explain why interest revenue is not included in the company's gross profit computation.

LOI4-6

EXERCISE 14.6

ROI

Shown below are selected data from a recent annual report of **Kimberly-Clark Corporation**, a large consumer products provider. (Dollar amounts are in millions.)

	Beginning of the Year	End of the Year
Total assets	$19,373	$19,873
Total stockholders' equity	4,985	5,249
Operating income		2,686
Net income		1,828

a. Compute for the year **Kimberly-Clark**'s return on average total assets. (Round computations to the nearest two-tenths of 1 percent.)

b. Compute for the year **Kimberly-Clark**'s return on average total stockholders' equity. (Round computations to the nearest two-tenths of 1 percent.)

c. What is the most likely explanation why **Kimberly-Clark**'s total stockholders' equity for the year increased?

LOI4-1, LOI4-6

EXERCISE 14.7

Computing and Interpreting Rates of Change

Selected information from the financial statements of Remmer, Inc., includes the following:

	2015	2014
Net sales	$2,200,000	$2,000,000
Total expenses	2,005,000	1,800,000

a. Compute the percentage change in 2015 for the amounts of (**1**) net sales and (**2**) total expenses.

b. Using the information developed in part **a**, express your opinion as to whether the company's *net income* for 2015:

1. Increased at a greater or lower percentage rate than did net sales.

2. Represented a larger or smaller percentage of net sales revenue than in 2014. For each answer, explain your reasoning *without* making any computations or references to dollar amounts.

LOI4-6

EXERCISE 14.8

Research Problem

Obtain from your library, the Internet, or other source the most recent annual report of a publicly owned company of your choice.

a. Using the annual report data, compute the basic measures of liquidity, long-term credit risk, and profitability summarized in Exhibit 14–26. Compare these measures with the appropriate industry norms available in your library or other source. Briefly comment on your findings.

b. Using the financial pages of a daily newspaper (such as *The Wall Street Journal*), determine (**1**) the current market price of your company's common stock, (**2**) its 52-week high and low market prices, and (**3**) its p/e ratio. Briefly comment on your findings.

c. On the basis of your analysis in parts **a** and **b**, make a recommendation as to whether investors should buy shares of the stock, hold the shares they currently own, or sell the shares they currently own. Defend your position.

LOI4-3, LOI4-4, LOI4-6

EXERCISE 14.9

Home Depot, Inc., Management's Discussion and Analysis

The financial statements of large public companies are often accompanied by a multiple-year summary of key financial and other information that is helpful in understanding the company. Appendix A of this text includes the financial statements of **Home Depot, Inc.**, and selected other information from the company's 2012 annual report. Included is a five-year Summary of Financial and Operating Results for the period 2008–2012. Locate this summary in Appendix A and respond to the following.

a. Considering the "store data" section of the five-year summary, what conclusions can you draw about the change in size of **Home Depot, Inc.**, during the five-year period?

b. Comment on the five-year trend in net earnings as a percentage of sales and what this trend means to you as an investor in the company.

c. Has the company's liquidity improved or diminished over the five-year period? Justify your answer.

LO14-4, LO14-6
EXERCISE 14.10
Evaluating Employment
Opportunities

Assume that you will soon graduate from college and that you have job offers with two pharmaceutical firms. The first offer is with Alpha Research, a relatively new and aggressive company. The second is with Omega Scientific, a very well established and conservative company.

Financial information pertaining to each firm, and to the pharmaceutical industry as a whole, is as follows:

Financial Measure	Alpha	Omega	Industry Average
Current ratio	2.2 to 1	4.5 to 1	2.5 to 1
Quick ratio	1.2 to 1	2.8 to 1	1.5 to 1
Return on assets	17%	8%	10%
Return on equity	28%	14%	16%
P/e ratio	20 to 1	10 to 1	12 to 1

The Omega offer is for $46,000 per year. The Alpha offer is for $42,000. However, unlike Omega, Alpha awards its employees a stock option bonus based on profitability for the year. Each option enables the employee to purchase shares of Alpha's common stock at a significantly reduced price. The more profitable Alpha is, the more stock each employee can buy at a discount.

Show how the above information may help you justify accepting the Alpha Research offer, even though the starting salary is $4,000 lower than the Omega Scientific offer.

LO14-7
EXERCISE 14.11
Ratios for a Retail Store

Selected financial data for Quick Sell, Inc., a retail store, appear as follows:

	2015	2014
Sales (all on account)	$750,000	$610,000
Cost of goods sold	495,000	408,000
Average inventory during the year	110,000	102,000
Average receivables during the year	150,000	100,000

a. Compute the following for both years:
   1. Gross profit percentage.
   2. Inventory turnover.
   3. Accounts receivable turnover.

b. Comment on favorable and unfavorable trends.

LO14-7
EXERCISE 14.12
Computing Ratios

A condensed balance sheet for Bradford Corporation prepared at the end of the year appears as follows:

Assets		Liabilities & Stockholders' Equity	
Cash	$ 105,000	Notes payable (due in	$ 40,000
Accounts receivable	145,000	6 months)	
Inventory	270,000	Accounts payable	110,000
Prepaid expenses	60,000	Long-term liabilities	360,000
Plant & equipment (net)	570,000	Capital stock, $5 par	300,000
Other assets	90,000	Retained earnings	430,000
Total	$1,240,000	Total	$1,240,000

During the year the company earned a gross profit of $1,116,000 on sales of $2,950,000. Accounts receivable, inventory, and plant assets remained almost constant in amount throughout the year, so year-end figures may be used rather than averages.

Compute the following:

a. Current ratio.

b. Quick ratio.

c. Working capital.

d. Debt ratio.

e. Accounts receivable turnover (all sales were on credit).

f. Inventory turnover.

g. Book value per share of capital stock.

LO14-6, LO14-7

EXERCISE 14.13

Current Ratio, Debt Ratio, and Earnings per Share

Selected items from successive annual reports of Middlebrook, Inc., appear as follows:

	2015	2014
Total assets (40% of which are current)	$400,000	$325,000
Current liabilities	$ 80,000	$100,000
Bonds payable, 12%	100,000	50,000
Capital stock, $5 par value	100,000	100,000
Retained earnings	120,000	75,000
Total liabilities & stockholders' equity	$400,000	$325,000

Dividends of $16,000 were declared and paid in 2015.

Compute the following:

a. Current ratio for 2015 and 2014.

b. Debt ratio for 2015 and 2014.

c. Earnings per share for 2015.

LO14-7

EXERCISE 14.14

Ratio Analysis for Two Similar Companies

Selected data from the financial statements of Italian Marble Co. and Brazil Stone Products for the year just ended follow. Assume that for both companies dividends declared were equal in amount to net earnings during the year and therefore stockholders' equity did not change. The two companies are in the same line of business.

	Italian Marble Co.	Brazil Stone Products
Total liabilities	$ 200,000	$ 100,000
Total assets	800,000	400,000
Sales (all on credit)	1,800,000	1,200,000
Average inventory	240,000	140,000
Average receivables	200,000	100,000
Gross profit as a percentage of sales	40%	30%
Operating expenses as a percentage of sales	36%	25%
Net income as a percentage of sales	3%	5%

Compute the following for each company and state a brief conclusion about which company is in the stronger financial position.

a. Net income.

b. Net income as a percentage of stockholders' equity.

c. Accounts receivable turnover.

d. Inventory turnover.

LOI4-6, LOI4-7
EXERCISE 14.15
Ratio Analysis for Feature
Company

Johnson & Johnson's 2012 financial statements include the following items (all dollars in millions):

	2012	2011
Balance sheet		
Current assets	$46,116	$54,316
Current liabilities	24,262	22,811
Total assets	121,347	113,644
Income statement		
Sales	$67,224	$65,030
Gross profit	45,566	44,670
Net earnings (income)	10,514	9,672

Compute the following ratios and comment on the trend you can observe from the limited two years of data you have available.

a. Gross profit rate.

b. Net income as a percentage of sales.

c. Current ratio.

Problem Set A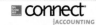

LOI4-I, LOI4-5
PROBLEM 14.1A
Comparing Operating
Results with Average
Performance in the Industry

Outdoor World, Inc., manufactures camping equipment. Shown below for the current year are the income statement for the company and a common size summary for the industry in which the company operates. (Notice that the percentages in the right-hand column are *not* for Outdoor World, Inc., but are average percentages for the industry.)

	Outdoor World, Inc.	Industry Average
Sales (net)	$20,000,000	100%
Cost of goods sold	9,800,000	58
Gross profit on sales	$10,200,000	42%
Operating expenses:		
Selling	$ 4,200,000	16%
General and administrative	3,400,000	20
Total operating expenses	$ 7,600,000	36%
Operating income	$ 2,600,000	6%
Income tax expense	1,200,000	3
Net income	$ 1,400,000	3%
Return on assets	23%	14%

Instructions

a. Prepare a two-column common size income statement. The first column should show for Outdoor World, Inc., all items expressed as a percentage of net sales. The second column should show the equivalent industry average for the data given in the problem. The purpose of this common size statement is to compare the operating results of Outdoor World, Inc., with the average for the industry.

b. Comment specifically on differences between Outdoor World, Inc., and the industry average with respect to gross profit on sales, selling expenses, general and administrative expenses, operating income, net income, and return on assets. Suggest possible reasons for the more important disparities.

LO14-3, LO14-5
PROBLEM 14.2A
Analysis to Identify Favorable and Unfavorable Trends

The following information was developed from the financial statements of Donelson, Inc. At the beginning of 2015, the company's former supplier went bankrupt, and the company began buying merchandise from another supplier.

	2015	2014
Gross profit on sales	$1,008,000	$1,134,000
Income before income tax	230,400	252,000
Net income	172,800	189,000
Net income as a percentage of net sales	6.0%	7.5%

Instructions

a. Compute the net sales for each year.

b. Compute the cost of goods sold in dollars and as a percentage of net sales for each year.

c. Compute operating expenses in dollars and as a percentage of net sales for each year. (Income taxes expense is not an operating expense.)

d. Prepare a condensed comparative income statement for 2014 and 2015. Include the following items: net sales, cost of goods sold, gross profit, operating expenses, income before income tax, income taxes expense, and net income. Omit earnings per share statistics.

e. Identify the significant favorable and unfavorable trends in the performance of Donelson, Inc. Comment on any unusual changes.

LO14-3, LO14-4
PROBLEM 14.3A
Measures of Liquidity

Some of the accounts appearing in the year-end financial statements of Rogand Grocery, Inc., appear below. This list includes all of the company's current assets and current liabilities.

Sales	$1,880,000
Accumulated depreciation: equipment	370,000
Notes payable (due in 90 days)	70,000
Retained earnings	241,320
Cash	69,400
Capital stock	150,000
Marketable securities	175,040
Accounts payable	128,100
Mortgage payable (due in 15 years)	320,000
Salaries payable	7,570
Dividends	25,000
Income taxes payable	14,600
Accounts receivable	230,540
Inventory	179,600
Unearned revenue	10,000
Unexpired insurance	4,500

Instructions

a. Prepare a schedule of the company's current assets and current liabilities. Select the appropriate items from the preceding list.

b. Compute the current ratio and the amount of working capital. Explain how each of these measurements is computed. State, with reasons, whether you consider the company to be in a strong or weak current position.

LOI4-3, LOI4-4, LOI4-7
PROBLEM 14.4A
Liquidity of Kroger

The Kroger Company is one of the world's largest supermarket chains. These selected items were adapted from a recent Kroger balance sheet. (Dollar amounts are in millions.)

Cash (including deposit-in-transit)	$1,193
Receivables	1,051
Merchandise inventories	5,146
Other current assets	569
Property, plant and equipment (net of depreciation)	14,875
Retained earnings	9,787
Total current liabilities	11,057

Instructions

a. Using the information above, compute the amounts of Kroger's total current assets and total quick assets.

b. Compute the company's (1) current ratio, (2) quick ratio, and (3) working capital. (Round ratios to two decimal points.)

c. From these computations, are you able to conclude whether Kroger is a good credit risk for short-term creditors or on the brink of bankruptcy? Explain.

d. Is there anything unusual about the operating cycle of supermarkets that would make you think that they normally would have lower current ratios than, say, large department stores?

e. What *other types of information* could you utilize in performing a more complete analysis of Kroger's liquidity?

LOI4-3, LOI4-4, LOI4-7
PROBLEM 14.5A
Balance Sheet Measures of Liquidity and Credit Risk

A recent balance sheet of Sweet Tooth, Inc., included the following items, among others. (Dollar amounts are stated in thousands.)

Cash	$ 50,230
Marketable securities (short-term)	55,926
Accounts receivable	23,553
Inventories	32,210
Prepaid expenses	5,736
Retained earnings	121,477
Notes payable to banks (due within one year)	20,000
Accounts payable	5,912
Dividends payable	1,560
Accrued liabilities (short-term)	21,532
Income taxes payable	6,438

The company also reported total assets of $353,816 thousand, total liabilities of $81,630 thousand, and a return on total assets of *18.1 percent.*

Instructions

a. Compute Sweet Tooth's (1) quick assets, (2) current assets, and (3) current liabilities.

b. Compute Sweet Tooth's (1) quick ratio, (2) current ratio, (3) working capital, and (4) debt ratio. (Round to one decimal place.)

c. Discuss the company's liquidity from the viewpoints of (1) short-term creditors, (2) long-term creditors, and (3) stockholders.

LO14-4, LO14-5, LO14-7

PROBLEM 14.6A

Financial Statement
Analysis

Shown below is selected information from the financial statements of Dickson, Inc., a retail
furniture store.

From the balance sheet:

Cash	$ 30,000
Accounts receivable	150,000
Inventory	200,000
Plant assets (net of accumulated depreciation)	500,000
Current liabilities	150,000
Total stockholders' equity	300,000
Total assets	1,000,000

From the income statement:

Net sales	$1,500,000
Cost of goods sold	1,080,000
Operating expenses	315,000
Interest expense	84,000
Income tax expense	6,000
Net income	15,000

From the statement of cash flows:

Net cash provided by operating activities		
(including interest paid of $79,000)		$ 40,000
Net cash used in investing activities		(46,000)
Financing activities:		
Amounts borrowed	$ 50,000	
Repayment of amounts borrowed	(14,000)	
Dividends paid	(20,000)	
Net cash provided by financing activities		16,000
Net increase in cash during the year		$ 10,000

Instructions

a. Explain how the interest expense shown in the income statement could be $84,000, when the
interest payment appearing in the statement of cash flows is only $79,000.

b. Compute the following (round to one decimal place):
1. Current ratio
2. Quick ratio
3. Working capital
4. Debt ratio

c. Comment on these measurements and evaluate Dickson, Inc.'s short-term debt-paying ability.

d. Compute the following ratios (assume that the year-end amounts of total assets and total
stockholders' equity also represent the average amounts throughout the year):
1. Return on assets
2. Return on equity

e. Comment on the company's performance under these measurements. Explain *why* the return
on assets and return on equity are so different.

f. Discuss (1) the apparent safety of long-term creditors' claims and (2) the prospects for
Dickson, Inc., continuing its dividend payments at the present level.

LOI4-4, LOI4-5, LOI4-7
PROBLEM 14.7A
Basic Ratio Analysis

Medtronics is a world leader in medical technology. The following selected data are adapted from a recent annual report. (Dollar amounts are stated in millions.)

	Beginning of the Year	End of the Year
Total current assets	$ 9,150	$ 9,515
Total current liabilities	4,726	5,857
Total assets	30,675	33,083
Total stockholders' equity	15,968	17,113
Operating income		4,145
Net income		3,617

The company has long-term liabilities that bear interest at annual rates ranging from 6 percent to 8 percent.

Instructions

a. Compute the company's current ratio at (1) the *beginning* of the year and (2) the *end* of the year. (Carry to two decimal places.)

b. Compute the company's working capital at (1) the beginning of the year and (2) the end of the year. (Express dollar amounts in thousands.)

c. Is the company's short-term debt-paying ability improving or deteriorating?

d. Compute the company's (1) return on average total assets and (2) return on average stockholders' equity. (Round average assets and average equity to the nearest dollar and final computations to the nearest 1 percent.)

e. As an equity investor, do you think that **Medtronic's** management is utilizing the company's resources in a reasonably efficient manner? Explain.

LOI4-5, LOI4-7
PROBLEM 14.8A
Ratios; Consider Advisability of Incurring Long-Term Debt

At the end of the year, the following information was obtained from the accounting records of Harrison Electronics, Inc.

Sales (all on credit)	$2,750,000
Cost of goods sold	1,781,000
Average inventory	375,000
Average accounts receivable	282,000
Interest expense	45,000
Income tax expense	84,000
Net income	159,000
Average investment in assets	1,800,000
Average stockholders' equity	895,000

Instructions

a. From the information given, compute the following:
   1. Inventory turnover.
   2. Accounts receivable turnover.
   3. Total operating expenses.
   4. Gross profit percentage.
   5. Return on average stockholders' equity.
   6. Return on average assets.

b. Harrison Electronics has an opportunity to obtain a long-term loan at an annual interest rate of 10 percent and could use this additional capital at the same rate of profitability as indicated by the given data. Would obtaining the loan be desirable from the viewpoint of the stockholders? Explain.

LO14-5, LO14-7, LO14-8
PROBLEM 14.9A

Ratios: Evaluation of Two Companies

Shown below are selected financial data for Another World and Imports, Inc., at the end of the current year:

	Another World	Imports, Inc.
Net credit sales	$675,000	$560,000
Cost of goods sold	504,000	480,000
Cash	53,000	22,000
Accounts receivable (net)	75,000	70,000
Inventory	84,000	160,000
Current liabilities	105,000	100,000

Assume that the year-end balances shown for accounts receivable and for inventory approximate the average balances of these items throughout the year.

Instructions

a. For each of the two companies, compute the following:
  1. Working capital.
  2. Current ratio.
  3. Quick ratio.
  4. Number of times inventory turned over during the year and the average number of days required to turn over inventory (round computation to the nearest day).
  5. Number of times accounts receivable turned over during the year and the average number of days required to collect accounts receivable (round computation to the nearest day).
  6. Operating cycle.

b. From the viewpoint of a short-term creditor, comment on the *quality* of each company's working capital. To which company would you prefer to sell $25,000 in merchandise on a 30-day open account?

Problem Set B

LO14-1, LO14-5
PROBLEM 14.1B

Comparing Operating Results with Average Performance in the Industry

Decor, Inc., manufactures bathroom equipment. Shown below for the current year are the income statements for the company and a common size summary for the industry in which the company operates. (Notice that the percentages in the right-hand column are *not* for Decor, Inc., but are average percentages for the industry.)

	Decor, Inc.	Industry Average
Sales (net)	$12,000,000	100%
Cost of goods sold	7,320,000	69
Gross profit on sales	$ 4,680,000	31%
Operating expenses:		
Selling	$ 1,800,000	10%
General and administrative	720,000	13
Total operating expenses	$ 2,520,000	23%
Operating income	$ 2,160,000	8%
Income tax expense	120,000	2
Net income	$ 2,040,000	6%
Return on assets	19%	12%

Instructions

a. Prepare a two-column common size income statement for Decor, Inc. The first column should show for Decor, Inc., all items expressed as a percentage of net sales. The second column should show the equivalent industry average for the data given in the problem. The purpose of this common size statement is to compare the operating results of Decor, Inc., with the average for the industry. (Round to the nearest percent.)

b. Comment specifically on differences between Decor, Inc., and the industry average with respect to gross profit on sales, selling expenses, general and administrative expenses, operating income, net income, and return on assets. Suggest possible reasons for the more important disparities.

LOI4-3, LOI4-5

PROBLEM 14.2B

Analysis to Identify Favorable and Unfavorable Trends

The following information was developed from the financial statements of Free Time, Inc. At the beginning of 2015, the company's former supplier went bankrupt, and the company began buying merchandise from another supplier.

	2015	2014
Gross profit on sales	$720,000	$800,000
Income before income tax	200,000	220,000
Net income	150,000	170,000
Net income as a percentage of net sales	8%	10%

Instructions

a. Compute the net sales for each year.

b. Compute the cost of goods sold in dollars and as a percentage of net sales for each year.

c. Compute operating expenses in dollars and as a percentage of net sales for each year. (Income taxes expense is not an operating expense.)

d. Prepare a condensed comparative income statement for 2014 and 2015. Include the following items: net sales, cost of goods sold, gross profit, operating expenses, income before income tax, income tax expense, and net income. Omit earnings per share statistics.

e. Identify the significant favorable and unfavorable trends in the performance of Free Time, Inc. Comment on any unusual changes.

LOI4-3, LOI4-4

PROBLEM 14.3B

Measures of Liquidity

Some of the accounts appearing in the year-end financial statements of Glaven, Inc., appear below. This list includes all of the company's current assets and current liabilities.

Sales	$2,500,000
Accumulated depreciation: equipment	180,000
Notes payable (due in 120 days)	85,000
Retained earnings	240,000
Cash	61,000
Capital stock	250,000
Marketable securities	175,000
Accounts payable	105,000
Mortgage payable (due in 20 years)	650,000
Salaries payable	7,200
Dividends	20,000
Income taxes payable	14,400
Accounts receivable	217,000
Inventory	195,000
Unearned revenue	15,000
Unexpired insurance	8,000

Instructions

a. Prepare a schedule of the company's current assets and current liabilities. Select the appropriate items from the above list.

b. Compute the current ratio and the amount of working capital. Explain how each of these measurements is computed. State, with reasons, whether you consider the company to be in a strong or weak current position.

LO14-3, LO14-4, LO14-7
PROBLEM 14.4B
Liquidity of Cheese, Inc.

Chezo, Inc., is a large cheese store chains. Shown below are selected items adapted from a recent Chezo, Inc., balance sheet. (Dollar amounts are in the millions.)

Cash	$ 72.4
Receivables	150.4
Merchandise inventories	1,400.0
Prepaid expenses	98.0
Fixtures and equipment	3,150.0
Retained earnings	295.0
Total current liabilities	2,500.0

Instructions

a. Using the information above, compute the amounts of Chezo's total current assets and total quick assets.

b. Compute the company's (1) current ratio, (2) quick ratio, and (3) working capital. (Round to two decimal places.)

c. From these computations, are you able to conclude whether Chezo is a good credit risk for short-term creditors or on the brink of bankruptcy? Explain.

d. Is there anything unusual about the operating cycle of cheese stores that would make you think that they normally would have lower current ratios than, say, large department stores?

e. What *other types of information* could you utilize in performing a more complete analysis of Chezo's liquidity?

LO14-3, LO14-4, LO14-7
PROBLEM 14.5B
Balance Sheet Measures of Liquidity and Credit Risk

A recent balance sheet of Sweet as Sugar included the following items, among others. (Dollar amounts are stated in thousands.)

Cash	$ 49,630
Marketable securities (short-term)	65,910
Accounts receivable	25,330
Inventories	44,000
Prepaid expenses	5,850
Retained earnings	350,000
Notes payable to banks (due within one year)	28,000
Accounts payable	4,900
Dividends payable	1,800
Accrued liabilities (short-term)	21,500
Income taxes payable	8,500

The company also reported total assets of $600,000, total liabilities of $90,000, and a return on total assets of 20 percent.

Instructions

a. Compute Sweet as Sugar's: (1) quick assets, (2) current assets, and (3) current liabilities.

b. Compute Sweet as Sugar's: (1) quick ratio, (2) current ratio, (3) working capital, and (4) debt ratio. (Round to one decimal place.)

c. Discuss the company's liquidity from the viewpoints of (1) short-term creditors, (2) long-term creditors, and (3) stockholders.

LOI4-4, LOI4-5, LOI4-7
PROBLEM 14.6B
Financial Statement
Analysis

Shown below are selected data from the financial statements of Hamilton Stores, a retail lighting store.

From the balance sheet:

Cash	$ 35,000
Accounts receivable	175,000
Inventory	225,000
Plant assets (net of accumulated depreciation)	550,000
Current liabilities	190,000
Total stockholders' equity	500,000
Total assets	1,300,000

From the income statement:

Net sales	$2,400,000
Cost of goods sold	1,800,000
Operating expenses	495,000
Interest expense	80,000
Income tax expense	4,000
Net income	21,000

From the statement of cash flows:

Net cash provided by operating activities		
(including interest paid of $72,000)		$ 50,000
Net cash used in investing activities		(54,000)
Financing activities:		
Amounts borrowed	$ 56,000	
Repayment of amounts borrowed	(25,000)	
Dividends paid	(24,000)	
Net cash provided by financing activities		7,000
Net increase in cash during the year		$ 3,000

Instructions

a. Explain how the interest expense shown in the income statement could be $80,000, when the interest payment appearing in the statement of cash flows is only $72,000.

b. Compute the following (round to one decimal place):
   1. Current ratio   3. Working capital
   2. Quick ratio   4. Debt ratio

c. Comment on these measurements and evaluate Hamilton's short-term debt-paying ability.

d. Compute the following ratios (assume that the year-end amounts of total assets and total stockholders' equity also represent the average amounts throughout the year):
   1. Return on assets
   2. Return on equity

e. Comment on the company's performance under these measurements. Explain *why* the return on assets and return on equity are so different.

f. Discuss (1) the apparent safety of long-term creditors' claims and (2) the prospects for Hamilton Stores continuing its dividend payments at the present level.

LOI4-4, LOI4-5, LOI4-7
PROBLEM 14.7B
Basic Ratio Analysis

Rochester Corporation is engaged primarily in the business of manufacturing raincoats and umbrellas. Shown below are selected information from a recent annual report. (Dollar amounts are stated in thousands.)

	Beginning of the Year	End of the Year
Total current assets	$ 43,000	$ 82,000
Total current liabilities	54,000	75,000
Total assets	230,000	390,000
Total stockholders' equity	120,000	205,000
Operating income		74,000
Net income		51,000

The company has long-term liabilities that bear interest at annual rates ranging from 8 percent to 12 percent.

Instructions

a. Compute the company's current ratio at (1) the beginning of the year and (2) the end of the year. (Carry to two decimal places.)

b. Compute the company's working capital at (1) the beginning of the year and (2) the end of the year. (Express dollar amounts in thousands.)

c. Is the company's short-term debt-paying ability improving or deteriorating?

d. Compute the company's (1) return on average total assets and (2) return on average stockholders' equity. (Round average assets and average equity to the nearest dollar and final computations to the nearest 1 percent.)

e. As an equity investor, do you think that Rochester's management is utilizing the company's resources in a reasonably efficient manner? Explain.

LO14-5, LO14-7

PROBLEM 14.8B

Ratios: Consider Advisability of Incurring Long-Term Debt

At the end of the year, the following information was obtained from the accounting records of Solar Systems, Inc.:

Sales (all on credit)	$4,800,000
Cost of goods sold	3,000,000
Average inventory	420,000
Average accounts receivable	380,000
Interest expense	50,000
Income tax expense	80,000
Net income	280,000
Average investment in assets	2,600,000
Average stockholders' equity	1,000,000

Instructions

a. From the information given, compute the following:

1. Inventory turnover.   4. Gross profit percentage.

2. Accounts receivable turnover.   5. Return on average stockholders' equity.

3. Total operating expenses.   6. Return on average assets.

b. Solar Systems has an opportunity to obtain a long-term loan at an annual interest rate of 8 percent and could use this additional capital at the same rate of profitability as indicated by the given data. Would obtaining the loan be desirable from the viewpoint of the stockholders? Explain.

LO14-5, LO14-7, LO14-8

PROBLEM 14.9B

Ratios: Evaluation of Two Companies

Shown below are selected financial data for THIS Star, Inc., and THAT Star, Inc., at the end of the current year:

	THIS Star, Inc.	THAT Star, Inc.
Net credit sales	$900,000	$840,000
Cost of goods sold	700,000	640,000
Cash	95,000	47,000
Accounts receivable (net)	100,000	90,000
Inventory	50,000	160,000
Current liabilities	120,000	110,000

Assume that the year-end balances shown for accounts receivable and for inventory also represent the average balances of these items throughout the year.

Instructions

a. For each of the two companies, compute the following:

1. Working capital.

2. Current ratio.

3. Quick ratio.

4. Number of times inventory turned over during the year and the average number of days required to turn over inventory (round computation to the nearest day).

5. Number of times accounts receivable turned over during the year and the average number of days required to collect accounts receivable (round computation to the nearest day).

6. Operating cycle.

b. From the viewpoint of a short-term creditor, comment on the *quality* of each company's working capital. To which company would you prefer to sell $50,000 in merchandise on a 30-day open account?

Critical Thinking Cases

LO14-1

CASE 14.1

Season's Greetings

Holiday Greeting Cards is a local company organized late in July of 2014. The company's net income for each of its first six calendar quarters of operations is summarized below. (Amounts are stated in thousands of dollars.)

	2015	2014
First quarter (Jan. through Mar.)	$ 253	–0–
Second quarter (Apr. through June)	308	–0–
Third quarter (July through Sept.)	100	$ 50
Fourth quarter (Oct. through Dec.)	450	500
Total for the calendar year	$1,111	$550

Hal Holcomb reports the business and economic news for a local radio station. On the day that Holiday Greeting Cards released the above financial information, you heard Holcomb make the following statement during his broadcast: "Holiday Greeting Cards enjoyed a 350 percent increase in its profits for the fourth quarter, and profits for the entire year were up by over 100 percent."

Instructions

a. Show the computations that Holcomb probably made in arriving at his statistics. (Hint: Holcomb did not make his computations in the manner recommended in this chapter. His figures, however, can be developed from these financial data.)

b. Do you believe that Holcomb's percentage changes present a realistic impression of Holiday Greeting Cards's rate of growth in 2015? Explain.

c. What figure would you use to express the percentage change in Holiday's fourth-quarter profits in 2015? Explain why you would compute the change in this manner.

LO14-3, through LO14-5

CASE 14.2

Evaluating
Debt-Paying Ability

You are a loan officer with Third Nebraska Bank. Joe West owns two successful restaurants, each of which has applied to your bank for a $250,000 one-year loan for the purpose of opening a second location. Condensed balance sheets for the two business entities are shown below.

NEBRASKA STEAK RANCH
BALANCE SHEET
DECEMBER 31, 2015

Assets		Liabilities & Stockholders' Equity	
Current assets	$ 75,000	Current liabilities	$ 30,000
Plant and equipment	300,000	Long-term liabilities	200,000
		Capital stock	100,000
		Retained earnings	45,000
Total assets	$375,000	Total liabilities & stockholders' equity	$375,000

THE STOCKYARDS BALANCE SHEET DECEMBER 31, 2015			
Assets		**Liabilities & Owners' Equity**	
Current assets	$ 24,000	Current liabilities	$ 30,000
Plant and equipment	301,000	Long-term liabilities	200,000
		Capital, Joe West	95,000
Total assets	$325,000	Total liabilities & owners' equity	$325,000

Both restaurants are popular and have been successful over the past several years. Nebraska Steak Ranch has been slightly more profitable, but the operating results for the two businesses have been quite similar. You think that either restaurant's second location should be successful. On the other hand, you know that restaurants are a "faddish" type of business and that their popularity and profitability can change very quickly.

Joe West is one of the wealthiest people in Nebraska. He made a fortune—estimated at more than $2 billion—as the founder of Micro Time, a highly successful manufacturer of computer software. West now is retired and spends most of his time at Second Life, his 50,000-acre cattle ranch. Both of his restaurants are run by experienced professional managers.

Instructions

a. Compute the current ratio and working capital of each business entity.

b. On the basis of the information provided in this case, which of these businesses do you consider to be the better credit risk? Explain fully.

c. What simple measure might you insist upon that would make the other business as good a credit risk as the one you identified in part **b?** Explain.

LO14-5

CASE 14.3

Strategies to Improve the Current Ratio

Nashville Do-It-Yourself owns a chain of nine retail stores that sell building materials, hardware, and garden supplies. In early October, the company's current ratio is 1.7 to 1. This is about normal for the company, but it is lower than the current ratios of several large competitors. Management feels that, to qualify for the best credit terms from its suppliers, the company's year-end balance sheet should indicate a current ratio of at least 2 to 1.

Instructions

a. Indicate whether taking each of the following actions would increase or decrease the company's current ratio. Explain your reasoning.

1. Pay some of the company's current liabilities.

2. Purchase large amounts of inventory on account.

3. Offer credit customers a special discount if they pay their account balance prior to year-end.

b. Propose several other ethical steps that management might take to increase the company's current ratio prior to year-end.

LO14-5

CASE 14.4

Evaluating Corporate Governance Quality

Assume that you are an intern working for the **California Public Employees Retirement System (CALPERS)** in its investments office and you have been asked to evaluate a number of companies for possible investment by **CALPERS**. You prepare an analysis of each company's prospects using the tools of financial statement analysis (e.g., trend analysis, common size statements, ratio analysis). Thinking you are done, you present your analysis to your boss. She tells you that, although your analysis of each company's financial information is fine, she is also interested in the quality of each company's corporate governance. Pick a public company, download their most recent proxy statement in support of the annual meeting of shareholders, and write a brief report on the quality of each company's board of directors in terms of board composition and structure, size, committees, and expertise.

LOI4-7, LOI4-8

INTERNET CASE 14.5

Evaluating Liquidity
and Profitability

Use the Internet search engine of your choice and do a general search on the name of a company of interest to you (e.g., General Motors, Johnson & Johnson, Coca-Cola, etc.). Explore the web site of the company you choose and locate that company's most recent financial statements. You may need to look under a category that provides general information about the company and/or investor information.

Instructions

a. Find and read the description of the company, including the type of business it is in. Why is gaining an understanding of the industry and type of business an important starting point for financial statement analysis?

b. Locate the company's primary financial statements. Find the summary table of ratios in this chapter in Exhibit 14–26. Calculate three of the listed ratios under each of the following categories: "Measures of short-term liquidity" and "Measures of profitability." Show your work in calculating these ratios. Write a brief statement describing what you have learned about your company's liquidity and profitability.

c. Why do you think the Internet has become such a widely used source of financial information by investors and creditors?

Internet sites are time and date sensitive. It is the purpose of these exercises to have you explore the Internet. You may need to use the Yahoo! search engine www.yahoo.com *(or another favorite search engine) to find a company's current web address.*

Answers to Self-Test Questions

1. c   2. a, c, d   3. a   4. d (see below)   5. b (see below)   6. d   7. c

Why answers a, b, and c in question **4** are incorrect:

a. The return on assets, 12 percent ($240,000 ÷ $2,000,000), exceeds the return on equity, which is 10 percent ($80,000 ÷ $800,000).

b. The current ratio is 1.6 to 1 ($480,000 ÷ $300,000).

c. Working capital amounts to $180,000 ($480,000 − $300,000).

Increase in net income required in question **5**: ($400,000 − $160,000) ÷ $160,000 = 150%

COMPREHENSIVE PROBLEM 4

Home Depot, Inc.

ANALYSIS OF THE FINANCIAL STATEMENTS OF A PUBLICLY OWNED CORPORATION

This Comprehensive Problem is to acquaint you with the content of the 2012 financial statements of **Home Depot, Inc.**, reproduced in Appendix A of this textbook. (The 2012 financial statements are for the fiscal year ended February 3, 2013.) The problem contains three major parts, which are independent of one another: *Part I* is designed to familiarize you with the general contents of a company's financial statements; *Part II* involves analysis of the company's liquidity; and *Part III* analyzes the trend in its profitability.

If you work this problem as a group assignment, each group member should be prepared to discuss the group's findings and conclusions in class.

A good starting point for understanding the financial statements of a company such as **Home Depot, Inc.**, is to understand the accounting policies used in preparing those statements. The first note accompanying the financial statements provides a brief description of the major accounting policies the company used. Most of the areas discussed in this note have been covered in this text.

Part I Annual reports include not only comparative financial statements but also other sources of information, such as:

- A multiyear summary of financial highlights, a summary of key statistics for the past 5 or 10 years.
- Several pages of *Notes* that accompany the financial statements.
- Reports by management and by the independent auditors in which they express their respective responsibilities for the financial statements.

Instructions

Answer each of the following questions and explain *where* in the statements, notes, or other sections of the annual report you located the information used in your answer.

a. How many years are covered in each of the primary comparative financial statements? Were all of these statements audited? Name the auditors. What were the auditors' conclusions concerning these statements?

b. **Home Depot, Inc.**, combines its statement of retained earnings with another financial statement. Where are details about changes in the amount of retained earnings found?

c. Over the three years presented, have the company's annual net cash flows been positive or negative from (**1**) operating activities, (**2**) investing activities, and (**3**) financing activities? Has the company's cash balance increased or decreased during each of these three years?

Part II Assume that you are the credit manager of a medium-size supplier of building materials and related products. **Home Depot** wants to make credit purchases from your company, with payment due in 60 days.

Instructions

a. As general background, read the first note to the financial statements, "Summary of Significant Accounting Policies." Next, compute the following for the fiscal years ending February 3, 2013, and January 29, 2012 (round percentages to the nearest tenth of 1 percent, and other computations to one decimal place):

1. Current ratio.
2. Quick ratio.
3. Amount of working capital.

4. Percentage change in working capital from the prior year.

5. Percentage change in cash and cash equivalents from the prior year.

b. On the basis of your analysis in part **a**, does the company's liquidity appear to have *increased* or *decreased* during the most recent fiscal year? Explain.

c. Other than the ability of **Home Depot** to pay for its purchases, do you see any major considerations that should enter into your company's decision? Explain.

d. Your company assigns each customer one of the four credit ratings listed below. Assign a credit rating to **Home Depot, Inc.**, and write a memorandum explaining your decision. (In your memorandum, you may refer to any of your computations or observations in parts **a** through **c**, and to any information contained in the annual report.)

POSSIBLE CREDIT RATINGS

A Outstanding Little or no risk of inability to pay. For customers in this category, we fill any reasonable order without imposing a credit limit. The customer's credit is reevaluated annually.

B Good Customer has good debt-paying ability but is assigned a credit limit that is reviewed every 90 days. Orders above the credit limit are accepted only on a cash basis.

C Marginal Customer appears sound, but credit should be extended only on a 30-day basis and with a relatively low credit limit. Creditworthiness and credit limit are reevaluated every 90 days.

D Unacceptable Customer does not qualify for credit.

Part III As general background, study the "Five-Year Summary of Financial and Operating Results."

Instructions

a. Compute the following for the fiscal years ending February 3, 2013, and January 29, 2012 (round percentages to the nearest tenth of 1 percent):

1. Percentage change in net sales (relative to the prior year).
2. Percentage change in net earnings.
3. Gross profit rate.
4. Net income as a percentage of sales.
5. Return on average total assets.
6. Return on average total equity.

b. Write a statement that describes your conclusion(s) concerning trends in **Home Depot**'s profitability during the period covered in your analysis in part **a** above. Justify your conclusion(s).

CHAPTER 15

Global Business and Accounting

AFTER STUDYING THIS CHAPTER, YOU SHOULD BE ABLE TO:

Learning Objectives

LO15-1 Define four mechanisms companies use to globalize their business activities.

LO15-2 Identify how global environmental forces—(a) political and legal systems, (b) economic systems, (c) culture, and (d) technology and infrastructure—affect accounting practices.

LO15-3 Explain why there is demand for harmonization of global financial reporting standards.

LO15-4 Demonstrate how to convert an amount of money from one currency to another.

LO15-5 Compute gains or losses on receivables or payables that are stated in a foreign currency when exchange rates fluctuate.

LO15-6 Describe techniques for "hedging" against losses from fluctuations in exchange rates.

LO15-7 Discuss how global sourcing increases product cost complexity.

LO15-8 Explain the importance of the Foreign Corrupt Practices Act.

INTERNATIONAL ACCOUNTING STANDARDS BOARD

The International Financial Reporting Standards Foundation's goal is to develop a single set of high-quality, understandable, enforceable, and globally accepted international financial reporting standards (IFRSs). They work to achieve this goal through a standard-setting body, the International Accounting Standards Board (IASB). Currently, the IASB has 16 full-time members. Meetings of the IASB are held in public and by webcast.

In fulfilling its standard-setting duties, the IASB engages with stakeholders around the world, including investors, analysts, regulators, business leaders, accounting standard-setters, and the accountancy educators and professionals. In determining standards, it is paramount that the board members understand the diversity of businesses, cultures, economic conditions,

political and legal structures, and infrastructures around the world. Recent interest in IFRS from the G-20 leaders[1] demonstrates the importance of considering global political and economic ramifications of creating and changing International Financial Reporting Standards.

Group of Twenty (G-20) was established in 1999 to bring together finance ministers and central bank governors from systemically important industrialized and developing economies to discuss key issues in the global financial economy. In 2013, the FASB and IASB prepared a report to the G-20 regarding progress on convergence between U.S. and International Financial Reporting Standards. The G-20 have confirmed the importance of an independent standard-setting body accountable to the public interest. ■

---

[1] The G-20 consists of 19 countries plus the European Union and represent 80 percent of global gross world product, 80 percent of world trade, and two-thirds of the world population.

The London-based International Accounting Standards Board began a mission in 1993 to develop financial reporting rules that all countries could use. The board has made significant progress. In this chapter we describe that progress and provide you with a foundation for understanding the richness and complexity of international accounting issues.

Accounting rules, procedures, and standards in almost any chosen country developed differently from those in the United States and those in other countries. Countries such as the United Kingdom, Japan, and Germany establish their own accounting rules, procedures, and standards. The goal of the International Accounting Standards Board is to identify a set of accounting standards that will be acceptable to all governments and their related securities markets. This is a very ambitious goal because accounting rules, procedures, and standards are affected by the political, legal, economic, and cultural systems in which they are embedded. Thus, the variations in these systems from country to country have a significant impact on how investors, creditors, and managers understand and use accounting information.

The objective of this chapter is to introduce you to the complexity of global business and to explore some of the accounting issues associated with global business. This is only a brief introduction. As your business education progresses, additional details will be added to the ideas introduced here.

Globalization

Globalization occurs as managers become aware of and engage in cross-border trade and operations. Think of globalization as a continuous process in which at the most basic level a purely domestic company's managers become aware that changes in foreign exchange rates, international technological advances, cultural diversity, or international political and economic

EXHIBIT 15–1

Location of the World's Largest Multinationals in 2009 and 2012

Country/Block		Number of 2009 Companies	Number of 2012 Companies	Percentage Change
European Union		163	138	−15%
United States		140	132	−6%
Japan		68	68	0%
China		37	73	+97%
Switzerland		15	15	0%
Canada		14	11	−21%
South Korea		14	13	−0.07%
Central/South America		11	13	+18%
Australia		9	9	0%
Russia		8	7	−12.5%
India		7	8	+14%
Others		14	13	−0.07%

Source: Adapted from "The Fortune Global 500," http://money.cnn.com/magazines/fortune/global500/countries.
In 2005, company headquarters were in Europe (195), the United States (176), Japan (80), and China (16).

issues will have an impact on their firm's ability to compete. An example of a higher level of globalization is a multinational enterprise that begins with raw material extraction and ends with final product assembly and sales in multiple foreign locations. In Exhibit 15–1 we show the location of the world's top multinational companies. The top 10 companies in 2012 include seven oil companies, one automobile company (Toyota), one retailer (Walmart), and one Chinese government-owned power company (State Grid).

Globalization typically progresses through a series of stages that include exporting, licensing, joint ventures, wholly owned subsidiaries, and, finally, global sourcing. **Exporting** is, at the simplest level, selling a good or service to a foreign customer. While *exporting* maintains control over product creation, *licensing* gives up some control for a monetary return. **International licensing** is a contractual agreement between a company and a foreign party allowing the use of trademarks, patents, technology, designs, processes, intellectual property, or other proprietary advantage. Most major multinational food manufacturing companies are involved in some form of international product licensing. An **international joint venture** is a company owned by two or more companies from different countries. A **wholly owned international subsidiary** is created when a company uses its own funds to construct or purchase 100 percent equity control of a foreign subsidiary. Finally, **global sourcing** is the close coordination of R&D, manufacturing, and marketing across national boundaries and typically includes exporting, licensing, joint ventures, and wholly owned subsidiaries in cross-border operations.

As shown in Exhibit 15–2, companies typically engage in globalization through an outward growth path. Those companies wishing to globalize typically progress through the following stages: (1) exporting domestically produced products, (2) establishing licensing and joint venture arrangements, (3) creating wholly owned subsidiaries, and (4) full-scale global sourcing. In practice, there are many subcategories that are not shown in the exhibit, and companies may pursue multiple globalization processes simultaneously.

L015-1

LEARNING OBJECTIVE
Define four mechanisms companies use to globalize their business activities.

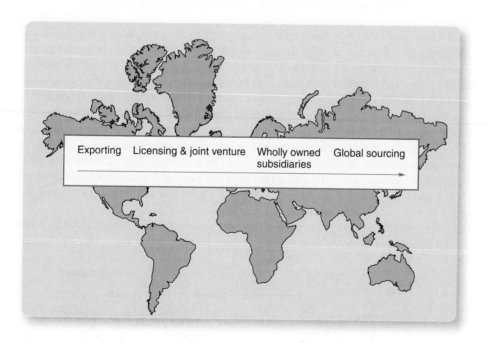

EXHIBIT 15–2
Processes for Increasing Globalization

Globalization has implications for the type of accounting information gathered, created, and reported. U.S. GAAP requirements for exporting, licensing, joint ventures, and wholly owned subsidiaries are very different. In addition, differences in currency exchange rates create financial reporting issues. Management decisions about how to globalize clearly impact a firm's accounting outputs, processes, and procedures.

Environmental Forces Shaping Globalization

LO15-2

LEARNING OBJECTIVE
Identify how global
environmental forces—
(a) political and legal systems,
(b) economic systems,
(c) culture, and (d) technology
and infrastructure—affect
accounting practices.

To help you understand how international environmental forces affect the accounting information measured, reported, and created, we consider environmental forces in four categories: (1) political and legal systems, (2) economic systems, (3) culture, and (4) technology and infrastructure.

These categories are not independent. A country's economy and culture have an influence on its political and legal structures. Culture affects and is affected by economics. As illustrated in Exhibit 15–3, the technological position of a country is dependent on political, demographic, and cultural issues.

POLITICAL AND LEGAL SYSTEMS

Managers operating in or planning operations in foreign settings must monitor associated political risks. Political risk occurs because governments have the ability to shift asset ownership from the company to the government or because the company may be asked to relinquish control over operations due to government intervention. For example, when Iran and Venezuela nationalized their oil industries in the late 1970s, many companies lost ownership of their assets invested in oil exploration, drilling, and oil delivery. United States GAAP requires companies to include in their financial reports discussions about political risk that may significantly impair assets or profits.

LO15-2a

LEARNING OBJECTIVE
Identify how political and
legal systems affect
accounting practices.

Laws enacted by foreign governments often have an impact on the net profits earned from international activities. Taxes, tariffs, and licensing fees vary substantially from country to country. Laws restricting the flow of currency can affect the amounts of foreign-earned profits that can be transferred out and used elsewhere. Ownership requirements are a common form of governmental control. For example, governments in China and India have ownership restrictions on foreign subsidiaries and joint ventures in their countries.

Other types of political intervention include content or value-added requirements and sourcing requirements. Trade agreements often specify the source of raw materials or labor content to allow preferential treatment in tariffs and customs for products or services that are produced in the regions covered by the agreement. For example, in order for a product to qualify for reduced tariffs, NAFTA (the North American Free Trade Agreement) specifies the amount of total cost that must be added in those countries that have signed the free trade agreement.

Another example of political intervention is the **foreign trade zone** within the United States. Goods imported into these zones are duty-free until they leave the zone. Companies that import raw materials frequently set up their factories in these trade zones. These companies are not required to pay duty on the imported raw materials until the finished product is shipped out of the zone. Using foreign trade zones can have an impact on revenue recognition and the cost of goods sold. In addition, a delay in paying the duty enlarges the company's working capital as discussed in Chapter 14.

As countries change and grow, governments try to manage that growth through political and legal means. For example, governments use tax incentives that encourage or discourage

EXHIBIT 15–3
Environmental Forces
Impacting Globalization

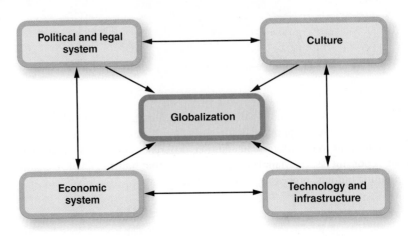

ownership of stocks. Policies also affect the level of individual savings, which impacts the availability of capital. Educational policies impact the literacy rate, the extent of formal education and training, and the number of accounting professionals. The political and legal structures of each country provide the framework for their economic structures.

ECONOMIC SYSTEMS

The economic systems under which businesses operate significantly affect the form and availability of accounting information. For example, in a **planned economy** the government uses central planning to allocate resources and determine output among various segments of the economy. Land and production facilities are government owned and controlled. The former Soviet Union and Soviet Eastern Bloc countries used central planning and had planned economies. China continues to use central planning extensively. Alternatively, in **market economies,** ownership of land and the means of production are private, and markets dictate the allocation of resources and the output among segments of the economy. Companies formerly operating in a planned economy can encounter significant difficulties when attempting to operate in a market economy. The reverse can also be true.

In some countries, businesses arrange themselves into **industrial organizations** as one method of raising capital. In South Korea and Japan, companies group themselves into conglomerates representing different industries. South Korean conglomerates, called *chaebol,* and Japanese conglomerates, called *keiretsu,* consist of companies that are grouped as customers and suppliers, and they usually contain a bank. Within these cartels of companies, suppliers receive loans, investment capital, technology, and long-term supply agreements from customers higher up on the pyramid. Suppliers integrate their operations with other suppliers and with their customers. Transactions between suppliers and customers are not arm's-length as in most U.S. transactions. In the United States, antitrust and price-fixing laws preclude the type of organized business groups found in Japan and South Korea.

INTERNATIONAL CASE IN POINT

Samsung, Hyundai, LG, and other Korean *chaebol* have reported impressive jumps in sales and profits in recent years. However, while the big Korean companies expand, the smaller- and medium-sized firms in the Korean economy are struggling. While the *chaebol* unquestionably have fueled the country's growth in recent decades, they're so powerful that they may be hampering innovation from smaller- and medium-sized companies that may harm Korea's long-run economic success. Economists worry that the *chaebol*'s deepening influence is hurting fair competition with suppliers and start-ups.

CULTURE

Think of culture as the mental mindset that affects the way individuals in a society act and perceive each others' actions.[2] U.S. cultural practices have a significant effect on the way foreign companies conduct business in the United States. Likewise, certain forms of advertising, methods of acquiring business, and hierarchical organizational structures, which are common practices in the United States, would not be culturally preferred elsewhere. Ignoring cultural variables can create significant business problems.

Experts have identified four cultural mindsets that significantly differ among international locations.

- *Individualism versus collectivism.* The degree of interdependence that a society maintains among individuals, where high interdependence connotes collectivism. Citizens of Asian countries typically score higher on collectivism than those in the United States.

[2] For a more detailed discussion of the information in this section, see G. Hofstede, *Cultures and Organizations: Software of the Mind* (Berkshire, England: McGraw-Hill, 1991), or www.geert-hofstede.com.

L015-2b

LEARNING OBJECTIVE
Identify how economic systems affect accounting practices.

L015-2c

LEARNING OBJECTIVE
Identify how culture affects accounting practices.

- *Uncertainty avoidance.* The extent to which members of a society feel uncomfortable or threatened by unknown or uncertain situations. Citizens of South American countries score high on uncertainty avoidance.
- *Short-term versus long-term orientation.* With a long-term orientation, perseverance, thriftiness, maintaining of order, and lasting relationships are highly valued. A short-term orientation focuses on the past and the present, ignores the future, and values personal stability.
- *Large versus small power distance.* Large power distance cultures accept unequally distributed power within and across institutions and organizations. The idea that everyone is created equal or should have an equal voice is more highly valued in small power distance societies.

Exhibit 15–4 provides a rough measure of the relative differences between selected countries.

EXHIBIT 15–4
Cultural Mindsets

Country	Individualism	Uncertainty Avoidance	Long-Term Orientation	High Power Distance
Japan	L	H	H	M
South Korea	L	H	H	H
Brazil	L	H	M	H
Italy	M	H	L	M
Germany	M	M	L	L
United States	H	M	L	M
Great Britain	H	L	L	L
Sweden	M	L	L	L

H = High, M = Medium, L = Low.

We can use Exhibit 15–4 to understand how cultural variables can affect both the type of accounting information that is produced and how that information is used. Studies have shown that in South Korea and Japan, where collectivism is high, less emphasis is placed on the transparency of financial statements for investors. The needs of creditors are given preference over the needs of investors. Thus, because financing for companies comes primarily from a bank in the keiretsu or chaebol, most accounting information is kept within the collectivist group. In addition, because of the strict government control of accounting regulations, the accounting profession in Asian countries has been slow to develop. The relative number of independent accountants is small, but increasing in many Asian countries.

TECHNOLOGY AND INFRASTRUCTURE

Other cross-border differences create global business challenges because of variations in infrastructure and education level. The ability to transfer information and knowledge between and among various geographic locations and peoples can be difficult. Frequently companies that create joint ventures or start wholly owned operations in foreign locations find few employees with the education and technical training available in the U.S. workforce.

LO15-2d

LEARNING OBJECTIVE
Identify how technology and infrastructure affect accounting practices.

INTERNATIONAL CASE IN POINT

Western-style management training is a recent development in many countries. Budapest has one of the oldest graduate management programs in eastern Europe, and it was founded in 1988. More specifically, because companies in formerly planned economies used centrally determined accounts and procedures, accounting as a profession did not exist in eastern Europe prior to 1988. Thus, companies establishing business operations in eastern European locations have difficulty locating trained accounting personnel. In addition, prior business records are unreliable. Before the early 1990s, there were no independent auditors, public accountants, or management accountants in most eastern European countries.

Differences in internal accounting systems can also create challenges for international business dealings. Culture, education, language, and software differences hinder the free flow of information. Potential benefits from acquired international operations are sometimes lost because of the inability to transfer valuable information within and between international companies.

Infrastructure impediments also pose problems for globalization. Poor access to communication equipment (for example, telephones, faxes, and computers), a lack of necessary R&D facilities (for example, specialized laboratory equipment, computer-aided design, or manufacturing), and fluctuating or unreliable power sources create significant hurdles to establishing international business in some locations. Manufacturing plants in many developing countries are not heated or cooled, which can create adverse operating environments for equipment that relies on lubricants and coolants. Inadequate transportation systems can slow the transfer of goods in and out of an international location. When estimating costs for inventory balance sheet items or cost of goods sold, accountants need to incorporate these unexpected costs into their computations to properly compute the cost of globally sourced products.

© AP Photo/Manish Swarup

Harmonization of Financial Reporting Standards

LO15-3

LEARNING OBJECTIVE
Explain why there is demand for harmonization of global financial reporting standards.

Cross-border differences in financial reporting standards create problems for analyzing and comparing accounting information. For example, financial reporting in the United States is based primarily on the principle of historical cost without adjustment for changes in general price levels. South and Central American countries such as Brazil or Mexico, on the other hand, have experienced such high rates of inflation that inflation-adjusted information is required. These differences cause the financial statements of a U.S. company and a Mexican company to be very different and difficult to compare.

As long as an enterprise operates solely within its own borders, differences in financial reporting practices between countries are not as significant a problem as they are if business activity extends across borders. For example, **cross-border financing,** in which a company sells its securities in the capital markets of another country, has become increasingly popular. Business activities that cross borders create the need for more comparable information between companies that reside in different countries.

The need for comparable information has led to an interest in the **harmonization of accounting standards**, a term used to describe the globalization of similar accounting methods and principles throughout the world. The **International Accounting Standards Board (IASB)** is particularly interested in harmonization and is charged with the responsibility of establishing and gaining acceptance of international financial reporting standards (IFRSs). This committee represents over 150 professional organizations from more than 120 countries and over 2 million accounting professionals worldwide. While the IASB has no regulatory authority in any country, it uses its influence to move the reporting standards of all countries closer together in hopes of better harmonizing those standards. For countries that do not have well-developed capital markets, the IASB standards provide a model that often has a significant influence on their early attempts to develop standardized accounting practices.

INTERNATIONAL FINANCIAL REPORTING STANDARDS: ADOPTION OR CONVERGENCE

Countries and jurisdictions have taken two approaches to implementing international accounting standards to achieve harmonization. First, some countries have chosen to adopt international financial reporting standards exactly as written and promulgated by the IASB. **Adoption** means abandoning the country's current financial reporting standards and replacing them with IFRS. The adoption approach was agreed to by the European Union in 2005 when all companies trading on European Union securities markets were required to adopt IFRS for their annual reports. Exhibit 15–5 shows that Chile, Mexico, and Canada have chosen to adopt IFRS.

Alternatively, Exhibit 15–5 shows that some countries or jurisdictions have currently chosen to converge their existing standards to IFRS. **Convergence** means changing the countries' existing standards so that they will produce IFRS "equivalent" financial reports. Convergence has been described as an ongoing process because, as IFRS changes, converging countries must reconsider whether their standards continue to be equivalent, or need to be changed. China, Japan, and Australia have chosen to amend their current financial reporting standards so that they will converge with IFRS.

EXHIBIT 15–5

IFRS Global Adoption and Convergence

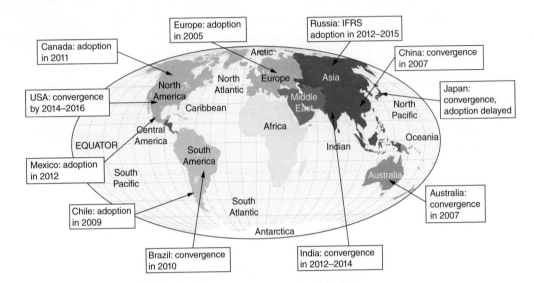

The United States has been working toward convergence of U.S. GAAP and IFRS for several years. However, progress has been slow and some companies and audit firms have called for the outright adoption of IFRS. The SEC suggested in 2010 that a small number of U.S. domestic companies might be allowed to use IFRS by 2015. However, more recent reports from the SEC suggest that time line is too ambitious. The SEC is currently debating the best approach to moving U.S. GAAP to be compliant with international standards.

Exhibit 15–6 provides a flavor of the differences that currently exist among financial reporting requirements around the world. The first column shows that the number of available auditors in any particular country varies significantly. This variation is a direct result of the environmental variables discussed earlier. The United States and the United Kingdom have the most highly developed capital markets in the world and the related auditing demands are evident in the table. Column two shows that fixed asset revaluations are only allowed under IFRS and U.K. GAAP. Variations in inventory valuation and goodwill practices are illustrated in columns three and four. The final column in Exhibit 15–6 displays differences in segment disclosure. Segment information has been in demand from investors in recent years. Countries such as Germany and Brazil, where capital is typically provided by banks, require lower levels

EXHIBIT 15–6   Global Variation in Accounting Practices

Country GAAP	Auditors per 100,000	Fixed Asset Revaluation Allowed	LIFO Allowed	Goodwill Impairment Test or Amortize	Depreciation Basis	Segment Disclosure Required
IFRS	—	Yes	No	Impairment	Economic	Yes
United States	168	No	Yes	Impairment	Economic	Yes
United Kingdom	352	Yes	No	Impairment	Economic	Yes
Japan	10	No	No	Amortize (20 yr)	Tax	Yes
Germany	26	No	No	Amortize (4 yr)	Tax	Limited
China	15	No	Yes	Impairment	Economic/tax	No
Brazil	1	Yes	No	Impairment	Economic	No
Russia	?	No	Yes	Amortized (20 yr)	Tax	No

of segment disclosure. These banks usually have access to inside information from their borrowers. Thus, demand for segment information to be included on required statutory financial reports is much lower in these countries.

Foreign Currencies and Exchange Rates

In addition to the environmental characteristics described above, companies with international business dealings encounter financial measurement challenges that result from using multiple currencies. Consider, for example, a Japanese company that sells merchandise to a U.S. corporation. The Japanese company will want to be paid in Japanese currency—yen—but the U.S. company's bank account contains U.S. dollars. Thus one currency must be converted into another.

© Ryan McVay/Photodisc/Getty Images

Most banks participate in an international currency exchange that enables them to buy foreign currencies at the prevailing *exchange rate.* Thus, a U.S. corporation can pay a liability to a Japanese company through the international banking system. The U.S. company will pay its bank in dollars. The bank will then use these dollars to purchase the required amount of yen on the international currency exchange and will arrange for delivery of the yen to the Japanese company's bank.[3]

EXCHANGE RATES

A currency **exchange rate** is the amount it costs to purchase one unit of currency with another currency. Thus the exchange rate may be viewed as the "price" of buying one unit of a foreign currency, stated in terms of the domestic currency (which for our purpose is U.S. dollars). Exchange rates fluctuate daily, based on the worldwide supply and demand for particular currencies. The current exchange rate between the dollar and most major currencies is published daily in the financial press. For example, a few of the exchange rates in *The Wall Street Journal* are shown in Exhibit 15–7.

Country/Region	Currency	Exchange Rate (in dollars)	Exchange Rate (in foreign currency)
Britain	Pound (£)	$1.5231	0.657
Europe*	Euro (€)	1.30506	0.766
Japan	Yen (¥)	0.01005	199.5
Mexico	Peso ($)	0.08155	12.262
India	Rupee (Rs)	0.01839	53.933

EXHIBIT 15–7

U.S. Dollar Equivalents for Five Foreign Currencies

*Many European countries, such as Austria, Belgium, Finland, France, Germany, Greece, Ireland, Italy, Luxembourg, the Netherlands, Portugal, and Spain, are using the euro.

Exchange rates may be used to determine how much of one currency is equivalent to a given amount of another currency. Assume that a U.S. company owes a Japanese company 1 million yen (expressed ¥1,000,000). How many dollars are needed to settle this obligation, assuming that the current exchange rate is $0.01005 per yen? To restate an amount of foreign currency in terms of the equivalent amount of U.S. dollars, we multiply the foreign currency amount by the exchange rate, as follows:[4]

Amount Stated in Foreign Currency		**Exchange Rate (in dollars)**		**Equivalent Number of U.S. Dollars**
¥1,000,000	×	$0.01005 per yen	=	$10,050

L015-4

LEARNING OBJECTIVE
Demonstrate how to convert an amount of money from one currency to another.

---

[3] Alternatively, the U.S. company may send the Japanese company a check (or a bank draft) stated in dollars. The Japanese company can then arrange to have the dollars converted into yen through its bank in Japan.

[4] To convert an amount of dollars into the equivalent amount of a foreign currency, we would *divide* the dollar amount by the exchange rate. For example, $10,050 ÷ $0.01005 per yen = ¥1,000,000.

Alternatively, consider that a Japanese company agrees to pay a U.S. company $10,000 for imported goods. To determine the equivalent amount of yen, the Japanese company needs to know the number of yen per dollar. The yen per dollar can be computed by dividing one dollar by the number of dollars per yen. Thus, $1 ÷ $.01005/yen = ¥99.5/dollar. Using the yen per dollar exchange rate, we can convert the dollars to yen as follows:

Amount Stated in U.S. Dollars	×	Exchange Rate (in yen)	=	Amount Stated in Foreign Currency (yen)
$10,000	×	¥99.5 per dollar	=	¥995,000

This process of restating an amount of foreign currency in terms of the equivalent number of dollars or restating a dollar amount into an equivalent amount of foreign currency is called *translating* the currency.

Exchange Rate Jargon In the financial press, currencies are often described as "strong" or "weak," or as rising or falling against one another. For example, an evening newscaster might say, "A strong dollar rose sharply against the weakening British pound, but fell slightly against the Japanese yen and the Swiss franc." What does this tell us about exchange rates?

To understand such terminology, we must remember that an exchange rate is simply the price of one currency *stated in terms of another currency*. Throughout this chapter, we refer to the prices of various foreign currencies stated in terms of *U.S. dollars*. In other countries, however, the U.S. dollar is a foreign currency, and its price is stated in terms of the local (domestic) currency.

To illustrate, consider the table from *The Wall Street Journal* shown in Exhibit 15–7. The exchange rate for the Japanese yen is $0.01005. At this exchange rate, $1 is equivalent to ¥99.5 (as shown above). Thus, while we would say that the exchange rate for the Japanese yen is *$0.01005,* the Japanese would say that the exchange rate for the U.S. dollar is *¥99.5.*

Now let us assume that the exchange rate for the yen (stated in dollars) rises to $0.0109. At this exchange rate, $1 is equivalent to only ¥92 ($1 ÷ $.0109 = ¥92). In the United States, we would say that the exchange rate for the yen has *risen* from $0.01005 to $0.0109. In Japan, however, they would say that the exchange rate for the dollar has *fallen* from ¥99.5 to ¥92. In the financial press, it might be said that "the yen has risen against the dollar" or that "the dollar has fallen against the yen." The two statements mean the same thing—that the yen has become more valuable relative to the dollar.

Now let us return to our original phrase, "A strong dollar rose sharply against the weakening British pound, but fell slightly against the Japanese yen and the Swiss franc." When exchange rates are stated in terms of U.S. dollars, this statement means that the price (exchange rate) of the British pound fell sharply, but the prices of the Japanese yen and the Swiss franc rose slightly. A currency is described as "strong" when its exchange rate is rising relative to most other currencies and as "weak" when its exchange rate is falling. Exchange rates fluctuate because of changes in the environmental forces discussed earlier in this chapter.

ACCOUNTING FOR TRANSACTIONS WITH FOREIGN COMPANIES

LO15-5

LEARNING OBJECTIVE
Compute gains or losses on receivables or payables that are stated in a foreign currency when exchange rates fluctuate.

When a U.S. company buys or sells merchandise in a transaction with a foreign company, the transaction price may be stipulated either in U.S. dollars or in units of the foreign currency. If the price is stated in *dollars,* the U.S. company encounters no special accounting problems. The transaction may be recorded in the same manner as are similar transactions with domestic suppliers or customers.

If the transaction price is stated in terms of the *foreign currency,* the company encounters two accounting problems. First, as the U.S. company's accounting records are maintained in dollars, the transaction price must be *translated* into dollars before the transaction can be recorded. The second problem arises when (1) the purchase or sale is made *on account* and (2) the exchange rate *changes* between the date of the transaction and the date that the account is paid. This fluctuation in the exchange rate will cause the U.S. company to experience either a *gain* or a *loss* in the settlement of the transaction.

Credit Purchases with Prices Stated in a Foreign Currency

Assume that on August 1 a U.S. company buys merchandise from a British company at a price of 10,000 British pounds (£10,000), with payment due in 60 days. The exchange rate on August 1 is *$1.63* per British pound. The entry on August 1 to record this purchase (assuming use of a perpetual inventory system) would be:

Inventory	16,300	
Accounts Payable		16,300
To record the purchase of merchandise from a British company for £10,000 when the exchange rate is $1.63 per pound (£10,000 × $1.63 = $16,300).		

The amount of a foreign currency credit purchase is determined by using the exchange rate on the date it is journalized

Let us now assume that by September 30, when the £10,000 account payable must be paid, the exchange rate has fallen to *$1.61* per British pound. If the U.S. company had paid for the merchandise on August 1, the cost would have been $16,300. On September 30, however, only *$16,100* is needed to pay the £10,000 liability (£10,000 × $1.61 = $16,100). Thus, *the decline in the exchange rate has saved the company $200.* This savings is recorded in the accounting records as a *Gain on Fluctuations in Foreign Exchange Rates.* The entry on September 30 to record payment of the liability and recognition of this gain would be:

Accounts Payable	16,300	
Cash		16,100
Gain on Fluctuations in Foreign Exchange Rates		200
To record payment of £10,000 liability to British company and to recognize gain from decline in exchange rate:		
Original liability (£10,000 × $1.63)	$16,300	
Amount paid (£10,000 × $1.61)	16,100	
Gain from decline in exchange rate	$ 200	

The foreign exchange rate gain for the credit purchase is determined by using the exchange rate on the payment date

Now let us assume that instead of declining, the exchange rate had *increased* from $1.63 on August 1 to *$1.66* on September 30. Under this assumption, the U.S. company would have to pay *$16,600* to pay off the £10,000 liability on September 30. Thus, the company would be paying *$300 more* than if the liability had been paid on August 1. This additional $300 cost was caused by the increase in the exchange rate and should be recorded as a loss. The entry on September 30 would be:

Accounts Payable	16,300	
Loss on Fluctuations in Foreign Exchange Rates	300	
Cash		16,600
To record payment of £10,000 liability to British company and to recognize loss from increase in exchange rate:		
Original liability (£10,000 × $1.63)	$16,300	
Amount paid (£10,000 × $1.66)	16,600	
Loss from increase in exchange rate	$ 300	

A foreign exchange rate loss occurs if the exchange rate increases between the purchase date and the collection date

In summary, having a liability that is fixed in terms of a foreign currency results in a gain for the debtor if the exchange rate declines between the date of the transaction and the date of payment. The gain results because fewer dollars will be needed to repay the debt than had originally been owed. An increase in the exchange rate, on the other hand, causes the debtor to incur a loss. In this case, the debtor will have to spend more dollars than had originally been owed in order to purchase the foreign currency needed to pay the debt.

Credit Sales with Prices Stated in a Foreign Currency

A company that makes credit *sales* at prices stated in a foreign currency also will experience gains or losses from fluctuations in the exchange rate. To illustrate, let us change our preceding example to assume that the U.S. company *sells* merchandise on August 1 to the British company at a price of £10,000. We shall again assume that the exchange rate on August 1 is $1.63 per British pound and that payment is due in 60 days. The entry on August 1 to record this sale would be:

Accounts Receivable	16,300	
Sales		16,300
To record sale to British company with sales price set at £10,000 (£10,000 × $1.63) = $16,300. To be collected in 60 days.		

In 60 days (September 30), the U.S. company will collect from the British company the U.S. dollar equivalent of £10,000. If the exchange rate on September 30 has fallen to $1.61 per pound, the U.S. company will collect only $16,100 (£10,000 × $1.61 = $16,100) in full settlement of its account receivable. Since the receivable had originally been equivalent to $16,300, the decline in the exchange rate has caused a loss of $200 to the U.S. company. The entry to be made on September 30 would be:

A foreign exchange rate loss occurs when the exchange rate decreases between the sales date and the collection date

Cash	16,100	
Loss on Fluctuations in Foreign Exchange Rates	200	
Accounts Receivable		16,300
To record collection of £10,000 receivable from British company and to recognize loss from fall in exchange rate since date of sale:		
Original sales price (£10,000 × $1.63) $16,300		
Amount received (£10,000 × $1.61) 16,100		
Loss from decline in exchange rate . . . . $ 200		

Now consider the alternative case, in which the exchange rate rises from $1.63 at August 1 to $1.66 at September 30. In this case, the British company's payment of £10,000 will convert into $16,600, creating a gain for the U.S. company. The entry on September 30 would then be:

Cash	16,600	
Accounts Receivable		16,300
Gain on Fluctuations in Foreign Exchange Rates		300
To record collection of £10,000 receivable from British company and to recognize gain from increase in exchange rate:		
Original sales price (£10,000 × $1.63) $16,300		
Amount received (£10,000 × $1.66) 16,600		
Gain from increase in exchange rate . . . . $ 300		

Adjustment of Foreign Receivables and Payables at the Balance Sheet Date

We have seen that fluctuations in exchange rates may cause gains or losses for companies with accounts payable or receivable in foreign currencies. Exchange rates fluctuate on a daily basis. For convenience, however, the company usually waits until the account is paid or collected before recording the related gain or loss. An exception to this convenient practice occurs at the end of the accounting period. An *adjusting entry* is made to recognize any gains or losses that have accumulated on any foreign payables or receivables through the balance sheet date.

To illustrate, assume that the transaction illustrated in Exhibit 15–8 occurs on November 10 when a U.S. company buys equipment from a Japanese company at a price of 10 million yen (¥10,000,000), payable on January 10 of the following year. If the exchange rate is $0.0100 per yen on November 10, the entry for the U.S. company to record the purchase would be:

| Equipment .... | 100,000 | |
| Accounts Payable .... | | 100,000 |

To record purchase of equipment from Japanese company at
a price of ¥10,000,000, payable January 10 (¥10,000,000 ×
$0.0100 = $100,000).

 Assets purchased on account must be recorded in dollars using the exchange rate on the date of purchase

EXHIBIT 15–8

Foreign Exchange Transaction: U.S. Company Buys Equipment from a Japanese Company

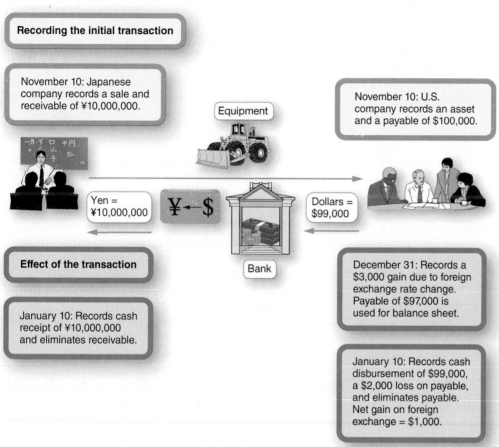

Recording the initial transaction

November 10: Japanese company records a sale and receivable of ¥10,000,000.

Equipment

November 10: U.S. company records an asset and a payable of $100,000.

Yen = ¥10,000,000

¥ ← $

Dollars = $99,000

Effect of the transaction

Bank

December 31: Records a $3,000 gain due to foreign exchange rate change. Payable of $97,000 is used for balance sheet.

January 10: Records cash receipt of ¥10,000,000 and eliminates receivable.

January 10: Records cash disbursement of $99,000, a $2,000 loss on payable, and eliminates payable. Net gain on foreign exchange = $1,000.

Now assume that on December 31, the exchange rate has fallen to $0.0097 per yen. At this exchange rate, the U.S. company's account payable is equivalent to only $97,000 (¥10,000,000 × $0.0097). Gains and losses from changes in exchange rates are recognized in the period *in which the change occurs*. Therefore, the American company should make an adjusting entry to restate its liability at the current dollar-equivalent and to recognize any related gain or loss. This entry, dated December 31, would be:

| Accounts Payable .... | 3,000 | |
| Gain on Fluctuations in Foreign Exchange Rates .... | | 3,000 |

To adjust balance of ¥10,000,000 account payable to amount
indicated by year-end exchange rate:

Original account balance	$100,000
Adjusted balance (¥10,000,000 × $0.0097)	97,000
Required adjustment	$ 3,000

 The foreign exchange rate gain on accounts payable is included in year-end statements

Similar adjustments should be made for any other accounts payable or receivable at year-end that are fixed in terms of a foreign currency.

If the exchange rate changes again between the date of this adjusting entry and the date that the U.S. company pays the liability, an additional gain or loss must be recognized. Assume, for example, that on January 10 the exchange rate has risen to $0.0099 per yen. As shown in Exhibit 15–8, the U.S. company must now spend $99,000 to buy the ¥10,000,000 needed to pay its liability to the Japanese company. Thus, the rise in the exchange rate has caused the U.S. company a $2,000 loss since year-end. The entry to record payment of the account on January 10 would be:

Accounts Payable	97,000	
Loss on Fluctuations in Foreign Exchange Rates	2,000	
Cash		99,000
To record payment of ¥10,000,000 payable to Japanese company and to recognize loss from rise in exchange rate since year-end:		
Account payable, December 31	$97,000	
Amount paid, January 10	99,000	
Loss from increase in exchange rate	$ 2,000	

Notice the *overall effect* of entering into this credit transaction stated in yen was a $1,000 gain due to fluctuations in the exchange rate for the yen between November 10 and the date of payment (January 10). The U.S. company recognized a $3,000 gain on fluctuations in the exchange rate from November 10 through the balance sheet date (December 31). This was partially offset in the next fiscal year by a $2,000 loss on fluctuations in the exchange rate between December 31 and January 10. The overall effect can be computed directly by multiplying the amount of the foreign currency times the *change* in exchange rates between the transaction date and the payment date (¥10,000,000 × [$0.0100 − $0.0099] = $1,000 gain). The $3,000 gain recorded at the balance sheet date and the $2,000 loss recorded at the date of payment have no associated cash flow effects.

Gains and losses from fluctuations in exchange rates on transactions carried out in a foreign currency should be included in the income statement. They typically are presented in a manner much like interest expense and gains and losses on the sale of plant assets.

CURRENCY FLUCTUATIONS—WHO WINS AND WHO LOSES?

Gains and losses from fluctuations in exchange rates are sustained by companies (or individuals) that have either payables or receivables that are *fixed in terms of a foreign currency.* United States companies that import foreign products usually have large foreign liabilities. Companies that export U.S. products to other countries are likely to have large receivables stated in foreign currencies.

As foreign exchange rates (stated in dollars) *fall,* U.S.-based importers will gain and exporters will lose. When a foreign exchange rate falls, the foreign currency becomes *less expensive.* Therefore, importers will have to spend fewer dollars to pay their foreign liabilities. Exporters, on the other hand, will have to watch their foreign receivables become worth fewer and fewer dollars.

When foreign exchange rates *rise,* this situation reverses. Importers will lose, because more dollars are required to pay the foreign debts. Exporters will gain, because their foreign receivables become equivalent to an increasing number of dollars.

Strategies to Avoid Losses from Rate Fluctuations

There are two basic approaches to avoiding losses from fluctuations in foreign exchange rates. One approach is to insist that receivables and payables be settled at specified amounts of domestic currency. The other approach is called *hedging* and can be accomplished in a number of ways.

To illustrate the first approach, assume that a U.S. company makes large credit sales to companies in Mexico, but anticipates that the exchange rate for the Mexican peso will gradually decline. The U.S. company can avoid losses by setting its *sales prices in dollars.* Then, if the exchange rate does decline, the Mexican companies will have to spend more pesos to pay for their purchases, but the U.S. company will not receive fewer dollars. On the other hand, the U.S. company will benefit from making credit *purchases* from Mexican companies at *prices stated in pesos,* because a decline in the exchange rate will reduce the number of dollars needed to pay for these purchases.

The interests of the Mexican companies, however, are exactly the opposite of those of the U.S. company. If the Mexican companies anticipate an increase in the exchange rate for the U.S. dollar, they will want to buy at prices stated in pesos and sell at prices stated in dollars. Ultimately, the manner in which the transactions will be priced simply depends on which company is in the better bargaining position.

Hedging

Hedging refers to the strategy of "sitting on both sides of the fence"—that is, of taking offsetting positions so that your gains and losses tend to offset one another. To illustrate the concept, assume that you make a large bet on a football game. Later you have second thoughts about the bet, and you want to eliminate your risk of incurring a loss. You could "hedge" your original bet by making a similar bet on the other team. In this way, you will lose one bet, but you will win the other—your loss will be offset by a corresponding gain.

A company that has similar amounts of accounts receivable and accounts payable in the same foreign currency automatically has a hedged position. A decrease in the foreign exchange rate will cause losses on the foreign receivables and gains on the foreign payables. If the exchange rate rises, the gains on the foreign receivables will be offset by losses on the foreign payables.

Most companies, of course, do *not* have similar amounts of receivables and payables in the same foreign currency. However, they may create this situation by buying or selling foreign currency **future contracts.** These contracts, commonly called *futures,* are the right to receive a specified quantity of foreign currency at a future date. In short, they are accounts receivable in foreign currency. Thus, for example, a company that has only foreign accounts payable may hedge its position by purchasing a similar dollar amount of foreign currency future contracts. Then, if the exchange rate rises, any losses on the foreign payables will be offset by a gain in the value of the future contracts.

Exchange Rates and Competitive Prices

Up to this point, we have discussed only the gains and losses incurred by companies that have receivables or payables stated in a foreign currency. However, fluctuations in exchange rates change the *relative prices* of goods produced in different countries. Exchange rate fluctuations may make the prices of a country's products more or less competitive both at home and to customers throughout the world. Even a small store with no foreign accounts receivable or payable may find its business operations greatly affected by fluctuations in foreign exchange rates.

Consider, for example, a small store in Kansas that sells a U.S.-made brand of television sets. If foreign exchange rates fall, which happens when the dollar is strong, the price of foreign-made television sets will decline. Thus, the store selling U.S.-made television sets may have to compete with stores selling imported television sets at lower prices. Also, a strong dollar makes U.S. goods *more expensive to customers in foreign countries.* Thus, a U.S. television manufacturer will find it more difficult to sell its products abroad.

The situation reverses when the dollar is weak—that is, when foreign exchange rates are relatively high. A weak dollar makes foreign imports more expensive to U.S. consumers. Also, a weak dollar makes U.S. products less expensive to customers in foreign countries.

L015-6

LEARNING OBJECTIVE
Describe techniques for "hedging" against losses from fluctuations in exchange rates.

YOUR TURN   You as a Consumer

Assume you are in the market for a new racing bicycle. You are considering buying an Italian, British, or U.S. racing bicycle. You have recently heard that the dollar is strengthening against the euro and is falling against the British pound. These trends are expected to continue for another month. How would this news affect your assessment of choices among racing bicycles?

(See our comments on the Online Learning Center website.)

In summary, we may say that a strong U.S. dollar *helps companies that sell foreign-made goods in the U.S. market.* A weak dollar, on the other hand, *gives a competitive advantage to companies that sell U.S. products both at home and abroad.*

CONSOLIDATED FINANCIAL STATEMENTS THAT INCLUDE FOREIGN SUBSIDIARIES

In Chapter 14, we discussed the concept of *consolidated* financial statements. These statements view the operations of the parent company and its subsidiaries as if the affiliated companies were a single business entity. Several special accounting problems arise in preparing consolidated financial statements when subsidiaries operate in foreign countries. First, the accounting records of the foreign subsidiaries must be translated into U.S. dollars. Second, the accounting principles in use in the foreign countries may differ significantly from U.S. generally accepted accounting principles.

These problems pose interesting challenges to professional accountants and will be addressed in later accounting courses. Readers of the financial statements of U.S.-based corporations, however, should know that the consolidated financial statements of these companies are expressed in U.S. dollars and conform to U.S. generally accepted accounting principles.

Global Sourcing

LO15-7

LEARNING OBJECTIVE
Discuss how global sourcing increases product cost complexity.

Differences in exchange rates can create significant complexities for firms practicing global sourcing. An article in the *Los Angeles Times* illustrated the additional problems associated with determining the cost of producing a doll using inputs from several countries. Exhibit 15–9 traces the multicountry path of a Barbie™ doll from its raw materials source in a Saudi

EXHIBIT 15–9

Global Sourcing for
Mattel Inc.'s Barbie™ Doll

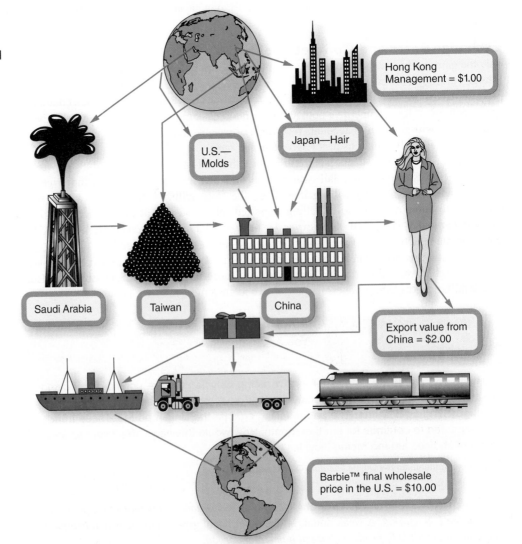

Hong Kong Management = $1.00

Japan—Hair

U.S.—Molds

Saudi Arabia

Taiwan

China

Export value from China = $2.00

Barbie™ final wholesale price in the U.S. = $10.00

Arabian oil field to U.S. toy stores. After the oil is refined to produce ethylene, Taiwan uses the ethylene to produce vinyl pellets that are shipped to Dongguan in China's Guangdong province. At the Chinese joint-venture factory, 5,500 workers, paid between $30 and $40 per month, make the plastic doll and her clothes. However, most of the machinery and tools, including the plastic mold injection machines, are imported from the United States, Europe, and Japan. The molds themselves come directly from the United States. Japan contributes Barbie's nylon hair. Hong Kong manages the entire process, arranging banking and insurance, supervising exporting and importing, and overseeing transportation back to the United States. Finally, U.S. domestic packaging, trucking, advertising, and other functions that employ thousands of U.S. workers result in a $10.00 Barbie™ wholesale price. **Mattel Inc.** has indicated that its typical profit from the sale of a Barbie™ is about $1.00.

Exhibit 15–10 illustrates the costs and exchange rate issues involved in the production of a Barbie™ doll. Panel A provides the currency exchange rates for the countries involved in global sourcing for the Barbie™ doll. Panel B includes estimated product export costs for the **Mattel Inc.** Barbie™ made at the Meitai factory in Dongguan, China. The estimated costs in the exhibit are based on a single day's reported exchange rates. Companies must choose a representative exchange rate to compute the cost buildup in their domestic currency.

EXHIBIT 15–10

Exchange Rates and Estimated Product Cost for Barbie™ Dolls

Estimated Product Cost for Barbie™*

Panel A: Exchange Rates†

Country	Currency	U.S. $ Equivalent
Saudi Arabia	Riyal	.2667
Taiwan	Taiwanese dollar	.0326
Hong Kong	Hong Kong dollar	.1286
Japan	Yen	.0095
China	Yuan	.1225

Panel B: Estimated Product Cost Buildup

Input	Foreign Currency Value	U.S. $ Equivalent
Raw materials:		
Saudi Arabia	0.6374 riyal	$0.17
Taiwan	4.908 Taiwanese dollars	0.16
Japan	22.11 yen	0.21
China	0.898 yuan	0.11
Direct labor:		
China	2.857 yuan	0.35
Overhead:		
Hong Kong	7.776 Hong Kong dollars	1.00
Total export cost		$2.00

*Estimates based on information provided in R. Tempest, "Barbie and the World Economy," *Los Angeles Times*, September 22, 1999, p. 1.

† Based on exchange rates from www.xe.com/ucc.

The information in the exhibit does not provide details about customs duties, import and export fees, multicountry tax laws, and tax treaties. These are also costs of doing business in a global environment. Many companies underestimate the cost of globalizing their business operations because they are not familiar with the environmental characteristics discussed at the beginning of this chapter. Making accurate estimates of costs for global sourcing is a challenge for companies wishing to become more global.

FOREIGN CORRUPT PRACTICES ACT

In many countries, product costs also include expenses incurred to expedite official paperwork. Kenyan business executives refer to *kitu kidogo* ("something small"), the Chinese pay *huilu,* Russians shell out *vzyatka,* and Middle Easterners pay *baksheesh.* In dozens of countries around the world, bribery is part of doing business. In many countries, this officially sanctioned corruption is not viewed as wrong or unethical. However, U.S.-based businesses are prohibited from influence peddling. The **Foreign Corrupt Practices Act** (FCPA), passed in 1977 and amended in 1986 and 1998 by the U.S. Congress, prescribes fines and jail time for managers violating its rules. For over 30 years, U.S. companies have complained about the advantage experienced by international competitors who are not bound by the FCPA.

Experiences in the past 5 to 10 years have changed international attitudes about the impact of corrupt practices on economic viability. In particular, the 1997–1998 Asian crisis was blamed partly on graft and influence peddling. According to some estimates, corruption associated with doing business in Indonesia can add 5 percent to operating costs. Corruption can be so rampant that companies refuse to operate in some foreign locations, causing countries to lose valuable direct foreign investment.

The International Monetary Fund and the World Bank instituted policies in the late 1990s to cut off funding to countries ignoring corrupt practices. In 2008, $33 million in contract payments for Philippine road projects were suspended until policies and procedures to prevent corruption were instituted. Many of the recommended policies and procedures are modeled after the FCPA. The scope of the FCPA is very broad. Under FCPA rules, it is illegal for all U.S. companies and foreign companies operating in the United States, their affiliates, and their agents to bribe a government official. Criminal and civil prosecution can lead to fines of up to $2 million for the company and $100,000 for executives involved, with prison terms of up to five years.

YOUR TURN   **You as a Head of International Acquisitions**

Assume you are the head of international acquisitions for a large multinational toy company traded on the New York Stock Exchange. You have been involved for several months in a deal to acquire a large facility in a midsize city in central China. This building will be remodeled by your company to produce a range of toy products for the Chinese market. For a variety of reasons, progress has been extremely slow on completing the acquisition. In particular, city administrators have continually delayed issuing the necessary paperwork. You decide to fly to China to meet with the city's top three officials. During your meeting it becomes clear that the three city officials would guarantee processing the associated paperwork much faster if your company would provide a significant payment to each of them to help expedite the necessary work. These administrators point out that a German company that acquired a facility in the city the previous year was willing to pay extra to expedite paperwork.

Your CEO has made it clear to you that the China project is very important and expediting it is critical for its long-run success. What should you do?

(See our comments on the Online Learning Center website.)

LO15-8

LEARNING OBJECTIVE
Explain the importance of the Foreign Corrupt Practices Act.

The FCPA has implications for accounting in two specific areas: record keeping and internal control procedures. The act requires that all payments, including improper payments, be recorded and disclosed. Further, the act requires an adequate system of internal controls that maintains the integrity of the company's assets, allowing only authorized personnel to have access to them. The 1986 amendment to the FCPA distinguished between *influence peddling,*

Ethics, Fraud, & Corporate Governance

The Foreign Corrupt Practices Act (FCPA) applies to U.S. companies and foreign companies operating in the United States, their affiliates, and their agents. Violations of the FCPA expose companies and individuals to both civil and criminal liability. For example, in 2012 the Securities and Exchange Commission (SEC) brought an enforcement action against Allianz SE, a Germany-based insurance and asset management company. Allianz SE was charged with violating (1) the books and records and (2) internal controls provisions of the FCPA for improper payments to government officials in Indonesia during a seven-year period.

The SEC's investigation uncovered 295 insurance contracts on large government projects that were obtained or retained by improper payments of $650,626 by Allianz's subsidiary in Indonesia to employees of state-owned entities. As a result, Allianz made more than $5.3 million in profits.

According to the SEC, the misconduct occurred while Allianz's share and bonds were registered with the SEC and traded on the New York Stock Exchange. Two complaints were alleged. First, unsupported payments were drawn from a "special purpose account" to make illegal payments to government officials to secure business in Indonesia. Second, Allianz failed to properly account for certain payments in the books and records when improper payments, disguised as an overpayment by the government holder of the insurance contract, were reimbursed by Allianz.

Without admitting or denying the findings, Allianz agreed to cease and desist from further violation and pay disgorgement of $5,315,649, prejudgment interest of $1,765,125, and a penalty of $5,315,649. The total penalty for violation of the FCPA was a whopping $12,396,423.

to motivate the awarding of business that would not otherwise have been awarded, and *facilitating payments,* to motivate officials to undertake actions more rapidly than they might otherwise. A facilitating payment might be given to a customs official to expedite imported merchandise through customs. This latter type of payment is not illegal under the act. Companies engaging in globalization must ensure that their cross-border employees comply with the FCPA.

Concluding Remarks

In this chapter we have established a framework to help you understand international financial reporting issues. You have learned how global environmental differences create demand for different types of financial information. However, other global forces, particularly global securities markets and large international firms, are pushing for a uniform set of international accounting standards for financial reporting. What does the development of international accounting standards foreshadow? We believe that significant progress toward harmonization is occurring. However, users of international financial statements should expect wide variation in disclosure levels and financial reporting practices for several years to come.

END-OF-CHAPTER REVIEW

SUMMARY OF LEARNING OBJECTIVES

LO15-1 **Define four mechanisms companies use to globalize their business activities.** Companies globalize their business activities through exporting, licensing, joint ventures, and wholly owned subsidiaries. Multinational companies use a global sourcing approach.

LO15-2 **Identify how global environmental forces— (a) political and legal systems, (b) economic systems, (c) culture, and (d) technology and infrastructure— affect accounting practices.** Countries use their political and legal systems to transfer and control business assets. Market versus centrally planned economic systems create different demands for financial reporting. Culture influences business relationships through beliefs and expectations of customers and business associates. The technology and infrastructure of each global location will affect the type and costs of business activities and related financial accounting reports.

LO15-3 **Explain why there is demand for harmonization of global financial reporting standards.** Cross-border differences in accounting and reporting create analysis and comparability problems between and among companies. The need for comparable information has led to the demand for harmonization.

LO15-4 **Demonstrate how to convert an amount of money from one currency to another.** To convert a foreign currency to an equivalent dollar amount, multiply the foreign currency by the foreign exchange rate. To convert a dollar amount into an equivalent amount of foreign currency, divide the dollar amount by the exchange rate.

LO15-5 **Compute gains or losses on receivables or payables that are stated in a foreign currency when exchange rates fluctuate.** The receivable or payable is recorded on the date the transaction is agreed to using the prevailing exchange rate. When exchanging cash completes the transaction, the exchange rate at the completion date is used to record the cash flow; the difference between the cash exchanged and the receivable or payable is recorded as a foreign exchange gain or loss.

LO15-6 **Describe techniques for "hedging" against losses from fluctuations in exchange rates.** Hedging is offsetting the potential for losses from foreign exchange rate fluctuations. It can be accomplished by having offsetting receivables and payables in the foreign currency or by buying or selling foreign currency future contracts.

LO15-7 **Discuss how global sourcing increases product cost complexity.** When some of the activities of designing, developing, producing, marketing, and servicing a product or service occur in more than one country, then global considerations affect product costs. These considerations include foreign exchange gains and losses, taxes, import and export duties, trade agreements, foreign trade zones, and limitations on currency flows.

LO15-8 **Explain the importance of the Foreign Corrupt Practices Act.** The FCPA prohibits influence peddling through bribery in international locations. The act requires companies engaged in global business activities to maintain good record keeping and adequate internal controls to safeguard company assets.

Key Terms Introduced or Emphasized in Chapter 15

adoption of IFRS (p. 691)   Means abandoning the country's financial reporting standards and replacing them with *International Financial Reporting Standards* (IFRS).

convergence with IFRS (p. 692)   A process by which a country's financial reporting standards are changed so that the use of their country GAAP standards will produce IFRS "equivalent" financial reports.

cross-border financing (p. 691)   Occurs when a company sells its securities in the capital markets of another country.

exchange rate (p. 693)   The amount it costs to purchase one unit of currency with another currency.

exporting (p. 687)   Selling a good or service to a foreign customer in a foreign country.

Foreign Corrupt Practices Act (p. 702)   Passed in 1977 and amended in 1986 and 1998 by the U.S. Congress, prescribes fines and jail time for managers violating its rules. It distinguishes between illegal influence peddling to motivate awarding of business that would not otherwise have been awarded and legal facilitating payments made to motivate officials to undertake actions more rapidly than they might otherwise.

foreign trade zones (p. 688)   Goods imported into these designated U.S. areas are duty free until they leave the zone.

future contracts (p. 699)   A contract giving the right to receive a specified quantity of foreign currency at a future date.

global sourcing (p. 687)   The close coordination of R&D, manufacturing, and marketing across national boundaries.

globalization (p. 686)   Occurs as managers become aware of and engage in cross-border trade and operations.

harmonization of accounting standards (p. 691)   The globalization of similar accounting methods and principles used throughout the world.

hedging (p. 699)   The practice of minimizing or eliminating risk of loss associated with foreign currency fluctuations.

industrial organizations (p. 689)   Exist when companies group themselves into conglomerates representing different industries. South Korean conglomerates, called *chaebol,* and Japanese conglomerates, called *keiretsu,* consist of companies that are grouped as customers and suppliers and usually contain a bank.

infrastructure (p. 691)   Access to communication, transportation, and utilities provided to businesses in each global location.

International Accounting Standards Board (IASB) (p. 691)   Charged with the responsibility of creating and promulgating international standards.

international joint venture (p. 687)   A company owned by two or more companies from different countries.

international licensing (p. 687)   A contractual agreement between a company and a foreign party allowing the use of trademarks, patents, technology, designs, processes, intellectual property, or other proprietary advantage.

market economy (p. 689)   Exists when ownership of land and the means of production are private and markets dictate the allocation of resources and the output among segments of the economy.

planned economy (p. 689)   Exists when the government uses central planning to allocate resources and determine output among various segments of the economy. Government ownership of land and the means of production characterize planned economies.

wholly owned international subsidiary (p. 687)   Created through a company's foreign direct investment; involves using domestically generated funds in another country to purchase 100 percent equity control of a foreign subsidiary.

Demonstration Problem

IronMan, Inc., is a U.S. company that manufactures exercise machines and distributes several lines of imported bicycles. Selected transactions of the company were as follows:

Oct. 4   Purchased manufacturing equipment from Rhine Mfg. Co., a German company. The purchase price was €400,000, due in 60 days. Current exchange rate, $0.770 per euro. (Debit the Equipment account.)

Oct. 18   Purchased 2,500 racing bicycles from Ninja Cycles, a Japanese company, at a price of ¥60,000,000. Payment is due in 90 days; the current exchange rate is $0.0098 per yen. (IronMan uses the perpetual inventory system.)

Nov. 15   Purchased 1,000 touring bicycles from Royal Lion Ltd., a British corporation. The purchase price was £192,500, payable in 30 days. Current exchange rate, $1.54 per British pound.

Dec. 3   Issued a check to First Bank for the U.S. dollar-equivalent of €400,000 in payment of the account payable to Rhine Mfg. Co. Current exchange rate, $0.771 per euro.

Dec. 15   Issued a check to First Bank for dollar-equivalent of £192,500 in payment of the account payable to Royal Lion Ltd. Current exchange rate, $1.52 per British pound.

Instructions

a.   Prepare entries in general journal form to record the preceding transactions.

b.   Prepare the December 31 adjusting entry relating to the account payable to Ninja Cycles. The year-end exchange rate is $0.0099 per Japanese yen.

c.   Identify some methods that IronMan, Inc., could use to decrease its exposure to foreign exchange rate fluctuations.

d.   Discuss environmental characteristics of Japan, Germany, and the United Kingdom that influence their exchange rate fluctuations.

Solution to the Demonstration Problem

a. The general journal entries to record the transactions are as follows:

	GENERAL JOURNAL		
Date	**Account Titles and Explanation**	**Debit**	**Credit**
Oct. 4	Equipment	308,000	
	Accounts Payable (Rhine Mfg. Co.)		308,000
	To record purchase of equipment from Rhine Mfg. Co. for €400,000, exchange rate $0.770 per euro (€400,000 × $0.770 = $308,000).		
Oct. 18	Inventory	588,000	
	Accounts Payable (Ninja Cycles)		588,000
	Purchased 2,500 bicycles from Ninja Cycles for ¥60,000,000, exchange rate $0.0098 (¥60,000,000 × $0.0098 = $588,000).		
Nov. 15	Inventory	296,450	
	Accounts Payable (Royal Lion Ltd.)		296,450
	Purchased 1,000 bicycles from Royal Lion Ltd. for £192,500, due in 30 days. Exchange rate $1.54 per pound (£192,500 × $1.54 = $296,450).		
Dec. 3	Accounts Payable (Rhine Mfg. Co.)	308,000	
	Loss on Fluctuations of Foreign Exchange Rates	400	
	Cash		308,400
	Paid €400,000 liability to Rhine Mfg. Co. (Original balance less amount paid equals loss: $308,000 − (€400,000 × $0.771) = −$400).		
Dec. 15	Accounts Payable (Royal Lion Ltd.)	296,450	
	Gain on Fluctuations of Foreign Exchange Rates		3,850
	Cash		292,600
	Paid £192,500 liability to Royal Lion Ltd. (Original balance less amount paid equals gain: $296,450 − (£192,500 × $1.52) = $9,625).		

b. The December 31 adjusting entry for the account payable to Ninja Cycles:

	GENERAL JOURNAL		
Date	**Account Titles and Explanation**	**Debit**	**Credit**
Dec. 31	Loss on Fluctuations in Foreign Exchange Rates	6,000	
	Accounts Payable (Ninja Cycles)		6,000
	To adjust balance of ¥60,000,000 liability to amount indicated by year-end exchange rate: (Original balance less adjusted balance equals loss: $588,000 − (¥60,000,000 × $0.0099) = −$6000).		

c. IronMan could use offsetting payables and receivables to control potential foreign exchange rate losses. For example, if IronMan could export its exercise equipment to Japan, then it would have a receivable to offset its payable. IronMan could also purchase future contracts maturing at the same time the liabilities were due. Gains and losses on the future contracts would offset gains and losses resulting from foreign currency fluctuations.

d. Germany has a lower volume and smaller capitalized equities market. Germany uses the euro and is part of the European Union. Banks are a major provider of capital to businesses in Germany. Japan has *keiretsu* organizations for many of its industrial groups. These organizations include manufacturers, distributors, wholesalers, retailers, and suppliers who work together and share resources. The accounting profession is much weaker in both Germany and Japan than in the United States. The United Kingdom is most like the United States, with active equity markets, a strong accounting profession, and similar accounting rules.

Self-Test Questions

The answers to these questions appear on page 720.

1. Which of the following statements are *true* about globalization methods?

   a. International licensing involves the creation of a new company that is owned by two or more firms from different countries.

   b. Exporting involves contracts that allow a foreign company to use a domestic company's trademarks, patents, processes, or technology.

   c. Global sourcing involves the close coordination of research and development, purchasing, marketing, and manufacturing across national boundaries.

   d. A wholly owned international subsidiary is created when a foreign government owns 100 percent of the equity in a U.S.-based firm.

2. Which of the following environmental factors can affect the cost of doing business in a foreign country? (Identify all correct answers.)

   a. The educational level of the workforce.

   b. Laws regulating the transfer of profits out of a country.

   c. Tax and tariff regulations.

   d. Restricted access to communication and transportation networks.

3. A country whose citizens are highly group oriented and who accept equal power distributions between and within organizations would be considered:

   a. Individualistic and low power distance.

   b. Collectivist and high power distance.

   c. Individualistic and high power distance.

   d. Collectivist and low power distance.

4. On March 1, Laton Products (a U.S. firm) purchased manufacturing inputs from a German supplier for 20,000 euros, payable on June 1. The exchange rate for euros on March 1 was $1.31. If the exchange rate decreases to $1.29 on June 1, what amount of gain or loss would be reported by Laton related to the currency exchange?

   a. $400 gain.

   b. $200 loss.

   c. $400 loss.

   d. $200 gain.

5. On January 1, a German company purchased merchandise from a U.S. firm for $50,000, payable on March 1. The exchange rate for the euro on January 1 was $1.10. If the exchange rate increases to $1.12 on March 1, what amount of gain or loss would the U.S. firm report related to currency fluctuations?

   a. $1,000 gain.

   b. $1,000 loss.

   c. $500 gain.

   d. No gain or loss would be reported.

ASSIGNMENT MATERIAL Discussion Questions

1. In general terms, identify several factors that prompt different countries to develop different accounting principles.

2. What is the International Accounting Standards Board? Why has the board been unable to obtain uniform global application of its standards?

3. An American company is considering entering into a joint venture with a Korean firm. Describe what cultural differences each party should consider.

4. Consider Exhibit 15–1. Identify the countries or regions with the highest and lowest percentage change in Fortune 500 companies. Provide an explanation for these percentage changes.

5. Why is it important to understand the economic system under which a company operates *before* entering into a business relationship?

6. Provide an example showing how the following environmental forces affect accounting practices:

   a. Political and legal systems.

   b. Economic systems.

   c. Culture.

   d. Technology and infrastructure.

7. Discuss two ways in which the Foreign Corrupt Practices Act has affected U.S. companies.

8. Explain two ways in which a company that makes purchases on account from foreign companies can protect itself against the losses that would arise from a sudden increase in the foreign exchange rate.

9. What does the *globalization* of business mean? Think of two companies with which you are familiar. How would you describe their level of globalization?

10. You've just read in *The Wall Street Journal* that the U.S. dollar has strengthened relative to the euro. All else equal, what would you expect to happen to the quantity of Italian leather jackets sold in the United States? Why?

11. What is the difference between an international licensing agreement and an international joint venture?

12. To maintain a high level of control over production operations and final product quality, what types of globalization activities could a company engage in?

13. How might the required financial reports differ between countries that are individualistic and countries that are collectivist?

14. A French furniture maker agrees to purchase wood stain from a U.S. paint manufacturer. If all payments are to be made in U.S. dollars, which company bears the risk of exchange rate gains and losses?

15. What is meant by the phrase *natural hedging against exchange rate risk?*

Brief Exercises

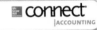

LO15-4 **BRIEF EXERCISE 15.1** Foreign Currency Translations	Translate the following amounts of foreign currency into an equivalent number of U.S. dollars using the exchange rates in Exhibit 15.7. **a.** £800,000. **b.** ¥350,000. **c.** €50,000.
LO15-4, LO15-5 **BRIEF EXERCISE 15.2** Purchases in a Foreign Currency	Assume that a U.S. company makes a purchase from a British company and agrees to pay a price of £2 million. **a.** How will the U.S. company determine the cost of this purchase for the purpose of recording it in its accounting records? **b.** Briefly explain how the U.S. company can arrange for the payment of pounds to the British company.
LO15-4 **BRIEF EXERCISE 15.3** Currency Strength	A recent newspaper shows the exchange rate for the British pound at $1.44 and the yen at $0.0108. Does this indicate that the pound is stronger than the yen? Explain.
LO15-5 **BRIEF EXERCISE 15.4** Exchange Rate Fluctuations	Explain how an increase in a foreign exchange rate will affect a U.S. company that makes: **a.** Credit sales to a foreign company at prices stated in the foreign currency. **b.** Credit purchases from a foreign company at prices stated in the foreign currency. **c.** Credit sales to a foreign company at prices stated in U.S. dollars.
LO15-5, LO15-6 **BRIEF EXERCISE 15.5** Currency Choice	You are the purchasing agent for a U.S. business that purchases merchandise on account from companies in Mexico. The exchange rate for the Mexican peso has been falling against the U.S. dollar and the trend is expected to continue for at least several months. Would you prefer that the prices for purchases from the Mexican companies be specified in U.S. dollars or in Mexican pesos? Explain.
LO15-4 **BRIEF EXERCISE 15.6** Currency Strength and Gains and Losses	CompuTech is a U.S.-based multinational corporation. Foreign sales are made at prices set in U.S. dollars, but foreign purchases are often made at prices stated in foreign currencies. If the exchange rate for the U.S. dollar has risen against most foreign currencies throughout the year, would CompuTech have recognized primarily gains or losses as a result of exchange rate fluctuations? Explain.
LO15-2 **BRIEF EXERCISE 15.7** Culture Effects on Business	When business transactions are conducted internationally, cultural differences must be taken into consideration. Geert Hofstede is a leading researcher on how cultural variables can affect such international arrangements. Hofstede has a website where he is quoted as saying: For those who work in international business, it is sometimes amazing how different people in other cultures behave. We tend to have a human instinct that "deep inside" all people are the same—but they are not. Therefore, if we go into another country and make decisions based on how we operate in our own home country—the chances are we'll make some very bad decisions.

Go to Hofstede's website (www.geert-hofstede.com) look under "national culture" and use the "applications" tab to find an example of how business dealings can be hindered by a lack of understanding of cultural differences.

LO15-5, LO15-6
BRIEF EXERCISE 15.8
Currency Fluctuation
Effects

Bosor Corporation has a receivable denominated in British pounds and a payable in Brazilian reals resulting from imports from Brazil. Bosor recorded foreign exchange losses related to both its pound-related receivable and its real-denominated payable. Did the foreign currencies increase or decrease in dollar value from the date of the transaction to the settlement date?

LO15-8
BRIEF EXERCISE 15.9
Foreign Corrupt
Practices Act

In 2011, Bridgestone Corporation agreed to plead guilty and pay a $28 million criminal fine for its role in rigging bids and making corrupt payments to foreign government officials in Latin America. Bridgestone, a Tokyo-headquartered company, participated in the conspiracies from January 1999 through May 2007. Bridgestone's local sales agents agreed to pay employees of state-owned customers a percentage of the total value of proposed sales. When Bridgestone secured a sale, it would pay the local sales agent a "commission" consisting of not only the local sales agent's actual commission, but also the corrupt payments to be made to employees of the state-owned customer. The local sales agent was responsible for passing the agreed-upon payment to the employee of the customer. At least nine individuals were convicted and sentenced to 4,557 days in prison. What U.S. law was violated and why?

LO15-4
BRIEF EXERCISE 15.10
Exchange Rate
Computation

A U.S. company purchased a shipment of fabrics from Bahrain for 3,500,000 dinars. According to the current exchange rate, what is the value of this contract in U.S. dollars?

Exercises

LO15-1 through LO15-8
EXERCISE 15.1
Global Business
Terminology

The following are nine global business terms used in this chapter:

Hedging	Foreign exchange risk	International Accounting Standards Board
Foreign Corrupt Practices Act	Planned economy	
	International licensing	Harmonization
Globalization		Exporting

Each of the following statements may describe one of these terms. For each statement, indicate the global business term described, or answer "None" if the statement does not correctly describe any of the terms.

a. The amount it costs to purchase one unit of currency with another currency.

b. Selling a good or service to a foreign customer.

c. A cross-border contractual agreement allowing one company to use the trademarks, patents, or technology of another company.

d. Distinguishes between illegal influence peddling and legal facilitating payments.

e. The practice of minimizing or eliminating risk of loss associated with foreign currency fluctuations.

f. Markets dictate the allocation of resources and output among segments of the economy.

g. The group charged with the responsibility of creating and encouraging the use of international financial reporting standards.

LO15-1, LO15-2
EXERCISE 15.2
External Financial Reports
and Globalization

With a group of two or three students, choose a publicly traded global company that you think you might want to invest in some time in the future. Use the Internet or annual report data to answer the following questions.

a. In which geographical regions does the company operate?

b. What is the proportion of total sales represented by foreign sales? How has this changed over the past five years?

c. What efforts has the company recently undertaken to increase/decrease globalization (for example, joint ventures, licensing agreements, etc.)?

d. What are the company's hedging practices/policies?

e. Have any overseas activities been unsuccessful, discontinued, or resulted in asset losses? If so, what happened?

f. Overall, how aggressively do you feel this company is pursuing globalization?

LO15-4
EXERCISE 15.3
Understanding Exchange Rate Conversions

For each of the following scenarios, use the current exchange rates in *The Wall Street Journal* or from an Internet site such as www.xe.com/ucc to compute the required amount:

a. A Citroën automobile is advertised in France for 17,990 euros. What is the dollar equivalent of 17,990 euros?

b. Jackk's food emporium is importing foreign hot sauce from Brazil for 7,000 reals. What is the dollar equivalent?

c. You are traveling on safari in South Africa and have brought $3,000 in spending money. How many South African rand will you receive for spending money?

d. While traveling in Europe, you cross the border between Germany and Switzerland. You have 150 euros left from your German travels when you spot a souvenir in a Swiss shop for 250 Swiss francs. Do you have enough spending money to buy the souvenir if you convert your euros to Swiss francs?

LO15-2, LO15-7, LO15-8
EXERCISE 15.4
Location International Business Information

The U.S. government maintains an Internet site containing information on various countries called The World Factbook. The site includes a database under the countries and regions tab. Use the data or other publicly available data to answer the following questions about Indonesia.

a. What are the country's main exports and imports?

b. What is the educational and job classification composition of the labor force?

c. How would you describe the infrastructure and technology base of the country?

d. What are the political and legal risks of doing business there?

e. If you were advising a U.S. company that wanted to locate a wholly owned subsidiary in Indonesia, what aspects of the country would you stress that management take into account when deciding whether to invest there and how to organize the subsidiary's manufacturing process?

LO15-2, LO15-5
EXERCISE 15.5
Currency Fluctuations: Who Wins and Who Loses?

Indicate whether each of the companies or individuals in the following independent cases would benefit more from a strong U.S. dollar (relatively low foreign exchange rates) or a weak U.S. dollar (relatively high foreign exchange rates). Provide a brief explanation of your reasoning.

a. Boeing (a U.S. aircraft manufacturer that sells many planes to foreign customers).

b. A Nikon camera store in Beverly Hills, California (Nikon cameras are made in Japan).

c. Citroën (made by Peugot, an auto manufacturer in France).

d. The Mexico City dealer for Caterpillar tractors (made in the United States).

e. A U.S. tourist visiting England.

f. A small store that sells U.S.-made video recorders in Toledo, Ohio (the store has no foreign accounts receivable or payable).

LO15-4, LO15-5
EXERCISE 15.6
Foreign Currency Transactions

The following table summarizes the facts of five independent cases (labeled **a** through **e**) of U.S. companies engaging in credit transactions with foreign corporations while the foreign exchange rate is fluctuating:

	Column			
	Type of Credit Transaction	Currency Used in Contract	Exchange Rate Direction	Effect on Income
Case	**1**	**2**	**3**	**4**
a	Sales	Foreign currency	Falling	_____
b	Purchases	U.S. dollars	Rising	_____
c	_____	Foreign currency	Rising	Loss
d	Sales	_____	Falling	No effect
e	Purchases	Foreign currency	_____	Gain

You are to fill in each blank space after evaluating the information about the case provided in the other three columns. The content of each column and the word or words that you should enter in the blank spaces are described as follows:

Column 1 indicates the type of credit transaction in which the U.S. company engaged with the foreign corporations. The answer entered in this column should be either *Sales* or *Purchases*.

Column 2 indicates the currency in which the invoice price is stated. The answer may be either *U.S. dollars* or *Foreign currency*.

Column 3 indicates the direction in which the foreign currency exchange rate has moved between the date of the credit transaction and the date of settlement. The answer entered in this column may be either *Rising* or *Falling*.

Column 4 indicates the effect of the exchange rate fluctuation on the income of the American company. The answers entered in this column are to be selected from the following: *Gain, Loss,* or *No effect.*

LO15-3
EXERCISE 15.7
Harmonization around the World

Visit the site at **www.iasplus.com/country/useias.htm.**

a. Name three governments that require companies to prepare their financial reports *only* in accordance with IFRS in order to list their stocks on the country's securities markets.

b. Name three governments that will not allow domestic companies to prepare their financial reports in accordance with IFRS to list their stocks on the country's securities markets.

LO15-4, LO15-5
EXERCISE 15.8
Foreign Currency Sale Journal Entries

Assume that on May 1, Zavior Corporation (a U.S. company) sells goods to a Portuguese corporation at a price of 100,000 euros, with payment due within three months. At the date of the sale, the exchange rate is $1.20 per euro. The Portuguese customer waits until the three months have passed and pays for the purchase on July 31, when the exchange rate is $1.18 per euro. What is the gain or loss on the transaction for Zavior? Show the journal entries that Zavior would record on May 1 and on July 31.

LO15-1, LO15-2
EXERCISE 15.9
Home Depot's International Expansion

In the **Home Depot** 2012 financial statements in Appendix A at the end of this textbook, read note 1. Find the information about **Home Depot**'s international store locations.

a. In what countries (other than the United States) does **Home Depot** have stores?

b. What environmental factors does it need to consider when expanding to foreign countries and why?

LO15-3
EXERCISE 15.10
Matching Foreign Exchange Gains and Losses

Match the following transactions, which are denominated in a foreign currency, with the appropriate foreign currency and exchange gain or loss effects.

Transaction		Matching Transaction Letter	Foreign Currency Effect	Foreign Exchange Gain or Loss
a.	Export sale			
b.	Import purchase	?	Appreciates	Loss
c.	Foreign currency receivable	?	Appreciates	Gain
d.	Payable in foreign currency	?	Depreciates	Gain
		?	Depreciates	Loss

LO15-6
EXRCISE 15.11
Foreign Currency Translation Effects

Find the Consolidated Statement of Comprehensive Income section of the **Home Depot** 2012 financial statements in Appendix A. Locate the translation adjustment for 2012. Was the effect of the adjustment positive or negative on Comprehensive Income? What is the implication of the translation adjustment?

LO15-4, LO15-7
EXERCISE 15.12
Global Sourcing Costs for **Mattel Inc.**

Reconsider Exhibit 15–10, panel B, in the chapter. Use current exchange rates to estimate the global costs of making a Barbie™ doll. Has the total cost increased or decreased as a result of changes in exchange rates?

LOI5-2, LOI5-3
EXERCISE 15.13
Financial Statement
Harmonization

Refer to Exhibit 15–6 in this chapter. Assume a United Kingdom company, Brits International, lists on both the London Exchange using U.K. GAAP and the New York Stock Exchange. Brits International must prepare a reconciliation from U.K. GAAP to U.S. GAAP. This reconciliation shows the following difference associated with revaluations of fixed assets:

	Net Income	Shareholder's Equity
U.K. balances	$783,200	$4,767,900
U.S. GAAP adjustments:		
a. Additional depreciation charges that result from revaluation of assets	47,600	326,533
b. Reversal of revaluation of fixed assets	_____	(523,740)
U.S. GAAP restatement	$830,800	$4,570,693

Required:

a. Explain why the adjustment to U.S. GAAP resulted in additions to net income.

b. Explain why there are additions to shareholders' equity and why those additions are greater than the additions to net income.

c. Explain why there is a deduction to shareholders' equity.

LOI5-3
EXERCISE 15.14
Honda Motor Company's
Use of IFRS or U.S. GAAP

Honda Motor Company reports that it has manufacturing facilities in over 25 locations around the world. Only five of those locations are in Japan. Several are in the United States, Europe, and South America. Identify the advantages and disadvantages for **Honda Motor Company** of reporting its financial results using either IFRS or U.S. GAAP.

LOI5-2
EXERCISE 15.15
Comparing Environmental
Factors

Research China and write a brief comparison of Chinese political-legal, economic, cultural, and infrastructure factors as contrasted to those in the United States. Explain how these factors might affect accounting practices in the two countries.

Problem Set A

LOI5-4, LOI5-5, LOI5-7
PROBLEM 15.1A
Exchange Rates
and Export Decision

Crackle Cookie Company is a relatively new company and so far has sold its products only in its home country, Denmark. In December, Crackle determined that it had excess capacity to produce more of its special Christmas cookies. It is trying to decide whether to use that capacity to ship a batch of cookies overseas. The marketing department has determined that the United States and Great Britain are the two most viable markets. Crackle has enough excess capacity to produce only one batch, which can be shipped to either country. The materials and labor cost to produce the batch amount to 8,500 kroner. The marketing department, which located a U.S. shipping company that could deliver to either location, also provided the following information:

	United States	Great Britain
Shipping cost	3,000 U.S. dollars	2,000 U.S. dollars
Duties/customs charges and miscellaneous selling expenses	400 U.S. dollars	480 British pounds
Total sales revenue	5,200 U.S. dollars	2,800 British pounds
Exchange rate data	1 krone = 0.166 U.S. dollars	1 krone = 0.115 British pounds

Instructions

a. If Crackle exports the batch to the United States, what is its estimated profit/loss in Danish kroner?

b. If Crackle exports the batch to Great Britain, what is its estimated profit/loss in Danish kroner?

c. If the British pound has exhibited rather large fluctuations relative to the Danish kroner recently, how might this impact Crackle's decision as to which country to ship to?

LO15-1, LO15-4 through LO15-6

PROBLEM 15.2A

Gains and Losses Journalizing Exchange Rate

Global Motors is a U.S. corporation that purchases automobiles from European manufacturers for distribution in the United States. A recent purchase involved the following events:

Nov. 12 Purchased automobiles from Stockholm Motors in Swedish kronor for Sk20,000,000, payable in 60 days. Current exchange rate, $0.1286 per krona. (Global uses the perpetual inventory system.)

Dec. 31 Made year-end adjusting entry relating to the Sk20,000,000 account payable to Stockholm Motors. Current exchange rate, $0.1288 per krona.

Jan. 11 Issued a check to World Bank for $2,566,800 in full payment of the account payable to Stockholm Motors.

Instructions

a. Prepare in general journal form the entries necessary to record the preceding events.

b. Compute the exchange rate (price) of the krona in U.S. dollars on January 11.

c. Explain a hedging technique that Global might have used to protect itself from the possibility of losses resulting from a significant increase in the exchange rate for the krona.

LO15-4

PROBLEM 15.3A

Exchange Rates and Performance Evaluation

A U.S.-based company, Global Products Inc., has wholly owned subsidiaries across the world. Global Products Inc. sells products linked to major holidays in each country.

The president and board members of Global Products Inc. believe that the managers of their wholly owned country-level subsidiaries are best motivated and rewarded with both annual salaries and annual bonuses. The bonuses are calculated as a predetermined percentage of pretax annual income.

Senora Larza, the president of Global Products of Mexico, has worked hard this year to make her Mexican subsidiary profitable. She is looking forward to receiving her annual bonus, which is calculated as a predetermined percentage of this year's pretax annual income earned by Global Products of Mexico. A condensed income statement for Global Products of Mexico for the most recent year is as follows (amounts in thousands of pesos):

Sales	MXN 20,000
Expenses	19,000
Pretax Income	MXN 1,000

The U.S. headquarters financial group translates each of its wholly owned subsidiary's results into U.S. dollars for evaluation. After translating the Mexican pesos income statement into U.S. dollars, the condensed income statement for Global Products of Mexico is as follows (amounts in thousands of dollars):

Sales	US$6,000
Expenses	6,600
Pretax Income	US$(600)

Instructions

a. Calculate the bonus amount based on (1) the Mexican pesos-based Pretax Income and (2) the U.S. dollar-based Pretax Income. Translate the pesos-based bonus to U.S. dollars using a current exchange rate.

b. Calculate the average exchange rate used to translate the Mexican pesos income statement into the U.S. dollar statement for the categories: (1) Sales and (2) Expenses.

c. Refer to the answers in parts **a** and **b**. Use those answers to explain why or how Global Products of Mexico's pretax income became a U.S.-dollar pretax loss.

d. Explain one reason why the dollar-based pretax income would be appropriate for evaluating Senora Larza and one reason why the pesos-based pretax income would be appropriate. Which would you choose and why?

LOI5-4, LOI5-7
PROBLEM 15.4A
Exchange Rates and Production Decisions

Ulsa Company has manufacturing subsidiaries in Malaysia and Malta. It is considering shipping the subcomponents of Product Y to one or the other of these countries for final assembly. The final product will be sold in the country where it is assembled. Other information is as follows:

	Malaysia	Malta
Average exchange rate	$1 = 4.30 ringgits	$1 = 0.40 lira
Import duty	5%	15%
Income tax rate	20%	10%
Unit selling price of Product Y	645 ringgits	70 liri
Price of subcomponent	215 ringgits	20 liri
Final assembly costs	200 ringgits	25 liri
Number of units to be sold	12,000 units	8,000 units

In both countries, the import duties are based on the value of the incoming goods in the receiving country's currency.

Instructions

a. For each country, prepare an income statement on a per-unit basis denominated in that country's currency.

b. In which country would the highest profit per unit (in dollars) be earned?

c. In which country would the highest total profit (in dollars) be earned?

LOI5-2, LOI5-7
PROBLEM 15.5A
NAFTA vs. AFTA

Form a group of students and research the ASEAN Free Trade Agreement (AFTA). A government website, www.ustr.gov, provides information on various trade agreements for the United States. Prepare a short presentation or a paper that explains how the North American Free Trade Agreement (NAFTA) differs from the AFTA. Explain how trade agreements help businesses and people in various countries.

LOI5-4 through LOI5-6
PROBLEM 15.6A
A Comprehensive Problem: Journalizing Exchange Rate Effects

Wolfe Computer is a U.S. company that manufactures portable personal computers. Many of the components for the computer are purchased abroad, and the finished product is sold in foreign countries as well as in the United States. Among the recent transactions of Wolfe are the following:

Oct. 28 Purchased from Mitsutonka, a Japanese company, 20,000 disk drives. The purchase price was ¥180,000,000, payable in 30 days. Current exchange rate, $0.0105 per yen. (Wolfe uses the perpetual inventory method; debit the Inventory of Raw Materials account.)

Nov. 9 Sold 700 personal computers to the Bank of England for £604,500 due in 30 days. The cost of the computers, to be debited to the Cost of Goods Sold account, was $518,000. Current exchange rate, $1.65 per British pound. (Use one compound journal entry to record the sale and the cost of goods sold. In recording the cost of goods sold, credit Inventory of Finished Goods.)

Nov. 27 Issued a check to Inland Bank for $1,836,000 in *full payment* of account payable to Mitsutonka.

Dec. 2 Purchased 10,000 gray-scale monitors from German Optical for €1,200,000, payable in 60 days. Current exchange rate, $0.7030 per euro. (Debit Inventory of Raw Materials.)

Dec. 9 Collected dollar-equivalent of £604,500 from the Bank of England. Current exchange rate, $1.63 per British pound.

Dec. 11 Sold 10,000 personal computers to Computique, a Swiss retail chain, for SFr23,750,000, due in 30 days. Current exchange rate, $0.6000 per Swiss franc. The cost of the computers, to be debited to Cost of Goods Sold and credited to Inventory of Finished Goods, is $7,400,000.

Instructions

a. Prepare in general journal form the entries necessary to record the preceding transactions.

b. Prepare the adjusting entries needed at December 31 for the €1,200,000 account payable to German Optical and the SFr23,750,000 account receivable from Computique. Year-end exchange rates, $0.7000 per euro and $0.5980 per Swiss franc. (Use a separate journal entry to adjust each account balance.)

c. Compute (to the nearest dollar) the unit sales price of computers in U.S. dollars in either the November 9 or December 11 sales transaction. (The sales price is the same in each transaction.)

d. Compute the exchange rate for the yen, stated in U.S. dollars, on November 27.

e. Explain how Wolfe Computer could have hedged its position to reduce the risk of loss from exchange rate fluctuations on (**1**) its foreign payables and (**2**) its foreign receivables.

LO15-8

PROBLEM 15.7A

FCPA Violations

Company A, a U.S. company, has a subsidiary located in Country Z, where various forms of bribery are accepted and expected. To oversee the operations of the subsidiary, Company A sent one of its top U.S. managers to Country Z. Manager M engaged in the following activities while in Country Z during recent months of operation:

a. Paid the equivalent of $200 to a government inspector to reschedule the inspection date of a new manufacturing facility from April 15 to February 15.

b. Paid an average of $50 each to four local police officers who are in charge of patrolling the area around the new manufacturing facility. The officers have agreed to increase the number of times they check the area.

c. Company N, a domestic company, is in competition with Company A for a government contract. Company A has learned that N has given approximately $5,000 to the official who will make the final contract decision. To remain in the running, Manager M authorized Company A to pay an equal amount to the official.

d. The electric utilities are government owned and operated. Due to the frequency of severe storms, there are often power outages due to downed lines. Manager M has paid the official in charge of coordinating repair crews $200 to ensure that the manufacturing plant's power is one of the first restored.

Under the Foreign Corrupt Practices Act, as amended, which of the above activities do you think would be considered illegal? From an operations standpoint, which of the above activities would be considered bad management practice? Are there solutions other than bribery?

LO15-1, LO15-2,

LO15-6, LO15-7

PROBLEM 15.8A

Home Depot's
Globalization

Consider note 1 to the 2012 financial statements of Home Depot, Inc., in Appendix A at the end of this textbook. Use this report to assess the globalization of Home Depot by answering the following questions:

a. What are the locations of Home Depot's international stores? What other global operations does Home Depot undertake?

b. Refer to note 1 under "Segment Information." What percentages of total assets and net sales revenue were associated with international operations in 2011? in 2012?

c. Read note 1 under "Foreign Currency Translation." What exchange rate is used to translate foreign assets and liabilities for reporting purposes?

d. Read note 1 under "Derivatives." Is there any evidence that management undertakes any formal hedging to attempt to reduce the impact of currency exchange risk?

e. Home Depot's provision for taxes for 2012 and 2011 was $2,686 and $2,185 million, respectively. Of the total taxes each year, $230 and $150 million, respectively, were paid to foreign governments. What percentage of taxes was paid to foreign countries each year?

f. Review note 2 to the consolidated financial statements and use the information gathered from the above questions to explain if you believe Home Depot, Inc., is a multinational company? Why or why not?

Problem Set B

LOI5-4, LOI5-5, LOI5-7

PROBLEM 15.1B

Exchange Rates and Export Decisions

Monster Cookie Company is located in Denmark. It is a relatively new company and so far has sold its products only in its home country. In December, Monster determined that it had excess capacity to produce more of its special Halloween cookies. It is trying to decide whether to use that capacity to ship a batch of cookies overseas. The marketing department has determined that the United States and Great Britain are the two most viable markets. Monster has enough excess capacity to produce only one batch, which can be shipped to either country. The materials and labor cost to produce the batch amount to 9,000 kroner. The marketing department, which located a U.S. shipping company that could deliver to either location, also provided the following information:

	United States	**Great Britain**
Shipping cost	2,800 U.S. dollars	1,900 U.S. dollars
Duties/customs charges and miscellaneous selling expenses	420 U.S. dollars	5000 British pounds
Total sales revenue	6,000 U.S. dollars	2,600 British pounds
Exchange rate data	1 krone = 0.16 U.S. dollars	1 krone = 0.09 British pounds

Instructions

a. If Monster exports the batch to the United States, what is its estimated profit/loss in Danish kroner?

b. If Monster exports the batch to Great Britain, what is its estimated profit/loss in Danish kroner?

c. If the British pound has exhibited rather large fluctuations relative to the Danish krone recently, how might this impact Monster's decision as to which country to ship to?

LOI5-1, LOI5-4 through LOI5-6

PROBLEM 15.2B

Gains and Losses Journalizing Exchange Rate

Euroam is a U.S. corporation that purchases motors from European manufacturers for distribution in the United States. A recent purchase involved the following events:

Dec. 1   Purchased tractors from WMB Motors for SFr4,000,000, payable in 45 days. Current exchange rate, $0.75 per Swiss franc. (Euroam uses the perpetual inventory system.)

Dec. 31   Made year-end adjusting entry relating to the SFr4,000,000 account payable to WMB Motors. Current exchange rate, $0.78 per Swiss franc.

Jan. 15   Issued a check to World Bank for $3,080,000 in full payment of the account payable to WMB Motors.

Instructions

a. Prepare in general journal form the entries necessary to record the preceding events.

b. Compute the exchange rate (price) of the Swiss franc in U.S. dollars on January 15.

c. Explain a hedging technique that Euroam might have used to protect itself from the possibility of losses resulting from a significant increase in the exchange rate for the Swiss franc.

LOI5-4

PROBLEM 15.3B

Exchange Rates and Performance Evaluation

A U.S.-based company, IBC, has wholly owned subsidiaries across the world. IBC is in the medical products market and sources most of its sales of medical devices from the United States, but sells most of those devices to the European market.

    The president and board members of IBC believe the managers of IBC's wholly owned country-level subsidiaries are best motivated and rewarded with both annual salaries and annual bonuses. The bonuses are calculated as a predetermined percentage of pretax annual income. Michael O'Brien, the president of IBC of Ireland, has worked hard to make the Ireland subsidiary profitable, although sales have lagged projections. He is looking forward to receiving his annual bonus, which is calculated as a predetermined percentage of this year's pretax annual income earned by IBC of Ireland. A condensed income statement for IBC of Ireland for the most recent year is as follows (amounts in thousands of euros).

Sales	40,000 euros
Expenses	39,500
Pretax Income	500 euros

The U.S. headquarters financial group translates each of its wholly owned subsidiary's results into U.S. dollars for evaluation. After translating the euros income statement into U.S. dollars, the condensed income statement for IBC of Ireland is as follows (amounts in thousands of dollars):

Sales	US$ 51,950
Expenses	50,300
Pretax Income	US$ 1,650

Instructions

a. Calculate the bonus based on the subsidiary's results in euros and U.S. dollars. Translate the euro result to U.S. dollars using a current exchange rate. Compare the results.

b. Calculate the average exchange rate used to translate the euro statement into the U.S. dollar-based statement for: (1) Sales and (2) Expenses.

c. Refer to the answers in parts **a.** and **b.** Use those answers to explain why or how IBC of Ireland's euro pretax income differs from the U.S.-dollar pretax income.

d. Explain one reason why the dollar-based pretax income would be appropriate for evaluating Michael O'Brien and one reason why the euros-based pretax income would be appropriate. Which would you choose and why?

LO15-4, LO15-7
PROBLEM 15.4B
Exchange Rates and
Product Decisions

Haliday Company has manufacturing subsidiaries in Thailand and Mexico. It is considering shipping the subcomponents of Product X to one or the other of these countries for final assembly. The final product will be sold in the country where it is assembled. Other information is as follows:

	Thailand	Mexico
Average exchange rate	$1 = 32.5 bhats	$1 = 12 pesos
Import duty	4%	12%
Income tax rate	30%	28%
Unit selling price of Product X	5055 bhats	2250 pesos
Price of subcomponent	1444 bhats	540 pesos
Final assembly costs	1805 bhats	900 pesos
Number of units to be sold	14,000 units	10,000 units

In both countries, the import duties are based on the value of the incoming goods in the receiving country's currency.

Instructions

a. For each country, prepare an income statement on a per-unit basis denominated in that country's currency.

b. In which country would the highest profit per unit (in dollars) be earned?

c. In which country would the highest total profit (in dollars) be earned?

LO15-2, LO15-7
PROBLEM 15.5B
NAFTA vs. CAFTA-DR

Form a group of students and research Dominican Republic–Central America–United States (CAFTA-DR) trade agreement for central America. A government website, www.ustr.gov, provides information on various trade agreements. Prepare a short presentation or a paper that explains how requirements for CAFTA-DR differ from those of the North American Free Trade Agreement (NAFTA). Explain how trade agreements help businesses and people in various countries.

LO15-4 through LO15-6
PROBLEM 15.6B

A Comprehensive Problem:
Journalizing Exchange Rate
Effects

Fox Games is a U.S. company that manufacturers computer game consoles. Many of the components for the consoles are purchased abroad, and the finished product is sold in foreign countries as well as in the United States. Among the recent transactions of Fox are the following:

Oct. 25 Purchased from Sutaki, a Japanese company, 15,000 parts. The purchase price was ¥120,000,000, payable in 30 days. Current exchange rate, $0.01 per yen. (Fox uses the perpetual inventory method; debit the Inventory of Raw Materials account.)

Nov. 15 Sold 500 consoles to British Vibes for £200,000, due in 30 days. The cost of the consoles, to be debited to the Cost of Goods Sold account, was $160,000. Current exchange rate, $1.60 per British pound. (Use one compound journal entry to record the sale and the cost of goods sold. In recording the cost of goods sold, credit Inventory of Finished Goods.)

Nov. 24 Issued a check to Inland Bank for $1,150,000 in *full payment* of account payable to Sutaki.

Dec. 4 Purchased 5,000 black cases from Swiss Plastics for SFr80,000, payable in 60 days. Current exchange rate, $0.70 per Swiss franc. (Debit Inventory of Raw Materials.)

Dec. 15 Collected dollar-equivalent of £200,000 from British Vibes. Current exchange rate, $1.55 per British pound.

Dec. 21 Sold 6,000 game consoles to Sounds, a Norwegian retail chain, for NOK40,000,000, due in 30 days. Current exchange rate, $0.20 per Norwegian krone. The cost of the consoles, to be debited to Cost of Goods Sold and credited to Inventory of Finished Goods, is $5,000,000.

Instructions

a. Prepare in general journal form the entries necessary to record the preceding transactions.

b. Prepare the adjusted entries needed at December 31 for the SFr80,000 account payable to Swiss Plastics and the NOK40,000,000 account receivable from Sounds. Year-end exchange rates, $0.68 per Swiss franc and $0.18 per Norwegian krone. (Use a separate journal entry to adjust each account balance.)

c. Compute (to the nearest dollar) the unit sales price of consoles in U.S. dollars in both the November 15 and the December 21 sales transaction. (The sales price may not be the same in each transaction.)

d. Compute the exchange rate for the yen, stated in U.S. dollars, on November 24.

e. Explain how Fox Games could have hedged its position to reduce the risk of loss from exchange rate fluctuations on (**1**) its foreign payables and (**2**) its foreign receivables.

LO15-8
PROBLEM 15.7B

FCPA Violations

Company P, a U.S. company, has a foreign subsidiary in Country Q, where various forms of bribery are accepted and expected. Company P sent one of its top U.S. managers to oversee operations in its subsidiary in Country Q. That manager engaged in the following activities while in Country Q:

a. Paid the equivalent of $200,000 to a government official to win the bid for a new manufacturing facility that opened on April 15.

b. Paid about $80 each to four local clerks at the import agency who agreed to move the company's import inspection process to expedite status, saving the company one week of inspection time.

c. The streets and sanitation department in Country Q is government owned and operated. Because of many hurricanes, downed trees and other debris frequently block access to the roads leading to the plant. The manager paid the official in charge of streets an additional $200 to ensure quick clearing of the streets leading to the plant.

d. After learning that a competing foreign company paid a government official in Country Q $10,000 to have priority consideration on a new contract to supply the military, the manager of Company P offered the official $20,000 for priority consideration for the same contract.

Under the Foreign Corrupt Practices Act as amended, which of the above activities would be considered illegal? From an operations standpoint, which of the above activities would be considered bad management practice? What alternative actions could you suggest for the manager?

Critical Thinking Cases

LO15-1, LO15-2

CASE 15.1

Decisions to Globalize Are Complex

Bristow Inc. is interested in establishing a presence in Country Y. Bristow is expecting demand for several of its products to increase in that country because a major customer, Kale Enterprises, is building a large manufacturing plant in Y. Bristow has been supplying Kale's other foreign manufacturing operations mainly through exporting. However, shipping costs and long delivery times have been somewhat troublesome to both companies in the past. Bristow has also identified several other companies native to Country Y as potential customers.

Bristow currently has operations only in the United States. Kale Enterprises is a successful global company with operations in over 20 countries. Bristow's managers have identified the following possible options:

a. Simply export to Country Y.

b. A company in Y has expressed an interest in licensing Bristow's technology and has the capability and capacity to produce the products used by Kale.

c. A joint venture with Kale may be possible, but managers for Kale would be willing to enter into an agreement only if substantial control for Bristow's operations is given to Kale managers.

d. Bristow's managers have located a company that could be purchased and operated as a subsidiary. The company currently produces products similar to Bristow, but it is using outdated technology.

Instructions

Discuss what factors should be considered when choosing among the above options. Develop a list of additional information you believe would be useful in making the decision.

LO15-2, LO15-3, LO15-5

CASE 15.2

Disclosure Requirements

The International Organization of Securities Commissions (IOSCO) is a group of top securities administrators from about 50 countries. The Securities and Exchange Commission (SEC) is a member of IOSCO. IOSCO is a primary supporter of the internationalization of financial reporting standards through the International Accounting Standards Board (IASB). At a recent meeting, a discussion of the pros and cons of internationalizing financial reporting standards included the following arguments:

Pro:

Having the same accounting standards for external financial reporting for all securities markets will reduce misunderstandings and create comparable information. For example, investors will be able to compare the financial reports of similar companies located in the United States with those located in China and decide where best to allocate their investments. One set of accounting standards will also save corporations money because they will not need multiple sets of books to track their international operations.

Con:

Requiring companies that list on all global securities exchanges to use the same external reporting requirements will mislead investors. For example, in countries where the majority of investment funds come from banks in the form of long-term borrowing, debt to equity ratios will look very different than those of comparable U.S. firms. Accounting information must reflect its environment. Besides, as all business becomes global, reporting requirements will naturally evolve to what investors demand.

Instructions

Write a one-page summary reflecting your opinion about the value of harmonizing accounting standards for global equity markets. Support your opinions by referencing comparable cross-country companies you have located on the Internet.

LO15-1, LO15-2, LO15-7

INTERNET CASE 15.3

U.S. Foreign Trade Zones

The National Association of Foreign Trade Zones (FTZs) maintains an Internet site containing information on U.S. foreign trade zones. Locate the site by searching under "foreign trade zone," or go to:

www.naftz.org

Instructions

a. Explain the key characteristics of a foreign trade zone (FTZ).

b. Identify an FTZ in your state. Where is it located? What types of business use it?

c. Other information is available at the site. Use that information to answer the following:

    1. How are FTZs created?

    2. What businesses utilize FTZs?

    3. What benefits can firms obtain from operating in FTZs?

LO15-2, LO15-3

CASE 15.4

International Demand for Corporate Governance

The international business community has been calling for stronger corporate governance for companies around the globe. As a result, in 1999 the Organization for Economic Cooperation and Development (OECD) issued some principles that deal with the ethical and fair treatment of shareholders, the importance of transparency, and adequate disclosure. These OECD principles were revised in 2004. The World Bank and the International Monetary Fund support these efforts. In particular, principle number five, called Disclosure and Transparency, states:

> The corporate governance framework should ensure that timely and accurate disclosure is made on all material matters regarding the corporation, including the financial situation, performance, ownership and governance of the company (see www.oecd.org).

Required

Form a group of four students. Visit the OECD website and use the information to write a one-page paper that explains why OECD corporate governance principle number five is important for international capital flows.

Internet sites are time and date sensitive. It is the purpose of these exercises to have you explore the Internet. You may need to use the Yahoo! search engine www.yahoo.com *(or another favorite search engine) to find a company's current web address.*

Answers to Self-Test Questions

1. c   2. a, b, c, d   3. d   4. a $(1.31 - 1.29) \times 20{,}000$

5. d (the transaction was denominated in dollars)

APPENDIX A

Home Depot 2012 Financial Statements

Home Depot Financial Statements Contents

Management's Responsibility for Financial Statements	A-1
Management's Report on Internal Control over Financial Reporting	A-1
Report of the Independent Registered Public Accounting Firm	A-2
Consolidated Statements of Earnings	A-3
Consolidated Statements of Comprehensive Income	A-4
Consolidated Balance Sheets	A-5
Consolidated Statements of Stockholders' Equity	A-6
Consolidated Statements of Cash Flows	A-7
Notes to the Consolidated Financial Statements—Note 1, Summary of Significant Accounting Policies; Note 2, China Store Closings	A-8–A-12
Five-Year Summary of Financial and Operating Results	A-13

Item 8. Financial Statements and Supplementary Data.

Management's Responsibility for Financial Statements

The financial statements presented in this Annual Report have been prepared with integrity and objectivity and are the responsibility of the management of The Home Depot, Inc. These financial statements have been prepared in conformity with U.S. generally accepted accounting principles and properly reflect certain estimates and judgments based upon the best available information.

The financial statements of the Company have been audited by KPMG LLP, an independent registered public accounting firm. Their accompanying report is based upon an audit conducted in accordance with the standards of the Public Company Accounting Oversight Board (United States).

The Audit Committee of the Board of Directors, consisting solely of independent directors, meets five times a year with the independent registered public accounting firm, the internal auditors and representatives of management to discuss auditing and financial reporting matters. In addition, a telephonic meeting is held prior to each quarterly earnings release. The Audit Committee retains the independent registered public accounting firm and regularly reviews the internal accounting controls, the activities of the independent registered public accounting firm and internal auditors and the financial condition of the Company. Both the Company's independent registered public accounting firm and the internal auditors have free access to the Audit Committee.

Management's Report on Internal Control over Financial Reporting

Our management is responsible for establishing and maintaining adequate internal control over financial reporting, as such term is defined in Rule 13a-15(f) promulgated under the Securities Exchange Act of 1934, as amended (the "Exchange Act"). Under the supervision and with the participation of our management, including our Chief Executive Officer and Chief Financial Officer, we conducted an evaluation of the effectiveness of our internal control over financial reporting as of February 3, 2013 based on the framework in *Internal Control—Integrated Framework* issued by the Committee of Sponsoring Organizations of the Treadway Commission (COSO). Based on our evaluation, our management concluded that our internal control over financial reporting was effective as of February 3, 2013 in providing reasonable assurance regarding the reliability of financial reporting and the preparation of financial statements for external purposes in accordance with U.S. generally accepted accounting principles. The effectiveness of our internal control over financial reporting as of February 3, 2013 has been audited by KPMG LLP, an independent registered public accounting firm, as stated in their report which is included on page 28 in this Form 10-K.

/s/ FRANCIS S. BLAKE	/s/ CAROL B. TOMÉ
Francis S. Blake	Carol B. Tomé
Chairman &	Chief Financial Officer &
Chief Executive Officer	Executive Vice President – Corporate Services

Report of Independent Registered Public Accounting Firm

The Board of Directors and Stockholders
The Home Depot, Inc.:

We have audited The Home Depot, Inc.'s internal control over financial reporting as of February 3, 2013, based on criteria established in *Internal Control—Integrated Framework* issued by the Committee of Sponsoring Organizations of the Treadway Commission (COSO). The Home Depot, Inc.'s management is responsible for maintaining effective internal control over financial reporting and for its assessment of the effectiveness of internal control over financial reporting, included in the accompanying Management's Report on Internal Control Over Financial Reporting. Our responsibility is to express an opinion on the Company's internal control over financial reporting based on our audit.

We conducted our audit in accordance with the standards of the Public Company Accounting Oversight Board (United States). Those standards require that we plan and perform the audit to obtain reasonable assurance about whether effective internal control over financial reporting was maintained in all material respects. Our audit included obtaining an understanding of internal control over financial reporting, assessing the risk that a material weakness exists, and testing and evaluating the design and operating effectiveness of internal control based on the assessed risk. Our audit also included performing such other procedures as we considered necessary in the circumstances. We believe that our audit provides a reasonable basis for our opinion.

A company's internal control over financial reporting is a process designed to provide reasonable assurance regarding the reliability of financial reporting and the preparation of financial statements for external purposes in accordance with generally accepted accounting principles. A company's internal control over financial reporting includes those policies and procedures that (1) pertain to the maintenance of records that, in reasonable detail, accurately and fairly reflect the transactions and dispositions of the assets of the company; (2) provide reasonable assurance that transactions are recorded as necessary to permit preparation of financial statements in accordance with generally accepted accounting principles, and that receipts and expenditures of the company are being made only in accordance with authorizations of management and directors of the company; and (3) provide reasonable assurance regarding prevention or timely detection of unauthorized acquisition, use, or disposition of the company's assets that could have a material effect on the financial statements.

Because of its inherent limitations, internal control over financial reporting may not prevent or detect misstatements. Also, projections of any evaluation of effectiveness to future periods are subject to the risk that controls may become inadequate because of changes in conditions, or that the degree of compliance with the policies or procedures may deteriorate.

In our opinion, The Home Depot, Inc. maintained, in all material respects, effective internal control over financial reporting as of February 3, 2013, based on criteria established in *Internal Control—Integrated Framework* issued by the Committee of Sponsoring Organizations of the Treadway Commission.

We also have audited, in accordance with the standards of the Public Company Accounting Oversight Board (United States), the Consolidated Balance Sheets of The Home Depot, Inc. and subsidiaries as of February 3, 2013 and January 29, 2012, and the related Consolidated Statements of Earnings, Comprehensive Income, Stockholders' Equity, and Cash Flows for each of the fiscal years in the three-year period ended February 3, 2013, and our report dated March 28, 2013 expressed an unqualified opinion on those consolidated financial statements.

/s/ KPMG LLP

Atlanta, Georgia
March 28, 2013

THE HOME DEPOT, INC. AND SUBSIDIARIES
CONSOLIDATED STATEMENTS OF EARNINGS

amounts in millions, except per share data	Fiscal Year Ended[1]		
	February 3, 2013	January 29, 2012	January 30, 2011
NET SALES	$ 74,754	$ 70,395	$ 67,997
Cost of Sales	48,912	46,133	44,693
GROSS PROFIT	25,842	24,262	23,304
Operating Expenses:			
Selling, General and Administrative	16,508	16,028	15,849
Depreciation and Amortization	1,568	1,573	1,616
Total Operating Expenses	18,076	17,601	17,465
OPERATING INCOME	7,766	6,661	5,839
Interest and Other (Income) Expense:			
Interest and Investment Income	(20)	(13)	(15)
Interest Expense	632	606	530
Other	(67)	—	51
Interest and Other, net	545	593	566
EARNINGS BEFORE PROVISION FOR INCOME TAXES	7,221	6,068	5,273
Provision for Income Taxes	2,686	2,185	1,935
NET EARNINGS	$ 4,535	$ 3,883	$ 3,338
Weighted Average Common Shares	1,499	1,562	1,648
BASIC EARNINGS PER SHARE	$ 3.03	$ 2.49	$ 2.03
Diluted Weighted Average Common Shares	1,511	1,570	1,658
DILUTED EARNINGS PER SHARE	$ 3.00	$ 2.47	$ 2.01

(1) Fiscal year ended February 3, 2013 includes 53 weeks. Fiscal years ended January 29, 2012 and January 30, 2011 include 52 weeks.

See accompanying Notes to Consolidated Financial Statements.

THE HOME DEPOT, INC. AND SUBSIDIARIES
CONSOLIDATED STATEMENTS OF COMPREHENSIVE INCOME

amounts in millions	Fiscal Year Ended[1]		
	February 3, 2013	January 29, 2012	January 30, 2011
Net Earnings	$ 4,535	$ 3,883	$ 3,338
Other Comprehensive Income (Loss):			
Foreign Currency Translation Adjustments	100	(143)	206
Cash Flow Hedges, net of tax	5	5	(116)
Other	(1)	(14)	(7)
Total Other Comprehensive Income (Loss)	104	(152)	83
COMPREHENSIVE INCOME	$ 4,639	$ 3,731	$ 3,421

(1) *Fiscal year ended February 3, 2013 includes 53 weeks. Fiscal years ended January 29, 2012 and January 30, 2011 include 52 weeks.*

See accompanying Notes to Consolidated Financial Statements.

THE HOME DEPOT, INC. AND SUBSIDIARIES
CONSOLIDATED BALANCE SHEETS

amounts in millions, except share and per share data	February 3, 2013	January 29, 2012
ASSETS		
Current Assets:		
Cash and Cash Equivalents	$ 2,494	$ 1,987
Receivables, net	1,395	1,245
Merchandise Inventories	10,710	10,325
Other Current Assets	773	963
Total Current Assets	15,372	14,520
Property and Equipment, at cost	38,491	38,975
Less Accumulated Depreciation and Amortization	14,422	14,527
Net Property and Equipment	24,069	24,448
Notes Receivable	140	135
Goodwill	1,170	1,120
Other Assets	333	295
Total Assets	$ 41,084	$ 40,518
LIABILITIES AND STOCKHOLDERS' EQUITY		
Current Liabilities:		
Accounts Payable	$ 5,376	$ 4,856
Accrued Salaries and Related Expenses	1,414	1,372
Sales Taxes Payable	472	391
Deferred Revenue	1,270	1,147
Income Taxes Payable	22	23
Current Installments of Long-Term Debt	1,321	30
Other Accrued Expenses	1,587	1,557
Total Current Liabilities	11,462	9,376
Long-Term Debt, excluding current installments	9,475	10,758
Other Long-Term Liabilities	2,051	2,146
Deferred Income Taxes	319	340
Total Liabilities	23,307	22,620
STOCKHOLDERS' EQUITY		
Common Stock, par value $0.05; authorized: 10 billion shares; issued: 1.754 billion shares at February 3, 2013 and 1.733 billion shares at January 29, 2012; outstanding: 1.484 billion shares at February 3, 2013 and 1.537 billion shares at January 29, 2012	88	87
Paid-In Capital	7,948	6,966
Retained Earnings	20,038	17,246
Accumulated Other Comprehensive Income	397	293
Treasury Stock, at cost, 270 million shares at February 3, 2013 and 196 million shares at January 29, 2012	(10,694)	(6,694)
Total Stockholders' Equity	17,777	17,898
Total Liabilities and Stockholders' Equity	$ 41,084	$ 40,518

See accompanying Notes to Consolidated Financial Statements.

THE HOME DEPOT, INC. AND SUBSIDIARIES
CONSOLIDATED STATEMENTS OF STOCKHOLDERS' EQUITY

amounts in millions, except per share data	Common Stock Shares	Amount	Paid-In Capital	Retained Earnings	Accumulated Other Comprehensive Income (Loss)	Treasury Stock Shares	Amount	Stockholders' Equity
Balance, January 31, 2010	1,716	$ 86	$ 6,304	$ 13,226	$ 362	(18)	$ (585)	$ 19,393
Net Earnings	—	—	—	3,338		—	—	3,338
Shares Issued Under Employee Stock Plans	6	—	42	—		—	—	42
Tax Effect of Stock-Based Compensation	—	—	2	—		—	—	2
Foreign Currency Translation Adjustments	—	—	—	—	206	—	—	206
Cash Flow Hedges, net of tax	—	—	—	—	(116)	—	—	(116)
Stock Options, Awards and Amortization of Restricted Stock	—	—	214	—	—	—	—	214
Repurchases of Common Stock	—	—	—	—	—	(81)	(2,608)	(2,608)
Cash Dividends ($0.945 per share)	—	—	—	(1,569)	—	—	—	(1,569)
Other	—	—	(6)	—	(7)	—	—	(13)
Balance, January 30, 2011	1,722	$ 86	$ 6,556	$ 14,995	$ 445	(99)	$ (3,193)	$ 18,889
Net Earnings	—	—	—	3,883		—	—	3,883
Shares Issued Under Employee Stock Plans	11	1	196	—		—	—	197
Tax Effect of Stock-Based Compensation	—	—	(2)	—		—	—	(2)
Foreign Currency Translation Adjustments	—	—	—	—	(143)	—	—	(143)
Cash Flow Hedges, net of tax	—	—	—	—	5	—	—	5
Stock Options, Awards and Amortization of Restricted Stock	—	—	215	—	—	—	—	215
Repurchases of Common Stock	—	—	—	—	—	(97)	(3,501)	(3,501)
Cash Dividends ($1.04 per share)	—	—	—	(1,632)	—	—	—	(1,632)
Other	—	—	1	—	(14)	—	—	(13)
Balance, January 29, 2012	1,733	$ 87	$ 6,966	$ 17,246	$ 293	(196)	$ (6,694)	$ 17,898
Net Earnings	—	—	—	4,535		—	—	4,535
Shares Issued Under Employee Stock Plans	21	1	678	—		—	—	679
Tax Effect of Stock-Based Compensation	—	—	82	—		—	—	82
Foreign Currency Translation Adjustments	—	—	—	—	100	—	—	100
Cash Flow Hedges, net of tax	—	—	—	—	5	—	—	5
Stock Options, Awards and Amortization of Restricted Stock	—	—	218	—	—	—	—	218
Repurchases of Common Stock	—	—	—	—	—	(74)	(4,000)	(4,000)
Cash Dividends ($1.16 per share)	—	—	—	(1,743)	—	—	—	(1,743)
Other	—	—	4	—	(1)	—	—	3
Balance, February 3, 2013	1,754	$ 88	$ 7,948	$ 20,038	$ 397	(270)	$ (10,694)	$ 17,777

See accompanying Notes to Consolidated Financial Statements.

THE HOME DEPOT, INC. AND SUBSIDIARIES
CONSOLIDATED STATEMENTS OF CASH FLOWS

amounts in millions	Fiscal Year Ended(1)		
	February 3, 2013	January 29, 2012	January 30, 2011
CASH FLOWS FROM OPERATING ACTIVITIES:			
Net Earnings	$ 4,535	$ 3,883	$ 3,338
Reconciliation of Net Earnings to Net Cash Provided by Operating Activities:			
Depreciation and Amortization	1,684	1,682	1,718
Stock-Based Compensation Expense	218	215	214
Goodwill Impairment	97	—	—
Changes in Assets and Liabilities, net of the effects of acquisitions and disposition:			
Receivables, net	(143)	(170)	(102)
Merchandise Inventories	(350)	256	(355)
Other Current Assets	93	159	12
Accounts Payable and Accrued Expenses	698	422	(133)
Deferred Revenue	121	(29)	10
Income Taxes Payable	87	14	(85)
Deferred Income Taxes	107	170	104
Other Long-Term Liabilities	(180)	(2)	(61)
Other	8	51	(75)
Net Cash Provided by Operating Activities	6,975	6,651	4,585
CASH FLOWS FROM INVESTING ACTIVITIES:			
Capital Expenditures, net of $98, $25 and $62 of non-cash capital expenditures in fiscal 2012, 2011 and 2010, respectively	(1,312)	(1,221)	(1,096)
Proceeds from Sale of Business, net	—	101	—
Payments for Businesses Acquired, net	(170)	(65)	—
Proceeds from Sales of Property and Equipment	50	56	84
Net Cash Used in Investing Activities	(1,432)	(1,129)	(1,012)
CASH FLOWS FROM FINANCING ACTIVITIES:			
Proceeds from Long-Term Borrowings, net of discount	—	1,994	998
Repayments of Long-Term Debt	(32)	(1,028)	(1,029)
Repurchases of Common Stock	(3,984)	(3,470)	(2,608)
Proceeds from Sales of Common Stock	784	306	104
Cash Dividends Paid to Stockholders	(1,743)	(1,632)	(1,569)
Other Financing Activities	(59)	(218)	(347)
Net Cash Used in Financing Activities	(5,034)	(4,048)	(4,451)
Change in Cash and Cash Equivalents	509	1,474	(878)
Effect of Exchange Rate Changes on Cash and Cash Equivalents	(2)	(32)	2
Cash and Cash Equivalents at Beginning of Year	1,987	545	1,421
Cash and Cash Equivalents at End of Year	$ 2,494	$ 1,987	$ 545
SUPPLEMENTAL DISCLOSURE OF CASH PAYMENTS MADE FOR:			
Interest, net of interest capitalized	$ 617	$ 580	$ 579
Income Taxes	$ 2,482	$ 1,865	$ 2,067

(1) *Fiscal year ended February 3, 2013 includes 53 weeks. Fiscal years ended January 29, 2012 and January 30, 2011 include 52 weeks.*
See accompanying Notes to Consolidated Financial Statements.

NOTES TO CONSOLIDATED FINANCIAL STATEMENTS

1. SUMMARY OF SIGNIFICANT ACCOUNTING POLICIES

Business, Consolidation and Presentation

The Home Depot, Inc. and its subsidiaries (the "Company") operate The Home Depot stores, which are full-service, warehouse-style stores averaging approximately 104,000 square feet of enclosed space, with approximately 24,000 additional square feet of outside garden area. The stores stock approximately 30,000 to 40,000 different kinds of building materials, home improvement supplies and lawn and garden products that are sold to do-it-yourself customers, do-it-for-me customers and professional customers. The Company also offers over 600,000 products through its Home Depot and Home Decorators Collection websites. At the end of fiscal 2012, the Company was operating 2,256 The Home Depot stores, which included 1,976 stores in the United States, including the Commonwealth of Puerto Rico and the territories of the U.S. Virgin Islands and Guam ("U.S."), 180 stores in Canada and 100 stores in Mexico. The Consolidated Financial Statements include the accounts of the Company and its wholly-owned subsidiaries. All significant intercompany transactions have been eliminated in consolidation.

Fiscal Year

The Company's fiscal year is a 52- or 53-week period ending on the Sunday nearest to January 31. The fiscal year ended February 3, 2013 ("fiscal 2012") includes 53 weeks and fiscal years ended January 29, 2012 ("fiscal 2011") and January 30, 2011 ("fiscal 2010") include 52 weeks.

Use of Estimates

Management of the Company has made a number of estimates and assumptions relating to the reporting of assets and liabilities, the disclosure of contingent assets and liabilities, and reported amounts of revenues and expenses in preparing these financial statements in conformity with U.S. generally accepted accounting principles. Actual results could differ from these estimates.

Fair Value of Financial Instruments

The carrying amounts of Cash and Cash Equivalents, Receivables and Accounts Payable approximate fair value due to the short-term maturities of these financial instruments. The fair value of the Company's Long-Term Debt is discussed in Note 11.

Cash Equivalents

The Company considers all highly liquid investments purchased with original maturities of three months or less to be cash equivalents. The Company's cash equivalents are carried at fair market value and consist primarily of money market funds.

Accounts Receivable

The Company has an agreement with a third-party service provider who directly extends credit to customers, manages the Company's private label credit card program and owns the related receivables. The Company evaluated the third-party entities holding the receivables under the program and concluded that they should not be consolidated by the Company. The agreement with the third-party service provider expires in 2018, with the Company having the option, but no obligation, to purchase the receivables at the end of the agreement. The deferred interest charges incurred by the Company for its deferred financing programs offered to its customers are included in Cost of Sales. The interchange fees charged to the Company for the customers' use of the cards and any profit sharing with the third-party service provider are included in Selling, General and Administrative expenses ("SG&A"). The sum of the three is referred to by the Company as "the cost of credit" of the private label credit card program.

In addition, certain subsidiaries of the Company extend credit directly to customers in the ordinary course of business. The receivables due from customers were $42 million and $45 million as of February 3, 2013 and January 29, 2012, respectively. The Company's valuation reserve related to accounts receivable was not material to the Consolidated Financial Statements of the Company as of the end of fiscal 2012 or 2011.

Merchandise Inventories

The majority of the Company's Merchandise Inventories are stated at the lower of cost (first-in, first-out) or market, as determined by the retail inventory method. As the inventory retail value is adjusted regularly to reflect market conditions, the inventory valued using the retail method approximates the lower of cost or market. Certain subsidiaries, including retail operations in Canada and Mexico, and distribution centers, record Merchandise Inventories at the lower of cost or market, as determined by a cost method. These Merchandise Inventories represent approximately 24% of the total Merchandise Inventories balance.

The Company evaluates the inventory valued using a cost method at the end of each quarter to ensure that it is carried at the lower of cost or market. The valuation allowance for Merchandise Inventories valued under a cost method was not material to the Consolidated Financial Statements of the Company as of the end of fiscal 2012 or 2011.

Independent physical inventory counts or cycle counts are taken on a regular basis in each store and distribution center to ensure that amounts reflected in the accompanying Consolidated Financial Statements for Merchandise Inventories are properly stated. During the period between physical inventory counts in stores, the Company accrues for estimated losses related to shrink on a store-by-store basis based on historical shrink results and current trends in the business. Shrink (or in the case of excess inventory, "swell") is the difference between the recorded amount of inventory and the physical inventory. Shrink may occur due to theft, loss, inaccurate records for the receipt of inventory or deterioration of goods, among other things.

Income Taxes

Income taxes are accounted for under the asset and liability method. The Company provides for federal, state and foreign income taxes currently payable, as well as for those deferred due to timing differences between reporting income and expenses for financial statement purposes versus tax purposes. Deferred tax assets and liabilities are recognized for the future tax consequences attributable to temporary differences between the financial statement carrying amounts of existing assets and liabilities and their respective tax bases. Deferred tax assets and liabilities are measured using enacted income tax rates expected to apply to taxable income in the years in which those temporary differences are expected to be recovered or settled. The effect of a change in income tax rates is recognized as income or expense in the period that includes the enactment date.

The Company recognizes the effect of income tax positions only if those positions are more likely than not of being sustained. Recognized income tax positions are measured at the largest amount that is greater than 50% likely of being realized. Changes in recognition or measurement are reflected in the period in which the change in judgment occurs.

The Company and its eligible subsidiaries file a consolidated U.S. federal income tax return. Non-U.S. subsidiaries and certain U.S. subsidiaries, which are consolidated for financial reporting purposes, are not eligible to be included in the Company's consolidated U.S. federal income tax return. Separate provisions for income taxes have been determined for these entities. The Company intends to reinvest substantially all of the unremitted earnings of its non-U.S. subsidiaries and postpone their remittance indefinitely. Accordingly, no provision for U.S. income taxes for these non-U.S. subsidiaries was recorded in the accompanying Consolidated Statements of Earnings.

Depreciation and Amortization

The Company's Buildings, Furniture, Fixtures and Equipment are recorded at cost and depreciated using the straight-line method over the estimated useful lives of the assets. Leasehold Improvements are amortized using the straight-line method over the original term of the lease or the useful life of the improvement, whichever is shorter. The Company's Property and Equipment is depreciated using the following estimated useful lives:

	Life
Buildings	5–45 years
Furniture, Fixtures and Equipment	2–20 years
Leasehold Improvements	5–45 years

Capitalized Software Costs

The Company capitalizes certain costs related to the acquisition and development of software and amortizes these costs using the straight-line method over the estimated useful life of the software, which is three to six years. These costs are included in Furniture, Fixtures and Equipment as discussed further in Note 4. Certain development costs not meeting the criteria for capitalization are expensed as incurred.

Revenues

The Company recognizes revenue, net of estimated returns and sales tax, at the time the customer takes possession of merchandise or receives services. The liability for sales returns is estimated based on historical return levels. When the Company receives payment from customers before the customer has taken possession of the merchandise or the service has been performed, the amount received is recorded as Deferred Revenue in the accompanying Consolidated Balance Sheets until the sale or service is complete. The Company also records Deferred Revenue for the sale of gift cards and recognizes this revenue upon the redemption of gift cards in Net Sales. Gift card breakage income is recognized based upon historical redemption patterns and represents the balance of gift cards for which the Company believes the likelihood of redemption by the customer is remote. During fiscal 2012, 2011 and 2010, the Company recognized $33 million, $42 million and $46 million, respectively, of gift card breakage income. This income is included in the accompanying Consolidated Statements of Earnings as a reduction in SG&A.

Services Revenue

Net Sales include services revenue generated through a variety of installation, home maintenance and professional service programs. In these programs, the customer selects and purchases material for a project, and the Company provides or arranges professional installation. These programs are offered through the Company's stores and in-home sales programs. Under certain programs, when the Company provides or arranges the installation of a project and the subcontractor provides material as part of the installation, both the material and labor are included in services revenue. The Company recognizes this revenue when the service for the customer is complete.

All payments received prior to the completion of services are recorded in Deferred Revenue in the accompanying Consolidated Balance Sheets. Services revenue was $3.2 billion, $2.9 billion and $2.7 billion for fiscal 2012, 2011 and 2010, respectively.

Self-Insurance

The Company is self-insured for certain losses related to general liability (including products liability), workers' compensation, employee group medical and automobile claims. The expected ultimate cost for claims incurred as of the balance sheet date is not discounted and is recognized as a liability. The expected ultimate cost of claims is estimated based upon analysis of historical data and actuarial estimates.

Prepaid Advertising

Television and radio advertising production costs, along with media placement costs, are expensed when the advertisement first appears. Amounts included in Other Current Assets in the accompanying Consolidated Balance Sheets relating to prepayments of production costs for print and broadcast advertising as well as sponsorship promotions were not material at the end of fiscal 2012 and 2011.

Vendor Allowances

Vendor allowances primarily consist of volume rebates that are earned as a result of attaining certain purchase levels and advertising co-op allowances for the promotion of vendors' products that are typically based on guaranteed minimum amounts with additional amounts being earned for attaining certain purchase levels. These vendor allowances are accrued as earned, with those allowances received as a result of attaining certain purchase levels accrued over the incentive period based on estimates of purchases.

Volume rebates and certain advertising co-op allowances earned are initially recorded as a reduction in Merchandise Inventories and a subsequent reduction in Cost of Sales when the related product is sold. Certain advertising co-op allowances that are reimbursements of specific, incremental and identifiable costs incurred to promote vendors' products are recorded as an offset against advertising expense. In fiscal 2012, 2011 and 2010, gross advertising expense was $831 million, $846 million and $864 million, respectively, and is included in SG&A. Specific, incremental and identifiable advertising co-op allowances were $85 million, $94 million and $90 million for fiscal 2012, 2011 and 2010, respectively, and are recorded as an offset to advertising expense in SG&A.

Cost of Sales

Cost of Sales includes the actual cost of merchandise sold and services performed, the cost of transportation of merchandise from vendors to the Company's stores, locations or customers, the operating cost of the Company's sourcing and distribution network and the cost of deferred interest programs offered through the Company's private label credit card program.

The cost of handling and shipping merchandise from the Company's stores, locations or distribution centers to the customer is classified as SG&A. The cost of shipping and handling, including internal costs and payments to third parties, classified as SG&A was $ 435 million, $430 million and $410 million in fiscal 2012, 2011 and 2010, respectively.

Impairment of Long-Lived Assets

The Company evaluates its long-lived assets each quarter for indicators of potential impairment. Indicators of impairment include current period losses combined with a history of losses, management's decision to relocate or close a store or other location before the end of its previously estimated useful life or when changes in other circumstances indicate the carrying amount of an asset may not be recoverable. The evaluation for long-lived assets is performed at the lowest level of identifiable cash flows, which is generally the individual store level.

The assets of a store with indicators of impairment are evaluated by comparing its undiscounted cash flows with its carrying value. The estimate of cash flows includes management's assumptions of cash inflows and outflows directly resulting from the use of those assets in operations, including gross margin on Net Sales, payroll and related items, occupancy costs, insurance allocations and other costs to operate a store. If the carrying value is greater than the undiscounted cash flows, an impairment loss is recognized for the difference between the carrying value and the estimated fair market value. Impairment losses are recorded as a component of SG&A in the accompanying Consolidated Statements of Earnings. When a leased location closes, the Company also recognizes in SG&A the net present value of future lease obligations less estimated sublease income. The Company recorded impairments and lease obligation costs on closings and relocations in the ordinary course of business, as well as for the closing of seven stores in China in fiscal 2012, which were not material to the Consolidated Financial Statements in fiscal 2012, 2011 or 2010.

Goodwill and Other Intangible Assets

Goodwill represents the excess of purchase price over the fair value of net assets acquired. The Company does not amortize goodwill but does assess the recoverability of goodwill in the third quarter of each fiscal year, or more often if indicators warrant, by determining whether the fair value of each reporting unit supports its carrying value. The Company assesses qualitative factors to determine whether it is more likely than not that the fair value of each reporting unit is less than its carrying amount as a basis for determining whether it is necessary to complete quantitative impairment assessments. During fiscal 2012, for all reporting units other than the China reporting unit, the Company used qualitative factors to determine that its goodwill balances for each reporting unit were not impaired. For the China reporting unit, the Company recorded a charge of $97 million to impair all of the goodwill associated with that reporting unit in fiscal 2012. Impairment charges related to the remaining goodwill were not material for fiscal 2012, 2011 or 2010.

The Company amortizes the cost of other intangible assets over their estimated useful lives, which range up to ten years, unless such lives are deemed indefinite. Intangible assets with indefinite lives are tested in the third quarter of each fiscal year for impairment, or more often if indicators warrant. Impairment charges related to other intangible assets were not material for fiscal 2012, 2011 or 2010.

Stock-Based Compensation

The per share weighted average fair value of stock options granted during fiscal 2012, 2011 and 2010 was $9.86, $7.42 and $6.70, respectively. The fair value of these options was determined at the date of grant using the Black-Scholes option-pricing model with the following assumptions:

	Fiscal Year Ended		
	February 3, 2013	**January 29, 2012**	**January 30, 2011**
Risk-free interest rate	**1.2%**	2.0%	3.1%
Assumed volatility	**27.0%**	27.3%	26.4%
Assumed dividend yield	**2.3%**	2.7%	2.9%
Assumed lives of options	**5 years**	5 years	5 years

Derivatives

The Company uses derivative financial instruments from time to time in the management of its interest rate exposure on long-term debt and its exposure on foreign currency fluctuations. The Company accounts for its derivative financial instruments in accordance with the Financial Accounting Standards Board Accounting Standards Codification ("FASB ASC") Subtopic 815-10.

Comprehensive Income

Comprehensive Income includes Net Earnings adjusted for certain gains and losses that are excluded from Net Earnings under U.S. generally accepted accounting principles. Adjustments to Net Earnings and Accumulated Other Comprehensive Income consist primarily of foreign currency translation adjustments.

Foreign Currency Translation

Assets and liabilities denominated in a foreign currency are translated into U.S. dollars at the current rate of exchange on the last day of the reporting period. Revenues and expenses are generally translated using average exchange rates for the period and equity transactions are translated using the actual rate on the day of the transaction.

Segment Information

The Company operates within a single reportable segment primarily within North America. Net Sales for the Company outside the U.S. were $ 8.4 billion, $8.0 billion and $7.5 billion for fiscal 2012, 2011 and 2010, respectively. Long-lived assets outside the U.S. totaled $ 3.1 billion and $3.1 billion as of February 3, 2013 and January 29, 2012, respectively.

Reclassifications

Certain amounts in prior fiscal years have been reclassified to conform with the presentation adopted in the current fiscal year.

2. CHINA STORE CLOSINGS

In fiscal 2012, the Company closed its remaining seven big box stores in China. As a result of the closings, the Company recorded a total charge of $145 million, net of tax, in fiscal 2012. Inventory markdown costs of $10 million are included in Cost of Sales, and $135 million of costs related to the impairment of Goodwill and other assets, lease terminations, severance and other charges are included in SG&A in the accompanying Consolidated Statements of Earnings.

Five-Year Summary of Financial and Operating Results
The Home Depot, Inc. and Subsidiaries

amounts in millions, except where noted	2012[1]	2011	2010	2009	2008
STATEMENT OF EARNINGS DATA[2]					
Net sales	$ 74,754	$ 70,395	$ 67,997	$ 66,176	$ 71,288
Net sales increase (decrease) (%)	6.2	3.5	2.8	(7.2)	(7.8)
Earnings before provision for income taxes	7,221	6,068	5,273	3,982	3,590
Net earnings	4,535	3,883	3,338	2,620	2,312
Net earnings increase (decrease) (%)	16.8	16.3	27.4	13.3	(45.1)
Diluted earnings per share ($)	3.00	2.47	2.01	1.55	1.37
Diluted earnings per share increase (decrease) (%)	21.5	22.9	29.7	13.1	(39.6)
Diluted weighted average number of common shares	1,511	1,570	1,658	1,692	1,686
Gross margin - % of sales	34.6	34.5	34.3	33.9	33.7
Total operating expenses - % of sales	24.2	25.0	25.7	26.6	27.5
Interest and other, net - % of sales	0.7	0.8	0.8	1.2	1.1
Earnings before provision for income taxes - % of sales	9.7	8.6	7.8	6.0	5.0
Net earnings - % of sales	6.1	5.5	4.9	4.0	3.2
BALANCE SHEET DATA AND FINANCIAL RATIOS[2]					
Total assets	$ 41,084	$ 40,518	$ 40,125	$ 40,877	$ 41,164
Working capital	3,910	5,144	3,357	3,537	2,209
Merchandise inventories	10,710	10,325	10,625	10,188	10,673
Net property and equipment	24,069	24,448	25,060	25,550	26,234
Long-term debt	9,475	10,758	8,707	8,662	9,667
Stockholders' equity	17,777	17,898	18,889	19,393	17,777
Book value per share ($)	11.97	11.64	11.64	11.42	10.48
Long-term debt-to-equity (%)	53.3	60.1	46.1	44.7	54.4
Total debt-to-equity (%)	60.7	60.3	51.6	49.9	64.3
Current ratio	1.34:1	1.55:1	1.33:1	1.34:1	1.20:1
Inventory turnover	4.5x	4.3x	4.1x	4.1x	4.0x
Return on invested capital (%)	17.0	14.9	12.8	10.7	9.5
STATEMENT OF CASH FLOWS DATA					
Depreciation and amortization	$ 1,684	$ 1,682	$ 1,718	$ 1,806	$ 1,902
Capital expenditures	1,312	1,221	1,096	966	1,847
Cash dividends per share ($)	1.160	1.040	0.945	0.900	0.900
STORE DATA					
Number of stores	2,256	2,252	2,248	2,244	2,274
Square footage at fiscal year-end	235	235	235	235	238
Increase (decrease) in square footage (%)	—	—	—	(1.3)	1.3
Average square footage per store (in thousands)	104	104	105	105	105
STORE SALES AND OTHER DATA					
Comparable store sales increase (decrease) (%)[3]	4.6	3.4	2.9	(6.6)	(8.7)
Weighted average weekly sales per operating store (in thousands)	$ 627	$ 601	$ 581	$ 563	$ 601
Weighted average sales per square foot ($)	319	299	289	279	298
Number of customer transactions	1,364	1,318	1,306	1,274	1,272
Average ticket ($)	54.89	53.28	51.93	51.76	55.61
Number of associates at fiscal year-end (in thousands)[2]	340	331	321	317	322

(1) Fiscal year 2012 includes 53 weeks; all other fiscal years reported include 52 weeks.
(2) Continuing operations only.
(3) Includes Net Sales at locations open greater than 12 months, including relocated and remodeled stores and excluding closed stores. Retail stores become comparable on the Monday following their 365th day of operation. Comparable store sales is intended only as supplemental information and is not a substitute for Net Sales or Net Earnings presented in accordance with generally accepted accounting principles. Net Sales for the 53rd week of fiscal 2012 are not included in comparable store sales results for fiscal 2012.

The Time Value of Money
Future Amounts and Present Values

AFTER STUDYING THIS APPENDIX, YOU SHOULD BE ABLE TO:

Learning Objectives

LOB-1   Explain what is meant by the phrase *time value of money.*

LOB-2   Describe the relationships between *present values* and *future amounts.*

LOB-3   Explain three basic ways in which decision makers apply the time value of money.

LOB-4   Compute future amounts and the investments necessary to accumulate future amounts.

LOB-5   Compute the present values of future cash flows.

LOB-6   Discuss accounting applications of the concept of present value.

The Concept

One of the most basic—and important—concepts of investing is the *time value of money*. This concept is based on the idea that an amount of money available today can be safely invested to accumulate to a larger amount in the future. As a result, an amount of money available today is considered to be equivalent in value to a *larger sum* available at a future date.

In our discussion, we will refer to an amount of money available today as a *present value*. In contrast, an amount receivable or payable at a future date will be described as a *future amount*.

To illustrate, assume that you place $500 in a savings account that earns interest at the rate of 8 percent per year. The balance of your account at the end of each of the next four years is illustrated in Exhibit B–1.

LOB-1

LEARNING OBJECTIVE
Explain what is meant by the phrase *time value of money.*

LOB-2

LEARNING OBJECTIVE
Describe the relationships between *present values* and *future amounts.*

EXHIBIT B–1
The Values of Money Over Time

Future values are bigger, but are they worth more? This is the real issue.

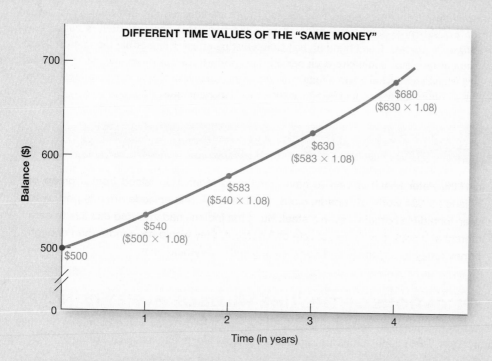

DIFFERENT TIME VALUES OF THE "SAME MONEY"

$680
($630 × 1.08)

$630
($583 × 1.08)

$583
($540 × 1.08)

$540
($500 × 1.08)

$500

Balance ($) — *Time (in years)*

These balances represent different time values of your $500 investment. When you first open the account, your investment has a *present value* of only $500. As time passes, the value of your investment increases to the *future amounts* illustrated in the graph. (Throughout this appendix, present values will be illustrated in **red**, and future amounts will be shown in **blue**.)

RELATIONSHIPS BETWEEN PRESENT VALUES AND FUTURE AMOUNTS

The difference between a present value and any future amount is the *interest* that is included in the future amount. We have seen that interest accrues over time. Therefore, the difference between the present value and a future amount depends on *two factors:* (1) the *rate of interest* at which the present value increases and (2) the *length of time* over which interest accumulates. (Notice in our graph, the farther away the future date, the larger the future amount.)

Present Values Change over Time   The present value of an investment gradually increases toward the future amount. In fact, when a future date *arrives,* what once was a future amount becomes the present value of the investment. For example, at the end of the first year, $540 will no longer be a future amount—it will be the present value of your savings account.

The Basic Concept (Stated Several Different Ways)   Notice that the present value of our savings account is *always less than its future amounts.* This is the basic idea underlying the time value of money. But this idea often is expressed in different ways, including the following:

- A present value is always *less than* a future amount.
- A future amount is always *greater than* a present value.
- A dollar available today is always worth *more* than a dollar that does not become available until a future date.
- A dollar available at a future date is always worth *less* than a dollar that is available today.

Read these statements carefully. All four reflect the idea that a present value is the "equivalent" of a larger number of dollars at a future date. This is what is meant by the time value of money.

COMPOUND INTEREST

The relationships between present values and future amounts assume that the interest earned on the investment is *reinvested,* rather than withdrawn. This concept often is called *compounding the interest.* Compounding has an interesting effect. Reinvesting the interest causes the amount invested to increase each period. This, in turn, causes more interest to be earned in each successive period. Over a long period of time, an investment in which interest is compounded continuously will increase to surprisingly large amounts.

CASE IN POINT

In 1626, Peter Minuit is said to have purchased Manhattan Island from a group of Indians for $24 worth of "beads, cloth, and trinkets." This episode often is portrayed as an incredible bargain—even a steal. But if the Indians had invested this $24 to earn interest at a compound interest rate of 8 percent, they would have more than enough money today to buy the island back—along with everything on it.

APPLICATIONS OF THE TIME VALUE OF MONEY CONCEPT

Investors, accountants, and other decision makers apply the time value of money in three basic ways. These applications are summarized below, along with a typical example.

LOB-3

LEARNING OBJECTIVE
Explain three basic ways in which decision makers apply the time value of money.

1. To determine the amount to which an investment will accumulate over time. *Example:* If we invest $5,000 each year and earn an annual rate of return of 10 percent, how much will be accumulated after 10 years?
2. To determine the amount that must be invested every period to accumulate a required future amount. *Example:* We must accumulate a $200 million bond sinking fund over the next 20 years. How much must we deposit into this fund each year, assuming that the fund's assets will be invested to earn an annual rate of return of 8 percent?
3. To determine the present value of cash flows expected to occur in the future. *Example:* Assuming that we require a 15 percent return on our investments, how much can we afford to pay today for new machinery that is expected to reduce production costs by $20,000 per year for the next 10 years?

We will now introduce a framework for answering such questions.

Future Amounts

A future amount is simply the dollar amount to which a present value *will accumulate* over time. As we have stated, the difference between a present value and a related future amount depends on (1) the interest rate and (2) the period of time over which the present value accumulates.

Starting with the present value, we may compute future amounts through a series of multiplications, as illustrated in our graph in Exhibit B–1. But there are faster and easier ways. For example, many financial calculators are programmed to compute future amounts; you merely enter the present value, the interest rate, and the number of periods. Or you may use a *table of future amounts*, such as Table FA–1 in Exhibit B–2.

EXHIBIT B–2

The Future Value of $1

Table FA–1
Future Value of $1 after *n* Periods

Number of Periods (*n*)	1%	1½%	5%	6%	8%	10%	12%	15%	20%
1	1.010	1.015	1.050	1.060	1.080	1.100	1.120	1.150	1.200
2	1.020	1.030	1.103	1.124	1.166	1.210	1.254	1.323	1.440
3	1.030	1.046	1.158	1.191	1.260	1.331	1.405	1.521	1.728
4	1.041	1.061	1.216	1.262	1.360	1.464	1.574	1.749	2.074
5	1.051	1.077	1.276	1.338	1.469	1.611	1.762	2.011	2.488
6	1.062	1.093	1.340	1.419	1.587	1.772	1.974	2.313	2.986
7	1.072	1.110	1.407	1.504	1.714	1.949	2.211	2.660	3.583
8	1.083	1.126	1.477	1.594	1.851	2.144	2.476	3.059	4.300
9	1.094	1.143	1.551	1.689	1.999	2.358	2.773	3.518	5.160
10	1.105	1.161	1.629	1.791	2.159	2.594	3.106	4.046	6.192
20	1.220	1.347	2.653	3.207	4.661	6.727	9.646	16.367	38.338
24	1.270	1.430	3.225	4.049	6.341	9.850	15.179	28.625	79.497
36	1.431	1.709	5.792	8.147	15.968	30.913	59.136	153.152	708.802

Approach to computing future amount

THE TABLES APPROACH

A table of future amounts shows the future amount to which *$1* will accumulate over a given number of periods, assuming that it has been invested to earn any of the illustrated interest rates. We will refer to the amounts shown in the body of this table as *factors,* rather than as dollar amounts.

To find the future amount of a present value *greater* than $1, simply multiply the present value by the factor obtained from the table. The formula for using the table in this manner is:

Future Amount = Present Value × Factor (from Table FA–1)

Let us demonstrate this approach using the data for our savings account, illustrated in Exhibit B–1. The account started with a present value of $500, invested at an annual interest rate of 8 percent. Thus, the future values of the account in each of the next four years can be computed as follows (rounded to the nearest dollar):

LOB-4

LEARNING OBJECTIVE
Compute future amounts and the investments necessary to accumulate future amounts.

Using the table to compute the amounts in our graph

Year	Future Amount	Computation (Using Table FA–1)
1	$540	$500 × 1.080 = $540
2	$583	$500 × 1.166 = $583
3	$630	$500 × 1.260 = $630
4	$680	$500 × 1.360 = $680

Computing a future amount is relatively easy. The more interesting question is: How much must we *invest today* to accumulate a required future amount?

Computing the Required Investment   At the beginning of Year 1, Metro Recycling agrees to create a fully funded pension plan for its employees by the end of Year 5. It is estimated that $5 million will be required to fully fund the pension plan. How much must Metro invest in this plan *today* to accumulate the promised $5 million by the end of Year 5, assuming that payments to the fund will be invested to earn an annual return of 8 percent?

Let us repeat our original formula for computing future amounts using Table FA–1:

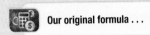
Our original formula . . .

$$\text{Future Amount} = \text{Present Value} \times \text{Factor (from Table FA–1)}$$

In this situation, we *know* the future amount—$5 million. We are looking for the *present value* which, when invested at an interest rate of 8 percent, will accumulate to $5 million in five years. To determine the *present value,* the formula shown above may be restated as follows:

$$\text{Present Value} = \frac{\text{Future Amount}}{\text{Factor (from Table FA–1)}}$$

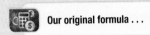
restated to find the present value

Referring to Table FA–1, we get a factor of 1.469 at the intersection of five periods and 8 percent interest. Thus, the amount of the required investment at the beginning of Year 1 is $3,403,676 ($5 million ÷ 1.469). Invested at 8 percent, this amount will accumulate to the required $5 million at the end of five years as illustrated in Exhibit B–3.

EXHIBIT B–3

The Future Amount of a Single Investment

THE FUTURE AMOUNT OF AN ANNUITY

In many situations, an investor will make a *series* of investment payments rather than a single payment. As an example, assume that you plan to deposit $500 into your savings account at the end of each of the next five years. If the account pays annual interest of 8 percent, what will be the balance in your savings account at the end of the fifth year? Tables, such as Table FA–2 in Exhibit B–4, may be used to answer this question. Table FA–2 presents the future amount of an *ordinary annuity of $1,* which is a series of payments of $1 made at the *end* of each of a specified number of periods.

To find the future amount of an ordinary annuity of payments greater than $1, we simply multiply the amount of the periodic payment by the factor appearing in the table, as shown here:

Approach to computing the future amount of an annuity

$$\begin{matrix}\text{Future Amount} \\ \text{of an Annuity}\end{matrix} = \text{Periodic Payment} \times \text{Factor (from Table FA–2)}$$

In our example, a factor of 5.867 is obtained from the table at the intersection of five periods and 8 percent interest. If this factor is multiplied by the periodic payment of $500, we find that your savings account will accumulate to a balance of $2,934 ($500 × 5.867) at the end of

Table FA–2
Future Amount of $1 Paid Periodically for *n* Periods

Number of Periods (*n*)	Interest Rate								
	1%	1½%	5%	6%	8%	10%	12%	15%	20%
1	1.000	1.000	1.000	1.000	1.000	1.000	1.000	1.000	1.000
2	2.010	2.015	2.050	2.060	2.080	2.100	2.120	2.150	2.200
3	3.030	3.045	3.153	3.184	3.246	3.310	3.374	3.473	3.640
4	4.060	4.091	4.310	4.375	4.506	4.641	4.779	4.993	5.368
5	5.101	5.152	5.526	5.637	5.867	6.105	6.353	6.742	7.442
6	6.152	6.230	6.802	6.975	7.336	7.716	8.115	8.754	9.930
7	7.214	7.323	8.142	8.394	8.923	9.487	10.089	11.067	12.916
8	8.286	8.433	9.549	9.897	10.637	11.436	12.300	13.727	16.499
9	9.369	9.559	11.027	11.491	12.488	13.579	14.776	16.786	20.799
10	10.462	10.703	12.578	13.181	14.487	15.937	17.549	20.304	25.959
20	22.019	23.124	33.066	36.786	45.762	57.275	72.052	102.444	186.688
24	26.974	28.634	44.502	50.816	66.765	88.497	118.155	184.168	392.484
36	43.077	47.276	95.836	119.121	187.102	299.127	484.463	1014.346	3539.009

EXHIBIT B–4

Future Value of an Ordinary Annuity

five years. Therefore, if you invest $500 at the end of each of the next five years in the savings account, you will accumulate $2,934 at the end of the five-year period.

While computing the future amount of an investment is sometimes necessary, many business and accounting problems require us to determine the *amount of the periodic payments* that must be made to accumulate the required future amount.

Computing the Required Periodic Payments
Assume that Ultra Tech Company is required to accumulate $10 million in a *bond sinking fund* to retire bonds payable five years from now. The *bond indenture* requires Ultra Tech to make equal payments to the fund at the end of each of the next five years. What is the amount of the required periodic payment, assuming that the fund will earn 10 percent annual interest? To answer this question, we simply rearrange the following formula for computing the future amount of an annuity:

$$\text{Future Amount of an Annuity} = \text{Periodic Payment} \times \text{Factor (from Table FA–2)}$$

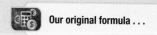 Our original formula . . .

In our example, we know that Ultra Tech is required to accumulate a future amount of $10 million. However, we need to know the amount of the periodic payments that, when invested at 10 percent annual interest, will accumulate to that future amount. To make this calculation, the formula may be restated as follows:

$$\text{Periodic Payment} = \frac{\text{Future Amount of an Annuity}}{\text{Factor (from Table FA–2)}}$$

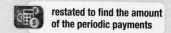 restated to find the amount of the periodic payments

The amount of each required payment, therefore, is $1,638,000 ($10 million ÷ **6.105**). If payments of $1,638,000 are made at the end of each of the next five years to a bond sinking fund that earns 10 percent annual interest, the fund will accumulate to $10 million, as shown in Exhibit B–5.

EXHIBIT B–5 Future Amount of a Series of Investmentsç

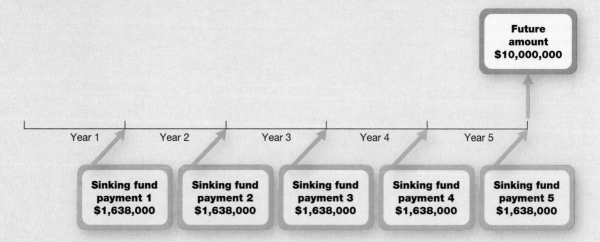

INTEREST PERIODS OF LESS THAN ONE YEAR

In our computations of future amounts, we have assumed that interest is paid (compounded) or payments are made annually. Therefore, in using the tables, we used *annual* periods and an *annual* interest rate. Investment payments or interest payments may be made on a more frequent basis, such as monthly, quarterly, or semiannually. Tables FA–1 and FA–2 may be used with any of these payment periods, *but the rate of interest must represent the interest rate for that period.*

As an example, assume that 24 monthly payments are to be made to an investment fund that pays a 12 percent annual interest rate. To determine the future amount of this investment, we would multiply the amount of the monthly payments by the factor from Table FA–2 for 24 periods, using a *monthly* interest rate of 1 percent—the 12 percent annual rate divided by 12 months.

Present Values

LOB-5

LEARNING OBJECTIVE
Compute the present values of future cash flows.

As indicated previously, the present value is *today's* value of funds to be received in the future. While present value has many applications in business and accounting, it is most easily explained in the context of evaluating investment opportunities. In this context, the present value is the amount that a knowledgeable investor would pay *today* for the right to receive an expected future amount of cash. The present value is always *less* than the future amount, because the investor will expect to earn a return on the investment. The amount by which the future cash receipt exceeds its present value represents the investor's profit.

The amount of the profit on a particular investment depends on two factors: (1) the rate of return (called the *discount rate*) required by the investor and (2) the length of time until the future amount will be received. The process of determining the present value of a future cash receipt is called *discounting* the future amount.

To illustrate the computation of present value, assume that an investment is expected to result in a $1,000 cash receipt at the end of one year and that an investor requires a 10 percent return on this investment. We know from our discussion of present and future values that the difference between a present value and a future amount is the return (interest) on the investment. In our example, the future amount would be equal to 110 percent of the original investment, because the investor expects 100 percent of the investment back plus a 10 percent return on the investment. Thus, the investor would be willing to pay *$909* ($1,000 ÷ 1.10) for this investment. This computation may be verified as follows (amounts rounded to the nearest dollar):

Amount to be invested (present value)	$ 909
Required return on investment ($909 × 10%)	91
Amount to be received in one year (future value)	$1,000

As illustrated in Exhibit B–6, if the $1,000 is to be received *two years* in the future, the investor would pay only *$826* for the investment today [($1,000 ÷ 1.10) ÷ 1.10]. This computation may be verified as follows (amounts rounded to the nearest dollar):

Amount to be invested (present value)	$ 826
Required return on investment in first year ($826 × 10%)	83
Amount invested after one year	$ 909
Required return on investment in second year ($909 × 10%)	91
Amount to be received in two years (future value)	$1,000

The amount that our investor would pay today, $826, is the present value of $1,000 to be received two years from now, discounted at an annual rate of 10 percent. The $174 difference between the $826 present value and the $1,000 future amount is the return (interest revenue) to be earned by the investor over the two-year period.

EXHIBIT B–6

Present Value of $1,000 to be Received in a Single Sum in Two Years

USING PRESENT VALUE TABLES

Although we can compute the present value of future amounts by a series of divisions, tables are available that simplify the calculations. We can use a table of present values to find the present value of $1 at a specified discount rate and then multiply that value by the future amount as illustrated in the following formula:

$$\text{Present Value} = \text{Future Amount} \times \text{Factor (from Table PV–1)}$$

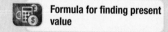 Formula for finding present value

Referring to Table PV–1 in Exhibit B–7, we find a factor of .826 at the intersection of two periods and 10 percent interest. If we multiply this factor by the expected future cash receipt of $1,000, we get a present value of *$826* ($1,000 × .826), the same amount computed previously.

WHAT IS THE APPROPRIATE DISCOUNT RATE?

As explained earlier, the *discount rate* may be viewed as the investor's required rate of return. All investments involve some degree of risk that actual future cash flows may turn out to be less than expected. Investors will require a rate of return that justifies taking this risk. In today's market conditions, investors require annual returns of between 2 percent and 6 percent on low-risk investments, such as government bonds and certificates of deposit. For relatively high-risk investments, such as the introduction of a new product line, investors may expect to earn an annual return of perhaps 15 percent or more. When a higher discount rate is used, the present value of the investment will be lower. In other words, as the risk of an investment increases, its value to investors decreases.

EXHIBIT B-7

Present Value of $1

Table PV-1
Present Values of $1 Due in *n* Periods

Number of Periods (*n*)	Discount Rate								
	1%	1½%	5%	6%	8%	10%	12%	15%	20%
1	.990	.985	.952	.943	.926	.909	.893	.870	.833
2	.980	.971	.907	.890	.857	.826	.797	.756	.694
3	.971	.956	.864	.840	.794	.751	.712	.658	.579
4	.961	.942	.823	.792	.735	.683	.636	.572	.482
5	.951	.928	.784	.747	.681	.621	.567	.497	.402
6	.942	.915	.746	.705	.630	.564	.507	.432	.335
7	.933	.901	.711	.665	.583	.513	.452	.376	.279
8	.923	.888	.677	.627	.540	.467	.404	.327	.233
9	.914	.875	.645	.592	.500	.424	.361	.284	.194
10	.905	.862	.614	.558	.463	.386	.322	.247	.162
20	.820	.742	.377	.312	.215	.149	.104	.061	.026
24	.788	.700	.310	.247	.158	.102	.066	.035	.013
36	.699	.585	.173	.123	.063	.032	.017	.007	.001

THE PRESENT VALUE OF AN ANNUITY

Many investment opportunities are expected to produce annual cash flows for a number of years, instead of one single future cash flow. Let us assume that Camino Company is evaluating an investment that is expected to produce *annual net cash flows of* $10,000 in *each of the next three years.*[1] If Camino Company expects a 12 percent return on this type of investment, it may compute the present value of these cash flows as follows:

Year	Expected New Cash Flows	×	Present Value of $1 Discounted at 12%	=	Present Value of Net Cash Flows
1	$10,000		.893		$ 8,930
2	10,000		.797		7,970
3	10,000		.712		7,120
Total present value of the investment					$24,020

This analysis indicates that the present value of the expected net cash flows from the investment, discounted at an annual rate of 12 percent, amounts to $24,020. This is the maximum amount that Camino Company could afford to pay for this investment and still expect to earn the 12 percent required rate of return, as shown in Exhibit B–8.

In the preceding analysis, we computed the present value of the investment by separately discounting each period's cash flows, using the appropriate factors from Table PV–1. Separately discounting each period's cash flows is necessary only when the cash flows vary in amount from period to period. Since the annual cash flows in our example are *uniform in amount,* there are easier ways to compute the total present value.

Many financial calculators are programmed to compute the present value of an investment after the interest rate, the future cash flows, and the number of periods have been entered.

---

[1] "Annual net cash flows" normally are the net result of a series of cash receipts and cash payments occurring throughout the year. For convenience, we follow the common practice of assuming that the entire net cash flows for each year occur at *year-end.* This assumption causes relatively little distortion and greatly simplifies computations.

EXHIBIT B–8

Present Value of Three $10,000 Cash Flows Discounted at 12%

Another approach is to refer to a *present value annuity table,* which shows the present value of *$1 to be received each period for a specified number of periods.* An annuity table labeled Table PV–2 appears in Exhibit B–9.[2]

To illustrate the use of Table PV–2, let's return to the example of the investment by Camino Company. That investment was expected to return $10,000 per year for the next three years, and the company's required rate of return was 12 percent per year. Using Table PV–2, we can compute the present value of the investment with the following formula:

Present Value of an Annuity = Periodic Cash Flows × Factor (from Table PV–2)

As illustrated in Table PV–2, the present value of $1 to be received at the end of the next three years, discounted at an annual rate of 12 percent, is 2.402. If we multiply 2.402 by the expected future annual cash receipt of $10,000, we get a present value of $24,020, which is the same amount produced by the series of calculations made earlier.

 Formula to find the present value of a series of cash flows

EXHIBIT B–9

Present Value of an Ordinary Annuity

Number of Periods (n)	Table PV–2 Present Values of $1 to Be Received Periodically for *n* Periods								
	Discount Rate								
	1%	1½%	5%	6%	8%	10%	12%	15%	20%
1	0.990	0.985	0.952	0.943	0.926	0.909	0.893	0.870	0.833
2	1.970	1.956	1.859	1.833	1.783	1.736	1.690	1.626	1.528
3	2.941	2.912	2.723	2.673	2.577	2.487	2.402	2.283	2.106
4	3.902	3.854	3.546	3.465	3.312	3.170	3.037	2.855	2.589
5	4.853	4.783	4.329	4.212	3.993	3.791	3.605	3.352	2.991
6	5.795	5.697	5.076	4.917	4.623	4.355	4.111	3.784	3.326
7	6.728	6.598	5.786	5.582	5.206	4.868	4.564	4.160	3.605
8	7.652	7.486	6.463	6.210	5.747	5.335	4.968	4.487	3.837
9	8.566	8.361	7.108	6.802	6.247	5.759	5.328	4.772	4.031
10	9.471	9.222	7.722	7.360	6.710	6.145	5.650	5.019	4.192
20	18.046	17.169	12.462	11.470	9.818	8.514	7.469	6.259	4.870
24	21.243	20.030	13.799	12.550	10.529	8.985	7.784	6.434	4.937
36	30.108	27.661	16.547	14.621	11.717	9.677	8.192	6.623	4.993

---

[2] This table is for an *ordinary* annuity, which assumes that the periodic cash flows occur at the *end* of each period.

DISCOUNT PERIODS OF LESS THAN ONE YEAR

The interval between regular periodic cash flows is called the *discount period.* In our preceding examples, we have assumed cash flows once a year. Often, cash flows occur on a more frequent basis, such as monthly, quarterly, or semiannually. The present value tables can be used with discount periods of any length, *but the discount rate must be for that length of time.* For example, if we use Table PV–2 to find the present value of a series of *quarterly* cash payments, the discount rate must be the *quarterly* rate.

There are many applications of the present value concept in accounting. In the next several pages, we will discuss some of the most important of these applications.

Valuation of Financial Instruments

LOB-6

LEARNING OBJECTIVE
Discuss accounting applications of the concept of present value.

Accountants use the phrase *financial instruments* to describe cash, equity investments in another business, and any contracts that call for receipts or payments of cash. (Notice that this phrase applies to all financial assets, as well as most liabilities. In fact, the only common liabilities *not* considered financial instruments are unearned revenue and deferred income taxes.)

Whenever the present value of a financial instrument *differs significantly* from the sum of the expected future cash flows, the instrument is recorded in the accounting records at its *present value*—not at the expected amount of the future cash receipts or payments.

Let us illustrate with a few common examples. Cash appears in the balance sheet at its face amount. This face value *is* a present value—that is, the value of the cash today.

Marketable securities appear in the balance sheet at their *current market values.* These too are present values—representing the amount of cash into which the security can be converted *today.*

Accounts receivable and accounts payable normally appear in the balance sheet at the amounts expected to be collected or paid in the near future. Technically, these are *future amounts,* not present values. But they usually are received or paid within 30 or 60 days. Considering the short periods of time involved, the differences between these future amounts and their present values simply are *not material.*

INTEREST-BEARING RECEIVABLES AND PAYABLES

When a financial instrument calls for the receipt or payment of interest, the difference between the present value and the future amounts *does* become material. Thus, interest-bearing receivables and payables initially are recorded in accounting records at the *present value* of the future cash flows—also called the "principal amount" of the obligation. This present value often is *substantially less* than the sum of the expected future amounts.

Consider, for example, $100 million in 30-year, 9 percent bonds payable issued at par. At the issuance date, the present value of this bond issue is $100 million—the amount of cash received. But the future payments to bondholders are expected to total *$370* million, computed as follows:

Future interest payments ($100 million × 9% × 30 years)	$ 270,000,000
Maturity value of the bonds (due in 30 years)	100,000,000
Sum of the future cash payments	$ 370,000,000

Thus the $100 million issuance price represents the present value of $370 million in future cash payments to be made over a period of 30 years.

In essence, interest-bearing financial instruments are "automatically" recorded at their present values simply because we do not include future interest charges in the original valuation of the receivable or the liability.

"NON-INTEREST-BEARING" NOTES

On occasion, companies may issue or accept notes that make no mention of interest, or in which the stated interest rates are unreasonably low. If the difference between the present value of such a note and its face amount is *material,* the note initially is recorded at its present value.

To illustrate, assume that on January 1, 2015, Elron Corporation purchases land from U.S. Development Co. As full payment for this land, Elron issues a $300,000 installment note payable, due in three annual installments of $100,000, beginning on December 31, 2015. This note makes *no mention* of interest charges.

Clearly, three annual installments of $100,000 are not the equivalent of $300,000 available today. Elron should use the *present value* of this note—not the face amount—in determining the cost of the land and reporting its liability.

Assume that a realistic interest rate for financing land over a three-year period currently is 10 percent per annum. The present value of Elron's installment note, discounted at 10 percent, is *$248,700* [$100,000, 3-year annuity × 2.487 (from Table PV–2) in Exhibit B–9]. Elron should view this $248,700 as the "principal amount" of this installment note payable. The remaining $51,300 ($300,000 − $248,700) represents interest charges included in the installment payments.

Elron should record the purchase of the land and the issuance of this note as follows:[3]

Land	248,700	
Notes Payable		248,700
Purchased land, issuing a 3-year installment note payable with a present value of $248,700.		

(U.S. Development Co. should make similar computations in determining the sales price of the land and the valuation of its note receivable.)

Elron also should prepare an *amortization table* to allocate the amount of each installment payment between interest expense and reduction in the principal amount of this obligation. This table, based on an original unpaid balance of $248,700, three annual payments of $100,000, and an annual interest rate of 10 percent, is illustrated in Exhibit B–10.

EXHIBIT B–10

Amortization Table for a Discounted Note Payable

AMORTIZATION TABLE					
(3-YEAR, $300,000 INSTALLMENT NOTE PAYABLE, DISCOUNTED AT 10% PER ANNUM)					
Interest Period	Payment Date	Annual Payment	Interest Expense (10% of the Last Unpaid Balance)	Reduction in Unpaid Balance	Unpaid Balance
Issue date	Jan. 1, 2015				$248,700
1	Dec. 31, 2015	$100,000	$24,870	$75,130	173,570
2	Dec. 31, 2016	100,000	17,357	82,643	90,927
3	Dec. 31, 2017	100,000	9,073*	90,927	–0–

*In the last period, interest expense is equal to the amount of the final payment minus the remaining unpaid balance. This compensates for the use of a present value table with factors carried to only three decimal places.

The entry at December 31, 2015, to record the first installment payment will be as follows:

Interest Expense	24,870	
Notes Payable	75,130	
Cash		100,000
Made annual payment on installment note payable to U.S. Development Co.		

---

[3] There is an alternative recording technique that makes use of an account entitled Discount on Notes Payable. This alternative approach produces the same results and will be explained in later accounting courses.

MARKET PRICES OF BONDS

The market price of bonds may be regarded as the *present value* to bondholders of the future principal and interest payments, discounted at the prevailing market rate of interest at the time of issuance. To illustrate, assume that Driscole Corporation issues $1,000,000 of 10-year, 10 percent bonds when the going market rate of interest is 12 percent. Because bond interest is paid semiannually, we must use 20 *semiannual* periods as the life of the bond issue and a 6 percent *semiannual* market rate of interest in our present value calculations. The discounted present value of the bond's future cash flows, discounted for 20 semiannual periods at 6 percent, is $885,500, computed as follows:

Present value of future principal payments:	
$1,000,000 due after 20 semiannual periods, discounted at 6%:	
$1,000,000 × .312 (from Table PV–1)	$312,000
Present value of future interest payments:	
$50,000 per period ($1,000,000 × 10% × ½) for 20 semiannual periods, discounted at 6%: $50,000 × 11.470 (from Table PV–2)	573,500
Expected issuance price of bond issue	$885,500

Note that, because the market rate of interest exceeds the bond's coupon rate, the bonds are issued at a $114,500 discount ($1,000,000 face value − $885,500 issue price). Thus, we know that these bonds were sold to an underwriter at 88.55 (meaning 88.55 percent of their face value).

As illustrated in Chapter 10, the entire amount of the discount is debited to an account titled Discount on Bonds Payable at the time the bonds are issued. The entry to record the issuance of this bond is:

Cash	885,500	
Discount on Bonds Payable	114,500	
Bonds Payable		1,000,000
Issued 10%, 10-year bonds with $1,000,000 face value to an underwriter at a price of 88.55.		

When the bonds mature in 10 years, Driscole must pay bondholders the *full* $1 million face value of the bond issue, or $114,500 *more* than it received at the time the bonds were issued. As discussed in Chapter 10, the additional $114,500 due at maturity represents a portion of the company's total *interest expense* that must be amortized over the 10-year life of the bond. Thus, Driscole will incur interest expense of $55,725 every six months, computed as follows:

Semiannual interest *payment* (1,000,000 × 10% × ½)	$50,000
Add: Semiannual amortization of bond discount ([$114,500 ÷ 10 years] × ½) ..	5,725
Semiannual interest expense	$55,725

The entry to record $55,725 of semiannual interest expense is:

Bond Interest Expense	55,725	
Cash		50,000
Discount on Bonds Payable		5,725
To record semiannual interest expense and to recognize six months' amortization of the $114,500 discount on 10-year bonds payable.		

Notice that, while the amortization of the discount increases semiannual interest expense by $5,725, it does not require an immediate cash outlay. The $114,500 of additional interest expense for the *entire* 10-year period will not be paid until the bonds mature.

CAPITAL LEASES

We briefly discuss capital leases in Chapter 10, but do not illustrate the accounting for these instruments. This appendix gives us an opportunity to explore this topic in greater detail.

A capital lease is regarded as a sale of the leased asset by the lessor to the lessee. At the date of this sale, the lessor recognizes sales revenue equal to the *present value* of the future lease payments receivable, discounted at a realistic rate of interest. The lessee also uses the present value of the future payments to determine the cost of the leased asset and the valuation of the related liability.

To illustrate, assume that, on December 1, Pace Tractor uses a *capital lease* to finance the sale of a tractor to Kelly Grading Co. The tractor was carried in Pace Tractor's perpetual inventory records at a cost of $15,000. Terms of the lease call for Kelly Grading Co. to make *24* monthly payments of *$1,000* each, beginning on December 31. These lease payments include an interest charge of *1 percent* per month. At the end of the 24-month lease, title to the tractor will pass to Kelly Grading Co. at no additional cost.

Accounting by the Lessor (Pace Tractor)

Table PV–2 shows that the present value of $1 to be received monthly for 24 months, discounted at 1 percent per month, is 21.243. Therefore, the present value of the 24 future lease payments is $1,000 × 21.243, or *$21,243*. Pace Tractor should record this capital lease as a sale of the tractor at a price equal to the present value of the lease payments, as follows:

Lease Payments Receivable (net)	21,243	
Sales		21,243
Financed sale of a tractor to Kelly Grading Co. using a capital lease requiring 24 monthly payments of $1,000. Payments include a 1% monthly interest charge.		
Cost of Goods Sold	15,000	
Inventory		15,000
To record cost of tractor sold under capital lease.		

Notice that the sales price of the tractor is only $21,243, even though the gross amount to be collected from Kelly Grading Co. amounts to $24,000 ($1,000 × 24 payments). The difference between these two amounts, $2,757, will be recognized by Pace Tractor as interest revenue over the term of the lease.

To illustrate the recognition of interest revenue, the entry on December 31 to record collection of the first monthly lease payment (rounded to the nearest dollar) will be:

Cash	1,000	
Interest Revenue		212
Lease Payments Receivable (net)		788
Received first lease payment from Kelly Grading Co.: $1,000 lease payment received, less $212 interest revenue ($21,243 × 1%), equals $788 reduction in lease payments receivable.		

After this first monthly payment is collected, the present value of the lease payments receivable is reduced to $20,455 ($21,243 original balance, less $788). Therefore, the interest revenue earned during the *second* month of the lease (rounded to the nearest dollar) will be *$205* ($20,455 × 1%).[4]

---

[4] Both Pace Tractor and Kelly Grading Co. would prepare *amortization tables* showing the allocation of each lease payment between interest and the principal amount due.

Accounting by the Lessee (Kelly Grading Co.)

Kelly Grading Co. also should use the present value of the lease payments to determine the cost of the tractor and the amount of the related liability, as follows:

Leased Equipment	21,243	
Lease Payments Obligation		21,243

To record acquisition of a tractor through a capital lease from Pace Tractor. Terms call for 24 monthly payments of $1,000, which include a 1% monthly interest charge.

The entry on December 31 to record the first monthly lease payment (rounded to the nearest dollar) will be:

Interest Expense	212	
Lease Payments Obligation	788	
Cash		1,000

To record first monthly lease payment to Pace Tractor: $1,000 lease payment, less $212 interest expense ($21,243 × 1%), equals $788 reduction in lease payments obligation.

OBLIGATIONS FOR POSTRETIREMENT BENEFITS

As we explain in Chapter 10, any unfunded obligation for postretirement benefits appears in the balance sheet at the *present value* of the expected future cash outlays to retired employees. The computation of this present value is so complex that it is performed by a professional actuary. But the present value of this obligation normally is far less than the expected future payments, as the cash payments will take place many years in the future.

ASSIGNMENT MATERIAL   ## Discussion Questions

1. Explain what is meant by the phrase *time value of money.*
2. Explain why the present value of a future amount is always *less* than the future amount.
3. Identify the two factors that determine the difference between the present value and the future amount of an investment.
4. Describe three basic investment applications of the concept of the time value of money.
5. Briefly explain the relationships between present value and
   (a) the length of time until the future cash flow occurs, and
   (b) the discount rate used in determining present value.

6. Define *financial instruments.* Explain the valuation concept used in initially recording financial instruments in financial statements.
7. Are normal accounts receivable and accounts payable financial instruments? Are these items shown in the balance sheet at their present values? Explain.
8. Assuming no change in the expected amount of future cash flows, what factors may cause the present value of a financial instrument to change? Explain fully.

Problems

LOB-1, LOB-2, LOB-4
PROBLEM B.1
Using Future Amount Tables

Use Table FA–1 (in Exhibit B–2) and Table FA–2 (in Exhibit B–4) to determine the future amounts of the following investments:

a. $50,000 is invested for 10 years, at 6 percent interest, compounded annually.
b. $240,000 is to be received five years from today, at 10 percent annual interest.

c. $20,000 is invested in a fund at the end of each of the next 10 years, at 8 percent interest, compounded annually.

d. $80,000 is invested initially, plus $6,000 is invested annually at the end of each of the next three years, at 12 percent interest, compounded annually.

LOB-3, LOB-4

PROBLEM B.2

Bond Sinking Fund

Tilman Company is required by a bond indenture to make equal annual payments to a bond sinking fund at the end of each of the next 20 years. The sinking fund will earn 8 percent interest and must accumulate to a total of $500,000 at the end of the 20-year period.

Instructions

a. Calculate the amount of the annual payments.

b. Calculate the total amount of interest that will be earned by the fund over the 20-year period.

c. Make the general journal entry to record redemption of the bond issue at the end of the 20-year period, assuming that the sinking fund is recorded on Tilman's accounting records at $500,000 and bonds payable are recorded at the same amount.

d. What would be the effect of an increase in the rate of return on the required annual payment? Explain.

LOB-1, LOB-2, LOB-5

PROBLEM B.3

Using Present Value Tables

Use Table PV–1 (in Exhibit B–7) and Table PV–2 (in Exhibit B–9) to determine the present values of the following cash flows:

a. $15,000 to be paid annually for 10 years, discounted at an annual rate of 6 percent. Payments are to occur at the end of each year.

b. $9,200 to be received today, assuming that the money will be invested in a two-year certificate of deposit earning 8 percent annually.

c. $300 to be paid monthly for 36 months, with an additional "balloon payment" of $12,000 due at the end of the 36th month, discounted at a monthly interest rate of $1\frac{1}{2}$ percent. The first payment is to be one month from today.

d. $25,000 to be received annually for the first three years, followed by $15,000 to be received annually for the next two years (total of five years in which collections are received), discounted at an annual rate of 8 percent. Assume collections occur at year-end.

LOB-3, LOB-5, LOB-6

PROBLEM B.4

Present Value and Bond Prices

On June 30 of the current year, Rural Gas & Electric Co. issued $60,000,000 face value, 9 percent, 10-year bonds payable, with interest dates of December 31 and June 30. The bonds were issued at a discount, resulting in an effective *semiannual* interest rate of 5 percent.

Instructions

a. Compute the issue price for the bond that results in an effective semiannual interest rate of 5 percent. (Hint: Discount both the interest payments and the maturity value over 20 semiannual periods.)

b. Prepare a journal entry to record the issuance of the bonds at the sales price you computed in part a.

c. Explain why the bonds were issued at a discount.

LOB-3, LOB-5, LOB-6

PROBLEM B.5

Valuation of a Note Payable

On December 1, Showcase Interiors purchased a shipment of furniture from Colonial House by paying $10,500 cash and issuing an installment note payable in the face amount of $28,800. The note is to be paid in 24 monthly installments of $1,200 each. Although the note makes no mention of an interest charge, the rate of interest usually charged to Showcase Interiors in such transactions is $1\frac{1}{2}$ percent per month.

Instructions

a. Compute the present value of the note payable, using a discount rate of $1\frac{1}{2}$ percent per month.

b. Prepare the journal entries in the accounts of Showcase Interiors on:

1. December 1, to record the purchase of the furniture (debit Inventory).

   2.   December 31, to record the first $1,200 monthly payment on the note and to recognize interest expense for one month by the effective interest method. (Round interest expense to the nearest dollar.)

   c.   Show how the liability for this note would appear in the balance sheet at December 31. (Assume that the note is classified as a current liability.)

LOB-3, LOB-5, LOB-6

PROBLEM B.6

Capital Leases: A
Comprehensive Problem

Custom Truck Builders frequently uses long-term lease contracts to finance the sale of its trucks. On November 1, 2015, Custom Truck Builders leased to Interstate Van Lines a truck carried in the perpetual inventory records at $33,520. The terms of the lease call for Interstate Van Lines to make 36 monthly payments of $1,400 each, beginning on November 30, 2015. The present value of these payments, after considering a built-in interest charge of 1 percent per month, is equal to the regular $42,150 sales price of the truck. At the end of the 36-month lease, title to the truck will transfer to Interstate Van Lines.

Instructions

a.   Prepare journal entries for 2015 in the accounts of Custom Truck Builders on:

   1.   November 1, to record the sale financed by the lease and the related cost of goods sold. (Debit Lease Payments Receivable for the $42,150 present value of the future lease payments.)

   2.   November 30, to record receipt of the first $1,400 monthly payment. (Prepare a compound journal entry that allocates the cash receipt between interest revenue and reduction of Lease Payments Receivable. The portion of each monthly payment recognized as interest revenue is equal to 1 percent of the balance of the account Lease Payments Receivable, at the beginning of that month. Round all interest computations to the nearest dollar.)

   3.   December 31, to record receipt of the second monthly payment.

b.   Prepare journal entries for 2015 in the accounts of Interstate Van Lines on:

   1.   November 1, to record acquisition of the leased truck.

   2.   November 30, to record the first monthly lease payment. (Determine the portion of the payment representing interest expense in a manner parallel to that described in part **a.**)

   3.   December 31, to record the second monthly lease payment.

   4.   December 31, to recognize depreciation on the leased truck through year-end. Compute depreciation expense by the straight-line method, using a 10-year service life and an estimated salvage value of $6,150.

c.   Compute the net carrying value of the leased truck in the balance sheet of Interstate Van Lines at December 31, 2015.

d.   Compute the amount of Interstate Van Lines's lease payment obligation at December 31, 2015.

LOB-5, LOB-6

PROBLEM B.7

Valuation of a Note
Receivable with an
Unrealistic Interest Rate

On December 31, Richland Farms sold a tract of land, which had cost $930,000, to Skyline Developers in exchange for $150,000 cash and a five-year, 4 percent note receivable for $900,000. Interest on the note is payable annually, and the principal amount is due in five years. The accountant for Richland Farms did not notice the unrealistically low interest rate on the note and made the following entry on December 31 to record this sale.

Cash	150,000	
Notes Receivable	900,000	
Land		930,000
Gain on Sale of Land		120,000
Sold land to Skyline Developers in exchange for cash and five-year note with interest due annually.		

Instructions

a. Compute the present value of the note receivable from Skyline Developers at the date of sale, assuming that a realistic rate of interest for this transaction is 12 percent. (Hint: Consider both the annual interest payments and the maturity value of the note.)

b. Prepare the journal entry on December 31 to record the sale of the land correctly. Show supporting computations for the gain or loss on the sale.

c. Explain what effects the error made by Richland Farms's accountant will have on (**1**) the net income in the year of the sale and (**2**) the combined net income of the next five years. Ignore income taxes.

Page numbers followed by n refer to notes.

A

AAA. *See* American Accounting Association (AAA)
Abbott Labs, 481
ABG Supply, 587
Accelerated depreciation
    declining-balance method, 395–397
    deferring income taxes through, 586
    defined, 392
    MACRS (Modified Accelerated Cost Recovery System), 395n, 586n
    straight-line depreciation vs., 392–393, 397, 400
    tax considerations, 395n, 397, 586
    units-of-output method, 400
Account, 115
Accountability, 88, 115
Accounting, as language of business, 5, 26
Accounting cycle
    accounting records, role of, 88
    adjusted trial balance, 159–160, 194, 195
    adjusting entries. *See* Adjusting entries
    after-closing trial balance, 205–207
    closing temporary accounts, 200–204
    defined, 88, 115
    financial statement preparation, 194–198
    journalized transactions, 91–95, 109–111
    in perspective, 112
    posting journal entries to ledger accounts, 92
    procedures vs. accounting knowledge, 112
    relationships among financial statements, 54–56, 198–200
    steps in, 88
    summary of, 208
    trial balance, 111–112
    worksheets, 209–212, 587–591
Accounting education, 26
Accounting equation
    about, 45–46
    double-entry accounting and, 90–91
    effects of business transactions on, 50–51, 52
Accounting information
    as communication of economic events, 5
    cost of producing, 8
    cultural variables and, 689–690
    decisions based on, 4–5
    externally reported, characteristics of, 13–14
    external users of, 10, 59–61
    financial. *See* Financial accounting
    general-purpose, 6
    integrity of, 17–24
    internal control and, 8–9
    internal users of, 14–15, 60–61
    as language of business, 5, 26
    management. *See* Management accounting
    standards for preparation of, 17–18
    tax, 6
    types of, 5–6
    user's perspective on, 5

Accounting periods
    adjusting entries and, 142, 143, 144
    defined, 99, 115
    different, preparing financial statements covering, 207
    length of, 99–100
    multiple, expenditures benefitting, 101
    time period principle, 99–100
    unprofitable, 156
Accounting principles
    about, 18
    adequate disclosure in, 60, 198–200, 208
    adjusting entries and, 156–158
    conservatism, 101, 349
    consistency, 349, 398
    cost principle, 43
    economic substance, 438
    entity principle, 42
    GAAP. *See* Generally accepted accounting principles (GAAP)
    going-concern assumption and, 43
    matching principle. *See* Matching principle
    materiality, 157–158, 262
    objectivity principle, 43–44, 101
    realization principle, 100, 156
    special journals and, 264–265
    stable-dollar assumption, 44
    time period principle, 99–100
    worldwide, 18
Accounting process, 5
Accounting records, 88
    bank records vs., 293–295
    updating, 296–297
Accounting Standards Codification (ASC), 18–19
Accounting systems
    accounting as information system, 7
    basic functions of, 8
    cost-effectiveness of, 8
    defined, 6–7, 30
    design/installation of, 8
    information needs, determining, 7–8
    internal control components of, 8–9
    merchandising companies, 250–251
    modifying, 264–265
Accounts, defined, 88. *See also specific types of accounts*
Accounts payable
    defined, 44
    foreign exchange transaction adjustments, 696–698
    as a liability, 44–45, 433
    merchandising companies, 253, 257
    other, 433
    payment of, 95, 253, 257
    subsidiary ledgers, 250
    to suppliers, 253, 257
    trade, 433
    valuation of, B-10
Accounts receivable. *See also* Notes receivable
    aging, 304–306
    collection of, 49, 253, 257
    credit card sales, 308–309

    defined, 300
    direct write-off method, 307
    factoring, 307–308
    foreign exchange transaction adjustments, 696–698
    internal control over, 301
    merchandising companies, 253, 257
    monthly estimates of credit losses, 304–306
    past due, 311
    recovery of, previously written off, 306–307
    subsidiary ledgers, 250
    uncollectible. *See* Uncollectible accounts
    valuation of, B-10
Accounts receivable turnover, 360–361
Accounts receivable turnover rate
    about/example, 311–312
    computing, 649–650, 649n
    defined, 315
    as measure of debt-paying ability, 456, 654
Accrual basis, 569, 593
Accrual basis of accounting, 102
    accrue, defined, 115, 152, 163
    accrued expenses (liabilities), 45
        adjusting entries for, 143, 144, 158–160
        income taxes, 155–156
        interest expense, 153–154
        payroll liabilities, 435–437
        wages (or salaries) expense, 152–153
    accruing uncollected revenue, 143, 144, 154–155
    accruing unpaid expenses, 143, 144, 152–154
    cash basis vs., 569
    converting to cash basis, 572–573
Accrue, 115, 152, 163
Accrued, defined, 45
Accrued expenses, 45
Accrued liabilities, 435, 463
Accrued revenue, 154
Accumulated depreciation, 150, 163, 409
Ace Hardware Stores, 259
Acid-test ratio, 632
Actuary, 459, 463
Additional Paid-in Capital, 491–492, 504
Adelphia Communications, 27
Adequate disclosure, 60, 198–200, 208, 213
Adidas, 538
Adjustable-rate mortgages, 439n
Adjusted trial balance, 159–160, 163, 194, 195, 208
Adjusting entries, 142–160, 163
    accounting periods and, 142–143
    accounting principles and, 156–160
    accruing income tax expense, 155–156
    accruing uncollected revenue, 143, 144, 154–155
    accruing unpaid expenses, 143, 144, 152–154
    adjusted trial balance, 159–160, 194, 195
    for Allowance for Doubtful Accounts, 303–304
    characteristics of, 143–144
    converting assets to expenses, 142–143, 144, 145–148

converting liabilities to revenue, 143, 144, 151–152
deferral of expenses, 142–143
deferral of revenue, 143
for depreciation, 148–150
effects on financial statements, 158–160
foreign receivables/payables, 696–698
income taxes expense, 155–156
for inventory shrinkage, 253–254, 351
materiality and, 157–158
need for, 142
reconciling net income with net cash flows, 580–581
timing differences, 142, 143, 580
types of, 142–143
unadjusted trial balance, 145
worksheets and, 209–212
year-end, 145
Adoption of IFRS, 691–693, 704
AFLAC, Incorporated, 171
After-closing trial balance, 205–207, 208, 213
Aging accounts receivable, 304–306, 315
Allete, Inc., 311–312
Allianz SE, 703
Allowance for Doubtful Accounts, 303–304, 305n, 313, 315
Allowances, 262–263, 266
Amazon, 584, 621
American Accounting Association (AAA), 21, 30
American Airlines, 67, 170, 482, 559
American Cancer Society, 15, 16
American Express, 308, 318
American Greetings, 481
American Institute of CPAs (AICPA)
    about, 20–21
    Auditing Standards Board, 21
    Code of Professional Conduct, 23
    CPA examination, 25
    defined, 30
    survey of depreciation methods, 400
America West Corporation, 171
Amortization, 403
    of bond discount, 446–447, B-12
    of bond premium, 448–450
    of discounted note payable, B-11
    goal of, 409
    negative, 439n
    of patents, 406
    tables for calculating, 438–440
Amortization table, 438, 463
Annual net cash flows, B-8n
Annual reports, 194, 633
    defined, 659
    legal requirements for, 487–488
    Management Discussion and Analysis (MD&A) sections, 208
Annuities
    future value of, B-4–B-6
    present value of, B-8–B-11
Apple Computer, 122, 288, 319, 321–322, 481
Arthur Andersen, 457
Articles of incorporation, 488
Articulation, 41, 55
Asset accounts, 90, 390–391
Assets
    converting to expenses, 142–143, 144, 145–148, 158
    cost principle and, 43

current, 57, 198, 629–631
defined, 12, 42, 64
depreciable, 148, 388
depreciation and, 148–150
financial. See Financial assets
going-concern assumption and, 43
intangible. See Intangible assets
liquid, 60
natural resources, 388, 408–409
objectivity principle and, 43–44, 101
plant. See Plant assets
prepaid expenses, 146–148
purchasing and financing part of the cost, 47–48
purchasing for cash, 47, 93
purchasing on account, 48, 94
quality of, 629
quick, 632
sale of, 48, 95
stable-dollar assumption, 44
trading in used for new, 402
write-downs of, 351–352, 399
AT&T, 486
Atlantic Richfield Company (ARCO), 559
Audits
    AICPA's Auditing Standards Board, 21
    defined, 20, 30
    of financial statements, 20, 194
    Government Accountability Office (GAO), 25
    Internal Revenue Service (IRS), 25
    lying to external auditors, 538
Australia, 686, 692
Autonomy (company), 3–4, 9
Available for sale securities, 297
Average-cost method, 350
    defined, 363
    evaluation of, 348
    in periodic inventory system, 355
    in perpetual inventory system, 344–345
Average stockholders' equity, 206

B

Balance sheet, 56
    accounting equation, 45–46, 50–51, 52
    adjusting entries, effects of, 158–160
    assets. See Assets
    business entity and, 42
    business transactions, effects of, 46–51
    cash presentation, 291–292
    classified, 198, 629–631
    defined, 12, 13, 30, 64, 40, 197
    earning of revenue and, 49–50
    features of, 42
    inventory errors and, 357–358
    liabilities. See Liabilities
    marketable securities, 300
    owners' equity, 45, 58–59
    payment of expenses and, 50
    preparing, 197–198
    purpose of, 41
    recording transactions in, 92–95
    reporting ownership equity in, 58–59
    sample, 196
    separate subtotals, 198
    statement of cash flows and, 578
    stockholders' equity, 491, 492, 537–538

Bally Total Fitness Corporation, 171
Bank credit cards, 308
Bankrate.com, 339
Bank reconciliation, 293–297, 315
Bankruptcy, 454, 454n, 463
Bank statements, 293–297
Bar-coded merchandise, 258
Basic earnings per share, 530, 540
Bearer bonds, 442n
Belk, Inc., 341
Best Buy, 193, 222
Best Buy Europe, 193
Board of directors, 488
    defined, 504
    dividend action by, 531
    functions of, 489
Boeing Aircraft, 34, 248, 519, 710
Bond certificates, 441
Bond premium
    accounting for, 447–450
    amortization of, 448–450
    in perspective, 450
    reduction in cost of borrowing, 448
BondsOnline, 482
Bonds payable
    accounting for, 442
        accrual of interest payable, 443–444
        amortization of bond discount, 446–447, B-12
        amortization of bond premium, 448–450
        bonds issued at discount, 450, B-12
        bonds issued at discount or premium, 444–447
        bonds issued at premium, 447–450
        bonds issued between interest dates, 444
    bonds, defined, 440–441
    carrying value of, 448
    convertible, 442
    defined, 463
    early retirement of, 452–453
    explained, 440–442
    issuance of, 441
    junk, 442
    market prices of, 441, 451–452
    present value of, 450–451, B-12
    statement of cash flows and, 578
    tax advantage of bond financing, 442
    transferability of, 441
    types of, 441–442, 442n, 450n
    yield rate, 648
Bookkeeping, 26, 30
Book value, 150, 392
    defined, 163
    disposal of plant/equipment and, 400–402
    market price and, 498
    per share of stock, 495–496, 655
Book value per share, 495, 504
Borrowing transactions, 577–578
Boston Red Sox, 67
Brazil, 691, 692
Bridgestone Corporation, 709
Bristol-Myers Squibb, 662
Buildings. See also Plant assets
    acquisition of, 388–391
    depreciation of, 149–150, 409
Bush, George W., 9, 61, 636

Business entity, 42, 46, 64
Business organizations. *See* Forms of business organization
Bylaws, corporate, 488

C

California Public Employees Retirement System (CALPERS), 34, 680
Callable bonds, 442
Call price, 442
Canada, 686, 691, 692
Capital expenditures, 390–391, 412
Capitalization
   defined, 412
   GAAP vs. IFRS, 102
   improper, 410
   plant assets and, 390–391
   of retained earnings, 532–533
Capital leases, 458, 463, B-13–B-14
Capital stock, 59, 487
   accounting by investor, 497
   accounting by issuer, 496–497
   authorization/issuance of, 490–492, 578
   book value of, 498
   buyback programs, 501
   common stock. *See* Common stock
   defined, 64, 504
   dividends. *See* Dividends
   earnings per share (EPS), 638
   market value of, 496–498
   no-par stock, 492
   par value of, 491–492
   preferred stock. *See* Preferred stock
   stock splits, 498, 534
   treasury stock, 499–501
Careers in accounting
   accounting education, 26
   accounting major and, 26–27
   bookkeeping, 26
   governmental accounting, 25
   management accounting, 25
   as a profession, 24
   public accounting, 24–25
   as a stepping-stone, 26
Carnival Corporation, 54, 387
Carrying value, 150. *See* Book value
Cash. *See also* Cash flow
   on balance sheet, 291–292
   bank reconciliation, 293–297
   current value of, 290
   defined, 291
   internal control over
      cash budgets, 292, 585
      control listing of cash receipts, 292
      petty cash funds, 292
   management of, 292. *See also* Cash flow management
   over and short, 293
   reductions in, 579
   restricted, 291–292
   on statement of cash flows, 569, 571–572
   valuation of, 290–291
Cash basis accounting
   accrual basis vs., 569
   converting from accrual basis to, 572–573
   defined, 102, 594

Cash budgets and budgeting, 292, 585, 594
Cash discounts
   as investment opportunity, 260n
   relating to purchases, 259–261
   sales, 263, 266
Cash dividends
   accounting for, 531–532
   in arrears, 493–494
   closing dividends accounts, 532
   debit-credit rules for, 103
   declaration and payment of, 531–532
   defined, 540
   dividend dates, 531–532
   liquidating dividends, 532
   from marketable securities, 298–299
   paid to stockholders, 578
   preferred stock and, 493–494, 497–498, 527–528
   receipts of, as operating activity, 572–573
   requirements for payment of, 531
   statement of cash flows and, 578
   statement of retained earnings, 197
   stock dividends vs., 532
   stockholders' rights to, 488
Cash equivalents,
   in balance sheet, 291
   defined, 315, 569, 594
   statement of cash flows and, 569, 571–572
Cash flow, 566, 594. *See also* Statement of cash flows
   discounted, B-6–B-10
   free, 583–584, 655
   management of. *See* Cash flow management
   negative, 41
   net
      annual, B-8n
      increasing, 585–587
      from operating activities, 583, 654
      reconciling with net income, 652–653, 654
     from operations to current liabilities, 652–653, 654
     positive, 41
Cash flow analysis, 652–653
Cash flow management, 584
   cash budgets, 292, 585
   complementary products, 586
   income tax deferral, 586
   increasing cash flows, 585–587
   peak pricing, 586
   product mix development, 586
Cash flow prospects, 10, 30
Cash inflows, 207
Cash management, 292, 315. *See also* Cash flow management
Cash obligation, 207
Cash outlays, 207
Cash over and short, 293
Caterpillar, 710
Central America, 686, 691
Central planning, 689
Certified Internal Auditor (CIA), 22, 30
Certified Management Accountant (CMA), 21, 22, 30
Certified public accountants (CPAs)
   AICPA. *See* American Institute of CPAs (AICPA)

   audits by, 20, 194
   competence and, 22–24
   CPA examination, 25
   defined, 30
   licensing of, 23
Chaebol, 689, 705
Check register, 264
Chief accounting officer (CAO), 25
Chief executive officers (CEOs), 26, 489
   certification of financial statements, 61
   fraud and, 27
   SEC enforcement action involvement, 27
Chief financial officers (CFOs), 26, 489
   certification of financial statements, 61
   fraud and, 27
   SEC enforcement action involvement, 27
Chile, 691, 692
China, 686, 689, 692
China Airlines, 34
Cisco Systems, Inc., 39, 84
Citicorp, 519
Citroën, 710
Classified balance sheet, 198, 213, 629–631
Classified financial statements
   balance sheet, 629–631
   defined, 624, 659
   income statement, 635–641
Clear Channel Communications, Inc., 171
Closely held corporations, 487, 504, 528n
Closing entries, 208
   cost of goods sold, 254
   defined, 200, 213
   dividend accounts, 203–204, 532
   expense accounts, 202
   Income Summary account, 203
   periodic inventory systems, 255–257
   perpetual inventory systems, 254, 257
   revenue accounts, 201
   summary of closing process, 204
   temporary (nominal) accounts, 200–204
Closing procedures, 255
Club Med, Inc., 481
Coca-Cola Company, 266, 297, 298–300, 406, 414, 584, 621, 681
Codes of ethics, 23, 410
Colgate-Palmolive Company, 523
Collateral, 432, 463
Collectivism, 690
Commissions Earned, 100
Commitments, 454, 463
Committee of Sponsoring Organizations of the Treadway Commission (COSO), 9, 21–22, 30
Common size income statement, 627
Common stock, 492, 504. *See also* Capital stock
   book value per share, 495–496, 655
   dividends. *See* Dividends
   earnings per share (EPS), 527, 644, 655
   financial analysis by holders of, 644–646
   market price of, 498, 532, 655
   stock splits, 498, 534
Communication, internal control and, 9
Comparable store sales, 265, 268
Comparative financial statements, 624, 625–629, 659
Compensating balance, 292, 315

Competence, 22–24
Complementary products, 586, 594
Component percentages, 627
Compound interest, B-2
Compound journal entry, 201
Comprehensive income, 536, 540
CompuTech, 708
Computerized terminals, 258
Conservatism principle, 101, 115, 349
Consistency (in inventory valuation), 363
Consistency principle, 349, 398
Consolidated financial statements, 624, 654, 659, 700
Continuing operations, 524–525
Continuity of existence, 486
Contra-asset account, 150, 163, 303, 409
Contract (interest) rate, 441, 451
Contra-equity accounts, 499
Contra-revenue account, 262, 266, 268
Contributed capital, 490, 504. *See also* Capital stock
Control accounts, 250, 268
Control activities, 9, 30. *See also* Internal control
Control environment, 9, 30
Controller, 25, 489
Control listing, 292
Convergence with IFRS, 356–357, 691–693, 704
Conversion privilege, 494
Convertible bonds, 442, 463
Convertible preferred stock, 493, 494, 530
Copyrights, 388, 407
Corporate bonds. *See* Bonds payable
Corporate charter, 488
Corporate governance
  adequate disclosure, 208
  allowance for, 313
  capital vs. revenue expenditures, 410
  cash flow manipulation, 587
  certification of financial statements by senior executives, 61
  codes of ethics and, 23–24, 410
  debt understatement, 457
  defined, 27, 30
  Foreign Corrupt Practices Act (PCPA), 702–703
  foreign officials, improper payments to, 702–703
  illegal/unethical orders from superiors, 113, 266, 410
  income overstatement, 161, 538
  inventory valuation, 361
  merchandising companies, 266
  pump-and-dump schemes, 502
  rating quality of, 656
  sales discounts/allowances, understating, 266
  Sarbanes-Oxley and. *See* Sarbanes-Oxley Act (SOX) of 2002
  SEC enforcement actions. *See* Securities and Exchange Commission
  shell companies, 502
  special purpose entities (SPEs), 457
  weak, fraud and, 27
Corporate Governance Quotient (CGQ), 656
The Corporate Library (TCL), 656
Corporate officers, 489
Corporations

accounting practices, 59
advantages/disadvantages of, 486, 634
board of directors, 488, 489
characteristics of, 58
closely held, 487, 528n
defined, 40, 58, 64, 486, 504
double taxation, 486
formation of, 488–490
income tax rate for, 155
limited liability of, 58
limited personal liability, 486, 634
multinational. *See* Globalization
officers, 489
organization chart, 489
organization costs, 488
owners' equity in, 59
paid-in capital, 490–496. *See also* Capital stock
parent company, 624
publicly owned, 487–488, 502
reasons for incorporating, 486–487, 634
small, loan guarantees for, 634
stockholder records, 490
stockholders' rights, 488–489
subsidiaries, 624, 687, 700
treasury stock, 499–501
Corruption, Foreign Corrupt Practices Act and, 702–703
COSO. *See* Committee of Sponsoring Organizations of the Treadway Commission (COSO)
Cost-effectiveness, 8
Cost flow assumptions, 343, 363
  average-cost method, 344–345, 350, 355
  FIFO. *See* First-in, first-out (FIFO) method
  LIFO. *See* Last-in, first-out (LIFO) method
Cost layer, 343, 363
Cost of goods sold. *See also* Inventory valuation
  closing process, 255–257
  computing, for periodic inventory, 255
  defined, 249, 268
  estimating techniques, 358–359
  gross profit method, 358–359
  matching revenue and, 353
  merchandising companies
    about, 249–250
    closing entries, 254, 255–257
    creating account, 256
    periodic inventory systems, 254–257
    perpetual inventory systems, 251–254
    year-end balance, 257
  on multiple-step income statement, 636
Cost principle, 43, 64
Cost ratio, 358–359, 363
Coupon bonds, 442n
CPAs. *See* Certified public accountants (CPAs)
Credit balances, 89–90
Credit card sales, 308–309
Credit losses, 304–306
Credit memoranda, 295, 295n
Creditors, 45
  defined, 10, 44, 64
  evaluating claims of, 454–456
  expectations of, 11
  financial statement use by, 40, 432, 648–652, 654–655
  short-term, 60

Credit ratings, 454, 457
Credit risk, 634, 655
Credits
  credit balances in liability and owners' equity accounts, 90
  defined, 89, 115
  determining balance of T account, 89–90
  in double-entry accounting, 90–91
  rules for, 102–103
Credit terms, 259–261
Cross-border financing, 691, 704
Culture
  accounting practices and, 689–690
  globalization and, 689–690
Cumulative preferred stock, 493–494, 527–528
Current assets, 198, 300
  accounts receivable. *See* Accounts receivable
  cash. *See* Cash
  cash equivalents, 291, 571–572
  defined, 57, 213, 659
  described, 629–631
  inventory. *See* Inventory
  marketable securities, 290, 298, 576
  notes receivable, 309–311
  prepaid expenses, 146–148
Current liabilities
  accounts payable. *See* Accounts payable
  accrued expenses, 152–154
  accrued liabilities, 435
  cash flows from operations to, 652–653, 654
  current assets and, 631
  current portion of long-term debt, 434–435, 440
  defined, 214, 631, 659
  financial analysis by short-term creditors, 648–652
  income tax payable, 155–156
  notes payable, 44, 433–434
  payroll, 152–153, 435–437
  sales tax payable, 264
  on separate balance sheet, 198
  unearned revenue, 151–152, 437
Current ratio, 651, 654
  defined, 57, 659
  creditors' use of, 456
  as measure of liquidity, 207, 631–632

D

Database warehousing, 14
Date of declaration, 531
Date of payment, 531
Date of record, 531, 541
Days to collect average accounts receivable, 654
Days to sell the average inventory, 655
Debenture bonds, 441
Debit balances, 89–90
Debit memoranda, 295, 295n
Debits
  debit balances in asset accounts, 90
  defined, 89, 115
  determining balance of T account, 89–90
  in double-entry accounting, 90–91
  rules for revenue and expenses, 102–103
Debt. *See also* Liabilities
  appropriate level of, 455

Debt—*Cont.*
　equity vs., 432
　leverage, 455, 647
　relative amount of, 629
　understatement of, 457
Debt ratio, 456, 632, 648, 655, 659
Debt service, 438, 463
Decelerated depreciation, 399
Declining-balance depreciation, 393, 395–397
Default, 311, 315
Deferrals
　of expenses, 142–143, 145–146, 158, 460–461
　of income taxes, 460–461, 586
　intangibles as, 407
　of revenue, 143, 144, 151–152, 158
Deferred expenses
in adjusting entries, 142–143, 145–146
converting assets to expenses and, 142–143, 145–146
to improve cash flow, 586
income taxes, 460–461, 586
Deferred Income Taxes, 460–461, 463
Deferred revenue, 151–152
Deflation, 44, 64
Delivery expenses, 263
Dell Computer Corporation, 350, 456, 647
Deloitte, 37
Depletion, 408–409, 412
Deposits in transit, 293
Depreciable assets, 148, 163, 388
Depreciation
　of buildings, 149–150, 409
　causes of, 392
　computing
　　accelerated methods, 392–393
　　accumulated method, 150
　　decelerated methods, 400
　　declining-balance method, 395–397
　　double-declining balance
　　　method, 395, 396
　　half-year convention, 394–395
　　MACRS (Modified Accelerated Cost
　　　Recovery System), 395n, 400, 586n
　　most-used methods, 397, 400
　　150 percent declining-balance method,
　　　395n, 396–397
　　straight-line method, 149, 393–395, 397
　　sum-of-the-years' digits (SYD) method, 400
　　units-of-output method, 399
　cost allocation over years of use, 391–392
　defined, 148, 163, 391, 412
　of equipment, 409
　as estimate, 148–149
　financial statement disclosures, 199, 398–399
　financial statements disclosure, 199
　for fractional periods, 394–395
　goal of, 409
　impairment losses, 399
　as noncash expense, 150
　process of, 391
　property subject to, 388
　residual value, 149n, 393–394, 398
　tax considerations, 395n, 397, 586
　tools and equipment, 150
　useful life and, 148–149, 398
　valuation vs., 392
Depreciation rate, 394, 395

DeVry, Inc., 171
Diluted earnings per share, 530, 541
Direct method, 566n
Direct write-off method, 307, 315
Disclosure. *See also* Adequate disclosure
　Best Buy example, 193
　defined, 64
　importance of, 60, 198–200
　inadequate, 208
Discontinued operations, 525, 541
Discounted cash flows, B-6–B-10
Discount period, 259–261
Discount rate, 451, B-6, B-7, B-8
Discounts
　on bonds payable, 444–447, 450, B-12
　on purchase transactions, 259–261
　on sales transactions, 263, 266
　understating sales discounts, 266
Dividend accounts, closing, 203–204
Dividends
　accounting for, 108, 531–532
　cash. *See* Cash dividends
　debit–credit rules, 103
　defined, 98, 103, 115, 504
　dividend dates, 531–532
　liquidating, 532–534
　statement of retained earnings, 197
　stock, 532–534
Dividend yield, 497, 504, 644, 655
Dodd-Frank Act of 2010, SEC payment of
　monetary awards to whistleblowers, 266
Dollar changes, financial statement
　analysis, 625–626
Dollar volume, 58
Double-declining balance depreciation, 395, 396
Double-entry accounting, 90–91, 115
Double taxation, 486, 504
Dow Chemical Co., 408
Due date, 309
Due diligence procedures, 4
Due on demand liabilities, 432n
Dun & Bradstreet, Inc., 628n, 633, 656
DuPont, 408, 470
Dynergy Inc., 266, 586–587

E

Earnings, overstating, 161
Earnings per share (EPS), 638, 655
　analysis by common stockholders, 644
　basic, 530
　defined, 527, 541, 659
　diluted, 530
　income statement presentation, 528–530
　net, 530
　preferred dividends and, 527–528
　weighted-average, 527
Earnings statement, 194. *See also* Income
　statement; Statement of retained earnings
Economic substance, 438
Economic systems, globalization and, 689
EDGAR database (SEC), 84, 382
Effective rate of interest, 451
Eli Lilly & Co., 408
Enron, 9, 27, 113, 161, 410, 457, 636
Entity principle, 42

Equipment, 388. *See also* Plant Assets
　acquisition of, 389
　cost determination, 389
　depreciation of, 150, 409. *See also*
　　Depreciation
　disposal of, 400–402
　trading in used for new, 402
Ernst & Young, 34
Estimated liabilities, 433, 453, 463
Estimated quarterly payments, 155
Estimated useful life, 149
Estimates
　Allowance for Doubtful Accounts, 303
　cost of goods sold, 358–359
　credit losses, 304–306
　depreciation as, 148–149
　　fractional periods, 394–395
　　useful life, 398
　ending inventory, 358–359
　in externally reported financial information, 13
　goodwill, 404–405
　income tax expense, 155–156
　liabilities, 432–433, 453
　predictive information for operations, 524
　residual value, 149n, 393–394, 398
　uncollectible accounts, 304–306
Ethical behavior, 22–24
Ethics. *See also* Corporate governance
　AICPA code of professional conduct, 23–24
　corporate codes of, 410
　integrity and, 23–24
E-Trade Financial, 297
Europe, 692
European Union, 686
Exchange rates, 693, 704
　competitive prices and, 699
　fluctuations in, 698–699
　foreign currency transactions, accounting
　　for, 694–698
　global sourcing and, 700–701
　jargon, 694
Ex-dividend date, 531, 532, 541
Expense account, 260
Expenses
　accrued, 45, 143, 144, 152–154, 158
　benefiting more than one accounting period, 101
　cash payments for, 104, 107, 574
　closing entries for expense accounts, 202
　converting assets to, 142–143, 144, 158
　debit and credit rules for, 102–103
　deferred, 142–143, 145–146, 460–461, 586
　defined, 51, 64, 100–101, 115, 524
　delivery expenses, 263
　depreciation. *See* Depreciation
　in financial statement analysis, 645–646
　impairment, 193
　in income statement, 98–99
　income taxes, 155–156
　insurance policies, 146–147
　interest, 152–154
　matching principle, 101
　noncash, 150, 580
　nonoperating items, 637
　payment of, 50
　prepaid, 146–148, 251
　unpaid, accruing, 143, 152–154, 158
　wages (salaries), 152–153

Exporting, 687, 704
External financial reporting
  characteristics of, 13–14
  objectives of, 10–13
External users, of accounting information, 10, 13–14, 30, 59–61
Extraordinary items, 524, 525–527, 541
ExxonMobil, 486

F

Face amount, 310
Facilitating payments, 703
Factoring, 307–308
Fair value accounting, 299–300, 315
Fannie Mae, 37
FASB. *See* Financial Accounting Standards Board (FASB)
Fastow, Andrew, 457
Federal Trade Commission (FTC), 10
Fees Earned, 100
Fila, 538
Finance charge, 260
Financial accounting. *See also* Financial statements
  about, 6
  defined, 10, 30
  external users of information, 10, 13–14, 59–61
  information characteristics, 13–14
  internal users of, 14–15, 60–61
  objectives of, 10–13
Financial Accounting Standards Board (FASB), 30
  about, 18–19
  accounting principles and, 18
  Accounting Standards Codification (ASC) and, 18–19
  capital lease criteria, 458
  cash flow statement, 568
  comprehensive income, 536
  direct method of cash flows, 581
  disclosure framework, 199
  extraordinary items, 526
  FASB/IASB convergence project, 19, 356–357, 691–693
  goodwill reporting requirements, 406
  inflation adjustments, 44
  interest payments/receipts classifications, 568
  preferred stock reporting, 493
  R&D accounting, 407
  SEC and, 18
Financial assets, 315
  accounts receivable. *See* Accounts receivable
  cash. *See* Cash
  defined, 290
  financial analysis of, 311–312
  marketable securities, 298–300
  notes receivable, 309–311
  short-term investments, 297
  valuation of, 290–291, 299–300
Financial Executives International, 22
Financial position, 7
Financial reporting
  building from the general to the specific, 12
  conceptual framework for, 18–19
  externally reported, 13–14
  financial statements vs., 12–13, 56

fraudulent, 27. *See also* Corporate governance
  objectives of, 10–13
  SEC as "watchdog" of, 25
  time line for, 55
Financial statement, 30, 64
Financial statement analysis, 622–623
  accounts receivable turnover, 360–361
  accounts receivable turnover rate, 311–312, 456, 649–650, 654
  cash flow analysis, 652–653
  by common stockholders, 644–646
  comparative financial statements, 624
    component percentages, 627
    dollar and percentage changes, 625–626, 655
    quality of assets, 629
    quality of earnings, 628–629
    ratios, 627
    relative amount of debt, 629
    standards for comparison, 627–628, 633
    trend percentages, 626–627
  comprehensive illustration, 641–655
  corporate governance, rating quality of, 656
  cost ratio, 358–359
  by creditors, 40, 648–652, 654–655
  current ratio, 57, 207, 456, 631–632, 651, 654
  debt ratio, 456, 632, 647, 648, 655
  fundamental analysis, 657
  gross profit margins, 265, 636–637
  industry standards and, 628, 633
  interest coverage ratio, 455, 456, 648, 655
  inventory turnover, 360
  inventory turnover rate, 456, 650, 654
  inventory valuation, 360–361
  liquidity and credit risk measures, 59–60, 454–456, 629–634, 654–655
  liquidity measures, 206–207
  by long-term creditors, 648, 655
  for merchandising businesses, 265
  net flows from operating activities, 456, 583–584, 654
  net income percentage, 206, 655
  net sales, 262, 265
  past performance and, 628
  price-earnings (p/e) ratio, 529–530, 638, 644, 655
  profitability measures, 205–206, 501, 634–641, 655
  quick ratio, 456, 632, 651, 654
  R&D to sales, 407
  return of common stockholder's equity, 501, 646, 655
  return on assets (ROA), 455n, 501, 640, 646, 655
  return on equity (ROE), 206, 455n, 640–641, 655
  return on investment (ROI), 639–640, 646
  revenue and expense analysis, 645–646
  by short-term creditors, 648–652
  summary of measures, 654–655
  working capital, 207, 433, 456, 631, 649, 654
Financial statement order, 111
Financial statements
  adequate disclosure in, 60, 198–200, 208
  adjusting entries, effects of, 158–160

articulation and, 41, 55
  audits of, 20, 194
  balance sheet. *See* Balance sheet
  CEO/CFO certification of, 61
  classified, 624, 635
  comparative, 624, 625–629
  consolidated, 624, 654, 700
  covering different time periods, 12, 207
  deferred income taxes in, 461, 586
  defined, 12, 40
  economic substance, 438
  external users of, 40–41, 59–61
  filing with SEC, 25
  financial reporting vs., 12–13, 56
  forms of business organization, 57–59
  Home Depot statements, A–A-13
  income statement. *See* Income statement
  Intel Corp., 39
  interim, 12, 207
  introduction to, 40–41
  inventory cost flows through, 251, 342–351
  inventory errors and, 357–358
  loss contingencies in, 453–454
  management's interest in, 60–61, 265
  notes accompanying. *See* Notes accompanying financial statements
  preparing, 194–198, 209–212
  purpose of, 624
  relationships among, 54–56
  of Sony Corporation, 6
  statement of cash flows. *See* Statement of cash flows
  statement of financial position. *See* Balance sheet
  statement of retained earnings, 194, 196, 197, 534–536
  statement of stockholders' equity, 536–537
  time line for, 55
  types of, 12–13, 40–41
  uncollectible accounts, 302
  window dressing, 61, 633–634
  worksheets for, 209–212, 587–591
Financing activities
  cash flows from, 53, 566, 568, 571, 577–578
  defined, 64, 594
  noncash, 54
  transactions with stockholders as, 496
  treasury stock transactions, 501
First-in, first-out (FIFO) method
  as cost flow assumption, 344
  defined, 363
  evaluation of, 348
  financial reporting standards, 356
  in inventory valuation, 350
  in periodic inventory system, 355
  in perpetual inventory system, 345–346
  shrinkage and, 351
Fiscal year, 100, 115, 194n
Fixed-percentage-of-declining-balance depreciation, 393, 395–397, 412
F.O.B. destination, 353, 363, 433
F.O.B. shipping point, 353, 363, 433
Food Lion, 418
Ford Motor Company, 242, 297, 371, 491, 639
Forecasts, 292
Foreign Corrupt Practices Act (PCPA), 702–703, 704

Foreign currency
    consolidated financial statements, 700
    exchange rates, 693–694
        about, 693–694
        accounting for foreign currency transactions,
            694–698
        competitive prices and, 699
        fluctuations in, 698–699
        global sourcing and, 700–701
        jargon, 694
    future contracts, 699
    hedging, 699
Foreign trade zones, 688, 704
Forms of business organization
    corporations. *See* Corporations
    liquidity/credit risk and, 634
    owners' equity reported by type, 58–59
    partnerships, 58–59, 634, 634n
    sole proprietorships, 57–58, 634
404 certification. *See* Sarbanes-Oxley Act (SOX)
    of 2002; Section 404 certification
Franchises, 388, 406–407
Fraud. *See* Corporate governance
Free cash flow, 583–584, 594, 655
Frito-Lay, 624
Fully funded pension fund, 459
Fundamental analysis, 657, 659
Future contracts, 699, 704
Future value, B-2–B-6. *See also* Present value

G

G-20. *See* Group of Twenty (G-20)
GAAP. *See* Generally accepted accounting
    principles (GAAP)
Gain, 298–299, 315, 401, 526
GAO. *See* Government Accountability Office
    (GAO)
The Gap, Inc., 241, 248, 329
Gatorade, 624
GE Capital, 360
General/administrative expenses, 637
General credit obligations, 432
General Electric Company, 157, 157n
General journal, 91, 96, 109, 115, 159, 264
General ledger, 250
General ledger software, 209, 214
Generally accepted accounting principles
    (GAAP), 30
    about, 18
    adequate disclosure in, 60, 198–200, 208
    convergence with IFRS, 356–357, 691–693
    FASB and, 19
    financial statements reporting, 198
    IFRS vs., on idle capacity and spoilage
        costs, 102
    international financial reporting
        standards vs.
        consolidated statements, 654, 700
        expensed/capitalized costs, 102
        inventory valuation, 356–357
        reversals of inventory write-downs, 254
        segment reporting, 692–693
        true and fair override, 198
    valuing inventory, 254
General Motors Corporation, 100, 248, 481,
    486, 681

General partners, 634n
General-purpose accounting
    information, 6, 13–14, 30
Georgia-Pacific Corporation, 559
Germany, 686, 692
Getty, J. Paul, 99
Globalization, 704
    environmental forces
        culture of, 689–690
        economic systems, 689
        political/legal systems, 688–689
        technology/infrastructure, 690–691
    Foreign Corrupt Practices Act (PCPA), 702–703
    foreign currencies and exchange rates. *See*
        Foreign currency
    global sourcing, 687, 700–701, 704
    harmonization of financial reporting standards.
        See Harmonization of financial reporting
        standards
    multinational companies, locations of, 686
    stages of, 687
Global sourcing, 687, 700–701, 704
Going-concern assumption, 43, 64
Good faith effort, 200
Goods in transit, 353
Goodwill, 388, 403–406, 412
Goodyear Tire & Rubber, 324
Government Accountability Office
    (GAO), 25, 30
Governmental accounting, 25
Gross invoice price, 260–261
Gross price method, 260–261
Gross profit, 250, 268, 636–637
Gross profit margin, 265, 268,
    636–637, 655
Gross profit method, 358–359, 363
Gross profit rate, 265. *See also* Gross profit margin
Group of Twenty (G-20)
    members, 685n
    purpose of, 685
Guarantees, loan, 634

H

Half-year convention, 394–395, 412
Harmonization of accounting standards, 19
Harmonization of financial reporting standards
    adoption of IFRS, 691–693
    convergence with IFRS, 356–357, 691–693
HealthSouth, 27, 61
Hedging, 699, 705
Held-to-maturity securities, 297n
Hershey's, 191
Hewlett, Bill, 3
Hewlett-Packard (HP), 3–4, 9
hhgregg, 233
Historical cost, 43, 44, 150
H. J. Heinz Co., 417
Hofstede, Geert, 689n, 708–709
The Hollywood Park Companies, 481, 781
Home Depot, Inc., 36, 70, 127, 173, 194, 198,
    200, 226, 265, 276, 326, 372, 419, 472, 512,
    533, 536, 549–550, 584, 605, 624, 639, 666,
    682–683, 711, 715, A–A-13
Honda Motor Company, 712
Horizontal analysis, 628
Hyundai, 689

I

IASB. *See* International Accounting Standards
    Board (IASB)
IBM, 248, 297, 451, 486, 497, 507
Idle capacity, 102
IIA. *See* Institute of Internal Auditors (IIA)
Illiquid, 454
IMA. *See* Institute of Management Accountants
    (IMA)
Immaterial items, 157, 163, 258
Impairment expense, 193
Impairment loss, 399, 412
Income
    from continuing operations, 524–525
    from interest, 309–311, 568, 572–573
    net. *See* Net income
Income statement, 53, 56
    about, 51
    accounting periods and, 99–100
    accrual basis of accounting and, 102
    adjusting entries, effects of, 158–160
    classifications in, 635
    common size, 627
    comprehensive income and, 536
    continuing operations, 524–525
    debit and credit rules for revenue and expenses,
        102–103
    defined, 12, 13, 30, 40–41, 51, 64, 98, 115,
        194–195
    discontinued operations, 524, 525
    earnings per share (EPS), 527–530, 638
    expenses, 98, 100–101, 102–103
    extraordinary items, 525–527
    income must be related to specified period of
        time, 99
    interim, 12, 207
    inventory errors and, 357–358
    limitations of, 195, 197
    merchandising companies, 249–250
    multiple-step, 635–637
    predictive information, 524
    preparing, 194–197
    preview of, 98–100
    profitability measures. *See* Profitability
    realization principle, 100
    recording transactions, 103–108
    restructuring charges, 526
    revenue, 98, 102
    sample, 98–99, 196
    service company, 249
    single-step, 635
    time period principle, 99–100
    unusual gains/losses, 526–527
Income statement approach, 306
Income Summary
    closing, 203
    closing temporary accounts, 200–204
    defined, 200, 214
    expense accounts transferred to, 202
    revenue account balances transferred to, 201
Income tax expense. *See also* Taxes
    accruing, 155–156
    deferred, 460–461, 586
    estimated quarterly payments, 155
    negative, 156
    as nonoperating item, 637

in unprofitable periods, 156
unrealized gains/losses and, 300
Indenture contracts, 432
India, 686, 692
Indirect method, 566n
Individualism, 690
Industrial organizations, 689, 705
Industry standards, in financial statement
analysis, 628, 633
Inflation, 44, 64
Influence peddling, 702–703
Information and communication, 9, 30
Infrastructure, globalization and, 690–691, 705
Installment notes payable, 438–440
Institute of Internal Auditors (IIA), 21, 30
Institute of Management Accountants
(IMA), 21, 30
Insurance policies, as prepaid expense, 146–147
Intangible assets, 388, 412
amortization of, 403
characteristics of, 403
copyrights, 407
corporate organization costs, 488
deferred charges, 407
financial analysis of, 407–408
franchises, 406–407
goodwill, 403–406
operating expenses vs., 403
other types, 407
patents, 406
research and development (R&D)
costs, 407–408
trademarks/trade names, 406
Integrated Electrical Services, Inc. (IES), 313
Integrity, 30. *See also* Corporate governance
AICPA Code of Professional Conduct, 23
competence and, 22–24
ethical behavior and, 22–24
institutional features, 17–20
judgment and, 22–24
professional organizations and, 20–22
Intel Corporation, 31, 39, 40, 584
Interest
on bank accounts, 294
compound, B-2
computing, 310
FASB/IASB standards for
classifying, 568
on liabilities, 432
from marketable securities, 298–299
nature of, 309–310
as operating activity, 568
present value and, B-1–B-2
simple, 310
Interest-bearing liabilities, 647
Interest coverage ratio, 455, 456, 463, 648, 655
Interest expense, 152–154, 637
accruing, 153, 443–444
on bonds payable, 443–444
cash payments for, 575
computing interest, 310
on discontinued notes payable, B-10–B-11
FASB/IASB standards for classifying, 568
on installment notes payable, 438–440
on liabilities, 434, 438–440
on notes payable, 434n
as operating activity, 568

plant assets and, 388–389
as tax deduction, 442
Interest income
bank credits for, 294
computing interest, 310
FASB/IASB standards for
classifying, 568
on notes receivable, 309–311
as operating activity, 572–573
Interest rates
bond prices and, 451–452
preferred stock and, 497–498
present value and, B-1–B-2
Interest revenue
computing interest, 310
on notes receivable, 309–311
Interim financial statement, 12, 207, 214
Internal control
components of, 8–9
defined, 8–9, 30
Foreign Corrupt Practices Act (FCPA) and,
702–703
over cash, 292–293
over receivables, 301
Sarbanes-Oxley Act and, 9, 22
Internal Control—Integrated Framework: 2013
(COSO), 9, 22
Internal Revenue Service (IRS), 25, 30
Internal users, of accounting information, 14–15,
30, 60–61
International Accounting Standards Board
(IASB), 30, 705
about, 19
accounting principles and, 18
cash flow statement categories, 568
FASB/IASB convergence project, 19, 356–357,
691–692
goodwill reporting requirements, 406
interest payments/receipts classifications, 568
International Financial Reporting Standards
(IFRSs), 19
LIFO prohibited, 355
standard-setting duties, 685–686
International Association of Machinists and
Aerospace Workers, 34
International Financial Reporting
Standards (IFRS)
about, 19
adoption of, 691–693
consolidated statements, 654
convergence with, 19, 356–357, 691–693
financial statement analysis, 653–654
financial statements reporting, 198
GAAP vs. *See* Generally accepted accounting
principles (GAAP)
goal of, 685
inventory valuation, 254, 356–357
plant asset revaluation, 403
plant assets, depreciation, and reevaluation
process, 402–403
segment reporting, 692–693
United States and, 19
U.S. GAAP vs., on idle capacity and spoilage
costs, 102
International joint ventures, 687, 705
International licensing, 687, 705
International Monetary Fund, 702

Inventory, 268. *See also* Inventory systems;
Inventory valuation
accounting for, 251
defined, 248
purchase-related transactions, 252, 255, 257,
259–262
sales-related transactions, 252–253, 257,
262–264
subsidiary ledger, 250–251, 343, 345, 346, 347
write-downs and, 254
Inventory costs, flow of, 251
Inventory fraud, 361
Inventory shrinkage, 253–254, 268,
351, 354n
Inventory subsidiary ledger
FIFO basis, 346
illustrated, 343, 345
LIFO basis, 347
for merchandising companies, 250–251
modified, 345
Inventory systems
compared, 257–258, 259
just-in-time (JIT), 349–351
modification of, 359
periodic. *See* Periodic inventory system
perpetual. *See* Perpetual inventory system
selecting, 258–259
Inventory turnover, 360, 363
Inventory turnover rate, 456, 650, 654
Inventory valuation
accuracy, importance of, 357–358
consistency in, 349
corporate governance issues, 361
cost flow assumptions, 343
average-cost method, 344–345, 345, 348,
350, 355
FIFO. *See* First-in, first-out (FIFO) method
LIFO. *See* Last-in, first-out (LIFO) method
in periodic inventory system, 354–356
errors in, 357–358
estimating
gross profit method, 358–359
retail method, 359
evaluation of methods, 347–351
financial analysis and, 360–361
international standards, 254, 356–357
inventory methods affecting
performance, 349
losses from fire/theft, 254n
lower-of-cost-or-market (LCM) rule, 351–352
at market prices, 342n
performance impacted by, 349
periodic inventory systems, 353–356
perpetual inventory systems, 342
physical inventory, 253–254, 351–359
specific identification method, 350
evaluation of, 347–348
periodic inventory systems, 354–355
perpetual inventory systems, 344
summary of methods, 350
tax considerations, 349, 356
write-downs, 351–352
year-end cutoff transactions, 352–353
year-end pricing by computer, 356
Invested capital, 492
Investing activities, 566
cash discount as, 260n

Investing activities—*Cont,*
    cash flows from, 568, 570, 575–577
    defined, 53, 64, 594
    noncash, 53–54, 409
Investment analysis, 11. *See also* Financial
    statement analysis
Invoices, 259
Iran, 688
Irregular items, 524, 525
IRS. *See* Internal Revenue Service (IRS)
ISS Governance Services, 656

J

Japan, 686, 689, 690, 692, 693–694
JCPenney, 100, 379–380, 399
Johnson & Johnson, 623, 669, 681
Journals, 208
    compound entries, 201
    defined, 91, 115
    general, 91–92, 96, 109, 115, 159, 264
    posting entries to ledger accounts, 92–95,
        103–111
    recording transactions in, 91
        balance sheet transactions, 92–95
        bonds payable, 442–444
        cash dividends, 531–532
        closing temporary accounts, 200–204
        income statement transactions, 103–108
        notes payable, 434
        payroll activities, 436–437
    special, 264–265, 268
Judgment, 22–24
Junk bonds, 442, 463
Just for Feet, Inc., 538
Just-in-time (JIT) systems, 349–351, 363

K

Keiretsu, 689, 705
Kenya, 702
Kimberly-Clark, 387, 666
Kozlowski, Dennis, 27
KPMG LLP, 34, 624
Kraft Foods Group, Inc., 87, 371–371
Kroger Company, 671

L

Land, 388, 389
Last-in, first-out (LIFO) method
    about/example, 346–347
    defined, 344, 363
    evaluation of, 348–349
    financial reporting standards, 356–357
    in periodic inventory system, 355–356
    prohibited by IASB, 355
    shrinkage and, 351
    summary of, 350
    tax benefits, maximizing, 356
Leases, 457–458, B-13–B-14
Ledgers
    defined, 88, 115
    illustrated, 110
    journal entries posted to, 92–103, 208
    ledger accounts after posting, 96–97, 109–111
    subsidiary, 250–251, 268

Legal capital, 491, 504
Legal systems, globalization and, 688–689
Lessee, 457, 463, B-14
Lessor, 457, 463, B-14
Leverage, 455, 463, 647
LG, 689
Liabilities, 42
    advance collections as, 151–152
    commitments, 454
    converting to revenue, 143, 144, 151–152, 158
    credit balances in liability accounts, 90
    creditors' claims, evaluating, 454–456
    current, 198. *See* Current liabilities
    deferred income taxes, 460–461
    defined, 44, 64, 432
    due on demand, 432n
    estimated, 432–433, 452
    financial statements disclosure, 199
    interest-bearing, 647
    lease payment obligations, 457–458
    long-term. *See* Long-term liabilities
    loss contingencies, 453–454
    maturity dates of, 199
    nature of, 432–433
    non-interest-bearing, 647
    order of repayment of, 45
    owners' equity vs., 432
    payment of, 49
    pensions/postretirement benefits, 458–460, B-14
    short-term, 45n, 456
    special purpose entities (SPEs), 457
    unfunded, 460
Liability
    of corporations, 58, 486, 634
    in credit balances and, 90
    limited, 58
    limited personal, 58, 486, 504, 634
    of partnerships, 58, 634, 634n
    personal, 57–58, 634
    of sole proprietorships, 57–58, 634
    unlimited, 58
Licensing, international, 687, 705
Limited Brands, Inc., 329
Limited liability, 58
Limited partnerships, 634n
Limited personal liability, 58, 486, 504, 634
Lines of credit, 292, 315, 456, 651–652
Liquid assets, 60
Liquidity, 629
    defined, 59, 64
    evaluating, 206, 454–456
    legal issues, 634
    measures of, 206–207
    short-term, 60, 632, 654–655
Loan guarantees, 634
Loans, 576
Long-term bond prices, 451–452
Long-term debt-paying ability, 456
Long-term liabilities, 45n, 437–453
    bonds payable. *See* Bonds payable
    current portion of, 434–435, 440
    financial analysis by long-term
        creditors, 454–456
    installment notes payable, 438–440
    maturing obligations intended to be refinanced,
        437–438
    secured claims, 648

Long-term orientation, 690
Los Angeles Times, 700
Loss, 298–299, 315, 401, 526
Loss contingencies, 453–454, 463
Lower-of-cost-or-market (LCM)
    rule, 351–352, 363
Lump-sum purchases, 389–390
Lynch, Mike, 3

M

MACRS (Modified Accelerated Cost Recovery
    System). *See* Modified Accelerated Cost
    Recovery System (MACRS)
Maker of the note, 309
Management, interest in financial
statements, 60–61
Management accounting
    about, 6
    career opportunities, 25
    Certified Management Accountant (CMA), 21
    defined, 30
    information characteristics, 16–17
    Institute of Management Accountants
        (IMA), 21
    internal users of information, 14–15, 60–61
    objectives of, 15–16
Management advisory services, 24–25
Management Discussion and Analysis (MD&A),
    208, 633, 659
Management intimidation, 113, 266
Management training, 690
Managerial accounting. *See* Management
    accounting
Mandated costs, 435–436
Manufacturing operations
    just-in-time (JIT) systems, 349–351
    merchandising companies vs., 248
    operating cycle of, 248
Marketable securities
    accounting for, 298–300, 569, 576
    balance sheet presentation, 300
    current value of, 290
    defined, 315
    dividend/interest revenue recognition,
        298–299
    purchase of, 298
    sale of, 299–300, 576
    valuation of, 299–300
Market economies, 689, 705
Market rate of interest, 451
Market share, 636, 659
Market value
    accounting by investor, 497
    accounting by issuer, 496–497
    of assets, 150
    of bonds, 441, 451–452, B-12
    book value and, 498
    of common stock, 498
    of financial instruments, 655
    of marketable securities, 299–300
    of preferred stock, 497
Martin Marietta Materials, Inc., 563
MasterCard, 291, 308, 318
Matching principle, 101
    accrual accounting, 102
    bond discounts, 445

defined, 115, 163
depreciation, 148
estimated liabilities, 453
income taxes, 460–461
materiality and, 157
sales of merchandise and, 252
transportation costs, 262
uncollectible accounts, 302, 304
Material errors, 535
Materiality concept
adjusting entries and, 157–158
defined, 157, 163
prior period adjustments, 535–536
professional judgment and, 157–158
transportation costs, 262
Mattel, Inc., 700–701, 711
Maturity dates
bond retirement prior to, 452–453
defined, 463
liabilities and, 432
of liabilities, in financial statement notes, 199
notes receivable and, 309
Maturity value, 441
Maxtor Corporation, 361
McDonald's, 406
McDonnell Douglas, Inc., 519
McKesson Corporation, 71
Media General Financial Services, 633
Medicare taxes, 435, 436, 436n, 437
Medtronics, 673
Memorandum entries, 498
Merchandising companies
accounting system requirements, 250–251
corporate governance issues, 266
cost of goods sold, 249–250
closing entries, 254, 257
creating account, 256
periodic inventory systems, 255–257
perpetual inventory systems, 251–254
year-end balance, 257
financial analysis of, 265
income statement of, 249–250
inventory systems
compared, 258–259
periodic, 254–259
perpetual, 251–254, 342–353
selecting, 258–259
manufacturing activities vs., 248
modifying an accounting system, 264–265
operating cycle of, 248–249, 361, 650–651
performance measures, 265
purchase-related transactions, 252, 255,
259–262
retailers, 248–249
returns of unsatisfactory merchandise, 261
sales-related transactions, 252–253, 262–264
service companies vs., 249
wholesalers, 249
Merck, 662
Merrill Lynch, 297
Mexico, 44, 691, 692, 698–699
Mexico's Bolsa, 297, 487n
Microsoft Corporation, 39, 297, 323, 408, 579
Middle East, 702
MiniScribe Corporation, 361
Minuit, Peter, B-2
Mission statement, 15

Modified Accelerated Cost Recovery System
(MACRS), 395n, 400, 412, 586n
Monitoring activities, 9, 30
Moody's Investors Service, 454, 457, 656
Morgan Stanley, 297
Mortgage bonds, 441
Moving average method, 344–345, 363
Multinational companies. See Globalization;
International Financial Reporting Standards
(IFRSs)
Multiple-step income statement, 635–637

N

NAFTA. See North American Free Trade
Agreement (NAFTA)
NASDAQ, 361, 410, 487n
National Association of Foreign Trade Zones
(FTZs), 720
National Association of Securities Dealers'
Automated Quotations (NASDAQ). See
NASDAQ
National Commission on Fraudulent Financial
Reporting, 21–22
Natural resources, 388, 408–409, 412
Negative amortization, 439n
Negative cash flows, 41, 64
Negative income taxes, 156
Net assets, 495
Net cash flows
annual, B-8n
increasing, 585–587
from operating activities, 456, 583–584, 654
reconciling with net income, 580–581
Net cost method, 260, 261, 261n
Net earnings per share, 530
Net identifiable assets, 404, 412
Net income
about, 98–103
adequacy of, 639
defined, 41, 51, 98, 115
in multiple-step income statement, 636, 637
percentage changes in, 626–627, 655
as percentage of net sales, 655
reconciling with net cash flows, 580–581
trend in, 456
Net income percentage, 206, 655
Net loss, 41, 51, 98, 115
Net realizable value
in balance sheet, 43, 291
defined, 315
uncollectible accounts and, 301, 302
Net sales, 262, 265, 268, 636
New York Bond Exchange, 441
New York Stock Exchange (NYSE), 208, 266,
297, 410, 457, 487n, 489, 497
New York Times Company, The, 151,
171, 481
Nicolaisen, Donald T., 592n
Nike, 538
Nikon, 710
Nominal (temporary) accounts, closing, 200–204
Noncash charge/expense, 150, 409, 412, 460, 580
Noncash expense, 150
Noncash investing and financing transactions,
53–54, 409
Non-interest-bearing liabilities, 647, B-10–B-11

Nonoperating items, 637
No-par stock, 492
North American Free Trade Agreement (NAFTA),
688
Notes accompanying financial
statements, 214
adequate disclosure in, 60, 198–200, 208
commitments, 454
depreciation methods, 199. See also
Depreciation
dividends in arrears, 494
loss contingencies, 453–454
Management Discussion and Analysis
(MD&A), 208
maturity dates of liabilities, 199
notes, 199
restrictions of retained earnings, 535–536
sample, 643
usefulness of, 653
Notes payable, 433–434
defined, 44
installment notes, 438–440
liabilities and, 44–45
non-interest bearing, B-10–B-11
Notes receivable, 309–311
NSF checks, 294–295, 315

O

Oakwood Corporation, 319
Objectivity principle, 43–44, 101, 115
Obsolescence, 392
Off-balance sheet financing, 458, 463
Olis, Jamie, 587
150 percent declining-balance depreciation, 395,
395n, 396–397
Operating activities
cash flows, 566–568, 572–573
defined, 53, 64, 594
net cash flows from, 456, 583–584, 654
statement of cash flows, 570
Operating cycle
current assets and, 630–631
defined, 248, 268, 659
of manufacturing companies, 248
of merchandising companies, 248, 361,
650–651
as short-term liquidity measure, 456, 655
Operating expense ratio, 645–646, 655
Operating expenses, 403, 437
Operating income
computation method, 655
defined, 659
in multiple-step income
statements, 636, 637
Operating leases, 457–458, 463
Oracle, 408
Organization chart, 15
Other accounts payable, 433
Outside directors, 489
Outstanding checks, 293
Outstanding shares, 490, 527
Overall gross profit margin, 265
Overstatement, of earnings, 161
Owners' equity, 42, 64
on balance sheets, 197
on corporate balance sheet, 59

Owners' equity—*Cont.*
  credit balances and, 90
  debit and credit rules for, 90, 102–103
  decreases in, 45, 90, 93, 101, 102–103
  increases in, 45, 90, 93, 98, 100, 102–103
  net income and, 98
  reporting by type of business organization, 58–59

P

Pacific Bell, 441
Pacific Telesis, 441
Packard, Dave, 3
Paid-in capital, 490, 504. *See also* Capital stock
Parent company, 624, 659
Parmalat, 27
Partners' equity, 58–59
Partnerships
  defined, 58, 64
  general partners, 634n
  liability in, 58
  liability of partners, 634, 634n
  partners' equity, reporting, 58–59
Par value, 491–492, 504
Past due receivable, 311
Patents, 388, 406
Payables. *See* Accounts payable; Bonds payable;
    Notes payable
Payee of the note, 309
Payroll liabilities
  accrued, 152–153, 435
  cash payments, 574
  fringe benefits, 436n
Payroll taxes, 435–436, 463
PCAOB. *See* Public Company Accounting
    Oversight Board (PCAOB)
PC Connection, 139, 274
Peak pricing, 586, 594
Pension funds, 458–459, 464
Pension liabilities, 458–459, B-14
PepsiCo, Inc., 266, 565, 624
Pepsi-Cola Puerto Rico (Pepsi PR), 266
Percentage changes, financial statement
    analysis, 625–626, 636, 655, 659
Percentage of net sales, 637, 655
Performance evaluation
  inventory method and, 349
  merchandising operations, 265
Performance measures, 265
Periodic inventory system, 251
  average-cost method, 355
  closing entries, 255–257
  cost flow assumptions, 354
  defined, 254, 268
  FIFO, 355
  flow assumptions in, 354
  LIFO, 355–356
  operation of, 254–255
  perpetual inventory systems vs., 257–258
  physical inventory, 254–255
  selecting, 258–259
  shrinkage losses in, 354n
  transactions in, 255
Permanent accounts, 200
Perpetual inventory system
  closing entries, 257
  cost flow assumptions, 344

defined, 251, 268
FIFO, 344, 345–346
LIFO, 346–347
periodic inventory systems vs., 257–258
periodic inventory system
    vs., 257–258, 259
physical inventory, 253–254, 351–352
selecting, 258–259
specific identification method, 344
transactions in, 252–253
Personal guarantees, 634
Personal liability, 57–58, 634
Petty cash funds, 292
Peugot, 710
Pfizer, Inc., 297, 408
Physical deterioration, 392
Physical inventory, 363
  in periodic inventory system, 254
  in perpetual inventory system, 253–254,
    351–352
Planned economies, 689, 705
Plant
  cost of, 388
  intangible, 388
Plant assets
  acquisitions of, 388–391, 576
  capital expenditures, 390–391, 410
  categories of, 388
  corporate governance issues, 410
  cost determination, 389
  defined, 388, 412
  depreciation. *See* Depreciation
  disposal of, 400–402, 577
  impairment of, 399
Plant assets—*Cont.*
  intangible. *See* Intangible assets
  international accounting standards and,
    402–403
  land, 388, 389
  natural resources, 388, 409–410
  revenue expenditures, 390–391
  statement of cash flows and, 409, 576–577
  as stream of future services, 388
  tangible, 388
  trading in used for new, 402
Point-of-sale (POS) terminals, 264, 268
Political systems, globalization and, 688–689
Positive cash flows, 41, 64
Post-closing trial balance, 205
Posting
  defined, 92, 115
  of journal entries to ledger accounts, 92–95,
    103–111, 208
  ledger accounts after posting, 96–97
Postretirement benefits, 459, 464
Postretirement liabilities, 458–460, B-14
Power distance, 690
PPL Corporation, 324
Predictive information, 524
Preferred stock, 492. *See also* Capital stock
  book value per share, 495–496
  convertible, 493, 494, 530
  cumulative, 493–494, 527–528
  defined, 504
  dividends and, 493–494, 497–498, 527–528
  earnings per share (EPS), 527–528
  market price of, 497–498

Premium, on bonds payable, 447–450
Prepaid expenses, 146–148, 163, 251
Present value, 450
  of annuities, B-8–B-9
  bond prices and, 451
  capital leases, B-13–B-14
  compound interest, B-2
  defined, 412
  discounting future cash flows, B-6–B-10
  discount periods of less than one
    year, B-10
  discount rate, B-6, B-7–B-8
  financial instrument valuation, B-10–B-14
  future amounts, 464, B-2–B-6
  interest-bearing
    receivables/payables, B-10
  market prices of bonds, B-12
  non-interest bearing notes, B-10–B-11
  pension/postretirement liabilities
    and, 459, 460
  postretirement benefits obligations, B-14
  tables for calculating, B-7–B-8
  time value of money concept, B-1–B-2
Price-earnings (p/e) ratio, 529–530, 541, 638,
    644, 655, 659
Principle amount, of note payable, 433–434,
    438–440, 464
Prior period adjustments, 535–536, 541
Procter & Gamble (P&G), 15–16, 431, 486, 639
Product mix, 586, 594
Professional judgment
  Allowance for Doubtful Accounts
    estimates, 303
  extraordinary vs. unusual gains/losses, 527
  inflation adjustments, 44
  loss contingency accounting, 454
  materiality, 157–158
Professional organizations, 20–22
Profitability
  of activities, 102
  defined, 59
  gross profit, 250
  income tax expense in unprofitable periods,
    156
  measures of, 206. *See also individual entries*
    earnings per share (EPS), 527, 638, 644
    gross profit rate, 636–637
    income statement, classifications
      in, 635
    multiple-step income statement, 637
    net income, adequacy of, 639
    price-earnings (p/e) ratio, 638, 644
    return on assets (ROA), 640, 646
    return on common stockholders'
      equity, 646
    return on equity (ROE), 640–641
    return on investment
      (ROI), 639–641, 646
    single-step income statements, 635, 639
    short-run vs. long-run, 59
Profit and loss statement, 194. *See also* Income
    statement
Project Alpha, 587
Promissory notes, 309
Property subject to depreciation, 388
Proxy statements, 489
Public accounting careers, 24–25

Public Company Accounting Oversight Board (PCAOB)
  about, 30–31
  auditing firm registration with, 194
  creation of, 20
Public information, 487, 504
Publicly owned companies, 194, 208
Publicly owned corporations, 487–488, 502, 504
Publix Super Markets, Inc., 275
Pump-and-dump schemes, 502
Purchase discounts, 259–261
Purchase transactions
  on account, 48, 94, 259–261
  cash, 47, 93, 573, 576
  credit terms, 259–261
  cash discounts, 259–261
  involving foreign currency, 695
  lump-sum purchases, 389–390
  marketable securities, 576
  merchandise inventory, 252, 255, 257, 573
  plant assets, 576
  recording purchases at gross invoice price, 260–261
  returns of unsatisfactory merchandise, 261
  through cash and financing, 47–48, 94
  transportation costs on purchases, 261–262

Q

Quaker Foods, 624
Quick assets, 632, 659
Quick ratio, 456, 632, 651, 654, 659
Qwest, 27

R

Rate of inflation, 636
Ratios, 627. *See also individual ratios*
  evaluating, 632–634
  liquidity, 456, 631–634, 654–655
  market price of common stock, 655
  profitability, 655
  usefulness/limitations of, 633–634
Real accounts, 200
Realization principle, 100, 115, 156, 163
Receivables. *See* Accounts receivable; Notes receivable
Reconciling bank statements, 293–297
Recovery of bad debts, 306–307
Refinanced liabilities, 435n, 437–438
Registered bonds, 442n
Research and development (R&D) costs, 407–408
Residual amount, 45
Residual owners, 495
Residual value, 149n, 393–394, 398, 412
Restricted cash, 291–292
Restructuring charges, 526, 541
Results of operations, 6. *See also* Income statement
Retailers, 248–249. *See also* Merchandising companies
Retail method, 359, 363
Retained earnings
  about, 98
  capitalizing, 532–533
  capital stock vs., 59

defined, 64, 115, 197, 504
  dividend account closed to, 203–204
  dividend payments and, 197, 530–531
  liquidating dividends and, 532
  prior period adjustments, 535–536
  restrictions of, 535–536
  results of operations and, 524–530
  statement of, 196, 197, 534–536
  stock dividends and, 532–534
  stockholders' equity and, 490
  transferred from Income Summary account, 203
Return of investment, 10, 31
Return on assets (ROA), 455n, 501, 640, 646, 655, 659
Return on common stockholders' equity, 501, 646, 655
Return on equity (ROE), 206, 455n, 640–641, 655, 659
Return on investment (ROI), 10, 31, 639–640, 646
Returns
  of merchandise, 261
  sales, and allowances, 262–263
Revenue, 98. *See also* Income statement
  accrued, entries for, 106
  cash, entries for, 103, 106
  closing entries for revenue accounts, 201
  converting liabilities to, 143, 144, 151–152, 158
  debit and credit rules for, 102–103
  defined, 100, 115, 524
  earning of, 49–50
  in financial statement analysis, 645–646
  from interest, 309–311
  investment, 298–299
  matching costs to, 156–157, 353
  on multiple-step income statement, 636
  nonoperating items, 637
  realization principle, 100, 156
  uncollected, accruing, 143, 144, 154–155, 158
  unearned, 151–152, 437
  when earned, 141, 142
Revenue expenditures, 390–391, 412
Revenues, 51, 64
Reverse mergers, 502
Risk assessment, 9, 31. *See also* Credit risk; Liquidity
Risk Metrics Group, 656
Robert Morris Associates, 628n
Royal Caribbean, 141, 170, 171
Running balance, 96
Russia, 686, 692, 702

S

Safeway, Inc., 275, 382
Saks Fifth Avenue, 247
Saks Fifth Avenue Off 5th, 247
Saks Inc., 247, 248, 265
Salaries (wages) expense. *See* Payroll liabilities
Sales, 100. *See also* Sales transactions
  evaluating percentage changes in, 626, 655
  on income statement, 249–250
  net, 262, 265, 636
  per square foot of selling space, 265
Sales allowances, 262–263, 266
Sales discounts, 259–260, 263, 266

Sales per square foot of selling space, 265, 268
Sales returns, 262–263
Sales taxes, 264n
Sales taxes, accounting for, 264
Sales transactions
  accounting for sales taxes, 264
  of assets, 48
  assets, sale of, 95, 400–402
  cash, 572
  credit card, 308–309
  delivery expenses, 263
  discounts, 263
  discounts and allowances, 266
  involving foreign currency, 695–696
  marketable securities, 299–300, 576
  merchandise inventory, 257
  merchandising companies, 252–253, 262–264
  net sales, 262
  plant assets, sale of, 400–402
  returns and allowances, 262–263
  sales discounts, 263
  sales returns and allowances, 262–263
  year-end, 353
Salvage (residual) value, 393–394, 412
Same-store sales, 265
Sam's Club, 258
Samsung, 689
Sarbanes-Oxley Act (SOX) of 2002
  about, 9, 31
  CEO/CFO certification of financial statements, 61
  compliance to financial reporting, 636
  corporate disclosure of code of ethics, 410
  illegal/unethical orders from superiors, 113
  internal control and, 9, 22
  lying to external auditors, 538
  passage of, 9, 20, 61, 410
  penalties for fraud, 113
  Public Company Accounting Oversight Board (PCAOB), 20
  purpose of, 113
  responsibilities dictated by, 20
  sanctions for misstated financial statements, 26
  Section 404 certification, 9
  whistleblower protection, 266
Scrap value, 351
SEC enforcement action involvement. *See* Securities and Exchange Commission (SEC)
Secretary, corporate, 489
Section 404 certification, 9
Secured claims, 648
Securities and Exchange Commission (SEC), 25, 31, 624
  about, 18
  accounting principles and, 18
  annual reports of public companies, 208
  EDGAR database, 84, 382
  enforcement actions
    Allowance for Doubtful Accounts, 313
    cash flow manipulation, 587
    debt understatement, 457
    foreign officials, improper payments to, 703
    improper capitalization of operating expense, 410
    income overstatement, 161, 266, 538

Securities and Exchange Commission—*Cont.*
   inventory fraud, 361
   MD&A, inadequate disclosure in, 208
   against senior executives, 27
   shell companies, 502
   understatement of sales discounts and
      allowances, 266
   FASB and, 18
   filing with, 7
   financial reporting oversight by, 25, 194
   global accounting standards and, 19
   publicly owned companies, filing requirements
      for, 194
   sales discounts/allowances, understating, 266
   Statement in Support of Convergence and
      Global Accounting Standards, 19
Segment of the business
   defined, 541
   discounting or selling, 525
   segment reporting, 654, 692–693
Selling expenses, 637
Service charges/fees, bank, 294
Service companies, 249
Shareholder's equity, 59
Shell companies, 502
Shop supplies, 146
Short-term bond prices, 451–452
Short-term borrowing transactions, 577–578
Short-term creditors, 60
Short-term debt-paying ability, 456
Short-term investments. *See* Marketable securities
Short-term liabilities, 45n, 456
Short-term liquidity, 60, 632, 654–655
Shrinkage losses, 253–254, 351, 354n, 363
Simple interest, 310
Single-step income statements, 635, 639
Sinking funds, 435n, 442, 464
Skilling, Jeffery, 113
Smith, Weston, 61
Social Security taxes, 435, 436, 436n, 437
Software, general ledger, 209, 214
Sole proprietorships, 57–58, 64, 634
Sony Corporation, 6, 208
Sony Music Entertainment, 208
Sony Pictures Entertainment, 208
South America, 686, 691
South Korea, 686, 689, 690, 705
Soviet Union, former, 689
SOX. *See* Sarbanes-Oxley Act (SOX)
   of 2002
Special journal, 264–265, 268
Special purpose entities (SPEs), 457, 464
Specific identification method, 343, 344,
   350, 363
   evaluation of, 347–348
   periodic inventory systems, 354–355
Spoilage costs, 102
Sprint, 321
Stable-dollar assumption, 44, 64
Standard & Poor's, 454, 457, 656
Standards, for preparation of accounting
   information, 17–18
Standards for comparison, financial statement
   analysis, 633
*Standards for the Professional Practice of
   Internal Auditing* (IIA), 21
Staples, Inc., 382, 520

Stated (par) value, 491–492, 504
State Grid, 687
Statement in Support of Convergence and Global
   Accounting Standards, 19
Statement of cash flows, 56
   about, 53–54
   corporate governance issues, 587
   defined, 12, 31, 64
   direct method
      additional information, 569–570
      cash and cash equivalents, 569, 571–572
      cash payments for merchandise/expenses,
         573–575
      classification of cash flows, 566–569
      financing activities, 571, 577–578
      indirect method vs., 579–580
      investing activities, 568, 570, 575–577
      operating activities, 566–568, 570, 572–573,
         652–653
      supplementary schedule required for,
         581–583
   expanded, 581–583
   free cash flows, 583–584, 655
   importance of, 41
   indirect method vs., 579–581
   plant transactions and, 409
   postretirement liabilities and, 460
   preparing, 569–583, 587–591
   purpose of, 566
   reconciling net income with net cash flows,
      580–581
   relationship with balance sheet, 578
   stockholder transactions and, 496
   treasury stock transactions, 500–501
   worksheet for, 587–591
Statement of financial position. *See also* Balance
   sheet
   defined, 12, 13, 31, 40, 64
   reporting ownership equity in, 58–59
Statement of operations, 194. *See also* Income
   statement
Statement of retained earnings, 195, 534
   defined, 541
   preparing, 197
   prior period adjustments, 535–536
   restrictions of, 535–536
   retained earnings, defined, 197
   sample, 196
Statement of stockholder's equity, 536–537, 541
State of incorporation, 488, 504
Static analysis, 628
Stock. *See* Capital stock
Stock buyback programs, 501
Stock certificates, 58, 488, 504
Stock dividends, 532–534, 541
Stock exchanges, 487n
Stockholders
   defined, 58, 64, 486, 504
   personal guarantees by, 634
   records for, 490
   rights of, 488–489
Stockholders' equity, 59, 64, 197
   average, 206
   balance sheet presentation, 491, 492, 537–538
   comprehensive income and, 536
   paid-in capital, 490–496
   statement of stockholders' equity, 536–537

   total, 495
   treasury stock purchase and, 499–501
   Unrealized Holding Gain (or Loss) on
      Investments, 299–300
Stockholders' meetings, 488–489
Stockholders subsidiary ledger, 490, 504
Stock market, 487n
Stock option plans, 499
Stock registrar, 490, 504
Stock splits, 498, 504, 534
Stock transfer agent, 490, 504
Straight-line method, of depreciation, 149
   accelerated depreciation vs., 392–393, 397, 400
   defined, 163, 412
   for fractional periods, 394–395
   residual value, 393–394
Subsidiaries, 624, 659
   foreign, on consolidated financial
      statements, 700
   wholly owned international, 687, 705
Subsidiary ledger, 252
   accounts payable, 250
   accounts receivable, 250
   defined, 250, 268
   inventory, 250–251, 343, 345, 346, 347
   marketable security, 298
   stockholders, 490
Sum-of-the-years' digits (SYD) depreciation,
   400, 412
Supplementary schedule, statement of cash flows,
   581–583
Switzerland, 686

T

T accounts, 89–90, 204
Take-home pay, 436
Taking a physical inventory, 253, 268. *See also*
   Physical inventory
Tangible plant assets, 388, 412. *See also* Plant
   assets
Target Corporation, 360–361, 485
Tax accounting, 6
Taxes
   audits of, 25
   bond financing advantage, 442
   cash payments for, 575
   corporate income, 155
   depreciation and, 395n, 397, 397n
   direct write-off method and, 307, 307n
   double taxation, 486
   income tax expense. *See* Income tax expense
   inventory methods and, 349
   inventory valuation and, 356
   Medicare, 435, 436, 436n, 437
   payroll, 435–437
   sales, accounting for, 264
   sales, 264, 264n
   Social Security, 435, 436, 436n, 437
Tax refunds, 156n
Technology, globalization and, 690–691
Temporary (nominal) accounts, closing, 200–204
3M (Minnesota Mining and Manufacturing Co.),
   311–312
Time line, 55
Timeliness, 16–17
Time period principle, 99, 115

Times interest earned, 648
Time value of money. *See* Present value
Timing differences, adjusting entries for, 142, 143, 160, 580
Tokyo Stock Exchange, 297, 487n
Tools, depreciation of, 150
Total stockholder's equity, 495
Toyota, 687
Trade accounts payable, 433
Trademarks, 388, 406
Trade names, 406
Trading securities, 297n
Transferability of ownership, 58, 486, 487
Transportation costs, on purchases, 261–262
Transportation-in, 261–262
Treadway, James C., Jr., 21–22
Treasurer, corporate, 489
Treasury stock, 498–501, 504
Trend in cash flows from operating activities, 456, 583–584, 655
Trend in net income, 456
Trend percentages, 626–627
Trial balance
    adjusted trial balance, 159–160, 194, 195
    after-closing, 205–207
    defined, 111, 115
    preparing, 208
    unadjusted, 145, 155
    uses and limitations of, 112
Tropicana, 624
Turnover
inventory, 360
receivables, 360–361
Turnover rates
    accounts receivable, 311–312, 315, 456, 649–650, 654
    creditors' use of, 356
    inventory, 360, 456, 650, 654
2DoTrade, Inc., 502
200 percent declining-balance depreciation, 395
Tyco, 27

U

Unadjusted trial balance, 145, 155
Uncertainty avoidance, 690

Uncollected revenue, 154–155
Uncollectible accounts
    aging accounts receivable, 304–306
    Allowance for Doubtful Accounts, 303–304, 305n
    allowance method, 303, 307n
    balance sheet approach, 304–306
    direct write-off method, 307, 307n
    estimating credit losses, 304–306
    income statement approach, 306
    recovery of previously written off, 306–307
    reflected in financial statements, 302
    writing off, 303–304, 307n
Underwriters, 441, 464, 490–491, 504
Unearned (deferred) revenue, 151–152, 158, 163, 437
Unearned revenue, 151–152, 437
Unfunded postretirement costs, 460
Union Carbide Corp., 559
United Kingdom, 686, 692, 695
United Parcel Service (UPS), 387
U. S. Bankruptcy Court, 410, 454n
U. S. Justice Department, 502, 538
Units-of-output depreciation, 399, 412
Unlimited liability, 58
Unlimited personal liability, 58
Unprofitable accounting period, 156
Unrealized Holding Gain (or Loss) on Investments, 299–300, 315
Useful life, 148–149, 163, 398

V

Valuation accounts, 303
Value Line Investment Survey, 656
Venezuela, 688
Ventitex, Inc., 519
Verizon Communications, 501
Vertical analysis, 628
Visa, 291, 308, 318

W

Wages (salaries) expense. *See* Payroll liabilities
Walgreen Co., 660
Wall Street Journal, 13, 529–530, 693, 694

Walmart, 98, 100, 249, 258, 265, 372, 376, 687
The Walt Disney Company, 100
Walton, Sam, 258
Waste Management, 161
Wausau Paper Mills Company, 481
Weis Markets, 321
Wells Fargo & Company, 481
Wet Seal, Inc., 292
Whistleblower protection, 266
White Electric Supply, 322
Wholesalers, defined, 294. *See also* Merchandising companies
Wholly owned international subsidiaries, 687, 705
Window dressing, 61, 64, 633–634, 659
Withholdings, payroll, 436, 436–437
Workers' compensation, 436, 464
Working capital, 207, 433, 456, 631, 649, 654, 659
Worksheets, 209–212, 214, 587–591
World Bank, 702
WorldCom, 9, 27, 161, 410, 636
Write-down, 3, 363
    impairment of plant assets, 399
    of inventory, 351–352
    lower-of-cost-or-market (LCM) rule, 351–352
    reversals of, 254
Write-off, 3, 311
    against the allowance, 303–304, 307n
    direct, 307, 307n
    recovery of bad debts, 306–307

Y

Yield
    bond, 648
    dividend, 497, 644, 655

Z

Zero-coupon bonds, 450n